Kurt Lipstein

Collection of Essays

Kurt Lipstein, Squire Law Library, Cambridge, 2006

Kurt Lipstein

Collection of Essays

Edited by

Peter Feuerstein
Heinz-Peter Mansel

Mohr Siebeck

Peter Feuerstein († 2013) was an International Legal Consultant (USA), Rechts-anwalt (Germany), and student of Kurt Lipstein.

Heinz-Peter Mansel is the director of the Institute of Private International and Foreign Private Law of the University of Cologne.

ISBN 978-3-16-152062-4

The Deutsche Nationalbibliothek lists this publication in the Deutsche National-bibliographie; detailed bibliographic data are available on the Internet at *http://dnb.d-nb.de*.

© 2014 by Mohr Siebeck, Tübingen. www.mohr.de

The book was typeset by pagina in Tübingen, printed on non-aging paper by Gulde-Druck in Tübingen and bound by Großbuchbinderei Spinner in Ottersweier.

Printed in Germany.

Vorwort

Kurt Lipstein hat durch seine wunderbare Persönlichkeit, sein Lehren und seine Schriften gewirkt. Hier wird eine Auswahl seiner Veröffentlichungen vorgelegt. Die Herausgeber hoffen, durch diesen Band den Zugang seinem Werk und damit zu dem bleibenden wissenschaftlichen Vermächtnis von Kurt Lipstein zu erleichtern.

Peter Feuerstein (1946–2013) nahm meine Würdigung Kurt Lipsteins, die in *Rabels Zeitschrift* veröffentlicht worden war, zum Anlass, an mich mit dem Plan der Herausgabe dieses Werkes heranzutreten. Ich habe das Unternehmen gerne aufgenommen, stehen mir doch die Erinnerungen an eine letzte Begegnung mit Kurt Lipstein in seinem blühenden Garten in Cambridge noch immer klar vor Augen.

Peter Feuerstein hatte bei Kurt Lipstein in Cambridge während eines Forschungsaufenthalts (1972–1974) als Fellow des Claire Colleges im Rahmen seiner Promotion an der Philipps-Universität Marburg studiert; auch danach riss der Kontakt zu seinem verehrten akademischen Lehrer nicht ab. Ihm ist für die Festschrift für Kurt Lipstein aus Anlass seines 70. Geburtstages (Multum non multa, 1980) zu danken, die er zusammen mit Clive Parry herausgab. Ohne ihn wäre auch dieser Band nicht erschienen. Peter Feuerstein lebte seit 1998 als International Legal Consultant in den USA. Bis zu seinem Tode begleitete er die Herausgabe der Gesammelten Schriften, half bei Aufbringung von Druckbeihilfen und Abdruckgenehmigungen.

Die Herausgeber danken der *Universität Würzburg*, der *Bayer Stiftung für Deutsches und Internationales Arbeits- und Wirtschaftsrecht*, Leverkusen, dem *William Senior Fonds*, Cambridge, dem *Max-Planck-Institut für ausländisches und internationales Privatrecht* in Hamburg und der *Gesellschaft für Auslandsrecht e. V.* in Köln für die Aufbringung von Druckbeihilfen, ohne die der Band nicht hätte veröffentlicht werden können.

Sie danken ferner den Verlagen, Institutionen und Rechteinhabern, die mit der Erteilung von Abdruckgenehmigung zu diesem Band beigetragen haben, insbesondere dem *Cambridge Law Journal*, der Haager *Académie de droit international*, *Springer Science+Business Media B.V.* und *Oxford University Press* sowie Herrn Colin Turpin, der die Kosten für einen der Beiträge übernommen hat.

VI

Der herzliche Dank der Herausgeber geht an Herrn Wiss. Mit. Tobias Lutzi (LL.M., Maître en droit), der mit größter Zuverlässigkeit und Sorgfalt die Drucklegung dieses Bandes redaktionell betreute. Dem Verlag *Mohr Siebeck* und insbesondere Herrn Dr. Gillig sind die Herausgeber für die Aufnahme der Gesammelten Schriften in das Verlagsprogramm und die angenehme Zusammenarbeit zu Dank verpflichtet.

Köln, im Frühjahr 2014   Heinz-Peter Mansel

Preface

Kurt Lipstein was a highly influential scholar, whose wonderful personality, teaching, and writing had lasting impact. This is a selection of his publications. The editors hope that it will provide an opportunity for readers to access his oeuvre and gain insight into his academic legacy.

It was Peter Feuerstein (1946–2013) who contacted me, following the publication of my remembrance of Kurt Lipstein in *Rabels Zeitschrift*, to propose that we edit the present collection. I agreed to undertake this project without hesitation, still remembering clearly my last meeting with Kurt Lipstein in his blooming Cambridge garden.

Peter Feuerstein was a student of Kurt Lipstein during his stay in Cambridge as a visiting researcher and fellow of Claire College. Even after his postgraduate studies, which he concluded with a PhD from the Philipps University of Marburg, Peter Feuerstein kept in contact with his admired academic teacher. He deserves credit for the Festschrift for Kurt Lipstein (Multum non multa, 1980), which he edited together with Clive Parry on the occasion of Kurt Lipstein's 70th birthday. If it were not for him, this volume too would not have been published. Since 1998, Peter Feuerstein lived and worked as an international legal consultant in the United States. Until his death, he participated actively in the work on this collection and helped to organise the necessary grants and printing permissions.

The editors would like to thank the *University of Würzburg*, the *Bayer Stiftung für deutsches und internationals Arbeits- und Wirtschaftsrecht*, Leverkusen, the *William Senior Fund*, Cambridge, the *Max Planck Institute for comparative and international Private Law*, Hamburg, and the *Gesellschaft für Auslandsrecht*, Cologne, for the award of the grants that made it possible to publish this volume.

The editors would further like to thank all of the publishers, institutions, and rights holders that contributed to this collection by allowing the reproduction of Kurt Lipstein's essays. In particular, we thank the *Cambridge Law Journal*, the *Hague Academy of International Law*, *Springer Science+-Business Media B.V.*, *Oxford University Press*, and Mr Colin Turpin, Cambridge, who generously underwrote the fees associated with one of the essays.

VIII

Finally, the editors wish to express their sincere gratitude to Mr Tobias Lutzi (LL.M., Maître en droit), research assistant in Cologne, who attended to the printing of this volume's publication with the utmost reliability and diligence. We would also like to thank the publishing house *Mohr Siebeck* and in particular Dr Franz-Peter Gillig for including the present volume in their publishing programme and for the pleasant collaboration on this project.

Cologne, spring 2014   Heinz-Peter Mansel

Acknowledgments

The publishers would like to thank all publishing houses, institutions, and right holders that contributed to this collection by allowing the reproduction of Kurt Lipstein's essays. In particular, we thank the Cambridge Law Journal, the Hague Academy of International Law, Springer Science+Business Media B.V., Oxford University Press, and Mr Colin Turpin, who generously paid the fees for one essay.

Table of Contents

XII

Kurt Lipstein
(1909–2006)*

Kurt Lipstein was born in Frankfurt am Main, Germany, on 19th March 1909. He died aged 97 on 2nd December 2006, in Cambridge, England. This year marks the 100th anniversary of his birth and provides an occasion to remember Kurt Lipstein, the legal scholar, the man and his work.*

In 1934, at the age of 24, Lipstein left Germany to escape persecution, finding his new home in Cambridge. His academic career evolved from this point on and by the end of his life Lipstein came to be regarded in Cambridge as "one of the greatest academic lawyers of our time."[1] Kurt Lipstein's influence extends well beyond the boundaries of England. He has made lasting

---

[HEINZ-PETER MANSEL, RabelsZ 73 (2009), 441–454 translated to English by Dr. iur. Maya Mandery, LL.M., LL.B. (Hons), University of Auckland]

* The following will be noted in abbreviated form: *Christian v. Bar,* Kurt Lipstein, The Scholar and the Man, in: Jurists Uprooted, German-speaking Emigre Lawyers in Twentieth-century Britain, in *Jack Beatson/Reinhard Zimmermann* (eds.) (2006) 749–760; *Christopher Forsyth,* Kurt Lipstein (*1909): *ibidem* 463–481; *Kurt Lipstein,* Acta et Agenda: Cambrige L.J. 36 (1977) 47–61; *idem.,* Cambridge 1933–2002, in: Jurists Uprooted (above) 761–770.

Further accounts can be found in *Lipstein ,* Cambridge 1933–2002; *idem.,* Acta et Agenda 47–61; *Lesley Dingle/Daniel Bates,* Conversations with Kurt Lipstein, Emeritus Professor of Comparative Law, Some reminiscences over seventy years of the Squire Law Library and the Faculty of Law, University of Cambridge: Int. J. Leg. Inform. 35 (Spring 2007) 93–133, also available at: www.squire.law.cam.ac.uk/eminent_scholars. This website of the Eminent Scholar Archive of the Squire Law Library of the University of Cambridge also makes the following available: audio files of the mentioned interview, (an incomplete and at times incorrect) bibliography, video file of Kurt Lipstein's last lecture on English Legal Methods (held on 17 July 2006), and additional further information and photocopies on Lipstein. See also, *v. Bar* 749–760; *Peter Feuerstein/Clive Parry,* Foreword by the editors, in: Multum non multa, FS Lipstein (1980) S. VII–X; *Reinhard Zimmermann,* Happy Birthday, Kurt Lipstein!: IPRax 1999, 296–297; *Bob Hepple,* Kurt Lipstein-Teacher, Colleague and Friend: The Claire Association Annual 2006/2007, 18–23; *idem.,* Obituary: Kurt Lipstein, Refugee from the Nazis and pioneer of comparative law: The Guardian from 29.1.2007, p. 33; *Andrew v. Hirsch,* Obituary: Kurt Lipstein: Wolfson College Magazine 31 (2006/2007) 156– 157.

[1] *Gordon Jonson,* From the President: Wolfson College Magazine 31 (2006/2007) 1–3 (3).

contributions within the area of private international law, in particular, within the English conflict of laws. He established the study of European Law as a discipline in England and kept close ties with German law and jurisprudence.

I. Frankfurt – Berlin

His father was born in Königsberg, East Prussia, and was a well-known successful senior physician in Frankfurt am Main. His mother was born into the long-established banking family Sulzbach that had family ties with Max Warburg's family.[2] The Gebrüder Sulzbach[3] private bank was one of the founders of Deutsche Bank AG. Kurt Lipstein learnt the English language from very early on as his grandmother had been raised in England. Together with Sir Otto Kahn-Freund (born 1900), he attended the revered Goethe-Gymnasium, which had been established as a reformed grammar school in his home town. In 1927, he commenced his study of law spending his first semester at the University of Grenoble. That same year, he transferred to the Friedrich Wilhelm University in Berlin.

He attended lectures held by Theodor Kipp, lectures on French Law by Martin Wolff who had immigrated to Oxford in 1938, and attended Roman Law seminars held by Ernst Rabels who had fled to Ann Arbor in the US in 1939. Later on, in his first valedictory lecture, Kurt Lipstein spoke of the profound influence his three Berlin lecturers had on his academic thinking.[4]

In 1932, Lipstein passed his first state examination in law and began his practical legal training as *Referendar* at the district Court of Appeal of Frankfurt. The statute of 7th April 1933, cynically entitled "Gesetz zur Wiederherstellung des Berufsbeamtentums"[5] (Law for the Restoration of the Professional Civil Service), effectively brought his career to an end. He was prevented from entering the courts and was forced to submit an application for leave.[6] He realised that he was no longer safe in Germany.

English relatives provided him with contact to Patrick Duff, at the time a Fellow, and later Professor of Civil Law in Cambridge. Thereupon, Kurt Lipstein travelled to England and on Martin Wolff's recommendation met

---

[2] Max M. Warburg (1867–1946).
[3] On the history of the bank, see *Hans-Dieter Kirchholtes*, Jüdische Privatbanken in Frankfurt am Main (1989) 29 et seq.
[4] *Lipstein*, Acta et Agenda 47.
[5] RGBI. 1933 I 175.
[6] On this, see *Lipstein*, Cambridge 1933–2002, 761; *v. Bar* 752.

with his brother-in-law H.F. Jolowicz in London. He later travelled on to Cambridge. Writing on his visit to Trinity College many decades later, Kurt Lipstein describes: "On a summer evening with the evening sun striking the court, the impression was overwhelming, and my mind was made up: it was to be Cambridge."[7]

II. Cambridge and the World

In 1934, Kurt Lipstein immigrated to England. Up until 1936, he had travelled back to Germany six times, trips which were to still cause him nightmares decades later.[8] The last message he was to receive from his parents came from the concentration camp Theresienstadt.[9]

Lipstein was one of the first doctoral students of the then newly established PhD degree. He obtained a place at Trinity College. Among his colleagues were Rene David and Glanville Williams with whom he was to forge a life-long friendship. His dissertation on Roman Law, supervised by Duff and Jolowicz, was completed in 1936. He obtained a work permit with the help of the influential Harold Cooke Gutteridge,[10] whom Lipstein regarded as his "friend and father". Gutteridge who later held the first chair of Comparative Law at the University of Cambridge appointed Lipstein as his personal assistant from 1937 to 1941.

Following the outbreak of World War II, Lipstein volunteered for British Military Service, but was never required to serve. In May 1940, he was interned as an enemy alien together with several other immigrants to Cambridge, many of whom were later to become part of England's academic elite.[11] At the end of October 1940,[12] he was released from the camp and subsequently employed as Faculty Secretary to the Board of Law.[13]

---

[7] *Lipstein,* Cambridge 1933–2002, 761.

[8] *Lipstein,* Cambridge 1933–2002, 764.

[9] *Hepple,* Orbituary (above n. 1) 33.

[10] See *Kurt Lipstein,* Harold Cooke Gutteridge 1876–1963: RabelsZ 28 (1964) 201–207.

[11] Generally on the contribution of German refugees in England, see *Kurt Lipstein,* The history of the contribution to law by German-speaking Jewish refugees in the United Kingdom, in: Second Chance, Two Centuries of German-speaking jews in the United Kingdom, in: W. E. Mosse et al. (eds.) (1991) 221–227; also, Jurists Uprooted; *Gunther Kuhne,* Entwurzelte Juristen: JZ 2006, 233– 241. A general overview of German lawyers persecuted by the NS-regime and their contribution abroad can be found in *idem.,* Die Erforschung der Juristen-Emigration 1933–1945 und der Beitrag der deutschen Emigranten zur Entwicklung des Rechtswesens in Israel, in: Justo iure, Festgabe Otto Sandrock (1995) 385–400 (385–388).

[12] *Lipstein,* Cambridge 1933–2002, 766: „On the day when the battle of Britain was won."

[13] *Feuerstein/Parry* (above n. 1) S. IX.

His university appointments were not as rapid as the spread of his scholarly influence in Cambridge and beyond. He was appointed university lecturer in 1946, and, later in 1962, he was appointed Reader in Conflict of Laws. It was not until 1972 that he received the Professorship in Comparative Law, formerly held by Harold Gutteridge. At the age of 68, the University of Cambridge awarded him his LL.D. This was in 1977, the year of his formal retirement, but by no means meant an end to his teaching and supervising of students.

He was given membership of Clare College in 1940 and was elected Fellow in 1956. Later he also became a Member of Trinity College and in 1998, was made Honorary Fellow of Wolfson College. His legal training, activities and accolades were: 1938 his enrolment as student of the Middle Temple, 1950 call to the Bar, and 1966 Honorary Master of the Bench of the Middle Temple. In 1998 he was made an Honorary Queen's Council.

The provision of legal services and advice was not the main area of Kurt Lipstein's work. But even within this field of work he left his mark. Perhaps the most significant trial he was involved in was the famous Nottebohm Case, Liechtenstein v Guatemala[14] heard before the International Court of Justice in The Hague. He became one of Liechtenstein's lawyers (alongside Erwin H. Loewenfeld, Georges Sauser-Halland, James E.S. Fawcett), after inheriting the case from Hersch Lauterpacht who had been unable to continue following his appointment as judge at the International Court of Justice. The case was concerned with the question of diplomatic protection of a German born but naturalized citizen of Liechtenstein, against Guatemala and raised fundamental issues of Public International Law. It was later to impact on issues of private international law, despite the decision itself not involving any conflict of laws issues.[15]

Kurt Lipstein's sphere of academic influence steadily spread well beyond England. He was made Director of Research at the International Association of Legal Science from 1954 to 1959 and worked on the reception of western law in Turkey and India.[16] He was Visiting Professor at the University of

---

[14] [1955] ICJ Reports 4; on this, see *Kurt Lipstein/Erwin H. Loewenfeld*, Liechtenstein gegen Guatemala: Der Nottebohm-Fall, in: Gedächtnisschrift Ludwig Marxer (1963) 275–325; *Lipstein*, Acta et Agenda 55 et seq.

[15] On this see, e.g. *Heinz-Peter Mansel*, Personalstatut, Staatsangehörigkeit und Effektivität (1988) 148–149; *Ralf Michaels*, Public and Private International Law, German Views on Global Issues: J. Priv. Int. L. 4 (2008) 121–138 (125).

[16] *Kurt Lipstein*, The reception of western law in Turkey: Annales Fac. Dr. Istanbul 1956, 11–27, 225–238; *idem.*, The reception of western law in Turkey: Social Science Bulletin 1957, 70–95; *idem.*, The reception of western law in countries of a different economic and social background with special regard to problems arising out of industrialisation: Annales Fac. Dr. lstanbul 1961, 3–13 19 et seq.; *idem.*, The reception of western law in countries with a different social and economic background: India: Rev. Inst. Der. Comp. 1957/1958, 8–11, 69–81; 213–255; *idem.*, The reception of western law in countries with a different social and economic background: India: Indian Yb. Int. L. 6 (1957) 277–293.

Pennsylvania and twice at Northwestern University (Chicago) in 1962, 1966 and 1968. He was Professeur Associé in Paris at the Sorbonne and lectured English Contract Law in 1977. Lipstein was for many decades reporter on English conflict of laws in 'Clunet'.[17]

In 1972, he was invited to lecture[18] at The Hague Academy of International Law. In 1993, he was elected to the world-renowned *Institut de Droit International*,[19] established in 1873. He was one of only 130 members accorded with this honour. His success as rapporteur of the *Institut* will be discussed further below. In an interview given in 2005, he lists the three highlights of his academic career to be: his appointment to Cambridge Faculty, receiving the title of Queen's Council (1998), and becoming a member of the *Institut* de Droit International.[20]

Lipstein also participated in the legislative process with great enthusiasm: "Nothing gives more satisfaction than the knowledge that at the end of one's work the legal system has been added to for the common good."[21] He succeeded Harold Gutteridge in 1952, becoming Member of the United Nations, where he was involved with the draft of the New York Convention on Maintenance Obligations of 20th June 1956.[22] Later, he also participated as Member of the Committee appointed by the Lord Chancellor and the Secretary for Scotland to advise on the conclusion of treaties prepared by The Hague Conference of Private International Law and in the negotiation of several Hague Conventions for the British Government. He was involved in the implementation of Conventions into English laws, specifically The Hague Convention on Jurisdiction, Applicable Law and Recognition of Decrees Relating to Adoptions,[23] and the 1973 Convention concerning the International Administration of the Estates of Deceased Persons[24]. He paid

---

[17] *Kurt Lipstein*, Chronique de jurisprudence britannique: Clunet 115 (1988) 803–845, 1051–1099.

[18] *Kurt Lipstein*, The general principles of private international law: Rec. des Cours 135 (1972-l) 97–230 (cited: General principles); further published in: Principles of the Conflict of Laws, National and International (1981) XII and 144 S.

[19] On the Institut and Session, in which Kurt Lipstein presented his draft resolution, see *Karl Doehring*, Tagung des Institut de Droit international in Berlin vom 17. bis 25.8.1999: NJW 1999, 3249–3250; *Erik Jayme*, Tagung des Institut de Droit international in Berlin: IPRax 2000, 61–62 (cited: Tagung). On the Institute generally, see *Fritz Munch*, Das Institut de Droit international: Arch. VolkR 28 (1990) 76–105.

[20] See *Dingle/Bates* (above n. 1) 93– 133.

[21] *Lipstein*, Acta et Agenda 54.

[22] *Kurt Lipstein*, A draft convention on the recovery abroad of claims for maintenance: Int. Comp. L.Q. 3 (1954) 125–134.

[23] Hague Convention on Jurisdiction, Applicable Law and Recognition of Decrees Relating to Adoptions of 15 Nov. 1965; on this see *Kurt Lipstein*, The Tenth Session of the Hague Conference: Cambridge L.J. 23 (1965) 224–230; *idem.*, Adoption in private international law: Int.Comp.L.Q.12 (1963) 835–849.

[24] Hague Convention concerning the International Administration of the Estates of

particular attention to the Hague Conventions.[25] Later, he examined and guided the developments in both private international law and the law of procedure.[26] He frequently called for efforts to introduce supranational rules of law, either through the unification of laws or through the development of general principles of law. He sought to free the conflict of laws from its national constraints as much as possible, referring to the difficulties of a uniform application of laws on a supranational level. Consequently, Lipstein initiated the establishment of private law specialised chambers within the European Court of Justice.[27]

It was primarily the last third of his life during which he received the bulk of both his academic and other public acknowledgments. In addition to the above mentioned distinctions, Kurt Lipstein received the research award from the Alexander von Humboldt Foundation and in 1995 an honorary doctorate from the Law Faculty of the University of Würzburg.

Kurt Lipstein was deeply rooted in Cambridge. It was here that he married Gwyneth Herford[28] in 1944, leading a fulfilled married life until her death in 1998. They had two daughters, Eve and Diana, and six grandchildren. Their house, which he had moved into in 1947/1948 near the University, was surrounded by and hidden in greenery. Those that visited him there following the death of his wife would nevertheless notice the strong presence she still had in his life.

Kurt Lipstein was a person with lasting relationships. He clearly had a very strong affiliation with the University of Cambridge, evidenced in an interview that he gave in 2005.[29] A reception was held by the Law Faculty on the 20th November 2006, celebrating the 70th anniversary of his PhD in Cambridge. His Memorial Service was held shortly thereafter.

Deceased Persons of 2. Oct. 1973; on this see *Kurt Lipstein,* Das Haager Abkommen über die internationale Abwicklung von Nachlassen: RabelsZ 38 (1975) 29– 55.

[25] For a specific overview, see *inter alia Kurt Lipstein,* The Hague Convention on private international law, public law and public policy: Int. Comp. L.Q. 8 (1959) 506–522.

[26] On international contract law, see references given below under n. 61; and further, e.g. *Kurt Lipstein,* Chapter 39: The EEC Convention on the jurisdiction and the enforcement of civil and commercial matters of 27 September 1968, in: The Cambridge Lectures 1981, in *N. E. Eastham/B. Krivy* (eds.) (1981) 412–431.

[27] See in particular, the case study in *Kurt Lipstein,* Enforcement of judgments under the jurisdiction and judgments convention: safeguards: Int. Comp. L.Q. 36 (1987) 873–878 (878).

[28] On her life, see the brief description given by *v. Bar* 754. Gwyneth Lipstein was on the board of Cambridge council from 1967 to 1990, as evidenced by other documents.

[29] *Dingle/Bates* (above n. 1) 93–133.

III. Academic Achievements

Kurt Lipstein's scholary estate was made public with the generous donation of academic papers, including letters and manuscripts to Clare College by his heirs. These were then passed on to the Eminent Scholars Archive of the Squire Law Library for curation. It was the Lipstein Estate that gave the impulse to the creation of the Eminent Scholars Archive. The core collection of more than 2000 items occupies the ground floor of the JANUS-Archive established in 2007. The publicly available database has recorded the collection, which includes additional material such as picture, audio and video files.[30] The critical assessment of the whole of Kurt Lipstein's estate was a particularly worthwhile task.

Kurt Lipstein's academic achievements have been presented and analysed many times.[31] His bibliography,[32] not including the numerous and comprehensive book reviews and case comments, comprises well over one hundred autonomous and joint publications, published in several western European languages. The thematic spectrum of his work is impressive, ranging from substantive, comparative and private international law, to European law and public international law. His most important publications, particularly those in private international law, deserve special mention.

The above mentioned unpublished thesis[33] on the *beneficium cedendarum actionum* has been described by Christopher Forsyth, based on the text of an elegy by Thomas Grey, as a "flower born to blush unseen". Namely, that modern standard works would benefit from taking into consideration the work of Kurt Lipstein.[34] Although he lectured in Roman Law for many decades, it was not his main field of publication.

Even before the United Kingdom joined the European Economic Community in 1973, he had an interest in European Law. Following the accession, he published his detailed study on the law of European Community, the first of its kind written in English.[35] It was written from the point of view of a civil lawyer. It was Kurt Lipstein's specific aim to present not only the EC Treaty as primary law, but also to assess the influence of secondary law and the case law of the European Court of Justice on the national laws of the

---

[30] On this see above n. 1.

[31] See Kurt Lipstein's own report on his retirement: *Lipstein*, Acta et Agenda 47–61, covering the period until 1976; see further *v*. Bar 749–760; *Forsyth* 463–481.

[32] Partial bibliographies can be found in: Multum non multa, FS Lipstein (1980) 379–382 (up until the beginning of 1981), as well as (beyond 1981) on the internet, above n. 1.

[33] *Kurt Lipstein*, Critical Studies upon the Beneficium cedendar um actionum and vendito nominis (unpublished Ph.D. thesis, University of Cambridge) (1936) 188 pages.

[34] *Forsyth* 467.

[35] *Kurt Lipstein* , The Law of the European Economic Community (1974); see e.g. the reviews by *Éric Stein*, C.M.L. Rev. 11 (1974) 445–447.

Member States. The interpretation of the specific Treaty provisions is supplemented by the systematic presentation of the corresponding secondary sources of law. With this major work, he was able to establish the study of European Law as a scholarly discipline in England. He later published further works on European law[36] but the focus of his work was private international law: "The conflicts of law, however, attracted me more than any other topic".[37]

Lipstein's first substantial article within the field of private international law was published together with Harold Gutteridge on unjustifiable enrichment in English law.[38] The conclusions of their study were subsequently integrated into the relevant section in *Dicey/Morris*, The Conflict of Laws.[39] This continued to be a main source of reference in English law, until the enactment of the legislative provision in Art. 10 of the Rome II Regulation.[40] Kurt Lipstein was co-author of this major work from the 6th to the 8th edition, published respectively in 1948, 1958 and 1967.[41] The paper also had influence within German conflict of laws[42] and is to this day still referenced in argument.[43] When comparing the 6th edition to the previous edition, it appears that several substantive amendments were made that are attributable to Kurt Lipstein. This is also clearly evidenced in his paper on "Conflict of Laws 1921–1971, the way ahead".[44] The study is in many respects a comprehensive draft of the Hague Lectures which will be discussed further below. The development of the English conflict of laws is masterfully presented and analysed. He draws attention to[45] the omission of the theory of acquired rights, upon which Dicey had justified the application of foreign law, which from the 6th edition onwards (for which Lipstein was

---

[36] *Kurt Lipstein*, Some practical comparative law, The interpretation of multi-lingual treaties with special regard to the EEC-Treaties: Tul. L. Rev. 48 (1974) 907–915; *idem.*, The legal structure of Association Agreements with the EEC: Brit. Yb. Int. L. 49 (1974/75) 201–226; *idem.*, Conflicts of law in matters of social security under the EEC Treaty, in: European Law and the Individual, *F. G. Jacobs* (ed.) (1976) 55–77; *idem.*, Un juriste anglais dans la Communauté européenne: Rev. int. dr. comp. 30 (1978) 493–504.

[37] *Lipstein*, Acta et Agenda 48.

[38] *Kurt Lipstein/Harold Cooke Gutteridge*, Conflicts of law in matters of unjustifiable enrichment: Cambridge L.J. 7 (1941) 80–93.

[39] See also *Lipstein*, Acta et Agenda 48; and further *Forsyth* 468.

[40] EG Regulation No. 864/2007 of the European Parliament and of the Council of 11 July 2007 on the law applicable to non-contractual obligations, ABl. EU 2007 L 199/40.

[41] The current version is the 14th edition from 2006.

[42] See *Konrad Zweigert*, Bereicherungsansprüche im internationalen Privatrecht: Süddeutsche Juristenzeitung 2 (1947) 247–253; specifically *v. Bar* 755.

[43] See *Geoffrey C. Cheshire/Peter North/James J. Fawcett*, Private International Law[14] (2008) 829.

[44] *Kurt Lipstein*, Conflict of laws 1921–71, The way ahead: Cambridge L.J. 31 (1972) 67–120.

[45] *Lipstein*, Conflict of laws 1921–71 (above) 67 et seq.; see also *idem.*, Acta et Agenda 54.

also responsible) was no longer considered to be a general principle within the conflict of laws. He emphasises the circular nature of the arguments and restrictions of the theory.[46]

Kurt Lipstein published extensively within the conflict of laws. His research ranged from adoption in private international law,[47] issues concerning intellectual property and procedural law,[48] European Community law,[49] to the law concerning international insolvency.[50] But it was the general theory and basic rules and principles within the conflict of laws that fascinated him. This was the area within which Lipstein consistently produced groundbreaking research. The relationship between private international law and public international law, as well as private and public law served as a distinct area of research on which he was able to continuously throw new light through his comparative assessments.[51] A particular interest of Lipstein's was to follow the development of the conflict of laws for and through international (arbitration) tribunals. Given that they do not possess a *lex fori*, international tribunals must either ascertain that a certain system of municipal law applies with the help of its own international rules of the conflict of laws, or develop jurisdiction-selecting rules on a comparative basis if the basic legal order does not identify such.

He discovered, described and analysed this development several times,

---

[46] See the detailed examination in *Lipstein*, Principles of the Conflict of Laws (above n. 19) 23 et seq.

[47] *Kurt Lipstein*, Adoption in private international law: Int. Comp. L.Q. 12 (1963) 835–849.

[48] *Kurt Lipstein*, Intellectual property: jurisdiction or choice of laws: Cambridge L.J. 61 (2002) 295–300; *idem.*, Intellectual property, Parallel choice of law rules: Cambridge L.J. 64 (2005) 593–613; see Forsyth 478.

[49] *Kurt Lipstein*, The law relating to the movement of companies in the European Community, in: FS Erik Jayme (2004) 527–531.

[50] *Kurt Lipstein*, Jurisdiction in bankruptcy: Mod. L. Rev. 12 (1949) 454–476; *idem.*, Jurisdiction to wind-up foreign companies: Cambridge L. J. 11 (1952) 198–208; *idem.*, Early treaties for the recognition and enforcement of foreign bankruptcies, in: Cross Border Insolvency, Comparative Dimensions?, in: Comparative Law XII Chap. 14, in E. E. *Fletcher (ed.)* (1990) 223–236; *idem.*, Bankruptcy and the Hague Conventions, in: FS Hans Hanisch (1994) 149–152.

[51] See in particular *Kurt Lipstein*, General principles (above n. 19) 167 et seq.; and *idem.*, Decisions of English courts during 1948–1949 involving questions of public or private international law: Brit. Yb. Int. L. 26 (1948/49) 469–493; *idem.*, Decisions of English courts during 1949–1950 involving questions of public or private international law: Brit. Yb. Int. L. 27 (1949/50) 466–482; *idem.*, Characterization, in: Int. Enc. Comp. L. III: Private International Law (1999) Chap.5, 65–67. See *idem.*, Conflict of public laws, Visions and realities, in: FS Zajtay (1982) 357–378; *idem.*, Öffentliches Recht und internationales Privatrecht, in: Internationales Privatrecht, internationales Wirtschaftsrecht, in *W. Holl/U. Klinke* (ed.) (1985) 39–54; *idem.*, Conflict of laws and public law, in: United Kingdom law in the 1980s, in *E. K. Banakas* (ed.) (1990) 38–58.

first in his essays completed in 1941 and 1943, then in his Hague lectures of 1972,[52] and finally in his paper of 2001.[53]

A seminal work of Lipstein's, which was based on his many earlier works[54] and was to become an important point of reference, is his lecture[55] at the Hague Academy of International Law in 1972. The lecture was later developed, updated and published in 1981.[56] In particular, the extension of the application of the Hague Convention was recognised and considered. The development of European contract law in the Rome Convention on the law applicable to contractual obligations[57] was not fully considered in the updated version of the Hague lecture. In contrast to earlier published versions he further refined the explanations on the significance of public policy in public international law and the limitation provisions of substantive law. He tackled issues such as the application of methodologically biased connections and overriding mandatory rules (from the *lex fori* or the law of a third state) through the application of the general jurisdiction-selection method in order to implement public policy interests. He re-examined these issues time and time again from differing perspectives.[58]

Kurt Lipstein's renowned Hague lecture[59] presents a concise yet comprehensive philosophical and historical perspective of the development of private international law and its defining principles. His work was largely carried out on a comparative basis. He examined the modern American revolutionary theories that sought to replace the outdated choice-of-law-selection system through value judgment. Lipstein's conclusions on this are conservative, mirroring his careful consideration of the need for the translation of his results into practice. The law must be coherent in practice. This is evidenced by foreseeability and predictability of results and certainty of the law.

---

[52] *Kurt Lipstein*, Conflict of laws before international tribunals I, in: Transactions of the Grotius Society 27 (1941) 142–181 and II: *ibidem*. 29 (1943) 51–83; *idem.*, General principles (above n. 19) 173 et seq.

[53] *Kurt Lipstein*, Conflict of laws before international tribunals sixty years later, in: Aufbruch nach Europa, 75 Jahre Max-Planck-Institut für Privatrecht (2001) 713–723.

[54] It has already been noted that Lipstein's major study Conflict of laws 1921–71, The way ahead (above n. 45) provides a comprehensive draft of his Hague lectures of 1972.

[55] *Lipstein*, General principles (above n. 18) 97–230; on this see also *idem.*, Acta et Agenda 52 et seq.

[56] *Lipstein*, Principles of the Conflict of Laws (above n. 18).

[57] Rome Convention on the law applicable to contractual obligations of 19 June 1980, consolidated version, ABl. EG C 27/34.

[58] Individual studies are e.g. *Kurt Lipstein*, Les normes fixant leur propre domaine d'application; les expériences anglaises et américaines, in: Droit international privé, Travaux du comité français de droit international privé (1977/1979) 187–201 (Centre National de la Recherche Scientifique); *idem.*, Inherent limitations in statutes and the conflict of laws: Int. Comp. L. Q. (1977) 884–902 (see in particular 898 et seq.).

[59] See the comprehensive review in *Forsyth* 470 et seq.

From very early on, Lipstein was not only concerned with European law, but also with the question of whether and how private international law and more specifically international contract law should be unified within the European Community.[60] Again, his forward thinking and practice oriented views become apparent.

It was a particularly auspicious choice when the editors of the *International Encyclopedia of Comparative Law*, appointed Kurt Lipstein as chief editor of the third volume on Private International Law. Once again he adopted a comparativist approach to private international law. Lipstein's work never ignored the link to positive law, nor did it simply provide a mere restatement and discussion of it. His views were in depth and focused on the subject specific field of international conflict of laws.

As editor of the private international law volumes, Lipstein was responsible for their publication and continued with this task until his death. With his meticulous scholarly style, linguistic elegance and extensive knowledge he was able to improve the substantive content of numerous contributions from around the world. He published three of his own, central sections, namely: interpersonal conflict of laws,[61] trusts,[62] and characterization.[63] In the first and particularly in the last contribution, Lipstein was able to build on the fundamental principles he had established in his Hague lectures. Once again, characteristic of these contributions is Lipstein's unique comparativist approach. He reaches the conclusion that characterization is not based on facts, but rather on the underlying legal relationship and that its function and purpose, not its technical connotation, is the object of the inquiry.

Another theoretical problem to which Lipstein has turned his attention on several occasions, is the relationship of foreign characterization and *renvoi*. In his most recent contribution on the issue,[64] he reaches uniquely reasoned and sophisticated conclusions. Lipstein was also drawn to the specific

[60] *Kurt Lipstein,* Comments on Art. 1 to 21 of the Draft Convention, in: European Private International Law of Obligations, in *Ole Lando/Bernd v. Hoffmann/Kurt Siehr* (eds.)(1978) 155–164; *idem.,* Preliminary Draft Convention on the Law Applicable to Contractual and Non-Contractual Obligations, in: Harmonisation of Private International Law by the E.E.C., in *Kurt Lipstein* (ed.) (1978) 1–14; *idem.,* Characteristic performance, A new concept in the conflict of laws in matters of contract for the EEC: Northwestern J. Int. L. Bus. 3 (1981) 402–414.

[61] *Kurt Lipstein/I. Szászy,* Interpersonal conflict of laws, in: Int. Enc. Comp.L. III: Private International Law (1985) Chap. 10,3 – 35.

[62] *Kurt Lipstein,* Trusts, in: Int. Enc. Comp. L. III: Private International Law (1994) Chap. 23,3 – 40.

[63] *Lipstein,* Characterization (above n. 52) 3–67.

[64] *Kurt Lipstein,* Unusual bedfellows – renvoi and foreign characterization joined together, Private law in the international arena, Liber amicorum Kurt Siehr (2000) 405–412; see above *idem.,* Two basic problems of private international law revisited: King's College L.J. 10 (1999) 167–176.

issue of the *renvoi* problem and presented his examinations from invariably differing perspectives on numerous occasions. As part of his work at the *Institut de Droit International*, Lipstein was able to focus on the issue extensively. Only a few years following his election to the *Institut*, Lipstein was given the honourable appointment of rapporteur to the 4th Commission. He prepared a resolution[65] on the *renvoi* issue[66], the formulation of which is based on an examination by Wilhelm Wengler.[67] But Lipstein's approach is considerably different to that of Wengler. Lipstein pragmatically refrains from a theoretical overhaul of the *renvoi* problem, instead focusing on the prevalence of *renvoi* in the conflict of law rules in national systems. The quintessence of the resolution is that *renvoi* generally is applicable, and only where there are alternative connections, or where there is a free choice of law, should *renvoi* be excluded. This is in accordance with German private international law, which in Art 4 II, Art 35 I 1 EGBGB treats a choice of law as being a choice of the applicable substantive provisions of law; and, where alternative connections exist, excludes *renvoi*,[68] according to Art 4 I 1 EGBGB on the basis that it is incompatible with the meaning of the referral. The Articles of the Resolution are not presented in the form of binding rules, but instead as recommendations. This approach and the omission of further legal aspects related to the recognition of foreign private international law enabled Kurt Lipstein's largely unchanged draft to be adopted as the resolution. What was not accepted was his recommendation to reject "hidden" *renvoi*.[69] Nevertheless, the adoption of the resolution by the Institute must be considered a great personal triumph of the then 90 year old Kurt Lipstein. He was able to achieve that which had failed on two previous attempts. On those two occasions, in the years between 1896–1900 and 1957–1965, the Commission attempted to reach a majority on the issue of a resolution on the

---

[65] *Kurt Lipstein*, Taking Foreign Private International Law to Account, Session de Berlin, 1999: Ann. Inst. Dr. int. 68 (1999–11) 89–153; Resolution also given in: IPRax 2000, 51–52; on the resolution, see *Jayme*, Tagung (above n. 20) 61–62.

[66] The preparatory works including the responses by the Commission Members are published in: The taking into consideration of foreign private international law, Travaux préparatoires, 4th Commission, Session de Berlin, 1999 – Première partie: Travaux préparatoires: Ann. Inst. Dr. int. 68 (1999-I) 13–56; on this see *Erik Jayme*, Völkerrecht und Internationales Privatrecht: Interdependenz und Interaktion: IPRax 1998, 139 et seq. (citation: Völkerrecht).

[67] *Wilhelm Wengler*, Die Beachtlichkeit des fremden Kollisionsrechts, Eine Bestandsaufnahme und Besinnung zum Renvoi-Problem: Internationales Recht und Diplomatie 1956, 56–74; referenced in *Jayme*, Völkerrecht (above) 140.

[68] *Heinz Georg Bamberger/Herbert Roth (-Stephan Lorenz)*, Kommentar zum BGB[11] (2008) Art. 4 EGBGB marg. no. 8 with further references.

[69] See *Lipstein*, in: The taking into consideration of foreign private international law (above n. 67) 46 et seq.; cf. *Jayme*, Tagung (above n. 20) 62. On hidden renvoi, see critically Münchener Kommentar zum BGB (-Hans-Jürgen Sonnenberger) (2006) Art. 4 EGBGB marg. no. 42 et seq. with further references.

issue of *renvoi*.[70] It was Kurt Lipstein's profound comparativist knowledge, his common sense, negotiation skills and his personality, which all contributed to the success of his resolution.

V. Kurt Lipstein, the Teacher

Much can be learnt about Lipstein as a teacher by reading the many comments and condolences dedicated to Kurt Lipstein on the Squire Law Library website. He is honoured and remembered with great fondness by different generations of former students. Kurt Lipstein was a true gentleman who treated everyone that he met with the same respect. To teach was for him to illustrate rather than instruct. Those who spoke with him are just as unlikely to forget his friendly interest and patience, composure and modesty, generosity and warmth, charm and humour, as his intellectual brilliance, the clarity of his reasoning, and wealth of knowledge. His ability to share his love and passion for the law with others earned him the status of a much admired and successful teacher.

From the beginning of his time in Cambridge Kurt Lipstein was a teacher. He began in 1936 with supervisions and continued with these well beyond his retirement. The Lord Justice of Appeal Michael Kerr (1921–2001) expressed his gratitude for his supervisor Kurt Lipstein.[71] He held his last supervisory session just two weeks before his death. He held lectures and seminars on a wide range of subjects from Roman Law – at the beginning of his academic career and to which he later returned to lecture –, European Law, Comparative Law, Private International Law and Public International Law, to Contract, Torts and English Legal Methods. The website of the Eminant Scholar Archive of the Squire Law Library has posted a video of Kurt Lipstein's last lecture in Legal Methods, held on the 17th July 2006.[72]

In addition to lecturing and supervision, Kurt Lipstein also taught in the Squire Law Library, which was only four years older than him, and over the many years worked in all three of the Squire Law Library's homes. For 72 years Kurt Lipstein faithfully followed, influenced and was devoted to the development of this Library. He often vividly described[73] how he helped new (and old) users of the Library to find their way around. Many discussions on substantive issues of law would transpire, from which users would

---

[70] See in-depth assessment in *Forsyth* 476 et seq.; *Jayme*, Tagung (above n. 20) 62.
[71] *Michael Kerr*, As far as I remember (2002) Chap. 30. On the internation of both Michael Kerr and Kurt Lipstein see also *Lipstein*, Cambridge 1933–2002, 765.
[72] At www.squire.law.cam.ac.uk/eminent_scholars.
[73] For specific memories see *Hepple*, Kurt Lipstein (above n. 1) 19, *v. Bar* 749 et seq, and *Zimmermann* (above n. 1) 296–297.

gain inspiration and ideas that were gratefully remembered decades later. This gratitude is documented in the introductory footnotes and forewords of numerous publications. The "Times"[74] obituary notes amongst his pupils in Cambridge six Lords Of Appeal in Ordinary, more Lords Justices of Appeal and "seemingly innumerable High Court Judges". He taught a countless number of non-English lawyers at the very successful courses at the International Summer School in English Legal Methods in Cambridge of which he was a co-founder.[75] It is they who carry on the memory of Kurt Lipstein, a remarkable man, a teacher and his work.

---

[74] The Times from 18 Jan. 2007.
[75] For an account of a seminar by Kurt Lipstein in the Summer School 1999, see *Thomas Hirschmann:* JuS 1999, Issue 11 (cover pages).

The Proper Law of the Contract[*]

More than any other branch of the law, the science of Conflict of Laws lends itself to a fruitful study from a comparative point of view.[1] For though its character is that of municipal law, it tends to find the most practical solutions in cases where a clash of two different systems of law seems unavoidable. Rigid national principles are scarce and the science seems altogether unorthodox. Within existing systems of Conflict of Laws, it is the principle of the law governing contracts which is open to the greatest number of diverse

---

[Editorial note: essay by *Kurt Lipstein, Jean S. Brunschig, Fredrick Jerie,* and *Karl M. Rodman*; first published in St John's Law Review 12 (1938), 242–246.]

[*] This article concerns itself with a comparative study of some aspects of the Continental and Anglo-American Systems.

Note: The authors wish to express their sincere gratitude to Professor H. C. Gutteridge, LL.M., K.C., Fellow of Trinity Hall of the University of Cambridge, under whose guidance this material was gathered during a seminar on the subject Lent Term 1938 at the University of Cambridge.

[1] See Kuhn, Comparative Commentaries on Private International Law; 4 Ficker, Rechtsvergleichendes Handwoerterbuch (1933) 371–390.

It is impossible to enter into the question of the relation between international law and conflict of laws. Reference may be made to the discussion by Arminjon (1928) (I) Rec. des cours 433–509; (1929) Revue de droit international et de legislation comparee 680–98 and a forthcoming article by Dr. Lipstein containing a full bibliography. We regard the attempt to find the basis of a system of conflict of laws in the conception of sovereignty as unfortunate; for either it means nothing more than that every state may introduce such rules of conflict of laws as it thinks fit. Or it may mean that every system of laws has to respect the sovereignty of other systems. Though this may be adequate (but not theoretically sound) in situations wholly connected with one territory, it fails to fulfill its task in cases connected with several systems of law. For what is the meaning of »respecting sovereignty«? Does it mean the universal recognition of the *lex patriae* (so Zitelmann, Frankenstein, Pillet) the *lex domicilii* (so v. Bar), or the *lex loci contractus*?

No answer can be given here; but it may be pointed out that it ends in a dispute upon questions of *a priori*.

solutions. This, because of the fact that contracts, more than any other legal institution, are less static than dynamic. Moreover, they are created by the free will of the parties. Thus, we believe, that a study of the solutions used in a number of European countries might be of use to the legal profession of the United States even though practice and doctrine are far more established there than in Europe.

Conflict of Laws or Private International Law, as it is more commonly called in Europe, has played the part of Cinderella in the codifications of most European systems, and | within the few systems that have attempted a codification of it, the rules governing contracts have often been consciously omitted. Thus we find detailed rules only in the Austrian aGBB² and the parts of Czechoslovakia and Yugoslavia which formerly belonged to the old Austrian Empire, in addition to Italy³ and Poland.⁴ In France, Germany and Switzerland the matter has been left to the courts as in the case of England and the United States. But as the role of precedent in Europe is a different one from that in the Common Law of England, case law has not been quite successful in introducing undisputed rules. For precedents are not binding upon any but the highest courts and even these are empowered to overrule their own precedents under certain conditions. This power is, of course, also exercised by Anglo-American courts but so rarely as not to seriously shake the ruling power of case precedents. In practice, however, European case law does establish a certain continuity, if only for the reason that inferior courts are reluctant to contradict cases decided by the supreme courts for fear of being overruled and thus to hamper the chances of promotion of the judges concerned.⁵ On the whole we may therefore say that a certain practice has been established, but exceptions exist and there is always a certain chance of being able to criticize, attack and finally bring about a change in this sphere of no man's land.

Writers have been only too willing to accept this task, and during the past forty years an immense literature has sprung up. Of recent text-book writers who have not limited themselves to a descriptive discussion we have to mention Arminjon, Niboyet, Frankenstein, Nolde, Sauser-Hall, Jeanprêtre and Haudek⁶ who have brought into bold relief the | problem as it exists on

---

² 4, 34–37.

³ Art. 9, § 2. disp. rel. c.c.; art. 58, c. comm. (1933).

⁴ Arts. 7–10, Statute of 2.8.1926.

⁵ The career of judges, on the continent of Europe, is distinct from that of other professional lawyers. After having completed their course of education, they have to decide whether they intend to go to the Bar or to the Bench, where they start as Assistant Judges, both in Regional and County Courts.

⁶ 2 Arminjon, Precis de droit international prive (2d ed. 1934) 231 sq.; Niboyet, Manuel de droit international prive (2d ed. 1928) 789 sq. no. 681; (1927) (I) Rec. des cours 1–12; 2 Frankenstein, Internationales Privatrecht (1929) 123 sq. no.; Jeanpetre, Les conflits de lois

the Continent. In England the influence of Story, the great American jurist, has, during the last century, largely been replaced by the work of the late Professor Dicey, but of late the writings and teachings of Professor H. C. Gutteridge and Dr. G. C. Cheshire[7] have been well received by scholars and practitioners alike. American legal thought on the subject, initiated by Judge Story, is now best represented by the work of Professors Beale, Lorenzen and Cook.[8] Before expressing the views and tendencies outlined by these writers, it seems advisable to touch on the position of the law as it stands today.

The French Code Civile does not contain any pertinent provisions but the courts have taken a steady course and a well established »jurisprudence« (case law)[9] enables us to draw definite conclusions.[10] The governing principle is that of autonomy of will, *i.e.,* of free choice of law by the parties.[11] However, it happens, and not only occasionally, that the parties have omitted to express their intention. It is then that canons of interpretation come into play. First, the judge is called upon to investigate whether a tacit reference to any system of law places that contract under the rules of that system.[12] Failing this, he has to apply certain tests, whether|as canons of interpretation or as objective tests cannot be stated with any certainty.[13] These tests are as follows: (1) If both parties are of the same nationality then the *lex patria* or the law of their nationality governs. If the parties are domiciled in any other country than that of their nationality then the law of their domicile gov-

---

en matiere d'obligations contractuelles selon la jurisprudence et la doctrine aux Estats-Unis (1936); Haudek, Die Bedeutung des Parteiwillens im Internationalen Privatrecht (1931); Sauser-Hall, Zeitschrift fuer Schweizerisches (1925) 271a–320a; Nolde, *Annuarie de l'Institut de Droit International* (1925) (32) 50–145, 501–508; (1927 (I) *id.* at 937–954; (II) *id.* at 194–225, 336.

[7] Professor H. C. Gutteridge (1936) Cambridge L. J. 19; Dr. G. C. Cheshire, Private International Law (2d ed. 1938) 241 *et seq.*

[8] Beale, A Treatise of the Conflict of Laws (1936); Beale, Cases on Conflict of Laws (1909); Lorenzen, Cases on Conflict of Laws; Lorenzen, A Comparative Study of the Law of Bills and Notes (1919).

[9] Precedent, in continental Europe, as we have stated above, does not carry the same weight as in Anglo-American law. Binding upon the supreme courts, but subject to overruling by a special form of judgment by the full court, it is only of persuasive authority with regard to inferior courts. The latter are not bound by their own previous decisions.

[10] This would not appear so from the attitude taken by text-book writers who attempt to introduce their own solution into the existing law.

[11] Cass. req. 28.12 (1936); (1937) Rev. crit. 684, with note by Battifol; Cass. civ. 31.5 (1932); (1934) Rev. crit. 909, with note by Niboyet; Cass. civ. 12.5 (1930); (1931) Clunet 164; *cf.* (1930) Clunet 417. See also Cass. civ. 5.12 (1910); Sirey (1911) 1, 129, with note by Lyon-Caen; (1911) Rev. Darras 395; Cass. req. 19.5 (1884); Sirey (1885) 1, 113, with note by Lacointa; *cf.* Haudek, *op. cit. supra* note 6, at 59.

[12] Battifol (1935) Rev. crit. 629; Cour d'Appel of Colmar (1934) Clunet 976; Lyon-Caeon, Sirey (1911) 1, 130; Cass. req. 10, 12 (1907); Sirey (1910) 1, 132.

[13] See Niboyet (1936) Rev. crit. 464.

erns.[14] (2) If the parties are of different nationalities then the *lex loci contractus* or the law of the place of contracting governs.[15] (3) If the place of contracting is difficult to ascertain then the law of the place of performance will be applied.[16] (4) Finally, the court will apply that system which would uphold or look with the greatest favor on the contract.[17]

Arminjon suggests a slight change in this order reversing the position of tests numbers two and three. Moreover, he suggests that in the case of test number three the *lex patria* of the debtor should supercede the *lex solutionis*, the law of the place of performance, provided it is a unilateral contract.[18] These contentions, however, have not found much favor in the decided cases.

| In Switzerland the law governing the essential validity of contracts has been summed up in the following words by the Tribunal Federal, the highest court of that country, in a recent case:

»Following a long line of decisions of the Tribunal Federal concerning the essential validity of contracts, we hold that that system of law is applicable which the parties intended submission to when the contract was concluded or lacking an express declaration, that system of law which they would have intended to apply if they had considered this question at all. The system of this presumed intention is the system of that country with which the contract in question has the closest local connection.«[19]

---

[14] *Cf.* Lyon-Caen, note to Sirey (1911) 1, 129, and to (1900) 1, 161, quoting many older cases. See Cass. req. 19.5 (1894); Sirey (1885) 1, 113; Cour d'Appel, Douai 2.11 (1933); Sirey (1934) 2, 109 (2).

[15] Cour d'Appel, Colmar, 162 (1937); (1937) Rev. crit. 687, with note by Battifol; cf. note to Sirey (1913) 4. See Cass. req. 28.12 (1936); (1937) Rev. crit. 684; Cass. civ. 15.5 (1935); (1936) Rev. crit. 464; Battifol (1937) Rev. crit. (1937) 434; Cass. civ. 31.5 (1931); (1934) Rev. crit. 911; Sirey (1933) 1, 17, with note by Niboyet; Cass. civ. 15.12 (1910); Sirey (1911) 1, 129; (1911) Rev. Darras 395; Cass. civ. 6.2 (1900); Sirey (1900) 1, 161; Cour d'Appel, Paris, 25.6 (1931); (1932) Clunet 933 (5); Cour d'Appel, Colmar, 11.3 (1933); (1934) Rev. crit. 138; Cour d'Appel, Douai, 2.11 (1933); Sirey (1934) 2, 109 (regarding it as the presumed intention of the parties, contrary to the well established doctrine of the Cour de Cassation). See also Colmar 17.2 (1937); Battifol (1934) Rev. crit. 639/40.

[16] Decisions favouring the *lex loci solutionis* are gaining ground. Cour d'Appel, Paris, 26.3 (1936); (1936) Rev. crit. 487; Battifol (1937) Rev. crit. 435; Cass. civ. 31.5 (1932); (1934) Rev. crit. 909; Cour d'Appel, Paris, 28.2 (1935); (1935) Rev. crit. 748, with note; Cour d'Appel, Metz, 12.4 (1934); (1935) Clunet 988 (the court purports to interpret the intention of the parties); Cour d'Appel, Colmar (Belfort) 2.5 (1933); (1934) Clunet 424; (1934) Rev. crit. 163; Battifol (1935) Rev. crit. 631. But. cf. Colmar, 30.1 and 13.3 (1933); (1934) Clunet 951; Battifol, *op. supra* note 12, at 630 (where the court was unable to locate the place of execution of the contract).

[17] Weiss, Manuel de droit international prive (9th ed. 1925) 571 sq.; 2 Arminjon, *op. cit: supra* note 6, at 248 sq. No cases can be quoted in favour of this proposition.

[18] 2 Arminjon, *op. cit. supra* note 6, at 250.

[19] Arret du Tribunal Federal, Receuil officiel (A. T. F.) 40-II–391 and 63-II–307. But free choice of law exists only at the time the contract is concluded. It does not go so far as to allow the parties to state, during the litigation, that they intended to apply Swiss law when

The Swiss courts then, we can say, attempt to find the proper law of the contract – that law which is most closely connected with the contract. It is interesting to note that this has usually been held to be the law of the place of performance of the contract.[20] In cases where the places of performance are situated in more than one country, and one of the places happens to be Swiss, then Swiss law will be applied.[21] In the case of a unilateral contract the law governing will be held to be the law of the debtor's domicile. In the same manner when a Swiss firm enters into a type of contract known as a »massenvertraege« or a »contrad' adhesion« [editorial note: contrat d'adhésion] – a standard contract by one debtor with a large number of creditors in various countries, the law of the debtor's domicile is applied, *i.e.*, the Swiss law.[22] In the event the court is unable to find | the »proper law of the contract«, then it will apply the *lex fori* or the law of the forum.[23]

Contracts concluded in Czechoslovakia between nationals and foreigners are governed by Czech law even if the contract is to be performed in a foreign country or the debtor is a foreigner.[24] The same system of law, *i.e.*, the *lex loci contractus*, is applied even though the contract is between foreigners, if the contract has been concluded in Czechoslovakia. However, foreigners have the option of stipulating, in their contract, that another system of law is to apply and this choice is binding on the Czech courts. They are limited in their choice to a system of law which has some connection with the contract.[25] Although on the Continent it is the general rule that the law of a man's nationality follows him wherever he goes, Czech law permits its citizens autonomy of will in making contracts outside of Czechoslovakia. This permission extends not only to a Czech and a foreigner but to two Czechs contracting in a foreign land. However, if the contract is to be performed in Czechoslovakia then Czech law will be applied.[26] Where two foreigners conclude a contract in a foreign land to be performed in Czechoslovakia they are permitted a free choice of the law governing that agreement. These rules apply to Austria as well.[27]

---

the circumstances of the case point to a different system. The declaration by the parties during the case to apply a certain system of law not specified in the contract can serve only as an indication to the judge of what they intended when entering into the contract. But this presumption or guide is in no way binding upon the judge. A. T. F. 63-II–44; A. T. F. 62-II–125; A. T. F. 60-II–300.

[20] A. T. F. 63-II–308.

[21] A. T. F. 57-II–72.

[22] A. T. F. 44-II–432.

[23] A. T. F. 44-II–492.

[24] Obcansky Zakonnik (Czech Code) § 36.

[25] *Ibid.*

[26] *Supra* note 24, § 4.

[27] *Supra* note 24, § 35. Unilateral contracts concluded by foreigners, being the debtors, are governed by Czech law or by the law of the nationality of the foreigners, depending upon which law is more favorable to the contract.

According to Italian law, contracts are governed by the *lex loci contractus* but if the parties are of the same nationality then by their *lex patria*. But it is always open to the parties to prove a different choice of law.[28]

The Polish Statute of 1926 provides an infinite variety of rules. The parties are free to choose for their contract one of the following systems: the *lex patria*, the *lex domicilii*, the *lex loci contractus*, the *lex loci solutionis*, or the *lex res sitae*.[29] Lacking a choice by the parties, the following system | is applicable: in contracts referring to stock exchange and other markets, the law governing the market concerned; as to land, the *lex res sitae;* for retail commerce, the law of the residence of the vendor; all insurance contracts, the law governing the insurance company; professional contracts, the law where the profession is exercised; labor contracts generally, the law of the place where the labor was done.[30] In all other contracts not mentioned above: if the parties are domiciled in the same country, the law of the domicile; if not domiciled in the same country, then the law of the debtor's domicile in the case of unilateral contracts; in the case of bilateral contracts, or if the domicile of the debtor is unknown, the *lex loci contractus*. For the purpose of this statute the *lex loci contractus* is the law of that place where the offeror receives the acceptance.[31]

More general rules, in this respect, are applied in Germany. In the first instance, the principle of free choice of law by the parties is recognized.[32] However, this does not mean that the parties may choose any law they may desire. A decision of the Reichsgericht, the highest court of the country, handed down in 1895, before the introduction of the new code of 1900, but which is still regarded as authority today, held that a marriage brokerage contract between two domiciled Saxons, executed and performed in Saxony, could not be submitted by the parties to the law of Prussia.[33] It is therefore suggested that the parties may choose the system of law they desire only so far as their contract has a certain connection with the system chosen.

In case the court is unable to find an expressed intention in the contract it

---

[28] Art. 9, § 2, disp. prel. c.c.; Art. 58, c. comm. Udina, 6 Repertoire de droit international 510–12.

[29] Art. 7, Statute of 2.8 (1926); cf. Makarov. in Leske-Loewenfeld: 8 Die Rechtsverfolgung im Internationalen Verkehr (1929) 145 sq. no.

[30] *Id.* art. 8.

[31] *Id.* art. 9.

[32] *E.g.,* Gz. 145, 121 (1934); IPR. Rspr. (1934) n. 29; I. W. 3121 (1935) 33; Bull. Inst. Jur. Int. 71, no. 8792; (1935) Rev. crit. 447, with note by Mezger surveying the cases; RGZ. IPR. Rspr. (1934) n. 19; RGZ. 142, 417, 23; (1933) n. 21; (1931) nn. 30–32; (1930) nn. 30–31, 40, 48; (1929) nn. 31, 36, 43. It must suffice to refer to these cases and to Lewald, Das Deutsche Internationale Privatrecht nos. 260–268, 10; Repertoire de droit international 71, n. 5; 73, n.–12; Haudek, *op. cit. supra* note 6, with numerous quotations at 47, n. 2.

[33] RGZ. 44, 300; Lewald, *op. cit. supra,* at 212, n. 269; 10 Rep. 79, n. 39.

has to look for a tacit one. Lacking this, | the court is entitled to find the intention of the parties from the circumstances of the case and what system of law the parties would have chosen if they had ever considered the matter.[34] In addition the court may, in the last instance, apply the test of the *lex loci solutionis* – the law of the place of performance.[35] It is difficult to say when and how the courts apply one or the other of these tests, as it is nearly always possible to construe a fictitious intention and find that intention to be the *lex loci solutionis*.[36] It may be stated with some confidence that they are applied vicariously and that the *lex loci solutionis* is used as the last resort.

It is universally agreed that the English rule with respect to the essential validity of a contract calls for the application of the proper law of the contract. This, according to Professor Dicey's Rule 155, is the rule that governs, and he states it to be: »The proper law [of the contract] is the law by which the parties to a contract intend the contract to be governed, or the law or laws to which the parties intended to submit themselves.«

The English courts have paid, and still continue to pay, great deference to the authority of Dicey, but no case has yet arisen wherein there was an express intention that a specific system of law should apply, with the possible exception of the case of the *Torni*,[37] but this is a doubtful case at best. Inevitably the courts are forced to deduce a presumed intention. This, of course, is really an objective test. Cheshire and Westlake[38] both contend that the courts adopt the objective test in every instance and therefore reject Dicey's theory of the proper law.[39]

In attempting to find this proper law of the contract the courts have availed themselves of a number of rebuttable presumptions. The first of these presumptions is the *lex loci contractus* or the law of the place where the contract was | made. This is always indulged in when the contract is to be performed where it was made or where no place of performance is specified.[40] If, on the other hand, the agreement between the parties is to be performed at a place other than that of the making, the presumption is that the law of the place of performance was intended by the parties.[41] Thirdly,

---

[34] See *supra* note 32; RGZ. IPR. Rspr. (1930) nn. 32–33, 34; RGZ. 126, 196 (1929) n. 45. Lewald, *op. cit. supra* note 32, at 212, n. 269; 221, n. 276; 10 Rep. 74–75, nn. 14–17 and the cases quoted there.

[35] See *supra* note 32; RGZ. IPR. Rspr. (1932) n. 27; (1930) nn. 30, 31; (1929) nn. 33, 37, 38, 47, 48, 49; Lewald, *op. cit. supra* note 32, at 224, n. 281, with references.

[36] See Lewald, *loc. cit. supra* note 32.

[37] The Torni (1932) Probate 27 at 78.

[38] Cheshire, Private International Law, 249 *et seq.*; Westlake, Private International Law (7th ed. Bentwich) 299 *et seq.*

[39] Dicey, Conflict of Laws (5th ed. Keith) Rule 155 at 647 *et seq.* and 958 *et seq.*

[40] P. & O. v. Shand (1865) 3 Moo P. C. (N. s.) 272.

[41] Chatonay v. Brazilian Submarine Telegraph Co. (1891) 1 Q. B. 79; Benain v. Debono (1924) A. C. 514.

and this is a very rare case, where, in the case of maritime contracts, specific reference is made by the parties to the law of the flag of the ship as the governing rule, a court will adopt that law as conforming with the intent of the contracting parties.[42]

Although throughout the numerous jurisdictions that comprise the United States, support can be found for almost every doctrine concerning the law governing the essential validity of contracts, it seems to be widely held, if in fact it is not the majority rule, as stated by Corpus Juris: »A contract is governed as to its intrinsic validity and effect by the law with reference to which the parties intended, or fairly may have presumed to have intended, to contract, the real place of the contract being a matter of mutual intention except in exceptional circumstances evincing a purpose in making the contract to commit a fraud on the law.«[43] »The intention of the parties may be either expressed or implied from their acts and conduct at the time of making the contract.«[44] However, express provisions as to the law they desire to govern their contract must be made in good faith by the parties or the court will not give effect to them.[45]

When construing this intent, the American courts have usually presumed, when no further statement was made, that the law of the place of contracting was intended by the parties because of the fact that they made their contract in that place, or, as it has been put, the contract is governed by the *lex loci contractus* unless a contrary intent appears to have been in the minds of the parties.

| However, where the contract is made in one country or place, to be performed, wholly or in part, in another place, the proper law, particularly as to performance, may be presumed to be the law of the place of performance.[46]

Neither of these main presumptions is, as to the leading rules, conclusive as to the intention of the parties but they are important indicia of that fact.[47] Professor Beale does not see the intention of the parties as the basis of the law which ought govern contracts. His interpretation of the American cases does not place the intention of the parties as the leading rule. Considerable may be said for that opinion as it is often very difficult to find out,

---

[42] Lloyd v. Gilbert (1865) L. R. 1 Q. B. 115.

[43] 13 C. J. 277, § 19 *et seq.*

[44] Bertonneau v. Southern Pacific Co., 17 Cal. App. 439, 120 Pac. 53 (1911).

[45] 2 Beale, *op. cit. supra* note 8, § 332.23 *et seq.*

[46] Northwestern Mutual Life Ins. Co. v. McCune, 223 U. S. 234, 32 Sup. Ct. 220 (1911); Am. Spirits Mfg. Co. v. Albany, 164 Ill. 186, 45 N. E. 442 (1896); Hall v. Cordell, 142 U. S. 116, 12 Sup. Ct. 154 (1891); Doughery v. Equitable Life Ins. Co., 266 N. Y. 171, 193 N. E. 897 (1891); Old Dominion Copper Mining Co. v. Bigelow, 203 Mass. 159, 89 N. E. 193 (1909).

[47] Mayer v. Rochw., 15 A. 235.

from the mere reading of a case, whether the judge applied the *lex loci contractus* as a rigid rule, or found that rule to have been intended by the parties.[48] It is sufficient to say, however, that rigid rules are applied in some of the states of the Union and the question of whether the rule which seeks to find the intention of the parties or one which lays down an unalterable legal principle is the leading rule is merely an academic quibble. A discussion of the relative merits of the two opposing camps is, however, imperative, and is dealt with in detail below.

Capacity

In French law, capacity to enter into contractual relations is governed by the *lex patria*, or the law of the nationality of the contracting parties, according to the statutory provisions of Article 3, Section 3 of the Code Civile. To this is added the reservation that a foreigner dealing with French citizens in France cannot avail himself of his incapacity if he acted fraudulently and the Frenchman acted in good faith and with due caution.[49]

| Likewise in Swiss Law, the question of contractual capacity is governed by the *lex patria*. But foreigners, capable according to Swiss Law, cannot claim exemption afforded them by their national law.[50] This is also the rule according to the law of Germany.[51]

In accord with the general rule of the Continent as exampled above, the law of Czechoslovakia applies the *lex patria* concerning the question of capacity of foreigners to contract in Czechoslovakia.[52]

Capacity, in Italy, is also governed by the *lex patria* with the reservation that the law of the place of making the contract shall govern commercial contracts.[53] In Poland the *lex patria* is always applied.[54]

The Anglo-American common law here makes a rather sharp break with the Continental tendency and refuses to recognize the doctrine of a personal law following a man wherever he may go. In England, Dicey supported the

---

[48] 2 Beale, *op. cit. supra* note 8, § 332.53 *et seq.*

[49] de Lizardi v. Chaise, Cass. req. 16.1 (1861); Sirey (1861) 1, 305, with note by Massé; Lyon, 30.4 (1907); (1908) Clunet 146; (1908) Rev. Darras 630; Cassin (1930) (IV) Rec. des cours 794, n. 94; Niboyet, *op. cit. supra* note 6, at 712, n. 600.

[50] Code civil suisse, Title Final, art. 59; 12 a 14.

[51] *Id.* art. 7, § 3 EGBGB; Lewald, *op. cit. supra* note 32, at 58, nn. 73–77, with cases.

[52] *Id.* § 36. Where foreigners are incapable according to the law of their nationality although this fact was not known to the other party, the contract cannot be enforced but the innocent party has a claim for damages.

[53] Idina, 6 Rep. de droit international 510, n. 127, quoting App. Milan 1.7 (1914); (1914) Rivista di diritto internazionale 610.

[54] Art. 1, Statute of 2.8 (1926).

view that the law of the domicile of the parties should govern, but made vital exceptions to that rule, particularly in the case of mercantile contracts. In the case of these latter contracts, all agree that the *lex loci contractus* must apply although Dr. Cheshire would apply the proper law of the contract to this phase of its validity as well.[55]

There is little doubt that in the United States the capacity of the parties to make a contract is, as a general rule, to be determined by the law of the place where the contract is entered into.[56] However, the law of the place of making the contract will not be given effect, as regards capacity, if it is contrary to the public policy of the forum.[57]

| Form

In French law formalities are governed by the law of the place where the transaction takes place.[58] This is also the rule in Swiss law.[59]

But in Germany, Poland and Czechoslovakia the law governing form is the proper law of the contract. Both countries, however, will recognize the formal validity of the contract if the *lex loci contractus* has been complied with.[60] In Italy the rule prevailing is the *locus regit actum* – the place where the act occurred – but if the parties are of the same nationality it is sufficient that the *lex patria* of the parties has been complied with.[61]

Dr. Cheshire, in his recent work, appeals for the proper law of the contract as governing with respect to form, but he has no authority for that proposition.[62] It is usually held to be the English rule that the *locus regit actum* governs, although no cases seem to exist on the question of the law governing the formal validity of a contract, outside of marriage and revenue cases.

The American rule follows the general trend as stated above.[63] However, as respects formalities in the nature of the Common Law Statute of Frauds, Professor Williston suggests that such requirements be considered a matter of validity instead of a requirement of procedure or evidence, since the parties to a contract normally observe the formalities required to make it en-

---

[55] Cheshire, *op. cit. supra* note 38, at 205 *et seq.*

[56] Mathews v. Murchison, 17 Fed. 760 (Cir. Ct. N. C. 1883); Union Nat. Bank v. Chapman, 169 N. Y. 538. 162 N. E. 672 (1902).

[57] Geneva First Nat. Bank v. Shan, 90 Tenn. 237, 59 L. R. A. 498.

[58] Cass. req. 19.5 (1884); Sirey (1885) 1, 113, with note (4) by Lacointa, quoting many cases.

[59] A. T. F. 46-II-490.

[60] Art. 11, EGBGB; art. 5, Statute of 2.8 (1926).

[61] Art. 9 (1) disp. prel. c.c.

[62] Cheshire, *op. cit. supra* note 7, at 243.

[63] Roubicek v. Haddad, 5 L. A. 938.

forceable in the place where they are contracting. For if the Statute of Frauds is held to be a procedural matter that is the concern of the *lex fori* and as we have stated it is invariably difficult and often impossible to determine in advance what the forum will be. The cases are, on this point, somewhat divided.[64]

| Reference to Material Parts of Foreign Systems

Not infrequently parties domiciled in the same country and of the same nationality, making a contract to be performed at the domicile, happen to include in their contracts some reference to a foreign system of law. This does not mean that the system is now governed entirely by some foreign system of law wholly unconnected with the contract. In fact it amounts to nothing more than that the parties, instead of inserting as contractual provisions all those rules of that foreign system in question, pertinent to their contract, have taken the shorter course of referring to those rules as such. A recent tendency to introduce such a limited choice of law (liberté des conventions)[65] – limited to a defined set of foreign material rules has, however, been stopped by the Cour de Cassation, the highest French court.[66] Thus it remains open to the court to determine whether such contracts are to be governed by municipal or foreign law.

The reference of the parties to some defined set of rules of foreign law appears to exempt the contract altogether from the sphere of the application of German law owing to the wide discretion left to the parties and owing to the liberal interpretation of the parties' intention to subject the contract to some other system of law. It appears therefore that a *liberté des conventions*, such as proposed by French and German lawyers, and as dismissed by French courts, will only lead to the desired results if the parties refer expressly to that limited part of the foreign system of law they wish to apply as a contractual provision of their contract. They must also express their wish not to take the contract out of the system which would govern it but for the reference to|some rules of foreign law.[67] A slightly less rigid attitude is taken in Switzerland,[68] Austria and Czechoslovakia.[69]

---

[64] 1 Williston, Contracts § 600.

[65] Arminjon, *op. cit. supra* note 6, at 310 sq.; Niboyet (1927) (I) Rec. des cours 57.

[66] Haudek, *op. cit. supra* note 6, at 41, n. 5, quotes; Cour d'Appel, Rennes, 16.7 (1926); (1927) Clunet 659; (1927) Rev. Darras 523; ca. Cass. civ. 19.2 (1930); (1931) Clunet 90; (1930) Rev. Darras 282; Limoges, 12.10 (1928); (1929) Clunet 355; 3 Jahrbuch fuer Schiedsgerichtswesen 374; *cf.* Mann (1937) (17) British Yearbook of International Law 101.

[67] Haudek, *op. cit. supra* note 6, at 49 and n. 1, 50; Lewald, *op. cit. supra* note 32, at 202–207, nn. 262–264; 10 Rep. 72, nn. 6–9; RGZ. IPR. Rspr. (1933) n. 21.

[68] Haudek, *op. cit. supra* note 6, at 54, with quotations.

[69] Haudek, *op. cit. supra* note 6, n. 1, quoting OGH. 26.5 (1908); GIUNF XI no. 4249.

In England the parties may by reference incorporate some part of foreign law into their contract, which as such, will remain to be governed by the proper law. Thus in the *Dobell* v. *Steamship Rossomore Co.* case,[70] a bill of lading incorporated sections of the Harter Act by reference. Kay, J., said, »This bill of lading must be read as if the words of the Harter Act were set out at length in it.« Also in *Rowett Leaky and Co. v. Scottish, Provident Institution*,[71] there were policies which Astbury, J., declared to be an English contract and construable by English law. The words »bona fide onerous holder« occurred and his Lordship said that he thought expert evidence was admissible to show the precise meaning of the phrase. He eventually decided the case by saying the result was the same whether he looked at the evidence or not. The words quoted above being a common usage in Scots law.

There is no reason why parties in the United States cannot, instead of putting certain specific clauses in their contract, merely refer to a foreign rule of law, if that rule is not contrary to the public policy of the forum.[72] This would be true of course in states which permit the free choice of law of the parties and those which seek to find the proper law of the contract, but it should also be true in those states applying a rigid rule, for the reason that what the parties are really doing is inserting a particular clause in their contract which should be enforced as any other clause in the contract is enforced.

Renvoi

If choice of law is taken in the sense that it means nothing more than including into a contract, governed by a de|fined and unchangeable system of law, of references to a substantially different set of rules of another system, instead of providing for each separate case by special clause containing the material solution of the foreign system, the question of *renvoi* cannot arise. For instance, the parties may feel inclined to provide for the parting of the risk in a sale at a time different from that provided in their own system. They may define this in a number of provisions or they may refer to a set of rules in another system of law which would comply with their wish and would save them the trouble of reembodying all these provisions in the form of their contract. In such a case the contract is not taken out of the system of law governing it originally as decided by the law of the forum. But when the parties decide to take the contract as a whole out of that system, including its

---

[70] L. 895 2 Q. B. 403.
[71] 42 T. L. R. 331.
[72] See *supra* note 46.

rules of municipal conflict of laws and public policy upon which the latter insists in all contracts governed by it, then reference to the foreign system of law does not differ at all from the reference by that foreign municipal system of conflicts of law to still another system. This means that we have to consider the question of *renvoi*.

Lewald states that he has only come across three cases in German law dealing with this matter, and in all of them *renvoi* is denied. No other system of law on the Continent has been discovered by us to contain a similar case.[73] *Prima facie* one feels inclined to say that if the parties did refer to a system of law, they meant it, and did not consider that this system could refuse to accept the reference to it.[74] But does this reason not hold as well when the law of the forum itself prefers another system? Perhaps one may say that the parties, when referring to a foreign system of law, made that selection because it was more convenient to them; if the law refers to a foreign system, it does so for the sake of justice and good administration, but it remains always in the background as a subsidiary system, only too willing to lend its | aid, as municipal law is always ready to be applied by municipal courts. The question of *renvoi*, in the law of contracts, is a comparatively new field, and many countries have not had occasion, as yet, to deal with the matter.

In England a controversy, or rather an extreme doubt, existed for some time as to whether or not the doctrine of *renvoi* was a part of the common law. Four cases[75] give a rather disputed and none too clear decision on the question. However, both Dr. Cheshire and the late Professor Mendelsohn-Bartholdy held that the doctrine was not part of English law. In the case of *In re Ross*, an English woman who died domiciled in Italy leaving a will valid according to Italian law but void as to English law, Luxmoore, J., held that under English Private International Law the will was good as the *lex domicilii* must apply. This is the same result that would have been reached had the doctrine of *renvoi* been followed, but the court did not follow that line of reasoning.[76]

In the case of *In re Annesley*[77] Russell, J., had a similar situation of an

---

[73] At 206, n. 264: OLG. Colmar, 19.5 (1893); (1895) Clunet 141; 4 ZIR. 152; LG. Hamburg, 2.1 (1903); 14 ZIR. 82; 2.1 (1903); OLG. Braunschweig, 7.2 (1908); (1909) Clunet 520; 16 OLG. Rspr. 362.

[74] 2 Arminjon, *op. cit. supra* note 6, at 311–312, n. 102; Niboyet (1927) (I) Rec. des cours 58/61, whom Arminjon quotes in support of his opinion takes a different view, starting from his conception of *liberté des conventions.*«

[75] *In re* Ross (1930) 1 Ch. 337; *In re* Anneseley (1926) Ch. 692; *In re* Askew (1930) 2 Ch. 259; Collins v. Attorney-General (1931) 145 L. T. 551.

[76] Cheshire, *op. cit. supra* note 38, at 45 et *seq;* Bendelsohnn-Bartholdy, Renvoi in Modern English Law 67 et seq.

[77] See note 75, *supra.*

English woman dying in France, having her *de facto* domicile there. The court here did not accept the remission to English law but applied what may be termed a double *renvoi* and applied the law of the domicile – as a French court would have done it. Although the doctrine of *renvoi,* being a part of English law, was not discussed, the words of the judge do not leave the matter clear. However, the other two cases clearly point out that *renvoi* is not a part of English law and although the decisions since that time have not been in perfect unanimity, writers are inclined to agree that English law has not adopted the doctrine as a ruling principle.[78]

In America there seems to be a dearth of authority on this point, with only two cases in the entire country cited on the principle. The case of *Harral* v. *Harral*[79] does not seem | to be a real problem of *renvoi*. However, the case of *Carter* v. *Mutual Life Insurance Co.* not only discussed the question, but the court held that a reference by the parties to the law of New York (from Hawaii) included the whole of the law – conflict of laws as well.[80] No support seems to have come for the principle laid down in this case although a thorough search of its subsequent history was beyond our power.

The objections against autonomy of will or free choice of law by the parties is two-fold.[81] Firstly, it can be said that it is more than anomalous that instead of the law governing the parties the parties should govern the law. In fact a choice exercised without a system allowing the parties to do so is an invalid attempt at a legislative act. But it may be said with some confidence that there is always a system which *ex poste* determines whether the parties could or could not take their choice. This is the law of the forum which now has jurisdiction over the case on some disputed point of the contract. It may not be very satisfactory to have this question deferred until an actual dispute arises because it is often impossible to determine in advance what the forum will be. It is our opinion that one of the purposes of law is stability through certainty, which certainty cannot be had where free choice is allowed. Secondly, there is a far more serious objection to be dealt with. If the parties are free to take their contract out of one system and to submit it to another, they are empowered to avoid all those rules of municipal law which parties contracting under this system are not entitled to stipulate away.[82] But then we

---

[78] See note 76, *supra.*

[79] 39 N. J. Eq. 279 (1884).

[80] Carter v. Mutual Life Ins. Co., 10 Hawaii 559 (1900). However, in the case of *In re* Talmadge, 109 Misc. 696, 181 N. Y. Supp. 336 (1919), the New York court held that reference to another system of law did not include reference to its system of conflicts. See Lorenzen (1910) 10 Col. L. Rev. 190.

[81] 2 Frankenstein, *op. cit. supra* note 6, at 158; Niboyet, *op. cit. supra* note 6, at 50–69; 2 Arminjon, *op. cit. supra* note 6, at 253–262, nn. 78–80; Lewald, *op. cit. supra* note 32, at 199–202, nn. 260–261; Haudek, *op. cit. supra* note 6, at 5–6, with references.

[82] Haudek, *op. cit. supra* note 6, at 3; Niboyet (1927) (I) Rec. des cours 53–69.

find a new tendency outlined above to distinguish between absolute free choice of law and *liberté des conventions*. This is a sign that the courts have become aware of a possible solution, namely, free choice of law where the contract is connected with several systems|of law and *liberté des conventions* where only connected with one system – connexion having a very wide meaning and including every conceivable test. This, for the reason that it is believed that the law is an institution for the convenience of the parties and therefore that every possible convenience and freedom be given the contracting parties. In the case, therefore, of two Swiss contracting in London it should be permissible for them to stipulate that Swiss law govern the contract inasmuch as they are familiar with the provisions of their own law. In the event of future litigation in the English courts, Swiss law should be applied.[83]

The *lex loci contractus* is likewise open to criticism. If the contract is concluded between present parties, the rule works smoothly. However, on the Continent, because of the relative smallness of the countries and the great diversity as to nationality and legal rules, this solution results very often in a chance application of a system of law which has no interest in the parties or the subject matter of the contract. For example: two Englishmen on a train traveling through Luxemborg conclude a contract concerning subject matter in England. Under the above rule the contract would be governed according to the law of the place where it was made. In the case of contract concluded between absent parties (absentes) it is difficult to determine where the contract has been concluded. A contract concluded by telephone between a Swiss in Geneva, making the offer, and a Frenchman in Paris, accepting the offer, is a contract between present parties (presentes) in Swiss law, and absentes in French law.[84] The result is that, according to Swiss law, the residence of the acceptor is where the contract was concluded, while, according to French law, the residence of the offeror where the contract acceptance was received is the place of the making. In the same manner if a contract were made, by previous arrangement through the mail, between a man in Tucson, Arizona, accepting an offer made by a man in Frankfort, Germany, the contract would be concluded – ac|cording to the law of Arizona when the acceptor there posted his acceptance, while under German law the contract would not be made until the acceptance was received. The result is that a different system of law will be applied depending on where the action is brought. This solution, which might be feasible in the case of common law jurisdictions, is unsatisfactory in Europe.

---

[83] *Cf.* Schnitzer, Handbuch des Internationalen Privatrechts 278–279; Mann, *op. cit. supra* note 66, at 98.

[84] Niboyet, *op. cit. supra* note 6, at 87–89; Lewald, *op. cit. supra* note 32, at 223, n. 279; 2 Arminjon, *op. cit. supra* note 6, at 267, n. 83; 2 Frankenstein, *op. cit. supra* note 6, at 153–158.

The *lex loci solutionis* has also come in for its share of attack.[85] It is again a question of classification (qualification) in the various countries which constitute the eventual forum, coupled with the additional difficulty that even municipal systems are not always unequivocal as to what ought be understood by the *lexus executionis*.[86] For example, a contract is made in England for the sale of goods which are to be delivered in several countries. Here performance takes place in any number of places and it is impossible to determine the *lex loci solutionis*. Some courts have attempted to solve this matter by using the place of the breach as the law governing but there may be more than one breach and the difficulty is still with us.[87] In bilateral contracts the use of this rule may lead to a splitting up of the contract[88] concerning which we shall have more to say below.

The *lex patria* is suggested, and in a number of places actually applied.[89] The number of its adherents is small, that of its opponents great.[90] The foundation of this doctrine is not empirical but rational. Zitelmann, arguing from the point of view of international law, commands nationals through the medium of their state to fulfill their obligations; Frankenstein believes that, primarily, every person is connected only with his *lex patria*. It is not necessary here to go further into this dispute between the national and inter|national schools and further reference may be had in the note.[91]

Attaching the contract to the law of the debtor's domicile in cases other than unilateral contracts means again splitting up the contract, but apart from that, the solution is not altogether unsound when it coincides with either the law of the place of making or performing the contract. It is generally considered good legal advice to a client to sue his debtor where he may be found. But this is open to the old objection of rigidity and often being unconnected with the contract, as well as to classification of disputes.[92]

---

[85] Niboyet, *op. cit. supra* note 6, at 89; Lewald, *op. cit. supra* note 32, at 224, nn. 281–285; 2 Arminjon, *op. cit. supra* note 6, at 268, n. 84; 2 Frankenstein, *op. cit. supra* note 6, at 132–152; Mann, *op. cit. supra* note – [editorial note: 66], at 100 sq.

[86] Lewald, *op. cit. supra* note 32, n. 285.

[87] 2 Beale, *op. cit. supra* note 8, at 1089.

[88] For in a bilateral contract we find two debtors.

[89] Czechoslovakia, Austria, Italy, Poland.

[90] To quote the most outstanding: 2 Zitelmann, Internationales Privatrecht 366; Pillet, Traité de droit international, p. 441, n. 232; (1896) Clunet 5 sq.; Frankenstein; ca.: *e.g.,* Niboyet, *op. cit. supra* note 6, at 85–86; 2 Arminjon, *op. cit. supra* note 6, at 269, n. 85; Lewald, *op. cit. supra* note 32, at 229, n. 256 (RGZ. 95–164); Schnitzer, *op. cit. supra* note 83, at 276.

[91] See above note 1a; Balladore-Pallieri (1936) (6) Rivista di diritto privato 217–54; Ago (1934) (17) Rivista di diritto internazionale 197–232; (1936 (IV) Rec. des cours 252–278; Gutzwiller (1934) (8) Zeitschrift fuer Auslaendisches und Internationales Privatrecht 652; 4 Makarov, Rechtsvergleichendes Handwoerterbuch 338. For an enumeration of older writers and writings see: Potu (1913) Clunet 482.

[92] Lewald, *op. cit. supra* note 32, at 230, n. 287; Schnitzer, *op. cit. supra* note 32, at 277; 2

To submit the contract to the municipal law of the forum is a way out which can only be characterized as rough and regrettable because it would be impossible to determine where the plaintiff would bring his suit.[93]

This leaves us to deal with proposals brought forward by some of the writers which are not covered by the above discussion. Arminjon, not satisfied with all the splits outlined above – capacity, form, essential validity, etc. – has thought it advisable to suggest a further splitting up of the contract into even more phases of possible litigation (entering into, avoiding, object of a contract, cause, invalidity, nullity).[94]

We adhere to the ideal of the French school, which, in order to save the unity of the contract, deemed the free choice of law by the parties the best method of obtaining that unity. For this reason we cannot accept this proposal as it introduces unnecessary complications without increasing the certainty of the rule. Niboyet has offered a solution which up to a certain point deserves serious consideration. First of all he introduces definite tests similar to the Polish statute|of 1926[95] discussed above; *e.g.*, the sale of immovables to be governed by the *lex res sitae* or the place where the thing is situated; state contracts governed by the law of the state; transactions on the stock exchanges and other markets by the law governing such market; retail sales by the *lex loci contractus*, etc.[96] But once he has reached the stage of having ascertained the law applicable he proceeds to add the privilege of *liberté des conventions*. Another rather imposing objection to the suggestions of Professor Niboyet is that it is almost impossible to determine, especially for a foreign lawyer, what rules of the municipal system of law involved may be stipulated away and what rules may not be so stipulated (or in other words what rules of that Continental system are called *droit imperatif* and what are called *droit superlatif*). The solution advanced by the Polish statute has, however, much to be said in favor of it. It is an objective test and avoids questions of classifications by making the rule of law governing the case determinable by the proof of a fact, *e.g.*, the locale of the stock exchange, instead of making it a question of law, *e.g.*, as to what in the particular case might be the *lex loci solutionis*. Such were the tests applied by the Mixed Arbitral Tribunal which, like the Permanent Court of International Justice, has no *lex fori* to apply for classification purposes. The Mixed Arbitral Tri-

---

Arminjon, *op. cit. supra* note 6, at 273; Niboyet, *op. cit. supra* note 6, at 86; Neumeyer (1925) (32) Annuaire de l'institut de droit international 99–101; Cassin (1930) (IV) Rec. des cours 795, n. 95.

[93] Niboyet, *op. cit. supra* note 6, at 84; Schnitzer, *op. cit. supra* note 83, at 278; ca. 2 Arminjon, *op. cit. supra* note 6, at 294, n. 92.

[94] 2 Precis 291 sq.

[95] See above 5a; see also Int. Law Assn. (1928), proposals cited by Niboyet, *op. cit. supra* note 6, at 100, n. 1; Nolde (1927) (I) Ann. de l'inst. de droit int. 939.

[96] (1927) (I) Rec. des cours 91 sq.

bunal applies the objective test in many cases[97] while the Permanent Court prefers to leave the choice entirely in the hands of the parties. Those solutions appear, from one point of view, to be equally advantageous as they offer a uniform system of law governing the contract as a whole.

Conclusions

1. It is our belief that the first and most important step in the solving of these intricate questions is through the me|dium of international co-operation by means of convention. This for the reason that such matters as the infinite variety of public policies (*ordre publique*) and the rules which may be stipulated away by the parties and those which may not be (*droit imperatif* and *droit superlatif*) make it obvious that some measure of compromise be effected for the purpose of uniformity.[98] Secondly, the law governing contracts lends itself peculiarly to international convention because it contains few if any of those elements of national policy, racial and religious opinion, that have proved themselves to be insuperable barriers to international agreement in the matter of marriage and divorce.[99]

2. We believe that free choice of law by the parties is a workable solution provided the system chosen has some connexion, however remote, with the circumstances of the case.

3. In case the parties have not exercised their freedom of choice of law when making the contract, we submit that the proper law of the contract should be applicable as a purely objective test and not by the interpretation of the intention of the parties. By the proper law of the contract we mean that system of law which is most closely connected with the contract. The convention might, if it saw fit, lay down definite factual tests for the determination of the proper law somewhat along the lines of the Polish statute set out above.[100]

4. Formalities of the contract should be governed, in our opinion, either by the law governing the contract or by the *lex loci actus*. If the provisions of either of these systems were complied with, the contract should be regarded as formally valid.

5. The law governing the capacity of the parties to enter into a contract

---

[97] *E.g.*, Recueil des decisions des tribunaux arbitraux mixtes 2, 294; 3, 275; 3,800; 3, 380; 3, 365; 4,268; 4, 315; 4, 321, 82; 5, 168; 5, 349; 5, 779; 5, 14; 5, 1083; 6, 138; 6, 229; 6, 320; 6, 635; 6, 634; 6, 727; 7, 347; 7, 468; 7, 512.

[98] Arr. 14, p. 42; arr. 15, p. 121; *cf.* TAM 5, 200; 3, 1020.

[99] In spite of the resignation expressed by the Institut de Droit International (1927) (III) annuaire 336.

[100] *Id.* at 5a.

should be governed by the personal law of the parties or by the law of the place where the transaction took place. A man would therefore be capable of contracting, if he were capable according to either of those two systems.

It is to be noted that no reference is made to the system | of law that should govern contract where an attempt at rescission is made on the ground of fraud, error, etc., nor have we discussed the question of illegality. These were conscious omissions as we felt them to be beyond the scope of the present article.[101]

---

[101] At this point the American member must, however reluctantly, make known his dissent from some of the conclusions of his eminent and learned Continental colleagues.

It is his belief that free choice of law by the parties and the so-called »proper law« are theoretically unsound and somewhat destructive in practice. They allow the parties to perform a legislative act – make their own law – an anomaly in the law. He believes that his colleagues have put the cart before the horse and selected these solutions because of the fact that they make it easier for the judge to settle the case. This ignores the fact that it is the purpose of law to prevent litigation, not to settle matters easily after the dispute has already come before the courts. Every case wherein a new rule of law is laid down represents a failure of the law to perform its proper function.

With respect to the »proper law« more particularly, his objection is that it is difficult to determine what the proper law is and so counsel may never, with confidence, say to his client what law will govern the prospective contract in the event of suit. He never knows what the future forum will be and what the judge of that forum will decide the proper law to be. This is far too uncertain for practitioners; however, it may please academics.

The alternate solution with respect to form introduces two possible systems governing an already complicated problem. An Englishman contracting with a Czech who is incapable according to English law, must investigate the intricacies of Czech law to decide whether or not he may enter into a contract. Why introduce the second system at all Is not the first the best from a commercial and almost every point of view?

Besides the above objections, the dissentor finds himself in fundamental disagreement with his fellows of the Continent on the question of Personal and Territorial Sovereignty and the logical and legal bases of Conflict of Laws. Discussions on this point, however, engendered such considerable heat and such very little light that it was thought best to omit any discussion of the matter and leave each reader to his own opinion.

The American member regrets exceedingly the necessity for this note, but was encouraged to include it by his colleagues in this undertaking who, by force of physical majority, controlled the thought of the textual conclusions and recommendations. He therefore wishes to express his thanks to them for this opportunity to touch on some of the views which he holds so strongly. He also wishes to express his appreciation to Mr. G. G. Tilsley (LL.B., Birmingham) for his invaluable aid in the preparation of the English law included in this paper.

Editor's note: Inasmuch as the completed article arrived from Cambridge, England while the rest of volume XII, number 2, of this review was at press, it was impossible, in the time allowed, to edit the footnotes according to the regular law review form.

Conflicts of Law in Matters of Unjustifiable Enrichment[1]

The situation which is created when rules of quasi-contract are in conflict has been neglected by English writers and has also received little attention on the Continent. It is possible, no doubt, to explain this lack of interest on the ground that the question is not one which occurs very often in practice. The various Continental rules relating to quasi-contract do not, in substance, differ widely from one another. Further, the somewhat narrow view of quasi-contractual liability hitherto taken by English law has probably discouraged foreign creditors from pressing claims of this type in our Courts. In particular, English law does not, in principle, recognise the rights of a *negotiorum gestor*[2] and the right to the restoration of an unjustified enrichment at common law must still be regarded as the subject-matter of a controversy in which we do not propose to take sides. It would, however, be unwise to dismiss the question of conflict as being in this instance of no practical importance when we have regard to the growth of interest in qua-

---

[Editorial note: essay by *H.C. Gutteridge* and *Kurt Lipstein*; first published in Cambridge Law Journal 7 (1939), 80–93.]

[1] This attempt to deal with the question is a by-product of the discussions in the Cambridge Seminar on Comparative Law during the Michaelmas Term, 1938, and the Lent Term, 1939. We desire to take this opportunity of expressing our gratitude to the members of the Seminar for the help which we have received from them and in particular to E. Lange (Trinity College and the University of Upsala) and E. von Hantelmann (Trinity College and the University of Göttingen).
[2] See *Leigh* v. *Dickeson* (1885) 15 Q. B. D. 60.

si-contract which has been a feature of the literature of English law during the last two or three years,[3] and to the possibility that English law may undergo revision in this direction. Changes in the rules of a system of law cannot be made *in vacuo*, and due regard must be had to possible repercussions in the international sphere.

The objects we have in mind are to attempt an exploration along comparative lines of such rules of conflict as can be found in the different systems and to make certain suggestions as to | the principles which, in our view, are best adapted to secure a satisfactory solution of the problem which is involved when a claim submitted to an English Court is based on an unjustifiable enrichment arising abroad. The first part of our study will deal with the position at Common Law, whilst the second part will be concerned with the rules of Continental Law. The third part will contain the conclusions at which we have arrived, though not without considerable hesitation.

The Attitude of the Common Law

The English text-book writers have very little to say about conflicts in matters of quasi-contract. Dicey,[4] who devotes only a short note to the question, is chiefly concerned with the problem of 'classification' and leaves it, otherwise, very much in the air. He refers in a footnote, without any discussion of its import, to a solitary case[5] and gives no indication as to the rules which should, in his opinion, govern the matter. Westlake[6] treats the question with more respect but with a lack of precision. He does not attempt any analysis of the different states of fact which may give rise to the problem in practice, nor does he discuss in any detail the rules to be applied. He confines himself to the statement that there can be little doubt that the proper law of a quasi-contractual obligation ought generally to be drawn from the place with which the act that occasions it has the most real connexion. Burge's Colonial and Foreign Law contains a somewhat obscure passage[7] dealing with a very recondite aspect of the matter, but is otherwise confined to a short statement of the views of certain Continental authors.[8] Baty dismisses the question as

---

[3] See Winfield, The Province of the Law of Tort; Lord Wright, *Sinclair* v. *Brougham*, 6 C. L. J. 305; Jackson, The History of Quasi-Contract; Friedmann, 'The Principle of Unjust Enrichment', Canadian Bar Review, xvi, 247, 369; Logan, 'Restatement on Restitution', 2 Modern Law Review, 153. Cf. Holdsworth, 'Unjustifiable Enrichment', 55 L. Q. R. 37; Gutteridge and David, 'Unjustified Enrichment', 5 C. L. J. 204.

[4] Conflict of Laws, 5th ed. at p. 783.

[5] *Batthyany* v. *Walford* (1887) 36 Ch. D. 269.

[6] Private International Law, 7th ed. § 235. He refers to *De Greuchy* v. *Wills* (1879) 4 C. P. D. 362.

[7] 2nd ed. vol. ii, p. 39.

[8] *Ibid.* pp. 484 and 485.

being 'comparatively unimportant'.[9] Foote and Cheshire ignore the problem altogether, as also do the editors of the relevant title in the Hailsham edition of Halsbury's Laws of England.[10]

|In the American Restatement of the Conflict of Laws the choice of law in quasi-contract is said to depend in the case of a benefit on the law of the place where the benefit is conferred[11]; in cases of unjustifiable enrichment the law of the place of enrichment is the determining factor.[12] American writers do not, however, deal with the question at any length. Beale's treatment of the matter is somewhat guarded. He says: 'It seems clear that a right arising on quasi-contract is determined by the law of the place where the benefit or other enrichment is rendered. There seem to be no cases in which the question of Conflict of Laws has been raised.'[13] Wharton deals very briefly with the point, but is inclined to favour the application of the *lex loci actus* giving rise to the claim.[14] Story and Goodrich are silent.

Certainly, so far as English law is concerned, there is an absence of authority which, however inconvenient it may be, has at least the advantage of leaving the way open for a solution which seeks to reconcile the requirements of logic with those of expediency. It is not always possible to deal with matters of conflict in a way which is either elegant in the legal sense or logical. Rules which are designed to have extra-territorial effect must often be moulded on lines which offend an orderly mind because their purpose may be to meet a situation which is complicated by differences in the structure of society and differing economic methods.

It is possible to simplify the problem somewhat by the elimination of certain aspects of maritime law which are said to possess a quasi-contractual character. Whether general average and salvage are quasi-contractual in nature does not seem to be open to doubt,[15] but, in any event, maritime law has, in this instance, found its own solution of questions of conflict[16] and it would

---

[9] Polarized Law, pp. 51 and 52.

[10] Dr. Frankenstein (Internationales Privatrecht, ii, p. 392, note 31) suggests that *Re Bonacina* [1912] 2 Ch. 394, may, perhaps, be treated as a case of the application of the doctrine of unjustified enrichment, but this was not the issue and the decision proceeded on other grounds.

[11] § 452.

[12] § 453.

[13] Treatise on the Conflict of Laws, 1935, vol. ii, p. 1429.

[14] Treatise on the Conflict of Laws, 2nd ed. at p. 484.

[15] See Winfield, The Province of the Law of Tort, p. 139; Holdsworth, 'Unjustifiable Enrichment', 55 L. Q. R. 37. Cf. C. L. J. vol. v at pp. 224, 225.

[16] In the case of general average the accepted rule is that the proper law is that of the port at which the adventure is lawfully terminated. Moreover the York-Antwerp Rules, 1924, which are the product of unification, are applicable in the majority of instances of conflict. Salvage is covered to some extent by international agreement. (See Maritime Conventions Act, 1911, ss. 6 and 7; Air Navigation Act, 1920, s. 11.) The outstanding problems are being

seem that no useful purpose is served by the introduction of rules of conflict into questions which are so essentially | international in character that conflicts are best solved by the process of unification of the law.

So far as English law is concerned it is also possible to eliminate the test of the nationality of the parties which has been suggested by Continental jurists as applicable in certain circumstances. A solution of this nature would be unacceptable for reasons which have been stated so often that it is unnecessary to repeat them.

This objection does not apply to the test of the domicil of the parties, but domicil raises difficulties of classification which should be avoided whenever possible. It is submitted that as the law now stands an English judge has a free hand to select any test by which conflicts of quasi-contract may be resolved, but discussion of the principles which, in our view, should govern his choice are, we think, best deferred until the rules of Continental law have been examined. There are, however, certain questions of a special character which arise if the problem is regarded solely from the angle of English law, and it will be convenient to deal with these at once.

In the first place, difficulties may conceivably arise as to the classification by an English Court of quasi-contractual claims of foreign origin. In *Batthyany* v. *Walford*[17] it was argued that the claim was not quasi-contractual but delictual both in Austrian and in English law, in which event the English Statutes of Limitation would have barred the claim. It is submitted, however, that an English Court applying either the *lex fori* or the foreign law to the classification would find no difficulty in assigning to the realm of quasi-contract foreign obligations, imposed by law, which do not belong either to the domain of contract or of tort.

There are, it is true, certain claims of a quasi-contractual nature which are recognized in Continental law but have no counterpart in our system, *e.g.*, claims by a *negotiorum gestor* or the claim by the holder of a bill of exchange who has lost his remedy on the bill owing to the absence of protest or notice of dishonour. Will an action lie in England to enforce claims of this kind? The answer would seem to be in the affirmative. The matter was put very clearly by Cardozo, J., when he said that 'a right of action is property. If a foreign statute gives the right, the mere fact that we do not give a like right is no reason for refusing to help the plaintiff in getting what belongs | to him. We are not so provincial as to say that every solution of a problem is wrong because we deal with it otherwise at home'.[18] In *Batthyany* v. *Walford*[19] an

---

considered by the International Maritime Committee and C. I. T. E. J. A. (See Bulletin No. 102 of the International Maritime Committee, 1938.)

[17] *Ubi supra*. See also Dicey, *op. cit.* p. 783 and Beckett, 'Classification in Private International Law', British Year Book of International Law, 1934, vol. xv, p. 62, note 4.

[18] *Loucks* v. *Standard Oil Co.*, 224 N. Y. 99, cited by Unger, 'The Place of Classification

English Court was requested to give effect to a rule of Austrian law imposing liability for deterioration of the property on the life tenant of an estate in Hungary subject to a *Fideikommis*. There is no strict analogy in English law to this liability, though it is, perhaps, akin to liability for 'waste', but the Court of Appeal found no difficulty in enforcing it. It was treated as being quasi-contractual in nature and therefore not subject to the English Statutes of Limitation.

A further problem arises which is of some difficulty owing to the absence of direct authority. If the English Court decides that it will enforce the quasi-contractual right based on foreign law, what is the remedy to which the plaintiff is entitled? Is he entitled to the remedy given to him by the foreign law or must he be content with the remedy, if any, provided by the *lex fori*?

The point may be illustrated in the following way. Let us suppose that, as the result of the labours of the Law Revision Committee, the rule in *Chandler* v. *Webster*[20] were to be altered so as to allow the recovery of money paid in advance under a contract which is subsequently frustrated. Let us also suppose that the reforming English statute lays it down that in such a case the person paying in advance is entitled to recover the whole of his advance, but that under the foreign law which the English Court decides is to be applied to the quasi-contract in the circumstances of the case, the claimant is entitled to recover only the amount of his advance less any expenses incurred by the other party in connection with the transaction. Which rule is to prevail? This is a question which we propose to examine when framing our conclusions.

---

in Private International Law', The Bell Yard, No. xix, p. 7. It cannot be said that it is contrary to the policy of English law to enforce quasi-contractual rights based on unjustifiable enrichment. Many claims based on this ground are in fact recognized. See 5 C. L. J. at p. 226 and L. Q. R. vol. 55 at p. 44.

[19] *Ubi supra.*

[20] [1904] 1 K. B. 493.

The Attitude of the Continental Legal Systems

Every approach to the problems of private international law from a comparative point of view must of necessity envisage | the differences of basic conceptions between English and Continental law. Quasi-contractual obligations in Continental law are based on a universally recognized principle of natural justice,[1] and if they are often classified as being quasi-contractual, this expression is used to distinguish them from obligations arising in contract or tort rather than for the purpose of assimilating them to contract. In particular the action for unjustifiable enrichment is an action *ex lege* which is frequently resorted to in order to smooth out hardships created by the rigidity of the law, and though it is often applied in connexion with contracts it does not presuppose a contract.

The classification of unjustifiable enrichment as a quasicontract and its frequent connexion with a contract have induced some Continental writers to regard claims arising out of such enrichment as contractual. Laurent[2] and Weiss[3] favour the French rules of conflict which are applied to contracts, *i.e.* the national law, if both parties are of the same nationality, and the *lex loci contractus* if they are not. Despagnet,[4] however, makes the pertinent observation that, apart from any intention of the person who is impoverished to recover what he has paid if it should prove not to be due, the intention of the person enriched must also be considered. As it is highly improbable that the latter, can ever have intended to return that which he receives whether it be due or not, for otherwise he would not have accepted it, a presumption of intention becomes necessary in practice.[5] If the person enriched acts in bad faith the transaction takes on the complexion of a tort rather than that of a contract. In any event it will be necessary to imply a contractual relationship, and this involves a cumulation of fictions which seems to be inadmissible. Laurent's attempt to introduce his doctrine into Belgian municipal law was unsuccessful as a draft law prepared by him for this purpose was rejected.[6]

In Germany the problem appears in a somewhat different form. Gutzwiller[7] and Wolff[8] hold the view that every | case of enrichment flows from

---

[1] Fiore (1900), Clunet 27, 451; Pillet-Niboyet, Manuel de droit international privé, ii, 610; Cass. civ. 23.2.1891; D. 1892. 1. 29; S. 1895. 1. 78.

[2] Droit civil international, viii, p. 9, quoted by Fiore, *op. cit.* 455.

[3] Traité théorique et pratique de droit international privé, iv, pp. 387–90.

[4] Précis de droit international privé, 5th ed. p. 933.

[5] See Planiol et Ripert (Esmein), Traité pratique de droit civil français (1931), vii, p. 65 (no. 767). As to German law see the judgment of the German Supreme Court of (at p. 174) 5.7.1910 in Reichsgerichtsentscheidungen (RGZ), vol. 77, p. 171.

[6] See Weiss, *op. cit.* iii, p. 190, note; Lainé in Bulletin de la Société de Législation comparée, 1889–90, vol. xix, p. 554.

[7] Internationalprivatrecht (in Stammler: Das gesamte Deutsche Recht) at p. 1624.

[8] Internationales Privatrecht, p. 104–5.

some previous transaction, *e.g.* a donation or the acquisition of a right of property by prescription. According to them each case of enrichment has its proper law which it derives from the previous transaction. It seems to follow from this that in the majority of cases the proper law is the *lex rei sitae* in the case of land or chattels and the *lex loci actus* in other cases. This solution certainly seems to demand serious attention where the *locus* of the transaction resulting in enrichment can be ascertained without difficulty.

Where there has been what an English lawyer would term a failure of consideration or where performance of a contract is frustrated there is a body of opinion on the Continent which advocates that any questions of enrichment which arise should be determined in all cases in accordance with the law of the original contract.[9] This solution comes dangerously near to the doctrine of Laurent which has already been referred to and is otherwise open to criticism. Even if the proper law is the correct test of the existence or non-existence of a contract it appears to be illogical to extend this test to the *sequelae* of the contract when the proper law of the contract results in a finding that the contract has ceased to exist.[10]

The majority of Continental writers favour the *lex loci actus* (the *locus* being unspecified), whether the enrichment is connected or not with a pre-existing contract which has been determined. This principle is supported by a body of opinion which is almost overwhelming in character.[11] It is adopted as a test by codified law in many instances[12] and is also given effect to by judicial practice in many countries.[13] Whether this, notwithstanding its widespread recognition, is the correct principle to apply to conflicts in the case of quasi-contract is a matter which will be discussed hereafter.

Other tests which have been suggested are those of the personal law of the parties based either on nationality or domicil. The nationality of the parties is adopted by Zitel‖mann[14] as a general principle and, as a preliminary rule of factual connexion (*Anknüpfung*), by Frankenstein.[15] It is also sponsored by

---

[9] Arminjon, Précis de droit international privé, 2nd ed. ii, p. 339. This view is also supported by two recent decisions of the German Supreme Court of May 4, 1932, IPRspr. 1932, p. 86, no. 38, and May 15, 1930 IPRspr. 1930, p. 120, no. 50. See also the decision of the Supreme Court of the Netherlands quoted in the Répertoire de droit international (Pays Bas), vol. vi, no. 251.

[10] Schnitzer, Handbuch des Internationalen Privatrechts, p. 290.

[11] The majority of French, Swiss and Dutch writers favour this view. Opinion is divided in Germany.

[12] For the relevant statute law see Ficker in Rechtsvergleichendes Handwörterbuch, vol. iv (sub tit. Quasikontrakte) p. 387.

[13] See the articles in Répertoire de droit international, vols. vi and vii, under the heading of Belgium, Bulgaria, Italy, The Netherlands and Switzerland. In Germany the practice varies.

[14] Internationales Privatrecht, ii, p. 523, cited by Frankenstein, ii, p. 391, note 29.

[15] Internationales Privatrecht, ii, pp. 392, 393.

Rolin[16] and Poullet[17] where the parties are of the same nationality. The domicil of the person enriched is the test preferred by Walker[18] and it has also been accepted by the Austrian[19] and the Czecho-Slovak Courts.[20] Von Bar[21] also advocates the law of the domicil, though he does not make it clear whether he means the domicil of the person enriched or the person impoverished. Arminjon[22] accepts the test of domicil if it is common to both parties.

The *lex loci solutionis* has been adopted by the German Courts.[23] It is submitted that this was done partly because the *lex loci solutionis* is a very convenient supplementary test in cases of debts of any kind and partly because it coincides, as a rule, with the law of the debtor's residence.

There remains the test of the *lex fori* which was adopted by the Anglo-German Mixed Arbitral Tribunal in a case presenting the same problem as *Chandler* v. *Webster*.[24] The Tribunal rejected the test of the *lex loci actus* and applied the principle of unjustifiable enrichment as embodied in Scots and German law. This conclusion was arrived at by treating the principle of unjustifiable enrichment as a matter of international public policy (*ordre public externe*) and applying it in this way as the *lex fori* of the Tribunal.[25] Of writers on private international law Valéry[26] and perhaps Pillet-Niboyet[27] support the application of the *lex fori* on grounds of national public policy (*ordre public interne*) and the only French decision in point seems to favour this solution.[28]

The position in Continental law may perhaps be summarized in this way. In spite of the general acceptance of the principle | of unjustifiable enrichment as based on natural justice, conflicts occur and there is no certainty or uniformity in the solutions which have been arrived at. From the standpoint of the English system of private international law these solutions are very useful in so far as they furnish a background against which the difficulties of the problem stand in relief. But their value as a guide to the principles which should prevail is more doubtful.

---

[16] Principes de droit international privé, vol. i, p. 568.

[17] Manuel de droit international privé belge, 2nd ed. p. 395.

[18] Internationales Privatrecht, 2nd ed. p. 467.

[19] Répertoire de droit international (Autriche), vol. vi, no. 178.

[20] *Ibid.* (Tchécoslovaquie), vol. viii, no. 184.

[21] Theorie und Praxis des Internationalen Privatrechts, 2nd ed., vol. ii, pp. 123, 124, 113.

[22] *op. cit.*, p. 339.

[23] Supreme Court of July 5, 1910, RGZ, vol. 77, p. 171; see also of March 16, 1928, IPRspr. 1928, p. 37, no. 58.

[24] [1904] 1 K. B. 493.

[25] Décisions des Tribunaux Arbitraux Mixtes, vi, pp. 13, 58, 607, 639.

[26] Manuel de droit international privé, p. 970.

[27] *op. cit.* p. 610.

[28] Cass. civ. 23.2.1891, D. 1892. 1. 29; S. 1895. 1. 78 and the decision of the Court of Appeal of Athens cited in Clunet, vol. 34 (1907), p. 503.

Conclusions[1]

In view of the absence of authority an English judge who is called upon to adjudicate in a dispute of a quasi-contractual nature, which contains a foreign element, has, it is submitted, a free hand as regards choice of law. He has it in his power to select one or other of the following tests: –

(A) The domicil either (i) of the party who is impoverished, or (ii) of the party who has been enriched.
(B) The *lex loci actus, i.e.,* either (i) the law of the place in which the unjustifiable enrichment occurs, or (ii) the law of the place in which the transaction takes place which subsequently results in the enrichment.
(C) The proper law of the quasi-contractual obligation ascertained by means of the presumed intention of the parties and by way of analogy to the case of a contract.
(D) The *lex fori, i.e.,* English law.

Which of these solutions is to be preferred is a question of some considerable difficulty, and the submissions which follow are made with great diffidence. The difficulty is enhanced by the fact that the principle on which relief in quasi-contract is based in English law must be regarded as uncertain until the House of Lords has pronounced on the matter. If the views held by Lord Wright and Professor Winfield are accepted an element will disappear which may possibly give rise to difficulties of classification, *i.e.,* the antithesis between quasi-contract founded on the principle of *ex aequo et bono* and a right dependent on the possibility of implying a contract to pay for a benefit or to restore an unjustifiable enrichment. But subject to this | an examination of the solutions outlined above appears to lead to the following conclusions.

The Law of the Domicil

This seems to be inappropriate. Suppose that A, a domiciled Frenchman, enters into a contract with B, a domiciled Englishman, for the hire of a seat from which to view a coronation procession in London. A pays 500 francs in advance to B in Paris, but the procession is subsequently abandoned. To apply either French law (the law of A's domicil) or English law (the law of B's domicil) would seem to be arbitrary, for why should either domicil be

---

[1] No reference is made to the *lex patriae* because it appears to be inappropriate to the decision of conflicts submitted to an English Court except in so far as it might possibly be introduced into the matter by the operation of the doctrine of renvoi. Lack of space has precluded us from dealing with the subsidiary problems of classification or renvoi which may arise. Our concern has been to present the problem in its broad outlines.

preferred to the other? Moreover, it is conceivable in cases of this kind that A might be unaware of the exact domicil of B or *vice versa* or that the parties would, in the present state of the law, have to take counsel's opinion before they could in any way be sure of their ground.

The Lex Loci Actus

This test, which seems to offer the best solution from a practical point of view is nevertheless open to criticism. To begin with what do we mean by the *locus*? Is it the place of enrichment or the place of impoverishment or the place in which the transaction occurs which results in an enrichment? There seems to be little doubt that the *locus* is the place in which the payment of money or transfer of property occurs which constitutes the unjustifiable enrichment. This is the solution which has been adopted by the American Restatement,[2] and, in substance, it also appears to cover most of the cases envisaged by Wolff and Gutzwiller.[3] The application of this test may, how-ever, lead to a result which is not easily reconcilable with the principle of *ex aequo et bono*. Neuner[4] instances the case in which there is a contract made between a domiciled German and a domiciled Englishman which is fru-strated. Subsequently a claim is made by the German for the restitution of an advance payment under the contract. Here the law of the place in which payment is made may be of paramount importance. If the German has paid in England he cannot recover owing to the operation of the rule in *Chandler* v. *Webster*.[5] If he is careful to pay in Germany or in France he will be able to recover by | virtue of Art. 812 of the German Civil Code and Arts. 1183–4 of the French Code Civil.[6] Nevertheless, it would seem that the law of the place in which the money is paid or in which the property becomes vested in the person who is enriched will in the great majority of instances be the law which has the closest connexion with the enrichment. It operates indepen-dently of the nationality or domicil of the parties. It avoids the employment of a cumulation of legal fictions and does not lend itself, save in exceptional cases, to attempts to turn a rule of conflict to the profit of one or other of the parties. It meets the cases of restitution *ex aequo et bono* and also the cases in which a contract to restore is implied by law. These are extremely cogent reasons for its adoption.

---

[2] § 453.
[3] *Ante*, p. 85.
[4] Zeitschrift fuer auslaendisches und internationales Privatrecht (1928), vol. ii, p. 122, note 1.
[5] *Ubi supra*.
[6] See Cass. civ. 4.5.1898; D. 1898. i. 457.

The Proper Law

The test based on the presumed or objective intention of the parties – for such it must necessarily be – is in this instance highly artificial in character. It involves a cumulation of fictions: the first fiction being the assimilation of quasi-contract in the strict sense, and the second fiction being the presumption of an intention that restitution should take place. This would in some cases involve a distortion of the attitude which the parties would have adopted if they had thought about the matter. If we may revert to the last illustration given, the German, having in mind his own law, would have thought that he was entitled to restitution whilst the Englishman would consider that he was entitled to retain the advance payment. An attempt to presume a common intention in these circumstances is to work the theory of a proper law to death. It may be added that if English law should adopt the principle that quasi-contractual rights arise *ex aequo et bono* the search for a fictitious intention would be otiose. Such intention would be irrelevant because restitution would rest on an overriding principle of law and not on any legal fiction.

Where the enrichment springs from a previous contract, the solution which would apply the law of the original contract is attractive, but it might lead to an impasse. Certain systems of law, *e.g.*, French law, regard frustration as avoiding a contract *ab initio*. If the proper law of the contract in such a case is held to be French law there is *ex hypothesi* no contract and an English Court would have to seek for some other solution.

| The Lex Fori

This test has few supporters. Its champions on the Continent base their opinion on municipal public order (*ordre publique interne*) by which is meant the principle that it is contrary to the policy of any system of law to permit a man to retain that which he receives by way of unjustifiable enrichment. This is also, when applied to the international sphere, the principle underlying the decision of the Anglo-German Mixed Arbitral Tribunal, to which reference has been made.[7] But this solution is not a practical one so far as choice of law by an English Court is concerned, since it does not base the right to recover on public policy. Moreover, the test of the *lex fori* is open to serious objection on other grounds. It would lead to a manoeuvring for position by the parties which should be avoided whenever possible in matters of conflict. The facts in *Chandler* v. *Webster*[8] furnish a case in point. If

---

[7] *Ubi supra.*
[8] *Ubi supra.*

the plaintiff and the defendant in that case had been resident in different jurisdictions we might well have witnessed a scramble, wholly incompatible with the dignity of the law, by each party to commence proceedings in that country whose law was most favourable to him. The adoption of the *lex fori* as a test would also serve as an encouragement to the type of recalcitrant debtor who has carried to a fine art the practice of evading those jurisdictions in which he might be held liable. On the other hand, the test possesses certain merits. It gives uniform treatment irrespective of the personal law of the parties or of any fortuitous elements which may be present in any particular case. It also relieves the trial judge of the unenviable task of probing into perplexing questions of foreign law.

The Remedy

There still remains the thorny problem of the law which is to be applied in determining the quantification of the relief to be granted by an English Court in a case of unjustifiable enrichment which contains a foreign element. There is no direct authority in point, but the order made by the Court of Appeal in *Batthyany* v. *Walford*[9] shows that the Court was of the opinion that the questions of *quantum* which arose fell to be determined by the law governing the quasi-contract. On principle it would seem that the extent of an obligation must | be fixed by the law from which the obligation takes its source.[10] The quantification of the amount which is due by way of restitution from the person who is enriched is not a procedural matter as in the case of the assessment of damages. It is rather in the nature of a debt the amount of which must be ascertained by the law governing the obligation and not by the *lex fori*.[11]

It is unlikely that the remedy given by the law of the obligation will be one unknown to our law, since relief must take the form of the restitution of property or the repayment of money. But where the remedy prescribed by the law of the obligation is the restitution of something other than money (*e.g.* the re-conveyance of an immovable or the delivery up of a chattel) it is more than doubtful if an English Court would apply the remedy. It would certainly not do so if the property is abroad and its decree would be entirely ineffectual. Moreover, until it is settled whether a claim for an unjustifiable enrichment rests upon a 'supereminent equity' or not[12] the elements which

---

[9] *Ubi supra.*

[10] Cheshire, *op. cit.* pp. 657, 658.

[11] Valéry, who favours the application of the *lex fori* to claims for restitution admits that the quantification of the sum to be restored must be governed by the law of the obligation.

[12] See *per* Lord Dunedin, *Cantiare San Rocco* v. *Clyde Shipbuilding and Engineering Co.* [1914] A. C. at p. 434.

must be present before an English Court will order the restitution of property as being retained against conscience appear to be lacking. The matter is, however, one which cannot be pursued in this place.[13]

The Choice of Law

The respective merits and demerits of the various solutions which have been proposed are somewhat evenly balanced, but it would seem that the law of the domicil and the law of the forum should be ruled out. The law of the domicil raises technical difficulties which, in our submission, are fatal to its adoption. The *lex fori* lends itself too readily to abuse to be regarded as a satisfactory test. If the 'proper law' of the obligation means the search for an objective intention, then, as we have endeavoured to show, it is inappropriate in the circumstances which lead to a claim for the restitution of an enrichment.

Our submission is that conflicts of law in matters of unjustifiable enrichment should be resolved in accordance with the law of the place in which the payment of money or the | vesting of property occurs which constitutes the enrichment. This is the solution adopted by the American Restatement and we venture to think that it is supported both by theoretical considerations and by the fact that it seems to be the rule best calculated to do justice in the majority of cases which, after all, must be the chief aim of any system of the Conflict of Laws.

Finally, if we have laid ourselves open to the charge that we have made a mountain out of a molehill, may we plead in extenuation that the subject-matter is one which seemed to us to afford an unusual opportunity for the application of the comparative method to the conflict of laws owing to the absence of direct authority in any national system. We venture to express our belief that if private international law is to be rescued from the condition of malaise which affects it throughout the world at the present time the remedy must be sought in the comparative method of study. Otherwise its claim to be international in character can never be more than a fiction and we hope that this will be taken into consideration in mitigation of any sentence that may be pronounced.

---

[13] See, generally, Dicey, *op. cit.* p. 207 *passim*; Cheshire, *op. cit.* p. 563 *passim*.

Conflict of Laws before International Tribunals*

A study in the Relation between International Law and Conflict of Laws

[Editorial note: first published in Transactions of the Grotius Society 27 (1941), 142–175].

*The decisions of the Mixed Arbitral Tribunals (M.A.T.) are cited according to Gidel, *Recueil des décisions des Tribunaux Arbitraux Mixtes*, 9 vols. (1921–80). References are to the volume and page of the *Recueil*. The names of the parties are omitted for reasons of space.

I

The Relation between International Law and Conflict of Laws

The question of the relationship between international law and conflict of laws has formed the subject of many discussions during the last fifty years. There is a substantial school of thought whom for convenience's sake we shall call »Internationalists.«[1] Compared with these, the so-called »national school« believes that the sovereignty of the state is, in the absence of specific rules of international law, as untrammelled in matters of private international law as on any other subject. The question resolves itself into two: firstly, whether there actually exist rules of international law bearing upon conflict of laws and, secondly, whether such rules, if existing, are capable of exercising | any influence upon municipal systems of conflict of laws. This second problem requires some explanation. Apart from treaty, states are not bound to introduce uniform rules of private law. It may be remembered that international responsibility for denial of justice is not incurred for the mere reason that a state does not possess any particular rule or any particular category of rules of private law. But there is denial of justice when the fundamental principles of law as observed by all civilised nations are violated. International law furnishes the criteria by which to judge whether the private law of a state complies with the requirements of international law. It does not lay down rules of private law proper. In other words, discussion on this subject has hitherto been directed towards ascertaining whether any rules of international law (to which I will, in this paper, refer as »preliminary rules«) prescribe any specific rules of municipal conflict of laws.[2] But it has been

---

[1] See Huber, *Praelectiones juris romani. De conflictu legum diversarum in diversis imperiis* (1707), t. ii, p. 23, quoted by Arminjon, *Hague Recueil*, 44 (1938), p. 9. For an enumeration of its adherents see Makarov, *Rechtsvergleichendes Handwörterbuch*, 4 (1933), p. 338; Kahn, *Abhandlungen zum Internationalen Privatrecht*, i (1928), p. 8, note 2; p. 269, note 28; p. 270, note 29; Gutzwiller, *Zeitschrift für ausländisches und internationales Privatrecht*, 8 (1934), p. 652; Potu, *Clunet*, 40 (1913), p. 482. For recent surveys see Ago, *Rivista di diritto internazionale*, 26 (1934), pp. 197–232; *ibid.*, 29 (1937), pp. 442–444; *Hague Recueil*, 58 (1936), pp. 252–278; Arminjon, *Hague Recueil*, 21 (1928), pp. 433–509; *Revue de droit international et de législation comparée*, 1929 (3rd ser. vol. x), pp. 680–698; Balladore-Pallieri, *Rivista di diritto privato*, 6 (1936), pp. 217–254; Neumeyer in *Strupp, Wörterbuch des Völkerrechts*, i (1924), pp. 567–570. See also Oppenheim, *International Law*, 5th ed. (1987), i, p. 6.

[2] See Kahn, loc. cit., p. 286; Arminjon, *Hague Recueil*, 21 (1928), pp. 433 ff. especially pp. 459 ff.; *Revue de droit international et de législation comparée*, loc. cit., pp. 680–698; Lorenzen, 20 (1920) *Col. L. Rev.*, p. 278; 33 (1923–24) *Yale L.J.*, p. 740, note 17; p. 741, note 20; p. 748, note 40; W. W. Cook, 28 (1918–19) *Yale L.J.*, p. 69, note 7; 33 *ibid.*, 457, at pp. 485–486. See also the summaries in Beale, *Conflict of Laws*, iii (1935), pp. 1948–1957; Streit, *Hague Recueil*, 20 (1927), pp. 23–39. De Lapradelle, »*De la délimitation du droit international public et du droit international privé,*« *Nouvelle Revue de droit international*

overlooked that such rules are not self-executory and that the non-compliance with such preliminary rules of international law relating to conflict of laws does not have any immediate effect on municipal law,[3] although in the international sphere their disregard would entail the responsibility of the state in question.[4] Apart from private | international law in that sense, that is to say, private international law conceived as a system of preliminary rules of international law in the matter of conflict of laws as applied within the state, there is another conception of private international law. This is private international law as a separate branch of international law. A system of conflict of laws as a separate branch of international law must be, of necessity, law governing the relationship between states as such who have taken up the case of their subjects,[5] or a system between states acting as subjects of private law. It must be admitted that these cases are, in substance, cases of private law. Up to the present time, such cases have very rarely arisen before international tribunals, though not so rarely as is often believed.[6] Until now, they have received little attention[7] on the part of international lawyers. These rules of International Conflict of Laws are the subject of this paper. I do not propose to discuss here the position of the »national« and »international« school in Private International Law. But it is necessary to give a brief summary of their principal tenets.

---

privé, 1934, pp. 9 ff., was not available. See also Westlake, *Transactions of the Juridical Society*, 1 (1855–58), p. 173, at p. 177.

[3] Ago, *Hague Recueil*, 58 (1936), p. 291, note 1, says: »*Il ne s'agirait donc jamais de l'existence de cette norme coutumière internationale concernant directement le droit international privé*«; Maury, *ibid.*, 57 (1936), p. 351 ff.; pp. 429 ff.; Balladore-Pallieri, loc. cit., p. 228, note; pp. 242–254; Raape in *Staudinger, Kommentar zum Bürgerlichen Gesetzbuch*, 9th ed. (1931), vi, 2, pp. 51–52; perhaps also Starke, 52 (1936) *L.Q.R.*, p. 396 at p. 400.

[4] Balladore-Pallieri, loc. cit., p. 251, quoting Bruns, *Fontes Juris Gentium*, ser. B, sectio i, tomus 1, pp. 454–455; Niboyet, *Mélanges Fillet* (1929), i, pp. 153–177; *Hague Recueil*, 40 (1932), pp. 157–231; Basdevant, *Revue de droit international privé*, 1 (1905), pp. 817–822; *ibid.*, 2 (1906), pp. 861–873; Maury, *Hague Recueil*, 57 (1936), p. 355; Kuhn, *Comparative Commentaries on Private International Law* (1937), pp. 25–26; Kahn, loc. cit., i, p. 285 ff. Contra: Aubry, *Clunet*, 28 (1901), p. 651; Rundstein, *Revue de droit international et de législation comparée*, 1936 (3rd ser., vol. xvii), p. 586 ff.; Melchior, *Die Grundlagen des Deutschen Internationalen Privatrechts* (1932), p. 86; Beckett, *B.Y.I.L.*, 7 (1926), p. 84.

[5] M.A.T., 4, p. 673.

[6] See e.g. Schmitthoff, *Journal of Comparative Legislation*, 1987 (3rd ser. vol. xix), p. 179 ff., and see also the proposals of Coquoz, *Revue générale de droit aérien*, 7 (1938), pp. 39–40.

[7] See below, note 33.

The National School in Conflict of Laws. The English View

England and the United States may be described as strongholds of the »national school.« From the days of Story[8] onwards, conflict of laws was regarded in these countries as a branch of municipal law, subject, at best, to considerations of international comity. This view was subsequently fully accepted by English writers. Says Westlake[9]: »the place of private international law is in the division of national law.« Harrison[10] states: »Private international law is a substantive part of municipal law.« He excepts such topics as nationality, extradition and international criminal law, which form part of international law, although they are often included in treatises on conflict of laws. His views have been elaborated by Mr. Beckett,[11] who may be | described as an adherent of the »national school.« He says[12]: »When all the topics which are not properly part of private international law are excluded, it does not appear that amongst what remains there is anything which as between states is regulated by the law of nations. Private international law is therefore not only municipal and not international law, but it treats only of matters which are, by the existing law of nations, within a state's exclusive sovereignty to legislate upon as it pleases.« And again: »There is no system of rules of private international law at present existing with obligatory force between nations.«[13] Wharton[14] forms an exception to that general trend; he states: »The law of nations is part of the common law and private international law is part of the law of nations.« However, he does not substantiate his contention. With the publication of Dicey's *Conflict of Laws*, the controversy has shifted to a different ground. Private international law is henceforth treated as governed by the paramount principle of acquired (or vested) rights. Thus we find Dicey stating: »Any right which has been duly acquired under the law of any civilised country is recognised and in general enforced by English courts and no right which has not been duly acquired is enforced or, in general, recognised by English courts.«[15] And again: »The incidents of a right of a type recognised by English law acquired under the law of any civilised country, must be determined in accordance with the law under which it is acquired.«[16] That doctrine governed the Eng-

---

[8] *Conflict of Laws*, 8th ed. (1883), pp. 32–33.
[9] *Private International Law*, 7th ed. (1925), p. 4.
[10] *On Jurisprudence and the Conflict of Laws* (1919), p. 180.
[11] *B.Y.I.L.*, 7 (1926), p. 76.
[12] *B.Y.I.L.*, 7, p. 94.
[13] *Ibid.*, p. 81.
[14] *Conflict of Laws*, 2nd ed. (1881), p. 5.
[15] *Ibid.*, 5th ed. (1932), p. 17.
[16] *Ibid.*, p. 43.

lish approach to private international law for a period of nearly half a century. It must now be regarded as obsolete. Dr. Cheshire, one of the leading authorities on conflict of laws of today, has described this theory – to quote his words – as insignificant, untrue and as begging the question.[17] This criticism has been generally accepted. The theory of acquired rights does in fact beg the question, for private international law, which, it is said, must respect acquired rights, must determine by its own rules of conflict of laws whether a |right has been acquired or not. This is a vicious circle.[18] Dr. Cheshire attacks with equal vigour the »international school.« He says: »Many objections may be raised to the theory of the internationalists, but the one that is both the simplest and the most fatal is that the general customary law of which they speak exists only in their own minds.«[19] Dr. Cheshire favours the view that conflict of laws is municipal law unfettered by any rules of international law. He states: »Anglo-American tribunals have always attempted to reach a just decision in accordance with their own conception of utility and justice.«[20]

This utilitarian and national conception of conflict of laws has also been put forward by the most representative American writers like Beale,[21] Lorenzen,[22] Goodrich[23] and W. W. Cook.[24]

The International School in Conflict of Laws

Before proceeding, it will be convenient to state the principal tenets of the »international school.« They are as follows:

(1) Every state must have a system of private international law.
(2) States may not exclude the application of foreign law altogether.
(3) No state may impose its own rules as to status upon persons who are merely temporary residents.
(4) With regard to immovables, the *lex rei sitae* must be applied and rights acquired according to a previous *lex rei sitae* must be recognised and respected.

---

[17] *Private International Law*, 2nd ed. (1938), pp. 86–87.
[18] Savigny, *System des heutigen Römischen Rechts*, 8 (1849), p. 132 (par. 361 (5)); W. W. Cook, 33 (1923–24) *Yale L.J.*, p. 457 at pp. 468–469, 485; Arminjon, *Revue de droit international et de législation comparée*, 1929 (3rd ser. vol. x), p. 680 ff.; *Hague Recueil*, 44 (1933), pp. 5–105.
[19] *Private International Law*, p. 84.
[20] *Ibid.*, p. 91; see also Foster, *Hague Recueil*, 65 (1938), pp. 399–423; Llewelyn Davies, *ibid.*, 62 (1937), pp. 427–488; Holland, *Jurisprudence*, 13th ed. (1924), p. 422.
[21] *Conflict of Laws*, i (1935), p. 52.
[22] 33 (1923–24) *Yale L.J.*, p. 736.
[23] *Conflict of Laws*, 2nd ed. (1938), pp. 9–11.
[24] 33 (1923–24) *Yale L.J.*, p. 457.

(5) Form is governed by the *lex loci actus.*[25]

| Of these five points, the first three are what I have previously described as preliminary rules. They do not prescribe a definite rule of municipal law, but only a certain tendency to be followed by states. They do not decide a particular case, such as whether the law of nationality or of the domicile is to govern personal status.[26]

The last two rules set out above do represent, it must be admitted, the practice of municipal systems of laws. But that does not necessarily mean that they are rules of international law.[27] Nothing but a complete transformation of such rules of private law can create rules of international law. (Reference may be had to the process of adaptation of Roman law principles into rules of international law by the founders of that science.) In spite of the dearth of rules of private international law common to all states, and regardless of the fact that these rules are not necessarily rules of international law, it has been contended that rules of international law in matters of conflict of laws exist. It must suffice here to set out the leading principles of this doctrine.

It is said that private international law is international law as to its substance; that international law proper does not contain rules of private international law and that, in the absence of such rules, municipal law is permitted to supplement international law by laying down its own rules of private international law. Such rules, it is contended, are municipal law as to form and source only, but, in substance, they are rules of international law.[28]

---

[25] Kahn, loc. cit., i, pp. 284–287; Diena, *Principi di diritto internazionale*, 2nd ed. (1930), ii, p. 27; Balladore-Pallieri, loc. cit., p. 238; Ago, *Hague Recueil*, 58 (1936), p. 286, note 2, note 3; Rundstein, loc. cit., p. 544, note 1; Verdross, *Die Verfassung der Völkerrechtsgemeinschaft* (1926), p. 167. But see the decision of the Court of Appeal of Brussels, of January 9, 1937, *Clunet*, 65 (1938), p. 367, to the contrary effect.

[26] Kahn, loc. cit., i, p. 283; Jitta, *Revue de droit international privé*, 4 (1908), p. 567; *ibid.*, 5 (1909), p. 486; Rundstein, loc. cit., p. 548, underrates the importance of these preliminary rules.

[27] Jitta, loc. cit., 4 (1908), p. 555; 5 (1909), p. 497; Rundstein, loc. cit., p. 325, citing Ago, *Teoria del diritto internazionale privato* (1934), p. 129: »*Si rischia di confondere un semplice comportamento uniforme degli Stati nella propria attività legislativa dettata unicamente da esigenze pratiche e da necessità reali con l'adempimento di un obbligo internazionale*«; Balladore-Pallieri, *Rivista di diritto privato*, 6 (1936), pp. 223, 238; Wolff, *Internationales Privatrecht* (1933), p. 5; Streit, *Hague Recueil*, 20 (1927), p. 36 with further literature; Maury, *ibid.*, 57 (1936), p. 428 ff.; Ago, *ibid.*, 58 (1936), p. 289; Rundstein, loc. cit., p. 528. See also *Giesler* v. *Giesler Heirs*, decided July 11, 1035, by the Swiss Federal Tribunal, *Annual Digest and Reports of Public International Law Cases*, 1935–37, case no. 1. *Contra*: Kahn, loc. cit., i, pp. 286, 291–292.

[28] Anzilotti, *Studi critici di diritto internazionale privato* (1898), p. 120; *Il diritto internazionale nei giudizi interni* (1905), p. 122, cited by Balladore-Pallieri, *Rivista di diritto privato*, 6 (1936), p. 219; Maury, *Hague Recueil*, 57 (1936), p. 366; but see Anzilotti, *Corso di diritto internazionale privato* (1925), p. 5 ff., *Corso di diritto internazionale*, p. 54 ff.

| On the other hand, it is stated that international law contains a set of subsidiary rules in matters of private international law. These rules are applied by municipal courts to supplement their own rules of private international law.[29]

Seeing that the existence of such systems is not borne out by the practice of states, these sweeping contentions must be regarded as attempts to establish *a priori* systems.[30]

Recognition and Application of Foreign Law

Neither is it possible to agree that there is support for the »internationalists« in the fact of the connection between recognition and the application of foreign law.[31]

(1) It is one thing to say that foreign law must not be applied unless the foreign state is recognised. This means simply that prior to recognition only the predecessor state's law may be applied.

(2) It is another thing to contend that foreign law must be applied, if the foreign state is recognised.

This second sweeping statement represents the law as laid down in *Luther* v. *Sagor*.[32] However high the authority of this rule may be, it is not unassailable, but there is no time to go into | that here. A short statement must suffice. The effect of recognition can be only to establish that the new legal order of a state is regarded as law by the recognising state and that the old law of the recognised state has been superseded. In other words, recognition estab-

---

(transl. Gidel, p. 56 ff.), where the author sides with the »national« school. Balladore-Pallieri, *Le origini internazionali del diritto internazionale privato, Temi Emiliana*, 1980, i, p. 89, and the same author's article »*L'élément international dans le droit international privé,*« reviewed by Maury, *Revue critique de droit international*, 32 (1938), p. 167, were not available.

[29] Zitelmann, *Internationales Privatrecht*, i, pp. 72, 122; ii, p. 13, cited by Balladore-Pallieri, *Rivista di diritto privato*, 6 (1936), p. 225, note 1; see also the summaries in Streit, *Hague Recueil*, 20 (1927), p. 34; Ago, *ibid.*, 58 (1936), pp. 253–254; Rundstein, *Revue de droit international et de legislation comparée*, 1986 (3rd ser. vol. xviii), p. 320; Beale, *Conflict of Laws*, iii (1935), pp. 1953–1957: »The private international law in force in each state is therefore composed: first of statutes passed by the state itself, and concerned with private international law; second, of rules of the supra-state private international law which bind the parties and the judge in default of statute« (at p. 1954).

[30] See *e.g.* Lorenzen, 88 (1928–24) *Yale L.J.*, pp. 736, 750; W. W. Cook, *ibid.*, p. 460; Arminjon, *Revue de droit international et de législation comparée*, 1929 (3rd ser. vol. x), p. 688; Rundstein, *ibid.*, 1986 (3rd ser. vol. xvii), pp. 820, 514.

[31] For a critical discussion see Sereni, *Rivista di diritto internazionale*, xxx (1938), pp. 102–141; Balladore-Pallieri, loc. cit., p. 240; Rundstein, loc. cit., p. 822; Melchior, loc. cit., p. 85, p. 151, note 1; I hope to give a survey of pertinent decisions in another article.

[32] [1921] 8 K.B. 582.

lishes which of two systems succeeding each other must be applied if the private international law of the recognising state refers to the law of the recognised state. Recognition establishes which of several foreign systems must be applied. It does not prescribe when foreign law must be applied.

International Conflict of Laws

It would exceed the limits of this paper to survey the practice of all international tribunals, but it is convenient to study the practice in this matter of that long series of tribunals usually referred to as Mixed Arbitral Tribunals, which were set up after the first World War for the performance of a variety of functions.

In the light of the introductory remarks, we may investigate to what extent the practice of the Mixed Arbitral Tribunals has had the result of producing a coherent body of rules of international law in matters of conflict of laws.[33]

Absence of lex fori

It is to be noted that both the Mixed Arbitral Tribunals and international tribunals in general have no | *lex fori*[34] in the sense of being bound by mu-

---

[33] See also: Basdevant, *Revue de droit international privé*, 1 (1905), pp. 817–832; *ibid.*, 2 (1906), pp. 861–873; Blühdorn, *Hague Recueil*, 41 (1932), p. 226; Gutzwiller, *Jahrbuch für Schiedsgerichtswesen*, 3 (1931), pp. 123–152; Hammarskjöld, *Revue critique de droit international*, 29 (1934), pp. 315–844; Niboyet, *Hague Recueil*, 40 (1932), pp. 157–231; *Mélanges Pillet*, 1 (1929), pp. 153–177; *Revue de droit international privé*, 24 (1929), pp. 478–489; Rabel, *Zeitschrift für ausländisches und internationales Privatrecht*, 1 (1927), pp. 33–47; Witenberg, *Clunet*, 56 (1929), pp. 991–1003. See also: Maury, *Hague Recueil*, 57 (1936), p. 861; Neumeyer, *Juristische Wochenschrift*, 1922, p. 753. See also Oppenheim, *International Law*, 6th ed. (1940), ii, p. 51, note 2.

The following books were not available: Geier, *Das Internationale Privatrecht der gemischten Schiedsgerichtshöfe* (1930); Weselowski, *Les conflits de lois devant la justice internationale*, thèse, Paris (1936).

For the purpose of this study, it appears permissible to assume that the Mixed Arbitral Tribunals, not being municipal courts, must be regarded as international tribunals. See M.A.T., 2, p. 268; 6, p. 243 (246); *ibid.*, p. 342; *ibid.*, p. 499; 7, p. 47 (53); *ibid.*, p. 865; *ibid.*, p. 871; *ibid.*, p. 877; 8, p. 195; but see M.A.T., 7, p. 743; 8, p. 195, to the contrary effect.

See also Niboyet, *Sirey*, 1921, Part 2, p. 81; *Revue de droit international et de legislation comparée*, 1928 (3rd ser. vol. ix), p. 809, note 1; Rühland, *Zeitschrift für ausländisches und internationales Privatrecht*, 5 (1931), p. 754; Blühdorn, loc. cit., pp. 144–146; Rabel, loc. cit., pp. 33–40.

In the absence of treaty provisions, these tribunals apply rules of private law; M.A.T., 8, p. 568.

[34] M.A.T., 4, p. 73 (75); 5, p. 200 (211); see Niboyet, *Revue de droit international privé*,

nicipal rules of procedure or of substantive law. The procedure of the Mixed Arbitral Tribunals was laid down either in the Peace Treaties setting up the tribunal in question, or by the courts themselves.[35] The relevant international conventions do not attempt to formulate rules of substantive law and the courts have felt little inclined to formulate general rules of their own.[36] They prefer to apply municipal law[37] and to reserve for themselves the decision of the question what municipal system is to apply according to the circumstances of the case; in other words, they create a system of conflict of laws for their own use.

But while private international law within the state chooses between the application of the municipal law of the court concerned and foreign law as a subsidiary source of law, international courts, owing to the absence of a *lex fori*, must elect between two or more systems, none of which can claim the privileged position of *lex curiae*. Consequently, it is impossible for the courts to decide in favour of one system of conflict of laws in preference to any other.[38] As there is no *lex fori* and no *lex curiae*, a municipal system of conflict of laws based upon the particular conceptions of public policy of the municipal law concerned would be of little avail.[39]

The courts, therefore, have felt it necessary to have recourse to general principles in order to lay down their own rules of conflict of laws. With regard to the Mixed Arbitral Tribunals, | two trends can be distinguished: a strictly municipal and a comparative trend, according to whether the principal aim of the court was to ascertain the municipal law most apposite to be exclusively applied in the circumstances, or whether it aimed at achieving a degree of harmony between the municipal systems available for choice. The great advantage of the comparative method consists in dispensing altogether with the application of private international law. As a rule, the Mixed Arbitral Tribunals were only competent to deal with, and consequently were confronted with litigation between nationals of the states which set up these

---

22 (1927), p. 103 ff.; *ibid.*, 24 (1929), pp. 480, 482; Mendelssohn Bartholdy, *Juristische Wochenschrift*, 1922, p. 154; *Contra:* Gutzwiller, loc. cit., p. 128; Dreyfus, *Clunet*, 48 (1921), p. 484, who holds that the *lex fori* of the defendant must be applied.

[35] M.A.T., 4, p. 6.

[36] For exceptions see below, note 123; note 192; M.A.T., 3, p. 291 (295); 4, p. 645; 6, p. 13; for the application of an international Convention see M.A.T., 6, p. 922; see also M.A.T., 8, p. 6, where municipal law applicable according to the rules of private international law of the tribunal was disregarded on the ground that the Treaty of Versailles contained an overriding provision; see also M.A.T., 6, p. 556; 8, p. 71; *ibid.*, p. 75. According to the Anglo-Bulgarian Mixed Arbitral Tribunal, M.A.T., 4, p. 671, the court may administer »analogies of municipal law and general principles of jurisprudence.«

[37] As applied and interpreted by municipal courts: M.A.T., 4, p. 852 (p. 854); *P.C.I.J.*, arr. 14, p. 46; arr. 15, p. 124; Niboyet, *Revue de droit international privé*, 24 (1929), p. 488.

[38] M.A.T., 6, p. 246; for exceptions see below, notes 62, 63.

[39] See below, p. 156 ff.

tribunals. The easiest method which, at first sight, eliminates hardship, and secures the greatest amount of justice, is that of coupling rules of substantive law of the countries concerned.[40]

In resorting to the comparative approach, the tribunals either apply the method of expressly coupling municipal systems,[41] or they invoke a conception of *»droit commun«* which in reality consists of a cumulation, comparison and merger of the national systems concerned.[42] The same tendency influences the courts when applying »analogies of municipal law and general principles of jurisprudence,«[43] *»principes généraux,«*[44] *»principes d'équité et de justice,«*[45] *»règle en tous pays,«*[46] and, sometimes, though not always, when judging according to *»règles généralement admises,«*[47] *»jurisprudence traditionelle de tous les pays,«*[48] | *»principes ordinaires du droit,«*[49] *»principes universellement adoptés,«*[50] *»principi elementari di diritto.«*[51]

This comparative method is illustrated by the case of *Bonnet-Dupeyron* v. *Ephraim Meyer* decided by the Franco-German Mixed Arbitral Tribunal. The facts were as follows. Before the first World War, the plaintiff, a French national, had appointed a German national his agent for the purpose of carrying out banking transactions with the defendants, bankers of German nationality. During the war the agent continued to transact such business on behalf of his principal. The plaintiff contended that these transactions were not binding upon him. The Mixed Arbitral Tribunal held that the transactions were binding upon the plaintiff. The Tribunal said: »Even admitting that the contract of agency has become invalid for one reason or another, the ordinary business transactions carried out between the agent on behalf of the

---

[40] See Gutzwiller, loc. cit., p. 141, with further literature.

[41] M.A.T., 1, p. 587; *ibid.*, p. 847; *ibid.*, p. 899 (903); 2, p. 89; *ibid.*, p. 235; *ibid.*, p. 247; *ibid.*, p. 753; *ibid.*, p. 786; 8, p. 155; *ibid.*, p. 220; *ibid.*, p. 286; *ibid.*, 296; *ibid.*, p. 328; *ibid.*, p. 340; *ibid.*, p. 387; *ibid.*, p. 408; *ibid.*, p. 534; *ibid.*, p. 570; *ibid.*, p. 872; *ibid.*, p. 988 (991); *ibid.*, p. 1020; 4, p. 366; *ibid.*, p. 417; 5, p. 200 (213); *ibid.*, p. 224; *ibid.*, p. 846; *ibid.*, p. 637; *ibid.*, p. 790; 6, p. 565; *ibid.*, p. 671; 7, p. 221; *ibid.*, p. 429; *ibid.*, p. 589; *ibid.*, p. 792; *ibid.*, p. 881; 8, p. 933; *ibid.*, p. 1000; 9, p. 424; *ibid.*, p. 560; doubtful: 3, p. 806 (808).

[42] See *e.g.* M.A.T., 2, p. 247; *ibid.*, p. 251; *ibid.*, p. 641; 4, p. 530; 5, p. 520; 6, p. 943; 7, p. 17; *ibid.*, p. 25; *ibid.*, p. 57; *ibid.*, p. 601; *ibid.*, p. 785 (792); 8, p. 994; 9, p. 302.

[43] M.A.T., 4, p. 671.

[44] M.A.T., 2, p. 89; *ibid.*, p. 784; 3, p. 274; 5, p. 410; 8, p. 5; *ibid.*, pp. 171–172; *ibid.*, p. 173. See also 7, p. 23; 9, p. 694; *ibid.*, p. 697, where the tribunals applied *»principes reconnus tant dans le droit national que dans le droit international.«*

[45] See the rules of the Mixed Arbitral Tribunals, *e.g.* 1. p. 57 (art. 98); *ibid.*, p. 73 (art. 92). See also M.A.T., 3, p. 291 (295).

[46] M.A.T., 3, p. 291 (295).

[47] M.A.T., 3, p. 570; 4, p. 366; 8, p. 325; see also 5, p. 887; 8, p. 114; *ibid.*, p. 403.

[48] M.A.T., 8, p. 374; *ibid.*, p. 570; 5, p. 58.

[49] M.A.T., 8, p. 111.

[50] M.A.T., 8, p. 993; *ibid.*, p. 1000.

[51] M.A.T., 8, p. 871.

plaintiff and the bank remained valid in all circumstances, in virtue of the general principles to be found both in German and in French law to the effect that third persons acting in good faith are protected.«[52]

As already pointed out, this tendency aims expressly at harmonising two equally applicable systems of municipal law,[53] but it was stated very correctly by the German-Roumanian Tribunal in the case of *Negreanu* v. *Meyer and Sons* that far from resulting invariably in a reconciliation of municipal systems of laws, this method endangers the strict application of even one municipal system, let alone of two.[54]

Thus in the case of *Société Communale des Tramways de Bucarest* v. *Phoenix S.A.* the same Tribunal had to decide whether the defendants were liable for a delay in the performance of a contractual duty. Both Roumanian and German law laid down in identical terms that there is no delay on the part of the debtor unless the creditor has claimed performance by means of serving a notice upon the debtor. But upon further investigation it | appeared that according to German law service of notice had to be presumed if the time when the performance of the contract was due could be ascertained. Roumanian law, on the other hand, did not know of such a presumption.[55]

Where a quick glance shows an apparent identity of solutions, their specific application may reveal far-reaching differences. The comparative method does not, in such cases, yield the expected results and the tribunals have to apply the rules of conflict of laws.

The second method aims at elaborating such rules of conflict of laws. The sources of such rules are usually referred to by the tribunals as »*principes de droit international,*«[56] »principles of international law,[57] »*droit international commun,*«[58] »comity of nations,«[59] »*doctrine et jurisprudence,*«[60] »*principes généraux de droit international privé,*«[61] or, in short, »private international law.«[62] I propose in this paper to examine the nature of these rules so variously described.

It is clear, in the first instance, that in thus applying private international law, the tribunals are not »sitting as English, French, or German

---

[52] M.A.T., 2, p. 89.
[53] M.A.T., 5, p. 218. See also Neumeyer, *Juristische Wochenschrift,* 1922, pp. 753, 1566.
[54] M.A.T., 5, p. 200 (210); *ibid.*, p. 226.
[55] M.A.T., 5, p. 218 (226).
[56] M.A.T., 3, p. 800; see also 2, p. 783.
[57] M.A.T., 7, p. 518.
[58] M.A.T., 7, p. 128 (134); *ibid.*, p. 140 (147).
[59] M.A.T., 4, p. 6, at p. 9.
[60] M.A.T., 3, p. 261; 6, p. 943.
[61] M.A.T., 1, p. 22 (26); 6, p. 247; *ibid.*, p. 806.
[62] M.A.T., 4, p. 655.

courts.«[63] The few cases in which they have not adhered to this principle and in which they have adopted a particular municipal system of private international law as such, either without giving any reasons,[64] or on the ground that it was the law of the debtor's domicile,[65] have led to unnecessary complications.

The objections raised here are well brought out in the case of *Luttges and Company* v. *Ormiston and Glass Company*,[66] decided by the Anglo-German Mixed Arbitral Tribunal, where the facts were as follows. The defendants, British nationals, had bought | 477 dozens of knives from the plaintiffs, German nationals. The plaintiffs now sued for payment. The defendants contested the claim and contended that property in the knives had not passed. The claim was dismissed. The Tribunal held, first, that English private international law applied (it will be noted that this is a first choice of law); secondly, the Tribunal found that according to English private international law »the passing of the property should be decided according to the law of the country where the goods are situate at the time when acts relied upon as passing the property have taken place« (this is a second choice of law). The Tribunal then found that the property in the goods had not passed under German law, when they were dispatched in Germany, nor according to Dutch law, while they were in transit, nor according to English law, when they arrived in England. It will be noticed that this decision was reached by a circuitous and complicated process of reasoning. First of all, it is not clear why English private international law was chosen in preference to German private international law. Secondly, this choice did not solve the question before the Tribunal. The Tribunal then applied the rule – alleged to be one of English private international law proper – that movables are governed by the law of the place where they are situate. The simpler course which, in addition, would have excluded the possibility of further complications (to be discussed later on), would have been to regard the principle that the *lex rei sitae* governs movables as a rule of international conflict of laws directly binding upon international tribunals.

The above case illustrates the objections which can be raised against the indiscriminate application of municipal systems of private international law. The adoption of municipal systems of conflict of laws, without any test, or even applying the test of the domicile of the debtor, is a purely arbitrary procedure.[67] The same applies to the cumulation of two systems of conflict

---

[63] Sir Herbert Jenner in *Collier* v. *Rivaz* (1841), 2 Curt. 855, at p. 859; Luxmoore J., in *re Ross, Ross* v. *Waterfield*, [1930] 1 Ch. 377, at p. 403.

[64] M.A.T., 5, p. 670; 6, p. 565 (569); *ibid.*, p. 637; 7, p. 421; *ibid.*, p. 435; *ibid.*, p. 512; 8, p. 67.

[65] M.A.T., 6, p. 543; 7, p. 345 (348).

[66] M.A.T., 6, p. 564.

[67] In fact, municipal systems of private international law are usually disregarded. See

of laws.[68] The adoption of a municipal system of conflict of laws as a whole means in fact the exercise by the Tribunal of a primary choice of law. It means that in order to decide the particular | case in question, the Tribunal must then, sitting as a municipal court and applying municipal conflict of laws, exercise a secondary choice of law in accordance with the private international law first adopted, together with the possibility of a reference back (*renvoi*) as a third. This peculiar situation did in fact arise, if only in a few cases.[69] Thus in the case of *Weiser and Company* v. *Heirs of L. Dürr*,[70] decided by the Anglo-German Mixed Arbitral Tribunal, the plaintiffs, British nationals, claimed a sum of money arising out of transactions in stocks and shares in England from the defendants, German nationals. The claim was resisted on the ground that it was barred by prescription. The Tribunal found that the contract was governed by English law and that under English law the rules of prescription were rules of procedure only. The claim was dismissed on the ground that it was barred by the German law of prescription. The Tribunal said: »The debtor, being a German national, resident in Germany, the Tribunal have to apply the principles of German private international law. According to these principles, the question of prescription is to be decided in accordance with the law governing the contract, the *lex contractus*. If the *lex contractus* is a foreign law, that foreign law has to be applied. If, however, the provisions of prescription of that foreign law are part of the law of procedure only, these foreign rules of procedure are not applicable under German private international law, and one has to fall back on the provisions of German domestic law.«

It will be noticed that the Tribunal adopted the rules of German private international law and sat as a German court. German private international law referred to English law. English law did not accept the reference, as it regarded rules of prescription as procedural rules, and referred the case back. Since the Tribunal had adopted German private international law in the first instance, and was thus sitting as a German court, the law of procedure of the court was German law, including its law of prescription.

Such an identification of an international tribunal with the courts of a particular country, so as to adopt the law of that country as *lex curiae*, before embarking upon the real question | of choice of law, appears contrary to the true character of international tribunals. It amounts to a capitulation of the international tribunal before the private international law of a particular country.[71]

M.A.T., 6, p. 243 (240); *contra*: Gutzwiller, loc. cit., p. 136, and the cases cited above notes 65 and 66.

[68] See *e.g.* M.A.T., 5, p. 670 (672).

[69] M.A.T., 4, p. 78 (75); 5, p. 687; 6, p. 548; *ibid.*, p. 682.

[70] M.A.T., 6, p. 632.

[71] Niboyet, *Mélanges Pillet*, 1 (1929), p. 166; *Hague Recueil*, 40 (1982), p. 229.

Public Policy

The second danger resulting from the application of a particular system of private international law for the solution of a case before the tribunal, is that the tribunal may be compelled to apply the rules of public policy of the substantive municipal law in question, aiming at excluding the application of yet another system.[72] No instances of this kind are to be found in the case law of the Mixed Arbitral Tribunals. But I may refer to the decisions of the Permanent Court of International Justice in the Serbian and Brazilian Loan Cases as illustrating this tendency. It is only necessary to read »private international law« instead of »municipal law« in the passage which follows. In the Brazilian Loan case the Court said[73]: »Once the Court has arrived at the conclusion that it is necessary to apply the municipal law of a particular country, there seems no doubt that it must seek to apply it as it would be applied in that country. It would not be applying the municipal law of a country if it were to apply it in a manner different from that in which that law would be applied in the country in which it is in force.« The Court referred to its statement in the Serbian Loan Case where it was held: »For the Court itself to undertake its own construction of municipal law, leaving on one side existing judicial decisions, with the ensuing danger of contradicting the construction which has been placed on such law by the highest national tribunal and which, in its results, seems to the Court reasonable, would not be in conformity with the task for which the Court has been established, and would not be compatible with the principles governing the selection of its members. It would be a most delicate matter to do so, especially in cases concerning public policy – a conception the definition of which in any particular country is largely dependent on the opinion | prevailing at any given time in such country itself – and in cases where no relevant provisions directly relate to the question at issue.«[74]

The flaws of this solution need not be stressed. International tribunals have no *lex fori*, save their own.[75] The public policy of any particular system of law is not the basis upon which international tribunals can properly proceed. There are express statements of the Mixed Arbitral Tribunals to the effect that they must not apply municipal public policy,[76] that mandatory

---

[72] Niboyet, *Revue de droit international privé*, 24 (1929), p. 488; *Mélanges Fillet*, loc. cit., p. 170; *Hague Recueil*, 40 (1982), p. 177 ff.; but see *P.C.I.J.*, arr. 14, pp. 41, 46; arr. 15, pp. 124–125.

[73] *P.C.I.J.*, arr. 15, p. 125.

[74] *P.C.I.J.*, arr. 14, p. 46.

[75] See above, note 34.

[76] M.A.T., 5, p. 200 (211); Gutzwiller, loc. cit., p. 151.

rules of municipal law may be disregarded[77] and that they are guided solely by their own »*ordre public international.*«[78]

Thus in the case of *Negreanu* v. *Meyer and Son,*[79] decided by the German-Roumanian Mixed Arbitral Tribunal, the Tribunal said: »According to established principles of private international law, the national law of one of the parties may be disregarded as a whole only if it conflicts with the rule of public policy of the *lex fori*. Mixed arbitral tribunals, not belonging to any state, and sitting wherever it is deemed expedient, do not possess a *lex fori*. Thus the national law of the parties can only conflict with the rules of »international public policy.« More specifically, in *Feldmann* v. *German Government,*[80] it was held by the same Tribunal that a contract concluded in Roumania during the first World War between a German and a Roumanian national was not necessarily void for an infringement of the Roumanian Trading with the Enemy Act. The Mixed Arbitral Tribunal was entitled to disregard rules of municipal public policy.

In one case, however, in accordance with the comparative method, a cumulation of two municipal public policies was attempted.[81]

Classification. – We have said that the reason why inter|national tribunals ought not to rely on a specific system of private international law is that there is no *lex fori*. The absence of a *lex fori* accounts also for the absence of difficulties of what is technically known as conflicts of classification.[82] At the risk of saying things which are known to this audience, perhaps I ought to say what the problem of classification means in this connection. The case of *In re Annesley,*[83] decided by Russell J. (as he then was), may serve as an illustration. Mrs. Annesley, a British subject, died in France, leaving movables in England. According to English private international law, movable property is to be distributed according to the law of the domicile at the time of the death of the *de cuius*. According to the English conception of domicile, Mrs. Annesley was domiciled in France. According to the French conception, she was domiciled in England. How, then, was the technical term of domicile to be interpreted? Russell J. held that before an English court the English interpretation of a technical rule of private international law was

---

[77] M.A.T., 1, p. 726 (729); 7, p. 112 (114).

[78] M.A.T., 4, p. 515, at pp. 524, 525.

[79] M.A.T., 5, p. 200, at p. 211.

[80] M.A.T., 7, p. 111, at p. 114.

[81] M.A.T., 1, p. 899 (903). In fact, this case turns upon the cumulation of the rules of illegality contained in two systems of laws. The tribunal was not concerned with the exclusion of a particular rule of foreign law, applicable in the circumstances. This, however, is the function of »*ordre public*« in the realm of private international law.

[82] Niboyet, *Revue de droit international privé*, 22 (1927), pp. 103 ff. with further literature; Gutzwiller, loc. cit., p. 149.

[83] [1926] Ch. 692.

alone admissible, on the ground that English law was the *lex fori*. In this respect, in the absence of a *lex fori*, the Mixed Arbitral Tribunals were in a more favourable position.

Except for international treaties and conventions,[84] the tribunals have been able to lay down their own rules of private international law in unequivocal terms and could, therefore, avoid the application of such tests as might have led to ambiguities, having regard to different meanings attributed to such tests by the various municipal systems. In applying international treaties and conventions, however, such conflicts could not be avoided nor could they be disregarded.[85]

Only in rare cases have the courts attempted to classify according to an arbitrarily chosen municipal system,[86] or by coupling the interpretation given by two systems,[87] or by opposing|them to a third.[88] Two tendencies can be observed: one based upon general conceptions of jurisprudence, and another based upon a somewhat unfortunate principle of private international law. In general, the tribunals classify according to »common juridical notion,«[89] »*principes universellement admis en matière législative,*«[90] »*portée générale,*«[91] »*sens large,*«[92] or they examine whether in the case in question institutions in both systems concerned tally in substance, despite the fact that they are classified under different headings.[93]

In matters of contract and succession, a tendency can be noticed to classify according to the law applicable to such contract or succession.[94] This practice may end in a vicious circle for the reason that the question what system of laws applies to the contract or succession may, in turn, depend upon the question according to what system of laws the tribunal classifies.

---

[84] Niboyet, *Revue critique de droit international*, 30 (1935), pp. 1–34, especially pp. 29 ff.

[85] M.A.T., 3, p. 305; 4, p. 842 (847); 9, p. 230 (233).

[86] M.A.T., 3, p. 274 (277); 5, p. 218 (224); *ibid.*, p. 235 (240); 6, p. 542; *ibid.*, p. 635 (637); *ibid.*, p. 665 (670). See also 7, p. 324 (326); but see 2, p. 211 (212); 3, p. 255 (256).

[87] M.A.T., 4, p. 390 (393); 5, p. 200 (214); *ibid.*, p. 429; *ibid.*, p. 670 (672); 7, p. 353 (iii); 8, p. 402.

[88] M.A.T., 1, p. 730 (733); 7, p. 353; *ibid.*, pp. 741 ff.

[89] M.A.T., 7, p. 353 (iii); *ibid.*, p. 947.

[90] M.A.T., 2, p. 395 (400).

[91] M.A.T., 1, p. 616 (619).

[92] M.A.T., 1, p. 600 (605).

[93] M.A.T., 3, p. 67 (72); *ibid.*, p. 223 (225); *ibid.*, p. 252; *ibid.*, 749 (753); 4, p. 59 (63); *ibid.*, p. 657 (660); 5, p. 303 (305); *ibid.*, p. 506 (512); *ibid.*, p. 635; 6, p. 2 (8); *ibid.*, p. 77 (80); *ibid.*, p. 228 (230); *ibid.*, p. 243 (248); *ibid.*, p. 655 (658); *ibid.*, p. 828 (830); 7, p. 403 (408). See also M.A.T., 2, p. 703; 6, p. 397 (399); 7, p. 280 (282); but see 8, p. 64 at p. 71, where the Anglo-German Mixed Arbitral Tribunal disregarded both the English and the German conception as to the time when a claim for general average falls due and substituted a conception of its own. See also Niboyet, *Revue de droit international privé*, 22 (1927), pp. 105–106.

[94] M.A.T., 2, p. 715 (718); 3, p. 232 (234); *ibid.*, p. 918 (922); 5, p. 305 (308); 6, p. 11 (13); 7, p. 516 (518) (Succession).

In a few cases, the law of the debtor's domicile provides the basis for the purpose of classification[95] – an arbitrary principle. Lastly, tribunals, on occasions, declare that their choice of law, including classification, is based upon »common ground.«[96] This seems to indicate a voluntary agreement of the parties on entering the litigation – a method which, although of practical importance,[97] need not be discussed in detail.

| II

Practice of Mixed Arbitral Tribunals

We have thus seen the dangers which beset any method based on the application of a specific system of municipal rules of private international law. International tribunals – and especially Mixed Arbitral Tribunals – have been alive to that danger and have, on the whole, decided cases by dint of the application of what may be called a system of private international law of their own. The object of the second part of this paper is to show by reference to specific questions how that method has been put into practice by the Mixed Arbitral Tribunals.

Nationality and Domicile

Both nationality and domicile have always been of great importance as tests with a view to ascertaining the status of persons. Tendencies in favour of the Anglo-American test of domicile or the Continental test of nationality are both to be noticed in the case law of the Mixed Arbitral Tribunals. When the test of domicile, familiar to English law though less to Continental law, is applied, it is applied in accordance with the meaning attached to it by English law.[98]

Nationality is, of course, determined by the law of the country in question.[99] The solution adopted by the Mixed Arbitral Tribunals in the case of

---

[95] M.A.T., 1, p. 730 (734); 2, p. 217 (219–220).

[96] See *e.g.* M.A.T., 6, p. 60 (62); *ibid.*, p. 75 (76); *ibid.*, p. 585 (587); *ibid.*, p. 643 (645); *ibid.*, p. 671 (674); 7, p. 330 (333); *ibid.*, p. 370; *ibid.*, p. 453.

[97] See *e.g.* M.A.T., 4, p. 530 (534); *ibid.*, p. 717; 5, p. 551 (563); 6, p. 573 (577); *ibid.*, p. 587; *ibid.*, p. 641; 8, p. 60; *ibid.*, p. 280; 9, p. 224; *ibid.*, p. 482; *ibid.*, p. 687.

[98] See the cases referred to above, note 86.

[99] M.A.T., 6, p. 220 (224); *ibid.*, p. 338 ff.; *ibid.*, p. 347; 7, p. 328; *ibid.*, p. 470; *ibid.*, p. 601; *ibid.*, p. 647; *ibid.*, p. 735; 8, p. 156; *ibid.*, p. 187; *ibid.*, p. 375; *ibid.*, p. 388; *ibid.*, p. 401; *ibid.*, p. 452; *ibid.*, p. 682; *ibid.*, p. 951; 9, p. 81 (85); *ibid.*, p. 253; *ibid.*, p. 438; *ibid.*, p. 593; *ibid.*, 620; *ibid.*, p. 627; *ibid.*, p. 763.

double nationality must be regarded as very satisfactory. For the purpose of these tribunals, nationality in such cases is to be determined by the law of that country with which a connection both of law and also of fact can be established,[100] a solution which found clear expression in the Hague Convention on Double Nationality of 1930.

The private status of persons has been very rarely the concern of the Mixed Arbitral Tribunals. Capacity appears to be governed by the *lex patriae*.[101] The law governing the relations between husband and wife was the object of three decisions. It is the | *lex patriae* of the spouses[102]; in a claim for maintenance it does not appear clearly whether the father's law is meant to be that of his *lex patriae* or of his domicile.[103] The position of a *curator absentis* is governed by the *lex rei sitae*.[104]

Nationality and Status of Corporate Bodies

The question whether corporations can possess a nationality has been the subject of much discussion for many years.[105] It is to be regretted that statements such as that by Lord Westbury in *Udny* v. *Udny*,[106] where he distinguished between the bonds of nationality and of domicile in matters of status, were originally confined to the status of individuals only. The Mixed Arbitral Tribunals have not been able to avoid confusion when confronted with this intricate question. But two outstanding decisions of the Franco-German Mixed Arbitral Tribunal have done much to elucidate it. In these cases, it was held that the essence of nationality consisted in the enjoyment of civic rights and in the bond of allegiance; that corporate bodies, unlike individuals, could not enjoy such rights and be subject to such duties and that, in order to ascertain the nationality of a corporate body, the corporate veil must be lifted. Seeing that the shareholders, being individuals, possessed a nationality, the majority of the shareholders determined the nationality of

---

[100] M.A.T., 6, p. 499 (503); *ibid.*, p. 806 (809), referring to *Annuaire de l'Institut de droit international*, 1888–89, p. 25; not quite clear: M.A.T., 2, p. 72; 7, p. 327 (329).

[101] Not quite clear: M.A.T., 9, p. 295.

[102] M.A.T., 1, p. 935; 6, p. 922 (925). See also 8, p. 553 (557).

[103] M.A.T., 6, p. 614.

[104] M.A.T., 2, p. 305; 3, p. 824 (828); 5, p. 502 (505); 9, p. 564.

[105] For a general survey see Travers, *Hague Recueil*, 33 (1930), pp. 1–109; Rühland, *ibid.*, 45 (1933), pp. 391–467 with further literature; Streit, *Revue de droit international et de législation comparée*, 1928 (3rd ser. vol. x), pp. 494–521. For a discussion of the practice of the Mixed Arbitral Tribunals on this question see Vaughan Williams and Chrussachi, 49 (1933) *L.Q.R.*, pp. 334–349; Gutzwiller, loc. cit., p. 130 with further literature; Ruze, *Revue de droit international et de législation comparée*, 1922 (3rd ser. vol. iii), pp. 54–60.

[106] [1869] L.R., 1 Sc. & Div., 441, at p. 457.

the corporate body.[107] In matters of private law, corporate bodies were subject to the law of their *»siège social.«* It must be admitted that this view did not meet with the unanimous approval of the other Mixed Arbitral Tribunals. Thus it was held by the Anglo-Bulgarian Mixed Arbitral Tribunal: »the recognition in the case of the *Daimler Company Limited* of the principle that a company constituted under the law of one power may, by reason of the conduct of its shareholders or of | those in control of its affairs, acquire the character of an enemy of that power from the standpoint of its laws regarding trading with the enemy, is in no way inconsistent with the recognition, as the test of nationality, of the law to the provisions of which the corporation owes its existence.[108]

In the cases decided by the Franco-German Mixed Arbitral Tribunal, a distinction is drawn between the public and the private status of corporations. This distinction, unnecessary in municipal private international law,[109] except in the case of war, is essential for international tribunals. Before them the nationality of a corporation must be established in order to ascertain, at the outset, the right of the corporation to sue or to be sued as a national of one of the states which have constituted the tribunals and which are subject to their jurisdiction.[110] For this purpose, and for this purpose alone, the test of control is applicable.[111] It enables the courts to arrive at a conclusion as to the nationality of the majority of the shareholders, as a corporation itself cannot be regarded as a national of any country for the reasons indicated in the decisions quoted above.[112] Control is a crude test at its best, as it does not take into account the nationality of the minority of the shareholders. However, it must be admitted that the test advocated here has

---

[107] M.A.T., 1, p. 427–428; 2, p. 384 (388); 3, p. 889, at pp. 892–893; 4, p. 803; but see 2, p. 72 (76); *ibid.*, p. 896; 7, p. 716 (723).

[108] M.A.T., 3, p. 534 (536). See also 1, p. 722 (723), 3, p. 265; 9, p. 665; McNair, *B.Y.I.L.*, 4 (1923–24), pp. 44 ff.; Holdsworth, *History of English Law,* 9, pp. 71, 103–104; Parry, 4 (1941) *Modern Law Review*, p. 168 ff.

[109] A widespread uncertainty can be observed in municipal private international law regarding the importance of nationality in the law of corporations. See the excellent discussion in *Répertoire de droit international*, vol. 10 (1931), s.v. *Sociétés en droit international*, nos. 12 ff., especially no. 27; Niboyet, *Revue de droit international privé*, 22 (1927), pp. 402–417.

[110] A change of nationality does not, therefore, affect the existence of a corporation. See M.A.T., 6, p. 172; 7, p. 473 (476); *ibid.*, p. 961; 9, p. 263 (265).

[111] See the cases cited above, note 107. See also M.A.T., 1, p. 401 (404); 5, p. 777 (779); 7, p. 890; 8, p. 518; 9, p. 189; *ibid.*, p. 508. However, the seat of the corporation or the place of its incorporation are also put forward as tests in order to ascertain the nationality of corporations. See M.A.T., 3, p. 535; 7, p. 837; *ibid.*, p. 876; *ibid.*, p. 953; 8, p. 539; *ibid.*, p. 587; *ibid.*, p. 670–671; *ibid.*, p. 701; 9, p. 403–404; *ibid.*, p. 453; *ibid.*, p. 539; *ibid.*, p. 667. Doubtful, 7, p. 895.

[112] See above, note 107.

not been universally admitted and a widespread uncertainty and discrepancy of solutions has ensued.[113]

| A different question is that of ascertaining the private status of corporations, *i.e.* the law governing their formation, representation, dissolution, their liability for debts of their predecessors, etc.[114] Very often a terminological confusion can be observed. The courts purport to ascertain the nationality of a corporation, while in reality they attempt to ascertain the law governing its private status.[115]

Unfortunately, a wide choice of tests has been suggested for this purpose. The test of control, applicable to the public status of corporate bodies, is again put forward.[116] The reason appears to be less a preference for this test than the wording of the Treaty of Peace,[117] and of municipal statutes passed during the Great War,[118] neither of which are concerned with the private status of corporations. Control is a dangerous test, as it may lead to heavy fluctuations in the law governing the private status of a corporation whenever dealings in its stock proceed. It is an unreliable test, if bearer shares are issued. It is an inaccurate test, as the shareholders, nationals of one country, can hardly influence through their control the private structure of a previously existing corporation in another country.

Two more tests are suggested and applied: the seat of the corporation[119] and the place of its creation.[120] It is submitted with some confidence that the law of the place of creation should be applied before international tribunals. Municipal systems of conflict of laws prefer the test of the »seat of the corporation.« Apparently, this preference is prompted by the fear on the part of municipal courts that if the test of creation were adopted, corporations created abroad would claim the benefit of the law of the place of their creation long after they had severed their relations with that country and although their present seat is|established within the jurisdiction of the courts concerned. In the case of International Tribunals this danger does not exist. On the other hand, the test of creation, as compared with that of the seat of

---

[113] See the cases cited above, notes 107 and 111; M.A.T., 4, p. 359. See also Gutzwiller, loc. cit., p. 180, note 15; Feller, *Zeitschrift für ausländisches öffentliches Recht und Völkerrecht*, ii, 2 (1930), p. 55.

[114] M.A.T., 7, p. 808.

[115] See e.g. M.A.T., 1, p. 611 (614); *ibid.*, p. 722 (724); 3, p. 570 (572) 5, p. 418 (421); *ibid.*, p. 779; *ibid.*, p. 849 (852); 7, p. 473.

[116] M.A.T., 5, p. 418 (421); 6, p. 810 (813); *ibid.*, p. 859 (861).

[117] M.A.T., 1, p. 401 (405); *ibid.*, p. 722 (725); 3, p. 534; *ibid.*, p. 954 (960); 5, p. 779; *ibid.*, p. 849 (852); 6, p. 859 (861). See art. 74 (i) and 297 (*b*) of the Treaty of Versailles.

[118] M.A.T., 2, p. 384 (388).

[119] M.A.T., 1, p. 422 (428); 3, p. 570 (573); *ibid.*, p. 889 (892); 5, p. 58 (68); *ibid.*, p. 430; 7, p. 476; *ibid.*, p. 856.

[120] M.A.T., 1, p. 722 (724); 3, p. 535; *ibid.*, p. 771; 5, p. 684. Doubtful: M.A.T., 2, p. 73 (75); *ibid.*, p. 895 (897); 3, p. 261 (265); 6, p. 611; 8, p. 586; 9, p. 046.

the corporation, offers the advantage of certainty, whenever a corporation consists of several branch establishments,[121] unless these branch establishments form separate entities.[122] The correctness of the view which distinguishes between public status (nationality) and private status (corporate structure) in matters of corporate bodies is also illustrated by the decisions regarding partnerships. While their private capacity is subject to the law governing the contract of partnership,[123] the nationality of partnerships is determined by that of its members.[124] They represent it proportionally, if of different nationality.[125] Claims vested in the partnership are apportioned among all of the partners. It is thus possible to ascertain the nationality of partnership claims.

Contracts; Conclusion of Contracts

A great amount of material and a great variety of solutions are to be found in decisions relating to contracts. I have already dealt in another place with the difficulty in municipal conflict of laws of ascertaining whether or not a contract is concluded.[126] Conflicts of classification may easily arise. This difficulty is even greater in the case of international tribunals which do not possess a *lex fori* to guide them. Sometimes the English solution is adopted,[127] sometimes Continental doctrines,[128] sometimes the plaintiff's and the defendant's | national system are coupled.[129] Once the law governing the contract, when concluded, is applied to determine whether it is concluded and whether the necessary formalities have been complied with.[130] This is a vicious circle. As long as it is unknown whether a contract has been concluded, the law governing the contract, where concluded, must be unknown, too.

---

[121] M.A.T., 1, p. 328 (333); *ibid.*, p. 795; *ibid.*, p. 864; *ibid.*, p. 872; *ibid.*, p. 986; 5, p. 781; 6, p. 413.

[122] M.A.T., 1, p. 722; 6, p. 834; *ibid.*, p. 840.

[123] M.A.T., 3, p. 261 (268); *ibid.*, p. 998 (1004); 8, p. 301; sometimes the law of the seat of the partnership or of the place where it was constituted is called upon to govern the private status of the partnership; see *e.g.* M.A.T., 8, p. 736. The Anglo-German Mixed Arbitral Tribunal favoured an independent solution and combined the rules of the English and the German law of partnership; see M.A.T., 3, p. 17; *ibid.*, p. 774. Not clear: M.A.T. 5, p. 387.

[124] M.A.T., 3, p. 688; 5, p. 855 (856); 8, 962.

[125] M.A.T., 3, p. 12 (17); *ibid.*, p. 19; 5, p. 376; *ibid.*, p. 664; 7, p. 370 (371); *ibid.*, p. 490; *ibid.*, p. 612. See also M.A.T., 2, p. 780 (783).

[126] 12 (1938) *St. John's Law Review*, p. 242, at p. 259.

[127] M.A.T., 2, p. 713.

[128] M.A.T., 3, p. 1024 (2); 5, p. 200 (213); *ibid.*, p. 218 (224); 6, p. 657; 7, 772; but see the obscure reasoning in M.A.T., 8, p. 66. See also Gutzwiller, loc. cit., p. 140, note 49. For a discussion of the various doctrines see Winfield, 55 (1939) *L.Q.R.*, p. 499 ff.

[129] M.A.T., 3, p. 1024.

[130] M.A.T., 8, p. 65, at p. 69.

Even if the vicious circle in matters of logic should be passed over, the last solution does not recommend itself for practical reasons. As we shall see later on, the law governing a contract may be the law of the place where the contract is concluded or the law of the place where the contract is to be performed. In the first case we are confronted once more with the problem whether and where the contract was concluded; in the second case, the attempt to ascertain the place of performance may give rise to a second conflict of classification, for the place of performance may differ according to what system of law is applied.[131] Having regard to the character of international tribunals it is advisable to eliminate opportunities for a conflict of classification as far as possible. Consequently, offer and acceptance should be governed by the law of the domicile of each party respectively.

Essential Validity

The question which test should be applied to contracts, their validity and execution, has been one of the most frequently discussed in private international law. Though certain general tendencies can be observed, the variety of solutions is astounding. General tests governing all obligations and special rules applicable to particular types of contracts, rules governing the contract as a whole and rules governing parts of it only (conclusion, interpretation, performance, illegality, etc.), all of these have been proposed and none of them rejected.

It is therefore not surprising to find some disagreement in the decisions of the Mixed Arbitral Tribunals, when concerned with conflict of laws in matters of contracts. The present writer has laid down elsewhere his reasons for preferring different rules for different types of contracts[132]; principally for the reason that conflicts of classification may thus be excluded. As indicated above, this argument applies with even greater force in the case of international tribunals. Accordingly, an attempt will be made in the present study to lay down rules applicable to different types of contracts, as far as the decisions permit it.

In general, however, international tribunals adhere to the orthodox doctrine and apply the same tests to all contracts regardless of their character. But even so, a variety of solutions is offered. Free choice of law is universally admitted.[133] If such a choice is not expressed, the courts try to establish the

---

[131] M.A.T., 5, p. 200 (214). See also Lewald, *Répertoire de droit international*, 10 (1931), p. 75, no. 23.

[132] 12 (1938) *St. John's Law Review*, p. 242, at p. 262.

[133] M.A.T., 1, p. 587 (589); *ibid.*, p. 727; *ibid.*, p. 927 (930); 3, 280 (283); *ibid.*, p. 543; *ibid.*, p. 578 (586); *ibid.*, p. 787; *ibid.*, p. 808; *ibid.*, p. 1025; 4, p. 858 (860); *ibid.*, p. 520; *ibid.*, p. 627 (633); 5, p. 200 (211); *ibid.*, p. 928; 6, p. 851; *ibid.*, p. 678.

presumed intention of the parties.[134] In this connection, or as a supplementary test, recourse is had to the *lex loci contractus*,[135] to the *lex loci solutionis*,[136] or to the proper law.[137] It is to be regretted that little use has been made of this test, which limits the parties in the exercise of their liberty of choice of law.[138] Contracts of a private law nature entered into by a state are not necessarily subject to the law of that state.[139]

In a remarkable judgment the German-Roumanian Mixed Arbitral Tribunal, fully conscious of the different outlook in the case of international tribunals, attempted, in the absence of a clear choice of law, to substitute yet another rule for the generally accepted principle that the *lex loci contractus* or the *lex loci solutionis*[140] applies. This Tribunal was aware of possible conflicts of classification. The definition of the *locus contractus* or *solutionis* may vary considerably according to what system of laws is applied as the law of the court. Moreover, in bilateral contracts, there may be two different places of performance. The Tribunal | tried to avoid this difficulty and advocated the application of the *lex loci contractus* in questions connected with the conclusion and the general effect of a contract, but of the respective *leges patriae* in matters of performance.[141]

While the courage of the court must be admired, it is questionable whether a dismemberment of the contract is the only solution to be recommended.[142] However, should this solution be adopted, it would appear that the law of the domicile of the respective parties should be applied in preference to their *leges patriae*.[143] The Mixed Arbitral Tribunal rejected this test in passing.[144]

With equal vigour, the German-Roumanian Tribunal disposed of the French doctrine of directory and mandatory laws which allows free choice

---

[134] M.A.T., 1, p. 587 (589); *ibid.*, p. 784, 3, p. 1025; 5, p. 200 (211); *ibid.*, p. 218 (225); *ibid.*, p. 923; 7, p. 459.

[135] M.A.T., 4, p. 717; 5, p. 73; *ibid.*, p. 588. See also the cases cited below, note 186.

[136] M.A.T., 3, p. 286 (289); *ibid.*, p. 1020 (1024); 4, p. 312 (315); 5, p. 218 (224); *ibid.*, p. 240; *ibid.*, p. 568; *ibid.*, p. 602; 7, p. 103 (110); *ibid.*, p. 787; *ibid.*, p. 750; *ibid.*, p. 772; 8, p. 917 (920).

[137] M.A.T., 3, p. 964 (966); *ibid.*, p. 1025; 4, p. 219; 5, p. 212 (5); 7, p. 854.

[138] See Niboyet, *Revue de droit international privé*, 22 (1927), p. 108.

[139] M.A.T., 7, p. 787; but see *P.C.I.J.*, arr. 14, p. 42; arr. 15, p. 121; Niboyet, *Hague Recueil*, 40 (1932), pp. 208–211.

[140] It is interesting to note that the Permanent Court disregarded these tests altogether; see above, note 189.

[141] M.A.T., 5, pp. 211, 214; 7, p. 745; *ibid.*, p. 772. See also *Revue de droit international privé*, 22 (1927), p. 97 with a note by Niboyet; Gutzwiller, loc. cit., p. 135.

[142] For a discussion of the same question in American conflict of laws, see Barbey, *Le conflit des lois en matière de contrats* (1938), p. 124, note 3, containing a survey of the literature.

[143] Lipstein, 12 (1938) *St. John's Law Review*, p. 261, and note 92.

[144] M.A.T., 1, p. 729.

of law within the framework of the proper law or of the *lex fori*.[145] This doctrine, the Tribunal observed with full justification, is unsuitable for international courts. To stress the importance of the *lex fori*, to refer to the proper law and to allow a second choice of law (*renvoi*, etc.) is not in keeping with the character of international tribunals.

Different Types of Contracts

The uncertainty of the courts regarding conflict of laws in matters of contract is illustrated by the variety of rules applied by the Mixed Arbitral Tribunals with regard to different types of contracts.

Wherever sale is involved, the following tests are suggested: the intention of the parties,[146] the *lex loci contractus*,[147] or the *lex loci solutionis*.[148] In the case of eviction the *leges patriae* of the parties are coupled,[149] or the *lex contractus* is applied.[150] Judicial review in case of »lésion« is governed by the law applicable to the contract.[151] Delivery is governed by the *lex loci solutionis*.[152]

| Two questions have attracted the particular interest of the tribunals: the passing of the risk and the passing of the property. In matters of risk,[153] the courts show an inclination towards the cumulation of national systems of laws.[154] It is not clear whether this is due to a preference for the comparative method or whether it is due to the fact that two *leges solutionis* may exist in bilateral contracts. Sometimes, and very correctly, the law of the contract is applied.[155]

In connection with the question whether ownership had passed in consequence of a sale, the courts had to decide whether this question must be classified as one of contract or of property.[156] Following the judgment of the Belgian-German Tribunal in *Bartelous* v. *German Government*,[157] the majority of the tribunals classified it as one of property and applied the *lex rei*

---

[145] M.A.T., 5, p. 211. For a discussion of this doctrine see Lipstein, loc. cit., p. 261 ff.

[146] M.A.T., 1, p. 589; 3, p. 283.

[147] M.A.T., 3, p. 277. See also 1, p. 614.

[148] M.A.T., 1, p. 464; 3, p. 289; 5, p. 224; *ibid.*, p. 240.

[149] M.A.T., 4, p. 367.

[150] M.A.T. 5, p. 462 (463); 6, p. 204.

[151] M.A.T., 5, 161 (163).

[152] M.A.T., 7, p. 355; but see 6, p. 654.

[153] See Gutzwiller, loc. cit., p. 146; Rabel and Raiser, *Zeitschrift für ausländisches und internationales Privatrecht*, 3 (1929), pp. 62–81.

[154] M.A.T., 2, p. 827; *ibid.*, p. 362; *ibid.*, p. 364; *ibid.*, p. 749; *ibid.*, p. 754; *ibid.*, p. 787; 3, p. 371; *ibid.*, p. 388; 7, p. 774; 8, p. 79; *ibid.*, p. 127.

[155] M.A.T., 3, p. 332; *ibid.*, p. 685–686; *ibid.*, p. 808; 7, p. 359. Not clear: M.A.T., 3, p. 381 (383); 7, p. 29; *ibid.*, p. 31 (33); 8, p. 79.

[156] See Rabel and Raiser, loc. cit., pp. 66 ff.

[157] M.A.T., 3, p. 274 (277); Gutzwiller, loc. cit., p. 144.

sitae[158]; other tribunals adhered to the *lex contractus*,[159] or attempted a cumulation[160] of the *leges patriae* of vendor and purchaser. However, it is doubtful whether the preference for the *lex rei sitae*, expressed in *Bartelous* v. *German Government*, is justified or necessary, as the prevalence of the *lex rei sitae* over every other test is less essential before international tribunals than before municipal courts, where the question of effectiveness is ever present.[161]

In cases of loans, the expressed or presumed intention of the | parties determines the law governing the contract.[162] Deposit is governed by the law chosen by the parties,[163] or by the debtor's law,[164] but it is not clear in one case what test was in fact applied.[165] A tendency towards cumulation can be observed in the cases on agency.[166] Some uncertainty exists with regard to contracts on the Stock Exchange and brokerage[167]; dealings with banks are governed by the law of the bank's seat.[168] The same test applies in the case of contracts of insurance.[169] The law of the debtor's domicile governs the liabilities arising from bills of exchange.[170]

The *lex rei sitae* is adopted in cases of lease.[171] Labour contracts are governed by the law applicable at the seat of the firm, but other tests are applied as well.[172] The expressed or presumed intention of the parties determines the law applicable to contracts of transport, especially by railway[173]; this is,

---

[158] M.A.T., 5, p. 58 (74); *ibid.*, p. 588; 6, p. 564 (569); 7, p. 117; *ibid.*, p. 348. Doubtful: M.A.T., 5, p. 218 (224); *ibid.*, p. 293; *ibid.*, p. 949; 7, p. 89; *ibid.*, p. 97; *ibid.*, p. 783; *ibid.*, p. 792; 8, p. 692. See also M.A.T., 5, p. 200, at p. 212, where the German-Roumanian Mixed Arbitral Tribunal approved the application of the *lex rei sitae* in respect of the rights of third parties only. See also Niboyet, *Revue de droit international privé*, 22 (1927), p. 108.

[159] M.A.T., 6, p. 62; *ibid.*, p. 76 (77); *ibid.*, p. 647; 7, p. 773; 9, p. 10.

[160] M.A.T., 1, p. 589; 8, p. 933; *ibid.*, p. 1000; 9, 428–429; *ibid.*, p. 525 (528).

[161] Niboyet, *Revue de droit international privé*, 22 (1927), pp. 108–109, suggests that the *lex rei sitae* should be applied, subject to the qualification that the *lex rei sitae* may refer to another system of laws, such as the law of the contract. This suggestion must be rejected for the reason that it introduces the element of *renvoi*.

[162] M.A.T., 5, 919 (923). Not clear: 1, p 849; 3, p. 875; 8, p. 282; *ibid.*, p. 805.

[163] M.A.T., 6, p. 351.

[164] M.A.T., 5, p. 753.

[165] M.A.T., 8, p. 920.

[166] M.A.T., 1, p. 464; 2, p. 93; 3, p. 1024; 7, p. 226.

[167] M.A.T., 5, p. 799; 6, p. 299. See also 1, p. 727; 2, p. 266; 3, p. 1; *ibid.*, p. 8; 7, p. 451; Gutzwiller, loc. cit., p. 143, note 60.

[168] Doubtful: M.A.T., 5, p. 602. For the law applicable in the case of cheques see M.A.T., 8, p. 792; 9, p. 687.

[169] M.A.T., 6, p. 55; *ibid.*, p. 659; for other solutions see M.A.T., 5, p. 347; 8, p. 644.

[170] M.A.T., 9, p. 573. See also 6, p. 586; 7, p. 461 (464); but see 2, p. 784; 4, p. 267.

[171] M.A.T., 2, p. 906; 5, p. 406. See also 2, p. 296; 5, p. 110; 7, p. 958; 8, p. 34 (36); Gutzwiller, loc. cit., p. 142, note 57.

[172] M.A.T., 4, p. 320; but see 2, p. 715; *ibid.*, p. 722; 4, p. 82; *ibid.*, p. 314.

[173] M.A.T., 1, p. 784; 2, p. 254.

generally, the law of the railways.[174] Free choice of law,[175] supplemented by the *lex loci contractus* and by the law of the flag, is adopted in matters of carriage of goods by sea.[176] Contracts for professional services by a lawyer are apparently connected with the law of the latter's domicile.[177] But in a rather singular case of a physician the proper law of the contract was applied.[178]

No clear test is laid down for cases concerning partnerships[179] | and sureties.[180] Trusts are governed by the law chosen by the parties or by the law of the debtor's domicile[181]; in one case a cumulation of the national laws of the parties took place.[182] Intention is also the test for compromises.[183] Subscription of shares appears to be connected with the law of the Company's seat.[184] The liability of shareholders is ascertained by a cumulation of the *leges patriae* of the parties.[185]

The question, much disputed in municipal private international law, what law to apply to quasi-contracts has given rise to equal difficulties before international tribunals. *Negotiorum gestio* appears to be governed by the law of the debtor's domicile,[186] or by the *lex loci actus.*[187] However, in actions for unjustified enrichment, the application of the *lex loci actus* entails great hardship whenever one of the parties is English.[188] Frequently it remains a mere matter of chance whether payment is made in England or abroad. If made in England, the rule in *Chandler* v. *Webster*[189] may apply and the action must fail. If payment is made abroad, the claim must succeed. Having regard to the decision in *Cantiare San Rocco* v. *Clyde Shipbuilding and Engineering Co. Ltd.*[190] and in view of the general tendency admitting claims for unjustified enrichment, as a principle of equity,[191] the Anglo-German Mixed Arbitral

---

[174] M.A.T., 2, p. 221; 3, p. 623; 9, p. 335.

[175] M.A.T., 1, p. 930; 4, p. 633.

[176] M.A.T., 4, p. 633. See also 3, p. 787.

[177] M.A.T., 7, p. 420; 8, p. 283 (284).

[178] M.A.T., 3, p. 964 (966).

[179] M.A.T., 2, p. 275; 6, p. 674; 7, p. 370; *ibid.*, p. 431; 8, p. 114; 9, p. 36 (39); Gutzwiller, loc. cit., p. 143, note 59.

[180] M.A.T., 5, p. 602; 8, p. 19; *ibid.*, p. 60; *ibid.*, p. 796 (799).

[181] M.A.T., 6, p. 12; 9, p. 18.

[182] M.A.T., 7, p. 880 (881).

[183] M.A.T., 4, p. 360.

[184] M.A.T., 6, p. 932 (935).

[185] M.A.T., 9, p. 57.

[186] M.A.T., 3, p. 925; 4, p. 345; 7, p. 374; *ibid.*, p. 383; *ibid.*, p. 420; *ibid.*, p. 435; *ibid.*, p. 497; *ibid.*, p. 500; 8, p. 10; 9, p. 247 (248); *ibid.*, p. 482.

[187] M.A.T., 7, p. 435; but see 4, p. 64; 7, p. 366; *ibid.*, p. 509; 8, p. 921; 9, p. 73; *ibid.*, p. 468.

[188] Gutteridge and Lipstein, 7 (1939) *Cambridge L.J.*, p. 89.

[189] [1904] 1 K.B. 493.

[190] [1924] A.C. 226.

[191] M.A.T., 3, p. 291 (295).

Tribunal allowed claims for unjustified enrichment, but no reference was made to any specific municipal system of laws.[192] The principle, there|fore, appears to apply as a rule of international public policy, a solution which recommends itself in the present case.

Illegality

It has been pointed out above that the practice of Mixed Arbitral Tribunals regarding rules of conflict of laws applicable to different types of contracts varies considerably. It varies even more in matters affecting the validity of contracts. Every conceivable test is applied in connection with the question of illegality: the law of the debtor's domicile or the *lex loci solutionis*,[193] the *lex loci contractus*,[194] the national laws of the parties,[195] and the law governing the contract.[196] The latter test recommends itself for the following reasons. Seeing that the parties may freely choose the law to be applied to their contract, it is undesirable to add the provisions in matters of illegality of yet another system. It must be admitted that, before municipal courts, the rules regarding illegality as established by the *lex fori* play an important part. On the other hand, no such rules apply before international tribunals owing to the absence of a *lex fori*. International public policy, being vague, cannot supersede the provisions on illegality contained in municipal systems of laws. Our conclusion is therefore that, before international tribunals, the parties are free to choose the system of laws applicable to their relations, but their freedom is limited by the rules of illegality laid down by that system of laws.

---

[192] M.A.T., 6, p. 18 (16); *ibid.*, p. 590; *ibid.*, p. 607; *ibid.*, p. 639, and 7, p. 514; 7, p. 399; 8, p. 111. See also M.A.T., 2, p. 245; 3, p. 448; 4, p. 534. The German-Roumanian Mixed Arbitral Tribunal, in accordance with its decision in the matter of the law governing contractual obligations (M.A.T., 5, p. 200, at p. 213), applied the national law of the debtor in the absence of a single system of laws governing all relations between the parties; see M.A.T., 7, p. 745; 8, p. 712.

[193] M.A.T., 3, p. 541 (543).

[194] M.A.T., 5, p. 919 (923). See also 6, p. 116.

[195] M.A.T., 1, p. 899 (903); 7, p. 467.

[196] M.A.T., 1, p. 726 (729); 6, p. 46 (48); *ibid.*, p. 715.

Error, Duress, Fraud, etc.

It is submitted that the law governing the contract should apply to questions of error,[197] duress,[198] and fraud,[199] as well as to questions of delay and interest. But the cases are obscure and offer a great variety of tests. For delay: the law of the contract,[200] and a cumulation of national systems.[201] For interest: the law of the contract,[202] or the *lex loci solutionis*.[203] For judicial review: the law of the contract,[204] or a cumulation of | systems of laws.[205] Equally, the law of the contract should be applied to questions of discharge[206] and set-off,[207] but other tests are also to be found.[208]

The decisions on assignment[209] and subrogation[210] permit of different interpretations. Consequently, no attempt shall be made here to lay down any working rule. By the Treaty of Peace[211] prescription was to be governed by the law of the debtor's country. After some difficulty in classifying owing to the procedural character of prescription in English law, the majority of the tribunals applied the debtor's national law, including its rules of conflict of laws which, at times, referred to another system of laws.[212] In a few cases the law of the contract furnished the rules of prescription.[213] This solution recommends itself. The solution adopted by the majority of the tribunals appears permissible in view of the treaty provisions, but exception has been taken above to the application of municipal systems of conflict of laws as a whole, including *renvoi*, whatever the circumstances may be.

---

[197] M.A.T., 4, p. 853 (860).

[198] M.A.T., 2, p. 586; 8, p. 428 (483).

[199] M.A.T., 4, p. 503 (505).

[200] M.A.T., 3, p. 286 (289); 4, p. 515 (528); 5, p. 226; *ibid.*, p. 241. See also 9, p. 125.

[201] M.A.T., 8, p. 570 (574); 8, p. 408–404. See also 8, p. 987.

[202] M.A.T., 8, p. 847 (853); 5, p. 827 (828).

[203] M.A.T., 5, p. 670 (672); *ibid.*, p. 675 (677). See also 4, p. 268.

[204] M.A.T., 8, p. 288; *ibid.*, p. 586; *ibid.*, p. 844. See above, note 151.

[205] M.A.T., 2, p. 641 (647); 7, p. 774; 9, p. 684.

[206] M.A.T., 4, pp. 534, 535; 6, p. 679 (685); 7, p. 468. See also 8, p. 310.

[207] M.A.T., 3, p. 847 (854); 6, p. 104 (105).

[208] For discharge: see M.A.T., 2, p. 882 (885); 8, p. 220 (223); 4, p. 48 (52); 6, p. 648 (650); 7, p. 383; *ibid.*, p. 391. For set-off see M.A.T., 3, p. 299.

[209] M.A.T., 5, p. 281; *ibid.*, p. 551 (572); 6, p. 637; 7, p. 512. See also 2, p. 882 (884); 5, p. 281; *ibid.*, p. 630; 6, p. 648 (650); 8, p. 26.

[210] M.A.T., 1, p. 772; 6, p. 128; 9, p. 682.

[211] Treaty of Versailles, art. 296, Annex, par 4. But see M.A.T., 9, p. 197.

[212] M.A.T., 4, p. 73 (76); 6, p. 542; *ibid.*, p. 634; 7, p. 428; 9, p. 19; *ibid.*, p. 58; *ibid.*, p. 688.

[213] M.A.T., 4, p. 717; 6, p. 542; 9, p. 335. See also 4, p. 530 (534); 9, p. 687.

Torts

The absence of jurisdiction of the Mixed Arbitral Tribunals in matters of tort[214] accounts for the absence of rules on this subject. In the only relevant case the *lex loci delicti commissi* was applied.[215]

Property

It has been pointed out that the *lex rei sitae* is applied in all cases where questions of property arise, whether in connection with contractual relations or not.[216] The same rule | applies to pledges,[217] mining rights,[218] and mortgage debts,[219] although a tendency can be noticed towards a cumulation of the national laws of the parties.[220] In particular, this tendency can be observed in the case of trusts.[221]

Succession

Difficulties arise in the law of succession. It has been pointed out above that before international tribunals the nationality of a claim is of paramount importance. The attention of the courts must be directed towards this question, quite apart from the question according to what system of laws the plaintiff's claim is to be decided. In the law of succession, however, these two questions are linked up closely. If the law of succession applicable in the circumstances recognises the position of executors or administrators, besides the beneficiary, a difference in nationality between the executor and the beneficiary may affect the jurisdiction of the tribunal according to whether, in the opinion of the tribunal, the right is vested in the executor or the beneficiary. The system of municipal law, applicable according to the rules of conflict of laws as established by international tribunals, may have to be disregarded and arbitrary solutions followed in order to vest the right in the person who is to be the final beneficiary and whose country is ultimately interested in the claim.[222]

---

[214] M.A.T., 7, p. 264; 8, p. 117; 9, p. 256; *ibid.*, p. 271; *ibid.*, p. 495.

[215] M.A.T., 5, p. 721.

[216] See above, note 157. See also M.A.T., 3, p. 660 (664).

[217] M.A.T., 3, p. 798 (800); 4, p. 656; 7, p. 712; 9, p. 778.

[218] M.A.T., 8, p. 593.

[219] M.A.T., 2, p. 879; 6, p. 682. See also 8, p. 875; 6, p. 65; 8, p. 804.

[220] M.A.T., 3, p. 328 (330).

[221] M.A.T., 7, p. 880 (881). See above, note 181.

[222] See below, note 233.

The rights of an heir are determined by the national law of the *de cuius*.[223] The tendency to adopt the law of the *de cuius* as a whole, including its rules of conflict of laws and *renvoi*,[224] must be rejected for the reasons set out above in connection with our discussion of *renvoi*. Sometimes, the test is »the personal law« of the *de cuius*,[225] i.e. the system the *de cuius* must be presumed to have chosen.[226] This rule is applied primarily in cases of intestacy. In one case it was suggested that succession to|immovables should be governed by the *lex rei sitae*.[227] This solution does not recommend itself. Unity of succession, without splitting the inheritance into parts devolving according to different systems of law, should be attempted always. The fact that the *lex rei sitae* is the law which is enforced at the place where the object is situated is an important consideration in municipal law, but it does not carry the same weight before international tribunals. Their decisions are enforced in consequence of treaty obligations and not by the comity of nations and according to municipal law.[228] The rule that the *lex rei sitae* shall apply is acceptable in the case of *bona vacantia*.[229]

The liability of heirs is determined by the personal law of the *de cuius*,[230] but no indication is given whether the national law of the *de cuius* or the law of his domicile is to govern as his personal law. The same uncertainty is to be observed in matters of legacies.[231]

The personal law of the *de cuius*, subject to the same doubts, but probably his national law, determines the position of executors.[232] However, in order to connect the claim with the nationality of the true beneficiary, the strict rules of conflict of laws were sometimes disregarded. Thus the English law of succession, applicable in the circumstances, allowing claims by executors in their own right, had to give way to Continental conceptions[233] according to which executors are denied an independent legal right and are granted a representative character only. Similar difficulties arise in the case of joint

---

[223] M.A.T., 3, p. 698 (699); 5, p. 637 (641); 7, p. 266 (272); *ibid.*, p. 422; *ibid.*, p. 589; 9, p. 663.

[224] M.A.T., 5, p. 637 (641); 7, p. 421 (423).

[225] M.A.T., 6, p. 247; Gutzwiller, loc. cit., p. 186.

[226] See above, note 225. For the law governing the interpretation of wills see M.A.T., 5, pp. 641–642.

[227] M.A.T., 8, p. 660 (664).

[228] See M.A.T., 6, p. 247; Rabel, *Zeitschrift für ausländisches und internationales Privatrecht*, 1 (1927), pp. 42–43.

[229] M.A.T., 6, p. 243 (248).

[230] M.A.T., 2, p. 211; 6, p. 600; 7, p. 481; 8, p. 783.

[231] M.A.T., 2, p. 286 (288); 4, p. 396 (898).

[232] M.A.T., 2, p. 190 (192); *ibid.*, p. 691; 4, p. 6 (8); 5, p. 637 (642); 7, p. 421 (423). See also above, note 231.

[233] M.A.T., 3, p. 762 (765); 4, p. 645 (648); 5, p. 637 (643).

heirs of different nationality claiming as joint owners.[234] The position of administrators is governed by the law of the *de cuius'* domicile.[235]

| Conclusions

In conclusion the following contentions may now be submitted:

(1) Rules of international law prescribing a certain tendency to be followed by municipal systems of conflict of laws, without laying down a single rule in detail, are not rules of international conflict of laws. They are minimum requirements addressed by international law to every branch of municipal law and thus also to municipal conflict of laws. To disregard these minimum requirements means to incur state responsibility for denial of justice.

(2) International tribunals have worked out rules of conflict of laws which may be called rules of international conflict of laws. These rules show two principal characteristics: firstly, the absence of a *lex fori*, resulting in the absence of mandatory rules of the court, except rules of international public policy, the lack of *renvoi* and a difficulty of classification. Secondly, they instance the importance of nationality, especially in questions of status, even besides other tests which determine the law applicable. For, apart from the question whether a right exists and according to what municipal system of laws, it is always necessary to decide whether the plaintiff and his claim are so intimately connected with one of the states subject to the jurisdiction of the tribunal as to confer the necessary competence upon the latter to adjudicate in the litigation.

(3) Even if the contents of the rules sometimes appear identical with those of municipal courts, the characteristics mentioned above are so strongly accentuated as to exclude any identity between international and municipal conflict of laws. Even if called upon to solve similar problems, they have to start from a different basis.

(4) For the same reason, the adoption of identical rules by the municipal systems of laws of all states of the community of nations can never result in the creation of rules of international conflict of laws.

(5) There is no hierarchy, in conflict of laws, of a supreme international and a secondary municipal system of conflict of laws. A difference of nature and of functions draws a line of demarcation which cannot be transgressed.[236]

---

[234] M.A.T., 9, pp. 663, 664.
[235] M.A.T., 5, p. 637 (644). See also M.A.T., 3, p. 340 (342); 4, p. 417 (424); *ibid.*, p. 720.
[236] I am indebted to Professor Lauterpacht for his kind help and advice.

|During the debate which followed the reading of the paper observations were made by –

Dr. Erwin H. Loewenfeld: The Paris Agreement No. II for the Settlement of Questions relating to the Agrarian Reforms and Mixed Arbitral Tribunals of April 28, 1930 (121 League of Nations Treaty Series, p. 80), concluded between Czechoslovakia, Jugoslavia, and Roumania of the one part and Hungary of the other part, provided that the Mixed Arbitral Tribunals (originally consisting of a neutral president and two national judges) were to be completed by the addition of two members, chosen by the Permanent Court of International Justice from countries which had been neutral in the World War.

This reinforcement of the Mixed Courts gave the President a far greater authority, particularly in the frequent case that the views of the national judges opposed each other.

The aforementioned Convention further introduced a Right of Appeal to the Permanent Court (art. 10).

It was to be exercised by written application by one of the Governments within three months from notification to its agent of the judgment of the Tribunal.

Article 10 was viewed by the Permanent Court as a special agreement of submission. Though the article conferred on the Court jurisdiction as a *Court of Appeal*, it was thought to be unnecessary to deal with the nature of this jurisdiction.

The fact that a judgment was given in a litigation to which one of the parties is a private individual does not prevent this judgment from forming the subject of a dispute between two states capable of being submitted to the Court in virtue of a special or general agreement between them.

However the Court was careful to declare that it had no power to control the way in which the Mixed Arbitral Tribunal had exercised its functions as regards procedure (see Judgment of the Permanent Court of December 15, 1933, relating to the *Peter Pazmany University* v. *Czechoslovakia*, Publications of the Court, Series A.B., no. 61, p. 222).

The reinforcement of the Mixed Courts by two further neutral judges and the introduction of the appeal to the Permanent Court have contributed to solve the complicated questions of connexity between genuine application of land reform of the Little Entente|to Hungarian landowners and disguised liquidation of landed property, prohibited by the Treaty of Trianon.

It would be desirable to introduce similar reforms into any scheme of Mixed Arbitral Tribunals to be re-established after the war.

Dr. Ernst Wolff: When I listened to the very interesting lecture, I had again the impression which I had before that the decisions of international tribunals on questions of conflict of laws are very often contradictory to one another and on the whole not very convincing. That is not meant as a reflection. Difficulties with which international tribunals have to meet in this respect are for the greater part insurmountable. As Dr. Lipstein pointed out, international tribunals have no *lex fori* unless the treaties or agreements under which they have been established contain some rules about conflict of laws, which, practically, is never the case. There are, of course, The Hague Conventions, but they are in force only between a restricted number of states and they do not cover a very wide field. In the absence of a *lex fori* international tribunals have to rest their decisions regarding problems of private international law on an international system of conflict of laws as distinct from the municipal law. But are there in fact some rules in the Law of Nations concerning conflict of laws? As Dr. Lipstein pointed out, the arbitral tribunals have tried to apply »*les principes généralement admis par les nations civilisées.*« In actual fact, however, there are very few such principles. As far as I can see there are only two which, in fact, are universally acknowledged. The one: *Locus regit actum*, and the other: *Lex rei sitae*, which applies to immovables and perhaps – but this is already controversial – to movables. With regard to other problems there is no common opinion. For instance, under the rules of conflict of laws of one country succession is governed by the law of domicile of the *de cuius*, whilst in the law of other no less civilised countries it is the law of the nationality which applies. I do not remember whether international tribunals, in particular the Mixed Arbitral Tribunals, had ever to deal with such problems of succession. If so, their decisions can have been only purely arbitrary, because there is no generally acknowledged principle regarding succession. The same difficulty applies to contractual obligations. Even with | regard to them one cannot speak of a generally acknowledged principle. The majority of the different systems of private international law agree that with regard to contractual obligations the intention of the parties decides what law has to govern their relations, but there are exceptions, and particularly the U.S.A. adhere to quite another system. Under the private international law of the U.S.A. it is not the intention of the parties that is decisive, but other points of attachment: the place where the contract has been made, the place where the performance has to be fulfilled, and so on. But even with regard to a system, as for instance the English system, under which it is the intention of the parties which prevails, there remain difficulties. It is generally acknowledged that the intention of the parties is without effect in so far as compulsory law is concerned. If, *e.g.,* the municipal law of a country declares void agreements between principal and agent under which the agent, after the end of his employment, is not allowed to make competition to his former employer, it is, of course, not open to the parties to avoid this nullity by submitting the agreement to another law as to the proper law of the contract. In such cases the intention of the parties is of no avail and international tribunals have to look for other points of attachment to find the proper law of the contract.

Sometimes there is a way out of these difficulties, namely, the comparative approach. If either the rules of the respective countries concerning conflict of laws or the rules of the substantive law are identical, there is no need to apply an international system of conflict of laws rules. If there is, for instance, a dispute about succession to which either French or German law is applicable, the tribunal will, no doubt, apply the law of the nationality, as the rules of both countries in question agree that succession is governed by the law of nationality of the *de cuius*. If the validity of an oral guarantee is in question, and under the laws of all countries concerned a guarantee is valid only if in writing, the tribunal will consider the guarantee as void without being compelled to examine what is the proper law of the guarantee. If I have rightly understood Dr. Lipstein, he is not in favour of such a comparative approach, because he thinks that it means shirking the real problem of private international law. However, I think, it commends itself from a practical point of|view, and it provides international tribunals with a more solid basis for their decisions than the international approach. This comparative approach is, however, restricted to a certain number of cases. When neither the respective municipal rules concerning conflict of laws nor the substantive rules are identical it is of no avail.

What can be done to supply international tribunals, instead of the international system of rules which, in my opinion, is almost non-existent, with another basis for their decisions concerning conflict of laws? If I say that an international system of conflict of laws is at present almost non-existent, that does not exclude, of course, that such a system can be created gradually by decisions of international tribunals, but, I am afraid, particularly the decisions of the Mixed Arbitral Tribunals instituted under the Treaty of Versailles have not contributed even the very first beginning in that direction. As set out by Dr. Lipstein, they are very often in contradiction with one another and, as no common Court of Appeal was provided for in the Treaty of Versailles against their decisions, it was impossible to obtain uniform decisions. On the other hand, the task is urgent, and it seems to me impossible to wait until in a more or less remote future a really international system of rules concerning conflict of laws will be created by the decisions of international tribunals. There is, as far as I can see, only one way out of this difficulty, viz., to provide rules concerning conflict of laws in the treaties instituting the tribunals. This task is comparatively easy if the subjects dealt with in these treaties are limited. In 1925, for instance, conventions were concluded between the Soviet Union and Germany, concerning, *inter alia*, succession of subjects of the one state residing in the other. They stipulated for certain eventualities which law should govern the succession. When disputes arising out of these conventions come before arbitral tribunals they have, of course, to apply the rules about conflict of laws contained in the conventions.

The task is a more difficult one if the tribunals will have to deal with problems of different provinces of the law. That will be the case, for instance, if, after the end of the present war, international tribunals of a similar kind to those instituted under the Treaty of Versailles should be instituted again. Obviously there | will be no sphere of law such tribunals could not have to deal with. In the great majority of the cases, it will be the law of obligations, but cases will and must occur which do not fall within the law of obligations, but will fall within the law of succession, of real property, and so on. No doubt, it would be a difficult task for the negotiators of the future peace treaty to work out rules about conflict of laws to be applied by the mixed arbitral tribunals. All the other problems to be dealt with by the future peace treaty are already so complicated and allimportant that it will not be possible for the future peace conference to work out in detail provisions about the conflict of laws. This alone would be a task which would take months and perhaps years. It will be remembered that the Conference of Private International Law at The Hague, instituted under the auspices of the League of Nations, has made little progress so far, and if – as it is to be hoped – it will be possible in the long run to create a really uniform international system of conflict of laws with the help of the League of Nations, the mixed arbitral tribunals under the future peace treaty will have to begin their work long before such a result can be obtained. What can be done to supply these tribunals with a basis for their decisions about conflict of laws? I wonder whether it would not be possible to adopt rules about conflict of laws for that purpose which are already in existence. I have in mind the Codici Bustamante, adopted by the majority of the members of the Pan-American Union in 1928. Its author, Mr. Bustamante, is a very distinguished lawyer of Cuba and for many years a judge of the Permanent Court of International Justice at The Hague. I am fully aware that the Code is subject to criticism in some respects. How could it be otherwise in such a complicated matter? Even the municipal conflict of law rules – may they be incorporated in statutes or contained in the decisions of the courts – are far from being complete and clear. I think, however, a Code, defective as it may be in some respects, is preferable to the actual state – *i.e.* to an almost complete absence of international rules whatsoever. It matters less – so it seems to me – what the law says with regard to conflict of laws, if only it says something definite. The municipal law is in close connection with the economic structure, the social life, the mental outlook of the people who live under | its rules, and therefore a law which is good for one country would perhaps be quite inappropriate for another. In the field of conflict of laws, however, such considerations are of much less importance. It is true that even in this province material interests can be affected. For a country like the United States, where comparatively many immigrants live who have not yet acquired American nationality, the law of domicile is more advantageous, whilst for a country from where many persons emigrate year by year – as *e.g.* Italy – the law of nationality is more convenient. But such cases where material interests are affected regarding conflict of laws are not very numerous. It seems to me therefore feasible, what would be hardly feasible with regard to substantive law – *i.e.* to adopt a codification already existing in other countries. The Code Bustamante has already stood the test of practice; a number of decisions of the courts of the states adhering to the Code have been rendered and recorded. That fact, too, would be of advantage should the Code be taken as a basis for the future mixed arbitral tribunals.

Conflict of Laws before International Tribunals (II)

[Editorial note: first published in Transactions of the Grotius Society 29 (1943), 51–83.]

I

The Application of Municipal Law by International Courts[*]

In a previous paper it was pointed out that public international law contains a category of rules of conflict of laws as a separate branch of international law.[1] These rules are designed to meet | the requirements of international courts in so far as these courts are confronted with questions of a private law nature. International rules of conflict of laws differ in their nature and in their functions from municipal private international law. They show two principal characteristics. First, they must operate without the assistance of a *lex fori*. Secondly, the test of nationality occupies a preponderant position, even besides other tests which may determine which system of laws is to apply. For unlike municipal courts, international tribunals must consider not only whether a right exists and according to which municipal system of laws, but they must also determine whether the plaintiff and his claim are so intimately connected with one of the States subject to the jurisdiction of the

---

[*] The following abbrevations will be used:

American-German Claims – Mixed Claims Commission, United States and Germany, Administrative Decisions and Opinions of a general nature and Opinions and Decisions in certain individual cases from October 1, 1926 to December 31, 1932.

Borchard = Borchard, *The Diplomatic Protection of Citizens Abroad*, 1915.

De Beus = De Beus, *The Jurisprudence of the General Claims Commission, United States and Mexico*, 1938.

Decisions I, II = *Decisions and Opinions of the Commissioners* in accordance with the Convention of November 19, 1926 between Great Britain and the United Mexican States, 2 vols., 1931, 1933.

Feller = Feller, *The Mexican Claims Commissions*, 1935.

Lapradelle and Politis = Lapradelle and Politis, *Recueil des Arbitrages Internationaux*, 2 vols., 1932.

Moore = Moore, *History and Digest of the Arbitrations to which the United States has been a Party*, 6 vols., 1898.

Nielsen = Nielsen, *International Law applied to Reclamations*, 1933.

Opinions I, II, III = Opinions of Commissioners under the Convention concluded September 8, 1923 between the United States and Mexico, 3 vols., 1927, 1929, 1931.

Panamanian Claims = American and Panamanian General Claims Arbitration under the Conventions between the United States and Panama of July 28, 1926 and December 17, 1932. Report of Bert L. Hunt. 1934.

Ralston = Ralston, *The Law and Procedure of International Tribunals*. Revised Edition. 1926.

Ralston, Supp. = Ralston, *Supplement to 1926 Revised Edition of the Law and Procedure of International Tribunals*, 1936.

Turkish Claims = American-Turkish Claims Settlement under the Agreement of December 24, 1923 and Supplemental Agreements between the United States and Turkey. Opinions and Report. Prepared by Fred K. Nielsen. 1937.

[1] *Transactions of the Grotius Society*, 27 (1942), pp. 142–175 and the literature quoted *ibid.*, p. 149, note 33. See also Ralston, Supp., pp. 48–50; Jenks, *B.Y.I.L.*, 19 (1938), pp. 67–103, especially p. 95 ff.

international tribunal as to confer upon the tribunal the necessary competence to take cognizance of the dispute.

In a previous paper it was admitted that cases involving the choice and application of municipal law are in substance disputes of a private law nature. It was conceded that a system of conflict of laws, as a Separate branch of international law, must be law governing the relationship between States who have taken up private law claims of their subjects, or a law between States acting as subjects of private law. This view, however, appears to be too restricted. It was true in respect of the Mixed Arbitral Tribunals, the practice of which formed the object of a previous essay. These tribunals were set up after the first World War to settle private law claims pending between nationals of the Allies on the one side and nationals of the Central Powers on the other side. An examination of the practice in matters of conflict of laws of international courts and tribunals in general, will show that an international system of conflict of laws is a branch of international law far wider in scope and importance than has been assumed hitherto.

Its sphere of application has been outlined by the American-Mexican Claims Commission in the *Illinois Central Railroad Co.* Case[2] in these words:

"International claims, needing decisions in accordance with the principles of international law, may belong to any of four types.

(i) Claims as between a national of one country and a national of another country. These claims are international, even in cases where international law declares one of the municipal laws involved to be exclusively applicable ... "

| This type of claims was discussed in my first paper.

(ii) "Claims as between two national governments in their own right ... "

This type of claims, in so far as it relates to disputes touching upon questions of private law, was envisaged in my previous paper but, owing to lack of material, no detailed examination could be attempted.

(iii) "Claims as between a citizen of one country and the government of another country in its public capacity.

(iv) "Claims as between a citizen of one country and the government of another country acting in its civil capacity. These claims, too, are international in their character and they, too, must be decided in accordance with the principles of international law, even in cases where international law should merely declare the municipal law of one of the countries involved to be applicable."[3]

---

[2] *Opinions*, I, p. 15, at pp. 17 ff; see also Feller, p. 173; De Beus, pp. 15–21; Ralston, p. 75; Borchard, p. 281.

[3] See also Lapradelle and Politis, II, pp. 258–59 (note doctrinale); *American Bottle Co.* Claim, *Opinions*, II, p. 162; Nielsen, p. 339, at p. 340. *Cook* Case, *Opinions*, II, p. 266 at

If we examine the nature of the claims described in the last two heads, it appears that claims listed in the fourth and last paragraph are either claims of a purely private law character or claims for denial of justice presented on the ground of a violation of private law rights by a State acting in its capacity as a subject of private law. The claims mentioned in the third paragraph are always based on a denial of justice. The State, acting in its capacity as a subject of public law, is charged with international responsibility for having acted illegally either in the sphere of private rights or of public law.

The international system of conflict of laws extends thus to claims of a private character between a national of one State and the government of another State. But, above all, it extends to claims for denial of justice if the violation of a property right is alleged. It is with this last type of claim that we are chiefly concerned in this paper. With reference to such claims, the Anglo-Mexican Claims Commission stated in the *Mexican Union Railway Claim*[4]:

"These claims bear a mixed character. They are public claims in so far as they are presented by one government to another government. But they are private in so far as they aim at the granting of a financial award to an individual or to a company. The award is claimed on behalf of a person or a corporation ..."

|The American-Turkish Claims Commission, in the *Hoachoozo Palestine Land and Development Co.*[5] Case, held with regard to the questions of private law involved in claims for denial of justice:

"In a case in which complaint is made that governmental authorities have confiscated contractual property rights, the preliminary question is one of domestic law as to the rights of the claimant under a contract in the light of the domestic proper law governing the legal effect of the contract. The next question for determination is whether in the light of principles or rules of international law rights under the contract have been infringed."

The same Commission held in the *Nicholas Marmaras* Claim:[6]

---

p. 269; Nielsen, p. 390, at p. 391; *Pomeroy's El Paso Transfer Co.* Case, Nielsen, p. 418, at p. 420; *Parker* Case, *Opinions*, I, p. 35; *Peerless Motor Car Co.* Case, *ibid.*, p. 303; *United Dredging Co.* Case, *ibid.*, p. 394; *National Paper and Type Co.* Case, *Opinions*, II, p. 3; *Parsons Trading Co.* Case, *ibid.*, p. 135; *P.C.I.J.*, ser. A. no. 20, pp. 18–20 (*Serbian Loans Case*); Jonkheer van Eysinga in *P.C.I.J.*, ser. A/B, No. 76, p. 38 (*Panevezys Saldutiskis* Ry. Case); Hudson *ibid.*, ser. A/B, no. 78, p. 184 (*Societé Commerciale de Belgique*); *ibid.*, ser. B. no. 6, p. 29 (*German Settlers in Poland*); Genet, *Revue générale de droit international public*, 36 (1929), pp. 682–685).

[4] *Decisions*, I, p. 157, at p. 162.

[5] *American-Turkish Claims*, p. 254, at pp. 259, 260. See also *The Norwegian Claims Case*, Scott *Hague Court Reports*, II, p. 39 at pp. 64, 65.

[6] *American-Turkish Claims*, p. 473, at pp. 479, 480. See also *P.C.I.J.* ser. A, no. 20, p. 19; *ibid.*, ser. A., No. 47, p. 42; and the observations of Anzilotti in a dissenting opinion, at pp. 26–27, and in *P.C.I.J.*, ser. A/B., no. 65, p. 60, at pp. 61–62. But see *P.C.I.J.*, ser. A/B, No. 76, p. 18; *ibid.*, ser. A/B, No. 77, p. 107 (per Urrutia, dissenting).

... the law by which the merits of the claim are ultimately decided is a law between States and not between a private person and a State. However, in addition to the national interest in the claim, it is assuredly pertinent to take account of the transactions out of which a claim arises and of the character and extent of rights asserted in behalf of a claimant in the presentation of a claim ... Opinions reveal that competent tribunals examine, preliminarily to any determination of questions of derogations of rules of substantive international law, the standing, so to speak, of the claimants. If property interests are involved ... the nature and value of such interests must be determined. Compensation will not be awarded unless a claimant shows possession by him of property rights which have been invaded, and compensation will be granted only in proportion to the measure of his loss resulting from injury to the rights possessed by him. It is believed that all competent international tribunals concern themselves with the question, as a preliminary one, whether there is before them a proper party entitled to compensation on and take account of the precise nature and extent of the interest of such a party in a claim."

Similar views were expressed by the American-Mexican Claims Commission.[7] In the *Cook* Case (No. 1), Nielsen, the American Commissioner, said:

"When questions are raised before an international tribunal ... with respect to the application of the proper law in the determination of rights grounded on contractual obligations, it is necessary to have clearly in mind the particular law applicable | to the different aspects of the case. The nature of such contractual rights or rights with respect to tangible property, real or personal, which a claimant asserts have been invaded in a given case is determined by the local law that governs the legal effects of the contract or other form of instrument creating such rights. But the responsibility of a respondent government is determined solely by international law ..."

Again, in the *Cook* Case (No. 2), the same Commissioner, in a dissenting opinion, said:[8]

"In this case, as it happens in many other international cases, the questions of domestic law are much more difficult than those involved in the application of the proper principles of international law ... If he (the claimant) had no rights (under Mexican law), it is of course unnecessary to proceed to the question whether in the light of any principle or rule of international law

---

[7] *Cook* Claim *Opinions*, I, p. 318, at p. 321; Nielsen, p. 196, at pp. 198–99; *Corrie* Claim, *Opinions*, I, p. 213, at pp. 214, 215, 217; Nielsen, pp. 159–160; *Venables* Case, *Opinions*, I, p. 331, at pp. 344, 366–67; Nielsen, p. 205, at pp. 224–25; *Debenture Holders of the San Marcos and Pinos Co. Claim, Decisions*, II, p. 135, at pp. 139–140; *Mexico Tramways Co. Claim*, ibid. II. p. 184, at p. 189.

[8] Nielsen, p. 389, at pp. 390–91, 395–96; *The Felix*, Moore, III, pp. 2800 at p. 2811.

such rights were infringed ... In dealing with an international case it should be borne in mind that the rights of a person to sue a government under domestic law is not conclusive with respect to rights that may be invoked in behalf of such a person under international law."

These quotations, expressing the experience of various international tribunals, bear out uniformly our principal proposition to the effect that international rules of conflict of laws occupy an important position in international courts. They are an essential factor in deciding claims for State responsibility on the ground of denial of justice in the wider sense, whenever property rights are involved, whether they be contractual or concerned with tangible property, real or personal. In these cases an international tribunal is confronted with two types of questions, the character of which differs diametrically. First, the tribunal must decide whether a private property interest exists in the light of domestic law and in whom such interest is vested. This decision necessitates a choice of municipal law. International rules of conflict of laws provide the guide as to which system of municipal private law applies, whether it allows a right of the character alleged to have been violated, and whether it confers this right upon the particular claimant. This stage may be conveniently called the preliminary investigation.[9]

Secondly, once the preliminary investigation has established the existence of a private law right, the tribunal must determine | whether the violation of the right acquired under municipal law constitutes an illegal act under international law. The American-Turkish Claims Commission held in the case of *Ina Hoffman and Dulcie Steinhardt*[10]:

"International tribunals have frequently rendered awards in cases involving the failure of a government to fulfil contractual oblications, although the law of nations does not embrace any 'law of contracts' such as is found in the domestic jurisprudence of nations and such cases are of course not actions on contracts in terms of domestic law. In such cases the right of a claimant under

---

[9] The American-German Mixed Claims Commission held correctly in *Knickerbocker Ins. Co. of New York v. Germany* that "all questions involving conflicts in the interests between American nationals or the transfer of interests in or to such original obligation, must be decided by municipal tribunals according to local jurisprudence," *American-German Claims*, p. 912, at p. 913. The municipal law applicable is the law existing at the time of the commission of the act complained of. See *Cook* Case (No. 1), *Opinions*, I, p. 311, at pp. 314, 317. Feller, pp. 177–184 is not very satisfactory.

[10] *Turkish Claims*, p. 286, at pp. 287–88; *Socony-Vacuum Oil Co.* Case, *ibid.*, p. 369, at pp. 374, 382; *Singer Sewing Machine Co.* Case, *ibid.*, p. 490, at p. 491; *Malamatinis* Case, *ibid.*, p. 603, at p. 605; *Dickson Car Wheel Co.* Claim, *Opinions*, III, p. 175, at pp. 199, 202; Nielsen, p. 505, at p. 515; *International Fisheries Co.* Case, *Opinions*, III, p. 207, at pp. 241–42; Nielsen, p. 520, at p. 539; *Salem* Case, Nielsen, p. 698; *Company General of the Orinoco* Case, Ralston, *French-Venezuelan Arbitration* (1902), p. 244. See also *Cook's Case, American Bottle Co's Claim, Pomeroy's El Paso Transfer Co's Claim*, cited above, note 3. See also Feller, p. 174.

a contract must be determined, in the first instance, by application of the proper domestic substantive law governing the rights of the parties to a contract. The ultimate question of international responsibility for acts of authorities with respect to contractual rights must be decided in accordance with international law ..."

Finally, the tribunal must ascertain whether the claimant State is entitled to maintain an action in an international court in respect of the alleged violation of international law. For, as stated in the *Cook* Case (No. 2):[11]

"In dealing with an international case, it should be borne in mind that the right of a person to sue a government under domestic law is not conclusive with respect to rights that may be invoked in behalf of such a person under international law."

International Claims and Unenforceable Private Rights

This statement requires some explanation. It may happen that the preliminary investigation establishes the existence of a property right under domestic law; in addition it is found that the right in question has been violated by the defendant State and that this violation is a breach of international law entailing State responsibility. The defendant State objects that, according to the system of municipal law governing the property right, no action could have been brought, seeing that the statute of limitations had begun to operate. Or, again, if an injury to a person, which constitutes a tort according to the municipal law applicable in the circumstances, is made the object of an international reclamation on behalf of the heir of the injured person, is the defence that the municipal law governing the tort liability allows the defence of *actio personalis moritur cum persona* also a good defence on the|part of the defendant State if sued in an international court? Lastly, if a person has suffered damages through acts of government officials for which, according to the municipal law applicable, the government may not be held liable or sued in its courts, is the absence of the right to sue the government under municipal law a bar to a claim in an international court for the violation of this right?

The answer seems clear. "The right of a person to sue a government under domestic law is not conclusive with respect to rights that may be invoked in behalf of such a person under international law."[12] The preliminary investi-

---

[11] Nielsen, p. 390, at pp. 395–96; see also *Thomas Morrison v. Mexico,* Moore, III, p. 2325, at p. 2326.

[12] See above, note 11; see also *P.C.I.J.,* ser. A, No. 20, p. 17 (*Serbian Loans* Case); *P.C.I.J.,* ser. A/B, no. 61, p. 232 (*Peter Pazmany University* Case).

gation is only concerned with the existence of a property right under municipal law. But the question whether a violation of the right thus ascertained is actionable must be decided, for the purposes of an international reclamation before an international tribunal, according to the principles of international law. Simple as this solution may appear, it has nevertheless caused some difficulty in practice.

Prescription

As far as the plea of prescription is concerned, it has been held with some uniformity that prescription is determined not by the system of municipal law governing the right the violation of which is alleged, but by the principles of international law. The American-Venezuelan Claims Commission expressed this view in two cases which concerned breaches of contracts concluded between an American citizen and Venezuela. It was held in *Williams'* Case:[13]

"It is a well settled principle in common law jurisdictions, and a recognised one in civil law countries that obligations are to be enforced according to the *lex fori* which here is the treaty and the public law ... It is left to the discretion of international law on the subject ...; prescription has a place in the international system and is to be regarded in these adjudications."

In the *Garcia Cadiz* Case[14], the same Commission applied the international law of prescription not because international law was regarded as the *lex fori*, but on the ground of international public policy. Since, as we shall see later on, international law is the *lex fori* of international tribunals and must therefore furnish the criteria of international public policy the awards in the *Williams'* and in the *Garcia Cadiz* Case are based upon the same considerations.

| The American-Mexican Claims Commission adopted the same view. In the *Cook* Case, Commissioner Nielsen, in a dissenting judgment, expressed it as follows[15]

"Domestic statutes of limitation take away at the end of prescribed periods the remedy which a litigant has to enforce rights before domestic courts ... The United States is not now debarred by any Mexican statute of limitations from recovering money wrongfully withheld from the claimant.

---

[13] Moore, IV, p. 4181 at pp. 4182, 4194–95; and see the critical note by Rolin in Lapradelle and Politis, II, p. 206.

[14] Moore, IV, p. 4199, at p. 4203.

[15] *Opinions*, I, p. 318, at p. 319; Nielsen, p. 196, at p. 197. See also to the same effect *McPherson's* Claim, Nielsen, p. 201, at p. 202; *Pomeroy's El Paso Transfer Co's* Case, *Opinions*, III, p. 1, at pp. 11–12; Nielsen, p. 418, at pp. 422–23.

The Mexican Government could not, by withholding payment for a period prescribed by a domestic statute of limitation, relieve itself from an obligation under international law to make restitution ..."

Actio Personalis Moritur cum Persona

A greater division of opinion may be observed in respect of the question whether the maxim *actio personalis moritur cum persona*, recognised by the common law countries, may be pleaded as a bar to an international claim for injuries to the person. In the case of *McHugh, Sherman* and *Brain*[16], the earliest award touching upon this question which I was able to find, the Anglo-American Claims Commission decided by a majority that the question was governed by international law. The Commission gave judgment in favour of the widow and the children in the *Sherman* case, but disallowed the action in the *McHugh* case where the deceased had died unmarried and leaving only collateral relatives, not dependent on him for support, entitled to inherit. It is not easy to understand why the Commission, having refused to consider the question whether according to municipal law heirs are entitled to maintain actions for personal injuries suffered by a *de cuius*, introduced a distinction between two categories of heirs, one of which is entitled to sue, and another which is not.[17] The American Commissioner, on the other hand, held that the law of the domicile of the deceased must decide whether the heir is entitled to sue. This opinion was easily refuted by the American-Mexican Commission in the *Russell* Case, where Commissioner Nielsen said:[18]

"It would be absurd reasoning that would justify a conclusion that, in a proceeding before an international tribunal, a claim predicated on a disregard of international law could be maintained against a country in which the principles of the civil law obtain, whereas the same kind of a claim against a

---

[16] Moore, IV, p. 3278.

[17] In one later case this distinction was maintained, although in a modified form. The American-Panamanian General Claims Commission, in the *Richeson* Claim, *Panamanian Claims.* p. 247, at p. 292, reduced the damages for the death of the *de cuius* to a minimum on the ground that the claimants were neither the parents nor the children of the *de cuius* nor persons supported by him. Boards of American Commissioners charged with the distribution of the Brazilian and other indemnities among American claimants had recourse to the law of the domicile of the deceased and disallowed claims of heirs for personal injuries suffered by the *de cuius*. But such boards cannot be regarded as international tribunals. See e.g. *Isaac Austin Hayes'* Case, Moore, V, p. 4622; but see *Hughes'* Claim, *ibid.*, III, p. 2972 *Plumer's* Case, Commissioners on Claims against Mexico, p. 182 to the contrary effect.

[18] Nielsen, p. 587, at p. 603 with further references; see also Feller, pp. 85, 104–106; De Beus, pp. 44–48; Ralston, Supp. pp. 67–69; Borchard, p. 632.

country | where the unaltered principles of the common law obtain, should be rejected in view of the provisions of local law. In such a situation, international delinquencies, which are defined by the same law among all countries, would be redressed or left unredressed according to the variations of domestic law. Rights of action accruing to wives and children, as well as other relatives of deceased persons, have been recognised in numerous cases before international tribunals."

It is submitted that this view is correct, provided it has been proved that the claimant is the heir according to the system of municipal law applicable in the circumstances.[19] The present trend was expressed by the American-Mexican Commission in the *Dujay* case,[20] where the tribunal said:

"The impropriety of giving application to any rule or principle of domestic law in relation to a subject of this kind is readily perceived. An international tribunal is concerned with the question whether there has been a failure on the part of a nation to fulfil the requirements of a rule of international law, or whether authorities have committed acts for which a nation is directly responsible under that law ... Domestic law ... is by its nature incompetent to prescribe what actions may be maintained before an international tribunal."

The same practice was followed by the American-Panamanian[21] and the American-Turkish Claims Commissions.[22]

Exemption of Governments from Liability

Lastly, we must examine the plea that a Government cannot be sued in an international court in respect of a breach of contract or of an act involving liability in tort if, according to the municipal law applicable in the circumstances, the claimant cannot bring an action against that government in contract or in tort. This plea was discussed by Commissioner Nielsen in the *Cook* Case (No. 1), where he said in a dissenting opinion:[23]

---

[19] *De Sabla Claim, Panamanian Claims*, p. 379, at p. 433; *Alter Levin's Case, Turkish Claims*, p. 688, at p. 690.

[20] Nielsen, p. 348, at p. 359 with further references at pp. 351–359. See also the opinion by Prof. Lauterpacht discussed in *"Ul" G.m.b.H. v Polish State*, decided by the Arbitral Tribunal for Upper Silesia, *Amtliche Sammlung von Entscheidungen des Schiedsgerichts für Oberschlesien*, Vol. III (1932), p. 118, at p. 124; Ralston, pp. 144–147; Borchard, p. 632. See also *Stephens' Case, Opinions*, I, p. 397, at p. 398; *Way* Claim, *ibid.*, II, p. 94; Nielsen, p. 302, at pp. 311–12; *Connelly* Claim *Opinions*, I, p. 159, at p. 161.

[21] *De Sabla Claim, Panamanian Claims*, p. 379, at p. 433 and the comment *ibid.*, at p. 455.

[22] *Alter Levin Case, Turkish Claims*, p. 688, at p. 690.

[23] Nielsen, p. 390, at p. 396. See also *Venable's Case, ibid.*, p. 205, at pp. 224–25; *Opinions*, I, p. 331, at pp. 366–67; Ralston, pp. 116–117.

"... the Government of the United States, and the Government of Great Britain, generally speaking, do not allow themselves to be sued in tort, nor do the tribunals of either of the two governments pass upon political acts of the government which created them. But redress guaranteed by international law for wrongful action can of course be obtained in behalf of aliens in other ways than by suits against the government, as | through diplomatic channels; or through the action of international tribunals. International reclamations for the most part grow out of what in terms of domestic law is described as tortious acts. So, likewise, in a case in which a government might not by its domestic law provide for suits in contract against itself, money due under a breach of contract could nevertheless be recovered in a proceeding before an international tribunal."

Miscellaneous

For the same reason, when a breach of contract or a tortious act is made the object of an international claim against a State, liability for damages, the measure of damages, the rate of exchange for assessing damages and the question of interest must be determined by international law and not by municipal law. The majority of international courts have adopted this view, but other solutions are also to be found. In the *Russell* Case, the American-Mexican Claims Commission said:[24]

"The principles underlying the law of each country may be useful in connection with the consideration of the subject of damages. But they cannot properly be invoked to any such degree as to attempt to make them controlling before an international tribunal in cases in which responsibility is fixed either in accordance with international law or in accordance with the stipulations of a treaty. A nation cannot by some municipal law denying pecuniary redress relieve itself from making compensation required either by stipulations of a treaty or a rule of international law ..."

The same argument was relied upon with regard to the measure of damages. The tribunals were generally guided by the principles of international law and, as far as damage to property was concerned, allowed compensation on the basis of the market price.[25] Moral damages were allowed as substantial

---

[24] Nielsen, p. 587, at pp. 644–45. See also *Janes'* Case, *Opinions*, I, p. 108 at pp. 115, 117; *P.C.I.J.* ser. A. No. 17, p. 28 (*Chorzow* Case (Merits)). But see the case of *Pelletier and Lazare*, Moore, II, p. 1749, at p. 1790, where the Tribunal attempted a cumulation of common and civil law. See also Feller, pp. 85, 150; De Beus, pp. 168 ff.; Jenks, *B.Y.I.J.*, 19 (1938), p. 67, at p. 84. Not clear: *Pirocaco v Turkey, Turkish Claims*, p. 232, at p. 236.

[25] *Melezer Mining Co.* Case, *Opinions*, II, p. 228; Nielsen, p. 363, at p. 369; *Illinois Central Railroad Co.* Case, Opinions, I, p. 187; *Venable* Case *ibid.*, p. 331, at pp. 345, 372;

satisfaction for serious dereliction of duty on the part of the government, even if such damages were inadmissible according to the *lex loci delicti commissi*.[26]

Some confusion can be observed with regard to the question what law determines the rate of exchange, once damages have been assessed. It is believed that the opinion expressed by the American-Mexican Claims Commission in the *Esther Moffitt* Case is correct. The tribunal said:[27]

| "Whatever may be said of the principles underlying the decisions of domestic courts in cases in which the rates of exchange have been fixed as of the date of judgment or as of the date when suit was brought, those principles do not appear to be susceptible of logical application in a case such as that pending before the commission. But the principle of applying the rate of exchange as of the date of the breach of an obligation appears to be one which the commission can properly apply."

The Anglo-Mexican Tribunal, in the *Watson* Case applied Mexican law, the law of the debtor State.[28]

It is believed that in claims for State responsibility in respect of contractual property rights, interest – we are not here concerned with a claim for arrears of interest – should be determined according to the principles of international law. This was the view of the American-Mexican Claims Commission, as expressed in the *Illinois Central Railroad Co.* Case.[29] However, in a substantial number of cases, the rate of interest was determined according to the *lex loci contractus*.[30]

U.S. v Germany, Consolidated Edition of Decisions (1925), pp. 61, 63; *MacAndrews* Case, Turkish Claims, p. 87, at p. 89; *Socony-Vacuum Oil Co., ibid.*, p. 369, at p. 370; *Bridges* Case, *ibid.*, p. 443, at p. 444; *Spencer Turner and Co., ibid.*, p. 454; *Wellington Sears and Co., ibid.*, p. 459; *Coumoulos* Case, *ibid.*, p. 460, at p. 462; *Texas Co.* Case, *ibid.*, p. 579, at p. 580.

[26] *Janes'* Case, *Opinions*, I, p. 108, at p. 116, 118; Nielsen, p. 92, at p. 110 with further references; *Stephens'* Case, *Opinions*, 1, p. 397, at p. 398 (3), with further references.

[27] Nielsen, p. 404, at p. 405, citing *Cook's* Case, *Opinions*, I, p. 318, at p. 322; Nielsen, p. 196, at p. 200; see also *Socony-Vacuum Oil Co. v. Turkey*, Turkish Claims, p. 369, at pp. 372–73; *Cook's* Case (No. 3), *Opinions*, III, p. 162, at pp. 164–66; Nielsen, p. 500, at pp. 502–505; see also De Beus, p. 272.

[28] *Decisions*, II, p. 92, at p. 95; *Pious Funds* Case, Scott, *Hague Court Reports*, I, p. 3, at p. 6.

[29] *Opinions*, I, p. 187, at p. 189; Nielsen, p. 141, at p. 143.

[30] *Hetty Green v. Mexico*, Moore, IV, pp. 3425, 4325; Lapradelle and Politis, I, p. 459; *The Tepeyac*, Lapradelle and Politis, I, p. 459. Not clear: *Youille, Shortridge and Co's* Case, Lapradelle and Politis, II, p. 78, at p. 108 and the note by Rolin *ibid.*, p. 226 ff. at p. 229 n. 1; *The Macedonian, ibid.*, II, p. 182, at p. 205; *The Masonic*, Moore, II, p. 1055, at p. 1068; *Jackson Maritims Ins. Co. of New York* Claim, *ibid.*, IV., p. 4324. See also Ralston, pp. 129–131.

Summary

It may be useful to sum up, at this point, the results of our investigations. In respect of claims involving State responsibility for denial of justice affecting property rights, international tribunals must apply both municipal law and international law. Municipal law determines whether a property right has been acquired and whether it is vested in the claimant. International law must decide whether the defendant State is liable for the violation of a property right so acquired, whether the claimant State is entitled to maintain the action in an international court and finally it must determine the measure of damages.

II

International Rules of Conflict of Laws. General Principles

We have said that international courts apply municipal law in the course of what we have called the preliminary investigation for the purpose of determining whether a property right, the violation of which is alleged, has been acquired. It is our task to examine the principles of conflict of laws which enable international tribunals to select the proper system of municipal law.

It is clear that international tribunals are not bound by decisions | in matters of private international law of municipal courts, which may be treated by them in the same manner as foreign judgments are treated by municipal courts.[31] Nor is it correct to hold with the Permanent Court of International Justice in the *Serbian and Brazilian Loan* Cases that international tribunals must apply municipal private international law, or rules of municipal private international law common to all nations, even if laid down by international conventions.[32] Nor are they called upon to act as appellate courts charged with controlling the proper application of municipal law including conflict of laws.[33] International tribunals, as shown previously, with regard to the Mixed Arbitral Tribunals and as it is proposed to demonstrate in this paper,

---

[31] *Idler v Venezuela*, Moore, IV, p. 3491, at pp. 3504 ff., but see pp. 3540–41.

[32] *P.C.I.J.*, ser. A, No. 20, p. 41; see also *Transactions of the Grotius Society*, 27, (1942), pp. 146–149, Jenks, l.c. p. 95.

[33] *Kennedy* Case, *Opinions*, I, p. 289, at p. 299; Nielsen, p. 188, at p. 191; *Capitation Tax Case*, Moore, II, p. 1412, at p. 1413; Lapradelle and Politis II, p. 485; *The Felix*, Moore, III, p. 2800, at p. 2811. Not quite clear: *The Henry Thompson*, Moore, IV, p. 3382; Lapradelle and Politis, I, p. 500; *O'Flaherty's Case, The William Turner*, Moore, IV, p. 3378; Lapradelle and Politis, I, p. 494 (the better report) with a note at p. 501 (iv); *Croft's* Case, Moore, V, p. 4979; Lapradelle and Politis, II, p. 1, at p. 22 and the *note doctrinale* at p. 33.

apply their own international rules of conflict of laws which are adapted to their own characteristics and designed to serve their own special needs. We must therefore examine these characteristics with a view to establishing an apposite international system of conflict of laws.

Absence of a lex fori

In the first place, international tribunals possess no *lex fori* in matters of private law. The *lex fori* of international tribunals consists of international law as developed by custom and treaties. The American-Venezuelan Commission said in *Williams'* Case[34]:

"it is a well settled principle in common law jurisdictions, and a recognised one in civil law countries, that obligations are to be enforced according to the *lex loci fori* which here is the treaty and the public law ..."

Thus, while private international law within the State may choose between the application of the municipal law of the court concerned and of foreign law as an alternative source, international courts, owing to the absence of a *lex fori* in matters of private law must elect between two or more systems of municipal law, none of which can claim the privileged position of *lex curiae*. Consequently the courts cannot rely on any municipal system of conflict of laws, seeing that a municipal system of conflict of laws is based upon the special policy conceptions of the *lex fori*.[35]

Renvoi

It follows, in the second place, that the doctrine of *renvoi* cannot apply. If an international system of conflict of laws accepted a reference back to the *lex fori* it would defeat its own ends, seeing that the reference back would lead to the application, not of muni|cipal, but of international law. It is therefore not surprising that not a single case involving *renvoi* can be found among the great number of international decisions.

On the other hand, it is conceivable that an international tribunal, having ascertained with the help of its own international rules of conflict of laws that a certain system of municipal law applies, adopts this system as a whole, including its rules of municipal private international law. These rules may

---

[34] Moore, IV, p. 4181, at p. 4182; see also *Eldredge's* Case, *ibid.*, p. 3460, at p. 3462.

[35] For a detailed discussion see the present writer's observations in *Transactions of the Grotius Society*, 27 (1942), p. 142 ff., especially at pp. 149–156; see also Neuner in *Canadian Bar Review*, 20 (1942), pp. 479–501.

refer to yet another system of municipal law, and so on. This situation arises at times in municipal private international law, where it is known as transmission or *Weiterverweisung*.[36] It is submitted with some confidence that this situation should not be allowed to arise in international courts. It would mean that an international tribunal identifies itself with the courts of a particular country, so as to adopt the law of that country as *lex curiae*, before embarking upon a final choice of law. This amounts to a capitulation of the international court before the private international law of a particular country.[37] A reference by international rules of conflict of laws to some system of municipal law must be final.

Public Policy

In the third place, it follows that in a system of international conflict of laws the principle of public policy must fulfil a different function than in municipal private international law. Within the latter system, the principle of public policy operates so as to substitute the municipal law of the *lex fori* for the system of foreign law ordinarily applicable. Seeing that the *lex fori* of international tribunals consists of international law alone, the function of public policy in an international system of conflict of laws can be only to exclude the operation of foreign private law. It is incapable of substituting another system of private law. Consequently, international public policy can only deny a property right, the violation of which forms the subject of an international reclamation. It can never allow a property right where the foreign law, ordinarily applicable, has denied its existence. It must be admitted that this contention is not borne out by the practice of the Permanent Court of International Justice. In the *Serbian and Brazilian Loan* Cases,[38] it was held that an international court, when applying the municipal law of a particular country, must seek to apply it as it would be applied by that country, including its principles of public policy.

|However, if an international court, with the help of its own international rules of conflict of laws, finds that a particular system of municipal law applies, it cannot serve any useful purpose to apply also the rules of public policy of that system which are directed against the application of yet anoth-

---

[36] Lorenzen, *Columbia Law Review*, 10 (1910), p. 190, at p. 197; and see *Cameron's Claim, Decisions*, I, p. 33, at p. 45. Another instance was discussed by the Franco-Mexican Claims Commission in the *Pinson* Case, where the Court was confronted by several systems of law in force within the State of Mexico; see *Revue générale de droit international public*, 39 (1932), p. 230, at p. 556 (43).

[37] See *Transactions of the Grotius Society*, 27 (1942), pp. 153–156.

[38] *P.C.I.J.*, ser. A, no. 20, pp. 41, 46; *ibid.*, no. 21, pp. 124–125.

er system of municipal law.[39] But it must be admitted that the answer would have to be different, if the principle of transmission or *Weiterverweisung*, which was rejected above, were to be accepted.

Generally speaking, the practice of international tribunals has not developed on the lines followed by the Permanent Court of International Justice. The case of *The Enterprize* decided by the Anglo-American Claims Commission,[40] represents a strong precedent in favour of our proposition that the principles of public policy, for the purposes of international courts, are furnished by international law. The facts were as follows. In 1835, an American vessel carrying slaves belonging to American owners took refuge in Bermuda, owing to stress of weather. The Court of Bermuda ordered the slaves to be freed pursuant to the Act of 3 and 4 Wm. IV c. 73 (1833) abolishing slavery in Great Britain and her dependencies. In the course of the claim for damages against Great Britain, the tribunal had to decide whether the court of Bermuda was entitled to apply the English statute in respect of *res in transitu* on board a vessel and which were ordinarily subject to American law as their former *lex rei sitae*, or as the law of the flag. It was clear that the Bermudan Court had applied the English statute on grounds of public policy. The question was therefore whether the principles of public policy to be considered by the international tribunal were those of the law of Bermuda which rejected slavery or of the *lex fori*, i.e., international law, which at that time did not. The Commission, including, it would appear, Hornby, the British Commissioner, who delivered a dissenting judgment,[41] decided that the principles of public policy were prescribed by international law and, by a majority, allowed the claim. Bates, the Umpire said:[42]

"It was well known that slavery had been conditionally abolished in nearly all the British Dominions about six months before ... No one can deny that slavery is contrary to the principles of justice and humanity and can only be established in any country by law. At the time of the transaction on which the claim is founded, slavery existed by law in several countries and was not wholly abolished in the British Dominions. It could not, then, be | contrary

---

[39] Transactions of the Grotius Society, 27 (1942), pp. 156–157; see also *The Norwegian Claims, Case*, Scott, *Hague Court Reports*, II, p. 38, at pp. 64, 65. See also, Kaeckenbeeck, *The International Experiment of Upper Silesia* (1942), p. 75 and n. 3, pp. 78, Niboyet, *Répertoire de droit international*, Vol. 10 (1931), s.v. *Ordre public*, especially nos. 439–457.

[40] Moore, IV, p. 4349; Lapradelle and Politis, I, 686; and see the *note doctrinale ibid.*, p. 705, at pp. 707–709. See also, to the same effect, the decisions of the same tribunal in *The Hermosa*, Moore, IV, p. 4374; Lapradelle and Politis, I, p. 688; *The Creole*, Moore, IV, p. 4375; Lapradelle and Politis loc. cit. But see *The Comet, The Encomium*, Moore, IV, 4349; Lapradelle and Politis, I, p. 691, to the contrary effect, seeing that the acts complained of occurred prior to the passing of the Act of 3 and 4 Wm. IV, c. 73.

[41] loc. cit., at pp. 4362–65.

[42] loc. cit., at p. 4373.

to the law of nations, and *The Enterprize* was as much entitled to protection as though her cargo consisted of any other description of property. The conduct of the authorities at Bermuda was a violation of the law of nations ..."

The remarks of Upham, the American Commissioner, are even more forceful, but it is submitted that they are too sweeping. He said:[43]

"There is but one ground on which it can be contended that the Act of 3 and 4 Wm. IV c. 73 overrules the principles that I have laid down [i.e., that the law of the port may not be applied to foreign vessels in port and to property on board] and that is that the municipal law of England is paramount to the absolute rights of other governments when they come in conflict with each other. Such a position virtually abolishes the entire code of international law. If one state can at pleasure revoke such a law, any other state may do the same thing, and the whole system of international intercourse becomes a mere matter of arbitrary will and of universal violence."

It may be useful to refer to a few more awards. In the case of *The Maria Luz*,[44] the Peruvian Government claimed damages from Japan on the ground that Japanese Courts had acted illegally in disallowing the claim of a Peruvian Captain for the restoration of escaped Chinese coolies who were under a contract to him. The arbitrator said:

"We have arrived at the conviction ... that the Japanese Government acted in good faith, in virtue of its own laws and customs, without infringing the general prescriptions of the law of nations or the stipulations of particular treaties."

Another example is furnished by the decision of the tribunal in *Reparation Commission v. U.S.A.*[45] The facts were as follows. Shortly before the outbreak of the war between the U.S.A. and Germany in 1917, the Standard Oil Co. sold its shares in a German Company to a German national in consideration of a sum the payment of which was deferred, supplemented by a deposit of securities as a guarantee. The securities were subsequently seized by the American Custodian of Enemy Property. The claim before the tribunal involved the question whether the contract of sale was valid and

---

[43] loc. cit., at p. 4361. But see the dissenting opinion of Hornby, the British Commissioner, loc. cit., at pp. 4362–4372. For a discussion of the relations between international law and municipal rules of conflict of laws see *Transactions of the Grotius Society*, 27 (1942), pp. 142–149.

[44] Moore, V, p. 5034; Lapradelle and Politis, I, p. 704; and see the *note doctrinale* by Strisower, *ibid.*, pp. 707–709 where he distinguishes between public policy in international law and in municipal law. See also the dissenting opinion of Mr. Little in *Henry Woodruff and Flanagan, Bradley, Clark and Co. v Venezuela*, Moore, IV, p. 3566; *Beales, Nobles Garrison v Venezuela*, Moore, IV, p. 3548, at p. 3560; see also *Camy v U.S.*, Moore, III, p. 2398, at p. 2400.

[45] *B.Y.I.L.*, 8 (1927), p. 156, at p. 158; *A.J.*, 22 (1928), p. 404, at p. 407.

whether the American Company had acquired a lien over the securities. The Tribunal said:

| "Whereas the ... securities ... were seized as enemy property by the Enemy Property Custodian, the latter, when opposition was lodged by the Standard Oil Co., asserted his belief in the good faith of the sale, but none the less by a decision ... declared it to be null and void. Whereas this decision, being prompted only by reasons of public order, could not lead the Tribunal to consider the sale as null ..."

Classification

In the fourth place, the absence of a *lex fori* in matters of private law explains why only a comparatively small number of cases involved difficulties of what is generally known as conflicts of classification. Such conflicts, it may be remembered, are not infrequent in municipal private international law. They may arise when a Court must interpret the meaning of a legal concept contained in a rule of private international law, such as immovables, capacity or matrimonial property. These terms may have one meaning according to the *lex fori* and another according to the law ordinarily applicable. The tribunals, the practice of which is under review today, have not followed any consistent line in matters of classification. In general they classified according to the law of one of the countries which were parties to the dispute.[46] But it is impossible to ascertain the reasons why the classification of one system of laws was chosen in preference to any other. Sometimes it cannot even be stated according to which system of laws the tribunals classified.[47]

---

[46] *Dusenberg v Mexico*, Moore, III, p. 2157, at p. 2158; *Knox v Mexico, ibid.*, III, p. 2166; *Robert v Mexico, ibid.*, III, p. 2468, at p. 2471; *Rivlin, Guardian of H. Sternberg v Turkey, Turkish Claims*, p. 622, at p. 626 (domicile classified according to American law); *Raeburn v Mexico, Decisions*, II, p. 54, at p. 59 (domicile classified according to English law); *Gleadell v Mexico, ibid.*, I, p. 55, at pp. 57, 63 (personal property, situs of choses in action classified according to English law); *The Enterprise*, Moore IV, p. 4349, at p. 4366 (rights over slaves classified according to American law); *Norwegian Claims* Case, Scott, *Hague Court Reports*, II, p. 38, at p. 67. And see the cases cited below, note 107. But see *P.C.I.J.*, ser. B. No. 10, at pp. 19–22 where the Court had to interpret private law terms contained in a treaty. For a discussion of this problem see *Transactions of the Grotius Society*, 27 (1942), p. 158 and the literature quoted *ibid.*, note 84. And see Niboyet, *Hague Recueil*, 31 (1930), pp. 68–99; *ibid.*, 40 (1932) p. 68; Kaeckenbeeck, *The International Experiment of Upper Silesia* (1942), pp. 51, 61; Jenks, *B.Y.I.L.* 19 (1938), p. 67, at p. 84.
[47] *The Montijo*, Moore, II, p. 1421, at p. 1430; *Raeburn v Mexico, Decisions*, II, p. 54, at p. 55.

Proof of Municipal Law

Finally, a word must be said concerning the method of proving foreign municipal law in international courts. The Permanent Court of International Justice held in the *Serbian and Brazilian Loan* Cases:[48]

"Though bound to apply municipal law when circumstances so require, the Court, which is a tribunal of international law and which, in this capacity, is deemed itself to know what this law is, is not obliged also to know the municipal law of the various countries. All that can be said in this respect is that the Court may possibly be obliged to obtain knowledge regarding the municipal law which has to be applied. And this it must do, either by means of evidence furnished it by the parties, or by means of any researches which the Court may think fit to undertake or to cause to be undertaken."

| And again

"For the Court itself to undertake its own construction of municipal law, leaving on one side existing judicial decisions, with the ensuing danger of contradicting the construction which has been placed on such law by the highest national tribunal and which, in its results, seems to the Court reasonable, would not be in conformity with the task for which the Court has been established ..."[49]

The Court based its conclusions with respect of French law on citations of publicists and judicial decisions of French Courts.[50] The same approach was chosen by the great majority of international tribunals,[51] although in some cases emphasis was laid upon the opinion of experts,[52] and in others upon the practice of municipal courts.[53] In the *Hudson Bay Co.* Claim[54] and in the *Puget Sound Agricultural Co.* Claim,[55] which involved disputes over titles to

---

[48] *P.C.I.J.*, ser. A, No. 21, at p. 124. See also *P.C.I.J.*, ser. A, No. 7, at p. 19 (German Interests in Upper Silesia).

[49] *P.C.I.J.*, ser. A, No. 20, p. 46; and see the observations of Anzilotti, *P.C.I.J.*, ser. A, No. 65, at pp. 63–64. (*Danzig Legislative Decrees*).

[50] But see the dissenting opinions of Bustamante, *P.C.I.J.*, ser. A, No. 20, at pp. 54–58; *ibid.*, No. 21, at pp. 131–136 and of Pessoa, *ibid.*, No. 20, at pp. 71 ff., especially at pp. 73–74; *ibid*, no. 21, at pp. 148–152. For the uncertainty of French law on the question discussed by the Court see Genet, *Revue générale de droit international*, 36 (1929), pp. 685–688. And see the *Lighthouse* Case (France v Greece), *P.C.I.J.*, ser A/B, No. 62, pp. 19–24, where the Court applied Turkish law. But see the observations of Prof. Hudson in *P.C.I.J.*, ser., A/B, No. 78, p. 184 (*Société Commerciale de Belgique*). See also Jenks in *B.Y.I.L.*, 19 (1938), p. 67 at pp. 69, 89.

[51] *Cook v Mexico, Opinions*, II, p. 162, at p. 165; Nielsen, p. 500, at p. 503; *Re Donnell's Executors, Re Hollins and McBlair*, Moore, IV, pp. 3545–46.

[52] *Reparation Commission v U.S.A., B.Y.I.L.* 8 (1927), p. 156, at p. 159; *A.J.*, 22 (1928), p. 404 at p. 408.

[53] *Dr. Baldwin's Case*, Moore, IV, p. 2859, at p. 2864.

[54] Moore, I, p. 250, at p. 259; Lapradelle and Politis, II, p. 503, at p. 511.

[55] Moore, I, p. 262, at p. 264, Lapradelle and Politis, II, p. 513, at p. 515 with a *note doctrinale* at p. 520.

land not yet under the sovereignty of any State, the tribunal applied the principles of natural justice.

Summary

Summing up the results of our investigations into the general principles of an international system of conflict of laws, we may state the following conclusions:–

(1) An international system of conflict of laws differs in essence from municipal systems of private international law inasmuch as it does not possess a *lex fori*.

(2) The doctrine of *renvoi* is inapplicable.

(3) Public policy is determined by international law and not by the system of municipal law to which international rules of conflict of laws refer.

(4) Conflicts of classification are rare. Guiding principles for their solution have not yet been elaborated.

III

International Rules of Conflict of laws. Special rules

Persons

We must now attempt to ascertain the particular rules of an international system of conflict of laws. In municipal private international law, private status is governed by the law of the domicile in common law jurisdictions, or by the *lex patriae* in civil law countries. In both jurisdictions, the public status of an individual is governed by the law of his nationality. Before intern|national tribunals, the private status of individuals is of little importance, except in the case of successions, seeing that international tribunals are only concerned with the question of municipal property rights. Whenever questions regarding the status of individuals arose, the tribunals applied the law of the domicile, while they classified domicile according to Anglo-American conceptions.[56]

Nationality, on the other hand, is of paramount importance for the purpose of international courts, in order to determine the nationality of the claim. International tribunals must always consider the nationality of the

---

[56] See above, note 46.

claimant himself in order to establish, at the outset, the right of the claimant's State to invoke the jurisdiction of the courts.[57] This distinction between the private status of a claimant which is governed by the law of his domicile, and his public status, which is governed by the law of his nationality, is superfluous in municipal private international law, except in time of war. Consequently, it is generally overlooked.

For the purposes of international tribunals and municipal courts alike, nationality is determined by the law of the country in question.[58] But it would appear that the tribunals are not bound to regard statements by the authorities of the country in question to the effect that a claimant possesses the nationality of that country as conclusive proof. There is ample and weighty support for the proposition that international tribunals are free to ascertain according to their own rules of evidence whether a claimant possesses the nationality of any particular country.[59] It is submitted that this opinion must be approved seeing that international tribunals, according to their own much reiterated statements, are not guided by domestic rules of evidence.[60] In the words of the American-Mexican Commission in the *Solis* Case:[61]

---

[57] *Dickson Car Wheel Co.* Case, Opinions, III, p. 175, at pp. 188, 191; *P.C.I.J.*, ser. A, No. 76, p. 16 (*Panevezys-Saldutiskis Railway* Case).

[58] *Willet's* Case, Moore, III, p. 2254, at pp. 2255–56; *Costello* Claim, *Opinions*, II, p. 252, at p. 265; Nielsen, p. 376, at p. 378 ff.; *Salem* Case, Nielsen, p. 649, at p. 659; *Belle M. Hendry* Case, *Opinions, III*, p. 97; *Mackenzie's* Claim, *American-German Claims*, p. 628, at p. 629; *Expropriated Religious Properties Case*, Scott, *Hague Court Reports*, II, p. 1 ff., *passim*; *P.C.I.J.*, ser. B, No. 4, p. 24 (*Tunis-Maroccan Nationality Decrees*); *ibid.*, ser. B, No. 10, p. 22 (*Exchange of Greek and Turkish Populations*). And see the following cases decided by the American-Turkish Claims Commission: *Benjamin, Turkish Claims*, p. 209; *Dimitroff and Constantinidi, ibid.*, p. 241; *Giwergiz, ibid.*, p. 272; *Greenfield and Sons, ibid.*, p. 394; *Weinberg, ibid.*, p. 538; *Yonan, ibid.*, p. 550, at p. 554; *Pirocaco, ibid.*, p. 587; Rivlin, *ibid.*, pp. 662; *Levin, ibid.*, p. 688 at p. 690.

[59] *Medina* Case, Moore, III, p. 2583; Lapradelle and Politis, II, p. 164, with a *note doctrinale* at p. 173; *Lizardi* Case, Moore, III, p. 2589; *Marquis de Potesdad, ibid.*, III, p. 2632; *Kuhnagel's* Case, *ibid.*, III, p. 2647; *Russell's* Case, Nielsen, p. 587, at p. 593; *Parker* Claim, *Opinions*, I, p. 33, at pp. 36–37; *Solis* Case, *ibid.*, II, pp. 48–50; Nielsen, p. 277, at p. 279; *Lynch* Claim, *Decisions*, I, p. 20, at p. 21; *Cameron* Claim, *ibid.*, I, p. 33, at p. 35; *Pinson* Claim, *Revue générale de droit international*, 39 (1932), p. 392, at p. 408 (20); *P.C.I.J.*, ser. A, No. 7, pp. 72–73 (*German Interests in Polish Upper Silesia*). But see the *Expropriated Religious Properties* Case, Scott, *Hague Court Reports* II, p. 1, at p. 25. See also Ralston, pp. 173–178; Feller, pp. 272–277; Borchard, pp. 490 ff., 522 ff.

[60] *Kling* Case, *Opinions*, III, p. 36, at pp. 44–45; Nielsen, p. 432, at pp. 441–42; *Mallén* Case, *Opinions*, I, p. 254, at p. 268; *Nielsen*, p. 177, at p. 181; *Russell's* Case, Nielsen, p. 587, at p. 635; *Parker* Case, *Opinions* I, p. 35, at pp. 37–39; *Dillon* Case, *ibid.*, II, p. 65; Nielsen, p. 291, at p. 293; *Mexico City Bombardment* Claims, *Decisions*, I, p. 100, at p. 109; *Cameron* Claim, *ibid.*, I, p. 33, at pp. 38, 48; *Pinson* Case, *Revenue générale de droit international*, 39 (1932), p. 556 (44); Feller, pp. 257–260.

[61] *Opinions*, II, pp. 48–50; Nielsen, p. 277, at p. 278. See also *Russell's* Case, Nielsen, pp. 593–596.

"The Commission is an international tribunal, and it is its duty to receive, and to appraise in its best judgment evidence presented to it in accordance with arbitral agreement and international practice."

The question what law determines nationality in the case of double nationality has attracted little attention on the part of international tribunals. Nationality was determined sometimes according to the principle of effectiveness,[62] sometimes according to the presumed preference of the claimant;[63] in one case the Anglo-Mexican Claims Commission left the question open and disallowed the claim | on the ground that the claimant was both a British and Mexican national.[64]

Corporations

In a previous paper the reasons were pointed out why before international tribunals the distinction drawn above between the private and the public status of individuals merits even greater attention in respect of corporations.[65]

The practice of the international tribunals under review has furnished only few decisions touching upon the problem what law governs the private status of corporations. It would appear that the law of the place where the company had been incorporated was applied.[66] But a considerable body of case law has grown around the question whether corporations possess a nationality and how it should be determined. In a well documented award, the Anglo-Mexican Claims Commission held in the *Flack* Claim[67] (per Flores, the Mexican Commissioner):

"The nationality of physical persons, i.e., the bond uniting a person to a particular nation, has never been laid open to doubt. On the contrary, doubt

---

[62] *Lebret's* Case, Moore, III, p. 2488, at p. 2498, 2505; *Willet's* Case, *ibid.*, III, p. 2254; *Heirs of H. Stevens Shreck*, *ibid.*, pp. 2450–2451; *re Lucien Lavigne*, *re Felix Bister*, *ibid.*, p. 2454; *Canevaro* Case, Scott, *Hague Court Reports*, I, p. 284, at p. 287. And see Borchard, pp. 587–90.

[63] *Re Hammer and De Brissot*, Moore, III, p. 2456, at pp. 2458–59.

[64] *Coralie Davis Honey v Mexico, Decisions*, II, p. 13, at p. 14.

[65] *Transactions of the Grotius Society*, 27 (1942), pp. 161–164; and see the literature quoted l.c., note 105. See also Beckett, *ibid.*, 17 (1932), pp. 175–194; De Visscher in *Revue de droit international et de législation comparée*, 61 (1934), pp. 624–51; 63 (1936), pp. 481–484; Feller, pp. 114–15 and the literature quoted at p. 114, n. 97, 98, p. 115, n. 101; De Beus, pp. 118–122; Ralston, p. 149 ff.; Borchard, pp. 617–26, especially at pp. 620 ff.

[66] *Melczer Mining Co.* Claim, Nielsen, p. 363, at p. 366; *International Fisheries Co.* Claim, *Opinions*, III, p. 207, at p. 214. Not quite clear: P.C.I.J., ser. A/B, No. 61, pp. 228–232 (*Peter Pazmany University* Case); *Spencer Turner v Turkey, Turkish Claims*, p. 454.

[67] *Decisions*, I, p. 80, at p. 87 ff., with further references at p. 90.

has arisen when the thought occurs that there may be a person without any nationality; in the case of artificial, or civil, or juridical persons, however, the problem is a different one. In the first case, the bond uniting the individual to the State consists in his submitting to its laws, so as to be able to appeal to the said State for protection in case of necessity. Rights and duties are correlative to one another. In the second case, artificial persons cannot always be considered as identical with physical persons; they cannot, for instance, at a given moment, render military service, as an individual can, or comply with any other similar requirement on the part of the Government to which they have submitted. And by reason of the lack of similarity between physical and artificial persons, and the legal fiction upon which the latter rest, the opinions of jurists have become divided, especially after the world war, some of them contending that limited companies should have no nationality at all ..."

The majority of the Commission determined the nationality of the Corporation by requiring that it must be incorporated by the law of the country, the nationality of which is claimed and, in addition, that its *siège social* must be established within the jurisdiction of | that country. The Mexican Commissioner required, moreover, that the nationality of the shareholders must be taken into account.

The test of incorporation combined with that of the *siège social* was applied by the Commission in a number of cases.[68] But in the *Mazapil Copper Co.* Claim[69] and in one other case[70] the same Commission applied the test of incorporation alone. To add to this confusion, the Anglo-Mexican Commission applied, in *Bowerman and Burberry's* Claim[71] the test of incorporation coupled with that of the nationality of the shareholders. Finally, in one case, the Commission allowed as British a claim by the shareholders – all British subjects – of a company incorporated under the laws of Arizona,[72] but it is submitted that this solution was adopted on equitable grounds only. The test of control was accepted by the American-German Mixed Claims Commission in the *Standard Oil Co. of New Jersey* Claim where the Commission held that a shareholder, an American national, could claim in respect of damage done to a corporation incorporated under the laws of Holland.[73] Control was also the test in the *International Fisheries Co.* Case

---

[68] *Madera Co.* Claim, *Decisions*, II, p. 67, at p. 71; *Interoceanic Ry. of Mexico* Claim, *ibid.*, II, p. 118, at p. 126.

[69] *ibid.*, I, p. 132, at p. 133.

[70] *Santa Gertrudis Jute Mill Co.* Claim, *ibid.*, I, p. 147, at p. 149. See also *MacAndrews and Forbes* Claim, *Turkish Claims*, p. 118, at p. 119; The *siège social* alone was the test in the *Barron* Claim, Moore, III, p. 2518, at p. 2523.

[71] *Decisions*, II, p. 17.

[72] *British Shareholders of the Mariposa Co.*, *ibid.*, II, p. 304, at p. 306.

[73] *American-German Mixed Claims Commission*, p. 877, at p. 878. See also *P.C.I.J.*, ser. A, No. 7, pp. 68–70 (*German interests in Polish Upper Silesia*).

decided by the American-Mexican Claims Commission.[74] In this case, however, the test of control was applied not in order to determine the nationality of the company as a claimant in its own right, but in order to allow the controlling interests to sue in their own name. This far reaching decision can be met by arguments which have found pungent expression in the decision of the special tribunal in *Reparation Commission v. U.S.A.* where it was stated:[75]

"... the decisions of principle of the highest courts of most countries continue to hold that neither the shareholders nor their creditors have any right to the corporate assets other than to receive, during the existence of the company, a share of the profits, the distribution of which has been decided by a majority of the shareholders, and after its winding up a proportional share of the assets ..."

The tribunal reviewed a number of relevant decisions of municipal courts and continued:

"... in none of these cases has it been a question of granting or assigning to claimant shareholders or debenture holders rights in any part of the corporate assets, but merely of granting them indemnity for damage caused by unjustified intervention on the part of the government ... It was specified that the shareholders and debenture holders were admitted, in view of | the circumstances, to be exercising not their own rights, but the rights which the company, wrongfully dissolved or destroyed, was unable thenceforth to enforce; .... they were, therefore, seeking to enforce not direct and personal rights, but indirect and substituted rights."

In view of the theoretical argument set out in the *Flack* Claim[76] to the effect that a corporation cannot possess any nationality, it is submitted that the nationality of claims brought on behalf of corporations is determined by that of the majority of the shareholders or must be divided proportionately between the shareholders of different nationality. But, having regard to the practical reasons advanced in *Reparation Commission v. U.S.A.,*[77] international claims in respect of corporations should not be allowed to be brought by shareholders in their own right.

It must be admitted that the solution here advocated is not entirely satisfactory. Control is a crude test, as it does not take into account the nationality of the minority of shareholders. But it serves to avoid three difficulties in addition to those mentioned above. First, in view of the absence of municipal laws regarding the nationality of corporations,[78] the tribunals would

---

[74] *Opinions,* III, p. 207, at p. 214; see also the observations in *MacAndrews and Forbes v. Turkey, Turkish Claims,* p. 118, at p. 119.

[75] *B.Y.I.L.,* 8 (1927), p. 156, at pp. 162–164; *A.J.,* 22 (1928), p. 404, at pp. 411–414.

[76] above, note 67.

[77] above, note 75. See also Feller, pp. 117–122.

[78] *Flack* Claim, *Opinions,* I., p. 80, at p. 93 (per Flores, Mexican Commissioner).

have to determine the nationality of corporations according to international principles of nationality. This would be contrary to the recognised principle of international law according to which nationality is determined exclusively by municipal law.[79] Secondly, as a result of the application of international principles of nationality, States would frequently find themselves entrusted with the protection of corporations which they themselves did not claim as nationals, or deprived of the right to protect corporations which they recognised as nationals. Thirdly, the recognition of an independent nationality on the part of legal entities may lead – and has led, in the case of partnerships – to double nationality of claims, once it is admitted that the rights of individual shareholders may form the basis of international claims.

Partnerships

The rights and duties of partnerships are determined by the law governing the contract of partnership.[80] The decisions regarding the nationality of claims brought on behalf of a partnership are conflicting. In the great majority of cases, the nationality of a partnership was determined by that of the partners, who were|regarded as representing it proportionately. Thus it was held in *Thomas Morrison v. Mexico*:[81]

"The right of the citizen to claim the protection of his own government … is a personal right confined to the citizen injured and cannot be by him extended or transferred. He cannot, by connecting himself with the citizens of another country in his business relation, throw over them the mantle of his own government or enable them to invoke its protection."

On the other hand, the American-Peruvian Claims Commission held in the case of *Ruden and Co.* that the nationality of business firms was that of the country where they resided, under whose laws they had been formed and by which they were governed.[82] In a number of cases these two tests were combined, with the result that the defendant State was threatened by two claims on the part of two States, but in respect of the same injury.[83] Once this double nationality of claims is admitted, it may even occur that a State is faced with a claim impressed with its own nationality.[84] This result must be

---

[79] P.C.I.J., ser. B, No. 4, p. 24 (*Tunis-Maroccan Nationality Decrees*).

[80] *Oldenbourg* Claim, *Decisions*, II, p. 163, at p. 165.

[81] Moore, III, p. 2325, at p. 2326. See also *Asiatic Raisin Trading Co. v. Turkey, Turkish Claims*, p. 196; *Greenfield and Sons v. Turkey, ibid.*, p. 394, at p. 397; *Deutz' Case, Opinions*, II, p. 213. See also Borchard, pp. 614–616.

[82] Moore, II, p. 1653, at p. 1654; Lapradelle and Politis, II, p. 589 with a *note doctrinale* at p. 590; Ralston, p. 139, Supp. p. 65.

[83] *Mexican Tramways Co.* Claim, *Decisions*, II, p. 184, at p. 193; *Frederick Adams* Claim, *ibid.*, p. 199, at pp. 200–201.

[84] *Spillane and Co. v. Mexico, Decisions*, II, p. 72, at p. 79.

avoided. It is submitted that the decision in *Thomas Morrison v. Mexico*[85] was correct. A partnership itself possesses no nationality of its own for the same reasons as those which led us to deny the existence of an independent nationality of corporations.

Contracts

Decisions bearing upon the question what law governs a contract are not as frequent as might be expected. The Permanent Court of International Justice in the *Serbian and Brazilian Loan* Cases[86] ascertained the law governing a contract "by reference to the actual nature of these obligations and to the circumstances attendant upon their creation", but admitted that account should also be taken "of the expressed or presumed intention of the parties." The American-Mexican Mixed Claims Commission relied in turn on free choice of law,[87] the *lex loci contractus*,[88] the *lex loci solutionis*[89], and the law of the place where the contract was situated.[90] Other Commissions applied, as a rule, the *lex loci contractus*[91] or, exceptionally, the proper law[92] Frequently it does not emerge clearly what test was applied.[93] At times, the Court refused to ascertain which system of domestic law governed the contract and applied "the general rules of domestic law"[94] or attempted a combination of the domestic laws of the parties.[95]

---

[85] See above, note 81. But see Feller, p. 116.

[86] *P.C.I.J.*, ser. A., no. 20, p. 41; *ibid.*, no. 21, p. 121. See also Borchard pp. 303–305.

[87] *North American Dredging Co.* Case, Opinions, I, p. 21, at p. 32.

[88] *Cook* Case, *Opinions*, I, p. 318, at p. 320; Nielsen, p. 196, at p. 198.

[89] *Dickson Car Wheel Co.* Case, *Opinions*, III, p. 175, at p. 185; Ralston, Supp., p. 51, No. 147a. For modalities of payment see *P.C.I.J.*, ser. A, no. 20, p. 44; no. 21, pp. 122–123.

[90] *Cook* Case, Nielsen, pp. 390–91. *American Tobacco Co. of the Orient* Case, *Turkish Claims*, p. 145, at p. 146.

[91] *Idler v. Venezuela*, Moore, IV, p. 3491, at p. 3510; *Donnell's Executors, Hollins and McBlair*, ibid., IV, pp. 3545, 3548; *Hetty Green v. Mexico*, Moore, IV, pp. 3425, 4325; Lapradelle and Politis, I, p. 459; *Chew v. Mexico, The Tepeyac*, Lapradelle and Politis, I, pp. 459–60. And see *Reparation Commission v. U.S.A., B.Y.I.L.*, 8 (1927), p. 156, at pp. 158, 159 where, before deciding the case in accordance with the *lex loci contractus*, the Tribunal applied the *lex loci contractus* in order to ascertain whether the contract was concluded or not. For a criticism of this method see *Transactions of the Grotius Society* 37 (1942), p. 165.

[92] *Marmaras v. Turkey, Turkish Claims*, p. 473, at p. 483; re *Achelis, American-German Claims*, p. 879.

[93] *Youille, Shortridge and Co.* Claim, Lapradelle and Politis, II, p. 78, at p. 102; *Cook* Case, Nielsen, p. 390, at p. 395; *McPherson* Case, *ibid.*, p. 201; *Opinions*, I, p. 325; *Home Insurance Co.* Case, *Opinions*, I, p. 51, at p. 56 (16), 58 (18); *Davies* Case, *ibid.*, p. 197, at p. 204; *Nielsen*, p. 145, at p. 151; *MacAndrews and Forbes* Claim, *Turkish Claims*, p. 120, at p. 125; *Malamatinis* Case, *ibid.*, p. 603, at p. 615; *Mexican Tramways Co.* Claim, *Decisions* II, p. 184, at p. 186; *Eagle Star Co.* Case, *ibid.*, p. 32, at p. 35.

[94] *Davies* Case, *Opinions*, I, p. 197, at p. 201; Nielsen, p. 145, at p. 148.

[95] *Socony-Vacuum Oil Co.* Case, *Turkish Claims*, p. 369, at p. 375; *Davies Case, Opinions*, I, at p. 199, Nielsen, at p. 147.

| In the matter of formalities, the Courts frequently asserted a wide discretion and disregarded the maxim *locus regit actum*, the only principle of municipal private international law which has been more or less universally accepted by the practice of nations.[96]

The majority of the relevant cases is inconclusive in respect of the question what law governs illegality. It appears that in a few cases recourse was had to the *lex loci contractus*.[97]

Interest seems to have been taken into consideration if acquired according to the law governing the contract or the *lex loci contractus*.[98]

Although the courts under review were concerned with contracts of such diverse character as sales, loans, leases, contracts of service, of partnership, of insurance, of transport by railway and claims for *quantum meruit* or unjustifiable enrichment, it is impossible to state that particular tests were applied with regard to any special type of contract.

Torts

The tribunals were seldom called upon to decide cases involving liability in tort. The few cases where this question was raised were concerned with collisions inside territorial waters between vessels of different nationality. In the *Daylight* Case, the American-Mexican-Claims Commission applied the *lex loci delicti commissi*.[99] But it was pointed out in the same case that, in respect of collisions with a state-owned vessel, the tribunal was free to apply the general rules of international law.[100] This latter solution was adopted by the American-Panamanian Claims Commission in the *Manzo* Case.[101] It is

---

[96] *Eldredge's* Case, Moore, IV, p. 3460, at p. 3462; Lapradelle and Politis, II, p. 264 with a *note doctrinale* at p. 266; *Pomeroy's El Paso Transfer Co.* Case, *Opinions*, III, p. 1, at p. 18; Nielsen, p. 418, at pp. 429–30; but see *Raeburn v. Mexico, Decisions*, II, p. 54, at p. 55; *Reparation Commission v. U.S.A., B.Y.I.L.*, 8 (1927), p. 156, at p. 159; *The Queen*, Lapradelle and Politis, II, p. 706, at p. 709; *Orinoco S.S. Co.* Case, American-Venezuelan Claims, Scott, *Hague Court Reports*, I, p. 240, at pp. 250, 268.

[97] *Cucullu's* Case, Moore, IV, p. 3477, at p. 3478; *Meade's* Case, *ibid.*, IV., p. 3430, at p. 3431. Doubtful: *Union Land Co.* Claim, Moore, IV, p. 3434, at p. 3450; *McRae* Claim, Lapradelle and Politis, I, p. 474.

[98] *Walter's* Case, Moore, IV, p. 3567, at p. 3568. Not clear: *Youille, Shortridge and Co.* Claim, Lapradelle and Politis, II, p. 78, at p. 108 with a *note doctrinale* at pp. 117, 229, n. 1.

[99] *Opinions*, I, p. 241, at pp. 245, 249; Nielsen, p. 171, at p. 172, referring to *The Canadienne*, Anglo-American Claims of 1910, American Agent's Report, p. 427, at p. 430, *The Sidra, ibid.*, p. 453, at p. 457, *A.J.*, 16 (1922), p. 110, at p. 113, *Institut de droit international, Annuaire*, 1888, p. 113. See also *Dr. Baldwin's* Case, Moore, III, p. 2859, at p. 2864; Lapradelle and Politis, I, pp. 465, 467; *The Brig "William,"* Moore, IV, p. 4226; Lapradelle and Politis, I, p. 470.

[100] l.c., at p. 250, Nielsen, p. 173 and the cases quoted there.

[101] *Panamanian Claims*, p. 679, at p. 694; not clear: *Castaneda* and *De Leon* Claim, *ibid.*, pp. 676, 677.

submitted, however, that in view of the general principles set out in the first part of this paper, recourse must first be had to *lex loci delicti commissi* before any liability under international law can be considered. In the case of torts committed by subordinate officials, States are liable under international law only if the redress afforded by the municipal law applicable in the circumstances is insufficient or if redress is excluded altogether. In the old case of *The Queen*,[102] the arbitrator applied the "general rules of maritime law" without referring to any particular system of municipal law.

Property

The selection of the test determining which system of laws is to govern in matters of property depends upon whether transfer|of property is classified as an incident of the contract to transfer property or as a separate transaction. In general, the tribunals classified all questions relating to the transfer of immovables as a separate category and applied the *lex rei sitae*.[103] It would appear that the same test was occasionally applied with regard to the transfer of movables.[104] But the American-Mexican and American-Turkish Claims Commissions established a constant practice to the effect that the title to movables is governed by the law of the transaction conferring the title, viz. the law governing the contract to transfer title.[105] In one case, the law governing the contract served to determine the title to immovables.[106] Trusts are probably governed by the *lex rei sitae*.[107]

---

[102] Lapradelle and Politis, II, p. 706, at p. 708 with a critical note at p. 712. See also *The Lindisfarne*, Anglo-American Claims Arbitration, *A.J.*, 7 (1913), p. 875, at p. 877.

[103] *Van Bokkelen* Case, Moore, II, p. 1807, at p. 1831; *Hoachoozo Palestine Land and Development Co.* Claim, *Turkish Claims*, p. 254, at p. 260; *Pirocaco* Claim, *ibid.*, p. 587, at p. 597; *American Board of Commissioners for Foreign Missions, ibid.*, p. 674, at p. 675; *Eleni Xydia* Case, *ibid.*, p. 84; *Caires* Case, *ibid.*, p. 164, at p. 165; *Shearer* Case, *Panamanian Claims*, p. 111, at p. 114; *Brown* Case, *ibid.*, p. 530, with a note at p. 532; *Chase* Claim, *ibid.*, p. 340, at p. 372; *P.C.I.J.*, ser. A/B, No. 61, p. 235 (*Peter Pazmany University* Case); *Yukon Lumber Co. Case, A.J.*, 7 (1913), p. 855, at p. 890.

[104] Not quite clear: *Romberg* Case, Lapradelle and Politis, II, p. 564 at p. 565; *Canevaro* Case, Scott, *Hague Court Reports*, I, p. 285, at p. 291.

[105] *Dickson Car Wheel Co.* Case, *Opinions*, III, p. 175, at p. 185; *Cook* Case, *ibid.*, p. 318, at p. 321; Nielsen, p. 196, at p. 198; *American Tobacco Co. of the Orient* Case, *Turkish Claims*, p. 145, at p. 146; *Nicholson File Co.* Case, *ibid.*, p. 445; *Spencer Turner* Case, *ibid.*, p. 454; *Wellington Sears* Case, *ibid.*, p. 459; *Reparation Commission v. U.S.A., B.Y.I.L.*, 8 (1927), p. 156, at p. 159; *A.J.*, 22 (1928), p. 404, at p. 408. Doubtful: *Caires* Case, *Turkish Claims*, p. 164, at p. 165; *Azoo* Case, *ibid.*, p. 193, at p. 194; *Alexandridis* Case, *ibid.*, p. 198, at p. 199; *Abrahams* Case, *ibid.*, p. 403, at p. 429; *Lagueruene* Case, Moore, III, p. 3027, at p. 3028; *Lavarello* Case, *ibid.*, V, p. 5021, at p. 5027.

[106] *Cook* Case, *Opinions*, I, p. 318, at p. 321; Nielsen, p. 196, at p. 198.

[107] *Hoachoozo Palestine Land and Development Co.* Case, *Turkish Claims*, p. 254, at

Successions

Particular difficulties arise in the law of succession. International law demands, first, that the property right, the violation of which forms the object of a claim, is vested in the claimant and, secondly, that the claimant possesses the nationality of the claimant State. In municipal law, however, and more specifically in common law jurisdictions, rights of succession may be said to be vested both in the persons of executors or administrators and in the person of the ultimate beneficiaries. If the executor and the beneficiary possess different nationalities, it may be necessary to disregard the rules of municipal law, applicable according to the international principles of conflict of laws, in order to vest the right in the person who is to be the final beneficiary. The nationality of the latter will determine the nationality of the claim.

In the *Gleadell* Case[108] the importance of this aspect was stressed with special lucidity. The facts were as follows. A British subject, acting as executor of a British *de cuius*, brought a claim before the Anglo-Mexican Claims Commission. The beneficiary was an American citizen. The Commission said:

"The question cannot be solved by the fact that the deceased ... was a British subject at the time of her death and that the husband acts on behalf of her estate. The necessity of the continuous national character of the claim ... does not allow to consider the estate as taking over and retaining the testator's nationality, as apart from the nationality of the heirs. It is essential to know in whose hands the assets of the estate have passed and whether this transition involved | a change of nationality in the person entitled to the claim ... This fact cannot be modified by the circumstance that the executor of the estate is a British subject."

This view of the Commission follows a firmly established practice to the effect that the *de cuius* and the beneficiary must both possess the nationality of the claimant State, while the person of the executor may have to be disregarded.[109] At times stress was laid upon the nationality of the *de cuius*[110] or of the beneficiary.[111]

---

p. 260; *Shimmer* Case, *ibid.*, p. 403, at p. 426; *American Board of Commissioners for Foreign Missions* Case, *ibid.*, p. 674, at p. 675.

[108] *Decisions*, I, p. 55, at pp. 56, 57; see also *Flack's* Case, *ibid.*, p. 80, at p. 81; *Eschauzier* Case, *ibid.*, II, p. 177; *Marmaras* Case, *Turkish Claims*, p. 473, at p. 479. See also Borchard, pp. 627–30, 634; Feller, pp. 86, 106–110, but see De Beus, p. 263.

[109] *Halley* Case, *Ferris* Case, Moore III, p. 2241–42; *Wiltz* Claim, *ibid.*, p. 2243, at p. 2246; *Clark* Case, *Opinions*, III, p. 94, at p. 95; Nielsen p. 472; *City Bank Farmers Trust Co.* Claim, *Turkish Claims*, p. 282, at p. 283; *Cachard and Harges, re Medora de Mores*, *American-German Claims*, p. 634, at p. 635.

[110] *Willet* Claim, Moore, III, p. 2254 at p. 2257; *Peck* Claim, *ibid.*, p. 2257; *Wiltz* Claim (dissenting opinion), *ibid.* p. 2252.

[111] *Belle M. Hendry* Case, *Opinions* III, p. 97, at p. 98; *Russell* Case, Nielsen, p. 587, at p. 602.

In general, the rights of an heir were determined by the law of the domicile of the *de cuius*.[112] At times, it is impossible to establish with any degree of certainty whether the *lex domicilii,* the *lex patriae,* or the *lex rei sitae* was applied.[113] In one case, the municipal law of the plaintiff and of the defendant State were combined.[114]

No clear test was laid down with regard to the interpretation of wills. In the *Gleadell* Claim[115] the Anglo-Mexican Claims Commission, when called upon to interpret a will made in England by a British subject domiciled abroad, followed the presumed intention of the testator and applied English law. The same Commission, by a majority, held in the *Raeburn* Case[116] that the formalities of a will must be governed by the *lex loci actus.* But it would appear that this rule was not strictly followed in the course of the decision. The British Commissioner, in a dissenting opinion, held, apparently under the influence of the principles of English private international law that, in respect of personal property, the formalities of a will were governed by the law of the testator's domicile.[117]

Sometimes the arbitration agreement permitted the signatory powers to lodge claims on behalf of executors. In these circumstances the law governing the status and the rights of the executor had to be ascertained. The American-German Mixed Claims Commission appears to have applied the *lex rei sitae.*[118] On the other hand, in the *Cameron* Claim,[119] decided by the Anglo-Mexican Claims Commission, the British Commissioner applied the law of the last domicile of the *de cuius.* However, he applied the law of the domicile as a whole, including its rules of private international law which referred to yet another system of municipal law. This tendency to adopt the law of the *de cuius* as a whole, including its private international law, results in the creation of *renvoi* and must be rejected for the reasons set out above in connection with our | discussion of *renvoi.*[120] The other Commissioners did not attempt to lay down any particular test.[121]

---

[112] *Glycofridis* Case, *Turkish Claims,* p. 293, at p. 294; *Marmaras* Case, *ibid.,* p. 473, at p. 478; Ralston, p. 146 with references to earlier cases; Borchard, p. 631.

[113] *Benjamin* Case, *Turkish Claims,* p. 440; *Malamatinis* Case, *ibid.,* p. 603, at p. 607; *Rivlin* Case, re *Sternberg, ibid.,* p. 622, at p. 625.

[114] *De Sabla* Case, *Panamanian Claims,* p. 379, at p. 433, with a note at p. 455.

[115] *Decisions,* I, p. 55, at p. 57.

[116] *ibid,* II, p. 54, at p. 55; and see the observations by G. G. Phillips in (1933) 49 *L.Q.R.* p. 226, at pp. 232, 233.

[117] l.c., at p. 59.

[118] *Achelis* Claim, *American-German Claims,* p. 914, at p. 915.

[119] *Decisions,* I, p. 33, at p. 45.

[120] See above.

[121] l.c. at p. 50.

Conclusions

We must now draw our final conclusions.

1. In claims involving State responsibility for denial of justice affecting property rights, international tribunals must apply both municipal and international law.

2. Municipal law determines whether a property right has been acquired and whether it is vested in the claimant.

3. International rules of conflict of laws enable international tribunals to ascertain which system of municipal law applies.

4. An international system of conflict of laws differs in substance from municipal private international law in four essential respects. It cannot rely on a *lex fori* in matters of private law; *renvoi* is inapplicable; public policy is determined by international law; conflicts of classification are rare.

5. The sphere within which international rules of conflict of laws are applied is mainly limited to contracts, property and successions.

6. The individual rules of conflict of laws which international tribunals proper have elaborated hitherto are neither as detailed nor as refined as those developed by municipal courts or even by the Mixed Arbitral Tribunals set up after the first World War. This may be due, in part, to the rougher practice of international tribunals. But the principal reason for the present short-comings of an international system of conflict of laws lies in the fact that it is still a very young branch of international law.

The Place of the Calvo Clause in International Law

Calvo Doctrine and Calvo Clause*

When, in 1868, Calvo first announced the doctrine which was to bear his name,[1] he claimed that European States should refrain from intervening, diplomatically or otherwise, in South America in so far as the protection of private property, including debts, was concerned.[2] In Calvo's opinion, States, and South American States in particular, were not to be embarrassed by international claims based on vicarious responsibility for acts of their officials, riots and insurrections which had resulted in damage to property

---

[Editorial note: first published in the British Yearbook of International Law 22 (1945), 130–145.]

* The following abbreviations will be used:
Decisions I, II = Decisions and Opinions of the Commissioners in accordance with the Convention of 19 November 1926, between Great Britain and the United Mexican States, 2 vols., 1931, 1933.
Moore, *Digest* = Moore, *A Digest of International Law*. 8 vols., 1906.
Moore, *Internat. Arb.* = Moore, *History and Digest of the Arbitrations to which the United States has been a Party*, 6 vols., 1898.
A.J. = *American Journal of International Law*.
Opinions I, II, III = Opinions of Commissioners under the Convention concluded 8 Sept., 1923, between the United States and Mexico, 3 vols., 1927, 1929, 1931.
Ralston, I = Ralston, *The Law and Procedure of International Tribunals*, Revised Edition, 1926.
[1] Calvo, *Le droit international théorique et pratique* (5th ed., 1896), I, par. 185–205, pp. 322–51; III, par. 1280–96, pp. 142–55; VI, par. 256, p. 231. See also Hershey in *A.J.*, 1 (1907), pp. 26–45; Saavedra Lamas, *Calvo* (*La doctrine de Calvo*), in *Académie Diplomatique Internationale*, I, p. 386; Fritsch in Strupp, *Wörterbuch des Völkerrechts*, I (1924), p. 177.
[2] Calvo, *loc. cit.*, I, par. 185–204, pp. 322–51.

belonging to aliens,[3] provided that the damage or the failure to repair it was not due to measures of a discriminatory character.[4] Claims of a proprietary nature were to be brought by the aliens themselves and were exclusively subject to municipal law and juridiction.[5]

These sweeping statements, put forward under the impact of British and French intervention in Argentina and Uruguay and of the French interference in Mexico,[6] failed to obtain the approval of international lawyers, both in Europe and in the United States. The modern procedure of international arbitration was attracting increasing attention, and the proposal to treat claims of a proprietary nature brought by aliens as claims in the nature of municipal law, subject to the exclusive jurisdiction of the courts of the defendant State, had little to commend itself. But even if Calvo's attempt to exclude claims on the ground of State responsibility for injuries to the person or to property, due to acts of subordinate officials, riots, and insurrections, was unsuccessful, it exercised a profound influence in the sphere of contracts concluded between States and aliens. Here, the Calvo doctrine, in the modified form of a contractual clause known as the Calvo Clause, has established itself and is still being incorporated in contracts | concluded between South-American States and alien contractors or concessionaries.[7]

The Elements of the Calvo Clause

An analysis of contracts containing this provision which have come before international tribunals, shows that the Calvo Clause, as employed with some uniformity by South American States during the last seventy years, contains a number of stipulations varying in character and bearing upon various aspects of the principal contract.

---

[3] Calvo, *loc. cit.*, III, par. 1280–96, pp. 142–55.

[4] Calvo, *loc. cit.*, III, par. 1280, p. 142; VI, par. 256, p. 231.

[5] Calvo, *loc. cit.*, I, par. 205, p. 351; III, par. 1280, p. 142.

[6] Calvo, *loc. cit.*, I, par. 185–204, pp. 322–51.

[7] See Borchard, *Diplomatic Protection of Citizens Abroad* (1917), par. 114 (2), p. 294; par. 371–9, pp. 792–810; *A.J.*, 20 (1926), p. 538; Eagleton, *Responsibility of States in International Law* (1928), pp. 168–76; Feller, *The Mexican Claims Commissions* (1935), p. 184; *A.J.*, 27 (1933), pp. 461–8; De Beus, *The Jurisprudence of the General Claims Commission, United States and Mexico* (1938), pp. 49–87; Freeman, *The International Responsibility for Denial of Justice* (1938), pp. 469–95; Dunn, *The Protection of Nationals* (1932), pp. 169–72; Summers in *Revue de droit international*, 7 (1931), pp. 567–81; Tantkidès in *Revue générale de droit international public*, 43 (1936), pp. 270–84; Harvard Research in International Law, *Responsibility of States*, art. 17, *A.J.*, 23 (1929), Supplement, pp. 202–15. See also *Journal of Comparative Legislation*, 3rd ser., 26 (1944), pp. 55–9.

(*a*) *Submission to Local Jurisdiction.* In the first place, the clause provides for the submission of the alien contractor to the jurisdiction of the courts of the contracting State. The parties agree that disputes shall be decided "by the judicial tribunals of Venezuela",[8] "by the ordinary tribunals of the Republic",[9] "by the competent tribunals of the respondent Government",[10] or "by the tribunals of the Republic".[11] They are subject "exclusively to the authorities",[12] or "to the decisions of the Courts of the Republic",[13] or, in short, "to the jurisdiction of the Courts of the Republic".[14]

Other contracts provide for private arbitration,[15] for submission to the courts of either party,[16] or attempt to solve the question of jurisdiction in such ambiguous terms as "they shall remain subject to the laws of the country".[17]

This part of the clause is in conformity with a well-established and worldwide practice which attempts, in contracts involving a foreign element, to determine in advance the jurisdiction of a particular municipal court, or of the courts of a particular country, by means of an express submission.[18]

(*b*) *Free Choice of Law.* In the second place, the clause includes an express | provision concerning the law applicable to the contract. The contract is "subject to the laws of the Republic".[19] In case of a dispute, it "shall be decided in accordance (or 'in conformity') with the laws of the Repu-

---

[8] *Flannagan, Bradley, Clark & Co.* v. *Venezuela*, Moore, *Internat. Arb.*, IV, p. 3564.

[9] *Coro and La Vela Ry. and Improvement Co.*, Ralston, I, no. 81, p. 65; *Woodruff* Case, Ralston, I, no. 75, p. 62.

[10] *French Company of Venezuelan Railroads*, Ralston, I, no. III, p. 84; *Fitzgerald Concession*, Ralston, I, no. 70, p. 58; *Turnbull* v. *Venezuela*, Moore, *Internat. Arb.*, VI, pp. 306–7.

[11] *Orinoco S.S. Co.* Case, Ralston, I, no. 79, p. 64, Scott, *Hague Court Reports*, I (1916), p. 226; *Martini* Case, Ralston, I, no. 85, p. 66; *Selwyn* Case, Ralston, I, no. 84, pp. 65–6; *American Electric and Manufacturing Co.* Case, Ralston, no. 78, p. 64.

[12] *Antofagasta and Bolivia Ry. Co.* Case; *Robert Stirling* Case, Ralston, I, no. 86, p. 68.

[13] *Pitol* Case, Feller, *The Mexican Claims Commissions* (1935), pp. 196–9.

[14] *International Fisheries Co.* Case, *Opinions* I, p. 21, at p. 22; *Mexican Union Ry.* Case, *Decisions*, I, p. 157, at p. 159; *Interoceanic Ry. of Mexico* Case, *Decisions*, II, p. 118, at p. 121 (5).

[15] *North and South American Construction Co.* v. *Chile*, Moore, *Internat. Arb.*, III, p. 2318; *Tehuantepec Ship and Canal Co.* Case, *ibid.*, III, p. 3132.

[16] *Tehuantepec Ship and Canal Co.* Case, *loc. cit.*

[17] *Nitrate Ry. Co. Ltd.* v. *Chile*, Ralston, I, no. 86, p. 67.

[18] Cheshire, *Private International Law* (2nd ed., 1938), pp. 594, 597; Dicey, *Conflict of Law* (5th ed., 1932), General Principle IV, and Rule 95 (3). See also *North American Dredging Co.* Case, *Opinions*, I, p. 21, at p. 27; *Mexican Union Ry.* Case, *Decisions*, I, p. 157, at p. 164 (12); *Interoceanic Ry. of Mexico* Case, *Decisions*, II, p. 118 at p. 122 (7).

[19] *Nitrate Ry. Co. Ltd.* v. *Chile*, Ralston, I, no. 86, p. 67; *Antofagasta and Bolivia Ry. Co.* Case; *Robert Stirling* Case, Ralston I, no. 86, p. 68.

blic",[20] or with "the common law"[21] or it shall be "determined in the ordinary course of law".[22]

This method of determining the law applicable to a contract is known, and to a greater or lesser degree accepted, by most systems of private international law under the heading of "free choice of law", and calls for no further comment.[23] However, in recent times this portion of the Calvo Clause which embodies the choice of law made by the parties has been couched in more sweeping terms. It is now generally provided that the alien contractors, their assignees and all persons having an interest in a foreign contracting corporation "shall not claim ... nor shall they have any rights or means to enforce the same than those granted by the laws of the Republic to Mexicans";[24] they "shall be considered as having all the rights and obligations which the Federal Constitution imposes on Mexicans and aliens respectively and shall enjoy the temporary exemptions provided by the present law."[25] In this form, the relevant provisions of the Calvo Clause are no longer concerned with the free choice of any particular system of municipal private law, but with the submission of the alien contractor to the law of the contracting government as a whole, including its administrative law and jurisdiction.

(c) *Sphere of Application.* Next follows a provision delimiting the subject matter in respect of which the submission to local jurisdiction and the free choice of law is to operate. Here a great variety of terms, ranging from the narrowest to the widest, can be found. Generally speaking, it may be said that the tendency has been towards increasing the sphere of the clause.

In its original version, the clause applied "for the ends of the contract"[26] to "all questions that may arise under this arrangement",[27] to "the contract or any decision upon matters growing out of it",[28] to "doubts and controversies

---

[20] *Turnbull* Case, Moore, *Internat. Arb.* VI, pp. 306–7; *Orinoco S.S. Co.* Case, Ralston, I, no. 79, p. 64; Scott, *Hague Court Reports*, I, p. 226; *Martini* Case, Ralston, I, no. 85, p. 66; *American Electric and Manufacturing Co.* Case, Ralston, I, no. 78, p. 64; *Fitzgerald Concession*, Ralston, I, no. 70, p. 58.

[21] *Woodruff* Case, Ralston, I, no. 75, p. 62.

[22] *Flannagan, Bradley, Clark & Co. v. Venezuela*, Moore, *Internat. Arb.*, IV, p. 3564.

[23] *North American Dredging Co.* Case, *Opinions*, I, p. 21, at p. 27.

[24] *North American Dredging Co.* Case, *Opinions*, I, p. 21, at p. 22; *International Fisheries Co.* Case, *Opinions*, III, p. 206, at p. 212; *Mexican Union Ry. Co.* Case, *Decisions*, I, p. 157, at p. 159; *Interoceanic Ry. of Mexico* Case, *Decisions*, II, p. 118, at p. 121; *El Oro Mining and Ry. Co. Ltd.* Case, *Decisions*, II, p. 141, at p. 146.

[25] *Pitol* Case, Feller, *The Mexican Claims Commissions* (1935), pp. 196–9.

[26] *North and South American Construction Co. v. Chile*, Moore, *Internat. Arb.*, III, p. 2318.

[27] *Tehuantepec Ship and Canal Co.* Case, Moore, *Internat. Arb.*, III, p. 3132.

[28] *Flannagan, Bradley Clark & Co. v. Venezuela*, Moore, *Internat. Arb.*, IV, p. 3564; *Woodruff* Case, Ralston, I, no. 75, p. 62.

arising from the provisions of the contract",[29] or to "all questions concerning the interpretation and execution of the contract".[30] In its | extended form, the clause was made to apply to "any doubts, differences, difficulties and mis-understandings that may arise from or have any connection with, or in any manner relate to, this contract, directly or indirectly".[31] It included "all matters within the Republic concerning the execution of such work and the fulfilment of this contract ... with regard to the interests and the business connected with this contract [or] in any manner related to this contract",[32] or "all matters the cause and action of which takes place within its territory ... with respect to matters connected with this contract".[33] Finally, in one case, the clause was to embrace "all questions which may arise".[34]

(d) *Waiver of Protection by Home State.* The next part of the clause appears to have been designed as a corollary of the provisions dealing with submission to local jurisdiction and the choice of the municipal law applicable to the contract. The grant, or imposition, of a *locus standi* in the courts of the contracting government is accompanied by a waiver of the right to appeal for the protection of the Home State. The alien contractor "renounces the protection of his government in support of his pretensions".[35] He submits to the demand that henceforth he shall be "without power to exercise diplomatic intervention"[36] and that "under no conditions shall the intervention of foreign diplomatic agents be permitted in any matter related to the contract".[37] Sometimes, "absolute exclusion of all foreign intervention" is even conceded.[38]

(e) *Surrender of Rights under International Law.* To a growing extent the contracting State requires not only a renunciation of the formal right to appeal for the protection of the Home State, but also the surrender, in sub-

---

[29] *French Company of Venezuelan Railroads* Case, Ralston, I, no. III, p. 84; *Turnbull* v. *Venezuela*, Moore, *Internat. Arb.*, VI, pp. 306–7; *Fitzgerald* Case, Ralston, I, no. 70, p. 58; and see the cases cited above, note 10.

[30] *Rogerio & Co.* v. *Bolivia*, Ralston, I, no 88, p. 69; *Orinoco S.S. Co.* Case, Ralston, I, no. 79, p. 64, Scott, *Hague Court Reports*, I (1916), p. 226; *Coro and La Vela Ry. and Improvement Co.* Case, Ralston, I, no. 81, p. 65; *Selwyn* Case, Ralston, I, no. 84, pp. 65–6.

[31] *Beales, Nobles and Garrison* Case, Moore, *Internat. Arb.*, IV, p. 3548.

[32] *North American Dredging Co.* Case, *Opinions*, I, p. 21, at p. 22; *Mexican Union Ry. Co.* Case, *Decisions*, I, p. 157, at p. 159; *Interoceanic Ry. of Mexico* Case, *Decisions*, II, p. 118, at p. 121; *El Oro Mining and Ry. Co.* Case, *Decisions*, II, p. 141, at p. 146.

[33] *International Fisheries Co.* Case, *Opinions*, III, p. 206, at p. 212.

[34] *Pitol* Case, Feller, *The Mexican Claims Commissions* (1935), pp. 196–9.

[35] *North and South American Construction Co.* v. *Chile*, Moore, *Internat. Arb.*, III, p. 2318.

[36] *Nitrate Ry. Co.* v. *Chile*, Ralston, I, no. 86, p. 67.

[37] *North American Dredging Co.* Case, *Opinions*, I, p. 21, at p. 22; see also *Mexican Union Ry. Co.* Case, *Decisions*, I, p. 157, at p. 159; *Interoceanic Ry. Co. of Mexico* Case, *Decisions*, II, p. 118, at p. 121; *El Oro Mining Co.* Case, *Decisions*, II, p. 141, at p. 146.

[38] *Pitol* Case, Feller, *The Mexican Claims Commissions* (1935), pp. 196–9.

stance, of all future claims of an international character. This demand has been expressed in various formulations, such as "in no case ... will any international claims be admitted on account of this concession",[39] "doubts and controversies [relating to the contract] shall never be the subject of international reclamations".[40] Finally, in some contracts an attempt has been made to combine the formal waiver of the right to appeal to the Home State with the surrender of all future claims in the international sphere. These contracts contain stipulations such as "the contractor ... shall be | considered as Mexican ..."; "he shall never claim ... any right as an alien under any form whatsoever".[41]

As pointed out above, the waiver of the right to appeal for the protection of the Home State and the surrender of all future rights under international law are meant to form the counterpart of the submission of the alien contractor to the local jurisdiction and of the contract to the municipal law of the contracting State. It would appear, however, that the counterpart of submission to the jurisdiction of the contracting State is the absence of jurisdiction on the part of all other municipal courts, while the choice of the law of the contracting State as governing the contract operates only to exclude all other municipal systems of private law. As a result, courts and writers have laboured for more than fifty years to reconcile the seemingly inconsistent provisions (i.e. submission to local jurisdiction; choice of local law; waiver of international jurisdiction; surrender of rights under international law) which form the usual contractual Calvo Clause.

Contractual Rights and International Law

(a) *In general.* Before discussing whether and to what extent a contracting individual can submit to the local jurisdiction of the contracting State in respect of international claims arising out of a contract and waive rights of an international nature ensuing from a contract, it is necessary to examine in what circumstances a contractual claim assumes an international character.

---

[39] *Coro and La Vela Ry. and Improvement Co.* Case, Ralston, I, no. 81, p. 65.

[40] *Woodruff* Case, Ralston, I, no. 75, p. 62; *Martini* Case, Ralston, I, no. 85, p. 66; *Orinoco S.S. Co.* Case, Ralston, I, no. 79, p. 64, Scott, *Hague Court Reports*, I (1916), p. 226; *Antofagasta and Bolivia Ry. Co.* Case; *Robert Stirling* Case, Ralston, I, no. 86, p. 68; *Flannagan, Bradley Clark & Co.* Case, Moore, *Internat. Arb.*, IV, p. 3564; *Beales, Nobles and Garrison* Case, Moore, *Internat. Arb.*, IV, p. 3548.

[41] *North and South American Construction Co.* v. *Chile*, Moore, *Internat. Arb.*, III, p. 2318; *North American Dredging* Co. Case, *Opinions*, I, p. 21, at p. 22; *Mexican Union Ry. Co.* Case, *Decisions*, I, p. 157, at p. 159; *Interoceanic Ry. of Mexico* Case, *Decisions*, II, p. 118, at p. 121; *El Oro Mining Co.* Case, *Decisions*, II, p. 141, at p. 146.

The great majority of writers are agreed that the failure of a State to fulfil a contractual obligation, unless such a failure is confiscatory or discriminatory in nature, does not automatically result in a breach of international law.[42] However, it has been contended that a breach of contract in municipal law is always to be regarded, in the international sphere, as a measure in the nature of confiscation entailing State responsibility. In the *International Fisheries Co.* Case, Nielsen, the American Commissioner, said in a dissenting opinion:

"In the ultimate determination of responsibility under international law ... an international tribunal in a case grounded on a complaint of a breach of contract can properly give effect to principles of law with respect to confiscation. ... International Law does not prescribe rules relative to the forms and the legal effect of contracts, but that law is ... concerned with the action authorities of a Government may take with respect to contractual rights."[43]

| Nielsen concludes that, in the view of international law, the failure of a Government to honour its contractual obligations constitutes a confiscation or destruction of property rights in the contract and, as it is confiscation without adequate compensation, that it leads to denial of justice in the wider sense. This doctrine fails to discriminate sufficiently between failure to perform a contract and confiscation, and confuses the absence of easily available remedies with denial of justice entailing State responsibility. If a State fails to honour its commercial obligations, alien creditors will find it difficult, in most countries, to obtain speedy justice in the courts of that State, seeing that most States have provided elaborate safeguards which are designed to protect them from being sued indiscriminately.[44] At the same time, the prevailing practice, which grants immunity to foreign States, whether engaged in

---

[42] Moore, *Digest*, VI, pp. 287 ff., pp. 295 ff., pp. 705–20, par. 996, pp. 723 ff., par. 997; *Internat. Arb.*, IV, p. 3425 ff.; Borchard, *Diplomatic Protection of Citizens Abroad* (1917), p. 799; Drago in *Revue générale de droit international public*, 14 (1907), p. 251, at pp. 255–6.

[43] *Opinions*, III, p. 206, at pp. 241–2. See also Nielsen, dissenting, in *Cook v. Mexico, Opinions*, II, pp. 266, 269, Nielsen's Reports, p. 390, at pp. 395, 396; *Ina M. Hoffmann and Dulcie H. Steinhardt v. Turkey*, American-Turkish Claims Settlement, p. 286, at pp. 287, 288; *Socony Vacuum Oil Co. Inc. v. Turkey, ibid.*, p. 369, at p. 374; *Dickson Car Wheel Co.* Case, *Opinions*, III, p. 175, at p. 199, Nielsen's Reports, p. 505, at pp. 512–15; *American Bottle Co's Claim*, Nielsen's Reports, p. 339, at p. 340; *Pomeroy's El Paso Transfer Co's* Case, Nielsen's Reports, p. 418, at p. 420, with further references; *Singer Sewing Machine Co. v. Turkey*, American-Turkish Claims Settlement, p. 490, at p. 491; *Malamatinis v. Turkey, ibid.*, p. 603, at p. 605.

[44] Jèze in *Hague Recueil*, 7 (1925), pp. 172 ff.; Strupp, *ibid.*, 8 (1925), p. 9, at p. 70; Fischer Williams in *Bibliotheca Visseriana*, II (1924), p. 1, at p. 15; *Chapters on Current International Law* (1929), p. 257, at p. 273; Séfériadès in *Hague Recueil*, 51 (1935), p. 5, at pp. 101, 109; Meurer in *Zeitschrift für Völkerrecht* 8 (1914), p. 1, at p. 20.

transactions of a public or of a private law nature, prevents alien creditors from suing a debtor State in a court of another country. In these circumstances it is understandable that strenuous efforts have been made to assist creditors by treating their claims as international. However, in the absence of rules of international law relating to contracts, contractual claims must be presented in the form of claims for denial of justice, and the failure to honour a contractual obligation constitutes a denial of justice only if it is due to a legislative or administrative measure, if all legal remedies have been exhausted or if none are available at all.

The United States, in a constant practice, have adhered to the generally accepted view and have refused to take up contractual claims of their nationals, except in cases of discrimination or denial of justice which result in what amounts to a confiscatory annulment of contractual rights and concessions.[45]

(*b*) *The Calvo Clause as limited to Contractual Relations proper.* If, then, a contract between an individual and a foreign State cannot, without further extraneous acts for which the foreign State is directly or vicariously liable, form the basis of an international reclamation, it may be argued that a clause in a contract whereby a party submits to local jurisdiction and stipulates not to appeal to the Home State for protection, is strictly confined to the sphere of private law in which alone the contract can be enforced and in which, according to the prevalent opinion, the power of foreign States to intervene does not operate. So understood, the Calvo Clause means what it says: The alien contractor agrees that the contract is to be governed by the law of the contracting State; he submits to the jurisdiction of its courts and acknowledges that the intervention of his Home State for the purpose of pressing his contractual claims is inadmissible.

A number of awards handed down during the last fifty years have so construed the clause and have, therefore, admitted its validity within this |limited sphere.[46] In the *North American Dredging Co.* Case,[47] the majority of the American-Mexican Claims Commission adopted this view in the following words:

---

[45] Wharton, *Digest of International Law*, II (1887), par. 231, pp. 654–6; par. 232, pp. 661–4; Moore, *Digest*, VI (1906), par. 995, pp. 705–17; par. 996, pp. 718–20; par. 997, pp. 723–32; Hackworth, *Digest of International Law*, V (1943), pp. 610–14; Harvard Research in International Law, *State Responsibility, A.J.*, Suppl., 23 (1929), art. 8.

[46] *North and South American Construction Co.* v. *Chile*, Moore, *Internat. Arb.*, III, p. 2318, at p. 2320; *Beales, Nobles and Garrison*, Moore, *Internat. Arb.*, IV, p. 3548, at pp. 3554, 3562; *Nitrate Ry. Co. Ltd.* v. *Chile*, Ralston, I, no. 86, p. 67; *Flannagan, Bradley, Clark & Co.* Case, Moore, *Internat. Arb.*, IV, p. 3564, at p. 3565.

[47] *Opinions*, I, p. 21, at p. 27 (14); p. 28 (15). See also *Mexican Union Ry.* v. *Mexico, Decisions*, I, p. 157, at p. 164 (12); p. 171 (6), *per* Percival, British Commissioner, dissenting; *International Fisheries Co.* v. *Mexico, Opinions*, III, p. 206, at p. 213.

"Its [the clause's] purpose was to bind the claimant to be governed by the laws of Mexico and to use the remedies existing under such laws ...; in executing the contract, in fulfilling the contract or in putting forth any claim regarding the interests or business connected with this contract the claimant should be governed by those laws and remedies which Mexico had provided for the protection of its own citizens. ... He did agree that in consideration of the Government of Mexico awarding him the contract, he did not and would not invoke or accept the assistance of his Government with respect to the fulfilment and interpretation of the contract and the execution of the work thereunder."

According to this view the Calvo Clause is an integral part of the contract, not only in form, but also in substance.[48]

(c) _Expansion of the Calvo Clause._ On the other hand, the sphere of the Calvo Clause has been constantly enlarged and has been made to include "all interests and the business connected with this contract". As far as this provision is restricted to questions of a private law nature arising out of the original transaction it is unobjectionable, seeing that a previous submission, however wide, is admissible in most systems of private law, if it remains limited to the original parties and to the transaction concluded between them. Difficulties arise, however, if the claim is based upon the breach of a collateral obligation.[49] In the great majority of cases these difficulties have been confused with the question whether, by means of a Calvo Clause, parties can legitimately oust the jurisdiction of international courts and waive the rights accruing under international law to their Home State. This approach is not surprising, seeing that breaches of collateral obligations consist mainly of what in municipal law are termed tortious acts for which a corresponding remedy in international law is readily available in the form of a claim for denial of justice.

(d) _The Calvo Clause and Collateral Obligations._ In the course of this discussion the preliminary question has generally been overlooked whether the clause is ever meant to apply to breaches of collateral obligations resulting from acts extraneous to the contract (such as confiscations, illegal acts of

---

[48] _Mexican Union Ry._ Case, _Decisions_, I, pp. 157, 160 (8), (9); _Rogerio_ v. _Brazil_, Ralston, I, no. 88, p. 69; _Rudloff_ Case, _ibid._, no. 77, p. 63; _Nitrate Ry. Co. Ltd._ v. _Chile, ibid._, no. 86, p. 67: _Beales, Nobles and Garrison_ Case, Moore, _Internat. Arb._, IV, p. 3548, at p. 3562; _Flannagan, Bradley, Clark & Co._ v. _Venezuela, ibid._, IV, p. 3564, at 3565; _Pitol_ Case, Feller, pp. 196–9.

[49] In the _Mexican Union Ry._ Case, _Decisions_, I, p. 157, at p. 159 (6), the Commission denied that the clause, in its more extensive wording, raised any additional problems. But in _Douglas Collie McNeill_ v. _Mexico, Decisions_, II, p. 21, at pp. 23 (5), 24 (5), the Commission refused to consider a clause which provided: "... The business will preserve its Mexican character and without rights of foreigners", on the ground that the precise right waived by the concessionnaire had not been properly specified.

officials) and for which the foreign State is directly or vicariously liable under international law. However, this aspect of the Calvo Clause has not | been entirely neglected. In the *Interoceanic Ry. of Mexico* Case, Stoker, the British Commissioner, in a dissenting opinion, pointed out that, among the cases before the Mexican Claims Commission which had involved an examination of the Calvo Clause, only the *North American Dredging Co.* Case had been based upon a breach of contract, while all others had been concerned with damage to property caused by revolutionary activities. Commissioner Stoker said:

"the judgment of the present Commission in the *Mexican Union Ry. Case* ... apply it [i.e. the principle in the *North American Dredging Co.* Case], in my opinion unnecessarily and irrelevantly, to the *Mexican Union Ry.* Case, as if that case were a case of alleged breaches of contract and not, as it was, a claim entirely distinct from the contract and one arising from revolutionary acts. The *Mexican Union Railway* Case has nothing to do with the position of the Mexican Union Railway as contractor and *qua* contract ... it was merely incidental that they were contractors. ... There was no question of contract or interpretation thereof, and the Mexican Union were not seeking to enforce a contract. ... The claim of the Mexican Union Railway was brought by them not as contractors, nor as seeking any rights under their contract, but as British subjects carrying on business in Mexico who had suffered loss ... through revolutionary causes. ... It is entirely outside any contract, whether it contained or did not contain a Calvo Clause."[50]

In the great majority of cases, however, international tribunals have held implicitly that a contractual Calvo Clause extends to damage done to property belonging to an alien contractor or concessionary in respect of which redress is accorded by an action in tort in municipal law and, correspondingly, by a claim based on State responsibility, direct or indirect, in the sphere of international law.

---

[50] *Decisions*, II, p. 118, at p. 132 (7), (8), and see the same Commissioner's dissenting opinion in *Veracruz (Mexico) Railways* v. *Mexico, ibid.*, II, p. 207, at p. 210. See also the dissenting opinion of Sir John Percival in the *Mexican Union Ry.* Case, Decisions, I, p. 157, at pp. 171 (6), 173 (11). And see *La Guaira Electric Light and Power Co.* v. *Venezuela*, Ralston, I, no. 83, p. 65; *American Electric and Manufacturing Co.* Case, Ralston, I, no. 78, p. 64; *Selwyn* Case, Ralston, I, no. 84, p. 65, at p. 66.

In *Douglas Collie McNeill* v. *Mexico, Decisons*, II, p. 21, at p. 24 (6), the tribunal rejected a plea to the jurisdiction set up by the respondent Government which relied on a Calvo Clause in a contract concluded between an alien contractor and the municipality of Colima (Mexico).

The Calvo Clause and International Jurisdiction

With regard to the effect of the Calvo Clause in the international sphere, the opinion of international tribunals is divided, but its validity has been maintained in recent years. However, the reasons given by the tribunals do not always agree with each other.

(a) *Contractual Aspect.* Some tribunals have examined the contractual aspects of the Calvo Clause and whether it excludes from the jurisdiction of international courts all questions of a private law nature of which municipal courts normally take cognizance. The majority of the tribunals investigated whether and to what extent the clause is compatible with international law.

The contractual view found its clearest expression in the *Turnbull Case*,[51] a much-criticised decision,[52] in which Barge, the Umpire, said:

"These damages can, according to the contract itself, only be declared due | in case the expressly designated judges decide that the fact, which according to the demanding party constituted such a breach of contract, really constituted such a breach, and therefore formed a good basis whereon to build a claim for damages. Parties have deliberately contracted themselves out of any interpretation of the contract and out of any judgment about the ground for damages for reason of the contract, except by the judges [designated] by the contract; and where there is no decision of these judges that the alleged reasons for a claim for damages really exist as such, parties according to the contract itself have no right to these damages and a claim for damages which parties have no right to claim, cannot be accepted."

According to this view, the Calvo Clause refers to questions of procedure and of substance, and international tribunals are not only precluded from entertaining a claim based upon the original contract, before the local remedies have been exhausted, but from giving judgment on any question of a private law nature arising out of the contract. However, the arguments of the umpire in the *Turnbull* Case are inconclusive, seeing that they fail to explain why a contractual clause relating to private law claims can affect an international reclamation, and the consequences of the decision are open to serious criticism.[53] Nevertheless, the underlying idea to the effect that international claims for State Responsibility on the ground of damage done to property can only succeed if the existence of a property right in municipal law has first been proved is correct.[54] It is difficult, however, to accept the view of the Umpire who believed that the question of private law was necessarily subject

---

[51] Ralston, I, no. 80, p. 64, Moore, *Internat. Arb.*, VI, pp. 306–7.

[52] Moore, *loc. cit.*, pp. 306–7.

[53] Moore, *loc. cit.* Thus an international reclamation would only be permissible if the municipal court has given a judgment in favour of the claimant.

[54] See *Transactions of the Grotius Society*, 29 (1944), p. 51, at pp. 55, 56.

to the jurisdiction of municipal courts, or that, in order to succeed in an international court, the same claim must have been allowed, and not dismissed, by a municipal court. It would appear that, in respect of claims involving State responsibility for denial of justice affecting property rights, international tribunals must themselves apply both municipal law and international law. Municipal law determines whether a property right has been acquired and whether it is vested in the claimant. International law must decide whether the defendant State is liable for the violation of a property right so acquired.[55]

With the exception of the tribunal in the *Turnbull* Case, however, international tribunals which have upheld the Calvo Clause in the international sphere on contractual grounds have only required that the local remedies must have been exhausted, but not that a judgment in favour of the claimant has been obtained in a local court. In support of this interpretation of the clause the tribunals have usually referred to the terms of the contract.[56] In | *Rogerio* v. *Bolivia*[57] the Court refrained from accepting jurisdiction "because it is not proper to divide the unity of a juridical act, sustaining the efficacy of some of its clauses and the inefficacy of others." In the *Rudloff* Case[58] the same argument was expressed in a slightly modified form, when the tribunal stated that it was prohibited from giving the benefit of its jurisdiction "to a claim based on a contract by which this benefit was renounced and thus absolving [the] claimants from their obligation whilst the enforcing of the obligation of the other party based on the same contract is precisely the aim of their claim."

(*b*) *Compatibility with International Law.* However, even when relying on the contractual effect of the Calvo Clause, international tribunals have never entirely neglected to examine whether the Clause is compatible with international law. In recent times the latter aspect of the problem has become

---

[55] *Transactions of the Grotius Society, loc. cit.*, at p. 61, and the cases quoted *ibid.*, at pp. 53–5 especially *Mexican Union Ry.* v. *Mexico, Decisions*, I, p. 167, at p. 162 (10); *North American Dredging Co.* Case, *Opinions, I*, p. 21, at p. 27 (14); *International Fisheries Co.* Case, *Opinions*, III, p. 206, at pp. 241, 273 (*per* Nielsen, dissenting). See also Sobolewski in *Revue générale de droit international public*, 38 (1931), p. 420, at p. 434; Genet, *ibid.*, 36 (1929), p. 669, at pp. 692–3; Ténékidès in *Revue de droit international et de législation comparée*, 57 (1930), p. 473, at p. 478; Rundstein in *Hague Recueil*, 23 (1928), p. 331, at p. 437.

[56] *Orinoco S.S.* Case, Ralston, I, no. 79, p. 64; *Day* Case, *ibid.*, I, no. 73, p. 59; *Woodruff* Case, *ibid.*, I, no. 75, p. 62; *French Co. of Venezuelan Railroads* Case, *ibid.*, I, no. III, p. 84; *Flannagan, Bradley, Clark & Co.* v. *Venezuela*, Moore, *Internat. Arb.*, IV, p. 3564, at p. 3565. And see *North and South American Construction Co.* v. *Chile*, Moore, *Internat. Arb.*, III, p. 2318.

[57] Ralston, I, no. 88, p. 69.

[58] Ralston, I, no. 77, p. 63. See also *Mexican Union Ry.* v. *Mexico, Decisions*, I, p. 157, at p. 162 (9).

predominant. The decisions of the tribunals show clearly that two principles have been recognized without reservation. In the first place, denial of justice always constitutes a violation of international law, if an alien is involved, and entitles the State of the alien to bring an international reclamation on his behalf.[59] In the second place, no individual can renounce the protection of his State and waive rights accruing to the State under international law.[60]

In the light of these principles the tribunals have examined whether the Calvo Clause is compatible with international law. In the words of the Commission in the *North American Dredging Co.* Case:

"What must be established is *not* that the Calvo Clause is universally accepted or universally recognized, but that there exists a generally accepted rule of international law condemning the Calvo Clause."[61]

The Calvo Clause is thus restricted to its contractual setting. The only opposition to this method of investigation has come from Commissioner Nielsen,[62] who asserted that it was necessary to establish not only that the Calvo Clause is compatible with international law, but that it has been adopted by the community of nations as a rule of international law proper. This approach is a natural consequence of the same Commissioner's conclusion, discussed above, to the effect that every breach of a contract on the part of a government automatically creates an international reclamation based on a violation of international law. In these circumstances it is necessary to prove the existence of a special, universally recognized rule of international | law permitting the individual to waive this international claim before the Clause can be regarded as valid, seeing that, according to international law, individuals cannot normally waive international claims. Nielsen's treatment of the Calvo Clause stands and falls with his premise, which was refuted above.[63] His attempt to elevate the Calvo Clause itself into the sphere of international law, if only in order to expel it therefrom, has failed.

---

[59] *North and South American Construction Co.* v. *Chile*, Moore, *Internat. Arb.*, III, p. 2318, at p. 2320; *Beales, Nobles and Garrison* Case, Moore, *loc. cit.*, IV, p. 3548, at p. 3562. See also *Flannagan, Bradley, Clark & Co.* v. *Venezuela*, Moore, *loc. cit.*, IV, p. 3564, at pp. 3665–66; *Woodruff* Case, Ralston, I, no. 75, p. 62; *North American Dredging Co.* Case, *Opinions, I*, p. 21, at p. 27 (14); *International Fisheries Co.* Case, *Opinions*, III, p. 206, at p. 219; *Mexican Union Ry. Co.* Case, *Decisions*, I, p. 157, at pp. 164 (12), 171 (6); *Interoceanic Ry. of Mexico* Case, *Decisions*, II, p. 118, at p. 122; *El Oro Mining Co.* Case, *Decisions, II*, p. 141, at p. 149 (7).

[60] *Nitrate Ry. Co. Ltd.* v. *Chile*, Ralston, I, no. 86, p. 67; *Martini* Case, *ibid.*, no. 85, p. 66; *North American Dredging Co.* Case, *Opinions*, I, p. 21, at p. 25 (11); *Mexican Union Ry.* Case, *Decisions*, I, p. 157, at pp. 162 (10), 171 (6); *Interoceanic Ry. of Mexico* Case, *Decisions*, II, p. 118, at p. 122 (7).

[61] *Opinions*, I, p. 21, at p. 24 (8).

[62] *International Fisheries Co.* Case, *Opinions*, III, p. 206, at pp. 235, 254–5, 259–61.

[63] Pp. 134, 135.

Courts of arbitration at the end of the nineteenth and the beginning of the present century were inclined to hold that the Calvo Clause cannot, in any circumstances, be set up as a defence against an international claim predicated on the ground of denial of justice.[64] However, the problem was given a new turn when the American-Mexican and the Anglo-American Mixed Claims Commissions were called upon to pronounce upon the validity of the Calvo Clause. These tribunals started from two premises, namely, first, that as a rule international claims in respect of breaches of contract can only be brought on the ground of denial of justice and after the local remedies have been exhausted and, secondly, that the Calvo Clause requires, similarly, that recourse must be had to the local courts.[65] Thus the contractual clause, being treated as identical with a condition imposed by international law, could be regarded as compatible with the latter.[66] Before commenting on the conclusion reached by these tribunals it may be useful to examine their premises.

In the first place, insufficient attention has been paid to the fact that claims for denial of justice in respect of breaches of contract on the part of a State do not necessarily require a previous exhaustion of local remedies. Denial of justice in the wider sense occurs not only if all local remedies have been exhausted or if no such remedies are provided. It also includes legislative and administrative measures for which a State is directly responsible. It is possible that the tribunals have failed to recognise this fact by reason of their tendency to treat contracts concluded between a State and an individual exclusively as acts *jure gestionis*, and all questions arising out of such contracts as disputes involving solely the application of municipal private law by municipal courts. Also, it may be due to the extension of the Calvo Clause to breaches of collateral obligations.

It is significant that the Anglo-Mexican and American-Mexican tribunals have never held a State to be directly responsible, even when the facts pointed to direct liability under international law, in spite of occasional statements that such liability was not excluded altogether.

---

[64] *North and South American Construction Co.* Case, Moore, *Internat. Arb.*, III, p. 2318, at pp. 2320–1; *Beates, Nobles and Garrison* Case, *ibid.*, IV, p. 3548, at p. 3562; *Flannagan, Bradley, Clark & Co.* v. *Venezuela*, *ibid.*, IV, p. 3564, at p. 3565; *Woodruff* Case, Ralston, I, no. 75, p. 62.

[65] *North American Dredging Co.* Case, *Opinions*, I, p. 21, at pp. 27 (15), 29 (20); *International Fisheries Co.* Case, *ibid.*, III, p. 206, at p. 218; *Interoceanic Ry. of Mexico* Case, *Decisions*, II, p. 118, at p. 122 (7); *El Oro Mining Co.* Case, *ibid.*, II, p. 141, at pp. 149 (7), 150 (9); *Mexican Union Ry.* Case, *ibid.*, I, p. 157, at p. 164 (12), (13).

[66] *Contra* Nielsen, dissenting, in *International Fisheries Co.* v. *Mexico*, *Opinions*, III, p. 206, at pp. 237 ff., citing, at p. 249 (IX), Commissioner Little, dissenting, in *Flannagan, Bradley, Clark & Co.'s* Case; and see pp. 251, 273. See also Sir John Percival, dissenting, in *Mexican Union Ry. Co.* v. *Mexico*, *Decisions*, I, p. 157, at p. 171 (6).

In the second place, the Calvo Clause itself has been subjected to a very restricted interpretation. As shown above,[67] the contracting alien is made |to waive the right to appeal for the protection of the Home State and is made to surrender all future rights under international law. The tribunals have held – rightly, it is believed – that a clause thus conceived is incompatible with international law. But instead of refusing to give effect to such a clause, the tribunals have reduced its compass and have attributed a meaning to it which the parties never intended. Only after this operation was it possible to reconcile the clause with the principle of international law. In other words, only by dint of over-emphasizing the importance, in the sphere of international law, of the principle that local remedies must be exhausted, and by reducing a far-reaching contractual provision to a simple submission to the jurisdiction of the courts of a particular State for the purpose of determining questions of private law proper, have international tribunals been able to maintain the validity of the Calvo Clause. Even if thus construed, the identity of the Calvo Clause with the principles of international law governing claims for denial of justice is more apparent than real. Submission to local jurisdiction under a Calvo Clause is a matter of procedure. The exhaustion of local remedies required by international law before a claim for denial of justice can be brought constitutes a material prerequisite of the claim and is thus a matter of substance.

Yet it may be doubted whether the effect of thus reconciling the Calvo Clause with the principles of international law justifies the labour of the tribunals concerned. If it is true that the exhaustion of local remedies is always required by international law before a claim for State responsibility in respect of breaches of contract can be brought, the insertion of a Calvo Clause in a contract is superfluous. If the exhaustion of local remedies is not always a necessary prerequisite according to international law, no contractual Calvo Clause can make it a prerequisite. Thus there is some substance in the statement of those tribunals which have held that the Calvo Clause is altogether ineffective in the international sphere.[68]

---

[67] P. 133 (*e*).

[68] Commissioner Little (dissenting) in *Flannagan, Bradley, Clark & Co.* v. *Venezuela*, Moore, *Internat. Arb.*, IV, p. 3564, at p. 3566; *Nitrate Ry. Co. Ltd.* v. *Chile*, Ralston, I, no. 86, p. 67; *Selwyn* Case, Ralston, I, no. 84, p. 65, at p. 66; *Coro and La Vela Ry. and Improvement Co.* Case, Ralston, I, no. 81, p. 65. And see above, p. 139, n. 4, p. 140, n. 2.

It is clear that municipal legislation embodying the Calvo Clause is equally ineffective, subject to the additional proviso that the contract must be governed by the law of the country adopting the clause. For an enumeration of such municipal legislation see Borchard, *Diplomatic Protection of Citizens Abroad* (1917), pp. 795–6, note 6, and Summers in *Revue de droit international*, 7 (1931), p. 567, at p. 568.

The Calvo Clause and Private Law Claims in International Courts

In recent years the tendency has grown among States to entrust international tribunals with the decision of questions of private law proper arising out of transactions between the defendant State and a national of the plaintiff State. The effect of the Calvo Clause on these reclamations is determined by the answer to the question whether they are international not only in form but also in substance.

There is a substantial measure of agreement that transactions of a private law nature concluded between a State and an alien are transactions governed by municipal law.[69] Also, it is generally accepted that, even in the absence | of an international claim based on a denial of justice, the States concerned may bring disputes arising out of such transactions before international tribunals by special agreement (e.g., under Art. 36 (1) of the Statute of the Permanent Court of International Justice), without previously exhausting the local remedies.[70] Confronted with disputes of this nature, the Permanent Court of International Justice in the *Serbian and Brazilian Loan* Cases[71] held, nevertheless, that these disputes were international in substance, and not only in form, that jurisdiction existed under Art. 36 (2) of the statute, and that in accordance with Art. 38, international law was applicable. The Court argued that every diplomatic dispute between two States in respect of a contract concluded between one of them and a national of the other was a legal dispute concerning "the existence of any fact which, if established, would constitute a breach of an international obligation".[72] Since it is clear

---

[69] Schwarzenberger in *Juridical Review*, 54 (1942), p. 25, at p. 27; Strupp in *Hague Recueil*, 8 (1923), p. 5, at p. 64; Rundstein in *Hague Recueil*, 23 (1928), p. 331, at p. 376, but see p. 402; Séfériadès in *Annuaire de l'institut de droit international*, 1929 (I), p. 505, at p. 525.

[70] Borchard in *Harvard Law Review*, 44 (1931), p. 1322; Watrin in *Revue de droit international*, 8 (1931), p. 161, at pp. 184, 185; Sobolewski in *Revue générale de droit international public*, 38 (1931), p. 420, at p. 435; Rundstein in *Revue de droit international et de législation comparée*, 56 (1929), p. 431, at pp. 440–1; Ténékidès, *ibid.*, 57 (1930), p. 473, at pp. 478–9; 59 (1932), p. 89, at pp. 95–7; Séfériadès in *Hague Recueil*, 51 (1935), p. 5, at p. 66; Mercier and De La Barra in *Annuaire de l'institut de droit international*, 1927 (II), p. 565, at p. 607; Strupp in *Hague Recueil*, 8 (1925), p. 9. *Contra*: Fischer Williams, *Chapters on Current International Law* (1929), p. 257, at p. 259; *Bibliotheca Visseriana*, II (1924), p. 1, at p. 3; *Hague Recueil*, 5 (1924), pp. 113–14 (only after denial of justice); similarly Rundstein in *Hague Recueil*, 23 (1928), p. 331, at pp. 344, 437, 453, but see pp. 406, 420; *Revue de droit international et de législation comparée*, 66 (1929), p. 431, at pp. 431–2, but see pp. 451–2, 761–3, 764–7, 771; Borchard in *A.J.*, 24 (1930), pp. 361–5.

[71] Ser. A, nos. 20, 21. See also *Illinois Central Railroad Co.* v. *Mexico, Opinions*, I, p. 15, at p. 17.

[72] Ser. A, no. 20, pp. 16–20; no. 21, p. 101. Similarly Séfériadès in *Hague Recueil*, 51 (1935), p. 5, at pp. 22, 102, but see p. 99; *Annuaire de l'institut de droit international*, 1929 (I), p. 505, at p. 547; Travers in *Clunet*, 52 (1925), p. 29, at p. 35; Rundstein in *Revue de droit international et de législation comparée*, 66 (1929), p. 431, at p. 433.

that neither the formal existence of a diplomatic dispute nor the seizure of an international tribunal by two States acting in agreement is "a fact which would constitute a breach of an international obligation", it would appear that the Court treated a breach of contract on the part of a State as constituting automatically a breach of international law. As shown above, this view must be rejected as far as ordinary commercial contracts are concerned.[73] The fact that the dispute concerned public loans and not ordinary commercial contracts is of no decisive importance. Public loans are governed by municipal law, public or private,[74] and, like all other claims governed by municipal law, they give rise to international reclamations only after a denial of justice in the wider sense has occurred. However, a considerable body of opinion holds that such loans are governed exclusively by international law, but it is impossible to go into this question here.[75]

| Apparently the Permanent Court itself found it difficult to adhere to the sweeping view expressed earlier in the judgment and applied not international but municipal law on the basis of a system of Private International Law the nature of which has been discussed elsewhere.[76] The reluctance of the Court to admit that it was applying nothing but municipal law is understandable, for apart from raising a difficult question of principle, it touched upon serious problems of a practical nature, such as proof of foreign mu-

---

[73] *Supra*, pp. 134, 135; not quite clearly Lauterpacht in *Hague Recueil*, 62 (1937), p. 99, at pp. 223–6.

[74] For a good survey of the problem see Borchard in *Proceedings of the American Society of International Law* (1932), p. 135, at p. 148; see also Fischer Williams, *Chapters on Current International Law* (1929), pp. 346–7; *Bibliotheca Visseriana*, II (1924), p. 57; Meurer in *Zeitschrift für Völkerrecht*, 8 (1914), p. 1, at p. 21. And see *R. v. International Trustee for the Protection of Bondholders Aktiengesellschaft* [1937] A.C. 500.

[75] (*a*) Not directly a claim under international law: Moore, *Internat. Arb.*, IV, p. 3614, at pp. 3615, 3641; Hackworth, *Digest of International Law*, V (1943), p. 610, at pp. 623–4; *Bluntschli and Pflug*, cited by Borchard, *loc. cit.*; Schwarzenberger in *Juridical Review*, 54 (1942), p. 21, at p. 22; Nussbaum, *Money in the Law* (1939), pp. 387–91, citing Domke in *Clunet*, 63 (1936), p. 547; Schmitthoff in *Journal of Comparative Legislation*, 3rd ser., 19 (1937), p. 179; Note in *Yale Law Journal*, 46 (1937), p. 891; Jacoby in *A.J.*, 30 (1936), p. 233, at p. 236; Strupp in *Hague Recueil*, 8 (1925), p. 5, at p. 64; Sobolewski in *Revue générale de droit international public*, 38 (1931), p. 420, at p. 435; Ténékidès in *Revue de droit international et de législation comparée*, 59 (1932), p. 89, at p. 98.

(*b*) Directly governed by international law: Moore, *Internat. Arb.*, IV, pp. 3631, 3649–50; Wuarin, *Essai sur les emprunts d'états* (1907), p. 35; Freund, *Rechtsverhältnisse der öffentlichen Anleihen* (1907), v. Liszt, cited by Borchard, *loc. cit.*; Watrin, *Revue de droit international*, 8 (1931), p. 161, at pp. 188–9; Séfériadès in *Hague Recueil*, 51 (1935), p. 5, at pp. 100, 102.

(*c*) Exceptional class, extra-legal, extra-national: Drago in *A.J.*, 1 (1907) at pp. 695–6; Fischer Williams in *Bibliotheca Visseriana*, II (1924), p. 1, no. 1; *Chapters*, p. 257, at p. 258, n. 3; Politis, *Les emprunts d'état en droit international* (1894), cited by Strupp, *loc. cit.*, p. 66, and the writers cited by Borchard, *loc. cit.*, pp. 144–5.

[76] *Transactions of the Grotius Society*, 29 (1944), pp. 51–83.

nicipal law. On the other hand, there seems to be no reason why States should not entrust international courts with the decision of disputes involving questions of private law alone, and not merely incidentally as a preliminary question in the sense discussed above,[77] seeing that States are clearly at liberty to refer to any municipal court disputes turning upon questions of international law.

Nevertheless, the practice of States, as expressed in treaties concerning the protection and the settlement of claims arising from contracts and from State loans, has not fully realized that this course is open and has refrained from explicitly imposing upon international tribunals the duty to apply municipal law for the decision of these disputes. Article 1 of the Hague Convention (No. II) respecting the Limitation of the Employment of Force for the Recovery of Contract Debts, of 18 October 1907, binds States not to have recourse to armed force for the recovery of contract debts, claimed from the government of one country by the government of another country as being due to its nationals, unless, *inter alia*, when the debtor State refuses or neglects to reply to an offer of arbitration. According to Article 2 the award under an arbitration, as envisaged in Article 1, "shall determine, except where otherwise agreed between the parties, *the validity of the claim, the amount of the debt, and the time and mode of payment* [italics mine].[78]

The wording of Article 2 suggests that the arbitration is to concern itself chiefly with questions of private law proper. This verbal interpretation is strengthened by the following juridical considerations. First, as stated above, international law contains no branch dealing with contracts. If a breach of contract is to form the basis of a claim based on international law, it must constitute a tortious act in the nature of a denial of justice. However, it is generally understood that claims for injuries done to resident aliens | are not affected by the Convention.[79] Secondly, if the Convention envisaged claims for denial of justice connected with injuries to aliens and arising out of breaches of contract, the absence of the requirement that local remedies must be exhausted coupled with the obligation immediately to resort to arbitration would restrict the range of claims covered by the Convention. For thus only breaches of contract in consequence of legislation or of administrative

---

[77] P. 138.

[78] See also Art. 53 (2) of Convention I for the Pacific Settlement of International Disputes.

[79] Pearce Higgins, *Hague Peace Conferences* (1909), pp. 191–6; Fischer Williams in *Bibliotheca Visseriana, II* (1924), p. 1, at pp. 42, 44; *Chapters*, p. 257, at pp. 310, 313; Strupp in *Hague Recueil*, 8 (1925), p. 5, at pp. 100–1. The following reservations were made: (1) denial of justice must have occurred. Argentine, Salvador, Guatemala; (2) local remedies must have been exhausted: Columbia; (3) the contract must not fall under the jurisdiction of the ordinary courts: Peru, Uruguay; (4) unless the contract or local laws provide to the contrary: Greece, Bolivia.

acts which are not subject to review would be directly affected, while claims on the ground of non-performance of contracts would not fall within the compass of the Convention. That the text of the Convention was not so understood by the contracting parties appears clearly from the action of certain South American States which signed subject to the reservation that the local remedies must have been exhausted. These States were anxious to restrict the Convention to claims based on international law, although arising from contracts, while the other signatories were attempting to meet the case of contractual claims proper.

Where claims of a private law nature form the object of an international reclamation, the proceedings are international in form, but not in substance. Consequently, it is necessary to examine whether the conclusions reached above, to the effect that the Calvo Clause is ineffective where international reclamations based on international law are concerned, require any qualification where the claims are predicated on the basis of private law.

The problem presented itself to the American-Mexican and the Anglo-Mexican Claims Commissions in the following circumstances:

Article V of the American-Mexican Claims Convention of 8 September, 1923, provided "that no claim shall be disallowed or rejected ... by the application of the general principle of international law that the legal remedies must be exhausted as a condition precedent to the validity or allowance of any claim".[80] Dealing with this article in the *North American Dredging Co.* Case[81] the American-Mexican Claims Commission held that it excluded the operation of the Calvo Clause where claims are presented on the ground of a breach of international law, but not where contractual claims are predicated on the basis of municipal law. The Commission said:

"If it (i.e. the claimant) had a claim for denial of justice, for delay of justice or gross injustice, or for any other violation of international law, committed by Mexico to its damage, it might have presented such a claim to its government which, in turn, could have espoused it and presented it here. But where a claimant has expressly agreed in writing ... that in all matters pertaining to the execution, fulfilment and interpretation of the contract he will have resort to local tribunals and then wilfully ignores them by applying to his government, he will be bound by his contract. ..."[82]

| Since the claim was one of contract proper, the Commission applied the Calvo Clause and declined jurisdiction. Such claims could not be "rightfully presented" prior to the exhaustion of local remedies.

---

[80] Art. VI of the Anglo-Mexican Convention of 19 Nov. 1926 was to the same effect.

[81] *Opinions*, I, p. 21, at pp. 29 (20), 31 (22); see also the majority opinion in the *Mexican Union Ry. Co.* Case, *Decisions*, I, p. 157, at pp. 163 (11), 164 (12). See also *Nitrate Ry. Co.* v. *Chile*, Ralston, I, no. 86, p. 67; *Rudloff* Case, Ralston, I, no. 77, p. 63.

[82] *Loc. cit.*, at pp. 29 (20), 31 (22) (23).

At first sight this argument may seem attractive. If the claim is predicated on grounds of private law and if, as shown above, the Calvo Clause is restricted to and applicable in the sphere of municipal law, it is difficult to escape the conclusion that effect must be given to its terms. Yet this conclusion is fallacious. The provisions of the Calvo Clause, as far as they concern submission to the jurisdiction of the contracting State, result in the absence of jurisdiction on the part of the courts of all other States.[83] They do not and cannot invalidate an agreement between the contracting State and the State of the contracting alien establishing the jurisdiction of an international tribunal for the decision of private law disputes arising out of a contract.[84] The jurisdictional provisions of the Calvo Clause are a matter of procedure, and not of substance.

Conclusions

(1) In the sphere of municipal courts administering municipal law the Calvo Clause is a legitimate expression of the liberty to contract accorded to the parties. It embodies a choice of the law governing the contract, submission to the jurisdiction of the contracting State, and an acknowledgment that recourse to the State of which the alien contractor is a national is inadmissible for the purpose of pressing a contractual claim.

(2) Before international tribunals the Calvo Clause is ineffective.

(*a*) In so far as international law requires the exhaustion of local remedies before a claim predicated upon State responsibility can be brought, the Calvo Clause is superfluous. Where the exhaustion of local remedies is not required by international law, no contractual Calvo Clause can supplement the law of nations.

(*b*) If, in virtue of an agreement between States, international tribunals are given jurisdiction to entertain claims alleged to be based on municipal law, the provisions of the treaty conferring jurisdiction must prevail over those of the contract which deny it.

---

[83] See above, p. 134.

[84] *Martini* Case, Ralston, I, no. 85, p. 66; *Selwyn* Case, *ibid.*, *I*, no. 84, p. 65, at p. 66; *Robert Stirling* Case, Ralston, I, no. 86, p. 68; *Antofagasta and Bolivia Ry. Co.* Case, Ralston, I, no. 86, p. 68; Nielsen (dissenting) in *International Fisheries Co.* v. *Mexico, Opinions*, III, p. 206, at p. 247. See also Ténékidès in *Revue générale de droit international public*, 43 (1936), p. 270, at pp. 281–3.

The Doctrine of Precedent in Continental Law with Special Reference to French and German Law

I

A casual glance at present-day textbooks of Continental law might lead to the conclusion that a system of precedent, whether of a binding or of a persuasive character, is entirely unknown to Continental lawyers. However, a study of the history, the foundations and the substance of Continental systems of law shows that this conclusion, if unqualified, would be misleading. Such a study reveals, in addition, the reasons for which Continental law was unable to develop a specific doctrine of binding precedent and to recognize precedents as a source of law. If all these factors are considered, it will be seen that, from the point of view of substantive law, case law forms an important part of Continental law and is of persuasive authority, but that its formal place within a legal system | has not been determined satisfactorily.[1]

[Editorial note: first published in Journal of the Society of Comparative Legislation 28 (1946), 34–44.]

[1] See e.g., Lambert, *La fonction du droit civil comparé*, I, (1903), pp. 153 ff. For a detailed list of the literature on this topic see Deák in (1934), 8 *Tulane Law Review* 337, at p. 340, note 6; Duguit, *Traité de Droit Constitutionnel*, I (3rd ed., 1927), pp. 166–69; see also Pound in (1923) 86 *Harv. L.R.* 641, at pp. 647, 649. And see Henry in *A.B.A. Journal*, 15 (1929), p. 11; Gray in (1895) 9 *Harv. L.R.* 27; Von Moschzisker (1924) 37 *Harv. L.R.* 409; Winder

For reasons of space and owing to a scarcity of material, it is proposed to examine mainly German law, but it is believed that the conclusions reached here apply *mutatis mutandis* to Continental systems of law in general.

1. Present Attitude of Textbook Writers

Textbook writers are agreed that the only sources of French, Italian and German law are statute law and customary law. At the same time it is recognized that neither statute law nor customary law can offer express guidance in respect of every one of the manifold problems which the courts are called upon to decide. When confronted with gaps in the law, the courts must attempt to fill them, but it is emphatically denied by the overwhelming majority of writers that the courts, in supplementing apparent gaps, create new rules of law. The method of supplementing gaps has been carefully developed. The courts must find the appropriate rule of law by means of studying the purpose of the statutory provision which would be applicable were the facts of the case somewhat different. For this purpose they may employ the process of analogy and the *argumentum e contrario*, or they may rely upon the reports and debates of the Parliamentary Committee which drafted the statute. If all these means should fail, the courts must decide "according to sound discretion, having regard to all economic and ethical considerations."[2] This principle has found legislative sanction in article 1 (2) of the Swiss Civil Code, which provides: "If the statute does not contain an appropriate rule, the judge must follow customary law, and in the absence of the latter, he must decide according to the principle which he would enact were he a legislator. In so doing he must follow the recognized doctrine and practice."

But whatever rule the courts may find and apply in the case for decision, this rule does not become a rule of law for the sole reason that it is applied by a court, except in the exceedingly rare case where the court applies what it regards as a previously existing rule of customary law.[3] It is necessary, therefore, to ascertain the place of judicial decisions on a novel point of law.

---

in (1940) 56 *L.Q.R.* 457 and in *Journal of Criminal Law,* 5 (1941), p. 242; Comment (1941) 50 *Yale L.J.* 1448; Holdsworth in (1934) 50 *L.Q.R.* 180; Goodhart, *ibid.,* p. 196; Allen (1935) 51 *L.Q.R.* 333; Holdsworth, *ibid.,* p. 443; note in (1944) 94 *L.J.* 396; Kessler in *Tulane Law Rev.* 19 (1944), p. 32, at p. 51.

The following were not available: – Kocourek, *Renovation of the Common Law through Stare Decisis,* 24 *Ill. L.R.* 984; Borchard, *Some Lessons from the Civil Law* (1916) 64 *U. Pa. L. Rev.* 570; Moore and Oglebay, *Stare Decisis and the Law of the Case* (1943).

[2] Enneccerus-Kipp-Wolff, *Lehrbuch des Bürgerlichen Rechts,* I, 1 (30–34. ed. 1928), pp. 87–88. See also Lambert, *La fonction du droit civil comparé,* p. 16. For a good survey of French, Austrian, Hungarian, Swiss and German rules dealing with this question see Samuel in *Toronto Law Journal,* 5 (1943), p. 148.

[3] Enneccerus-Kipp-Wolff, *loc. cit.,* pp. 87–88; p. 119; Lambert, *La fonction du droit civil*

2. Decisions of Courts and Customary Law

From the 18th century onwards writers were agreed with few exceptions[4] that a single decision, resulting in a course of decision, if other courts follow suit, may lead to the establishment of a constant practice of the courts (*Gerichtspraxis*), notwithstanding the fact that an individual court is precluded from laying down general principles purporting to cover similar cases arising in the future.[5] In these circumstances, it is said, a customary rule of law may spring up which must be observed henceforth by all courts. No writer has been able to show at what stage and under what | conditions a constant practice of the courts becomes a rule of customary law,[6] but it is significant that von Tuhr, writing in 1910,[7] brushed aside the suggestion that any one decision, or any course of decision of the German Supreme Court in respect of the Civil Code of 1900 had, at that time, obtained the force of customary law.[8]

Gény, on the other hand, writing in respect of French case law after the Civil Code had been in force for over one hundred years, admitted, without according case law the force of customary law, that it was necessary to treat it as "une règle de droit, vraiment obligatoire, comme issue de cette source formelle, la coutume."[9] Similarly, Lambert expressed the view that "... la jurisprudence est-elle l'agent nécessaire de la transmutation du sentiment

---

comparé, pp. 144 ff. Gény II, *Methode d'Interprétation* (2nd ed., 1919); p. 45, n. 1; (ca. Planiol, Lambert), p. 261.

[4] For the views of some dissenting writers, see Gény, II, p. 66 ff.

[5] Gény, I, p. 210, II, p. 38; 72; Portalis quoted by Lambert, l.c. 164.

[6] Dernburg, Bürgerliches Recht, I (3 ed., 1906), p. 84, citing Kohler, *Lehrbuch des Bürgerlichen Rechts,* I, p. 112; Esmein, *Histoire Générale du Droit Francais,* I (1904), p. 27. Gierke, *Deutsches Privatrecht,* I (1895), p. 179; Gény I, pp. 331, 337, note, p. 445, note 4 with further references, but see p. 362; II, pp. 29 ff., p. 70 ff. Lambert, pp. 800, 802, 19, 143, 145, n. 3. It is interesting to note that the opinions on the function of case law expressed by judges and writers in England during the 17th and 18th centuries are strongly influenced by the doctrine of customary law as developed in Canon Law. See, e.g., the statements cited by Holdsworth, (1934) 50 *L.Q.R.,* 180.

[7] *Allgemeiner Teil des Bürgerlichen Rechts,* I, p. 47.

[8] It is believed that a body of such rules having the force of customary law has not been developed as yet in any one of the Continental legal systems. On the other hand, the courts have established many new principles supplementing statutory provisions. Even if the place of these rules cannot be adequately determined (see Gény, II, p. 3 ff., pp. 10, 32, Ancel in *Journal of Comparative Legislation,* 3rd Ser., XVI (1934), p. 1) an examination of their substance, preferably on a comparative basis, is much needed. It will show that the contribution of the courts is very considerable. See Gény, I, pp. 362, 370, 386, 402–3, 413–14, 416, 424, n. 2; II, p. 50; Vauthier in *Revue de droit international et de législation comparée,* 23 (1908), p. 247, at pp. 267–70. For studies on the development of law by the courts see e.g., Ripert, *La règle morale dans les obligations civiles* (3rd ed., 1935), and *Le régime démocratique et le droit civil moderne* (1936), by the same author.

[9] II, p. 51.

juridique en normes de droit. Son intervention est indispensable pour mé-tamorphoser les simples usages, les habitudes de commerce, les convenances, en véritables coutumes juridiques sanctionnées par l'ordre permanent d'exécution."[10] Going further still, Planiol and Ripert[11] stated that "les cours ... reconstituent perpetuellement en dehors des Codes et des lois, un droit coutumier de nouvelle formation" but by adding that "le pouvoir judiciaire n'est jamais lié par sa jurisprudence antérieure" they rendered the preceding sentence practically meaningless, notwithstanding the proviso: "en fait il s'y conforme le plus souvent et la stabilité de ses décisions équivant *pour les particuliers* à l'existence d'une législation obligatoire" (italics mine).

Although it must be conceded that a single decision of a German, French or Italian court is not a binding precedent, it is nevertheless of high persuasive authority.[12] The reasons for this are three:[13]

First, a principle of mental economy leads judges to follow the opinions of their predecessors rather than to develop their own views, untrammelled by authority. Regard for the authority of other courts is also instrumental in bringing about a respect for precedents.

Second, legal certainty requires a uniform application of the same rules by all courts of law. Reasons of expediency force the courts to take cognizance of previous case law, whether it emanates from higher courts or from courts of co-ordinate, or even of subordinate, jurisdiction.

Third, the decisions of the Supreme Court, although not of binding authority, exercise an influence not less marked than those of a court in a common-law jurisdiction.

3. Decisions of Supreme Courts of Appeal

In Germany, two grounds may be distinguished which, together, established the preponderant position of the Supreme Court (*Reichsgericht*). First, by means of its jurisdiction in appeal, which enabled the Court either to quash a decision and to order a new trial or, in exceptional circumstances, to give final judgments (similar to the jurisdiction of the House of Lords), the

---

[10] Lambert, *loc. cit.,* p. 802.

[11] Planiol et Ripert, *Traité élémentaire de Droit Civil* (12th ed., 1989), I, p. 7; Josserand, *Cours de Droit Civil Positif Français,* I (3rd ed., 1938), p. 79, no. 99 (4); but see, e.g., Baudry-Lacantinerie et Houques Fourcade, *Traité Théorique et Pratique de Droit Civil,* I (3rd ed., 1907), p. 199, nos. 245 ff. Aubry et Rau, *Cours de Droit Civil,* I (6th ed., 1936, by Bartin), p. 241, Colin et Capitant, *Cours élémentaire de Droit Civil Français,* I (9th ed., 1939), pp. 86–39, no. 28.

[12] Gény, II, p. 47 ff.; *Laurette* v. *Sicard,* decided by the French Court of Cassation on March 11, 1884, s. 1884. 1. 288.

[13] Von Tuhr, *loc. cit.,* p. 46; Planiol et Ripert, *loc. cit.,* p. 48, nos. 122 ff., p. 89, no. 204.

Reichsgericht was in a position to impose its views upon the Courts of Appeal. For it would be indeed a stubborn Court of Appeal which would constantly refuse to accept the views of the Supreme Cdurt and which would prefer to be over-ruled again and again in matters concerning the same question of law. The position is the same in those countries where the highest court exercises a jurisdiction of *cassation* whereby decisions of the lower courts can only be quashed and if quashed must be referred back for a new trial (e.g., France, Italy). This factual supervision of the legal development must not be under-estimated even if, from the point of view of judicial hierarchy, the Supreme Court (*Reichsgericht, Cour de Cassation*) cannot, as a rule, directly impose its views upon the great number of small courts of first instance against the decisions of which an appeal lies to the Court of Appeal of the district, which may be final (Germany) or not (France). Second, the doctrine of precedent was embodied, to a limited extent, in articles 136 ff. of the German Law concerning the Organization of the Courts (*Gerichtsver-fassungsgesetz*).[14] According to this provision one division (civil or criminal) of the Supreme Court, if intending to dissent from a rule established by another division of the same court, must state a case for all civil or criminal divisions in joint session (since 1935 the Great Senates consisting of 9 judges). If a criminal division wished to deviate from a principle laid down by a civil division, or *vice versa,* all divisions (since 1935 the combined Great Senates) were to be summoned. By a similar provision, Courts of Appeal with a final jurisdiction in matters of land registration were forced to state a case for the Supreme Court, if they wished to disregard a decision on the same point of another Court of Appeal possessing the same jurisdiction in matters of land registration.[15] Although the concept of *sections réunies,* or *sezioni riunite,* is known in French[16] and Italian[17] law, the function of these plenary sessions combining the many divisions of the court is different, inasmuch as they are designed not so much to safeguard uniformity as to give additional weight to decisions of the Court of Cassation which has quashed a decision, referred it back and is seized with a second appeal. In fact, such decisions enjoy the highest authority and are usually followed without further discussion in subsequent cases.

It will be noted, however, that decisions of the Supreme Court, and for

---

[14] For a more detailed discussion of this law prior to the reform in 1935 see Cohn in (1935) 5 *Cambridge L.J.,* 366.

[15] For proposals to the same effect with regard to Provincial Courts of Appeal in Canada see C.A.W. in *Canadian Bar Review,* 13 (1935), 183.

[16] Decree of 27 ventôse, an VIII, Art. 78; law of April 1, 1837, art. 1, 2. See Gény, II p. 37; see e.g., the important decision of February 13, 1930, D. 1930. 1. 57 (strict liability in tort).

[17] *Codice de Procedura Civile,* Art. 547. See e.g., *De Meeus v. Forzano,* decided on January 18, 1940, *Foro Italiano,* 1940, I, p. 336 (diplomatic immunity).

that matter of Courts of Appeal possessing final jurisdiction, are not binding upon lower courts. Not even the provisions which limit the power of any division of the German Supreme Court to dissent from any previous decision of another division of co-ordinate jurisdiction prevent (*a*) the division concerned | from overruling any previous decision of its own or (*b*) the full court (or Great Senates) from overruling any previous decision given by the full court (or Great Senates). No rule exists similar to that laid down by the House of Lords in *London Street Tramways, Ltd., v. L.C.C.*[18] Our conclusion is, therefore, that, as between divisions of the German Supreme Court and between German Courts of Appeal in matters of land registration, the binding force of precedent is recognized to a limited extent. In other Continental countries not even this restricted operation of precedent is recognized. Moreover, no court is bound by its own decisions, nor are lower courts under any obligation to follow previous decisions of higher courts.

4. Historical Background of the German Rule

In order to stress the exceptional character of the provisions concerning the German Supreme Court, it may be convenient to give a sketch of the historical development which found its final expression in article 136 of the German Law concerning the Organization of the Courts. In the 18th century, the Supreme Court of the German Empire (*Reichskammergericht*)[19] and the *Oberappellationsgericht* of Kassel[20] were bound by their own decisions, but these decisions were not binding upon the lower courts. The Prussian Code of 1794[21] provided that judicial pronouncements should not be credited with any binding force, but this rigid rule was found to be unworkable and a decree of 1836 provided a procedure similar to that at present followed by the *Reichsgericht.* If a division of the Prussian Supreme Court (*Obertribunal*) wished to disregard a decision pronounced by another division of the same court, a case had to be stated for consideration by the full court. The ensuing judgment of the full court was binding upon all divisions of the *Obertribunal,* but not upon the lower courts.[22] On the other hand, the decisions of the local Supreme Courts of Appeal were given binding force also as regards the lower courts in Bavaria by the *Codex Maximilianeus Bava-*

---

[18] [1898] A.C. 375.

[19] Stobbe, *Handbuch des Deutschen Privatrechts,* I (1871), pp. 6, 144, and note 6.

[20] *Regulation of 1746,* Stobbe, *loc. cit.,* pp. 144, 145.

[21] *Allgemeines Landrecht,* Introduction, par. 6; Stobbe, *loc. cit.,* p. 145; Dernburg, *loc. cit.,* p. 13; Savigny, *System des heutigen Römischen Rechts,* I (1840), p. 198; Gény, II, p. 59.

[22] The Prussian Supreme Court, like the German Reichsgericht, was thus given little scope for developing a doctrine of precedent.

ricus of 1756[23] and by a statute of 1837,[24] in Hanover by a statute of 1838,[25] in the jurisdiction of the *Oberappellationsgericht* of Jena,[26] in Austria by an order of 1850,[27] and in Brunswick by a law of 1853.[28] However, a decree of 1872 abolished the rule of *stare decisis* for Austria.[29]

II

5. Reasons for the Absence of a Doctrine of Precedent: The Reception of Roman Law

The question must therefore be raised why a doctrine of precedent did not develop despite the appearance in Prussia, Austria, Bavaria, Hanover and elsewhere of provisions which in one form or another rendered the decisions | of a division of the Supreme Court binding either upon courts of co-ordinate or of subordinate jurisdiction. The answer will be found in the peculiar development of Continental law in the period between 1500 and 1800, the influence of the historical school[30] in the first half of the 19th century, the technique of interpreting statutes and the resulting modern approach to the theory of the sources of law.

There is a certain amount of evidence to show that during the early Middle Ages Germanic law, both in France and Germany, relied upon precedent, which was identified with custom, as the most important source of law.[31] But in the 15th and 16th centuries a "reception" of Roman law took place in

---

[23] I, c. 2. par. 14; see Stobbe, *loc. cit.*, p. 145; Gierke, *Deutsches Privatrecht*, I, (1895), p. 177. note 3; Gény II, p. 59.

[24] See note 21.

[25] Stobbe, *loc. cit.*, Gierke, *loc. cit.*

[26] Rules of Organization and Procedure, 1816, Stobbe, *loc. cit.*; Gierke, *loc. cit.*

[27] Decree of August 7, 1850; Gierke *loc. cit.;* Samuel in *Toronto Law Journal*, 5 (1943), p. 148 at p. 153.

[28] Law of July 5, 1853; Gierke, *loc. cit.*

[29] Gierke, *loc. cit.* For the practice of the *Reichskammergericht* and of the higher courts of several German States in the early 19th century to give rulings (*Gemeine Bescheide*) on disputed questions of general importance see Wächter, *Handbuch des Württembergischen Privatrechts*, II (1842), p. 44. For *arrêts de règlement* in France before 1790 which fulfilled a similar function, see Gény II, p. 35, n. 1, p. 36; Lambert, *loc. cit.*, p. 166; Baudry-Lacantinerie, *loc. cit.*, I, p. 202, no. 247.

[30] See e.g., Ehrlich, *Fundamental Principles of the Sociology of Law* (transl. Moll, 1936), *passim.*; Lambert, *La Fonction du Droit Civil Comparé*, I (1903), pp. 107–174, Gény, II, p. 56 ff.

[31] Lambert, *loc. cit.*, pp. 717–798; Brissaud, *Cours d'Histoire générale du Droit Français Public et Prive* (1904), I, pp. 297–307; Esmein, *Cours élémentaire d'Histoire du droit Français*, (14 ed., 1925), p. 686 (for the territories living according to the *droit écrit*), 689 (*droit coutumier*); p. 704 ff.

Central Europe, as a result of which Roman law was superimposed upon national systems of law. Inappropriate rules, such as those dealing with slavery, were omitted, but Roman law in its final stage of development, as codified by Justinian, assumed the function of a Central European Common law. The deficiencies of such a "reception" are patent. Roman law of 533 A.D. was not capable of meeting the requirements of society in the 17th and 18th centuries. Moreover, not being a living system, it was not open to a further homogeneous development. These difficulties were overcome in Germany by the "method of construing" or "jurisprudence of conceptions." Roman law, which had become the law of the land, was presumed to be a complete system of laws covering all possible situations. It was only necessary to find, by means of interpretation and generalization, the rule of Roman law applicable to the particular case in question. It is clear that in such a system all creative power was denied to the courts whose sole task was to employ the mechanical process of judicial syllogism and to apply the general and abstract rules of Roman law to the facts of the case.[32] It is true that customary law was recognized as a source of law, but its validity rested chiefly upon the fact that the provisions of Roman law granted statutory authority to customary law. The interpretation and application of statutes were the principal object of practitioners and writers alike. This reliance upon the authority of statutes, whether it be express or implied, direct or delegated, barred the way to an independent consideration of previous decisions, and it is interesting to note that one of the foremost treatises of the late 18th century rejected categorically the suggestion that judicial pronouncements should be treated as binding.[33] How deeply this conception of the function of the judge remained rooted in the minds of German lawyers even during the 19th century can be gleaned from Windscheid's statement, in his well-known textbook, where he said: "It is essential to divide up conceptions into their component parts and to show the elements contained in them. ... For not only a complete knowledge of the law, but also the certainty of its appli|cation depends upon an exhaustive grasp of the contents

---

[32] See also Goodhart, *Precedent in English and Continental Law,* (1934) 50 *L.Q.R.* 40, at p. 62, but on the ground that Roman law was a highly developed system. And see Esmein, *Cours élémentaire,* p. 686. For the influence, on this question, of the historical school upon Austin and upon American legal thought see Pound in (1923), 36 *Harv. L.R.,* 802, at p. 811.

[33] Glück, *Ausführliche Erläuterung der Pandecton,* I (2nd ed., 1797) pp. 218–224, pp. 440–492. For further references see Windschied-Kipp, *Lehrbuch des Pandektenrechts,* I (8th ed., 1900), p. 64, note 1.

For a somewhat different development in France prior to 1789 see Gény, II, p. 14. The paper by Meynial, *Remarques sur le rôle joué par la doctrine et la jurisprudence dans l'oeuvre d'unification du droit en France depuis la rédaction des coutumes jusqu'à la révolution, en particulier dans la succession aux propres,* read before the Congress of Comparative Law in 1900, was not available.

of the conceptions embodied in legal rules. ... The ultimate decision is the result of a calculation, the factors of which are represented by these legal concepts."[34]

6. The Influence of the Historical School

In France the technique of rigidly restricting legal science to the application and interpretation of statute law established itself only in the wake of the introduction of the Civil Code of 1804, but the effect of this technique (that developed by the so-called "école des interprètes du code civil") was not less marked than the corresponding practice which had grown in Germany under the ægis of Roman law.[35] With the advent of the historical school legal theory attached increasing importance to customary law. Savigny and his followers gave first place to customary law for the reason that, since in their view all law was based upon the "conviction (or consciousness) of the people,"[36] customary rather than statutory law represented the best expression of this conviction. However, the Historical School faced a difficult task, for it had to explain how the conviction of the people had embraced Roman law as the common law of the German States.[37] On the basis of its own theory the Historical School could have come to the conclusion that Roman law was not the common law of the German States, but this result was ruled out, seeing that Savigny's principal work was his treatise on the reception of Roman law in central Europe during the middle ages. In fact, the reception of Roman law was due, not to the "conviction of the people," but to the exertions of judges and of practitioners trained in Italy. Facts and theory were reconciled in the thesis first supported by the *glossa ordinaria*[38] that during the later stages of legal development courts and judges represent the "conviction of the people."[39]

---

[34] *Lehrbuch des Pandektenrechts* I, (6th ed. 1887) pp. 65 ff. (8th ed.), pp. 93–94; see also Jones, *Historical Introduction to the Theory of Law* (1940), pp. 68, 107. Present day Italian textbooks still adopt the same attitude.

[35] Lambert, *loc. cit.*, p. 206, note, contends that the English technique corresponds to that employed by the "école des interpretes du code civil." This statement is misleading. In Germany, soon after the introduction of the Civil Code, in 1900, a new wave of criticism arose against conceptualistic interpretation. See e.g., Heck in *Archiv für die Zivilistische Praxis*, 112 (1914), p. I ff., and the literature quoted there.

[36] For the various meanings attributed to this term and the many theories derived from it, see e.g., Zitelmann in *Archiv für die Zivilistische Praxis*, 66 (1883), pp. 324 ff.

[37] See Kantorowicz, (1937), 53 *L.Q.R.*, p. 326, at p. 338.

[38] Lambert, *loc. cit.*, pp. 144 ff., especially at p. 153.

[39] See also Jones, *loc. cit.*, pp. 56, 60. For similar theories in Mohammedan Law see Lambert, p. 337.

Inasmuch as the Historical School rejected both statute as well as customary[40] law as the predominant legal source, it could have opened the way to a new appreciation of the function of the courts, but by relying exclusively upon the conscience of the people as the only source of law it excluded a proper understanding of judge-made law[41] which is not based on the assent or the belief of the people, but on force.[42] The flaws of Savigny's doctrine were exposed by Beseler (1843), who drew attention to the distinction between customary law (*Volksrecht*) and case law (lawyer-made law, *Juristenrecht*).[43] But in so distinguishing disservice was done to lawyer-made law, for in Germany the latter became finally identified with Roman law and with the special technique of interpretation outlined above. *Juristenrecht* was thereby identified with a system of abstract rules which was foreign by origin and which had been imposed by a body of learned theorists. It never became associated with the idea of progress and of organic legal development. Although the two schools differed with|regard to the sources of law they both rejected precedent as a source. Nevertheless, since Roman law texts expressed opinions on the function of judicial decisions, it was necessary, as a technical problem, to examine what place Roman law had allotted to case law.

Both supporters and opponents of the doctrine of precedent relied on D. 1. 3. 38,[44] and C. 8. 52. 1.[45] Savigny[46] noted, in connection with these texts, that *res judicatae* were treated by the rhetors, although not by lawyers, as a source of law, but he, and with him the majority of writers,[47] rejected the

---

[40] See e.g., Lambert, p. 141.

[41] Gény, II, pp. 58, 60 ff.; Lambert, p. 146.

[42] See e.g., the observations of Cézar-Bru in *Revue générale du droit, de la legislation et de la Jurisprudence*, 28 (1904), p. 330, *et* p. 346.

[43] For a modern discussion of this distinction see Duguit, *Traité de Droit Constitutionnel*, I (3 ed., 1927), pp. 159, 160 ff.

[44] *D. 1. 3. 38.* Nam imperator noster Severus rescripsit in ambiguitatibus quae ex legibus proficiscuntur consuetudinem aut rerum perpetuo similiter iudicatarum auctoritatem vim legis optinere debere.

[45] *C. 8. 52. 1.* (a. 224) Praeses provinciae probatis his, quae in oppido frequenter in eodem genere controversiarum servata sunt, causa cognita statuet. nam et consuetudo praecedens et ratio quae consuetudinem suasit custodienda est, et ne quid contra longam consuetudinem fiat, ad solicitudinem suam revocabit praeses provinciae.

[46] Savigny, *System des heutigen Römischen Rechts*, I. (1840), p. 148 ff., and note (*h*), p. 136, and note (*r*), p. 173; p. 96, and note (*b*). The observations of Gray, (1895), 9 *Harv. L.R.*, 27, at p. 31, concerning the binding force of *decreta* are concerned with the legislative rather than with the judicial function of imperial *constitutiones*. See Wlassak, *Kritische Studien zur Theorie der Rechtsquellen* (1884), p. 134.

[47] Savigny *loc. cit.*; Wächter, *Handbuch des im Königreich Württemberg geltenden Privatrechts*, II (1842), p. 42, note 6, and the writers quoted there. *Contra*: e.g., Thibaut, *System des Pandekten-Rechts*, I (9th ed., 1846), par. 16. (pp. 14–15); Mühlenbruch, *Lehrbuch des Pandekten-Rechts*, I (4th ed., 1844), par. 41 (pp. 112/113), especially note 2. Some wished to accord binding force only to those decisions which had decided doubtful ques-

view that these texts sanctioned the principle of *stare decisis*.[48] Further than this, they refused to accord any significance to the *mos judiciorum* (*Gerichtsgebrauch*), even in so far as it might affect the practice of subordinate courts.[49]

The question of the *mos judiciorum*, with special regard to the application of the principle of *stare decisis*, was considered in detail in 1840 in an article written by a leading authority,[50] but his conclusions were altogether negative. Should the principle of precedent bind the court alone which had pronounced the decision, should it bind courts of co-ordinate jurisdiction, or should judgments of higher courts bind the courts of subordinate jurisdiction?[51] Was it conceivable that a constant practice of the lower courts could bind the higher court?[52] Furthermore, assuming that a constant, although different, practice had arisen in the lower and in the higher court, could the law of the land differ according to whether the lower or the higher court was seized?[53] For an English lawyer these questions do not appear to raise any difficult problems, and the answers provided by English law are clear.

But the writer of the article was unable to find a solution, and therefore inclined towards the orthodox view which held that the *mos judiciorum* was not binding upon any court, unless it had developed into a rule of customary law. He admitted, however that the *mos judiciorum* was of persuasive authority.

7. The Organization of the Courts and the Doctrine of Precedent

One effect of precedent in English law, i.e., that a superior court is bound by its own | decisions, was excluded by the rigid Continental doctrine of the 19th century which refused to recognize any source of law other than statute and customary law. It should be remembered, however, that even in England

---

tions or cases for which no solution was provided by the courts. On the whole, modern writers incline towards Savigny's view. See Krüger, *Geschichte der Quellen und Litteratur des Römischen Rechts*, (2nd ed., 1912), pp. 103, 305; but see Jolowicz, in *Journal of the Society of Public Teachers of Law,* 1937, pp. 1–15: Collinet in *Études Gény,* I, pp. 23–31.

[48] They referred to C. 7. 45. 13 (a. 529); C. 1. 14. 11. (a. 474) and distinguished C. 1. 14. 12 (a. 529) as referring exclusively to decisions by the Emperor himself. For texts quoted by their opponents see C. 7. 45. 4 (a. 229); C. 4. 1. 12. 6 (a. 529; irrelevant); C. 8. 10. 3 (a. 224); C. 9. 35. 11 (a. 478; *Mos iudiciorum*).

[49] This doctrine has not been accepted. For Rome see Kaser, *Zeitschrift der Savigny Stiftung, Rom. Abt.,* 59 (1939), p. 52. at pp. 99–100; Lambert, *loc. cit.,* pp. 693 ff.

[50] Wächter, in *Archiv für die Zivilistische Praxis,* 23 (1840), pp. 432–46. For further literature see Lambert, *loc. cit.,* p. 150 ff.; Gény, I, p. 385.

[51] *ibid.,* pp. 439–40.

[52] *ibid.,* pp. 440–43.

[53] *ibid.,* pp. 440–41.

the rule whereby the House of Lords and the Court of Appeal are bound by their own decisions is a product of the 19th and of the 20th centuries,[54] and that in the realm of Chancery the principle of precedent proper was only able to assert itself at a very late date.[55]

Another effect of precedent acknowledged in English law, viz., that the decisions of superior courts are binding upon the courts of subordinate jurisdiction,[56] was recognized in some German jurisdictions during the first half of the 19th century, but failed to obtain general support and was finally disregarded.

In view of these developments the absence on the Continent of precedent in the second sense is due, perhaps, not so much to the widely differing characteristics of English and Continental law[57] as to certain features of the judicial hierarchy.

First, a judicial hierarchy in the English sense did not exist in France up to the end of the 18th century and in Germany before the middle of the 19th century. Precedent in these circumstances would have meant numerous different bodies of precedent, each of which would have applied within a very restricted jurisdiction. As far as they emanated from courts administering

---

[54] *London Street Tramways Ltd.* v. *L.C.C.* [1898] A.C. 375; *Young* v. *Bristol Aeroplane Co.* [1944] K.B. 718; see also *Adair* v. *Birnbaum* [1939] 2 K.B. 149; Allen, *Law in the Making* (3rd ed., 1939), pp. 223, 226, n. 3, 273. Lord Wright in (1943) 8 *Cambridge L.J.*, 117–145; Salmond in (1900) 16 *L.Q.R.*, 377, at p. 340, note 3; Kotzé in *South African Law Journal*, 34 (1917), 280, at p. 296; Laird in *Canadian Bar Review*, 13 (1935), 1. For an interesting attempt to connect this development with the slowing up of the process of expansion in the era of liberalism, see Kessler in 19 (1944), *Tulane L.R.*, 82, at p. 50.

[55] Winder in (1941), 57 *L.Q.R.*, 245–279.

[56] For the practice in Scotland, which up to the 19th century developed on continental lines, compare Erskine, *Principles of the Law of Scotland*, I, 1 (1 ed., 1754), para. 17 (p. 7); *An Institute of the Law of Scotland*, (New ed., 1872), I, para. 47 (p. 20); Gloag and Henderson, *Introduction to the Law of Scotland*, (3rd ed., 1939), pp. 9–10; Gardner in (1940), 26 *A.B.A. Journal*, 774; (1940), 52 *Jur. Rev.*, 144, *ibid.*, 53 (1941), p. 132. For South Africa, see Kotzé, *loc. cit.*, at p. 311; Anders, *ibid.*, 27 (1910), at p. 372; Kovalsky in *South Africa Law Times*, 4 (1935), p. 95. For Canada, see Laird, *loc. cit.*, at p. 12. For Quebec, see Mignault in *Canadian Bar Review*, 3 (1925), p. 1; Kennedy in *South African Law Times*, 1 (1932), pp. 196; 197; for Louisiana, see Davidson in *Tulane Law Review*, 7 (1932), p. 100; for Mississippi, see Alexander in *Mississippi Law Journal*, 17 (1945), p. 170, at p. 176.

[57] English law shows that it is possible to combine a codification of a particular branch of law (e.g., Workmen's Compensation Acts) with the retention of the doctrine of precedent in the same field. See Allen, *loc. cit.*, p. 152; Goodhart, *loc. cit.*, p. 62. But see Pound in (1923), 36 *Harv. L.R.*, 641, at p. 647. Von Moschzisker in (1924), 37 *Harv. L.R.*, 409, at p. 422, and note 37, and Henry, cited above, note 1, for the disadvantages of combining these methods. It must be remembered that in accordance with Continental statutory technique and interpretation, courts applying civil law system deliver their judgments in terms of general propositions. Consequently, adherence to the principle of *stare decisis* would amount to the recognition of the power of the courts to modify the law to a far greater extent than that admitted in common law jurisdictions, at least in so far as the interpretation of statutes, as distinct from the implementation of gaps is concerned.

Roman law or the *droit écrit* all these precedents, even if conflicting, would have purported to represent the law common to the whole country.[58] The picture conjured up here resembles to a marked degree that which Professor Goodhart | has drawn of the present position of precedent in the United States.[59] It is clear that in these circumstances a doctrine of precedent would have been unworkable.

Second, in the 20th century, when Continental law had become unified, codified and centrally administered, the great number of Courts of Appeal (26 in Germany, 27 in France) rendered the application of the doctrine of precedent difficult as far as these courts were concerned, and restricted it, within the limits of law and fact set out above,[60] to the decisions of the Supreme Courts. Otherwise, in the absence of guidance by the Supreme Court, conflicting decisions handed down by the numerous Courts of Appeal could have established different bodies of precedent which, although serving as a stabilizing factor within the jurisdiction of each Court of Appeal, would have endangered the uniform application of the law. The only possible alternative, that of attributing binding authority to the pronouncements of the Supreme Court, could have been adopted, although not without some difficulty, seeing that Continental Supreme Courts sit in many divisions.[61] That it has not been adopted may be due, in part, to the rigid doctrine regarding the sources of law, which also prevented the development of precedent in the first sense discussed above (p. 38). In part it may be due to an understandable reluctance to treat individual decisions turning solely on the interpretation of statutes on an equal footing with statutory and customary law. No such reluctance is felt where a course of decision has developed; case law then exercises its authority in no uncertain manner.

---

[58] All attempts in this direction were doomed in the absence of official or private law reports. It appears that law reporting was introduced in Germany in the middle of the 19th century. See Ehrlich, *loc. cit.*, p. 177 ff. For suggestions in this direction made by writers in the 18th century, see Savigny, *Vom Beruf unserer Zeit für Gesetzgebung und Rechtswissenschaft* (2nd ed., 1828), p. 127. For France, see Meynial, *Les Recueils d'arrets et les Arretistes*, in *Le Code Civil*, 1804–1904, Vol. I, (1904), pp. 173–204. For an attempt by the German jurist Mynsinger (1514–88) to report the decisions of the Imperial Court, see Jones, *loc. cit.*, p. 45, note 2.

[59] *Essays in Jurisprudence* (1937), pp. 50–74; see also Lambert, *loc. cit.*, p. 209, note, and the earlier literature quoted there.

[60] *supra*, pp. 6–9.

[61] Attempts to solve conflicts between the practice of the Supreme Court and the Courts of Appeal by reference to the legislation (*référé au législateur*) were made in France by a law of August 24, 1790, amended by a law of September 16, 1807, and abrogated by a law of April 1, 1837 (see above, p. 37, note 16); and in Naples. See Jones, *loc. cit.*, p. 53; de Ruggiero *Instituzioni di Diritto Civile*, I (5th ed., 1928), p. 128, and note 2; Planiol et Ripert, *Traité élémentaire*, I, p. 91, no. 210; see also Savigny, *Vom Beruf unserer Zeit für Gesetzgebung und Rechtswissenschaft* (2nd ed., 1828), ff. 88–89, and the suggestions made by him at p. 131.

However, since Continental courts are concerned with the interpretation of statutes, and since the primary evidence for the existence of a rule of Continental law must be found in statutes, case law is principally of importance where the courts are called upon to fill apparent gaps in the statute which the legislature, intentionally or by oversight, has left for the consideration of the judiciary. Aided by very flexible systems of interpretation, the courts are well equipped to decide cases *primae impressionis.* They have assumed this task with an ever-increasing eagerness and, as a result, the function of case law to create new rules outside statutory law has been more in the foreground than its role in applying and interpreting statutes.[62] It would be a mistake, however, to attach excessive significance to this feature when attempting to explain the absence of a fully developed doctrine of precedent.

III

Conclusions

To sum up, the main reasons for the absence of a doctrine of binding precedent in the English sense are three. First, a different approach to the sources of law in consequence of the reception of Roman law has so far | prevented the adoption of the principle in *London Street Tramways, Ltd.,* v. *L.C.C.*[63] In view of the doubts recently expressed in England whether the strict theory of precedent is justified,[64] it is unlikely that in years to come it will find many supporters on the Continent. Second, the adoption of the principle that courts of subordinate jurisdiction must follow the decisions of superior courts is rendered difficult, although not impossible, by the fact that Continental Supreme Courts of Appeal sit in many divisions. Third, in view of the great number of Courts of Appeal, the principle cannot easily be applied to Courts of Appeal and to other courts of subordinate jurisdiction without jeopardizing the uniform application of law rather than enhancing it.

---

[62] Gény, II, p. 11. Consequently Continental writers have inclined either to stress unduly the binding force of precedent in English law or to over-estimate its creative force. See e.g., Gerland, *Englische Gerichtsverfassung,* II, (1910), pp. 771–773, 994; Esmein in *Revue trimestrielle de droit civile,* I (1902), p. 5, at p. 8; *Cours d'Histoire Générale de Droit Français,* I (1904), p. 27; Josserand, *Cours de Droit Civil Positif Français,* I (3rd ed., 1938), p. 80, no. 99; Lambert, *loc. cit.,* pp. 97 ff.; Staudinger, *Kommentar zum Bürgerlichen Gesetzbuch,* I (9th ed., 1925), pp. 31–34, with further literature. See also Goodhart in (1934), 50 *L.Q.R.,* 44, at p. 54; Deák, *loc. cit., supra,* note 1; Jones, *loc. cit.,* p. 297, note 4.

[63] [1898] A.C. 875.

[64] Lord Wright in (1943), 8 *Cambridge L.J.,* 117, at p. 144.

Jurisdiction in Bankruptcy

A Study in the Interrelation between Choice of Law Clauses and the Conflict of Laws

I. Legislation 1825–1914

In recent years choice of law clauses in domestic legislation have attracted considerable attention.[1] Some have been examined in considerable detail, but others have scarcely been noticed. Among the latter, the provisions contained in the Bankruptcy Act, 1914, are of particular interest not only from the theoretical but also from the historical point of view. Moreover, the Court of Appeal has recently had the rare opportunity of discussing and applying them.[2]

The Bankruptcy Act, 1914, provides:–

1.–(1) A debtor commits an act of bankruptcy in each of the following cases:–

(a) If in England or elsewhere he makes a conveyance or assignment of his property to a trustee or trustees for the benefit of his creditors generally;

[Editorial note: first published in Modern Law Review 12 (1949), 454–476.]

[1] Morris, (1946) 62 L.Q.R. 170; Robertson, *Characterisation in the Conflict of Laws* (1940), p. 99, Nussbaum, *Principles of Private International Law* (1942), p. 70.
[2] *Re a Debtor (No. 335 of 1947)* [1948] 2 All E.R. 533; 64 T.L.R. 446.

(*b*) If in England or elsewhere he makes a fraudulent conveyance, gift, delivery, or transfer of his property, or of any part thereof;

(*c*) If in England or elsewhere he makes any conveyance or transfer of his property or any part thereof, or creates any charge thereon, which would under this or any other Act be void as a fraudulent preference if he were adjudged bankrupt;

(*d*) If with intent to defeat or delay his creditors he does any of the following things, namely, departs out of England, or being out of England remains out of England, or departs from his dwelling-house, or otherwise absents himself, or begins to keep house;

(*e*) If execution against him has been levied by seizure of his goods under process in an action in any court, or in any civil proceeding in the High Court, and the goods have been either sold or held by the sheriff for twenty-one days:

Provided that, where an interpleader summons has been taken out in regard to the goods seized, the time elapsing between the date at which such summons is taken out and the date at which the proceedings on such summons are finally disposed of, settled, or abandoned, shall not be taken into account in calculating such period of twentyone days;

| (*f*) If he files in the court a declaration of his inability to pay his debts or presents a bankruptcy petition against himself;

(*g*) If a creditor has obtained a final judgment or final order against him for any amount, and, execution thereon not having been stayed, has served on him in England, or, by leave of the court, elsewhere, a bankruptcy notice under this Act, and he does not, within seven days after service of the notice, in case the service is effected in England, and in case the service is effected elsewhere, then within the time limited in that behalf by the order giving leave to effect the service, either comply with the requirements of the notice or satisfy the court that he has a counter-claim set off or cross demand which equals or exceeds the amount of the judgment debt or sum ordered to be paid, and which he could not set up in the action in which the judgment was obtained, or the proceedings in which the order was obtained:

For the purposes of this paragraph and of section two of this Act, any person who is, for the time being, entitled to enforce a final judgment or final order, shall be deemed to be a creditor who has obtained a final judgment or final order;

(*h*) If the debtor gives notice to any of his creditors that he has suspended, or that he is about to suspend, payment of his debts.

1.–(2) In this Act, the expression 'a debtor', unless the context otherwise implies, includes any person, whether a British subject or not, who at the time when any act of bankruptcy was done or suffered by him–

(*a*) was personally present in England; or

(*b*) ordinarily resided or had a place of residence in England; or

(*c*) was carrying on business in England, personally, or by means of an agent or manager; or

(*d*) was a member of a firm or partnership which carried on business in England.

4.–(1) A creditor shall not be entitled to present a bankruptcy petition against a debtor unless

(*d*) the debtor is domiciled in England, or within a year before the date of the presentation of the petition has ordinarily resided, or had a dwelling-house or place of business, in England, or (except in the case of a person domiciled in Scotland or Ireland or a firm or partnership having its principal place of business in Scotland or Ireland) has carried on business in England, personally or by means of an agent or manager, or (except as aforesaid) is or within the said period has been a member of a firm or partnership of persons which has carried on business in England by means of a partner or partners, or an agent or manager, nor, where a deed of arrangement has been executed, shall a creditor be entitled to present a bankruptcy petition, founded | on the execution of the deed, or on any other act committed by the debtor in the course or for the purpose of the proceedings preliminary to the execution of the deed, in cases where he is prohibited from so doing by the law for the time being in force relating to deeds of arrangement.

Choice of law clauses incorporated in domestic statutes purport to establish the limits of operation of these statutes. The origin of these clauses can be traced back to the Dutch doctrine of the seventeenth century which held that conflicts of laws could be solved by restricting the competence of every country to legislate for its own subjects, local residents and goods situate within its territory.[3] This doctrine failed, for it did not determine in what circumstances one country must apply the laws of another where the facts are connected with several countries. It could claim a limited success in respect of all actions where it was not envisaged that foreign law should ever be applied by the *forum* and where the question was solely whether the forum had jurisdiction. Such questions arise, for instance, in administrative law, criminal law and the law of bankruptcy. Choice of law clauses determine either the circle of persons, the class of objects or the type of transaction to which the statute is to apply.

The Bankruptcy Consolidation Act, 1825,[4] defined, in the first place, the circle of persons subject to the Act. They were only traders exercising one of the trades enumerated in section 2. The Act did not state that the trade must

---

[3] Cp. Huber, *Praelectiones Juris Romani et Hodierni*, vol. 2, bk. 1, tit. iii, par. 2. See also Story, *Conflict of Laws* (8th ed. 1883), pp. 21–25 (paras. 18, 20, 23).

[4] 6 Geo. 4, c. 16.

be carried out in England, but the insistence on trading appears to have excluded foreign traders who did not carry on trade in England. This question was clarified by subsequent legislation. In the second place the Act provided a list of transactions which were to be treated as acts of bankruptcy.[5] This list foreshadowed that now contained in section 1 (1) of the Bankruptcy Act, 1914. However, the only reference to acts done abroad occurred in section 3 of the Act of 1825, which like section 1 (1) (b) of the Act of 1914 mentioned fraudulent conveyances in England or elsewhere.

The Act of 1825, therefore, defined the circle of persons to which it was to apply by referring to their personal qualifications. By implication the Act restricted itself to those trading in England, until the Act of 1849, section 90, expressly confirmed this view. As regards the nature of the transaction, sections 3–6 contained no territorial restrictions. The provision in section 3 meant naturally in this connection conveyances made abroad by a person trading in England, and thus having effect, if only indirectly, in England, either by reducing the assets in England, or, if operative abroad, by curtailing the rights of the English creditors to assets abroad.

|It is understandable that section 4 of the Act of 1825, which dealt with the conveyance of all property to trustees for the benefit of creditors, did not refer to conveyances made abroad,[6] for it was well established that universal assignments by persons domiciled in England extend to property abroad[7] and that universal assignments of movables made by persons domiciled abroad are effective in England, if made in accordance with the law of the assignor's domicile.[8] Thus, whether the assignor was domiciled in England or abroad, any universal assignment in accordance with the law of his domicile was recognised according to the English rules of private international law. The Bankruptcy Act only determined the question of jurisdiction by requiring that the assignor must be trading in England.

The Insolvent Debtors Act, 1842,[9] must be mentioned next. This Act applied chiefly to non-traders, and allowed only petitions by debtors them-

---

[5] Sections 3–8.

[6] But see the Bankruptcy Act, 1914. ss. 1 (1) (a), 167.

[7] *Sill* v. *Worswick* (1791) 1 H.Bl. 665; *Hunter* v. *Potts* (1791) 4 T.R. 182; *Phillips* v. *Hunter* (1795) 2 H.Bl. 402; Dicey, Rule 54, p. 328, n. 15, pp. 329, 330, n. 26, p. 331, n. 27.

[8] *Solomons* v. *Ross* (1764) 1 H.Bl. 131 (n.); *Jollet* v. *Deponthieu* (1769) 1 H.Bl. 132 (n.); Dicey, Rule 99 and p. 440, n. 17; Nadelmann (1946) 9 M.L.R. 154. It should be noted that today the rule is no longer accepted in this restricted form. A foreign assignment in the course of proceedings in bankruptcy in a court to whose jurisdiction the debtor is subject, although he is not domiciled there, is a valid assignment of the movables of the bankrupt in England. See *Re Davidson's Settlement Trusts* (1873) L.R. 15 Eq. 383; *Re Lawson's Trusts* [1896] 1 Ch. 175; *Re Anderson* [1911] 1 K.B. 896; compare Dicey, Rule 99, p. 440, n. 20, and the cases cited there.

[9] 5 & 6 Vict. c. 116.

selves. A debtor had to publish notices in the *London Gazette* and in some newspapers circulating in the county wherein he resided.[10] It is thus clear that the debtor, in order to enjoy the benefit of the Insolvent Debtors Act, 1842, had to be resident in England. These two statutes form the basis of the present law relating to jurisdiction in bankruptcy. The Bankruptcy Consolidation Act, 1849, s. 65,[11] virtually reproduced the list of persons who were made subject to the bankruptcy law in virtue of section 2 of the Act of 1825. Similarly, the catalogue of acts of bankruptcy underwent little change, except that detailed provisions were added regulating acts of bankruptcy by nonpayment after summons. Debtor's petitions were introduced,[12] and creditor's petitions were normally to be prosecuted in the court for the district in which the trader had resided or carried on business for six months next before the petition.[13]

The Bankruptcy Act, 1861,[14] attempted to place traders and non-traders on a more equal footing by amalgamating the Bankruptcy Act and the Insolvent Debtors Act. No new catalogue of | acts of bankruptcy was enacted. The old catalogue remained in principle applicable to traders, but a number of acts were set out, some of which were to be acts of bankruptcy if committed by a trader only,[15] others if committed by traders and non-traders,[16] and some if committed by non-traders only.[17] It must be noted that section 70, in so far as it extended the provisions relating to fraudulent conveyances[18] to non-traders, omitted to include conveyances 'elsewhere'. This omission may have been influenced by the insertion in the definition section[19] of a provision that '"property" shall mean all the real and personal estate within the Realm and abroad, but this provision, and its successors, envisaged the universality of the effect of an English bankruptcy and did not necessarily refer to the acts which may cause a bankruptcy.[20]

By omitting to require that a non-trading debtor must have resided in England and by introducing a distinction between (a) fraudulent convey-

---

[10] Section 1.

[11] 12 & 13 Vict. c. 106.

[12] *Ibid.*, s. 93.

[13] *Ibid.*, e. 90.

[14] 24 & 25 Vict. c. 134.

[15] Section 73: suffering execution to be levied for the recovery of a sum exceeding £50.

[16] Sections 71, 72, 75, 76, 77, 85: lying in prison or escaping out of prison; declaration of inability to pay debts; bankruptcy petition and adjudication in dominion court; judgment debtor summons for more than £50; debtor's petition.

[17] Section 70: with intent to defeat or delay creditors to depart the realm, or being out of the realm to remain abroad; fraudulent conveyance.

[18] Bankruptcy Consolidation Act, 1849, s. 67; Bankruptcy Consolidation Act, 1825, s. 3.

[19] Section 229. See now Bankruptcy Act, 1914, s. 167: and compare Bankruptcy Act, 1883, s. 168.

[20] Compare Topham, (1903) 19 L.Q.R. 295 at p. 296.

ances in England or elsewhere committed by traders, and (b) fraudulent conveyances pure and simple committed by non-traders, the Act of 1861 laid the foundation for further confusion and difficulties. Some additional guidance can be obtained from section 78 of the same Act which provided that judgment summonses against traders and non-traders alike were to be issued (a) out of the Court of Bankruptcy for the district in which the debtor usually lived, provided the debtor was then in England, and (b) out of the court for the district in which was the debtor's *usual or last* known abode in England, provided the debtor was not then in England. It may be assumed from this provision that a debtor, whether trader or not, must normally reside in England.[21]

Modern bankruptcy legislation begins with the Bankruptcy Act, 1869.[22] This Act, in its definition section, no longer included in the term 'property' all the real and personal estate within the realm or abroad. Instead, it suppressed every reference to the location of the property. The catalogue of acts of bankruptcy was | amalgamated with the provisions regulating creditor's petitions.[23] The catalogue of acts of bankruptcy referred, in respect of conveyances to trustees and of fraudulent conveyances, to acts done in England and elsewhere, but contained no restrictions in space in so far as all other acts of bankruptcy were concerned. The provisions regulating creditor's petitions gave no indication whether the debtor had to be resident in England at the time when the act of bankruptcy was committed. Only the provisions governing debtor's summonses[24] pointed indirectly to the requirement that the debtor must have resided or traded in England.[25] Further, section 59 of the Act of 1869 defined the jurisdiction of the courts. The London Bankruptcy Court was to have jurisdiction (a) over persons residing or carrying on business in London, and (b) over persons not resident in England.

The wording of this Consolidating Act was unfortunate, for it encouraged many doubts. Formerly it was reasonably clear that a person, in order to be caught by the Bankruptcy or Insolvent Debtors Acts, must have resided or traded in England. It seemed to follow, further, that any act, in order to be an act of bankruptcy in England, must have been committed in England, unless (1) the statute provided otherwise, or (2) the act was one which was effective

---

[21] It should be noted, further, that the Act of 1861 added debtor's petitions of traders to the catalogue of acts of bankruptcy, thus achieving uniformity in respect of the act of bankruptcy now set out in the Bankruptcy Act, 1914, s.1 (1) (f). The conditions under which a creditor's petition could be brought were regulated by s. 89 of the Act of 1861.

[22] 32 & 33 Vict. c. 71.

[23] Bankruptcy Act, 1869, s. 6.

[24] *Ibid.*, s. 6 (6).

[25] Compare Bankruptcy Act, 1861, s. 78, discussed above.

in England according to the ordinary rules of private international law. After the passing of the Act of 1869 it could be argued that even persons abroad were subject to English bankruptcy legislation, and that any act of the kind enumerated in the catalogue of acts of bankruptcy was an act of bankruptcy for the purposes of the Bankruptcy Act, 1869, no matter whether it was committed in England or abroad.

The Bankruptcy Act, 1883,[26] made some changes, but they affected more the form than the substance of the Act. The catalogue of acts of bankruptcy received its final form,[27] and included conveyances in England or abroad which would be void as fraudulent preferences if the debtor were adjudged bankrupt.[28] The provisions concerning creditor's petitions were separated from the catalogue of acts of bankruptcy and laid down that the debtor must have been domiciled in England, or within a year before the date of the presentation of the petition have ordinarily resided or had a dwelling-house or place of business in England.[29] This attention to the question of jurisdiction over the debtor was timely. However, by linking jurisdiction, at least in part, with the domicile of the debtor in preference to residence, by restricting the jurisdictional requirements to creditor's petitions and by separating | them from the catalogue of acts of bankruptcy, the Act left it open whether English bankruptcy legislation took notice of acts of bankruptcy by British subjects and others, wherever committed, even if the act of bankruptcy had no direct effect in England.[30]

The Bankruptcy Act, 1914,[31] attempted to remedy this defect by inserting a provision[32] defining the categories of debtors who were subject to the Act, irrespective of the somewhat more limited provisions defining the jurisdiction of English courts in respect of creditor's petitions.[33] Inasmuch as this provision relied strongly on residence or trading in England, it was a step in the right direction. However, it defined the sphere of operation of the English Bankruptcy Act by reference to jurisdiction over the person of the debtor and failed to establish satisfactorily to what extent acts of bankruptcy committed abroad attract the operation of the English bankruptcy legislation. Thus the question to what extent acts committed abroad are acts of bankruptcy in England remained open and continued to attract the attention of English courts. It was solved with the help of rules of the conflict of laws which the courts developed gradually.

---

[26] 46 & 47 Vict. c. 52.
[27] *Ibid.*, s. 4, now Bankruptcy Act, 1914, s. 1 (1).
[28] *Ibid.*, s. 4 (c), now Bankruptcy Act, 1914, s. 1 (1) (c).
[29] *Ibid.*, s. 6, now Bankruptcy Act, 1914, s. 4 (1) (d).
[30] See Foote in *Clunet*, II (1884), p. 225 at p. 230.
[31] 4 & 5 Geo. 5, c. 59.
[32] Section 1 (2).
[33] Section 4 (1) (d).

II. Jurisdiction in Bankruptcy and the Courts

As set out above, the Bankruptcy Act, 1883, and, with the exception of fraudulent preference, the Act of 1869, enumerating the acts of bankruptcy in terms identical with those employed in section 1 (1) of the Act of 1914, defined only the types of transactions which were affected by them. Among these, conveyances for the benefit of creditors generally, fraudulent conveyances and conveyances constituting fraudulent preferences, fell under the jurisdiction of English courts if made in England or elsewhere. In so far as the jurisdiction in bankruptcy was extended to these transactions, now contained in section 1 (1) (*a*)–(*c*) of the Act of 1914, no matter where they had taken place, it was too wide; in so far as concerned all other acts of bankruptcy, such as departing out of England, or being out of England and remaining out of England with intent to defeat creditors (section 1 (1) (*d*) of the Act of 1914), no choice of law clauses were attached. The result was that jurisdiction could be assumed on a strictly territorial basis or that it could be extended to persons and acts abroad, no matter how slender their connection with England. Thus the courts were forced to develop their own rules of conflict of laws.

1. Rules of the Conflict of Laws: section 1 (1) (d). First Phase

To take the second alternative first. In the case of *Re Crispin*,[34] Mellish L.J. stated that a foreign trader committing an act of|bankruptcy in England was subject to English bankruptcy laws, even if he did not reside or carry on business here. He held that physical presence attracted the bankruptcy laws and that a departure in the sense of section 1 (1) (*d*)[35] of the Act of 1914 was an act of bankruptcy for the purpose of the Act. On the other hand, this case established that a foreigner not domiciled in England and not carrying on trade in England who quits England without having committed an act of bankruptcy cannot subsequently be made a bankrupt. For the same reason a person who remains out of England cannot be subject to the English bankruptcy laws if he is a foreigner remaining in his own home, but he is subject to these laws if he has his home or place of business in England.

---

[34] (1873) L.R. 8 Ch. 374, 380, 381.
[35] Bankruptcy Act, 1869, s. 6 (3); Bankruptcy Act, 1883, s. 4 (1) (*a*).

(a) Nationality and Jurisdiction in Bankruptcy

It will be noticed that the vague term 'foreigner', otherwise unknown in the conflict of laws, was employed by the court. It may be interpreted as a reference to the nationality or the domicile of a person, but it would appear that the Court of Appeal in *Re Crispin* relied on the debtor's nationality. This conclusion is borne out by the decision in *Ex p. Blain, re Sawers,*[36] where the principle, alleged to be one of public international law, that every State is competent to legislate within certain limits only[37] was made the basis of the jurisdiction of English courts under the Bankruptcy Act. Cotton L.J. said: 'all laws of the English Parliament must be territorial; they apply to and bind all subjects of the Crown who come within the fair interpretation of them, and also all aliens who come to this country and who during the time they are here do any act which ... comes within its provisions' (at p. 531). James and Brett L.JJ. concurred (at pp. 527, 529), but Brett was inclined to allow jurisdiction over a foreign national domiciled in England, even if he had not committed an act of bankruptcy in England. The views expressed in these two cases were followed by the Court of Appeal in *Re Pearson.*[38]

Thus in the period between 1873 and 1892 the principles of the conflict of laws in matters of bankruptcy were enriched by the following rule:

Where the bankruptcy legislation does not provide otherwise (as it does by the proto-typical provisions which are now to be found in section 1 (1) (*a*)–(*c*)), its provisions extend–

(1) to all British subjects, no matter where the act of bankruptcy is committed;

(2) to those foreign nationals who commit an act of bankruptcy while present in England, or, possibly, who are domiciled | in England and commit an act of bankruptcy in England or abroad.

Lord Davey in *Cooke* v. *Chas. Vogeler* Co.,[39] like Brett L.J. before him in *Ex p. Blain,*[40] was well aware of this development when he said:

'... *Ex p. Crispin* laid down that a foreigner ... in England is subject to the bankruptcy laws, but it is the act of bankruptcy which gives the court jurisdiction, and in the case of a foreigner that act of bankruptcy must be committed in this country ...'.

---

[36] (1879) 12 Ch. D. 522.
[37] For the meaning of the term 'legislative competence', see *Thakur Jagannath Baksh Singh* [1946] A.C. 327 at p. 336 (P.C.).
[38] [1892] 2 Q.B. 263.
[39] [1901] A.C. 102, 113, 114.
[40] (1879) 12 Ch.D. 522, 529.

(b) Present rule: s. 1 (2)

Inasmuch as the new rule claimed that the Bankruptcy Act applied to all British subjects irrespective of where they were domiciled or resident, and irrespective of where the act of bankruptcy was committed, it was clearly too wide. The interaction of the principle extending the Act to a limited class of aliens and of the principle claiming jurisdiction over every British subject created the balanced rule which is embodied in section 1 (2) of the Act of 1914. The general effect of section 1 (2) is not to extend the jurisdiction over foreigners appreciably beyond that previously allowed by the courts,[41] but to restrict that over British subjects to the same extent as that exercised over foreigners. This subsection is a proper rule of the conflict of laws, which determines whether the English Bankruptcy Court has jurisdiction over the person of a particular debtor. However, one effect of the codification was that the criterion whether jurisdiction exists over the person of the debtor[42] was divorced from the additional requirement in the case of foreigners that the act of bankruptcy must be committed in England. As a result, this latter requirement has been neglected at times. As will be shown in the next paragraph it cannot be contended that it has been abrogated by section 1 (2), notwithstanding the fact that the express provisions of section 1 (2) are to a great extent identical with those developed by the courts in respect of section 1 (1) (d).

2. Rules of the Conflict of Laws: s. 1 (1) (d). Second Phase

There was, on the whole, no need to develop a further rule of the conflict of laws to determine what objects or what types of transactions were subject to English bankruptcy legislation.[43] A | British subject fell under the operation of the English bankruptcy laws no matter where the act of bankruptcy was committed. An alien of the limited class subject to the operation of the English bankruptcy laws had to commit an act of bankruptcy in England.[44] However, one provision (section 1 (1) (d) of the Act of 1914) did not fit into the scheme for it provides that an act of bankruptcy is committed–

'if with intent to defeat or delay his creditors he ... departs out of England, or being out of England remains out of England ...'.

---

[41] But note the introduction of s. 1 (2) (c) and (d), which confers jurisdiction in bankruptcy in respect of acts done in England by means of an agent carrying on business there, or by members of a firm or partnership trading in England.

[42] This jurisdiction is sometimes called jurisdiction *ratione persona*. See Judge Hudson (dissenting) in the *Panevezys-Saldutiskis Railway Case*, P.C.I.J., ser. A/B, No. 76, at p. 44.

[43] This jurisdiction is sometimes called jurisdiction *ratione materiæ*. See Hudson, *loc. cit.*

[44] For the exceptions in the cases now specified in s. 1 (a)–(c), see below.

Here the distinction, based upon the division of legislative competence over British subjects anywhere and aliens resident in England, broke down. Not all British subjects are resident in England, and resident aliens frequently show a desire to return home.

Yet both classes of persons appear at first sight to run the risk of committing an act of bankruptcy in England by showing a preference for their foreign home. The Court of Appeal in *Ex p. Crispin*[45] negatived this view by stating:

'If a domiciled Englishman, who is being pressed by his creditors, and has been served with a writ, were to leave England, and so to escape being served with a debtor's summons, there would be strong evidence that he intended to defeat or delay his creditors, because England is the proper, if not the only place for him to be made a bankrupt in, and if he cannot pay his debts, he has no right to avoid being made a bankrupt there.[46] But we do not think that the same reasoning applies to a foreigner who comes to England for a temporary purpose and leaves England to return to his own home ...'.

'A foreigner not domiciled in England, and not carrying on trade in England, who quits England without having committed an act of bankruptcy, cannot be made a bankrupt upon an alleged act of bankruptcy committed out of England'.[47] 'He can be followed to his own home'.[48] It may be argued that the distinction drawn in *Re Crispin* in respect of acts of bankruptcy in the sense of section 1 (1) (*d*) of the Act of 1914[49] concerns only the burden of proof.[50] It may be said that the intention to delay or to defeat creditors is more easily established when a person resident or trading in England departs from England than in the case of a person resident and trading abroad. However, the act of | bankruptcy defined in section 1 (1) (*d*) consists of an objective and of a subjective element. It would appear that the objective element is restricted to persons resident or trading in England at the time when the subjective element, the intent to defeat creditors, arises, and to those debtors resident or trading abroad who, upon leaving England, go underground abroad instead of returning to their usual place of residence or business. The objective element consists of departing out of England, or being out of England to remain out of England. In the first place, it would seem that a person not resident or trading in England who, being out of England remains out of England, cannot commit an act of bankruptcy in the

---

[45] (1873) L.R. 8 Ch. 374 at p. 381.
[46] See also *Re Brandon* (1884) 25 Ch.D. 500, 502.
[47] At p. 379. See also *Ex p. Pascal, re Myer* (1876) 1 Ch.D. 509, 512 (C.A.); *Cooke v. Chas. Vogeler Co.* [1901] A.C. 102.
[48] At p. 381. See also *Re Brandon* (1884) 25 Ch.D. 500, 502.
[49] Bankruptcy Act, 1869, s. 6 (3); Bankruptcy Act, 1883, s. 4 (1) (*d*).
[50] As regards burden of proof in s. 1 (1) (*d*), see *Re Wood* (1872) L.R. 7 Ch.App. 302.

sense of section 1 (1) (*d*), even if he intends to delay or defeat his creditors. It would seem to follow, in the second place, that a person who departs out of England, where he is not domiciled and after he has ceased to reside or trade in England, does not usually commit an act of bankruptcy either, if he goes home or sets up a new home abroad, seeing that both situations are treated in the same provision. The only exception would appear to be that the debtor was resident or trading in England when the debt arose, or was about to mature, and the debtor subsequently returned to his former home country or any other country abroad, having meanwhile given up his domicile, residence or business in England. To hold otherwise would mean to impose upon persons not resident or trading in England, a duty to appear in England in order to face their creditors, or to remain in England if they have reason to believe that there are English creditors.

An examination of the practice of English courts does not yield a clear-cut result. In most cases where section 1 (1) (*d*) or its forerunners were invoked the debtor was a trader domiciled and carrying on business in England[51] who had gone abroad where he had no residence or business. In these cases it was held uniformly that the departure or the sojourn abroad coupled with the inevitable delay suffered by the creditors was an act of bankruptcy, seeing that a person must be deemed to have intended the natural consequences of his acts. However, in several cases the debtor carried on business in England and abroad and left England in order to return to his foreign house of trade.

In *Williams* v. *Nunn*[52] the debtor traded in England and in Ireland, where he resided. However, during the whole time of his residence in Dublin he continued to keep his former house in London; his name was upon the door and his wife and family resided there continually. The petition was heard upon the debtor's departure for Ireland. Chambre J. directed the jury that the | statute was not restrained to such persons only who resided in England but extended to all natural born subjects.[53] Upon a motion for a new trial, Mansfield C.J. expressed himself more cautiously. He said: 'It does not exactly appear how long he was here before he again returned to Ireland, but on the facts of this case he is as little a resident out of this country and as little entitled to take that objection as can well be supposed. ... While he is in England, a creditor is, as plaintiff thinks, about to arrest him. He instantly quits England and returns to Ireland. Is not this an act of bankruptcy? ... he may be arrested here and ... *if he lies in prison for two months he will be a*

---

[51] See, *e.g., Re Woodier* (1739) Bull.N.P. 39; *Raikes* v. *Poreau* (1786) Cooke's Bankrupt Laws 80; *Re Osborne* (1813) 2 V. & B. 177; *Ex p. Kilner, re Bryant* (1837) 3 M. & A. 722; *Ex p. Bunney* (1857) 1 De G. & J. 309; *Ex p. Goater, re Finney* (1874) 30 L.T. 620; *Ex p. Campbell, re Campbell* (1887) 4 Mor. 198.

[52] (1809) 1 Taunt. 270.

[53] Mansfield C.J. observed that it also extended to aliens.

bankrupt. To avoid an arrest he runs away, and it is said that this makes a distinction. I will suppose that in returning to Ireland he is going to his house or place of trade; but he does not go as for the purpose of going home; by his own confession it is to avoid arrest. If he was not liable to the bankrupt laws of this country immediately upon his landing here, how long was it necessary that he must stay before that liability would accrue? Everyman coming hither knows that he must be subject to the law, and any personal contact which he makes may be enforced according to law. It seems ... to be ... a necessary consequence ... that *if to avoid the process of the country he goes away so that no proceedings by action can be taken against him he shall be nevertheless liable to the other mode which the law points out, namely, a commission of bankruptcy'.*

The same question arose in *Windham* v. Paterson[54] where Lord Ellenborough said: 'He might be going for the very purpose of procuring funds for the payment of his creditors. If he departed with a bona fide intention to return he committed no act of bankruptcy, although in fact he never did return. No doubt a trader must be presumed to contemplate the consequences of his absence. *A creditor certainly has a right to the person of his debtor for the purpose of application and importunity,*[55] but still, if he departs with an honest intention compatible with business he does not commit an act of bankruptcy'.

Gibbs C.J. in *Warner* v. *Barber*[56] expressed himself in the same sense when he said:

'That (he) withdrew himself from such creditors as were disposed to arrest him is clear from the facts; the question is: was the going abroad an act of bankruptcy? It is undeniable that (his) creditors were delayed. But if there be no intent to delay, the circumstance of departing from the realm whereby delay is occasioned is no act of bankruptcy. (He) had a right to go abroad to look after his property. If he went abroad from this motive, though delay was a consequence, yet, if not intended, it is not an act of | bankruptcy, but *if he went abroad from the other cause, the fear of arrest,* though it concurred with the first and justifiable motive ... it is an *act of bankruptcy'.*

It appears that in these cases the courts were guided by two considerations. First, by departing the realm, the debtor deprived his creditors of their most effective means, at that time, of obtaining a commission of bankruptcy. It was provided by 1 Jac. 1, c. 15, and by subsequent Bankruptcy Acts until the modern codification in 1869[57] that lying in prison for a specified period as a result of being arrested and committed to prison for debt, of any attach-

---

[54] (1815) 1 Stark. 144; 2 Rose 466.
[55] See also *Holroyd* v. *Whitehead* (1814) 3 Camp. 530.
[56] (1816) Holt N.P. 175.
[57] See 6 Geo. 4, c. 16 (1825), s. 5; 12 & 13 Vict. c. 106, s. 69; 24 & 25 Vict. c. 134, s. 71.

ment for non-payment of money or of detention for a debt, was an act of bankruptcy. By his departure the debtor effectively prevented the creditors from taking steps towards obtaining a commission of bankruptcy. The introduction of debtor's summonses[58] and the possibility, created in 1883,[59] of serving bankruptcy notices abroad removed the greater part of the obstacles which formerly prevented the courts from assuming jurisdiction in bankruptcy once the debtor had departed the realm. Second, the provisions of the Common Law Procedure Act, 1852, c. 76, ss. 18, 19, allowing service of notices of writs abroad, now developed in Order XI of the Rules of the Supreme Court, enabled creditors in a great number of instances to take proceedings by action against debtors who had gone abroad. This removed the additional ground, set out in *Williams* v. *Nunn*,[60] for treating a debtor's departure from England as an act of bankruptcy. As a result it was to be expected that the courts would adopt a more lenient attitude towards debtors who departed from England. This change becomes apparent in those cases where the debtor, although domiciled in England, had a residence abroad to which he returned. In *Ex p. Brandon, re Trench*,[61] the Earl of Selborne L.C. said:

'The question whether such an act of bankruptcy has been committed must be considered with regard to the circumstances of the foreign residence of the debtor. ... Assuming that he retained his English domicile, still the original constitution of his foreign residence cannot, as far as the evidence goes, be said to have taken place with the intention of defeating or delaying his creditor.

'*I cannot leave out of consideration that France is a civilized country in which creditors can sue their debtors.* It does not appear that the petitioning creditors have been in any way baffled by the debtor in the pursuit of their remedy against him. Can we, upon | the principle that man must be taken to intend the natural consequences of his acts, say that he remained out of England with intent to defeat or delay his creditors? *If a debtor had left this country in order to place himself beyond the reach of its laws*, the presumption that by so doing he intended to defeat or delay his creditors might arise, but the present case is entirely different'.

Thus it would appear that in the absence of special circumstances a debtor who returns to his foreign residence where he can be sued and served with notices concerning proceedings in England does not, and possibly cannot,

---

[58] Now s. 1 (1) (g) of the Bankruptcy Act, 1914.

[59] Bankruptcy Rules, 1883, r. 148 (see 53 L.J.Ch. 2), now Bankruptcy Rules, 1915, r. 158. It is interesting to note that *Re Crispin* was decided prior to the introduction of this provision.

[60] (1809) 1 Taunt. 270.

[61] (1884) 25 Ch.D. 500 (C.A.).

commit thereby an act of bankruptcy in the sense of section 1 (1) (*d*). This view is supported by the decision of the Court of Appeal in *Ex p. Langworthy, re Langworthy.*[62] Here the debtor, who was domiciled in England and had a residence in Argentina, where he had a business, left England for Buenos Ayres but broke his journey in France and Portugal. In these circumstances Lindley L.J. said: '... no doubt the debtor meant to go to Buenos Ayres to his property there, but he went to France and to Portugal with intent to defeat or delay the creditor who was before the court'.

The principle arising from these cases may be formulated in one of two ways, one of which stresses the subjective, the other the objective element in section 1 (1) (*d*) of the Act of 1914.

(1) It may be said that in the case of a debtor resident or trading in England a departure from England raises a presumption that the debtor intended to defeat or delay his creditors and that no such presumption arises in the case of a debtor, whether trading in England or not, who returns home. In the latter case evidence of the intent to delay or defeat creditors must be adduced.

(2) Alternatively it may be said that in the absence of special circumstances the act of returning home, if the debtor resides abroad, is not a departure in the sense of section 1 (1) (*d*) and that a debtor residing abroad cannot commit an act of bankruptcy in the sense of section 1 (1) (*d*) unless he goes abroad without returning to his home.

The combined effect of the cases appears to be that in spite of the somewhat obscure language employed by the court in *Re Crispin* – notably its use of the terms 'Englishman' and 'foreigner' – a further rule of the conflict of laws was added in respect of what is now section 1 (1) (*d*). Owing to the nature of the act of 'departing out of England, or being out of England, to remain out of England', the rule combines the features of a rule of jurisdiction in respect of the person and of a rule concerning the nature of the subject-matter.

In its original form, before section 1 (2) of the Act of 1914 introduced a uniform principle of jurisdiction in respect of the person of the debtor, it may perhaps be paraphrased as follows:

| In order to commit an act of bankruptcy in the sense of section 1 (1) (*d*)–

1. A British subject or alien domiciled[63] and resident in England must have left England with intent to delay or defeat his creditors. This intent is presumed if creditors have been in fact delayed.

2. A British subject domiciled but not resident in England must have left

---

[62] (1885) 3 T.L.R. 544.

[63] It appears that in the cases discussed above, and in particular in *Re Crispin* and in *Re Brandon*, the term domicile was not necessarily used in its technical sense.

England for a destination other than his ordinary residence or place of business.

3. An alien not domiciled in England and not resident or carrying on trade in England must have left England after having committed an act of bankruptcy in England.[64] But

4. An alien not domiciled in England and not resident or carrying on trade in England who has left England before committing an act of bankruptcy does not commit an act of bankruptcy by departing from or by remaining out of England.

The first and second propositions were discussed in *Re Brandon*[65] and in *Re Langworthy*[66] where the court pointed out that the foreign residence of the debtor must be considered. The third proposition was originally laid down in *Re Crispin (supra)* and was followed in *Ex p. Gutierrez*[67] which involved a debtor's summons against an alien who had come to England for a temporary purpose and had then returned home. James L.J. said: 'I should not have thought it possible, after the distinction between an Englishman and a foreigner had been so clearly explained by Mellish L.J. in *Ex p. Crispin* that such an order could have been made'.[68]

Section 1 (2) of the Act of 1914 modified the rule only in so far as it abolished the distinction between British subjects and aliens and clarified doubts by replacing 'domicile' by 'residence'. The term 'person' must therefore be substituted for 'British subject' and 'alien'. There is *jurisdiction* over British subjects and aliens alike if at the time when the act of bankruptcy they (a) were personally present in England or (b) were ordinarily resident or had a place of residence in England, or (c) carried on business in England personally or by means of an agent or manager, or (d) were members of a firm or a partnership which carried on business in England.

An *act of bankruptcy* in the sense of section 1 (1) (*d*) is committed if with intent to delay or defeat their creditors they depart from England or remain out of England in the circumstances defined in clauses (*a*)–(*d*) of section 1 (2). It has been shown|that a person residing abroad who fulfils the requirements establishing jurisdiction according to section 1 (2) (*c*) and (*d*) does not easily commit the act of departing out of England if he carries on his business by means of an agent or manager, or if, while residing abroad, he is a member of a firm or a partnership carrying on business in England. Certainly such a person does not commit an act of bankruptcy by remaining out of England. The requirements of section 1 (2) and section 1 (1) (*d*) overlap, but they do not coincide.

---

[64] Thus the effect of s. 1 (1) (*d*) is purely nominal in this case.
[65] (1884) 25 Ch.D. 500, 502.
[66] (1885) 3 T.L.R. 544.
[67] (1879) 11 Ch.D. 298.
[68] At p. 312.

3. Section 1 (1) (a)–(c)

We must now turn to section 1 (1) (*a*)–(*c*) of the Act of 1914 whereby certain transactions in England or elsewhere are declared to be acts of bankruptcy for the purpose of the Act. It is clear, in the first place, that this choice of law clause does not define the circle of persons who are affected by the operation of the provision. This was not done until 1914, when the rule of the conflict of laws which is now embodied in section 1 (2), and which was discussed above, was made to extend to the transactions mentioned in section 1 (1) (*a*)–(*c*). It is clear, in the second place, that in the absence before 1914 of a rule of the conflict of laws determining jurisdiction over the person of the debtor the choice of law clauses in respect of the transactions set out in section 1 (1) (*a*)–(*c*) were too wide. Here again, the Court of Appeal in *Re Crispin* provided the corrective by adding a proviso to the choice of law clause. Not every conveyance in England or elsewhere of the kind enumerated in section 1 (1) (*a*)–(*c*) is an act of bankruptcy. No doubt it is an act of bankruptcy if carried out in England, but if executed abroad, it is so only if the conveyance is to operate according to English law. This was the view expressed by Mellish L.J.,[69] who drew from this premise the following conclusions:–

Only a conveyance executed abroad by a person domiciled in England is caught by the Act, being a conveyance governed by English law. A conveyance executed abroad by a person domiciled abroad is not an act of bankruptcy, being governed by foreign law. The House of Lords in *Cooke* v. *Chas. Vogeler Co.*[70] approved the rule and the Court of Appeal in *Re Debtor (No. 836 of 1935)*[71] followed this view.

Nevertheless, it would appear that the choice of law clause in its amended form, like every choice of law clause which is expressed in terms of domestic law and not of the conflict of laws, has only partially achieved its purpose. As the law now stands, a conveyance abroad of movables in England may be an act of bankruptcy for the purpose of section 1 (1) (*a*)–(*c*) if executed by a person | domiciled in England. Again, every conveyance abroad of immovables, and possibly of individual movables, in England, whether executed by a person domiciled in England or abroad, may constitute an act of bankruptcy. On the other hand, no universal assignment abroad by a person domiciled abroad of movables in England is caught by the Act, notwithstanding that the conveyance may operate in England as a universal assignment.[72] This omission could have been remedied if the words of Mellish L.J.

---

[69] (1873) L.R. 8 Ch.D. 374, 380.
[70] [1901] A.C. 102, 113.
[71] [1936] Ch. 622.
[72] But see *Dulany* v. *Merry* [1901] 1 Q.B. 536.

had been understood to include every conveyance which is to operate according to English law, including its rules of the conflict of laws. However, it is probably too late to remedy this defect and certainly too late to substitute for the test laid down by Mellish L.J. to the effect that the conveyance must operate according to English law, the more general criterion that it must operate in England, *i.e.*, according to English domestic law or the English rules of conflict of laws. In its present form the rule in *Cooke* v. *Chas. Vogeler Co.* (*supra*) is perhaps to be explained on the ground that it purports to apply the principle of the division of legislative competence. If the bankruptcy laws apply to all British subjects who fulfil the conditions of section 1 (2), and if English law governs all British subjects (which it does not), then the rule is in accordance with principle. The same applies to the converse rule applicable in the case of aliens. However, the premise is false, since British nationality does not attract the application of English law.

Once the original choice of law clause in the Bankruptcy Acts of 1869 and 1883 had been thus restricted, the need for a choice of law clause determining jurisdiction over the person of the debtor had practically disappeared, but it would seem that the 'negative and restrictive provision'[73] now contained in section 1 (2) of the Act of 1914, while creating a uniform jurisdiction in respect of the persons subject to the Act for all situations covered by section 1 (1), has not altered the substance of the choice of law clause in respect of the type of the transaction in any substantial degree.

To sum up

(1) Section 1 (2) provides a rule of the conflict of laws determining the jurisdiction over the person of the debtor which applies to all acts of bankruptcy enumerated in section 1 (1).

(2) Section 1 (1) (*a*)–(*c*) is limited by a rule of the conflict of laws in respect of the type of transaction covered by the Act.

(3) Section 1 (1) (*d*) is limited by a separate rule of the conflict of laws which combines the features of a rule determining the type of transaction and the class of debtor covered by the Act.

---

[73] *Cooke* v. *Chas. Vogeler Co.* [1901] A.C. 102, 113, *per* Lord Davey.

| III. Recent Trends

In the light of the principles developed above it is now possible to examine the conclusions of the Court of Appeal in *Re a Debtor (No. 335 of* 1947).[74]

A Roumanian citizen, who had a place of residence in England where he carried on a business, appealed against assessments in respect of unpaid excess profits tax. On the day when the assessments were confirmed he left England for Eire and did not return. He sent his wife a power of attorney in exercise of which she sold the business.

The Crown obtained an order giving leave to serve a bankruptcy petition out of the jurisdiction in accordance with rule 158 of the Bankruptcy Rules, 1915. This order was discharged on the ground that leave to serve out of the jurisdiction could not be granted seeing that the debtor was a foreigner residing abroad and therefore not subject to the jurisdiction of the bankruptcy laws.

The Court of Appeal held that there was jurisdiction.

The case involved three questions. First, does the Bankruptcy Act, 1914, extend to aliens? The wording of section 1 (2) of the Bankruptcy Act answered this question in the affirmative. Second, was the debtor a 'debtor' in the sense of section 1 (2) of the Act which provides: '... the expression "a debtor", unless the context otherwise implies, includes any person, whether a British subject or not, who at the time when any act of bankruptcy was done or suffered by him ... (*c*) was carrying on business in England, personally, or by means of an agent or manager'? The Court of Appeal held that notwithstanding that he had left England before the act of bankruptcy occurred and had sold the business, he was so carrying on business for he had unpaid debts. The court relied on the combined operation of the Married Women's Property Act, 1882, s. 1 (5), the Bankruptcy and Deeds of Arrangement Act, 1913, s. 12 (1), the Bankruptcy Act, 1914, s. 25, as well as on *Re Dagnall*[75]; *Re Clark*.[76] Third, was an act of bankruptcy in the sense of section 1 (1) (*d*) of the Bankruptcy Act committed by the debtor, an alien, who, having given up his business and his residence in England, remained out of England? The Court of Appeal had no doubt that a strong prima facie case had been made out.[77]

---

[74] [1948] 2 All E.R. 533; 64 T.L.R. 446.

[75] [1896] 2 Q.B. 407.

[76] [1914] 3 K.B. 1095.

[77] The petition did not rely on the first part of s. 1 (1) (*d*), *viz.*, that the debtor had departed out of England with intent to defeat or delay his creditors. This ground was excluded by s. 4 (1) (*c*), in view of the delay in the presentation of the petition.

1. Jurisdiction in respect of the person of the debtor

As shown above, it was recognised more than seventy years ago that the bankruptcy laws extend to aliens. Section 1 (2) of the | Act of 1914 which repeats this rule is merely declaratory of an established practice. Inasmuch as section 1 (2), which defines the term 'debtor' for the purpose of the Act, added the requirement that the debtor must fulfil a residence qualification or must have traded in England, the Act adopted and extended a principle enunciated in older statutes and in previous decisions where it was restricted to aliens. It now appears that its express application to British subjects has opened a dangerous path. The principle purported to reflect the division of jurisdictions among different countries, as derived from a division of legislative competence. The Court of Appeal held that it was impossible 'that the reference to carrying on business in the definition of a debtor is to be construed in a different way from the corresponding reference in relation to married women' (section 125, which was repealed by 25 & 26 Geo. 5, c. 30, Second Schedule) and thus extended the meaning of 'carrying on business' in England to that of 'having unpaid debts'[78] in England.

These considerations, taken from the domestic rule as to whether or not a woman in England was to remain subject to the Bankruptcy laws after having ceased to trade, are applied by the Court of Appeal to determine international jurisdiction where the question was whether a trader who had given up his business and had gone abroad remained subject to English courts. The work of the courts during the past seventy years is disregarded, restricting and defining the conditions under which a foreigner is subject to English bankruptcy law – described above as the 'First Phase' – and a situation is restored which existed before the decision in *Re Crispin*. The words of James L.J. in *Re Gutierrez* (*supra*) ring true once again: 'I should not have thought it possible, after the distinction between an Englishman and a foreigner had been so clearly explained by Mellish L.J. in *Ex p. Crispin* that such an order could have been made'.

The fact that the Married Women's Property Act had not been passed when *Re Crispin* was decided does not appear to affect the issue for the reason set out above.

---

[78] At p. 537.

2. Jurisdiction in respect of the type of transaction

(a) Section 1 (1) (d)

By reading the words concerning jurisdiction over the person of the debtor of section 1 (2) in their extended form as developed by the Court of Appeal into the relevant subsection (*d*) of section 1 (1), which defines the acts of bankruptcy, the court precluded itself from considering the rule of the conflict of laws concerning the type of transaction which was developed during what has been described above as the 'Second Phase'.

At the time when the alleged act of bankruptcy was committed | by remaining out of England with intent to defraud his creditors, the appellant was neither present nor resident in England, and even if it should be assumed with the Court of Appeal that for the purpose of establishing jurisdiction according to section 1 (2) the appellant must be deemed to be carrying on business in England because he had unpaid debts there, it cannot be assumed that he must be deemed to be carrying on business *in person*. Personal trading, however, is necessary in order to constitute an act of bankruptcy in the sense of section 1 (1) (*d*), while trading by means of an agent or through members of a firm or partnership and, it is believed, by means of a notional business, does not.

The authorities are somewhat inconclusive seeing that they either date from the time before the decision in *Re Crispin*,[79] or that the debtor, being domiciled and ordinarily resident in England went underground abroad after having departed in good faith on legitimate business.[80] However, it would appear that, in the absence of continued personal trading in England, no act of bankruptcy is committed if the debtor returns to his home abroad and remains there, if he can be reached. It may therefore be relevant whether the debtor returned to his established residence abroad and whether he could either be served there with a bankruptcy notice arising out of an act other than that mentioned in section 1 (1) (*d*), or whether notice of a writ could be served upon him and whether he could be sued there. In the absence of a previous residence abroad and failing the means of reaching him or enforcing a claim there, it may well be that an act of bankruptcy in the sense of section 1 2(1) (*d*) was committed. But it would appear that in the absence of evidence to this effect the appellant had not committed an act of bankruptcy in the meaning of section 1 (1) (*d*). To assume the contrary would be to act in the teeth of the decision of the same court in *Re Brandon* (*supra*).

---

[79] (1873) L.R. 374.
[80] Compare *Ex p. Kilner, re Bryant* (1837) 3 M. & A. 722; *Ex p. Bunney* (1857) 1 De G. & J. 309 at p. 314, with *Re Campbell* (1887) 4 Mor. 198.

As shown above, it is a well-established principle 'that a foreigner ... in England is subject to the bankruptcy laws, but it is the act of bankruptcy which gives the court jurisdiction, and in the case of a foreigner that act of bankruptcy must be committed in this country'.[81] The Court of Appeal held that for this proposition to be true today 'there must be implied somewhere in the relevant words a restriction of the operation of these provisions in the case of a person being out of England who is not a British subject. ... it is quite impossible to make such an implication and the argument that a British statute does not apply to an act done by a foreigner out of this country seems to me to be entirely misplaced, because in this case the British legislature has said that | it shall apply'.[82] However, as shown above, the rule concerning jurisdiction over the person of the debtor laid down in section 1 (2) did not add an extension of the Bankruptcy Act to foreigners by equating it to the jurisdiction exercised over British subjects. Generally speaking, it did the reverse, by restricting the jurisdiction over British subjects to the limit of jurisdiction exercised over foreigners. Moreover, it did not extend English jurisdiction as developed in respect of the nature of the act of bankruptcy.

(b) Section 1 (1) (a)–(c)

The rules of the conflict of laws concerning the types of transactions covered by the Act as developed by the courts in respect of section 1 (1) (a)–(d) were not touched by the Act of 1914. This was recognised by the Court of Appeal inasmuch as Lord Greene discussed at length the relevant passages in *Cooke v. Chas. Vogeler Co. (supra)* and *Re Debtors (No. 836 of* 1935) *(supra)* which laid down that the conveyances envisaged in section 1 (1) (a)–(c) must operate according to English law. If this rule was not abrogated by the Act of 1914 it would appear that the rule of the conflict of laws developed with regard to section 1 (1) (d) by the decisions in *Re Crispin, Ex p. Pascal, Re Brandon* and *Ex p. Gutierrez* and others should also have been taken into account, for the petition before the court was based on section 1 (1) (d) and not on section 1 (1) (a)–(c).

The observations of the court in respect to *Cooke v. Chas. Vogeler Co.* and *Re Debtors (No. 836 of* 1935) to the effect that conveyances abroad in order to be caught by section 1 (1) (a)–(c) must operate according to English law were merely obiter. However, in view of the criticisms raised above when discussing the rule laid down in these cases, it is interesting to note that by stressing the importance of an English domicile, the sphere of operation of section 1 (1) (a)–(c) remains severely restricted. The hope that universal

---

[81] *Per* Lord Davey in *Cooke v. Chas. Vogeler Co.* [1901] A.C. 102, 113.
[82] [1948] 2 All E.R. 533 at p. 539.

assignments by a person domiciled abroad of movables in England may be caught by section 1 (1) (*a*)–(*c*) would thus appear to be more remote than ever, although in every other respect such an assignment will be recognised here. However, in two passages Lord Greene referred to the test whether the assignment is intended to operate by the laws of England.[83] Since intention is irrelevant in the conflict of laws regarding movables, and since it is agreed that universal assignments of movables are not governed by the *lex situs*, there is some ground for holding that these words have the following meaning: a conveyance by a person domiciled abroad may be caught by section 1 (1) (*a*)–(*c*) if the assignor intends to assign movables in England and the assignment operates here whether in virtue of English domestic law or of |foreign law which is applicable according to the English rules of the conflict of laws.

Following *Ex p. Blain, re Sowers*,[84] the court discussed the question whether an English statute which extends to a limited number of foreigners is contrary to the comity of nations, and found that it was not. This question can arise only if we accept the original Dutch doctrine which assumed a division of legislative competence. Today this doctrine is on the whole discarded, and it is recognised that each country is free to determine when its own law and when foreign law is to be applied. The only limit is that imposed by international law which prohibits illegal discrimination and requires the observance of the minimum standards of civilised nations. Be that as it may, an English court is bound to apply an English statute even if contrary to international law, but if possible the statute must be interpreted so as not to conflict with international law.[85] Nevertheless, as shown above, the doctrine may be still useful where it is necessary unilaterally to limit the application of English administrative, criminal and bankruptcy law, and the development traced here has been much influenced by it. However, no cases can be found where foreign countries have complained when the usual limits of jurisdiction over persons and transactions were exceeded. The Court of Appeal examined this question in the light of possible violations of the comity of nations. It may be that this term embraces the principles here discussed under the head of international law. If the court wished to refer to the principle of comity developed by the Dutch school where it served to explain why foreign law must be applied by the courts of the forum, it is difficult to see how this principle can be applied here.

---

[83] [1948] 2 All E.R. 533 at pp. 540, 542.
[84] (1879) 12 Ch.D. 522, 527, 529.
[85] *Mortensen* v. *Peters* (1906) 14 S.L.T. 227; 43 S.L.R. 872. Lauterpacht in (1939) 25 Transactions of the Grotius Society, 51 ff.

To sum up: If the principles here advanced are applied to *Re a Debtor* (*No.* 335 *of* 1947),[86] it follows that English courts had no jurisdiction on the ground that there was no jurisdiction–

(a) over the person of the debtor according to section 1 (2) of the Act of 1914; and

(b) in respect of the transaction according to section 1 (1) (*d*) of the same Act, in the absence of evidence of the nature indicated above (III (2) (a)).

In these circumstances it is impossible to seek for an alternative remedy in the provisions of section 122 of the Act of 1914 (which still applies in Eire), according to which bankruptcy courts in the Empire act as auxiliaries to each other. There is also little comfort in the advice given by the Court of Appeal in *Re Crispin* (*supra*)[87] | and in *Re Brandon* (*supra*)[88] to the effect that the creditor can follow the debtor to his own home, seeing that the claim in the case under review was based on a revenue law which may possibly be disregarded abroad.

---

[86] [1948] 2 All E.R. 533; 64 T.L.R. 446.
[87] At p. 381.
[88] At p. 503.

Recognition of Governments and the Application of Foreign Laws

The aim of this paper is to re-open an old problem which, for the purposes of English Courts, appears at first sight to have been put at rest by the Court of Appeal in *Luther* v. *Sagor*.[1] This decision can claim to have increased its authority by lapse of time, but it has not yet been endorsed by the House of Lords, except perhaps by *some dicta* in *Russian Commercial and Industrial Bank* v. *Comptoir d'Escompte de Mulhouse*.[2] However, if these dicta are taken literally, the *ratio decidendi* in this case is not easily to be reconciled with that of the same House in *Lazard Bros.* v. *Midland Bank*[3] and, as will be shown below, there is no compelling reason for holding that *Luther* v. *Sagor* in its undiluted form cannot now be interpreted restrictively. In a leading

---

[Editorial note: first published in Transactions of the Grotius Society 35 (1949), 157–188.]

[1] [1921] 3 K.B. 532; see also *Brazosco* v. *Sagor* (1921) 8 LL.L.R. 388; *Walneff* v. *All-Russian Co-operative Society* (1921) 9 LL.L.R. 527.
[2] [1925] A.C. 112, 123–24, per Viscount Cave; see Wortley in *Transactions of the Grotius Society*, 33 (1948), pp. 25, 32.
[3] [1933] AC. 289.

textbook,[4] the rule in *Luther* v. *Sagor*[5] is | summed up thus: "Recognition being retroactive and dating back to the moment at which the newly recognized Government established itself in power, its effect is to preclude the Courts of law of the recognizing State from questioning the legality or validity of the acts both legislative and executive, past and future, of that Government; it therefore validates, as far as concerns those courts of law, certain transfers of property and other transactions which before recognition they would have treated as invalid." The case, it will be remembered, dealt with a consignment of timber shipped to England from Russia. The timber was originally the property of the plaintiffs, but the Russian Government had confiscated it, and sold it to the defendants. In the Court of Appeal in England the title of the defendants prevailed over that of the plaintiff. The reasons which led the Court of Appeal to this conclusion are usually summed up in terms similar to those set out in Oppenheim, but it is suggested here: (1) that this interpretation overstresses the arguments of Warrington, L. J. to the detriment of those of Bankes and Scrutton, L. J. J.; (2) that even if the leading principle should be that laid down by Warrington, L. J., such a principle was absent in English law prior to this decision, and did not necessarily follow from the American cases upon which the Court of Appeal, relied; (3) that the principle, as stated at present is: (a) vague and ill-defined and constitutes a slogan rather than a rule, if recognition has been accorded, and that it requires a new restrictive interpretation; (b) too rigid and leads to unjust or even absurd results if recognition has not been accorded.

Analysis of the decision in Luther v. Sagor

Warrington, L. J., in a judgment which has caught the imagination of Courts and writers alike said: "It is well settled that the validity of the acts of an independent sovereign Government in relation to property and persons

---

[4] Oppenheim, *International Law* (7th ed. 1948), Vol. I., p. 133, and Note 2 (literature), p. 296; See also Lauterpacht, *Recognition in International Law* (1947), pp. 145–157; McNair, *Legal Effects of War* (3rd ed. 1948), pp. 358–374. Hervey, *Legal Effects of Recognition in International Law* (1928), pp. 138–155; Spiropoulos, *Die de facto Regierung im Völkerrecht* (1926), pp. 140–158; Kunz, *Die Anerkennung von Staaten und Regierungen im Völkerrecht* (1928), pp. 152–164; Noel-Henry, *Les Gouvernements de Fait devant le Juge* (1927), p. 95, No. 90–, p. 109, No. 102; p. 122, No. 112; p. 133, No. 123 – p. 145, No. 129; p. 149, No. 137 – p. 170, No. 149; p. 174, No. 153 – p. 179, No. 157; Kleist, *Die Völkerrechtliche Anerkennung Sowjetrusslands* (1934), pp. 48–66; Schlüter, *De Facto Anerkennung im Völkerrecht* (1936), pp. 114–130; Stierlin, *Die Rechtsstellung der Nichtanerkannten Regierung im Völkerrecht* (1940), pp. 48–111; Tenekides, *Clunet.* 52 (1925), p. 1143.

[5] See above, Note 1.

within its jurisdiction cannot be questioned in the Courts of this country ... Every sovereign State is bound to respect the independence of every other sovereign State, and the Courts of one country will not sit in judgment on the acts of the Government of another within its own territory."[6] On the other hand, Bankes, L. J. approached the question from a point of view which recalls principles of private rather than of public international law. He said: "The question | is as to the title of goods lying in a foreign country which a subject of that country has sold under a f.o.b. contract ... to this country. The Court is asked to ignore the law of the foreign country under which the vendor acquired title and to lend its assistance to prevent the purchaser dealing with the goods."[7] It is probably permissible to assume that by these words Bankes L. J. wished to express in guarded language that he was apply- ing the *lex rei sitæ*.[8] Scrutton, L. J., followed an independent and, it is be- lieved, indefensible train of thought. He discussed the rules relating to the immunity of foreign Governments as laid down in *The Parlement Belge*,[9] *Vavasseur* v. *Krupp*[10] and *Morgan* v. *Larrivière*.[11] From these he concluded: "What the Court cannot do directly, it ... cannot do indirectly. If it could not question the title to goods brought by that Government to England, it can- not indirectly question it in the hands of a purchaser from that Government by denying that the Government could confer title to the property."[12] This argument is fallacious and has been disproved by subsequent events. In the first place, as the House of Lords has pointed out in *R.* v. *International Trustee Bondholders, A.G.,*[13] exemption of a foreign Government from ju- risdiction does not necessarily require the application of the law of that Government to all its transactions. In the second place, the Court of Appeal, in the *Jupiter*[14] saw no obstacle to the determination by an English Court of the title of a purchaser from the Russian Government which had obtained possession of a ship belonging to private persons and had sold it subsequent- ly. There is, it must be admitted, a distinction between the *Jupiter* and *Luther* v. *Sagor*, for in the former the ship was not in Russia at any relevant moment, while the timber which formed the object of the claim in *Luther* v. *Sagor* had been situated in Russia. On the other hand, the Russian Government, in

---

[6] at pp. 548–49, see also Scrutton and Sankey, L. JJ. in *Princess Olga Paley* v. *Weiss* [1929] 1 K.B. 725, 728.

[7] at p. 545.

[8] The reference on p. 545 to *Santos* v. *Illidge* (1860), 8. C.B. (N.S.), 861, 876 bears out this view.

[9] (1880) Q. 5 P.D. 197, 217.

[10] (1878) 9 Ch. D. 351.

[11] (1875) 7 H.L. 423, 430.

[12] at p. 555.

[13] [1937] A.C. 500.

[14] [1927] P. 250.

selling the *Jupiter*, must have purported to make title according to Russian law, whereby ships abroad may, or may not|have been confiscated.[15] Be that as it may: the question before the Courts in *Luther* v. *Sagor* and in the *Jupiter* was either a question of private international law, or it was a question whether executive acts of foreign Governments in their own country and abroad are entitled to the respect of English Courts. If the latter is correct, we are confronted with a problem of the conflict of laws in matters of administrative law, about which little is known as yet. Both Bankes and Warrington, L. J. J., appear to have considered the problem as one more in the nature of private than of public international law, for they both discussed whether Russian law was excluded in the circumstances as contravening English principles of public policy. They both denied that the relevant rule of Russian law was contrary to English public policy; Bankes, L. J. did so after considering the character of the Russian legislation;[16] Warrington, L. J.[17] sought guidance in the previous cases on public policy. He dismissed *Kaufmann* v. *Gerson*[18] as inapplicable and cited with approval *Santos* v. *Illidge*[19], which would probably not be followed in modern conditions. Scrutton, L. J., on the other hand, preferred to base himself upon public international law. He said: "Should there be any Government which appropriates other people's property without compensation, the remedy appears to be to refuse to recognize it as a sovereign State. Then the Courts could investigate the title without infringing the comity of nations ... But it appears a serious breach of international comity if a State is recognized as a sovereign independent State to postulate that its legislation is contrary to essential principles of justice and|morality. Such an allegation might well with a susceptible foreign Government become a *casus belli*; and should ... be the action of the sovereign through his ministers and not of the judges in reference to a State which their sovereign has recognized."[20] He concluded by finding that, in any case, the legislation in question was not against public policy. It goes

---

[15] It is irrelevant here that in the opinion of the Court of Appeal the Russian legislation in virtue of which the transfer of title to the Russian Government could have been asserted did not purport to affect property outside Russia. What is relevant is that the Court of Appeal relied primarily on a test established by private international law which may have been the law of the flag or the *lex situs*. For before it can be examined whether certain Russian laws according to their tenor purported to affect a factual situation which was under review by an English Court, it must be established that according to the English rules of conflict of laws Russian law applies at all.

[16] at p. 546.

[17] at pp. 548–49; compare Neumeyer, *Internationales Verwaltungsrecht* IV. (1936), p. 252.

[18] [1904] 1 K.B. 591.

[19] (1860) 8 C.B. (N.ü.) 861.

[20] at pp. 556, 558, 559; following *Oetjen* v. *Central Leather Co.* (1918), 246 U.S. 297, 304. But see Habicht in *A.J.*, 21 (1927), p. 238, Idelson, *Clunet*, 51 (1924), p. 28, at p. 37 n. 15.

without saying that, were Scrutton's view part of English law, the doctrine of public policy would have no place in it, and the only question would be not whether but in what circumstances the acts of foreign Governments, be they legislative, executive and judicial, must be respected by English Courts.

The Historical Basis of Luther v. Sagor

The decision in *Luther* v. *Sagor* is remarkable for the fact that the Court of Appeal was unable to refer to any English authorities and had to reply exclusively on the persuasive force of American decisions. This is, of course, a not unusual occurrence,[21] but it is doubtful whether the authorities relied upon by the Court of Appeal do in fact support the sweeping rules laid down by that Court. It is therefore appropriate to examine in some detail the three American decisions which have made English law. The first case was *Williams* v. *Bruffy* (1878).[22] This was an action of assumpsit for goods sold by the plaintiff to Jason N. Bruffy, since deceased. The action was brought some time after the Civil War had come to an end through the collapse of the Confederate States. The defendant pleaded, *inter alia*, that he was relieved by an Act of the Confederate States whereby all property belonging to persons resident in the North was sequestrated and all payments due to alien enemies had to be made to a receiver appointed by the Confederate Government. The plaintiff resided at all times in Pennsylvania and the defendant paid his debt to the receiver. There was no doubt that the law applicable in Virginia applied to the contract. The only question was whether the law of the Confederate States or of the United States governed the contract as the law applicable in Virginia. Upon appeal from the Supreme Court of Appeals in Virginia the United States | Supreme Court held, in the first place, that the enactment referred to was unconstitutional. In the second place, the Court rejected the argument that the enactment of the Confederation was valid, notwithstanding the United States Constitution, on the ground that it was legislation of an independent Government. The Supreme Court distinguished between a *de facto* Government exercising power over the whole of the country, such as the Commonwealth Government in England, and a secessional movement which was neither recognized by other countries nor succeeded in maintaining its separate existence. The Court was only concerned with the latter for the purpose of deciding the case under review. With respect to the latter, the Court said: "The validity of its Acts, both against the parent State and its citizens ... depends entirely upon its ultimate success. If

---

[21] See Kiralfy, *Tulane Law Review*, 23 (1848–49), pp. 209–217.
[22] 96 U.S. 176, 24. L. Ed. 716 (1878).

it fail to establish itself permanently, all such Acts perish with it. If it succeed, and become recognized, the Acts from the commencement of its existence are upheld as those of an independent *nation* ... It would be a strange thing if the nation, after succeeding in suppressing the rebellion and re-establishing its authority over the insurrectionary district should, by any of its tribunals, recognize as valid the attempt of the rebellious organisation to confiscate a debt due to a loyal citizen or a penalty for his loyalty ... When its military forces were overthrown, it utterly perished, and with it all its enact-ments."[23] It may be doubted whether there is a distinction in character, for the purpose of the problem before the Court, between a revolutionary Gov-ernment exercising authority over an entire country and a secessional Gov-ernment. It has been suggested that this distinction was motivated by the wish to differentiate between a foreign Government and a rebellious Gov-ernment within the boundaries of a Federal State. However, it is difficult to read such an opinion into the words of the decision.[24] A second possibility suggests itself. The Commonwealth Government of England was recog-nised as a Government; the Confederate Government was | not. It is true that the Supreme Court alluded to the fact that the Confederate States had not been recognised as a Government by any other Power, but the decisive factor was that it had not survived. It may therefore be suggested that the *ratio decidendi* in *Williams* v. *Bruffy*[25] was the purely negative principle to the effect that if according to the ordinary principles of the conflict of laws, the law of a particular country is to be applied, the enactments of insurrec-tionist authorities may be disregarded, if they have never been recognised and have not survived. Insofar as the Supreme Court referred to revolution-ary authorities which had been able to establish themselves permanently, and had become recognized, its observations are purely *obiter*. Nevertheless, it may be useful to recall these observations here. The Court said: "... such a Government is treated as in most respects possessing rightful authority; its contracts and treaties are usually enforced; its acquisitions are retained; its legislation is in general recognized; and the rights acquired under it are, with few exceptions, respected after the restoration of the authorities which were expelled." The words, expressed, it is believed, as *obiter dicta*, provided the basis of further developments. It should be noted, however, that the Su-preme Court went no further than to state that the legislation of a *de facto* recognized Government is in general recognised. This means, probably, that

---

[23] But see *United States* v. *Home Insurance Co.* 22 Wall. 99, 89 U.S. 99.
[24] But see Noel-Henry, loc. cit., p. 103, No. 98, pp. 174–177, Nos. 154, 154; *Texas* v. *White*, 7 Wall. 700, 703, 19 *L. Ed.* 227 (1869); *Sprott* v. *U.S.* 20 Wall, 459, 22 L.Ed. 371 (1874); *U.S.* v. *Home Insurance Co.*, 22 Wall, 9, 22 *L. Ed.* 816 (1875); *Baldy* v. *Hunter* 171 U.S. 388; 43 *L. Ed.* 208 (1898): note in (1924–25) 38 *Harv., L. R.* 816, 818.
[25] 96 U.S. 176.

such legislation will be applied, if the law of the foreign country concerned is applicable, and need not be applied if it is against public policy. The Supreme Court did not, and could not, lay down that the law of a foreign country must always be applied if its Government is recognised and if its legislation purports to apply to situations abroad. The principle was examined afresh in *Underhill* v. *Hernandez* (1897).[26] The pleadings do not emerge clearly from the report, but it appears to have been an action for damages brought in the United States for false imprisonment in Venezuela. Thus according to the general principles of the conflict of laws in the United States, the *lex loci delicti commissi* applied;[27] this was Venezuelan law. It follows that the action failed if the act of detention was lawful in Venezuela. The detention was carried out at the orders of | the defendant, an insurrectionist military commander. In due course, the insurrectionist Government was recognised by the United States. The action failed. The question was clearly whether the legality of the detention was to be decided by the law of Venezuela as it would have applied at the time of the detention (when the detention was unlawful seeing that the defendant was not the agent of a Government and that the orders of his superiors had not the force of law in Venezuela) or as it applied at the time of the action (when the detention was lawful with retroactive effect inside Venezuela, seeing that by then the defendant was an agent of the Government and the orders of his superiors had the force of law in Venezuela). For, as Mr. Justice Holmes said in *American Banana Co.* v. *United Fruit* Co.[28] "The very meaning of sovereign is that the decree of the sovereign makes law[29] ... the acts of the soldiers and officials of Costa Rica are not alleged to have been without the consent of the Government and must be taken to have been done by its order. It ratified them, at all events ... "[30] The Supreme Court held, rightly it is believed, that this was not a question of intertemporal conflict of laws, and applied the law of Venezuela as it would have applied had the insurrectionists already been recognized. In other words, the question was not whether the law of Venezuela applied or not; the question was only what the law of Venezuela was. In this respect, the Court added a second limb to the principle in *Williams* v. *Bruffy*.[31] This case had decided that acts of an unrecognised foreign government which failed to establish itself could not be regarded as laws or as lawful acts of the foreign

---

[26] 168 U.S. 250, 42 L. Ed. 456 (1897).

[27] Story, *Conflict of Laws* (*8th ed.* G. Bigelow), S. 625, p. 844, Note (a)

[28] 213 U.S. 347, 358, 53 L. Ed. 826 (1909).

[29] citing *Kawananaksa* v. *Polyblank.* 205 U.S. 349, 353; 51 L. Ed. 834, 836.

[30] citing *O'Reilley de Camara* v. *Brooke,* 209 U.S. 45, 52, 52 L. Ed. 676, 678; *The Paquete Habana,* 189 U.S. 453, 465, 247, L. Ed. 901, 903; *Dempsey* v. *Chambers,* 154 Mass. 330, 332, 26 Am. St. Rep. 249.

[31] 96 U.S. 176.

country so far as an American Court was concerned. It was now decided that such acts obtained the force of law or became lawful acts with retroactive effect, once recognition was granted. Once this question was also settled, an American Court had to treat the orders of the new Government as law, subject to the overriding power of American public policy. But it was not open for the plaintiff to complain before an American Court|that the law of Venezuela violated International Law by disregarding the minimum standards of justice or by introducing discriminatory treatment for aliens.[32] This is a matter of state responsibility which involves the home countries of plaintiff and defendant. It may lead to a claim for damages in an international tribunal or it may give rise to diplomatic intervention, but it does not permit or require the attention of American Courts when applying Venezuelan law. These considerations make it possible to read the observations of Fuller, C. J. in their proper light. He said: "Every sovereign State is bound to respect the independence of every other sovereign State, and the Courts of one country will not sit in judgment on the acts of the Government of another done within its own territory. Redress or grievance by reason of such acts must be obtained through the means open to be availed of by sovereign Powers as between themselves. Nor can the principle be confined to lawful or recognised Governments, or to cases where redress can manifestly be had through public channels. The immunity of individuals from suits brought in foreign tribunals for acts done within their own States, in the exercise of Governmental authority ... must necessarily extend to the agents or Governments ruling by paramount force as a matter of fact ... If the party seeking to dislodge the existing Government succeeds, and the independence of the Government it has set up is recognised, then the acts of such Government from the commencement of its existence are regarded as those of an independent nation." The langue of the Supreme Court which employs terms drawn from the exemption of States from the jurisdiction of foreign Courts is a little ambiguous, but it may be summed up as follows: First, as long as a foreign Government has not been recognised, complaints regarding *illegal* acts, such as false imprisonment, can be brought against the individual tortfeasor in an American Court. Second, once the Government has been recognised, complaints regarding alleged illegal acts, such as false imprisonment, carried out in the exercise of governmental duties and in accordance with local law, can no longer be entertained in an American Court. The question whether an act lawful by the *lex loci delicti* is illegal according to international law must be considered by Governments and international tribunals.

|The third case was *Oetjen* v. *Central Leather Co.* (1918).[33] The facts were

---

[32] Compare *Johnstone* v. *Pedlar* [1921] 2. A.C. 262, at p. 290.
[33] 246 U.S. 297, 62 L. Ed. 726 (1918).

similar to those in *Luther* v. *Sagor*.[34] The goods were seized in Mexico by a revolutionary force which subsequently obtained *de facto* and then *de jure* recognition by the United States. Assignees from the former owner claimed title in the goods against the defendants who had purchased the goods from the revolutionary Government. The plaintiff contended that the seizure was illegal on the ground that it violated Hague Convention IV Respecting Laws and Customs of War on Land which constituted a treaty between the United States and Mexico. It seems to have been acknowledged on all sides that the question whether title to the goods had passed while they were situated in Mexico must be governed by Mexican law, which was the *lex situs*. Thus there were only two questions to be answered: first, what was the law of Mexico applicable to the case and, second, did the fact that Mexican law violated international law exclude the application of Mexican law by a Court in the United States. The first question raised a problem which had been decided before, in the case of *Underhill* v. *Hernandez*[35] which laid down a rule which we have described as the second limb of the rule in *Williams* v. *Bruffy*[36] The Court said: "We have a duly commissioned military commander of what must be accepted as the legitimate Government of Mexico ... seizing and selling in Mexico ... the property in controversy ... Plainly this was the action, in *Mexico*, of the legitimate Mexican Government when dealing with a Mexican citizen ... such action is not subject to re-examination and modification by the Courts of this country." The second question had also been answered in *Underhill* v. *Hernandez*.[37] It is not possible to complain in a domestic Court of a violation of international law committed by a foreign country. Thus the Court said: "The principle that the conduct of one independent Government cannot be successfully questioned in the Courts of another is as applicable to a case involving the title to property brought within the custody of the Court ... as ... to the cases ... in which claims for damages were based upon acts done in a foreign | country; for it rests upon the highest considerations of international comity and expediency. To permit the validity of the acts of one sovereign State to be re-examined and perhaps condemned by the Courts of another would very certainly 'imperil the amicable relations between Governments and vex the peace of nations'." The Court then pointed out that the plaintiff's remedy was to be found in a Mexican Court (presumably for the reason that these Courts may be able to examine the compatibility with international law of Mexican legislative and executive acts), or in diplomatic intervention.[38]

---

[34] *Supra.*
[35] 168 U. S. 250, 253.
[36] 96 U.S. 176.
[37] 168 U.S. 250, 42 L. Ed. 456; see also *American Banana Co.* v. *United Fruit Co.*, 213 U.S. 347, 53 L. Ed. 826.
[38] See also *Stark* v. *Howe Sound* Co. (1938), 271 N.Y.S. 1097, 5 N.Y.S. (2nd) 551; *Ter-*

Summary of the American Cases

Three rules were thus established by the American Supreme Court: First, the enactment of a non-recognized foreign revolutionary authority which fails to establish itself are not to be treated as law, when American conflict of laws refers to the law of the foreign country. Second, the enactments and acts of a foreign revolutionary authority which has obtained recognition are to be treated retroactively as the laws and executive acts of a lawful Government, when American conflict of laws refers to the law of the foreign country. Thirdly, the laws of a recognised foreign Government, applicable according to the American rules of conflict of laws, cannot be examined by an American Court for the purpose of deciding whether these laws violate international law. They cannot be treated as invalid on the ground that they are in conflict with international law nor can a claim for damages succeed if based upon the allegation that such a conflict exists.

We must now consider to what extent the Court of Appeal in *Luther* v. *Sagor* has applied or extended the principles first laid down by the American Supreme Court.

Critique of the Rule in Luther v. Sagor

The rule which purports to introduce certainty in the application of foreign Acts of State by English Courts to an unprecedented degree, raises at least as many doubts as it intends to lay at rest.

| Foreign Judgments and the Recognition of Governments

In the first place, it is not clear whether the Court of Appeal wished to include legislative and executive as well as judicial acts. It seems reasonably certain that foreign judgments are not included. For these, whether they are *in personam* or *in rem*, English private international law provides detailed rules which determine when they are to be recognized in England. Yet even here recognition may be relevant. Thus in *Krimtschansky* v. *Officier de l'Etat Civil, Liège*,[39] decided on March 21, 1929, by the Court of First In-

---

razas v. *Holmes,* 115 Tex. 32, 46; *Annual Digest,* 1925–26, Case No. 43; *Cia. Ramos* v. *Bartlesville Zinc,* 115 Tex. 21; *Annual Digest,* 1925–26, Case No. 47; *Peltzer* v. *United Dredging* Co. (1922), 193, N.Y. Sup. 675; 118 Misc. 210, and see Stierlin, cited below, p. 45, n. 3.; Dickinson (1923), *R.D.I.L.C.,* 3rd ser., vol. 4, pp. 145, 149; P. M. Brown in *A.J.* 30 (1936), 689, 690.

[39] *Annual Digest,* 1929–30, Case No. 26; *Clunet* 56 (1929), p. 1158. Cp. *Digmeloff* v.

stance of Liège, it was held that a divorce given by a Court in Odessa, competent according to Belgian private international law, was to be disregarded on the ground that the Russian Government, which had set up the Court, was not recognised. Conversely, in *Tcherniak* v. *Tcherniak*[40] decided by the Swiss Federal Tribunal on June 15, 1928 the Court was asked to determine whether Swiss Courts had jurisdiction in divorce over Russian citizens, having regard to the rule of Swiss law that Swiss Courts may exercise such jurisdiction only if the decree is recognised by the national Courts of the parties. There was evidence that the Soviet Russian Courts would recognise the Swiss decree, but Switzerland had not recognised the Soviet Government. The Federal Tribunal held that non-recognition was irrelevant. The Court said: "… la non-reconnaissance des Soviets par la Suisse déploie ses effets dans une autre domaine et … le droit russe n'en existe pas moins pour le juge suisse en tant qu'il n'est pas contraire à l'ordre public … la circonstance que les actes et jugements des autorités bolchévistes sont dépourvus de force exécutive sur territoire fédéral n'empêche nullement les parties de prouver et les juges suisses de retenir le fait que l'Etat russe admettrait la validité des divorces d'époux russes prononcés en Suisse."

|These decisions throw some light on the problem as a whole. Within their own setting, which was jurisdiction in divorce, they lead to the following conclusion: Insofar as foreign judgments are concerned, English private international law determines whether a foreign Court has jurisdiction, and the recognition of a foreign Government does not bind English Courts always to recognize or to enforce the decisions of the Courts of that Government. On the other hand, recognition of a foreign Government determines whether the attribute of "Courts" can be given to new bodies set up abroad or whether the old order established by the previous Government must still be regarded as subsisting. If this is correct our first conclusion is this: Recognition of a foreign Government does not determine whether the jurisdiction of the Courts must be accepted by English Courts but it does determine whether the Courts established by the predecessor Government or the bodies set up by the new Government are Courts the pronouncements of which can be respected or enforced in England, if the Courts of the foreign country have jurisdiction according to English private international law. Recognition enables an English Court to determine which of two jurisdic-

---

Officier de l'Etat Civil of Josse – Ten Noode decided by the Court of First Instance of Brussels on June 16, 1928, *Belgique Judiciaire,* 1928, col. 470; Clunet 55 (1928), p. 1253; *Annual Digest,* 1927–28, Case No. 45; *Jelnikova* v. *De Serbouloff,* decided by the same Court on June 5, 1925: Pas. Belge, 1926, III, 131; *Clunet* 54 (1927) p. 189; *Annual Digest,* 1925–26, Case No. 20. And see Clunet 53 (1925), pp. 367–318. See also *Pelzer v. United Dredging Co.* 194 N.Y. Suppl. 965, 196 N.Y. Suppl 342, 202 Appl. Div. 58.

[40] *Entscheidungen des Schweizerischen Bundesgerichts,* 54, II, 225, at pp. 230 (4), 231.

tions competing among themselves within one country may be regarded as clothed with authority. This formulation may be new, but it should hardly be controversial for, as stated before, it has never been contended that recognition of a foreign Government binds English Courts to enforce foreign judgments indiscriminately.[41]

Foreign Legislation and the Recognition of Foreign Governments

Our difficulties increase once we approach the field of legislation. The application of foreign law is determined by the principles of the conflict of laws. Whatever Courts and writers in other countries may have believed, it has been held by English Courts consistently from the time of Lord Mansfield onwards that the principles of the conflict of laws are part of English law[42] and are not rules of international law or subject to specific directions by international law.[43] Yet Warrington, | L. J. stated: (the appellants) "are resisting an endeavour on the part of the respondents to induce the Court to ignore and override legislative and executive acts of the Government of Russia and its agents affecting title to property in that country – it is that which, in my opinion, we are not at liberty to do."[44] It is therefore not surprising to see the same statement appear in Oppenheim[45] in a form which is both more extensive and more restrictive. It is more extensive, inasmuch as it is not limited to legislation by the *lex rei sitæ* in respect of property situate there; it is more restricted inasmuch as it merely prohibits English Courts from questioning the validity or legality of the legislation of the newly recognised Government. The question is threefold: (1) Does recognition exercise a positive function? Does it bind English Courts (a) to apply the law of the recognised Government in respect of all situations which arise in that foreign country or (b) only to apply the *lex situs* to movable and immovable property. The latter view appears to have been taken by Warrington, L. J., or (2) Does recognition exercise a negative function? Are English Courts precluded from investigating the validity and legality of foreign legislation if English rules of conflict of laws refer to the law of a particular foreign country? This appears to be the view of Oppenheim; it has been described by Dr. Mann[46] as a principle of immunity *ratione materiæ*, inasmuch as it purports

---

[41] Cp. the somewhat redundant discussion in *Kadler* v. *Kadler* decided on February 5, 1931 by the Polish Supreme Court, *Annual Digest*, 1931–32, Case No. 72.

[42] *Dalrymple* v. *Dalrymple* (1811) 2 Hagg. Cous. 54; *Holman* v. *Johnson* (1775), 1. Cowp. 341.

[43] *Transactions of the Grotius Society*, 27 (1942), pp. 142–148.

[44] at p. 549.

[45] *loc. cit.*, p. 134.

[46] (1943) 59 L.Q.R. 42, 155.

to state that foreign legislation, being an emanation of a foreign Government, enjoys the same immunity as the Government itself. According to this view, then, an English Court cannot examine the content of foreign law, but it must be noted that, according to this view, English Courts are not bound to apply the foreign legislation. Immunity implies exemption from local jurisdiction, not an invasion of local jurisdiction by foreign legislation; or (3) Is recognition totally unconnected with the question whether English Courts must apply foreign law? Instead, is the reliance upon recognition merely a technical device used by the Courts in order to determine which of two legal systems which compete with or have succeeded each other in one and the same country must be regarded as the "law of the country" at a given moment?

The positive function of recognition

Let us consider the | first alternative. Nobody to-day would claim that foreign law must be applied in its entirety, once a foreign Government is recognised. It must be admitted that in former days the question would not have been entirely misplaced, but it was not raised then. In times when the doctrine of the statutists was accepted on the Continent[47] and again after the doctrine of the territoriality of laws which asserted jurisdiction to legislate over all subjects at home or abroad and over all property situate within the country had been proclaimed by Huber[48] and by Story,[49] a principle such as that laid down in *Luther* v. *Sagor* could have been of considerable use. For, apart from the difficulty of ascertaining whether statutes enacted by foreign countries were personal, and could claim extraterritorial effect, or real and therefore limited to the country where they were enacted, the question remained why the extraterritorial effect of foreign legislation was to be recognised by other countries. The failure to show why the forum was under a liability to apply foreign law was the reason why all systems of private international law of a universal character were unable to hold their ground. On the other hand, the principle that recognition of a foreign Government binds the recognizing Government to apply the laws of the recognised Gov-

---

[47] The legal basis of the doctrine of the Statutists was refuted by Wächter, *Archiv für die Zivilistiche Praxis*, vols. 24 (1841), pp. 230–311; 25 (1842), pp. 162–200, 361–419; that of the Territorialists has been rejected by many contemporary writers. See, e.g. Lorenzen (1923), 33 *Yale, L. J.*, 736; *Essays in the Conflict of Laws* (1947) pp. 1. ff; W. W. Cook (1923), 33 *Yale, L. J.*, 457, *The Logical and Legal Bases of the Conflict of Laws* (1942), pp. 1. ff.

[48] *Praelectiones Juris Romani et Hodierni*, II. C.K. I. tit. iii. s. 2; see Llewelyn Davies, *B.Y.I.L.* 18 (1937), p. 48.

[49] *Conflict of Laws* (8th ed., 1883, by Bigelow), ss. 18–23, pp. 21–26.

ernment enacted within their sphere of competence to legislate, can only have a concrete meaning if there exists a generally accepted universal system of private international law whereby competence to legislate is regulated with effect towards all. To-day, foreign law is applied in English Courts because English rules of private international law so demand, and neither the Court of Appeal in *Luther* v. *Sagor* nor writers have ever attempted to attribute such a far-reaching effect to recognition as that indicated above. Instead Bankes L. J., treated the effect of recognition with respect to the title to | goods lying in a foreign country, and the learned editor of Oppenheim limits this statement by referring only to "certain transfers of property" and extends it to "other transactions", which are not enumerated. But even this statement is not correct in its absolute form. It is true that most countries apply the *lex rei sitæ* to questions involving transfers of movables *inter vivos*, but they do not necessarily follow this rule in matters of succession or where any other kind of universal assignment is involved. Thus, according to English private international law, succession to movables is governed by the law of the last domicile of the deceased, and by Italian law the *lex patrice* applies. It is interesting to speculate what conclusions the Court of Appeal would have reached if the goods forming the object of the claim in *Luther* v. *Sagor* had been part of the estate of a person who had died domiciled in England and if they had been seized in Russia by the Russian Government under a provision of Russian law granting the Russian Government a share in the estate, not in virtue of a title to *bona vacantia*, but in virtue of a right to take a share of the estate beneficially.[50]

Moreover, English Courts have professed to apply foreign law in consequence of recognition not only where title to movables was concerned[51] but also where the question was whether a corporation which was registered abroad had been dissolved or not.[52] It must be noted that recognition was only relevant when this was *de facto*. When there was only one Government and if this was recognised *de jure* (such as the Russian Government after 1924), English Courts have applied foreign law in accordance with their own rules of private international law without any reference to recognition. The result has been the same as in the cases which involved an examination of recognition: again the *lex rei sitæ* was applied to questions involving transfers of movables;[53] the law of the place of incorporation | was employed to deter-

---

[50] See *Re Bold*, Surrogates Court, N.Y. County, 14 February 1940; 18 N.Y.S. (2nd) 291; *Annual Digest*, 1938–40, Case No. 26.

[51] *Luther* v. *Sagor* [1921] 3 K.B. 532 (C.A.); *Princess Paley Olga* v. *Weisz* [1929] 1 K.B. 728 (C.A.).

[52] *Russian Commercial and Industrial Bank* v. *Comptoire d'Escompte de Mulhouse* [1925] A.C. 112, 123–124; *Bank of Ethiopia* v. *National Bank of Egypt & Liguori* [1937] Ch. 513; *Banco de Bilbao* v. *Rej.* [1938] 2 K.B. 176 (C.A.).

[53] *The Jupiter* (No. 3) [1927] P. 122, 250.

mine whether a corporation incorporated in Russia had been dissolved.[54] On the other hand the legislation of the recognised Russian Government was not applied to debts payable in England.[55] The reason is, of course, that the debt was governed by English law, although the Court relied to a certain extent on the alleged intention of the relevant Russian legislation not to operate abroad.

It would appear, therefore, that the recognition of the foreign Government is not the factor which determines whether foreign law applies.[56] Recognition, it may be said, determines only which of two competing sets of regulations within one country must be regarded as the law of the foreign country, once English private international law has determined that the law of a particular foreign country applies. This conclusion, reached with regard to the question whether recognition determines that the law of the recognised Government must be applied, is in conformity with the conclusions reached previously when the relation between recognition and the enforcement of foreign judgments was examined. It is also in conformity with the practice of other countries. There is general agreement that after recognition the legislation of the new Government must be regarded as law and not as the arbitrary command of an unorganised body and must be applied, provided always that the private international law of the forum requires the application of foreign law. To formulate the same principle differently: the legislation of a recognised Government cannot be rejected out of hand and *in toto*. The practice of French Courts provides the best illustration. French Courts have always insisted that the French rules of private international law and not the recognition of the foreign government determines whether foreign law is to be applied. Consequently, they have never had any doubts – such as the Court of Appeal in *Luther* v. *Sagor* had – that French Courts are free to reject the application of the foreign law normally applicable, if it | conflicts with French public policy. Thus, faced with a claim by the Russian owners of a ship which had been seized by the Soviet Government outside Russia, the Court of Cassation held in *Russian State* v. *Ropit*[57]: "Although the principle must be admitted that the Courts of a State faced with a juridical situation governed by foreign law should apply foreign law, this rule is only obligatory insofar as the application of foreign law and the respect for the rights

---

[54] *Lazard Bros.* v. *Midland Bank* [1933] A.C. 289; *Re Russian and English Bank* [1932] 1 Ch. 663; *Employers' Liability Assurance Corp.* v. *Sedgwick Collins & Co.* [1937] A.C. 95; *First Russian Ins. Co.* v. *London & Lancashire Ins. Co.* [1928] Ch. 922.

[55] *Re Russian Bank for Foreign Trade* [1933] Ch. 745, 767.

[56] See Stone, C.J. (diss.) in *U. S.* v. *Pink* (1942) 315 U.S. 203, at p. 252. See also *The Maret* C.C.A. (3rd), 17 October 1944, 145 F. (2nd) 431; *Annual Digest*, 1943–45, Case No. 9.

[57] 5 March, 1928, S. 1929. 1. 217 with note by Audinet; Clunet, 55 (1928), p. 674; *Revue Darras*, 24 (1929), p. 288 with note by Niboyet; *Annual Digest* 1927–28, Case No. 43.

acquired thereby are not incompatible with those principles and provisions of their own law which are regarded as essential from the point of view of public policy." As regards the effect of recognition, the Court of Aix,[58] the decision of which was upheld, had said: "Although, as a result of recognition *de jure*, the judge is no longer at liberty to ignore Soviet laws and to reject them *en bloc*, the recognition has not the effect of preventing him from examining them in each individual case and from refusing to give them legal effect if they contravene French political and social organisation." Again, where French private international law referred to Russian law in order to determine whether corporations registered in Russia and having a seat in France, continued to have a corporate existence, the Courts expressed themselves clearly. The Court of Appeal of Bordeaux said:[59] "Le gouvernement français a reconnu l'Union des U.S.S.R. Qu'il suit de là que l'autorité judiciaire française ne peut pas tenir comme non-avenue en bloc toute la nouvelle législation russe: mais qu'en cas de contestations entre particuliers mettant en opposition les lois françaises et les lois russes, le conflit doit être résolue suivant les règles de droit international privé ... sans doute ... la législation russe ne saurait s'imposer aux tribunaux français dans tous les cas où elle est incompatible avec l'ordre public français." In a similar case, the Court of Appeal of Paris devoted special attention to the | effects of recognition and said:[60] "The recognition of the Soviet Government by the French Government cannot result in the application in France of legislation adopted in Russia since 1918, when it is incompatible with the general principles of French law and *ordre public* in France. ... However, although the decree of December 13, 1918 [which nationalised the corporation] is incompatible with French public policy and therefore inapplicable in France, it is not the concern of a foreign Government to interfere with legislation validly adopted in the territory of a Government invested with the right to legislate within that territory." French Courts have had occasion to treat this question not only in connection with ownership of movables and corporations, but also in applying Russian divorce law[61] and other laws concerning status. Further,

---

[58] 23 December, 1925; S. 1926, 2. 1. with note Audinet; *Clunet*, 53 (1926), p. 667: *Revue Darras*, 21 (1926), p. 56; *Annual Digest* 1925–26. Case No. 17.

[59] *Banque de Commerce de Sibérie* v. *Vairon*, 2 January, 1928, S. 1928, 2. 161 with note Niboyet; D. H. 1929, p. 451; *Clunet*, 56 (1929), p. 115: *Revue Darras*, 24 (1929), p. 93 with note Niboyet.

[60] *Cie Nord de Moscou* v. *Phénix Espagnol*, 13 June, 1928; S. 1928. 2. 161 with note Niboyet; *Clunet*, 56 (1929), p. 119 with note by Picard and Tager; *Revue Darras*, 24 (1929), p. 97 with note Niboyet; *Annual Digest*, 1927–1928, Case No. 42; on appeal from Trib. Civ. Seine, 9 May 1925, *Clunet*, 53 (1926) p. 128.

[61] *Chiger* v. *Chiger*, C.A. Paris, 30 April, 1926, S. 1926, 2. 89 with note Niboyet; D. 1927, 2. 1. with note Savatier; *Revue Darras*. 22 (1927), p. 242, *Clunet*, 53 (1926), p. 943; *Annual Digest*. 1925–26, Case No. 18; *De Mayenne* v. *Joutal*, Trib. Civ. Suisse, 24 December, 1926, *Clunet*, 55 (1928), p. 710; *Annual Digest* 1927–28. Case No. 68.

when a claim under a Russian copyright was brought in France, Soviet Russian law was applied, subject to the overriding provisions of French public policy.[62] The practice of the French Courts proceeds on the basis of arguments which are exclusively drawn from private international law. In adopting this approach it differs, at least in outward appearance, from the practice adopted by the Court of Appeal in *Luther* v. *Sagor*, about which Professor Niboyet had the following to say:[63]

| "Il y a là, outre une méconnaissance des exigences de l'ordre public, une confusion entre deux ordres de questions très distinctes, celle de la reconnaissance des Soviets et de l'application de leurs lois. La première est une question d'opportunité politique ... Mais la reconnaissance d'un gouvernement n'oblige pas à appliquer celle de ses lois qui heurtent l'ordre public. S'il en était autrement l'ordre public n'interviendrait jamais puisqu'il joue toujours entre pays entretenant des relations suivies ..." However, these strictures apply only if the reasons given in *Luther* v. *Sagor* are accepted literally. As shown here, the Court of Appeal cannot have intended to say more than that according to English private international law the *lex rei sitæ* applied to movables and that in the particular circumstances of the case Soviet Russian law, which was applicable, was not excluded on grounds of public policy.

Little guidance can be obtained in the matter from German and Italian practice.[64] Both countries recognised the Soviet Russian Government *de jure*

---

[62] *Basil and Bessel* v. *Cools*, Trib. Comm. Suisse, 20 December, 1929, *Clunet*, 57 (1930), p. 681; *Annual Digest*, 1929–30, Case No. 24.

[63] *Revue Darras*, 24 (1929), p. 117; See also *ibid.*, 22 (1927), pp. 245 ff. at p. 247; *R.D.I.L.C.* (3rd ser.) IX (1928), p. 753 at p. 784. See also Dickinson, *A.J.* 19 (1925), pp. 263, 268; Van Prague, *R.D.I.L.C.* (3rd ser.) 4, (1923), p. 436, at p. 450; Champ communal *Revue Darras* 19 (1924), pp. 321, 364, 525; Delehelle *Revue Darras*, 22 (1927), pp. 193, 216; Trachtenberg, *ibid.*, p. 561; *Clunet*, 53 (1926), p. 572; Audré-Prudhomme, *Clunet* 52 (1925), p. 318; Melchior, *Die Grundlagen des Deutschen Internationales Privatrechts* (1932), pp. 35, 85, 151, n.l.; Frankenstein, *Internationales Privatrecht*, III. (1934), p. 19 n. 31; IV (1935), p. 333 n. 181, 182.

[64] For Germany see Supreme Court, 16 October, 1925, I.W. 1926, II, p. 1986 and compare *Caucassian Liquorice* v. *Katz*, L.G. Hamburg, 13 June, 1924, 1 Ostrecht 165; *Keil* v. *Nathan*, L.G. Hamburg, 26 December 1924, ibid., p. 170; and see *Sphan and Son* v. *Selbig and Lange*, decided by the German Supreme Court on 20 May 1930, RGZ. 129, p. 98, *Darras*, 26 (1931), p. 716; *Ginsberg Bros.* v. *Deutsche Bank*, decided by the Court of Appeal of Berlin on 27 October 1927, Darras 23 (1928), p. 678; I.W. 1925, I, 1300; 1928, II, 1232; *Prince Dabischa-Kotromaniz* v. *Lepke*, decided on 1 November 1928 by the Court of Berlin, *Clunet*, 56 (1929), p. 184. See also *Zeitschrift für ausländisches und internationales Privatrecht*, 2 (1928), p. 791. And see Frankenstein, *loc. cit.* IV p. 333, n. 182; Freund, *Clunet*, 51 (1924), p. 51; 52 (1925), p. 331. For Italy see: *Italian Black Sea Co.* v. *U.S.S.R.* Court of Appeal Milan, 26 July 1922; *Giur. It.* 1922, I. 2, 444; *Riv. dir. internaz.* 1921–22, p. 562; *Annual Digest* 1919–22, Case 11; *Federazione Italiana Consorzi Agrari* v. *Commissariat of the U.S.S.R.*, 25 June, 1924; *Giur It.* 1924, I. 1, 559; *Foro It.* 1924, I. 777; *Annual Digest* 1923–24, Case No. 5. Philonenko *Clunet*, 56 (1929), p. 13. at p. 23.

at an early date and concluded treaties[65] with Russia whereby the title of the Russian Government to property obtained by means of confiscation was to be respected in Germany and Italy. The Courts of most of the other European countries adopted an attitude similar to that of | the French Courts.[66]

The practice of the Courts in the United States before 1933 was only concerned with the effect of non-recognition which will be discussed below. After 1933 only two problems arose, namely first, whether the rule in *Luther* v. *Sagor* permitted the application of the local rules of public policy to defeat a title obtained in Russia in virtue of confiscatory legislation[67] and, second, whether the treaty concluded between the United States and the Soviet Union of November 16, 1933, rendered the local rules of public policy inapplicable.[68] To this may be added another problem which does not really fall within the compass of this paper. It is whether, after the conclusion of the above mentioned treaty, Soviet Russian confiscatory legislation affected also property outside the U.S.S.R., or at least | if situated in the United States.[69] In fact, the problem was a different one, namely, whether by treaty the United States Government had acquired the right to appropriate the property in the United States belonging to dissolved Russian corporations.[70]

---

[65] Italy: 26 December, 1922; Germany: 6 May, 1921, 16 April 1922 (Rapallo); 5 November 1922.

[66] *Sweden: Forsikringsaktieselskapet Norske Atlas* v. *Undén-Cullberg,* Supreme Court, 18 October 1929, Nytt Juridisk Arkiv 1929, p. 471; *Ann. Dig.* 1929, Case 61;

Netherlands: Court of Doordrecht, 12 January 1927, *ibid.* 1927–28, Case No. 47; *Papadopoulos* v. *N. V. Konniklijke Stoomboot Maatschappij etc., ibid.,* 1927–28, Case No. 17.

Hungary: Supr. Court, 23 February 1927, *ibid.,* 1927–28, Case No. 19.

Brazil: C.A. Rio, 10 June 1932, Clunet, 59 (1932), p. 1124.

[67] *Contracts: Dougherty* v. *Equitable Life Assurance Soc.* 266 N.Y. 71; *Ann. Dig.* 1933–34, Case No. 28; cp. *Columbia L. R.* 35 (1935), 292; *Cornell L. Q.,* 20 (1935), 499; *U. Pa. L.R.,* 83 (1935), 917; *Vladikavkazky Ry.* v. *New York Trust* Co., 263 N.Y. 369 (1934), *Ann. Dig.,* 1933–34, Case No. 67; *Hiller* v. *Russo-Asiatic Bank,* 273 N.Y.S. 594 (1934); *Issaia* v. *Russo-Asiatic Bank,* 280 N.Y. S. 735 (1935).

Property: United States v. *Bank of New York and Trust Co.* (1936) 77 F. (2d) 866, 296 U.S. 463; *Ann. Dig.,* 1933–34, Case No. 29: *Moscow Fire Ins. Co.* v. *Bank of New York & Trust Co.,* Court of Appeals, New York, 19 April 1939, 294 N.Y.S. 648; 280 N.Y. 286; *Ann. Dig.* 1938–40, Case No. 53, ff. 309 U.S. 624; *Bollack* v. *Soc. Gén. etc.* Supreme Court, N.Y., App. Div., 27 March, 1942; 33 N.Y.S. (2d) 986, 263 App. Div. 601; *Ann. Dig.* 1941–42; Case No. 36. cp. *Holzer* v. *Deutsche Reichsbahn Gesellschaft* 277 N.Y. 474, 14 N.E. (2d.) 798; *ibid.,* 1938–40, Case No. 71.

[68] *U.S.* v. *Belmont,* 301 U.S. 324; *ibid.* 1935–37, Case No. 15, disregarding the question raised by the Circuit Court of Appeals 85 F. (2d.) 542, whether Russian law was applicable. See *A.J.* 31 (1937) 537, 481, 675, *Harv. L.R.* 51 (1937) 162; *Yale, L. J.* 47 (1937), 292; *U. Chi. L.R.,* 5 (1937), 280; *California L.R.* 26 (1937) 117; *Guarantee Trust Co. v. U.S.* 304 U.S. 126, *Annual Digest,* 1938–40, Case No. 69.

[69] *U.S.* v. *Pink* 86 S.Ct. 459, 315 U.S. 203; *Ann. Dig.,* 1941–42, Case No. 13, *A.J.,* 36 (1942), 275, 282; *Yale L.J.,* 51 (1942), 848 and see *Ann. Dig.* 1943–45, Case No. 7. *Cp. U.S.* v. *Belmont; Moscow Fire Ins. Co.* v. *Bank of New York & Trust Co.* (*supra*).

[70] *Guarantee Trust Co.* v. *U.S.* 304 U.S. 126, 143 *U.S.* v. *Belmont,* 301 U.S. 324.

It is now possible to answer our first question, i.e. whether recognition exercises a positive effect and binds English Courts (1) to apply the law of the recognised Government to all situations which arise in that foreign country or (2) to apply the *lex situs* to movables and inmmovables situated there. Recognition has no positive effect. There is no obligation to apply the law of a recognised Government to all situations which arise in that foreign country or to all movables and immovables situated there. Foreign law is applied not because a particular Government is recognised but because English private international law refers to the law of that particular country in preference to that of any other country or of the *lex fori*.[71]

The negative function of recognition

We must now turn to our second alternative which we have called the negative function of recognition. According to Warrington, L. J. "the validity of the acts of an independent sovereign Government in relation to property and persons within its jurisdiction cannot be questioned in the Courts of this country." As shown above, this principle was first laid down by the American Supreme Court. Its original purport was, first, that the enactments of a recognised Government were to be treated as law and, second, that the legislation and executive acts of a recognised Government cannot be questioned, as regards their validity, or made the object of a claim for damages on the ground that they violate rules of public international law. It is necessary now to examine whether the Court of Appeal in *Luther* v. *Sagor*[72] laid down a wider principle. In the first | place, it has been shown above that English private international law, and not the recognition of a foreign Government by the British Government, determines whether foreign law is to be applied. In the second place, it must be remembered that foreign law must be proved by the parties. If they fail to do so, the Court cannot apply foreign law. In the third place, if the evidence on foreign law is conflicting, an English Court must determine for itself what the law of the foreign country is. It has been contended, at times, that this involves only a process of sifting the evidence and not of deciding a question of foreign law.[73] In effect, however, the English Court must give a decision on a disputed point of foreign law, even if that law is treated as a fact. It may be that the Court cannot examine sources and materials other than those given in evidence, but this will usually

---

[71] See also Beitzke in *Festschrift für Raape*, pp. 93–111, at p. 105; Note in (1937–38), 5 *University of Chicago Law Review* 280–295.

[72] [1921] 3 K. 532.

[73] *Lazard Bros.* v. *Midland Bk.* [1933] A.C. 289, 298; *De Bode's Case* (1845) 8. Q.B. 208, 266; *Sunea Peerage Case*, (1844) 11 Cl. & F. 85, 116.

include the relevant provisions of foreign statute law, and the Court may attempt an independent interpretation of the relevant provision, if there is a dispute.[74] In form, this decision may well determine a conflicting issue of evidence. In substance it determines a point of foreign law, if only indirectly. It follows that if evidence of foreign law is given, and if this evidence is contradicted on the ground that the relevant rule of foreign law violates the constitution or an enabling Act, if delegated legislation is proved, and is invalid, an English Court must give a decision. In *Re Amand*[75] English Courts have done so, and in *Shapleigh v. Mier*[76] the American Supreme Court indicated willingness to do the same. Only where foreign law reserves for a special Court the decision | whether a particular statute violates the constitution and is void, it would appear that an English Court is precluded from assuming the function of the foreign Court. The reason is clear: until the foreign Court has spoken the law in question is valid even in the foreign country concerned; after the foreign Court has spoken, the law has ceased to operate. However, if the foreign legal system grants the right of scrutiny to all its Courts, English Courts may also exercise this right. If the right of scrutiny is excluded altogether by foreign law, an English Court cannot question the validity of foreign legislation.[77] Thus, an English Court may well be in a position to question the constitutional validity of foreign law, and the rule in *Luther* v. *Sagor*[78] is too wide. Moreover, the rule is too wide even if understood in the restricted sense as originally understood by the American Supreme Court. English and American Courts cannot dismiss a domestic statute on the ground that it contravenes international law.[79] According to the American Supreme Court they cannot do so either when the application of a foreign statute is involved. However, if according to foreign

---

[74] *De Sora* v. *Phillips* (1863) 10 H.L.C. 624, 636; *Coucha* v. *Murrieta* (1889), 40 Ch. D. 543, *De Béeche* v. *South American Stores* [1935] AC. 148, 157.

[75] [1941] 2 K.B. 239; [1942] 1 K.B. 445. cp. *King of the Hellenes* v. *Brostrom* [1923] 16 Ll. L.R. 190, and see the note in *Ann. Dig.*, 1935–37, p. 201. cp. McNair, *Legal Effects of War* (3rd. ed. 1948), pp. 374–77.

[76] 299 U.S. 468; *A.J.*, 31 (1937), p. 528, on appeal from 83 F. (2d) 673, *Annual Digest*, 1935–37, Case No. 14; but see *Eastern States Petroleum Co.* v. *Asiatic Petroleum Corporation*, District Court, Southern District, N.Y., 13 April 1939, 28 F. Suppl 279; *Ann. Dig.* 1938–40, Case No. 35. Compare in respect of the jurisdiction of foreign courts, *Rose* v. *Himely* (1808) 4 Cranch 241, 271, 276.

[77] For a discussion of this problem see Niboyet, *Revue de Droit International et de Législation Comparée* (3rd ser.), IX (1928), pp. 753–812; Mussbaum, *Principles of Private International Law* (1942), p. 258, note 46, Fedozzi, *Hague Recueil* 27 (1929, II), p. 145, at p. 221.

[78] (1921) 3 K.B. 532.

[79] *Mortensen* v. *Peters* (1906) 14 S.L.T. 227; 43 S.L.R. 872; Kunz in Niemeyer's *Zeitschrift für Internationales Recht*, 32 (1924), pp. 26–35; Neumeyer, *Internationales Verwaltungsrecht*, IV (1936), p. 221 ff. Lauterpacht in (1939) 25 *Transactions of the Grotius Society*, 51 ff.

law or according to the constitution of the foreign country all legislation is void which contravenes international law, and if the right of scrutiny is granted by the foreign law or constitution to all its Courts, it would appear that an English Court may exercise this right, provided the validity of the foreign legislation is questioned in evidence. To sum up: the negative function of the rule in *Luther* v. *Sagor* is too wide. The validity of foreign law may be questioned in an English Court. This scrutiny may extend to the compatibility with foreign constitutional or international law, provided such a scrutiny is permissible according to foreign law and is not reserved for determination by a special Court.

Recognition as a device to ascertain foreign law

There remains a third alternative. Is recognition merely employed by | the Courts as a device in order to ascertain which of several legal orders competing within the same country is to be applied as law in an English Court? It would appear that for the purpose of the conflict of laws recognition is only relevant if there are at least two Governments, one recognised *de jure* and the other *de facto*, which lay claim to legislate for the same country. If there is only a *de jure* recognised Government, the question does not seem to arise. Nor would it seem to arise necessarily where the *de jure* recognised Government has succumbed and there is only one government which has obtained *de facto* but not *de jure*.[80] recognition or which has not obtained any recognition at all. Thus in the Russian Bank cases, English Courts have considered the recognition of the Soviet Russian Government while only recognised *de facto*[81] but not any longer after the same Government had obtained *de jure* recognition.[82] And in *King of the Hellenes* v. *Bostrom*,[83] Rowlatt, J., attached sole importance to the question whether the legislation cited to him was *de facto* in force. English Courts are only interested to ascertain whether the orders and regulations of some foreign organisation are to be regarded as law. This presupposes that these regulations are pleaded by one party as representing the foreign law applicable in the circumstances, and that the opponent pleads a different set of rules enacted by another Government. Confronted with conflicting evidence as to what is the rule of foreign law, a Court may feel inclined to form its own opinion, or it may rely on the attitude of the executive, as is the practice in immunity cases.[84] English and

---

[80] See below, p. 42 ff; cp. Hershey, loc. cit., p. 96.
[81] See above, note 2.
[82] See above, note 3.
[83] (1923) 16 Ll.L.R. 190, 192.
[84] *Mighell* v. *Sultan of Johore* [1894] 1 Q.B. 149; *Duff* v. *Government of Kelantan* [1924] A.C. 797; *Engelke v. Musmann* [1928] A.C. 433.

American Courts[85] as well as the Courts of many other countries follow the executive. There is less reason to do so when there is only a *de facto* recognised Government or no recognised Government at all. Yet it must be remembered that it is not the existence of two Governments but the fact that the parties rely on different bodies of legislation in their evidence which forces the Court to take sides. It is therefore understandable that even|in the latter type of situation the Courts rely on the guidance which can be obtained from the attitude of their own executive. This was done in *Luther* v. *Sagor*.[86] It is another question whether the practice of certification, as Dr. Mann has called it,[87] creates more difficulties than it solves. To treat the Foreign Office certificate as conclusive rather than as relevant under the best evidence rule may be erroneous. Courts in other countries have reserved somewhat greater freedom of action for themselves in cases where the only Government in existence was unrecognised by the executive. This practice will be discussed later on.

It is now possible to state a positive conclusion: In the sphere of private international law, recognition of a Government is an aid in determining which of several sets of regulations enacted by competing factions within the same country and pleaded in an English Court is to be regarded as the law of the country at a given moment.

Foreign Executive Acts and the Recognition of Foreign Governments

The question remains whether the doctrine in *Luther* v. *Sagor*[88] is restricted to the executive acts of a foreign Government, which affect private property, such as acts of confiscation or of winding up. Some observations of the Court of Appeal in *Luther* v. *Sagor*[89] invite such an interpretation. If it were so, the question would have to be considered whether there is a special branch of law which may be called international administrative law. Such a law would present the conflict of laws in its purest form. No country would be asked to enforce the law of any other country, and every country would be required to respect and recognise the effect abroad of all executive acts

---

[85] *Jones* v. *United States*, 137 U.S. 202, 34 L.Ed. 691; cp. Lyons in *B.Y.I.L.*, 23 (1946), pp. 240–281; 24 (1947), pp. 117–147. Hervey, *The Legal Effects of Recognition in International Law* (1928), pp. 38 ff.

[86] [1921] 3 K.B. 532.

[87] (1943) 29 *Transaction of the Grotius Society*, 145 at p. 158, 159; (1943) 59 L.Q.R. 42, 155, at p. 167.

[88] [1921] 3 K.B. 532.

[89] See Note I.

carried out in the foreign country in respect of things and persons within its territorial or, possibly, its personal jurisdiction. But such a system does not exist, and it is inadmissible to speak of any extra-territorial effect of foreign law in whatever sense, except in virtue of some rule of English private international law.[90] It is well known that English | Courts have had great difficulties in deciding in what circumstances foreign bankruptcies are to be recognised in England.[91] Nor are English Courts likely to recognise an executive decree of the King of Denmark dissolving a marriage of two Danes resident in Denmark but domiciled in England.[92] Further, if recognition by the Crown were automatically to bring into indirect operation, in England, all the executive acts of a foreign Government, the question would arise whether an enabling Act is required so far as British subjects are concerned.[93]

To sum up: it may be stated with some confidence that the effect of the recognition of a foreign Government is not restricted to its executive acts. Nor does recognition confer upon the executive acts of a foreign Government any greater binding force than upon its legislative or judicial acts.

Non-recognition and the application of foreign law

So far our conclusion has been that reliance upon recognition is a useful device employed by the Courts in deciding which of two competing legal orders within the same country is to be treated as the law of the foreign country for the purpose of applying it in an English court. As Mann[94] has indicated, too rigid an adherence to the statement of the executive by applying the legislation of the *de facto* recognised Government, to the exclusion of the *de jure* Government, as the law of the country in question may have undesirable effects. Foreign Offices certificate should be treated as the best evidence, but not as conclusive. The same problem arises if one of the competing authorities has not been recognised by the British Government. If the rule in *Luther* v. *Sagor*[95] is applied according to strict logic, the regulations of an authority not recognised by the British Government can never be applied

---

[90] See, *e.g.*, Fedozzi, *Hague Recueil*, 27 (1929, II), p. 145, at pp. 164, 172–180, 183–196, 267–210, 215, 223: Hannab Schwartz, *Die Anerkennung ausländischer Staatsakte* (1935), pp. 38 ff.; Neumeyer, *Internationales Verwaltungsrecht*, IV (1936), passim, especially pp. 432, 436 ff., 492 ff.

[91] See Dicey, *Conflict of Laws* (6th ed. 1949), Rule 99, p. 440 and note 20.

[92] Compare C.A. Douai, 29 January, 1924, S. 1924, 2. 113 with a note by Niboyet; Neumeyer, loc. cit. p. 223.

[93] See McNair in B.Y.I.L. 9 (1928), 61, 62, note 4.

[94] Above, note 87.

[95] [1921] 3. K.B. 532.

in an English Court. Thus, in respect of the period, before the Soviet Russian | Government had been recognised, French,[96] Belgian,[97] Italian,[98] Hungarian,[99] Rumanian[100] and Egyptian[101] Courts applied pre-Soviet Russian law. This was either Czarist law, or the law in force under the Government of Kerensky. The practice of English[102] and, at first, of American Courts,[103] was the same. This could lead to absurd results inasmuch as Czarist law was | still applied when this legal system had ceased to operate altogether. Even the application of the *lex fori* would have yielded better results than that of a dead legal system. It is therefore not surprising that the robust commonsense of Swiss courts led them to apply consistently Soviet Russian law although Switzerland had never recognised the Soviet Government.[104] Courts of other

---

[96] *Bonnatrau* v. *Optorg,* Trib. Civ. Seine, 12 December 1923, Gaz. Pal. 6 July, 1924; Gaz. Trib. 27 January, 1924, Darras 19 (1924), p. 282 (movables); *Vlasto* v. *Banque Russe-Asiatique*; Trib. Comm. Seine, 26 April 1922, Clunet 50 (1923), p. 933 (Corforation); *Kharan* v. *Banque Russe,* Trib. Civ. Seine, 20 May, 1921, Clunet 50 (1923), p. 523 (cheque).

[97] *Jelnikova* v. *De Serbouloff,* Trib. Civ. Brussels, 5 June, 1925; *Pas. Belge,* 1926, III, 131; *Clunet,* 54 (1927), p. 189; *Annual Digest, 1925–26,* Case No. 20 (divorce); *Digmeloff* v. *Officier de l'Etat of Josse-Ten Noode,* Trib. Civ. Brussels, 16 June, 1928, *Belgique Jud.* 1928, col. 470; *Clunet* 55 (1928), p. 1253; *Annual Digest 1927–28,* Case No. 45 (status); *Krimschansky* v. *l'Officier de l'Etat Civil de Liège, Lhoest-Siniawskaia* v. *the same* Trib. Civ. Liège, 21 March, 1929, *Clunet* 56 (1929), p. 1158, *Annual Digest 1929–30,* Case 26 (divorce) and see the critical note in *Clunet* 57 (1930), p. 473. Cp. *Benoit* v. *National City Bank,* Court of Appeal, Brussels, 11 July 1936; *Revue Critique de droit international,* 32 (1937), 121.

[98] *Nomis* v. *Federation of Seamen,* C.A. Genoa, 7 March 1930. *Clunet* 58 (1931), p. 761; *Annual Digest 1929–30,* Case No. 23; *Katsikis* v. *Soc. Fotis Svoroni di Follone,* Court of Genoa; 19 May 1922, *Clunet* 56 (1923), p. 1021; *Revue de droit maritime Comparé* 1 (1923), p 546.

[99] Royal Hungarian Court of Appeal, 20 April 1925, *Annual Digest 1925–26,* Case No. 22 (marriage); but see the note *ibid.,* regarding a different practice of the same Court which excluded Soviet Russian law on grounds of public policy.

[100] *Re Sustov,* Cass. 13 February 1929, *Annual Digest 1929–30,* Case No. 28; Cass. 5 December 1932, *Clunet* 62 (1935), p. 718; *Annual Digest 1933–34,* Case No. 34.

[101] *Hanawi* v. *Credit Lyonnais,* Mixed Court Alexandria, 24 January 1925, *Clunet* 52 (1925), p. 475; *Annual Digest 1925–26,* Case No. 21: *National Navigation Co.* v. *Tavoularidis,* Mixed Court, Alexandria, 9 November 1927, *Clunet* 57 (1930), p. 203, *Annual Digest 1927–28,* Case No. 110; *Gregorian* v. *Gregorian,* Mixed Court, Alexandria, 29 May 1929; *Annual Digest, 1929–30,* Case No. 27. *Gross* v. *Gretchenko,* 30 April 1924, *Clunet* 51 (1924), p. 1112; But see *Dahan & Dorra Bros.* v. *Tchoureff,* 24 June 1934, *Annual Digest 1935–37,* Case No. 34.

[102] *Luther* v. *Sagor* [1921] 1 K.B. 456.

[103] *Pelzer* v. *United Dredging Co.* Supreme Court, New York (1922). 193 N.Y. Sup. 675: *Joint Stock of Volgakama Oil* v. *National City Bank of New York,* New York C. Appeals (1925) 206 N.Y. Sup. 476; 240 N.Y. 368; *Bourne* v. *Bourne* (1924) 204 N.Y. Sup. 866; *Agency of Canadian Car Foundry Co.* v. *American Can Co.* C.C.A. (2d,) 21 April 1919, 258 F. 263, see Dickinson, *A.J.* 9, pp. 263, 268. *Petrogradsky Meschdunarodny Kommertschesky Bank* v. *National Bank of New York,* New York Court of Appeals, 11 February 1930, 253 N.Y. 23; 170 N.E. 479. *Clunet* 57 (1930), p. 782; *Annual Digest 1929–30,* Case No. 20.

[104] High Court, Zürich, 12 September 1921, *Blätter für Zürichsche Rechtssprechung*

countries occasionally followed the same course.[105] But it fell to the American Courts to assign its proper place to the rule in *Luther* v. *Sagor* which purported to reproduce American law. In the first place, if recognition|of a revolutionary body invests the regulations of that body with the character of law, it does not follow necessarily that non-recognition denies that character to such regulations. In the second place, if the conclusion follows with logical necessity, then logic and commonsense are at variance, and commonsense must prevail. Such were the reasons given by American Courts in later cases which applied Soviet Russian law before the Soviet Government was recognised by the United States in 1933.[106] To this may be added two further reasons: First, if recognition is the best evidence as to which of several competing legal orders is the law of a country, the absence of recognition should

---

1921; *Hausner* v. *Banque Internationale de Commerce de Petrograd,* Federal Court, 10 December 1924, N.G.E. 50, II, 507; *Annual Digest* 1925–26, Case No. 97 *Revue Darras,* 20 (1925), p. 118; *Wilbuschewitsch* v. *Zurich,* 13 July 1925, B.G.E. 51, II, 259; *Annual Digest* 1925–26, Case No. 75 (corporations); *Schintz* v. *High Court of Zürich,* 4 June 1926, B.G.E. 52, I, 218; *Annual Digest* 1925–26, Case No. 23 (contract); *Tcherniak* v. *Tcherniak,* 15 June 1928, B.G.E. 54, II, 225; *Annual Digest* 1927–28, Case No. 39 (status); *Pr. Sch.* High Court Zürich, 18 December 1928, Clunet, 57 (1930), p. 1159; *Prochorow* v. *Upper Court of Zürich,* 26 October 1929, B.G.E. 55, I, 289, *Clunet* 57 (1930), p. 1164; *Annual Digest* 1929–30, Case No. 62 (corporation); *Lempert* v. *Borfol,* 15 June 1934, B.G.E. 60, I, 67; *Annual Digest* 1933–34, Case No. 115, See Stierlin, *Die Rechtsstellung der nichtanerkannten Regierung im Völkerrecht* (1940), *passim.*

[105] *D'Aivasoff* v. *De Rædemækers,* Trib. Civ. Brussels, 28 February 1927, *Pas Belge* 1927, III, 38; *Annual Digest* 1927–28; Case No. 46: *Vseobtchaia Stroitelnaia Ko. of Petrograd* v. *Smit,* District Court, Doordrecht, 12 January 1927, *ibid* 1927–28, Case No. 47; *Papadopoulos* v. *Monastery of Mount Sinai,* Mixed Court of Appeal, Egypt, 23 June 1927, *ibid* 1927–28, Case No. 41 (*obiter*). For Germany see Mann, *Transactions of the Grotius Society,* 29 (1943), 145, at p. 158, note 102, with cases and literature; Freund, Clunet 51 (1924), p. 51; *ibid.,* 52 (1925), p. 331. For the Netherlands, see the decision of the Court of Appeal of The Hague, 3 June 1937, *Annual Digest* 1935–37, Case No. 75. And see Sereni, *Rivista di diritto internazionale,* (3rd ser. XVII), 1938, p. 102, at pp. 112, ff, 132.

[106] *Sokoloff* v. *National City Bank of New York.* New York Court of Appeals, 25 November 1924, 239 N.Y. 158; 145 N.E. 917; *Annual Digest* 1923–24, Case No. 19 (per Cardozo, J.); *Fred James & Co.* v. *Second Russian Insurance Co.* by the same Court (1924); 239 N.Y. 248; 146 N.E. 369; *Annual Digest,* 1925–26, Case No. 42; *Russian Reinsurance Co* v. *Stoddard,* decided by the same court, 7 April 1925, 240 N.Y. 149; 147 N.E. 703 (per Lehman, J.); *Annual Digest* 1925–26, Case No. 40; *Banque de France* v. *Equitable Trust Co. of New York,* District Court, S. District, New York, 21 March 1929, 33 F. (2nd.) 202, *Annual Digest* 1929–30, Case No. 22; *Salimoff* v. *Standard Oil Co of New York,* New York Court of Appeals, 11 July 1933, 262 N.Y. 220; 186 N.E. 679; *Annual Digest* 1933–34, Case No. 8; see Dickinson, A. J. 19 (1925) 753; *ibid.,* 27 (1933) 743; *Harv. L. R.* 39 (1925), 127; 3 *Yale L. J.* 35 (1925) 98; *Cornell L.Q.* 11 (1925) 99; *Boston L.R.* 5 (1925) 255; *Clunet* 61 (1934) 564; *Werfel* v. *Zirnoslenska Bank,* New York, Supreme Court, Appellate Division, 20 December 1940, 23 N.Y.S. (2d), 1001; *Ann. Dig.* 1938–40, Case No. 32; C.A.N.Y. 27 November 1941, 287 N.Y. 91, *Annual Digest* 1941–42, Case No. 17; See also *Oliver American Trading Co.* v. *Govt. of Mexico* C.C.A. (2nd.) (1924) 44 S.Ct. Rep. 390; *Re Mariano Viamonte y Fernandez* Superior Court, Essex County, with note by Wright, A.J. 17 (1923) 742, 743, *The Maret,* 145 F. (2d) 431, *Annual Digest* 1943–45, Case No. 9.

lead to the admission of other evidence. This should show that the regulations of the revolutionary Government are in fact applied as law over the entire area of the country which the authorities concerned purport to govern. Second, it must be remembered that the decisions in *Underhill* v. *Hernandez*[107] and *Oetjen* v. *Central Leather* Co.,[108] upon which the doctrine in *Luther* v. *Sagor*[109] rests, laid down a rule of a very special nature. It was that the legislation of a *de facto* recognised Government must be applied, even if it should|contravene rules of international law. The reason is, of course, that the *de facto* recognised Government has sufficient international personality to be made responsible by diplomatic means or before an international tribunal. It does not follow from this rule that the legislation of a non-recognised Government can never be applied for the reason that it cannot be held responsible, irrespective of whether or not the particular rule pleaded by the party violates international law. If it should contravene the latter, there may be reason for not applying it. But it seems unnecessary to link the application of foreign law in domestic Courts with the responsibility of States in international law.[110]

Conclusions

1. The rule in *Luther* v. *Sagor* reproduces in general terms the specific principles which were developed by the American Supreme Court.

2. The first principle is: when the domestic rules of the conflict of laws refer to the law of a particular foreign country, the regulations of a foreign revolutionary Government are not applied as the law of the foreign country, unless that Government has been recognised and has succeeded in establishing itself.

3. The second principle is: when the domestic rules of the conflict of laws refer to the law of a particular foreign country, the regulations of a foreign revolutionary Government are applied as the law of the foreign country and the acts of its organs are treated as the executive acts of a foreign Government, once that Government has been recognised and has succeeded in establishing itself.

4. The third principle is: if the domestic rules of conflict of laws refer to the law of a foreign country, the Court cannot examine whether the law of the foreign country conflicts with international law.

---

[107] 168 U.S. 250.
[108] 246 U.S. 296.
[109] [1921] 3 K.B. 532.
[110] Compare Beitzlle, *loc. cit.*, p. 105.

5. The rule in *Luther* v. *Sagor* does not bind English Courts to recognise unconditionally the decisions of the judicial authorities of the foreign Government.

6. The rule in *Luther* v. *Sagor* does not bind English Courts to apply the law of the foreign country whenever that law purports to affect property or persons within the territory or jurisdiction of the foreign country.

|7. The rule in *Luther* v. *Sagor* does not bind English Courts to recognise unconditionally the acts of the executive authorities of the foreign Government.

8. English Courts are free to examine whether a rule of foreign law, applicable according to the English principles of conflict of laws, is unconstitutional or conflicts with international law, provided such an examination is permissible according to foreign law and is not reserved for a special Court.

9. When English rules of Conflict of Laws refer to foreign laws recognition is the best evidence for determining whether the regulations of foreign authorities are to be regarded as the law of the foreign country, but it is not conclusive evidence.

10. The regulations of foreign authorities which have not been recognised may be applied as the law of the foreign country if they are in fact enforced in that country, notwithstanding that the authorities have not been recognised by Great Britain.

The Hague Conventions on Private International Law, Public Law and Public Policy

International and domestic conflict of laws

1. In 1929, the Permanent Court of International Justice considered, in relation to a claim for State responsibility arising out of an alleged breach of contract, what rules of Private International Law were to be applied by the court itself in order to determine the preliminary question whether a right of a proprietary nature according to municipal law had been violated.[1] The court was thus concerned with what may be called international rules of the conflict of laws.[2] Thirty years later, in the case of the *Application of the Convention of 1902 governing the Guardianship of Infants*,[3] the Interna-

---

[Editorial note: first published in International and Comparative Law Quaterly 8 (1959), 506–522.]

[1] *Serbian and Brazilian Loans Cases*, P.C.I.J., Ser. A, Nos. 14 and 15.
[2] Lipstein, *Transactions of the Grotius Society*, 29 (1944), pp. 51–83.
[3] *I.C.J. Reports*, 1958, p. 52.

tional Court of Justice examined the duty of a State to apply in its own courts certain rules of municipal conflict of laws which were embodied in a treaty, namely, the Hague Convention on Guardianship of June 12, 1902, of which the Netherlands (the plaintiff) and Sweden (the defendant) were parties. The guardianship in question involved a girl of Dutch nationality born in 1945 in Sweden of a Dutch father and a Swedish mother. The mother had died in December 1953, and in March 1954 the Dutch courts appointed the father guardian of the child in accordance with article 378 of the Dutch Civil Code. This was followed by the appointment of deputy guardians later on in 1954 in accordance with article 401 of the Dutch Code and the replacement of the father as guardian by another Dutch subject. The Swedish administrative authorities, by a series of measures approved by the Swedish administrative courts over the period between May 1954 and February 1956, ordered the protective upbringing of the child in Sweden in virtue of the Swedish law of June 6, 1924, on the ground that her mental health required it. At the same time the Swedish courts at first recognised the existence and validity of the Dutch guardianship as regards the care both of the person and of the property of the child,|but subsequently withdrew their recognition of the Dutch guardians in regard to the custody of the child. They held, however, that the two measures were complementary and not mutually exclusive, on the ground that the Hague Convention, which requires the recognition of a guardianship established according to the national law of the child, dealt with the private law aspects of guardianship, while the Swedish law was a measure of a public law character. The International Court of Justice, in a majority opinion, endorsed this view, while doubting whether the Convention included an implied reservation of public policy in favour of the *forum*. Judge Spender, who concurred, and Judge Winiarski, who dissented, appear to have been moved by the same considerations, though with different results. The recognition of an implied reservation of public policy formed, however, the reason of the concurring opinions of Judges Badawi, Spiropoulos, Moreno Quintana and Sir Hersch Lauterpacht, who relied, in addition, on public policy as a general principle of international law. Judge Cordova rejected the application of Swedish public policy and of Swedish public law in face of the terms of the Convention, article 7 of which only permitted the local authorities of the place of residence to take measures "in cases of urgency." In the light of the pleadings, however, no situation of urgency had been shown in his opinion. Judge Offerhaus followed the same line of thought. Judge Wellington Koo, on the other hand, accepted the need to take urgent measures as a justification of the Swedish action. Judge Kozevnikov relied on the maxim *pacta sunt servanda* without considering the substance of the dispute, which was that the Convention was open to differences of interpretation.

The court was thus called upon exclusively to determine a question of public international law, but in so doing it was inevitably compelled to express certain assumptions and to make pronouncements which fall within the sphere of domestic systems of the conflict of laws. Since these assumptions and pronouncements do not merely constitute evaluations of domestic law, which the court must treat as a fact,[4] but will form part of the body of rules of interpretation applicable to treaties establishing uniform rules of the conflict of laws, a somewhat detailed examination may be appropriate; the more so since some of the parties to the Hague Conventions on Private International Law have agreed to accept the jurisdiction of the International Court of Justice to determine disputes arising thereunder.[5]

| 2. The Hague Convention concerning the Guardianship of Infants of June 12, 1902,[6] proceeded upon two guiding principles. (1) The *lex patriae* of the child governs all questions of substantive law concerning the conditions for the establishment of guardianship and the powers of guardians over the person and the property of the child.[7] (2) The courts of the country of which the child is a national have primary, but not exclusive, jurisdiction to appoint a guardian. Subject to one exception,[8] which is of little interest here, the courts of the child's residence have subsidiary jurisdiction, which is ousted by the previous or subsequent appointment of a guardian by the law or by the courts having primary jurisdiction.[9] In addition, they may always exercise jurisdiction in case of urgency.[10]

In the exercise of this subsidiary jurisdiction the court of the child's residence follows its own procedure, while it must pay regard to the substantive provisions of the child's *lex patriae*.[11] However, there is some reason for the view that the *lex fori* applies without limitation if jurisdiction is exercised on

---

[4] P.C.I.J., Ser. A, No. 7, p. 19; Ser. A, Nos. 20–21, pp. 46, 124.

[5] Protocol of March 27, 1931, L.N.T.S., 167 (1936), p. 341; Hudson, *International Legislation*, 5, p. 933; for a list of the signatories, see Gutzwiller in *Schweizerisches Jahrbuch für Internationales Recht*, 2 (1945), p. 71, note 79.

[6] For the text and for literature, see Niboyet et Goulé, *Recueil des textes usuels de droit international*, II (1929), p. 147; Makarov, *Die Quellen des I.P.R.* (1929), p. 353; 95 *British and Foreign State Papers* 421; *Revue de droit international et de legislation comparée* (2nd ser.), 4 (1902), p. 485; Gutzwiller, *loc. cit.*, p. 60, note 40, pp. 92, 96–97; Lewald in Strupp, *Wöterbuch des Völkerrechts*, 1 (1924), p. 472; Van Hille in *Répertoire de droit international*, 10 (1931), p. 629, Nos. 182 *et seq.*; Plaisant, *Les règles de conflit de lois dans les traités* (1946) 312–329; Gutteridge, *Codification of Private International Law* (1951), p. 29.

[7] Arts. 1, 5, 6.

[8] Art. 2.

[9] Art. 9.

[10] Art. 7.

[11] Lewald in Strupp, *Wörterbuch des Völkerrechts*, I, p. 473; *Chabannes* v. *Chambre des tutelles*, decided on June 10, 1909, by the Swiss Federal Tribunal, B.G.E. 1909, I, 467, at p. 473; *Clunet* 38 (1911), p. 1348; Kosters-Bellemans, *Les Conventions de la Haye de 1902 et 1905* (1921), p. 786.

grounds of urgency,[12] or if it is impossible to ascertain the provisions of the *lex patriae*.[13]

Limits of the Convention: guardianship

3. The Convention applies whenever guardianship (*tutelle*) as distinct from custody (*puissance paternelle*) is an issue.[14] This involves, in the first place, that the courts of each contracting State are free to determine all questions of custody in accordance with their own rules of the conflict of laws, and that their jurisdiction is not subordinated to that of the courts of the child's nationality.[15] | It means, in the second place, that the Convention is applicable when custody is not exercised because both parents either have died or have been deprived of custody.[16] It is less easy to decide whether the Convention applies if only one of the parties has been deprived of custody or has died. The answer here must depend upon whether the matter is one of guardianship or of custody. Unfortunately, it does not appear possible to achieve a common definition of guardianship. The question whether custody (parental authority) or guardianship is in issue must finally come down to one of characterisation.

Characterisation in treaties

4. The fact that a particular legal system employs the term guardianship (*tutelle* or the like) in relation to some of the powers conferred upon a parent does not necessarily indicate the existence in that system of a guardianship within the meaning of the Convention, still less so, since, according to article 6 of the Convention, guardianship comprehends the care both of the child's

---

[12] Art. 7. Japiot in *Revue de droit international privé*, 8 (1912), 288, at p. 293.

[13] Tribunal of Nassoud (Roumania), September 20, 1926, *Clunet*, 54 (1927), 1174.

[14] *Re Badoud*, decided by the Tribunal of Geneva on May 6, 1912, *Clunet*, 40 (1913), 258; Kosters-Bellemans, p. 791; Court of Appeal, Berlin, November 28, 1913, cited by Lewald in Strupp, *Wörterbuch des Völkerrechts*, I, 472; *Internationales Privatrecht* (1930), Nos. 190, 216; Van Hille in *Répertoire de droit international*, 10 (1931), p. 630, No. 184 (d); The International Court of Justice, *I.C.J. Reports*, 1958, p. 65, brushed this distinction aside.

[15] For a draft of a Convention on Custody, see *International Law Association*, Dubrovnik Session, 1956, pp. 386–433. For the Dutch rules on custody, see the Dutch Civil Code, arts. 365–374 (e).

[16] Van Hille in *Répertoire de droit international*, 10 (1931), p. 630, No. 184 (d); Olivi in *Revue de droit international et de législation comparée* (2nd ser.) 6 (1904), 41, at p. 51; *Institut de Droit International*, Hamburg, 1891, *ibid.*, 23 (1891), 496, at p. 515.

person and of his property. When the case involves the application of a multilateral Convention, it would appear to be even less desirable or practicable to characterise private law institutions according to either the *lex fori* or to the *lex causae*, than it is in any system of municipal law, for both the *lex fori* and the *lex causae* are variable from the point of view of the Convention. Instead, it is necessary to examine the function of the provisions of the *lex causae* (which in the case of the Hague Conventions is normally the *lex patriae*, but may exceptionally be the law of the place of the residence of the child) and to interpret the terms of private international law employed by the Convention.

Guardianship: characterisation

5. European systems of guardianship may be conveniently classified in two ways.[17] First as to the method of appointment: this may be by operation of law, or by will, or by either a private body or a public authority. Secondly as to the class of persons who are to be treated as guardians: here the specific question is whether, upon the death of one spouse or upon his loss of custody (*puissance paternelle*), the other spouse succeeds to the custody, or is to be | regarded as a guardian. German, Swiss and Italian law require a guardianship only upon the death or incapacity of both parents.[18] Most systems which follow the French Civil Code concede *puissance paternelle* and *tutelle légale* to the father or, if he be dead, to the mother, but the use of the term *tutelle* should not be taken to imply that either parent is a guardian proper. Only the surviving parent is a guardian for certain purposes.[19] Austrian law requires a guardianship upon the death of the father, but not of the mother,[20] while Dutch and, it would appear, Swedish law make the appointment of the surviving parent a matter of guardianship proper.[21]

It appears, therefore, that guardianship is a broad, but not a uniform, institution in so far as either the class of persons or the method of appointment is concerned. It does not embrace the rights and duties of the parents, while both alive and qualified to act, in respect of the care and control of the

---

[17] Lehr in *Revue de droit international et de législation comparée* (2nd ser.) 4 (1902), pp. 315 *et seq.*; 9 (1907), pp. 52 *et seq.*, 171 *et seq.* (*out* of date in parts). *Cf.* Veith in Schlegelberger, *Rechtsvergleichendes Handwörterbuch*, 4 (1933), 770.

[18] Enneccerus-Kipp-Wolff, *Lehrbuch des Bürgerlichen Rechts*, II, 2 (6th ed., 1928), par. 101, I, p. 433; par. 106, I, 4; Swiss Civil Code, arts. 274, 346; Italian Civil Code, art. 343.

[19] Code Civil, arts. 373, 384 (*puissance paternelle*), 389, 390, 394 (*tutelle*); Ripert, Traité élémentaire de droit civil, I (3rd ed., 1946), No. 1983, p. 671, No. 2028, p. 683; Planiol et Ripert, *Traité pratique*, I (2nd ed., 1952), p. 486, No. 417, p. 487, No. 419.

[20] Austrian Civil Code, par. 187.

[21] Dutch Civil Code, art. 378.

child and of his property.[22] On the other hand, it is capable of covering any appointment subject to the special procedure applicable to guardians which is made by law, will or by any public or private authority in the absence, or upon the failure of the exercise of care and control of the infant by the parent entrusted primarily therewith. Since according to Dutch law a surviving parent becomes a guardian subject to the supervision of the court and is assisted by a deputyguardian,[23] there can be little doubt that the Convention applies to that case.

This conclusion is supported by an examination of the general structure of the Convention. The latter gives a subsidiary jurisdiction to the courts of the place of residence if no guardian has been appointed by the law or by the courts of the country of the child's nationality.[24] This presupposes, as the principal, if not the only, purpose of the Convention, the provision of machinery for the appointment of a guardian, if the parents who possess care and control by operation of law from the time of the birth of the child | have ceased to carry out their functions in this regard.[25] The main purpose is thus to fill any gap in the discharge of the office of guardian, and it may well be asked whether the distinction drawn in the Convention, between the primary role of the law and of the courts of the child's nationality, and the subsidiary function of the courts of the place of his residence is not unduly favourable to the former, since in reality the jurisdiction of the latter may be more important in practice.[26] No clear-cut answer can be given here, but the purpose of the Convention is achieved by two means: if a guardian has been appointed by the law or by the courts of the child's nationality, this appointment will be recognised automatically. In the absence of such an appointment, the courts of the child's residence are free to make appropriate temporary provision,[27] pending an appointment under the law or by the courts of the child's nationality.

---

[22] *Cf.* Olivi in *Revue de droit international et de législation comparée* (2nd ser.), 6 (1904), 41, at p. 51; *Institut de Droit International*, Hamburg 1891, *ibid.*, 23 (1891), 496, at p. 515; Veith in Schlegelberger, *Rechtsvergleichendes Handwörterbuch*, 4 (1933), 770, 773. For custody (*puissance paternelle*), see Marty in *Répertoire de droit international*, 10 (1931), p. 345, at p. 347, No. 8.

[23] Dutch Civil Code, arts. 378, 401, 402, 418.

[24] Arts. 3 and 7.

[25] See the observations by Lewald in Strupp. *Wörterbuch des Völkerrechts*, I, at p. 472; Guyot in *Répertoire de droit international*, 10 (1931), p. 695, No. 68.

[26] See Lewald, above, note 25.

[27] For the limits of a temporary guardianship, see below, no. 10.

Limits of the Convention: modern children's legislation

6. When the Convention on Guardianship was concluded in 1902, after it had first been proposed in 1894, the modern trend towards legislation for the protection of children in the general interest of society, irrespective of the rules of guardianship established by private law, had hardly made itself felt. True, legislation in various countries[28] had made provision for depriving parents of the care and control of their children in order to protect the latter from the criminal acts of the former. On the other hand, the need for provision for children whose moral or physical state calls for the intervention of public authorities in their education and upbringing was only to be realised later.[29] Therefore, it is not surprising that the Convention laid down no express rule as to the application of laws of this type, whether enacted by the country of which the child is a national or by the country where he resides. It was concerned only with the speedy appointment of a guardian if no person should be charged with the care and control of the child and with the |prevention of disputes between two or more persons who, under different legal systems, should be able to claim to act. Whether the courts of the place of residence have retained the power to apply their own children's legislation to foreign children who are nationals of other countries parties to the Convention, whether these laws must give way to the rules of general private law of the *lex patriae* or, finally, whether perhaps the children's legislation of the *lex patriae* itself must be applied, are thus questions which can only be answered upon a study of the principle involved and of the general structure of the Convention.

Conflict of laws and public law

7. It is generally agreed among writers that the conflict of laws itself is only concerned with ascertaining the rules of private law which are applicable,[30] and that different rules of choice of law apply in relation to public

---

[28] See, *e.g.*, the French laws, of July 24, 1889, April 19, 1898, June 27, 1904; German Civil Code, paras. 1666, 1838; Law of July 9, 1922, paras. 63 *et seq.* English Children Act, 1908, s. 58 (1), replacing the Industrial Schools Act, 1886, s. 17. Marty, above, note 22, at p. 350, No. 15, p. 362, No. 61. And see, for a survey, Neumeyer, *Internationales Verwaltungsrecht*, I (1910), 228–231.

[29] German Law of July 9, 1922; Belgium, Laws of December 15, 1912; June 14, 1920; France, Decree-Law of October 30, 1935; Ordinance of December 23, 1958; Decree of January 7, 1959; Dutch Civil Code, arts. 365–373; English Children and Young Persons Act, 1933, s. 61 (1) (a); Children Act, 1948, ss. 1, 2. And see Neumeyer, *loc. cit.*, pp. 235–243; Kraemer-Bach, *La Vie Judiciaire*, 1959, No. 675.

[30] As regards the Hague Conventions on Private International Law, see Anon. in *Revue*

law.[31] In other words, private international law or the conflict of laws determines the system of laws which governs the relations between individuals. It is concerned with relations between individuals and public authorities only if the latter act *jure negotii*, but not if they act *jure imperil*.[32] Laws dealing with the relation between individuals and public authorities in the sovereign exercise of public functions are subject to special rules of administrative, procedural or criminal conflict of laws.[33] These rules differ from the ordinary rules of the conflict of laws in civil matters inasmuch as they are strictly unilateral. The reason is that they have to do with a process of self-limitation and not with a true process of choice of law.[34] The question is never whether foreign public law is applicable; it is whether the public law of the *forum* is applicable in the particular circumstances of the case. Consequently, foreign laws of an administrative, procedural or criminal character are not enforced by the courts of other countries. | This principle is often expressed in the form of a proposition that foreign public laws are not applied.[35] However, some of their effects may have to be recognised if they have already occurred abroad. For instance, an act of expropriation abroad, a judgment *in rem* or a foreign adjudication in bankruptcy may have resulted in a transfer of title[36]; a foreign import or export regulation may render the performance of a contract illegal[37]; a foreign devaluation of currency may affect a debt governed by English law if the money of account is foreign[38]; the imposition of a tax abroad may attract relief from taxation in England.

---

de droit international privé 10 (1914), 5, at pp. 19–20; *ibid.*, 6 (1910), 193, at p. 184; *Chabannes v. Chambre des tutelles*, decided by the Swiss Federal Tribunal on June 10, 1909, B.G.E., 1909, I, p. 467; *Clunet* 38 (1911), p. 1348; Kosters-Bellemans 786, at p. 788.

[31] See, *e.g.*, Fedozzi, "Sur l'efficacité extraterritoriale des lois et des actes de droit public," in *Recueil des Cours de la Haye* 27 (1929, II), pp. 145–242; Barile. *Appunti sul valore del diritto pubblico straniero nel ordinamento nazionale* (1948); Sperduti, "Efficacia interna di atti stranieri di amministrazione pubblica," *Foro Padano*, 1951, 810; De Nova in *Diritto Internazionale* 13 (1959), 13, at p. 21, with further literature; Plaisant, *loc. cit.*, pp. 341–342, 366.

[32] See Dicey, *Conflict of Laws* (7th ed., 1958), Rule 21, and especially p. 162 (penal, revenue laws), p. 599 (foreign State claiming *bona vacantia*).

[33] See, *e.g.*, Neumeyer, *Internationales Verwaltungsrecht* (1910–36); Riezler, *Internationales Zivilprozessrecht* (1949); Morelli, *Diritto processuale civile internazionale* (2nd ed., 1954); Udina, *Diritto internazionale tributario* (1949); Giuliano, *Il fallimento nel diritto processuale civile internazionale* (1943).

[34] Lipstein in B.Y.I.L. 26 (1949), 553; and see below, p. 517.

[35] Maury in *Revue critique de droit international* 43 (1954), 7, at p. 10; Niboyet, *Traité de Droit International Privé Français* IV (1947), pp. 1098 *et seq.;* Dicey, Rule 21, p. 159, expresses the same principle in terms of jurisdiction.

[36] *Luther v. Sagor* [1921] 3 K.B. 532; *Castrique v. Imrie* (1870) L.R. 4 H.L. 414; Dicey, pp. 982–983; Rule 144, p. 703.

[37] *Ralli v. Compania Naviera Sota y Aznar* [1920] 2 K.B. 287; *Regazzoni v. Sethia* [1958] A.C. 301. And see Sir Percy Spender, *I.C.J. Reports*, 1958, 118–119.

[38] *Re Chesterman's Trusts* [1923] Ch. 466.

Children's protective upbringing. Characterisation

8. The only question is, therefore, whether in any particular case the rules concerning protective upbringing of children who are in need of care or protection must be characterised as falling within the sphere of guardianship, as envisaged by the Convention, or as falling within the sphere of administrative law. This depends upon the function of the rules within the framework of the law as a whole, and not upon whether they form part of a statute which regulates guardianship as such (as does the Dutch Civil Code).

Guardianship as an institution of private law maintains an intimate tie with the family. It maintains a link between the child and his nearest relatives, or a council composed of some of them; it recognises appointments by operation of law or by will; and it relies on the supervision of the guardian by the civil courts. In short, both in respect of the persons and the property concerned, the existence of the family is its basis, and the maintenance of the family is its purpose.

Protective upbringing, as an administrative measure, answers a different purpose. It separates the child from his parents or his normal guardians, does not aim at maintaining or strengthening the family ties, is concerned only with the physical and moral welfare of the child[39] and is often carried out by or under the supervision of administrative authorities.

| The distinction between guardianship, as an institution of private law, and the protective upbringing of children, as an administrative measure, results, as has been seen, in the application of different conflict rules. As regards administrative measures of upbringing, in the absence of an express treaty to the contrary,[40] each country is free to apply its own children's legislation, even if it overrides the powers of the foreign parent or guardian which are to be recognised according to the ordinary rules of the conflict of laws or in virtue of a treaty. At the same time, the negative effect of foreign children's legislation may have to be recognised in virtue of the ordinary rules of the conflict of laws or of a treaty, if the effect has been to deprive the parent or guardian of his function and to vest it in the foreign public authority or in a person designated by it.

---

[39] No argument to the contrary can be derived from the wording of the English Guardianship of Infants Act, 1925, s. 1. There the insistence upon the welfare of the child as the paramount consideration in awarding *custody* to either parent serves to stress that, since the rights of husband and wife to the custody of their children are equal, the right of neither is to prevail as such.

[40] German Supreme Court, June 30, 1927, RGZ. 117, p. 376; Court of Appeal, Karlsruhe, November 26, 1926; Niemeyer's *Zeitschrift für Internationales Recht* 37 (1927), p. 388; Lewald, *Internationales Privatrecht*, No. 216, p. 161; Neumeyer, *loc.* cit., pp. 243–247, esp. p. 245; Pillet in *Clunet* 19 (1892), 5, at p. 10. But see Staudinger-Raape, *Einführungsgesetz* (9th ed., 1931), p. 618, B. III. 8.

The Convention and public law

9. The question remains whether the Hague Convention excludes the application of the children's legislation of the *forum*, in derogation of the general principle outlined above, which distinguishes between conflicts of private and public law. It is suggested that the structure of the Convention itself provides the answer here.

(a) If the care and control of the child is vested in the parents in virtue of their parental power under foreign law, the imposition of protective upbringing by the courts of the child's residence is a measure depriving the parents of their parental power and substituting another authority to fill the gap. The deprivation of parental power is not covered by the Convention, and each country thus retains its freedom of action.[41] The appointment of a guardian, and *a fortiori* an order for protective upbringing, is permissible under the Convention in the absence of a previous appointment according to the *lex patriae* or in case of urgency.

(b) If the child is without a parent or guardian charged with his care according to the *lex patriae*, the courts of the child's residence are free to appoint a guardian according to the general law applicable by those courts (which is normally but not necessarily the *lex patriae*[42]) or in accordance with their own children's legislation.[43]

(c) If the child is in charge of a guardian previously appointed | by the law or by the authorities of the country of which he is a national, the courts of the child's residence retain nevertheless jurisdiction in cases of urgency and can apply their own law.[44]

It follows, as a general conclusion, that it is unnecessary, in so far as cases (a) and (b) are concerned, to distinguish within the framework of the Convention between the application of rules of private law and public law in matters of guardianship. As regards case (c) the same conclusion holds if the local action is determined by reasons of urgency, no matter whether it leads to the appointment of a guardian according to the private law of the *forum* or to an order for protective upbringing according to the public law of the *forum*. In the exceptional case, where no need arises for the appointment of a guardian according to private law, it is still possible that an order for protective upbringing may be urgently required.[45] In this situation only, the pro-

---

[41] Above, p. 508; *cf.* Neumeyer, *loc. cit.*, p. 245, but see p. 232.
[42] See above, para. 2, and notes 12, 13.
[43] Art. 3.
[44] Art. 7.
[45] This situation existed apparently in the case under review. In certain countries, such as Germany, the appointment of a guardian is required, before a measure of protective upbringing can be contemplated. Measures concerning compulsory upbringing are necessari-

visions of the public law of the *forum*, and not those of the Convention, must be considered exclusively (above, pp. 512–514).

Thus, it has been shown that the provisions of the *lex fori* on protective upbringing are applicable, in principle, because they are rules of public law, the sphere of operation of which is determined by conflict rules of their own, distinct from those on private law governed by the Convention. It has been shown, further, that the Convention does not exclude altogether, in terms, the application of the *lex fori*, whether public or private. The reason for the simultaneous operation of foreign private law and local public law within its framework emerges from the technique of the Convention. It not only determines the question of choice of law by requiring the application of the *lex patriae* in normal, though not in all, cases. It also divides jurisdiction between the courts of the nationality and those of the residence of the child. In so far as the latter are concerned, it is conceded that they can apply their own law as a whole in case of urgency, and in certain circumstances even when not acting for urgent reasons (above, No. 2). Thus, the children's legislation of the place of the child's residence is not excluded *in limine*. It requires strong evidence to prove that in all other cases where the courts of the residence exercise jurisdiction, they must, in virtue of the Convention, apply the private law of the *lex patriae* relating to guardianship, to the exclusion of both their own rules|of an administrative or welfare character relating to infants as well as those forming part of the *lex patriae*.[46] In the dispute between the Netherlands and Sweden, this consideration was obscured by the fact that the rules on protective upbringing figure in the Dutch Civil Code and are administered by the ordinary civil courts. However, this formal aspect should not affect the process of characterisation (above, No. 8) and the ensuing choice of law. Instead, having regard to the well-known phenomenon of *dépéçage* in the conflict of laws, the two sets of rules of foreign private law and local public or private law are complementary, as the following considerations confirm independently.

The relation between the lex patriae and the lex fori

10. It has been set out above (Nos. 2, 9) in what circumstances apart from ordering protective upbringing, the courts of the child's residence may take measures on their own to appoint a guardian in accordance with the *lex fori*.

---

ly urgent measures. *Cf.* Court of Appeal, Karlsruhe, November 26, 1926, Niemeyer's *Zeischrift für internationales Recht*, 37 (1927), 388, at p. 390.

[46] Compare Neumeyer, *loc. cit.*, p. 244; Rehbock in *Revue critique de droit international privé*, 31 (1936), 703, at p. 709, and see below, note 61.

In all these cases the Convention requires that the guardianship established in the country of the child's residence must cease, once a guardian has been appointed under the *lex patriae*.[47] There is, however, some evidence to show that the courts of the country of the child's residence can and must determine of their own motion not only whether but also when the time has arrived for releasing the locally appointed guardian.[48] It may be that this reservation of the *lex fori* is limited to cases where the local appointment was made for reasons of urgency, and does not apply to the general rule embodied in Article 4 of the Convention,[49] but there is not sufficient evidence in support of this restrictive interpretation.

Since both Sweden and the Netherlands failed to communicate the details of the case to the court, it was and is impossible to examine this aspect of it, both as regards the appointment of a guardian or an order for protective upbringing according to the *lex fori*. If it had been possible, this examination would have included the question whether, in finding grounds for applying measures of urgency according to the private or public law of the *forum* and for maintaining them over a number of years, the Swedish | authorities violated their duties under the treaty. In these circumstances, the presumption is in favour of the defendant Government, Sweden.

Limits of the Convention: public policy

11. The conclusion has been reached above that the *lex patriae* and the courts of the country of which the child is a national have primary jurisdiction, that the courts of the child's residence have subsidiary jurisdiction, that a choice of law rule concerning guardianship relates to guardianship as known in private law, that public measures of protective upbringing are governed by different conflict rules and, finally, that the Convention has preserved, to a certain extent, the principle of the application of their own law by the courts of the child's residence. In the light of these conclusions, it is strictly speaking unnecessary to discuss whether the appointment of a guardian in virtue of the *lex patriae* can be ousted on grounds of public policy. Nevertheless, it is necessary in interpreting the Convention, to consider whether the excep-

---

[47] Art. 4, third paragraph.

[48] *Foders* v. *Massac*, decided by the Tribunal Civil of Bordeaux on January 11, 1909; *Clunet*, 36 (1909), 1085, Kosters-Bellemans, p. 751, and by the Court of Appeal of Bordeaux on July 6, 1909, and again on May 30, 1910, *Clunet*, 37 (1910), 220; 38 (1911), 614; *Revue de droit international privé*, 6 (1910), 884; Kosters-Bellemans, pp. 755, 757; Lewald in Strupp, *Wörterbuch des Völkerrechts*, *I*, 472, at p. 473; Guyot in *Répertoire de droit international*, 10 (1931) p. 698, No. 78.

[49] Japiot in *Revue de droit international privé*, 8 (1912), 288, at p. 293.

tion of public policy has been retained, the more so since the judges of the International Court of Justice relied upon it to a certain extent.

Public policy – meaning

12. It may be recalled that the exception of public policy in the conflict of laws had two different meanings attributed to it in the course of the last century. As a purely negative notion, which can be traced back through the ages, it fulfils the function of excluding the application of foreign law normally applicable according to the ordinary rules of the conflict of laws, if its application in the particular case would be contrary to the fundamental notions of morality or policy on which the *lex fori* is based.[50]

On the other hand, following Mancini's distinction between necessary and voluntary rules of private law and rules of public policy,[51] a school of thought, mainly in countries influenced by | French and Italian doctrine, asserted that certain rules of the *lex fori*, alleged to be of the "ordre public international" may be of paramount importance and must be applied in all circumstances, to the exclusion of foreign law, whatever its character. Thus, public policy assumed a positive character. The mandatory nature of certain rules of the *lex fori*, whether of a public or private law character, was believed to require the application of the *lex fori* without any consideration as to whether or not foreign law is applicable in the first place. It is impossible to

---

[50] Dicey, *Conflict of Laws* (7th ed., 1958), General Principle No. 2, p. 12; Batiffol, *Traité élementaire de droit international privé* (2nd ed., 1955), Nos. 356 *et seq.*, p. 412; Niboyet, *Traité de droit international privé français*, III (1944), No. 1021, p. 493; No. 1021 *bis*, p. 503; Wolff, *Das Internationale Privatrecht Deutschlands* (3rd ed., 1954), p. 60; Dölle in *Deutsche Landesreferate zum III. Internationalen Kongress für Rechtsvergleichung*, London, 1950, pp. 397 *et seq.*; Staudinger-Raape, *Einführungsgesetz*, art. 30; Monaco, *L'efficacia della legge nello spazio* (1954), No. 41, pp. 81 *et seq.*; Schnitzer, *Internationales Privatrecht* (4th ed., 1958), I, 225, at pp. 230–232. For older writers, see Savigny, *System des heutigen Römischen Rechts*, 8 (1849), para. 349; Story, *Conflict of Laws* (8th ed., 1883), paras. 25, 32; Foelix, Droit *International Privé* (4th ed., 1866), I, p. 28, No. 15.

[51] *Clunet*, 1 (1874), 221, 284; Sereni, *The Italian Conception of International Law* (1943), pp. 164–166; and see the critique of Fedozzi, *Recueil des Cours de la Haye*, 27 (1929), II), 145, at p. 149; Brocher, *Nouveau Traité de droit international privé* (1876), pp. 52 *et seq.*; Pillet, *Principes de droit international privé* (1903), ss. 136 *et seq.*, pp. 292 *et seq.*; Weiss, *Traité théorique et pratique de droit international privé*, III (1898), 83 at pp. 90–96; Despagnet, *Précis de droit international privé* (5th ed., 1901), p. 357, at p. 361; Valéry, *Manuel de droit international privé* (1914), pp. 566 *et seq.*, especially pp. 570–583; and see the critique by Niboyet, *Traité*, III (1944), No. 1021, p. 491; Bartin, *Principes de droit international privé français*, I, paras. 91, 93, 94, pp. 243, 246, 262; Von Bar, *Theorie und Praxis des internationalen Privatrechts, I* (2nd ed., 1889), No. 30, p. 95, No. 36, p. 127; and compare the observations of Kahn-Freund, *Transactions of the Grotius Society*, 39 (1954). 39, at p. 41.

discuss here the fallacies of this doctrine which confuses mandatory rules of domestic private law with rules of the conflict of laws[52] and fails to perceive that administrative, criminal, fiscal and procedural laws – often grouped together as rules of public law – are governed by different, unilateral rules of self-limitation.[53] The difference of approach may be summed up thus: the function of public policy in the conflict of laws is to exclude foreign law, which is normally applicable because in the individual case its effect offends the local notions of morality or policy, because of its content and the degree of intensity with which the case is connected with the *forum*. Foreign public law is inapplicable *in limine*, and the question cannot arise of excluding it in a particular case. It must suffice to state that in the overwhelming majority of countries of continental Europe, the function of public policy is regarded today as purely negative.[54] In the ensuing discussion, public policy is understood in this sense.

The Convention on Guardianship

13. The question is, therefore, whether the Hague Convention on Guardianship permits the contracting parties to disregard the *lex patriae*, which is declared to be normally applicable, on the ground that its effect in a particular instance is incompatible with fundamental notions of morality and policy of the *forum*.

When the Hague Conventions on Private International Law came | into force, it was generally held that the specific designation by the terms of the Convention of a law applicable prevented the exclusion of that law for reasons of public policy.

This view produced a strong reaction on the ground that "cette affirmation du système de la personnalité des lois dans toute son étendue sans le correctif indispensable de l'ordre public devait forcément provoquer des résistances."[55] This resistance did not fail to materialise, and as early as 1914 France denounced the Conventions on Marriage, Divorce and Guardianship for this very reason. However, as regards the Convention on Guardianship it could be said with some justification: "la tutelle n'intéresse ... que d'une façon accidentelle l'ordre du pays où réside le pupille étranger ... il n'y

---

[52] This confusion manifests itself in the converse sense within private international law proper, when the objectivist school would allow free choice of law only if the rules of contract of the *lex fori* are merely *lois supplétives* and permit freedom of contract.

[53] Above, No. 7. But see Judge Moreno Quintana, *I.C.J. Reports*, 1958, at p. 105.

[54] For a recent summing up, see Maury in *Revue critique de droit international privé*, 43 (1954), 6 *et seq.*

[55] *Revue de droit international privé*, 10 (1914), 364, at p. 384; *cf. ibid.*, 12 (1912), 839.

a aucun interét à ce que cette assistance soit organisée plutôt d'après sa propre loi que d'après la législation des parties."[56]

Writers are divided on this subject. The overwhelming majority[57] believe that, in the absence of an express reservation of public policy by the Treaty, the conflict rules of the Treaty must prevail. Niboyet, who has examined this question closely,[58] inclines in principle to the contrary view where the treaty is silent, but recognises that the Hague Conventions, by specifically excluding the *lex patriæ* in certain circumstances, have thereby eliminated public policy as a general means of excluding foreign law.[59] Plaisant appears to share this view when he states[60]: "La réserve de l'ordre public ... doit être sous-entendue dans les traités qui ne contiennent aucune clause à cet égard et qui n'ont pas élaborés de telle sorte que la volonté formelle des contractants ait été de supprimer l'intervention de l'ordre public, des mesures ayant été prises par ailleurs pour donner des garanties suffisantes à la lex fori."

Thus all writers, with the possible exception of Plaisant, who | does not examine the Conventions on their facts, agree that within the framework of the Hague Conventions there is no reason for the operation of public policy. The attitude of the contracting States (especially France and Belgium) as well as the practice of the courts[61] bear out the same conclusion. The public policy

---

[56] Lehr in *Revue de droit international et de législation comparée* (2nd ed., ser.), 4 (1902), 315, at p. 337.

[57] Lewald, in *Revue de droit international privé*, 23 (1928), 149, at p. 164; *Répertoire de droit international*, 7 (1930), No. 49, p. 308; Melchior, *Die Grundlagen des Deutschen Internationalen Privatrechts* (1932), para. 238, p. 359; Wolff, *Das Internationale Privatrecht Deutschlands* (3rd ed., 1954), p. 70; Schnitzer, *Handbuch des Internationalen Privatrechts* (4th ed., 1958), I, 237; Dölle in *Deutsche Landesreferate* (above, note 50), at p. 415; Rehbock in *Revue critique de droit international privé*, 31 (1936), at p. 709.

[58] *Traité de droit international privé français*, III (1944), No. 1026, p. 522, III; No. 1032, p. 540. See also Batiffol, *Traité élémentaire de droit international privé*, no. 364, p. 421; Anon. in *Revue de droit international privé*, 10 (1914), 5, at pp. 19–20.

[59] *Traité*, III, no. 1026, pp. 515–522.

[60] *Les règles de conflit de lois dans les traités* (1946), p. 93, but see, *e.g.*, pp. 17, 301, 324, 349, 390.

[61] For Italy, see: *Ricci* v. *Panayotis*, decided on July 13, 1939, by the Court of Cassation, *Foro Italiano*, 1939, I, 1097, with a note; *Wedenisoff*, decided on June 14, 1928, by the Court of Cassation, *Giurisprudenza Italiana*, 1928, I, 1, 983, on appeal from the Court of Appeal of Milan, June 30, 1927, *Giur. It.*, 1927, I, 2, 472; *Manassei* v. *Kossatkin*, decided on December 30, 1911, by the Court of Cassation, Rome (United Sections), *Giur. It.*, 1912, I, 1, 5; *Zannoni* v. *Sbissa*, decided on December 29, 1920, by the Court of Appeal of Milan, *Giur. It.*, 1921, I, 2, 14, with further references; *Payola* v. *Ferro*, decided on March 3, 1921, by the Court of Appeal of Milan, *Giur. It.*, 1921, I, 2, 277; *Filo della Torre* v. *Alvarez de Toledo*, decided on August 4, 1920, by the Court of Appeal of Naples, *Giur. It.*, 1920, I, 2, 442; *Del Vecchio* v. *Connio*, decided on November 24, 1920, by the Court of Appeal of Milan, *Giur. It.*, 1920, I, 2, 446. For The Netherlands, see, to the same effect: Rb. Rotterdam, August 9, 1933, *W.* 12865; December 18, 1933, *W.* 12774; *N.J.* 1934, 546; The Hague, August 28, 1936, *W. and N.J.*, 1936, n. 920; Doordrecht, May 20, 1936, *W. and N.J.*, 1936, n. 456, *Bull. Inst. Int.*, 35, p. 84; *N.J.*, 1936, p. 816; Rotterdam, May 29, 1936; *W. and N.J.*, 1936, n. 454;

of the *forum* cannot be called in aid in order to exclude a guardianship proper established by the *lex patriae*. And, if it could, it would only lead to the application of the rules of the *lex fori* on guardianship proper, and not of the rules of protective upbringing, for their application depends upon different conflict rules, as was shown above (No. 7). Moreover, in the particular circumstances of the dispute between the Netherlands and Sweden it is difficult to see in what respect the operation of Dutch law, which confers the rights and duties of a guardian upon the legitimate father, can be incompatible with the fundamental notions of morality and policy of Swedish law. In fact, it would appear that Swedish law sanctions the same solution. In reality, as was shown above (No. 9), the Dutch guardianship is supplemented, but not ousted, by the Swedish measure ordering protective upbringing.

Public policy as a general principle of international law

14. One further aspect of public policy remains to be considered. In a concurring judgment Sir Hersch Lauterpacht argued that since public policy is recognised in all municipal systems of the conflict of laws, it forms a general principle of international law which may be applied in supplementing the interpretation of a treaty on conflict of laws. This argument must be examined by considering the formal and material aspects of the alleged general principle.

| The Convention and general principles of law

15. In the first place, public policy is a means of excluding foreign law which is normally applicable according to the conflict rules of the *forum*. Since municipal law is free to determine whether and in what circumstances foreign law is to be applied in the first instance,[62] the exception of public policy is merely an affirmation, in general terms, of that freedom. However, a State can fetter its freedom to apply its own law or that of any other country by entering into a treaty which binds it generally to apply a specific system of laws. Since the exception of public policy is merely the reverse aspect, in specific cases, of the freedom to apply or not to apply foreign law generally,

---

Bull. Inst. Int., 35, p. 81; *Revue critique de droit international privé*, 31 (1936), 703. But see "Hertogenbosch," June 16, 1936, *W. and N.J.*, 1936, n. 479; *Bull. Inst. Int.*, 35, p. 281; July 31, 1936, *W. and N.J.*, 1936, n. 360, *Bull. Inst. Int.*, 36, p. 40. And see *Zeitschrift für ausländisches und internationales Privatrecht*, 11 (1937), p. 206.

[62] Lipstein in *Transactions of the Grotius Society*, 27 (1942), pp. 142 *et seq.*

it may well be asked whether, in fettering its general discretion to apply or not to apply foreign law, a State has not also fettered its discretion to reject foreign law which has thus been rendered applicable. If a multilateral treaty in matters of conflict of laws is to have any meaning beyond that of an essay in drafting uniform conflict rules, and is to be effective between country and country, it is essential that the initial discretion, which has been fettered by the treaty, should not be restored by implication, in the absence of a clear indication in this direction.[63] The debates preceding the conclusion of the Hague Conventions show that this consideration was well in the foreground of the discussion[64] and led to the suppression of any reservation of public policy. If the treaty is capable of interpretation, if necessary by reference to the *Travaux préparatoires*, it does not require supplementation by general principles of law.

Common practice and general principles of law

16. In the second place, an apparent identity of terminology conceals a material diversity of notions as to what effects of foreign law are against public policy.[65] Formal unanimity does not supply a uniform set of material rules.[66] At best it may set a standard, the violation of which may constitute a denial of justice leading to international responsibility, but it is significant that hitherto neither the enactment of a particular conflict rule nor the refusal to apply foreign law which governs in virtue of such a rule has led to an international dispute.[67]

| Instead, the universal acceptance of public policy as a corrective controlling the normal application of foreign law shows that States cannot agree on any general standards of law in this field and that they recognise the fundamental diversity of laws resulting from their different cultural, social and economic background. This diversity manifests itself not only in the substantive law, but also in the concept of public policy, which excludes foreign law.

---

[63] See above, No. 13, especially notes 58 and 59, but see the cautious remarks of Lewald in *Revue de droit international privé*, 23 (1928), 149, at pp. 164–165, and of Niboyet, *Traité*, III (1944), No. 1026, p. 523.

[64] Niboyet, *Traité*, III (1944), No. 1026, pp. 515–519, and see above, No. 13.

[65] Niboyet, *loc.* cit., p. 521.

[66] Lipstein, *loc.* cit., p. 147, and note 27 with further literature.

[67] Lipstein, *loc. cit.*, p. 143, note 4, with further references.

Public policy in international law

17. However, even if a common basis of public policy in the conflict of laws could be found, it would not become a general principle of law in the terms of article 38 of the Statute of the Court. The function of public policy in the conflict of laws, as was pointed out above (No. 12), consists in the exclusion of the foreign private law which is normally applicable and in the substitution of the private law of the *forum*. However, international courts have no *lex fori* other than public international law, and this is incapable of replacing domestic rules of private law.[68] Nor is there any need to replace them. International courts are not called upon to apply private law, which for their purposes is a fact, and may, if it is patently unjust, support a claim for damages. Thus, domestic law is neither applied nor rejected by an international tribunal.

Meaning of public policy in international law

18. In the third place, if a common formal content of the principle of public policy is to be established which is significant in public international law, it is this: a country which is free to apply foreign law may also refuse to apply foreign law. So expressed, the principle reiterates the rule that, within the sphere of domestic jurisdiction, such as the conflict of laws, a State is free, subject only to the general rules of international law. In addition it may be concluded that, since rules of the conflict of laws fall within the sphere of domestic jurisdiction, a treaty which fetters the legislative powers of States in matters of the conflict of laws, must be interpreted restrictively. Thus public policy as a general principle of international law administered by international courts is either identical with international law as a whole or it expresses the principle that, within its own sphere, a State is sovereign and free, unless bound by a treaty. It adds nothing to the recognised general principles of law, municipal or international.

---

[68] Lipstein, *loc. cit.*, Vol. 87 (1942), pp. 149, 156–157, and note 67, with references; Vol. 29 (1944), pp. 63–66. See also Niboyet, *Traité*, III (1944), No. 1041, p. 562; Batiffol, *Traité élémentaire*, No. 368, p. 421; Schnitzer, *Handbuch*, I, p. 239.

Protected Interests in the Law of Torts

Introduction: The Problems

(1) Whichever is taken as the point of departure, a general principle of liability for injurious acts done intentionally or negligently, or a catalogue of individual protected interests, and whatever the wish to establish criteria of general liability, a comparison between some of the leading systems of the law of the Western World – both civil and common law – shows that it is impossible to get away from the individual situation, irrespective of the force of an existing, or the desire for the creation of, a general principle.

The reason is not far to seek. The protection of private interests against external interference must vary with the change in the evaluation of those interests in a changing society and economy. Where formerly the preservation of the physical integrity of the plaintiff and his servants against direct acts, and the protection of land and movable objects against similar interference ranked foremost, modern conditions require the protection against

[Editorial note: first published in Cambridge Law Journal 22 (1963), 85–103.]

indirect violations of the economic potential of the individual and of commercial or industrial enterprises. For modern conditions extend vastly the circle of personal and commercial relations and increase the area of dangerous or potentially dangerous activities.

Certain aspects have remained constant: there must be an act or omission which can be imputed to a person, which is illicit or not justified – one is tempted to say looking at the situation from the standpont of the victim: contrary to a duty, instead of contrary to law (*widerrechtlich*) or not justified[1] – and there must normally be damage. Yet certain areas remain grey:

(1) What is the duty?

(2) What circle of persons does it protect?

(3) Is the duty towards others compatible with the lawful exercise of a right–*i.e.*, is abuse of rights accepted?

(4) Is the burden of proof about to be shifted to the defendant, thus creating a risk-determined liability?

(5) Is damage required?

|Speaking of duty alone, one is tempted to say, therefore, that the content of duty is variable, while the principle of reparation for culpable illegal acts remains constant.

(2) Formerly, it could be stated that, unlike the representative systems of the civil law (French, German), English, and following it, American law, had concentrated to a much greater extent on the development of the law of tort, but events during the last eighty years in France and the increasingly rapid development in Germany (according to my impression particularly rapid in the last ten years) have closed the gap, and a comparison of the respective case law, *jurisprudence* and *Rechtsprechung* will prove useful. This will be all the more rewarding since the law of torts has not been examined as thoroughly on a comparative basis as other branches of legal learning. The reason is clear: case law is more difficult to compare than statute law, and the tenor of continental judgments does not make fine distinctions as readily available as the form of common law decisions.

In view of the foregoing it is proposed to take the common law as a starting point, for it offers a highly categorised and flexible system of rules and to examine then to what extent the civil law systems have reached similar, more extensive, or more restricted rules, or no rules at all. Such an investigation will reveal not only a variety of legal techniques, but also the differing valuation of interests deserving protection.[2]

---

[1] *Cf.* Esser, *Revue internationale de droit comparé*, 1961, p. 481 at p. 488, and see BGHZ 27, 137 (1958).

[2] For some recent discussions, see von Caemmerer, *100 Jahre Deutsches Rechtsleben* (1960), II, 49; Esser, *Revue internationale de droit comparé*, 1961, p. 481. Mazeaud & Tune, *Traité théorique et pratique de la responsabilité civile*, 5th ed., 1957–60; Seavey (1942) 56

Areas of Agreement: Direct Damage to Persons and Property Excluding Nervous Shock

(3) We will begin with those situations where agreement is obvious. The protection of the person himself against direct interference, be it intentional or negligent, is recognised throughout. It may be noted, however, at this stage, that in the United States, considerations of risk distribution and of redressing unjust enrichment have made their appearance (Keeton, James).

Thus the English tort of intentional application of force to another person (*battery*) has its counterpart elsewhere, subject to the question whether damage must be shown. But what is the | attitude towards *assault*, defined as an attempt to commit battery (*i.e.*, to apply force) against another person who reasonably believes that his assailant has the necessary present ability to effect this purpose?

Leaving aside the question of damage, this introduces the problem of fear induced by the act, and of shock. Incidentally it opens the more general question whether any intentional or negligent act causing damage gives rise to a claim.

As to the first: fear and shock, *Wilkinson* v. *Downton* [1897] 2 Q.B. 57 laid down that even statements, and not only acts, calculated to cause harm and doing so indirectly, can be actionable.[3] A German court has attempted to overcome this difficulty in giving a remedy under paragraph 823 BGB in these circumstances on the ground of criminal assault.[4] As for French law the question is more difficult to answer.

The matter is different where the shock inflicted on one person is the unintended consequence of a wilful or negligent injurious act against another. Here the literature[5] is divided, and the cases distinguish on the basis of the test whether a duty is owed to the person suffering the shock.[6] The reason is,

---

Harv.L.R. 72, 81; C. Wright (1948) 26 Can.Bar Rev. 46, 50; Braybrook (1957–59) 4 Annual L.R.U.W. Australia 209; Heuston (1959) 2 Univ. of Melbourne L.R. 34; F. James (1958) 8 Buffalo L.R. 315, 321, 325; Keeton (1959) 72 Harv. L.R. 401; Ward (1956) 42 Cornell L.R. 28; Pedrick, C. A. Wright and Heuston in (1961) *Journal of The Society of Public Teachers of Law*, 12–35; Reinhardt, *Juristenzeitung*, 1961, 713; Raiser, *ibid.* 1961, 464, 469.

[3] For American practice see Magruder (1936) 49 Harv.L.R. 1033 at p. 1045 *et seq.*

[4] Aachen, January 12, 1949, N.J.W. 1950, 759.

[5] Bohlen (1902) 41 Am.L.Reg. (N.S.) 141; Magruder (1936) 49 Harv.L.R. 1033; Prosser (1939) 37 Mich.L.R. 874; Goodhart (1953) 69 L.Q.R. 347; F. James (1958) 8 Buffalo L.R. 315, 335; C. Wright (1948) 26 Can.Bar Rev. 46, 65; (1957) 4 S.P.T.L. 30; Brody (1961–62) Villanova L.R. 232.

[6] *Janvier* v. *Sweeney* [1919] 2 K.B. 316; *Owens* v. *Liverpool Corp.* [1939] 1 K.B. 394; *Hambrook* v. *Stokes* [1925] 1 K.B. 141; *King* v. *Phillips* [1952] 2 All E.R. 459 (McNair J.); [1953] 1 Q.B. 429 (C.A.); *Bourhill* v. *Young* [1943] A.C. 92; *Bielitski* v. *Obadiak* (1922) 65 D.L.R. 627. But see *Mitchell* v. *Rochester Ry.*, 151 N.Y. 107; 45 N.E. 354 (1896), and the cases cited (1959) 11 Syracuse L.R. 126.

of course, that in these circumstances it is necessary to establish some limits in a chain of doubtful and not easily foreseeable causation. The less delicate nature of cattle (cows) and the easily ascertainable connection between shock and its symptoms on the one hand, and certain external acts, on the other, make cases of nervous shock of cattle fall into a different category.[7] As to the second: the situation is more anomalous in the common law which does not in principle allow an action based on malicious intent, let alone negligence, only,[8] than in the civil law which can rely on well established remedies. Recently, in *J. Bollinger* v. Costa *Brava Co.* [1960]|Ch. 262, 288, it was said: "But the law may be thought to have failed, if it can offer no remedy to the deliberate act of one person which causes damage to the property of another." This approach, which is to be found more frequently in the United States, where it is called the prima facie tort doctrine,[9] is rooted in three separate torts: interference with contractual relations (see below) and with prospective advantages (*i.e.*, unfair competition) and injurious false-hood.[10] Its basis is claimed to be a statement of Bowen L.J. in *Mogul SS. Co.* v. *McGregor,*[11] but it generally overlooked that his formulation was as follows:

"Intentionally to do that which is calculated in the ordinary course of events to damage and which does in fact *damage* another in that other person's *property or trade* is actionable if done without just cause or excuse," and he continued (pp. 616, 618) that in the case of an illegal combination either the act or the means must be unlawful. This leaves the matter very much where it was before, and restricted to damage to property at that. Our conclusion, up to here, is then that the common law does not recognise a general principle of liability for intentional or negligent indirect injuries to the person and that it is, to that extent, less generous than the civil law. On the other hand it must be pointed out that the absence of the requirement of damage in assault and battery makes these remedies more popular (though not necessarily more remunerative) than any comparable claim in German or French law.

On the other hand, common law and civil law are more in line in other respects, although the common law may appear to be more generous. *False imprisonment* by a private individual, whether exercising powers of arrest or

---

[7] *Gonsenhauser* v. *New York Central R.R. Co.*, 8 App.Div. (2d) 483; 188 N.Y.S. (2d) 901 (1959). See note in (1959) 11 Syracuse L.R. 126 with cases.

[8] G. L. Williams (1939) 7 C.L.J. 111, 125 *et seq.*, *e.g.*, spite fence: p. 129, note 71. *Capital & Counties Bank* v. *Henty* (1882) 7 App.Cas. 741, 766; Wills J. in *Allen* v. *Flood* [1898] A.C. 1, 46 but see Seavey (1942) 56 Harv.L.R. 72, 84.

[9] See Holmes in *Aikens* v. *Wisconsin* (1904) 195 U.S. 194, 204, and the cases cited in (1958) 10 Syracuse L.R. 53, 54, No. 11; Forkosch (1957) 42 Cornell L.R. 465; Hansen (1958) 7 Buffalo L.R. 305; (1952) 52 Cal.L.R. 503; (1956) 41 Cornell L.R. 567.

[10] *Cf.* (1958) 10 Syracuse L.R. 53.

[11] (1889) 23 Q.B.D. 598, 613; affirmed [1892] A.C. 25.

not, or by a police officer purporting to exercise such powers, have their counterpart in paragraphs 823, 847 of the German Civil Code, while in France the doctrine of *abus de droit* may help in certain circumstances.[12] Moreover, it must be remembered that a criminal prosecution may furnish a more appropriate remedy in Europe in the absence of a system of damages which is not limited to restitution and which provides satisfaction for the plaintiff while expressing disapproval of the defendant. We shall return to this question when discussing defamation.

|Procedural reasons, not unlike those which underlie the German *Unter-lassungsklage*,[13] rather than the prospect of damages, led English law to replace the equivalent of a *rei vindicatio* of land by the action of *trespass to land*. Where movables are concerned the flexible use of damages has favoured the actions for *detinue or conversion* which stress the loss of possession rather than interference with ownership as the ground of the action.

Thus both as to interference with land and chattels, the common law relies on principles which would seem also to be capable of satisfying a need expressed, as regards German law, by von Caemmerer[14] in respect of purchasers and tenants. It may be pointed out, however, that the particular cases[15] would be covered, at common law by an action for nuisance, if the interference resulted from an unreasonable use of the land.

New Areas: Indirect Financial Interests

(4) So far we have moved on fairly familiar ground. Difficulties arise if economic interests as such are affected through indirect acts not directly aimed at the person or the property of the victim. Here the question of the *legally protected interest* arises most clearly. It may be framed as a question of *breach of duty*, as English law does, or of a protected acquired right not representing a mere expectation,[16] as French writers formulate it. It may be expressed in the more casuistic German form whether a *Recht am eingerichteten und ausgeübten Gewerbebetrieb* is affected in so far as property interests are immediately involved, or a *Persönlichkeitsrecht*, if the damage flows from an invasion of the private sphere.

All these legal systems agree that this duty concerns the avoidance of certain hazards and risks, that it exists independently of any problem of

---

[12] Mazeaud, *Traité théorique et pratique de la responsabilité civile*, 5th ed., 1957, I, No. 591.

[13] von Caemmerer, *loc. cit.*, p. 49 at p. 52 *et seq.*; RGZ 60, 6 (1905).

[14] *Loc. cit.*, pp. 81–83.

[15] RGZ 59, 326, 328 (1904): petrol fumes; RGZ 105. 213, 218: soot and sulphur fumes.

[16] Mazeaud I, No. 275, p. 344.

causation and that it is only necessary to delimit these duties from case to case. However, there are significant differences of principle.

While *German* law is in search of new areas of *protected interests, English* and *French* law concentrate on the nature of *activities* by the defendant which interfere with recognised interests. Although this distinction is, on the face of it, one between rights and duties, this is only superficially so, since it is acknowledged that in the law of torts, protected interests are not identical with|subjective rights. It is, therefore, necessary to examine some of the new categories.

Duties of Care – Verkehrspflichten – Dangerous Premises – Goods Incapable of Intermediate Examination – Wrong Statements

(5) These categories have attracted much interest in the common law over a long period of time, for an urgent need made itself felt from early time onwards. The reason is that, unlike in civil law systems, it is impossible to encompass any such liabilities within the framework of contractual duty.[17] *Culpa in contrahendo*[18] is no answer to a common lawyer in the absence of a contract for want of consideration and *contracts in favorem tertii* are excluded for the same reason.[19]

Instead, in so far as injuries were suffered on *premises* which the injured party had entered, an elaborate system of delictual liability of occupiers of premises – now simplified in the Occupiers' Liability Act, 1957 – enables lawful visitors of premises to sue in respect of damage suffered while on the premises and arising out of the state of the premises, a liability which much exceeds that imposed by paragraph 836 BGB and article 1886 C.C.[20]

Similarly, where goods are put into circulation, whether by a manufacturer or by a repairer, it is impossible to construe a contract, at common law, between the manufacturer or repairer in favour of third parties, such as the puchaser buying from the retailer, and the *tort of negligence* takes the place of the nonexistent contract[21] even where the buyer himself is concerned –

---

[17] *Cf. Mummery d Savings Ptg. Ltd.* (1956) 96 C.L.R. 99; for contrats de securité see Mazeaud, Nos. 151–172.

[18] *Cf.* Mazeaud, No. 116; Paris, 30.6.1958, Gaz.Pal. 1958.2.348; Rev.trim. 1959, 89; Cass. 20.12.1960, D.1961, 141; Rev.trim. 1961, 309; BGHZ, N.J.W. 1962, 31.

[19] *Cf., e.g., Cavalier* v. *Pope* [1906] A.C. 428; Mazeaud, Nos. 136, 137; Cass. 16.2.1897, D.1897.1.96; Cass. 9.12.1932, D.1933.1.137.

[20] Mazeaud, No. 1042. Marsh (1953) 69 L.Q.R. 182, 359. And see the strange Louisiana case, *Williams* v. *Employers Liability Ass. Corp.*, 296 F. (2d) 569 (1961).

[21] *Donoghue* v. *Stevenson* [1932] A.C. 562; *Grant* v. *Australian Knitting Mills* [1936]

where German law might assume *Positive Vertragsverletzung*. It would appear, however, that this rule does not apply to damage | caused by immovables.[22] However, continental law, too, has made little use of the direct contractual approach[23] and has neglected the question whether the employer himself is liable for supplying defective equipment.[24]

On the other hand, such situations as those discussed by von Caemmerer,[25] namely, involving the responsibility of (a) a maker of a map who fails to set out an obstruction in the sea[26]; (b) of the broadcasting station which mistakenly publishes a false weather report with the result that innkeepers in holiday resorts who had made provision for an influx of visitors on Sunday fail to obtain their normal number of holiday customers; (c) of a person towards the employers of an actress whom he has injured; (d) the art expert who negligently gives as his opinion that a certain picture is genuine, would, it is believed, be treated as innocuous at common law in the absence of a duty towards the plaintiff, at least in so far as cases (a)–(c) are concerned.[27] As regards (d) a statement of opinion may not result in any liability to anybody.

However, apart from the narrower problem whether a duty exists towards the plaintiff in these cases, a more fundamental question arises. Does a negligent incorrect statement which is acted upon and leads to economic loss involve the maker of the statement in liability? English practice has, so far,

---

A.C. 85; *Herschtal* v. *Stewart & Ardern* [1940] 1 K.B. 155; *Stennett* v. *Hancock* [1939] 2 All E.R. 578; *Malfroot* v. *Noxal* (1935) 51 T.L.R. 551; *Macpherson* v. *Buick* (1916) 271 N.Y. 382; 111 N.E. 1050 and the lit. cited (1948) 26 Can.Bar Rev. 62, n. 51; 68 *et seq.*; Mankiewicz, Rev.int. de droit comparé, 1956, 241; Wilson (1955) 43 Cal.L.R. 614, 839; Mazeaud, No. 181. See also Paris 13.12.1954, D.1955, 96; Cass.Civ. 26.6.1953, D.1954, 181; Swiss BGE 64, II, 254 (1938).

[22] G. L. Williams (1942) 5 M.L.R. 1947; *Otto* v. *Bolton* [1936] 2 K.B. 46; *Davies* v. *Foots* [1940] 1 K.B. 116; *Travers* v. *Gloucester Corp.* [1946] 2 All E.R. 506. Note in (1959) 44 Minn.L.R. 144; *Kilmer* v. *White* (1950) 254 N.Y. 64; 171 N.E. 908: only for concealment *de lege ferenda*; Rest.Torts, para. 353.

[23] See the cases cited by E. von Caemmerer, *loc. cit.*, p. 72, note 102, p. 73; RGZ 163, 21, 26; RG D.R. 1940, 1293; BGH 13/6/1952; 25/4/1956; 15/3/1956; BGE 64, II, 254. Note, however, the indirect contractual approach in RGZ 127, 14, 18: negligent omission to perform a contract, the failure of which is likely to endanger life may be a tort.

[24] *Davie* v. *New Merton Board Mills* [1959] A.C. 604 – or of liability if the third party performed under a contract of sale: G. L. Williams (1961) 24 M.L.R. 113.

[25] *Loc. cit.*, p. 66.

[26] *Cf.* Asquith L.J. in *Candler* v. *Crane, Christmas* [1951] 1 All E.R. 426, 442; Winfield, *Torts*, 4th ed., p. 387; *Old Gates Estates* v. *Toplis Hartnig & Russell* [1939] 3 All E.R. 209; *Heskell* v. *Continental Express* [1950] 1 All E.R. 1030, 1041; *Le Lievre* v. *Gould* [1893] 1 Q.B. 491.

[27] For the negligent failure of a bank not bound by a legally binding contract, which interfered with the plaintiff's prospective economic advantage, namely, the lapse of an insurance through failure to pay premiums, see *Walker Bank & Trust Co.* v. *First Sec. Corp.* (1939) 341 P. 944; (1960) 12 Stanford L.R. 509.

answered this question in the negative.[28] Illogical as the position may be, it would appear that, at common law as seen from Australia and New Zealand, there is a duty not to cause certain specified kinds of harm, including physical damage to the person or, possibly | property, but excluding harm to a person's economic position not resulting from physical injury.[29] An attempt to bridge this gap was made in England by Salmon J. in *Clayton* v. *Woodman*,[30] at least in so far as wrong advice (by an architect) led to physical injury. Some indications as to the German attitude are provided by the cases dealing with untrue testimonials negligently given by employers to their employees or to other prospective employers.[31] Intentional action of this character will render the writer liable, as it will in English law, possibly in deceit. French law is more willing to impose liability in tort for statements made negligently.[32]

Addressee of the Duty of Care

(6) Yet where are the limits of the class of persons to whom the duty is owed? Pre-natal injuries of the kind envisaged recently by the *Bundesgerichtshof*[33] are not, according to the established English practice, to be taken into account.[34] However, it may well be that they would be today, if the defendant was under a duty towards the plaintiff. As *Bourhill* v. *Young*[35] shows, the foreseeability of the *type* of damage is irrelevant for determining the first question which is whether the plaintiff's person and his interests fall within the circle of persons whose interests the defendant is required to consider in the conduct of his own affairs. This consideration supports the *German Power Cable Case*[36] and the American practice.[37]

---

[28] Mainly on the basis of *Derry* v. *Peek* (1889) 14 App.Cas. 337 – liability for statements in a prospectus. But see Companies Act, 1948, s. 43.

[29] Braybrook, *loc. cit.*

[30] [1961] 3 All E.R. 249; reversed on other grounds [1962] 2 All E.R. 33; [1962] 1 W.L.R. 585.

[31] Olg. Hamburg 14/12/54. N.J.W. 1956, 348. *Cf.* von Caemmerer, pp. 73, 114; as to the U.S. see Seavey (1942) 56 Harv.L.R. 72, 87; no duty: *Ultramares Corp.* v. *Touche, Niven & Co.* (1931) 255 N.Y. 170, 174, 176, 179, 181, 185, 188; 174 N.E. 441.

[32] Mazeaud, No. 501; Cass.Req. 2.12.1930, D.H. 1930, 18; Paris, 5.2.1952, D. 1952, 275.

[33] BGHZ 8, 243, 248 (1953).

[34] *Dulieu* v. *White* [1901] 2 K.B. 669, 675. See also *Chester* v. *Waverly Corp.* (1939) 62 C.L.R. 1. Similarly the practice in the U.S.: Seavey (1942) 56 Harv.L.R. 72, 90; F. James (1958) 8 Buffalo L.R. 315, 335, but see *Woods* v. *Lancel*, 303 N.Y. 349; 102 N.E. (2d) 691 (1951); (1951) 50 Mich.L.R. 166. And see *Montreal Tramways* v. *Leveille* [1933] S.C.R. 456; [1933] 4 D.L.R. 337; *Annual Survey of American Law*, 1955, p. 448; 1956, p. 369; 1957, p. 389. See also C.A.L. (1962) 110 U.Pa.L.R. 554.

[35] [1943] A.C. 92; see also *King* v. *Phillips*, above, note 6.

[36] BGHZ, 29, 65; von Caemmerer, pp. 93, 94; below (8 (d)).

[37] *Palsgraf* v. *Long Island Ry.* (1928) 248 N.Y. 339; 162 N.E. 99.

Increased Protection Against Dangerous Objects and Installations

(7) French law is most conspicuous for having created an *increased liability* based on a presumption of responsibility (not fault) in|respect to *motor-cars*, thus reversing the burden of proof.[38] Belgian practice, at one period, went even further in presuming fault whenever a motor-car was involved in an accident,[39] and German law has achieved the same object by special legislation concerning railways and motor-cars. On the other hand, English law has conspicuously refrained from following a similar course,[40] except that a person who accumulates on his land anything likely to do damage, if it escapes, is liable for any consequences, subject to the defence, *inter alia*, of Act of God.[41] Yet this liability has been restricted so as not to include injuries to persons on the land.[42]

Generally speaking, it seems that where dangerous goods are being handled, the person involved must be more careful, having regard to the nature of the object, but this is only a particular aspect of the general duty of care.[43]

It would thus seem that the civil law is more inclined to extend protection against dangerous objects and installations than the common law, subject to the proviso (developed originally for a different purpose) that in conducting an enterprise involving dangerous activities governed by statutory regulations, the management cannot rely on the fact that duties imposed by these regulations were delegated.[44]

Nevertheless, it must be noted that, at least in so far as injuries suffered by workmen are concerned, a trend has been strongly felt ever since the last decade of the nineteenth century to mitigate the severity of a fault-determined liability of employers and that compulsory insurance schemes have filled the gap.[45] Moreover, in the United States, risk-shifting as a judicial

---

[38] Mazeaud, Nos. 88, 89, 1139–1147; Cass. Req. 18/2/1930, D. 1930.1.57; Cass. 16/6/96, S. 1897. 1.17.

[39] Mazeaud, No. 385, p. 452; for rebuttable presumptions in Canadian law see Wright (1948) 26 Can.Bar Rev. 46, 72; V. C. Macdonald, *ibid.* (1935), Vol. 13, p. 535.

[40] Accord: G. L. Williams (1961) 24 M.L.R. 115; Keeton (1959) 72 Harv.L.R. 401, 407.

[41] *Rylands* v. *Fletcher* (1866) L.R. 1 Ex. 265; (1868) L.R. 3 H.L. 330; in fact this constitutes a reversal of proof. Mazeaud, No. 626.

[42] *Read* v. *Lyons* [1947] A.C. 156.

[43] As to damage flowing from ultra-hazardous activities in the U.S. see Seavey (1942) 56 Harv.L.R. 72, 86; Wright (1948) 26 Can.Bar Rev. 46, 77. As regards the medical profession: Mazeaud, No. 510 *et seq.*

[44] *Wilsons & Clyde Coal Co.* v. *English* [1938] A.C. 57. C. Wright (1948) 26 Can.Bar Rev. 46, 47; G. L. Williams (1961) 24 M.L.R. 112.

[45] France: Law, October 10, 1946, replacing Law of April 9, 1898. Mazeaud, No. 649.

policy, redressing an unjust enrichment (in the widest sense), and in certain circumstances involving dangerous or hazardous operations an attitude to consider the insurance cover[46] have come into prominence. This tendency is | to a certain extent the reflex of a normal or compulsory practice on the part of persons exercising such operations to insure.

Protection of Enterprises (Recht am eingerichteten und ausgeübten Gewerbebetrieb)

(8) The enterprise as a nascent protected interest, which is recognised in German law[47] but which has not hitherto been accepted in the common law,[48] may have crystallised into a general clause, but for the present purpose the practice will be examined analytically.

(a) Two decisions – BGHZ 3, 278 and 14, 171 – concern situations in which the defendant wilfully published statements which were derogatory of the plaintiff's publications and which were intended to discourage the parishioners from buying them. At common law, short of the tort of injurious falsehood, *i.e.*, a false and malicious statement about a person, his property or business which inflicts damage, an action for defamation would be the only remedy. This action is, however, subject to the defences of qualified privilege, justification and fair comment on a matter of public interest, and in the present case no action would lie. In short, a business interest is not altogether sacrosanct, but is open to injurious honest statements to persons having an interest in receiving them or if the person exercises a business "which may fairly be said to invite comment or challenge public attention."

(b) BGHZ 8, 142 – circulating for reward a list of bad or slow debtors among members of a trade association has its counterpart in English law.[49] At common law, if the information is untrue, the informant is liable for defamation, unless he himself is a trade association and, possibly, if the information was not supplied for purposes of gain only.[50] These special circumstances will exclude liability on grounds of qualified privilege.

---

[46] Ehrenzweig, *Negligence without Fault* (1951); *Full Aid Insurance for the Traffic Victim* (1954); (1941) 8 U.Chicago L.R. 729; (1944) 30 Cornell L.R. 179; (1950) Law & Contemp.Prob. 445; (1950) 72 Juristische Blätter 253; (1950) 3 Bol. del Instituto de Derecho Comparado 3; (1955) 43 Cal.L.R. 1. Mazeaud, No. 339 *et seq.*

[47] BGHZ 29, 65 with history and cases; BGHZ 27, 137; 23, 157, 163; N.J.W. 1959, 1424; Fabricius (1961) *Archiv für die civilistische Praxis*, 273–336 at p. 304.

[48] Wright (1948) 26 Can.Bar Rev. 46, 54; Tilley (1935) 33 Mich.L.R. 829; *Bourhill* v. *Young* [1943] A.C. 93, 110, *per* Lord Wright.

[49] *Macintosh* v. *Dun* [1908] A.C. 390; *London Ass. for Protection of Trade, Ltd.* v. *Greenlands, Ltd.* [1916] 2 A.C. 15.

[50] But see Winfield, p. 352. *Cf.* Mazeaud, No. 501, p. 556.

Conclusion

These two cases would be considered in English law as falling within the general sphere of defamation and not within a specific | province of protecting business interests. The greater use of the tort of defamation to protect those interests which consist principally in commercial reputation is to be explained in the developed system of damages which operates irrespectively of the actual damage suffered, as measured in strictly financial loss. It may be that the German reliance on the *eingerichtete oder ausgeübte Gewerbebetrieb* is an attempt to find some *economic* interest, against which to measure damages, when the common law is free to award damages without proof of special damage. Perhaps the new trend in German law to award "immateriellen Schadensersatz"[51] points the way in the same direction.

(c) BGHZ 24, 200, 205 – invitation by a newspaper to boycott a shop, because the owner has refused to accept a returning prisoner of war as a member of his tenant's household – is a difficult case. In principle an invitation to boycott a business is lawful according to the common law, unless the means employed or the purpose are unlawful.[52] Here only the latter question can arise. If the purpose is to persuade the owner, *qua* landlord, to allow the ex-prisoner of war to continue to reside, such a purpose does not benefit the defendant's own interests. While charitable on the face of it, it is in reality an attempt to force another party to make a contract with a third party, the interest of neither of whom is identical with that of the defendant. My conclusion is that, at common law, if any protection were afforded to the owner of the business, it would be because the attempt to force him into a tenancy agreement is unlawful,[53] and not because his business is affected, but the damages would be expressed in terms of loss suffered by the business.

(d) BGHZ 29, 65[54] – cutting a power cable with the result that a factory stops work – does not, according to any of the legal systems concerned, involve the liability of the tortfeasor towards one or all of the customers of the Electricity Works.[55] This situation falls within the ambit of the general question whether, in face of a contractual link between the plaintiff and a third party (the Electricity Works), a second claim in tort is to be allowed against the perpetrator of the injurious act. In view of the usual exemption clause, the contractual claim will be of little value.

---

[51] BGHZ 18, 149, 156; paras. 824, 847 B.G.B. For France see Mazeaud, I. Nos. 292–335, pp. 376–417.

[52] This principle applies also to strikes. *Cf.* BAG 2, 75 – N.J.W. 1955, 1373; BAG 1, 291, N.J.W. 1955, 882; JZ 1955, 386. Mazeaud. No. 590 (2).

[53] *Cf.* G. L. Williams (1939) 7 C.L.J. 111, 123–124; *Allen* v. *Flood* [1898] A.C. 1, 9.

[54] N.J.W. 1959, 1423, 670.

[55] von Caemmerer, pp. 88, 93; Mazeaud, No. 1872 (dommage "par ricochet").

|The answer is to be found in the determination of the objective limit of the duty of care (see above (5)), but these limits are by no means clear.[56]

While the new trends in protecting business enterprises have arisen in civil law countries, attention must be drawn to some remedies of the common law which do not appear to have attracted attention elsewhere.

Liability for inducing a breach of contract[57] protects a contracting party against interference by outsiders, subject, possibly, to a distinction that, if the interference is lawful, a prima facie tort may have been committed in the United States.[58] It is more doubtful whether a breach of contract as such gives rise to a tort.[59]

Privacy – Persönlichkeitsrecht

(9) The right of privacy occupies an important place in German and Swiss law.[60] In the countries of the common law its present place is indeterminate, and the interest, raised thirty years ago, in this institution has receded.[61] It must be remembered that the law of defamation, which protects reputation, provides a satisfactory remedy against false and derogatory statements, subject however to some important defences. Other types of interference in the personal sphere are properly protected by actions for false imprisonment,[62] assault, negligence, injurious falsehood or contempt of court,[63] and malicious prosecution[64] which includes both in English | and in French law

---

[56] von Caemmerer, p. 96. But see *Cattle* v. *Stockton Waterworks* (1875) L.R. 10 Q.B.D. 453 and the Canadian cases cited (1948) 26 Can.Bar Rev. 57, note 34. As for possibilities of subrogation see G. L. Williams (1961) 24 M.L.R. 103. But see *Tooth & Co.* v. *Tillyer* (1956) 95 C.L.R. 605; *Lister* v. *Romford* [1957] A.C. 555.

[57] *Lumley* v. *Gye* (1853) 2 E. & B. 216; *Thomson & Co.* v. *Deakin* [1952] 1 Ch. 646; J. G. Starke (1955–57) 7 Res Judicatae 136; Sayre (1923) 36 Harv.L.R. 663, 671; Mazeaud, No. 144, Note 3, No. 1956, Note 4. Threats to induce a breach of contract; *Rookes* v. *Barnard* [1962] 2 All E.R. 579; [1962] 3 W.L.R. 260; Wedderburn (1961) 24 M.L.R. 572; (1962) 25 *ibid.* 513; Mazeaud, No. 144, Note 3, No. 590.

[58] (1959) 10 Syracuse L.R. 53, 66 and note 108.

[59] *Schisgall* v. *Fairchilds Publications Inc.*, 207 Misc. 224; 137 N.Y.S. (2d) 312 (1955); and note (1956) 41 Cornell L.Q. 507.

[60] Switzerland: Rätelmann (1961) *AcP.* 367; France: Martin, *Rev.trim.* 1959, 227; Germany: Löffler, N.J.W. 1959. 1.

[61] Winfield (1931) 47 L.Q.R. 23; Gutteridge, *ibid.* 203; but see the Right of Privacy Bill introduced in the House of Lords on February 14, 1961, by Lord Mancroft; Warren & Brandeis (1890) 4 Harv.L.R. 193; Feinberg (1948) 48 Cal.L.R. 713, 717: life history, likeness, name; Bohlen (1937) 50 Harv.L.R. 725, 731; Wright (1948) 26 Can.Bar Rev. 48, 93; Nizer (1941) 39 Mich.L.R. 526.

[62] Such as certifying a person as a lunatic not justified by law. *De Freville* v. *Dill* (1927) 96 L.J.K.B. 1056; *Everett* v. *Griffiths* [1921] 1 A.C. 631; *Harnett* v. *Fisher* [1927] A.C. 573, 579–580; RGZ 72, 175.

[63] *Cf. McGovern* v. *Van Riper*, 137 N.J.Eq. 24, 45 A (2d) 514 (1945).

[64] *Cf.* Mazeaud, No. 500, 591.

cases involving prosecutions without reasonable and probable cause.[65] German practice appears to take the same attitude in the latter respect,[66] but it also appears to admit responsibility in respect of negligent preliminary proceedings, such as for injunctions and precautionary seizure.[67]

Leaving aside these aspects, German practice seems to go much beyond the protection afforded by the common law. Thus letters[68] and pictures[69] which are given or sold to others leave no residuary rights in the author or painter, except those which are protected by his copyright, but this, according to English practice, is normally conveyed to the purchaser. Thus to overpaint a picture and to exhibit it as a work of the artist who signed it may, once again, give rise to an action for defamation, but to no other. The situation in BGHZ 13, 855 (letter of Schacht's lawyer) is more complex, but in no circumstances would BGHZ 30, 7 (10) – *Constance Valente* Case[70] – be followed in England. The mention of a name of a well-known artist in an advertisement, if it does not create the impression that the artist has lent his name to the advertisement for cash, thus lowering his reputation, does not lead to liability in tort or otherwise.[71] A wholly favourable reference by way of comparison lies outside altogether. Matters are different as regards BGHZ 26, 349, which may be compared with *Tolly* v. *Fry*.[72] Nevertheless, the difference of approach is significant. To reproduce the picture of a prominent citizen and sportsman in an advertisement for sexually strengthening medicines may be defamatory according to English law, since it implies, first, that the sportsman takes money for lending his name to the advertisement, thus prejudicing his status as an amateur, and secondly, that he is in need of medicines of this kind. The absence of an equally developed rule in the German law of defamation and the impossibility, hitherto, of awarding damages appropriate to the offence but much exceeding the actual, insignificant damage may have been a reason for extending the law of privacy this far. But now, since German courts allow reparation for *immateriell-rechtlichen Schaden*[73] and since the French courts have always been | willing to compensate for *dommage moral*[74] which may be regarded as equivalent to

---

[65] Mazeaud, No. 591, p. 663; No. 667, n. 5, under the heading, of *abus de droit*.

[66] von Caemmerer, pp. 97–98.

[67] von Caemmerer, p. 97, n. 218.

[68] BGZ 69, 401, 403.

[69] BGZ 79, 397, 398. Cologne, N.J.W. 1962, 48. *Cf. Sports & Press Agency Co.* v. *Our Dogs Publishing Co., Ltd.* [1916] 2 K.B. 880; [1917] 2 K.B. 125.

[70] *Cf.* BGHZ 13, 334, 338; 15, 249, 257, 258; 20, 345, 351; 24, 72, 76; 27, 284, 285, 286; N.J.W. 1959, 525.

[71] G. L. Williams (1939) 7 C.L.J. 111, 121.

[72] [1931] A.C. 333.

[73] BGHZ 18, 149; 20, 345.

[74] Mazeaud, No. 818; *Camoin* v. *Syndicat de la Propriété artistique*, Trib.Seine 15/11/1927. S. 1928. 2.137 which seems to protect new rights. See restrictively Req. 2/2/1931, S. 1931. 1.123; D. 1931. 1, 38. Mazeaud, No. 325.

general damages, the result, if not the grounds for reaching it, is much the same in all legal systems.

Ideas relative to the protection of the reputation, rather than of the name, seem to have influenced the decision BGHZ of December, 5, 1956[75]: removal of the name of a fallen soldier from a memorial tablet. It is interesting to compare this decision with *Ralston* v. *Ralston*[76] in which defamation was the only element.

BGHZ 24, 72 – the indiscreet medical expert of an insurance company – is difficult to analyse. In terms of English law a statement alleged to have been defamatory was made on the privileged occasion. Apart from that, a breach of medical secrets may be a violation of professional etiquette or a breach of contract, but no more.

At the same time attention may be drawn to one French[77] and one American[78] case – historian of certain scientific developments omits to mention a relevant invention while naming others; failure to list the plaintiff's song among the hundred best songs of the year. It is difficult to see what interest, except reputation, has been violated. As regards the latter, only an innuendo would be in issue according to English law.

To sum up

The unrestricted granting of remedies where the name, person or voice of an individual is mentioned exceeds by far the protection accorded at common law, where the law of contract, defamation, passing off and of copyright are the sole limits to the unrestrained recording of the impact of a person upon society.[79]

Abuse of Rights

(10) Abuse of right[80] differs from all other torts inasmuch as malicious intent and damage are normally supposed to be sufficient to constitute this tort,

---

[75] N.J.W. 1959, 525.

[76] [1930] 2 K.B. 238.

[77] *Branly* v. *Turpain*, Cass. 27.2.1951, D. 1951, 329. Mazeaud, No. 515 (5).

[78] *Advance Music Corp.* v. *American Tobacco* Co. (1946) 296 N.Y. 70; 70 N.E. (2d) 401; (1958) 8 Buffalo L.R. 307.

[79] Except if done with the intention of injuring another in his property, business or profession. *Dockrell* v. *Dougall* (1899) 80 L.T. 556, 558; *Walter* v. *Ashton* [1902] 2 Ch. 282, 293.

[80] Gutteridge (1933) 5 C.L.J. 22; Leake (1933) 7 Tulane L.R. 426; G. L. Williams (1939) 7 C.L.J. 111, 125 *et seq.* Mazeaud, Nos. 547–592.

even in the absence of a breach of duty. It is evident that it is difficult to establish a duty, if the defendant | exercises a right, and abuse of right is an attempt to reconcile rights of one party with duties towards another. The purely subjective approach of paragraph 826 BGB (an *actio doli*) is counterbalanced by the French doctrine which requires, objectively, that the right should have been exercised without legitimate interest,[81] whether intentionally or negligently.

Although the common law has, so far, refused to acknowledge a similar principle based upon malice or a balance of interests, it has, in its typically action-minded approach, recognised a limited number of cases which may be examined with profit.

It may be useful to leave on one side those cases where a malicious act in the exercise of an acknowledged discretion[82] renders an otherwise unprotected interest a protected one. Instances are: the wilful appropriation of a name, malicious prosecution, inducing a breach of contract. Instead, it is necessary to concentrate on situations where the defendant exercises a clear right. Thus an act done by illegal means or for an illegal purpose, even if done in the exercise of a right, such as a strike or boycott,[83] renders the perpetrator liable. Whether the exercise of a property right can ever lead to an actionable wrong merely because it is carried out with a malicious purpose is still doubtful.[84] Nuisance, where the question is whether the interference is the result of a reasonable or of an unreasonable exercise of a property right, appears to carry the seeds of the doctrine within it or, as others would say, to adopt the doctrine of fault.[85]

Finally it must be asked whether abuse of rights extends to the law of contract.[86]

On the whole it would seem that the common law is more inclined to allow damages in respect of lawful activities maliciously carried out in the exercise of social activities than in the exercise of proprietary rights.

---

[81] *Forissier* v. *Chaverot*, S. 1903, 1, 11; D. 1902, 1.454; Mazeaud, No. 548, p. 623; No. 549, p. 638.

[82] Rouast, Rev.trim.droit civil, 1944, 1.

[83] *Crofter Handwoven Harris Tweed* v. *Veitch* [1942] A.C. 435. Mazeaud, No. 566.

[84] *Mayor of Bradford* v. *Pickles* [1895] A.C. 587, 594; *Christie* v. *Davey* [1893] 1 Ch. 316; *Hollywood Silver Fox Farm* v. *Emmett* [1936] 2 K.B. 468, 475; *Abbott* v. *Sullivan* [1952] 1 K.B. 189, *per* Denning L.J.; Fridman (1958) 21 M.L.R. 484, 493; *cf. Langan* v. *First Trust & Deposit Co.* (1944) 293 N.Y. 604; 59 N.E. (2d) 424: foreclosing mortgage in order to buy property cheaply, and compare *Victoria Park Racing & Recreation Grounds Co.* v. *Taylor* (1937) 58 C.L.R. 479, 505, 508, 510.

[85] Mazeaud, No. 577.

[86] For France see, *e.g., Clement-Bayard*, Cass. 3/8/1915. S. 1920.1. 300; Mazeaud, Nos. 559, 583–587 (3).

| Claims by Dependants

(11) It is common to all the legal systems under review to allow actions in favour of a certain circle of members of the family as a result of an injury to a member of the family on whom they depend financially. The problem of recovery of *dommage moral* in French law is equivalent to that for shock discussed above (3). English law appears to go further, inasmuch as it allows a claim on behalf of the deceased for loss of expectation of life. On the other hand, English law allows claims of dependants only if the person who provided the maintenance has died, and not when he has only been injured.[87] A problem, which appears so far to have arisen in France only, may be noted here which is whether a concubine and illegitimate children should be protected too.[88]

The more extravagant protection of the unity between husband and wife by actions for damages against a co-respondent in an action for divorce against a wife (but not in the converse case),[89] for enticing or harbouring and for loss of consortium[90] and by the wife for enticing only, seem to have their roots in a conception of the family which is no longer current.[91] This applies even more strongly to actions by parents for the loss of services of their children. On the other hand, it is difficult to support the former English rule (a historically determined fact) that a wife can only sue her husband in tort for the violation of proprietary interests,[92] but not of her person, with certain exceptions.[93] Similarly, it is difficult to understand the decision of the German Federal Court[94] allowing an action by a wife against her husband's concubine living in the matrimonial home, but limiting the claim to the protection of the matrimonial home, if it is to be supported by any one of the principles set out here.

---

[87] Williams (1961) 24 M.L.R. 104.

[88] Mazeaud, Nos. 277–277 (8).

[89] Distinguish the action against a guilty spouse in a divorce suit in France; Loi April 2, 1941, approved by Ord. 12/4/45 adding Art. 301 (2) C.C.

[90] *Best* v. *Samuel Fox* [1952] A.C. 716; *Behrens* v. *Bertram Mills Circus* [1957] 2 Q.B. 1; *Kirkham* v. *Boughey* [1957] 3 All E.R. 153; *McNeill* v. *Johnstone* [1958] 3 All E.R. 16; *Birch* v. *Taubmans, Ltd.* (1956) 74 W.N. (N.S.W.) 70 (total loss of sexual intercourse); *Tookey* v. *Hallier* [1955] A.L.R. 302 (partial loss); Note (1955–57) Res Judicatae 211. For Germany see Fabricius (1961) 160 *Archiv für die zivilistische Praxis* 273, 316, 335.

[91] G. L. Williams (1939) 7 C.L.J. 111, 120; (1961) 24 M.L.R. 107, 110 (U.S. Practice).

[92] G. L. Williams (1961) 24 M.L.R. 101.

[93] *Curtis* v. *Wilcox* [1948] 2 K.B. 474. Now Law Reform (Husband and Wife) Act, 1962.

[94] BGHZ 6, 360, 364, 365.

Some Special Torts Without Equivalent

(12) Attention may be finally drawn to types of situations in which the common law is more willing to provide protection than the|civil law. Inducing a breach of contract is one (see above (8) and note 56), conspiracy is another (and a very effective remedy at that); on a minor scale, namely for the loss of the services of menial servants the action *quoad servitium amisit* provides means of redress.[95] However, the unauthorised appropriation of an idea by the organisers of a radio programme would not according to English law require any remedy,[96] nor would an unauthorised autopsy and removal of organs of a deceased husband justify an action by the widow.[97]

Conclusions

I. Whether a general principle of liability for culpable injurious acts or a system of individual protected interests is accepted as the basis of tortious liability, in the end it is necessary to look to the individual situation. The reason is that the range of protected interests changes with the evaluation of those interests in a changing society.

II. Where formerly the preservation of physical integrity and the protection of land and movable objects against direct interference ranked foremost, today the law of tort is more concerned with (1) indirect violations of the economic potential of the individual and of commercial and industrial enterprises and (2) with the creation of responsibility in respect of an increasing area of dangerous or potentially dangerous activities.

III. Within this new sphere of protection, the rapid growth of protected interests raises the following questions:

(a) what are the duties to be observed?

(b) to whom are they owed?

(c) how is the existence of such duties compatible with the exercise of a right?

---

[95] *Att.-Gen. of New South Wales* v. *Perpetual Trustee Co.* [1955] A.U.C. 457; *Commonwealth* v. *Exever* (1944) 68 C.L.R. 227; *Receiver of Metropolitan Police* v. *Croydon Corp.* [1957] 2 Q.B. 154; *I.R.C.* v. *Hambrook* [1956] 2 Q.B. 641, 656; the suggestion of a loss-shifting device was followed in *Blundell* v. *Musgrove* (1956) 96 C.L.R. 73.

[96] But see *Belt* v. *Hamilton National Bank* (1953) 108 F.Supp. 689, 690, affd. 210 F. (2d) 706; Ward (1956) 42 Cornell L.Q. 28, 37; (1957) 43 Cornell L.Q. 115; Wright (1948) 26 Can. Bar Rev. 46, 93; Brandeis & Warren (1890) 4 Harv. L.R. 193; Nizer (1941) 39 Mich.L.R. 526.

[97] *Cf. Deeg* v. *City of Detroit* (1956) 345 Mich. 371; 76 N.W. (2d) 16; Note (1957) 55 Mich.L.R. 610 with cases; Magruder (1936) 49 Harv.L.R. 1033 at p. 1064; Prosser (1939) 37 Mich.L.R. 874 at pp. 885–886. As to property in and possession of a dead body according to English law, see Williams *On Executors and Administrators* (14 ed. 1960), Vol. I, p. 438, para. 735.

(d) is the burden of proof shifting, thus leading, perhaps indirectly, to a risk-determined liability?

| (e) to what extent must the damage be specified in terms of ascertained pecuniary loss?

IV. The previous gap between a highly developed casuistic common law of torts and a less refined civil law of general reparation is being or has already been closed.

V. Within the classical field of liability for personal injury, the questions of proof of damage, emotional shock, especially if inflicted intentionally, not as a concomitant of a physical act, but of statements, and of physical acts committed against third parties rank foremost.

VI. The absence of a general principle of liability at common law remains counterbalanced by

(a) a greater protection of the more intangible aspects of personal integrity

(b) by a more flexible system of assessing damages.

VII. In all the systems under review the indirect protection of economic interests has been accepted, but the form and the extent of the protection vary. By way of generalisation, it seems that English and French law look to the nature of the activities which may lead to responsibility, while German law tries to define the new protected interests.

VIII. One aspect of this new tendency is that it concerns *Verkehrspflichten*, dangerous premises, goods put in circulation which are incapable of intermediate examination, and wrong statements. In this sphere, the common law of tort has a much greater diversity of remedies because it cannot look to the law of contract (*culpa in contrahendo*, contracts in favour of third parties) to fill the gaps. On the other hand, liability for wrong statements appears to create much greater difficulties in the common law than in the civil law.

IX. At the same time the question arises how the circle of protected persons must be defined where, for instance, pre-natal injuries are concerned.

X. Increased protection against dangerous objects and installations is required everywhere, but apart from special legislation protecting workmen the remedy seems to lie in a strict application of the principles of culpability rather than in the recognition of liability for risk.

XI. A most notable feature is the German principle of the *Protection of Enterprises*, which has no equivalent elsewhere. Some of its features are covered by the common law of defamation or conspiracy. Others may be covered by the fact that in this | sphere the common law may allow damages without proof of special damage, and the new German trend may simply represent an attempt to find an economic asset against which the damages can be assessed. The common law tort of inducing a breach of contract, on the other hand, does not appear in the civil law.

XII. The *Persönlichkeitsrecht* of German law appears to go much beyond any similar protection of comparable rights elsewhere. At common law the right of privacy as such is not gaining much new support, but actions for false imprisonment, assault, negligence, injurious falsehood, defamation and malicious prosecution fulfil a comparable purpose. Letters and pictures are not as strongly protected, unless a copyright or passing off is involved. It may be, however, that the recent recognition of *immateriell-rechtlicher Schaden* may reduce the field of privacy in German law by bringing actions based on defamation into the fore.

XIII. Abuse of right in the meaning of an *actio doli* (par. 826 BGB) does not appear to find favour elsewhere, where an objectively unreasonable exercise of the right is required, thus striking an objective balance between the exercise of rights and the corresponding sacrifice of other rights.

XIV. The protection of rights of dependent persons appears to be solved on very similar lines almost everywhere, whilst the protection of masters and employers, as it figures in the common law, appears to be dying out.

Recognition of Foreign Divorces: Retrospects and Prospects

During the last decade the legislation and the practice in the Commonwealth have shown a tendency to extend the recognition of foreign decrees of divorce either in line with an enlarged jurisdiction or in contrast to a more restricted jurisdiction of the courts of the forum. In the light of a recent decision of the House of Lords, the author examines the assumptions on which extended jurisdiction is recognized and the consequences which arise therefrom. He suggests that a more diversified system of rules is called for, which distinguishes between an extended recognition of divorces granted abroad to parties who are domiciled in the recognizing country and a very restricted recognition if the parties are domiciled in a third country.

I. The Background

For some twenty-five years up to 1953 it seemed to be finally established that, at common law, a foreign divorce could be recognized only if the foreign decree had been pronounced by the courts of the domicile of the spouses[1] or, in case it had been pronounced elsewhere, if the decree would be

---

[Editorial note: first published in Ottawa Law Review 2 (1967), 49–70.]

[1] Conway v. Beazley, 3 Hagg. Ecc. 639, 645, 648, 651–52, 162 Eng. Rep. 1292, 1295–97 (Ecc. 1831); Tollemache v. Tollemache, 1 Sw. & Tr. 557, 561 (Div. & Mat. Causes Ct. 1859); Palmer v. Palmer, I Sw. & Tr. 551, 552 (Div. & Mat. Causes Ct. 1859); Pitt v. Pitt, 4 Macqueen App. Cas. 627, 635, 636 (H.L. 1864); Shaw v. Gould, L.R. 3 H.L. 55, 69, 76. 83, 87 (1868); Harvey v. Farnie, 8 App. Cas. 43, 50, 57 (1882); Le Mesurier v. Le Mesurier,

recognized by the courts of their domicile, which was that of the husband.[2] No exception was permitted at common law, even if the husband had deserted the wife and had acquired a domicile elsewhere,[3] or if a decree of judicial separation had been granted to the wife[4] or if the parties had separated by agreement.[5] The narrowness and rigidity of this rule was matched by a similar self-restraint on the part of the courts in England | to assume jurisdiction unless the spouses were domiciled in England.[6] Both rules reflect the consideration, to be examined later on, that a judicial decree of divorce is not merely a judgment which attracts the common-law rules of the conflict of laws concerning the recognition and enforcement of foreign judgments, but affects status. Since status is governed by the law of the domicile, the courts of the domicile alone can decide whether the status is to be changed by applying their *lex fori* or whatever law their own choice of law rules declare to be applicable.[7]

Isolated attempts by a few individual judges, in the form of an obiter dictum[8] or as a course of decision amounting at least to a practice,[9] to attribute to a deserted wife a separate domicile for the purpose of justifying the assumption of jurisdiction in divorce by English courts – though not where the recognition of foreign divorces was in issue – remained unsuccessful in England. In Scotland, on the other hand, jurisdiction was assumed if the last matrimonial home, in the sense of the place of residence of the married pair, was in Scotland where they were then domiciled. In the view of the Scottish courts, it is irrelevant that: the husband had deserted the wife;[10] the wife had

---

[1895] A.C. 517, 527 (P.C.); *See also* Brett, L.J., in Niboyet v. Niboyet, 4 P.D. 1, at 14, 19, 20 (1878).

[2] Armitage v. Attorney-General, [1906] P. 135.

[3] Herd v. Herd, [1936] P. 205; H. v. H., [1928] P. 206. at 212.

[4] Attorney-General for Alberta v. Cook, [1926] A.C. 444 (P.C.).

[5] Lord Advocate v. Jaffrey, [1921] 1 A.C. 146; In Scot., *sub nom.* Mackinnon's Trs. v. Inland Revenue, [1920] Sess. Cas. 171.

[6] Wilson v. Wilson, L.R. 2 P. & D. 435, 441–42 (1872).

[7] Shaw v. Gould, L.R. 3 H.L. 55, at 70, 83 (1868); Wilson v. Wilson, L.R. 2 P. & D. 435 (1872); Harvey v. Farnie, 8 App. Cas. 43, at 50, 57 (1882); Le Mesurier v. Le Mesurier, [1895] A.C. 517, at 526–27 (P.C.).

[8] *E.g.*, Niboyet v. Niboyet, 4 P.D. 1, at 14 (1878) (per Brett, L.J.); Armytago v. Armytago, [1898] P. 178, 185 (per Sir Gorrell Barnes, P.); Bater v. Bater, [1906] P. 209, 216; Ogden v. Ogden, [1908] P. 46, at 82.

[9] Le Sueur v. Le Sueur, 1 P.D. 130, 142 (1876); Stathatos v. Stathatos, [1913] P. 46 (per Bargrave Deane, J.); De Montaigu v. De Montaigu, [1913] P. 154 (per Sir Samuel Evans, P.) and, probably, a number of undefended cases. *See* Lord Wilberforce *in* Indyka v. Indyka, [1967] 3 W.L.R. 510, at 553 (H.L.), *citing* the Report of the Royal Commission on Divorce, Cd. No. 6478 (1912). The ground on which jurisdiction was assumed in the curious case of San Teodoro v. San Teodoro, 5 P.D. 79, 83 (1880), does not emerge clearly from the report.

[10] Jack v. Jack, 24 Sess. Cas. (2d s.) 467, 483, 485 (Scot. 1862); Humo v. Humo, 24 Scss. Cas. (2d s.) 1342, 1343 (Scot. 1862); *See also* Warrender v. Warrender, 2 Cl. & F. 488, 556 (H.L. 1835); Ringer v. Churchill, 2 Sess. Cas. (2d s.) 307, 313, 315 (Scot. 1840).

given the husband grounds for leaving her, taking up a domicile abroad;[11] the wife had refused to follow her husband when he went abroad,[12] provided only, so it would appear, that the parties had not separated voluntarily.[13] This jurisdiction is not determined by the circumstance that the marriage had been concluded in Scotland[14] or that the matrimonial offence had taken place there,[15] but is grounded on the existence of a proper home or residence of the parties in Scotland[16] which the husband had not transferred abroad.[17] Despite | protestations that this test is couched in "phraseology calculated to mislead, is figurative and wants judicial precision"[18] and does not exist in law,[19] it has maintained itself in Scotland. The test serves not only to relieve the hardship which might be caused to a wife who would have to seek out the proper jurisdiction abroad,[20] but also enables a husband to seize the jurisdiction of Scottish courts, if for instance the courts of his present domicile deny him a remedy.[21] Shorn of any technical language which is expressed in terms of a wife's separate domicile or of a "matrimonial domicile," the Scottish rule permits Scottish courts to entertain proceedings in divorce, if the last common home was in Scotland (always provided that the spouses did not part by agreement). Such a principle comes near to the jurisdictional test adopted in a number of continental countries.[22] At the same time it must be noticed that the courts in Scotland appear to be unwilling to concede a similar jurisdiction to courts abroad, if the parties are domiciled in England.[23]

---

[11] Shields v. Shields, 15 Sess. Cas. (2d s.) 142, 144, 146 (Scot. 1852).

[12] Jack v. Jack, 24 Sess. Cas. (2d s.) 467, at 485 (Scot. 1862).

[13] Lord Advocate v. Jaffrey, [1921] 1 A.C. 146, at 161 (per Viscount Cavo); Jack v. Jack, 24 Sess. Cas. (2d s.) 467, at 485 (Scot. 1862).

[14] Jack v. Jack, 24 Sess. Cas. (2d s.) 467, at 475 (Scot. 1862).

[15] Stavert v. Stavert, 9 Sess. Cas. (4th s.) 519, 529 (Scot. 1882); Jack v. Jack, 24 Sess. Cas. (2d s.) 467, at 474, 478, 482 (Scot. 1862); *but see* Shields v. Shields, 15 Scss. Cas. (2d s.) 142, at 146, 147 (Scot. 1852).

[16] Jack v. Jack, 24 Sess. Cas. (2d s.) 467, at 475, 477, 478, 482 (Scot. 1862); Humo v. Humo, 24 Sess. Cas. (2d s.) 1342, at 1343 (Scot. 1862).

[17] Jack v. Jack, 24 Sess. Cas. (2d s.) 467, at 471 (Scot. 1862).

[18] *Id.* at 473 (per Lord Deas).

[19] Stavert v. Stavert, 9 Sess. Cas. (2d s.) 519, at 530 (Scot. 1882) (per Lord Dcas), 533 (per Lord Shand); Lord Advocate v. Jaffrey, [1921] 1 A.C. 146, at 161, at 168 (per Lord Shaw of Dunfermline).

[20] Redding v. Redding, 15 Sess. Cas. (2d s.) 1102, 1104 (Scot. 1888); Robertson v. Robertson, [1915] 2 Scots L.T.R. 96, [1916] 2 Scots L.T.R. 95; Ramsay v. Ramsay, [1925] Sess. Cas. 216. 219. 220; Hannah v. Hannah, [1926] Scots L.T.R. 370; Lack v. Lack, [1926] Scots L.T.R. 656; Crabtree v. Crabtree, [1929] Scots L.T.R. 675.

[21] Shields v. Shields, 15 Sess. Cas. (2d s.) 142, at 146 (Scot. 1852).

[22] *E.g.*, Germany, ZPO § 606(a) (2).

[23] Warden v. Warden, [1951] Sess. Cas. 508; *but see* A. Dicey, Conflict of Laws 313, n. 32 (8th ed. J. Morris 1967).

In 1937 and 1949, the jurisdiction of English courts was extended, following a similar development in other parts of the Commonwealth,[24] to permit the courts to entertain a petition by a wife who had been deserted by her husband or whose husband had been deported from the United Kingdom, if the husband was immediately before the desertion or deportation domiciled in England[25] or by a wife who is resident in England and has been ordinarily resident there for a period of three years immediately preceding the commencement of the proceedings, and the husband is not domiciled in Scotland, Northern Ireland, the Channel Islands or the Isle of Man.[26] Within a short time thereafter the question arose whether this extension of English jurisdiction in divorce was matched by a comparable concession of jurisdiction to other countries.

| The gradual evolution between 1955 and 1958 of a number of technical rules enlarging these jurisdictional rules of English courts into rules for the recognition of foreign decrees need be set out here in outline only. First, by converting the unilateral rules of English statute law into bilateral rules, recognition was accorded to decrees based on provisions of foreign law which are substantially identical with those of English law.[27] Then the principle of equivalence was adopted, which permitted the recognition of decrees, if the facts before the foreign court were such that, had they occurred in England, English courts would have been able to exercise jurisdiction.[28] Finally, the artificial restriction, developed in English divorce proceedings, that the court could only exercise this extraordinary jurisdiction on the basis of a petition by a wife, to the exclusion of any cross-petition by the husband,[29] was engrafted on the exceptional rule of recognition of foreign divorces.[30]

---

[24] Griswold, *Divorce Jurisdiction and Recognition of Divorce Decrees – A Comparative Study*, 65 Harv. L. Rev. 193, at 200–07 (1951); *see also* Griswold, *The Reciprocal Recognition of Divorce Decrees*, 67 Harv. L. Rev. 823 (1954).

[25] Matrimonial Causes Act, 1937, 1 Edw. 8, 1 Geo. 6, c. 57. § 13; Matrimonial Causes Act, 1950, 14 & 15 Geo. 6, c. 25, § 18(1) (a); Matrimonial Causes Act 1965, c. 25, § 40(1) (a); and see A. Dicey, *op. cit. supra* note 23, at 295, n. 20, for the legislation in other pans of the United Kingdom and in the Commonwealth; for Canada, *see* The Divorce Jurisdiction Act, Can. Rev. Stat. c. 84 (1952).

[26] Law Reform (Miscellaneous Provisions) Act, 1949, 12 & 14 Geo. 6, c. 100, § 1; Matrimonial Causes Act, 1950, 14 & 15 Geo. 6, c. 25, at § 18(1)(b); Matrimonial Causes Act 1965. c. 25, at § 40(1)(b); see A. Dicey, *op. cit. supra* note 23, at 296, n. 21 for the legislation in other parts of the United Kingdom and in the Commonwealth.

[27] Travers v. Holley, [1953] P. 246; Dunne v. Saban, [1955] P. 178; *see also* Carr v. Carr, [1955] 1 W.L.R. 422 (P.D. & A.).

[28] Arnold v. Arnold, [1957] P. 237; Manning v. Manning, [1958] P. 112; Robinson-Scott v. Robinson-Scott, [1958] P. 71.

[29] Russell v. Russell, [1957] P. 375.

[30] Levett v. Levett, [1957] P. 156 (C.A.).

II. Analysis and Critique of the Present Rules

The result cannot be described as satisfactory. In the first place, the technical process of interpreting a statute extensively, so as to read a unilateral rule of jurisdiction as a bilateral rule, or even as sanctioning the principle of equivalence, may be acceptable to continental lawyers, whose systems of private international law have been greatly enhanced by this device, but cannot easily be reconciled with the English canons of statutory interpretation. In the second place, it has been alleged that the principle extending the recognition of foreign decrees in the circumstances described above purports to be based on the common law,[31] and, in particular, on the ground that the English rules on the recognition of foreign decrees of divorce have no positive but only a negative content. English courts will not recognize foreign judgments affecting status given in circumstances in which *mutatis mutandis* English courts themselves would not have jurisdiction, and it is the policy of English law to avoid the creation of limping marriages. If this is true, the charge must be levelled that sight has been lost of the function of the rule which restricted the recognition of foreign divorces to decrees given by the courts of the foreign domicile of the parties, no matter whether the courts of the forum (whether English or foreign) were empowered by provisions "exorbitant de droit commun" to assume jurisdiction on a broader basis.[32]

|This charge must now be developed in some detail. The original rule that jurisdiction in divorce is attributed exclusively to the courts of the domicile of the spouses, which is that of the husband, found its justification in the idea – first developed in Northwestern Europe during the fourteenth century and has maintained its relevance to this day – that jurisdiction is to be entrusted to the courts of the country with which the parties are most closely connected. Thus jurisdiction and choice of law were co-extensive. While this consideration is important in commercial and personal matters, it is paramount in matters of divorce. A decree of divorce does not simply record the breakdown of the marriage, the existence of certain obligations of maintenance, the award of custody and, possibly, the settlement of property. The spouses can separate by agreement, or a spouse may disappear, and the marriage comes equally to an end; maintenance obligations and custody can be determined in proceedings other than for a divorce, and so can a settlement of property. The essence of a decree of divorce is its final acknowledgement of the breakdown of the marriage by conferring on both parties to the

---

[31] Indyka v. Indyka, [1966] 3 W.L.R. 603, at 609, 613 (C.A.) (per Lord Denning, M.R., and Diplock, L.J.).

[32] *Cf.* Le Mesurier v. Le Mesurier, [1895] A.C. 517, at 527 (P.C.).

marriage the capacity to marry again. Thus the favourite catchword that a divorce affects status must be understood to refer not so much to the existing marital status as to the newly acquired capacity to enter into another marriage.

It follows that, ideally, the same law should determine the dissolution of a previous marriage and the capacity of either spouse to marry again. Leaving aside, for the moment, the difficulty that the parties may have acquired a new domicile after the dissolution of their previous marriage, the postulate set out above can be given concrete expression by linking the two aspects of the validity of a divorce, on the one hand, and of capacity to marry on the other, either by requiring the observation of the same choice of law rule in both situations[33] or by concentrating the judicial process in the same jurisdiction as that which must determine, by its domestic law, the capacity of the spouses to marry again.

The rules of private international law in England and elsewhere do not differentiate between capacity to marry in general and any such capacity arising from a decree of divorce, and thus capacity to marry depends upon the laws of the respective domiciles of the spouses.[34] As a result of the failure to perceive the function of jurisdiction in divorce and its link with choice of law in the private international law of common-law (as distinct from civil-law) countries, the danger of limping divorces and of limping marriages is increased. This danger was absent when the ecclesiastical courts administered matrimonial jurisdiction in England on the assumption, | however unfounded it may have been even at that time, that the law applied by these courts was universal in character. Thus Lord Justice James in *Niboyet v. Niboyet*[35] could contemplate with equanimity the exercise of jurisdiction on the basis of residence only, by the courts of the diocese of Winchester over spouses domiciled in the Channel Islands, or by the courts of the province of York over those domiciled in the Isle of Man, even if the law of the Channel Islands and of the Isle of Man differed from the law of England. If divorces granted by courts other than those of the domicile of the spouses are recognized by the courts of the forum but not by the courts of the foreign domicile of the spouses, the policy, if it should exist, of avoiding the creation of limping marriages is disregarded and certainly not observed.

In the absence of any jurisdictional choice of law rule in section 40(1)(a) and (b) of the English Matrimonial Causes Act, 1965 (and of its predecessors) which would enjoin English courts to recognize foreign decrees of

---

[33] Cheshire, *The International Validity of Divorces*, 61 L.Q.R. 352 (1945); *cf.* Matrimonial Causes and Personal Status Code § 14(b) (West. Austl. 1948).

[34] Sottomayor v. de Barros (No. 1), 3 P.D. 1 (C.A. 1877); A. Dicey, *op. cit. supra* note 23, rule 31, at 254.

[35] 4 P.D. 1, at 5 (1878).

divorces granted by foreign courts other than those of the domicile in circumstances identical with, or equivalent to, those laid down by the statute extending the jurisdiction of English courts, the question has been put whether the interpretation placed on this section in *Travers v. Holley*[36] was self-evident. If limping divorces and subsequent limping marriages are to be avoided, the operation of the provisions of this section must be restricted to spouses who are domiciled in England, in so far as the recognition of foreign divorces granted on the basis of identical legal provisions or equivalent circumstances is concerned.[37] The rule in *Travers v. Holley* would then merely constitute an aspect of the rule in *Armitage v. Attorney-General*[38] limited to the divorce of spouses domiciled in England. Thus a divorce granted in Ontario by virtue of the Divorce Jurisdiction Act, 1930, on the ground that the petitioning wife had been deserted by her husband[39] who, immediately prior to the desertion, had been domiciled in Ontario, would be recognized in England only if the husband had subsequently acquired a domicile in England. Similar recognition would be accorded to an Australian divorce under the Australian Matrimonial Causes Act, 1959, section 24(2) on the ground that the petitioning wife was resident in Australia and had been so resident for the period of three years immediately|preceding that date only if the husband had subsequently acquired a domicile in England or had been so domiciled throughout. Of course, English courts themselves are bound to entertain a petition brought by a wife whose husband has deserted her or has been deported from the United Kingdom, if the husband was immediately before the desertion or deportation domiciled in England, even if the husband has acquired a new domicile abroad at the time the wife brings a petition for divorce in England.[40] Similarly, English courts themselves are bound to entertain a petition brought by a wife who is resident and has been ordinarily resident in England for a period of three years preceding the commencement of the proceedings.[41] In both cases the likelihood is great that the divorce will not be recognized by the law of the husband's domicile, but as

---

[36] [1953] P. 246.

[37] Sec Sinclair, Note, 30 Brit. Y.B. Int'l L. 527 (1953); Latham, Letter to the Editor, 33 Can. B. Rev. 514 (.1955); Lipstein, Comment, [1959] Camb. L.J. 10, at 12; Lipstein, Comment, [1967] Camb. L.J. 42, at 44. *But see*: Griswold, *Divorce Jurisdiction and Recognition of Divorce Decrees – A Comparative Study*, 65 Harv. L. Rev. 193, at 228, n. 108 (1951); Griswold, *The Reciprocal Recognition of Divorce Decrees*, 67 Harv. L. Rev. 823, at 827 (1954); Webb, *Recognition in England of Non-Domiciliary Divorce Decrees*, 6 Int'l & Comp. L.Q. 608, at 615 (4955); A. Dicey, *op. cit. supra* note 23, at 314.

[38] [1906] P. 135.

[39] The requirement that the petitioning wife must have lived separate and apart from her husband for a period of two years would be disregarded by the courts of England.

[40] Matrimonial Causes Act 1965, c. 25, § 40(1) (a).

[41] *Id.* at § 40(1) (b).

Lord Watson pointed out in *Le Mesurier v. Le Mesurier,*[42] the *lex fori* can exceed in its jurisdictional provisions the limits set by what he believed to be a precept of international law or at least an acknowledged international custom, and can permit the exercise of jurisdiction, even if the domicile of the spouses is not in the country of the forum. In short, the *lex fori* may permit the assumption of jurisdiction on an exceedingly wide range of facts, but it does so at the risk of nonrecognition abroad. The failure to gear the special jurisdictional provisions of the English Matrimonial Causes Act, 1965, to the rule of the conflict of laws which determines capacity to marry by reference to the law of the domicile of the parties may lead, but has not led so far, to an unusual conflict. If the wife, who has obtained a divorce in the circumstances described above wishes to marry again in England, the refusal by the law of her domicile (which is that of the former husband) to recognize the divorce will normally be held to be irrelevant, since a wife who remains in England after her husband has deserted her or has been deported, has abandoned his English domicile and has acquired a new domicile abroad, will be regarded as having acquired a separate domicile of her own in England at the moment the decree of divorce became absolute.[43] The same applies if a wife, whose husband is domiciled abroad, obtains a divorce in England after having been ordinarily resident in England for three years. Matters become more complicated if the husband, domiciled abroad, wishes to avail himself of the decree obtained by his wife in England. Confronted with an English decree of divorce, which purports to sever any existing marital ties, and the provisions of the law of the husband's foreign domicile, which refuses to recognize the decree, the question remains open whether an English court must give full effect to the English decree, or treat it as unilateral and as pronounced in favour of the wife only, or must determine the incidents of the decree, in so far as capacity to marry again is concerned, | by reference to the law of the husband's foreign domicile, in disregard of the decree.[44] It is suggested, though with considerable hesitation, that English courts will adopt the last-mentioned course of action.

Although the view that recognition in virtue of the rule in *Travers v. Holley*[45] should be restricted to divorces abroad of spouses who are domiciled in England either at the time of the foreign divorce or of the conclusion of a new marriage has not commended itself to the English courts, some support for it can be derived from other legislation which has extended the

---

[42] [1895] A.C. 517 (P.C.).

[43] *Cf. Re* Scullard. [1957] Ch. 107; Miller v. Teale, 92 Comnw. L.R. 406, 419 (Austl. High Ct. 1952).

[44] *Cf.* M. Wolff, Private International Law § 358, at 379, & n. 3 (with references) (2d cd. 1950).

[45] [1953] P. 246.

jurisdiction in divorce of English courts in exceptional circumstances. Thus the Indian Divorces (Validity) Act, 1921, and the Indian and Colonial Divorce Jurisdiction Act, 1926, section 1(1) extended the recognition of Indian divorces, granted in circumstances amounting to less than domicile, to divorces pronounced in respect of spouses domiciled in England or Scotland. Again, the Matrimonial Causes (War Marriages) Act, 1944, operated only in favour of women who, prior to their marriage, had been domiciled in England or Scotland and had not taken up residence in the country of their husband's domicile.[46] It must be admitted that, in the last instance, the English domicile is that of the wife before the marriage and after the divorce. Nevertheless, that connection with England, apart from exclusive residence in England, is significant, not only because it introduces the notion of domicile into the rule of jurisdiction, but also because the relevant domicile is that of the wife after the divorce. As was suggested above, the same factor is relevant in considering the effect of an English divorce granted to the wife by virtue of paragraph (a) or (b) of section 40(1) of the Matrimonial Causes Act, 1965. Its existence raises the question whether the recognition of foreign divorces is an independent principal question in the conflict of laws, or whether it constitutes a preliminary question.

III. Recognition of Foreign Divorces: Preliminary or Main Question

An affirmative answer in favour of the second alternative was given by Mr. Justice MacKay in *Schwebel v. Ungar*[47] when he said: "To determine that status ... our inquiry must be directed not to the effect to be given under Ontario law to the divorce proceedings in Italy, but to the effect to be given to these proceedings by the law of the country in which she was domiciled at the time of the marriage to the plaintiff in 1957, namely | Israel." The Court of Appeal of Ontario relied on the law of the domicile at the time of the marriage in issue, *i.e.*, on the law governing capacity to enter into a new marriage, as well as on the rules of the conflict of laws of the latter, and treated the recognition of the Italian divorce as a preliminary question. Thus it was able to hold that a previous informal divorce in Italy between spouses who at the time were domiciled in Hungary (where the divorce could not be recog-

---

[46] The Matrimonial Causes (Dominion Troops) Act, 1919, 9 & 10 Geo. 5, c. 28, was an imperial statute which claimed recognition throughout the British Empire, as it then was.
[47] [1964] 1 Ont. 430, at 441, 42 D.L.R.2d 622, at 633 and *also* see the valuable comment by Lysyk, 43 Can. B. Rev. 363 (1965); Webb, *Bigamy and Capacity to Marry*, 14 Int'l & Comp. L.Q. 659 (1965).

nized) was nevertheless effective in dissolving the previous marriage since the divorce was recognized by the law of the subsequent domicile of the spouses, Israel. If the court had regarded the question of the recognition of the divorce in Italy as a main question, independent of, and on an equal footing with, the question whether the wife, who had been so divorced, could marry again, it would have had to deny recognition of the divorce in Ontario since, at common law, only the courts of the domicile at the time of the divorce have jurisdiction to pronounce such a decree.

The Supreme Court,[48] employing a pragmatic approach, did not dissociate itself from the approach adopted by the Ontario Court of Appeal and may thus be said to have approved this approach, at least within the narrow limits of the facts of the case.

It was probably unnecessary in the particular circumstances to draw this distinction and to consider the recognition of the informal divorce in Italy as anything else but a principal question. The court was confronted with a conflict of laws in time. According to Hungarian law, which was applicable according to the Ontario rules of the conflict of laws as the law of the domicile of the spouses at the time of the divorce, the divorce in Italy was ineffective. Therefore the marriage subsisted. At the moment when the parties obtained a domicile in Israel, the marriage terminated, since the law of Israel recognizes extrajudicial divorces of Jews pronounced in the presence of any Rabbinical court. Thus, whether the wife was domiciled in Israel or in Ontario at the time when she entered into a new marriage in Ontario, she was an unmarried woman capable of marrying again.

In the particular circumstances of *Schwebel v. Ungar*, the result is the same irrespective of whether the recognition of the divorce in Italy is treated as a main or as a preliminary question incidental to the determination of the question whether the divorced wife has capacity to enter into a new marriage. However, the problem must be put in more general terms: Is the question of the recognition of a foreign divorce always a main question, with the result that the conflict rules of the forum determine uniformly in all disputes concerning a foreign divorce (such as capacity to marry, duty to maintain, custody) whether the divorce must be recognized or not? Alternatively, is the question of the recognition of a foreign divorce (at | times) a preliminary question with the result that at one time the conflict rules of the forum and at other times the conflict rules of the *lex causæ* of the particular main question determine, for the purposes of the particular issue before the court only, whether the divorce must be recognized or not? So formulated, the problem is whether the divisible divorce is a reality outside the United States.

---

[48] Schwebel v. Ungar, [1965] Sup Ct. 148, 48 D.L.R.2d 644.

The House of Lords, in *Shaw v. Gould*,[49] set a course whereby each legal issue is determined in historical sequence, and the rules of the conflict of laws of the forum apply to each issue successively. Thus, in the circumstances before the House of Lords, the issues, in a historical order of events, were: the marriage of Elizabeth to Buxton in England, the recognition of the decree of divorce obtained in Scotland while the spouses were domiciled in England, the validity of the subsequent marriage of Elizabeth in Scotland to Shaw, who was domiciled in Scotland, and the legitimacy of the children born in Scotland of the second union. If these issues had not been treated, one and all, as main questions, but some of them as preliminary questions, the result would have been the opposite. If the main issue is the legitimacy of the children born of the second union in Scotland, it must be decided in accordance with the law of the alleged lawful father's domicile, which is Scotland. The law of Scotland as the *lex causæ*, including its rules of the conflict of laws, must determine the capacity of Elizabeth and Shaw to enter into a marriage as well as the validity of the previous divorce in Scotland. On the strength of these considerations, the children would have been legitimate, not illegitimate as the House of Lords held them to be. However, the last mentioned approach was used by Mr. Justice Romer in *Re Bischoffs-heim*.[50]

The problem is, therefore, which approach is to be preferred in determining whether a foreign divorce is to be recognized. The solution lies, it is believed, in the answer to the question whether the institution (legitimacy, divorce) differs considerably from country to country, or is uniform. When English domestic law regarded as legitimate only those children who were born in lawful wedlock, while foreign law took notice of legitimacy arising from legitimation by subsequent marriage or otherwise, and as a consequence of a putative marriage, it is understandable that English private international law, as part of the *lex fori*, insisted on compliance with its own tests and was loath to subordinate this determination to the rules of the conflict of laws of a foreign *lex causæ*. A lawful marriage according to the English rules of private international law had to exist, not a general status of legitimacy. Today, when legitimation by subsequent | marriage[51] and legitimacy arising from a putative marriage[52] have become part of English domestic law, insistence on proof of a valid marriage according to the rules of English private international law has become pointless. It remains to apply these conclusions to the problem of divorce, bearing in mind that what appears at first sight

---

[49] L.R. 3 H.L. 55, at 80 (1868); *but see id.* at 97 (per Lord Colonsay).

[50] [1948] Ch. 79.

[51] Legitimacy Act, 1926, 16 & 17 Geo. 5, c. 60, § 1; Legitimacy Act, 1959, 7 & 8 Eliz. 2, c. 73, § 1.

[52] Legitimacy Act, 1959, 7 & 8 Eliz. 2, c. 73, § 2.

to be a problem of jurisdiction may conceal a real choice of law. As long as divorce was unknown in English law, and perhaps even when the earliest English provisions on divorce had been enacted, it is understandable that English private international law, as part of the *lex fori*, insisted on compliance with its own tests. Moreover, capacity to marry became subject to the rigid test of domicile only in 1877,[53] while it was formerly determined by the fortuitous circumstance that the marriage took place in a certain country. Today, when the institution of divorce has assumed fairly uniform features throughout the world, the time may have come, not for diversifying and enlarging the English rules on the recognition of foreign jurisdictions to pronounce divorces, but to subordinate this recognition, as a preliminary question, to the law governing the capacity to remarry, including its rules of the conflict of laws.

Such a change of attitude would not operate as a panacea and would leave a number of problems unsolved. In some instances, it would relieve existing difficulties, as the following example will show. *H*, an Italian national, is married to *W*, who has retained her original Swiss citizenship. They are domiciled in Switzerland. On a petition for divorce brought by *W* in Switzerland, the Swiss court assumes jurisdiction on the ground, admitted by Swiss law, that *W* is a Swiss national, applies Swiss law and pronounces a decree of divorce. *H* wishes to marry again. According to Swiss private international law[54] capacity to marry is governed by the *lex patriæ, i.e.*, Italian law. Italian law does not recognize foreign divorces of Italian nationals.[55] Since Switzerland and Italy are parties to the Hague Convention on Marriage of 12 June 1902, Swiss courts are precluded, in the circumstances, from disregarding on the ground of public policy *H's* incapacity to enter into a second marriage. *H* is validly divorced in Switzerland, but he cannot marry there. *H*, wishing to marry *X*, a German national domiciled in Germany, comes to England. According to English private international law, the Swiss divorce will be recognized since *H* was domiciled in Switzerland at the relevant time; moreover, *W* was ordinarily resident there all her life and was a Swiss national. *H's* capacity to marry is governed by the law of his domicile, Switzerland, and renvoi is excluded here. A Swiss divorce | confers capacity to marry again. Thus *H* is free to marry in England, but the marriage is invalid in Switzerland.[56] If the validity of the divorce were to be treated as a

---

[53] Sottomayor v. de Barros (No. 1). 3 P.D. 1 (C.A. 1877).

[54] Gesetz betr. die zivilrechtlichen Verhältnisse der Niedergelassenen und Aufenthalter art. 7(c) (Law of June 25, 1891, Swit.).

[55] Pro. Gen. App. Bari v. Trizio, *in* [1957] Rivista di diritto internazionale 147 (Corte di Cassazione 1955); Proc. Gen. App. Turin v. Ghinolfi, *In* [1957] Rivista di diritto internazionale 575 (Corte di Cassazione 1956).

[56] Caliaro v. Canton de Argovie, 80 Pt. I. BGE 427 (1954), [1957] Revue critique de droit international privé 52. *See also* Reymond, Comment, 5 Int'l & Comp. L.Q. 144 (1956).

preliminary question, it would be found to be ineffective in Switzerland, at least in so far as *H*, though not *W*, is concerned, and a greater harmony of decision would be achieved.

In other instances, the technique of treating the question of the recognition of foreign divorces as a preliminary question may create a dangerous state of uncertainty and confusion. Thus a divorce obtained abroad in circumstances such as those in *Travers v. Holley*[57] would be ineffective in England, if one of the spouses, being domiciled abroad where such a divorce is not recognized, wished to enter into a new marriage in England, and he would be precluded from doing so. If that spouse subsequently acquired a domicile in England and died there intestate, without having entered into a new marriage, his former wife would be precluded from claiming a share under the Intestate Estates Act, 1952,[58] since English law governs the succession, and English private international law governs the preliminary question.

In most other situations it will make little difference whether the recognition of a foreign divorce is treated as a preliminary or as a main question, since English law will be both the *lex fori* and the *lex causæ*. Such is the case when one of the spouses brings a petition for judicial separation or for restitution of conjugal rights. The recognition of a foreign divorce is clearly a main question – and perhaps the only instance of such recognition being a main question – when an action for a declaration that the divorce is valid is brought in England. However, a prudent practice requires the petitioner in such proceedings to be domiciled in England.[59]

IV. Preliminary Conclusions

The conclusion, so far, has been this: In view of the close link between divorce and capacity to marry,

(1) The recognition of foreign divorces can be determined by broad rules, in so far as the spouses are domiciled in the forum (England); if the spouses are not domiciled in the forum a rigid rule which coordinates the recognition of the foreign divorce with the law governing capacity to marry is desirable. At the time when the foreign proceedings are instituted, this is the law of the domicile of the parties at that time, and no allowance can be made with respect to a possible change of this domicile after the divorce. Therefore, jurisdiction should be | concentrated on the courts of the foreign domicile;

---

[57] [1953] P. 246.
[58] Intestates' Estates Act, 1952, 15 & 16 Geo. 6, 1 Eliz. 2, c. 64 as amended.
[59] Har-Shefi v. Har-Shefi (No. 1), [1953] P. 161; *cf.* Garthwaite v. Garthwaite, [1964] P. 356.

alternatively, the recognition of such foreign divorces should be treated as a preliminary question to be decided according to the law of the foreign domicile, including its rules of the conflict of laws, of the spouse who wishes to marry again or the distribution of whose estate is in issue.

(2) The exercise of jurisdiction by the courts of the forum (England) on a broad basis, such as that provided by section 40(1)(a), (b) of the English Matrimonial Causes Act, 1965, causes little difficulty and will normally enable the wife to marry again.[60] The case of the divorced husband, who is domiciled abroad, is more difficult. Here the choice lies between allowing him to marry again on the strength of the English decree in disregard of his personal law, if this should not recognize the English divorce, or of observing the precepts of his personal law, which continues to regard him as married, and of denying him the right to marry again, in disregard of the English decree of divorce.

V. Recognition of Foreign Divorces in the Commonwealth

It is interesting to observe that the development in the Commonwealth has followed the opposite course. Recognition has been accorded to foreign divorces on a scale which exceeds by far the limits within which the courts in the Commonwealth can exercise jurisdiction themselves.

Little need be said about the Canadian legislation[61] and practice. In matters of recognition of decrees granted outside Canada it would seem that the English rules known as the rules in *Le Mesurier v. Le Mesurier*[62] and *Travers v. Holley*[63] have been taken over.[64] Whether recognition of divorces pronounced in other provinces follows from the federal character of the extending local jurisdiction, or whether such recognition requires, once more, recourse to the doctrine in *Travers v. Holley* appears to have remained an open question.[65] In addition, the rule in *Armitage v. Attorney-General*[66] ap-

---

[60] *See* discussion in text at 54–56 *supra*.

[61] The Divorce Jurisdiction Act, Can. Rev. Stat. c. 84 (1952).

[62] [1895] A.C. 517 (P.C.).

[63] [1953] P. 246.

[64] Bednar v. Dep'y Reg. of Vital Statistics, 31 W.W.R. (n.s.) 40. 24 D.L.R.2d 238 (Alta. Sup. Ct. 1960) (separate domicile); *Re* Allarie, 41 D.L.R.2d 553 (Alta. Sup. Ct. 1963); Yeger v. Reg. of Vital Statistics, 26 W.W.R. (n.s.) 651 (Alta. Sup. Ct. 1958); *but see* La Pierre v. Walter. 31 W.W.R. (n.s.) 26, 24 D.L.R.2d 483 (Alta. Sup. Ct. 1960). For the rule in *Le Mesurier v. Le Mesurier*, see J. Castel, Private International Law 122 (1960), and the cases cited in n. 85.

[65] *Cf.* Kennedy, Comment, 32 Can. B. Rev. 211, at 213 (1954); Payne, *Recognition of Foreign Divorce Decrees in the Canadian Courts*, 10 Int'l & Comp. L.Q. 847 (1961); Griswold, *Divorce Jurisdiction and Recognition of Divorce Decrees – A Comparative Study*, 65 Harv. L. Rev. 193, at 219 (1951).

[66] [1906] P. 135.

plies.[67] These rules, together with the principle that the|courts of the domicile of the spouses have general jurisdiction in divorce, make up a balanced system, in which the local exercise of jurisdiction is matched by the recognition of the same, or similar or equivalent jurisdiction abroad.

No such neat balance as that to be found in Canadian conflict of laws is expressed in the modern legislation which has been recently enacted in New Zealand[68] and in Australia.[69] These acts distinguish clearly between the conditions under which New Zealand and Australian courts respectively can exercise jurisdiction and those under which foreign decrees can be recognized in New Zealand and Australia. Before this legislation can be analysed, it must be noted that, for the purposes of jurisdiction in divorce, whether exercised by Australian or New Zealand courts, or by courts elsewhere, a married woman is accorded a separate domicile. The two acts achieve this result by somewhat different means. The New Zealand act states generally[70] that, for the purposes of the act, the domicile of a married woman, wherever she was married, shall be determined as if she were unmarried and, if she is a minor, as if she were an adult. The term "domicile" bears the meaning attributed to it by the law of New Zealand. The Australian act provides that a deserted wife, who was domiciled in Australia either immediately before her marriage or immediately before the desertion, shall be deemed to be domiciled in Australia and that a wife, who is resident in Australia at the date of instituting proceedings and has been so resident for the period of three years immediately preceding that date, shall be deemed to be domiciled in Australia at that date.[71] This unilateral rule, which establishes only a separate domicile of married women in Australia, has its exact counterpart in Part X of the Australian act, which deals with the recognition of foreign divorces and accords to wives a separate foreign domicile under the same conditions.[72] Thus both acts attribute to a wife a separate domicile for purposes of jurisdiction in divorce. Only the New Zealand act employs the general rules on domicile, by way of the fiction that the wife is a *feme sole*. The Australian act relies on the modern criteria of desertion and on a previous domicile in the country concerned, or on residence for a period of three years. The only notable differences between these provisions seem to consist in the treatment of deserting wives and of wives who have separated from

---

[67] Wyllie v. Martin, [1931] 3 W.W.R. 465 (B.C. Sup. Ct.): Burnflel v. Burnfiel, [1926] 1 W.W.R. 657, [1926] 2 D.L.R. 129 (Sask.); Lyon v. Lyon, [1959] Ont. 305; Walker v. Walker, [1950] 2 W.W.R. 411, [1950] 4 D.L.R. 253 (B.C.).

[68] Matrimonial Proceedings Act, Act No. 71 of 1963 (N.Z.). [Hereinafter cited N.Z. Act.].

[69] Matrimonial Causes Act, Act No. 104 of 1959 (Austl.). [Hereinafter cited Austl. Act.].

[70] N.Z. Act at § 3.

[71] Austl. Act at § 24.

[72] Austl. Act at § 95(3).

their husbands by agreement. While such married women appear to be able to acquire a separate domicile at any time according to the law of New Zealand, they cannot enjoy the benefit of a fictitious domicile of their own under the Australian act, except after three years' ordinary residence in the country concerned.

|With these notions of a separate domicile of a married woman in mind, it is possible to examine the jurisdictional provisions of these acts. A foreign divorce is recognized:

(a) If one or both of the parties were domiciled in the foreign country concerned.[73]

It is irrelevant, for the present purpose, that according to the New Zealand act, the party or parties concerned must have been domiciled in the foreign country at the time of the decree, while the Australian act requires the domicile to have existed at the time when the proceedings were instituted. It is noteworthy, however, that according to the Australian act, the party at whose instance the dissolution was effected, or if it was effected at the instance of both parties, either of those parties, must have been so domiciled. This may be an attempt to perpetuate, unnecessarily it is believed, the rule in *Levett v. Levett*[74] which was itself the product of a liberal technique of statutory interpretation.

(b) If one or both of the parties were resident in the foreign country and had been so resident for a continuous period of not less than two years at the time when the proceedings were commenced.[75]

In this form the provision is only to be found in the New Zealand act. The Australian act, however, in so far as it relies on residence, refers to residence by a wife for a period of three years immediately preceding the institution of the proceedings.[76]

(c) If one or both of the parties were nationals or citizens of the foreign country or of the sovereign state of which that country forms part.[77]

This provision is peculiar to New Zealand and has no counterpart in the law of Australia.

(d) If the wife was deserted by her husband, and the husband was immediately before the desertion domiciled in the foreign country[78] or if the wife was so domiciled immediately before her marriage or immediately before her desertion.[79]

---

[73] N.Z. Act at § 82(1)(a); Austl. Act at § 95(2)(a).
[74] [1957] P. 156 (C.A.).
[75] N.Z. Act at § 82(1)(b)(i).
[76] Austl. Act at § 95(3)(b).
[77] N.Z. Act at § 82(1)(b)(ii).
[78] N.Z. Act at § 82(1)(b)(iii).
[79] Austl. Act at § 95(3)(a).

These provisions reflect, respectively, the techniques of the New Zealand and Australian legislation to attribute to a wife a separate domicile, either generally or in specific circumstances. They are recalled here, separately, | since their factual basis rather than their legal characterization is significant in the present context.

(e) If the husband was deported and the husband was immediately before the deportation domiciled in the foreign country.[80]

No such provision is to be found in the Australian act.

(f) If the wife was legally separated from her husband, by order of a competent court or by agreement, and the husband was at the date of the order or agreement domiciled in that country.[81]

This provision, the purpose of which seems to be to eliminate the effect of *Lord Advocate v. Jaffrey*[82] and *Attorney-General of Alberta v. Cook*,[83] has no equivalent in the Australian act.

(g) If the rule in *Armitage v. Attorney-General*[84] applies.

Since the New Zealand act acknowledges the existence of a separate domicile of the wife in matters of divorce, the act is satisfied if the foreign divorce is recognized by the courts of the country where one of the parties to the marriage is domiciled.[85] The Australian act, on the other hand, attempts to cut down a possible extended effect of the rule by requiring that the foreign decree must be recognized by the courts of the country where the parties were domiciled at the time of the dissolution of the marriage.[86] While the Australian act has thus succeeded in eliminating the operation of the rule in *Armitage v. Attorney-General*[87] in circumstances comparable to those in *Mountbatten v. Mountbatten*,[88] but which are of greater importance in Australia, given the broad range of foreign jurisdictions which are recognized by the act, it may be doubted whether it has achieved this result in situations such as that which presented itself in *Schwebel v. Ungar.*[89]

(h) If the divorce obtained abroad is recognized under the common-law rules of private international law in addition to the rules incorporated in the act.[90]

---

[80] N.Z. Act at § 82(1)(b)(iii).

[81] N.Z. Act at § 82(1)(b)(iv).

[82] [1921] 1 A.C. 146, at 161.

[83] [1926] A.C. 444 (P.C.).

[84] [1906] P. 135.

[85] N.Z. Act at § 82(1)(c); Gould, *The Matrimonial Proceedings Act, 1963 and the Conflict of Laws, in* A. G. Davis Essays 26, at 34 (J. Northey ed. 1965).

[86] Austl. Act at § 95(4).

[87] [1906] P. 135.

[88] [1959] P. 43.

[89] [1964] 1 Ont. 430, 42 D.L.R.2d 622 and authorities cited in notes 47 & 48 *supra.*

[90] N.Z. Act at § 82(2); Austl. Act § 95(5).

In face of this extensive array of provisions permitting the courts of New Zealand and Australia to recognize foreign divorces in a great variety of circumstances, even if the parties are not domiciled in New Zealand or Australia, it is even more striking to observe the strict limits within which | these same courts can exercise jurisdiction themselves. In New Zealand, where the wife is accorded a separate domicile of her own, the petitioner or the respondent must be domiciled in the country. In a limited number of circumstances, residence for at least two years immediately preceding the filing of the petition is required in addition.[91] In Australia, the petitioner must be domiciled in the country.[92] For this purpose, a deserted wife who was domiciled in Australia either immediately before her marriage or before the desertion, and a wife who is resident in Australia at the date of instituting proceedings and has been so resident for three years, are deemed to be domiciled in Australia.[93]

VI. New Trends: England

In the light of the development sketched above and of the theoretical and practical conclusions drawn therefrom, it is now necessary to turn to the recent decision of the House of Lords in *Indyka v. Indyka*.[94] Its practical effect is difficult to gauge at present, but it is clear that, as regards recognition of foreign divorces, the evolution which covered the last hundred years has been given a new direction.

In 1938, while domiciled in Czechoslovakia, the husband married there. As a result of the war, he found himself in England and, in 1946, acquired an English domicile. The wife, who had stayed behind, obtained a divorce from a Czech court in January, 1949 on the ground of profound disruption of matrimonial relations. In 1959, the husband entered into a new marriage in England. In subsequent proceedings brought by the second wife, the validity in England of the Czech divorce was in issue. In 1937, the Matrimonial Causes Act, 1937, section 13 (now section 40(1) (a) of the Matrimonial Causes Act, 1965) enabled a deserted woman, whose husband had been domiciled in England immediately before the desertion, to resort to the English courts for the purpose of obtaining a divorce. On December 16, 1949, the Law Reform (Miscellaneous Provisions) Act, 1949, came into force, section 1(1) of which (now section 40(1)(b) of the Matrimonial Causes

---

[91] N.Z. Act at § 20, in conjunction with § 21 (m), (n) & (o).
[92] Austl. Act at § 23(4).
[93] *Id.* at § 24(1) & (2).
[94] [1966] 2 W.L.R. 892 (P.D.A.) (per Latcy, J.); [1966] 3 W.L.R. 603 (C.A.); [1967] 3 W.L.R. 510 (H.L.).

Act, 1965) permitted a woman who had been ordinarily resident in England for three years to petition for a decree in England, although the husband was domiciled abroad. In 1953, it was decided in *Travers v. Holley*[95] that these provisions, as consolidated in section 18(1)(a), (b) of the Matrimonial Causes Act, 1950, operated as a bilateral rule. The question was whether the Czech decree of January, 1949, could be recognized, by virtue of the rule in *Travers v. Holley*, in the reciprocal application of | section 40(1) (a) or (b), notwithstanding that the forerunner of this section had been first enacted after the divorce had been pronounced in Czechoslovakia. Both Mr. Justice Latey, who refused to recognize the decree, and the Court of Appeal, which held that it was effective in England, considered the problem to be one of applying the rule in *Travers v. Holley* in a conflict of laws in time. The former did so by way of statutory interpretation; the latter on the strength of alleged principles of the common law.[96]

The House of Lords held that the Czech decree must be recognized, but the reasons differed from those adduced in the courts below. Their Lordships drew a clear distinction between jurisdiction in divorce and the recognition of foreign decrees of divorce.[97] In order to do so, they had to dissociate themselves from a long line of authorities beginning in 1868 and ending in 1936.[98] They did so partly by reference to the statutory extensions of English jurisdiction and comparable enlargements of the jurisdiction of foreign courts,[99] partly by reference to unsuccessful attempts in the past by English courts to enlarge their jurisdiction,[100] partly on the reports and recommendations of two royal commissions[101] and partly by means of frontal assaults on some old favourites of the conflict of laws. Since the first two aspects were examined before, and the third was not canvassed to any extent, it is only necessary to concentrate on the last.

In their Lordships' view, the advice of the Privy Council in *Le Mesurier v. Le Mesurier*[102] was the main obstacle barring a more generous approach towards the recognition of foreign judgments. Although *Le Mesurier* was concerned with jurisdiction and not with the recognition of foreign judgments, and only with the jurisdiction of the courts in Ceylon in virtue of

---

[95] [1953] P. 246.

[96] For a critical appraisal see Lipstein, Comment, [1967] Camb. L.J. 42.

[97] [1967] 3 W.W.R. 510, at 519D, 524F (per Lord Reid), 531E, 532A (per Lord Morris), 535D (per Lord Pearce), 548B, C (per Lord Wilberforce); *but see* at 557B.

[98] *See* authorities cited in notes 1–5 *supra*.

[99] *See* discussion in text at 54–56 *supra*.

[100] *See* authorities cited in notes 7 & 8 *supra*.

[101] Report of the Royal Commission on Divórce, Cd. 6478 (1912); Report of the Royal Commission on Marriage and Divorce, Cmd. 9678 (1956); see [1967] 3 W.L.R. at 534, 545, 553.

[102] [1895] A.C. 517 (P.C.).

Roman-Dutch law there in force, it must be admitted that the generality of the principle formulated by the Privy Council applied equally to both aspects. However, in criticising the Privy Council for having misconstrued the authority of von Bar,[103] Lords Reid and Pearce did less than justice to the acumen of Lord Watson and gave too much credit to a translation.[104] In fact, von Bar, dealing with choice of law in matters of divorce, said this:

Divorce and permanent separation pronounced by a court (*separatio a thoro et mensa, séparation de corps*) ... are also subject to the national (domiciliary) law of the spouses

...

| The dilemma that, on the one hand, the national law, and, on the other hand, the *lex fori* applies is solved, however, by the device that in matrimonial causes only the national courts have jurisdiction, leaving aside any legislation to the contrary .... Therefore a decree of divorce pronounced by any other courts than a Court of the *home state* is to be regarded in all other countries as inoperative.[105]

Speaking of jurisdiction in proceedings affecting status, and of proceedings for a declaration that a divorce is invalid, von Bar said:

Consequently the courts of the States to which the parties belong must have *exclusive jurisdiction*. It is true that this exclusive jurisdiction may create great inconvenience, if the distance between the home State and the place of the foreign domicile is considerable and especially if the domicile is of long standing .... Nevertheless it is necessary, as a matter of principle, to insist on this exclusive jurisdiction, if questions of status are to be governed at all by the law of the nationality.[106]

Thus von Bar was treating jurisdiction of local and of foreign courts on an equal footing and according to the same principles. He envisaged only one, exclusive jurisdiction, namely, that of the courts of the country, the law of which was the personal law of the parties. In his view, this was the *lex patriae*,[107] but the words in brackets, cited above, show that he was prepared, as an alternative, to make a concession in favour of the courts of the country of the domicile, if the law of the country concerned relied on the *lex domicilii* to determine personal status. By postulating an exclusive jurisdiction, he forged the link between jurisdiction and the personal law which, in the absence of an exclusive jurisdiction, can only be achieved by postulating a uniform rule of choice of law. As a realistic student of comparative private

---

[103] L. von Bar, Private International Law § 173, at 382 (Gillespie transl. 1892).

[104] [1967] 3 W.L.R. at 523B (per Lord Reid), 537A (per Lord Pearce).

[105] 1 L. von Bar, Theorie und Praxis des Internationalen Privatrechts § 173. at 482–84 (2d ed. 1889). (Writer's transl., emphasis added.).

[106] 2 *id.* § 421, at 435; *see also* 1 *id.* § 178. at 497. (Writer's transl., emphasis added.).

[107] *See also* J. Westlake, Private International Law § 41, at 76 (2d ed. 1880).

international law he acknowledged that the exclusive jurisdiction must be *either* that of the country of the nationality *or* that of the country of the domicile of the spouses. The Privy Council, in *Le Mesurier*, followed this train of thought faithfully. The other two authorities of considerable weight, *Shaw v. Gould*[108] and *Harvey v. Farnie*[109] were hardly given more than passing attention,[110] and all these decisions were regarded as coloured by the subsequent ossification of the concept of domicile.

In the opinion of their Lordships, the statutory expansion of the jurisdiction of English courts required to be matched, but not copied, by broad rules permitting the recognition of foreign decrees of divorce. Unfortunately, the clarity with which this need was expressed was not equalled | by precise indications of the criteria to be employed henceforth. Moreover, since all members of the House[111] approved of the result reached by the Court of Appeal in recognizing the Czech divorce in reliance on the rule in *Travers v. Holley*, it is not easy to say which, if any, of the new criteria can be regarded as a *ratio decidendi*. They will now be reviewed in succession.

In the first place, the courts of the domicile of the spouses have jurisdiction.[112] The majority understood this to mean the domicile of the husband,[113] but Lord Pearson was prepared to recognize the jurisdiction of foreign courts which had acted on a different characterization of domicile consonant with their own notions.[114] Such a conclusion strikes at the roots of any system of conflict of laws, for if any principle is accepted today, it is that the characterization of connecting factors must rely on the notions of the *lex fori*, no matter whether rules of choice of law or of jurisdiction are concerned.[115]

In the second place, the courts of the nationality of the spouses have jurisdiction.[116] This suggestion was put forward tentatively only by some

---

[108] L.R. 3 H.L. 55 (1868).

[109] 8 App. Cas. 43 (1882).

[110] Indyka v. Indyka, [1967] 3 W.L.R. 510, at 532G (per Lord Morris), 536C (per Lord Pearce), 548F, 550D (per Lord Wilberforce).

[111] *Id.* at 515D, 517H (per Lord Reid), 533A-F, 534C (per Lord Morris), 540G, 542F, 546D (per Lord Pearce), 559B, F (per Lord Wilberforce), 561G, 562E, 564H (per Lord Pearson).

[112] *Id.* at 525A (per Lord Reid), 531E (per Lord Morris), 541F, 545E (per Lord Pearce), 548A, 556F, 557D (per Lord Wilberforce), 563C, G (per Lord Pearson).

[113] *Id.* at 557D (per Lord Wilberforce).

[114] *Id.* at 563G.

[115] *E.g., Re* Annesley, [1926] Ch. 692; A. Dicey, *op. cit. supra* note 23, at 31, n. 62, 718 & n. 58; Entores, Ltd. v. Miles Far East Corp., [1955] 2 Q.B. 327, [1955] 2 All E.R. 493 (C.A.).

[116] Indyka v. Indyka, [1967] 3 W.L.R. 510, at 527E (per Lord Reid), 534D (per Lord Morris), 537A, 545F (per Lord Pearce), 551C, 557G (per Lord Wilberforce), 563D, F. 565A (per Lord Pearson); *but see* Shaw v. Gould, L.R. 3 H.L. 55, at 84 (1868), rejecting the interpretation by J. Story, Commentaries on the Conflict of Laws § 205, at 254, especially n. 1 (6th cd. I. Redfield 1865).

members,[117] by others as indicating a substantial connection[118] and by one or possibly two as including jurisdiction based on the nationality of one spouse only, if the nationality of the spouses should differ.[119]

In the third place, their Lordships were agreed that the rule in *Armitage v. Attorney-General*[120] is to be maintained in supplementing the jurisdiction of the courts of the domicile and, possibly, also of the nationality of the spouses[121] or even of one of them only.[122]

In the fourth place, their Lordships were attracted by the test of residence, but their conception of residence was not uniform. Lord Reid relied on the notion of the matrimonial home;[123] Lord Pearce and Lord|Wilberforce were impressed by this notion, having regard to the position of resident wives in England;[124] Lord Wilberforce considered residence either generally or in the particular case of wives living apart from their husband,[125] though with some hesitation, unless some substantial connection is found to exist.[126] Lord Pearson expressed similar sentiments.[127]

The somewhat hesitant allusions to residence probably reflect, negatively, a detachment from the present rigidly technical notion of domicile and, positively, the existence of the limited jurisdiction in England in virtue of section 40(1)(a), (b) of the Matrimonial Causes Act, 1965. However, Lord Reid's reliance on the matrimonial home, if it means the same as the matrimonial domicile in Scots law, requires further examination and definition, since in former times this concept perplexed Lord Deas[128] and was said by Lord Watson to be "vague."[129] As shown above,[130] the courts in Scotland have exercised jurisdiction, if the spouses were formerly domiciled in Scotland, if the last common place of residence was there and the husband has moved abroad, irrespective of whether he acquired a domicile in the foreign country, provided only that the parties had not separated by agreement. The matrimonial home or domicile is thus the last domicile where the parties

---

[117] Indyka v. Indyka, [1967] 3 W.L.R. 510, at 527E, 521D, 523C (per Lord Reid), 557G (per Lord Wilberforce).

[118] *Id.* at 534D (per Lord Morris), 558A, G (per Lord Wilberforce).

[119] *Id.* at 563G (per Lord Pearson), 558A (per Lord Wilberforce).

[120] [1906] P. 135.

[121] Indyka v. Indyka, [1967] 3 W.L.R. 510, at 532A (per Lord Morris), 541G (per Lord Pearce), 557F (per Lord Wilberforce).

[122] *Id.* at 546A (per Lord Pearce).

[123] *Id.* at 523B, 525F–526B, 527A, G.

[124] *Id.* at 546C, 547F.

[125] *Id.* at 557D, 558B.

[126] *Id.* at 558C, G.

[127] *Id.* at 564C, G.

[128] *See* authorities cited in notes 18 & 19.

[129] Le Mesurier v. Le Mesurier, [1895] A.C. 517, at 538 (P.C.).

[130] *See* discussion in text at 49–51 *supra*.

lived together. Far from replacing the domicile it perpetuates it. If, as it seems most likely, this notion moved Lord Reid, his statements, couched in modern terms of English law, amount to this: in proceedings for divorce not only the wife, but also the husband, may seize the courts of the former domicile, if either the husband has deserted the wife or if the wife has given the husband grounds for leaving her. If this is and has been a rule of English law, the introduction, in 1937, of what is now section 40(1)(a) of the Matrimonial Causes Act, 1965, was *otiose*. If, on the other hand, Lord Reid intended to refer to the place of the present common residence of the spouses, shorn of the ballast of the requirement of a domicile of the husband in that country, it would mean that the decision of the majority in *Niboyet v. Niboyet*[131] had been restored. However, this interpretation is excluded, seeing that Lord Reid rested his judgment on the notion of a matrimonial home, in circumstances where no such home had existed for ten years.

Finally, it is possible, but unlikely, that Lord Reid envisaged the place of the last common residence of the spouses, not being their domicile, as a proper forum for proceedings in divorce, even if one or both of the spouses reside in another country at the time when the proceedings are|begun. Such a notion would not be in keeping with Scots law or with the opinion of the majority in *Niboyet v. Niboyet*.

VII. Conclusions

The principles for determining the recognition of foreign decrees of divorce formulated by the House of Lords do not differ to any noticeable extent from those which have been expressed by the legislature in New Zealand and in Australia. Like the latter, they fail to relate the recognition of foreign decrees of divorce to the resulting choice of law affecting capacity. As stated above, this correlation can only be achieved in one of two ways: either by concentrating jurisdiction in the country the law of which determines the ensuing capacity to marry or by linking jurisdiction, however extensive, to the requirement that the personal law must have been applied. The solutions in England, Australia and New Zealand fulfil neither of these conditions, and the danger of creating limping marriages has been greatly increased.

As pointed out above, this danger does not arise if recognition on an extensive scale is accorded to foreign decrees of divorce only if the spouses are domiciled in the recognizing country, *i.e.*, in the present case in England. In other words, if extensive recognition is to be accorded, a much more sophisticated system of rules must be devised which differentiates on the

---

[131] 4 P.D. 1 (1878).

lines set out above between divorces granted abroad to spouses who are domiciled in the recognizing country and to those who are not.

The objections raised against the decision of the House of Lords in *Indyka v. Indyka*,[132] therefore, lose much of their force, if the decision can be restricted to the particular facts of the case, where the husband was domiciled in England at all relevant times. However, the generality of the statements made there renders this conclusion difficult. The danger of limping divorces may have been reduced, but this will have been achieved at the expense of the intended beneficiaries who may well be condemned to unmarried celibacy or exposed to the threat of nullity proceedings if they succeed in entering into a second marriage.

---

[132] [1967] 3 W.L.R. 510.

Conflict of Laws 1921–1971
The Way Ahead

I

(1) Legal Basis

When the first issue of the Cambridge Law Journal appeared in 1921, the English rules of the conflict of laws were those stated and reformulated by Dicey[1] and by the editors of Westlake[2] and Foote.[3] Their progress between 1858 and 1912 had been charted by Dicey himself in a survey published in 1912.[4] The legal basis for the application of foreign law in England was and remained Lord Mansfield's pronouncement in *Holman* v. *Johnson*: "Every

---

[Editorial note: first published in Cambridge Law Journal 31 (1972), 67–120.]

[1] *Conflict of Laws* (3rd ed., 1922), pp. 1–33; (1890) 6 L.Q.R. 1; (1891) 7 L.Q.R. 113.
[2] *Private International Law* (7th ed., 1925, by N. Bentwich).
[3] *Private International Law* (5th ed., 1925, by H. Bellott).
[4] (1912) 28 L.Q.R. 341.

action here must be tried by the law of England, but the law of England says that in a variety of circumstances ... the law of the country where the cause of action arose shall govern."[5] Dicey never waivered in his adherence to this rule of English law,[6] but he supplemented it with an argument drawn from the doctrine of acquired rights[7] which bedevilled English lawyers for a long time, until in 1949 the editors of the sixth edition of Dicey took what they believed to be a bold, but substantially honest, step by restricting the concept to its proper boundaries and thus by depriving it of its capacity to serve as a general principle of the Conflict of Laws.[8]

Recent research has justified this change of approach to the basis of the English conflict of laws. The doctrine of acquired rights is of some antiquity and can be traced to the Postglossators,[9] though it is|doubtful whether they wished to apply it to questions of the conflict of laws.[10] It has been refuted again and again by eminent writers,[11] but until recently its sudden emergence in England under the auspices of Dicey has been a baffling phenomenon. The researches of Nadelmann[12] have shown that Dicey formulated his view for the first time in a review of Piggott's Foreign Judgments,[13] developed it as his "General Principle No. 1" in 1891[14] and then, in 1896, transported it verbatim into his "Digest of the Law of England with reference to the Conflict

---

[5] (1775) 1 Cowp. 161, 171. See also *Harford* v. *Morris* (1776) 2 Hag.Ecc. 423, 430, 434; *Dalrymple* v. *Dalrymple* (1811) 2 Hag.Con. 54, 58, 59. But see Lord Mansfield in *Robinson* v. *Bland* (1760) 1 W.Bl. 234, 246.

[6] (1890) 6 L.Q.R. 1, at pp. 3, 4, 6, 12, 13, 18, 20, 21; *Conflict of Laws* (3rd ed., 1922), pp. 3, 4, 6, 7, 13, 14, 20.

[7] *Ibid.*, pp. 10, 11, 13 without any detailed discussion, but noting Savigny's critique of circuity; *cf.* (1891) 7 L.Q.R. 113, at p. 114, 115; *Conflict of Laws* (3rd ed., 1922), pp. 11, 12, 14, p. 23 (General Principle No. 1), p. 25, and in particular p. 26.

[8] Foreshadowed in the 3rd ed. (1922), p. 33. See also Cheshire, *Private International Law* (2nd ed., 1938), pp. 85–86.

[9] Horst Müller, *Der Grundsatz der wohlerworbenen Rechte im Internationalen Privatrecht* (1935), reviewed by Gutzwiller (1936) 10 *Rabels Z.* 1056; Weiller, *Der Schutz der wohlerworbenen Rechte im Internationalen Privatrecht* (1934).

[10] See Gutzwiller *loc. cit.*, above, note 9.

[11] Wächter (1841) 24 *Archiv für die civilistische Praxis*, 230, at p. 300 and note 146; 25 (1842) 361, at p. 391; Savigny (1849) 8 *System des heutigen Römischen Rechts*, par. 361 (5), p. 132, Guthrie's transl. (2nd ed., 1880), pp, 147 *et seq.*; von Bar (1889) 1 *Theorie und Praxis des Internationalen Privatrechts*, p. 67, par. 23; Lorenzen (1924) 33 Yale L.J. 736; *Selected Articles* (1947) 1; W. W. Cook (1924) 33 Yale L.J. 745; *The Logical and Legal Basis of the Conflict of Laws* (1942) 1; Arminjon, *Hague Rec.* 44 (1933 II) 1.

[12] *Ius et Lex*, Festgabe für Gutzwiller (1959) 263 at pp. 276–279.

[13] (1885) 1 L.Q.R. 246, 248: "the rules of ... private international law are based on the recognition of actually acquired rights, *i.e.*, of rights which when acquired could be really enforced by the sovereign of the state where they have their origin."

[14] (1891) 7 L.Q.R. 113.

of Laws."[15] Dicey[16] acknowledged his indebtedness to Holland, whose *Elements of Jurisprudence* included the statement that the conflict of laws is in reality concerned with the recognition by English courts of rights created and defined by foreign law.[17] It is difficult to see how Holland reached his conclusion for his reference to Vattel is spurious and that to Wächter reverses the latter's thoughts.[18] It is possible that Holland owed it to Huber whom he cited in the second edition of his work.[19]

In juxtaposition with the common law rule expressed in *Holman*|v. *Johnson*[20] the principle of the protection of acquired rights makes little sense and lays itself open to the charge of circuity.[21] If the rules of the conflict of laws are part of English domestic law the latter, and not an overriding principle alleged to be of universal validity (such as that of personal and real statutes), determines the application of foreign law. Moreover, the legal nature of this allegedly international principle remains uncertain. Despite certain indications mentioned above,[22] Huber saw the problem in a different light, for his Third Principle proclaimed that "those who exercise sovereign authority so

---

[15] p. 22; *Conflict of Laws* (3rd ed., 1922), p. 23 *et seq.*, especially p. 27; see also (1891) 7 L.Q.R. 113, at pp. 113 *et seq.*, 114. In (1890) 6 L.Q.R. 1, at pp. 3, 5, 11, 14, 17, 18, 19–21, *Conflict of Laws* (3rd ed.), p. 3 note (e), p. 5 note (f), pp. 12, 15 and note (9), 19, 20, 21, 23, he speaks of the extraterritorial operation of law or recognition of rights. This phrase is copied from Holland, *Jurisprudence* (1880), p. 288; see below, note 18. And see the critique of Pillet, *Principes de droit international privé* (1905) 514, note.

[16] *Conflict of Laws*, p. VII.

[17] 1st ed. (1880), p. 288 and note 1; Dicey, *Conflict of Laws* (3rd ed., 1922), pp. 3, 5, notes.

[18] Nadelmann, *loc. cit.* (above, note 12), 277, 278; for the revision of these references in subsequent editions see Nadelmann, p. 277, note 90, and p. 278. The wording of Dicey's Principle I (1891) 7 L.Q.R. 113, *Conflict of Laws* (3rd ed., 1922) p. 23: "duly acquired" recalls a similar passage in Pillet, *Principes* (above p. 68, note 15) p. 496, no. 273; *Hague Rec.* 8 (1925 III) 489, at p. 496 who speaks of "un droit étant supposé acquis regulièrement dans un pays, c'est-à-dire conformément à la loi en vigueur dans ce pays," which is limited to a well-defined situation. See p. 497, no. 274; p. 510, note.

[19] *Praelectiones ad Pandectas* II, 1, 3.15, who may have envisaged a doctrine of acquired rights in order to counter the doctrines of the statutists; see *ibid.*, II, 1, 3.2. Thus the respect for acquired rights may have served as a motive for the application of foreign law which could not apply *proprio motu*, as the statutists would have it, but not as a principle requiring the application of foreign law replacing a similar doctrine of the statutists. *Cf.* Dicey (1891) 7 L.Q.R. 113, at p. 118; *Conflict of Laws* (3rd ed., 1922), p. 33.

[20] See above p. 67, note 5.

[21] See the writers cited above p. 68, note 11, and Dicey's own admission in (1891) 7 L.Q.R. 113, at 118; *Conflict of Laws* (3rd ed., 1922), p. 33. And see in particular the formulation adopted in *Conflict of Laws* (3rd ed., 1922), p. 27: "The word 'duly' [acquired] ... fixes in effect the limit of the application of General Principle I. This principle is ... only that rights which have been, in the opinion of *English courts* (italics mine), properly and rightly acquired are ... enforceable here." This restriction appeared first in Dicey article (1891) 7 L.Q.R. 113, at pp. 118–119, but in a less explicit sense, when it was stated: "This grant of 'due acquisition' may arise either from A's own conduct, or from the conduct of the [foreign] sovereign either as a legislator or as judge."

[22] Above p. 68, note 19.

act from comity that the laws of each nation which are enforced within its own boundaries should retain their effect everywhere. ....[23] It may be that the stress laid on comity was meant to underline that foreign law need not be enforced as such and that no more than a general respect for foreign acquired rights inspired the unfettered right of states to apply or not to apply foreign law.[24] The meaning of "comity" as Huber employed it is not clear. Taken as a minimum requirement it is equal to courtesy.[25] Taken as a maximum requirement it must be identical with legal duty. Some help can be derived from Huber himself in *Heedensdaegse Rechtsgeleertheyt*,[26] when he added, after formulating his three principles[27]:

From this it is clear that the decision of such cases is a part of the law of nations and not, properly speaking, of civil law, inasmuch as it does not depend on the individual pleasure of the | higher powers of each country, but on the mutual convenience of the sovereign powers and their tacit agreement with each other.[28]

Thus according to Huber there was no duty arising by the nature of private law to apply foreign law (as the statustists assumed). Instead, customary international law (the tacit pact between states) established a duty to give full effect to a right existing according to foreign law, once a state has decided to apply foreign law in the particular circumstances. Thus understood the doctrine of acquired rights does not suffer from the flaws expressed by its critics, limited as it is to providing a motive or explanation for applying foreign law and for applying it consistently, once chosen, but it has also become meaningless as a theory.[29] There are indications that Dicey was fully aware of this

---

[23] *Praelectiones* II, 1.3, 2; *Heedensdaegse Rechtsgeleertheyt* (1686) I, 3.4–6; *De jure civitatis* I, 4.1 (3rd ed.); III, 10 (1st ed., 1684).

[24] Meijers, *Hague Rec.* 49 (1934 III) 547, at p. 670, citing *Praelectiones* II, 1, 3.3, *Heedensdaegse Rechtsgeleertheyt* I, 3.8 and 10; Kollewijn, *Geschiedenis van de Nederlandse Wetenschap van het I.P.R.* tot 1880 (1937) 145, 146, but see pp. 138, 142; Yntema, *Vom deutschen zum europäischen Recht* II (1963) 65, at p. 75 *et seq.*; (1966) 65 Mich.L.R. 1, at p. 19 *et seq.*

[25] Meijers *loc. cit.*, at p. 664 demonstrates the difference between the use of the terms "de summo jure," "de necessitate," on the one hand, and of "de humanitate," "de comitate," on the other hand. See also Yntema, *op. cit.*, II, p. 76, n. 30; p. 79, n. 40, n. 44. For Dicey's view, see (1890) 6 L.Q.R. 1, at pp. 9 *et seq.*, 14, *Conflict of Laws* (3rd ed., 1922), pp. 10–11.

[26] I, 3.7. See also *Praelectiones* II, 1.3. para. 1: "quamquam ipsa quaestio magis ad jus gentium quam ad jus civile pertineat quatenus quid diversi populi inter se servare debeant, ad juris gentium rationes pertinere manifestum est." See Meijers, p. 668, note.

[27] *Praelectiones* II, 1.3. para. 2; *Heedensdaegse Rechtsgeleertheyt* I, 3.4–6.

[28] For the "tacit pact" of states, see Grotius, *De Jure Belli ac Pacis*, Prolegomena 1, 15, 16, 17, 26, 40: Yntema, *op. cit.*, II, pp. 76, 81, 83, 84, and 85 n. 65. See also Kollewijn *loc. cit.*, p. 133. But see Huber, *De jure civitatis* III, 10 nos. 1 and 2: "etsi non teneantur ex pacto vel necessitate subordinationis " (Meijers *loc. cit.*, 667, n. 2).

[29] See Pillet, *Principes* 135: "The respect for acquired rights is a ... fundamental notion of Private International Law, provided that the applicable law has been determined previously and applied"; see also *Hague Rec.* 8 (1925 III) at p. 503; Lainé, *Introduction au droit*

when he qualified his principle by the addition of the word "duly."[30] The example given by Dicey when he proclaimed the doctrine is limited, moreover, to a situation in which all the facts of the case in issue have arisen in the same country abroad. Such an example provides the strongest motive for not applying the *lex fori* and a clear incentive for relying on the law of the country where all the facts took place. The choice of law is accompanied by a sequence in time. But it provides a weaker motive and a less clear incentive if the facts have not arisen in one single country, and if no time sequence can be observed (*e.g.*, two separate wills made in two different countries by the same person).[31] Nevertheless a doctrine of | acquired rights in the sense considered here may support the object of rules of Private International Law and may claim some practical merits which may have influenced Dicey when he said:

> ... the principle of the enforcement of vested rights does not supply such a universal test. To admit this, however, is quite consistent with maintaining that this principle does define the object in the main aimed at by rules having reference to the conflict of laws or to the extra-territorial effect of rights.[32]

The court in England is invited, not to ascertain and to apply foreign law of its own motion when faced with a factual statement of claim, but to decide whether a claim brought in the light of some legal system can be sustained. It is for the parties to submit a claim based on some legal system, and it is for the court in England to determine whether the claim as framed according to foreign law is framed in accordance with that legal system which applies according to the English rules of the Conflict of Laws.[33] In the end, there-

---

international privé II (1892) 108; Gutzwiller (1936) 10 *Rabels Z.* 1064; Kollewijn, *loc. cit.*, p. 133: "... it follows from the character as natural law of his *jus gentium* that inasmuch as the rule has come into existence which requires the application of foreign law, no country can withdraw from this of its own motion." *Cf.* Dicey (1890) 6 L.Q.R. 1, at p. 11; (1891) 7 L.Q.R. 113, at p. 118. *Conflict of Laws* (3rd ed., 1922), at pp. 12, 24, 333.

[30] See above p. 69, note 21. It was only the last step in the logical argument when the editors of the sixth edition (1949), pp. 11, 12, replaced the qualification that the right must have been "duly" acquired by the requirement that it must have been acquired "according to the English rules of the conflict of laws." For comments, see Falconbridge (1950) 66 L.Q.R. 104, 106; Mann (1949) 12 M.L.R. 518, 520; Cavers (1950) 63 Harv.L.R. 1278, 1280; Rheinstein (1950) 35 N.Y.U.L.R. 180, 181.

[31] If it is assumed that a division of legislative competences exists between states, and that this division must be respected, the doctrine of acquired rights assumes the character of a legal principle based upon an overriding international duty. But such was not Dicey's point of departure, which is firmly based upon the practice of English courts as initiated by Lord Mansfield (see above, p. 67, note 5). Nevertheless traces of such a doctrine are to be found in Dicey's General Principle II (1891) 7 L.Q.R. 113, at pp. 118, 119; *Conflict of Laws* (3rd ed., 1922), pp. 27, 28; *cf.* Gutzwiller (1936) 10 *Rabels Z.* 1062.

[32] (1891) 7 L.Q.R. 113, at p. 118; *Conflict of Laws* (3rd ed., 1922), p. 33.

[33] (1891) 7 L.Q.R. 113, at p. 115: "The object for which courts exist is to give redress for the infringement of rights"; see also p. 117; *Conflict of Laws* (3rd ed., 1922), pp. 26, 27.

fore, a choice of law must be made, and it must be made according to English Private International Law, but the initiative lies with the parties who submit claims, counterclaims or defences which rely not merely on facts but combine facts with reliance on some foreign system of laws. Technically, this insight proves useful in many respects, as will be shown later on in connection with the discussion of characterisation and *renvoi*. If this was Dicey's view, his juxtaposition of a system of English rules of the conflict of laws, unfettered by any overriding considerations or principles, and of a doctrine of respect for acquired rights is justifiable. The former provides the legal basis; the latter serves to explain a technical device.

(2) Function of rules of the Conflict of Laws – Choice of Law Rules in Statutes; Spatially Conditioned Rules

Students of the conflict of laws have not been content, however, with the insight that the rules of the conflict of laws are part of English law. Instead, attempts have been made again and again to determine the jurisprudential or philosophical background of these rules. Apparently the insight that they are technical rules which have no substantive content of their own and only point to some legal system as being applicable was felt to be insufficient. There is some reason for such discontent, for a crucial question has remained unsolved: In the absence of a specific rule of the conflict of laws (*e.g.*, as regards quasi-contracts), is the court to develop a new rule by | way of analogy or otherwise, or is it to apply English domestic law as such on the ground that in the particular circumstances there is no reference to foreign law?

Graveson is one of the few English writers who has faced this problem.[34] For him, the underlying principle of the conflict of laws is justice, but this insight does not disclose a specific principle or philosophy which is not common to English law as a whole or which provides an answer to the question posed above. Webb,[35] following in Ehrenzweig's footsteps, finds some support for a trend towards the application of the *lex fori*, the validation of transactions and the exercise of free choice of law. However, these policies do not add up to a general principle, let alone philosophy. Kahn-Freund[36] detects a trend towards internationalism through the development of bilateral rules of the conflict of laws which are of general application and a move away from a purely jurisdictional approach. At the same time a movement in the opposite direction has been observed by a series of writers.[37] So-

---

[34] (1964) 78 L.Q.R. 337; *XXth Century Comparative and Conflicts Law* (1961) 307.
[35] (1961) 10 I.C.L.Q. 818.
[36] *The Growth of Internationalism in English Private International Law* (1962).
[37] Nussbaum, *Private International Law* (1942) 70–73; Morris (1946) 62 L.Q.R. 170;

called legislatively localised laws[38] or particular choice of law rules,[39] functionally restricting rules[40] or spatially conditioned internal rules[41] determine the application in space of particular rules of domestic law. Technically this is achieved by adding a choice of law provision to the particular rule of domestic law instead of formulating rules of the conflict of laws in broad categories which are then applied to claims formulated according to some system of laws, whether it be foreign law or the domestic law of the court. In English law this trend has become more distinct during the period under review.[42]

| It has been recognised for a long time that there are certain branches of law, primarily of a public law nature, where the problem is one of establishing the respective frontiers of legislation, but never that of applying foreign substantive law. Rules of the conflict of laws may be unilateral or bilateral, but when concerned with the application of private law they must always deal with the twofold problem of when the *lex fori* and when foreign law must be applied. It is to be noted, however, that there are certain branches of the conflict of laws which rely exclusively upon unilateral rules, for the reason that they are concerned with a process of self-limitation and not with a process of choice of law. The law of procedure is such a branch, and the law of bankruptcy is another, as are the law of taxation and administrative law.[43] Modern anti-trust legislation follows the same technique of self-limitation.[44] The forum never applies such foreign laws, but they can be taken into account as facts or data.[45] The ancient principle of territoriality based

---

Francescakis, *Théorie du renvoi* (1958) 11–16, nos. 7–11 with references to earlier literature; *Rev.crit.d.i.p.* 1966; 1; (1967) 3 Riv.dir.int.e.proc.priv. 691; Graulich, *Mélanges Dabin* II (1963) 629; De Nova, *Dir.int.* 1959, 13, 500; *Mélanges Maury* I (1960) 377; *Studi Ghisleriana*, Ser. I, Vol. IV: *Studi giuridici* (1967) 126–135; (1966) 54 Calif.L.R. 1569; von Overbeck in *De Conflictu Legum* (in honour of Kollewijn and Offerhaus) (1962) 362; Ballarino, Mosconi and Pocar in (1967) 3 Riv.dir.int.priv.e.proc. 707, 730, 734; Kelly (1969) 18 I.C.L.Q. 249; Danson (1963) 1 Harv.J.of Legislation 71; Tommasi di Vignano, *Lex fori e diritto straniero* (1964) 122–133.

[38] Unger (1952) M.L.R. 88; (1959) 43 *Transactions of the Grotius Society* 37; (1967) 83 L.Q.R. 427; Mann, *Hague Rec.* 111 (1964, I) 1, at pp. 69–70; Cavers, *The Choice of Law Process* (1965) 221. Francescakis calls these rules "règles d'application immédiate."

[39] Morris, *loc. cit.*

[40] De Nova, *loc cit.*

[41] Nussbaum, *loc. cit.*

[42] Examples are: Wills Act 1861, ss. 1, 2; Merchant Shipping Act 1894, s. 265; Carriage of Goods by Sea Act 1924, s. 1; Legitimacy Act 1926, ss. I, 8; Inheritance (Family Provisions) Act 1938, s. 1 as amended; Law Reform (Frustrated Contracts) Act 1943, s. 1 (1); Adoption Act 1958, s. 1 (1) (5); Legitimacy Act 1959, s. 2 (2); Marriage (Enabling) Act 1960, s. 1 (3); Matrimonial Causes Act 1965, ss. 14 (2) (*a*) (*b*), 24 (1) (2), 25 (1), 26 (1), 39 (1) (4), 40 (1) (*a*) (*b*); Contracts of Employment Act 1963, s. 9 (1) (2) and Sched. 1, para. 1 (3); Redundancy Payments Act 1965, ss. 17, 56 (4); Mann (1966) 82 L.Q.R. 316; see also (1964) 80 L.Q.R. 29.

[43] See Lipstein (1949) 26 B.Y.I.L. 553–555.

[44] Tommasi di Vignano, *Lex fori e diritto straniero* (1964), pp. 79–97.

[45] See, *e.g.*, *Re Bettinson's Question* [1956] Ch. 67; *Regazzoni* v. *Sethia* [1958] A.C. 301,

upon the division of legislative spheres of states fulfils its proper function here.

Spatially conditioned internal rules of the kind mentioned above are of a different kind. They are rules of private or public law to which personal or territorial limitations are attached.

The interplay between the application of ordinary rules of the conflict of laws and self-limiting choice of law rules concerning the application of domestic public law can be observed in such situations as the *Bold Case (Netherlands v. Sweden).*[46] The application of ordinary rules of the English conflict of laws coupled with the recognition of the operation abroad of foreign self-limiting rules of public law is a frequent feature in English Private International Law.[47] The interplay between the application of ordinary rules of the conflict of laws and spatially conditioned internal rules is much rarer. Thus it was suggested by Glanville Williams,[48] following Gutteridge and Lipstein,[49] that the wording of section 1 (1) of the Law Reform|(Frustrated Contracts) Act 1943, which restricts the operation of the Act to claims arising under a contract governed by English law, lets in the old rule in *Chandler v. Webster*[50] through the operation of the ordinary rule of the conflict of laws. If in claims for unjustifiable enrichment the latter should refer to the law of the place of enrichment, English common law applies, if the enrichment is conferred in England. It is irrelevant that the contract is not governed by English law (in which case the Act of 1943 applies) but by foreign law. This case serves well as an illustration, even if the conclusion that the law of the place of enrichment invariably determines claims for unjustifiable enrichment is erroneous.[51] The spatially conditioned internal rule is, in this instance, identical with the general rule of the conflict of laws. The law governing the contract applies. The Wills Act 1861 (Lord Kingsdown's Act), which is now defunct, provides a better example. While the Act applied to wills of personalty made by British subjects (and incidentally provided choice of law rules for them in these limited circumstances), the general conflicts rule, relying on the law of the domicile, applied in all other circumstances, no matter whether the testator was domiciled in England or not.

---

and *Ralli Bros.* v. *Cia Naviera Sota y Aznar* [1920] 2 K.B. 287, as interpreted by Mann (1937) 18 B.Y.I.L. 97; *The Halley* (1868) L.R. 2 P.C. 193, 202, and the cases cited by Lipstein in *Ius Privatum Gentium* I (1969) 411, at pp. 420–422.

[46] *I.C.J. Reports* 1958, p. 52; Lipstein (1959) 8 I.C.L.Q. 506, 512.

[47] See above n. 45.

[48] *Law Reform (Frustrated Contracts)* 1943 (1944), pp. 18–20 with reference to s. 1 (1); see Falconbridge, *Conflict of Laws* (2nd ed., 1954), pp. 428–431.

[49] [1939] 7 C.L.J. 80.

[50] [1904] 1 K.B. 492.

[51] See Dicey, *Conflict of Laws* (6th ed., 1949), pp. 754–757; (7th ed., 1958), pp. 927–931; (8th ed., 1967), pp. 903–908.

The problem is more complicated if the English rules of the conflict of laws refer to foreign law, and the foreign law applicable contains either a unilateral conflicts rule or a spatially conditioned rule of domestic law. In the former case the question is, first, whether the unilateral conflicts rule has been interpreted as a bilateral one, and, if so, secondly, whether *renvoi* applies. If it has not been interpreted as a bilateral rule, the reference to foreign law remains one to foreign domestic law. If, however, the foreign domestic rule is a spatially conditioned rule, a considerable difficulty arises.[52] What law applies, if the spatially conditioned rule of the foreign *lex causae* fails to apply in the circumstances? *Ex hypothesi* the foreign *lex causae* does not contain a rule of domestic law which purports to apply where the spatially conditioned rule does not operate. Sometimes it may be possible to detect a rule of the conflict of laws which refers to a legal system other than that of the *lex causae*. In practice the problem does not appear to arise frequently, and since spatially conditioned rules of domestic law are often special legislation, general rules of domestic law can be relied upon. Article 992 of the Dutch Civil Code (which states that Dutch nationals must make their wills in notarial form, even if the will is made abroad) and article 170 of the French Civil Code | (which requires French nationals marrying abroad to comply with certain formalities of French law) merely extend to situations abroad certain formal requirements of Dutch and French law concerning wills and marriages which apply peremptorily in the Netherlands and in France. Thus a reference by the English rules of the conflict of laws to Dutch or French law involving these articles as the *lex loci actus* or the *lex loci celebrationis* will mean a reference to Dutch or French law as such.[53] However, a spatially conditioned rule of domestic law may indicate the need to characterise the rule differently from a similar rule of domestic law which is not spatially conditioned. Thus it has been asserted that the requirement of form expressed in Article 992 of the Dutch Civil Code is to be characterised as one of substance, namely, capacity, and it remained for the Wills Act 1963[54] to exclude this practice.[55] The English Carriage of Goods by Sea Act 1924 and the Carriage of Goods by Sea Ordinances of Palestine and of Newfoundland, which provided the basis of the litigation in *The Torni*[56] and the *Vita*

---

[52] See also Unger (1967) 83 L.Q.R. 427, 444.

[53] See the decisions of the German Federal Supreme Court of 12 January 1967, *NJW* 1967, 1177; *IPRspr.* 1966–67, no. 19, p. 64, and of 19 December 1958, BGHZ 29, 137, *IPRspr.* 1958–59, no. 112; Kropholler, *NJW* 1968, 1561 with further references; Wengler, *Rev.crit.d.i.p.* 1954, 661, at 683, n. 2.

[54] s. 3. And see the Hague Convention of 1961 on the Form of Wills, s. 5.

[55] See Robertson, *Characterization in the Conflict of Laws* (1940), pp. 235–237; Beckett (1934) 15 B.Y.I.L. 46, at 73, n. 1; Falconbridge, *Conflict of Laws* (2nd ed., 1954), pp. 90–94; Lorenzen, *Selected Articles*, pp. 129–130; (1941) 50 Yale L.J. 743, at 755, 756; and the former practice of the German Supreme Court, RG., *JW* 1913, 333.

[56] [1932] P. 78.

Food Case,[57] concern shipments out of these countries and leave it to the ordinary rules of domestic law to solve questions arising under contracts of carriage by sea into England, Palestine and Newfoundland.

None of these techniques solves the general question formulated at the beginning of this paragraph, which is whether there are any general principles according to which the balance must be struck between the application of English law, the *lex fori*, and foreign law. Upon analysis, this raises the question whether laws are limited in space or operate outside the jurisdiction which enacted them. It is clear that foreign law, by itself, cannot claim to be applied elsewhere, including England. It is incapable of exporting itself on its own, and it cannot be imported into England, except by virtue of a precept of English law embodied in a rule of English Private International Law. The problem is, therefore, to determine the range of the latter by examining the relationship between English domestic law and foreign law.

If English domestic law is a closed and self-sufficient system, it follows that English law applies even to situations containing a foreign element which form the object of litigation in England,[58] | unless a specific rule of English Private International Law restricts the operation of English law and, at the same time, introduces foreign law as an exception. On this view English law is of universal application, unless it is cut down by exceptional rules of Private International Law.[59]

If English domestic law is primarily restricted to situations having a connection with England on personal or territorial grounds it follows that a broad range of rules of Private International Law must determine which foreign law is applicable. Otherwise no legal system might be applicable, or only English domestic law, thus restoring the closed and universal character of English domestic law.

No clear answer can be given, since English domestic law applies in a subsidiary capacity if foreign law, which is applicable according to the English rules of Private International Law, has not been proved. It would seem, however, that during the last century and even during the first three or four decades of the present century the former approach prevailed. Dicey believed that claims based on principles of foreign law which are unknown in English domestic law could not be enforced in England,[60] and this approach can still be met, if rarely.[61] It is rough and mechanical. However, even then it

---

[57] [1939] A.C. 277.

[58] *Cf.* Pillet, *Principes*, p. 253, no. 110; p. 255, no. 112; but see p. 250.

[59] See Unger (1957) 43 *Transactions of the Grotius Society* 87, at p. 94.

[60] (1891) 7 L.Q.R. 113, 120, General Principle II, Exception (2); see also Fillet, *Principes* 516, 36, 42.

[61] See *Phrantzes* v. *Argenti* [1960] 2 Q.B. 19; for an earlier pronouncement, see *Sottomayor* v. *De Barros (No. 2)* (1879) 5 P.D. 94 (personal incapacity not recognised by English law).

was not without exceptions.[62] Today, with the help of a more subtle process of characterisation, the second approach appears to be more favoured. Thus the introduction of adoption in England in 1926 coupled with the formulation of jurisdictional rules involving an implicit choice of law led to the development of a bilateral rule resulting in the recognition of foreign adoptions in England[63]; the enactment of what is now section 40 (1) of the Matrimonial Causes Act 1965 enlarging the jurisdiction in divorce of English courts has since resulted in the recognition of an equivalent jurisdiction abroad,[64] appropriate rules of the conflict of laws have been developed for quasi-contracts and arbitration proceedings, and are being developed for trusts. Theoretically the approach based on the initial univer|sality of English domestic law is attractive, and even the present trend towards bilateral rules of jurisdiction and choice of law can be accommodated within it. In no circumstances can it be said that the foreign law so referred to is incorporated into English law.[65]

(3) Characterisation

Although the problem of characterisation had been introduced into Anglo-American literature in 1920,[66] English writers did not take note of it until the thirties,[67] and the courts applied the *lex fori* to an unconscious process of characterisation. This technique has been firmly approved where the interpretation of connecting factors forming part of rules of Private International Law of the forum is concerned.[68] The same process may also seem natural in

---

[62] Legitimation by subsequent marriage was recognised long before this institution was introduced in England; see *Re Goodman's Trusts* (1881) 17 Ch.D. 266, and foreign judicial decrees of divorce were recognised before they became possible in England; see *Warrender* v. *Warrender* (1835) 2 Cl. & F. 488; foreign proxy marriages are recognised although they are unknown in English law: see *Apt* v. *Apt* [1948] P. 83.

[63] *Re Wilson* [1954] Ch. 733; *Re Marshall* [1957] Ch. 507; *Re Valentine's Settlement* [1965] Ch. 831, at 844, 846, 848, overruling *Re Wilby* [1956] P. 174.

[64] *Travers* v. *Holley* [1953] P. 246; *Arnold* v. *Arnold* [1957] P. 237; *Manning* v. *Manning* [1958] P. 112; *Robinson-Scott* v. *Robinson-Scott* [1958] P. 71, limited by the considerations in *Levett* v. *Levett* [1957] P. 156.

[65] The doctrine of "rinvio ricettizio" in its various forms is not part of English law, and foreign law, when applied by English courts, remains the law of a foreign country. The principles on proof of foreign law bear out this contention.

[66] Lorenzen (1920) 20 Col.L.R. 20.

[67] Beckett (1934) 15 B.Y.I.L. 46; Unger (1937) 19 *Bell Yard* 3; Robertson, *Characterization in the Conflict of Laws* (1940); (1939) 52 Harv.L.R. 747; see also Falconbridge (1937) 53 L.Q.R. 235, 537; revised (1952) 30 Can. Bar Rev. 103; *Conflict of Laws* (2nd ed., 1954), pp. 50 *et seq.*

[68] *Re Annesley* [1926] Ch. 692; for a strict differentiation between the interpretation of connecting factors and characterisation of operative facts, see Makarov (below, n.70) p. 151, n. 8.

any legal system when it comes to the interpretation of the operative facts,[69] and it is seemingly imperative in those legal systems where the courts are believed to be called upon to apply foreign law of their own motion to a set of facts pleaded by the parties.[70] In reality no suit involving a foreign element is introduced in which the plaintiff (and subsequently the defendant) has not considered his rights (or his defences) according to some legal system; in English law, moreover, a party must plead not only the facts but also the law, if foreign, on which he intends to rely. In other words, the plaintiff introduces his claim in the light of some foreign law according to which he alleges to have a right against the defendant.[71] The same applies to a defendant who may wish to plead that some other law, whether English or foreign, applies. The court, relying on its set of rules of the conflict of laws, must ascertain which rule of English Private International Law covers | the claim.[72] Difficulties arise from the fact that the claim is, *ex hypothesi*, expressed in substance and in form in terms of foreign law. The operative facts of English rules of Private International Law are formulated sometimes in terms of English domestic law,[73] but more frequently in terms peculiar to English Private International Law,[74] yet the court must apply its own rules of Private International Law to claims presented in terms of foreign domestic law, if it is to determine whether the law pleaded by the party applies.[75] For this purpose each must be interpreted in terms of the other.[76] This process of

---

[69] For the use of this term, see Rabel, *Conflict of Laws* I (1945), p. 42; (2nd ed., 1958), p. 47; Falconbridge, *Conflict of Laws* (2nd ed., 1954), p. 44; and see Makarov (below, n. 70) at p. 150, n. 7.

[70] See also Makarov, *Vom deutschen zum europäischen Recht* II (1963), 149, at p. 154; Wengler, *Rev.crit.d.i.p.* 1954, 66 at pp. 670, 673, 682, rejecting for such countries the approach advocated here – see *loc. cit.*, pp. 666–667, 671, 674; see also Wengler, *Festschrift für Martin Wolff* (1952) 337, at pp. 340, 356.

[71] As was suggested above, Dicey's theory of acquired rights may perhaps have been derived from such an analysis of the process in an English court leading to a choice of law. The court in England does not apply foreign law as such. It determines whether a particular claim based on foreign law is supported by the English choice of law rules.

[72] *Cf.* Robertson, p. 127; Falconbridge, *Conflict of Laws* (1947), p. 101; (2nd ed., 1954), p. 59, believes that the court provisionally consults foreign law before finally characterising the question for the purpose of selecting the proper law. See the valid critique in Dicey, *Conflict of Laws* (8th ed., 1967), p. 27. The present account avoids this pitfall by analysing the concrete situation.

[73] *e.g.*, contract, tort, succession, capacity to marry, formality.

[74] *e.g.*, status, rights in movables or immovables, evidence, procedure, property relations between spouses.

[75] It is assumed that the application is opposed by the other party, who alleges that another legal system is applicable.

[76] In order not to complicate and to confuse this analysis no mention is made at each stage that the same process applies, if the defendant relies for his defence on English law. Here again the court must apply its own rules of Private International Law (which are not always expressed in terms of English domestic law) in order to determine whether English

subsuming claims formulated in accordance with one legal system under one of several rules of the conflict of laws of the forum by way of interpreting each in terms of the other is the essence of characterisation. The process of interpreting rules involving at least two, and possibly more, legal systems must necessarily rely on some legal notions, and over the years reliance on those of the *lex fori*, the *lex causae* and of comparative jurisprudence has been canvassed in turn. The present analysis must discard the approach from the *lex fori*, which assumes that facts alone must be characterised and not facts presented in the light of some legal system, or at least in the light of a plea based on English domestic law.[77] Where English | courts have followed this technique the result has been unfortunate.[78] However, the present analysis also does not embrace the approach from the alleged *lex causae*, which has come in for acute criticism by the present writer,[79] but it takes the *lex causae* into consideration. According to the view set out here, abstract rules of law alone are not characterised. The courts analyse the nature of a claim (or defence) expressed according to foreign (or English) law in the light of the function (not the technical connotation) of that rule within the particular legal system. They relate the claim so analysed to that among their conflicts rules which, upon a broad interpretation (not restricted to notions of English domestic law), is capable of covering the claim in question. This interpretation of disparate notions in terms of each other is the process of characterisation. The result is an indication of the law applicable which may or may not be that which has been pleaded by the parties.

Technically the problem of characterisation involves one of three situa-

---

law applies: see *British Linen Co.* v. *Drummond* (1830) 10 B. & C. 903; *Huber* v. *Steiner* (1835) 2 Bing.N.C. 202, 210, 213; *Don* v. *Lippman* (1837) 5 Cl. & F. 1, 13, 16; *Leroux* v. *Brown* (1852) 12 C.B. 801, 823; *Bristow* v. *Sequeville* (1850) 5 Ex. 275; *Re Martin, Loustalan* v. *Loustalan* [1900] P. 211, 230, 233, 240; *S. A. de Prayon* v. *Koppel* (1933) 77 S.J. 80; *Re Cutcliffe's Will Trust* [1940] Ch. 565; *Re Middleton's Settlement* [1947] Ch. 329, 583 (C.A.); [1949] A.C. 418; *Re Priest* [1944] Ch. 58; *Adams* v. *National Bank of Greece* [1961] A.C. 255, 287; see also *Dreyfus (C. and H.) Foundation Inc.* v. *I.R.C.* [1956] A.C. 39; *Rae (Inspector of Taxes)* v. *Lazard Investment Co. Ltd.* [1963] 1 W.L.R. 555; *Baron Inchyra* v. *Jennings (Inspector of Taxes)* [1966] Ch. 37.

[77] This seems to be the view expressed by Inglis (1958) 74 L.Q.R. 493, at pp. 509, 513, who argues from the decisions in *Re Cohn* [1945] Ch. 5 and *Re Maldonado* [1954] P. 223 that where conflicting claims are made which rely respectively on English and foreign law, only the claim based on English law is characterised. If English law is then found to be inapplicable according to the relevant English rule of Private International Law, the claim based on foreign law is not characterised and is admitted without further consideration. The cases cited do not bear out this contention. Tommasi di Vignano, *Lex fori e diritto straniero* (1964) 217, holds that a relationship alleged to be governed by foreign law remains a factual relationship.

[78] *Ogden* v. *Ogden* [1907] P. 46 (C.A.), and the comments in Dicey and Morris, pp. 237–239; Westlake, *P.I.L.* (2nd ed., 1925), p. 61; *Phrantzes* v. *Argenti* [1960] 2 Q.B. 19.

[79] Note to *Re Maldonado* [1954] P. 223; [1954] C.L.J. 123.

tions: either the claim or defence is identical in form and in substance with similar claims or defences in English domestic law[80] or it is unknown in substance and in form in English law[81] or it corresponds in form to a similar claim under English law but the formal similarity conceals a material difference.[82]

The process of characterisation set out here was in effect adopted by Uthwatt J. (as he then was) in *Re Cohn*[83] and by Scarman J. in *Re Fuld*,[84] though it has not been formulated in the terms submitted here.[85]

|It is now clear that a party must plead foreign law for two purposes: first, in order to enable the court to embark upon a selection of law, and, secondly, in order to enable the court to apply that law, once it has been found to be applicable. The court, in turn, must consider the law pleaded by the parties at two stages; first, in order to apply its own rules of Private International Law, which may or may not result in the selection of the foreign law pleaded by the party and, secondly, in order to apply the particular foreign law which has been selected by its own rules of Private International Law.[86] Of course foreign law is pleaded only once and proved only once, even if it must be considered at two stages of the process of judicial reasoning. The first stage

---

[80] See the cases cited above n. 76, and see *Re Wilks* [1935] Ch. 645; *Re Kehr* [1951] 2 T.L.R. 788; [1951] 2 All E.R. 812; *Re Barnett's Trusts* [1902] 1 Ch. 842; *Mahadervan* v. *Mahadervan* [1964] P. 233, 241–242.

[81] *Batthyany* v. *Walford* (1887) 36 Ch.D. 269, 278; *De Nicols* v. *Curlier* [1900] A.C. 21; *Re Bonacina* [1912] 2 Ch. 394, 396 (C.A.) *Phrantzes* v. *Argenti* [1960] 2 Q.B. 19, 36 and the comments in (1960) 9 I.C.L.Q. 508; (1960) 23 M.L.R. 446.

[82] *Ogden* v. *Ogden* [1908] P. 46, and see also *Bliersbach* v. *McEwen* 1959 S.C. 43; *Lodge* v. *Lodge* (1963) 107 S.J. 437, and see the comments by Anton (1959) 3 Jur.Rev.(N.S.) 253, 277; Carter in (1960) 36 B.Y.I.L. 417; *Re Maldonado* [1954] P. 223, 231, 244 *et seq.*, but see Lipstein [1954] C.L.J. 22. See also Garde Castillo, *La Institución Desconocida en el d.i.p.* (1947), pp. 46–47.

[83] [1945] Ch. 5. According to Master Jacob in Smit, *International Cooperation in Litigation (Europe)* (1965), p. 103 n. 205, the parties in this case agreed not to plead foreign law and to leave the question of foreign law to the court.

[84] [1966] 2 W.L.R. 717, at pp. 735, 736–738.

[85] It is useful to note the approach adopted in recent times by the German Federal Supreme Court in a decision of 12 January 1967, *NJW* 1967, 1171, *IPRspr.* 1966–67, no. 19, p. 64. The court said: "The subsumption of these rules [*i.e.*, Art. 992 of the Dutch Civil Code] must be made in accordance with German law. In this connection the following principles of interpretation must be observed: the rules of foreign law must be examined with a view to their meaning and purpose, they must be analysed from the standpoint of foreign law and must be compared with the institutions of the German legal order. On the basis of this knowledge they must be subsumed by the German rules of Private International Law, the characteristics of which are shaped by the notions and delimitations of German law." See also B.G.H.Z. 29, 137, *IPRspr.* 1958–59, no. 112, p. 389; and see Castel (1961) 39 Can. Bar Rev. 93, 192, citing *Lively* v. *Horst* [1924] S.C.R. 605; [1925] 1 D.L.R. 159.

[86] Compare *Huber* v. *Steiner* (1835) 2 Bing.N.C. 203 at pp. 212, 213; Robertson, *op. cit.* p. 248; Falconbridge, *Conflict of Laws* (1947), pp. 101, 106.

alone involves the process of interpretation known as characterisation or qualification. The second stage, which is exclusively concerned with the application of foreign law, is no longer concerned with the fact that foreign domestic law or foreign Private International Law would adopt a different process of characterisation, if the case had arisen abroad.[87] The reason is, as stated above, that a choice of law in English Private International Law is initiated by pleadings which contain not only the facts but include the individual rule or set of rules of foreign law on which the party relies and which are alleged to be applicable. Thus English Private International Law is at no stage concerned with foreign law in the abstract or with the categories of foreign law in general, while it is concerned with the functional analysis of a particular rule within its own setting. Consequently no additional reliance on the characterisation of foreign law as practised abroad by the courts of the country of the alleged *lex causae* for the purpose of applying their own rules of Private International Law is required. There is no need to reduce the foreign law applicable to concrete rules[88] and to individualise the rules of foreign|law a second time. They are individualised in the pleadings once and for all.[89]

Transposition, Substitution and Adaptation of laws are unknown as such in the English conflict of laws, but in practice these phenomena, first observed by continental writers,[90] can be found in English Private International Law as well. The line of demarcation between them is not always clear.[91] Certain it is that none of them concerns a choice of law; in all of them the choice of law has taken place, but owing to the fact that different aspects of a

---

[87] Only if the English court, in deference to the English doctrine of *renvoi*, sits as a foreign court, it must have regard to the characterisation, if different, by the foreign *lex causae*. The present conclusions constitute, therefore, a rejection of secondary characterisation. For this problem, see Robertson, *op. cit.*, pp. 118–134, 255–279; Cheshire, *Private International Law* (3rd ed., 1947), pp. 71–85; Falconbridge, *Conflict of Laws* (1st ed., 1947), pp. 98 *et seq.*, 107, 161 *et seq.;* 184 *et seq.*, but see (2nd ed., 1954), p. 68, note g; (1939) 17 Can. Bar Rev. 369; (1941) 19 Can. Bar Rev. 311, at 334.

[88] Falconbridge, *Conflict of Laws* (2nd ed., 1954), pp. 59, 60, 134, is inclined to think in terms of abstract rules.

[89] The popular analysis which detects a process in three stages is thus accepted subject to the explanations given above that: (i) analysis of the function of the rule of foreign (or English) law within its own setting and (ii) interpretation of the operative facts of the rules of Private International Law of the forum alleged to be relevant must be carried out simultaneously followed by (iii) application of the rule of foreign law found to be applicable. *Cf.* Dicey, *Conflict of Laws* (8th ed., 1967), p. 30; Falconbridge, *Conflict of Laws* (2nd ed., 1954), pp. 50 *et seq.*, 133–136; Inglis (1958) 74 L.Q.R. 493, 503.

[90] These categories were first discussed by Lewald, *Hague Rec.* 69 (1939, III) 1, at p. 129.

[91] According to Neuhaus, *Grundbegriffe des Internationalen Privatrechts* (1962) 251, n. 604, the category described as transposition merges into the other two. There is some substance in this contention, at least as far as any overlap between transposition and substitution is concerned.

situation may be governed by different legal systems a reconciliation between various institutions of the several legal systems applicable in the circumstances may be called for.

Transposition was the technique employed in *Studd* v. *Cook*[92] and in *Re
Piercy*[93] when the events enjoined the creation at the *situs* of interests as
nearly as possible identical with those created by a will governed by another
legal system and expressed in terms of different institutions.

Substitution may be illustrated by a reference to section 16 (1) and (2) of
the Adoption Act 1958, which provides:

(1) Where at any time after the making of an adoption order, the adopter ... dies intestate ... that property shall devolve ... as if the adopted child
were the child of the adopter born in lawful wedlock. ...

(2) In any disposition of ... property made ... after the date of an adoption
order ... any reference ... to the child or children of the adopter shall ... be
construed as ... a reference to the adopted person.

As enacted, section 16 (1) and (2) envisages English adoptions. The question is whether it can include foreign adoptions. The practice of the courts in
England shows that such adoptions, made by the authorities which are competent according to English Private Inter|national Law and which place
adopted children in a position substantially equivalent to natural children,
conferring comparable rights upon the parties as exist under English law,
will be treated as adoptions for the purpose of this section.[94]

It will have been noticed that problems of transposition and substitution
arise only after a choice of law has been made in accordance with the Private
International Law of the *forum* which has led to the application of different
systems of law to different aspects of the case. In the case of *transposition* the
disparate institutions representing the different aspects of the case are adjusted to each other. In the case of *substitution* the question is whether the
institutions representing the different aspects of the case correspond to each
other to such an extent as to be interchangeable.[95] In both cases the problem
is one of comparing institutions of domestic law in order to integrate the
different aspects of the case after the operation of the conflicts rules of the
forum has led to the application of different legal systems to these various
aspects.

Adaptation raises entirely different questions. If different aspects of a case
are governed by different legal systems, the operation of different laws may
create hardship and material injustice. The following example may serve as

---

[92] (1883) 8 App.Cas. 577, at pp. 591, 600, 604.
[93] [1895] 1 Ch. 83, 89.
[94] *Re Marshall* [1957] Ch. 507 (C.A.), overruling *Re Wilby* [1956] P. 174.
[95] See, *e.g.*, *Tursi* v. *Tursi* [1958] P. 54: effect of a foreign separation order upon a state of
desertion according to English law.

an illustration.[96] Spouses were domiciled in a common law State of the United States during their working life. Upon their retirement they acquire a domicile in California. The husband dies. According to the law of California matrimonial property relations are governed by the law of the domicile of the spouses at the time of the marriage; succession to movables is governed by the law of the last domicile. According to the law of the common law State, the matrimonial régime was separation of goods, but the surviving spouse is accorded a share in her spouse's estate on the latter's death. According to the law of California spouses live according to a régime of community of goods, but a spouse is not entitled to a share in the other's estate by virtue of the law of succession. The result is that both the law of the common law State and the law of California grant a spouse some share in the assets of the other, but by applying the common law rule to matrimonial property relations (because it was the law of their domicile at the time) and the law of California to the succession (because it is the law of the last domicile of the deceased) the surviving spouse goes away with empty hands. In the converse case she collects twice | over.[97] The result is not due to a faulty technique of the conflict of laws, but to the fact that each legal system is a coherent whole. Choice of law, which leads to the application of different laws to different aspects of the case, may cause a disequilibrium of solutions, but it is for the domestic law of succession to redress the balance by a process of adaptation.[98]

(4) Renvoi

Renvoi was well known as a problem fifty years ago[99] and it was solved in practice on the strength of Westlake's theory of desistment.[100] Subsequent decisions have relied on other grounds,[101] and it has become clear that *renvoi* applies only in certain specific situations.[102] The problem has not been put to

---

[96] It is superficially reminiscent of situations such as that decided in the arrêt *Bartholo, Clunet* 1891, 1171; Robertson, *Characterization in the Conflict of Laws* (1940), p. 158 *et seq.*

[97] *Baudoin* v. *Trudel* [1937] 1 D.L.R. 216; [1937] O.R. 1.

[98] See the California Probate Code, s. 201.5 (California Statutes 1957, c. 490). And see the cases cited by Lewald, pp. 140–148.

[99] *Re Johnson* [1903] 1 Ch. 821; *Re Bowes* (1906) 22 T.L.R. 711.

[100] *Private International Law* (4th ed., 1905), pp. 33, 40, (5th ed., 1912), pp. 32, 34; Falconbridge, *op. cit.*, pp. 212–215, esp. p. 214, note (y).

[101] *Re Annesley* [1926] Ch. 692; *Re Ross* [1930] 1 Ch. 377 (foreign court theory); *Re Askew* [1930] 2 Ch. 259 (acquired rights).

[102] Status: *Re Askew* [1930] 2 Ch. 259; succession to movables: *Re Annesley* [1926] Ch. 692, and to immovables: *Re Ross* [1930] 1 Ch. 377; *Re Duke of Wellington* [1947] Ch. 506, [1948] Ch. 118 (C.A.); capacity to marry: *R.* v. *Brentwood Superintendent Registrar of*

rest, however, as to what are its limits in practice, if it is a desirable institution at all.

The present discussion starts from the premise that an English court does not apply foreign law, unless it is pleaded and proved in the individual case. If the parties fail to prove foreign law, the court must apply English law, and if the parties discharge the burden of proof the court cannot scrutinise the content of foreign law except|in two circumstances, one of which is important here.[103] If the parties lead conflicting evidence the court must determine the disputed question of foreign law.[104] The evidence may be conflicting because one party proves a rule of foreign domestic law while the other proves foreign domestic law coupled with foreign Private International Law which leads to a reference back to the *lex fori* or on to a third legal system. In this situation, the English court is compelled to determine, as a question of English Private International Law, what is, in its view, the correct solution according to the foreign *lex causae*. Now it would appear that in principle the parties must prove how the particular dispute involving a foreign element, which is before the English court, would be decided by the foreign law which is the *lex causae*. The parties are not called upon to prove how a similar case would be decided by the foreign *lex causae*, if no foreign element were involved. To hold otherwise would mean to allow proof of foreign law as applied to a hypothetical case, while what is required is proof of the hypothetical judgment of the foreign court in the actual case before an English

---

Marriages, ex p. Arias [1968] 2 Q.B. 956; formalities of marriage: *Taczanowska* v. *Taczanowski* [1957] P. 301, 305. *Renvoi* does not apply to contracts: *Re United Railways of Havana* v. *Regla Warehouses Ltd.* [1960] Ch. 52, at pp. 96–97, 115 (C.A.), but see [1958] Ch. 724, 760 (Wynn-Parry J.); Hall (1959) 109 L.J. 645; see also *Rosencrantz* v. *Union Contractors Ltd.* (1960) 23 D.L.R. (2d) 473; Castel (1961) 39 Can. Bar Rev. 93; (1961) 21 Rev. du Barreau de Quebec 181, 199; Sherwood (1956) 5 A.J.Comp.L. 120–125. The question remains open for discussion whether it should be admitted in the law of contract, if the parties have not exercised an express or implied choice. See the survey by Graue, *Aussenwirtschaftsdienst des Betriebsberaters* 1968, 121; Gamillscheg (1962) 27 *Rabels* Z. 591; Maier, 1962 *NJW* 323, 325; Kreuzer, *Das Internationale Privatecht des Warenkaufs* (1964) 284; Hartwig, *Renvoi im internationalen Privatrecht* (1967) 152, 156; Vischer, *Internationales Vertragsrecht* (1962) 111; Batiffol, *Conflits de Lois en matière de contrats* (1938) no. 53; *Traité de d.i.p.* (4th ed., 1967), no. 311, p. 358 and note 52 *bis*: Kegel in *Soergel's Kommentar* (10th ed., 1970), note 34 to article 27; Kelly (1969) 18 I.C.L.Q. 249, at p. 257, n. 39. And see the following cases: *Mason* v. *Rose* 176 F. (2d) 486 (2 Cir. 1949); *Siegelman* v. *Cunard* 221 F. (2d) 189 (1 Cir. 1955); *University of Chicago* v. *Dater*, 227 Mich. 658, 279 N.W. 175 (1936); *ca: Lann* v. *United Steel Works Corpn.*, 166 Misc. 465, 1 N.Y.S. (2d) 951, 957; C. A. Frankfurt, 13 November 1956, *IPRspr.* 1956–57 No. 24, affirmed by the German Supreme Court, 14 February 1958, *NJW* 1958, 750, *AWD* 1958, 57, *IP Rspr.* 1958–59 no. 39, p. 155 and of 9 June 1960, *NJW* 1960, 1720, *AWD* 1960, 183, *IPRspr.* 1960–61 no. 23, p. 94; but see Swiss Federal Tribunal, 21 October 1955, BGF 81, II 391.

[103] The other concerns the rejection of foreign law on the ground of public policy.

[104] *Lazard Bros.* v. *Midland Bank* [1933] A.C. 289, at 298; *A. S. Talinna Laevauhisus* v. *Esthonian S.S. Line* (1946) 80 Lloyd's List Law Report 99, at p. 107 *et seq.*

court. In short, it would appear that an English court must accept that evidence which purports to show how a dispute involving identical facts, and therefore a foreign element, would be determined by the foreign law which is applicable according to English Private International Law.[105] It follows that an English court is bound to accept foreign rules of Private International Law as part of the evidence of foreign law. English law is, of course, free to reject *renvoi* explicitly, and the question discussed above in what circumstances *renvoi* is admitted is only the reverse of the question when it is excluded. It is a question of practical convenience and not of legal theory.

It remains to consider the newly discovered, so-called "concealed," *renvoi*.[106] This is said to arise when the conflicts rule of the *forum* refers to foreign law, and the foreign law (mainly common law) regards the question as one of jurisdiction, treats jurisdiction and | choice of law as co-extensive and attributes jurisdiction to the *forum*. In these circumstances it is said that the refusal to assume jurisdiction and the attribution of jurisdiction to the courts of the *forum* equals a reference back to the *lex fori* as well.

In the case when a civil law country, *e.g.*, Germany, is the *forum*, instances include proceedings in Germany between American or English spouses domiciled there concerning the custody of a child of the marriage. A reference to the personal law of the spouses (to the law of a state of the U.S.A. or England) is said to be met by a jurisdictional attribution of competence to the courts in Germany, and thus to imply a reference to German law. Similar situations, it is argued, may arise in connection with divorces and ancillary claims arising therefrom, as well as in cases of adoptions governed by English law. It is questionable whether in such circumstances a reference to the English law of divorce or adoption can be more than a reference to the English domestic law of divorce or adoption, and not the law of jurisdiction. It is true that English courts, if seized, would have had to decline jurisdiction, and thus also to decline the application of English law. But the refusal to assume jurisdiction is not equal to a reference back or on to another jurisdiction, and, *ex hypothesi*, the English court has never been seized at all. In

---

[105] The desire to reach a decision identical with that which would be reached in the country of the *lex causae* induced Dicey, *Conflict of Laws* (3rd ed., 1922), p. 775, to relate *renvoi* to jurisdiction.

[106] See Hanisch, *NJW* 1966, 2085 with lit. and cases p. 2086, n. 15; see especially Neuhaus, *Grundbegriffe des I.P.R.* (1962) 190–194; JZ 1954, 704; Gündisch, *Fam. R.Z.* 1961, 352; Jayme, *Dir. Int.* 22 (1968), pp. 84, 88, notes 33, 34, with lit.; Ehrenzweig, *Treatise on the Conflict of Laws* (1962) 404. For a case of concealed reference on (transmission) see the decision of the Court of Mainz of 21 October 1966, StAZ 1967, 24; *IPRspr.* 1966–67, no. 159, p. 502, reported by Jayme, *loc. cit.*, and in (1969) 21 Florida L.R. 290; Soergel-Kegel, *Kommentar zum BGB*, Vol. VII (10th ed., 1970), note 14 to art. 27. Von Mehren in *XXth Century Comparative and Conflicts Law* (1961), pp. 380, 382, uses the term in a different sense.

other words, the reference by German law to the English law of divorce or adoption is a reference to the substantive law of England, and the refusal of English courts to assume jurisdiction is not a reference back or on in the field of jurisdiction, and still less in the field of substantive law. It is equally true that English courts will recognise a German decree of divorce or an adoption order, if made by a court having jurisdiction, irrespective of what law was applied.[107] Thus in the first case the jurisdictional problem has not arisen and cannot arise; if it did, it must be remembered that the English rule of jurisdiction is strictly unilateral[108] and does not purport to shift jurisdiction and thus, by implication, the law applicable. In the second case a choice of law problem does not arise. Thus *renvoi*, even of the concealed kind, does not come into play. It is difficult to envisage a situation in which this problem could be raised in an English court, except in the circumstances of section 1 of the Adoption Act 1958 or of *Armitage* v. *Att.-Gen.*[109] The former would equal a choice of the foreign law of the domicile. If according to the latter (say Ontario law), the courts of the parties' residence (*e.g.* England) have juris|diction, the reference back to English law is said to be implied. In reality, the English court cannot assume jurisdiction on a reference by foreign law, and the implied reference back to English law does not operate. If English courts recognise a divorce granted by the courts in South Dakota, because it is recognised by courts of the domicile, New York, a question of recognising a foreign decree, but not a reference on by foreign (New York) law is involved.

(5) Public Policy

It has always been admitted that any right, power, capacity, disability or legal relationship arising under foreign law need not be enforced, or even recognised, if it conflicts with the fundamental public policy of English law.[110] Enforcement is refused, in the first place, in respect of those rules of foreign law to which English rules of the conflict of laws do not extend, because they are penal or revenue laws, but not merely because they are confiscatory.[111] It is refused, in the second place, if it conflicts with English

---

[107] The situation is not unlike that in *Armitage* v. *Att.-Gen.* [1906] P. 135, which is not regarded as one involving *renvoi*. See Dicey and Morris, *Conflict of Laws*, pp. 61–62.

[108] See above p. 73.

[109] [1906] P. 135. See also *Abate* v. *Abate* [1961] P. 29; *Mather* v. *Mahoney* [1968] 1 W.L.R. 1773; [1968] 2 All E.R. 223.

[110] Dicey, Rule 2.

[111] *Luther* v. *Sagor* [1921] 3 K.B. 532; *Princess Paley Olga* v. *Weisz* [1929] 1 K.B. 718; *Re Banque des Marchands de Moscou (Koupetchesky), Royal Exchange Assurance* v. *The Liquidator* [1952] 1 All E.R. 1269, 1271; *Re Banque des Marchands de Moscou (Koupet-*

political or social institutions. In recent years these principles have been attacked at their foundations by a series of cases which were principally concerned with the recognition of foreign decrees of nullity and divorce,[112] but in one instance with a foreign diminution of status imposed by an order of a foreign court.[113] According to the judgments in these cases, English courts have a residual discretion, at least in the particular circumstances, to refuse to recognise the operation of the applicable foreign law or of the competent foreign jurisdiction, if the recognition would be improper or unjust or unconscionable in the circumstances of the particular case.[114] If these judicial pronouncements were to indicate that any such principle had found its way into English Private International Law, the strictures of Morris that "the whole of the conflict of laws, or even that part which is concerned with status [is reduced] to the | level of judicial discretion,"[115] must apply, and English Private International Law would have returned to the starting point of all Private International Law in the late twelfth century.[116] However, at present these pronouncements have not operated to the exclusion of the application of the law normally applicable by an English court itself, and the basis of the alleged power is weak, derived as it is from a misinterpretation of earlier cases.

In *Re Langley's Settlement Trust*[117] Lord Evershed M.R. relied on a passage in *Baindail* v. *Baindail*[118] where Lord Greene M.R. said in respect of the recognition of a foreign polygamous marriage:

---

chesky) (*No. 2*) [1954] 1 W.L.R. 1108, 1113; *Re Russian Bank for Foreign Trade* [1933] Ch. 745, 766. They will be disregarded if the confiscatory law is penal: *Novello* v. *Hinrichsen* [1951] Ch. 595, 1026 (C.A.). If the foreign confiscatory legislation purports to operate in respect of assets in England, the rule that English law as the *lex situs* must be applied, and not the confiscatory character of the foreign law, leads to the disregard of the foreign law; see *Bank voor Handel* v. *Slatford* [1953] Q.B. 248, 261; *Banco de Vizcaja* v. *Don Alfonso de Borbon y Austria* [1935] 1 K.B. 140.

[112] *Gray* v. *Formosa* [1963] P. 259; *Lepre* v. *Lepre* [1965] P. 52.

[113] *Re Langley's Settlement Trust* [1962] Ch. 541.

[114] *Re Langley's Settlement Trust* [1962] Ch. 541, 555, 557–558 (C.A.); *Russ* v. *Russ* [1963] P. 87, 100; [1964] P. 315, 327–328; 334, 335 (C.A.); *Cheni* v. *Cheni* [1965] P. 85, 98; *Gray* v. *Formosa* [1963] P. 259, 269, 270, 271 (C.A.); *Lepre* v. *Lepre* [1965] P. 52, 63; *Qureshi* v. *Qureshi* [1971] 1 All E.R. 325, 343 (55), 346 (63), [1971] 2 W.L.R. 518, 536 (4), 540.

[115] Dicey and Morris, pp. 76–77; Grodecki (1962) 11 I.C.L.Q. 578, 582; Nygh (1964) 13 I.C.L.Q. 39, 51; Cheshire, 151–152.

[116] Aldricus (1170–1200): quaeritur si homines diversarum provinciarum. quae diversas habent consuetudines, sub uno eodemque judice litigant, utram earum judex qui judicandum suscepit sequi debeat. Respondeo earn quae potior et melior videtur. Debet enim judicare secundum quod melius ei visum fuerit secundum Aldricum. See Gutzwiller, *Hague Rec.* 29 (1929, IV) 291, 301 n. 1; Neumeyer, *Die gemeinrechtliche Entwickelung des internationalen Privat- und Strafechts bis Bartolus*, II (1916) 67; Meijers, *Bijdrage*, p. 87; Niederer in *Festschrift für Hans Fritzche* (1952) 115; Rev. crit.d.i.p. 49 (1960) 137, 141.

[117] [1961] Ch. 541, 554.

[118] [1946] P. 122 (C.A.).

The practical question in this case appears to be: Will the courts of this country, in deciding upon the validity of this English marriage, give effect to the status possessed by the respondent? That question we have to decide with due regard to common sense and some attention to reasonable policy. We are not fettered by any concluded decision on the matter. The learned judge set out … some of the consequences which would flow from disregarding the Hindu marriage for present purposes.[119]

Thus Lord Greene rejected, on grounds of common sense and reasonable policy, the sweeping contention that all polygamous marriages must be disregarded for all purposes on grounds of public policy. He distinguished between status as such and some of its incidents (such as the right to matrimonial remedies). Public policy, as a means of rejecting the application of foreign law which is normally applicable, must be used cautiously. The judicial discretion must temper an all-out rejection of foreign law.[120] In *Re Langley's Settlement Trust*,[121] this observation of Lord Greene was torn out of its context[122] and was used to justify exactly the opposite process, namely, to disregard the foreign law which is normally applicable, despite the fact that the foreign status of incompetence was not penal or governed by English law as being procedural.

What was meant to restrict the uncritical use of public policy by | drawing its fire upon particular, offensive, aspects of the foreign status, and by calling in aid the limiting factor of judicial discretion, now assumed the appearance of an absolute discretion to disregard foreign law which is applicable and not as such contrary to English public policy.

However, the wording of the pronouncements by Lord Evershed M.R.[123] and Donovan L.J. (as he then was)[124] shows that they were moved by Rules 28 and 29 of Dicey's *Conflict of Laws*[125] which read:

… the existence of a status under the law of a person's domicile is recognised by the court, but such recognition does not necessarily involve giving effect to the results of such status. The court will not give effect to the results of a status existing under a foreign law which is penal.

These rules embody the principles enshrined in *Worms* v. *De Valdor*[126] and *Re Selot's Trusts.*[127] According to the individual preference of interpretation put upon these two cases, such incidents of foreign status which are penal or

---

[119] At p. 129.
[120] See also Scarman J. in *Russ* v. *Russ* [1963] P. 87, 99–100, [1962] 2 W.L.R. 708, at 714–715; *In the Estate of Fuld* [1966] 2 W.L.R. 717, 737.
[121] [1962] Ch. 541, 554.
[122] Despite Lord Greene's warning: [1946] P. 122, 125.
[123] At pp. 554–555.
[124] At pp. 557–558.
[125] 7th ed., (1957), p. 225; see now (8th ed., 1967), pp. 225–231.
[126] (1880) 49 L.J.Ch. 261.
[127] [1902] 1 Ch. 488.

procedural[128] may be disregarded, without affecting the recognition of the status itself.

No such restrictive meaning can be attributed to the pronouncements in *Gray (Formosa)* v. *Formosa*.[129] Here a decree of nullity of marriage was refused recognition, although as a decree *in rem* its validity could not be questioned, unless the foreign court lacked jurisdiction or was induced by fraud to assume jurisdiction or violated natural justice.[130] In proceedings for divorce, natural justice was formerly thought to have been violated if the court assumed jurisdiction although the respondent failed to receive sufficient notice of the proceedings because the petitioner falsely stated that he was ignorant of the respondent's address.[131] It was never believed that the court in England could refuse to recognise a foreign decree on the ground that the foreign court had exercised a choice of law which conflicted with English rules of Private International Law or that the rules of foreign law, applied by the court abroad, differed from those of English law.

However, in *Gray (Formosa)* v. *Formosa*[132] the Court of Appeal did just this by refusing to recognise a Maltese decree of nullity of an English secular marriage on the ground that the Maltese party | lacked capacity to marry otherwise than in religious form. Leaving aside the possibility that in the view of the court English law should have been applied to determine capacity, either because the husband was domiciled in England at the relevant time or in deference to the time-honoured, though discredited rule in *Sottomayor* v. *De Barros (No. 2)*,[133] because the wife was domiciled in England, where the marriage took place, the only possible reason is that English law does not require a compulsory religious marriage. The result, as has been pointed out,[134] is that according to the present practice a foreign decree based on the incapacity of a Jewess to marry a Christian[135] or on the celebration of a religious marriage ceremony, when the local law required a civil marriage, can be recognised. Equally a religious marriage abroad, sufficient according to the personal law of the parties and the *lex fori*, but insufficient according to the *lex loci celebrationis*, can be regarded as invalid.[136] But when the decree

---

[128] (1880) 49 L.J.Ch. 261, 262; [1902] 1 Ch. 488, 492.

[129] [1963] P. 259.

[130] Dicey, *Conflict of Laws* (8th ed., 1967), pp. 317–318, 376–377.

[131] Dicey, Rule 40 (4), pp. 318–319.

[132] [1963] P. 259, followed to this extent by *Lepre* v. *Lepre* [1965] P. 52.

[133] (1879) 5 P.D. 94; Dicey and Morris, Rule 31, Exception 3, pp. 269–270, supported by Cotton L.J. in *Sottomayor* v. *De Barros (No. 1)* (1877) 3 P.D. 1, at p. 7, where he said: "No country is bound to recognise the law of a foreign state when they work injustice to its own subjects." See also *Cheni* v. *Cheni* [1965] P. 85, at p. 98.

[134] Dicey and Morris, p. 370.

[135] *Corbett* v. *Corbett* [1957] 1 W.L.R. 486.

[136] *Berthiaume* v. *Dastous* [1930] A.C. 79.

involves an English secular marriage and a personal law requiring a religious marriage, such a law must be disregarded, and a decree based on such a law cannot be tolerated in England and must not be recognised.[137]

It is difficult to accept this result, or the reasoning on which it is based. Lord Denning M.R.[138] relied on English ideas of justice, Donovan L.J. (as he then was) on a residual discretion to avoid flagrant injustice,[139] while Pearson L.J. (as he then was) found support in *Pemberton* v. *Hughes*,[140] where it was said that "our courts never inquire whether a competent foreign court has exercised its *jurisdiction* improperly, provided that no *substantial injustice* according to our notions has been committed " (italics mine). It may be asked whether the concern with the exercise of jurisdiction expressed in *Pemberton* v. *Hughes* does not extend to the proviso as well and whether its extension to the application of foreign law was ever envisaged. Be that as it may, it remains surprising that a foreign law governing capacity to marry which is satisfied by an additional religious marriage ceremony and does not *require* an exclusive religious marriage ceremony should be regarded as shocking.

| Perhaps it was regarded as shocking because one of the spouses was domiciled in England at the time of the marriage there and because the latter's expectations were defeated. This would elevate the rule in *Sottomayor* v. *De Barros* (*No. 2*)[141] to a principle of English public policy, might eliminate the rule in *De Massa* v. *De Massa*[142] and in *Galene* v. *Galene*,[143] and could enlarge the range of limping marriages by disregarding foreign incapacities of a religious[144] or family nature unknown to English law.

(6) Preliminary Question and Datum

It has been known for a long time that different aspects of a case involving foreign elements may be governed by different systems of laws (*dépecage*). Thus the form of a marriage is governed by the *lex loci celebrationis* and

---

[137] It is interesting to note that in the 7th ed. (1958) of Dicey, at p. 57, characterisation is illustrated by reference to this example.

[138] At p. 269.

[139] At p. 270.

[140] At p. 27, citing [1899] 1 Ch. 781, at p. 790, approved in *Salvesen* (or *von Lorang*) v. *Administrator of Austrian Property* [1927] A.C. 641, at pp. 659, 663.

[141] (1879) 5 P.D. 94; *cf.* Kahn-Freund (1953) 39 *Transactions of the Grotius Society* 39, at p. 53.

[142] [1939] 2 All E.R. 150n.

[143] [1939] P. 237.

[144] Imposed upon Roman Catholics not only in Malta but also in Spain, Código civil, art. 42; also in Greece, Civil Code, art. 1367.

capacity by the law of the respective domiciles of the parties. Sometimes these various aspects may have to be considered in the same case, and at times they may be connected by a relationship in which one of the aspects is of primary importance because it embodies the substance of the claim, while another affects the solution because it answers a preliminary or incidental question. Thus a claim to share in the estate of a deceased may depend upon the legitimacy of the claimant, upon the validity of a marriage to the deceased or of an adoption. The validity of a marriage may depend upon the validity of a previous divorce, and the legitimacy of a child may in turn depend upon both.

Until the beginning of the 1930s all these questions were regarded as posing essentially the same problem, namely, what law applies to each individual aspect of the case according to the rules of private international law of the *forum*. Following the researches of Melchior[145] and Wengler,[146] Robertson introduced the problem in England[147] whether the choice of law for the solution of a preliminary or incidental question was to be determined, not by the conflicts rules of the *lex fori*, but of the *lex causae* of the principal question.[148]

The English cases are inconclusive, since the *lex fori* always | coincided with the *lex causae*.[149] A choice between the two alternatives raises not only a technical question, however, but one of practical importance. If the Private International Law of the *lex fori* applies, the individual substantive question which forms the object of the preliminary or incidental question in the case before the court will be determined uniformly in the *forum*, irrespective of whether or not the substantive problem arises as a principal or as a preliminary question. If the Private International Law of the *lex causae* governing the principal question applies, the individual substantive question which

---

[145] *Die Grundlagen des deutschen internationalen Privatrechts* (1932), p. 249 *et seq.*

[146] (1934) 8 *Rabels Z.* 148; (1963) 17 *Dir. Int.* I, 50. See also van Hoogstraten in *Mélanges Kollewijn* (1962), p. 209; Lagarde, *Rev. crit. d. i. p.* 1960, 459, with further lit. at n. 1. For a survey, see Voskuil (1965) 19 *Dir. Int.* I, 183.

[147] *Characterization in the Conflict of Laws* (1940) 135–156; (1939) 55 L.Q.R. 565, at p. 584.

[148] It is generally agreed that neither the domestic law of the *forum* nor that of the *lex causae* can furnish the solution.

[149] *Birtwhistle* v. *Vardill* (1840) 7 Cl. & F. 940; *Re Wright's Trusts* (1856) 2 K. & J. 595; *Mette* v. *Mette* (1859) 1 Sw. & Tr. 416; *Brook* v. *Brook* (1861) 9 H.L.C. 193; *Shaw* v. *Gould* (1868) L.R. 3 H.L. 55; *Re Goodman's Trusts* (1881) 17 Ch.D. 266; *Re Andros* (1883) 24 Ch.D. 637; *Re Grove* (1888) 40 Ch. D. 216; *Re Bozelli* [1902] 1 Ch. 751; *De Wilton* v. *Montefiore* [1909] 2 Ch. 481; *Skottowe* v. *Young* (1871) L.R. 11 Eq. 474; *Atkinson* v. *Anderson* (1882) 21 Ch.D. 100; *Cantiere San Rocco* v. *Clyde Shipbuilding etc. Co.* [1924] A.C. 226; *Fibrosa Spolka Akcyjna* v. *Fairbairn Lawson Combe Barbour Ltd.* [1943] A.C. 32; *Kahler* v. *Midland Bank* [1950] A.C. 24. In the case of suretyship Voskuil, p. 192, distinguishes between preliminary and incidental questions.

forms the object of the preliminary or incidental question in the case before the court will be determined differently according as the substantive problem is raised as a principal or as an incidental question. In the former case the Private International Law of the *forum*, in the latter the Private International Law of the *lex causae* applies. It would seem that the second alternative is to be preferred. Excessive importance should not be attached to the result that the same substantive question is determined by a different legal system as the circumstances lay in which it is raised before the court, even if the same person may thus be legitimate for one purpose and not for another. Such was the result of the decisions of the Canadian courts in *Schwebel* v. *Ungar,*[150] although the reasons given here are not adduced expressly.

It may be asked why this problem is raised when a preliminary or incidental question comes up for decision, and not in other situations calling for the application of foreign law. It must be remembered that the alternative as to whether one system of foreign law or another is to be applied can be considered only if one party pleads the law of country A, while the other pleads that of country B. This would appear to be a possibility in one of three situations.

|(1) One single legal question only is in issue – *e.g.*, as to what law governs a succession. Here the view was taken above that in principle the *lex causae* including its rules of Private International Law should be taken into account unless the *lex fori* includes *renvoi* expressly; the reasons are set out above.[151]

(2) Several legal questions are in issue – *e.g.*, because claimants to the estate of a deceased person rely in part on the law governing matrimonial property relations and in part on the law governing the succession. These legal questions are of equal importance and independent of each other. Although it would be desirable to dovetail the results which follow from the application of one legal system to determine the question based on the matrimonial property régime and another based on the law of succession, no technical manipulation of the rules of Private International Law can achieve this harmony; sometimes the process of adaptation may help.[152]

---

[150] [1963] 37 D.L.R. (2d) 467; (1964) 42 D.L.R. (2d) 622, 633; [1964] O.R. 430, 441 (C.A.) [1965] S.C.R. 148, [1965] 48 D.L.R. (2d) 644. The decision could have been supported on another ground, drawn from the principle of the conflict of laws in time: see Lipstein (1967) 2 Ottawa L.R. 49, 56, relying on arguments developed in [1967] C.L.J. 42. If this approach had been chosen, the problem would have involved two principal questions of equal standing, *i.e.*, the recognition of a divorce in Italy of Hungarian domiciliaries and the capacity to marry of a person domiciled in Israel who had been divorced, on the strength of a decree recognised in Ontario. See also Lysyk (1965) 43 Can. Bar Rev. 365; Webb (1965) 14 I.C.L.Q. 659.

[151] Above section (4).

[152] See above the observations on the problem of adaptation.

(3) Several legal questions are in issue, of which all but one form preliminary or incidental questions.

It has been shown above that in these circumstances problems of substitution may occur (such as when a right of succession depends upon the validity of a foreign adoption). But in such a case the selection of the law applicable has taken place already. The question for discussion here arises at an earlier stage, if at all. To take a classic example: the court in England is called upon to determine the following case: the *de cuius*, a Greek national who died domiciled in Greece leaving movables in England, had married the claimant in a civil marriage ceremony in England. According to Greek law, a Greek national who is a member of the Greek Orthodox Church cannot marry otherwise than in a Greek Church, and the marriage is void. Consequently the claim of the wife fails. If English Private International Law is applied to both questions, the succession is governed by Greek law as the *lex ultimi domicilii*, and the validity of the marriage is (possibly) governed by English law as the *lex loci celebrationis*.[153] It is conceivable, however, that the requirement of a religious marriage ceremony laid down by Greek law is to be characterised as a matter of capacity – and Greek law is applied to this question as well. The same result will be reached if the *lex causae* governing the succession (*i.e.*, Greek law) including its rules of Private International Law is applied. In these circumstances a functional characterisation renders the need unnecessary to rely on the conflict rules of the law governing the main question. A further | advantage of this technique is that it ensures a uniform course of decision in the *forum*, irrespective of whether the question is posed as a main question or as a preliminary question.

The difference in treatment by the conflict rules of the *forum* and of the *lex causae* may however be due to factors other than a difference of characterisation of the preliminary question. Differences in the use and characterisation of connecting factors, in the approach to *renvoi* and possibly in a number of other cases exercise an effect.[154] Here the question arises whether the *forum* should adhere to its own conflict rule to determine the preliminary question. This must depend not so much on the *lex causae* than on the evaluation of the importance of the conflict rule of the *forum*. If the latter does not express a principle which is of paramount importance to the *lex fori* as a whole, the *lex causae* including its conflicts rules should prevail over those of the *lex fori*.[155] The principle which has been developed above in connection with *renvoi* can be called in aid a second time.[156] If, however, the

---

[153] See Wolff, *Private International Law* (2nd ed., 1950), ss. 196, 198, pp. 206–209.

[154] Gottlieb (1955) 33 Can. Bar Rev. 523, 528.

[155] Lipstein (1967) 2 Ottawa L.R. 49, at p. 58; see also Unger (1957) 43 *Transactions of the Grotius Society* 86, at p. 94.

[156] *Cf.* Wolff, *Private International Law* s. 196.

conflicts rule of the *forum* is determined by considerations of paramount importance to the *forum*, the fact that the *lex causae* and its conflicts rule would reach a different result is irrelevant.[157] The following example may serve as illustrations.

For a long time legitimacy in English law depended exclusively upon the existence of a valid marriage of the parents and was regarded as identical with birth in lawful wedlock according to English domestic, or, later, also according to English Private International Law. Consequently, in *Shaw* v. *Gould*[158] which turned on the legitimacy of issue to, take under a will, succession presented the main question: the validity of the marriage of the parents was treated as a preliminary question, since it alone determined legitimacy according to English law. For this purpose the English rules of the conflict of laws were applied to determine its validity, and the further preliminary question whether a previous divorce in Scotland was to be recognised was also determined according to English Private International Law.[159]

The same principle would have been applied if either legitimacy or the recognition of a foreign divorce had arisen as a principal question. In either situation the criteria constituting the operative | facts of the two rules were regarded as being of paramount interest to English law. Today, when legitimacy in English domestic law is no longer determined exclusively by the existence of a valid marriage and when children of voidable,[160] void[161] or subsequent[162] marriages may enjoy this status, the time may have come to regard the intimate link between marriage and legitimacy as severed in English law and to treat them as distinct questions governed by two separate conflicts rules of the *forum*, which concern legitimacy on the one hand[163] and the validity of the marriage on the other hand.[164] Also, the time may be ripe to concede to the foreign *lex causae* governing legitimacy the faculty to apply its own criteria for determining legitimacy by applying the conflicts rules of the foreign law governing legitimacy to determine any preliminary questions. The learned editor of Dicey[165] seeks to rely on either of these criteria as

---

[157] Wengler (1958) 22 Rabels Z. 535, at 544, is more pragmatic.

[158] (1869) L.R. 3 H.L. 55.

[159] According to Inglis (1957) 6 I.C.L.Q. 202, at p. 214, *Shaw* v. *Gould* turned on the validity of the first marriage, and therefore on English law as that of the domicile of the children. However, in this case the presumption of legitimacy would have applied.

[160] Matrimonial Causes Act 1965, s. 11.

[161] Legitimacy Act 1959, s. 2.

[162] Legitimacy Act 1926, s. 1; Legitimacy Act 1959, s. 1.

[163] See in a different context, but in a similar vein, Melchior, *Grundlagen* p. 260, and notes 3 and 4; Lagarde, *Rev.crit.d.i.p.* 1960, 459, at p. 468, who speaks of "eloignement." And see Wolff, *Private International Law*, paras. 362, 363.

[164] Dicey and Morris, Rule 60, p. 418.

[165] Dicey and Morris, Rule 60, p. 418.

alternatives, but this formulation bars the way to the conclusion that legitimacy and the validity of the marriage of the parents according to English domestic or Private International Law may now be separate questions. It is true that the law governing legitimacy may rely upon the validity of the marriage of the parents, but in this case the validity of the marriage has become a preliminary question to be determined by the conflicts rules governing the main question, namely, legitimacy.[166] On this view it is no longer possible to state with certainty that a marriage which is valid according to English Private International Law will result in the legitimacy of the children.[167]

The principles developed here may be tested against the instructive example given by Wolff.[168]

An Italian couple (A and B) validly married under all laws concerned is domiciled in England. B obtained from the English court a decree of divorce under English Law on the ground of her husband's adultery. Then both parties marry again in England. Later A goes with his second wife C to Italy, acquires a domicile there and dies leaving movable property in England.

Italian law does not admit or recognise divorces of Italian citizens.[169] In proceedings in England, the determination of the | preliminary question whether B or C is the wife of the *de cuius* entitled to a share in his estate, if made in accordance with the rules of Private International Law of the main question, must result in the recognition of B as the sole wife of A. It would seem, however, that where a marriage entered into in England after a divorce there is concerned, English courts will determine the validity of such a marriage according to the English rules of Private International Law. The grant of a decree of divorce in England, followed by a marriage ceremony here, especially if the other spouse is domiciled in England, appears to justify the paramountcy of English law including English Private International Law. It is true that the opposite conclusion was reached in *R. v. Brentwood Superintendent Registrar of Marriages, ex p. Arias*[170] but even a superficial analysis shows, first, that the divorce in question was granted abroad and that neither party to the intended marriage appears to have been domiciled in England.[171] However, the Hague Convention of 1968 on the Recognition of

---

[166] Subject to the modifications set out above, see Lipstein in (1954) I *Festschrift für Rabel* 611.

[167] e.g., a marriage valid in England under the rule in *Sottomayor* v. *De Barros* (*No. 2*) (1879) 5 P.D. 94.

[168] *Private International Law* (2nd ed., 1950), s. 200.

[169] On 18 December 1970 divorce was introduced in Italy. (Law No. 898 of 1 December 1970). According to art. 3 of the Law, a marriage abroad after a decree of divorce granted abroad will be recognised in respect of parties subject to Italian law.

[170] [1968] 2 Q.B. 956.

[171] *Ibid.* p. 966, 967.

Foreign Divorces[172] has created a régime of the type advanced here.[173] Incidental or preliminary questions in the conflict of laws have hitherto been regarded as restricted to questions of private law. However, this is not necessarily so, for they may also involve matters outside private law which are commonly said to be of a public law nature. In this case the preliminary question may be said to constitute a datum, seeing that foreign public law cannot be applied.[174] Thus a foreign rule of the road or of the high seas[175] may have to be taken into account in order to determine whether or not a person whose liability is governed by another legal system has offended against a standard of care. Similarly, in order to ascertain whether a foreign pilot was a compulsory pilot it may be necessary to examine whether according to foreign law a duty existed to accept the pilot and to submit to his orders,[176] and a foreign prohibition forbidding the performance of certain transactions may excuse the failure to perform a contract governed by English law.[177] The question has been put whether | the last-mentioned conclusion reflects the respect for a foreign datum[178] or an English rule of the conflict of laws.[179] While the practical consequence is the same, no matter which explanation is preferred, if the contract is governed by English law, it is of importance when the contract is governed by a foreign legal system other than that of the place of performance. If the prohibition in the country of performance is taken into account by an English court, because an English rule of the conflict of laws so requires, the result must be the same if the contract is governed, *e.g.*, by French law. But if the prohibition is treated as a datum, it can only be taken into consideration if the law governing the contract attaches consequences to it.

The answer to the question of which solution is the correct one must depend upon whether or not a prohibition by the law of the place of per-

---

[172] s. 11. For the text, see (1969) 18 I.C.L.Q. 658. It has been incorporated in the English Recognition of Divorces and Legal Separations Act 1971, s. 7.

[173] *Cf.* Lipstein, (1967) 2 Ottawa L.R. 49.

[174] See Lipstein, *Ius Privatum Gentium* I (1969) 411, at pp. 420–421.

[175] *The Halley* (1868) L.R. 2 P.C. 193, at p. 203; *cf. S.S. Diana, The Cliveden* [1894] A.C. 625, 629; *The Youri* v. *The Spearman* (1885) 10 App.Cas. 276; *The Talabot* (1890) 15 P.S. 194; *The Kaiser Wilhelm der Grosse* [1907] P. 36, 43–44; *The City of Berlin* [1908] P. 110.

[176] *The Augusta* (1887) 57 L.T.R. 326, 327; *The Darlington* [1903] P. 77, 78, 80; *The Prinz Hendrick* [1899] P. 177, 181; *The Guy Mannering* (1882) 7 P.D. 132, 135; *The Agnes Otto* (1887) 12 P.D. 56, 57; *The Andoni* [1918] P. 14, 18; *The Waziristan* [1953] 2 All E.R. 1213; *The Peerless* (1860) Lush. 30; *The Arum* [1921] P. 12, 18, 20.

[177] *Ralli Bros.* v. *Compania Naviera Sota y Aznar* [1920] 2 K.B. 287.

[178] Mann (1937) 18 B.Y.I.L. 97, 107–113; Falconbridge, *Conflict of Laws* 387, pp. 391–394; Morris (1953) 6 Vanderbilt L.R. 505 at 510; Rabel II, 536; Cheshire and North 228–229. See also Serick (1953) 18 *Rabels Z.* 633, 647 with reference to the decision of the German Supreme Court RGZ 161, 296, 300; 93, 182, 184 and the lit. cit. in n. 79.

[179] Dicey and Morris, Rule 132, Exception, pp. 761–762.

formance is regarded as so intimately linked to the contract and thus to the law governing the contract that it must be treated as a preliminary or incidental question. On the other hand, if such a prohibition is regarded as always relevant in an English court, no matter whether the contract is governed by English or foreign law, it is obvious that a separate English rule of the conflict of laws is required. The present attitude of English law, as it is evidenced by the decision of the House of Lords in *Regazzoni* v. *Sethia*,[180] is not clear, but the second view deserves full consideration.[181]

(7) Conflict of Laws in Time

Although the problems raised by the time factor have come before the courts over a long period, the literature has been attracted by them only recently.[182] In substance there are three: changes in the conflicts rule of the forum, changes in the connecting factor and changes in the *lex causae*. Of these, changes in the *lex causae* present much the most important and difficult problems of time in the conflict of laws, especially when the change purports to have retrospective effect.[183] It is generally believed that the *lex causae* should be applied|in its entirety,[184] and much thought has been expended by writers on domestic private law to determine in what circumstances supervening legislation is to be applied, with or without retroactive effect, to situations which have materialised previously, in the absence of specific indications that the rule is to have retrospective effect. The results of this investigation in what may be called the two-dimensional field can be put to use where the situation becomes three-dimensional through the addition of space in the form of rules of Private International Law.[185] If it is admitted at

---

[180] [1958] A.C. 301.

[181] Morris (1953) 6 Vanderbilt L.R. 505, at p. 510 with references.

[182] See Dicey and Morris, p. 40, n. 1, with lit., esp. Mann (1954) 31 B.Y.I.L. 217; Grodecki (1959) 35 B.Y.I.L. 58.

[183] Dicey and Morris, p. 44. *Cf.* Mann, 217, at p. 219. In reality the so-called retroactive effect discussed by writers resolves itself into two separate effects. Either the subsequent legislation purports to affect *ex nunc* the previously existing situation (*e.g.*, s. 8 (1) of the Legitimacy Act 1926) or *ex tunc*. Only the latter effect can properly be regarded as retroactive. Thus two different questions arise: the first is whether the law applies to an existing legal relationship and, secondly, whether it applies *ex tunc*. The former involves a question of the conflict of laws in time; the latter involves the interpretation of domestic law found to apply to an existing legal relationship. No retroactive effect was envisaged by the statutes in issue in *Lynch* v. *Government of Paraguay*, *Re Aganoor's Trusts* and *Nelson* v. *Bridport* (see *infra*).

[184] Critical Wengler (1958) 23 *Rabels* Z. 535, 552, 558 *et seq.*

[185] See my review of Roubier, *Le droit transitoire* (2nd ed., 1960) in [1961] C.L.J. 123. The term is used in a simpler sense than that adopted by Mendes da Costa (1958) 7 I.C.L.Q. 217, 251.

the outset that in the sphere of one legal system alone, subsequent legislation applies to past occurrences, if they represent a continuous relationship,[186] the question whether such subsequent legislation applies in space presupposes, once again, that the relationship is continuous. If it is not, as for instance in the case of a succession where the law of the domicile of the deceased at the time of his death operates upon the death and because of it, or in the law of tort where the *lex fori* and to a certain extent the *lex loci delicti*, are determining, any subsequent legislation must be disregarded,[187] because it does not apply to an event which has spent itself and does not constitute a continuous relationship. At the same time it must be remembered that even where a relationship is continuous, subsequent legislation may not be applicable because it may have to be characterised differently, with the result that the subsequent legislation is covered by another rule of the conflict of laws, and that some other legal system applies[188] If these principles are accepted, Paraguayan law as it stood at the death of the deceased was applied correctly to a will in *Lynch* v. *Government*|of *Paraguay*[189] for both reasons indicated above: the death crystallised the law of succession, and the subsequent legislation had to be characterised not as falling within the field of succession but of expropriation. The latter was governed by the *lex situs*, English law, and not by the law of the last domicile of the deceased, which was Paraguayan.[190]

With equal justification Austrian law at the time of the death of the testatrix was applied in *Re Aganoor's Trusts*,[191] although the will contained a settlement in the nature of substitutions which were invalidated by subsequent legislation by the Italian successor state. The fund was situated in England, where it had been paid into court and where successive interests were lawful. Thus the will, valid according to the law of the testatrix's domi-

---

[186] *e.g.*, contracts, matrimonial relations both of a personal and of a proprietary nature and other family relationships. For the use of this distinction, see Wengler (1958) 22 *Rabels* Z. 535, 543; for its practical application, see *Parkasho* v. *Singh* [1968] P. 233.

[187] Unless a positive rule of Private International Law requires the contrary, as does the rule in *Phillip* v. *Eyre* (1870) L.R. 6 Q.B. 1, at p. 28.

[188] Wengler (1958) 23 *Rabels* Z. 535; *Adams* v. *National Bank of Greece S.A.* [1961] A.C. 255, and see Lipstein [1960] C.L.J. 169. The objection that the reference to the domicile "at the time of his death" refers to the connecting factor domicile is irrelevant in the present context, which concerns a different problem. *Ca.* Dicey and Morris, p. 46, with lit. n. 37; Mann, *loc. cit.*, p. 234, but see pp. 237, 242; Grodecki, *loc cit.*, p. 66; Makarov (1957) 22 *Rabels* Z. 200, who speaks of the "petrification" of the law applicable. But see Wengler, *loc. cit.*, at pp. 548, 554. And see *In the Estate of Musurus* [1936] 2 All E.R. 1666, with a note by M. Schoch (1939) 5 *Giur.Comp.d.i.p.* n. 103, p. 308.

[189] (1871) L.R. 2 P. & D. 268, esp. p. 272.

[190] See now *Bank voor Handel etc.* v. *Slatford* [1953] 1 Q.B. 248, at p. 257 *et seq.* Diplock L.J. in *Adams* v. *National Bank of Greece and Athens* [1958] 2 Q.B. 59, 76, 77, but see Lord Reid in *Adams* v. *National Bank of Greece S.A.* [1961] A.C. 255, 282.

[191] (1895) 66 L.J.Ch. 521.

cile at the time of her death, could be given effect in England, since the *lex situs*, English law, which determined the nature of the proprietary interests in the hands of the beneficiaries, allowed interests in the nature of substitutions.[192] On the other hand, in *Nelson v. Bridport*[193] Sicilian law as it stood at the time of the action (and prohibited substitutions) and not as it stood at the time of the testator's death (when substitutions were lawful) was applied to a settlement of land in Sicily. However, Sicilian law was both the law governing the succession and the *lex situs* governing the nature of the proprietary interests in the hands of the beneficiaries. Thus a subsequent change of Sicilian law changing the nature of the proprietary interests created some time previously and now vested in the successors had to be noticed because proprietary rights are governed by the *lex situs*, irrespective of the validity of the will. The latter remained valid but had become ineffective. Thus the popular contention that *Re Aganoor's Trusts*[194] and *Nelson v. Bridport*[195] are conflicting decisions cannot be supported.

Both cases show once again that subsequent legislation which modifies previous law may have to be characterised differently from the law which it purports to modify. The former may concern a question of succession, the latter may vary the nature of proprietary interests available to be held *inter vivos*, or it may involve expropriation (as in the case considered first). The *lex situs* applies as the law which determines the nature of permitted proprietary interests.

|The fact that the succession as such may also be governed by the *lex situs* should not be allowed to obscure this insight, and *Re Aganoor's Trusts*[196] serves to confirm it, for here the *lex situs* was not identical with the *lex successionis*.

For the purpose of ascertaining what interests have devolved on the death of the deceased the law applicable to successions must be applied as it stood at the time of the death, when the estate crystallised. Any charge of "petrification" is inappropriate since the *lex situs* can impose modifications of the proprietary interests in the hands of the beneficiaries at any time.

Philipps v. *Eyre*[197] does not add anything to the discussion by holding specifically that in matters of tort the *lex loci delicti* at the time of the act and subsequently must be taken into consideration in so far as it authorises,

---

[192] *Ca.* Dicey and Morris, p. 45; Mann 234, who argues that Italian law altered the beneficial interests in the trust fund. According to the view taken here it altered the nature of proprietary interests in general capable of being held according to Italian law as the *lex situs*. See also Grodecki, 69.

[193] (1846) 8 Beav. 547.

[194] (1895) 66 L.J.Ch. 521.

[195] (1846) 8 Beav. 547.

[196] (1895) 66 L.J.Ch. 521.

[197] (1870) L.R. 6 Q.B. 1, 28.

enjoins or ratifies the act. If according to English Private International Law the *lex loci delicti* as such determined liability in torts for acts committed abroad, the *lex loci delicti* at the time of the act and not at the time of the suit would have to apply, since the cause of action arises from a single act and not from a continuous relationship.[198] In fact, the *lex fori* applies and the *lex loci delicti* has always been resorted to for the limited purpose of justification only. *Phillips* v. *Eyre*[199] confirms a special rule designed to discourage gold-digging actions in England based on English law, if at any time the act committed abroad was or became justifiable abroad.[200]

It is evident that contracts, since they constitute a continuous relationship until performed, are subject to any subsequent changes in the law applicable.[201] Of course the position is different if foreign law is only incorporated into a contract which is, itself, governed by some other legal system.[202]

Starkowski v. *Att.-Gen.*[203] may be regarded as illustrating that a single act, namely the formal celebration of a marriage, which has spent itself,[204] is governed by the law of the place of celebration at the time when the marriage took place, but may be affected by subsequent legislation in certain circumstances notwithstanding the fact that it is not a continuous relationship. The reason may be that the parties to the act have remained subject to the legal system|concerned through the operation of another, subsidiary, connecting factor (such as domicile etc.).[205] In *Starkowski* v. *Att.-Gen.* the marriage ceremony was celebrated on 19 May 1945 in Austria. At that time it was invalid according to Austrian law, but on 30 June 1945 it was potentially validated by subsequent Austrian legislation. The parties, Polish refugees, left Austria in July 1945.[206] It may be said, therefore, that when the subsequent legislation was enacted, the marriage of the parties was still exclusively subject to Austrian law, because the parties were still resident there. In short, their legal position at that time was still two-dimensional, Austrian law applied to them, and the only question was whether it purported to operate *ex nunc* or *ex tunc*.[207] By removing themselves in time they could have fru-

---

[198] Lipstein in *Ius Privatum Gentium* I (1969) 411, at p. 426, and note 88 with lit.

[199] (1895) 66 L.J.Ch. 521.

[200] *Ibid.*, pp. 411, 422.

[201] *R.* v. *International Trustee for the Protection of Bondholders A.G.* [1937] A.C. 500, and the cases cited in Dicey and Morris, p. 47, n. 44; Grodecki, *loc. cit.*, p. 78. See also Wengler (1958) 23 *Rabels Z.* 335, at p. 355.

[202] Cf. *Rossano* v. *Manufacturers' Life Insurance Co.* [1963] 2 Q.B. 352, 362.

[203] [1954] A.C. 155; see Mann, *loc. cit.*, p. 243.

[204] Ca. Mann, *loc. cit.*, pp. 242, 244, who stresses the continuance *de facto* of the marriage; Grodecki, p. 72.

[205] See Wengler, *loc. cit.*, at pp. 535, 560.

[206] [1954] A.C. 155, 157, and see pp. 169, 172 (Lord Reid: "remedial legislation was promptly enacted"), pp. 173, 176 (Lord Tucker) p. 177 (Lord Asquith of Bishopstone) – but see Mendes da Costa, p. 256.

[207] Mendes da Costa, p. 257 overlooks this point, but states rightly (at p. 254) that the

strated the purpose of the new law, in so far as it purported to affect them, by transforming the problem, from one of pure domestic law into one of conflict of laws in time.

II

While it has been possible to show that during the last fifty years the theory and the general principles of English Private International Law have been refined and analysed, the most dynamic developments affected particular aspects of the conflict of laws. At the beginning of our period it could be said that the English rules of the conflict of laws were among the most orthodox. Today, thanks to a vigorous revival of interest in this subject, they are again in the forefront of development.

(8) Domicile

The concept of domicile as a connecting factor and its application have undergone little change, despite official efforts to modify its proof and some of its dependent rules.[208] Nor has the tendency, noticeable in recent Hague Conventions, to rely on the notion of habitual residence,[209] exercised much influence as yet, but the incorporation of the Conventions on the Form of Wills of 1961 and on | Adoption of 1965[210] has posed the question. However, the Convention on the Recognition of Divorces and Legal Separations of 1970, which relies heavily on this connecting factor[211] has introduced a concession[212] to common law countries by allowing the country where the matrimonial cause is tried to substitute the notion of domicile for that of habitual residence in determining its jurisdiction under the Convention.[213] This makeshift solution does not appear to have eliminated the problem altogeth-

---

court did not rely clearly on the time when the subsequent legislation came into force, but did not either rely wholeheartedly on the time when the marriage was registered subsequently.

[208] Dicey and Morris, p. 118; First Report of the Private International Law Committee (1954) Cmd. 9068; Seventh Report (1963) Cmnd. 1955.

[209] See Lipstein [1965] C.L.J. 224, at p. 225, and note 3; Wills Act 1963, s. 1; Recognition of Divorces and Legal Separations Act 1971, s. 3.

[210] See the Convention on the Form of Wills, art. 1 (d), Wills Act 1963, s. 1; Convention on Jurisdiction, Applicable Law and Recognition of Decrees relating to Adoption of 1965, see arts. 2, 3, 7; Adoption Act 1968, s. 11.

[211] Art. 2.

[212] Art. 3.

[213] Art. 3.

er in so far as English courts are concerned. It would seem that where a divorce pronounced in a Convention country comes up for recognition in England, the courts in England must accord recognition if, on the facts found abroad, the prerequisites for a finding of domicile have been found to be present by the foreign court, even if they would not have supported a finding of domicile according to English notions.[214]

The domicile of origin retains its strong attractive force; it is less easily abandoned than a domicile of choice,[215] and the acquisition of a first domicile of choice is correspondingly more difficult to achieve.[216] Of late, considerations which gave rise to the adoption of the notion of an Anglo-Indian domicile[217] have been resurrected with a different geographical denominator.[218] The transition from a domicile of dependence of a minor to a domicile of his own has been elucidated[219] and the change of a residence of a soldier or official in virtue of an office or duty to that of a domicile of choice has been made possible.[220]

(9) Marriage and divorce

In the field of matrimonial relations, polygamous marriages have attracted attention[221] perhaps to a greater degree than their importance and frequency within English legal life justifies.

|Polygamous marriages are recognised, except as a basis for the initiation of matrimonial proceedings in England.[222] Their nature remains initially determined by the *lex loci celebrationis*, but their validity in substance is now known to depend upon the capacity of the parties to enter into such a union[223] and their future character may depend upon it too. It is accepted that

---

[214] This conclusion seems to follow from art. 6, last para. of the Convention and is apparent from s. 3 (2) and s. 5 (2) of the Act of 1971 (above p. 100, n. 7).

[215] *Re Lloyd Evans* [1947] Ch. 695; *Re Flynn* [1968] 1 W.L.R. 103, 112–115 [1968] 1 All E.R. 49, 56–58; *Qureshi* v. *Qureshi* [1971] 2 W.L.R. 518, 530.

[216] Leaving aside the cases influenced by conditions in wartime; see *May* v. *May* (1943) 168 L.T. 42; *Cruh* v. *Cruh* [1945] 2 All E.R. 545.

[217] Laid to rest in *Casdagli* v. *Casdagli* [1919] A.C. 145.

[218] *Qureshi* v. *Qureshi* [1971] 2 W.L.R. 518, 531–533.

[219] *Harrison* v. *Harrison* [1953] 1 W.L.R. 865; *Henderson* v. *Henderson* [1967] P. 77.

[220] *Donaldson* v. *Donaldson* [1949] P. 363. *Cruickshanks* v. *Cruickshanks* [1957] 1 W.L.R. 564; [1957] 1 All E.R. 889; *Stone* v. *Stone* [1958] 1 W.L.R. 1287; [1959] 1 All E.R. 194; *Sears* v. *Sears* (1962) 106 S.J. 529.

[221] Beginning with articles by Beckett (1932) 48 L.Q.R. 341; Vesey-Fitzgerald (1931) 47 L.Q.R. 253; (1948) *Current Legal Problems* 222 *et seq.*; Morris (1952–53) 66 Harv.L.R. 961; *Festschrift für M. Wolff* (1952) 287–336, and others.

[222] *Baindail* v. *Baindail* [1946] P. 122; *Risk* v. *Risk* [1951] P. 50; *Sowa* v. *Sowa* [1961] P. 70. But see the proposals of the Law Commission, Report on Polygamous Marriages (Law Com. No. 42 (1971)); Morris, *Conflict of Laws* (1971), p. 128.

[223] Morris, *loc. cit.*, *Ali* v. *Ali* [1968] P. 564.

an initial incapacity of a husband to enter into a union enabling him to marry more than one wife renders the union void, even if he never marries more than one wife.[224] Today, it may be that such a union is monogamous from the beginning, since it has been decided that a valid polygamous union *becomes* monogamous upon a change of domicile to a country which prohibits polygamy. Yet it seems to be acknowledged that the character of a marriage celebrated in England between parties who are both capable of entering into a polygamous marriage is determined exclusively by English law, the *lex loci celebrationis*, and is monogamous.[225] It may be that English law is not disposed to allow the conclusion of other than monogamous marriages in England, but it has never been possible to neglect the fact that a husband domiciled in a foreign country permitting polygamy can, by going there, acquire one or more partners who are his lawful wives.[226] The question remains whether in these circumstances the marriage is not only monogamous, but a valid monogamous marriage. If the answer is in the affirmative,[227] the valid conclusion of a second marriage by the husband in the country of his domicile would have to be treated as adultery. It may be doubted whether a decree of divorce could be granted in England, seeing that adultery as such is no longer a ground for dissolving a marriage,[228] and since it can hardly be argued that it is intolerable for a woman, the law of whose matrimonial domicile permits polygamy, to find that she is not the sole wife.[229] In practice the special legislation in India and Pakistan regulating the conclusion of monogamous marriages by persons otherwise entitled to marry polygamously probably takes some of the sting out of the problem, but it remains real where the law of the domicile does not provide similar legislation.

| The greatest changes occurred in the law relating to divorce. At the beginning of our period, English courts only assumed jurisdiction on the basis of domicile,[230] and recognised foreign decrees of divorce only if they were pronounced by the courts of the domicile of the spouses[231] or were recog-

---

[224] *Re Bethell* (1887) 38 Ch.D. 220.

[225] *Qureshi* v. *Qureshi* [1971] 2 W.L.R. 518, 537, 538; Pearl [1971] C.L.J. 41, at p. 43.

[226] *Cf. Lendrum* v. *Chakravarti*, 1929 S.L.T. 96; *McDougall* v. *Chitnavis*, 1937 S.C. 390.

[227] *Cf. Chetti* v. *Chetti* [1909] P. 67; *Sottomayor* v. *De Barros* (*No.* 2) (1879) 5 P.D. 94.

[228] Divorce Reform Act 1969, s. 2 (1) (*a*).

[229] For this problem, see now the Law Commisson's Report, No. 42 (1971), paras. 42–75.

[230] *Wilson* v. *Wilson* (1872) L.R. 2 P. & D. 435, 441–442; *Harvey* v. *Farnie* (1882) 8 App.Cas. 43, 50, 57; *Le Mesurier* v. *Le Mesurier* [1895] A.C. 517, 526–527. The assumption of jurisdiction in favour of a deserted wife whose previous domicile was in England, foreshadowed in *Armytage* v. *Armytage* [1898] P. 178, 185; *Ogden* v. *Ogden* [1908] P. 46, 83, and put into practice in *Stathatos* v. *Stathatos* [1913] P. 46; *De Montaigu* v. *De Montaigu* [1913] P. 154, did not survive for a number of reasons. *Cf.* Dicey, *Conflict of Laws* (3rd ed., 1922), Appendix Note 13, p. 826, and Rule 63, Exception, p. 294.

[231] *Shaw* v. *Gould* (1868) L.R. 3 H.L. 55, 69, 79, 83, 87, and the cases cited above, note 28.

nised by them.[232] The wife shared her husband's domicile for this purpose, even if the spouses were separated.[233] Today the jurisdiction has been enlarged by statute[234] to permit the courts to entertain a petition by a wife who had been deserted by her husband or whose husband had been deported from the United Kingdom, if the husband was domiciled in England immediately before the desertion or deportation,[235] or by a wife who is resident in England and has been ordinarily resident there for a period of three years immediately preceding the commencement of the proceedings, provided that the husband is not domiciled in Scotland, Northern Ireland, the Channel Islands or the Isle of Man.[236] Three years' ordinary residence by the wife coupled with the mandatory application of English domestic law[237] has increased the danger of limping divorces followed by limping marriages,[238] but does not seem to perpetuate any personal incapacity to marry again of a respondent husband who is domiciled in a foreign country where the English divorce, or possibly any divorce whatsoever, cannot be recognised. Even if his capacity to marry is governed by the law of his foreign domicile and if the effect of the English divorce is treated as a preliminary question governed by the foreign *lex domicilii* including its conflicts rule, and not as a separate question, such a husband can probably marry *in England*, at least within the limits of the rule in *Sottomayor* v. *De Barros (No. 2)*.[239] Consequently he is little worse and no better off than the petitioning wife who stands little chance of being able | to conclude a second marriage outside England on the strength of the English decree.[240] Within a short time the question arose whether this extension of English jurisdiction in divorce is matched by a comparable concession of jurisdiction to other countries. In the short time between 1953 and 1958 the unilateral rules of English statute law were converted into bilateral rules. First, recognition was accorded to decrees based on jurisdictional provisions of foreign law which were substantially identi-

---

[232] *Armitage* v. *Att.-Gen.* [1906] P. 135.

[233] *Lord Advocate* v. *Jaffrey* [1921] 1 A.C. 146.

[234] Matrimonial Causes Act 1937, s. 13 = M.C. Act 1950, s. 18 (1) = M.C. Act 1965, s. 40 (1) (*a*). And see the Matrimonial Causes Bill 1921; Westlake, *Private International Law* (7th ed., 1925), p. 89; Dicey, *Conflict of Laws* (3rd ed., 1922), App. Note 14, p. 835.

[235] Matrimonial Causes Act 1937, s. 13 = M.C. Act 1950, s. 18 (1) = M.C. Act 1965, s. 40 (1) (*a*). And see the Matrimonial Causes Bill 1921; Westlake, *Private International Law* (7th ed., 1925), p. 89; Dicey, *Conflict of Laws* (3rd ed., 1922), App. Note 14, p. 835.

[236] Law Reform (Miscellaneous Provisions) Act 1949, s. 1 = M.C. Act 1950, s. 18 (1) (*b*) = M.C. Act 1965, s. 40 (1) (*b*).

[237] Matrimonial Causes Act 1965, s. 40 (2).

[238] For this possibility, see Lord Watson in *Le Mesurier* v. *Le Mesurier* [1895] A.C. 517, at p. 528; Wolff, *Private International Law* (2nd ed., 1950), para. 358, p. 379 and n. 3.

[239] (1879) 5 P.D. 94.

[240] For this possibility, see Lord Watson in *Le Mesurier* v. *Le Mesurier* [1895] A.C. 517, at p. 528; Wolff, *Private International Law* (2nd ed., 1950), para. 358, p. 379 and n. 3.

cal with those of English law.[241] Then the principle of equivalence (falsely called "reciprocity ") was adopted, which permitted the recognition of the decrees, if the facts before the foreign court were such that, had they occurred in England, English courts would have been able to exercise jurisdiction.[242] Shortly afterwards the restriction, developed in English divorce proceedings; that the court can only exercise this extraordinary jurisdiction on the basis of a petition by the wife to the exclusion of any cross-petition by the husband[243] was engrafted on the exceptional rule of recognition of foreign divorces.[244] Finally, the House of Lords has indicated a variety of situations[245] in which foreign decrees will be recognised which seem to express the principle that one of the spouses must have been substantially connected with the country concerned.[246]

The difficulties arising from the exercise by English courts of an enlarged jurisdiction in divorce were exposed above. They stem|from the severance of domicile as the exclusive basis of jurisdiction in divorce from domicile as the law governing status, including divorce, and the resulting capacity to marry. As was shown above, this severance between jurisdiction and the law governing status does little harm if the jurisdiction in divorce is exercised by the courts in England although the husband is domiciled abroad. The situation is very different if a similarly enlarged jurisdiction is accorded to foreign courts. Even if such decrees will be recognised in England according to the English rules of private international law, their recognition by the law gov-

---

[241] *Travers* v. *Holley* [1953] P. 246; *Dunne* v. *Saban* [1955] P. 178; see also *Carr* v. *Carr* [1955] 1 W.L.R. 422.

[242] *Arnold* v. *Arnold* [1957] P. 237; *Manning* v. *Manning* [1958] P. 112; *Robinson Scott* v. *Robinson Scott* [1958] P. 71.

[243] *Russell* v. *Russell* [1957] P. 375.

[244] *Levett* v. *Levett* [1957] P. 156 (C.A.).

[245] Domicile of the spouses, nationality of the spouses with or without qualifications, possibly residence, if coupled with a substantial connection such as nationality even of one of the spouses only; the last matrimonial home, in virtue of the rule in *Armitage* v. *Att.- Gen.* or of the rule in *Travers* v. *Holley.* See the analysis in Dicey and Morris, First Supplement to 8th ed. (1968), p. 315; Graveson, *Conflict of Laws* (6th ed., 1969), p. 325; Cheshire and North (8th ed., 1970), pp. 363–365; Morris, *Conflict of Laws* (1971), pp. 143–144.

[246] (*a*) *Travers* v. *Holley; Tijanic* v. *Tijanic* [1968] P. 181; [1967] 3 All E.R. 976; *Brown* v. *Brown* [1968] P. 518; (*b*) habitual residence (1 year) and nationality: *Angelo* v. *Angelo* [1968] 1 W.L.R. 401; [1967] 3 All E.R. 314; (*c*) habitual residence (2 plus or 3 years): *Welsby* v. *Welsby* [1970] 1 W.L.R. 45; [1970] 2 All E.R. 467; (*d*) if respondent has a real connection with the country: *Mayfield* v. *Mayfield* [1969] P. 119; [1969] 2 All E.R. 219 – see also *Angelo* v. *Angelo, supra* (*b*); *Turczak* v. *Turczak* [1970] P. 198; [1969] 3 All E.R. 317; *Brown* v. *Brown, supra* (*a*); (*e*) if the petitioning husband formerly had a real connection with the country: *Blair* v. *Blair* [1969] 1 W.L.R. 221; [1968] 3 All E.R. 639, 642; (*f*) if the petitioning husband has established a substantial connection of one year's duration through residence: *Munt* v. *Munt* [1970] 2 All E.R. 516, 518; (*g*) or if the country with which the wife is connected will recognise the decree given elsewhere: *Mather* v. *Mahoney* [1969] 3 W.L.R. 1046; [1968] 3 All E.R. 223.

erning the capacity of the parties to marry again cannot be ensured by the same means, unless the parties are domiciled in England.

However desirable in the result, it cannot be contended at present with any degree of authority that the extended recognition of foreign divorces is restricted to decrees dissolving the marriage of parties domiciled in England.[247] If it were so, the extended recognition which began with *Travers* v. *Holley*[248] and culminated in *Indyka* v. *Indyka*[249] would be no more than an extension of the rule in *Armitage* v. *Att.-Gen.*[250] English law is of course at liberty to regard persons domiciled in England to have been released from the bonds of matrimony by any means or by any courts anywhere in the world which it chooses to recognise. If, however, the recognition is also accorded to such divorces of persons domiciled in third countries, where these decrees are not recognised, the recognition of such divorces in England will be ineffective, if a party to such a divorce wishes to marry again in England; such will certainly be the result if both parties to the marriage are domiciled abroad[251]; and even if the other party is domiciled in England, it may be doubted whether the rule in *Sottomayor* v. *De Barros (No. 2)*[252] will help. Moreover, if the validity of a marriage concluded in these circumstances in some foreign country which recognised the divorce and allowed a subsequent marriage were subsequently to become the object of proceedings in England, English courts would have to treat the marriage as void, if the law of the domicile of the divorced party at the time of his subsequent marriage did not recognise the divorce.

| The conclusion to be drawn from this examination is clear: any broad recognition of foreign divorces in disregard of the law of the domicile of the parties, if foreign, will be ineffective to allow the parties to the foreign divorce to marry again in England, *unless* the English rule of Private International Law concerning capacity to marry is changed, at least in part, to permit parties to a foreign divorce, recognised in England, to marry again, even if the law governing their capacity to marry in general does not recognise the decree and prevents a second marriage.

The Hague Convention on the Recognition of Divorces and Legal Sepa-

---

[247] See the literature cited by Lipstein (1967) 2 Ottawa L.R. 49, 54, n. 37.

[248] [1953] P. 246.

[249] [1969] A.C. 33.

[250] [1906] P. 135; consequently *Mountbatten* v. *Mountbatten* [1959] P. 43 would stand and *Mather* v. *Mahoney* [1968] 1 W.L.R. 1773; [1968] 3 All E.R. 223 would be wrongly decided. See Lipstein (1967) 2 Ottawa L.R. 49, 54, 56, 70, and see Unger (1957) 43 *Transactions of the Grotius Society* 86, 93–94.

[251] *R.* v. *Brentwood Superintendent Registrar of Marriages, ex p. Arias* [1968] 2 Q.B. 956.

[252] (1879) 5 P.D. 94; the incapacity of the foreign party is not one of a kind to which the English party might not be subject, even if it does not affect the English party in the particular case.

rations of 1 June 1970[253] seeks to achieve this result and to eliminate the pitfalls set out above when it provides (art. 11) that "A State which is obliged to recognise a divorce under this Convention may not preclude either spouse from remarrying on the ground that the law of another State does not recognise the divorce." Once again jurisdiction in matters of divorce and capacity to marry are linked, but with one difference. While formerly jurisdiction was linked to capacity by relying exclusively on the law and the courts of the domicile, the Hague Convention links capacity to jurisdiction by looking to the law and the courts of a variety of countries. The English Recognition of Divorces and Legal Separations Act 1971, s. 7, has given effect to this innovation.

(10) Nullity of marriage

Jurisdiction in matters of nullity of marriage has undergone great changes in the last fifty years. At the beginning of this period, only one rule existed: the courts of the place of celebration have jurisdiction.[254] *Salvesen's* case established the jurisdiction of the courts of the domicile of the parties[255]; *White* v. *White* drew the logical consequence and accorded jurisdiction to the courts of either party.[256] Writers with "academic sophistry"[257] and the President of the Probate, Divorce and Admiralty Division with cold practical sense[258] have maintained this principle in face of attempts to whittle it down.[259]

| Common residence was added for historical reasons.[260] Finally the same statutory extensions as in matters of divorce were introduced here as well[261] In 1931 the distinction, known to English domestic law, between void and voidable marriages was transplanted into the conflict of laws, and an attempt, successful for twenty-five years, was made to restrict jurisdiction to annul marriages on the ground that they are voidable to the courts of the domicile of the parties.[262] The trend has now been reversed and common

---

[253] Which provides in art. 2 a set of rules for the recognition of foreign divorces which does not differ greatly from those adumbrated in *Indyka* v. *Indyka* [1969] 1 A.C. 33. For the text, see, *e.g.*, Cmnd. 3991 (1968); (1969) 18 I.C.L.Q. 658.

[254] *Simonin* v. *Mallac* (1860) 2 Sw. & Tr. 67; *Ogden* v. *Ogden* [1908] P. 46, 57, 67, 75, 76, 78, 80; *Ross-Smith* v. *Ross-Smith* [1963] A.C. 280; *Padolecchia* v. *Padolecchia* [1968] P. 314.

[255] *Salvesen* v. *Administrator of Austrian Property* [1927] A.C. 641.

[256] [1937] P. 11; *Mehta* v. *Mehta* [1945] 2 All E.R. 690; Morris (1946) 62 L.Q.R. 117.

[257] *Gray (or Formosa)* v. *Formosa* [1962] P. 259, *per* Lord Denning M.R. at p. 269.

[258] *Lepre* v. *Lepre* [1965] P. 52.

[259] *Chapelle* v. *Chapelle* [1950] P. 134.

[260] *Ramsay-Fairfax* v. *Ramsay-Fairfax* [1956] P. 115; *Ross-Smith* v. *Ross-Smith* [1963] A.C. 280, 311, 317; *Szechter* v. *Szechter* [1970] 3 All E.R. 905, 912; note that in 1925 the editor of Westlake believed that residence of the respondent was sufficient (p. 94).

[261] Matrimonial Causes Act 1965, s. 40 (1) = Matrimonial Causes Act 1950, s. 18 (1).

[262] *Inverclyde* v. *Inverclyde* [1931] P. 29.

residence,[263] though not the place of celebration,[264] confers jurisdiction, which has also been further enlarged by statute.[265]

The recent trend to rely on the distinction between marriages alleged to be void or voidable is not without danger, both where the jurisdiction of English courts and the recognition of foreign nullity decrees is concerned. When the jurisdiction of English courts is in issue, any grounds of nullity drawn from foreign law have to be translated into the categories of English law. This exercise is not always easy.[266] In addition, the question has been debated whether the English choice of law rules which distinguish between the law applicable to formalities of marriage and capacity to marry must be augmented by another, to determine the grounds rendering the marriage voidable. This would rely on the law of the matrimonial domicile, which is that of the husband at the time of the marriage.[267] It is not clear whether the reference to the law of the matrimonial domicile in the sense described above serves only to determine the jurisdiction of English courts.[268] According to Dr. Morris[269] the development from *De Reneville* v. *De Reneville*[270] to *Ross-Smith* v. *Ross-Smith*[271] shows that English law alone determines whether the marriage is void or voidable. Taken literally, this statement is open to question since it is undoubted that the grounds | on which a petition for nullity may be based can be drawn from foreign law, from the *lex loci celebrationis* or the law of the respective domiciles of the parties, or possibly from that of the husband alone at the time of the marriage, and not merely on English law. Nor need they coincide with those of English law. However, it would seem that the operative facts of the English rule of jurisdiction must be characterised according to English domestic law and not, as is usual in the case of rules of the conflict of laws, on a broader, comparative basis.[272] This does not dispense the parties from having to plead the foreign law containing the grounds on which they seek to rely,[273] but they are not obliged to plead it. If

---

[263] *Ramsay-Fairfax* v. *Ramsay-Fairfax* [1956] P. 115; see also *Easterbrook* v. *Easterbrook* [1944] P. 10; *Hutter* v. *Hutter* [1944] P. 95; possibly also the residence of the respondent alone: *Magnier* v. *Magnier* (1968) 112 S.J. 233.

[264] *Ross-Smith* v. *Ross-Smith* [1963] A.C. 280.

[265] See above, n. 58.

[266] Cohn (1948) 64 L.Q.R. 324, 337, 533; Grodecki (1957) 20 M.L.R. 566, 575; (1958) 74 L.Q.R. 225, 234–235.

[267] *De Reneville* v. *De Reneville* [1948] P. 100; Dicey and Morris, Rule 45, pp. 359–367; Morris (1970) 19 I.C.L.Q. 424. In *Ponticelli* v. *Ponticelli* [1958] P. 204, the law of the husband's domicile at the relevant time coincided with the *lex fori*.

[268] See Dicey and Morris, *loc. cit.*; Morris, *loc. cit.*, p. 55, n. 5.

[269] (1970) 19 I.C.L.Q. 424.

[270] [1948] P. 100.

[271] [1963] A.C. 280.

[272] See above, Section (3).

[273] This may be the law governing the formalities of marriage, the capacity to marry or,

they fail to do so, foreign law will be deemed to be the same as English law.[274] Thus parties may be able by pleading or by refraining from pleading the foreign law determining the alleged defect of the marriage as void or voidable to determine the jurisdiction of English courts and, in the end, the outcome of the proceedings. This possibility, which became a reality in the cases cited above, draws attention to a serious danger of *forum* shopping, of miscarriage of justice and of limping nullity decrees.

If the recognition of foreign nullity decrees is made to depend upon the same tests formulated by English domestic law, similar problems of transposing foreign notions of nullity into English categories arise, subject to the important difference that English domestic law can never apply.[275] Consequently it may be that the English distinctions of voidability and voidness do not apply here. In practice it means that the jurisdiction of the foreign *forum celebrationis* may be recognised in circumstances in which, had they occurred in England, English courts could not have assumed jurisdiction, because the marriage is regarded as voidable.[276]

| (11) Contracts

The law of contract has progressed steadily on lines which were foreseeable fifty years ago. The *quaestio aurea* whether or not free choice of law is possible has been answered by many with different situations in mind. When the parties have not made any express choice of law, it matters little whether the subjective or the objective doctrine is adopted[277] and the courts have

---

possibly the law relating to certain grounds for rescinding the marriage for reasons appearing after the marriage ceremony. All require a formal determination by a court; for a so-called non-marriage not requiring a decree according to foreign law, see *Merker* v. *Merker* [1963] P. 283; [1963] C.L.J. 50; *Berthiaume* v. *Dastous* [1930] A.C. 79, as explained by Cohn (1948) 64 L.Q.R. at p. 339. Thus the test should be ideally whether the decree operates *ex nunc* or *ex tunc,* but the wording of the corresponding English decrees precludes this solution. However, see now the Nullity Act 1971, s. 5.

[274] As happened in *De Reneville* v. *De Reneville* [1948] P. 100; *Hill* v. *Hill* [1960] P. 130; *Ross-Smith* v. *Ross-Smith* [1963] A.C. 280; *Easterbrook* v. *Easterbrook* [1944] P. 10; *Hutter* v. *Hutter* [1944] P. 95; Falconbridge, *Conflict of Laws* (2nd ed., 1954), pp. 695–698; (1948) 26 Can. Bar Rev. 907, at pp. 915–917; (1944) 22 Can. Bar Rev. 923; F. H. (1944) 60 L.Q.R. 115, 116.

[275] See *Lepre* v. *Lepre* [1965] P. 52, 60.

[276] *Mitford* v. *Mitford* [1923] P. 130, and the explanation given by Westlake (7th ed., 1925), p. 57. See the wording of Dicey and Morris, Rule 46, pp. 371, 375, text to note 77, and see *Corbett* v. *Corbett* [1957] 1 W.L.R. 486, 490. But contrast the conclusions of Sir Jocelyn Simon P. in *Merker* v. *Merker* [1963] 283, 297, relying on *Ross-Smith* v. *Ross-Smith* [1963] A.C. 280.

[277] For some differences, see Mann (1950) 3 Internat. Law Quarterly 60, 597, and see Morris, *ibid.*, p. 197.

given formal expression to this insight.[278] A presumed intention is always a hypothetical intention determined objectively.

Nevertheless, the problem is not entirely academic; the objective doctrine seeks to establish the connection of the contract with a particular territorial unit; the subjective doctrine, by implying a choice of law, looks to the connection with a particular legal system.[279] The latter approach is to be preferred for, as will be shown below, the choice of law to govern a contract may be affected by considerations which are only indirectly connected with the contract itself and wholly independent of the territorial boundaries within which it is intended to operate. The question has a real meaning when the parties have made an express choice. Although it appears to have been solved by the decision in the *Vita Food* case,[280] the qualifications to the effect that the choice must be bona fide, legal and not against public policy[281] leave much unanswered. These conditions are negative, but it has never been possible to establish positively the circumstances in which the choice may be exercised. Yet it is not impossible to offer an answer of general validity, once it is realised that freedom to contract and its limits *within a system of domestic law* are only of importance *after it has been decided that the particular system of law applies.* It is a freedom which forms part of substantive domestic law. Freedom to select a particular system of laws as a problem of Private International Law must be considered at a stage which precedes the consideration or application of any domestic rules of law. It can only be exercised if the contract contains a foreign element, either directly in consequence of some personal or proprietary elements, or indirectly because the contract is | intimately connected with another transaction bearing a foreign character, such as a contract of resale, or of insurance. In short, free choice of law is a connecting factor attached to the operative facts known compendiously as "contract," forming together a rule of Private International Law.[282] As in the case of any other connecting factor, its adoption and formulation with or without qualifications is a matter of policy to be decided by each country for itself.

---

[278] *Bonython* v. *Commonwealth of Australia* [1951] A.C. 201, 219; *The Assunzione* [1954] P. 150, 179–180, 194, but see p. 164.

[279] *Rossano* v. *Manufacturers Life Ins. Co.* [1963] 2 Q.B. 352, 360–361, 369; *Whitworth Estates* v. *Miller* [1969] 2 All E.R. 210, 212G, *per* Lord Denning M.R., at p. 215 *per* Widgery L.J.; [1969] 1 W.L.R. 377, 381, 384; but see Lord Wilberforce in the House of Lords: [1970] 1 All E.R. 808D; *Cie. Tunisienne de Navigation S.A.* v. *Cie. d'Armament Maritime S.A.* [1969] 3 All E.R. 589, at p. 591, *per* Lord Denning M.R.; *cf. Pick* v. *Manufacturers Life Ins. Co.* [1958] 2 Lloyd's Rep. 93.

[280] *Vita Food Products Inc.* v. *Unus Shipping Co. Ltd.* [1939] A.C. 277.

[281] *Ibid.*, p. 290.

[282] This view was first put forward by Haudek, *Die Bedeutung des Parteiwillens im Internationalen Privatrecht* (1930), p. 5.

In England, experience has shown that disputes as to what law applies are rare when the parties have exercised a free choice[283] and frequent where they have not. Of course the situation may arise where the contract thus subjected to the law of one country offends that of another. If that law is the *lex loci solutionis* it will be taken into account in so far as the performance of the contract is illegal in that country.[284] If that law is the *lex loci contractus*, the question must be put whether the law of the place of contracting has any claim to preferential treatment. The answer must depend upon the Private International Law of the *forum* which may give precedence to the *lex loci contractus* over the exercise of free choice of law by the parties, and may admit the latter only if the *lex loci contractus* permits such a choice,[285] thus opening the way to *renvoi*. Free choice of law and the application of the *lex loci contractus* are alternatives which are mutually exclusive. Finally the *lex fori* can always intervene in the guise of rules of public policy, of public law and of procedure.[286]

(12) Tort

During the last four decades, until *Boys* v. *Chaplin*[287] came before the courts in England, the conflicts rule in matters of tort remained firmly that which had been enunciated by Dicey himself and is known as the rule in *Phillips* v. *Eyre*.[288] Writers were much intrigued by the niceties of the problems involving torts in the conflict of laws.[289]

| The function of the *lex fori*, the *lex loci delicti*, a combination of both[290] and the proper law of the tort all attracted attention. But the working rule

---

[283] *Vita Food Products Inc.* v. *Unus Shipping Co.* [1939] A.C. 277; *The Torni* [1932] P. 78; *Ocean Steamship Co.* v. *Queensland State Wheat Board* [1941] 1 K.B. 402; *Jones* v. *Oceanic Steam Navigation Co.* [1924] 2 K.B. 730; *cf. Pena Copper Mines* v. *Rio Tinto Co. Ltd.* (1912) 105 L.T. 846; *Kirchner* v. *Gruban* [1909] 1 Ch. 413. And see Lord Wilberforce in *James Miller* v. *Whitworth Estates* [1970] 1 All E.R. 796, at p. 809B.

[284] *Ralli Bros.* v. *Cia Naviera Sota y Aznar* [1920] 2 K.B. 287 (C.A.); Dicey and Morris, Rule 132, Exception, pp. 760–766.

[285] See the observations in Dicey (7th ed., 1958), p. 782, omitted in the 8th ed. (1967), referring to *The Torni* [1932] P. 78 (C.A.). But see the Uniform Laws on International Sales Act 1967, s. 1 (4), which states that no provision of English law shall be regarded as mandatory, in contradistinction to art. 4 of the Convention itself.

[286] Dicey and Morris, p. 758.

[287] [1967] 2 All E.R. 615 (Milmo J.); [1968] 2 Q.B. 1 (C.A.); [1971] A.C. 356 (H.L.).

[288] (1870) L.R. 6 Q.B. 1, 28, on appeal from (1869) L.R. 4 Q.B. 225.

[289] See the lit. cited by Dicey and Morris, p. 909, n. 1, and by Lipstein, *Ius Privatum Gentium* I (1969) 411, n. 4.

[290] *The Mary Moxham* (1876) 1 P.D. 107, 110, 113; *Chartered Mercantile Bank of London, India and China* v. *N.I. Steam Navigation Co.* (1883) 10 Q.B.D. 521, 536, 537; *The Tolten* [1946] P. 135, 165.

remained that the act must be actionable as a tort in England and must not be justifiable abroad. The relationship between the two limbs was never properly resolved, and each situation as it arose was accommodated within the formal framework of the rule, without much regard to its function. In reality, the rule in *Phillips* v. *Eyre* covers only a negative aspect of the conflicts rule, *i.e.*, where the act complained of is authorised, enjoined or ratified by the *lex loci delicti*.[291] It leaves the question unanswered as to the legal position if the *lex loci actus* takes a neutral attitude towards the act complained of by not treating it as wrongful[292] If more than a neutral attitude of the *lex loci delicti* is required, must a positive condition be fulfilled; must the remedy be the same in substance according to the *lex fori* and the *lex loci*, or is it sufficient if the *lex loci* treats the act as actionable to some extent, even in proceedings other than civil, or does it suffice if the act is criminal only (a situation which in the present state of the law in the world is unlikely to occur)?[293]

Originally jurisdiction in matters of tort and choice of law were co-extensive, subject to some doubts as to whether aliens abroad could be held responsible, if they were not bound to observe the King's Peace.[294] There are indications, if only *obiter*, that as between British subjects (probably, in the meaning of that time, English domiciliaries) an action in England will succeed on the strength of English law alone,[295] thus letting in the proper law of a tort, restricted to those governed by English law. Implicitly, the problem presents itself whether in all other circumstances some degree of actionability according to foreign law is required.

The *lex fori* in the form of general maritime law was applied by Phillimore J. in the Admiralty Division to determine the liability of shipowners for a Belgian compulsory pilot arising out of a collision in foreign waters which were part of the high seas according to maritime law.[296] Foreign and English statute law were both inapplic|able in the circumstances. The *lex loci delicti* as such was irrelevant, except that the *locus delicti* served to exclude British legislation modifying general maritime law. Nevertheless, as a second line of argument, Phillimore J. relied on the *lex loci delicti* in order to introduce Belgian law, which was itself identical with general mari-

---

[291] The following discussion is based on Lipstein in *Ius Privatum Gentium* I (1969) 411–432; see pp. 412, 422–426.

[292] *Mostyn* v. *Fabrigas* (1775) 1 Cowp. 161, 176. Such is the problem posed by Lord Pearson [1971] A.C. 394E-F; [1969] 2 All E.R. 1106G-H.

[293] For Brazilian law, see Rabel, *Conflict of Laws* II (2nd ed., 1960), p. 240; for Neapolitan law in 1862, see Crompton J. in *Scott* v. *Seymour* (1862) 1 H. & C. 219, at p. 235.

[294] *Mostyn* v. *Fabrigas* (1775) 1 Cowp. 161, 176.

[295] *Scott* v. *Seymour* (1862) 1 H. & C. 219, *per* Wightman J. at p. 234, mildly supported by Willes J. at p. 236.

[296] *The Halley* (1867) L.R. 2 Adm. & Ecc. 3, at p. 7.

time law.[297] This process of reasoning was strictly unnecessary and based on little supporting authority.[298] Instead the phrase occurs "this tort was committed, or this obligation was incurred, in the territory of another state."[299] Thus a triple assumption, namely, that the act was a tort abroad, that it created an obligation and that all obligations are governed by the conflicts rule dealing with contracts, led to the adoption of the rule that the *lex loci delicti* applies. However, the Privy Council restored the *status quo* by applying the *lex fori* to the claim, which it treated as concerning vicarious liability at common law.[300] Considerations of liability according to the *lex loci delicti* were disregarded on the ground that British subjects and aliens alike had been allowed for a long time to sue in tort in England in accordance with English law.[301] It is necessary, however, to note the narrower suggestion made *obiter* that "aliens may sue in England for personal injuries done to them by other aliens, when such injuries are actionable both by the law of England, also by that of the country where they are committed."[302] Thus the principle that the act must be actionable as a tort in England and in the place where it was committed appears for the first time, but does not form the *ratio decidendi.* Foreign (Belgian) law was taken into account but, to use modern terms, as a *datum* only. It controlled the terms of appointment of the compulsory pilot and the defendant owners' power of control. Their nature determined whether, for the purpose of vicarious liability according to English law, he was a servant of the defendants or not.[303]

In 1897 the question, raised above, whether in all circumstances, other than one involving English domiciliaries only, some degree of actionability according to foreign law is required was answered by turning the negative condition formulated in *Phillips* v. *Eyre* into a positive one.[304] While the emphasis remained on actionability according to English law, the function of the *lex loci delicti* was re-defined.

| Unlawfulness according to the latter was required and sufficient, no matter whether the act was a criminal offence or a civil wrong and irrespec-

---

[297] *Ibid.*, at pp. 6, 9.

[298] *Ibid.*, p. 17 *et seq.*

[299] *Ibid.*, p. 6. This passage expresses for the first time the *obligatio* theory generally attributed to Mr. Justice Holmes; see *Slater* v. *Mexican National Railways,* 194 U.S. 120 (1904); see also *Phillips* v. *Eyre* (1870) L.R. 6 Q.B. 1, at pp. 28–29, *per* Willes J.

[300] (1868) L.R. 2 P.C. 193, at p. 201.

[301] *Ibid.*, at pp. 201, 203.

[302] *Ibid.*, at pp. 202–203.

[303] For the application of this principle, see the cases cited above, p. 95, n. 76.

[304] *Machado* v. *Fontes* [1897] 2 Q.B. 231 (C.A.), foreshadowed by the observations of Wightman J. in *Scott* v. *Seymour* (1862) H. & C. 219, 234 and of Cockburn C.J. in *Phillips* v. *Eyre* (1869) L.R. 4 Q.B. 225, 239–240.

tive of whether it could form the object of civil or criminal proceedings. Until 1968 the only development to be registered ranged over situations where the act fell into an area outside criminality and actionability.[305]

The judgment of the House of Lords in *Chaplin* v. *Boys*[306] has probably removed the rule in *Machado* v. *Fontes*,[307] but opinions vary as to what it decided. Although no more than two out of the five members of the House of Lords who heard the case agreed on any one *ratio decidendi*, the following conclusions appear to be justified, bearing in mind that the plaintiff, domiciled in England, succeeded on the strength of English law, the *lex fori*, in an action against a defendant who was also domiciled in England on a claim which was also actionable according to the *lex loci delicti*, Maltese law, but only in respect of a much more limited set of heads of damages.

(1) As a general principle, *Phillips* v. *Eyre* stands.[308]

(2) It is insufficient if the act constitutes a crime abroad, but not a tort.[309]

(3) In general the act complained of must be actionable both in England and in the *locus delicti*, but the extent of the claim need not be the same in both jurisdictions.

This principle is stated either expressly[310] or by implication, if it said that the extent of damages both as to heads and quantification are matters of procedure to be determined by the *lex fori*.[311] It constitutes a "double actio-

---

[305] *Walpole* v. *Canadian Northern Ry.* [1923] A.C. 113, 119; *McMillan* v. *Canadian Northern Ry.* [1923] A.C. 120.

[306] [1971] A.C. 356 (H.L.), affirming *Boys* v. *Chaplin* [1968] 2 Q.B. 1; [1968] 1 All E.R. 283 (Diplock L.J. diss.), dismissing an appeal from Milmo J. [1967] 2 All E.R. 665; and see the comments by North and Webb (1970) 19 I.C.L.Q. 24; Karsten, *ibid.*, p. 35; Pearl [1968] C.L.J. 219; McGregor (1970) 33 M.L.R. 1; Graveson (1969) 85 L.Q.R. 505; Reese (1970) 18 A.J.Comp.L. 189; Webb (1967) 16 I.C.L.Q. 1145.

[307] *Machado* v. *Fontes* [1897] 2 Q.B. 231 (C.A.), foreshadowed by the observations of Wightman J. in *Scott* v. *Seymour* (1862) H. & C. 219, 234 and of Cockburn C.J. in *Phillips* v. *Eyre* (1869) L.R. 4 Q.B. 225, 239–240.

[308] Lord Donovan [1971] A.C. 383(D); [1969] 2 All E.R. 1096 end, 1097(A); Lord Pearson [1971] A.C. 398(B), 400(E), 406(D); [1969] 2 All E.R. 1109(E), 1111(F), 1116(E); Lord Wilberforce [1971] A.C. 385(B), 387(B); [1969] 2 All E.R. 1098(F), 1100(B).

[309] Lord Hodson [1971] A.C. 377(C); [1969] 2 All E.R. 1091(F); Lord Wilberforce [1971] A.C. 388(D); [1969] 2 All E.R. 1101(C); *ca* Lord Donovan [1971] A.C. 383(F); [1969] 2 All E.R. 1097(C); Lord Pearson [1971] A.C. 406(A); [1969] 2 All E.R. 1116(D). No such case is likely to arise in the future since in most legal systems – that of Brazil in 1897 and at present included – a criminal act gives rise to an action in tort either in civil proceedings or by means of *partie civile* proceedings in connection with criminal proceedings. *Cf.* Rabel, *Conflict of Laws* II (2nd ed., 1960), p. 240.

[310] Lord Guest [1971] A.C. 381(E); [1969] 2 All E.R. 1095(D); Lord Wilberforce [1971] A.C. 389(F); [1969] 2 All E.R. 1102(B); *ca* Lord Donovan [1971] A.C. 383(D); [1969] 2 All E.R. 1097(B); Lord Pearson [1971] A.C. 398(C), 399 (E-F), 405(E); [1969] 2 All E.R. 1109(F), 1110(F), 1115(H).

[311] Lord Guest [1971] A.C. 381(G), 382(E, F); [1969] 2 All E.R. 1095(F), 1096(D).

nality" rule in the limited sense that the | act must lead to pecuniary redress abroad in some proceedings, but not necessarily civil proceedings. It does not constitute a "double tort" rule in the sense that the grounds and the heads of damages must be the same as in English law.[312] The *obiter dictum* in *The Halley*[313] has become a *ratio decidendi*, but not, as originally conceived, restricted to claims between aliens alone.

(4) Alternatively, or possibly by way of a subsidiary rule supplementing the general principle, claims by and against Englishmen (*i.e.*, by parties who are domiciled or, perhaps, ordinarily resident in England) are governed by the *lex fori*, English law.[314] Thus the *obiter dicta* in *Scott* v. *Seymour*[315] assume the character of a *ratio decidendi* in a slightly modified form. Viewed historically, such a rule is supported by the consideration that those who owe allegiance to the Crown owe a duty to observe the Queen's Peace in England, the alleged violation of which formed the basis of trespass. Thus, in historical perspective, the general principle (above 3) applies when one or both parties are domiciled or ordinarily resident outside England. The exception is restricted to parties subject to English law and does not introduce the notion of the proper law of a tort.[316] Nor does it necessarily require, as a corollary, that actions in tort between two parties who are domiciled or ordinarily resident in the same country abroad should be governed by their personal law, even though two of their Lordships were prepared to consider this proposition.[317] It has been said that in these circumstances, the *lex fori*, English law, is disinterested and that the personal law of the parties, if they belong to the same country, is the only legal system which has an interest in determining the case.[318] This fashionable argument would be persuasive if there existed an overriding division of legislative competence and a corresponding duty of mutual respect, such as the systems developed by the

---

[312] See for a first consideration of this solution Cussen J. in *Varawa* v. *Howard Smith (No. 2)* [1910] V.L.R. 509, 529, 533.

[313] (1868) L.R. 2 P.C. 193, at pp. 202–203; Lipstein in *Ius Privatum Gentium* I (1969) 411, at p. 419.

[314] Lord Hodson [1971] A.C. 378(E), 379(G); [1969] 2 All E.R. 1092(G), 1093(H); Lord Wilberforce [1971] A.C. 392(C); [1969] 2 All E.R. 1104(F).

[315] (1862) H. & C. 219, 235.

[316] Lord Hodson [1971] A.C. 377(H); [1969] 2 All E.R. 1092(B); Lord Guest [1971] A.C. 381(C-D); [1969] 2 All E.R. 1095(B); Lord Donovan [1971] A.C. 383(G); [1969] 2 All E.R. 1097(D); Lord Wilberforce [1971] A.C. 391(D); [1969] 2 All E.R. 1102(F); Lord Pearson [1971] A.C. 405(H); [1969] 2 All E.R. 1116(A).

[317] Lord Hodson [1971] A.C. 377(F – G), 380(A); [1969] 2 All E.R. 1092(B), 1094A; Lord Wilberforce [1971] A.C. 392(B); [1969] 2 All E.R. 1104(E). English Private International Law relies on domicile in personal matters, but not all legal systems agree. If the parties to an accident in Italy are German nationals domiciled in Italy, neither German nor Italian law would regard Italian law as preponderantly involved.

[318] Karsten (1970) 19 I.C.L.Q. 35.

statutists or which the territorialists purported to establish. However, no such system exists, and even if it were|assumed to exist, no firm criterion can be visualised which determines in what circumstances a legal system has an interest in the particular subject-matter. Such criteria might be sought and found in the nature of the laws, following the attempts of the statutists, or in the territorial connection of persons and objects, not unlike the axiomlike connecting factors in Beale's system. However, all of them would constitute *a priori* principles. If no such overriding system of legislative competence exists,[319] it is well to remember Wächter's observations put forward in reply to the alleged duty to respect foreign acquired rights because the respect for the foreign territorial sovereign demanded it[320]: the courts in one country are incapable of determining whether in the view of another country the latter's sovereignty (or, as might be said in the present context, its interests) are affected by a particular factual situation. Even if courts purport to act in deference to any such criteria, they are in fact determining on their own whether to apply foreign law and, if so, which, by imputing an intention to exercise sovereignty or to safeguard an interest. Thus, in the end, the solution is one of policy to be adopted by English Private International Law. This policy has been over the last two centuries to apply English law, but to exclude liability if the *lex loci delicti* authorised, enjoined or ratified the act. The desire to exclude *forum* shopping has now added the double actionability rule, except in the case of parties who are connected by personal ties with England and its jurisdiction. But the overriding position of the *lex fori* in the English conflict of laws has not been undermined or modified nor has the need been shown to introduce the foreign personal law of the parties, if the same for both. In the first place, it may be asked whether the personal law should take precedence over the *lex loci delicti*, if different, especially when it falls to be decided whether an act which is authorised, enjoined or ratified by the latter is to be taken into account. Here the rule in *Phillips* v. *Eyre* serves the purpose much better. In the second place, it may be asked whether the personal law is to be determined by the residence, the domicile or the nationality or any other personal quality of the parties, such as family ties or implied contractual relationships.

It is equally impossible to rely on another fashionable slogan which decries so-called "false conflicts."[321] In English Private International Law, at least, questions of the conflict of laws arise because the pleadings indicate

---

[319] It can exist in a federal state governed by a written constitution; *cf.* Morris, *Conflict of Laws* (1971), pp. 531–532, 533.

[320] (1841) 24 *Archiv für die zivilistische Praxis* 230, at pp. 299, 304; (1842) 25 *ibid.* 150, at p. 162.

[321] Karsten, *loc. cit.*, p. 40; Morris, *Conflict of Laws* (1971), pp. 542–546; and see the observations above.

that each of the parties to the dispute relies on a | different legal system to support its claim or defence which is rejected by the other party. Thus a real conflict must exist before the court can exercise a choice of law. And if the view taken here is adopted that, in principle, every legal system is complete unless it curtails its own operation either by allowing foreign law in through its rules of the conflict of laws or in restricting its own scope by spatially conditioned rules, legal systems conflict generally.

(13) Matrimonial property relations

In recent years the question has been reopened as to what law determines matrimonial property relations. Previously few doubts existed that the principles now set out in Rules 110 and 111 of the present edition of Dicey and Morris as regards movables and in Rule 80, Exception 2, as regards immovables determined this branch of the law. If there is a marriage contract or settlement, the proper law applies to movables and also to any immovables (if situated in England). In the absence of a marriage contract or settlement movables are governed by the law of the matrimonial domicile, which is that of the husband's domicile at the time of the marriage. Immovables are governed by the *lex situs*. Nevertheless, the last (8th) edition of Dicey's *Conflict of Laws* reflects a recent discussion which was in part solved and in part occasioned by the decision of Roxburgh J. in *Re Egerton's Will Trust*.[322] The matrimonial domicile is not, as had been contended by Cheshire,[323] the intended but the actual domicile at the time of the marriage.[324] But the present wording of Rule 110, which refers to the law of the husband's domicile at the time of the marriage, *in the absence of special circumstances*, lets in the rejected notion in a hovel form which may have far-reaching consequences. For it must be remembered, further, that the practice of English courts has not yet settled the question whether, in the absence of a marriage contract or settlement, a change of domicile changes the law governing matrimonial property relations or not, and the present Rule 112 giving effect to such a change subject to the protection of acquired rights is tentative.[325]

The recent doubts arise from the fact that while subscribing to the principle that the law of the husband's domicile at the time of the marriage applies in the absence of a marriage contract or settlement, Roxburgh J. was

---

[322] [1956] Ch. 593.

[323] *Private International Law* (4th ed., 1952), pp. 492–494; see now 8th ed. (1970) by Cheshire and North, pp. 564–566.

[324] Subject, possibly, to limited exceptions; see Dicey and Morris, p. 639; *Re Egerton* [1956] Ch. 593, at pp. 604–605.

[325] *Cf.* Westlake, *Private International Law* (7th ed., 1925), p. 73.

prepared to consider an exception, if it is possible: "to infer that the parties intended their proprietary rights to be | regulated by the law of the new domicile from the moment of their marriage."[326]

It has been shown elsewhere[327] that when there is *ex hypothesi* no marriage settlement or contract, it is difficult to imply a choice of law, especially where the common law applies. At common law there is either a contract or there is none. In civil law systems the freedom to enter into marriage settlement is, generally speaking, more restricted, but the parties can choose one of several models, and if this choice is not exercised, the adoption of one of these models may be implied by law as an implied contract[328] or by operation of law. Thus it may be possible to characterise foreign statutory régimes as contractual, and to imply a choice of law as well. But an implied choice of law alone, without implying a contract in substance as well, is a choice *in vacuo*, where foreign legal systems offer a choice of matrimonial régimes, unless the inference of a choice of law is coupled with an inference of the adoption of a substantive matrimonial régime by the use of a double fiction.

Matters are simpler if only common law systems are in issue. The existence of one single statutory system[329] excludes the necessity of a double fiction. It has been argued that, by the use of an implied or constructive choice, the statutory régime of separation of goods must be treated as contractual.[330] As a result it is argued that the rule of Private International Law concerning marriage contracts or settlements applies always to the exclusion of that which governs the situation when no marriage contract or settlement has been concluded. This would mean in practice that English Private International Law would be forced into adopting the principle of the immutability of matrimonial property régimes, contrary to the only relevant (though antiquated) authority.[331] It may be doubted whether such a development is in accordance with modern aims and trends, which tend to relax the immutability of matrimonial régimes, at least in domestic law.[332] Neither the principle of mutability nor that of immutability | succeeds in eliminating injus-

---

[326] [1956] Ch. 593, 605; see also p. 603, last six lines. It is to be noted that Westlake's editor stated in 1925 (at p. 72) that the application of the law of the matrimonial domicile in the sense of the husband's domicile at the time of the marriage may be replaced by that of any domicile "which may have been acquired immediately after the marriage in pursuance of an agreement to that effect made before it." The difference in the wording is to be noted: here an agreement to set up the matrimonial domicile elsewhere, there an agreement to adopt the law of a future domicile.

[327] *Clunet* 1961, p. 1152, but see Morris, *Revue critique d.i.p.* 1957, p. 78, at pp. 87–90.

[328] *e.g.*, as regards French law, in *De Nicols* v. *Curlier* [1900] A.C. 21.

[329] In England the Married Women's Property Acts 1882–1964.

[330] See Goldberg (1970) 19 I.C.L.Q. 557.

[331] *Lashley* v. *Hog* (1804) 4 Paton 581, as analysed and explained by Goldberg, *loc cit.*, pp. 580–584.

[332] For the recent reforms in France, see L. Neville Brown (1965) 14 Am.J.Comp.L. 308.

tices which may arise if spouses move from one country to another. Some can be mitigated by the device of recognising proprietary rights acquired under a previous matrimonial régime.[333] Others arise because the conflict of laws splits up certain legal questions for determination by different legal systems (*dépeçage*). Consequently questions of matrimonial property rights may be determined by one legal system and those touching succession by another. As a result, the close gearing of the rules on matrimonial property and on succession in any one legal system is broken, and a surviving spouse may either receive the same as he would have received if one legal system applied alone,[334] or too much,[335] or possibly too little or nothing.

(14) Succession – immovables

If any two interrelated principles have retained their claim to validity throughout the centuries, the rules that succession to movables is governed by the law of the last domicile of the deceased and that to immovables by the *lex situs* qualify for this title. Nevertheless Dr. Morris has recently put forward a powerful plea for the uniform application of the law of the last domicile of the *de cuius* both to movables and immovables and, correspondingly, for the relegation into the realm of history of the hitherto undisputed predominance of the *lex situs*.[336] The examples given by Dr. Morris are impressive. By combining English, Scots and Northern Irish law respectively as the *lex domicilii* and the *lex situs* applicable to the estate of a *de cuius* whose estate consists of movables in one of these countries and immovables in another, leaving him surviving his widow and his mother, he shows that the share of the widow will vary greatly, and that of the mother will fluctuate from a portion to nil. Such a result clearly fails to achieve that harmony of decision which rules of the conflict of laws are supposed to pursue and even offends the sense of justice.[337] It should not make any difference in ascertaining the shares attributable to the widow and to the mother whether the deceased died domiciled in England, Scotland or Northern Ireland respectively, if his immovable property is situated in Scotland, Northern Ireland or England or in any combination of these or in any one of these countries

---

[333] See Dicey and Morris, Rule 112.

[334] *Bartholo Case*, C.A. Algiers, 24 December 1889, Clunet 1891, 1171; Robertson, *Characterization in the Conflict of Laws* (1940), p. 158 *et seq.*

[335] *Beaudoin* v. *Trudel* [1937] O.R. 1; [1937] 1 D.L.R. 216.

[336] (1969) 85 L.Q.R. 339.

[337] It does not appear to have done so when the same person acquired the movable estate in England and took the Scottish immovables as heir: *Balfour* v. *Scott* (1795) 6 Bro.P.C. 550, 566.

alone. One way of achieving uniformity is to determine | succession to movables and to immovables uniformly according to the law of the last domicile of the deceased. However, on further analysis, two further features gain prominence. (i) In the first place, the peculiar results demonstrated by Dr. Morris follow from the fact that the statutory rights of a surviving spouse in English, Scottish and Northern Irish law (as distinct from the common law right of *legitim* in Scots law) are expressed in terms of fixed sums of money or of individual homes. This feature is prevalent in common law countries, while civil law systems rely on the technique of reserving a quota for the surviving spouse or a life interest in a portion of the estate. One way of resolving the apparent injustice which follows from the present practice of according the same statutory sum twice over, or of setting off the value of the matrimonial home, if in England, but not in Scotland (if valued under £15,000), would be to make the beneficiary account for any sums received in any one of the other jurisdictions. In practice, this may cause some difficulties, since the final settlement would have to be concentrated in the personal representatives of the deceased, but these may be different persons in the country of the last domicile of the deceased and in that of the *situs*. Within the United Kingdom, general legislation by Parliament at Westminster may overcome this difficulty, but the existing problem will remain troublesome in relation to any other country where the deceased left assets.

(ii) In the second place, the difficulties could be overcome if the statutory rights of a surviving spouse in England, Scotland and Northern Ireland were modified by legislation so as to represent a claim to a portion of the estate (not unlike the *ius relictae* in Scots law). If this position is assessed separately for each estate, as it is at present in order to determine the statutory right, the right of the surviving spouse is geared to the value of the estate. As a result, the existence of separate estates situated in different countries will not lead necessarily to the duplication of the statutory right, but only to its proportional increase. Here again, the intervention of Parliament in Westminster will be necessary, and the present difficulties will remain, where some of the assets are situated in a country outside the United Kingdom.

(iii) As shown above, the solution advocated by Dr. Morris and the measures suggested above have one aspect in common. Any change of existing principles can only be effective if overriding legislation resolves the overlap of statutory rights either (as Dr. Morris wants it) by discarding the *lex situs* altogether in respect of foreign immovables, or (as suggested above (i) and (ii)) by adjusting the nature of the statutory rights in domestic law. Thus any such measures would have to be confined to the United Kingdom. As within the | United Kingdom itself, so in relation to countries outside, the mere fact that the *forum* discards the principle of the *lex situs* in matters of succession to immovables is ineffective, unless the *forum* is also the *situs*. Since the administration at the *situs* can, and normally will, be independent of that at the place of the last domicile of the deceased, it is unlikely to submit of its own to the administration at the latter place. The question is therefore whether countries will be ready to relinquish the *lex situs* rule in respect of successions, the movable assets of which are governed by some other law according to this notion.

Recent experience at the Hague during the preparatory meetings for a Convention concerning the International Administration of the Movable Estate of Deceased Persons has shown that states are not ready to recognise a foreign administration in the place of the last domicile of the deceased unless the rules of Private International Law at the domicile and at the *situs* lead to the application of the same law. They will lead to the application of different laws not only if both countries follow the scission principle, which distinguishes between succession to movables and to immovables, but also if both countries follow the principle of unity of succession, but rely respectively on domicile and nationality as the uniform connecting factor. In order to achieve the result desired by Dr. Morris outside the United Kingdom, it will therefore be necessary to agree not only on the abolition of the rule that succession to immovables is governed by the *lex situs*,[338] but also on the adoption of a uniform single connecting factor for the determination of succession to movables. In the present state of the world's systems of Private International Law, such an agreement is unlikely to be forthcoming. It is only possible to contemplate it within the framework of the United Kingdom, and it may be doubted whether an ineffective uniform rule or a two-tier system, which distinguishes between inter-United Kingdom and international rules of Private International Law in matters of succession, will serve a useful purpose. If a change is desirable in order to achieve more equitable results in the conflict of laws, a modification of domestic law on the lines indicated above may lead to the desired improvement. As in the case of matrimonial property relations, the break in the gearing of rules of domestic law by the operation of different rules of the conflict of laws which result in the application of several legal systems to different aspects of the same question cannot be mended by using or refining the techniques of the conflict of laws alone.

---

[338] Outside common law countries, few states rely on this principle; France and Belgium apply the *lex domicili* to the succession to movables; Austria relies on the *lex patriae*.

The General Principles
of Private International Law

[Editorial note: first published in Académie de droit international de la Haye, Recueil des cours 135 (1972), 99–229.]

| Biographical Note

Kurt Lipstein, born 19 March 1909 in Frankfurt am Main; studied in Grenoble, Berlin and
   Cambridge.
Gerichtsreferendar (1931); Ph.D. (Cantab) 1936; assistant to Professor H. C. Gutteridge
   1937–1941; Secretary, Faculty Board of Law 1944–1948; University Lecturer in Law 1946;
   Reader in the Conflict of Laws 1962; Professor of Comparative Law elect 1972– ; Fellow of
   Clare College 1956; of the Middle Temple barrister-at-law 1950; Hon. Bencher 1966; Director
   of Research, International Association of Legal Science 1954–1959; Visiting Professor of Law,
   University of Pennsylvania 1962; Northwestern University, Chicago 1966, 1968; Member of
   the Committee appointed by the Lord Chancellor and the Secretary for Scotland to advise on
   the conclusion of treaties prepared by the Hague Conferences on Private International Law;
   Member of the International Academy of Comparative Law.

| Principal Publications

Books

One of the editors of *Dicey's Conflict of Laws*, 6–8 ed. 1948, 1958, 1967.
One of the editors of Leske-Loewenfeld, *Das Eherecht der europäischen Staaten*, 2 ed.
Editor of Volume III (Private International Law) of the *International Encyclopaedia of Com-
   parative Law.*
The Law of the European Economic Community (in preparation).

Articles

"The Proper Law of the Contract" (with J. Brunschvig, F. Jerie, K. Rodman), (1938) 12 *St John's Law Rev.* 242–264.

"Unjustified Enrichment in the Conflict of Laws" (with H. C. Gutteridge), (1939) 7 *Cambridge Law Journal* 80–93.

"Conflict of Laws before International Tribunals I, II" (1942) 27 *Transactions of the Grotius Society* 142–175.

– (1944) 29 *Transactions of the Grotius Society*, 51–83.

"The Doctrine of Precedent in Continental Law", (1946) 28 *Journal of the Society of Comparative Law* 34–44.

"The Calvo Clause", (1945) 22 *British Year Book of International Law* 130–145.

"Bentham, Foreign Law and Foreign Lawyers", in *Jeremy Bentham and the Law*, (1947) 202–221.

"Italian Law", *Chambers Encyclopaedia* 1947.

"Spanish Law", *Chambers Encyclopaedia* 1947.

"Jurisdiction in Bankruptcy", (1949) 12 *Modern Law Rev.* 454–476.

"Recognition of Governments and the Application of Foreign Law", (1950) 35 *Transactions of the Grotius Society* 157–188.

"Jurisdiction to Wind-up Foreign Companies", (1952) 11 *Cambridge Law Journal* 198–208.

"The Review of Legislative, Executive and Judicial Acts of an Occupying Power", (1952) 4 *Communicazioni e Studi* 115–141.

"The Fundamental Categories of English Law", *Cuadernos de derecho anglo-americano* 1953.

"Legitimacy and Legitimation in English Private International Law", *Festschrift für Rabel* I, (1954) 611–630.

"A Draft Convention on the Recovery Abroad of Claims for Maintenance", (1954) 3 *International & Comparative Law Quarterly* 125–134.

The Reception of Western Law in the Countries with a Different Social and Economic Background: Turkey, I, II. Annales de l'Institut de droit de l'Université d'Istanbul t. 5, No. 6 (1956) 11–27, 225–238.

– t. 11, Nos. 16–17 (1961), 3–13, (1957) 9 *Social Science Bulletin* 70–95.

"The Reception of Western Law in Countries with a Different Social and Economic Background: India", *Revista del Instituto de derecho comparado*, Barcelona, 8–9 (1957) 69–81, 213–225.

– (1957) 6 *Indian Yearbook of International Law* 277–293.

"The Ambatielos Case, Last Phase", (1957) 6 *I.C.L.Q.* 643–656.

| "The Hague Conventions on Private International, Public Law and Public Policy" (1959) *International and Comparative Law Quarterly* 508–522.

"The Anglo-French Treaty on the Recognition and Enforcement of Judgments in Civil and Commercial Matters", *Jurisclasseur de droit international* (1960) fasc. 593, 40 pp.

"Naturalization", *British Encyclopaedia* (1960).

"Protected Interests in the Law of Torts", (1963) *Cambridge Law Journal* 85–103.

"Adoption in Private International Law", (1963) 12 *I.C.L.Q.* 835–849.

(With E. Loewenfeld) "Liechtenstein gegen Guatemala, Der Nottebohm Fall", in *Gedächtnisschrift für Ludwig Marxer*, (Zurich 1963) 275–325.

"Common Law Marriage and Private International Law", *Revue critique de droit international privé*, 1964, 106–111.

"Harold Cooke Gutteridge 1876–1953", *Rabels Z.* 28 (1964) 201–207.

"English Family Law", in Leske-Loewenfeld, *Das Eherecht der europäischen Staaten*, Vol. I, Pt. 3, (1965) pp. 379–462.

"Research in Family Law", (1966) 9 *Journal of the S.P.T.L.* 217–225.

"Recognition of Foreign Divorces, Retrospects and Prospects" (1967) 2 *Ottawa L.R.* 49–70.

"Recognition of Foreign Divorces", (1967) *Cambridge Law Journal* 42–45, 182–186.

"The Tenth Session of the Hague Conference", (1966) *Cambridge Law Journal* 224–230.

"Reflexions on the Roumanian Family Code", in *Etudes juridiques en l'honneur du Prof. I. Ionescu, Revue roumaine des sciences sociales* 12 (1968) 259–264.

"Proof of Foreign Law, Scrutiny of its Constitutionality and Validity", (1967) 42 *British Year Book of International Law* 265–270.

"The Protection of Bondholders", in *Studi Ascarelli*, Vol. 3, (1969) 1159–1171.

"*Phillips* v. *Eyre*, a Re-interpretation", in *Jus Privatum Gentium, Festschrift für Max Rheinstein*, I (1969) 411–432.

"Conflict of Laws 1921–71, The Way Ahead" [1972 B] 31 *Cambridge L.J.* 67–120.

"Powers of Appointment in the Conflict of Laws", *Festschrift für Wengler* (1972).

| Part I. The Nature and Function of Private International Law

Section 1. Introduction

1. "Gentlemen, this subject is very important. I have earned 15000 ducats by opinions given in this matter" (Baldus);[1] "the nature of the conflict of laws is a dismal swamp, filled with quaking quagmires and inhabited by learned but eccentric professors who theorize about mysterious matters in a strange and incomprehensible jargon. The ordinary court or lawyer is quite lost when engulfed or entangled in it."[2]

Unlike Baldus, I do not promise you golden rewards, but unlike Dean Prosser I hold out the prospect of exciting journeys into areas of great practical and intellectual interest. The general and specific aspects of this subject have been explored many a time in the Hague Lectures,[3] sometimes by speakers who relied exclusively on their own law, but also by those who took into account those other legal systems which are most representative in this field. For reasons which will become clear later on, the present discussion will not be confined to one legal system only and will attempt to weave into a pattern ideas and practices as they have left their mark over the centuries.

---

[1] Savigny, *Geschichte des Römischen Rechts im Mittelalter*, VI (2 ed.) 229; Gutzwiller in *Festschrift für Tuor* (1946), pp. 145, 167, n. 55; Meijers, *Hague Rec.* 49 (1934 III), 543, at p. 614.

[2] Prosser, (1953) 51 *Mich. L. Rev.* 959, 971; De Nova, *Hague Rec.* 118 (1966 II), 434.

[3] See the bibliography in Ehrenzweig, *Hague Rec.* 124 (1968 II), 169, at p. 179, n. 2; to these should now be added:

(2) *Latin-American:* Vieira, 130 (1970 II), 351; *Yougoslavia:* Katičič, 131 (1970 III), 393; *USA:* Cavers, 131 (1970 III), 75.

(5) *Constitutional Aspects:* Castel, 126 (1969 I), 1; *Rivers:* Koutikov, 127 (1969 II), 247; *Contracts between State and Individual:* Weil, 128 (1969 III), 94; *Nationality and domicile:* de Winter, 128 (1969 III), 346; *Maritime Law* (flag): Bonassis, 128 (1969 III), 504; *Restrictive Practices:* Goldman, 128 (1969 III), 631; *Agency:* Schmitthoff, 130 (1970 I), 109.

(8) *Conventions:* Vitta, 126 (1969 I), 110.

2. Private International Law or the Conflict of Laws comprises that body of rules which determines whether local or foreign law is to be applied and, if so, which system of foreign law. Both names are imprecise and misleading. This branch of the law is neither international nor private in character[4] and any conflict is notional only.[5] According|to some, mainly continental, writers it also includes the law of nationality.[6] According to Anglo-American notions it comprises the rules which delimit the jurisdiction of local courts and determine the recognition and enforcement of foreign judgments. The reason is that formerly jurisdiction and choice of law were coextensive at common law.[7] The definition raises as many questions as it answers. Firstly, why should foreign law rather than local law be applied at all? The answer is that it is, of course, possible to disregard foreign law altogether, but the result is frequently inconvenient or unjust if a factual situation which has certain legal consequences in the country where it occurred originally, is treated differently in another country merely because the *lex fori* takes a different view.[8] Again, the application of the *lex fori* to situations involving strong foreign elements may lead to what may seem an unnecessary and often ineffective extension of domestic law to matters which are outside the ambit of the *lex fori*. Secondly, are those rules of choice of law common to all countries, or does every legal system include its own rules of Private International Law? If they are not common to all countries, are they common in virtue of certain rules of Public International Law? If they are not common to all countries, what is the purpose of applying foreign law if not even a semblance of uniformity can be attained by this process? These are the basic questions which must be answered at some stage for the following reason. Modern Private International Law is only of comparatively recent growth, and gaps in the law manifest themselves frequently. Moreover, the solution of a particular question of choice of law raised by the introduction of a claim or defence according to a particular system of foreign law may have to be restricted to the particular case and may not provide guidance in another case based upon an identical set of facts, but involving a claim or defence based upon the law of another country. Nevertheless, Private International Law is capable of development on a firm basis of principle more than any other branch of law.

---

[4] See below sec. 20, pp. 164–166; sec. 25, pp. 192–194.

[5] See below sec. 21, pp. 167–173.

[6] But see now the Third French Draft of a law on P.I.L. amending the Civil Code. Foyer, *Clunet* 1971, 31; Reichelt, *Z.f.Rv.*, 12 (1971), 249; Nadelmann and von Mehren, (1970), 18 *AJCL*, 614.

[7] See below sec. 10, pp. 126–129.

[8] Huber, *Praelectiones Juris Romani et Hodierni* II, 1, 3, 2; Rodenburg, *de Statutorum Diversitate* I, 3, 4, cited by Story, *Commentaries*, para. 25.

Domestic law is the creation of national, territorial or religious units which desire to regulate in detail the social life of the community in accordance with certain social imponderables and conditions, with moral convictions and varying policies. Tradition, certainty and develop|ment are its driving forces. Private International Law, whatever its underlying purpose, has no material content. It does not offer any immediate solution for a particular dispute but operates indirectly. It only indicates the legal system which is to provide the rules to be applied in determining the particular issue.[9] It is a technique and not a system of substantive rules. Its philosophy is international or may be national, according to the view which is taken of the function and ambit of domestic law[10] and of the existence of rules of Public International Law in this matter.[11]

Because it is a technique, Private International Law, more than any other branch of the law, has been particularly susceptible to influence from abroad. Italy in the 12th, 13th and 14th centuries, France in the 14th, 15th and 16th centuries, the Netherlands in the 17th century, the United States in the first half of the 19th and the second half of the 20th century, France, Italy, Germany and England in the second half of the 19th century, have each contributed to the common technique, and it is impossible to ignore the literature and practice of foreign countries. For the same reason, the influence of writers has been more marked in this sphere of law than in any other;[12] indeed it would be possible to identify the various stages in the development of Private International Law with the names of one or a small number of persons and to trace its growth by describing the writings of various authors. A different course will be attempted here. The nature and function of Private International Law will be established by analysing the process whereby these rules were obtained over the course of centuries.

Section 2. Rome and Beyond

3. It is neither necessary nor profitable to examine whether ancient legal systems, such as those in Greece[13] and Rome[14] possessed rules of Private

---

[9] Evrigenis, *Hague Rec.* 118 (1966 II), 319, at p. 320, n. 2 with lit.

[10] See below sec. 25, pp. 192–194.

[11] See below sec. 21, pp. 167–173.

[12] Evrigenis, *loc. cit.*, p. 322 with lit.

[13] Lewald in *Archeion tou Idiotikou Dikaiou*, 13 (1946), 30–78; *Labeo*, 5 (1959), 335–369; *Rev. critique de droit international privé*, 1968, 419–440, 615–639; Taubenschlag, *The Law of Graeco-Roman Egypt in the light of the Papyri* (1944), *Opera Minora*, I, II (1959), *passim*; Maridakis, *Mélanges Streit*, I (1939), 575.

[14] Savigny, VIII, pp. 78 ff.; Baviera, "Diritto internazionale di Roma", *Arch. giur.*, 61 (1898), 243; for texts see Wächter, *Archiv f. d. civ. Praxis*, 24 (1841), 230 at pp. 242 ff.; Meili

International Law of the kind known to modern society. Even if they did exist – which is a matter for debate – it is certain that these rules did not influence the modern branch of this law.

| Section 3. The Period After the Division of the Roman Empire – Personality of Laws

4. Choice of law became a real problem when the Roman Empire was overrun and settled by Germanic tribes.[15] These carried their own laws and customs with them, but the introduction of Germanic, especially Lango-bard, law in areas which formerly were part of the Roman Empire did not supersede the native Roman law, for according to the Germanic concep-tion every person was governed by the law of the tribe to which he belon-ged. Thus conquerors vanquished and strangers lived according to their own laws. However, in so far as the laws of conqueror and vanquished applied within the same State, they applied not in virtue of a choice of law introducing a foreign system of laws, but because they were each of them part of the local law which was Langobard.[16] As in India and Pakistan today, so then, these personal laws constituted the local law. Matters were different where foreigners were involved. Here the difficulties in adminis-tering the law had become increasingly burdensome, as Bishop Agobard's famous complaint illustrates; commenting on the law of the Burgundians, he said:

---

in *Zeitschrift für internationales Privatrecht,* 9 (1899), pp. 3 ff.; Gutzwiller, *Hague Rec.,* p. 308, n. 1, and in *Festschrift für Tuor* (1946), 145 at p. 162, n. 32. And see David in *Sym-bolae van Oven* (1946), pp. 231–250; Niederer in *Festschrift für Fritzsche* (1952), pp. 115–132; *Rev. critique de droit international privé,* 1960, pp. 137–150; F. de Vischer, *Antiquité classique,* 13 (1945), 11; *ibid.,* 14 (1946), 29; *Rev. de la Soc. Jean Bodin,* 9 (1958), 195; Volterra, *Travaux et Conférences de la Faculté de droit de l'Université libre de Bru-xelles,* III (1955), 135–155; *Annuario di diritto internazionale,* 1 (1965), 553–562, and see the literature cited by de Nova, p. 443, n. 1.

[15] Savigny, *Geschichte,* I (1815), p. 90 ff.; Neumeyer, *Die gemeinrechtliche Entwicklung des internationalen Privat- und Strafrechts bis Bartolus,* I (1901), *passim;* Hamaker, *Rechts-geleerd Magazijn,* 22 (1903), p. 133; Stutz, *Zeitschrift der Savigny Stiftung* (Germ.Abt.), 26 (1905), p. 354; Beckmann, *Zeitschrift für vergleichende Rechtswissenschaft,* 1 (1907), pp. 394 ff.; Ernst Mayer, *Zeitschrift der Savigny Stiftung* (Germ.Abt.), 38 (1917), pp. 373 ff.; Meijers, *Bejdrage tot de geschiedenis van het International Privaat- en Strafrecht in Fran-krijk en de Nederlanden* (1914) = *Etudes d'histoire du droit international privé* (1967); *Hague Rec.* 49 (1934 III), 543, 548 ff.; same in *Tijdschrift voor Rechtsgeschiedenis,* 3 (1922), pp. 61 ff.; van Hove, *ibid.,* 3 (1922), p. 277; Stobbe, *Jahrbücher des gemeinen Rechts,* 6 (1863), pp. 21 ff.; Niederer, *Einführung* (2 ed. 1956), pp. 23–31, and see the literature cited by de Nova, *Hague Rec.* 118 (1966 II), at p. 443, n. 1.

[16] Subject to emerging local customs; Neumeyer, I, 40, but generally the dichotomy is clear: Neumeyer, I, 50, 80 ff., 121.

| "Tanta diversitas legum quanta non solum in singulis regionibus aut civitatibus, sed etiam in multis domibus habetur. Nam plerumque contingit ut simul eant aut sedeant duinque homines et nullus eorum communem legem cum altero habeat."[17]

When persons, subject to different legal systems, came into contact with each other, whether through commerce or intermarriage, a cumulation of laws was clearly impracticable and clear-cut solutions were required.[18] Convenience led to the device of a *professio juris* either in order to pinpoint[19] or to select, by one's own free will,[20] the law governing the transaction.

In the end, the appearance of the newly discovered classical Roman law as a common law of the Holy Roman Empire[21] reduced Langobard law, Frankish Imperial Capitularia and the customary Roman law to special local customs[22] and destroyed the personality of laws;[23] moreover, with the growth of circumscribed local law in the city states, the *lex fori* began to assume importance,[24] especially in respect of the substance of proprietary rights.[25] Nevertheless the application of what has become local customary law was not due originally to the emergence of a notion that laws are territorial; it was applied as the law applicable to all residents, but not to foreigners, who remained subject to their personal law or to the common law (which may be Roman or Langobard).[26] However, by the end of the 12th century, the law no longer attached to a person, and the same person could be subject to Langobard law, if in Florence, and to Roman law in Bologna.[27] "Thus the former | tribal laws had become elements of a conflict of laws, just as any other local law".[28]

---

[17] Agubardi ep. ad Lud. P.; see Boucquet, *Rerum Gallicarum et Franciarum Scriptores* (1738), Vol. 6, p. 356; Savigny, *Geschichte* (2 ed. 1834), Vol. I, p. 116; Neumeyer, I, 10, see also 62, 85–87, 144; Meijers, *Hague Rec.* at p. 561–562; *Mon. Germ., Epistolae* V, 159; Migne, 104 col. 116.

[18] E.g., nobody loses a right, except under his own law; claims arising out of a crime attract the law of the injured person.

[19] Neumeyer, I, 89, 111–112 ff., 119, 155.

[20] Neumeyer, I, 94, 98, 107, 155, 158.

[21] Neumeyer, I, 123, 136, 160, 168.

[22] Neumeyer, I, 58, 65, 92, 127, 141, 145, 156, 160.

[23] Neumeyer, I, 144, 146 (as a result of the disappearance of tribal divisions and loyalties), 160, 162, 165, esp. 166.

[24] Neumeyer, I, 106: first for criminal law, procedure, majority, 145, 169, 170 (continued co-existence of local and tribal law), 171.

[25] Neumeyer, I, 170.

[26] Neumeyer, I, 172.

[27] Neumeyer, I, 175; cp. I, p. 231.

[28] Neumeyer, I, 175.

Section 4. Feudalism and the Revival of Roman Law[29]

5. Two factors contributed to mould the Private International Law of the Middle Ages into a shape which differed radically from the earlier sphere of personality of laws. In the Netherlands and France feudalism left its imprint. In Italy, the new schools for the study of Roman Law had to grapple with a situation where local laws in force in the different regions or cities claimed exclusive application in disregard of the circumstance that the reason for the exercise of jurisdiction may have been purely adventitious.

[Section] 5. Feudalism

6. It would be wrong to assume that in a feudal society the *lex fori* applied to all cases which came before the local courts. True, in a feudal society the court always applied its own laws, provided that the court had jurisdiction, but the court exercised its jurisdiction only because the case was somehow factually connected with its territory. The fact counted that the defendant was resident,[30] that the act had taken place, that the contract had been concluded, or the object was situated there.[31] Jurisdiction and the application of law were co-extensive, but it was the convenience of applying the latter which determined the former and not the converse.

Thus, by the 12th century a system had been developed in the Germanic parts of France and the Netherlands which connected persons,|things, contracts and torts with a particular legal system indirectly by determining jurisdiction with the help of certain localising or connecting factors, such as place of birth, permanent residence, place of contracting or situs of objects. Effectiveness was the moving consideration, and the choice of law was coincident with the choice of jurisdiction. Feudalism and the remains of the system of personal law helped to establish it, but in the end principles of

---

[29] Meijers, *Hague Rec.* 49 (1934 III), p. 543, at pp. 567 ff.; Gutzwiller, *Hague Rec.* 29 (1929 IV), 29; see also Wächter, *A.c.P.*, 24 (1841), pp. 280 ff.; 25 (1842), pp. 1 ff.; pp. 361 ff.; Lainé, *Introduction au droit international privé*, I (1888), 1–296; Neumeyer, II (1916); same in *Zeitschrift für vergleichende Rechtswissenschaft*, 11 (1917), 190 ff.; Yntema (1953), 2 *A.J.Comp.Law*, 297–317; De Nova, *Hague Rec.* 118 (1966 II); for the canonist literature see Oudin, *Revue de droit international et de droit comparé*, 31 (1953), pp. 16–25.

[30] The proper court is that of the place where the interested party in personal matters or in matters of succession had his home. Meijers, *loc. cit.*, pp. 573, 575.

[31] Meijers, *Hague Rec.*, at p. 583. For movables the jurisdiction was vested in the court before which the original transfer had been made; see Wächter, *A.c.P.*, 24 (1841), p. 230, at p. 254, n. 1; Sachsenspiegel, III.33.1.30; Schwabenspiegel c. 286. No clear cut rules were developed for torts. Procedure was always governed by the *lex fori*, but evidence remained linked to the personal law of the parties.

choice of law emerged which bear a remarkable similarity to modern Private International Law. This was the contribution of Germanic legal thought in the 12th and 13th centuries. It has influenced the early development in England, before the Dutch school of the 17th century made itself felt, and today a similar technique has found favour with an influential American writer.[32]

Section 6. Italy – The Legists

7. While the northern countries were grappling with questions of choice between several legal systems, none of which could claim a preponderant place, and solved them by concentrating on jurisdiction, Italian legal science[33] had to face the problem that the new common law of the Holy Roman Empire – Roman Law – existed side by side with the indigenous laws and customs of cities and regions in Italy. An early instance of the problem is to be found in the writings of Carolus de Tocco (± 1200):[34]

"Hic nota quod alios noluit ligare nisi subditos imperio suo et est argumentum infra C.3.1.14.
Est autem hoc contra consuetudines civitatum quae etiam alios constringere volunt suis statutis. Et est argumentum si litigat Mutinensis contra Bononiensem in hac civitate quod statutum non noceat Mutinensi. Sed quidam contra hoc autem dicunt argumento illo quod Mutinensis hic forum sequitur conveniendo Bononiensem unde omnes leges illius fori recipiat."

The writer was not certain whether the court in Bologna must apply its own law, the *lex fori*, to all persons and cases before it, or whether an | equitable solution was required. The great lawyers of that period Azo[35] and Accursius (1228?)[36] still tended towards the application of the *lex fori*.[37] Yet this view had not gone unchallenged, and Aldricus (1170–1200) came out in favour of the "better law". He had said:

---

[32] Ehrenzweig.

[33] For the treaty practice of the Italian City States, which laid the foundations of their domestic practices, see Neumeyer, II, pp. 9–56; Meijers, *Hague Rec.*, at pp. 592 ff.

[34] Meijers, *Hague Rec.* 49 (1934 III), p. 594, n. 1; the attribution to Carolus de Tocco, rather than to Roffredus, Neumeyer, II, 75, was made by Meijers in *Atti del Congresso internazionale di diritto romano*, I (1934), 431, at p. 469.

[35] For texts setting out his opinion see Neumeyer, II, 58, n. 3; Baiduinus seems to have shared this opinion, at least initially; Neumeyer, II, 63, 76.

[36] Neumeyer, II, 61–63, 76 n. 1, for the authorship of the text which is regarded by Neumeyer as an addition after 1228 to the Accurian gloss; "Pone: duo litigant coram judice in casu determinato; una est consuetudo in loco rei, alia est consutudo in loco actoris, alia in loco judicis. Per quam consuetuetudinem terminabitur." See also Gutzwiller, p. 303; Bellapertica C 1.1.1. ad. legem cunctos populos, No. 14; Meijers, *Bijdrage*, Annex 5, xxxi; *Etudes de droit international privé*, p. 130.

[37] See the text and comment given by Meijers, *Hague Rec.*, p. 595.

"Quaeritur si homines diversarum provinciarum quae diversas habent consuetudines sub uno eodemque iudice litigant, utrum earum iudex qui iudicandum suscepit sequi debeat. Respondeo eam quae potior et utilior videtur. Debit enim iudicare secundum quod melius ei visum fuerit. Secundum Aldricum."[38]

Hugolinus, who expressed a similar opinion, may have limited its purport to the situation where plaintiff and defendant, being citizens of two different towns, litigate before a court in a third city.[39] Whatever its field of application, glossators and post-glossators were agreed that the clue to the solution of the problem was to be found in C.1.1.1.pr. (380 A.D.), C. Theod. 16.2.2. which provides:

"Cunctos populos quos clementiae nostrae regit temperamentum in tali volumus religione versari quam Divinum Petrum apostolum tradidisse Romanis religio usque ad nunc ab ipso insinuata declarat ..."

Hugolinus interpreted this passage as follows:

"Ex ista lege aperte colligitur argumentum quod imperator non imponit legem nisi suis subditis; nam extra territorium jus dicenti impune non paretur."[40]

An inapposite text was thus employed to solve problems which it never envisaged but the principle which it interpreted was made to express | was of far reaching importance. Neither the narrow application of the *lex fori*, nor the broad choice of the "better law" had in fact inspired the practice. To a certain extent the application of the *lex fori* was conditional upon the existence of jurisdiction. This could be assumed over non-residents if it was the *locus contractus, delicti, rei sitae* or in respect of counterclaims,[41] and the *lex fori* applied. Now a doctrinal basis was provided for these and other cases. Legislative power was understood to extend to all subjects, persons and objects within a particular city or State.[42] Neither the unbridled dominance of the *lex fori*, nor the uncertain operation of good sense and a feeling of justice determined the issue in the courts. An objective test, based upon personal or local allegiance (to use a modem expression), determines the choice of law. The fact that jurisdiction exists does not necessarily support the application of the *lex fori.* A first attempt in the history of Private International Law was thus made to determine the application of local and foreign law with the help of a doctrine which claimed to be of universal validity and was based upon the ties of personal and local allegiance.

---

[38] Neumeyer, II, pp. 66–68; see also the treaties (1181, 1191, 1237) cited p. 69, note; Tilsch, *Rev. dr. int. et de legisl. comparée* (2nd ser.), 13 (1911), p. 417; Gutzwiller, p. 301, n. 1.

[39] Neumeyer, II, pp. 70–71.

[40] Gutzwiller, p. 302.

[41] Neumeyer, II, pp. 80, 83, n. 1, 71, 84.

[42] Neumeyer, II, 89.

The doctrine suffered from a serious deficiency, for it failed to set out in *what circumstances* the claim to apply the *lex fori* on the ground of personal or local allegiance could be asserted. This gap was filled to a great extent during the 13th and 14th centuries. A first distinction was made by Jacobus Balduinus (± 1235), followed by Odofredus, between rules of procedure (*ad litis ordinationem*) and rules of substance (*ad litis decisionem*).[43] As regards the former, the rules of procedure of the *forum* apply always and in all suits. As regards the latter, the *lex fori* is not applicable in all circumstances and without restrictions. But Balduinus failed to show in what circumstances the local law had to withdraw[44] and his distinction was not accepted without opposition, especially on the part of Accusius.

Nevertheless, the contribution of Balduinus was of great significance. While the text of the Corpus Juris encouraged the application of law based upon a division of legislative competence, Balduinus introduced | a criterion to determine which legislative competence is involved. It relies on the *difference in nature* of rules of law. They are either rules of procedure or of substance, and their application in space is to be determined by the intrinsic character of the legal rules themselves.

It will be shown below that this new test is unworkable, except in the limited circumstances which attracted the attention of Balduinus himself. In those particular instances the test is still employed in modern Private International Law, where the principle applies at the present time that, where rules of procedure are in issue, the forum must follow its own rules. It became the fundamental test in the Middle Ages when, with further refinements added to it, it became known as the doctrine of the statutists.

Section 7. The Doctrine of the Statutists[45]

8. It is proper to connect the further development of the statutists doctrine with the French schools in Orléans, Toulouse and Montpelier, where the influence of Accursius, who favoured the unrestricted application of the *lex fori*, was less marked than in Italy. Here Balduinus' tenet[46] that the appli-

---

[43] Neumeyer, II, 85–87; Lainé, I, 253, see also 121, 135, 177, 189, 204; Gutzwiller, *Hague Rec. 29* (1929 IV), p. 304; Meijers, *ibid.*, 49 (1939 IV), 597.

[44] Except for contracts concluded abroad (see Revigny cited below, p. 113, n. 46; for the application of foreign law during this period see the proposal of Aldricus, above p. 111; Neumeyer, II, p. 101. The conclusions are only negative in the sense that they restrict the operation of the *lex fori*; see Neumeyer, II, p. 99.

[45] See Meijers, *Hague Rec.*, p. 597 ff.

[46] Revigny (Ravanis) was a pupil of Jac. Balduinus – Lainé, I, 120; for Revigny see ad D.5.1.1 (1. si subiiciant), Meijers, *Nieuwe Bijdrage*, p. 82; *Etudes d'histoire du droit*, III, p. 139 (6); the *lex loci contractus, lex delicti, lex rei sitae*, all served as choice of law rules; see

cation of statutes in space depends upon their intrinsic nature is believed to have been given its final form. The achievements of the French school, its claim to originality and its function in the light of its political and historic background will be examined next.

9. *The French school.* One of the earliest French writers on this subject, Jean de Révigny (1270), in adding another choice of law rule to those already known in practice,[47] connected succession, both testate and intestate, with the law of the situs. In his own words –

"semper inspicienda est loci consuetudo in quo res sunt".[48]

| This hard and fast rule was qualified by his pupil Pierre de Belleperche or Bellapertica (± 1285) when he said –

"si consuetudo est realis".[49]

Thus a second distinction had been drawn in addition to that offered by Balduinus between *leges quae ad litis ordinationem spectant* and *leges quae ad litis decisionem spectant.* Now the rules of substantive law themselves are subdivided; they are either *statuta personalia* which follow the person or *statuta realia* which are strictly local in their operation. The *lex fori* as a *statutum personale* applies only to those subject to it; as a *statutum reale* it applies to all assets situated within its jurisdiction.[50] But it does not apply to foreigners and to objects situated abroad,[51] who are subject to the *jus commune* or to the incipient conflict rule that the *lex loci* applies to contracts.[52]

The difficulty was, however, to determine whether a statute was *personalis* or *realis*; "si consuetudo non sit contra personalem obligationem inducenda sed contra realem ..." said Lambert de Salins (± 1300).[53] The answer came

---

also p. 140 (8) ad D.13.4.2.1 (1. arbitraria actio); (9) ad C.7.33.12 (1. Quicum in longi temporis prescriptione), *Bijdrage*, Annex XX; *Etudes d'histoire du droit*, III, p. 140; *Etudes d'histoire du droit international privé*, p. 127 (4).

[47] See above n. 46.

[48] Ad legem Cunctos populos 1.1.1.1: Dominus meus dicit: semper est inspicienda loci consuetudo in quo res sunt (arg. legum allegatarum, D.26.7.42.2; D.26.5.27); Meijers, *Hague Rec.*, at p. 597; *Etudes d'histoire du droit international privé* (1967), p. 126 (1) end; *Etudes d'histoire du droit*, III (1959), 133, 135 (1) end; Meijers, *Nieuwe Bijdrage*, p. 86; *Etudes d'histoire du droit*, III, 146; and see Meijers, *Hague Rec.*, at p. 599: "pour Pierre de Belleperche, une coutume personnelle n'est rien qu'une coutume qui, à l'instar d'une action personnelle, prescrit de donner ou faire quelque chose. La coutume réelle donne, à l'instar de l'action réelle, une déclaration des droits réels de personnes intéressées."

[49] Lainé, I, 121–122; Meijers, *Hague Rec.*, p. 598. For Bellapertica's views on this distinction see ad Inst., 1, 2, n. 45–46.

[50] See, e.g., Bellapertica ad 1. Cunctos populos, Meijers, *Nieuwe Bijdrage*, p. 88; *Etudes d'histoire du droit*, III, pp. 141, 142 (8); *Etudes d'histoire du dr.i.p.*, p. 129, App. V, at p. 133.

[51] Neumeyer, II, pp. 78, 80.

[52] See above, p. 112, n. 44.

[53] Meijers, *Hague Rec.*, p. 599 and n. 2.

from Guillaume de Cun (1315–1316):[54] *statuta realia* are those which affect directly objects, *statuta personalia* are those which affect directly persons and which affect objects only indirectly. The distinction may seem plausible at first but, as will be shown below, it is often impossible to state in any particular instance whether a statute is *realis* or *personalis*.

10. *The historical background of the French doctrine.* The meaning and purpose of the new distinction, said to have been introduced in France, becomes clear if its historical and political background is examined. This was the time when the Emperor's supremacy was challenged by France and Naples. The authority of the Pope to legislate with bind|ing effect elsewhere had been challenged some 70 years before.[55] Shortly after 1250 political thinkers in France and Naples had challenged the principle that "everyone is subject to the Emperor without exception" by opposing to it the principle: *Rex in suo regno est imperator.*[56] According to this view, within his own territory and in respect of those subject to his allegiance, the King of France as the local sovereign can legislate with effects which override imperial legislation and the *jus commune.* The purpose of the distinction employed by the French writers is now clear. Its aim is to assert the sovereign power of France or Naples to enact exceptional legislation with regard to its own territory, but not beyond. What had been hitherto only a system of interprovincial conflict of laws, subject to the overriding common and imperial law, had become a set of inter-State rules.

Thus *statuta personalia* and *statuta realia* were not mutually exclusive, as it was held later on; they are special legislation with a built-in restriction of application comparable to a modern unilateral conflict rule. Thus understood, the distinction between real and personal statutes loses much of the importance which was attributed to it later on, but it gains in clarity and significance. Further refinements were added, such as the inclusion of formalities in *statuta personalia.*

---

[54] Meijers, *Hague Rec.*, p. 600.

[55] Ullmann (1949) 64 *English Historical Review*, 1 ff.; Gutzwiller, *Hague Rec.*, at p. 314, n. 3 and the writers cited there. The interpretation given by Mann, *Hague Rec.* 111 (1964 I), at pp. 24–25, is influenced by notions developed in later centuries.

[56] 1303; a thesis pronounced by the lawyers of Philippe le Bel; see Chénon, *Histoire générale du droit français public et privé, I* (1926), pp. 526, 817; Gutzwiller, *Hague Rec.*, at pp. 306 ff.; Neumeyer, II. ch. 3.

For the canonist view see Régout, *La doctrine de la guerre juste* (1935), pp. 54, 82 (Thomist theory), 87, 100, esp. 125 (Cajetanus), 145; Ives de la Brière, *Le droit de juste guerre* (1938), pp. 59–60, citing Alanus: *"Unus quisque enim (illorum) tantum juris habit in regno suo quantum imperator in imperio"*; see also J. Rivière, *Le problème de l'Eglise et de l'Etat au temps de Philippe de Bel* (1926), p. 428; van Hove, *Tijdschrift voor Rechtsgeschiedenis*, III (1922), p. 277; Gutzwiller, *Festschrift für Tuor* (1946), at p. 163, n. 4; Oudin, *Rev. de droit international et de droit comparé*, 31 (1954), Suppl., pp. 16–25; Belgian Reports to the 4th Congress of the International Academy of Comparative Law. But see Meijers, *Hague Rec.*, at p. 630 and n. 1.

11. *The Statutists Doctrine in Italy–14th Century.* It is commonly said that the statutist doctrine was given its final form by Bartolus,[57] | followed by Baldus (1314–1357)[58] who took over the teachings of the French school. Drawing on the canonist and civilian writers in Italy[59] and France[60] he re-affirmed the statutist doctrine,[61] but developed at the same time what may be called the equivalent of modern conflicts rules, to govern especially contracts,[62] delicts,[63] and the form of wills more particularly where the foreign *lex causae* is the *jus commune.* Unlike his predecessors, however, he no longer treated the qualification of statutes as real and personal as a personal or territorial limitation of the *lex fori qua lex specialis.* Instead these tests now served to determine also whether foreign special legislation in the nature of personal or real statutes are to be applied in the courts of the forum. The notion now serves a bilateral purpose[64] and conflicts between a foreign *statutum personale* and a local *statutum reale* can present themselves.[65]

At the same time restrictions upon a foreign personal statute which was otherwise applicable now became necessary. Foreign prohibitive statutes are excluded if they are a *consuetudo odiosa*[66] – a forerunner of the modern doctrine of public policy:

"Quidquid disponitur contra naturam rel rationem naturalem ilium odiosum appellabitur."[67]

---

[57] For lit. see Gutzwiller, *Hague Rec.*, 316, n. 3, especially as regards editions of texts: Meili, *Die theoretischen Abhandlungen des Bartolus und Baldus über das internationale Privat- und Strafrecht, Niemeyer's Z.*, 4 (1894), pp. 258, 340, 446; Guthrie's transl. of Savigny, *System des heutigen römischen Rechts*, Vol. 8 (2 ed. Edinburgh, 1880), App. I; Beale, *Bartolus on the Conflict of Laws* (Cambridge, Mass. 1914), but see the critique of Ehrenzweig (1963), 12 *A.J.Comp.L.*, 384; Meili in *Festschrift für Laband* (1908); Lainé, I, 131; Surville in *Clunet* 1921, p. 5.

[58] For lit. see Meijers, *Hague Rec.*, at p. 606; Gutzwiller, *Hague Rec.*, p. 320, n. 2, and in *Festschrift für Tuor* (1946), pp. 145–178; Meili, *loc. cit.*, above n. 57; Lainé, I, 166; Bonolis, *Questioni di diritto internazionale in alcuni consigli inediti di Baldo* (1908).

[59] Gutzwiller, *loc. cit.*, p. 305. Meijers, *Hague Rec.*, pp. 600 ff.

[60] Meijers, *Bijdrage*, Annex XVI; *Hague Rec.*, pp. 602, 603, 605; *Etudes d'histoire de droit*, III (1959), 283, 286 n. 7; *Tijdschrift voor Rechtsgeschiedenis*, 16 (1939), 114, 117, n. 3.

[61] Statutum reale: quod disponit circa rem; statutum personale: quod disponit circa personam.

[62] Lainé, I, 137.

[63] Lainé, I, 138.

[64] Bartolus, *Commentarii in Codicem* (C.1.11.), Nos. 32, 39, 40, 41; Cp. Lainé, I, 132, 146, 150.

[65] Cp. Lainé, I, 153 ff., 171 ff.

[66] Bartolus, *loc. cit.*, No. 33; Lainé, I, 157; Meijers, *Hague Rec.*, at pp. 601, 608, 630 ff.

[67] Baldus C.1.1.1.1., No. 91; Angelus cons. 210; Meijers, p. 531. Many doubts existed: was the rule which postponed females to males in intestate succession, or the prohibition of gifts between spouses, whether *inter vivos* or by will, *odiosa* or *favorabilis*, seeing that the disability imposed upon one party is always balanced by a benefit conferred upon another. See Meijers, *Hague Rec.*, pp. 618–610, 630; Bartolus, *loc. cit.*, No. 33.

| Baldus introduced a new line of thought when he put forward the doctrine of acquired rights as a motive and a justification for the application of foreign law.[68]

The shift towards a bilateral notion of real and personal statuta introduced the idea – not yet express in Bartolus – that all laws are either real or personal, stand on a level of equality and are mutually exclusive. Thus their application in space outside the country where they form the domestic law must depend upon whether they bear the character of the former or of the latter. *The nature of rules of domestic law determines their application in space.*

This new approach to questions of Private International Law showed itself most clearly in the controversy which raged at the beginning of the 14th century as to what law governed a succession. One party of the French school[69] believed that all rules of succession were real; another party[70] held that no hard and fast rule could be laid down; it all depended upon the wording of the statute.[71] The problem, in one form or another, has exercised the minds of lawyers up to the present day. Upon the answer to it depends whether a succession which includes assets in several countries is governed by several laws (if all laws of succession are real) or by one legal system only (if all laws are personal). The principle that a succession may be governed by several systems of law is adopted today in England and France; Germany and Italy follow the principle of unity. Bartolus followed the middle course advocated by Guillaume de Cun: *"verba consuetudinis attendenda sunt"*.[72] In so doing he exposed unwittingly the weakness of the entire structure erected by the statutists, for he argued as follows: In the case of an interstate succession of a deceased who died domiciled in England, where the principle of primogeniture applied, and who left land in Italy, where the rules of Roman law dividing the land in equal shares between the next of kin obtained, the solution must depend upon the wording of the English rule. If English law provided:

| "bona decendentium veniant in primogenitum"

the statute was *realis*, and thus restricted to the assets in England, and the Italian assets must be divided in equal shares

---

[68] Meijers, *Hague Rec.*, at p. 607.

[69] Revigny, Belleperche, ad 1. Cunctos populos; Meijers, *Bijdrage*, Annex XXI; *Etudes d'histoire du droit*, III, 141, 144; *Etudes d'histoire du d.i.p.*, p. 129, at 132.

[70] Guillaume de Cun, ad 1. Cunctos populos, Meijers, *Etudes d'histoire du d.i.p.*, p. 135, at 136, 137.

[71] "Verba consuetudinis attendenda sunt"; see Meijers, *Bijdrage*, Annex XXVIII; *Etudes d'histoire du droit international privé*, Appendix VI, p. 135, at P. 137.

[72] Bartolus, *loc. cit.*, No. 42; Meijers, *Hague Rec.*, at p. 608.

"quia jus afficit res ipsas".

If English law provided –

"primogenitus succedat"

then the statute was *personalis*[73] and the eldest son takes, subject to the exception that such a law must be regarded as an odious statute.[74] No distinction could be more fortuitous, no result could be more arbitrary.[75] The fault does not lie with Bartolus. It lies in the doctrine which he was attempting to apply. It is impossible to obtain guidance from the nature, and still less from the wording, of a statute or rule of law as to the extent to which it must be applied in space. The doctrine is unworkable in practice.[76]

It is not surprising, therefore, that Baldus refused to follow Bartolus and came down squarely in favour of the nature of all rules of succession as *statuta realia*.[77] Others, similarly bent upon avoiding the absurd result to which Bartolus' doctrine was bound to lead, invoked for the first time the intention of the deceased.[78]

To sum up: compared with the practice in Northern France and in the Netherlands, which relied on jurisdiction to be determined by clearcut connecting factors based on residence, place of contracting, to mention one or two, reflecting the primitive concept of personality of | laws, feudal ties and practical expediency, the doctrine of the statutists is strictly legal and formalistic. It had serious defects, but it was based on principles, some of which were of lasting value.

In the first place, it was international.[79] It attempted to furnish an explanation why foreign law is applied. This it found in the division of legislative powers between autonomous territorial units. Thereby a link was forged between the exercise of sovereign powers by States in International Law and the application of domestic or foreign law. However, the link was more

---

[73] Bartolus, *loc. cit.*, No. 43. The French school regarded the law of the domicile of choice as the *lex personalis*; the Italian school relied on the law of the domicile of origin.

[74] Bartolus, *loc. cit.*, No. 43; Lainé, I, 156; see a similar solution given by Guillaume de Cun, above, p. 117, n. 71.

[75] For the treatment of this question by Bartolus see Gutzwiller, *Hague Rec.*, p. 319; Lainé, I, 154 ff., 158. For the lit. on the "English question" see Gutzwiller, *Hague Rec.*, at pp. 315, n. 1, 319; in *Festschrift für Tuor* (1946), p. 145, at 164; Meijers, *Bijdrage*, Annex XVIII and text, p. 92; Bellapertica ad 1. Cunctos populos cited above, p. 117, n. 69. D'Argentré's comment was: *Nihil potest dici futilius*, cited by Wächter, *A.c.P.*, 24 (1841), p. 230, at p. 274, n. 79; Hertius: *Verum in iis definiendis mirum est quam sudent Doctores*; Wächter, *loc. cit.*, p. 278, n. 90, and generally pp. 278 ff. Another example is: *conjux conjugi ne donato*; Wächter, *loc. cit.*, at p. 257; Meijers, *Hague Rec.*, p. 617 and n. 4; Lainé, I, 160–161.

[76] For cases see Meijers, *Hague Rec.*, at pp. 617 ff.

[77] Meijers, *Hague Rec.*, at pp. 308–309, and n. 1.

[78] Meijers, *loc. cit.*, p. 609.

[79] See also Meijers, *Hague Rec.*, at p. 629.

apparent than real, for while the doctrine justified the power of States to legislate with extra-territorial effect, subject only to the right of other States to enact *statuta realia* which stifled the effect of foreign law, it was unable to explain why one country must apply the extra-territorial legislation of any other country. The recognition that legislative powers are divided justifies the right to export local law; it does not establish the duty to import foreign law. An answer to this problem was only offered towards the end of the 17th century by the Dutch school of writers.[80]

In the second place, it was *universalistic*. The statutist doctrine attempted to provide principles of universal application which were to indicate when foreign law was applicable. However, these attempts to determine the application in space of laws from the nature of these laws as real or personal were impracticable, since the criteria were unreal.[81] Nevertheless, the claim that these criteria were common to all legal systems laid the foundations for the development of uniform rules of Private International Law.

In the third place, it relied on *natural law*, if only to counteract the first and second tenets.[82] The principle that *statuta odiosa*, repugnant foreign laws, need not be applied by courts of other countries, drew upon general standards derived from reasoning outside the limited sphere of the domestic law of the court called upon to apply foreign law.

In the fourth place, if only in order to evade its own pitfalls, the statutist theory gave an opportunity to the parties to indicate a *choice of law*, either expressly or by implication, in a limited number of circumstances. It established the importance of choice of law by the parties.[83]

| These four elements, the international, the universalistic, the ethical and the voluntaristic, have all contributed to the subsequent development of Private International Law.

Section 8. The French School in the 16th Century – Dumoulin and D'Argentré

12. The French school of the 16th century made its own contribution to the further refinement of the statutist doctrine, but its principal importance lies in the fact that it handled the technique of the statutists in a manner which prepared a later and entirely new approach. Its outstanding representatives,

---

[80] See below, sec. 9, pp. 121–126.
[81] See Gutzwiller, *Hague Rec.*, at p. 312.
[82] See Meijers, *Hague Rec.*, p. 630.
[83] Meijers, *ibid.*, p. 633 ff.

Dumoulin (1500–1566)[84] and D'Argentré (1519–1590),[85] showed highly individual, though opposing tendencies.[86] Dumoulin relied (though only in a limited number of cases) on the express or implied intention of the parties to select the law applicable. He is largely responsible for the introduction of the free choice of law into Private International Law.[87]

D'Argentré, under the influence of feudal ideas, expanded the range of rules which he regarded as *statuta realia* and restricted, correspondingly, the number of rules which, in his opinion, were to be treated as *statuta personalia*.[88] The French school of the 16th century, which was centred in the North, thus completed a development which had begun in the southern part of France *in* the late 13th and early 14th centuries. There Révigny and Belleperche had asserted the right of the local sovereign to enact special legislation overriding the *jus commune* and foreign law. D'Argentré pushed this development to a stage where the principles were reversed. If possible a statute is to be regarded as *realis*; only in exceptional circumstances is a personal character to be attributed to it. With the disappearance of the unilateral character of *statuta personalia* and *realia* this means no longer that every court must | disregard foreign law and must apply the *lex fori*. Since the doctrine of *statuta personalia* and *realia* now covers foreign law as well, it means, in the great majority of cases, courts, wherever situate, must apply the *lex situs* on the ground that most rules of law are by their nature *statuta realia* designed to affect property and are by their nature restricted in space so as to operate only in the country in which they have been enacted. Yet neither Dumoulin nor D'Argentré abandoned the statutist doctrine as such, much as their own teachings suggested such a course. In particular, like the Italian, the French school failed to show why foreign laws, whether personal or real, could claim to be applied by courts outside the territory for which they had been enacted. The answer to this question was given by the Dutch writers of the 17th century.

---

[84] Gutzwiller, *Hague Rec.* 29 (1929 IV), p. 230; Meylan in *Mélanges Fournier* (1929), p. 511; Meili in *Niemeyer's Z.*, 5 (1895), pp. 362, 452; Lainé, I, 223; Laborderie, *Clunet* 1921, p. 79; Gamillscheg, *Der Einfluss Dumoulin's auf die Entwicklung des Kollisionsrechts* (1955).

[85] Gutzwiller, *loc. cit.*; Meili, *loc. cit.*, at p. 371; Lainé, I, 311; Barbey, *Rev. hist. de droit français et étranger*, 19–20 (1940–41), 397 ff.; de Nova, *Hague Rec.* 118 (1966 II), at pp. 447–448.

[86] For details see especially Meijers, *loc. cit.*, at pp. 639, 640, n. 3, 641; Wächter, *A.c.P.*, 24 (1841), at p. 295, n. 132; p. 302, n. 147; 25 (1842), p. 190, n. 136, p. 384.

[87] For details see Meijers, *loc. cit.*, pp. 645, 649, 652, who attributes (p. 610) the earliest reliance on the intention of a party to Butrigarius.

[88] For details see Meijers, *Hague Rec.* 49 (1934 IV), pp. 637, 641.

Section 9. The Dutch School – Comity

13. With one notable exception, the Dutch school[89] of the late 17th century shows a strange discord. In all matters of practice Dutch writers adhered to the technique of the statutists, but they also showed another side. They were much exercised by the question why the courts of one country apply the laws of another country, be they personal or real. As shown above, this question had never been put either by the Italian or the French writers, who relied on the division of legislative powers as a principle of Private International Law, embodied originally in a rule of Roman law,[90] the universal validity of which was never questioned. Yet this problem was not merely a theoretical one. D'Argentré's attitude, which insisted that, with few exceptions, all statutes are real, had seriously undermined the universalistic approach to Private International Law. If most statutes purport only to operate within the territory of the legislature which enacted them, it becomes impossible to justify the application of those laws elsewhere by relying on the extraterritorial effect of personal statutes to which *statuta realia* formed an exception.[91] It must not be forgotten either, that the Dutch writers in the second half of the 17th century were acquainted with Bodin's[92] | and Grotius'[93] works. These confirmed the division of legislative powers between States but did not bear out any specific duties of States to apply the laws of other countries in given circumstances. There was a division of legislative competence but no system of mutual enforcement of laws. The universalistic approach to Private International Law to the effect that foreign laws of a particular character apply everywhere by reason of their nature had been refuted. There remained only a division of competence between States to legislate and a true conflict of laws. The application and enforcement of the law of other States, like all other international intercourse was determined by rules of international law.

An answer was attempted by P. Voet (1619–1677) when he said –

"nonnunquam dum populus vicinus vicini mores *comiter* vult observare et ne multa bene gesta turbarentur, de moribus statuta territorium statuentis, inspecto effectu, solent egredi"[94]

---

[89] For lit. see Gutzwiller, *Hague Rec.* 29 (1929 IV), p. 325, n. 2; see also Meijers, *Hague Rec.* 49 (1934 III), at pp. 663–670; de Nova, *Hague Rec.* 118 (1966 II), at pp. 448–451 and the writers cited below in n. 92 and at p. 123, n. 97.

[90] See above, p. 111.

[91] Gutzwiller, *Hague Rec.*, at p. 326.

[92] See Yntema, in *Vom deutschen zum europäischen Recht*, II (1963), p. 65 at p. 74; (1966), 65 *Mich.L.R.*, 1 at p. 18; (1963), 12 *A.J.Comp.L.*, 474.

[93] See Huber, *Praelectiones Juris Civilis Romani et hodierni* (1689), II. 1. 3. 12.

[94] *De statutis eorumque concursu* (1661), 4. 2. 17; Gutzwiller, *loc. cit.*, p. 326, n. 1; Meijers, *Hague Rec.*, p. 664, n. 1 with further texts; Yntema, *loc. cit.*, p. 78, n. 37; Grotius, *De jure belli ac pacis* lib. 1, cap. III, para. 21.2.

and again –

"statuta cuiuscunque sint generis, jus dicentis territorium neque propalam neque per consequentiam egredi. Nisi ex comitate. Ideo malui, id est tutius esse judicabam, ad solam humanitatem recurrere, qua populos vicinus vicini decreti comiter observat".[95]

His son Johannes (1647–1714) proclaimed the same principle:

"de statutis personalibus non ita per generales regulas definiri potest, quousque alter alteriius, statuta ac decreta ex comitate servet".[96]

It is usual to credit Huber (1624–1694) with the presentation of the new doctrine of comity. While this is not strictly accurate, the credit must go to Huber for having combined the local doctrine of comity, which replaced the universalistic concept of Private International Law, with the international doctrine based upon a division of legislative competence. His doctrine is well expressed in the three maxims which restate the teachings of the Dutch school:

| (1) The laws of every sovereign authority have force within the boundaries of its State and bind all subject to it, but not beyond.[97]

(2) Those are held to be subject to a sovereign authority who are found within the boundaries, whether they be there permanently or temporarily.[98]

(3) Those who exercise authority so act from comity that the laws of each nation which are enforced within its own boundaries should retain their effect, so far as they do not prejudice the power or rights of another State of its subjects.[99]

---

[95] *Mobilium et immobilium natura* (1666); Gutzwiller, *loc. cit.*, p. 326, n. 1.

[96] Gutzwiller, p. 327, n. 1. See Yntema, *loc. cit.*, 79.

[97] *Praelectiones*, II. 1.3.2; *Heedendaegse Rechtsgeleertheit*, I. 3.4; *De jure civitatis*, III. 4.1.14. For the text of the *Praelectiones* see Lorenzen (1919), 13 *Ill.L.R.*, 375; *Selected Articles* (1947), pp. 136 ff.; Llewelfryn Davies (1937), 18 *British Yb.Int.L.*, 49; Meili, *Zeitschrift für Internationales Privatrecht*, 7 (1898), p. 189; see also 3 *Dallas* 370–377 (1797) – see Nadelmann in *Jus et Lex, Festgabe für Gutzwiller* (1959), 263 at p. 267; Lainé, II, 199; Gutzwiller, *loc. cit.*, p. 327, n. 1. For variants in the text of *De jure civitatis* see Kollewijn, *Geschiedenis van de Nederlandse Wetenschap van het International Privaatrecht tot 1880* (1937), p. 132.

[98] *Praelectiones*, II, 1. 3.2; *Heedendaegse Rechtsgeleertheit*, I.3.5; *De jure civitatis, loc. cit.*; "intra terminos eius exercita" (Rodenburg). See Yntema, *loc. cit.*, p. 76.

[99] *Praelectiones*, II, 1.3.2; *Heedendaegse Rechtsgeleertheit*, I. 3, 6; *De jure civitatis*, III. 4.1 (3 ed.); III, 10 (1st ed.). The Dutch text (*Heedendaegse Rechtsgeleertheit*) is significant: it says: "de hooge machten van yder landt bieden elkander de handt ten einde de rechten van yder op elk syn onderdanen, schoon elders zynde soo verre gelden, als het niet is strydig met de macht of het recht van des anderen in syn bedryf"; cp. Asser, *Schets van het International Privaatrecht*, Intr.s. 5: international benevolence, Evrigenis, *loc. cit.*, p. 326.

14. *The theoretical basis of Huber's doctrine.* The *international* basis of Huber's doctrine emerges from his first rule which proceeds from the division of legislative competence among States and points to the jurisdiction of each State to legislate for its own subjects and in relation to its own territory. The *territorial* character of this legislative jurisdiction emerges from the second rule which limits the range of subjects to persons who are permanently or temporarily resident within the territory. The *local nature* of rules of Private International Law is set out in Huber's third rule. There are no principles of Private International Law which can claim universal validity.

The significance of the third rule is, however, obscured by Huber's reliance on comity. Doubts about its meaning have detracted from the effectiveness of the rule, a defect which was all the more serious since Huber's influence upon the development of English and American Pri|vate International Law was decisive. Taken as a minimum requirement it is equal to courtesy.[100] Taken as a maximum requirement it must be identical with legal duty.[101] Some help can be obtained from Huber himself in *Heedendaegse Rechtsgeleertheit*[102] when he added, after formulating his three principles,

"From this it is clear that the decision of such cases is part of the law of nations and not, properly speaking, of civil law, inasmuch as it does not depend on the individual pleasure of the higher powers of each country, but on the mutual convenience of the sovereign powers and their tacit agreement with each other".[103]

Thus according to Huber there was no duty arising by the nature of foreign private law to apply it (as the statutists assumed). Instead, customary international law (the tacit pact between States)[104] established a duty to give full

---

[100] Meijers, *Hague Rec.*, at p. 664, demonstrates the difference between the terms "de summo jure", "de necessitate" on the one hand, and of "de humanitate", "de comitate" on the other hand. See also Yntema, *op. cit.*, II, p. 76, n. 30; p. 79, n. 40, n. 44.

[101] For early examples of the notion that comity equals legal duty see *Warrender v. Warrender* (1835) 12 Ch. & F. 488 at p. 530: *not ex comitate sed ex debito justitiae; Watson v. Renton* (1972) 1 Bell's Cases 92, 102, cited by Nadelmann in *Jus et Lex, Festgabe für Gutzwiller* (1959), 263, at p. 275; Livermore, *Distinctions on the questions which arise from the Contrariety of the Positive Laws of different States and Nations* (New Orleans 1828); Gutzwiller, *Hague Rec.* 29 (1929 IV), pp. 340, 348; van Wesel, *Commentarii ad Novas Constitutiones*, Art. 13, n. 28: international legal duty; cp. Suyling, *De Statutentheorie in Nederland gedurende de 17de Eeuw* (1893), p. 52.

[102] I. 3. 7.

[103] See also *Praelectiones*, II. 1.3.1: "quamquam ipsa quaestio magis ad jus gentium quam ad jus civile pertineat quatenus quid diversi populi inter se servare debeant, ad juris gentium rationes pertinere manifestum est"; see also Meijers, *loc. cit.*, p. 668, note.

[104] For the "tacit pact" of States see Grotius, *De jure belli ac pacis, Prolegomena*, 1, 15–17, 26, 40; Yntema, *op. cit.*, II, pp. 76, 81, 83, 84 and 85, n. 65. See also Kollewijn, *loc. cit.*, p. 133. But see Huber, *De Iure civitatis*, III, 10, Nos. 1 and 2: "etsi non teneantur ex pacto vel necessitate subordinationis". And see Meijers, *loc. cit.*, p. 667, n. 2.

effect to foreign law, *once a State has decided generally to apply foreign law in the particular circumstances.*

Put in another way, the stress laid on comity served to underline that foreign law need not be enforced as such and that no more than a general respect for foreign law, once chosen to apply in the particular circumstances of the case, was called for. Thus Huber may have envisaged a doctrine of acquired rights[105] for the limited purpose of | countering the doctrine of the statutists rather than as the basis for establishing a duty to recognise private rights under customary international law.[106] Thus understood the respect postulated for foreign acquired rights may have served only as a motive for the consistent application of foreign law which would not apply *proprio motu*, as the statutists would have had it, but not as a principle requiring the application of foreign law as a matter of duty.[107]

15. Huber put his axioms into practice in his little treatise on the Conflict of Laws, as he aptly called the subject strictly in accordance with the legal situation as he saw it. In this treatise he abandons completely the statutist technique. The facts of the case are linked to one of several legal systems which may be applicable with the help of connecting factors such as domicile, place of contracting, place of performance, situs, place of action and the intention of the parties. For reasons which will be set out below it can pass as an introduction to Private International Law in England and in all countries which have adopted the common law. Nevertheless, as understood by Anglo-American writers and courts, Huber's doctrine was not entirely consistent. On the one hand it recognised the territoriality of laws based upon the international division of legislative competence and proclaimed an international custom to apply foreign territorial law which has operated in a particular instance. On the other hand, it rejected the statutist doctrine which determined the application of laws in space by reference to the nature of rules of law, but offered no substitute rules for determining when foreign law must be regarded as having operated territorially. Huber's treatise provided a number of examples with solutions showing the individual connecting factors, but no set of detailed independent rules of Private International Law. It was reasonably clear that, if all the facts arose within the legislative competence of country A, the courts of country B were to apply the law of A. If, however, the facts showed connections with several countries, the doctrine

---

[105] *Praelectiones*, II, 1.3.3.

[106] Cp. Meijers, *loc. cit.*, at p. 670, citing in addition to *Praelectiones*, II, 1.3.3, *Heedendaegse Rechtsgelerthejt*, I. 3.8. and 10; Kollewijn above p. 123, n. 97, at pp. 145, 146, but see pp. 138, 142; Yntema, *Vom deutschen zum europäischen Recht*, II (1963), 65 at pp. 75 ff.; (1966), 65 *Mich.L.R.*, at pp. 19 ff.

[107] This insight may prove helpful when the place of the doctrine of acquired rights in English and American law must be examined.

of territoriality as such, sanctioned by comity, could not provide a reliable guide for a choice of law. Instead, guidance had to be found, once again, *either* in tests chosen by any one system of municipal law according to its own |notion of policy and justice *or* in tests chosen *a priori* upon the basis of certain fundamental principles alleged to be of international origin and validity.

The Dutch school gave birth to modern Private International Law. Special rules of the *lex fori*, and not the nature of domestic and foreign rules of private law determine whether municipal or foreign law must be applied. The question remained open, however, whether the Private International Law of the forum is strictly domestic law or whether it is *either* determined *or* controlled by Public International Law.

Section 10. The Subsequent Development of the Doctrine of Huber – England[108]

16. In its own time, the Dutch doctrine failed to gain adherents in continental Europe, where courts and writers remained faithful to the statutist doctrine up to the middle of the 19th century. It succeeded in England and in the United States, whence it returned to stimulate continental Private International Law. It could gain an easy foothold in England because the specific problems of Private International Law which had exercised the minds of lawyers in continental Europe for the last 500 years had not attracted much attention in England and because, when they did present themselves, English courts could approach them in accordance with the most recent Dutch technique, unfettered by the ballast of statutist learning which hindered progress abroad.

Until then, questions of choice of law had been sidestepped and had been answered without the help of rules of Private International Law. Either they were treated as questions of jurisdiction or they were solved by the application of a uniform system of laws deemed to be of universal application. If treated as questions of jurisdiction, and if English common law courts were competent, English law applied as a matter of course; if the English common law courts were not competent the case did not come up for trial at all in England. Alternatively, if the courts of Staple and Piedpowder, which heard disputes of foreign merchants in England, the Court of Admiralty, which exercised jurisdiction in cases arising on the high seas or abroad, or the courts of arbitration set up by the merchants themselves, assumed jurisdiction, they relied | on the *Law Merchant* as a uniform system of universal applicati-

---

[108] Sack in *Law, A Century of Progress*, III (1937), pp. 322 ff.; Gutzwiller, *Hague Rec.* 29 (1929 IV), pp. 332 ff.

on.[109] They never developed a system of choice of law.[110] It is true that earlier the Norman and the English part of the population had lived according to their personal law. It is also clear that in matters of distribution of personality, the ecclesiastical courts, which were charged with the administration of this branch of law in England, applied the law of the ecclesiastical province in which the accused had last resided, if the custom at the place of residence of the deceased and of the situs of the goods differed from each other.

Since English law was always applicable if the common law courts had jurisdiction, actions involving a foreign element only could not be tried in the absence of a venue in England. As in the Netherlands and Northern France in early feudal times,[111] jurisdiction and choice of law were closely connected. The contest was therefore an internal one between the jurisdiction of the common law courts and the Admiralty Court; indirectly it was between common law and law merchant, between English domestic law and uniform law, both of which were applicable in England. In the 18th century the attitude towards the exclusion of foreign law began to change. The common law courts began to apply the law merchant, first as a fact, and then as law. Lord Mansfield completed the process by incorporating the law merchant into English law. Thereby it lost its international and assumed a national character. Thus it became necessary to determine what law applied in cases involving a foreign element which were formerly decided according to the law merchant. This movement was assisted by other factors, among them the circumstance that foreign judgments had become enforceable in England (1607) and that the Privy Council now had occasion to hear cases from foreign possessions. Sitting as a court of appeal from a colonial court, it applied the local law as the law of the court. Throughout the first three-quarters of the 18th century cases were few,[112] and | the reasons for applying foreign law were drawn from foreign writers.[113]

---

[109] The same applied to the Curia Regis, the Chancellor's court, the Star Chamber and the Council.

[110] If it was unavoidable to consider foreign law, the experts in civil law were consulted.

[111] See above sec. 5, No. 6, pp. 109–110.

[112] *Dungannon* v. *Hackett* (1702), 1 Eq.Ca.Abr. 289; *Daws* v. *Pindar* (1675), 2 Mod. 45; *Blanskard* v. *Galdy* (1693), 4 Mod. 222; *Robinson* v. *Bland* (1760), 2 Burr. 1077; 1 W.Bl. 234, 256: contract; *Mostyn* v. *Fabrigas* (1774), 1 Cowp. 161, 171: tort; *Scrimshire* v. *Scrimshire* (1752), 2 Hag. Cons. 395: marriage; *Pipon* v. *Pipon* (1744), Amb. 25, 799; *Thorne* v. *Watkins* (1750), 2 Ves. sen 35: succession; *Solomon* v. *Ross* (1764), 1 H.Bl. 131; Wallis-Lyne, *Irish Chancery Reports* (1839), 59 n.; *Jollet* v. *Deponthieu* (1769), 1 H.Bl. 132 (n); *Neale* v. *Cottingham* (1770), 1 H.Bl. 132 n.; Wallis-Lyne, *Irish Chancery Rep.* (1839), 54: bankruptcy.

[113] Voet, Huber, Gail, Mynsinger and others; see Anton (1956), 5 *I.C.L.Q.*, 534, 538 ff.

17. The general principle behind these cases which has inspired English Private International Law was formulated by Lord Mansfield in *Holman* v. *Johnson:*[114]

"Every action here must be tried by the law of England, but the law of England says that in a variety of circumstances ... the law of the country where the cause of action arose shall govern".[115]

Following Huber and the Dutch school, Lord Mansfield acknowledged that all laws are territorial and that it is for English law to determine whether and in what circumstances foreign law is to be applied in England. Having affirmed the local character of choice of law rules, Lord Mansfield's subsequent reference to the place of birth of the action abroad, while intended once more to emphasise the territorial character of law, introduced a static and undefined element inasmuch as it could be regarded as attributing a territorial character to a cause of action on the strength of an overriding division of territorial competences, and not on the basis of the Private International Law of the forum only. The Dutch school did not provide any general clues for ascertaining the place where a cause of action arises, and relied instead on connecting factors (such as domicile, place of contracting, place of performance, situs, etc.) freely adopted by the local choice of law rules. While these serve well the dual purpose of appearing as local rules and of pinpointing the territorial law where the cause of action arose, they cannot be said to fulfil necessarily both these tests if the situation or transaction in issue is centred in two or more countries. A marriage settlement made in one country by persons domiciled in two other countries whose property is situated in yet another provides such an example. Here the doctrine of territoriality does not provide an answer. It serves a useful purpose only as long as all the facts of a case arise in one | country, while the action is brought in another. This ambiguity in Lord Mansfield's formulation was soon to lead to a new search for a general overriding principle which permitted to localise causes of action; otherwise a vicious circle might be perpetuated, for English law, which was said to refer to the law of the country where the cause of action arose, would itself have to define whether a cause of action arose abroad.[116]

The next 60 years witnessed only a slow growth in England of this new branch of the law. Few cases came before the courts; writers, too, were

---

[114] (1775), 1 Cowp. 341, 343; see also Lord Stowell in *Dalrymple* v. *Dalrymple* (1811), 2 Hag. Con. 54.

[115] At p. 343. Cp. *Harford* v. *Morris* (1776), 2 Hag. Ecc. 423, 430, 434. But see Lord Mansfield in *Robinson* v. *Bland* (1760), 1 W.Bl. 234, 246 (local, personal statutes).

[116] See below, sec. 13, No. 22, pp. 135–138, for this aspect of the doctrine of acquired rights.

incapable of giving a lead, and the literature in England up to the middle of the 19th century was insignificant. The sterile statutist doctrines still held their own.[117]

Section 11. The United States

18. In the United States, the diversity of State legislation encouraged a vigorous interest in this new branch of the law.[118] Within the short period of 6 years three major works[119] appeared, one of which was of outstanding importance. Story's *Commentaries on the Conflict of Laws* | was based on English and American law and on the writings of the French and Dutch schools. It was the first modern treatise on this subject, but on general principles Story had little to say, and what he said was not far removed from his Dutch forerunners. His maxims were these:

(1) "The first ... maxim ... is that every nation possesses an exclusive sovereignty and jurisdiction within its own territory. The direct consequence ... is that the laws of every State affect and bind directly all property ... within its territory, and all persons who are resident within it ... and all contracts made and acts done within it."[120]

---

[117] Jabez Henry, *The Judgment of the Court of Demarara in the case of Odwin v. Forbes, ... To which is prefixed a Treatise on the Difference between Personal and Real Statutes and its Effects on Foreign Judgments, Contracts, Marriage and Wills*, XVI, 296 pp. (1823); see also de Nova, *Hague Rec.*, at p. 469. Clarke, *Summary of Colonial Laws* (1834); Burge, *Commentaries on Colonial and Foreign Laws generally, and in their Conflict with each other and with the Law of England* (1838): Wheaton, *Elements of International Law*, I (1836), p. 136; Reddie, *Inquiries in International Law* (1842); Hosack, *Treatise on the Conflict of Laws in England and Scotland* (1847); see Lorenzen (1934), 48 *Harv. L.R.*, 15, at p. 19; Harrison, *Clunet*, 1880, p. 429. Prater, *Cases illustrative of the Conflict of Laws between the Laws of England and Scotland* (1835); Dwarris, *General Treatise on Statutes* (1830–1831), Pt. II, pp. 647–665.

[118] See the early cases cited by Nadelmann in *Ius et Lex, Festgabe für Gutzwiller*, 263, at p. 265.

[119] Livermore, *Distinctions on the questions which arise from the Contrariety of Positive Laws of different States and Nations*, New Orleans, 1828, and the comments by De Nova (1964), 8 *Am. J. of Legal History*, 136; *Diritto internazionale*, 16 (1962), I. 207; Kent, *Commentaries on American Law*, 1826–1930; Story, *Commentaries on the Conflict of Laws, Foreign and Domestic, in regard to Contracts, Rights and Remedies, and especially in regard to Marriages, Divorces, Wills, Successions and Judgments* (1834), 2 ed. (1841), XXXIV and 927 ff.; see the comments by Lorenzen, 48 *Harv.L.R.*, 15 (1934), *Selected Articles* (1947), P. 181; *Rev.crit.d.i.p.*, 1935, 295; Nadelmann in *Jus et Lex, Festgabe für Gutzwiller* (1959), 263, at p. 272; (1966), 65 *Mich.L.R.*, 1; (1961), 5 *Am. J. of Legal History*, 230. See also Gardner, *Institutes of International Law*, public and private, as settled by the Supreme Court of the United States, New York, 1860.

[120] Paras. 18, 20, 23. See Lorenzen (1923), 33 *Yale L.J.*, 736; (1934), 48 *Harv. L.R.*, 15, at p. 37; *Selected Articles*, p. 1, at p. 3, p. 181, at p. 199.

(2) "Another maxim ... is that no State ... can by its own law directly affect or bind property out of its own territory or bind persons not resident therein ... it would be ... incompatible with ... the sovereignty of all nations that one nation should be at liberty to regulate either persons or things not within its own territory."[121]

(3) "From these two maxims ... flows a third ... that whatever force ... the laws of one country have in another depends solely upon the laws ... of the latter ... upon its own express or tacit consent."[122]

This statement of principle comes very near to that of Huber, but Story's maxims are both fuller and more precise. The first maxim combines Huber's first and second principles. It expresses the international principle of territoriality in respect of persons, objects and acts. The second maxim has no counterpart in Huber's work. It rejects the statutist doctrine of the extra-territoriality of *statuta personalia.* The third reduces the doctrine of comity from an international duty to a domestic motive. There is no duty imposed by customary international law to apply foreign law. Private International Law is domestic law unfettered by any external rules. The era of 19th-century Private International Law had arrived.[123] However, while this principle provides an acceptable working basis|for conflicts of laws involving several independent countries, it may be that Story, a Federal Judge, failed to give sufficient attention to the specific problems which can arise in the United States, a Federal State, where private law is not uniform. Here the insight that Private International Law is municipal law unfettered by overriding principles of international law may be counterbalanced by the requirements of the Constitution. This specifically American problem has since been presented by recent American writers as 20th-century Private International Law.[124]

Section 12. Modern Private International Law – Wächter, Savigny

19. The success of Story's work in England and on the Continent of Europe, where the statutist doctrine had lingered on, was immediate.[125] The French

---

[121] See Lorenzen (1923), 33 *Yale L.R.*, 736, at p. 740; (1934), 48 *Harv.L.R.,* 15, at p. 37; Selected Articles p. 1, at pp. 5 ff.; 181, at p. 201, but see the critique by Mann, *Hague Rec.* 111 (1964 I), 1, at pp. 31–33.

[122] See also paras. 25, 33, 34, 35, 36, 38; see also Evrigenis, *loc. cit.,* at p. 326.

[123] The conclusions of Mann, *Hague Rec.* 111 (1964 I), 1, at p. 33, are diametrically opposed, but it is believed that they treat Story's approach to the conflict of laws in isolation, torn out of its historical setting and in the light of rules of Public International Law which had not yet reached the stage of refinement imputed to them by Mann.

[124] See below sects. 15–19, paras. 29–39, pp. 144–163.

[125] See, e.g., *Huber* v. *Steiner*, (1835), 2 Bing N.C. 200, at p. 211; Savigny, *System des heutigen gemeinen Rechts*, 8 (1849), p. 25 n. (a); Fœlix, *Traité de droit international privé*, (1843) ss. 9–11.

Civil Code of 1804 does not follow any particular doctrine of Private International Law, and it is a matter of doubt whether it adopted the statutist or the Dutch doctrine,[126] while the Austrian provisions in the Code of 1811 are regarded as statutist in conception.[127] In Germany, Wächter, in a thought-provoking article, reviewed the development of the conflict of laws in that country.[128] He was able to show that in the 17th and 18th centuries the classical doctrine of the statutists had been attacked by German writers[129] on the ground that it was "illdefined, capable of different meanings, uncertain and varying"[130] and had been modified in its fundamentals.[131] Even if laws are territorial,| it is not the duty of other countries to follow them,[132] no matter whether the territorial law is the *lex domicilii*[133] or the *lex situs*.[134] Moreover, the fact that a foreign country is competent according to international law to legislate within its own territory, does not prove that such country necessarily desires to subject every person and every object within it to its own laws,[135] and it may well be that it wishes to exclude them from their operation. The doctrine of acquired rights does not provide a solution since its only effect is to prohibit retroactive legislation.[136] If the doctrine of acquired rights, understood in a wider, territorial sense, were correct, every country would be obliged to pay unlimited respect to the laws of other countries, where such rights are alleged to have arisen, but such a submission to foreign law had never been asserted even by its protagonists.[137] The true purpose of the doctrine of acquired rights as a motive for the adoption of some choice of law rules and not as a legal precept requiring the application of foreign law in

---

[126] Gutzwiller, *Hague Rec.* 29 (1929 IV), p. 337, with lit. n. 3.

[127] Gutzwiller, *ibid.*, p. 337, n. 4.

[128] *Archiv für die zivilistische Praxis*, 24 (1841), pp. 230–311 (cited as Wächter, I), 25 (1842), pp. 150–200; 361–491 (cited as Wächter, II); see Nadelmann (1964), 13 *Am.J.Comp.L.*, 414; De Nova, *Hague Rec.* 118 (1966 II), 437, at pp. 452–456; and cp. Wengler (1961), 28 *Law & Contemp. Problems*, 822, 829, n. 31; Baade, *ibid.*, p. 675, n. 9, as regards Wächter's influence on Currie.

[129] I, 280 and notes 94–98 (lit.).

[130] I, 286.

[131] I, pp. 274, 275, n. 81 (lit.), 256–257: "Der neue Sprachgebrauch dagegen, der sich allmählig, ohne dass man Abweichung von Aelteren betrachtet zu haben scheint, bildete ist ein ganz anderer. *Statuta personalia* sind nach ihm die sämtlichen Gesetze welche am Wohnort einer Person gelten, von welchem Gegenstand, ob von Personen, Sachen oder Formen eines Geschäftes sie handeln mögen, *statuta realia*, das Recht welches am Orte gilt wo eine gewisse Sache liegt, *statuta mixta* das Recht welches am Orte gilt wo eine gewisse Handlung vorfiel."

[132] I, 287–288, 307, 310; II, 378.

[133] I, 287, 290, 292.

[134] I, 292.

[135] I, 299, 304, 310–311; II, 162.

[136] I, 300–301 and n. 145; II, 391.

[137] I, 301; II, 162, 170.

particular circumstances defined by some overriding legal principles had even been admitted by one of its exponents.[138] Wächter thus perceived that neither the claim of foreign law to apply (as the statutists believed) nor their foreign territorial character (as some supporters of the Dutch school thought) offered a guide for the court seized with the dispute. Such a court was faced with the determination of a –

"legal relationship which had either its origin abroad or in which foreigners participated or which otherwise has contacts abroad".[139]

From this he concluded: the court must follow its own domestic law[140] unless the statute law of the forum provides definite criteria for exercising a choice of law[141] or (it would seem) unless the common law|contains choice of law rules[142] or spatially conditioned rules.[143] In advocating a solution which pays particular regard to the limitations in space of the substantive rules of private law of the *forum*, Wächter took a dangerous step backwards towards the early practice of the postglossators; especially by insisting that the *lex fori* must be applied always, if it is mandatory in character *(jus cogens)*[144] he fell back on the learning of the statutists.[145] Finally, it was difficult to proclaim the existence of a general overriding principle, if it is the task of the parties to prove foreign law and not of the court to find it *proprio motu.*[146]

20. The credit for having shown a new approach goes normally to Savigny,[147] but in the main arguments he was preceded by Wächter. Savigny, too, refused to determine the application of laws in space in virtue of the nature of such laws;[148] he, too, refused to attach any importance to the alleged terri-

---

[138] I, 299 ff., especially pp. 301, 302–303 citing Maurenbrecher, *Deutsches Privatrecht* (2 ed.), I, 315: "die Regierung muss den Status des Fremden schützen so gut wie ihre Personen und ihre Vermögen, so weit sie diese überhaupt als wohlerworbene Rechte bei sich anerkannt ..."

[139] I, p. 236–237: "Rechtsverhältnis welches entweder im Auslande begründet wurde oder bei welchem Ausländer beteiligt sind, oder welches sonst mit dem Auslande in einer Beziehung steht."

[140] I, 237, 261, 264–266; II, 162.

[141] I, 239–241, 267, 268.

[142] I, 242, 255, 267, 268; II, 170, 180, n. 302.

[143] I, 262, 264, 268; II, 362, 364, 385, 387.

[144] I, p. 266; II, 405.

[145] II, 362 (property relations between spouses, personal statute), p. 364 (succession – real statutes); pp. 384–386 (movables – real statutes).

[146] I, 310.

[147] *System des heutigen Römischen Rechts*, 8 (1849); for lit. see Gutzwiller, *Der Einfluss Savigny's auf die Entwicklung des Internationalprivatrechts* (1923); *Hague Rec.* 29 (1929 IV), pp. 352 ff., Neuhaus, *Rabels Z.*, 15 (1949), pp. 364–381; Yntema (1952), 2 *A.J.Comp.L.*, 297, 309; Maridakis in *Festschrift für Lewald* (1953), 309; Coing, *Eranion Maridakis*, III (1964), 19; De Nova, *Hague Rec.* 118 (1966 II), 437, 456–464.

[148] Savigny, pp. 2, 122 ff.

toriality of laws[149] on the ground, firstly, that no one territory alone is normally involved and, secondly, that the doctrine of acquired rights is fallacious.[150] Both Wächter and Savigny offered a new solution. The legal relationship before the court was the starting point. The court must determine what law applies. At this stage, however, the two scholars parted company. Wächter relied on the rules of domestic and conflict of laws of the forum.[151] Savigny believed that the rules of conflict of laws were of universal application based on the –

"international community of nations in interchange with each other".[152]

| The test was simple. He believed that–

"for each legal relationship that legal system must be ascertained to which this legal relationship pertains or is subject having regard to its particular nature".[153]

The legal relationship and its seat were thus made the elements of all rules of Private International Law. It was only necessary to give formal expression to the tests (now known as connecting factors) according to which the seat was determined by the community of nations.

The number of legal relationships which require to be connected with a particular system of laws is of course infinite, and it may be, as will be shown below, that an almost infinite choice of law or spatially conditioned choice of law rules can and should be ascertained and developed. However, ever since Huber had written his account of the conflict of laws it was clear that for the purpose of the latter legal relationships had been reduced to a limited number of typical situations which relate to the person, property, contract, tort, succession and a small number of others.[154] Each of these can be attributed a centre at a place which can be determined with some certainty: domicile, residence, situs, place of contracting, place of performance, place where an act has been completed and so on. These tests are now known as connecting factors. Savigny believed that they were of universal application. Story and Wächter, whose opinion turned out to be right, thought that they were not, but differed from country to country.[155]

---

[149] P. 25.

[150] P. 132, para. 361 (5).

[151] See above, p. 132; cp. Savigny, p. 127.

[152] "Völkerrechtliche Gemeinschaft der mit einander verkehrenden Nationen", see Savigny, pp. 28, 118.

[153] "Dass bei jedem Rechtsverhältnis dasjenige Recht aufgesucht wurde welchem dieses Rechtsverhältnis seiner eigentümlichen Art nach angehört oder unterworfen ist"; see Savigny, p. 27.

[154] Neuhaus, *loc. cit.*, 364, at p. 371.

[155] Cp. Neuhaus, *loc. cit.*, 364, 368.

21. At first sight it might seem that Wächter and Savigny halted halfway when they made the legal relationship the starting point. It might even be argued that the statutist notion according to which all laws are personal or real had been transposed into the individual case; all legal situations have a personal, proprietary, contractual or delictual character, or they fall within the realm of succession or procedure. It might be objected that legal relationships exist only in virtue of some system of laws and that an attempt to ascertain the law applicable to a particular situation by linking a legal relationship to a legal system which|is to apply to it anticipates the choice of law.[156] Ideally only a set of facts can be connected with a legal system before it can be stated that a legal relationship exists. In reality no pure factual situation before the court induces a choice of law. The need to determine whether foreign, rather than domestic, law must be applied arises in practice if the plaintiff frames his claim or the defendant his reply according to some foreign law. Foreign law is not selected in the abstract but only in respect of a particular claim or defence. Thus the legal relationship is rightly treated as the object on which the rules of Private International Law operate. This conclusion opens up a new problem. Since legal relationships in the *abstract* form the principal element of domestic choice of law rules, which connect these relationstips with a particular system of laws with the help of connecting factors, and since the object of the dispute is a *concrete* legal relationship expressed in the form of a claim or defence, the integration of the concrete relationship into the abstract relationship formulated in the choice of rule causes a problem of interpretation which is known as characterization, or qualification.[157]

Whatever new problems came into being with it, the modern technique of handling questions of Private International Law had emerged.[158] Immediately following its birth, however, the search began again for some overriding firm principles which could determine when the forum should apply its own or foreign law.

Section 13. Modern Doctrines of Territoriality or Pseudo-Territoriality – Acquired Rights

22. The teachings of Story and Savigny exercised much influence upon Westlake[159] and Dicey[160] in England whose practical, empirical approach was in

---

[156] See von Bar, *Theorie und Praxis des internationalen Privatrechts*, I (2 ed. 1889), 107.

[157] See below sec. 27, Nos. 56–58, pp. 198–204.

[158] Neuhaus, *loc. cit.*, p. 366: "auf der Kopernikanischen Wende in der Fragestellung von einer schematischen Klassifizierung der Gesetze zur individualisierenden Suche nach dem natürlichen 'Sitz' jedes einzelnen Rechtsverhältnisses".

[159] *Private International Law* (1858).

[160] (1890), 6 *L.Q.R.*, 1; (1891), 7 *L.Q.R.*, 113; *Conflict of Laws* (1 ed. 1894).

sympathy with them. The legal basis of the English conflict of laws remained Lord Mansfield's pronouncement in *Holman* v. *Johnson*[161] to the effect that English rules of the conflict of laws, as part of English domestic law, refer to foreign law in certain circum|stances. Dicey never waivered in his adherence to this rule of English law.[162] However, he supplemented his firm belief in the local character of choice of law rules by an express reliance on the doctrine of acquired rights.[163] This doctrine is of some antiquity and can be traced to the postglossators,[164] though it is doubtful whether they wished to apply it to questions of the conflict of laws.[165] In juxtaposition with the common law rule expressed in *Holman* v. *Johnson*,[166] the principle of the protection of acquired rights makes little sense and is open to the charge of circuity. It has been refuted again and again by eminent writers who have shown that since rights exist only in virtue of some system of laws, the protection of foreign acquired rights assumes that foreign law has been applied; thus Private International Law which, it is said, must respect foreign acquired rights, must first determine by its own rules of the conflict of laws whether a right has been acquired.[167]

The researches of Nadelmann have traced the development of this idea by Dicey.[168] He acknowledged his indebtedness to Holland, whose *Elements of Jurisprudence* included the statement that the conflict of laws deals in reality with the recognition of rights created and defined by foreign law.[169] It is difficult to see how Holland reached this conclusion for his reference to Vattel is spurious and that to Wächter reverses the latter's thoughts.[170] It is possible that Holland derived it from Huber[171] whom he cited in the second edition of his work.

---

[161] (1775), 1 Cowp. 341, 343; see above p. 128.

[162] (1890), 6 *L.Q.R.*, 1, at pp. 3, 4, 6, 12, 13, 18, 20, 21; *Conflict of Laws* (3 ed. 1922), pp. 3, 4, 6, 7, 13, 14, 20.

[163] (1890), 6 *L.Q.R.*, 10, 11, 13.

[164] Horst Müller, *Der Grundsatz der Wohlerworbenen Rechte im internationalen Privatrecht* (1935), reviewed by Gutzwiller, *Rabels Z.*, 10 (1936), 1056.

[165] See Gutzwiller, *loc. cit.*

[166] (1775), 1 Cowp. 341, 343; see above, p. 128.

[167] Wächter, *Archiv für die zivilistische Praxis*, 24 (1841), 230, at p. 300 and note 146; 25 (1842), 361, at p. 391; Savigny, *System des heutigen Römischen Rechts* (1849), para. 361 (5), p. 132, Guthrie's transl. (2 ed. 1880), pp. 147 ff.; Lorenzen (1924) 33 *Yale L.J.* 736, *Selected Articles* (1947) 1; W. W. Cook (1924) 33 *Yale L.J.* 457, *The Logical and Legal Basis of the Conflict of Laws* (1942) 1; Arminjon, *Hague Rec.* 44 (1933 II) 1; Caswell (1959), 8 *I.C.L.Q.*, 268, at pp. 285–286.

[168] For details see Nadelmann, in *Ius et Lex, Festgabe für Gutzwiller* (1959), 263, at pp. 276–279; Yntema in *Festschrift für Rabel*, I (1953), 513, at p. 526, n. 29; Lipstein [1972 B], 31 *Cambridge L.J.*, 67–71.

[169] 1 ed. (1880), p. 288, and note 1; Dicey, *Conflict of Laws* (3 ed. 1922), pp. 3, 5, notes.

[170] Nadelmann, *loc. cit.* (above n. 168), 277, 278; for the revision of these references in subsequent editions see Nadelmann, p. 277, note 90, and p. 278.

[171] *Praelectiones*, II, 1.3.3; see above p. 124 and n. 105.

There are indications that Dicey was aware of the limited function|of the doctrine of acquired rights in Huber's system when he qualified his principle by stating:

"The word 'duly' [acquired] ... fixes in effect the limit of the application of General Principle I. This principle is ... only that rights which have been *in the opinion of English courts* [italics mine] properly and rightly acquired are ... enforceable here."[172]

Thus understood the doctrine of acquired rights does not suffer from the flaws expressed by its critics, limited as it is to providing a motive or explanation for applying foreign law and for applying it consistently, once chosen, but it has also become meaningless as a theory. Nevertheless a doctrine of acquired rights in the sense considered here may support the object of rules of Private International Law and may claim some practical merits which may have influenced Dicey when he said:

"... the principle of the enforcement of vested rights does not supply such a universal test. To admit this, however, is quite consistent with maintaining that this principle does define the object in the main aimed at by rules having reference to the conflict of laws or to the extra-territorial effect of rights."[173]

The court, in England at least, is invited, not to ascertain and to apply foreign law of its own motion when faced with a factual statement of claim, but to decide whether a claim brought in the light of some legal system[174] can be sustained. It is for the parties to submit a claim based on some legal system, and it is for the court in England to determine whether the claim as framed according to some foreign law is framed in accordance with that legal system which applies according to the English rules of the conflict of laws.[175] In the end, a choice must be made, and it must be made in accordance with English Private Inter|national Law, but the initiative lies with the parties who submit claims, counterclaims and defences which rely not merely on facts but combine facts with reliance on some foreign system of laws. Technically this insight may prove useful in many respects, as will be shown later on in connection with the discussion of characterisation and *renvoi*. If this was Dicey's view, his juxtaposition of a system of domestic rules of the conflict

---

[172] Dicey, *Conflict of Laws* (3 ed. 1922), pp. 23, 27; see also (1891), 7 *L.Q.R.*, 113, at p. 118. It was only the last step in the logical argument when the editors of the sixth edition (1949), pp. 11, 12, replaced the qualification that the right must have been "duly" acquired by the requirement that it must have been acquired "according to the English rules of the conflict of laws". For comments see Falconbridge (1950), 66 *L.Q.R.*, 104, 106; Mann (1949), 12 *M.L.R.*, 518, 520; Cavers (1950), 63 *Harv.L.R.*, 1278, 1280; Rheinstein (1950), 35 *N.Y.U.L.R.*, 180, 181.

[173] (1891), 7 *L.Q.R.*, 113, 118; *Conflict of Laws* (3 ed. 1922), p. 33.

[174] See above p. 135.

[175] Cp. Dicey, *Conflict of Laws* (3 ed. 1922), pp. 26, 27; (1891), 7 *L.Q.R.*, 113, 115.

of laws, unfettered by any overriding considerations or principles, and of a doctrine of acquired rights is not inconsistent. The former provides the legal basis; the latter serves to explain a technical device.

23. An additional practical observation is appropriate here. Private International Law is not exclusively concerned with the enforcement of rights by way of judicial process; it also serves to instruct the parties who are about to conclude some transaction, such as marriage or contract, whether to comply with the rules of this or that system of laws.[176] Any doctrine that Private International Law is exclusively concerned with the protection of foreign acquired rights would only be justifiable on one of two assumptions:

The first alternative assumption is that an international system of conflict of laws determines in what circumstances foreign law must be applied. In this case local courts would only be called upon to enforce rights which had been brought into existence by a legal system operating with universal effect. However, no such system exists in the international sphere; within a Federal State an overriding system of federal conflict of laws can provide such a framework, though no such system is believed to exist at the present time. At best, the experience in the United States shows that the law of a particular State can or cannot apply in the presence or absence of a clear connection with the State concerned.[177]

The second alternative assumption is that a strict system of territoriality exists coupled with the duty to enforce foreign rights which had come into being in accordance with the territorial laws of the particular country. The first part of this hypothetical principle formed the substance of the Dutch doctrine. As was shown above, only a small number of situations involving a foreign element arise exclusively within the confines of one particular territorial system of laws and, secondly, | that legal system does not necessarily wish to apply to the case in question. The second part of the hypothetical rule involves the question, also raised by the Dutch doctrine, whether foreign law which operates territorially must be applied by the courts in other countries as a matter of legal obligation of an international character, or whether the choice of law is a matter for the *lex fori*, in deference to its own sense of policy and convenience.[178] As will be shown later on[179] there are no overriding rules of international law which force one country to *apply* the territorial law of another country, even if the entire factual situation is centred in the latter. It follows that the duty to apply foreign law on the ground

---

[176] Arminjon, *loc. cit.*, p. 39.

[177] See below, sec. 16, No. 31, pp. 148–154.

[178] See above p. 124. For some modern views on comity see Cardozo J. in *Loucks* v. *Standard Oil* (1918), 224 N.Y. 99, 111, 120, N.E. 198, 201–202; *Dean* v. *Dean*, 241 N.Y. 240, 243; 149 N.E. 844, 846 (1924); Cheatham (1948), 51 *Harv.L.R.*, 361, 376 n. 39.

[179] Below sec. 21, Nos. 41–42, pp. 167–171.

that the cause of action arose within the legislative competence of a particular foreign country can only be found in some provision of the domestic law of the *forum*. The legal system which purports to protect rights which were acquired in a foreign country must first bring these rights into being.

24. A doctrine of Private International Law which is based upon a doctrine of territorially acquired rights and which avoids the pitfalls of a vicious circle must therefore assume that all causes of action are necessarily centred within the territory of one country only and that foreign law which has operated territorially must be applied everywhere if the cause of action arose within its legislative competence.

Such a doctrine was supplied by Beale[180] and through him inspired the First Restatement of the Conflict of Laws. In the first place, he overcame the difficulty that in most cases involving a foreign element the cause of action does not arise exclusively in one country by relying on tests selected arbitrarily upon *a priori* considerations.[181] In the second place, he identified the duty to apply the law of the foreign country with the duty to respect foreign sovereignty. The fallacy of this reason|ing is clear[182] if it is remembered, first, that the cause of action is initially located in the foreign country by the application of *a priori* principles provided by the author himself and, second, that the wish or disinclination of the foreign sovereign to determine the cause of action by his own laws is never considered. The *forum* is first made to confer legislative competence upon the foreign sovereign and is then employed to determine the material exercise of those powers. Nevertheless, as was indicated above[183] and will be shown below,[184] such a doctrine embodying a distribution and mutual respect of territorial legislative powers may be useful in controlling the ambit and the application of choice of law rules in a Federal State, such as the United States, where a maximum of respect is due to the law of Member States.[185]

---

[180] *A Treatise on the Conflict of Laws*, I (1935), para. 42.1, p. 274, para. 5.4, P. 53; III, pp. 1968, 1972; (1896), 10 *Harv.L.R.*, 168, at 170; and see the comments by de Sloovère (1936), 13 *N.Y.U.L.R.*, 333, 338, 342, 345; McClintock (1936), 84 *U.Pa.L.R.*, 309; Cook (1935), 35 *Col.L.R.*, 1154; Read (1935), 49 *Harv.L.R.*, 346, 347; Cheshire (1936), 52 *L.Q.R.*, 540; Falconbridge (1935), 13 *Can. Bar Rev.*, 531, 533; Rheinstein in *Festschrift für Rabel*, I (1954), 539, 585–586.

[181] See, e.g., as to contracts, *Treatise*, II, para. 322.4; torts, *Treatise*, II, para. 378.1. And see Cavers, *The Choice of Law Process* (1965), pp. 6–7.

[182] Cp. Beach (1917–1918), 27 *Yale L.J.*, 656–667, but see Taney C.J. in *Bank of Augusta v. Earle*, 13 Pet. 519, 589, 10 L.Ed. 274, 308 (1839).

[183] See p. 138.

[184] No. 38, p. 162.

[185] Rheinstein, *Festschrift für Rabel*, I (1954), 539–589; (1954–1955), 22 *U.Chi.L.R.*, 775–824; Cheatham (1953–1954), 28 *Vanderbilt L.R.*, 581; Cook, *Logical and Legal Basis*, p. 41; see *Commercial Travellers* v. *Wolfe* (1947), 331 US 586 91 L.Ed. 1687; *Alaska Packers Association* v. *Industrial Accident Comm'n*, 294 US 532 (1933); *Richards* v. *US*, 369 US 1

25. In the period between the two World Wars, the pendulum in the United States has swung in the opposite direction. Where formerly the doctrine of the territoriality of laws and of the protection of acquired rights had been most firmly entrenched, several new schools of thought took its place. It was the merit of Lorenzen to have led the way towards the dethronement of Beale's doctrine of acquired rights together with the dogmatic tests linking certain types of legal relations (operative facts) with particular countries or territories.[186] Thus Private International Law, especially in the Anglo-American world, reached its full maturity, a part of domestic law unfettered by any shackles, except | those which Public International Law imposed upon domestic law in general.[187]

Proceeding from the same basis as Lorenzen, the "local law" theory[188] put forward by W. W. Cook, that the forum neither applies foreign law nor enforces foreign acquired rights, but rights created by the *lex fori* in a form which approximates as closely as possible to similar rights abroad. In the words of W. W. Cook:

"The forum, when confronted by a case involving foreign elements, always applies its own law to the case, but in doing so adopts and enforces as its own law a rule of decision identical, or at least highly similar, though not identical, in scope with a rule of decision found in the system of law in force in another state[189] with which some or all of the foreign elements are connected ... The rule thus 'incorporated' into the law of the forum ... the forum ... enforces not a foreign right but a right created by its own law."[190]

1962; *Clay* v. *Sun Insurance etc.*, 377 US 179 (1964); *Hughes* v. *Fetter*, 341 US 609 (1951); *Allendorf* v. *Elgin, etc., Ry*, 8 Ill. 2d. 164, 133 N.E. (2d) 288 (1956); *Wells* v. *Simon Abrasive Co.*, 345 US 514 (1953); *Watson* v. *Employers, etc.*, 348 US 66 (1954); foreign law: *Home Ins. Co.* v. *Dick*, 281 US 397 (1930); de Sloovère (1935–1936), 13 *N.Y.U.L.R.*, 333 at p. 354 and notes 92, 93; Beach (1917–1918), 27 *Yale L.J.*, 565, at p. 662, 665; *Bond* v. *Hume*, 243 US 15, 21 (1916); Jackson (1945), 45 *Col.L.R.*, 1; Weintraub (1958–1959), 44 *Iowa L.R.*, 449; Ehrenzweig, *P.I.L.*, p. 63, n. 2, p. 34; Bernstein, *N.J.W.* 1965, 2273.

[186] (1924), 33 *Yale L.J.*, 736; *Selected Articles* (1947), pp. 1 ff. See also Goodrich (1950), 50 *Col.L.R.* 881–899; Harper (1947), 56 *Yale L.J.*, 1055–1077.

[187] See below No. 41, pp. 167–169.

[188] Cook, *The Logical and Legal Basis of the Conflict of Laws* (1942), 1 ff., at pp. 20–22; (1924), 33 *Yale L.J.*, 457 at pp. 475, 489; (1943), 21 *Can. Bar Rev.*, 249; (1943), 37 *Ill.L.R.*, 418; for comments see Rheinstein (1943), 10 *U.Chi.L.R.*, 446; Cavers (1943), 56 *Harv.L.R.*, 1170; Lorenzen (1943), 52 *Yale L.J.*, 680; Hancock (1944), 44 *Col.L.R.*, 579 = (1944), 5 *U. of Toronto L.R.*, 476; Cheatham (1944), 93 *U.Pa.L.R.*, 112; (1945), 58 *Harv.L.R.*, 366, at pp. 386–387; Keith (1943), 59 *L.Q.R.*, 378; Morris, *ibid.*, p. 379; Falconbridge (1943), 21 *Can. Bar Rev.*, 329 = (1943), 37 *Ill.L.R.*, 375; see also Lorenzen (1924), 33 *Yale L.J.*, 736, *Selected Articles* (1947), p. 1 ff.; in (1943), 52 *Yale L.J.*, 680, 681, he traces the doctrine back to Hohfeld (1909), 9 *Col.L.R.*, 492, (1910), *ibid.*, 283, 520.

[189] At pp. 20–21.

[190] See the words of Cardozo J. in *Loucks* v. *Standard Oil Co.* (above, p. 139, n. 178), para. 4: "A foreign statute is not law in this state ... No law can exist as such except the law of the land but ... vested rights shall be protected."

In so far as Cook denied that *a priori* considerations lead to the location of a cause of action or right in a foreign country and that such rights must be recognised or enforced elsewhere, he accomplished the same task as Lorenzen. The attempt to substitute "locally created rights" for the vanished "foreign created rights" adds no new insight, once it is accepted with Lorenzen that Private International Law is unadulterated domestic law. It adds no new insight into the question why foreign law is applied, though it does seek to explain how it is applied.

26. The manner in which foreign law is introduced into the law of the forum has occupied writers, especially in Italy, who found it difficult | to reconcile the notion that the forum is exclusively subject to its own law with the postulate that the former may have to apply law which is foreign in origin. Doctrines of incorporation, such as those of the *rinvio ricettizio o materiale*[191] or the adoption of "special" rules of domestic law side by side with those of domestic law proper,[192] have sought to provide a solution to a problem which has little practical importance.[193]

27. In the light of this evaluation of the local law theory it is unnecessary to examine the contention that in reality two separate local law theories have been expounded.[194] It must suffice to indicate that the local law doctrine adopted by Learned Hand in the District Court for the Southern District of New York and in the Circuit Court of Appeals[195] may be less radical. According to the latter, a right must have come into existence within the legislative competence of a foreign territorial sovereign in accordance with *a priori* considerations suggested by Beale, but the enforcement of such a right is not a legal duty incumbent upon other countries as a legal duty. Instead they grant relief which is as nearly as possible identical with the right created abroad. Thus Learned Hand J. may have accepted the doctrine of the terri-

---

[191] Monaco, *L'efficacia della legge nello spazio* (2 ed. 1964), para. 13, pp. 28–31, and note 1 with lit. See also Ehrenzweig, *P.I.L.*, p. 61.

[192] Monaco, *loc. cit.*, p. 30 and note 2; Ago, *Teoria del diritto internazionale privato* (1934), pp. 99–100; *Hague Rec.* (1936 IV) 243, pp. 294 ff., at 301 ff., 304; *Lezioni di diritto internazionale privato* (1939), p. 73 ff.; Maury, *Hague Rec.* 57 (1936 III), 325, at pp. 381–383; Sperduti, *Saggri di teoria generale del diritto internazionale privato* (1967), pp. 91–95; Bernadini, *Produzione di norme giuridiche mediante rinvio* (1966), *passim.*

[193] Except for the answer to the question whether the correctness of the application of foreign law by a lower court can be the object of an appeal on points of law only; see Zaytay, *Contribution à l'étude de la condition de la loi étrangère en droit international privé français*, pp. 163–173, *idem* in *Anwendung ausländischen Rechts im international Privatrecht* (Dierk Müller ed., 1968), pp. 193–213; C. David, *La loi étrangère devant le juge du fond* (1965), p. 195, No. 258.

[194] Cavers (1950), 63 *Harv.L.R.*, 822–832.

[195] *Guiness* v. *Miller*, 291 F. 769, 770 (S.D.N.Y. 1923); see also *Direktion der Diskontogesellschaft* v. *U.S. Steel Corporation*, 300 F. 741 (S.D.N.Y. 1924); *Louis-Dreyfus* v. *Paterson Steamship Ltd.*, 43 F. (2d) 824 (C.C.A. 2. Circ. 1930); *Siegmann* v. *Meyer*, 100 F. (2d) 367 (2 Circ. 1938).

toriality of laws but rejected the duty to respect foreign acquired rights or foreign sovereignty. In so doing he may have expounded a local law doctrine of a second degree. In the search for an answer to the question why foreign law is to be applied and whether any specific rules outside the discretion of the *lex fori* determine the choice, the local law doctrine | does not assist. It affirms that Private International Law is part of domestic law and is determined by the traditions and policies inherent in the latter.

Section 14. Sociological Neo-Statutists

28. During the second half of the 19th century and during the early part of the 20th century, codifications of Private International Law in Europe and elsewhere, except in common law countries and in Scandinavia, were much influenced by the sociological approach of Mancini.[196] It centres on nations, as shaped by territory, race, language, custom, history, laws and religion as the nuclei of modern international organisation. The link between the individual and a particular nucleus is not created by residence within one nation but by the tie of allegiance created by the possession of a given nationality; permanent residence and nationality may not coincide[197] but, unlike in the common law,[198] civil and political status are both determined by the same criterion. Accordingly the *lex patriae* applies, but if "voluntary" as distinct from "necessary" private law is involved the *lex patriae* may give way to another system of laws to be selected by the parties. Whether a law is "necessary" or "voluntary" depends upon the nature of the rule of law concerned. More specifically it depends upon whether the rule is an expression of the special characteristics of the nation composing the State by which it was created. These characteristics are said to make themselves felt most strongly in the law relating to status, capacity, family relations and succession. Finally local rules which bear the character of public policy,[199] especially those affecting property within the jurisdiction, have an overriding effect.

---

[196] *Della nazionalità come fondamento del diritto delle genti* (1851); see also *Clunet* 1 (1874), pp. 221, 285; see Sereni, *The Italian Conception of International Law* (1943), pp. 160–181; de Nova (1963), 28 *Law and Contemporary Problems,* 808; Nadelmann (1969), 17 *Am.J.Comp.L.*, 418.

[197] Contrast the approach to the same question by English law in the 19th century: Sinclair (1950), 27 *British Year Book of International Law,* 125, at pp. 131–137; Mervyn Jones (1956), 5 *International and Comparative Law Quarterly,* 230, at p. 243; Parry, *Hague Rec.* 90 (1956 III), at pp. 704–705.

[198] *Udny* v. *Udny* (1866), L.R. 1, Sc. & Div. 441.

[199] Such rules would be described today as spatially conditioned rules of domestic law or as rules *d'application immédiate* – see below sec. 28, No. 59.

Thus, the statutist notion of the nature of laws determining their operation in space and the criterion of the "but social"[200] are called in | aid to establish fixed principles which determine, indirectly through the connecting factors nationality and situs, which law is to apply or whether free choice is allowed. In the different climate of the United States a similar cord was struck by Currie.[201]

Others, similarly bent on developing a system of international application, relied on the notion of sovereignty. On the assumption that sovereignty extends over all property within its sway, and over all nationals within and without the territorial reach, it is asserted that the *lex patriae* governs all matters affecting persons and that the *lex situs* governs all matters concerning things.[202] It is only one further step to assert that the *lex patriae* and the *lex situs* are the only two systems of law to which the Private International Law of the forum may refer. In face of the fact that the world's systems of Private International Law have developed different and more sophisticated connecting factors, it is admitted that the *lex patriae* and the *lex situs* themselves can, by their own rules of Private International Law, refer to other systems of law with the help of such connecting factors as domicile, residence, place of contracting and place of performance. Thus the Private International Law of the forum is severely restricted in its choice, the emphasis is shifted to the Private International Law of the *lex causae* and *renvoi* is elevated to a position of paramount importance. In effect every country could, and probably would, provide two systems of Private International Law. One would apply to foreign nationals and to objects situated abroad and would be bound to rely solely on the *lex patriae* and the *lex situs*; the other, much more differentiated and unfettered, using other connecting factors, could apply to its own nationals and to all objects situate within its own jurisdiction.

Section 15. Wächter redivivus – Ehrenzweig

29. In a series of consecutive studies[203] culminating in three major works, Ehrenzweig[204] has mounted a frontal attack against what he | alleges is the

---

[200] Pillet, *Principes* (1903), pp. 265 ff.

[201] See below sec. 17, Nos. 33–34.

[202] Zitelmann, *Internationales Privatrecht*, I (1899); *Festgabe für Karl Bergbohm* (1919), 207 = *Diritto Internazionale*, 15 (1961), I, 152; Frankenstein, *Internationales Privatrecht*, I (1926); Briggs (1953), 6 *Vanderbilt L.R.*, 667, 707; (1955), 39 *Minn.L.R.*, 517; (1955), 4 *Int. and Comp. L.Q.*, 329; (1948), 61 *Harv.L.R.*, 1165; (1945), 15 *Miss.L.J.*, 77; and see the comments by Cavers, *The Choice of Law Process* (1965), pp. 211–273; Sohn (1942), 55 *Harv.L.R.*, 978, 982, 1003.

[203] For a survey see *Hague Rec.* 124 (1968 II), 170–173.

[204] *Treatise on the Conflict of Laws* (1962); *Private International Law* (1967); *Specific Principles of Private Transnational Law*, Hague Rec. 124 (1968 II), 170.

present tendency towards conceptualism, internationalism and a mechanical application of foreign law regardless of the practical realities. In its latest formulation he puts forward seven propositions:[205]

Firstly, choice of law is a matter for the law of the forum, unfettered by any overriding principle except treaties or, in a Federal State, overriding rules of the Constitution;[206]

secondly, where no specific or emerging choice of law rule can be identified in practice, the question whether foreign law applies must be determined by references to the substantive rule of law of the forum, which must be interpreted as regards its claim to apply in space;[207]

thirdly, the interpretation of the substantive rules of the forum often results in their own application even in respect of situations involving a foreign element;[208]

fourthly, if no choice of law rule, either express or implied by the process of interpretation set out above, which leads to the application of foreign law can be isolated, the substantive rule of the forum applies as a residuary law;[209]

fifthly, the *lex fori* applies to questions of procedure, rules of factual interpretation,[210] standards of behaviour such as negligence, public policy and by virtue of an agreement to this effect by the parties;[211]

sixthly, the recognition of the existence of certain rules of foreign law does not necessarily indicate that a choice of law rule of the forum has given it effect;[212]

seventhly, existing choice of law rules often operate subject to considerable modifications in practice brought about by judicial interpretation, | the characterisation of the operative facts, the circumstance that the *lex fori* and the *lex causae* are identical in substance or, while differing in substance, lead to identical results.[213]

Finally, the operation of choice of law rules is limited, as a matter of

---

[205] *Hague Rec., loc. cit.*, at pp. 214–215; 255–260; (1963), 28 *Law & Contemporary Problems*, 700; *Treatise*, pp. 352–353.

[206] Ehrenzweig, Proposition 3; see also *Hague Rec.*, pp. 200–213.

[207] Ehrenzweig, Proposition 6.

[208] Ehrenzweig, Proposition 7.

[209] Ehrenzweig, Proposition 1.

[210] See Ehrenzweig, *P.I.L.*, ss. 33, 138. From these it would appear that in practice courts interpret the intention of the parties as if this concerned a pure question of fact, although the intention of the parties may have been expressed and intended to be understood in the light of some foreign system of law. Such a conclusion overlooks the need to interpret words in the light of a foreign language and of their meaning in foreign law: *Studd* v. *Cook* (1883), 8 App. Cas. 577, 600, 604.

[211] Ehrenzweig, Proposition 2.

[212] Ehrenzweig, Proposition 4.

[213] Ehrenzweig, Proposition 5.

policy, by the "principle of validation" and the respect for the autonomous choice of law by the parties.[214]

Of these propositions, the first four concern the basis of Private International Law. The principal tenets are not new; they reproduce Wächter's notions[215] that primarily established choice of law rules and spatially conditioned rules of the forum must provide guidance and that, failing such rules, the substantive law of the forum applies. The advance beyond Wächter lies in the second proposition which emphasises the role played by the interpretation of the substantive rule of the forum in order to determine its operation in space. The assumption is that the interpretation of a rule of substantive law can yield an answer to the question whether it applies within the territory of the forum or also beyond. Such an assumption was made by the statutists, whose tests, namely whether the law affected persons or things, proved unworkable.[216] It may be that modern interpretation seeking to ascertain the purpose of a rule[217] can succeed where the postglossators failed. Yet several lacunae remain. In interpreting a rule of domestic substantive law it may be possible to read into it a spatially conditioned rule, or a unilateral choice of law rule, but not a bilateral rule. Thus it would only be possible to ascertain whether the substantive rule of the *lex fori* applies or not; if it does not apply, the question remains whether the case is to be dismissed, or whether some rule of foreign law applies in virtue of a choice of law rule which is to be found extraneously of the rule of domestic substantive law. In the former case, jurisdiction and choice of law are made to coincide; in the latter case, the system of Ehrenzweig is less far reaching than it seems. Ehrenzweig himself realises that in giving preponderance to the substantive law of the *forum*, the choice of jurisdiction assumes overriding importance and that rules of jurisdiction must be devised which exclude manipulations of the choice of law by an easy access to | the local courts.[218] If, therefore, rules of jurisdiction are to be formulated which, through the identity of jurisdiction and choice of law, result in the application of what appears to be desirable rule of law, such rules of jurisdiction must embody those rules which formerly determined the desired choice of law. Thus the problem of choice of law continues to exist; only it has been transposed and becomes a problem of jurisdiction. Such a system, which was described above[219] existed in the middle ages in Northern France and in the Netherlands. It has left its imprint in English Private International Law, especially in the sphere of status and of title to

---

[214] Ehrenzweig, *Treatise* (1962), 465–490.
[215] Above No. 19, pp. 131–133.
[216] See above p. 118.
[217] See, e.g., *Pugh* v. *Pugh* [1951], p. 482.
[218] Ehrenzweig (1963), 28 *Law & Contemporary Problems*, 700, 703.
[219] Above No. 6, pp. 109–110.

immovable property and in certain provisions relating to assumed jurisdiction,[220] until the rigidity of the older jurisdictional rules was relaxed. Its merits are simplicity and the reduced need to apply foreign law. Its defect is not only the denial of a remedy but also of a court if the narrow jurisdictional requirements cannot be met.

The attempt to attach choice of law rules to individual substantive rules of the *lex fori* opens up interesting prospects, despite the shortcomings inherent in Ehrenzweig's present exposition. As an alternative to the present technique which relies on broad choice of law rules[221] it merits attention for its subtlety and flexibility, provided that the choice of law is not conceived in unilateral terms only.

30. By relying on the continental approach which starts from the local rules of the conflict of laws and by stressing the need to connect the individual rule of substantive law with the legal system to be applied, this doctrine from the United States follows traditional lines of thinking in this field. It must be noted, however, that the propositions set out above allow a special reservation for overriding rules of public international and constitutional law. The former, more general problem will be discussed later on.[222] The latter, which is confined to the United States where it has influenced much modern thought purporting to be of universal validity, must be set out here, before it is possible to consider the most recent doctrines emanating from the North American continent.

| Section 16. Conflict of Laws and the American Constitution

31. For the present purpose, which is to determine whether any overriding rules of the conflict of laws can be discovered in the constitutional law of the United States[223] it is unnecessary to examine the history and aims of the various provisions of the Constitution of the United States which affect the choice of law by State and Federal courts,[224] their development following the

---

[220] E.g., contracts: R.S.C., O. 11 = Rule 1 (1) (f); torts: R.S.C., O. 11 = Rule 1 (1) (h).

[221] For their analysis see below Part III, Nos. 53–63, pp. 195–209.

[222] See below sec. 21, Nos. 41–43, pp. 167–173.

[223] See Rheinstein in *Festschrift für Rabel*, I (1954), 569–589; W. B. Cowles, *Nordisk Tidschrift for international Ret*, 31 (1951), 51; Brainerd Currie, *Selected Essays on the Conflict of Laws* (1963), 188–360, 445–583; for surveys of the practice see 74 *A.L.R.*, 710; 100 *A.L.R.*, 1143; 134 *A.L.R.*, 1472; 137 *A.L.R.*, 965; annotation in 95 L. ed. 1212; Baxter (1963), 16 *Stanford L.R.*, 1 and the lit. cited by Cavers, *Choice of Law Process* (1965), 117, n. 3.

[224] Rheinstein, *loc. cit.*, pp. 541, 547, 555, 559, i.e., the 14th Amendment (due process of law); art. IV s. 1 of the Constitution (Full Faith and Credit) and art. 1, s. 10 (1) of the Constitution (contract clause).

changing tendencies of the Supreme Court of the United States to curtail or to encourage the vigorous growth of local legislation and its effective exercise, or the emergence of the rule that there is no federal common law and therefore no federal conflict of laws to be administered in the Federal courts.[225] It must be stressed, however, that even if after the decision in *Klaxon* v. *Stentor*[226] the common law is not the law common to the Federation, but applies with variants, and modified by local legislation, as separate systems of law in the Member States, nevertheless the common core has remained such that in most matters of private law conflicts arise principally because legislative measures in some States have modified the rules of the common law, especially in matters of contract and tort.

One conclusion is clear. The Supreme Court of the United States cannot determine the applicable law,[227] given that, subject to the Constitution, the Member States are sovereign and stand to each other in a | relationship governed by international law.[228] The respect for the territorial competence of Member States in legislative and judicial matters furnishes the basis of this relationship.

"Prima facie every State is entitled to enforce in its own courts its own laws, unless ..."[229]

This guarantee of independence in legislative and judicial matters is matched by that accorded to other Member States. As a result conflicting overlaps[230] or cumulative abstentions[231] may occur. At first the Fourteenth Amendment served to protect rights acquired on the strength of foreign

---

[225] Rheinstein, *passim; Klaxon* v. *Stentor Electric Manufacturing Co.*, 313 US 487; 85 L.ed. 1447 (1941); *Griffin* v. *McCoach*, 313 US 498, 85 L.ed. 1481 (1941); for the approach to conflict rules in a federal court see *Richards* v. *US*, 369 US 1, 12; 7 L.ed. 2d 492, 500 (1962).

[226] Above, note 225.

[227] *Klaxon* v. *Stentor*, above n. 225, at p. 497. It did so, nevertheless, when it posited the application of the law of procedure and evidence of the forum on the ground that these matters are subject to the *lex fori: Hawkins* v. *Barney's Lessee, 5* Pet. 457, 466, 467, 8 L.ed. 190, 193, 194 (1831); *McElmoyle* v. *Cohen*, 13 Pet. 312, 324, 325, 10 L.ed. 177, 183, 185 (1839) and *(obiter) Home Insurance Co.* v. *Dick*, 281 US 397, 407, 74 L.ed. 926, 933 (1930); *Wells* v. *Simonds Abrasive Co.*, 345 US 514, 516, 517, 97 L.ed. 1211, 1215 (1953); *Order of United Commercial Travelers* v. *Wolfe*, 331 US 586, 607, 91 L.ed. 1687, 1700 (1947).

[228] Rheinstein, pp. 580–581.

[229] *Alaska Packers Ass.* v. *Industrial Accident Commission*, 294 US 532, 544, 546, 547, 79 L.ed. 1044, 1050, 1051, 1052 (1935); *Pink* v. *A.A.A. Highway Express*, 314 US 201, 209, 86 L.ed. 152, 158 (1941); *Pacific Employers* v. *Ins. Co. Industrial Accident Commission*, 306 US 493, 500, 83 L.ed. 940, 944 (1939); *Magnolia Petroleum Co.* v. *Hunt*, 320 US 430, 436, 88 L.ed. 149, 154 (1943); *Bradford Electric Co.* v. *Clapper*, 286 US 145, 156, 76 L.ed. 1026, 1033 (1932); Rheinstein 583.

[230] *Alaska Packers Ass.* v. *Industrial Accident Commission* (above n. 229), at p. 538.

[231] At p. 542; Cavers, *The Choice of Law Process* (1965), p. 105; De Nova, 28 *Law & Contemporary Problems* (1963), 808, 818–820.

territorial jurisdiction,[232] but in due course the Full Faith and Credit Clause which secured the enforcement of judgments given by a court of a Member State, if competent according to the principles of the Constitution, was called in aid to safeguard the application of the substantive law of a Member State.[233] Thus a basic conflict could arise between –

| "the strong unifying principle embodied in the Full Faith and Credit Clause looking towards maximum enforcement in each state of the obligations or rights created or recognized by the statutes of sister states ... and the policy of [the forum]".[234]

This conflict is not to be solved by supplanting the *lex fori* by foreign law every time that a sister State has acted within its competence and by obliging the courts of the forum in these circumstances always to apply law other than its own[235] to persons and events within the *forum*,[236]

"... the full faith and credit clause does not require one state to substitute for its own statute, applicable to persons and events within it, the conflicting statute of another state, even though that statute is of controlling force in the courts of the state of its enactment with regard to the same persons and events",

even if the law of the sister State is of controlling force in the latter State in respect of the same persons and events.[237]

---

[232] Rheinstein, *loc. cit.*, pp. 573–575, 547, 552, 554. The problem as to when a right has been acquired was more difficult. Beale (above No. 24, p. 139) solved it by a doctrinal approach, and the US Supreme Court did so, too, in a few decisions by the application of abstract and rigid choice of law rules; *lex loci delicti: Western Union Telegraph* v. *Chiles*, 214 US 274; 53 L.ed. 994 (1909); *Western Union* v. *Brown*, 234 US 542, 58 L.ed. 1457 (1913); see also *Slater* v. *Mexican Railways*, 194 US 120, 48 L.ed. 900 (1904); *lex loci contractus: N.Y. Life Insurance Co.* v. *Dodge*, 246 US 357, 62 L.ed. 772 (1918); *Mutual Life Ins. Co.* v. *Liebing*, 259 US 209, 66 L.ed. 900 (1922); *Hartford Accident and Indemnity Co.* v. *Delta Pine*, 292 US 134, 78 L.ed. 1178 (1934).

In other cases the exercise of territorial jurisdiction was believed to be concentrated on persons and events within the territorial reach: see p. 150, n. 236 and see *Bradford Electric Co.* v. *Clapper* (above n. 229) at p. 184 (per Stone J. diss.): "The Full Faith and Credit clause has not hitherto been thought to do more than compel recognition outside the state of operation and effect of its laws upon persons and events within it."

[233] Rheinstein, pp. 555–567; for the contract clause (US Const., art. I, s. 10 (1)) in a conflict of laws in time see *Watson* v. *Employers Liability Assn Corp.*, 348 US 66, 70, 90 L.ed. 74, 81 (1954).

[234] *Hughes* v. *Fetter*, 341 US 609, 612, 613; 95 L.ed. 1212 (1951).

[235] *Pink* v. *A.A.A. Highways Express*, at pp. 209–210; *Alaska Packers Ass.* v. *Industrial Accident Commission*, at pp. 546, 548; *Milwaukee County* v. *White*, 296 US 268, 273, 274, 80 L.ed. 220, 225, 226 (1935); *Order of United Commercial Travelers* v. *Wolfe*, at p. 607; *Broderick* v. *Rosner*, 294 US 629, 642, 70 L.ed. 1100, 1107 (1935).

[236] *Pacific Employers Ins. Co.* v. *Industrial Accident Commission*, at p. 502; *Watson* v. *Employers Liability Assn. Co.*, 348 US 66, 73, 99 L.ed. 74, 82; *Clay* v. *Sun Ins. Office*, 377 US 179, 181, 12 L.ed. 229, 231 (1964).

[237] *Magnolia Petroleum Co.* v. *Hunt*, at p. 436; see also *Bradford Electric Co.* v. *Clapper*, at p. 156; *Quong Ham Wah Co.* v. *Industrial Accident Commission*, 255 US 445, 65 L.ed. 723 (1921).

"The purpose of the Full Faith and Credit Clause was to alter the status of the several states as independent sovereignties, each free to ignore obligations created under the laws ... of the others, and to make them integral parts of a single nation throughout which a remedy upon a just application might be demanded as of right, irrespective of the state of origin. That purpose ought not lightly to be set aside out of deference to a local policy ..."[238]

It is necessary to balance the claims of the competing laws to apply:

| "... but the room left for the play of conflicting policies is a narrow one ... For the States of the Union the constitutional limitation imposed by the Full Faith and Credit clause abolished in large measure the general principle of international law by which local policy is permitted to dominate rules of comity."[239]

In a series of decisions the balance has been struck by the test which focuses on the interest of the States concerned[240] and –

"by appraising the governmental interests of each jurisdiction and turning the scale of decision according to their weight".[241]

In striking the balance, it is accepted that the forum has power to determine its own affairs and may disregard claims based on the law of a Member State which otherwise merit recognition and enforcement,[242] not merely if its own policy is different, but if the law of the sister State is clearly contrary to the public policy of the forum.[243]

---

[238] *Milwaukee County* v. *White* (above n. 235), at pp. 276, 277; *Hoopeston Canning Co.* v. *Callen*, 318 US 313, 87 L.ed. 777 (1943); *Alaska Packers Ass.* v. *Industrial Accident Comm.*, 294 US 532, 79 L.ed. 1044.

[239] *Broderick* v. *Rosner* (above p. 150, n. 235), at pp. 642, 643.

[240] *Bradford Electric* v. *Clapper*, at p. 162.

[241] *Alaska Packers Ass.* v. *Industrial Accident Commission* (above p. 149, n. 229), at pp. 542, 549; *Hartford Accident and Indemnity Co.* v. *Delta Pine Land Co.*, 292 US 143, 150, 78 L.ed. 1178, 1181 (1934); *Carroll* v. *Lanza*, 349 US 408, 99 L.ed. 1183 (1955); *Vanston Bondholders Protective Committee* v. *Green*, 329 US 156, 161, 162, 91 L.ed. 162, 165, 166 (1946); *Richards* v. *US*, 369 US 1, 15, 7 L.ed. 2d 492, 501 (1962).

[242] *Watson* v. *Employers Liability Assur. Corp.*, 348 US 66, 72, 99 L.ed. 74 82 (1954); *Osborn* v. *Ozlin*, 310 US 53, 84 L.ed. 1074 (1940).

[243] *Converse* v. *Hamilton*, 224 US 243, 260, 56 L.ed. 749, 755 (1911); *Griffin* v. *McCoach*, 313 US 498, 503, 506, 85 L.ed. 1481, 1445, 1456 (1941); such as: *Bond* v. *Hume*, 243 US 15, 21, 61 L.ed. 565, 567 (1917); imputing capacity to contract to a married woman contrary to the *lex fori*: *Union Trust* v. *Grosman*, 245 US 412, 62 L.ed. 368 (1918); doing a prohibited act in the country of the forum: *Bothwell* v. *Buckbee Mears & Co.*, 275 US 274, 278, 72 L.ed. 277, 280 (1927); enforcing penal law: *Huntington* v. *Altrill*, 146 US 657, 16 L.ed. 1123 (1892); *Hughes* v. *Fetter* (above p. 150, n. 234), at p. 612; *Order of Commercial Travelers of America* v. *Wolfe* (above p. 148, n. 227) at p. 624; *Home Insurance Co.* v. *Dick*, 281 US 397, 410, 74 L.ed. 926, 934 (1930); *Bradford Electric Co.* v. *Clapper* (above p. 149, n. 229), at p. 157; *Hartford Accident and Indemnity Co.* v. *Delta Pine Land Co.* (above n. 241) at p. 149.

The term recalls a similar phrase (manifestly against public policy) employed by the Hague Conventions on Private International Law.

It is clear that the absence of any contact between the relationship upon which the claim is based and the forum precludes the *lex fori* from being applied on the sole ground that one of the parties to the relation|ship is a citizen.[244] The relationship itself furnishes the criterion, and it is relevant whether it existed before the cause of action arose (such as a contract) or whether it came into being at the same time as the cause of action (such as a tort).[245] As regards contracts the protection of acquired rights has even been put forward as a restrictive test or motive.[246] Yet the *lex loci delicti* has been allowed to apply rather than the *lex contractus*, and the *lex fori* rather than the *lex loci delicti.*[247] In giving licence to the *lex fori* in preference to some other law, it matters whether the plaintiff can effectively sue the defendant elsewhere.[248] In maintaining the application of the law of a sister State it matters whether that law affords the defendant a defence of which he would be deprived if the *lex fori* applied.[249]

While it might have been possible to argue at the outset that in "appraising the governmental interests of each jurisdiction",[250] the Supreme Court of the United States proposed to examine the grouping of the connecting factors[251] so as to determine which Government is principally involved and to ascertain the seat of the relationship, thus replacing Story by Savigny, the subsequent development has shown that the court seeks to establish no more by this process than to strike a balance between the claims of the various jurisdictions and to safeguard | justice between party and party in a very limited number of factual situations[252] by analysing the rules of law in issue.

---

[244] *Home Insurance Co.* v. *Dick* (above n. 243) – an international claim not subject to the Full Faith and Credit Clause, but see also *John Hancock Mutual Life Ins. Co.* v. *Yates*, 299 US 178, 81 L.ed. 106, at p. 182 (1936); *Hartford Accident and Indemnity Co.* v. *Delta and Pine Land Co.* (above p. 151, n. 241), at p. 149; *Watson* v. *Employers Liability Assur. Corp.*, 348 US 66, 71, 88 L.ed. 76, 81 (1954).

[245] *Hughes* v. *Fetter* (above p. 150, n. 234), at p. 617 (per Frankfurter, Reed, Jackson, Minton JJ. diss.); see also *Alaska Packers Ass.* v. *Industrial Accident Commission* (above p. 149, n. 229), at p. 541; *Carroll* v. *Lanza*, 349 US 408 at 412, 419, 99 L.ed. 1183, 1188, 1192 (1955), per Frankfurter diss.

[246] *Pacific Employers Ins. Co.* v. *Industrial Accident Commission* (above p. 149, n. 229), at p. 502, but see the restriction imposed upon the alleged principle at p. 503; *Griffin* v. *McCoach* (above p. 148, n. 225), at p. 506; *Bradford Electric Company* v. *Clapper* (above p. 149, n. 229), at pp. 159, 164; *Hartford Accident and Indemnity Co.* v. *Delta Pine Land Co.* (above p. 151, n. 241), at p. 149.

[247] See the statement in *Magnolia Petroleum Co.* v. *Hunt* (above p. 149, n. 229), at p. 436; *Clay* v. *Sun Ins. Office*, 377 US 179, 181, 12 L.ed. 229, 231 (1964).

[248] Thus the plaintiff's substantive rights are not impaired: *Hughes* v. *Fetter* (above p. 150, n. 234), at p. 617 (diss.); *Alaska Packers Ass.* v. *Industrial Accident Commission* (above p. 149, n. 229), at p. 540.

[249] *Bradford Electric Co.* v. *Clapper* (above p. 149, n. 229), at p. 159.

[250] Above p. 151 and note 241.

[251] *John Hancock Mutual Life Ins. Co.* v. *Yates* (above n. 244), at p. 183. For this term see Cavers, *The Choice of Law Process* (1965), p. 82, and n. 44.

[252] See Fraukfurter J. diss. in *Carroll* v. *Lanza*, 349 US 408 at pp. 416 ff., 99 L.ed. 1183, 1191 (1955).

Not unnaturally the problems which beset the statutists reappeared arising out of modern legislation and couched in the technical language of to-day.[253] Once again an attempt was made to rely on the notion of territoriality of laws, now presented in terms of federal constitutional law as one of legis-lative jurisdiction. Once again it proved impossible, in situations which show local contact with several territorial units or legislative jurisdictions, to state with certainty that the relationship or cause of action has arisen in any one individual territory. Unable to rely on fixed rules of Private Internation-al Law, be they only of the dogmatic nature provided by Beale, the Supreme Court of the United States fell back on principles which attempt to deter-mine the application of law in space through an analysis of the nature of the law in issue and of its claim to apply within its own territory or also without. Yet a Federal Supreme Court may succeed where the statutists failed because neither the writers themselves nor the courts which they served could claim overriding authority. Unable to determine in individual cases with contacts in several States of the Union which territorial sovereignty and therefore which legislative jurisdiction was involved, the Supreme Court seeks to reach the same determination by considering the aims and consequences of the rules|put forward respectively by the parties. The selection of the proper legislative jurisdiction is achieved by an analysis or evaluation of the rules themselves. It is not surprising, therefore, that the most recent doctrine in the United States has taken as its themes the two general guide-lines which the Supreme Court has established for itself in order to carry out its duties under the Constitution – appraising governmental interests involved – justice be-tween the parties – and has sought to give them a new life as general princi-

---

Tort, survival of actions: *Hughes* v. *Fetter* (above p. 150, n. 234); Workmen's Compen-sation: *Alaska Packers Ass.* v. *Industrial Accident Commission* (above p. 149, n. 229); *Pacific Employers Ins. Co.* v. *Industrial Accident Commission* (above p. 149, n. 229); *Bradford Electric Co.* v. *Clapper* (above p. 149, n. 229);

Contract: *John Hancock Mutual Life Ins. Co.* v. *Yates* (above p. 152, n. 244); *Griffin* v. *McCoach* (above p. 151, n. 243); *Home Ins. Co.* v. *Dick* (above p. 151, n. 243); *Bradford Electric Co.* v. *Clapper* (above p. 149, n. 229) at p. 158; *Alaska Packers Ass.* v. *Industrial Accident Commission* (above p. 149, n. 229); *Pacific Employers Ins. Co.* v. *Industrial Acci-dent Commission* (above p. 149, n. 229) at p. 503;

Companies: *Pink* v. *A.A.A. Highways Express* (above p. 149, n. 229); *Order of United Commercial Travelers of America* v. *Wolfe* (above p. 150, n. 235); *Broderick* v. *Rosner* (above p. 150, n. 235); *Converse* v. *Hamilton* (above p. 151, n. 243);

For the problem of characterising contracts and torts see *Alaska Packers* v. *Industrial Accident Commission* (above p. 149, n. 229) at p. 542; *Broderick* v. *Rosner* (above p. 150, n. 235) at p. 644; *John Hancock Mutual Life Ins. Co.* v. *Yates* (above p. 151, n. 244) at p. 182; *Home Ins. Co.* v. *Dick* (above p. 151, n. 243) at p. 407.

The problem arose as a preliminary question in *Pink* v. *A.A.A. Highway Express* (above p. 149, n. 229).

[253] Cp. Rheinstein (1962), 11 *Am.J.Comp.L.*, 632, 633.

ples of universal application for determining the purpose and limitations of Private International Law or the Conflict of Laws.

32. These doctrines do not seek to develop and refine the principles which the Supreme Court of the United States has followed in controlling the choice of law rules forming part of the law of the Member States in order to ensure their compliance with the overriding principles of the Constitution which were analysed above. Undoubtedly the new doctrines did not exclude this goal in their general purpose which was to provide the courts of the Member States in the Federation with rules of general validity capable, incidentally, of serving as rules of universal application in other countries not subject to a federal system. In the ensuing discussion the distinction between these two separate uses must be constantly borne in mind.

Section 17. Governmental Interests as Conflict resolving Factors – Currie – Neo-statutists

33. The first of these two doctrines seeks to determine the application of law in space by analysing the governmental interests underlying the rules of law which are said to conflict. It is connected with the name of Brainerd Currie.[254] It rejects orthodox rules of the conflict of laws which are part of the *lex fori* and refer the forum to foreign law in particular situations. It is obvious, however, that not all available legal systems and their rules can or may be scrutinised in order to ascertain their governmental interest to apply.

The question must be put why the rules of law of some legal systems can be examined for the purpose of determining the governmental interests involved, while others are not. Two possibilities exist. Either the | consideration of rules of law belonging to foreign legal systems is determined by the *lex fori* or by overriding principles. The answer is not made any easier if it is realised that the new system is evolved exclusively from conflicts of law in matters of tort and contract, limited, moreover, to conflict of laws in the United States. Here the *lex fori*, the *lex actus,* the *lex injuriae* and the law of the respective home countries of the parties as well as the *lex loci solutionis* offer a baffling plethora of choice. At the same time all those laws originate in territorial units and, unlike rules of law selected by a free choice of law, can be regarded as claiming to be applied either generally within their own area, or with limitations only, or to extend to persons and events abroad. The assertion of the doctrine that it examines all governmental interests con-

---

[254] *Selected Essays in the Conflict of Laws* (1963); see also, e.g., de Nova, *Hague Rec.* 118 (1966 II), 591–606, with lit. p. 590, n. 1–3; Shapira, *The Interest Approach to Choice of Law* (1970); Kegel, *Hague Rec.* 112 (1964 II), pp. 95–207.

cerned seems to point to the conclusion that rules forming part of these various legal systems are taken into account because Member States of the United States must respect the sovereign powers of other Member States. If this is the case, the choice of law is determined in the first instance by considerations of American Constitutional Law, which does not contain, and cannot easily admit, fixed rules of conflict of laws and requires respect for the law of other Member States. The doctrine would, in these circumstances, be primarily national, and its value internationally must form the object of a special examination.

It must be admitted, however, that in looking to the legal systems of the restricted range of jurisdictions, this doctrine starts from the premise that a choice of law is primarily entrusted to the *lex fori*, but that in evolving sophisticated rules which may play fast and loose with orthodox choice of law rules, the autonomy of the *lex fori* must be reconciled with the claims of other States to see their law applied. Although such an interpretation starts from a premise which is the opposite to that examined before, it ends, once again, in according priority to aspects of American Constitutional Law. The only difference is that according to the first interpretation, an overriding system of the conflict of laws is emerging; according to the second interpretation, the limits of free choice of law are explored. In attempting to solve the question which of these two approaches inspires Currie's doctrine, some insight can be obtained from the stress which is laid on what it calls "false conflicts". Although it is not easy to determine all the facets of this new notion,[255] it seems to be agreed that a case presents a false conflict if either the | rules of law of the various legal systems concerned are the same or if they should differ in content, nevertheless produce the same result or do not purport to apply. It would seem that in practice, parties to a dispute do not plead the different rules in such circumstances, and no conflict of laws arises. The situation assumes another complexion if an overriding principle, which may be in the nature of constitutional law, requires imperatively that a selection must be made. Such would appear to be the assumption made by the adherents of the doctrine of governmental interests.

34. Whichever view is adopted, when it comes to determine the governmental interests involved in particular rules belonging to different legal systems, it is well to remember the experience gained in previous centuries that rules of substantive law can, but do not usually, indicate their claim to be applied extensively or restrictively in space. When they do, it is possible to respect this wish.[256] When they do not, attempts to ascertain the application

---

[255] See, e.g., Cavers, *Choice of Law Process* (1965), pp. 167, 89; Morris, *Conflict of Laws* (1971), pp. 542 ff., 490.

[256] In Europe unilateral choice of law rules and spatially conditioned internal rules serve this purpose. For the various techniques see below No. 59, pp. 204–206.

of rules in space by reference to the nature of the rules themselves, such as those made by the statutists, have failed. The doctrine which is associated with Currie may not seek directly to determine the claim to apply in space and its limits, but in seeking to unearth the respective unexpressed governmental interests underlying the rules concerned in order to allow one of these to prevail over another[257] it does so indirectly. Nor can it be expected that such an assessment of foreign governmental interests can be reached on objective rather than subjective grounds. Wächter's observations, put forward in reply to the alleged duty to respect foreign acquired rights because the respect for the foreign territorial sovereign demanded it, must be recalled here: the courts in one country are incapable of determining whether in the view of another country the latter's sovereignty (or, as it might be said in the present context, its interests) are affected and, if so, to what extent.[258] Any attempt to determine such interests must remain | an exercise by the courts of the *forum* in interpreting foreign law, and the various explanations given to the relevant Ontario law on claims by guest passengers in order to support the decision in *Babcock* v. *Jackson*[259] bear out this contention. The task may not seem to be insuperable in the United States, where the differences in the law of tort and contract of the Member States are represented by legislation which modifies, enlarges, restricts, and generally improves the rules of the common law which forms the basis in all but one of the States. It assumes an entirely different dimension, if the rules in question are drawn from the common law, civil law in the form of different codifications, and Germanic law. The novelty of this doctrine is its exclusive reliance on unilateral rules of conflict of laws or on spatially conditioned rules. Failing any express guidance by such rules, their absence is replaced by an interpretation of the substantive rules of law. However, substantive law cannot be translated into spatially conditioned rules without doing violence to the rules of substantive law themselves and without the use of artificial devices.

Moreover, the doctrine assumes that legal systems wish to restrict or to extend their application in general and of individual rules in particular to certain areas or classes of persons. It remains to be examined later on whether such an analysis is universally valid or whether it is restricted to the special conditions of a Federal State.[260] It must be pointed out at this stage, however, that in the international sphere individual legal systems may perhaps be regarded as closed and self-sufficient, subject only to express limitations imposed by their own law.

---

[257] If one of the possible systems involved shows a governmental interest to be applied in the circumstances, that legal system must be applied. If several show a concurrent interest, the *lex fori* takes over; it is the same, if no legal system shows an interest.

[258] *Archiv für die zivilistische Praxis*, 24 (1841), 299, 304; 310–311; *ibid.*, 25 (1842), 162.

[259] 12 N.Y. 2d 473, 191 N.E. 2d 279 (1963).

[260] See below Nos. 36, 39, pp. 161–163.

Section 18. Result selecting Principles – Cavers

35. After a long period when the protagonist of the "result selecting" doctrine, Cavers, was regarded in company with others[261] as a disciple of Aldricus[262] who favoured the application of the "better law" in the individual case, it is now clear that this doctrine seeks to establish new choice of law principles and does not renounce upon them altogether.[263]

| The existing rules are taken for granted.[264] Only when the need arises to fill gaps, the old technique is to be abandoned either to subsume the new problem under the established categories of choice of law rules or to construct a new choice of law rule limited to new categories of rules (such as trusts or quasi-contracts), and a result selecting principle is advanced. This doctrine is therefore less ambitious than that of Currie.[265] Moreover, it retains the notion of choice of law rules. Like the doctrine of governmental interests, it looks to the rules of substantive law, and only to the rules of substantive law, of a restricted number of legal systems.[266] It considers only the personal law, which is that of the home State and territorial law, which is the law in which a certain activity or result has manifested itself.[267] Thus the question arises, once again, whether the initial selection of potentially applicable laws is made on the strength of overriding principles, namely those of the American Constitution, or in virtue of the unfettered discretion of the *lex fori*. Once again it would seem that an overriding principle forms the basic assumption, and once again the reliance on the notion of false conflicts supports this conclusion.[268] In a conflict between these rival laws, all of which can claim attention (so it would seem) by virtue of the overriding principle, that rule is to be applied which, after weighing the purposes of the various rules for selection[269] deserves to be preferred. Such preferences, expressed in abstract propositions, are expected to supply a sufficient number of principles of preference combining spatial and substantive criteria within a frame-

---

[261] Frankel, *Rabels Z.*, 4 (1930), 239; see also Cavers (1933), 47 *Harv.L.R.*, 173.

[262] Above, p. 111.

[263] Cavers, *Choice of Law Process* (1965), pp. 76, 8, 9, esp. 76, 113, 122; *Hague Rec.* 131 (1970 III), 75–308.

[264] *Ibid.*, pp. 137, 200, 215.

[265] *Ibid.*, p. 15.

[266] Cp. as regards German law, EGBGB, art. 12.

[267] *Ibid.*, pp. 134, 136, 142, 150. For a discussion of any preference between the two see p. 156.

[268] See above, pp. 155–156 with lit., esp. Cavers, p. 89.

[269] Cavers, pp. 89, 98, 100–101, but see p. 171.

work of creative justice which accommodates conflicting laws[270] and provides predictability.[271]

Five such principles are put forward by way of example. Shorn of their special terminology and expressed in terms of orthodox rules of conflict of laws, they proclaim –

(1) In a conflict between the *lex personalis (lex larium et penatium)* of the defendant, the *lex loci actus* and the *lex loci injuriae*, the | *lex loci injuriae* applies if it requires a higher standard of conduct or accords higher financial protection than the other two laws.[272]

Exception: if the injured person and the person causing the injury stand in a special relationship towards each other, the law governing their relationship applies.

(2) In a conflict between the *lex personalis* of the plaintiff (see above (1)), the *lex loci actus* and the *lex loci injuriae*, the laws of the *lex loci actus* and the *lex loci injuriae*, if the same, apply, if they set a lower standard of conduct or of financial protection than the *lex personalis*.[273]

Exception: the same exception as in Principle (1).

Proviso *(a)*: If the *leges personale* of the injured party and the tortfeasor are both more exacting than the *lex loci delicti*, the latter applies.[274]

Proviso *(b)*: In a conflict between the *lex personalis* of the injured party and the *lex loci delicti*, concerning claims for wrongful death and survival of actions in tort, the *lex personalis* applies.[275]

(3) In a conflict between the *lex loci actus* and the *lex loci injuriae*, the *lex loci actus* applies if it has "established special controls, including the sanction of civil liability", even if the standards of conduct and financial protection of the *lex loci injuriae* are less exacting.[276]

Proviso: if the *lex loci actus* enacts a law with the dual purpose of regulating an activity and of safeguarding property, the latter purpose, if predominant, excludes the application of the *lex loci actus* in favour of the *lex loci injuriae* which is less exacting.[277]

---

[270] Cavers, pp. 120, 124; the *lex fori* must determine it: *ibid.*, pp. 106, 218–219; *Hague Rec.* 131 (1970 III), pp. 75–308.

[271] Cavers, p. 222.

[272] Cavers, p. 139; the personal law of the plaintiff does not seem to attract attention, possibly on the irrelevant ground of lack of jurisdiction of the plaintiff's State. For the meaning of "home State" see Cavers, p. 154. Neither is the question taken into account as to the burden of proof of all these rules taken from different legal systems.

[273] Cavers, p. 146.

[274] Cavers, p. 153.

[275] Cavers, pp. 156–157.

[276] Cavers, p. 159; this principle expresses the rule in *Schmidt v. Driscoll Hotel Inc.*, 249 Minn. 376, 82 N.W.Ld. 365 (1957) – for meaning of "special controls" see p. 164.

[277] Cavers, pp. 160–162.

(4) In a conflict between the law of the State in which a relationship has its seat and the *lex loci delicti*, the law governing the relationship|applies if it has imposed on one party to the relationship a standard of conduct or of financial protection for the benefit of the other party which is higher than that imposed by the *lex loci delicti.*[278]

Proviso: In a conflict between the personal laws of the parties and the *lex loci delicti* on the one hand and the law of the State in which a relationship between the parties has its seat, on the other hand, the former, if less exacting, applies.[279]

(5) In a conflict between the law of the State in which a relationship has its seat and the *lex loci injuriae*, the law governing the relationship applies if it has imposed on one party to the relationship a standard of conduct or of financial protection for the benefit of the other party which is lower than that imposed by the *lex loci injuriae.*[280]

(6) In a conflict between the *lex personalis*, which protects a person from his own incompetence, heedlessness, ignorance and unequal bargaining power by restricting that person's power to contract or to convey or encumber property, and any other law, the personal law applies, if the transaction or property concerned is centred in the State which provides the personal law or if it is not so centred by chance or due to *fraude à la loi.*[281]

Proviso 1: If the protective law envisages certain types of transactions and not classes of persons, the law of the place applies where the transaction is centred,[282] presumably if the latter law does not coincide with the *lex personalis.*

Proviso 2: If the personal law of the promisor provides protection and the law of the place where the transaction is centred denies protection, the law which denies special protection to the promisor and upholds the agreement may have to be applied.[283]

|(7) Free choice of law is admitted if the law so chosen is reasonably related to the transaction, and permits the performance of it, although neither party has his home in the State, the law of which is chosen, and although the

---

[278] Cavers, p. 166. This principle expresses the rule in *Babcock* v. *Jackson*, 12 N.Y. 2d 473, 482, 191 N.E. 2d 279, 284 (1963); *Haumschild* v. *Continental Casualty Co.*, 7 Wis. 2d 130, 95 N.W. 2d 814 (1959). Cavers stresses rightly that this relationship must not be characterised as contractual so as to make the claim sound in contract (p. 173). However, it may be that it savours sufficiently of a contract to rebut the defendant's plea that the *lex loci delicti* rather than the law governing their relationship as host driver and guest passenger must be applied.

[279] Cavers, p. 175.

[280] Cavers, p. 177.

[281] Cavers, p. 180; for the notion of "centring" see pp. 183, 188.

[282] Cavers, p. 183.

[283] Cavers, p. 189.

transaction is not centred there, provided that no protective law applicable under Principle No. (6) is in issue or that the transaction concerns land and is contrary to mandatory rules of the *lex situs*. The legal effect of the transaction on third parties with independent interests is not determined by this principle.[284]

Section 19. The International Use of the New Doctrines

36. The modern American doctrines promulgated by Currie, Cavers and a number of other writers[285] with some variations can now be examined in their setting.

Both doctrines look to substantive law in order to make a choice; Currie relies on the expression of governmental interests, weighs them and applies the law which represents the preponderant interest or the *lex fori*. Cavers looks to the purpose of the various rules of law and selects that rule which produces the better result.[286] Both doctrines look to a number of laws or rules which are drawn from a variety of legal systems, which is, however, limited. The limitation is determined by a number of tests (known as connecting factors, to be discussed below) calling on the consideration of the laws of States which are concerned either because the transaction or event is connected with their territory or because the parties involved have their home in one or the other of these States. The need to consider all these laws appears to be dictated by an overriding principle of the American Constitution requiring equal respect for the laws of all Member States together with that of the forum.

37. Faced with a choice imposed by an overriding principle, Currie examines the governmental interests shown by the rules of the States concerned and resolves the problem either by relying on the *lex fori* or the *lex gravitatis unicae*; Cavers embarks upon a cumulation of the | rules embodied in the various legal systems which are potentially applicable, and seeks one in accordance with a preference expressed by the *forum* in the terms of a choice of law rule. The difference between orthodox choice of law rules (to be analysed, *infra*, Part III) and those advocated here is that the former are expressed in terms of formal categories of rules which are connected with particular countries by a series of formal connecting factors; the latter are in

---

[284] Cavers, p. 194.

[285] De Nova, *loc. cit.*, p. 604.

[286] The question does not appear to have attracted sufficient attention whether this is always the rule of the *lex validitatis*, or the law which protects a party from his own follies, the law which accords a right to the plaintiff or a defence or counter-claim to the defendant.

addition, expressed in terms of substantive categories of rules advantageous or disadvantageous to the plaintiff. Both doctrines thus seek to pinpoint a rule forming part of a particular system of laws out of a number available for consideration. The need to consider foreign legal systems, otherwise than by an act of initial discretion (as European systems of Private International Law do), and the aim to apply objective criteria of choice which are not arbitrary and accord full respect to the rules in a number of legal systems is explained by the practice of the Supreme Court of the United States of America. The court, as will be remembered, requires the rules of the conflict of laws of the Member States to be so constructed that they give weight to the various governmental interests involved while administering justice between the parties. Both doctrines which were examined above seek to satisfy these requirements; Currie attaches preponderant importance to governmental interests, while Cavers is moved by the need to do justice in the individual case without jettisoning principle and certainty.

38. The conclusion must be, therefore, that the doctrines reflect the need in the federal system of the United States to adapt general, unfettered choice of law rules, as they are known in the Private International Law dealing with conflicts of laws between different States, to the demands of the Constitution. The conclusion suggested here, namely that these doctrines were conceived in order to satisfy the particular needs of the conflict of laws under the American Constitution, is borne out by another consideration. Both make much play with so-called "false conflicts" which must be disregarded. In fact they are disregarded in Europe and elsewhere, because no party will raise an issue of conflict of laws if the rules in both systems of law are identical in form or in their effect or do not purport to apply. On the other hand, the failure to consider the law of a sister State which is the same or has the same effect as that applied by the forum may stimulate a constitutional complaint. The fact that in the opinion of the court only one country has an interest in the case may be a good reason for denying consti|tutional review if a rule taken from that legal system is applied, but outside the United States the existence or not of an established rule of Private International Law counts first, except *de lege ferenda.*

39. The two doctrines may be suited to the needs of the United States where orthodox rules of the conflict of laws form part of the domestic law of the Member States, must operate concurrently with other rules of the conflict of laws in sister States and are subject to the overriding control of the Constitution. The homogeneous character of American private law, which is based on the common law, except in Louisiana, may assist in fostering their success, and the relative small number of situations involving the application of foreign law (mainly in the field of contract and tort) may help. In these areas the need is clear for the development of new, detailed and so-

phisticated rules of conflict of laws. The problem remains whether the standards of control developed by the Supreme Court of the United States can
serve themselves as rules of the conflict of laws or at least as the basis for such
rules in the law of the Member States and in the federal courts or whether the
principles elaborated by the Supreme Court are and remain general standards to which individual systems of conflict of laws must conform, while
retaining their individual identity. Apparently, the Supreme Court itself has
expressed the belief at least on one occasion[287] that a new system of conflict of
laws is emerging; many modern writers seem to think so, but it will be for the
practice and, if need be, the legislature to formulate such rules. As shown
above, the task is not an easy one.

It is quite another problem whether countries outside the federal system
of the United States should heed the voices from the United States. This will
depend in part on the result of the discussion whether Private International
Law outside a federal system is subject to overriding principles of Public
International Law.[288] In part it has been answered above[289] when it was
pointed out that the differing character of legal systems outside the United
States makes it possible, at best to ascertain their function[290] and to characterise them, but makes it impracticable to determine the real interests and
ulterior purposes of rules of foreign law.

|*Section 20. Conclusions*

40. Private International Law, like any other branch of domestic law, is
determined partly by tradition and partly by policy. Since it is of recent
growth, the importance of policy in its development is greater than in other
branches of law which can look back to a longer history. For the same reason
it has relied more upon doctrine than is usual in domestic law. Only Public
International Law has drawn on writers to an even greater extent. Although
these factors make for diversity rather than uniformity the following trends
emerge:

First, there is a tendency to hold that all rules of domestic law contain their
own limitations in space. These limitations are said to arise from the nature
of these rules, from the fact that they concern persons or property, from their
social purpose or governmental interest or from the expression of charac-

---

[287] *Richards* v. *U.S.*, 369 US 1; 7 L.ed. 2d 492 (1962).
[288] See below Nos. 41–43, pp. 167–173.
[289] See p. 157.
[290] See below Nos. 56–58, pp. 198–204.

teristics peculiar to the nation to which a person belongs. By their nature these doctrines are universalistic.

Second, there is a tendency to hold that all rules of law, whether local or foreign, are applied in accordance with the territorial division of legal systems and in deference to the sovereign character of States. Some believe that this division determines with universal effect when local and when foreign law applies. Others, taking a more one-sided view, believe that the territorial division of legal systems can only determine whether local law applies and where its sphere of application ends.[291] Others again, relying more upon the tie of sovereignty than upon the territorial division of States as a link between the law of a country, its territory and its subjects, assert that it is thus possible to determine the sphere of local law to situations at home and abroad. Still others, by way of generalising the last assumption, state that the division of sovereignties determines not only whether local law applies to situations which arise abroad but also whether foreign law applies to situations which arise locally. All these doctrines rely upon the division of sovereignty or the territoriality of law. They are all international no matter whether they purport to lay down with universal validity general principles of Private International Law or unilateral rules determining when local law and when foreign law must be applied, or whether they claim to be particularist by determining exclusively when local law must be applied to situations abroad without touching | upon the question when foreign law must be applied to situations which arise locally or abroad.

While t is not possible to accept these doctrines as a general basis of private International Law, it must be admitted that they are of limited validity.

In the first place modern systems of Private International Law were first developed within States which possessed composite systems of law.[292] The existence of a central authority with overriding powers to delimit the sphere of operation of individual legislation and the application of law by the courts in the member States encourages the doctrine of territoriality of laws. Modern American doctrines reflect this historical inheritance coupled with an unconscious return to an even older way of thinking.

In the second place, there are certain branches of law, primarily of a public law nature,[293] where the problem is one of establishing the respective frontiers of legislation, but never that of applying foreign substantive law. In

---

[291] For a discussion of this view see de Nova, *loc. cit.*, pp. 570–590.
[292] Italy, France, Netherlands, Germany, Great Britain, United States.
[293] Mann, *Hague Rec.* 132 (1971 I), 107, at pp. 115–121.

general, rules of Private International Law can be unilateral or bilateral, but when concerned with the application of private law they must always deal with the two-fold problem of when the *lex fori* and when foreign law must be applied. Certain branches of Conflict of Laws, however, rely exclusively upon unilateral rules, for the reason that they are concerned with a process of selflimitation and not with a process of choice of law. The law of procedure is such a branch, and the law of bankruptcy is another, as are the law of taxation, administrative law and modern anti-trust and currency legislation. The forum never applies such foreign laws. It is only concerned with the limits of operation of local and foreign laws bearing the character of public law, but the latter can be taken into account as a fact or datum.[294] The principle of territoriality based upon the division of legislative spheres fulfils its proper function here.

Third, there is a trend from the time of Wächter onwards to regard Private International Law as part of domestic law, determined by considerations of domestic policy, circumscribed by domestic legislation and unfettered by limitations arising from the person, area or nature and purpose of a rule of law as such. Its task is to introduce categories | of rules of foreign law, or individual rules of foreign law to be applied to types of situations or to particular situations or events. The only legal controls are exercised by Public International Law among the community of States and by constitutional law among the Member States of a specific Federal State. The restrictions on an unbridled choice of law which can be imposed by constitutional law in a Federal State were discussed above when the influence of the Constitution upon and the practice of the Supreme Court of the United States were examined as they affect rules of the conflict of laws in the United States.[295] It remains, therefore, to turn last to the relationship between Public International Law and Private International Law.

---

[294] See Lipstein, [1972 B] *Cambridge L.J.*, 67, at p. 73; Mann, pp. 134–144 and see below, p. 171 and n. 28. But see Frank, *Rabels* Z., 34 (1970), 56.

[295] The practice in other Federal States yields less significant results from the point of view of a general theory of the conflict of laws; see Castel, *Hague Rec.* 126 (1969 I), 1–109.

| Part II. The Relationship between Public and Private International Law

Section 21. The Influence of Public International Law upon Domestic Private International Law

41. During the last 100 years the question has been raised frequently whether Private International Law is regulated by certain overriding principles of Public International Law.[1] Upon analysis this question resolves itself into two. The first is whether there exist rules of international law bearing upon the conflict of laws; the second is whether such rules, if existing, can exercise any direct influence upon domestic systems of conflict of laws.

The second problem requires some explanation. International Law, being a system of laws governing the relation between States, does not contain any specific rules of private law. Apart from treaty obligations (which may be extensive) in the field of Private International Law[2] States are not bound to introduce any uniform rules of private law, criminal law or any other branch of law, such as Private International Law. International responsibility for denial of justice is not incurred | for the mere reason that a country failed to adopt a particular rule or set of rules of domestic law. But there is denial of justice when the fundamental principles of law as observed by all nations are violated. Such are, *inter alia*, the rules: *audi alteram partem*,[3] *nemo judex in*

---

[1] For an account of the problem up to the Second World War see Lipstein (1942), 27 *Transactions of the Grotius Society*, 142, at pp. 142–149 with lit. notes 1–4 and see Maury, *Hague Rec.* 57 (1936 III), 329 at 356; Makarov in *Mélanges Streit* (1939), 535; Balogh, *ibid.*, p. 71; Niederer in *Schweizerisches Jahrbuch für Internationales Recht*, 5 (1948), p. 63; *Einführung in das internationale Privatrecht* (2 ed. 1956), pp. 102–114; Stevenson (1952), 52 *Col.L.R.*, 561; Maridakis, *Ius et Lex, Festgabe für Gutzwiller* (1959), 253; Wortley, *Hague Rec.* 85 (1954 I), 245; Riphagen, *ibid.*, 102 (1961 I), 219; Hambro, *Varia Juris Gentium, Liber Amicorum François* (1959), 132, *Hague Rec.* 105 (1962 I), 1; Makarov in Strupp-Schlochauer, *Wörterbuch des Völkerrechts*, II (1961), 129–133; Schnitzer in *Mélanges Guggenheim* (1968), p. 102.

[2] Attention must be drawn to the great number of treaties concluded by the Hague Conferences on Private International Law (see for the treaties in force, as regards those conducted before 1914 Gutzwiller, *Schweizerisches Jahrbuch für Internationales Recht*, 2 (1945), pp. 48–99; Kegel, *Internationales Privatrecht* (3 ed. 1971), pp. 87 ff.; for the period after 1945 see *ibid.*, pp. 87–90; *Rev.crit.*, 1971, 153–157; Conférence de La Haye, *Recueil des Conventions de La Haye*); by the Socialist States of Eastern Europe: Drobnig, *Osteur. R.* (1960), 154; Uschakow, *ibid.*, 7 (1961), 161; Makarov, *ibid.*, (1969) 1; by the Benelux countries: Rigaux, *Clunet* 1969, 334; *Rev.crit.* 1968, 812; de Winter, *ibid.*, 597. Scandinavian Treaties: see Philip, *Hague Rec.* 96 (1959 I), 245. South and Central American States: Vitta, *Hague Rec.* 126 (1969 I), at pp. 128–133; Makarov, *Quellen des internationalen Privatrechts* (1960 II), Nos. 1–5.

[3] Wortley, *loc. cit.*, p. 318; Hambro, *Hague Rec., loc. cit.*, p. 12, citing Ago, *Hague Rec.* 58 (1936 IV), 289–290.

propria causa,[4] *ut res magis valeat quam pereat,*[5] restitution equals reparation,[6] and the prohibition of self-help,[7] but contrary to the belief of some[8] they are not rules bearing upon the substance of domestic law including Private International Law. They may well constitute criteria which Public International Law furnishes in order to assess whether a system of private law of a particular country complies with certain international standards. But Public International Law does not lay down rules of private law proper. However, even if there existed rules of Public International Law which prescribed the adoption of any specific rules of domestic law, including rules of the conflict of laws, such rules could not be self-executing. Failure to comply with what might be called "preliminary" rules of Public International Law would not have any immediate effect in domestic law;[9] in the international sphere it would lead to State responsibility resulting in damages. In the words of Ago: "Il ne s'agirait donc jamais de l'existence de cette norme coutumière internationale concernant directement le droit international privé".[10]

In addition to the principles discussed and dismissed above, the supporters of the internationalist school of Private International Law, in their search for rules of Private Law embodied in Public International Law, have only been able to detect a very limited range of rules, altogether not more than 6 in number.[11] Upon examination, they are either not principles of Public International Law or they are not principles of Private International Law. They are:

| (1) Every State must have a system of Private International Law;
(2) States must not exclude the application of foreign law altogether;[12]
(3) States may exclude foreign law on grounds of public policy;[13]

---

[4] Wortley, *loc. cit.*, p. 316.
[5] Hambro, *loc. cit.*, p. 12.
[6] Wortley, *loc. cit.*, p. 319.
[7] Wortley, *loc. cit.*, p. 320.
[8] See above note 3.
[9] Lipstein, *loc. cit.*, p. 143, n. 3.
[10] *Hague Rec.* 58 (1936 IV), p. 291, n. 1.
[11] Lipstein, *loc. cit.*, p. 146 and note 25 with lit. to which should be added: von Bar, *Theorie und Praxis des international Privatrechts,* I (2 ed. 1889), paras. 2–5; Pillet, *Principes de droit international privé* (1903), p. 55; *Traité pratique,* I (1923), pp. 18–21; Murad Ferid, *Vom Deutschen zum Europäischen Recht, Festschrift für Doelle* (1963), II, 119 at pp. 127–129.
[12] Kahn, *Abhandlungen zum internationalen Privatrecht,* I (1928), 286; see now the observations of Mann, *Hague Rec.* 111 (1964 I), at p. 56, n. 12.
[13] *Boll Case (Netherlands v. Sweden), I.C.J. Reports 1958,* p. 52; Lipstein (1959), 8 *International and Comparative Law Quarterly,* 506, at p. 520; Batiffol and Francescakis, *Rev.crit.d.c.p.* 1959, p. 259; von Overbeck, in *Ius et Lex, Festgabe für Gutzwiller* (1959), 325; Makarov, *ibid.,* p. 303; Kollewijn, *Nederlands Tijdschrift voor international Recht* 1959, 311 = *Diritto, Internazionale,* 14 (1960), 103; M. Weser, *Riv.dir.int.* 1959, 426.

(4) No State may impose its own rules relating to status upon persons who are merely temporary residents;

(5) Immovables are governed by the *lex situs*, and rights in movables acquired in virtue of a previous *lex situs* must be respected;

(6) Form is governed by the *lex loci actus*.[14]

42. Of these six principles the first four are preliminary or directory rules of Public International Law. They indicate a certain tendency to be followed by States. They do not prescribe the application of any one particular rule of Private International Law, such as whether the law of nationality or of domicile governs status, or which law is to apply to a contract or tort, or whether one legal system is to govern a succession as a whole or whether succession to movables is to be governed by the personal law of the deceased (and, if so, whether this is the law of his nationality or his domicile), while succession to immovables is governed by the lex situs.[15] Instead, the universal acceptance of public policy as a corrective controlling the normal application of foreign law shows that States cannot agree on any general standards of law in this field. In fact most countries possess a system of Private International Law and no country refuses categorically to recognise or to apply foreign law altogether. This attitude is not, however, identical with the implementation of a duty prescribed by Public International Law to introduce any particular rule of Private International Law, let alone with adoption of a uniform set of rules of Private International Law. It merely reflects obedience to the general principles of Public Inter|national Law which require the observation of minimum standards of justice and abstention from illegal discrimination.

The last two principles set out above are, it must be admitted, true principles of Private International Law, but they are not rules of Public International Law. In the first place, they are not universally applied[16] and yet no complaint has ever been raised on this ground.[17]

In the second place, even if these principles were applied by all countries in identical circumstances, such a course of action may lead to a uniform practice only. It would not necessarily provide evidence of the existence of prin-

---

[14] See Mann, above, note 12; P. Klein, *Archiv für bürgerliches Recht*, 29 (1906), 102.

[15] See Lipstein (1942), 27 *Transactions of the Grotius Society*, 143, at p. 147 with lit. at n. 26.

[16] According to Art. 23 of the Introductory Law to the Italian Civil Code of 1942, succession to movables and to immovables is governed by the *lex patriae*. In England, before the Wills Act 1861, the formalities of wills of personalty generally and, after 1861, the formalities of wills of personalty made by aliens were governed, until 1963, by the law of the last domicile of the deceased.

[17] See the lit. cited by Lipstein (1942), 27 *Transactions of the Grotius Society*, 142, at p. 143, n. 4, especially Bruns, *Fontes Juris Gentium*, ser. B sectio I, tomus I, pp. 454–455; Nussbaum (1942), 42 *Col. L.R.*, 189.

ciples of International Law to the same effect,[18] although it must be admitted that a new standard of conduct may have crystallised.[19]

However, in the *Boll* Case[20] decided by the International Court of Justice, Judge Sir Hersch Lauterpacht asserted that the principle of Public Policy had acquired this character and that it is also applicable by an International Court or Tribunal.[21] The latter assertion will be discussed later on where the role of rules of the conflict of laws in international tribunals must be examined.[22] Here the question is only whether public policy is a fixed principle of the conflict of laws forming part of Public International Law, or whether it is only a preliminary or directory rule enunciated by Public International Law and addressed to domestic systems of law. Public Policy is a means of excluding foreign law which is normally applicable according to the rules of Private International Law of the Forum. Since domestic law is free to determine whether and in what circumstances foreign law is to be applied in the first instance, the exception of public policy is merely an affirmation in general terms of that freedom to apply foreign or domestic law within the framework of Public International Law, i.e., subject to the observance of the minimum standards of justice and without illegal discrimination.[23] Thus the principle of public policy is neither a rule nor a standard forming part of Public International Law. Moreover, even if a common basis of public policy in the conflict of laws could be found, it would not become a general principle of law in the meaning of Article 38 of the Statute of the Court. The function of public policy in the conflict of laws consists in the exclusion of the foreign private law which is normally applicable, and in the substitution of the private law of the forum. However, international courts have no *lex fori* other than Public International Law, and this is incapable of replacing domestic rules of private law.[24] Thus public policy as a general principle of international law is either identical with international law as a whole or it expresses the principle that, within its own sphere, a State is sovereign and free, unless bound by a treaty. It adds nothing to the recognised principles of law, municipal or international.

---

[18] Lipstein, *loc. cit.*, p. 147 with lit. n. 27.

[19] Hambro, *loc. cit.* (above p. 167, n. 1); for a series of theories on the relationship between Public and Private International Law which bear no relation to any actual practice see Lipstein, *loc. cit.*, p. 148, and notes 28–30 with lit.; de Nova, *Hague Rec.* 118 (1966 II), 438, at pp. 473–477 with lit.; Mann, *Hague Rec.* 111 (1964 I), at p. 22, n. 37.

[20] Above, p. 87, n. 13.

[21] *I.C.J. Reports 1958*, p. 52, at pp. 79 ff., esp. pp. 89 ff.

[22] Below, sec. 22, Nos. 44–45, pp. 173–183.

[23] See Lipstein (1959), 8 *International and Comparative Law Quarterly*, 506, at pp. 520–521.

[24] Lipstein, *Transactions of the Grotius Society*, 27 (1942), pp. 149, 156–157, and note 67 with references; 29 (1944), pp. 63–66; see also Niboyet, *Traité*, III (1944), No. 1041, p. 562; Batiffol, *Traité élémentaire* (5 ed. 1970), No. 362, p. 431; Schnitzer, *Handbuch des Internationalen Privatrechts* (4 ed. 1950), I, p. 228.

43. *Legislative Jurisdiction according to Public International Law and Choice of Law* rules. Recently it has been asserted by an authoritative voice[25] that the distribution of legislative (sometimes called prescriptive) jurisdiction by Public International Law must determine the substance or content of rules of Private International Law.[26] By stressing the importance of legislative jurisdiction and of its control by Public International Law, emphasis is placed upon the power of a State to impose its law on persons and situations at home and abroad. Seen in this light, the process of choice of law is one of self-limitation, not of applying foreign law. This process, it will be remembered,[27] is appropriate to the determination of the range of public law of any one country, seeing that foreign public law is never applied by the *forum* though it may be taken into account as a datum irrespective of whether the *lex fori* or foreign law applies.[28] It is notable that the recent prota-
| gonist of the internationalist doctrine of jurisdiction draws his inspiration from criminal law,[29] labour law,[30] tax law,[31] the law of bankruptcy,[32] antitrust legislation,[33] procedure and jurisdiction[34] and exchange control legislation,[35] all of which are only concerned with the boundaries of their own operation to the exclusion altogether of foreign law bearing this character. In applying the principle of legislative jurisdiction to Private International Law proper, which involves the choice between local and foreign law, Dr. Mann resuscitates Beale[36] and seeks, once again, to pinpoint the sovereign whose power to exercise legislative jurisdiction according to Public International Law must be respected by Private International Law. Even if the "legally relevant contact" is made the criterion, as Dr. Mann suggests,[37] the result is

---

[25] Mann, *Hague Rec.* 111 (1964 I), pp. 1–162.

[26] See also above, p. 144.

[27] See also above, p. 165, but see Frank, *Rabels Z.*, 34 (1970) 56.

[28] See, e.g., *Re Bettinson's Question*, [1956] Ch. 67; *Regazzoni* v. *Sethia*, [1958] A.C. 301 and *Ralli Bros.* v. *Cia Naviera Sota y Aznar*, [1920] 2 K.B. 287 as interpreted by Mann (1937), 18 *B.Y.I.L.*, 97; *The Halley*, (1868) L.R., 2 P.C. 192, 202 and the cases cited by Lipstein in *Ius Privatum Gentium*, I (1969), 411, at 420–422; cp. Mann, 132; *Hague Rec.* 132 (1971 I), 109 at 189, but see p. 193, n. 47.

[29] Mann, *loc. cit.*, at p. 29, n. 30, p. 33; *The Lotus, P.C.I.J., Ser. A, No. 10 (1927)*, at pp. 36, 39, 47, n. 90; *Reg.* v. *Jameson*, [1896] 2 Q.B. 425, 430; pp. 82 ff.

[30] At p. 47, n. 90: *Lauritzen* v. *Larsen*, 345 US 571, 578 (1953).

[31] At p. 29, n. 29: *Amsterdam* v. *Min. of Finance* (Israel), International Law Reports 1952, 229, 231; p. 37; p. 48 n. 92: *Trustees & Executors Agency Co.* v. *Federal Commissioner of Taxation* (1933), 49 C.L.R. 220, 325, 239; see also Mann, pp. 109–119.

[32] At p. 29, n. 28: *Ex p. Blain* (1879), 12 Ch.D. 522, 528.

[33] At pp. 95–108 with cases.

[34] At pp. 73 ff.

[35] At pp. 122–126.

[36] See above, p. 139.

[37] At pp. 44, 49, 50; see also pp. 19, 21, 9, but see the curious case posited at pp. 39–40. The criterion seems to have been inspired by the practice of the American Supreme Court set out above, sec. 16.

not more encouraging than it was to Beale's successors in the United States.[38] Torts are said by Public International Law to fall within the legislative jurisdiction of the *locus delicti* because of the admonitory character of the law of tort.[39] However, this leaves all the well-known problems wide open: where is the *locus delicti* in interstate torts; what is the effect of rules sounding in tort which are compensatory?

Title to property is said to be governed by the *lex situs*, but as was pointed out above,[40] this principle is not universally applied, especially where general assignments on marriage, death or bankruptcy are con|cerned, and Dr. Mann must allow here an exception in favour of the personal law.[41]

These discrepancies between theory and practice lay the Neo-Bealians open to the same charge as that which was raised against Beale himself. If vague generalities cannot serve the purpose, only *a priori* rules satisfy an overriding doctrine of legislative jurisdiction which seeks to determine when domestic and when foreign law is to be applied in order to solve questions of choice of private law. It is quite another matter when the spatial operation of public law (criminal, labour, tax, anti-trust, procedure) must be determined. Here the need to delimit the actual operation of such laws may well be served best by reliance on the division of legislative competence of States according to Public International Law as a yardstick.[42]

Section 22. Private International Law as Part of Public International Law – Choice of Law before International Tribunals

44. It has been shown above that Public International Law does not contain any specific rules bearing on Private International Law. It is quite another question whether Private International Law has a role to play in Public International Law. If an international dispute arises involving State responsibility for damage to the proprietary interests in the broadest sense, whether they be contractual or are represented by title to property, movable or immovable, alleged to be vested in an alien or in a foreign State, an international tribunal must ascertain, first of all, whether a right of a proprietary nature in

---

[38] See above, Nos. 25–27, pp. 140–143.

[39] At p. 57, but see p. 37.

[40] See above, p. 170, n. 16.

[41] *Loc. cit.*, at p. 62.

[42] Contra Mann, *loc. cit.*, pp. 71–72, but see *passim*, esp. pp. 63–71 and *Hague Rec.* 132 (1971 I), 109–196. It is another matter whether enforcement orders may be made which purport to affect conduct in another country; Mann, *loc. cit.*, p. 97, pp. 127 ff., esp. pp. 145 ff.

the sense described above is vested in the alien or in the foreign State concerned. This question must be determined before it is possible to turn to the principal problem, which is whether in the light of Public International Law a right of a proprietary nature has been infringed so as to constitute an international wrong.[43] For this purpose the International Tribunal | must exercise a choice of law in accordance with a set of rules of Private International Law. The problem is only which system of Private International Law is to supply these rules. In response to this need the practice of international tribunals over the last century has developed independent rules of Private International Law which may be called "Rules of International Conflict of Laws".[44] These rules cover a broad | range of situations and do not appear to

---

[43] See *Illinois Central Railroad Case*, Opinions of Commissioners under the Convention concluded September 8, 1923, between the United States and Mexico, I, p. 15 at pp. 17 ff., cited as *Opinions*, I, II, III (3 vols., 1924, 1929, 1931); see also Feller, *Mexican Claims Commission* (1935), p. 173; De Beus, *The Jurisprudence of the General Claims Commission, United States* v. *Mexico* (1938), pp. 15–21; Ralston, *The Law and Procedure of International Tribunals* (1926), p. 75; *Mexican Union Railways Claim*, Decisions and Opinions of the Commissioners in accordance with the Convention of November 19, 1926, between Great Britain and the United Mexican States (2 vols., 1931, 1933), I, p. 157, at p. 162, henceforth cited as *Decisions*, I, II; *Hoachozo Palestine Land and Development Co. Case*, American-Turkish Claims Settlement under the Agreement of December 24, 1923 (ed. Nielsen, 1937), cited as *American-Turkish Claims*, p. 254, at pp. 259, 260; *Nicholas Marmaras Claim, ibid.*, p. 473, at pp. 479, 480; *Cook* Case (No. 1), *Opinions*, I, p. 318, at p. 321; *Nielsen*, p. 196, at pp. 198–199; *Cook* Case (No. 2), *Opinions*, II, p. 266, at p. 269; Nielsen, *International Law applied to Reclamations* (1933), henceforth cited as Nielsen, p. 389, at pp. 390–391, 395–396; *Ina Hoffman and Dulcie Steinhardt*, American-Turkish Claims, p. 286, at pp. 287–288; see also *Norwegian Claims Case*, Scott, *Hague Court Reports*, II, p. 39, at pp. 64, 65; *Corrie* Claim, *Opinions*, I, p. 213, at pp. 214, 215, 217; Nielsen, pp. 159–160; *Venables* Case, *Opinions*, I, p. 331, at pp. 344, 366–367; Nielsen, p. 205, at pp. 224– 225; *Debenture Holders of San Marcos and Pinos Co.* Claim, *Decisions*, II, p. 135, at pp. 139, 140; *Mexican Tramways Co.* Claim, *ibid.*, II, p. 184, at p. 189; *The Felix*, Moore, *International Arbitrations* (1898) – henceforth cited as Moore– III, p. 2800, at p. 2811; *Socony-Vacuum Oil Co.* Case, American-Turkish Claims, p. 369, at pp. 374, 382; *Singer Sewing Machine Co.* Case, *ibid.*, p. 490, at p. 491; *Malamatinis* Case, *ibid.*, p. 603, at p. 605; *Dickson Car Wheel Co.* Claim, *Opinions,* III, p. 175, at pp. 199, 202; Nielsen, p. 505, at p. 515; *International Fisheries Co.* Case, *Opinions*, III, p. 207, at pp. 241–242; Nielsen, p. 520, at p. 539; *Salem* Case, Nielsen, p. 698; *Company General of the Orinoco Case*, Ralston, *French-Venezuelan Arbitrations* (1902), p. 244.

  See also Lapradelle and Politis, *Recueil des Arbitrages internationaux* (2 Vols. 1932) – henceforth cited as Lapradelle and Politis – II, pp. 258–259 (note doctrinale); *American Bottle Co.* Claim, *Opinions*, II, p. 162; Nielsen, p. 339, at p. 340; *Pomeroy's El Paso Transfer Co.* Case, Nielsen, p. 418, at p. 420; *Parker Case*, *Opinions*, I, p. 35; *Peerless Motor Car Co.* Case, *ibid.*, p. 303; *United Dredging Co.* Case, *ibid.*, p. 394; *National Paper & Type Co.* Case, *Opinions*, II, p. 3; *Parsons Trading Co.* Case, *ibid.*, p. 135; *P.C.I.J., Ser. A. No. 20*, pp. 18–20 (*Serbian Loans* Case); *P.C.I.J., Ser. A/B, No. 76*, p. 18 (*Panevezys Saldutiskis Ry.* Case); Hudson, *ibid., Ser. A/B, No. 78*, p. 184 (*Société Commerciale de Belgique); ibid., Ser. B, No. 6*, p. 28 (*German Settlers in Poland); P.C.I.J., Ser. A, No. 7*, at p. 42 (*German Interests in Poland*), but see *Ser. A/B No. 77*, p. 107 (per Urrutia, dissenting *Electricity Co. of Sofia*); Genet, *Revue générale de droit international public*, 36 (1929), pp. 682–685.

[44] Lipstein (1942), 27 *Transactions of the Grotius Society*, 142–176; (1944), 29 *ibid.*,

differ much from domestic rules of Private International Law, were it not for some overriding special characteristics. In the first place, international tribunals do not possess a *lex fori* in matters of private law. The *lex fori* of international tribunals consists of Public International Law as developed by custom and treaties. The American-Venezuelan Commission said in *William's* Case:[45]

"it is a well-settled principle in common law jurisdictions, and a recognised one in civil law countries, that obligations are to be enforced according to the *lex fori* which here is the treaty and the public law".

Thus, while Private International Law within a State may choose between the application of the municipal law of the court concerned and of foreign law as an alternative source, international courts, owing to the absence of a *lex fori* in matters of private law, must elect between two or more systems of municipal law, none of which can claim the privileged position of *lex curiae*.[46]

It follows, in the second place, that the doctrine of *renvoi* cannot apply. If an international system of conflict of laws accepted a reference back to the *lex fori* it would defeat its own ends, seeing that the reference back would lead to the application, not of municipal, but of international law. It is therefore not surprising that not a single case involving *renvoi* can be found among the great number of international decisions.

On the other hand, it is conceivable that an international tribunal, having ascertained with the help of its own international rules of the conflict of laws that a certain system of municipal law applies, adopts this system as a whole, including its rules of municipal private international law. These rules may refer to yet another system of municipal law by a process known as remission or *Weiterverweisung*.[47] Such a | situation should not be allowed to arise in international courts. It would mean that an international tribunal identi-

---

51–81; (1959), 8 *International and Comparative Law Quarterly*, 506, at p. 522; the following cases should now be added:

    Diverted Cargoes Case, *International Law Reports* 1955, 820; (1956), 5 *International and Comparative Law Quarterly*, 471; *Rev. crit. d.i.p.* 1956, 427; *Ann. français de droit international* 1956, 427.

    Alsing Case (1954), *International Law Reports* 1956, 633, with comments by Schwebel (1959), 8 *International and Comparative Law Quarterly*, 320.

    Aramco Case (1958), 27 *International Law Reports*, pp. 117 at 153 ff.

    Sapphire Case (1963), 35 *International Law Reports*, pp. 136 ff., esp. 170 ff.

[45] Moore, IV, p. 4181, at p. 4182; see also *Eldridge's* Case, *ibid.*, p. 3460, at p. 3462.

[46] See Lipstein, *Transactions of the Grotius Society*, 27 (1942), p. 142, especially at pp. 149–156.

[47] *Cameron's* Claim, *Decisions*, I, p. 33, at p. 45; see also the *Pinson* Case, decided by the Franco-Mexican Claims Commission, *Revue générale de droit international public*, 39 (1932), p. 230, at p. 556 (43).

fies itself with the courts of a particular country, so as to adopt the law of that country as the *lex curiae*, before embarking upon a final choice of law. This would amount to a capitulation of the international court before the Private International Law of a particular country. A reference by international rules of the conflict of laws to some system of municipal law must be final.

In the third place, it follows that in a system of international conflict of laws the principle of public policy must fulfil a different function than in municipal private international law. Within the latter system, the principle of public policy operates so as to substitute the municipal law of the *lex fori* for the system of foreign law ordinarily applicable. Seeing that the *lex fori* of international tribunals consists of international law alone, the function of public policy in an international system of conflict of laws can be only to exclude the operation of foreign private law. It is incapable of substituting another system of private law. Consequently, international public policy can only deny a property right, the violation of which forms the subject of an international reclamation. It can never allow a property right where the foreign law, ordinarily applicable, has denied its existence. It must be admitted that this contention is not borne out by the practice of the Permanent Court of International Justice. In the *Serbian and Brazilian Loan Cases*,[48] it was held that an international court, when applying the municipal law of a particular country, must seek to apply it as it would be applied by that country, including its principles of public policy.

However, if an international court, with the help of its own international rules of conflict of laws, finds that a particular system of municipal law applies, it cannot serve any useful purpose to apply also the rules of public policy of that system which are directed against the application of yet another system of municipal law.[49] But it must be admitted that the answer would have to be different, if the principle of transmission or *Weiterverweisung*, which was rejected above, were to be accepted.

Generally speaking, the practice of international tribunals has not | developed on the lines followed by the Permanent Court of International Justice. The case of *The Enterprize* decided by the Anglo-American Claims Commission,[50] represents a strong precedent in favour of our proposition

---

[48] *P.C.I.J., Ser. A, No. 20*, pp. 41, 46; *ibid., No. 21*, pp. 124–125.

[49] (1942), 27 *Transactions of the Grotius Society*, pp. 156–157; see also the *Norwegian Claims* Case, Scott, *Hague Court Reports*, II, p. 38, at pp. 64, 65. See also Kaeckenbeeck, *The International Experiment of Upper Silesia* (1942), p. 75, and n. 3, p. 78; Niboyet, *Répertoire de droit international*, Vol. 10 (1931), s.v. *ordre public*, especially Nos. 439–457.

[50] Moore, *International Arbitrations*, IV (1898), p. 4349; Lapradelle and Politis, *Recueil des Arbitrages internationaux*, I (1932), 686, and see the *note doctrinale, ibid.*, p. 705, at pp. 707–709. See also, to the same effect the decisions of the same tribunal in *The Hermosa*, Moore, IV, p. 4374; Lapradelle and Politis, I, p. 688; *The Creole*, Moore, IV, p. 4375; Lapradelle and Politis, *loc. cit.* But see *The Comet, The Encomium*, Moore, IV, 4349; La-

that the principles of public policy, for the purposes of international courts, are furnished by international law. The facts were as follows. In 1835, an American vessel carrying slaves belonging to American owners took refuge in Bermuda, owing to stress of weather. The Court of Bermuda ordered the slaves to be freed pursuant to the Act of 3 and 4 Wm. IV c. 73 (1833) abolishing slavery in Great Britain and her dependencies. In the course of the claim for damages against Great Britain, the tribunal had to decide whether the court of Bermuda was entitled to apply the English statute in respect of *res in transitu* on board a vessel and which were ordinarily subject to American law as their former *lex rei sitae*, or as the law of the flag. It was clear that the Bermudan Court had applied the English statute on grounds of public policy. The question was therefore whether the principles of public policy to be considered by the international tribunal were those of the law of Bermuda which rejected slavery or of the *lex fori*, i.e., international law, which at that time did not. The Commission, including, it would appear, Hornby, the British Commissioner, who delivered a dissenting judgment,[51] decided that the principles of public policy were prescribed by international law and, by a majority, allowed the claim. Bates, the Umpire said:[52]

"It was well known that slavery had been conditionally abolished in nearly all the British Dominions about six months before ... No one can deny that slavery is contrary to the principles of justice and humanity and can only be established in any country by law. At the time of the transaction on which the claim is founded, slavery existed by law in several countries and was not wholly abolished in the British Dominions. It could not, then, be contrary | to the law of nations, and *The Enterprize* was as much entitled to protection as though her cargo consisted of any other description of property. The conduct of the authorities of Bermuda was a violation of the law of nations ..."

The remarks of Upham, the American Commissioner, are even more forceful, but it is submitted that they are too sweeping. He said:[53]

"There is but one ground on which it can be contended that the Act of 3 and 4 Wm. IV c. 73 overrules the principles that I have laid down [i.e., that the law of the port may not be applied to foreign vessels in port and to property on board] and that is that the municipal law of England is paramount to the absolute rights of other governments when they come in conflict with each other. Such a position virtually abolishes the entire code of international law. If one state can at pleasure revoke such a law, any other state may do the same thing, and the whole system of international intercourse becomes a mere matter of arbitrary will and of universal violence."

---

pradelle and Politis, I, p. 691, to the contrary seeing that the acts complained of occurred prior to the passing of the Act of 3 and 4 Wm. IV, c. 73.

[51] Moore, *loc. cit.*, at pp. 4362–4365.

[52] Moore, *loc. cit.*, at p. 4373.

[53] Moore, *loc. cit.*, at p. 4361. But see the dissenting opinion of Hornby, the British Commissioner, *loc. cit.*, at pp. 4362–4372.

It may be useful to refer to a few more awards. In the case of *The Maria Luz*,[54] the Peruvian Government claimed damages from Japan on the ground that Japanese Courts had acted illegally in disallowing the claim of a Peruvian Captain for the restoration of escaped Chinese coolies who were under a contract to him. The arbitrator said:

"We have arrived at the conviction ... that the Japanese Government acted in good faith, in virtue of its own laws and customs, without infringing the general prescriptions of the law of nations or the stipulations of particular treaties."

Another example is furnished by the decision of the tribunal in *Reparation Commission v. U.S.A.*[55] The facts were as follows. Shortly before | the outbreak of war between the U.S.A. and Germany in 1917, the Standard Oil Co. sold its shares in a German Company to a German national in consideration of a sum the payment of which was deferred, supplemented by a deposit of securities as a guarantee. The securities were subsequently seized by the American Custodian of Enemy Property. The claim before the tribunal involved the question whether the contract of sale was valid and whether the American Company had acquired a lien over the securities. The Tribunal said:

"Whereas the ... securities ... were seized as enemy property by the Enemy Property Custodian, the latter, when opposition was lodged by the Standard Oil Co., asserted his belief in the good faith of the sale, but none the less by a decision ... declared it to be null and void. Whereas this decision, being prompted only by reasons of public order, could not lead the Tribunal to consider the sale as null ..."

In the fourth place, the absence of a *lex fori* in matters of private law explains why only a comparatively small number of cases involved difficulties of what is generally known as conflicts of characterisation. Such conflicts, it may be remembered, are not infrequent in municipal private international law. They may arise when a Court must interpret the meaning of a legal concept contained in a rule of private or of private international law. These terms may have one meaning according to the *lex fori* and another according to the law ordinarily applicable. The tribunals, the practice of which is under review today, have not followed any consistent line in matters of characterisation. In general they characterised according to the law of one of the coun-

---

[54] Moore, V, p. 5034; Lapradelle and Politis, I, p. 704; and see the *note doctrinale* by Strisower, *ibid.*, pp. 707–709, where he distinguishes between public policy in international law and municipal law. See also the dissenting opinion of Mr. Little in *Henry Woodruff and Flanagan, Bradley, Clark & Co. v. Venezuela*, Moore, IV, p. 3566; *Beales, Nobles Garrison v. Venezuela*, Moore, IV, p. 3548, at p. 3560; see also *Camy v. U.S.*, Moore, III, p. 2398, at p. 2400.

[55] (1927), 8 *British Year Book of International Law*, 156, at p. 158; (1928), 22 *American Journal of International Law*, 404, at p. 407.

tries which were parties to the dispute.[56] But it is impossible to ascertain the reasons | why the characterisation according one system of laws was chosen in preference to any other. Sometimes it cannot even be stated according to which system of laws the tribunals characterised.[57]

In the fifth place the method of proving foreign municipal law in international courts must be noted. The Permanent Court of International Justice held in the *Serbian and Brazilian Loan* Cases:[58]

"Though bound to apply municipal law when circumstances so require, the Court, which is a tribunal of international law and which, in this capacity, is deemed itself to know what this law is, is not obliged also to know the municipal law of the various countries. All that can be said in this respect is that the Court may possibly be obliged to obtain knowledge regarding the municipal law which has to be applied. And this it must do, either by means of evidence furnished it by the parties, or by means of any researches which the Court may think fit to undertake or to cause to be undertaken."

And again:

"For the Court itself to undertake its own construction of municipal law, leaving on one side existing judicial decisions, with the ensuing danger of contradicting the construction which has been placed on such law by the highest national tribunal and which, in its results, seems to the Court reasonable, would not be in conformity with the task for which the Court has been established ..."[59]

The Court based its conclusions with respect to French law on citations of publicists and judicial decisions of French Courts.[60] The | same approach was

---

[56] *Dusenberg* v. *Mexico*, Moore, III, p. 2157, at p. 2158; *Knox* v. *Mexico, ibid.*, III, p. 2166; *Robert* v. *Mexico, ibid.*, III, p. 2468, at p. 2471; *Rivlin, Guardian of H. Sternberg* v. *Turkey*, American-Turkish Claims, p. 622, at p. 626 (domicile characterised according to American notions); *Raeburn* v. *Mexico, Decisions*, II, p. 54, at p. 59 (domicile characterised according to English law); *Gleadell* v. *Mexico, ibid., I*, p. 55, at pp. 57, 63 (personal property, situs of choses in action characterised according to English law); *The Enterprize*, Moore, IV, p. 4349, at p. 4366 (rights over slaves characterised according to American notions); *Norwegian Claims* Case, Scott, *Hague Court Reports*, II, p. 38, at p. 67. But see *P.C.I.J., Ser. B, No. 10* at pp. 19–22, where the Court had to interpret private law terms contained in a treaty. For a discussion of this problem see (1942), 27 *Transactions of the Grotius Society*, 158, and the literature quoted, *ibid.*, p. 84. And see Niboyet, *Hague Rec.* 31 (1930 I), pp. 68–99; *ibid.*, 40 (1932 II), pp. 180 ff.; Kaeckenbeeck, *loc. cit.* (above p. 176, n. 49), pp. 51, 61; Jenks (1938), 19 *British Year Book of International Law*, 67, at p. 84.

[57] *The Montijo*, Moore, II, p. 1421, at p. 1430; *Raeburn* v. *Mexico, Decisions*, II, p. 54, at p. 55.

[58] *P.C.I.J., Ser. A, No. 21*, at p. 124; see also *P.C.I.J., Ser. A, No. 7*, at p. 19 *(German Interests in Upper Silesia)*.

[59] *P.C.I.J., Ser. A, No. 20*, p. 46; see also the observations of Anzilotti, *P.C.I.J., Ser. A, No. 65*, at pp. 63–64 *(Danzig Legislative Decrees)*.

[60] But see the dissenting opinions of Bustamente, *P.C.I.J., Ser. A, No. 20*, at pp. 54–58; *ibid., No. 21*, at pp. 131–136, and of Pessoa, *ibid., No. 20*, at pp. 71 ff., especially at pp. 73–74; *ibid., No. 21*, at pp. 148–152. For the uncertainty of French law on the question in issue see Genet, *Revue générale de droit international.* 36 (1929), pp. 685–688. And see

chosen by the great majority of international tribunals,[61] although in some cases emphasis was laid upon the opinion of experts,[62] and in others upon the practice of municipal courts.[63] In the *Hudson Bay Co.* Claim[64] and in the *Puget Sound Agricultural Co.* Claim,[65] which involved disputes over titles to land not yet under the sovereignty of any State, the tribunal applied the principles of natural justice.

Finally, nationality is of paramount importance, for unlike municipal courts, international tribunals must consider not only whether a right exists and according to which system of law, but they must also determine whether the plaintiff and his claim are so intimately connected with one of the States subject to the jurisdiction of the tribunal as to confer upon it the necessary competence to adjudicate.

45. If the preliminary investigation establishes the existence of a property right under domestic law and that the right has been violated by the defendant State in breach of Public International Law involving State responsibility, a defence based on a domestic statute of limitations,[66] a domestic rule that *actio personalis moritur cum persona*[67] or a domestic rule that the State is not liable for the acts of its officials[68] is of no avail.

"The right of a person to sue a Government under domestic law is not conclusive with respect to rights that may be invoked in behalf of such a person under international law."[69]

| The same applies to the measure of damages, the rate of exchange and the question of interest.[70]

---

the *Lighthouse* Case *(France* v. *Greece), P.C.I.J.,* Ser. *A/B, No. 62,* pp. 19–24. where the Court applied Turkish law. But see the observations of Judge Hudson in *P.C.I.J.,* Ser. *A/B, No. 78,* p. 184 *(Société Générale de Belgique).* See also Jenks in (1938), 19 *British Year Book of International Law,* p. 67, at pp. 69, 89.

[61] *Cook* v. *Mexico, Opinions,* II, p. 162, at p. 165; Nielsen, *International Law applied to Reclamations* (1933), p. 500, at p. 503; *Re Donnell's Executors, Re Hollins and McBlair,* Moore, IV, pp. 3545–3546.

[62] *Reparation Commission v. U.S.A.* (1927), 8 *British Year Book of International Law,* 156, at p. 159; (1928), 22 *American Journal of International Law,* 404, at p. 408.

[63] *Dr Baldwin's* Case, Moore, IV, p. 2859, at p. 2864.

[64] Moore, I, p. 250, at 259; Lapradelle and Politis, II, p. 513, at p. 515, with a *note doctrinale* at p. 520.

[65] Moore, I, p. 262, at p. 264; Lapradelle and Politis, II, p. 503, at p. 511.

[66] See (1944), 29 *Transactions of the Grotius Society,* 51, at pp. 57–58, and notes 13–15 with cases.

[67] See *ibid.,* pp. 58–59, and notes 16–22 with cases.

[68] See *ibid.,* pp. 59–60, and note 23 with cases.

[69] Nielsen, p. 390, at pp. 395–396; see also *Thomas Morrison* v. *Mexico,* Moore, III, p. 2325, at p. 2326; *P.C.I.J.,* Ser. *A, No. 20,* p. 17 *(Serbian Loans* Case); *P.C.I.J.,* Ser. *A/B, No. 61,* p. 232 *(Peter Pázmány University Case).*

[70] (1944), 29 *Transactions of the Grotius Society,* 51, at pp. 60–61, and notes 24–30 with cases.

The preliminary investigation is only concerned with the existence of property rights under municipal law. The question whether a violation of the right thus ascertained is actionable must be decided, for the purposes of an international reclamation before an international tribunal, according to the principles of international law. The Rules of International Conflict of Laws cover a fairly wide range of situations including proof of foreign law,[71] corporations[72] and partnerships,[73] contracts and quasi-contracts,[74] torts,[75] property[76] and successions.[77]

Even if the content of these rules of International Conflict of Laws appear more often than not to be the same as those of domestic Private International Law, the special characteristics set out above (para. 44) are so strong as to exclude any identity of these two systems of Private International Law. For the same reason there exists no hierarchy, in the conflict of laws, of a supreme international and subordinate municipal systems of Private International Law.

At the same time the existence of Rules of International Conflict of Laws, much neglected hitherto, eliminates the need to make provision in international agreement of a private law nature between States or between a State or an individual for the application of "general principles of law" observed by all nations.[78] If it is the purpose of this device to eliminate any difficulties arising out of the absence of any particular system of domestic Private International Law which can determine the law applicable to the preliminary question as to whether a right of a proprietary nature exists, the answer must be that the Rules of International Conflict of Laws, which were outlined above, are sufficiently developed to dispose of these difficulties. If this device is used because the parties are unwilling to allow any one legal system to apply which | is connected with the transaction and seek to exclude the application of specific domestic law altogether,[79] it must be asked whether

---

[71] *Ibid.*, pp. 61–62, and notes 31–33 with cases.

[72] *Ibid.*, pp. 69–71, and notes 65–79 with cases.

[73] *Ibid.*, pp. 71–72, and notes 80–85 with cases.

[74] *Ibid.*, pp. 72–73, and notes 86–98 with cases.

[75] *Ibid.*, p. 73, and notes 99–102 with cases.

[76] *Ibid.*, pp. 73–74, and notes 103–107 with cases.

[77] *Ibid.*, pp. 74–76, and notes 108–121 with cases.

[78] If restricted to principles common to the legal systems of both parties, this provision amounts to no more than a call for cumulating the two legal systems concerned.

[79] For this problem see *Abu Dhabi* case, *International Law Reports* 1951, Case No. 37; *Petroleum Development (Quatar) Ltd.* v. *Ruler of Quatar*, *International Law Reports* 1951, Case No. 38; *Ruler of Quatar* v. *International Marine Oil Ltd*, *International Law Reports* 1953, p. 534; for lit. see McNair (1957), 31 *British Year Book of International Law*, 1; Mann (1944), 21 *ibid.*, 11 ff.; (1959), 35 *ibid.*, 34; (1967) 42 *ibid.*, 1, at pp. 2 ff.; in *Jus et Lex, Festgabe für Gutzwiller* (1959), 465; (1960) 54 *American Journal of International Law*, 572. See also *Davies Case (U.S.* v. *Mexico)*, *Opinions*, I, p. 197, at p. 201; Nielsen, p. 145, at p. 148.

the parties can do so effectively. In an international tribunal the rules of international conflict of laws, in domestic courts the rules of domestic Private International Law continue to apply and may perhaps override the choice of general principles of law.[80]

Section 23. Recognition and the Application of Foreign Law[81]

46. It is necessary to draw attention at this stage to the principle, alleged to have been developed in English and American Law, which has been summed up as follows some 25 years ago:

"Recognition, being retroactive and dating back to the moment at which the newly recognised Government established itself in power, its effect is to preclude the courts of law of the recognising State from questioning the legality or validity of the acts, both legislative and executive, past and future, of that Government."[82]

This principle is known in England as the rule in *Luther* v. *Sagor*[83] and in the United States as the "Act of State" doctrine represented most recently by the *Sabbatino* Case,[84] preceded by many other decisions to the same effect. It is less rigidly applied or even unknown in other | countries.[85] Read literally, it only prohibits courts from "questioning the legality or validity of legislative and administrative acts". If this interpretation is followed, the rule is restricted to the prohibition to allow an action in tort in England or the United

---

[80] See Lipstein in *Rabels Z.*, 27 (1962), 359, at p. 361.

[81] Mann (1943), 59 *Law Quarterly Review*, 42, 155; (1954), 70 *ibid.*, 217; (1955) 40 *Transactions of the Grotius Society*, 25; (1965), 51 *Virginia Law Rev.*, 604; *Hague Rec.* 132 (1971 I), 109, at pp. 145–156; Lipstein (1950), 35 *Transactions of the Grotius Society*, 157–188; Stevenson (1951), 51 *Col.L.R.*, 710; Zander (1959), 53 *American Journal of International Law*, 826; Greig (1967), 83 *Law Quarterly Review*; Bernstein (1967), 65 *Mich.L.R.*, 924; Sauveplanne, *Nederlands Tijdschrift voor Internationaal Recht*, 7 (1960), 17; Simmonds (1965), 14 *International and Comparative Law Quarterly*, 452.

[82] Oppenheim, *International Law* (7 ed. 1948), Vol. I, p. 133, and note 2, p. 296.

[83] [1921] 3 K.B. 532 (C.A.).

[84] *Banco Nacional de Cuba* v. *Sabbatino*, 376 US 398; 11 L.ed. 2d 804 (1964).

[85] See, e.g., Kegel in Sörgel, *Kommentar zum BGB*, Vol. 7 (10 ed. 1970), para. 101, before Art. 7, EGBGB, and note 1 with lit.; Wengler, *Festschrift für Lewald* (1953), 615–632; Sauveplanne, *loc. cit.*, p. 23 ff., and the Civil Court of Rome, 13 Sept. 1954 in *Anglo-Iranian Oil Co. Ltd* v. *S.U.P.O.R. Co.*, 1955 *International Law Reports* 23, at p. 42, with cases, notes 1–3; *Foro it.*, 1955, I, 256; *Riv. dir. int.*, 39 (1955), p. 97. The judgment of the Civil Court of Antwerp of 21 February 1939, *Annual Digest* 1938–1940, Case No. 11; *La Belgique Judiciaire*, 1939, Nos. 11, 12 col. 371; that of the Court of Appeal of Arnhem of 12 June 1939; *Annual Digest* 1919–1942 (Suppl. vol.), 19 *W. & N.J.* 1940, No. 20, and of the District Court of New York (S.D.) of 13 April 1939, *Ann. Dig.* 1938–1940, Case No. 35, 28 F. Supp. 279 definitely deny that any court is entitled to decide on the lawfulness of an expropriation carried out by a foreign government; the same conclusion was reached by the Court of Tokyo in its judgment of 21 September 1953, 1953 *International Law Reports* 305.

States on the strength of an allegation that a foreign legislative or administrative act is illegal under the foreign law concerned, but does not oblige the *lex fori* to apply the foreign law concerned or to give effect to the foreign administrative act. Unfortunately the development has gone far beyond this point, due perhaps to the fact that in common law countries actions, which in civil law countries enforce title to goods by a *rei vindicatio*,[86] are framed in tort even if directed against a third party. Thus the prohibition to institute an action in tort as a result of legislation or of an administrative act by a recognised government has a much more far reaching effect. Conceived as a barrier to prevent individuals with a grievance against a foreign government from by-passing the normal channels, i.e., from proceeding against that government in its own courts in respect of acts of a public law nature, or from pressing claims based on a violation of international law in respect of aliens,[87] the principle may have its origin[88] in the English doctrine of acts of State, which prohibits actions in tort brought in England by aliens in respect of acts abroad by individuals whose acts are authorised or ratified by the |Government in the United Kingdom.[89] As it appears today in the books, it may not stand up to scrutiny[90] and will perhaps assume finally its proper role, which has now become two-fold. This role is, firstly, to preclude a claim for damages in tort against an individual for a violation of foreign Public or Public International Law committed by a Government and, secondly, to determine which of two competing sets of rules enacted or which measures taken by rival authorities in the same country are to be regarded as the law and the acts of the Government of that country, but no more. Thus understood the principle does contain a choice of law rule; it concerns the proof of foreign law and the exclusion of Public International Law as a basis of an action in tort, in disregard of foreign law which is normally applicable, against persons who carried out the act or who acquired property in consequence of the act. It is believed that this is the proper function and meaning of the rule.

47. In England and in the countries which look to the common law of England, the judgment of the Court of Appeal in *Luther* v. *Sagor*[91] gave the

---

[86] See, e.g., *Anglo-Iranian Oil Co. Ltd* v. *S.U.P.O.R.*, Civil Court of Rome, 13 Sept. 1954, 1955 *International Law Reports*, 23, 25; *Foro it.* 1955, I, 256; *Riv. dir. int.*, 39 (1955), 97.

[87] This may have been the ground for the decision in *Duke of Brunswick* v. *King of Hanover* (1848), 2 H.L.C.I. at pp. 17, 21, 27, discussed by Mann, *Hague Rec.* 132 (1971 I), at pp. 145–146.

[88] See Mann, *loc. cit.*, p. 152.

[89] *Buron* v. *Denman* (1848), 2 Ex. 167; see Mann, *loc. cit.*, p. 156, but see Sauveplanne, p. 33.

[90] See also Mann, *loc. cit.*, pp. 151, 153, 156; it is certainly not a principle of Public International Law.

[91] [1921] 3 K.B. 532.

lead; but it was a case *primae impressionis* and its interpretation depends much on the stress which is laid upon the respective arguments adduced by the three Lords Justices who decided it.[92] If authority is to be sought for this decision, it is to be found in three judgments of the Supreme Court of the United States on which the English Court of Appeal relied.

Of these *Williams* v. *Bruffy*[93] established a purely negative rule. *If the ordinary principles of the conflict of laws refer to the law of a particular foreign country*, the enactments of insurrectionist authorities may be disregarded, if these authorities were never recognised and did not survive.[94] *Underhill* v. *Hernandez*[95] established a positive and a negative rule. *If the ordinary principles of the conflict of laws refer to* | *the law of a particular foreign country*, the enactments and acts of revolutionary authorities are treated retroactively as the law of the foreign country and as the executive acts of a foreign government, once these revolutionary authorities have been recognised as the government by the executive of the forum. In a conflict of laws in time, the rules and acts of the government which was recognised last prevails. The fact that prior to recognition the measures were illegal acts of individual rebels is irrelevant. Furthermore the question whether an act, lawful by the *lex loci*, constitutes a breach of Public International Law can only be considered by governments and by international tribunals.

Oetjen v. *Central Leather Co.*[96] enlarges upon the principle established in *Underhill* v. *Hernandez*.[97] *If the ordinary principles of the conflict of laws refer to the law of a particular foreign country*[98] the government of which has

---

[92] Per Warrington L.J. at pp. 548–549: territoriality of laws; Bankes, L.J. at p. 545: *lex situs*; Scrutton L.J. at pp. 555, 556, 558, 559: sovereign immunity and a restrictive application of public policy by the forum. See Lipstein, *loc. cit.*, p. 158.

[93] (1878) 96 U.S. 176.

[94] An *obiter dictum* suggests that the legislation of a de facto recognised government would, in general, have been recognised.

[95] (1897) 168 U.S. 250.

[96] (1918), 246 U.S. 297. See also *Ricaud* v. *American Leather Co.* (1918), 246 U.S. 304, 310: "It is irrelevant whether the property was owned by an American or a foreign national". H. Lauterpacht [1954], *Cambridge Law Journal,* 20, seeks to draw a distinction according as the objects of the executive measure are nationals of the foreign country or not, referring to *Princess Paley Olga* v. *Weiss* [1929], 1 K.B. 718. This distinction is not only unsupported by the authorities, but it would lead to the result that in the case of a violation of Public International Law by foreign law which is normally applicable, the rule of foreign law would have to be disregarded where nationals of the country of the *forum*, possibly where nationals of third countries, but never where stateless persons or nationals of the country of the *lex causae* are involved. Such a discriminatory application of local public policy does violence to the notion of public policy itself. Cp. *Banque des Marchands de Moscou (Koupetschesky), Royal Assurance Association* v. *The Liquidator* [1952], 1 All E.R. 1269; [1951], 1 T.L.R. 739. See also, e.g., *Koh-i-Noor, L. H. Hardtmuth* v. *Koh-i-Noor Tužkárna L. H. Hardmuth* decided by the Austrian Supreme Court on 2 June 1958, *SZ* XXXI (1958), p. 280; 26 *International Law Reports*, 40.

[97] (1897), 168 U.S. 250.

[98] This need to make a preliminary choice of law is now acknowledged by the decision in

been recognised by the executive of the forum, the enactments and acts of that government cannot be examined by the courts of the forum for the purpose of determining whether damages are to be awarded against an individual on the ground of a breach of international law. The much discussed decision of the Supreme Court of the United States in *Banco Nacional de Cuba* v. *Sabbatino*,[99] has added little, but its existence has been the first reason for its erosion by the Hickenlooper | Amendment attached to the Foreign Assistance Act, 1964, enacted in the United States.[100]

48. It is now necessary to consider the rule, as commonly understood, its limits and its justification at the present time.

In the first place, recognition is not the factor which determines whether foreign law is to be applied by the courts of the forum.[101] Otherwise the laws of all recognised governments could claim respect. It is the task of the rules of Private International Law of the forum to determine this conflict. Recognition determines only which of two competing sets of regulations within one country must be regarded as the law of the foreign country, once the Private International Law of the forum has referred to the law of the particular foreign country.[102]

At the same time recognition of a government confers upon the acts and measures of the recognised authority the character of an act by a public authority and attributes to it the character of a datum, which has to be taken into account by the courts of the forum whenever the operation of foreign public law must be considered.

In the second place, the rule does not apply to the decisions of foreign courts. Here again recognition determines only whether the courts established by the predecessor government or the bodies set up by the new government are courts, the pronouncements of which can be recognised and enforced by the forum, *if* the courts of the foreign country have jurisdiction according to the law of the court of the recognising country.[103]

In the third place, despite the past and present trend to the contrary in

---

Tabacalera Severiano Jorge S.A. v. *Standard Cigar Co.*, 392 F. 2d. 706, L. 714 (5. Circ. 1968), cert. denied, 393 U.S. 924, 21. L.ed. 2d 260 (1968).

[99] 376 U.S. 398, 11 L.ed. 2d 804 (1964); the literature is enormous; here it is only necessary to add Hopkins [1964], *Cambridge Law Journal*, 282; *Banco Nacional de Cuba* v. *Farr, Whitlock & Co.*, 383 F. 2d 166 (1967), cert. denied, 390 U.S. 956, 19 L.ed. 2d 1151 (1968).

[100] 78 Stat. 1013, am. 79 Stat. 653, 22 U.S.C. § 2370 (e) (2).

[101] See Stone C.J. (diss.) in *U.S.* v. *Pink* (1942), 315 U.S. 203, at p. 252. But see, e.g., *The Maret*, 145 F.Ld 431 (5. Circ.); (1944–1945), 58 *Harv.L.R.*, 612; (1944–1945) 93 *Univ. of Pennsylvania L.R.*, 323; and cp. *Carl Zeiss Stiftung* v. *Carl Zeiss V.E.B.*, 293 F. Supp. 892 at p. 900–901, 915–916; affd. 433 F. 2d 686, 699 (2 Cir. 1970).

[102] See also Bernstein (1967), 65 *Mich.L.R.*, 924.

[103] See Lipstein (1950), 35 *Transactions of the Grotius Society*, 157, at pp. 183–187.

common law countries,[104] it would seem that the regulations of foreign bodies which have not been recognised can nevertheless be applied in accordance with the rules of Private International Law of the forum, | if they are in fact enforced in the foreign country concerned.[105] Recognition by the government of the forum is the best evidence for determining whether the regulations and measures of foreign bodies are to be regarded as the law of the foreign country and the acts of public authorities, but it is not conclusive evidence.

In the fourth place, recognition does not bind the courts of the recognising State unconditionally to respect the law of the recognised State, if the rules of Private International Law of the forum refer to that law, or to accept the effects, in private law, of the acts of the executive organs of the recognised government. The existence of the latter cannot be denied, and they constitute a datum or data,[106] but no more. This latter aspect must be developed in some detail.

Section 24. Scrutiny of, and Refusal to Apply or to Respect, the Law and the Executive Acts of a Foreign Recognised Government

49. The contention that the rule known as the act of State principle or the rule in *Luther* v. *Sagor*[107] is concerned, at least in part, with proof of foreign law when the court is confronted by two conflicting sets of rules enacted by rival authorities in a State, is borne out by the practice and literature on the scrutiny of the constitutional validity of foreign law.[108] On a lower level the same problem is posed, if the rule of foreign law is to be found in delegated legislation and it is alleged that such legislation contravenes an Enabling Act of the *lex causae*. Again, it may be alleged that a treaty entered into by the State of the *lex causae*, has not been incorporated into the law of the State

---

[104] See *Carl Zeiss Stiftung Ltd* v. *Rayner and Keeler* [1967], 1 A.C. 853, but see the observations of Lord Reid at p. 906 and of Lord Wilberforce at pp. 953, 954.

[105] See above, p. 184, n. 85 and see Lipstein, *loc. cit.*, p. 185; Sauveplanne (above p. 183, n. 81), at p. 21, with cases notes 17, 20, 24, 46; *Carl Zeiss Stiftung* v. *V.E.B.C. Zeiss Jena*, 293 F. Supp. 892, 900–901, 915–916 (1968), (1969) 63 *Am. J. of International Law*, 638; (1969), 3 *Int. Lawyer*, 525; (1968), *U.S. P.Q.*, 97; Treves, *Rev. crit. d.i.p.*, 1967, p. 23; *Riv. dir. int. priv. e proc.*, 3 (1967), 437; 6 (1970), 451, with references to the practice of the courts in continental Europe; affd. 433 F. 2d 686, 699 (2 Cir. 1970); Bernstein (1972), 20 *American Journal of Comparative Law*, 299.

[106] See, e.g., *The Miriella*, decided by the Tribunal of Venice on 11 March 1953, *Foro it.*, 1953, I, 719, 721, 1955 *International Law Reports*, 19, 21.

[107] [1921], 3 K.B. 532.

[108] See Lipstein (1967), 42 *British Year Book of International Law*, 265–270, and notes 2 and 3 with lit.; for the cases see p. 268 and notes 2–8; and see Mann, *Hague Rec.* 132 (1971 I), 151–152; Batiffol, *Aspects philosophiques du droit international privé* (1956), p. 114, n. 1.

which is applicable, although the Constitution of that State so requires, if the treaty is to be effective. Conversely it may be argued that, according to | the constitutional law of the foreign *lex causae*, a previous treaty has been superseded by subsequent domestic legislation. Finally, the question may present itself in two stages, if it is contended, firstly, that the applicable rule of foreign law violates a precept of public international law and, secondly, that the constitution of the foreign State concerned invalidates all provisions of its domestic law which are contrary to the principles of Public International Law accepted by that State.[109]

If the foreign law concerned permits the judicial control of the constitutional validity of its statutes, the forum may also exercise this control, unless the foreign law concerned reserves for a special court[110] the determination, with binding effect *erga omnes*, whether a particular rule violates the constitution and is invalid.

Thus, in all these circumstances, the rule of foreign law applicable in the circumstances, may be disregarded and the foreign executive act can be treated as invalid because the forum may determine the constitutional validity according to the *lex causae*. This conclusion does not, however, lead necessarily to another, namely that an action in tort may be brought in the forum against a member of the foreign government or a third party who has acquired property on the strength of the foreign law or of the foreign executive act. The answer to the latter question must depend upon whether the executive measure simply ceases to be a datum or must henceforth be treated as an illegal act.

50. Those who believe that the foreign act of State doctrine is a precept of Public International Law[111] seek to mitigate its effects by asserting that a breach of Public International Law by the foreign government concerned either deprives the act of its validity altogether, or at least relieves the courts in other countries from giving effect to it.[112] The conclusion that a foreign government has committed a breach of Public International Law and that

---

[109] See, e.g., the Constitution of the German Federal Republic, Arts. 25, 100; of Italy, Arts. 101, 134–136; of Austria, Arts. 9, 140, 140a.

[110] See, e.g., the Constitutions of the German Federal Republic, Art. 100, subject to the exception of "Inzidente Normen Kontrolle", and of Italy, Art. 134, and of Austria, Art. 89.

[111] For a rejection of this view see, *inter alia*, Mann, above p. 185, n. 90.

[112] See, e.g., H. Lauterpacht [1954], *Cambridge Law Journal*, 20; Mann (1954), 70 *Law Quarterly Review*, 181; (1956), 19 *Modern Law Rev.*, 301; M. Mann (1956), 5 *International and Comparative Law Quarterly*, 245; E. Lauterpacht, *ibid.*, p. 301; Lipstein [1956], *Cambridge Law Journal*, 138; de Nova, *Rev. crit. d.i.p.*, 47 (1958), 519, 534; Gihl in *Liber Amicorum ... to Bagge*, 56; Kollewijn, *Nederlands Tijdschrift voor Internationaal Recht*, 6 (1959), 140; Schwarzenberger (1960), 9 Journal of Public Law (Emory University), 147, at p. 164; Mann, *Neue Juristische Wochenschrift* 1961, 705; Seidl-Hohenveldern, in *Recht im Wandel*, *Festschrift Carl Heymanns Verlag* (1966), pp. 591–619.

the foreign executive measure can be disregarded as void involves the appreciation and determination of extraneous factors and the application of a
system of law which is not, properly speaking, that of the forum. It is,
therefore, not surprising that | this result has only been reached rarely.[113] It
must be stressed, however, once more that the problem cannot be disposed
of by the argument that laws or executive measures are void if they conflict
with Public International Law.[114] Whether domestic law is void can only be
determined by reference to the constitutional law of the foreign country
concerned; as shown above, this scrutiny is only possible during the process
of proving foreign law and only if the foreign law concerned permits generally the judicial review of the constitutionality of its legislation.[115] In the
absence of such a finding by a competent court, the act remains at least a
datum. Any principle of the foreign law postulating the primacy of International Law is thus safeguarded.

51. It is another matter whether the forum will give effect to foreign law,
which is applicable according to its rules of Private International Law, or to
foreign executive measures, if they infringe Public International Law. Since
the choice and application of foreign law is in the discretion of the *lex fori* and
since the foreign act of State doctrine is equally a doctrine of domestic law, it
is clear that the forum need not apply foreign law or give effect to foreign
acts, if they offend manifestly against the public policy of the forum. The
problem is, therefore, whether a breach of Public International Law as such
offends against the public policy of the forum or whether it is only a factor to
be taken into account in deciding whether foreign law which is normally
applicable is to be applied in the particular case, or whether a foreign executive act is to be recognised and given effect.

| The answer is easy, if the foreign law or the foreign executive measure in
issue runs counter to a fundamental principle of the *lex fori* as embodied in
the Constitution of the latter[116] and, especially if the local Constitution sanc-

---

[113] *The Rose Mary, Anglo-Iranian Oil Co.* v. *Jaffrate*, decided on 9 January 1953 by the
Supreme Court of Aden [1953], 1 W.L.R. 246; 1953 *International Law Reports*, 316; (1953)
47 *American Journal of International Law*, 325; *Clunet* 1956, 713, and the decisions of
lower German courts cited there.

[114] See above, p. 188, n. 106.

[115] See above, pp. 188–189; only when the law in question has been promulgated, or the
executive measure has been executed by an Occupying Power, courts in other countries
must look exclusively to Public International Law in order to determine the validity of the
law or measure; see Lipstein, *Communicazioni e Studi*, IV (1952), 114–141.

[116] Gamillscheg, *Festschrift für Nipperdey* (1965), I, p. 323; *Gesetz über das Bundesver-
fassungsgericht* of 12 March 1951 (BGBl. 1951, I, p. 423, para. 13 (6), (11), (12)); Decision of
the Federal Constitutional Court, 1 (1951), p. 11; 6 (1957), pp. 291, 295; Morelli, *Studi
Perassi* (1957), II, 169, at pp. 180–186; Mosconi, *Diritto internazionale*, 14 (1960), 426 at
pp. 429, 435, restricts the effect of Art. 10 of the Italian Constitution incorporating the
supremacy of international law to the control of Italian legislation.

tions the primacy of Public International Law. In all other circumstances it would appear that, when confronted with a plea that the foreign law or the foreign executive act offends against Public International Law, courts in a variety of countries have considered the rules of Public International Law incidentally only as a facet of a broader notion of local public policy.[117] This attitude is to be approved since, in the absence of the principle of primacy of Inter|national Law in the *lex causae* or the *lex fori*, the substance of the individual rule of foreign law or of the particular executive act and not the formal violation of a rule of Public International Law must determine whether the rule or act offends against the basic social, political and moral foundations of the *lex fori*. At the same time, reliance on the negative function of public policy rather than on negative reaction to a breach of International Law makes it possible to deny effect to the foreign law or foreign executive measure in issue irrespective of whether the person affected is an alien, a stateless person or a national of the country of the *lex causae*. Thus the foreign law or the foreign measure is accorded or denied effect uniformly and without discrimination in accordance with the general standards of the

---

[117] England: *Re Helbert Wagg & Co. Ltd* [1956], Ch. 323, 344.

Italy: *The Miriella, Anglo-Iranian Oil Co.* v. *Società Petrolifera Orientale,* decided by the Tribunal of Venice on 11 March 1953, *Giur. it.* 1953, I, 2, 305; *Foro it.* 1953, I, 719; *Riv. dir. internaz.,* 36 (1953), 217; 1955 *International Law Reports,* 19; (1953), 2 *Internat. and Comp. L.Q.,* 628; *Anglo-Iranian Oil Co.* v. *S.U.P.O.R.,* decided by the Civil Court of Rome on 13 September 1954, *Giur. it.,* 1955, I, 2, 91, *Foro it.,* 1955, I, 256; *Riv. dir. internaz.,* 38 (1955), 97; *Rev. crit. d.i.p.,* 47 (1948), 519, 1955 *International Law Reports,* 23; Cass. 19 February 1960; *Kooh-i-Noor Tuzkarna* v. *L. & C. Hardtmuth, Foro it.,* 1960, I, 985, *Riv. dir. internaz.,* 43 (1960), 533; 40 *International Law Reports,* 17; *Svit Impresa Nazionale* v. *Cipera,* decided by the Court of Appeal of Bologna on 28 April 1956, *Riv. dir. internaz.,* 40 (1957) 264.

Germany: *N.V. Vereenigde Deli Maatschappijen N.V. Senembah Mij.* v. *Deutsche-Indonesische Tabak Ges.,* decided by the C.A. Bremen, on 21 August 1959, *Archiv für Völkerrecht,* 9 (1961), 318, at pp. 352–355; *Jahrbuch für Internationales Recht,* 9 (1960), 84, 28 *International Law Reports,* 16.

France: Cass. 23 April 1969, *Crédit Foncier d'Algérie* v. *Narbonne, Clunet* 1969, 914, see also *Revue crit. d.i.p.,* 1969, 917; 1970, 754.

Netherlands: *Bank of Indonesia* v. *Senembah Maatschappij* decided 4 June 1959 by the Court of Appeal of Amsterdam, *N.J.* 1959, No. 350, *Nederlands Tijdschrift voor Internationaal Recht,* 8 (1961), 79; 30 (1960), *International Law Reports,* 28, on appeal from a decision of the President of the District Court, Amsterdam, dated 22 December 1958, *N.J.* 1959, No. 73, *Nederlands Tijdschrift,* 7 (1960), 285, 403, *N.J.* 1959, p. 73 (1958 II), *International Law Reports,* 38; *Clark* v. *Bank voor Handel en Scheepvaart,* decided by the Dutch Supreme Court on 17 October 1969, *N.J.* 1969, p. 279, *International Legal Materials,* 9 (1970), 758.

Japan: *Anglo-Iranian Oil Co.* v. *Idemitsu Kosan Co.,* decided by the High Court, Tokyo in 1953 *International Law Reports,* 312; on appeal from District Court, Tokyo, 27 May 1953, *ibid.,* p. 305; *Japanese Annual of Internat. Law* 1957, 55.

lex fori. Only in the United States rigid adherence to the foreign act of State doctrine has made this course impracticable.[118]

Section 25. Conclusions

52. The result of the foregoing examination can be summed up thus: Private International Law as part of the law of individual countries is domestic law, unfettered by special rules of Public International Law and unrelated to the rules of International Conflict of Laws. Subject only to the general standards of Public International Law, it is determined by the policies, traditions and standards of justice of the individual countries, and free from controls except in Federal states, where the Constitution may impose curbs. Students of the conflict of laws have not been content, however, with this insight. Instead, attempts have been made again and again to determine the philosophical background of these rules. Apparently, the knowledge that they are technical rules which (in most instances)[119] have no substantive content of their own and only point to some legal system as being applicable was felt to be insufficient. There is some justification for such discontent, for a crucial question has remained unsolved: In the absence of a specific rule of Private International Law, is the court to develop a new rule by way | of analogy or otherwise, or is it to apply its own *lex fori* on the ground that in the particular circumstance there is no reference to foreign law?

The various attempts to find a fundamental approach which have been made in recent years have been surveyed elsewhere.[120] As an instrument of internationalisation,[121] reconciling conflicting interests, rational co-ordination or, generally to promote justice,[122] it does not appear to represent principles or to serve purposes which are not common to every legal system as a whole. It may be suggested here that the basic problem is whether the validity of laws is limited *ratione loci* and *ratione personae* or whether, in the

---

[118] *Bernstein* v. *Van Heyghen*, 163 F. 2d 246 (1947), cert. denied, 332 U.S. 772; 92 L.ed. 357 (1947); Mann, *Hague Rec.* 132 (1971 I), at pp. 149–150, 154, but see to the contrary *Bernstein* v. *N.V. Nederlandsche Amerikaansche, etc.*, 210 F. 2d. 375 (2 Cir. 1954), approved by the Supreme Court in *First National City Bank* v. *Banco Nacional de Cuba*, 40 U.S. Law Week, 6 June 1972; as regards England: *Frankfurter* v. *Exner* [1947], Ch. 629, on the ground that the measure was penal; see also *Novello* v. *Hinrichsen* [1951], Ch. 595, 1026.

[119] For exceptions see below, No. 59, pp. 204–206.

[120] Evrigenis, *Hague Rec.* 118 (1966 II), at pp. 410–422; Ehrenzweig, *Private International Law* (1967), pp. 57–74, ss. 21–29.

[121] Kahn-Freund, *The Growth of Internationalism in English Private International Law* (1962).

[122] Graveson, *Rev. crit. d.i.p.*, 1962, 397; (1964), 78 *L.Q.R.*, 337; *XXth Century Comparative and Conflicts Law* (1961), 307.

absence of any specific restriction, laws purport to operate outside the jurisdiction. It is clear that neither the *lex fori* nor foreign law can claim to be applied elsewhere. The former is incapable of exporting itself on its own and the latter cannot be imported into the forum except by a precept of the *lex fori* embodied in a rule of its Private International Law. The problem is, therefore, to determine the range of the *lex fori* by examining the relationship between the *lex fori* and foreign law.

If the *lex fori* is a closed and self-sufficient system, it follows that the *lex fori* applies even to situations containing a foreign element which form the object of litigation in the forum[123] unless a specific rule of Private International Law of the forum *restricts* the operation of the *lex fori* and, at the same time, *introduces* foreign law as an exception.[124]

If the *lex fori* is primarily restricted to situations having a connection with the country of the *forum* on personal or territorial grounds, it follows that a broad range of rules of Private International Law must determine which foreign law is applicable. Otherwise no legal system might be applicable, or only the *lex fori*, thus restoring the closed and universal character of the *lex fori*.

It is probably difficult to state with certainty which legal system in the world follows either view. Some indications are provided by the | rules of Private International Law themselves, whether they are rudimentary or detailed, whether they are expressed in terms of the ordinary conflict rules[125] or of spatially conditioned internal rules,[126] and whether renvoi is accepted or not.[127] The analysis of the practice and the literature in the United States[128] point to the assertion of closed and selfsufficient systems; an examination of the recent practice in England points in the opposite direction[129] in accordance with what appears to be a European trend. The development and refinement of orthodox rules of Private International Law[130] or alternatively an increased emphasis on spatially conditional internal rules[131] will follow from adherence respectively to the former or the latter trend. Given what is believed to be the trend in Europe to deny a universalistic character to each legal system, the American experience, based on a contrary trend, is not likely to assist greatly.

---

[123] See, e.g., Pillet, *Principes*, p. 253, No. 110; p. 255, No. 112; but see p. 250; Batiffol, *Aspects philosophiques ...*, p. 118, n. 53, note 1 with references to modern Italian literature.

[124] See in addition to the writers quoted above n. 123, Unger (1957), 43 *Transactions of the Grotius Society*, 87, at p. 94.

[125] See below, Nos. 53–54, pp. 195–196.

[126] See below, No. 59, pp. 204–206.

[127] E.g., Italy, Introductory Provisions to the Civil Code, Art. 30.

[128] See above Nos. 29–39, and in particular Ehrenzweig, above Nos. 29–30, pp. 144–147.

[129] See [1972 B], *Cambridge Law Journal*, 67, at p. 76.

[130] See below, p. 226.

[131] See below, p. 226.

| Part III. The Structure and Interpretation of Rules of Private International Law

Section 26. Structure

53. Ideally, every individual rule of Private Law should be served by its own rules of Private International Law.[1] The immense variety of rules of substantive law makes this a practical impossibility. Instead two techniques are employed, one general, one particular. The former is represented by the ordinary rules of Private International Law which may be unilateral by indicating directly only when the *lex fori* applies, or bilateral by using criteria which lead at times to the application of the *lex fori* and at times to that of other legal systems. In effect this technique always leads in the end to a system of rules which ensure the application of the *lex fori* or of foreign law in clearly determined circumstances. The latter is exceptional and is represented by the so-called "spatially conditioned internal rules"[2] or "legislatively localised laws",[3] "particular choice of law rules"[4] or "functionally restricting rules".[5]

54. *Operative Facts and Connecting Factors.* Usually sets of rules of substantive law are grouped together for the purpose of formulating one broad principle of Private International Law. This method of grouping adopts largely the time-honoured categories which were applied by the statutists. Today, however, these categories are no longer employed to describe the nature of the substantive law which claims to apply in space. Instead, the categories are detached from the rules of substantive law. They have come into their own, have spawned new categories and now form the backbone of the modern independent rules of Private International Law. Nevertheless, their character has remained the same, | and they are still few in number. They concern status,[6] capacity, marriage, divorce and judicial separation, nullity of marriage, maintenance, guardianship and adoption, corporations,[7] con-

---

[1] Robertson, *Characterization in the Conflict of Laws* (1940), pp. 243–244.

[2] Nussbaum, *Private International Law* (1942), pp. 70–73.

[3] Unger (1952), *Modern L.R.*, 88; (1959), 43 *Transactions of the Grotius Society*, 37; (1967), 83 *L.Q.R.*, 427; Mann, *Hague Rec.* 111 (1964 I), 1, at pp. 69–70; Cavers, *The Choice of Law Process* (1965), 221. Francescakis calls these rules "règles d'application immédiate". *Théorie du renvoi* (1958), 11–16, Nos. 7–11; *Rev. crit. d.i.p.*, 1966, 1. Riv. dir. int. priv. e proc., 3 (1967) 691.

[4] Morris (1946), 62 *Law Q.L.* 170.

[5] De Nova, *Dir. Int.* 1959, 13, 500; *Mélanges Maury*, I (1960), 377; (1966), 54 *Calif. L.R.*, 1569. See Lipstein (1949), 26 *B.Y.I.L.* 553–555 and the extensive lit. cited [1972 B], 31 *Cambridge L.J.*, p. 72, n. 37.

[6] Including legitimacy and legitimation.

[7] Including their creation, powers, existence and dissolution.

tracts,[8] quasi-contracts, torts,[9] interests in movables and in immovables,[10] formalities and procedure.

For want of a better expression these heads of typical legal situations will be called *operative facts.*[11]

These operative facts are linked to a particular system of domestic law by means of what are called *connecting factors.*[12] These are limited too and can be enumerated without difficulty. They are:

Nationality, domicile, residence, ordinary residence,[13] habitual residence,[14] place of contracting, place of performance, the place of the situation of the object, the intention of the parties, the centre of a relationship, the place where a transaction is concluded and the locality of the court seized of the dispute. Normally a rule of Private International Law consists of one set of operative facts and one connecting factor.[15] Sometimes one set of operative facts is coupled with two connecting factors which may function cumulatively[16] or alternatively.[17]

| *Section 27. Interpretation*

55. *Interpretation of Connecting Factors.* Like all rules of law, the rules of Private International Law require interpretation. This task is simple where it is limited to the connecting factors. It is highly complex when it involves the operative facts.

---

[8] Including their conclusion, validity, interpretation, discharge, damages.

[9] Including inter-spousal immunity, effect of death upon a ciaim in tort, contributory negligence, heads and measure of damages, to mention a few aspects.

[10] Created *inter vivos* and on death.

[11] See Rabel, *Conflict of Laws*, I (1945), p. 42; (2 ed. 1958), p. 47; Falconbridge, *Conflict of Laws* (2 ed. 1954), p. 44; Makarov, *Vom Deutschen zum Europäischen Recht, Festschrift für Dölle*, II (1963), 149, at p. 157, n. 7. Other terms in current use are *Rahmen-* or *System-* or *Sammel-* or *Verweisungsbegriffe* – see Neuhaus, *Grundbegriffe des Internationalen Privatrechts* (1962), p. 52; *catégories de rattachement synthétiques*: Rigaux, *Théorie des qualifications en d.i.p.* (1956), No. 157, p. 244; cp. Evrigenis, *Hague Rec.* 118 (1966 II), 309, at p. 318.

[12] *Points de rattachement, Anknüpfungsmomente.*

[13] See Mann, *Juristenzeitung* 1956, 466; Neuhaus, *Grundbegriffe*, p. 151.

[14] See Lipstein [1965], *Cambridge Law Journal*, 224, at pp. 225–226 with exemples; Neuhaus, *loc. cit.*, p. 155; Nadelmann (1969), 47 *Texas L.R.*, 765; De Winter, *Hague Rec.* 128 (1969 III), 346 at pp. 419–436.

[15] E.g., status is governed by the law of the domicile; title to movables is governed by the law of the *situs.*

[16] E.g., a foreign tort can be made the object of a suit in England, if it is actionable in England *and* abroad. See also Neuhaus, *loc. cit.*, pp. 96 ff.

[17] E.g., the formalities of a contract are governed *either* by the *lex loci actus or* by the law which governs the substance of the contract.

Each connecting factor indicates a particular legal system which is to apply to the individual legal situation. Since Private International Law is domestic law and forms part of the *lex fori*, it follows that the *lex fori* alone determines in what circumstances foreign law is to apply. Consequently, not only the selection of the appropriate connecting factor, but also its interpretation, is exclusively determined by the *lex fori*. Thus in an English court the question whether a person resident in France is domiciled there must be decided according to English and not according to French notions.[18] The place where a contract is concluded is fixed, in an English court, where and when the acceptance is posted, even if according to the law of the country where it was dispatched, it takes effect only where and when the offeror receives it.[19]

Three exceptions must be noted, however. In the first place the connecting factor nationality must be interpreted in accordance with the law of the country of which the person concerned is alleged to be a national. In the second place, connecting factors, such as habitual residence, which have been received into the domestic Private International Law of countries as a result of the adoption of an International Convention,[20] should, it is submitted, be interpreted with special regard to uniformity.[21] In the third place, in all cases involving *renvoi*, when | the forum applies foreign law including foreign Private International Law, the connecting factors of the foreign rules of Private International Law must be interpreted in accordance with the law of the foreign country.[22]

---

[18] For England see *Re Annesley* [1926], Ch. 692.

[19] *Badische Anilin und Soda Fabrik* v. *Basle Chemical Works Bindschedler* [1898], A.C. 200, 207; *Hanson* v. *Dixon* (1906), 23 T.L.R. 56; *Benaim* v. *Debono* [1924], A.C. 514, 520; see also *Cowan* v. *O'Connor* (1888), 20 Q.B.D. 640; *Clarke* v. *Harper* [1938], N.I. 162, 171; but contracts by telex or telephone are treated as made *inter praesentes* at the place where the answer is received: *Entores Ltd* v. *Miles Far East Corporation* [1955], 2 Q.B. 327; *N.V. Handel Mij. J. Smits* v. *English Exporters Ltd* [1955], 2 Ll.R. 69, 71; 317, 323, 324 (C.A.); and the place where it has been concluded according to these principles determines whether it has been validly concluded: *Albeko Schuhmaschinen A.G.* v. *The Kamborian Shoe Machine Co.* (1961), 111 L.J. 519; *Clunet* 1965, p. 459.

[20] See the Hague Conventions on the Form of Wills, 1961, Art. 1 *(d)*; on Jurisdiction, Applicable Law and Recognition of Decrees relating to Adoption of 1965, Arts. 2, 3, 7; and on the Recognition of Divorces and Legal Separations, 1970, Art. 2.

[21] See Makarov, *Mélanges Maury*, I (1960), 207 ff., at pp. 217, 223, and in *Vom Deutschen zum Europäischen Recht, Festschrift für Dölle*, II (1963), 149, at p. 167. The Hague Convention on the Recognition of Divorces and Legal Separations of 1970, Art. 3, has introduced a concession to common law countries by allowing the country where the matrimonial cause is tried to substitute the notion of domicile for that of habitual residence in determining its jurisdiction under the Convention; at the same time all other countries cannot refuse recognition on this ground (Art. 6, last para.).

[22] *Re Annesley* [1926], Ch. 692, but see *Re O'Keefe* [1940], Ch. 124; Falconbridge, *Conflict of Laws* (2 ed. 1954), p. 208, note m; (1941), 19 *Canadian Bar Rev.*, 320, 323; de Nova, *It Ricchiamo di ordinamenti Plurilegislativi* (1940), pp. 108 ff.

56. *Interpretation of Operative Facts–Characterisation.* The same process of characterisation, which relies on the *lex fori*, may also seem natural in any legal system when it comes to the interpretation of the operative facts[23] and is seemingly imperative in those legal systems where the courts are believed to be called upon to apply foreign law of their own motion to a set of facts pleaded by the parties.[24] In reality, so it would appear, no suit involving a foreign element is introduced in which the plaintiff (and subsequently the defendant) has not considered his rights (or his defences) according to some legal system. Despite outward appearances, it does not seem to make any difference whether the court may, or is bound to, ascertain of its own motion (as courts in civil law countries can) whether and, if so, which system of laws applies, and what the particular rule of foreign law is which must be taken into consideration, or whether a party must plead not only the facts but also the law, if foreign, on which he intends to rely (as is the practice in common law countries).[25] The only difference appears to be that courts in civil law countries can, and courts in common law countries cannot, go beyond the allegations of the parties. The difference is one of degree only.[26]

| In other words, cases raising a question of foreign law differ from purely domestic cases in the manner of their presentation. In purely domestic cases the facts are pleaded and a claim must be submitted. However, if the plaintiff or the defendant believes that foreign law is applicable he must introduce his claim in the light of some foreign law according to which he alleges to have a right against the defendant. The same applies to a defendant who may wish to plead that some other law – be it the *lex fori* or some other foreign legal system – applies and that according to the latter the claim is not well founded. The claim or defence must be framed in the light of a particular system of laws in order to induce the court to apply foreign law.[27] At this stage, proof of ordinary facts and proof of foreign law show different features. An allegation of foreign law forces the court to exercise a choice of law. The court, relying on its set of rules of conflict of laws, must ascertain which rule of its Private International Law covers the claim or defence.[28] Difficulties

---

[23] For a strict differentiation between the interpretation of connecting factors and characterization of operative facts see Makarov, *loc. cit.* (above n. 21), p. 151, n. 7.

[24] It is generally said that common law courts apply foreign law only if pleaded and proved by the parties while civil law courts apply foreign law of their own motion. Thus formulated the difference of the practice is too clear-cut.

[25] See Zajtay, *Riv. dir. int. e proc.*, 4 (1968), 233–301, esp. pp. 246–251, para. 14.

[26] See also Makarov, *loc. cit.* (above p. 197, n. 21), at p. 154; but see Wengler, *Rev. crit. d.i.p.*, 1954, 661, at pp. 670, 673, 682, rejecting for such countries the approach advocated here – see *loc. cit.*, pp. 666–667, 671, 674; and in *Festschrift für Martin Wolff* (1952), 337, at pp. 340, 356.

[27] Falconbridge, *Conflict of Laws* (2 ed. 1954), pp. 53 ff.; (1952), 30 *Can. Bar Rev.*, 103, at pp. 114, 116 and note 49, 117; Ledermann (1951), 29 *Can. Bar Rev.*, 3, 24.

[28] Cf. Robertson, p. 127; Falconbridge, *Conflict of Laws* (1947), p. 101; (2nd ed., 1954),

arise from the fact that the claim or defence is, *ex hypothesi,* expressed in substance and in form in terms of domestic law, primarily foreign. The operative facts of rules of Private International Law are formulated sometimes in terms of the domestic law of the *forum,*[29] but more frequently in terms peculiar to Private International Law;[30] yet the court must apply its own rules of Private International Law to claims presented in terms of foreign domestic law, if it is to determine whether the law pleaded by the party applies.[31] For this purpose each must be interpreted in terms of the other.[32] This process of subsuming claims | formulated in accordance with one legal system under one of several rules of the conflict of laws of the forum by way of interpreting each in terms of the other is the essence of characterisation. The process of interpreting rules involving at least two, and possibly more, legal systems must necessarily rely on some legal notions, and over the years reliance on those of the *lex fori,* the *lex causae* and of comparative jurisprudence has been canvassed in turn. The present analysis must discard the approach from the *lex fori,* which assumes that facts alone must be characterised, and not facts presented in the light of some legal system.[33] However, the present analysis does not embrace the approach from the alleged *lex causae,* but it takes the *lex causae* into consideration.[34] According to the view set out here, abstract rules of law as such are not characterised. The courts analyse the nature of a claim (or defence) expressed according to some system of laws (foreign law or the *lex fori*), in the light of the function (not the technical connotation) of that rule within the particular

------

p. 59, believes that the court provisionally consults foreign law before finally characterising the question for the purpose of selecting the proper law. See the valid critique in Dicey, *Conflict of Laws* (8th ed., 1967), p. 27. The present account avoids this pitfall by analysing the concrete situation.

[29] E.g., contract, tort, succession, capacity to marry, formality.

[30] E.g., status, rights in movables or immovables, evidence, procedure, property relations between spouses.

[31] It is assumed that the application is opposed by the other party, who alleges that another legal system is applicable.

[32] In order not to complicate or to confuse this analysis no mention is made at each stage that the same process applies, if the defendant relies for his defence on the *lex fori.* Here again the court must apply its own rules of Private International Law (which are not always expressed in terms of the domestic law of the forum) in order to determine whether the *lex fori* applies; for the English practice see Lipstein [1972 B], 31 *Cambridge Law Journal,* 67, at p. 78, n. 76.

[33] Where English courts have followed this technique the result has been unfortunate. See *Ogden* v. *Ogden* [1907], P. 46 (C.A.), and the comments in Dicey and Morris, pp. 237–239; Westlake, *P.I.L.* (2nd ed., 1925), p. 61; *Phrantzes* v. *Argenti* [1960], 2 Q.B. 19.

[34] See Lipstein, note to *Re Maldonado* [1954], P. 223; [1954], *Cambridge Law Journal,* 123; and compare *In re Utassi's Will,* 15 N.Y. 2d 436, 209 N.Y. 2d 65 (1965), discussed by Ehrenzweig, *Hague Rec.* 124 (1968 II), 169, at p. 234, see also Ehrenzweig in *XXth Century Comparative and Conflicts of Law* (1961), 395, at pp. 402, 403, n. 4, citing *Estate of Turton,* 20 Misc. 2d 569, 192 N.Y.S. 2d 254 (Surr. 1959).

legal system. They relate the claim or defence so analysed to that among their own rules of Private International Law which, upon a broad interpretation (not restricted to notions of the domestic law of the *forum*), is capable of covering the claim in question. This interpretation of disparate notions in terms of each other is the process of characterisation. The result is an indication of the law applicable which may, or may not, be that which has been pleaded by the party or parties.[35]

The process of characterisation set out here was expressed by the German Federal Supreme Court in these words:

"The subsumption of these rules [i.e., Art. 992 of the Dutch Civil Code] must be made in accordance with German law. In this connection the following principles of interpretation must be observed; the rules of foreign law must be examined with a view | to their meaning and purpose, they must be analysed from the standpoint of foreign law and they must be compared with the institutions of the German legal order. On the basis of this knowledge, they must be subsumed by the German rules of Private International Law, the characteristics of which are shaped by the notions and delimitations of German law."[36]

It was in effect adopted on two recent occasions in England, although the process was not formulated in the terms submitted here.[37] Technically it involves one of three situations: either the claim or defence is identical in form and in substance with similar claims or defences in the *lex fori*,[38] or it is unknown in substance and in form in the *lex fori*[39] or it corresponds in form

---

[35] Cp. Graulich, *Principes de droit international privé* (1961), No. 130, p. 99, whose solution comes near to that proposed here.

[36] BGHZ, 12 January 1967, N.J.W. 1967 1171, *I.P.Rspr.* 1961–1967, No. 19, p. 64; see also BGHZ 29, 137, *I.P.Rspr.* 1958–1959, No. 116, p. 389; and see Castel (1961), 39 *Can. Bar Rev.*, 93, 102 citing *Livesley* v. *Horst* [1924], S.C.R. 605; [1925] 1 D.L.R. 159.

[37] *Re Cohn* [1945], Ch. 5, where according to Master Jacob in Smit, *International Co-operation in Litigation* (Europe) (1965), p. 103, n. 205, the parties agreed not to plead foreign law and to leave the question of foreign law to the court; *Re Fuld* [1966], 2 W.L.R. 717, at pp. 735, 736–738. Ehrenzweig, *XXth Century Comparative and Conflicts Law* (1961), 395, at p. 408, n. 2, does less than justice to the former decision.

[38] For examples taken from English practice see *British Linen Co.* v. *Drummond* (1830), 10 B. & C. 903; *Huber* v. *Steiner* (1835), 2 Bing. N.C. 202, 210, 213; *Don* v. *Lippman* (1837), 5 Cl. & F. 1, 13, 16; *Leroux* v. *Brown* (1852), 12 C.B. 801, 823; *Bristow* v. *Sequeville* (1850), 5 Ex. 275; *Re Martin, Loustalan* v. *Loustalan* [1900], P. 211, 230, 233, 240; *S.A. de Prayon* v. *Koppel* (1933), 77 S.J. 80; *Re Cutcliffe's Will Trust* [1940], Ch. 565; *Re Middleton's Settlement* [1947], Ch. 329, 583 (C.A.); [1949], A.C. 418; *Re Priest* [1944], Ch. 58; *Adams* v. *National Bank of Greece* [1961], A.C. 255, 287; see also *Dreyfus (C. and H.) Foundation Inc.* v. *I.R.C.* [1956], A.C. 39; *Rae (Inspector of Taxes)* v. *Lazard Investment Co. Ltd* [1963], 1 W.L.R. 555; *Baron Inchyra* v. *Jennings (Inspector of Taxes)* [1966], Ch. 37; *Re Wilks* [1935], Ch. 645; *Re Kehr* [1951], 2 T.L.R. 788; [1951], 2 All E.R. 812; *Re Barnett's Trusts* [1902], 1 Ch. 842; *Mahadervan* v. *Mahadervan* [1964], P. 233, 241–242.

[39] For examples taken from English practice see *Batthyany* v. *Walford* (1887), 36 Ch.D. 269, 278; *De Nicols* v. *Curlier* [1900], A.C. 21; *Re Bonacina* [1912], 2 Ch.D. 394, 396 (C.A.); *Phrantzes* v. *Argenti* [1960], 2 Q.B. 19, 36 and the comments in (1960), 9 *I.C.L.Q.*, 508; (1960), 23 *M.L.R.*, 446.

to a similar claim in the *lex fori*, but the formal similarity conceals a material difference.[40]

| 57. Although foreign law must only be alleged and proved once during the proceedings, it must be considered at two stages of the process of judicial reasoning. The first stage alone involves the process of interpretation known as characterisation or qualification. Here the court (whether in civil or common law countries)[41] must not only consider the facts but the individual rule or set of rules either of the *lex fori* or of foreign law on which the party relies and which are alleged to be applicable. Thus the Private International Law of the forum is at no stage concerned with a reference to foreign law in the abstract or with the categories of foreign law in general; it is concerned with a functional analysis of a particular rule within its own setting. Consequently during the second stage, which is exclusively concerned with the application of foreign law, no additional reliance is required on the characterisation of the foreign law as practised abroad by the courts of the country of the *lex causae* for the purpose of applying their own rules of Private International Law, except in situations involving *renvoi*. The reason is that, upon proper analysis, there is no need to reduce the foreign law applicable to concrete rules and to individualise the rules of foreign law a second time. They are individualised in the allegations or pleadings of the parties once and for all. As the process of characterisation is understood here, there is no place for secondary characterisation.[42]

In particular, it is of no importance that for technical reasons, due, *inter alia*, to the wording of a statute which requires unconditional and uniform application by the courts of its own country and is therefore regarded as procedural (on the illogical ground that all procedural laws require uniform unconditional application by the forum), such laws as Statutes of Frauds and Statutes of Limitations in common law countries are characterised as procedural. What matters is the function of the rule within its own setting: does it only affect the remedy, or does it also affect the right?[43]

---

[40] For examples taken from English practice see *Ogden* v. *Ogden* [1908], P. 46, and see also *Bliersbach* v. *McEwen* (1959), S.C. 43; *Lodge* v. *Lodge* (1963), 107 S.J. 437, and see the comments by Anton (1959), 3 *Jur. Rev. (N.S.)*, 253, 277; Carter in (1960), 36 *B.Y.I.L.*, 417; *Re Maldonado* [1954], P. 223, 231, 244 *et seq.*, but see Lipstein [1954], *C.L.J.*, 22. See also Garde Castillo, *La Institucion Desconocida en el d.i.p.* (1947), pp. 46–47.

[41] See above, p. 198, No. 56.

[42] For this problem see Robertson, *op. cit.*, pp. 118–134, 255–279; Cheshire, *Private International Law* (3rd ed. 1947), pp. 71–85; Falconbridge, *Conflict of Laws* (1st ed. 1947), pp. 98 *et seq.*, 107, 161 *et seq.*, 184 *et seq.*; but see (2nd ed. 1954), p. 68, note *(g)*; (1939), 17 *Can. Bar Rev.*, 369; (1941), 19 *Can. Bar Rev.*, 311 at 334; Ago, *Teoria del diritto internazionale privato* (1934), 136 ff., at p. 154; *Hague Rec.* 58 (1936 IV), 313 ff.; Frankenstein, *Internationales Privatrecht*, I (1926), 276 ff.; Fedozzi, *Diritto internazionale privato* (2 ed. 1939), pp. 193–195.

[43] See, e.g., *Huber* v. *Steiner* (1835), 2 Bing. N.C. 202, 210, 213, per Tindall C.J.

Viewed from this angle, the famous sybilline riddles which have | plagued the German Supreme Court, fascinated writers, and generally, occupied three generations of lawyers lose their glamour.

If German law regards limitation of actions as a matter of substance and refers to the law governing the contract, while the law of New York which governs it regards it as procedural, the latter formal characterisation is irrelevant, if the function of the New York rule is the same as that envisaged by the German rule of Private International Law.[44]

If (at a time when breach of promise was an actionable contractual claim in England),[45] parties entered into an engagement to marry each other, which was governed by French law, and a breach occurred in England (where the same act was a breach of contract), once again the function of each rule must be analysed. Such an analysis will show that, notwithstanding its delictual configuration, the French rule, like the English, serves to provide a remedy in a situation which is derived from an agreement, but which cannot be called "contractual" in France, given the reluctance of French law to admit that an engagement to marry could be enforceable (if only by granting damages). Thus an English court can treat a claim based on French law as contractual and apply French law.[46]

58. The prevalence of situations of this nature (characterisation of Statutes of Frauds, Statutes of Limitations)[47] in the practice of the courts in the United States may account for the unwillingness of modern American writers to concede to characterisation its proper function, which is real in those situations which arise only rarely in the United States, due to the close affinity of the legal systems within the Union, when a claim or defence is either unknown in form or in substance in the *lex fori*, or if it corresponds in form to a similar claim or defence in the *lex fori*, but the formal similarity conceals a material difference.[48]

| At the same time, a greater readiness to acknowledge the more sophisticated function of characterisation, as understood here, could have enabled American courts to deal in a more orthodox manner, but with the same result, with cases such as *Babcock* v. *Jackson*.[49] Many obligations sounding at

---

[44] German Supreme Court, 6 July 1934, RGZ 145, 121, at pp. 128 ff.; but see RGZ 7, 21 of 4 January 1882; RGZ 24, 383, 393 of 18 May 1889 and see RGZ 21, 13 of 8 May 1880; RGZ of 21 November 1910, *Niemeyer's* Z., 21, p. 62.

[45] Before the enactment of the Law Reform (Miscellaneous Provisions) Act, 1970, s. 1.

[46] But contrast Wolff, *Private International Law* (2 ed. 1957), para. 156, p. 165. For a variant of this example, solved without difficulty by the writer, see Wolff, para. 155, p. 164.

[47] See above No. 57 and see, e.g., *Bernkrant* v. *Fowler* (1961), 55 Cal. 2d 588, 360 P. 2d 906; *Grant* v. *McAuliffe* (1953), 41 Cal. 2d 859, 264 P. 2d 944; *Bournias* v. *Atlantic Maritime Co. Ltd.*, 220 F. 2d 152 (2 Cir. 1955).

[48] See, e.g., Ehrenzweig, *Hague Rec.* 124 (1968 II), 169, at pp. 233 ff.; *Private International Law* (1967), pp. 113–219, paras. 52–55.

[49] 12 N.Y. 2d 473, 191 N.E. 2d 279 (1963).

first sight in tort arise from or are affected by previous agreements which may include an express or implied choice of law clause.[50]

Section 28. Spatially Conditioned Internal Rules

59. In contrast to ordinary rules of Private International Law, socalled spatially conditioned internal rules or legislatively localised laws, particular choice of law rules or functionally restricting rules[51] determine the application in space of particular rules of domestic law. Technically this is achieved by adding a choice of law provision to the particular rule of domestic law instead of formulating rules of the conflict of laws in broad categories which are then applied to claims formulated according to some system of laws, whether it be foreign law or the domestic law of the court.[52]

Spatially conditioned internal rules differ from the unilateral rules of self-limitation discussed above[53] which circumscribe the operation of certain branches of domestic law. In those latter branches of the law, the application of foreign law is never contemplated; spatially conditioned internal rules do not purport to exclude the application of equivalent rules of foreign law.

The interplay between ordinary rules of Private International Law | and unilateral self-limiting rules of domestic public law can be observed in such situations as that underlying the *Boll* Case (*Netherlands* v. *Sweden*).[54] There the ordinary Dutch choice of law rule on guardianship clashed with a Swedish self-limiting rule on the protection of children in need of care. The application of ordinary rules of Private International Law coupled with the recognition of the operation abroad of foreign self-limiting rules of public law is a frequent practice.[55] The interplay between ordinary rules of Private

---

[50] *Sayers* v. *International Drilling Co. N.Y.* [1971], 1 W.L.R. 1176; [1971], 3 All E.R. 163; Collins in (1972), 21 *International and Comparative Law Quarterly*, 320; and see Wengler in *Rev. crit. d.i.p.*, 1972, pp. 637–661; French Court of Cassation, 15 December 1969, *Thomas* v. *Cie. Erste Allgemeine, Rev. crit. d.i.p.*, 1971, p. 512, with lit.

[51] See above, p. 195, and notes 2–5 with lit.

[52] For England see: Wills Act 1861, ss. 1, 2; Merchant Shipping Act 1894, s. 265; Carriage of Goods by Sea Act 1924, s. 1; Legitimacy Act 1926, ss. 1, 8; Inheritance (Family Provisions) Act 1938, s. 1 as amended; Law Reform (Frustrated Contracts) Act 1943, s. 1 (1); Adoption Act 1958, s. 1 (1) (5); Legitimacy Act 1959, s. 2 (2); Marriage (Enabling) Act 1960, s. 1 (3); Matrimonial Causes Act 1965, ss. 14 (2) *(a) (b)*, 24 (1) (2), 25 (1), 26 (1), 39 (1) (4), 40 (1) *(a) (b)*; Contracts of Employment Act 1963, s. 9 (1) (2) and Sched. 1, para. 1 (3); Redundancy Payments Act 1965, ss. 17, 56 (4); Mann (1966), 82 *L.Q.R.*, 316; see also (1964), 80 *L.Q.R.*, 29.

[53] P. 165.

[54] *I.C.J. Reports 1958*, p. 52; for the lit. see above, p. 169, n. 13.

[55] See, e.g., Conforti, *L'execuzione delle obbligazioni nel diritto internazionale privato* (1962), *passim*; for the practice in England see, e.g., *Re Bettinson's Question* [1956], Ch. 67; *Regazzoni* v. *Sethia* [1958], A.C. 301, and *Ralli Bros.* v. *Cia Naviera Sota y Aznar* [1920], 2

International Law and spatially conditioned internal rules is much rarer.[56] The Wills Act 1861 (Lord Kingsdown's Act), which applied in Great Britain until 1963, provides a good example. While the Act applied to wills of personalty made by British subjects (and incidentally provided choice of law rules for them in those limited circumstances), the general rule of Private International Law, relying on the law of the last domicile, applied in all other circumstances, no matter whether the testator was domiciled in England or not.

The problem is more complicated, if the rules of Private International Law of the forum refer to foreign law, and the foreign law applicable contains either a unilateral rule of Private International Law or a spatially conditioned rule of domestic law. In the former case, the question is, first, whether the unilateral rule has been interpreted as a bilateral one and, if so, secondly, whether *renvoi* applies. If it has not been interpreted as a bilateral rule, and the case is not covered by the unilateral rule, the reference to foreign law remains one to foreign domestic law. If, however, the foreign domestic rule is a spatially conditioned rule a considerable difficulty arises.[57] What law applies, if the spatially conditioned rule of the foreign *lex causae* fails to apply in the circumstances? *Ex hypothesi* the foreign *lex causae* does not contain a rule of domestic law which purports to apply when the spatially conditioned rule does not operate. Sometimes it may be possible to detect|a rule of Private International Law which refers to a legal system other than that of the *lex causae*; also spatially conditioned rules of domestic law are often special legislation, and if they do not apply, general rules of domestic law can be relied upon. Article 992 of the Dutch Civil Code (which states that Dutch nationals must make their wills in notarial form,

even if the will is made abroad) and Article 170 of the French Civil Code (which requires French nationals marrying abroad to comply with certain formalities of French law) merely extend to situations abroad certain formal requirements of Dutch and French law concerning wills and marriages which apply peremptorily in the Netherlands and in France. Thus a reference by the Private International Law of the forum to Dutch or French law involving these articles as part of the *lex loci actus* or the *lex loci celebrationis* will mean a reference to Dutch or French law applicable to these formalities.[58] However, a spatially conditioned rule of domestic law may indicate

---

K.B. 287, as interpreted by Mann (1937), 18 *B.Y.I.L.*, 97; *The Halley* (1868), L.R. 2 P.C. 193, 202, and the cases cited by Lipstein in *Ius Privatum Gentium*, I (1969), 411, at pp. 420–422.

[56] See Lipstein [1972 B], 31 *Cambridge Law Journal*, 67, at pp. 73–74.

[57] See also Unger (1967), 83 *L.Q.R.*, 427, 444; Kelly (1969), 18 *Int. & Comp. L.Q.*, 249, at pp. 254 ff.

[58] See the decisions of the German Federal Supreme Court of 12 January 1967, *NJW*

the need to characterise the rule differently from a rule which is not spatially conditioned. Thus it has been contended that the requirement of form expressed in Article 992 of the Dutch Civil Code is to be characterised as one of substance, namely capacity to make a will, and it remained for the Hague Convention of 1961 on the Form of Wills[59] to exclude this practice.[60] The Carriage of Goods by Sea Act 1929 enacted in Great Britain and the Carriage of Goods by Sea Ordinances of Palestine and Newfoundland, which provided the basis of the litigation in *The Torni*[61] and the *Vita Food Case*[62] concern shipments out of these countries and leave it to the ordinary rules of domestic law to solve questions arising under contracts of carriage by sea into Great Britain, Palestine and Newfoundland.

| Section 29. Transposition, Substitution and Adaptation

60. Transposition, substitution and adaptation, first observed by continental writers,[63] are phenomena which can be found in all legal systems. The line of demarcation between them is not always clear.[64] None of them, however, is concerned with a choice of law; in all of them a choice of law has taken place, if a question of private law is in issue, or the operation of foreign public law has been acknowledged as a fact, if the issue is one involving public law.[65] Yet owing to the circumstance that different aspects of a situation may be governed by different legal systems a reconciliation between various institu-

---

1967, 1177; *IPRspr.* 1966–1967, No. 19, p. 64, and of 19 December 1958, BGHZ 29, 137, *IPRspr.* 1958–1959, No. 112; Kropholler, *NJW* 1968, 1561 with further references; Wengler, *Rev. crit. d.i.p.*, 1954, 661, at 683, n. 2; Ago, *Hague Rec.* 58 (1936 IV), 245, at pp. 326 ff.; Frankenstein, *Internationales Privatrecht*, I (1926), p. 285.

[59] S. 5; the Wills Act 1963, s. 3, enacted by the United Kingdom; the Netherlands did not ratify this Convention.

[60] See Robertson, *Characterization in the Conflict of Laws* (1940), pp. 235–237; Beckett (1934), 15 *B.Y.I.L.*, 46, at 73, n. 1; Falconbridge, *Conflict of Laws* (2nd ed., 1954), pp. 90–94; Lorenzen, *Selected Articles*, pp. 129–130; (1941), 50 *Yale L.J.*, 743, at 755, 756; and the former practice of the German Supreme Court, RG., *JW* 1913, 333.

[61] [1932], P. 78.

[62] [1939] A.C. 277.

[63] These categories were first discussed by Lewald, *Hague Rec. 69* (1939 III), 1, at 129. For lit. see Kegel, *Internationales Privatrecht* (3 ed. 1971), p. 125.

[64] According to Neuhaus, *Grundbegriffe des Internationalen Privatrechts* (1962), 251, n. 604, the category described as transposition merges into the other two. There is some substance in this contention, at least as far as any overlap between transposition and substitution is concerned.

[65] Where domestic and foreign public law are concerned, the recognition of the operation of foreign law takes the place of the so-called preliminary question; see below p. 220 and see Mann (1963), 79 *Law Quarterly Review*, 525; *Hague Rec.* 132 (1971 I), 109, at pp. 134–144.

tions of the several legal systems applicable in the circumstances may be called for. Thus a will which is to be interpreted according to German law may contain the appointment of a *Vorerbe* and a *Nacherbe* in respect of land in England where this institution is unknown. Here a transposition is called for. It will be necessary to interpret the will in the light of German law and to create interests in England which are as nearly as possible identical with those created by the will framed in accordance with another legal system and expressed in terms of different institutions.[66]

61. *Substitution* may be illustrated by reference to an intestate succession which is governed by a legal system equating adopted children with legitimate children by allowing them equal shares. If the deceased had adopted a child in accordance with another system of laws then, even if the adoption is recognised by the law governing the succession, it remains necessary to examine whether the foreign adoption represents an equivalent substitute for the type of adoption envisaged | by the law governing the succession by conferring upon the adopted person a status of a legitimate child in all respects. Such equivalence is not necessarily assured by the circumstance that both legal systems acknowledge adoption as an institution, for this can vary very much in character from country to country. *Adoptio plena, minus quam plena, légitimation adoptive* and other types, are all aspects of the genus adoption, but they may differ so much in effect as to exclude any interchange.[67] If the law governing the status of spouses permits the conversion of legal separations and divorces, the question may arise whether a previous legal separation abroad qualifies for this purpose.[68]

---

[66] *Studd* v. *Cook* (1883), 8 App. Cas. 577 at pp. 591, 600, 604; *Re Piercy* [1895], 1 Ch. 83, 89; *Piercy* v. *E.t.f.a.s.*, decided on 15 March 1956 by the Tribunale Oristano, *Foro it.* 1956, I, 1019; *Riv. dir. internaz.*, 1959, 687; *Re Ernst Meyer, Gutachten zum internationalen und ausländischen Privatrecht*, 1967 and 1968 (1970), No. 67, p. 707.

[67] See *Re Marshall* [1957], Ch. 507 (C.A. and, generally, Ancel, *L'adoption dans les législations modernes* (2nd ed. 1958), and the supplement in *Rev. internat. de dr. comp.*, 13 (1961), 561.

[68] See, e.g., *Tursi* v. *Tursi* [1958], P. 4; and the problems raised in the cases cited by Mann, *Hague Rec.* 132 (1971 I), at pp. 135 ff.: whether a woman validly married in a polygamous union in Pakistan according to the personal law of the parties is a wife for the purpose of receiving public assistance in England under the National Assistance Act 1948, *Imam Din* v. *National Assistance Board* [1967], 2 Q.B. 213, at p. 218; a French *société en nom collectif* a corporate body or partnership for the purpose of English tax legislation: *Dreyfuss* v. *Commissioners of Inland Revenue* (1929), 14 T.C. 560, at pp. 576, 577; life interest in the income of a New York trust fund; whether income from stocks, shares or rents, or from other possessions outside the United Kingdom for the purposes of English tax legislation: *Archer-Shee* v. *Garland* [1931], A.C. 212, with a valid criticism by Mann, *loc. cit.*, at p. 136; a distribution of shares in a subsidiary in Maryland to the shareholders of the parent company, treated as capital in Maryland; whether a distribution of income for the purposes of English tax legislation: *Rae* v. *Lazard Investment Co.* [1963], 1 W.L.R. 555, see also *Courtaulds Investment Ltd.* v. *Fleming* [1969], 1 W.L.R. 1683. For what would appear to be the

62. It is thus clear that problems of transposition and substitution arise not simply after a choice of law has taken place in accordance with the Private International Law of the *forum* which has led to the application of different systems of law to different aspects of the case. In the case of *transposition* the disparate institutions representing different aspects of the case must be translated in terms of each other. In the case of *substitution*, the question is whether the institutions representing the same aspect of the case correspond to each other to such an extent as to be interchangeable. In both cases the problem is one of comparing institutions of domestic law in order to integrate the different aspects of the case after the rules of Private International Law of the forum have led to the application of different legal systems to | these various aspects or, alternatively, if the rules of public law of various legal systems have operated in their various legal spheres.[69]

63. *Adaptation* raises questions of another kind.[70] If different aspects of a case are governed by different legal systems, the operation of different laws may create hardships and material injustice. The following example illustrates the problem well. Spouses are domiciled in a common law country such as England during their working life. Upon their retirement they acquire a domicile in California. The husband dies. According to the law of California matrimonial property relations between spouses are governed by the law of the domicile of the spouses at the time of the marriage; succession to movables is governed by the law of the last domicile. According to the law of the common law State, the matrimonial régime was separation of goods, but the surviving spouse is accorded a share in her spouse's estate on the latter's death. According to the law of California spouses live according to a régime of community of goods, but a spouse is not entitled to a share in the other's estate by virtue of the law of succcession. The result is that both the law of the common law State and the law of California grant a spouse some share in the assets of the other, but by applying the common law rule to matrimonial property relations (because it was the law of their domicile at the time) and the law of California to the succession (because it was the law of the last domicile of the deceased), the surviving spouse goes away with empty hands. In the converse case she collects twice over.[71] The result is not due to a faulty technique of the conflict of laws, but to the fact that each legal system is a coherent whole. Choice of law, which leads to the application of

---

correct answer in keeping with the attitude taken above in the text see *Baron Inchyra* v. *Jennings (Inspector of Taxes)* [1966], Ch. 37.

[69] See below p. 220.

[70] Cp. Lewald, *Hague Rec.* 69 (1939 III), 1, at pp. 139–148; Kegel, *Internationales Privatrecht* (3 ed. 1971), pp. 127 ff.; Raape, *Hague Rec.* 50 (1934 IV), 401, at pp. 496–517.

[71] *Baudoin* v. *Trudel* [1937], 1 D.L.R. 216; [1937], O.R. 1, but see Kegel, *Internationales Privatrecht* (3 ed. 1971), p. 129.

different laws to different aspects of the case, may cause a disequilibrium of solutions, but it is for the domestic law of succession to redress the balance by a process of adaptation.[72]

| Section 30. Renvoi

64. It is unnecessary to set out once more the various approaches to the application of foreign law; whether the reference is to the domestic law of the *lex causae* (one step), to the domestic and private international law of the *lex causae* (simple *renvoi*, two step) or to the law which would be applied by the *lex causae* in similar circumstances (total *renvoi*, the valse, commonly known as the foreign court theory of English courts). All of these have been analysed here over the years.[73] Instead it is proposed to examine the place of *renvoi* in a system of Private International Law.

Although all countries have rules of Private International Law, these differ from each other, especially in the choice of connecting factors. This is natural since, as was shown above, Private International Law is part of the law of each country and is unfettered by any overriding uniform principles. Thus if the Private International Law of the forum refers in a particular case to some foreign legal system, it could be assumed that this reference is final. International Law does not, and foreign law cannot, impose upon the forum the duty to apply any law other than that which these courts are bound to apply in virtue of their own laws. Yet this seemingly convincing answer is only acceptable, if the premise is correct, namely, that a reference to foreign law by the Private International Law of the forum must clearly be understood to exclude the Private International Law of the *lex causae*.

In practice, renvoi appears to arise when one party relies on the *lex causae*, and the other on the latter's rules of Private International Law; this practical experience is not restricted to common law countries where the parties must plead foreign law, but seems to be equally valid in countries where the court can make a choice of law *proprio motu*. Here the court takes the place of one of the parties. Faced with a choice between the foreign *lex causae* and another law (*lex fori* or the law of a third country) the question is whether the reference back or on is to be accepted. At this stage it is useful to recall the

---

[72] See the Californian Probate Code s. 201.5 (California Statutes 1957, c. 490); see also s. 201,7,6; 140.5 (1961) and see Kegel, *op. cit.*, pp. 131–133, with lit.; Cavers, *Hague Rec.* 131 (1970 III), 75, at p. 215, n. 57, 58; Abel, Berry, Halsted and Marsh, 47 *Calif. L.R.*, 211 (1959).

[73] See in this collection of courses Lewald, *Hague Rec.* 29 (1929 IV), 515–616; 69 (1939 III), 1 at 47–66; de Nova, *Hague Rec.* 118 (1966 II), 437, at pp. 485–531, and the lit. cited by Kegel, *op. cit.*, p. 139; Ehrenzweig, *Private International Law* (1967), p. 141, n. 6, with further references; *Hague Rec.* 124 (1968 II), 167, at pp. 238–244.

problem stated above:[74] is the law of the forum a closed and self-sufficient system, with the result | that it applies even to situations containing a foreign element which come before the courts, unless a specific rule of the Private International Law of the forum restricts the operation of the *lex fori* and at the same time introduces foreign law as an exception? Alternatively, is the law of the forum primarily restricted to situations having a connection with the forum on personal or territorial grounds with the result that a broad range of rules of Private International Law must determine which foreign law is applicable? Otherwise no legal system might be applicable or only the *lex fori.* No clear answer can be given, but today the second approach appears to be more favoured.

65. On this latter assumption it would seem that in the last resort the particular dispute involving a foreign element must be solved by the forum as it would be decided in the country of the *lex causae*, and not (as might be done if the first assumption were correct) by the *lex causae* if no foreign element were involved. To hold otherwise would mean to apply foreign law as applied to a hypothetical case and not as it would be applied in the individual fact situation before the court. Given this need, *renvoi* is not a problem of legal theory[75] but of practical necessity. Properly analysed, on the assumption that the *lex fori* is not closed and self-sufficient, the problem is therefore whether the *lex fori* rejects *renvoi* rather than whether it accepts it.

It must be admitted that, given the diversity of connecting factors employed by the world's systems of Private International Law, universal harmony of decision cannot be achieved. It must be stressed, however, that at least unilaterally, in one country, a fair degree of uniformity of decision with that in the country of the *lex causae* (selected by connecting factors peculiar to the *lex fori* and without universal validity) is reached by this method.

In practice the solutions in the various countries range from the complete rejection of *renvoi*, acceptance of simple *renvoi* to total or | double *renvoi* in a limited number of cases, but never in all situations. Thus there exists a fair measure of agreement that *renvoi* is excluded in the law of contract[76] and

---

[74] Pp. 193–194.

[75] Neither the need, existing in common law countries, for the parties to prove foreign law as it would be applied in the foreign country concerned and not abstract rules of law, nor the alleged preference of English judges for having foreign judges decide foreign cases – see de Nova, *Hague Rec.* 118 (1966 II), at pp. 500, 502–503, esp. 506, para. 25; Ehrenzweig, *Private International Law* (1967), p. 146, para. 70 – provide a well-founded theoretical explanation. It was precisely his previous refusal to try a case involving a succession concerning personalty including an English leasehold interest of a *de cuius* who had died domiciled in France: *De Bonneval* v. *De Bonneval* (1838), 1 Curt 856, which led the same Judge to "sit as a foreign court" in *Collier* v. *Rivaz* (1841), 2 Curt. 855.

[76] See, e.g., *Re United Railways of Havana* v. *Regla Warehouses Ltd.* [1960], Ch. 52 at pp. 96–97, 115 (C.A.); *Rosencrantz* v. *Union Contractors Ltd.* (1960), 23 D.L.R. (2d.) 473; Castel (1961), 39 *Can. Bar Rev.*, 93; (1961), 21 *Rev. du Barreau de Quebec*, 181, 189;

tort. At the present time unsolved problems in this field include that whether *renvoi* should be admitted in the Private International Law of contract, if the parties have not exercised an express or implied choice.[77] Another new problem is that concerning the so-called "concealed" *renvoi*.[78] This is said to arise when the Private International Law of the forum refers to foreign law, and the foreign law (mainly common law) regards the question as one of jurisdiction, treats jurisdiction and choice of law as co-extensive and attributes jurisdiction to the *forum*. In these circumstances it is said that the attribution of jurisdiction to the courts of the *forum* equals a reference back to the *lex fori*.

In the case when a civil law country, e.g., Germany, is the *forum*, | instances include proceedings in Germany between American or English spouses domiciled there concerning the custody of a child of the marriage. A reference to the personal law of the spouses (to the law of a state of the U.S.A. or England) is said to be met by a jurisdictional attribution of competence to the courts in Germany, and thus to imply a reference to German law. Similar situations, it is argued, may arise in connection with divorces and ancillary claims arising therefrom, as well as in cases of adoption governed by English or American law. It is questionable whether in such circumstances a reference to the English or American law of divorce or adoption can be more than a reference to the English or American domestic law of divorce or adoption, and not the law of jurisdiction. It is true that English or American courts, if

---

Sherwood (1956), 5 *Am.J.Comp.L.*, 120–125; Raape, *Neue Juristische Wochenschrift* 1959, 1013, 1016; but see *Mason* v. *Rose*, 176 F. (2d) 486 (2 Cir. 1949); *Siegelman* v. *Cunard*, 221 F. (2d) 189 (1 Cir. 1955); *University of Chicago* v. *Dater*, 227 Mich. 658, 279 N.W. 175 (1936); ca.: *Lann* v. *United Steel Works Corpn.*, 166 Misc. 465, 1 N.Y.S. (2d) 951, 957; C. A. Frankfurt, 13 November 1956, *IPRspr.* 1956–1957, No. 24, affirmed by the German Supreme Court, 14 February 1958, *NJW* 1958, 750, *AWD* 1958, 57, *IPRspr.* 1958–1959, No. 39, p. 155, and of 9 June 1960, *NJW* 1960, 1720, *AWD* 1960, 183, *IPRspr.* 1960–1961, No. 23, p. 94; but see Swiss Federal Tribunal, 21 October 1955, BGE 81, II, 391.

[77] See the survey by Graue, *Aussenwirtschaftdienst des Betriebsberaters* 1968, 121; Gamillscheg, 27 *Rabel's* Z. (1962), 591; Maier, *NJW* 1962, 323, 325; Kreuzer, *Das Internationale Privatrecht des Warenkaufs* (1964), 284; Hartwig, *Renvoi im international Privatrecht* (1967), 152, 156; Vischer, *Internationales Vertragsrecht* (1962), 111; Batiffol, *Conflits de Lois en matière de contrats* (1938), No. 53; *Traité de d.i.p.* (4th ed. 1967), No. 311, p. 358 and note 52 *bis*: Kegel in *Soergel's Kommentar* (10th ed., 1970), note 34 to article 27; Kelly (1969), 18 *I.C.L.Q.*, 249, at p. 257, n. 39.

[78] See Hanisch, *NJW* 1966, 2085, with lit. and cases p. 2086, n. 15; see especially Neuhaus, *Grundbegriffe des I.P.R.* (1962), 190–194; *JZ* 1954, 704; Gündisch, *Fam.R.Z.* 1961, 352; Jayme, *Dir. Int.*, 22 (1968), pp. 84, 88, notes 33, 34, with lit.; *Z.f.Rv.* 11 (1970), 253; Ehrenzweig, *Treatise on the Conflict of Laws* (1962), 404; *Private International Law* (1967), p. 147, para. 72. For a case of concealed reference on (transmission) see the decision of the Court of Mainz of 21 October 1966, StAZ 1967, 24; *IPRspr.* 1966–1967, No. 159, p. 502, reported by Jayme, *loc. cit.*, and in (1969), 21 *Florida L.R.*, 290; Soergel-Kegel, *Kommentar zum BGB*, Vol. VII (10th ed., 1970), note 14 to Art. 27. Von Mehren in *XXth Century Comparative and Conflicts Law* (1961), pp. 380, 382, uses the term in a different sense.

seized, would have had to decline jurisdiction, and thus also to decline the application of English or American law. But the refusal to assume jurisdiction is not equal to a reference back or on to another jurisdiction, and, *ex hypothesi*, the English or American court has never been seized at all. In other words, the reference by German law to the English or American law of divorce or adoption is a reference to the substantive law of those countries, and the refusal of English or American courts to assume jurisdiction is not a reference back or on in the field of jurisdiction, and still less in the field of substantive law. It is equally true that English or American courts will recognise a German decree of divorce or an adoption order.[79] Thus in the first case the jurisdictional problem has not arisen and cannot arise; if it did, it must be remembered that the common law rule of jurisdiction is strictly unilateral[80] and does not purport to shift jurisdiction and thus, by implication, the law applicable. In the second case a choice of law problem does not arise. Thus *renvoi*, even of the concealed kind, does not come into play. It is difficult to envisage a situation in which this problem could be raised in an English court, except in the circumstances of section 1 of the Adoption Act 1958 or of *Armitage* v. *Att.-Gen.*[81] The former would equal a choice of the foreign law of the domicile. If according to the latter (say Ontario law), the courts of the parties' residence (e.g., England) have jurisdiction, the reference back to English law is said to be implied. In reality, the | English court cannot assume jurisdiction on a reference by foreign law, and the implied reference back to English law does not operate. If English courts recognise a divorce granted by the courts in South Dakota, because it is recognised by courts of the domicile, New York, a question of recognising a foreign decree, but not a reference on transmission by foreign (New York) law is involved.

Section 31. Preliminary Question

66. It has been known for a long time that different aspects of a case involving foreign elements may be governed by different systems of laws (*dépeçage*). Thus the form of a marriage is governed by the *lex loci celebrationis* and capacity by the law of the respective domiciles of the parties. Sometimes these various aspects may have to be considered in the same case, and at times they may be connected by a relationship in which one of the aspects is of primary importance because it embodies the substance of the claim, while

---

[79] The situation is not unlike that in *Armitage* v. *Att.-Gen.* [1906], P. 235, which is not regarded as one involving *renvoi*. See Dicey and Morris, *Conflict of Laws*, pp. 61–62.

[80] See above, pp. 165, 204 ff.

[81] [1906], P. 135. See also *Abate* v. *Abate* [1961], P. 29; *Mather* v. *Mahoney* [1968], 1 W.L.R. 1773; [1968], 2 All E.R. 223.

another affects the solution because it answers a preliminary or incidental question. Thus a claim to share in the estate of a deceased may depend upon the legitimacy of the claimant, upon the validity of a marriage to the deceased or of an adoption. The validity of a marriage may depend upon the validity of a previous divorce, and the legitimacy of a child may in turn depend upon both.

Until the end of the 1930s all these questions were regarded as posing essentially the same problem, namely as to what law applies to each individual aspect of the case according to the rules of Private International Law of the *forum*. Following the researches of Melchior,[82] Wengler[83] and Raape,[84] Robertson[85] introduced the problem into the Anglo-American world whether the choice of law for the solution of a preliminary or incidental question was to be determined not by the Private International Law of the *lex fori*, but of the *lex causae* of the principal question.

| The examination of this problem is rendered more difficult by the fact that in the preponderant number of instances, the *lex fori* coincided with the *lex causae*.[86] A choice between the two alternatives raises not only a technical question, however, but one of practical importance. If the private International Law of the *lex fori* applies, the individual substantive question which forms the object of the preliminary or incidental question in the case before the court will be determined uniformly in the *forum*, irrespective of whether or not the substantive problem arises as a principal or as a preliminary question. If the Private International Law of the *lex causae* governing the principal question applies, the individual substantive question which forms the object of the preliminary or incidental question in the case before the court will be determined differently according as the substantive problem is raised as a principal or as an incidental question. In the former case the

---

[82] *Die Grundlagen des deutschen international Privatrechts* (1932), pp. 249 *et seq.*

[83] *Rabels Z.*, 8 (1934), 148; *Dir. Int.*, 17 (1963), I, 50; *Rev. crit. d.i.p.*, 1966, 165. See also van Hoogstraten in *Mélanges Kollewijn* (1962), p. 209; Lagarde, *Rev. crit. d.i.p.*, 1960, 459, with further lit. at n. 1. For a survey, see Voskuil (1965), 19 *Dir. Int.*, I, 183; de Nova, *Hague Rec.* 118 (1966 II), at pp. 557–569.

[84] *Hague Rec.* 50 (1934 IV), 401, at pp. 485–495.

[85] *Characterization in the Conflict of Laws* (1940), 135–156; (1939), 55 *L.Q.R.*, 565, at p. 584.

[86] For England see *Birtwhistle* v. *Vardill* (1840), 7 Cl. & F. 940; *Re Wright's Trusts* (1856), 2 K. & J. 595; *Mette* v. *Mette* (1859), 1 Sw. & Tr. 416; *Brook* v. *Brook* (1861), 9 H.L.C. 193; *Shaw* v. *Gould* (1868), L.R. 3, H.L. 55; *Re Goodman's Trusts* (1881), 17 Ch.D. 266; *Re Andros* (1883), 24 Ch.D. 637; *Re Grove* (1888), 40 Ch.D. 216; *Re Bozelli* [1902], 1 Ch. 751; *De Wilton* v. *Montefiore* [1909], 2 Ch. 481; *Skottowe* v. *Young* (1871), L.R. 11 Eq. 474; *Atkinson* v. *Anderson* (1882), 21 Ch.D. 100; *Cantiere San Rocco* v. *Clyde Shipbuilding etc. Co.* [1924], A.C. 226; *Fibrosa Spolka Akcyjna* v. *Fairbairn Lawson Combe Barbour Ltd.* [1943], A.C. 32; *Kahler* v. *Midland Bank* [1950], A.C. 24. In the case of suretyship Voskuil, p. 192, distinguishes between preliminary and incidental questions.

Private International Law of the *forum*, in the latter the Private International Law of the *lex causae* applies. It would seem that the second alternative is to be preferred. Excessive importance should not be attached to the result that the same substantive question is determined by a different legal system as the circumstances lay in which it is raised before the court, even if the same person may thus be legitimate for one purpose and not for another. Such was the result of the decisions of the Canadian courts in *Schwebel* v. *Ungar*,[87] although the reasons given here are not adduced expressly.

| 67. It may be asked why this problem is raised when a preliminary or incidental question comes up for decision and not in other situations calling for the application of foreign law. In order to provide an answer, three possible situations must be distinguished:

(1) One single legal question only is in issue – e.g., as to what law governs succession. Here the view was taken above that in principle the *lex causae* including its rules of Private International Law should be taken into account unless the *lex fori* excludes *renvoi* expressly; the reasons are set out above.[88]

(2) Several legal questions are in issue – e.g., because claimants to the estate of a deceased person rely in part on the law governing matrimonial property relations and in part on the law governing the succession. These legal questions are of equal importance and independent of each other. Although it would be desirable to dovetail the results which follow from the application of one legal system to determine the question based on the matrimonial property régime and another based on the law of succession, no technical manipulation of the rules of Private International Law can achieve this harmony; sometimes the process of adaptation may help.[89]

(3) Several legal questions are in issue, of which all but one form preliminary or incidental questions.

It has been shown above that in these circumstances problems of substitution may occur (such as when a right of succession depends upon the validity of a foreign adoption). But in such a case the selection of the law applicable has taken place already. The question for discussion here arises at

---

[87] [1963], 37 D.L.R. (2d) 467; (1964), 42 D.L.R. (2d) 622, 633; [1964], O.R. 430, 441 (C.A.); [1965], S.C.R. 148, [1965], 48 D.L.R. (2d) 644. The decision could have been supported on another ground, drawn from the principle of the conflict of laws in time: see Lipstein (1967), 2 Ottawa L.R. 49, 56, relying on arguments developed in [1967], *C.L.J.*, 42. If this approach had been chosen, the problem would have involved two principal questions of equal standing, i.e., the recognition of a divorce in Italy of Hungarian domiciliaries and the capacity to marry of a person domiciled in Israel, who had been divorced, on the strength of a decree recognised in Ontario. See also Lysyk (1965), 43 *Can. Bar Rev.*, 365; Webb (1965), 14 *I.C.L.Q.*, 659.

[88] See above p. 211, No. 65.

[89] See the observations above No. 63, p. 209, on the problem of adaptation.

an earlier stage, if at all. To take a classic example: the court in England is
called upon to determine the following case: the *de cuius*, a Greek national,
who died domiciled in Greece leaving movables in England, had married the
claimant in a civil marriage ceremony in England. According to Greek law, a
Greek national who is a member of the Greek Orthodox Church cannot
marry otherwise than in a Greek Church, and the marriage is void. Consequently, the claim of the wife to share in the estate fails. If English Private
International Law is applied to both questions, the succession is governed by
Greek law as the *lex ultimi domicilii*, and the validity of the marriage is
(possibly) governed by English law as the *lex loci celebrationis*.[90] It is con-
ceivable, | however, that the requirement of a religious marriage ceremony
laid down by Greek law is to be characterised as a matter of capacity – and
Greek law is applied to this question as well. The same result will be reached
if the *lex causae* governing the succession (i.e., the Greek law) including its
rules of Private International Law is applied. In these circumstances a functional characterisation renders the need unnecessary to rely on the conflict
rules of the law governing the main question. A further advantage of this
technique is that it ensures a uniform course of decision in the *forum*, irrespective of whether the question is posed as a main question or as a preliminary question.

The difference in treatment by the conflict rules of the *forum* and of the *lex
causae* may however be due to factors other than a difference of characterisation of the preliminary question. Differences in the use and characterisation of connecting factors, in the approach to *renvoi* and possibly in a number of other cases exercise an effect.[91] Here the question arises whether the
forum should adhere to its own conflict rule to determine the preliminary
question. This must depend not so much on the *lex causae* than on the
evaluation of the importance of the conflict rule of the *forum*. If the latter
does not express a principle which is of paramount importance to the *lex fori*
as a whole, the *lex causae* including its conflicts rules should prevail over
those of the *lex fori*.[92] The principle which has been developed above in
connection with *renvoi* can be called in aid a second time.[93] If, however, the
conflicts rule of the *forum* is determined by considerations of paramount
importance to the *forum*, the fact that the *lex causae* and its conflicts rule
would reach a different result is irrelevant.[94] The following example may
serve as an illustration.

---

[90] See Wolff, *Private International Law* (2nd ed., 1950), ss. 196, 198, pp, 206–209.

[91] Gottlieb (1955), 33 *Can. Bar Rev.*, 523, 528.

[92] Lipstein (1967), 2 *Ottawa L.R.*, 49, at p. 58; see also Unger (1957), 43 *Transactions of the Grotius Society*, 86, at p. 94.

[93] Cf. Wolff, *Private International Law*, s. 196.

[94] Wengler, *Rabels Z.*, 22 (1958), 535, at 544, is more pragmatic.

For a long time legitimacy in English law depended exclusively upon the existence of a valid marriage of the parents and was regarded as identical with birth in lawful wedlock according to English domestic, or, later, also according to English Private International Law. Consequently, in *Shaw* v. *Gould*,[95] which turned on the legitimacy of issue to | take under a will, succession presented the main question: the validity of the marriage of the parents was treated as a preliminary question since it alone determined legitimacy according to English law. For this purpose the English rules of the conflict of laws were applied to determine its validity, and the further preliminary question whether a previous divorce in Scotland was to be recognised was also determined according to English Private International Law.[96]

The same principle would have been applied if either legitimacy or the recognition of a foreign divorce had arisen as a principal question. In either situation the criteria constituting the operative facts of the two rules were regarded as being of paramount interest to English law. Today, a change of attitude has taken place in English law. Legitimacy is no longer determined exclusively by the existence of a valid marriage and children of voidable,[97] void[98] and subsequent[99] marriages may enjoy this status. The time may have come, therefore, to regard the intimate link between marriage and legitimacy as severed in English law and to treat them as distinct questions governed by two separate conflicts rules of the forum, which concern legitimacy on the one hand[100] and the validity of the marriage on the other hand.[101] Also, the time may be ripe to concede to the foreign *lex causae* governing legitimacy the faculty to apply its own criteria for determining legitimacy by applying the conflicts rules of the foreign law governing legitimacy to determine any preliminary questions. It is true that the law governing legitimacy may itself rely upon the validity of the marriage of the parents, but in this case the validity of the marriage has become a preliminary question to be determined by the conflicts rules governing the main question, namely, legitimacy.[102] On

---

[95] (1869), L.R. 3 H.L. 55.

[96] According to Inglis (1957), 6 *I.C.L.Q.*, 202, at p. 214, *Shaw* v. *Gould* turned on the validity of the first marriage, and therefore on English law as that of the domicile of the children. However, in this case the presumption of legitimacy would have applied.

[97] Matrimonial Causes Act 1965, s. 11.

[98] Legitimacy Act 1959, s. 2.

[99] Legitimacy Act 1926, s. 1; Legitimacy Act 1959, s. 1.

[100] See in a different context, but in a similar vein, Melchior, *Grundlagen*, p. 260, and notes 3 and 4; Lagarde, *Rev. crit. d.i.p.*, 1960, 459, at p. 468, who speaks of "éloignement". And see Wolff, *Private International Law*, paras. 362, 363.

[101] Dicey and Morris, Rule 60, p. 418.

[102] Subject to the modifications set out above, see Lipstein in *Festschrift für Rabel* (1954), 611.

this view it is no longer possible to state with certainty that a marriage which is valid according | to English Private International Law will result in the legitimacy of the children.[103]

The principles developed here may be tested against the instructive example given by Wolff.[104]

"An Italian couple (A and B) validly married under all laws concerned is domiciled in England. B obtained from the English court a decree of divorce under English law on the ground of her husband's adultery. Then both parties marry again in England. Later A goes with this second wife C to Italy, acquires a domicile there and dies leaving movable property in England."

Italian law did not at the time admit or recognise divorces of Italian citizens.[105] In proceedings in England, the determination of the preliminary question whether B or C is the wife of the *de cuius* entitled to a share in his estate, if made in accordance with the rules of Private International Law of the main question, must result in the recognition of B as the sole wife of A. It would seem, however, that where a marriage entered into in England after a divorce there is concerned, English courts will determine the validity of such a marriage according to the English rules of Private International Law. The grant of a decree of divorce in England, followed by a marriage ceremony there, especially if the other spouse is domiciled in England, appears to justify the paramountcy of English law including English Private International Law. In England[106] and in Germany,[107] the courts, when faced with a divorce of Italians in Switzerland and a subsequent attempt to enter into a second marriage in England or Germany respectively, have dealt with | these two problems as separate principal questions. The result was that the Swiss divorce was recognised, but the party whose divorce was thus accepted was not allowed to marry again, because Italian law at the time forebade divorces and remarriages of their nationals. Since neither English nor Ger-

---

[103] E.g., a marriage valid in England under the rule in *Sottomayor* v. *De Barros (No. 2)* (1879), 5 P.D. 94.

[104] *Private International Law* (2nd ed., 1950), s. 200.

[105] On 18 December 1970 divorce was introduced in Italy. (Law No. 898 of 1 December 1970.) According to Art. 3 of the Law, a marriage abroad after a decree of divorce granted abroad will be recognised in respect of parties subject to Italian law.

[106] *R.* v. *Brentwood Superintendent Registrar of Marriages, ex p. Arias* [1968], 2 Q.B. 956.

[107] L. G. Weiden, 28 February 1953, NJW 1953, *IPRspr.* 1952–1954, No. 104; Directive of the President of the OLG Hamburg, 5 August 1955, *IPRspr.* 1954– 1956, No. 84, *Rev. crit. d.i.p.*, 1957, p. 50; BGH, 12 February 1964, BGHZ 41, 136, at p. 143 (3) with lit. at p. 144, referring to OLG Karlsruhe, 3 September 1962, *IPRspr.* 1962–1963, No. 70; OLG Munich 17 December 1962, *IPRspr.* 1962– 1963, No. 72; LG Cologne, 10 January 1962, *IPRspr.* 1962–1963, No. 66; see also BGH, 14 July 1966, BGHZ 46, 87, at p. 93 – but see the conclusions to the contrary and concurring with those put forward above in the text by the court below.

man law had a paramount interest in making the effect of the Swiss divorce prevail over the incapacity to marry again according to Italian law, the result is explicable but not desirable. Consequently the Hague Convention of 1968 on the Recognition of Divorces and Legal Separations of 1 June 1970 has created a régime of the type advanced here.[108]

68. Incidental or preliminary questions in the conflict of laws have hitherto been regarded as restricted to questions of private law. However, this is not necessarily so, for they may also involve matters outside private law which are commonly said to be of a public law nature. In this case the preliminary question may be said to constitute a datum, seeing that foreign public law cannot be applied.[109] Thus a foreign rule of the road or of the high seas[110] may have to be taken into account in order to determine whether or not a person whose liability is governed by another legal system has offended against a standard of care. Similarly, in order to ascertain whether a foreign pilot was a compulsory pilot it may be necessary to examine whether according to foreign law a duty existed to accept the pilot and to submit to his orders,[111] and a foreign prohibition forbidding the performance of certain transactions may excuse the failure to perform a contract governed by English law.[112] The question has been put whether the last-mentioned conclusion reflects the respect for a foreign datum[113] or a rule of Private | International Law of the *forum*.[114] While the practical consequence is the same, no matter which explanation is preferred, if the contract is governed by the *lex fori*, it is of importance when it is governed by a foreign legal system other than that of the place of performance. If the prohibition in the country of performance is taken into account by the *forum*, because a rule of Private International Law of the *forum* so requires, the result must be the same if the contract is governed by a foreign *lex causae*. If, however, the prohibition is treated as a datum, it can only be taken into consideration if the law governing the contract attaches consequences to it.

---

[108] Lipstein (1967), 2 *Ottawa L.R.*, 49. For the new Swiss practice see BGE 97, I, 389 of 3 June 1971; Dutoit and Mercier, *Riv. dir. int. priv. e proc.*, 8 (1972), 5.

[109] See Lipstein, *Ius Privatum Gentium*, I (1969), 411, at pp. 420–421.

[110] *The Halley* (1868), L.R. 2 P.C. 193, at p. 203; cf. *S.S. Diana, The Cliveden* [1894], A.C. 625, 629; *The Youri* v. *The Spearman* (1885), 10 App. Cas. 276; *The Talabot* (1890), 15 P.D. 194; *The Kaiser Wilhelm der Grosse* [1907], P. 36, 43–44; *The City of Berlin* [1908], P. 110.

[111] *The Augusta* (1887), 57 L.T.R. 326, 327; *The Darlington* [1903], P. 77, 78, 80; *The Prinz Hendrick* [1899], P. 177, 181; *The Guy Mannering* (1882), 7 P.D. 132, 135; *The Agnes Otto* (1887), 12 P.D. 56, 57; *The Andoni* [1918], P. 14, 18; *The Waziristan* [1953], 2 All E.R. 1213; *The Peerless* (1860), Lush. 30; *The Arum* [1921], P. 12, 18, 20.

[112] *Ralli Bros.* v. *Compania Naviera Sota y Aznar* [1920], 2 K.B. 287.

[113] Mann (1937), 18 *B.Y.I.L.*, 97, 107–113; Falconbridge, *Conflict of Laws,* 387, pp. 391–394; Morris (1953), 6 *Vanderbilt L.R.*, 505 at 510; *Rabel*, II, 536; Cheshire and North, 228–229. See also Serick, *Rabels Z.*, 18 (1953) 633, 647, with reference to the decisions of the German Supreme Court RGZ 161, 296, 300; 93, 182, 184 and the lit. cit. in n. 79.

[114] Dicey and Morris, Rule 132, Exception, pp. 761–762.

The answer to the question which solution is the correct one must depend upon whether or not a prohibition by the law of the place of performance is regarded as so intimately linked to the contract and thus to the law governing the contract that it must be treated as a preliminary or incidental question. On the other hand, if such a prohibition is regarded as always relevant in the *forum*, no matter whether the contract is governed by the *lex fori* or foreign law, it is obvious that a separate rule of Private International Law of the forum is required.[115]

69. Conversely, incidental or preliminary questions of a private law character may be raised by rules of public law.[116] Since the latter are self-delimiting[117] and do not contain, or rely on, choice of law rules, the question whether any legal notions employed by them refer to institutions of domestic law only or also to the same institutions in foreign law must remain a matter of construction.[118] Yet irrespective of whether the notion employed by the rule of public law of the *forum* includes the same notions abroad or not, the latter must be taken into account in one form or another. If the reference to foreign law is clear, the foreign institution must be taken into account in virtue of the reference to it; if there is no reference to foreign institutions, any foreign situations | corresponding to the domestic notion will be taken into account as *data*. In either case it may be necessary to resort to the process of *substitution*[119] in order to determine whether the institutions are interchangeable.

Section 32. Conflict of Laws in Time[120]

70. In substance a conflict of laws in time can arise in one of three forms. The rule of Private International Law of the forum, or the situation attracting the connecting factor, or the *lex causae* may change. Of these, changes in the *lex causae* present much the most important and difficult problems of time in the conflict of laws, especially when the change purports to have retrospective effect[121] In fact, the so-called retroactive effect resolves itself into two separate effects. Either the subsequent legislation purports to affect *ex nunc*

---

[115] The present attitude of English law is not clear; see *Regazzoni* v. *Sethia* [1958], A.C. 301; Morris (1953), 6 *Vanderbilt L.R.*, 505, at p. 510, with references to earlier cases.

[116] Mann (1963), 79 *L.Q.R.*, 525; *Hague Rec.* 132 (1971 I), 109, at pp. 134–144.

[117] See above pp. 165–166, 171.

[118] Mann, *loc. cit.*, above note 116.

[119] See above p. 207, No. 61; Mann, *Hague Rec.* 132 (1971 I), at p. 144 (4).

[120] For the lit. see Rigaux, *Hague Rec.* 117 (1966 I), pp. 433–437, especially Affolter, Batiffol, Castel, Diena, Gavalda, Grodecki, Lysyk, Makarov, Mann, Morris, Olivi, Roubier, Szászy, Spiro, *loc. cit.*

[121] Dicey and Morris, *Conflict of Laws* (8 ed. 1967), p. 44.

the previously existing situation,[122] or *ex tunc.* Only the latter effect can properly be regarded as retroactive. Thus two different questions must be put: the first is whether the law applies to an existing legal relationship; if the first is answered affirmatively, the second is whether the law applies *ex tunc.* The first involves a question of the conflict of laws in time; the latter involves the interpretation of domestic law found to apply to an existing legal relationship.

It is generally believed that the *lex causae* should be applied in its entirety,[123] and much thought has been expended by writers on domestic law to determine in what circumstances supervening legislation is to be applied, with or without retroactive effect, to situations which have materialised previously, in the absence of specific indications that the rule is to have retrospective effect. The results of this investigation in what may be called the two-dimensional field can be put to use where the situation becomes three-dimensional through the addition of space in the form of rules of Private International Law.[124] If it is admitted that, | in the sphere of one legal system alone, subsequent legislation applies to past occurrences, if they represent a continuous relationship[125] the question whether such subsequent legislation applies in space presupposes, once again, that the relationship is continuous. If it is not, as for instance in the case of succession, where the law of the last domicile (or nationality) of the deceased operates upon his death (at least in respect of movables) and as a result of it, or in the law of tort where the *lex loci delicti* or the *lex fori* or even the law governing the relationship between the parties is determining, any subsequent legislation must be disregarded,[126] because it does not apply to an event which has spent itself and does not constitute a continuous relationship. If the relationship is continuous until performed, such as a contract, it is subject to any subsequent changes in the law applicable.[127] At the same time it must be remembered that even when a relationship is continuous, subsequent legislation may not be appli-

---

[122] Such as the English Legitimacy Act 1926, s. 8 (1), introducing *legitimatio per subsequens matrimonium.*

[123] Critically Wengler, *Rabels Z.,* 23 (1958), 535, at pp. 552, 558 ff.

[124] See my review of Roubier, *Le droit transitoire* (2 ed. 1960), in [1961], *Cambridge Law Journal,* 123.

[125] E.g., contracts, matrimonial relations, both of a personal and of a proprietary nature and other family relationships. For the use of this distinction see Wengler, *Rabels Z.,* 22 (1958), 535, at p. 543; for its practical, application see *Parkasho* v. *Singh* [1968], P. 233.

[126] Unless a positive rule of Private International Law requires the contrary, as does the rule in *Phillips* v. *Eyre* (1870), L.R. 6 Q.B. 1 at p. 28, see Lipstein [1972 B], 31 *Cambridge Law Journal,* 67, at p. 99.

[127] See, e.g., *Rex* v. *International Trustee for Bondholders A.G.* [1937], A.C. 500. Dicey and Morris, *Conflict of Laws* (8 ed. 1967), p. 47, n. 44, with cases; Grodecki, *loc. cit.,* p. 78. Of course the position is different if foreign law is only incorporated into the contract which is, itself, governed by some other legal system.

cable because it may have to be characterised differently, with the result that the subsequent legislation is covered by another rule of the conflict of laws and that some other legal system applies to the latter.[128] Thus the merger of two companies and the creation of a new company may be governed by the law of the country where the companies are incorporated; a subsequent statute enacted by the country of the place of incorporation discharging the new company of all debts incurred by the predecessor companies is governed by the law applicable to the respective contractual obligations.[129]

If these principles are accepted, the personal law of the deceased at the time of his death (Paraguayan law) was applied correctly to a will disposing of movable estate in England, and subsequent Paraguayan | legislation declaring the estate to be property of the Paraguayan nation was rightly disregarded,[130] for both reasons indicated above: the death crystallised the law of succession, and the subsequent legislation was characterised not as falling within the field of succession but of expropriation. The latter was governed by the *lex situs*, English law, and not by the law of the last domicile of the deceased, which was Paraguayan.[131]

With equal justification the personal law of the testatrix, Austrian law, as it was in force at the time of her death, was applied in *Re Aganoor's Trusts*[132] to a settlement in the nature of substitutions contained in the will which was valid according to Austrian law in force at the time but had been invalidated by subsequent legislation of the Italian successor State. The fund was situated in England, where it had been paid into court and where successive interests were lawful. Thus the will, valid according to the law of the testatrix's domicile at the time of her death, could be given effect in England since the *lex situs*, English law, which determined the nature of the proprietary interests in the hands of the beneficiaries, allowed interests in the nature of substitutions.[133]

On the other hand, in *Nelson v. Bridport*[134] Sicilian law as it stood at the time of the action (and prohibited substitutions) and not as it stood at the

---

[128] Wengler, *Rabels Z.*, 23 (1958), 535.

[129] *Adams v. National Bank of Greece S.A.* [1961], A.C. 255, and see Lipstein [1960], *Cambridge Law Journal*, 169.

[130] *Lynch v. Government of Paraguay* (1871), L.R. 2 P. & D. 268, esp. p. 272.

[131] *Bank voor Handel, etc. v. Slatford* [1953], 1 Q.B. 248, at pp. 257 *et seq.;* Diplock L.J. in *Adams v. National Bank of Greece and Athens* [1958], 2 Q.B. 59, 76, 77, but see Lord Reid in *Adams v. National Bank of Greece SA.* [1961], A.C. 255, 282.

[132] (1895), 66 L.J.Ch. 521.

[133] But see Dicey and Morris, *Conflict of Laws* (8 ed. 1967), p. 45; Mann, *loc. cit.*, who argues that Italian law altered the beneficial interests in the trust fund. According to the view taken here it altered the nature of proprietary interests in general capable of being held according to Italian law as the *lex situs*. See also Grodecki, 69.

[134] (1846), 8 Beav. 547.

time of the testator's death (when substitutions were lawful) was applied to a will containing a settlement of land in Sicily. However, Sicilian law was both the law governing the succession and the *lex situs* governing the nature of proprietary interests in the hands of the beneficiaries. Thus a subsequent change of Sicilian law altering the nature of the proprietary interests created some time previously and now vested in the succeeding beneficiaries had to be taken into account, because proprietary rights are governed by the *lex situs*, irrespective of the validity of the will. The latter remained valid but had become in|effective.[135] Any charge of "petrification" is inappropriate, since the *lex situs* can impose modifications of the proprietary interests in the hands of the beneficiaries at any time.

Both cases show once again that subsequent legislation which modifies previous law may have to be characterised differently from the law which it purports to modify. The former may concern a question of succession, the latter may vary the nature of proprietary interests available to be held *inter vivos*, or it may involve expropriation; the former may deal with the creation, merger or extinction of companies, the latter with the discharge of contracts entered into by these companies.

| Part IV. Conclusions

71. The purpose of these lectures was to examine the nature, the function and the structure of Private International Law. The need to determine the application of law in space has existed throughout the ages, but the aims and the methods which determine its sphere of operation have never crystallised. The nature of rules of private law, the discretion of individual legal systems, subject only to the overriding control of customary International Law, the international character of rules of Private International Law, constitutional principles which can balance the choice of law in a Federal State, sociological and teleological considerations have been called in to provide criteria of general or international validity.

The foregoing examination has shown that every one of these theories or basic ideas has re-appeared over the ages in a slightly modernised guise. Yet some fundamental insights have emerged. Unlike in the realm of public law, where governmental action is paramount and where the sphere of operation is necessarily circumscribed by the need not to impinge on the legitimate sphere of operation of other governments, private law is not so restricted. Its sphere of application, embodied in a set of rules of Private International

---

[135] The common contention that *Re Aganoor's Trusts* and *Nelson* v. *Bridport* are conflicting decisions cannot be supported.

Law, is only controlled in substance and not territorially by the general rules of Public International Law which prohibit illegal discrimination and demand the observance of minimum standards of behaviour. At the same time, Public International Law has developed a set of rules of the conflict of laws for the use of international tribunals, but these rules differ in nature and function from those which form part of domestic law, and there is no hierarchy of norms. Modern doctrines which rely on a balance of governmental interests or of substantive rules find their justification in the law and Constitution of the United States, where the law is homogeneous, the laws of the member States are on an equal footing, and the Supreme Court watches over the balancing act. Their usefulness outside such a special framework remains doubtful. In the end the exercise of discretion by individual legal systems in devising rules of Private International Law is only matched by the need to provide certainty from the outset, except perhaps where torts are involved.

In these circumstances each domestic legal system on its own, without any specific directives by Public International Law, must determine | whether it will regard itself as closed, self-sufficient and complete, except where it makes specific concessions to foreign law or whether it regards itself as primarily restricted to situations having a connection of a personal or territorial character with the country of the *forum*. The trend in the United States appears to be in the former direction; that elsewhere in the world points in the latter direction.

The structure of the rules of Private International Law reflects these trends. Their formulation in terms of orthodox rules of the conflict of laws, or as spatially conditioned internal rules, their detailed or rudimentary character provides a pointer. The view appears to receive growing support that foreign law occupies a place concurrently with domestic law and that the structure of domestic rules of Private International Law may not be able to take sufficiently into account the different character of foreign law and legal institutions as well as different choice of law rules. This realisation has led to a greater emphasis on the importance of characterisation (qualification) and of *renvoi* and to the development of sophisticated solutions, and has also accorded its proper place to the preliminary question by conceding a role to the rules of Private International Law of the foreign *lex causae*. At the same time, the foreign legal system chosen as the *lex causae* is not allowed unlimited power, and subsequent foreign legislation may find its match in local rules of conflict of laws in time.

| Bibliography

Ago, *Teoria del d.i.p.* (1934). "Règles générales de D.I.P.", *Hague Rec.* (1936 IV), 243.
Arminjon, "La notion des droits acquis en D.I.P.", *Hague Rec.* 44 (1933 II), *1.*
Batiffol, *Aspects philosophiques du droit international privé* (1956).
Batiffol (and Lagarde), *Droit international prive*, I (5 ed. 1970).
Cavers, "A Critique of the Choice-of-Law Process" (1933), 47 *Harv.L.R.*, 173.
– "Two Local Law Theories" (1950), 63 *Harv.L.R.*, 822.
– *The Choice of Law Process* (1965).
W. W. Cook, *The Logical and Legal Basis of the Conflict of Laws* (1942), esp. p. 1 ff.
Currie, B., *Selected Essays on the Conflict of Laws* (1963).
David, *La loi étrangère devant le juge du fond* (1965).
De Nova, "Historical and Comparative Introduction to Conflict of Laws", *Hague Rec.* 118 (1966, II), 434.
Dicey and Morris, *Conflict of Laws* (8 ed. 1967).
Ehrenzweig, *Treatise on the Conflict of Laws* (1962).
– *Private International Law* (1967).
– "Specific Principles of Private International Law", *Hague Rec.* 124 (1968 II), 169.
Evrigenis, "Les tendances doctrinales actuelles en D.I.P.", *Hague Rec.* 118 (1966 II), 309.
Falconbridge, *Conflict of Laws* (2 ed. 1954).
Gutzwiller, "Le developpement historique du D.I.P.", *Hague Rec.* 29 (1929 IV), 291.
Hambro, "Conflict Law as Part of International Law", in *Varia Juris Gentium, Liber amicorum J. P. François* (1959), 132.
– "The Relations between International Law and Conflict Law", *Hague Rec.* 105 (1962 I), 1.
Kahn-Freund, *The Growth of Internationalism in English Private International Law* (1962).
Kegel, *Internationales Privatrecht* (3 ed. 1971).
Lewald, "Règles générales des conflits de lois", *Hague Rec.* 69 (1939 III), 127.
– "Conflits de lois dans le monde grec et romain", *Rev. crit. d.i.p.*, 1968, 419–440, 615–639.
Lipstein, "Conflict of Laws before International Tribunals, I, II", (1942), 27 *Transactions of the Grotius Society*, 142. (1944) 29 *Transactions of the Grotius Society*, 51.
– "Recognition of Governments and the Application of Foreign Law" (1950), 35 *Transactions of the Grotius Society*, 157.
– "Conflict of Laws 1921–1971; The Way Ahead [1972 B]", 31 *Cambridge L.J.*, 67.
Lorenzen, *Selected Articles on the Conflict of Laws* (1947), esp. pp. 1 ff., 181 ff.
Mann, "The Doctrine of Jurisdiction in International Law", *Hague Rec.* 111 (1964 I), 1.
– "The Primary Question of Construction and the Conflict of Laws" (1963), 79 *Law Quarterly Review*, 525.
– "Conflict of Laws and Public Law", *Hague Rec.* 132 (1971 I), 109. Maury, "Règles générales des conflits de lois", *Hague Rec.* 57 (1936 III), 325.
| Meijers, "L'histoire des principes fondamentaux du D.I.P. à partir du Moyen Age …", *Hague Rec.* 49 (1934 III), 543.
Morris, *Conflict of Laws* (1971).
Monaco, *L'efficacia della legge nello spazio* (2 ed. 1964).
Nadelmann, "Some Historical Notes on the Doctrinal Sources of American Conflict Law", *Jus et Lex, Festgabe für Gutzwiller*, 263.
Neuhaus, *Grundbegriffe des Internationalen Privatrechts* (1962).
Neumeyer, *Die gemeinrechtliche Entwickelung des internationalen Privat- und Strafrechts bis Bartolus, I* (1901), II (1916).
Niederer, *Einführung in die allgemeinen Lehren des I.P.R.* (3 ed. 1963), cited 2 ed. 1956.
Rheinstein, "Das Kollisionsrecht im System des Verfassungsrechts der Vereinigten Staaten von Amerika", *Festschrift für Rabel*, I (1954), 539.
Robertson, *Characterization in the Conflict of Laws* (1940).
Sack, *Law, A Century of Progress*, III (1937), 322.

Shapira, *The Interest Approach to Choice of Law* (1970).
Sperduti, *Saggi di teoria generale del d.i.p.* (1967).
Stevenson, "Effect of Recognition on the Application of Private International Law Norms" (1951), 51 *Col.L.R.*, 710.
– "The Relationship of Private International Law with Public International Law" (1952), 52 *Col.L.R.*, 561.
Zajtay, *Contribution à l'étude de la condition de la loi étrangère en d.i.p. français* (1958).

Some Practical Comparative Law:
The Interpretation of Multi-Lingual Treaties with Special Regard to the EEC Treaties

F.H. Lawson, in whose honour these lines are written, has always been interested in every aspect of foreign law, whether it touches upon its substance or form. It is, therefore, not inappropriate to draw attention to a specific problem that requires both legal and linguistic techniques derived from foreign law. This is the problem of interpreting bilingual or multi-lingual treaties.[1]

Whenever a treaty, which was drafted either in a foreign language only or in a foreign language and that of the *lex fori,* is incorporated into domestic law, such a problem can arise. In recent times the Diplomatic Privileges Act of 1964, based on the Vienna Convention on Diplomatic Relations of 1961, has provided that diplomatic immunity cannot be pleaded, *inter alia,* in "a real action relating to private immovable property situated in the territory of the receiving State. ..."[2] The term "real action" no longer serves to indicate a type of action that is available in English courts,[3] and the type of remedy that

---

[Editorial note: first published in Tulane Law Review 48 (1974), 907–915.]

[1] *See* Dölle, *Eine Vor-Studie zur Erörterung der Problematik mehrsprachiger Gesetzes- und Vertragstexte,* in XXth Century Comparative and Conflicts Law 277 (1961); Dölle, *Zur Problematik mehrsprachiger Gesetzes- und Vertragstexte,* 26 Rabels Z. 4 (1961); Hardy, *The Interpretation of Plurilingual Treaties by International Courts and Tribunals,* 37 Brit. Y.B. Int'l L. 72 (1961); Dickschat, *Problèmes d'Interprétation des traités européens résultant de leur plurilinguisme,* [1968] Revue belge de droit international 40; Akehurst, *Preparing the Authentic English Text of the EEC Treaty,* in Introduction to the Law of the EEC 20 (B. Wortley ed. 1972); Stevens, *The Principle of Linguistic Equality in Judicial Proceedings and in the Interpretation of Plurilingual Legal Instruments: The Régime Linguistigue in the Court of Justice of the European Communities,* 62 Nw. U.L. Rev. 701 (1967); Bowyer, *Englishing Community Law,* 9 Comm. Mkt. L. Rev. 439 (1972). *See also* Riese, in II Vom Deutschen zum Europäischen Recht 507 (1963); Makarov, in Mélanges Guggenheim 403 (1968); Zuleeg, 4 Europarecht 97 (1969).

[2] Diplomatic Privileges Act, ch. 81, sched. 1, art. 31(1) (a) (1964) (reproducing The Vienna Convention on Diplomatic Relations of April 18, 1961, 500 U.N.T.S. 96).

[3] *See, e.g.,* G. Cheshire, Real Property 28 (11th ed. E. Burn 1972).

it represented in England in former days was never one with which the drafters of the Convention were familiar. In fact, they envisaged an action based on a proprietary title to recover immovable property, which is known in civil law systems as an action *in rem*.[4]

| Conversely, the Anglo-French Convention on the Mutual Recognition and Enforcement of Judgments in Civil and Commercial Matters of 18 January 1934[5] which reproduces the relevant provisions of the English Foreign Judgments (Reciprocal Enforcement) Act of 1933 contains a special jurisdictional provision concerning judgments *in rem* against movable property.[6] In its own setting this provision envisages proceedings *in rem*. Such proceedings have been described as an action "against a ship or other chattel in which the plaintiff seeks either to have the res adjudged to him in property or possession, or to have it sold, under the authority of the Court, and the proceeds, or part thereof, adjudged to him in satisfaction of his pecuniary claims."[7]

For this purpose, "the inquiry is, first, whether the subject matter was so situated as to be within the lawful control of the State under the authority of which the court sits; and, secondly, whether the sovereign authority of that State has conferred on the court jurisdiction to decide as to the disposition of the thing and whether the court has acted within the jurisdiction."[8] A leading French commentator, however, was not unnaturally induced to explain article 4(2) of the Convention in terms of French law as envisaging an action in the nature of a *rei vindicatio* to recover property.[9] The Treaty establishing the European Economic Community[10] and, to a lesser degree, the Treaty establishing the European Coal and Steel Community[11] have raised similar problems, albeit in a somewhat different setting. The Community Court, to whom the control of the interpretation and application of the Treaty is entrusted,[12] is itself charged as an institution of the Community with rendering the tasks of the Community[13] effective. It differs, thereby, from that of an

---

[4] *See* A. Dicey, Conflict of Laws 146 n. 23 (9th ed. J. Morris 1973) (where the English Act is interpreted with the help of French literature dealing with French civil procedure).

[5] S.R. & O. 1936 No. 609, in France J.O. 30 June 1936.

[6] *Id.* art. 4(2); English Foreign Judgments Act 1933, 23 Geo. 5, ch. 13, § 4(3) (a).

[7] The Henrich Björn, 11 App. Cas. 270, 276 (1886).

[8] Castrique v. Imrie, L.R. 4 H.L. 414, 448 (1870) (per Lord Chelmsford).

[9] J.-P. Niboyet, Traité de droit international privé francais Vol. VI, pt. 2, § 2092, at 243 (1950).

[10] 298 U.N.T.S. 4 (English); 294 U.N.T.S. 19 (French); 295 U.N.T.S. 19 (German); 296 U.N.T.S. 19 (Italian); 297 U.N.T.S. 19 (Dutch). For a synopsis in the four languages of the original Community see [1957] BGBl. II 753.

[11] 261 U.N.T.S. 140. For a synopsis of the official French and the unofficial German version see [1952] BGBl. II 448.

[12] EEC Treaty art. 164, 298 U.N.T.S. 3, 73.

[13] EEC Treaty art. 4, 298 U.N.T.S. 3, 16; ECSC Treaty art. 3, 261 U.N.T.S. 140, 147.

international tribunal proper, where the interpretation of agreements turns exclusively on the intention of the parties and is less functional.

| 1. Where differences occur in the formulation of the Treaty, they may provide, in the first place, a means of ascertaining the intentions of the parties. Thus, when invited to define the meaning of *barème (Preistafel)*,[14] the Court said:

> The Treaty is ... very clear in its language when it makes reference to "*the* price lists" and not "price lists." The price lists ... are, thus, not documents related merely to the Treaty and specially established for the purposes of the Treaty, but documents of a type accepted by the established trade practices and which ... have always, although in a general or provisional way ... the character of an offer to contract upon the basis of the prices which they set out.

> The price lists do not lose this character of an offer to contract, although the Treaty assigns to them those purposes of public interest which are specified by its provisions. ... [T]he expression "price list" retains in the Treaty its usual meaning and refers to the prices on the basis of which the enterprises declare themselves ready to sell their products.[15]

Article 33 (2) of the ECSC Treaty allows enterprises and associations to invoke the annulment jurisdiction of the Court against "les décisions et recommendations individuelles les concernant," while the (unofficial) German version speaks of "Klage gegen die sie individuell betreffenden Entscheidungen und Empfehlungen." While the French version appears to stress that the measure must be of individual concern to the plaintiff, the German version seems to lay much greater stress on the fact that the measure is directed towards the plaintiff individually. The Court said "it is sufficient ... that this decision ... is not general, but possesses the characteristics of an individual decision, without it being necessary that it should possess these characteristics with respect to the plaintiff."[16] In reaching this interpretation, the Court may have been influenced by the arguments of the Advocate-General (K. Roemer), who was able to point to an exact parallel in German administrative law.[17]

---

[14] ECSC Treaty art. 60 (2) (b).

[15] French Government v. High Authority, 1 Recueil de la Jurisprudence de la Cour 7, 26 (1955) [hereinafter cited as Rec.]; 2 Valentine, The Court of Justice of the European Communities 18, 29–30 (1965) [hereinafter cited as Valentine]. *See also* 1 Rec. 7, 48 (1955) (per Adv. Gen. M. Lagrange).

[16] Groupement des Industries Sidérurgigues Luxembourgeoises v. High Authority, 2 Rec. 53, 87 (1956).

[17] 2 Rec. at 120, referring to German Bundesverwaltungsgerichtsgesetz of September 23, 1952, [1952] BGBl. I 625, para. 15(3), replaced by the Verwaltungsgerichtsordnung of January 21, 1960, [1960] BGBl. I 17, para. 42(2), which requires the plaintiff to plead that a right of his has been infringed.

The wording of article 63(2) (a) of the ECSC Treaty, which speaks conjointly of agreements to "fixer ou déterminer" (festzusetzen oder zu bestimmen) prices, induced the Court to hold that

| the juxtaposition of the two assertions requires to delve more deeply into the subtle distinction between ... the "power to fix prices" and the power to "determine them." No such distinction appears explicitly anywhere in the Treaty ... the power to fix prices is for the seller who exercises it as a function necessitated by the objective situation and discharged by familiar means. The power to determine prices, however, connotes a power given to the seller to establish prices appreciably different from that established by the unaided effect of competition. ...[18]

The difference in the wording of article 85(1) of the EEC Treaty, which speaks of restrictive practices that are capable[19] of "affecter – beeinträchtigen – pregiudicare – ongunstig beinvloeten – le commerce entre Etats membres" has forced the Court to consider whether the neutral sense of the French version or the pejorative requirement in the other languages characterizes the nature of the practices that are prohibited. The question was first raised in *De Geus v. Bosch G.m.b.H.*[20] by the Advocate General, M. Lagrange,[21] who argued that, following the view put forward by the German Government, any influence, not necessarily involving a restriction of a harmful character, was sufficient, seeing that even favourable effects are constantly accompanied by harmful consequences. The matter has now been put to rest by the combined operation of the decisions in the *Consten and Grundig v. EEC Commission*[22] and *Société Technique Minière v. Maschinenbau Ulm G.m.b.H.*[23] cases. In the former it was held that

it is necessary, in particular, to know whether the agreement is capable of endangering, either directly or indirectly, in fact or potentially, freedom of trade between member States in a manner which could *harm* the attainment of the objects of a single market between States. Thus, the fact that an agreement favours an increase, even a large one, in the volume of trade between States, is not sufficient to exclude the ability of the agreement to "affect" trade in the above mentioned direction.

---

[18] Geitling v. High Authority, 8 Rec. 165, 200–01 (1962), 1 Comm. Mkt. L.R. 113, 151 (1962).

[19] "Susceptibles"–"geeignet"–"che possano"–"kunnen." *Contra*, ECSC Treaty art. 65 (2): "tendraient à, empêcher"–"die daruf abzielen würden," 260 U.N.T.S. 140, 194. *See also* Worms v. High Authority, 8 Rec. 377, 400, 409 (1962) (per Adv. Gen. M. Lagrange).

[20] 8 Rec. 89 (1962), 1 Comm. Mkt. L.R. 1 (1962).

[21] 8 Rec. 139–41 (1962).

[22] 12 Rec. 429, 495 (1966), 5 Comm. Mkt. L.R. 418, 471–72 (1966).

[23] 12 Rec. 337, 359 (1966), 5 Comm. Mkt. L.R. 357, 375 (1966). *See also* Völk v. Vervaecke, 15 Rec. 295, 302(5) (1969), 8 Comm. Mkt. L.R. 273 (1969); Cadillon v. Höss, 17 Rec. 351, 356(6) (1971), 10 Comm. Mkt. L.R. 420 (1971).

In the latter, the infringement of the objects of the Treaty became the determining consideration when the Court said:

| To fulfill this condition [art. 85(1)], the agreement in question must, on the basis of a complex of objective legal or factual elements, allow the expectation, with a sufficient degree of probability, that it will exercise a direct or indirect, actual or potential, effect upon the current of trade between member States.

The question whether sickness benefits in the meaning of Regulation 3 on Social Security for Migrant Workers[24] include payments made to the beneficiary in order to keep up his contributions to any such scheme of insurance[25] was answered in the negative on the strength of the German version of the Regulation, which was clearer than the French.[26]

2. In the second place, differences in the formulation of the various linguistic versions of the Treaty may inspire a construction that is unaffected by the legal connotations in the domestic laws of the member States. Thus, it was held that article 97 of the EEC Treaty allowing member States to levy a turnover tax on the German model, calculated by a cumulative multi-stage system to institute average rules (*taux moyen*),[27] conferred on the latter term a uniform meaning for the Community. It is irrelevant that, in assuming an independent meaning of its own, the relevant article of the Treaty draws wholly or in part on the domestic law of the member States.[28]

---

[24] Arts. 2(a), 22; J.O. 1958, 561.

[25] "Leistungen bei Krankheiten," which is equivalent to "prestations *en cas* de maladie" in French, while the French official text of Reg. 3 spoke obscurely of "prestations de maladie." *See* Dekker v. Bundesversicherungsanstalt für Angestellte, 11 Rec. 1111, 1116 (1965), 5 Comm. Mkt. L.R. 503 (1966).

[26] For the application of this technique see Guerra v. Institut Nat'l. d'Assurance Maladie-Invalidité, 13 Rec. 283, 289 (1967) (Reg. 3, art. 45(2) –"institutions" et "autorités"); Bestuur der Sociale Verzekeringsbank v. Van der Vecht, 13 Rec. 445, 456–58 (1967), 7 Comm. Mkt. L.R. 151, 165–67 (1968) ("een bedrijf ... waarbij zij gewoonlijk werkzaam zijn"–"un etablissment ou ils sont normalement occupés" "occupation"–"tewerkstelling"); EEC Comm'n v. Italy, 16 Rec. 93, 100, 101(5) (1970), 10 Comm. Mkt. L.R. 466, 473–74 (1971) (Reg. 24, art. 1(1) – whether "istituiscono un catasto viticolo" is identical with "fonder en droit"); Assider v. High Authority, 1 Rec. 263, 275, 278 (1955) (Protocol on the Statute of the Court, art. 37–"en cas de difficulté"–"entsteht ein Streit" – a "dificulté" is a broader term than a "contestation"); Humblet v. Belgium, 6 Rec. 1125, 1149 (1960) (Protocol on Immunities: "privilèges" (French)–"Vorrechte," "Voorrechten" (German, Dutch)); Stauder v. City of Ulm, 15 Rec. 419, 424(2), 429 (1969) (Commission Decision 69/71, J.O. E.E.C. 1969 L. 252/9: "bon individualisé" (French) –"auf ihren Namen ausgestellten," "op naam gestelde" (German, Dutch).

[27] *See generally* K. Lipstein, The Law of the European Economic Community 255 (1974) [hereinafter cited as Lipstein].

[28] Milch-, Fett- und Eierkontor G.m.b.H. v. Hauptzollamt Saarbrüken, 15 Rec. 165, 180(5) (1969), 8 Comm. Mkt. L.R. 390, 400–01 (1969).

Among the grounds for claiming the annulment of a Community meas-
ure, *détournement de pouvoir* (abuse of power) figures promi|nently.[29] In
one form or another, this ground figures in the domestic law of the original
six,[30] and its beginnings are to be found in French administrative law of the
latter part of the nineteenth century. The Community Court, in dealing with
ECSC article 33(2), was not called upon to pronounce on this notion, but the
survey provided by the Advocate General (M. Lagrange) bears out the impression that its features vary according as the notion itself has a predomi-
nantly objective or subjective content.[31] In the absence of a single notion of
détournement de pouvoir, both the subjective French[32] approach, which
fastens on the extraneous purpose of the measure,[33] and the German, which
employs a more objective standard and comes near to equating it to an
infringement of the law (*i.e.*, the Treaty),[34] has been considered by the Community, though inconclusively.

When called upon to interpret the meaning of "force majeure" in a Commission Regulation,[35] the Court acknowledged that this notion did not have
the same content in all the branches of law, and that it depended upon the
nature of the relationship under review. It then attempted a definition of its
own when it said:

[A]n importer who has used all the necessary endeavours is in principle released from
the obligation ... when circumstances beyond his control make it impossible for him
to carry out the importation within the necessary period .... [T]he cases enumerated
in art. 6(3) are obviously based on this criterion, since the circumstances on which
they | depend do not correspond with a concept of *force majeure* in the sense of an

---

[29] EEC Treaty art. 173, 294 U.N.T.S. 19, 108; ECSC Treaty art. 33, 260 U.N.T.S. 140,
166.

[30] The corresponding approach in English law is expressed in Schmidt v. Secretary of
State for Home Affairs, [1969] 2 Ch. 149, 166, 168; Reg. v. Governor of Brixton Prison, *Ex
Parte* Soblen, [1963] 2 Q.B. 243, 302.

[31] Assider v. High Authority, 1 Rec. 123, 149 (1955), 2 Valentine 45 (1965). In Nold v.
High Authority, 5 Rec. 89, 146 (Adv. Gen. K. Roemer), the parties agreed on the French
definition of "détournement de pouvoir." *See also* Wirtschaftsvereinigung Eisen- und
Stahlindustrie v. High Authority, 4 Rec. 261, 292 (1958).

[32] Also adopted in Belgium, Luxembourg, the Netherlands, and, substantially, in Italy.

[33] Netherlands v. High Authority, 1 Rec. 201, 226–27 (1955), 2 Valentine, *supra* note 15,
at 206–07; Groupement des Hauts Fourneaux et Aciéries Belges v. High Authority, 4 Rec.
223, 256 (1958), 2 Valentine, *supra* note 15, at 531–32; Compagnie des Hauts Fourneaux de
Chasse v. High Authority, 4 Rec. 129, 147 (1958), 2 Valentine, *supra* note 15, at 507–08;
Compagnie des Hauts Fourneaux de Chasse v. High Authority, 4 Rec. 155, 195, 2 Valentine, *supra* note 15, at 500–01; Gutmann v. EEC Comm'n, 12 Rec. 149, 171 (1966).

[34] Fédération Charbonnière de Belgique v. High Authority, 2 Rec. 199, 309–16 (1956), 2
Valentine, *supra* note 15, at 114–21; Chambre Syndicale de la Sidérurgie Francaise v. High
Authority, 11 Rec. 567, 584 (1965).

[35] Reg. 136/64 art. 6(2)–(4), J.O. E.E.C. 1964, 2601 (import certificates); Reg. 102/64 art.
8(1), J.O. E.E.C. 1964, 2125 (grain import and export certificates); 473/67 art. 9(1), J.O.
E.E.C. 1967, L. 204/16 (grain import and export certificates).

absolute impossibility, but with abnormal difficulties independent of the will of the importer arising in the course of the execution of the contract. However, the recognition of a case of *force majeure* presupposes not only the occurrence of an unusual event, but also that the consequences of this event were not avoidable. ...[36]

The responsibility of the Community in tort is engaged under the ECSC Treaty,[37] if a "faute de service"–"Amtsfehler" – of the Community has occurred. Under the EEC Treaty,[38] this liability is determined by the general principles common to the laws of the member States in respect of damages "causés par ses institutions ou par ses agents dans l'exercice de leurs fonctions"–"durch ihre Organe oder Bediensteten in Ausübung ihrer Amtstätigkeit verursachten." Given the dichotomy in continental law which distinguishes between the liability in tort of individuals, as determined by private law, and that of the state for its own acts and for those of its employees in the exercise of their duties, as determined by special rules of administrative law in France and in countries following the French system of administrative law, and by the general law of civil liability in others,[39] the question is whether the general principles common to the law of member States that are to be observed in the present context are confined to those enshrined in administrative law.[40] If this should be the case, the liability of the Community would be restricted to liability for bad organization or functioning of public services (including liability for its agents in so far as the faults of the latter can be attributed to bad organization or functioning of the service concerned). If, on the other hand, article 215 (2) includes in its reference to general principles those applying in civil law, it must be considered whether the general principle of primary liability of the administration, | albeit in civil proceedings, as expressed in the German Constitution[41] and in German civil law[42]

---

[36] Schwarzwaldmilch G.m.b.H. v. Einfuhr- und Vorratsstelle für Fette, 14 Rec. 549, 562–63 (1968), 8 Comm. Mkt. L.R. 406, 562–63 (1969); Einfuhr- und Vorratsstelle Getreide und Futtermittel v. Köster, Berodt & Co., 16 Rec. 1161, 1179 (37)–80(40), 11 Comm. Mkt. L.R. 255, 293–94 (1972); Internationale Handelsgesellschaft m.b.H. v. Einfuhr- und Vorratsstelle für Getreide und Futtermittel, 16 Rec. 1125, 1139(23)–40(25), 11 Comm. Mkt. L. R. 255, 286–87 (1972).

[37] Art. 40, para. 1, 261 U.N.T.S. 140, 170. For the jurisdiction in respect of personal fault of the agent in the exercise of his functions, see *id.* at para. 2.

[38] Art. 215, para. 2, 298 TJ.N.T.S. 3, 86–87 (English), 294 U.N.T.S. 19, 125 (French), 295 U.N.T.S. 19, 125 (German). For the limited jurisdiction in respect of the personal liability of the agents toward the Community only see *id.* at para. 3. For a comparison of ECSC art. 40 and EEC art. 215, para. 2 see Kampffmeyer v. EEC Comm'n, 13 Rec. 317, 351–64 (1967) (per Adv. Gen. J. Gand).

[39] FERAM v. High Authority, 5 Rec. 501, 516–18 (1959); *id.* at 523–27 (per Adv. Gen. M. Lagrange). *See also* Société Fives Lille Cail v. High Authority, 7 Rec. 559, 617–21 (1961) (per Adv. Gen. K. Roemer).

[40] *See* Lipstein, *supra* note 27, at 323 n. 2.

[41] Grundgesetz art. 34 (1949) (W. Ger.).

[42] BGB § 839(1).

can take its place here. The answer must probably be found in the broad notion of State responsibility for torts, and not in the procedural and jurisdictional niceties of the domestic law of the member States.[43]

Sometimes the answer is clear: the individual domestic law of each member State must interpret the provision according to its own notions. This solution applies to EEC Treaty article 37(1), which speaks of "organisme," "Einrichtungen," "organismo," and "lichaam," whereby a member State controls imports or exports between member States.[44] The same applies to article 48 (2), which limits freedom of movement on grounds of public order.[45]

Some notions clearly bear the stamp of a particular legal system; such is the distinction between *prestations familiales*[46] and *allocations familiales*[47] current in French law and adopted by Regulation 1408/71 on Social Security. The Convention of 27 September 1968 on the Jurisdiction and the Enforcement of Decisions in Civil and Commercial Matters,[48] made in accordance with article 220 of the EEC Treaty, relies on the individual laws of the member States when it makes the place where the parties are *domiciliés, ihren Wohnsitz haben,*[49] the basis of the jurisdiction to be exercised by the member States. Jurisdiction as the *forum connexitatis* when a *demande en garantie* has been issued reflects the law of all the original member States, except Germany.[50] Jurisdiction to *connaître du fond, in der Hauptsache,*[51] reflects the distinction in all the legal systems between procedural or interlocutory matters and all others. By including in judgments a *mandat d'exécution* and a *fixation par le greffier du montant des frais du procès,*[52] notions of | German law, namely the *Vollstreckungsbefehl*[53] and the *Kostenfestsetzungsbeschluss,*[54] are accorded a special place owing to their exceptional

---

[43] Kampffmeyer v. EEC Comm'n, 13 Rec. 317, 352 (1967) (per Adv Gen. J. Gand).

[44] 294–97 U.N.T.S. 19, 43. As to their duties, the four versions differ from each other when they speak respectively of "aménagent," "formen ... um," "procedono a un ... riordinamento," "passen ... aan." *Id.*

[45] *See* Lipstein, *supra* note 27, at 87 n. 1; *In re* Residence Prohibition on an Italian National, Verwaltungsgerichtshof Baden-Württemberg, (Dec. 23, 1965), 10 Comm. Mkt. L.R. 540, 543 & n. 8 (1971).

[46] Reg. 1408/7 art. 1(u) (i), O.J. E.E.C. 1971, L. 149/2.

[47] *Id.* art. 1(u) (ii).

[48] O.J. E.E.C. 1972, L. 299/32 [hereinafter cited as Convention]. *See generally* Lipstein, *supra* note 27, at 270 *et seq.*

[49] Convention, *supra* note 48, arts. 2, 52.

[50] *Id.* art. 6 (2); Lipstein, *supra* note 27, at 278 n. 12. A third party notice comes nearest to it.

[51] Convention, *supra* note 48, art 24; Lipstein, *supra* note 27, at 278 n. 13.

[52] Convention, *supra* note 48, art. 25; Lipstein, *supra* note 27, at 278 & nn. 3–4.

[53] ZPO §§ 699, 794(4).

[54] ZPO §§ 104, 794(2).

character. The same applies to *actes authentiques reçus et exécutoires,*[55] as well as *transactions conclues devant le juge au cours d'un procès et exécutoires dans l'Etat d'origine,*[56] which are unknown in French law, but represent the German *Vollstreckbare Urkunde*[57] and *Vergleich.*[58] By refusing recognition and enforcement to a judgment if the institution of proceedings has not been brought to the notice of the defendant by being *signifié ou notifié,*[59] the Convention relies on the general distinction between personal and substituted service,[60] expressed in technical terms of French law.

The wording of EEC Treaty article 172,[61] which confers on the Community Court in certain circumstances *compétence de pleine juridiction* (a term well known in French administrative law), is reflected in the Italian version of *competenza giurisdizionale anche di merito* and in the Dutch *volledige rechtsmacht,* but perhaps less happily in the German *Befugnis zu unbeschränkter Ermessensnachprüfung.* Only a detailed paraphrase can convey the purport of *exceptions* and *incidents* as interlocutory in the Rules of the Court.[62]

---

[55] Convention, *supra* note 48, art. 50.

[56] *Id.* art. 51.

[57] ZPO §§ 794(5), 797.

[58] *Id.* § 794(1).

[59] Convention, *supra* note 48, art. 27(2).

[60] Lipstein, *supra* note 27, at 280 n. 6.

[61] 294–97 U.N.T.S. 19, 108. *See also* arts. 178, 181, *id.* at 110–11.

[62] Rule 91, para. 1, translated in 1 Valentine, The Court of Justice of the European Communities 528 (1965), as applications for a ruling upon a preliminary objection or upon a preliminary issue of fact. *See* Lipstein, *supra* note 27, at 340–41.

Inherent Limitations in Statutes and the Conflict of Laws

When John Morris drew attention, in 1946, to choice of law clauses in statutes,[1] the problem was one of manageable proportions. A statutory provision either contained no choice of law clause, or a general choice of law clause, altering or restating a conflict of laws rule, or it offered what he called "a particular choice of law clause" purporting to delineate the scope of a rule of domestic law. The Carriage of Goods Act 1924,[2] the Inheritance (Family Provision) Act 1938[3] and the Law Reform (Frustrated Contracts) Act 1943[4] together with the Wills Act 1861,[5] now defunct, provided what were then some of the best examples[6] of such "particular" choice of law clauses. Then, as now,[7] statutory provisions containing a general choice of law clause

[Editorial note: first published in International and Comparative Law Quaterly 26 (1977), 884–902.]

[1] "The Choice of Law Clause in Statutes" (1946) 62 L.Q.R. 170–185. See now *Conflict of Laws* (1971), at pp. 235–236.

[2] s. 1; see *Vita Food Products Inc.* v. *Unus Shipping Co. Ltd.* [1939] A.C. 277; *Ocean Steamship Co.* v. *Queensland State Wheat Board* [1941] 1 K.B. 402.

[3] s. 1; now Inheritance (Provision for Family and Dependants) Act 1975, s. 1 (1).

[4] s. 1 (1).

[5] ss. 1, 2.

[6] The Merchant Shipping Act 1894, s. 265, is another. Its general reference to the law of the port of registration has been replaced in the Merchant Shipping Act of 1972, s. 100 (3) and Sched. 5 (see S.I. 1972 No. 1977), by innumerable references to the same test, but sometimes to others: see ss. 4 (2), 42 (2), 49.

[7] Legitimacy Act 1926, ss. 1, 8; Adoption Act 1958, s. 1 (1) (5), replaced by the Children Act 1975, ss. 10 (2) (*a*), 11 (2) (*a*), coupled with s. 9 of the Legitimacy Act ss. 14 (2) (*a*) (*b*), 24 (1) (2), 25 (1), 26 (1), 39 (1) (4), 40 (1) (*a*) (*b*), replaced, except 1959, s. 2 (2); Marriage (Enabling) Act 1960, s. 1 (3); Matrimonial Causes Act 1965, s. 26 (1) – as previously amen-

existed not infrequently, and they have assumed increasing importance where labour relations and consumer protection are concerned.[8]

|During the last 30 years these special rules of the conflict of laws as well as certain allegedly extensive or restrictive statutes[9] have attracted increasing attention from writers in various countries, albeit under different titles, such as "spatially conditioned internal rules,"[10] "legislatively localised laws" or "laws containing localising limitations,"[11] "functionally restricting rules,"[12] or perhaps "special substantive rules for multi-State problems."[13]

At the same time, domestic rules of another type, limiting or extending their own operation, have been discovered, or perhaps rediscovered.[14] In his book, *La Théorie du Renvoi,*[15] Francescakis pointed to the existence of rules which he called *"règles d'application immédiate"*; de Nova terms them *"normes fixant leur propre domaine d'application,"* or *"norme con apposita delimitazione della sfera di efficacia"*[16] or *"norme autolimitate,"*[17] while others describe them as *"norme di applicazione necessaria."*[18] They also circumscribe their sphere of operation, either restrictively or extensively, but unlike

---

ded – by respectively the Matrimonial Causes Act 1972, ss. 19 (2), 35 (1) (3), 36 (1), 45 (1), 46 (1) (2) – see also s. 54 (1) and Sched. 2, para. 5, or abolished by the Domicile and Matrimonial Proceedings Act 1973, s. 5 (2)–(4), subs. (6) of which amends the Matrimonial Causes Act 1973, s. 27 (2).

[8] Contracts of Employment Act 1963, s. 9 (1) (2) and Sched. 1, para. 1 (3), replaced by the Contracts of Employment Act 1972, s. 12 and Sched. 1, para. 1 (2); Redundancy Payments Act 1965, ss. 17, 56 (4); Mann (1966) 82 L.Q.R. 316; Hughes, 83 *ibid.* 180; Unger, *ibid.* 428–433; Equal Pay Act 1970, s. 1 (2) (7), as amended by the Sex Discrimination Act 1975, Sched. 1, Pt. I, para. 1 (4); Trade Union and Labour Relations Act 1974, Sched. 1, Pt. II, para. 9 (2); Sex Discrimination Act 1975, ss. 6, 10; Employment Protection Act 1975, s. 119 (5); Supply of Goods (Implied Terms) Act 1973, s. 5.

[9] For the Variation of Trusts Act 1958, see Morris, *Conflict of Laws* (1971), pp. 410–411, with cases.

[10] Nussbaum, *Principles of Private International Law* (1942), pp. 70–73; Morris, *op. cit. supra*, n. 9, at p. 170; De Nova (1969) 22 *Rev. Hellénique de droit international* 24–32; *Studi Ghisleriana Ser. Spec. per il IV Centenario* (1967), pp. 126–135.

[11] Unger (1952) 15 M.L.R. 88; (1959) 43 *Transactions of the Grotius Society* 37; (1967) 83 L.Q.R. 427; Cavers, *Choice of Law Process* (1965), p. 221; 131 (1970 II) *Hague Rec.* 77 at pp. 133–135.

[12] De Nova (1966) 54 Calif.L.R. 1569; (1967) 3 Riv.dir.int.priv. e proc. 699.

[13] Von Mehren (1974) 88 Harv.L.R. 347.

[14] Graulich in *Mélanges Dabin* II (1963), p. 629 at p. 630 attributes it to Kahn, *Beiträge* I, p. 161.

[15] (1958) at pp. 11, No. 7; 13, No. 10; 16, No. 12; 19, No. 13; 31–43, Nos. 26–39; see also (1966) Rev.crit.d.i.p. 1; (1974) *ibid.* 273; (1967) 3 Riv.dir.int.priv. e proc. 691; Graulich, *op. cit. supra*, n. 14.

[16] (1959) 13 *Diritto Internazionale* 13; *Melanges Maury* I (1960), p. 377.

[17] (1973) 5 *Adelaide L.R.* 1; *Multitudo Legum, Jus Unum: Festschrift für Wengler* II (1973), p. 617; (1971) 25 *Diritto Internazionale* 239.

[18] Ballarino (1967) 3 Riv.dir.int.priv. e proc. 707; Mosconi, *ibid.* 730; Pocar, *ibid.* 731.

spatially conditioned rules of the earlier type, they may also claim to apply exclusively, and their sphere of operation is not defined expressly.[19]

A situation has thus arisen where there exist side by side with the general rules of the conflict of laws, not only rules of the character first enumerated by Morris, which contain either a general choice of law clause, altering or restating a conflict of laws rule, or a particular choice of law clause. There exist also unilateral rules of | the conflict of laws which determine the application of those rules of the *lex fori* which are sometimes said to be of a public law character, such as rules of civil procedure, administrative and criminal law.[20] There exist, in addition, rules of private law which are spatially conditioned by implication only. These may be restricted *ratione personae, materiae* or *loci*, or they may purport to apply in all circumstances, irrespective of the presence or absence of particular connecting factors. For this reason they show a certain affinity with rules of public policy and with unilateral rules of the conflict of laws defining the exclusive application of those rules of the *lex fori* which are of a public law nature. And since the distinction between rules of public and private law is not one which is readily applicable in the conflict of laws in general and in English law in particular, the new categories of "self-limiting" or "immediately applicable" rules of domestic law may offer some attraction to students of the conflict of laws and to common lawyers.

The ensuing danger of confusion has not been rendered any less by the insight, developed in some detail by de Nova[21] and Kelly,[22] to the effect that rules which are spatially conditioned or which are said to claim immediate or direct application can form part either of the *lex fori* or of foreign law, which may or may not constitute the *lex causae* according to the ordinary rules of the conflict of laws of the *lex fori*. In these circumstances it seems indicated to examine separately the place of these rules according as they form part of the *lex fori* or of the *lex causae*.

---

[19] See, *e.g.*, the Fatal Accidents Act 1846: *The Esso Malaysia* [1975] O.B. 198 at p. 206; Dicey and Morris, *Conflict of Laws* (1972), pp. 956 and n. 12 with lit., and 974, n. 63; the Law Reform (Personal Injuries) Act 1948, s. 1 (3): *Brodin* v. *A/R Seljan and Another*, 1973 S.L.T. 198 at pp. 201, 202; Thomson (1974) 23 I.C.L.Q. 458; Hire Purchase and Small Debt (Scotland) Act 1932, s. 2 (2) (*d*): *English* v. *Donnelly*, 1959 S.L.T. 2; *Duncan* v. *Motherwell Bridge and Engineering Co.*, 1952 S.C. 131; Law Reform (Miscellaneous Provisions) Act 1970, s. 1 (1).

[20] Lipstein (1949) 26 B.Y.I.L.; (1959) 8 I.C.L.Q. 506 at pp. 512, 514.

[21] *Supra*, nn. 12, 16, 17.

[22] (1969) 18 I.C.L.Q. 249; *Localising Rules in the Conflict of Laws* (1974).

General Considerations

Before embarking upon this examination, it may be useful to set out some general observations which will guide this inquiry.[23] In the present writer's view, the fundamental problem underlying all choice of law rules of whatever kind is whether the validity of law is limited *ratione loci* or *ratione personae* or whether, in the absence of any specific restriction, law purports to operate outside the jurisdiction. Since neither the *lex fori* nor foreign law by itself can put into practice its claim to apply elsewhere, their range can only be determined by the attitude of the *lex fori* towards foreign law.

If the *lex fori* purports to be a closed and self-sufficient system, the *lex fori* applies even to situations containing a foreign element, unless a specific rule of Private International Law of the forum *restricts* the operation of the *lex fori* and, at the same time, *introduces* | foreign law as an exception. In the absence of such a reference to foreign law, a gap will exist, unless the *lex fori* contains a subsidiary rule replacing the reference to foreign law, or the spatially conditioned rule, by another substantive rule.

If, on the other hand, the *lex fori* is primarily restricted to situations having a connection with the country of the forum on personal or territorial grounds, a broad range of rules of Private International Law must determine which foreign law is applicable. Otherwise no legal system might be applicable, or only the *lex fori*, thus restoring the closed and universal character of the *lex fori*.[24]

It is difficult to state which legal system in the world follows either view. Some indications are provided by the rules of Private International Law themselves, whether they are rudimentary or detailed and accept *renvoi*, or whether they are expressed in terms of general conflict rules or of spatially conditioned domestic rules. The practice and literature in the United States points to the assertion of closed and self-sufficient systems. The practice in England points in the opposite direction. More particularly, in determining whether an Act of Parliament, not a rule of common law, contains spatial limitations, the presumption is accepted, in the absence of a clearly expressed intention to the contrary, that Parliament does not assert or assume jurisdiction which goes beyond the limits established by the common consent of nations. Territoriality, presence and allegiance are presumed to determine its range.[25] These considerations may affect the English approach to self-limi-

---

[23] See also Unger (1967) 83 L.Q.R. 427 at p. 444.

[24] See Lipstein 135 (1972 I) Hague Rec. 99 at p. 193.

[25] *Re Sawers, ex p. Blain* (1879) 12 Ch.D. 522 *per* James L.J. at pp. 527, 533; *per* Brett L.J. at p. 528; *per* Cotton L.J. at p. 532; *Cooke* v. *C.A. Vogeler Co.* [1901] 102; *Mount Albert Borough Council* v. *Australasian Temperance and General Mutual Assistance Society* [1938] 224 at pp. 242, 243; *Theophile* v. *Solicitor-General* [1950] A.C. 186; *Barcelo* v. *Elec-*

ting and immediately applicable statutes, where English law is the *lex fori*.[26]

Where spatially conditioned rules form part of English or Scottish law as the *lex fori*, it makes no difference to their application, as Morris himself has observed,[27] whether English or Scots law is the proper law or not. They may operate for either reason.

Rules Forming Part of the Lex Fori

Instructive modern examples are furnished by the practice of Australian courts. In *Barcelo* v. *Electrolytic Zinc Co. of Australasia*[28] | debentures were issued in Victoria, secured by a fixed charge over land in Tasmania and a floating charge over the debtor's property in other places. The trust deed provided that it was to "be construed according to the law of the State of Victoria." The question arose whether the interest payable was reduced by virtue of the Victoria Financial Emergency Act 1931. The High Court of Australia, on appeal from the Supreme Court of Victoria,[29] applied the Act principally, it would seem, because the parties had in their agreement referred to the law of Victoria as a whole, either as the law governing the debentures or the trust deed,[30] though Starke J. appears to have relied on the wording of the Act as such, at least to a certain extent.[31]

In *Wanganui-Rangitikii Electric Power Board* v. *Australian Mutual Provident Society*,[32] debentures were issued by a New Zealand local authority, secured by a charge on the local rates. Interest was payable in New South Wales. The question was once again whether by virtue of the local statute, the New South Wales Interest Reduction Act 1931 (the equivalent of the Vic-

---

tolytic Zinc Co. of Australasia [1932] 48 C.L.R. 391 at pp. 410, 424, 443–444; and see generally Mann 111 (1964 I) Hague Rec. 1 at p. 66.

[26] See *e.g. Re Price, Tomlin* v. *Latter* [1900] 1 Ch. 442 at p. 451.

[27] *Conflict of Laws*, pp. 236, 410–411, citing as to contracts: *Santos* v. *Illidge* (1860) 8 C.B. N5 (N.S.) 681; *Strichand* v. *Lacon* (1906) 22 T.L.R. 245: English statute not applied; see also *Velchand* v. *Manners* (1909) 25 T.L.R. 319; *contra: Boissevain* v. *Weil* [1950] A.C. 327; *Duncan* v. *Motherwell Bridge and Engineering* Co., 1952 S.C. 131; *English* v. *Donelly*, 1958 S.C. 494: statute of the *lex fori* applied.

[28] (1932) 48 C.L.R. 391.

[29] [1932] V.L.R. 193 at p. 346, *sub. nom. Electrolytic Zinc Co. of Australasia* v. *Knight*.

[30] *Per* Rich J. at p. 407: debentures governed by Victorian law; also *per* Dixon J. at pp. 425, 428; *per* McTiernan J. at p. 446; *per* Evatt J. at pp. 434 *et seq.*: free choice of Victoria law.

[31] At pp. 411, 413, 415, but contrast Rich J. at pp. 406–407: the transaction must be concerned with Victoria in a real and practical sense.

[32] (1933–34) 50 C.L.R. 581 on appeal from the Supreme Court of New South Wales (1933) 50 N.S.W.W.N. 207.

toria Financial Emergency Act 1931) the amount of interest had been reduced. The court was agreed that New Zealand Law was the proper law of
the debentures and of the charge[33] and held, further, by a majority, that on its
proper construction the New South Wales Act did not apply in the circumstances, even if there was no legal obstacle why the Act should not have
attempted to do so,[34] while Gavan Duffy C.J. and Starke J. found that the
wording of the Act permitted its application on the facts of the case.[35]

In *Kay's Leasing Corporation* v. *Fletcher*,[36] the Supreme Court of New
South Wales, faced with a hire purchase agreement concluded, it would
seem, in Victoria, between the plaintiff, a company incorporated in Victoria
but registered to carry on business in New South Wales, and the defendant
resident in New South Wales, found | that the parties had validly chosen
Victoria Law to govern their contract.[36a] Nevertheless, Walsh J. considered
in some detail whether the provisions of the New South Wales Hire Purchase
Agreements Act 1941–57 applied. He found that, while the Act was not
restricted to agreements *made* in New South Wales, yet in the absence of an
express statement in the Act of the criterion in what circumstances the Act
was to apply, the general rules of the conflict of laws must determine its
application. Thus Victoria law applied exclusively.[37] On appeal, the High
Court of Australia, affirming the decision of the court below, stressed that
statutes of the *lex fori* may have to be taken into account, even if the proper
law is foreign.[37a] To use the words of Kitto J.[37b]: "Where a provision renders
an agreement void for non-compliance by the parties or one of them with
statutory requirements, especially where the requirements can be seen to
embody a specific policy directed against practices which the legislature has
decreed oppressive or unjust, a presumption that the agreements in contemplation are only those of which the law of the country is the proper law
according to the rules of private international law has no apparent appropri-
ateness to recommend it ... It would mean that provisions enacted as salu-
tary reforms might be set at nought by the simple expedient ... of inserting in
an agreement a stipulation that validity should be a matter for the law of
some other country." In all these cases the courts were rightly not deterred
from considering the ambit of a statute of the *lex fori*, even if the transaction
was governed by foreign law in accordance with the general rules of the
conflict of laws.

---

[33] *Per* Gavan Duffy C.J. and Starke J. at pp. 594–596; *per* Dixon J. at p. 598; *per* Evatt J. at
pp. 604–606; *per* McTiernan J. at p. 611.

[34] *Per* Dixon J. at p. 601; *per* Evatt J. at p. 609; *per* McTiernan J. at p. 612.

[35] At p. 597.

[36] (1963–64) 64 S.R.(N.S.W.) 195.

[36a] *Ibid.* at pp. 201, 205.

[37] *Ibid.* at pp. 203–204.

[37a] (1964) 116 C.L.R. 124 at pp. 134–135 *per* Barwick C.J., McTiernan and Taylor JJ.

[37b] *Ibid.* at p. 143.

Rules Forming Part of Foreign Law

It is an entirely different matter if the case is being considered in the courts of a country other than that where the spatially conditioned or immediately applicable rule has been enacted or, in other words, if it is not part of the *lex fori* and is part of foreign law. In these circumstances, systematic considerations would suggest that the particular restrictive or extensive provision, if it is to be taken into account, must constitute part of the proper law which applies according to the general rules of the conflict of laws. However, the practice of the courts is meagre and offers little guidance.[37c]

|The most prominent case is probably *Mount Albert Borough Council* v. *Australasian Temperance and General Mutual Life Assurance Society*,[38] which is the counterpart of *Wanganui-Rangitiki Electric Power Board* v. *Australian Mutual Provident Society*[38a]; only the payment of interest was due in Victoria, and the application of the Victoria Financial Emergency Act 1931 (also relied upon in *Barcelo* v. *Electrolytic Zinc Co. of Australasia*[39]) was in issue, not that of the New South Wales Interest Reduction Act 1931. Upon appeal from the Court of Appeal of New Zealand Lord Wright, tendering the advice of the Privy Council, found that the debentures were governed by New Zealand law and that the charge on the local rates, being equivalent to a charge on land, was also governed by New Zealand law, which was the *lex situs*. Nevertheless he considered whether according to its tenor the Victoria Act applied so as to reduce the rate of interest payable. In the end, after a detailed examination of the Act's provisions, and especially art. 37 which states: "Nothing in this part shall apply to any mortgage or security for moneys raised by any public or local authority outside Australia," he concluded that the Victoria statute was inapplicable.[40] It is difficult to see on what grounds, except the mere fact of its existence in the locality where performance was due (a factor to be considered later on), the Victoria Act, a foreign statute, was relevant, seeing that the proper law of the transaction was New Zealand, and that according to Lord Wright himself the *lex loci solutionis* only affected the manner of performance.[41] Lord Wright repeated this exercise in the *Vita Food* case[42] where, sitting as a Nova Scotia court and

---

[37c] See Starke J. *obiter* in *Barcelo* v. *Electrolytic Zinc Co. of Australasia* (above, n. 28) at pp. 413, 414; *Vita Food Products Inc.* v. *Unus Shipping Co.* [1939] A.C. 277 at p. 292. Kelly, *Localising Rules* (*supra*, n. 22) pp. 67 *et seq.*; Deby-Gérard. *Role de la règle de conflit* (1973) pp. 54 *et seq.*; Lando (1976) 11 *Texas. Int.L.J.* 505, 519: Kahn-Freund, 143 (1974 III) *Hague Rec.* 141, 241.

[38] [1938] A.C. 224.

[38a] See *supra*, n. 32.

[39] (1932) 48 C.L.R. 391.

[40] [1938] A.C. 224 at pp. 237–239, 243.

[41] See Morris (1953) 6 Vanderbilt L.R. 505 at pp. 519 *et seq.*

[42] [1939] A.C. 277 at p. 292 *et seq.*

applying English law as the proper law of the contract, he considered nevertheless the Newfoundland Carriage of Goods by Sea Ordinance 1932, which formed at best part of the *lex loci contractus*. However, he had qualified his approach by acknowledging the difference of weight carried by a statute of the *lex fori* or of a foreign law.[43]

On the other hand, the High Court of Australia, on appeal from a judgment of Fox J. in the court of the Australian Capital Territory,[44] held in *Augustus* v. *Permanent Trustee Co. (Canberra) Ltd.*[45] that a voluntary settlement made in the Australian Capital Territory by payments of money made there, out of which stocks registered | mainly in the Australian Capital Territory were purchased, by a settler domiciled and resident in New South Wales in favour of beneficiaries there, the trustee being a company incorporated in the Australian Capital Territory and not registered to do business in New South Wales, in violation of the rule of remoteness in force in the Australian Capital Territory, but not of that [editorial note: in] force in New South Wales, was valid nevertheless. The court adopted the argument that a settlement is governed by its proper law as if it were a contract and that clause 5 of the trust deed, which provided that the trustees were to have the powers conferred on them by New South Wales law and the rights and liabilities of the trustee and the beneficiaries as between themselves and as against the trustee and the administration of the trusts of the settlement were to be regulated by that law, rendered the latter applicable. Once this conclusion was reached, it did not matter whether on a proper construction of the New South Wales Conveyancing Act 1919–67 the latter may perhaps (though the Court doubted it) purport to apply only to property situated in New South Wales.[46]

Critical Analysis

In so holding the court adopted on the face of it the view of the Australian High Court expressed, at least by some members, in the cases where the spatially conditioned or immediately applicable statute was part of the *lex fori*, possibly also of the *lex causae*, but not of foreign law.[47] In reality a considerable difference divides the two situations.[48] Where the spatially con-

---

[43] *Ibid.* 292; 296 and see below, n. 51.

[44] [1969] 14 F.L.R. 246.

[45] (1970–71) 124 C.L.R. 245; [1971] A.L.R. 661.

[46] *Ibid.* 259.

[47] See also *Merwin Pastoral Co.* v. *Moolpa Pastoral Co.* (1933) 48 C.L.R. 565 at p. 573.

[48] Sec also Unger (1967) 83 L.Q.R. 427 at p. 439; but see Mahn (1972–73) 46 B.Y.I.L. 117, 129.

ditioned or immediately applicable statute is part of the *lex fori* and the proper law is either found to be the *lex fori*[49] or foreign law,[50] the spatial restrictions or extensions of the statute are given full play. Where the spatially conditioned or immediately applicable statute is part of foreign law, and the proper law is the *lex fori* (or of yet a third legal system), the spatially conditioned or immediately applicable statute is not nor|mally taken into consideration.[51] When the spatially conditioned or immediately applicable statute is part of the proper law, being a law other than the *lex fori*, any spatial or other restrictions are disregarded on the ground that the initial reference to foreign law is final.

This conclusion has been the object of much doubt and discussion in the literature since it may appear to evoke the well-known problem as to whether a reference to foreign law is final or whether *renvoi* or transmission are to be admitted. It must be conceded, at the outset, that since *ex hypothesi* the spatially conditioned or immediately applicable statute forms part of foreign law as the proper law of the transaction and cannot claim that unquestioned observance which it could command if it were part of the *lex fori*, the question of its application in substance, including its extension *ratione personae, loci* or *materiae*, is one concerning the proof and application of foreign law.

Thus it is not surprising that such an eminent judge as Evatt J. in the High Court of Australia should have considered whether the question before him in *Barcelo* v. *Electrolytic Zinc Co. of Australasia*[52] *i.e.* whether the Victoria Financial Emergency Act 1931, as part of the proper law governing the debentures (which was also the *lex fori*) extended to the mortgage over land in Tasmania or desisted from purporting to apply introduced the problem of *renvoi*. If so, he was inclined to reject *renvoi* and to treat a reference to a legal system as a reference to its domestic law as such, irrespective of any terri-

---

[49] Such is the position in the United States in administering the Harter Act or the avoiding provisions on the common law which preceded it: *The Brantford*, 29 Fed.Rep. 373 (1886); *Liverpool and Great Western SS Co.* v. *Phoenix Insurance Co.*, 129 U.S. 397, 461 (1889); 32 L.ed. 788, 799 (1889). For the operation of the Fatal Accidents Act 1846 in England and the Law Reform (Personal Injuries) Act 1948 in Scotland see, *supra*, text related to n. 19.

[50] *Knott* v. *Botany Mills*, 179 U.S. 69, 71 (1900); 45 L.ed. 90, 93 (1900); *New York Central R.R. Co.* v. *Lockwood*, 17 Wall 357 (1873), 21 L.ed. 627 (1873); *Cia de Navigacion La Flecha* v. *Branci*, 168 U.S. 104, 117, 118 (1897); 42 L.ed. 398, 404, 405 (1897). For the Jones Act see *Lauritzen* v. *Larson*, 345 U.S. 571 (1953).

[51] *Vita Food Products Inc.* v. *Unus Shipping Co.* [1939] A.C. 277 at pp. 292, 296; *Re Missouri S.S. Co.* (1889) 42 Ch.D. 321 at pp. 339–340 *per* Cotton L.J.; 341–342 *per* Fry L.J. *The Montana* case referred to in that decision is *Liverpool and Great Western S.S. Co.* v. *Phoenix Insurance Co.* (*supra*, n. 49). For a similar case in France see Cass. Dec. 5, 1910, *American Trading Co.* v. *Quebec S.S. Co.*, S. 1911.1.129 with a note by Lyon-Caen; (1911) 7 *Rev. de droit international privé* 395 with further references. See generally Unger (1967) 83 L.Q.R. 427 at p. 442.

[52] (1932) 48 C.L.R. 391.

torial extensions or restrictions.[53] It is not surprising, either, that de Nova, an Italian writer, shares this view[54] when he concentrates on the parties' choice of law and describes the approach taken by Walsh J. in *Kay's Leasing Corporation* v. *Fletcher*[55] as a reference to the domestic law of New South Wales (*materiellrechtliche Verweisung*) and not as a reference to the conflicts rules of the latter (*Kollisionsrechtliche Verweisung*).

| In fact a reference to foreign law which includes a spatially conditioned statute or a rule of immediate application raises a problem which is distinct from that of *renvoi*, as both de Nova and Kelly acknowledge. The seeming link is the feature that a spatially conditioned rule limits its own sphere of operation in some form or another and thus may create the impression that it constitutes a living example of Westlake's *desistement* theory.[56] However, such a rule does not feature an abdication in favour of some other legal system. It only refuses to apply as part of its own system of laws, thus leaving a choice between three possible alternatives.

First, another rule forming part of the same legal system may take its place as a subsidiary principle. Thus, since the Marriage (Enabling) Act 1960, s. 1 (3) applies only to persons domiciled in England, it could be argued that a reference by some foreign court to English law in circumstances where *e.g.* the parties reside or married in England, means in the absence of the acceptance of *renvoi* by the foreign court a reference to English law as it stood before the passing of the Act. Consequently, the prohibition against marriages between a person and his or her divorced spouse's brother or sister would still apply. Such a solution displays a touch of the unreal.

Secondly, the spatial limitation could be disregarded on the ground, discussed above, that a reference to a foreign legal system is to that system as a whole, to the exclusion both of *renvoi* and, as it must be assumed also, of its spatially conditioned limitations. Such a solution is acceptable to those who subscribe to the belief that the *lex fori* is a closed and self-sufficient system and that any reference to foreign law only restricts the application of the *lex fori* to situations clearly defined by the latter, in disregard of foreign spatial restrictions or of *renvoi*.[57]

---

[53] *Ibid.* at p. 437, citing *Re Annesley* [1926] Ch. 692 at p. 709.

[54] (1973) 5 Adelaide L.R.I. at p. 8; (1971) 25 *Diritto Internazionale* 239 at p. 240 esp. 245; *Multitudo Legum, Jus Unum* II (1973) 617 at p. 625. See also *Mélanges Maury* I (1960) 377 at pp. 393 *et seq.*; (1959) 13 *Diritto Internazionale* 13, at pp. 28 *et seq.*

[55] (1963–64) 64 S.R.(N.S.W.) 195.

[56] *Private International Law* (1912), pp. 32–34; (1900) 18 *Annuaire de l'Institut de Droit International* 35–40.

[57] See *supra*, p. 885. Without subscribing to any assumption as basic as that set out here, de Nova adopts this view: *Mélanges Maury* I (1960) 377 at p. 395; (1959) 13 *Diritto Internazionale* 13 at p. 26; (1973) 5 Adelaide L.R. 1 at p. 7; *Multitudo Legum, Jus Unum* II (1973) 617 at p. 628; (1971) 25 *Diritto Internazionale* 239 at p. 245. See also Kelly (1969) 18 I.C.L.Q. 249 at pp. 254–259.

Thirdly, the presence of a spatially conditioned rule may lead to the conclusion that the *lex fori* should be applied in the absence of any indication of an intention of the *lex causae* to cover the situation. Such a solution is acceptable to those who hold that the *lex fori* is primarily restricted to situations having a connection with the country of the forum on personal or territorial grounds and that in all other cases foreign law is applicable in accordance with the general rules of Private International Law which, themselves, will | give way to any different or contrary reference by the foreign legal system to which they themselves refer.

If, on the other hand, the foreign law referred to includes a spatially conditioned rule which is extensive and not restrictive or claims to apply in all circumstances,[58] it might seem that a different problem is posed. For instance, de Nova confesses his inability to suggest any solution except perhaps by extending the operation of such a rule in the teeth of his opposition to *renvoi.*[59] In fact, such a rule is one which is of immediate application, to use the term coined by Francescakis. It applies as part of the *lex causae* in all cases governed by the *lex causae*, and the fact that it purports to extend its operation to situations or transactions in countries other than that of the forum or of the *lex causae* is irrelevant. If the legal system of which it forms part is the *lex causae* to which the conflict rule of the forum refers, the rule applies, no matter whether the facts arose within the territory of the *lex causae* or not.

Of course, difficulties can arise if according to the rules of Private International Law of the forum, having regard to a separate process of characterisation, another legal system applies to the situation which is centred in a third country. This difficulty is best illustrated by article 992 of the Dutch Civil Code which states peremptorily that Dutch nationals must make their wills in notarial form, even if the will is made abroad. Suppose that, according to the rules of Private International Law of the *lex fori*, capacity to make a will is governed by the *lex domicilii*, Dutch law, and the form of a will is governed by the *lex loci actus*, which is New York Law, the difficulty that the *lex domicilii* requires a will in notarial form and declares any other will to be void could be overcome by characterising the rule as pertaining to capacity.[59a] Thus the will would be rendered invalid in substance, although according to the *lex loci actus*, the law governing formalities, it is valid.

---

[58] See *e.g.*? 61 of the German Stock Exchange Act, as interpreted by the German Federal Supreme Court in a decision of June 4, 1975, *Recht der Internationalen Wirtschaft, Aussenwirtschaftsdienst des Betriebsberaters* (1975), 500; Reg. 2 of the Defence (Finance) Regulations 1939 (S.R. & O. 1939 No. 1620) as amended; *Boissevain* v. *Weil* [1950] A.C. 327.

[59] (1973) 5 Adelaide L.R. 1 at p. 7; *Multitudo Legum, Jus Unum* II (1973) 617 at p. 627; (1971) 25 *Diritto Internazionale* 239 at. p. 246.

[59a] The Hague Convention on the Form of Wills (1961), s. 3 and the Wills Act 1963, s. 3 now rule out this possibility.

It has been argued, however, that since the practice of Dutch courts requires an alien who makes a will in the Netherlands equally to comply with the requirement of notarial form or at least deposition, the rule is one of "immediate" application which is to be respected elsewhere whenever Dutch law is applicable to a succession | on whatever grounds.[59b] It shows characteristics hitherto attributed to rules of public law or public policy.

It must not be overlooked that, when it is alleged that a rule of the foreign *lex causae* is spatially conditioned or immediately applicable, the burden of proof is on the party alleging it. Experience has shown that, in the absence of an express clause forming part of the rule concerned, conclusions as to implied spatial or person restrictions are frequently vague, based on an obscure or vacillating practice in the country concerned or in its literature. Thus in *Sayers* v. *International Drilling Co. N. V.*[60] it was contended by the defendants that an exemption clause in a contract of employment governed by Dutch law was not void, because the prohibition of such exemption clauses was restricted to domestic situations and did not extend to so-called international contracts. On uncontroverted evidence of the defendant's expert, unsupported by any citation of Dutch practice, the court was forced to accept this interpretation, but even a brief examination of this practice shows that in this form the evidence was clearly incorrect.[61] However, it is equally clear that, quite generally, the determination of implied spatial restrictions contained in provisions of foreign law is a difficult task, if it can be carried out at all. If any further evidence is required, *Babcock* v. *Jackson*[62] supplies it. Here it was assumed on the strength of a student's note in a learned periodical[63] that the Ontario Highway Traffic Act, s. 105 (2),[64] which prohibited action in tort by guests against their host drivers, served the exclusive purpose of preventing "the fraudulent assertion of claims of passengers in col-

---

[59b] Ballarino (1967) 3 Riv.dir.int.priv. e proc. 707 at p. 724 distinguishing art. 170 of the French Civil Code (which requires French nationals marrying abroad to comply with certain formalities, but does not impose the same requirement in the case of aliens marrying in France). *Cf.* Simon-Depitre (1974) Rev.crit.d.i.p. 591 at pp. 595 *et seq.* But see the German Federal Supreme Court, Jan. 20, 1967, IPRspr. 1966–67 No. 19 p. 64; Krbpholler (1968) N.J.W. 1561; Ago 58 (1936 IV) Hague Rec. 244 at pp. 326–327.

[60] [1971] 1 W.L.R. 1176; [1971] 3 All E.R. 163 at p. 167; contrast *Brodin* v. *A/F Seljan*, 1973 S.L.T. 198.

[61] Lipstein in (1973) 100 Clunet 442 at p. 445 (3); de Nova (1973) 5 *Adelaide L.R.* 1 at p. 10 *et seq.*; *Multitudo Legum, Jus Unum* II (1973) 617, at 630 *et seq.*; (1971) 25 *Diritto Internazionale* 239 at 249 *et seq.*

[62] 12 N.Y. 2d. 473, 481; 191 N.E. 2d. 279, 283; 240 N.Y.S. 2d. 743, 745 (1963).

[63] (1936) 1 *Univ. of Toronto L.J.* 358, at pp. 365–366.

[64] Rev.Stat.Ontario 1960, ch. 175, s. 105 (2) as amended; now Rev.Stat.Ontario 1970, ch. 202, s. 132 (3): exclusive or contributory gross negligence of the driver negatives the exemption.

lusion with the drivers against insurance companies which have issued third party policies to the drivers and owners of motor vehicles." Subsequent research has not substantiated such a clear-cut conclusion.[65]

Spatially Conditioned and Mandatory Rules

| Spatially conditioned rules are to be distinguished from what are purely mandatory provisions. The former purport to apply by virtue of the express or implied clause regulating their sphere of operation. The latter apply whenever domestic law is applicable, and apply to situations containing a foreign element only if the ordinary rules of private international law refer to them.[66]

In either case, the assumption has been hitherto that a statutory provision is subject to some restriction in its application, either by virtue of its inherent limitation or of the general rules of private international law. It has, however, been contended also that some rules, said to be immediately applicable, apply by implication to all situations which can arise in the forum.[67] Perhaps the Limitation Act 1939 provides the most outstanding example of such legislation in English law. It is usually stated that the provisions of the Act are procedural, since they determine only whether a remedy is available and do not affect the right,[68] but the wording of the Act and of its predecessor is of a peremptory character and could well be explained as requiring directly, without the assistance of the rules of the conflict of laws, the application of the English provisions to the exclusion of all others. Thus it would be an exclusive statute requiring absolutely the application of the English rules of limitation of actions, but not necessarily procedural in character because all rules of procedure are exclusive and absolute. Recourse to the alleged procedural character of these English rules may have served as a device to explain their exclusive dominance in terms of general rules of the conflict of laws at a time when *règles d'application immédiate* were unknown and when any attempt to introduce principles which savoured of statutist learning would have been rejected. These considerations may throw a new and differ-

---

[65] See Rosenberg (1967) 67 Col.L.R. 459; Trautmann, *ibid.* 465, 466, n. 9, and 468 *et seq.*, with Canadian authorities; Willis Reese (1971) 71 *ibid.* 548 at p. 554 n. 22; Fuld C.J. in *Neumeier* v. *Kuehner*, 31 N.Y. 2d. 121, 286 N.E. 2d, 454 (1972); 335 N.Y.S. 2d. 64 (1972).

[66] *The Missouri* (1889) 42 Ch.D. 32, at pp. 336, 341–342; Eek, *The Swedish Conflict of Laws* (1965), p. 224.

[67] Francescakis, *supra*, n. 15.

[68] *British Linen Co.* v. *Drummond* (1830) 10 B. & C. 903; *Don* v. *Lippmann* (1837) 5 Cl. & F. 1. *Huber* v. *Steiner* (1835) 2 Bing.(N.C.) 202 at p. 218.

ent light on *Harris* v. *Quine*[69] and *Black-Clauson International Ltd.* v. *Papierwerke Waldhof-Aschaffenburg A.G.*[70]

Leaving aside the various arguments which can be raised in support of the judgment in the Court of Appeal,[71] the refusal to recognise a foreign judgment dismissing an action, on the ground that the period of limitation according to foreign law has been completed, in | the teeth of *Godard* v. *Gray*[72] and *Nouvion* v. *Freeman*[73] can perhaps be explained on the ground that English law as the *lex fori* has created in section 2 of the Limitation Act a rule of immediate application which requires observance everywhere. The close connection with the well known notion of public policy is obvious. Even then the question remains unanswered as to why a foreign judgment cannot be recognised if (as, it seems likely, it occurred in *Harris* v. *Quine*), the foreign court applied principles of limitation of actions identical with those of English law, and even more so, if they applied the English rules themselves or why such a judgment must be recognised if the foreign court gave judgment on the merits when the English period of limitation of action had run. Perhaps the answer must be that English law wishes to ensure that English courts should be available as far as possible for the adjudication of claims and will only abdicate this function when the claim has been determined *on the merits* by a judgment which either concedes to the plaintiff certain claims or deprives him of his alleged right once and for all. Even so "this expression, whether related to pleas or to judgments is a familiar one in English law; any practitioner would use it – even if it is not always understood."[74] It may well be asked where a judgment must range which declares once and for all that the plaintiff can no longer in the pending or in future proceedings in the same court prosecute the claim against the defendant. Some may say let him sue again, only time has been against him in foreign parts; he could and should sue here. But this begs the question; others may say: "Let him try again; his claim was regarded as unmeritorious abroad only."

---

[69] (1869) L.R. 4 Q.B. 653.
[70] [1975] A.C. 591.
[71] See (1974) 33 C.L.J. 229.
[72] (1870) L.R. 6 Q.B. 139 at p. 150.
[73] (1887) 37 Ch.D. 244 at p. 251: see also (1889) App.Cas. 1 at p. 9.
[74] *Per* Lord Wilberforce [1975] A.C. 591 at p. 631.

Recognition of Foreign Spatially Conditioned Rules

The foregoing discussion has shown that the number and importance of spatially conditioned rules and of what has been called "rules of immediate application" has grown in the last 30 years. When they form part of the *lex fori* they assert themselves side by side with the rules of the conflict of laws which may refer to some foreign *lex causae*; if of immediate application, they are often treated on the same footing as were formerly rules of public policy.

When they do not form part of the *lex fori* they do not normally apply, unless they are part of the *lex causae*. It seems, however, that the increased importance of these categories of rules may be due to the fact that they include both those which formerly claimed | (whether effectively or not) complete or limited exclusiveness as laws of a public law nature, such as revenue, labour,[75] currency protection or export/import licensing legislation, as well as certain types of mandatory rules of a mixed character, often regarded as showing some affinity with private law, such as rules prohibiting exemption clauses, introducing moratoria, maximum prices, controlling cartels and restrictive practices and the like, whereby legislation intervenes in private arrangements. Unlike continental law,[76] English private international law has been able to accommodate the latter, and some of the former, by various devices, of which *Ralli Bros.* v. *Cia. Naviera Sota y Aznar,*[77] *Banco de Vizcaya* v. *Don Alfonso de Borbon y Austria*[78]; *Re Helbert Wagg,*[79] *Jabbour* v. *Custodian of Israeli Absentee Property,*[80] *Re Banque des Marchands de Moscou (Koupetschesky), Royal Exchange Ass.* Co. v. *The Liquidator,*[81] *Re Emery's Investments Trust,*[82] *Regazzoni* v. *Sethia*[83] and *The Halley*[84] (where regard was paid to local traffic regulations) are outstanding examples. It may be argued that, within certain limits, foreign rules which claim to be peremptorily applicable and are thus rules of immediate appli-

---

[75] See Gamillscheg in *International Encyclopaedia of Comparative Law*, Vol. III, paras. 43–47, *Internationales Arbeitsrecht* (1959), pp. 203 *et seq.*; (1959) 23 *Rabels Z.* 819 at p. 843.

[76] See Zweigert (1965) Rev. drit. d. i. p. 645 at p. 646; Frank (1970) 34 *Rabels Z.* 56; de Nova, *Mélanges Maury* I (1960) 377 at pp. 400–401; (1959) 13 *Diritto Internazionale* 13 at p. 30, but see Conforti, *L'execuzione delle obbligazioni nel diritto Internazionale privato* (1962), *passim.*

[77] [1920] 2 K.B. 287.

[78] [1935] 1 K.B. 140.

[79] [1956] Ch. 323.

[80] [1954] 1 W.L.R. 139.

[81] [1952] 2 T.L.R. 739; [1952] 1 All E.R. 1269.

[82] [1959] Ch. 410.

[83] [1958] A.C. 301.

[84] (1868) L.R. 2 P.C. 193 at p. 202.

cation in the country where they have been introduced should also be respected elsewhere, even if they do not form part of the proper law. It has indeed been suggested in recent years by continental lawyers that the rigid disregard of foreign rules of a public law character is not justified. It has, however, not been possible to formulate any specific criteria to determine the application of such rules.

Little progress has been made in this quest since Wengler first required that there must be a sufficiently close contact between the legislation concerned and the facts which it intends to regulate.[85] It has been said that, in addition, the performance of the legal duty in issue must be centred totally or in part in the foreign country concerned.[86] The following considerations may perhaps assist in defining the sphere of operation of foreign public law or immediately applicable rules a little more closely.

| In the first place it is worth noting that apparently only foreign prohibitory rules are taken into account and not foreign rules which require action by those to whom they are addressed. In other words, at the present stage of development, foreign rules of public law or immediately applicable rules are not enforced.[86a] They are recognised.

In the second place, the recognition of such foreign rules arises in the form of an incidental or preliminary question. Unlike an incidental or preliminary question affecting matters of private law, it does not posit any problems of choice of law to be determined either by the *lex fori* or by the *lex causae*. The foreign rule of public law or of immediate application is *a fact* (in Ehrenzweig's terminology, a *datum*) which affects the execution of a legal duty according to the *lex causae* or creates a legal relationship, which is relevant for the determination of duties arising under the *lex causae*.

Foreign rules of public law or of immediate application prohibiting a certain conduct were first considered as facts by F. A. Mann.[87] He suggested that *Ralli's* case, far from establishing a subsidiary rule of the English conflict of laws to the effect that illegality of performance was governed by the *lex loci solutionis*, merely reflected the foreign rule of public law or of immediate application as a factual impossibility in England. It may be suggested that, in addition to such rules in the country where any aspect of the transaction in issue is to be realised or put into practice, the rules in force in countries with which a party is connected through personal ties may also have to be taken into consideration. This may involve a second look at cases such as *Klein-*

---

[85] (1941) 54 Z.f.vgl.Rw. 168 at p. 181.

[86] Zweigert (1965) Rev.crit.d.i.p. 645 at p. 649.

[86a] See *e.g.* the Shipping Contracts and Commercial Documents Act 1964; the Dutch Economic Competition Act of June 28, 1956, as amended, s. 39. And see Mann (1964) 13 I.C.L.Q. 1460.

[87] (1937) 18 B.Y.I.L. 97.

wort v. *Ungarische Baumwolle A.G.*,[88] but little harm should follow if it were to be reversed.[89]

As a source of establishing a legal relationship the method of appointment of a foreign pilot, and the position of the pilot towards the shipowner, as created either compulsorily or voluntarily according to foreign law, has been taken into account and been translated into terms of English law appropriate to the notions of master and servant in order to establish whether the shipowner was vicariously liable for the foreign pilot.[90]

| Limits of Recognition

Within the broader sphere of private law, the regard by courts elsewhere for foreign spatially conditioned or immediately applicable rules will, it would seem, have to be confined to statutes in common law countries (where statute law is *lex specialis* or consolidation), and to exceptional statutes in civil law countries (where all law is expressed in statutes). The reason is to be found in a basic consideration.

Spatially conditioned and immediately applicable rules of domestic law determine unilaterally the operation of their own sphere of operation. Outside of this consists a vacuum which in the absence, *ex hypothesi*, of subsidiary principles of common law in common law countries and of general statute law in civil law systems can only be filled in one of two ways. *Either*, account must be taken of all other legal systems which may have enacted spatially conditioned or immediately applicable rules to apply in the circumstances. *Or* general rules of the conflict of laws must determine with bilateral effect when the *lex fori* and when foreign law applies, whenever the *lex fori* cannot fall back on a spatially conditioned or immediately applicable rule, or the *lex causae* contains restrictive rules of this character.

The first of these solutions conjures up shades of recent American theory and practice, where the United States Supreme Court, since the middle of the 1930s, appraises the governmental interests of each jurisdiction and weighs them, thus avoiding a clash of claims to apply, as well as a cumulative abstention,[91] and can even discover countries whose laws are neutral in the

---

[88] [1939] 2 K.B. 678.

[89] The preliminary draft of a Convention on the Law applicable to Contractual and Non-Contractual Obligations prepared by the Commission of the EEC contains a provision to this effect (art. 10).

[90] *The Halley, supra* n. 84; *The Guy Mannering* (1882) 7 P.D. 132 at p. 135; *The Agnes Otto* (1887) 12 P.D. 56 at p. 57; *The Augusta* (1887) 57 L.T.R. 326 at p. 327; *The Prins Hendrick* [1899] P. 177 at p. 181. *The Darlington* [1903] P. 77: *The Andoni* [1918] P. 14 at pp. 18; 19, 20; *The Arum* [1921] P. 12 at pp. 18, 20; *The Waziristan* [1953] 2 All E.R. 1213.

[91] Lipstein, 135 (1972 I) Hague Rec. 99 at pp. 148–154.

particular circumstances. Such an approach, which runs contrary to either of what are here considered to be the two basic approaches to rules of the conflict of laws,[92] can only be explained on grounds of federal constitutional law.

In so far as conflicts have arisen in recent times in the courts of the Union, the practice of the courts in New York, especially the Court of Appeals, in cases involving not an interstate element (which is necessarily affected by the principles of constitutional law administered by the United States Supreme Court set out above), but in cases involving an international element, yields interesting results when examined from the point of view taken here.

In a conflict between a statute of a foreign *lex loci delicti* and rules of common law forming part of the *lex fori* and the *lex domicilii* of the parties, the New York Court of Appeals started by examining the purported range of the foreign statute and the interest of the | common law rules of the *lex fori* and the *lex domicilii* to apply.[93] After some vacillations,[94] the same court now admits that the application of its common law rules (*i.e.* those of the *lex fori*) is primarily determined by the general rules of the conflict of laws, subject to the overriding interest of the *lex fori* not to apply foreign statutes which are unfair or anachronistic, and that implied spatial restrictions are not lightly to be read into foreign statutes.[95] Thus even in the United States the tendency appears to be growing not to imply that common law rules carry implicitly a spatial restriction.

The other trend evidenced in New York, to imply spatial restrictions only sparingly in the case of statutes, is not shared as yet in *California* where the Supreme Court in *Hurtado* v. *Supreme Court of Sacramento County*[96] laid down a series of specific tests which are to determine, in Californian courts, on an objective basis, the interests of the litigants and of the *States involved.*[97]

---

[92] See *supra*, at p. 885.

[93] *Babcock* v. *Jackson*, 12 N.Y. 2d. 473 at pp. 481, 483; 191 N.E. 2d. 279 at pp. 283, 285; 240 N.Y.S. 2d. 743 at pp. 749, 751 (1963); see also *Macey* v. *Rozbicki*, 18 N.Y. 2d. 289, 221 N.E. 2d. 380, 274 N.Y.S. 2d. 591 (1966).

[94] *Kell* v. *Henderson*, 47 Misc. 2d. 992, 263 N.Y.S. 2d. 647 (Sup.Ct. 1965), affd. 26 App.Div. 2d. 595, 270 N.Y.S. 2d. 552 (Second Dept. 1966).

[95] *Neumeier* v. *Kuehner*, 31 N.Y. 2d. 121, 286 N.E. 2d. 454, 335 N.Y.S. 2d. 64 (1973).

[96] 11 Cal. 3d. 579, 114 Cal.Rptr. 106, 552 P. 2d. 666 (1974).

[97] In a suit brought on behalf of the dependants of the deceased, domiciled and resident in Mexico, who had been killed in a motor car accident in California, against defendants domiciled and resident in California, the defendants contended that the stricter measure of damages according to Mexican law should have been applied rather than the more generous standard of Californian law. The court was able to read two separate and disparate limitations into wrongful death statutes containing a limit of the amount of damages to be awarded.

The rule limiting damages was to protect defendants from excessive financial burdens or exaggerated claims. Thus the law of the defendant's domicile and residence determined its

However, even these disclose a certain break with the recent past. The Supreme Court of California did not, apparently, rely on any evidence as to the purpose of the Mexican law. In attributing different spatial limitations to different sections of a Wrongful Death Statute (whether Californian or Mexican) according as these sections | create a cause of action (when the *lex fori*, if also the law of the domicile and residence of the plaintiff, applies) or limit the amount of damages recoverable (when the law of the domicile and residence of the defendant applies), the court applied the well known technique of *depecage.* The only difference between its application in California and in countries outside the United States consists in the cumulative or alternative use of connecting factors and in the objective assessment of the interests to apply which recalls the technique of the statutists.

Historically the new tests may be inappropriate since the limitation of damages in Wrongful Death Statutes when they were first introduced was not to cut down the amount of damages accorded at common law, but to allow well defined damages where they were not available before. Nevertheless, the new trend in California attributes local interests, as the *forum* sees them, rather than acknowledges foreign interests, as the *forum* believes them to be estimated abroad, and thus defines itself the connecting factors. A first step towards the re-establishment of rules of the conflict of laws – perhaps of a more sophisticated kind than hitherto – may thus have been taken in California.

The second of the possible solutions suggested here recalls that set out previously,[98] which was there described as coming nearest to the English and the continental approach. After having considered the new tendency in the United States it may possibly be regarded as the better and the most acceptable one.[99]

---

application at pp. 670 [5], [8], 671 [10] and Californian, not Mexican law applied. The question whether Californian law had an interest to determine the basic liability for wrongful death, when the plaintiffs are domiciled and resident in Mexico was side-stepped by the finding that a State, in enacting such a law, does not only create a cause of action to compensate survivors – its own domiciliaries and residents – but also to influence conduct by deterrence (pp. 671 [10]; 672 [11]–[13]). See also *Bernhard* v. *Harrah' Club,* 16 Cal. 3d 313, 128 Cal.Rptr., 546 P. 2d. 719 (1976).

An English lawyer, using orthodox techniques, would have considered the matter in two stages. He would have analysed the rule of Mexican law in order to ascertain whether it sounded in tort or in succession, whether it purported to add a new rule extending the common law (in which case the limitation of damages was one of substance) or whether it merely restricted the normal assessment of damages (thus constituting a rule of procedure). He would then have ascertained whether the *lex fori* wished to cover the case or not, by examining its rules of Private International Law. This functional test seems preferable to one based on imputed interests, but as shown above, even the approach adopted by the Californian Supreme Court opens the door for the operation of rules of the conflict of laws as they have been known always.

[98] *Supra,* p. 885.

[99] Kegel, "Die Selbstgerechte Sachnorm," in Gedächtnisschrift für Albert A. Ehrenzweig (1976) could not be taken into account.

Acta et Agenda[*]

When I was first called upon to lecture during the darkest days of the war in 1941, because Hersch Lauterpacht was on some mission, I was still surrounded by my own teachers – Buckland, Duff, Gutteridge and McNair (Hazeltine had left). Of these Gutteridge and McNair influenced me most – the former by convincing me that foreign law was well worth studying, if not for its own sake, then in order to test the validity of one's own cherished notions and established techniques and to acquire the inspiration for new solutions, but not in order to discover an all pervading *droit commun législatif*. McNair impressed upon me the reality of the rules of international law in the practice of states and in the administration of law by domestic courts. Not monism of a doctrinaire kind, but the age old tradition of the common lawyer to interpret English law so as not to conflict with international law was his inspiration, which has guided me ever since. I must not omit two other formative influences from times long passed. My teachers in Berlin included the last "Pandectist" (Th. Kipp), the broadly based Romanist, Greek scholar and modern comparatist as well as innovator of private international law (Rabel), and the superb exponent of private and private international law (M. Wolff) whose nephew, I am happy to think, will continue the propagation of the work which has been carried out in Cambridge since 1930 by Gutteridge, Hamson and myself. Gutteridge, Rabel and Wolff, whose works in the English language have enriched the fund of the common law, probably gave me the foundations on which most of my own work is based. No scholar works in isolation, and it would probably be possible to draw up pedigrees of ideas, as it has been possible to establish pedigrees of civilians which trace their descent to Irnerius.

The combination of doctrinal interests and, what may seem to be, antiquarian learning, which is in reality an attempt to comprehend any principles of permanent and universal validity, directed my early work. Thus I still believe that I was right in suggesting that the *beneficium cedendarum actionum* in the Roman law of suretyship was a technical device, invented in the

[Editorial note: first published in Cambridge Law Journal 36 (1977), 47–61.]

[*]A Valedictory Lecture delivered on 20 May 1976 before the Faculty of Law, Cambridge University.

3rd century A.D. in order|to enable a paying surety to become the assignee of any pledges, given by the principal debtor to the creditor, which would have otherwise reverted to the debtor. Such a surety was not in need of an action against the debtor to recover the money on his behalf. The *Lex Publilia* and the *actio mandati contraria* offered sufficient remedies for that.

Again, much later in life I sought to show that the agnatic relationship is rooted in the law of succession where it serves to prevent family assets passing through females into another family on the death, intestate, of the *pater familias.*

The conflict of laws, however, attracted me more than any other topic, and my first steps in this direction were two studies. The first, with Gutteridge, investigated a hitherto neglected aspect, namely the rules relating to quasi-contract.[1] From its somewhat rudimentary conclusions emerged later on the new chapter in Dicey (6th ed., 1949)[2] which, in offering a troika of rules, has survived to appear unscathed in the ninth edition (1973).[3] The last word has not been written yet. The unsatisfactory, rough solution put forward by a committee of experts (Giuliano *et al.*) appointed by the EEC Commission to formulate a draft convention on the private international law of contract, quasi-contract and tort[4] calls for a minute examination of the various aspects of quasi-contract which may require separate treatment. The way has been pointed by Zweigert and Müller-Gindullis.[5] The second study, the product of a seminar held by Gutteridge, on problems of choice of law in matters of contract, carries the names of three other participants,[6] and thereby hangs a tale. As part of the article I had raised the question whether *renvoi* has a place in the conflict of laws relating to contracts and had denied it. The American participant (Karl Marx Rodman), who placed the article in a little known American legal periodical, took it upon himself to improve upon my exposition by explaining to|American readers what *renvoi* is, and in so doing he

---

[1] "Unjustified Enrichment in the Conflict of Laws" (1939) 7 *Cambridge Law Journal* 80–93.

[2] pp. 754–757, r. 167.

[3] pp. 924–929, r. 176.

[4] Preliminary Draft Convention, Doc. XIV/398/72, Rev. E; F; (1973) 21 Am.J. Comp.L. 587 (text with introduction by Nadelmann); 1973 Rev.crit.dr.i.p. 209 (text), 369 (analysis by Lagarde); (1973) 9 *Revista di diritto privato e processuale* (text and Report Giuliano); Siehr (1973) 19 *Aussenwirtschaftsdienst des Betriebsberaters* 569; Lando (1974) 38 *Rabels Z.* 6 (contractual and quasi-contractual aspects); von Overbeck and Volken, *ibid.*, 56 (torts); Cavers (1975) 48 So.Calif. L.R. 603; Nadelmann (1976) 24 Am.J.Comp.L. 1; Collins (1976) 25 I.C.L.Q. 35; Lando, von Hoffmann, Siehr (eds.), *European Private International Law of Obligations* (1975); A. Philip (1972) 42 *Nordisk Tidskrift for International Ret* 177, 220.

[5] (1973) 3 *International Encyclopaedia of Comparative Law*, Chap. 30.

[6] "The Proper Law of the Contract" (with J. Brunschwig, J. Jerie and K. M. Rodman (1938) 12 *St. John's Law Rev.* 242–264.

reversed the meaning of my conclusion. Lord Wright, who was then preparing his advice to be given in *Vita Food Inc.* v. *Unus Shipping Co.,*[7] saw a copy of the article thus transformed on Gutteridge's desk and took it home. When the advice was published it included a passage which suggests that *renvoi* can operate in these circumstances, and ever since writers and judges have been at pains to explain that this was a *lapsus calami.* But it was Karl Marx Rodman's, last heard of in Oakland (California). It is time that the myth which connects the authority of Lord Wright with this unfortunate pronouncement is dispelled forever.

The relationship between public and private international law with its various facets has occupied my mind more than any other problem, and if I can claim to have made any significant contributions, they are to be found here. Following studies by Niboyet[8] and Gutzwiller[9] who had first been interested in the treatment of questions of the conflict of laws by the Mixed Arbitral Tribunals set up under the Peace Treaties concluded after the First World War, I turned to the entire practice then available of International Courts and Arbitral Tribunals.[10] I found that these bodies had built up rules of the conflict of laws of their own, which I called rules of international conflict of laws. Their content may appear more often than not to be the same as those of domestic private international law; nevertheless the special characteristics of the international rules are so strong as to exclude any identity between these two systems of private international law – their *lex fori* is international law, *renvoi* is excluded because it is self-defeating by leading back to public international law, public policy can only operate negatively so as to exclude the operation of foreign private law referred to in the first place, but fails in its positive function, which is to replace the rejected foreign law by the *lex fori.*

For the same reason no hierarchy exists in the conflict of laws of a supreme international and subordinate municipal system of private international law. At the same time I was able to show that international law does not prescribe the adoption of specific rules of private international law proper. Instead, private international law, like any other branch of domestic law, must conform to the standards of public international law; it must therefore comply with the|minimum standards of civilised nations and must not discriminate illegally. This means, probably, that no country may exclude foreign law

---

[7] [1939] A.C. 277.

[8] (1932, II) 40 *Hague Recueil* 157–231; (1929) 1 *Mélanges Pillet* 153–177; (1929) 24 Rev.d.i.p. 478–489.

[9] (1931) 3 *Jahrbuch für Schiedsgerichtswesen* 123–152.

[10] "Conflict of Laws before International Tribunals I, II" (1942) 27 *Transactions of the Grotius Society* 142–175; (1944) 29, *ibid.* 51–83. See now (1972, I) 135 *Hague Recueil* 99, at pp. 167–194.

altogether but that every country is free to apply or to disregard foreign law according to its own general rules of private international law and its own notions of public policy. Of course it is possible for a consensus of domestic systems of private international law to create a standard which may become elevated to one which all nations must observe at the risk of incurring state responsibility leading to damages for failure to do so. What cannot occur is the emergence of a general principle of public policy in private international law which defines the limits of a country's power to disregard foreign law in order to supplement an alleged gap in customary international law, seeing that the freedom of domestic legal systems according to customary international law to apply or not to apply foreign domestic law implies the freedom to disregard it generally or in individual circumstances.

For these reasons I opposed Hersch Lauterpacht when he stated in the Boll Case[11] that the principle of public policy was a general principle of law in the meaning of Article 38 of the Statute of the Court which is to be applied by the International Court of Justice as part of customary international law.[12] As it serves no useful purpose in relation to the exercise of a choice of law by individual states, so it fails to have a function where the International Court of Justice itself applies its own rules of international conflict of laws. For here, as stated above, public policy by operating negatively in excluding the domestic law of a state so found to be applicable, fails in its positive function of replacing the rejected domestic law of a state by the *lex fori.* The latter is international law itself, in the eyes of which domestic law is only a fact. Thus public policy in its negative and positive function in an international tribunal administering international law is identical with customary international law.

If it be argued, as Lauterpacht did, that public policy as a general principle of law supplements not customary international law but the law of treaties, the following questions must be put. Are all treaties subject to the exception that states may disregard their individual provisions and substitute for the latter the provisions of their own domestic law when their sensitive areas are affected? Alternatively, are only those treaties subject to the exception which themselves lay down choice of law rules? While the answer to the |first question must clearly be in the negative, the answer to the second may seem doubtful at first sight since these treaties refer to unknown rules of foreign domestic law. If it is remembered, however, that according to customary international law states are free to determine when to apply or not to apply foreign domestic law, it seems strange that a treaty concluded for the

---

[11] *Netherlands* v. *Sweden* [1958] I.C.J. Reports 55, at pp. 79–101, esp. 92–100.

[12] "The Hague Conventions on Private International Law, Public Law and Public Policy" (1959) 8 I.C.L.Q. 508–522; but see Kahn-Freund (1974, III) 143 *Hague Recueil* 141 at 173, 195.

purpose of fixing with binding effect the criteria for a choice of law should have built into it a rule of customary international law which weakens its effect. Rather it would seem that a question of treaty interpretation is involved, and not one of strict customary international law. The question is, whether the treaty permits the operation of local public policy by domestic courts when applying the treaty. Given the flexible attitude of customary international law to the application of foreign domestic law by states, valid arguments can be marshalled both for and against a broad interpretation of a treaty on choice of law. The modern practice, which insists on the inclusion of a clause reserving the right of states to reject foreign domestic law which is applicable according to the treaty, if it is "manifestly" against public policy, supports the contention that in the absence of such a clause the reservation of public policy is not necessarily to be implied.

After examining the connection between recognition and the application of foreign law it has been possible to attribute its proper place to the rule in *Luther* v. *Sagor.*[13] Recognition is not the factor which determines automatically and with general effect whether foreign law is to be applied by English courts. This is the task of the rules of private international law of the forum. Recognition determines only which of two competing sets of regulations within one country must be regarded as the law of that country, once the private international law of the forum has referred to the law of the particular foreign country. It also confers upon the measures of the recognised authority the character of an act by a public authority and attributes to it the character of a datum which must be taken into account by the courts of the forum whenever the operation of foreign public law must be considered. On the strength of these facts I concluded[14] that recognition by the state of the forum is the best evidence for determining whether the regulations and measures of foreign bodies are to be regarded as the law of the foreign country and the acts of public authorities, but that is not conclusive evidence. Consequently I asserted that the regulations of foreign bodies which have not been recognised can nevertheless be applied|in accordance with the rules of private international law of the forum as the law of the foreign country concerned, and that, despite recognition, a reference to the law of a country does not bind that forum absolutely to apply the regulations of the body which has been recognised. The development in the United States, where the relationship between recognition of governments and the application of foreign law was first established, has borne out the latter conclusion,[15] but in England only Lord Wilberforce and perhaps Lord Reid alluded

---

[13] [1921] 3 K.B. 532.

[14] "Recognition of Governments and the Application of Foreign Law" (1950) 35 *Transactions of the Grotius Society* 157–188.

[15] See *Bernstein* v. *L.V. Nederlandsche Amerikaansche etc.* 210 F. 2d 375 (2 Cir. 1954)

to the possibility in *Zeiss Stiftung Ltd.* v. *Rayner & Keeler*[16] of applying the regulations of an unrecognised body as the law of the country referred to.

Closely related is the problem whether foreign law which is contrary to public international law can be said to be invalid. Since foreign law is a fact for the purpose of international courts and domestic courts elsewhere, the latter cannot normally determine its validity or invalidity. On the other hand, its validity can be challenged in the courts of third countries if the constitution of the country where it was enacted itself invalidates legislation which is contrary to public international law. I made it my concern to investigate to what extent such a scrutiny of the validity of foreign law which is applicable by their rules of private international law can be carried out by courts elsewhere in any other circumstances.[17] Only in one instance can international law claim to determine the choice of law unequivocally. The legislative, executive and judicial acts of an occupying power supersede the local law and are themselves controlled by public international law.[18]

The search for controlling principles of private international law naturally led to the search for general principles of the conflict of laws themselves. My Hague Lectures linked up these principles.[19] I concluded that there were none apart from the two guiding rules of public international law which control all municipal law: domestic rules of private international law must conform to the minimum standards and must not discriminate illegally. Neither the assertion that rules of domestic law contain their own limitation in space nor the alleged division of sovereignty or the territoriality of law pro|vides a sufficient explanation as to why and when foreign law is applied. True, in so far as rules of a public law nature, such as those concerning procedure, bankruptcy, taxation, monopolies, restrictive practices and administrative law are concerned, the principle of territoriality based upon a division of legislative spheres fulfils a proper function, for such foreign laws are never applied elsewhere at the present time. Here the task is only to delimit the frontiers of our own law. Similarly, in a federal state where there does not exist an overriding system of the conflict of laws, such as the United States, the Constitution can provide limitations of a substantive character as a substitute. Here, where all Member States are equal and can claim to apply

---

approved by the United States Supreme Court in *First National City Bank* v. *Banco Nacional de Cuba* 406 U.S. 759, 32 L.Ed. 2d 466, 92 S.Ct. 1808 (1972), rehearing denied 409 U.S. 897, 34 L.Ed. 2d 155, 93 S.Ct. 92 (1972).

[16] [1967] 1 A.C. 583 at pp. 906, 953.

[17] "Proof of Foreign Law, Scrutiny of Constitutionality and Validity" (1967) 42 B.Y.I.L. 265–270.

[18] "Esame degli atti legislativi, esecutivi e guidiziari di una Potenza Occupante" (1952) 4 *Communicazioni e Studi* 115–141.

[19] "The General Principles of Private International Law" (1972, I) 135 *Hague Recueil* 99–229.

their own law, while similarly bound to respect that of sister states, an attempt has been made (unsuccessfully, I believe) to avoid the danger of overlaps or cumulative abstentions by the technique of balancing the claims of the competing laws to apply. This is said to be achieved by an appraisal of the respective governmental interests in order to do justice between individual parties. This task may not be insuperable in a federal state, such as the U.S.A. where the differences between competing laws have been confined to legislative changes in contract and tort and where, on the whole, the common law is in force, modified, enlarged or restricted by local legislation. I doubt whether a technique of balancing claims by competing laws to apply, especially by relying on an appraisal of the respective governmental interests, is suitable outside a constitutional conglomerate of homogeneous laws where the *lex fori* is predominant and does not have to face competing laws on a basis of equality, especially if the choice of law involves common law and civil law, Germanic, Scandinavian and other systems. Instead I suggested that the fundamental problem for a system of private international law and its application by the courts is whether the *lex fori* regards itself as closed, self-sufficient and complete, except where it makes special concessions to foreign law, or whether it regards itself as primarily restricted to situations having a connection of a personal or territorial character with the country of the *forum* with the result that a bilateral or reciprocal application of foreign law is required.

In the course of these studies, it was possible to put forward a new and workable technique of characterisation. Leaving aside the interpretation of connecting factors, problems of characterisation arise when the claim, presented in terms of foreign or English law, must be subsumed under one or, more frequently, under one of several rules of the conflict of laws of the forum, the operative facts of which are expressed either in terms of English domestic law or of English private international law. For this purpose each must | be interpreted in terms of the other. The claim or defence must be analysed in the light of the function of the rule relied upon within the particular legal system. It must then be related to that local rule of private international law, interpreted broadly, which can accommodate the claim. Characterisation is thus the interpretation of disparate notions in terms of each other.

When I first proposed to excise from the sixth edition of Dicey the principle of acquired rights (long proved to be circuitous in the conflict of laws), I did not realise, as I found out later on,[20] that Dicey never intended the reference to the principle of the enforcement of vested rights to supply a

---

[20] "Conflict of Laws 1921–1971, The Way Ahead" [1972B] 31 C.L.J. 67–120, at pp. 67–71.

universal test but only to 'define the object in the main aimed at by rules having reference to the conflict of laws or to the extra-territorial effect of rights'.[21] It simply serves to explain the motives underlying a technical device– namely the existence of rules of the conflict of laws.

Nothing gives more satisfaction than the knowledge that at the end of one's work the legal system has been added to for the common good. When, in 1952, I was invited by the Secretary General of the United Nations Organisation to take the place of Gutteridge on a Committee charged with drafting a Convention on the Enforcement of Maintenance Obligations abroad, the legal adviser of the Home Office (Sir Leslie Brass) impressed upon me the need not to deviate from English law, *i.e.* the Maintenance Orders (Facilities for Enforcement Act) 1920. However, this proved unacceptable to the other members, and under the chairmanship of E. M. Meijers we drew up an instrument of a novel kind whereby claims of this kind are assembled in the country of the claimant and dispatched to that of the defendant, where the entire proceedings are concentrated.[22] It became the New York Convention on Maintenance Obligations of 20 June 1956[23] and was ratified by many countries, but only some years ago I had an opportunity to persuade one of the present legal advisers of the Home Office of its merits, and it has now become Part II of the Maintenance Orders Act 1972. More recently, at the XIIth Hague Conference in 1972, I played my part in formulating a convention which facilitates the use of letters of representation in collecting the assets abroad of deceased persons.[24] Since civil law countries as well as Scandinavia do not know the|distinction between administration and distribution, between personal representatives and legatees, and recognise instead heirs, who are personally liable for the debts of the deceased, English personal representatives have met with many obstacles abroad, and foreign heirs have found it difficult to establish their title in England. The Convention should ease this situation.

My excursions into public international law began with a study of the Calvo Clause.[25] Although not acceptable to lawyers in Central and South America, it has, I believe, stood the onslaught of time. My next encounter with Central American, *in casu* Guatemalan, law was less successful.[26] In

---

[21] (1891) 7 L.Q.R. 113, at p. 118; *Conflict of Laws* (3rd ed., 1922), p. 33.

[22] "A Draft Convention on the Recovery Abroad of Claims for Maintenance" (1954) 3 I.C.L.Q. 125–134: Doc. E/A.C. 39/1 of 18 September 1952.

[23] 268 U.N.T.S. 3; U.K.T.S. 85, 1975: Cmnd. 6084.

[24] "Des Haager Abkommen über die internationale Abwicklung von Nachlassen" (1975) 39 *Rabels* Z. 29–55.

[25] "The Calvo Clause" (1945) 22 B.Y.I.L. 130–145.

[26] *Liechtenstein* v. *Guatemala, The Nottebohm Case* (2nd Phase) [1955] I.C.J. Reports 1; *Gedächtnisschrift für Ludwig Marxer* (Zürich, Schulthess & Co., 1963), pp. 275–325 (with E. Loewenfeld).

preparing the reply on behalf of Liechtenstein, I was aware of the practice of the Franco-German Mixed Arbitral Tribunals after the First World War, which had developed the new notion of *"nationalité virtuelle."*[27] This attributed to a claimant a nationality which at the relevant time he did not possess and denied him a nationality which clearly adhered to him according to domestic law. However, it was decided not to argue this point (if only to reject it) in order not to confuse the court. Instead, the court *proprio motu*, without inviting the parties to express their views on this point, introduced a similar notion, based upon the effective link of a person with a country. This notion had been introduced in identical terms in 1905 by Judge Basdevant, then a young professor, when he sought to argue in respect of the *Stevenson* case before the Venezuelan Claims Commission that, contrary to the recognised opinion to the effect that double nationality excluded a claim by a national state of the claimant against another state, of which the claimant was also a national, such a claim was admissible, if an effective link existed between the claimant and the plaintiff state. More fundamentally, outside the sphere of double nationality Professor Basdevant, as he then was, believed that all nationality was based on this principle and that such effectiveness must have existed at the time when the nationality was acquired.[28]

Personally, I believe that the claim of Nottebohm had to fail, in so far as it was based on the assertion that the sequestration of neutral property as tainted with enemy character was unlawful (and this aspect was not pressed in the Reply), but stood a chance of success on the related ground that the liquidation for the same reasons was | illegal, if unaccompanied by adequate compensation. Now when the liquidation occurred. Nottebohm lived permanently in Liechtenstein, as he did when the Principality lodged the claim. According to the recognised principle of double actionability of claims in international law the test was satisfied since Nottebohm was a national of Liechtenstein, who even by the rigorous standards of Basdevant had the closest possible links with the claimant state at the time when the injury occurred and when the claim was brought. According to international law, *pace* Basdevant, a claim has never been affected by the nationality of the injured party at an earlier time. Indeed he could have possessed another nationality previously.

Apart from being irreconcilable with the rules on nationality of claims, the alleged new principle raises further difficulties; does it apply only to the acquisition of a new nationality by naturalisation or does it apply to all other assumptions of nationality, such as by way of marriage, legitimation and

---

[27] *Chamant* v. *Etat Allemand* (1922) 1 *Decisions des Tribunaux Arbitraux Mixtes* 361; *Heim* v. *Etat Allemand, ibid.* 381; see Triepel, *Virtuelle Staatsangehörigkeit* (1921), esp. pp. 17, 59.

[28] (1909) 5 *Rev. de droit international privé* 41, esp. p. 60.

adoption, and does it extend also to acquisition by operation of law of a single nationality by birth and to its loss?

The brief account of English family law published in Germany never saw the light of day in England and, after twelve years, only retains a historical value.[29] In discussing the place of research in Family Law,[30] I stressed that while in technical fields of law historical and systematic considerations form the starting point, and while inequitable, inconsistent or absurd results may raise problems of policy, nevertheless these are restricted to policy making with a technical result in view. Family law (as also the law of succession) is linked with deep seated social conventions and taboos, with religious convictions which touch those to whom the law is addressed in an entirely different manner than, say, the holder of a bill of exchange. Where religious precepts, natural law and philosophy provided a framework we may have to look to other agencies today. Clearly the sociologist can help where group reactions are concerned. To the study of the individual member of the family, his personality, especially the disturbed personality, his motivations, cultural patterns and social function, the psychologist and the psychiatrist may be able to contribute as well. Nevertheless, if the plea is for more interdisciplinary research, the initiative for the investigation of legal problems must remain with the lawyers. The psychoanalyst speaks in terms of motivation, the lawyer in terms of action, positive or negative. For instance, if the breakdown of a marriage, divorced from guilty behaviour, is to be the sole basis of divorce, the *real*│grounds for the breakdown must be investigated, and the procedure and remedies in matrimonial proceedings will have to be changed radically in order to ascertain and to take into account the new factors. When the expectation of life together was not much more than ten years, a union for life had a different meaning from that which it has today. This gives a new dimension to divorce. The change from a single unit of production, where each member of the family had his place, to one where the spouses no longer operate a single unit and where in an urban, as distinct from an agricultural, setting the wife, in the twentieth century, has often lost any economic function or pursues an economic activity of her own, while the protective marital activity of the man has vanished and when education and discipline of the children has passed into other hands, has, I believe, created the hitherto unknown problems concerning married women. The position of spinsters, on the other hand, creates much fewer problems in this century. Armed with these insights, the lawyers must devise the appropriate framework. To supply him with an unlimited discretion (Matrimonial

---

[29] "Das Eherecht Englands, in Leske-Loewenfeld" (1965) *Das Eherecht der europäischen Staaten* 379–462.

[30] Research in Family Law (1969) 9 J.S.P.T.L. 217–225.

Causes Act 1973, ss. 24, 25, 31), however, is either to alter the function of courts, as we understand it, or to leave to the latter the development of principles which the legislation failed to formulate either by creating a new set of guidelines[31] or by supervising the exercise of the discretion.

The comparison of legal systems has attracted me from my student days onwards. Quite recently, the accession of the United Kingdom to the EEC has made the study of foreign laws a necessary concomitant of any work within the Community.[32] It is an accepted fact that weak countries must try to balance their absence of power in negotiations and in court by a mastery of the foreign laws which inspire their opponents. The growth of comparative legal studies in Germany after the First World War bears out this conclusion, and we should draw one lesson from it. It is not sufficient, however laudable, to concentrate on the rules dealing with the application of foreign law (conflict of laws) or on uniform or harmonising provisions, primarily as they figure in EEC law; instead it is necessary to grasp the general principles of foreign private law, which permeate foreign legal thought. In Brussels and in Luxemburg we must be able to meet our partners on their ground. For this purpose we must strive to make the oral proceedings before the EEC Court more flexible in order to present more effectively and in greater detail our legal approach in terms comprehensible to civil lawyers and now also to a Scandinavian judge. It is all the more necessary since that | court, of its own motion, has transformed itself from an international tribunal administering a treaty between Member States as sole parties into a federal court which determines individual rights. By the device of declaring many provisions of the Treaty and even Directives to be directly applicable, it has arrogated to itself indirectly the role of administering law between individuals, far exceeding that which the Treaty accorded to the court when acting as an administrative tribunal.

This development, which involves the court in technical aspects of private law to an extent unforeseen by the Treaty, raises the question whether the time has come to establish a special Bar attending the court in order to ensure the submission of cases with the highest possible expertise, not unlike the special Bars attached to the highest court in most continental countries. The jurisdiction of the Community Court to give uniform rulings on the interpretation of the EEC Conventions dealing with private international law, including bankruptcy and patents, may similarly call for separate divisions of the court staffed by specialists. At the same time the submissions of counsel should be fully argued in the judgment of the court and not merely form part of the facts, as they do at present.

---

[31] *Wachtel* v. *Wachtel* [1973] Fam. 72.
[32] See my *Law of the European Economic Community* (1974), *passim.*

Perhaps the most valuable insights into the comparative process were obtained in the course of the investigations by the International Association of Legal Science into the possibilities of a reception of Western law by countries of a different cultural, social and economic background. The experience in Turkey[33] and in India[34] showed that, while it is easily possible to introduce novel rules of a technical character, there are two spheres where the imposition and administration of new legal rules may meet social conventions head on. In such a clash the law is the loser. These spheres are the family and, connected therewith, succession. They differ from property, contract and tort in that they affect the traditions of the family unit. If ever the *Volksgeist*, called in aid by Savigny to explain the reception of Roman law by the learned professions, plays its part, it is here. However, it is not creative, at least in modern times. Popular reaction can stifle legal innovations, but it does not create them. In the end the somewhat disturbing lesson emerged that even in face of such popular resistance economic inducements and a leadership | which is homogeneous in its composition will overcome the surviving impeding elements of the *Volksgeist*.

This does not mean that family law and the law of succession are the only branches of the law which require a sensitive insight into their basis, which is not only technical. It has always seemed to me that contract, tort and property, too, are founded on some fundamental assumptions which are disregarded at one's peril. What at first sight appear to be differences among legal systems reveal identical foundations grounded on substantive ideas of justice. From classical Roman law through the *usus modernus Pandectarum* to the present time and during the entire life of the common law, considerations which are not merely technical but which appear to be of permanent value have been expressed in the principles according to which one can conclude and execute arrangements involving duties to do, not to do or to give, according to which one owes compensation for the invasion of protected interests of others and one may exercise absolute rights over things. Continental administrative law is entirely based on such general principles. *Esso* v. *Mardon* decided on 6 February 1976[35] provides a good example. In admitting the existence of a contractual warranty in respect of words spoken in the course of pre-contract negotiations the Court of Appeal touched upon

---

[33] "The Reception of Western Law in Countries with a different social and economic background: Turkey I, II," *Annales de l'Institut de Droit de l'Université d'Istanbul*, t. 5, no. 6 (1956), pp. 11–27, 225–238; (1957) 9 *Social Science Bulletin* 70–95; t. 11, nos. 16–17 (1961), pp. 3–13.
[34] "The Reception of Western Law in Countries with a different social and economic background: India," *Revista del Instituto de derecho comparado*, Barcelona, t. 8–9 (1957), pp. 69–81, 213–225; (1957) 6 *Indian Yearbook of International Law* 277–293.
[35] [1976] Q.B. 801 (C.A.).

a question of principle, discovered in 1859 when it was named *culpa in contrahendo*.[36] However, no trace of any general considerations appears in the judgments of the three Lords Justices, and the conditions and consequences of pre-contractual warranties in a legal system where a contract requires consideration are not explored. A comparison with the position elsewhere shows that such contractual liability has been recognised to exist in four situations, namely where a party has engaged in expenses or lost a chance of making a gain in connection *either* with a void contract, *or* with an existing contract *or* in negotiations which did not lead to a contract *or* before a contract could be even contemplated. The need for such a contractual remedy is greater or lesser in the case of void contracts according as to whether a particular legal system makes it easier or more difficult to rely on grounds for annulling a contract. Thus it is easier in Germany and in France than in England to allege mistake effectively; in France contracts of sale are regarded as void, if the object is not the property of the vendor with the result that the remedies under the law of sale cannot apply. If a contract is valid, losses may have occurred, because wrong information was supplied negligently. If no contract results from the negotiations, bargains elsewhere may have been lost. This situation occurred more fre|quently in the nineteenth century, when offers could be freely revoked in civil law countries and arises only in Germany in situations such as that which presented itself in *Ward* v. *Tesco Stores Ltd.*,[37] because the liability in tort, but not in contract, of an employer for the acts of his servants is restricted. One or two of these cases may constitute a negligent misrepresentation according to English law, but in all cases damages are limited in Germany to losses suffered through reliance on the supposed existence or the terms of the contract or, if none ever came into being, of the precontract itself – as distinct from the illogical solution sanctioned by the Misrepresentation Act 1967 which allows expectation damages.[38] Thus a transplant must always take into consideration a considerable number of factors extraneous to the institution itself, which affect its existence and function. Changes have occurred, of course, but to my mind less in the sphere of commercial law where terms and customs of merchants anticipate needs for development. Even outside this narrow field, they have taken place within the existing framework through the development of general principles of law, such as the appearance of frustration in contract, abuse of rights in various forms in property and most noticeably in tort, where the protected interests change with changing conditions and needs. The devices by which this is achieved may differ from legal system to

---

[36] See Kessler (1964) 77 Harvard L.R. 401; Nirk (1953) 18 *Rabels* Z. 310.

[37] [1976] 1 W.L.R. 810 (C.A.). See also *Turner* v. *Arding & Hobbs Ltd.* [1949] 2 All E.R. 911, 912.

[38] But see *Esso Petroleum Ltd.* v. *Mardon* [1976] Q.B. 801, 820 (C.A.).

legal system. If in English law assumpsit as an action in tort replaced the old contractual claims of debt, covenant and account, continental law used other means to the same effect. In German law the actions for failure to perform or for delay in performing, which alone were available for breach of contract were supplemented by an action in contract for what may be compared to fundamental breach; on the other hand the absence of a duty of care or the availability of defences in case of vicarious liability have induced French and German law to expand contractual duties (*obligations de résultat*) where an action in tort will supply the remedy in England. Such developments sponsored by courts and lawyers have occurred throughout the ages. The Romans were experts in this art and modern common lawyers from Roscoe Pound who advocated Social Engineering, to Lord Denning, who tries it out, have practised this craft.

Re-allocation or re-distribution of resources is quite another matter. It is the province of Parliament. But behind it lurks a real danger to the law as I have tried to serve it by testing, shaping, reformulating it in accordance with general principles. In a statutory | process of allocation of resources, the substance of the law is determined by Parliament, the execution and procedure is left to the lawyers. As a result the provision of remedies against the acts and decisions of the executive and the control of procedure by constitutional and other guarantees have assumed a growing importance at the expense of the control of the law itself. *Anisminic Ltd.* v. *Foreign Compensation Commission*[39] and *Padfield* v. *Minister of Agriculture, Fisheries and Food*[40] are examples of this threatening development and show how the courts are attempting to counter it. A worthwhile activity, no doubt, but it has brought nearer to us the picture of the lawyer, as he is seen in the U.S.S.R. and elsewhere, an arm of the executive, not its ever watchful partner.[41] If this should happen here the common law, which applies to ruler and subject alike and does not accord a special place to "The State," will have disappeared, and the rule of law as we understand it can perhaps be restored within limits by the enactment of a Constitution and a Bill of Rights to which the executive and the legislature are subject once again. But should this really be necessary? "χρὴ πείδεσται τοῖς νόμοις" determined the submission of Socrates to death. The lawyer as I see him not only obeys the laws, but moulds them at every stage, guided by the general principles of law. Some will interject: a "*laudatio temporis acti.*" It is time for me to be silent.

---

[39] [1969] 2 A.C. 147.
[40] [1968] A.C. 997.
[41] But see the more optimistic attitude of Lord Devlin, *Samples of Law Making* (1962), pp. 25, 26.

One Hundred Years of Hague Conferences on Private International Law[*][1]

[Editorial note: first published in International and Comparative Law Quaterly 42 (1993), 553–653.]

[*][Kurt Lipstein] Emeritus Professor of Law and Fellow of Clare College, University of Cambridge. This article is published to coincide with the centenary of the establishment of the First Hague Conference in September 1993.

NB. In accordance with the house style the terms *idem* and *ibidem* have been employed interchangeably.

[1] Lit: Lewald, in Strupp, *Wörterbuch des Völkerrechts* (1924), Vol. I, p. 454; Heinsheimer, *idem*, p. 487; Makarov, *idem* (2nd edn, 1960), Vol. I, p. 745; Niederländer, *idem*, p. 751; Gutzwiller (1945) 2 A.S.D.I. 48; Offerhaus (1959) 16 A.S.D.I. 27; van Hoogstraten (1967 – III) 122 Rec. des Cours 337; von Overbeck (1971 – I) 132 Rec. des Cours 3. The series of articles in (1993) 57 Rabels Z 1–302 could not be taken into account.

I. Introduction

A. *The Background*

On 16 September 1881 the Italian Minister of Foreign Affairs, P. S. Mancini, supported by three resolutions of the Italian Parliament in 1863, 1866 and 1873, addressed a memorandum to the Italian diplomatic representatives in the major European and South American countries.[2] In it Mancini recalled that in 1867, when he was Minister of Public Instruction, he had been charged with the task of ascertaining to what extent it might be possible to establish some common rules concerning the civil status of aliens, the extension and guarantee of their rights and their easier participation in the benefits of the respective laws. While received favourably in France, Belgium and Germany no action had been taken on the earlier initiative until, in 1875, the Dutch government had proposed an agreement for the execution of foreign judgments based upon personal jurisdiction. A second memorandum followed on 19 September 1882.[3] In it Mancini now proposed not a general codification of the rules of private|international law, however desirable, but one limited to specific topics among countries whose laws showed a certain affinity, the practical importance of which would lead to further action. As objects of immediate interest he pointed to the divisive use of domicile and nationality as connecting factors in matters of status,[4] of domicile and *situs* for movable property in respect of title *inter vivos* and of succession and to the question of the extent of the principle *locus regit actum*. The problem of the unity of a succession or its division into that of movables and immovables governed by different laws also merited attention.

---

[2] Martens (1896) 16 Nouveau Recueil Général des Traités (2nd ser.) 89 (Italian version), 115 (abbreviated French version); see (1886) Clunet 36.

[3] Martens, *idem*, pp. 124, 239; (1886) Clunet 40 taking up ideas developed over two decades; (1874) 1 Clunet 221, 283; (1875) 7 Rev. dr. internat. et de législ. comparé 529–556.

[4] Martens, *idem*, pp. 91, 239, 241.

The response was lukewarm.[5] The British government reacted negatively by referring to the existence of legislation in most of these matters[6] enabling the conclusion of Conventions.[7] It conceded, however, that a convention establishing choice of law rules for marriage, divorce and the enforcement of foreign judgments would be useful in the first place.[8] It also consented to a preliminary conference on the project supported by the International Law Association for a convention on the enforcement of foreign judgments.[9] The Danish government merely set out the relevant Danish and Italian provisions[10] and believed that only uniformity of laws would serve, but was willing to participate in a preparatory conference, as was the Swedish government. The Belgian government referred to its own proposals in 1867 in response to the Italian memorandum of that date and pointed out that Belgian law complied with the aims of the memorandum.[11] The initiative taken in 1875 by the Dutch government figured prominently in both the Italian approach and the Dutch reply.[12] The French answer was encouraging.[13] It welcomed the formulation of technical proposals and suggested that the legal situation of commercial entities and the enforcement of judgments, including letters rogatory and the recognition of entries in registers of status, should be included. The Dutch answer,[14] in supporting the Italian initiative, referred to its own action in 1875. It rejected the device of bilateral treaties, supported the | conclusion of multilateral conventions, although not necessarily of a universal character, given the great diversity of laws,[15] and suggested as a first topic of codification an agreement on the personal and territorial jurisdiction as a basis for the international enforcement of judgments as well as

---

[5] Summarised by Mancini in *idem*, p. 242. See *idem*, pp. 108, 126, 133 (Germany), 109 (Belgium).

[6] *Idem*, p. 111; Naturalisation Act 1870; Foreign Law Ascertainment Act 1861; Wills Act 1861; Wills and Domicile Act 1861.

[7] Declaration between Great Britain and Switzerland relating to Succession and Legacy Duties to be levied on the Property of subjects of the United Kingdom and of citizens of the Canton of Vaud, 27 Aug. 1872, Art. I. *British & Foreign State Papers*, Vol. LXII, p. 20, Parry (1872–1873) 145 C.T.S. 71, 72.

[8] Martens, *op. cit. supra* n. 2, at pp. 160–161.

[9] *ILA Conference 1883*, pp. 165, 170.

[10] Martens, *op. cit. supra* n. 2, at pp. 116, 248.

[11] *Idem*, pp. 109(2), 140, 151, 152.

[12] *Idem*, p. 128.

[13] *Idem*, p. 147.

[14] *Idem*, pp. 129, 155 referring to a Pro-Memoria of 1874, 208.

[15] *Idem*, pp. 219–223; GB 175; Switzerland 168, 186; Austria 170; Greece 171; Belgium 176; Netherlands 183; France 183; Russia 185; Portugal 190, 194; Mexico 191; Peru 197; Colombia 199; Argentina 201; Uruguay 202; Guatemala 204, 214; San Salvador 205; Venezuela 207; Costa Rica 212; Honduras 213; *Actes de la Conference de la Haye 1893* (hereafter, *Actes 1893*), p. 6.

letters rogatory and other aspects of procedure. It also mentioned the establishment of general principles governing matters of private law.

The German government was not helpful.[16] Bismarck had doubts about the competence and impartiality of certain foreign courts. The US Attorney-General saw no need for a convention which restated the principles already operating at common law.[17] The majority of the governments were, however, willing to participate in a preliminary conference to consider the proposal for a treaty on the enforcement of foreign judgments submitted by the International Law Association.[18] Mancini expressed the hope that such a meeting would encourage the study of further topics, such as nationality, marriage, divorce, testate and intestate succession, letters rogatory, legal assistance and others.[19] In order to overcome the reluctance of the German government he suggested that instead of entering into a multilateral commitment it might conclude bilateral agreements on the basis of a multilateral draft treaty serving as a model.

When no conference had materialised by 1885, Mancini took up once more the subject of his memorandum of 16 September 1881,[20] but the initiative had passed into other hands. In response to Mancini's circular and his memorandum, Antonio Arenas, the Peruvian government's representative, drew attention to the fact that in 1875 the government of Peru had invited the American States[21] to a conference in Lima with the same purpose. Opened on 9 December 1877 it had concluded its work on 5 December 1878 by a treaty signed by a number of Central and South American States.[22] It covered capacity, property, contracts, marriage including matrimonial property, succession and jurisdiction.[23] It was|followed by a series of treaties between 1889 and 1989[24] and the comprehensive attempt at codification by the Bu-

---

[16] Martens, *idem*, pp. 169, 217, 221.

[17] *Idem*, p. 230, also Chile 206.

[18] *ILA Conference 1883*, p. 165.

[19] Martens, *op. cit. supra* n. 2, at p. 219.

[20] Memorandum 28 June 1885; Martens, *idem*, p. 236; for the reasons for the delay see p. 238; Gutzwiller (1945) 2 Ann. suisse dr. internat. 48, 55.

[21] Martens, *idem*, p. 169.

[22] Argentina, Bolivia, Chile, Costa Rica, Ecuador, Peru and Venezuela.

[23] Martens, *op. cit. supra* n. 2, at pp. 266, esp. 293.

[24] Montevideo, 12 Feb. 1889; Martens, *idem* (1893) 18 (2nd ser.) 414, 424, 432, 443; (1896) Clunet 441: Persons, family, property, contracts including property arrangements, succession, prescription, jurisdiction and foreign judgments and arbitral awards. Panama City, 30 Jan. 1975 (1975) 14 I.L.M. 325: Powers of attorney, taking evidence abroad, bills of exchange and promissory notes, cheques, commercial arbitration, letters rogatory. Montevideo, 8 May 1979 (1979) 18 I.L.M. 1211: Cheques, commercial companies, foreign companies, foreign judgments and arbitral awards, execution of preventive measures, proof of foreign law; domicile of natural persons; general rules of private international law,

stamante Code of 20 February 1928,[25] which does not appear to have met with success. On 21 July 1897 the Central American States concluded two conventions dealing respectively with conflict of laws and the recognition and enforcement of foreign judgments.[26]

At the same time the Institut de droit international, which first met in Ghent in 1873,[27] resolved to prepare projects of treaties, general or special, in matters of private international law,[28] and Bluntschli proposed a convention on questions of nationality.[29]

The Dutch government, whose earlier steps in 1874 and 1875 have already been noted, now took the initiative and called for a conference to be opened on 12 September 1893. Thirteen States accepted. In its proposals for a programme the Dutch government, apart from referring to some general aspects (formalities, obligations arising by law, property obligations), concentrated on family law (marriage, paternity, both legitimate or illegitimate, adoption, paternal authority, guardianship, including that of lunatics and spendthrifts, and succession, both testate and intestate.[30] (See the Table of Signatures and Ratifications of the Hague Conventions at the end of the article.)

B. Areas Covered

Historically, two productive periods can be distinguished. The first four conferences (1893, 1894, 1900, 1904) resulted altogether in six treaties | dealing respectively with civil procedure (1896),[31] the conclusion of marriages (1900),[32] choice of law and jurisdiction in matters of divorce and judicial

---

letters rogatory (additional protocol). La Paz, 24 May 1984 (1985) 24 I.L.M. 459: Adoption of minors, capacity of juridical persons, foreign judgments, taking evidence abroad, letters rogatory (additional protocol). Montevideo, 15 July 1989 (1990) 29 I.L.M. 62: International return of children, support obligations, international carriage of goods by road. And see generally Samtleben, (1980) 44 Rabels Z 368 (texts); (1992) 56 *ibid.* 1, 88, 142 *et seq.* (texts).

[25] 86 L.N.T.S. 120, 254; 4 Hudson Int. Legislation 2283.

[26] (1897) 185 C.T.S. 272, 275.

[27] (1877) 1 Ann. Inst. dr. internat. 12.

[28] *Idem*, pp. 123–140; (1878) 2, pp. 34, 103; (1879–80) 3, p. 192; (1874) 6 Rev. dr. internat. législ. comp. 582; (1875) 7, 529.

[29] (1870) 2 Rev. dr. internat. législ. comp. 107.

[30] *Actes 1893*, pp. 7–12.

[31] 14 Nov. 1896, Martens, *op. cit. supra* n. 2 (1898) 23 (2nd ser.) 398; (1896) 183 C.T.S. 470, rev. 27 July 1904, Martens, *idem* (1910) 2 (3rd ser.) 243; (1905) 199 C.T.S. 1; Additional Protocol 22 May 1897; Martens, *idem* (1900) 25 (2nd ser.) 226, rev. 1 Mar. 1954, 286 U.N.T.S. 265; 18 Mar. 1970, 847 U.N.T.S. 231; U.K.T.S. 20 (1977) Cmnd. 6727.

[32] 12 June 1902, Martens, *idem* (1904) 31 (2nd ser.) 706; (1902) 191 C.T.S. 253. Parties today: Portugal, Romania, Germany.

separation (1900),[33] guardianship of minors (1900),[34] the personal and pro-prietary relationships between spouses (1904),[35] compulsory guardianship of adults (1904)[36] and succession and wills.[37] The remaining time before the First World War was taken up by the Hague Peace Conferences,[38] and the work on private international law was resumed only in 1925.[39] The confer-ences were held in 1925 and 1928.[40] Succession, bankruptcy, sale, companies and the recognition and enforcement of judgments formed the object of detailed studies and debates,[41] but the only concrete result was a protocol dated 27 March 1931 accepting the jurisdiction of the International Court of Justice for the interpretation of the Hague Conventions.[42]

II. 1951 and After

After the Second World War the loose structure of the Hague Conference was given a firm legal basis by an agreement between 16 States (mainly European, but also Japan),[43] which affirmed the usages established by the Dutch government during five decades and indicated its permanent charac-ter by calling it "The Hague Conference on Private International Law".[44]

| Its aim was to be the progressive unification of the rules of private inter-national law. In addition to the founder members, membership is to be conferred by a majority of votes cast upon a proposal of two members. The Netherlands Standing Government Committee is to be in charge of opera-

---

[33] 12 June 1902, *idem*, pp. 715 and 259 respectively; parties today: Portugal, Romania.

[34] 12 June 1902, *idem*, pp. 724 and 264 respectively; partly replaced by the Convention of 5 Oct. 1961, 658 U.N.T.S. 143.

[35] 17 July 1905, Martens, *idem* (1912) 6 (3rd ser.) 480; (1905) 199 C.T.S. 17: parties today: Portugal, Romania.

[36] 17 July 1905, *Idem*, pp. 490 and 12 respectively.

[37] 17 July 1905, (1905) 199 C.T.S. 21.

[38] V Conference, *Actes 1926*, p. 15.

[39] For the literature regarding the V and VI Conferences see Gutzwiller, *op. cit. supra* n. 1 at pp. 67 n. 65, 71 n. 80.

[40] For the survival or revival of the pre-war treaties see (1967) Rev. crit. d.i.p. 209.

[41] *Actes 1926*, pp. 193, 341, 344; *Actes 1928*, p. 405; Gutzwiller, *op. cit. supra* n. 1, at pp. 83–85 and n. 120.

[42] *Actes 1926*, p. 332; *1928*, pp. 198, 229, 394, 424; parties: Belgium, Netherlands, Estonia, Portugal, 12 Feb. 1936; 167 L.N.T.S. 341; (1929–1931) 5 Hudson Internat. Legislation 933; Norway, Sweden, Denmark, Finland and Hungary also became parties.

[43] Now: Argentina, Austria, Australia, Belgium, Canada, Chile, Cyprus, Czechoslo-vakia, Denmark, Egypt, Finland, France, Germany, Greece, Hungary, Italy, Ireland, Is-rael, Luxembourg, Mexico, Netherlands, Norway, Poland, Portugal, Romania, Spain, Sweden, Switzerland, Turkey, UK, US, Venezuela.

[44] 220 U.N.T.S. 123; 226 U.N.T.S. 384; 510 U.N.T.S. 317; (1951) Rev. crit. d.i.p. 738.

tions through a Permanent Bureau which is to determine the action to be taken, the date and the agenda. Conferences are to be called every four years, with power to convene extraordinary sessions. The Permanent Bureau is to be appointed by the Netherlands government and is to consist of a secretary general and two secretaries of different nationalities charged with the preparation and organisation of the conferences.

During the years that followed, the Conference dealt with the topics of procedure, family matters, succession, commercial matters, torts and conflict of laws.

A. Procedure Conventions

1. 1 March 1954: Service Abroad of Judicial and Extrajudicial Documents, Letters Rogatory, *Cautio Judicatum Solvi*, Execution against the Person.[45]
2. 15 November 1965: Service Abroad of Judicial and Extrajudicial Acts in Civil and Commercial Matters.[46]
3. 5 October 1961: Abolition of the Requirement of Legalisation for Foreign Public Documents.[47]
4. 18 March 1970: Taking Evidence Abroad in Civil and Commercial Matters.[48]
5. 15 April 1958: *Prorogatio Fori* – International Sale of Goods.[49]
6. 25 November 1965: *Prorogatio Fori*.[50]
7. 1 February 1971: Recognition and Enforcement of Foreign Judgments in Civil and Commercial Matters and Additional Protocol.[51]
8. 25 October 1980: International Access to Justice.[52]

---

[45] 286 U.N.T.S. 265; (1951) Rev. crit. d.i.p. 732: 29 participants.

[46] 658 U.N.T.S. 163; 737 U.N.T.S. 408, 410; U.K.T.S. 50 (1969) Cmnd.3986; (1964) Rev. crit. d.i.p. 819.

[47] 527 U.N.T.S. 198, U.K.T.S. 32 (1965) Cmnd.2617.

[48] 847 U.N.T.S. 231, U.K.T.S. 20 (1977) Cmnd.6767. (1968) Rev. crit. d.i.p. 759. Report (1985) 24 I.L.M. 1668.

[49] (1956) Rev. crit. d.i.p. 750. Not in force.

[50] (1964) Rev. crit. d.i.p. 828. Not in force.

[51] 1144 U.N.T.S. 249, 269; (1966) Rev. crit. d.i.p. 329; (1967) 203 (additional protocol).

[52] Misc. 14/1981 Cmnd.8281; (1980) Rev. crit. d.i.p. 901: 12 participants.

B. Conventions on Family Matters

1. 14 March 1978: Celebration and Recognition of the Validity of Marriages.[53]
| 2. 1 June 1970: Recognition of Divorces and Judicial Separations.[54]
3. 5 October 1961: Powers of Authorities and Law Applicable in Respect of the Protection of Infants.[55]
4. 25 October 1980: Civil Aspects of International Child Abduction.[56]
5. 14 March 1978: Matrimonial Property Regimes.[57]
6. 24 October 1956: Law Applicable to Maintenance Obligations Towards Minor Children.[58]
7. 15 April 1958: Recognition and Execution of Decisions Involving Obligations to Support Minor Children.[59]
8. 2 October 1973: Law Applicable to Maintenance Obligations.[60]
9. 2 October 1973: Recognition and Enforcement of Decisions Relating to Maintenance Obligations.[61]
10. 15 November 1965: Applicable Law and Recognition of Decrees Relating to Adoption.[62]

C. Succession Conventions

1. 5 October 1961: Form of Testamentary Dispositions.[63]
2. 18 March 1970: International Administration of the Estates of Deceased Persons.[64]
3. 1 August 1989: Succession of the Estates of Deceased Persons.[65]

---

[53] Misc.11(1977) Cmnd.6830; (1977) 25 A.J.Comp.L. 399.
[54] 978 U.N.T.S. 393; (1975) U.K.T.S. 123, Cmnd.6248; (1968) Rev. crit. d.i.p. 790: 14 participants.
[55] 658 U.N.T.S. 143; (1960) Rev. crit. d.i.p. 125; (1973) 575.
[56] Misc. 14/1981; Cmnd.8281; U.K.T.S. 66 (1986); Cm.33; (1980) Rev. crit. d.i.p. 893: 27 participants.
[57] Misc.11(1977), Cmnd.6830; (1977) 25 A.J.Comp.L. 394, in force since 1 Sept. 1992, ratification by the Netherlands; French J.O. 25, Sept. 1992; S.J. leg. § 65739.
[58] 510 U.N.T.S. 161; (1956) Rev. crit. d.i.p. 733; 15 participants.
[59] 539 U.N.T.S. 27; (1956) Rev. crit. d.i.p. 755; 20 participants.
[60] 1056 U.N.T.S. 199; (1973) Rev. crit. d.i.p. 398; 34 participants.
[61] 1021 U.N.T.S. 187; (1980) U.K.T.S. 49; (1973) Rev. crit. d.i.p. 398; 11 participants.
[62] (1978) U.K.T.S. 94, Cmnd.7342; (1964) Rev. crit. d.i.p. 815; 3 participants.
[63] 510 U.N.T.S. 175; U.K.T.S. 5 (1964) at p. 14; 34 participants.
[64] Misc.6(1973); Cmnd.5225; (1972) Rev. crit. d.i.p. 806; 7 participants; not in force.
[65] (1989) 28 I.L.M. 150; (1988) Rev. crit. d.i.p. 807; 2 participants; not in force.

D. Commercial Conventions

1. 15 June 1955: International Sale of Goods.[66]
2. 1 June 1956: Recognition of Foreign Companies, Associations and Foundations.[67]
3. 15 April 1958: Transfer of Title in the case of International Sale of Movables.[68]
|4. 14 March 1978: Law Applicable to Agency.[69]
5. 20 October 1984: Law Applicable to Trusts and on their Recognition.[70]
6. 22 December 1986: Contracts for the International Sale of Goods.[71]

E. Torts Conventions

1. 4 May 1971: Traffic Accidents.[72]
2. 2 October 1973: Products Liability.[73]

F. Conflict of Laws

1. 15 June 1955: Conflict of Laws between Nationality and Domicile.[74]

In this period conferences were held in 1951, 1956, 1960, 1964, 1968, 1972, 1976, 1980, 1984 and 1988. The United Kingdom had joined them as an observer in 1925 but became a full member only after the Second World War. It is only a party to the following conventions: Form of Testamentary Dispositions, Legalisation for Foreign Public Documents, Adoptions, Service Abroad of Judicial and Extrajudicial Documents, Taking Evidence Abroad in Civil and Commercial Matters, Recognition of Divorces and Judicial Separations, International Administration of the Estates of Deceased Persons, Recognition and Enforcement of Maintenance Obligations, Civil As-

---

[66] 510 U.N.T.S. 147; (1951) Rev. crit. d.i.p. 725; (1956) 750; 12 participants.
[67] (1951) Rev. crit. d.i.p. 727; 5 participants; not in force.
[68] (1956) Rev. crit. d.i.p. 747; 2 participants; not in force.
[69] Misc.29(1977); Cmnd.7020; (1978) 26 A.J.Comp.L. 438; (1977) Rev. crit. d.i.p. 639.
[70] Misc.3(1985); Cmnd.8494; (1984) 23 I.L.M. 1389; (1984) Rev. crit. d.i.p. 770; 8 participants.
[71] (1985) 24 I.L.M. 1573; (1985) Rev. crit. d.i.p. 774; 3 participants.
[72] (1968) Rev. crit. d.i.p. 796; (1975) Clunet 963; 9 participants.
[73] 1056 U.N.T.S. 187; (1972) Rev. crit. d.i.p. 818.
[74] (1951) Rev. crit. d.i.p. 730; 5 participants.

pects of International Child Abduction, Law Applicable to Trusts and on their Recognition. It has ratified only the Wills, the Legalisation, the Procedure (1965), the Evidence, the Divorce, the Maintenance (Recognition), the Child Abduction and the Trust Conventions.

III. Conventions Prepared Before the First World War

A. Marriage

With one exception, the conventions concluded before the First World War were concerned with family law.

The Draft Convention on the Conclusion of Marriages,[75] following a proposal of the Institut de droit international of 5 September 1888,[76] | referred questions relating to the right[77] to enter into a marriage to the respective national laws of the parties,[78] but allowed a reference on (*renvoi*[79]) to the respective laws of their domicile or to the law of the place of celebration of the marriage (Article 1). The law of the place of celebration was, however, permitted to prohibit a marriage on the ground that a mandatory law[80] applying without regard to the national or international character of the marriage precluded the ceremony in view of the relationship of blood or affinity between the spouses or because a previous marriage had not been dissolved (Article 2).[81] The meaning of the last-mentioned impediment was open to various interpretations.[82] It could refer to the need for a foreign divorce to be recognised, but seems to have been directed against polygamous marriages and second marriages before a decree absolute.[83] Evidence of the capacity to marry was to be provided by the diplomatic or consular representatives or

---

[75] *Supra* n. 32. Lit: Lewald, *op. cit. supra* n. 1, at p. 459; Kahn, *Abhandlungen zum Internationalen Privatrecht* (1928), Vol. II, p. 61; Buzzati (1901) 3 (2 ser.) Rev. dr. int. leg. comp. 269; Kosters and Bellemans, *Conventions de la Haye 1902–1905 sur le Droit International Privé* (1921), pp. 22–41.

[76] I Conference, *Actes 1893*, p. 45. Inst. dr. internat. (Lausanne) (1888–89) 10 Ann. 56.

[77] This term was used to include problems of mistake and duress as grounds of nullity; III Conference, *Actes 1900*, p. 169.

[78] For the problems arising out of a seeming cumulation see Kahn, *op. cit. supra* n. 175, at pp. 62 *et seq.*, esp. the reflective effect of an incapacity. Cf. *Pugh* v. *Pugh* [1951] P. 482.

[79] In view of Swiss legislation which relied on domicile.

[80] For a critique see Kahn, *op. cit. supra* n. 75, at p. 85.

[81] This formulation was chosen in order to exclude the broad operation of public policy as unsuitable for a choice of law convention. It introduces substantive rules into a provision dealing with conflict of laws. See *idem*, p. 68; Buzzati, *op. cit. supra* n. 75, at p. 273.

[82] Kahn, *idem*, pp. 99, 100.

[83] *Actes 1893*, p. 47; *1900*, p. 169.

by the competent authorities (Article 3). The form of marriage was to be governed by the law of the place of celebration,[84] but if the marriage had been celebrated abroad in a form required by the *lex loci celebrationis* other than a religious one, or in the absence of publicity required by the *lex patriae*, the national authorities of the parties could refuse to recognise it (Article 4(1)).[85] The same applied if the national rules on publicity had been disregarded[86] (Article 4(2)). Diplomatic or consular marriages between foreigners of the same nationality[87] were to be recognised, if the law of the place of celebration permitted it (Article 5).[88]

| It became clear at an early stage that difficulties of characterisation involving form and capacity might ensue,[89] and that the importance of religious marriages at that time in Austria, Hungary and Russia had to be taken into account;[90] further, the inadvisability of allowing resort to public policy, if the convention was to be effective, was acknowledged.[91]

The draft reflected the concerns of its time: the novelty of *renvoi*, the importance in certain countries of religious marriages, and the reluctance to allow resort to public policy in order to exclude the applicable foreign law, in a choice of law convention.

The draft was revised in 1894. The reference by the *lex patriae* to the law of the domicile or of the place of celebration Article 1 was reworded.[92] They were to apply only if the *lex patriae* "allowed" it. The power of the law of the place of celebration (Article 2) was increased so as to refuse the celebration of a marriage on the ground, *inter alia*, that its law prohibited absolutely the remarriage of a party whose previous marriage had been dissolved because of his or her adultery.

---

[84] The application of the law governing the essential validity was rejected by the first draft: *Actes 1893*, p. 53. Cf. Kahn, *op. cit. supra* n. 75, at p. 124; Inst. dr. internat. (Heidelberg) (1887–88) 9 Ann. 95.

[85] *Actes 1893*, p. 48, now Art. 5(2) of the Convention, but see Inst. dr., *idem*, p. 101. Once again the choice of law rule contained substantive provisions: Kahn, *op. cit. supra* n. 75, at pp. 127, 136.

[86] Kahn, *idem*, p. 143.

[87] The possibility, supported by Prussian law, was considered and rejected that in the case of parties of different nationality those of the husband's nationality should be competent: *Actes 1893*, pp. 48–49, 54, 60.

[88] *Idem*, pp. 82–85; Kahn, *op. cit. supra* n. 75, at pp. 149, 166.

[89] *Actes 1893*, pp. 40, 59–60; a distinction was drawn between *formalités habilitantes* and *formalités substantielles* (*lex situs* for property) or *formalités d'exécution* (law of place of execution). See also *infra* n. 115.

[90] *Idem*, pp. 39, 43.

[91] *Idem*, pp. 37–38, for this problem see Jayme (1965) Neue J.W. 16; Makarov, in *Jus et Lex, Mélanges Gutzwiller* (1959), p. 303 but see the *Boll* case I.C.J. Rep. 1958, 52; Lipstein (1959) 8 I.C.L.Q. 506.

[92] Kahn, *op. cit. supra* n. 75, at p. 70; Buzzati, *op. cit. supra* n. 75, at p. 274.

The new subchapters (b and c) introduced related topics by dealing with the law governing the status of the wife and the children and with divorce and judicial separation: topics which the III Conference converted into separate draft conventions. Once again the law of the husband's nationality at the time of the marriage was to determine the *status* and the *capacity* of the wife and of the children of the marriage (subchapter b, Article 1).[93] That law also governed the duties of the spouses towards each other, but this enforcement was to depend upon whether the law of the place of enforcement allowed the same remedy (subchapter b, Article 2).[94] If the husband changed his nationality the personal relations between the spouses remained subject to the law of their last common nationality while the status of the children born after their father's change of nationality was governed by his new *lex patriae* (subchapter b, Article 3).

| A divorce could be granted only if both the *lex patriae* and the *lex fori* allowed it (subchapter c, Article 1).[95] The grounds had to be the same (Article 2). Judicial separation was subject to the same conditions (Articles 3 and 4), but if the *lex patriae* allowed only a divorce while the *lex fori* knew only judicial separation, a decree of separation was to be admissible (Article 3). Jurisdiction was to be exercised by the courts of the domicile of the spouses, but if by virtue of their *lex patriae* they had separate domiciles, the courts of the defendant's domicile were to have jurisdiction (Article 5(1)), the same article admitting an exception if the *lex patriae* prescribed the jurisdiction of ecclesiastical courts for religious marriages. Naturally the courts of the country of the parties' nationality were to have concurrent jurisdiction (Article 5(2)). If the parties possessed different nationalities, the law of their last common nationality was to be regarded as their national law (Article 6).[96]

The final draft adopted by the IV Conference in 1902[97] contained a number of modifications. *Renvoi* by the *lex patriae* to another law to determine the right to enter a marriage had to express.[98] The power of the law of the

---

[93] *Actes 1894*, p. 82. The Commission was not inclined to make the capacity of the wife to enter into commercial transactions depend upon the *lex loci actus*, contrary to a widely accepted practice for the benefit of a *bona fide* contracting party: see e.g. *De Lizardi* v. *Chaize*, D.P. 1861.1.19; S. 1861.1.365.

[94] The Conference, *Actes 1894*, p. 82, admitted that such measures as forcing a wife to return to the matrimonial home had become obsolete.

[95] See also Inst. dr. internat., *op. cit. supra* n. 76, at p. 78, Art. 17.

[96] *Actes 1894*, p. 85.

[97] *Actes 1900*, pp. 168, 237 reproduced by the Convention of 12 June 1902 (*supra* n. 32); cf. Inst. dr., *op. cit. supra* n. 84, at p. 62; n. 76, at p. 7.

[98] Art. 1; Kahn, Buzzati, *loc. cit. supra* n. 92; cf. the negative vote of the Inst. dr. internat. (Neuchatel) (1900) 18 Ann. 145. For the reasons for this exclusion see Kahn, *idem*, p. 76.

place of celebration to apply was further strengthened by adding as a ground of refusal to entertain a marriage if the parties had been condemned for having made an attempt on the life of the previous spouse of one of them,[99] but the range of this liberty was restricted to the laws of the contracting States.[100] The earlier provision that no previous marriage must have existed was abandoned[101] only to reappear in another, more rigid, form. Article 2 provided that no contracting party was to be obliged to allow a marriage of persons who were previously married or if religious reasons forbade it, but a marriage concluded in violation of this prohibition was to be invalid only in the country of celebration. However, a marriage concluded in violation of these provisions could nevertheless be recognised if it was valid according to the *lex patriae*,[102] and marriages in civil form could be disregarded in other contracting States where religious form was compulsory.[103] Conversely the *lex loci celebrationis* could allow a marriage prohibited by the *lex|patriae*, if the prohibition was based exclusively on religious reasons,[104] while all other contracting States were to be at liberty to treat it as invalid.[105]

Article 4 on proof of the *lex patriae* was improved and diplomatic or consular marriages were to be recognised, except if a party to it was a national of the country where it was celebrated and if the host State prohibited such marriages – however, the fact that a party had been previously married or religious reasons could not furnish a sufficient ground.[106] The Convention applied if one of the parties was a national of a contracting State (Article 8).

The Convention reflected the contemporary concerns of certain States in the observation of religious practices and the indissoluble character of marriages. In an attempt to respond to them rules were devised which sought to satisfy all the interested parties by a series of concurrent and therefore potentially conflicting choice of law rules which either reflected the existing controversies or added further complications.

---

[99] Art. 2(3). Note the use of the plural.

[100] *Actes 1900*, p. 171; Convention, Art. 8. Thereby the general principle of public policy was reduced to a set of specific substantive rules, known today as particular rules of public policy. For the reasons for this policy see *Actes 1893*, p. 41; Kahn, op. *cit. supra* n. 75, at p. 79.

[101] *Actes 1900*, p. 171.

[102] Convention, Art. 7; Kahn, *op. cit. supra* n. 75, at pp. 103 *et seq.*

[103] *Idem*, Art. 5, p. 136 respectively.

[104] Convention, Art. 3(1), but see the recommendation made in 1925 to add to this list military service obligations and conditions imposed by princely houses: *Actes 1925*, pp. 324, 333.

[105] Convention, Art. 3(2); Kahn, *op. cit. supra* n. 75, at pp. 112, 119.

[106] *Idem*, p. 108, Art. 6(i).

B. Effects of Marriage

The effect of marriage, limited to its personal aspects, was first discussed by the II Conference in 1894[107] in connection with the conclusion of marriage and limited to its personal effects. Extended to property relations it was considered separately and provisionally in 1900[108] and finally in 1904,[109] to be adopted in a modified form by the IV Conference.[110] The *personal* rights and duties of the spouses were to be governed by the law of their nationality at the time of the marriage, but the means of enforcement by the *lex patriae* and the *lex fori* had to be comparable.[111] A subsequent acquisition of another nationality by both spouses affected their personal relations as well as any subsequent change of a marriage settlement, thus sanctioning a restrictive principle of mutability. If the | spouses acquired different nationalities the law of their last common nationality was to apply.[112]

In accordance with an established practice a distinction was drawn between marriages accompanied by a marriage settlement and those without one. In the absence of an express contract (disregarding the French doctrine of a presumed contract) the law of the husband's nationality at the time of the marriage was to apply in respect of both movables and immovables,[113] and a subsequent change of the domicile of the spouses or of either of them was to have no effect, thus sanctioning immutability (Article 2). However, it would seem that they could subsequently enter into a marriage settlement if none had been concluded before (Article 4). The capacity to enter into such a contract was to be determined by the respective *leges patriae* of the spouses at the time (Article 3), and their national law was to determine whether such a contract could be either rescinded or modified subsequently (Article 4). The essential validity of the contract and its effects were to be determined by the husband's *lex patriae* at the time of the marriage, but by the (common) national law of the spouses, if concluded subsequently (Article 5(1)). The

---

[107] *Actes 1894*, pp. 47–49, 81. Final Protocol, p. 2(b), part 2; see also Inst. dr., *op. cit. supra* n. 84, at pp. 61, 72, 115.

[108] *Actes 1900*, pp. 219, 226 (report).

[109] *Actes 1904*, pp. 165, 177 (report), 186, 215 (text).

[110] 17 July 1904 (1905) 199 C.T.S. 17 (*supra* n. 35); Lewald, *op. cit. supra* n. 1, at p. 474, Audinet (1910) 6 Rev. dr. internat. priv. 289; Lainé (1905) Clunet 771, 803; (1906) 1; (1907) 897.

[111] Art. 1. *Quaere* whether Art. 1 covered the capacity of a married woman to act; Lewald, *idem*, p. 475; Audinet, *idem*, pp. 294, 311 but see Art. 8(2) of the Convention.

[112] Convention, Art. 9, limited to personal relations, making or rescinding a marriage settlement subsequently and its validity.

[113] Unity of the matrimonial regime was accepted by all contracting parties. Immovables were, however, to be subject to the operation of the *lex situs*, if it had established a special regime for land (Art. 7); *Actes 1900*, p. 226; *1904*, p. 178.

law governing essential validity was also to determine whether a choice of a different law was permissible (Article 5(2)), thus allowing *renvoi* – an attempt to insert the French contractual approach into the status approach accepted by the other contracting States. Article 9(1) allowed the parties to a marriage settlement to submit it to another law, and it must remain an open question whether in the absence of a contractual regime the power to enter into a new contractual regime conferred by Article 4 applies only to modifications or permits a new contract superseding the previous non-contractual regime.[114]

Compliance with the formalities of the *lex loci actus* was to suffice or with those of the *lex patriae* of each of the spouses at the time of the marriage or, if made subsequently, at the time of the contract (Article 6). However, the requirement of a particular form as a substantive condition required at the time of the marriage by the *lex patriae* of one of the spouses was to be respected, characterising such a requirement as one of substance.[115] Immovables subject to a special regime were to be governed by the formalities of the *lex situs* (Article 7).

| The right of States was reserved to require the observance of special formalities in bringing the existence of a matrimonial regime to public notice and to prescribe measures for the protection of third parties in their dealings with married women exercising a profession in the country of third parties (Article 8).

The Convention was restricted to the application of the law of contracting States (Article 10), but it is noteworthy that the elaborate provision of the draft safeguarding what are now termed *règles d'application immédiate* was not incorporated in the Convention.[116]

C. Divorce and Judicial Separation

Divorce and judicial separation had been detached as a separate section in the draft adopted by the II Conference in 1894,[117] but it was subsequently omitted as inconsistent with the object of a convention restricted in its final version to the conclusion of marriage. Instead a separate convention was

---

[114] Audinet, *op. cit. supra* n. 110, at pp. 302, 363; not clear: Trib.civ. Seine 21 June 1910, (1912) Clunet 867.

[115] Convention, Art. 6(2); *"formes habilitantes"*, Inst. dr. int. (Lausanne) (1927) 34 Ann. 335, Art. 3, limited in each case to that of the acting party; Lewald, *op. cit. supra* n. 1, at p. 477.

[116] *Actes 1904*, pp. 104–105; Draft Convention, Art. 11 (p. 187).

[117] *Actes 1894*, pp. 81, 83; Final Protocol, p. 2(c). See also Inst. dr. int., *op. cit. supra* n. 76, at p. 78.

prepared dealing with choice of law and jurisdiction in relation to divorce and separation.[118]

As in the earlier draft, both the *lex patriae* and the *lex fori* had to permit divorce or, as the case may be, judicial separation.[119] The previous draft permitting judicial separation, if the *lex fori* was restricted to judicial separation while the *lex patriae* knew only divorce, was abandoned.[120] Relaxing the stricter provisions of the earlier draft, both the *lex patriae* and the *lex fori* had to be satisfied only that a cause for divorce or separation existed, not that it was the same.[121] However, if the *lex fori* permitted it, a ground recognised by the *lex patriae* was to suffice by itself.[122] A new article excluded reliance on facts which had occurred while a former *lex patriae* applied which did not treat them as a ground for divorce or judicial separation.[123] Thus *fraude à la loi*, as evidenced by the *Bauffremont* case,[124] was to be avoided. The provisions on jurisdiction were amplified by permitting it to be exercised by the national courts of the spouses or by those of their domicile, if common, or by that of the|defendant, if separate, as well as by the courts of their last domicile, abandoned or changed before the cause of action arose.[125] As an exception, exclusive jurisdiction was accorded to the national courts, if so claimed, but other courts retained their jurisdiction upon a disclaimer of competence.[126] The courts of the parties' domicile had the power to take protective measures, even if they could not pronounce a decree of divorce or judicial separation.[127] Both judicial and administrative decrees of divorce and judicial separation were to be recognised,[128] subject to what had become the usual control of jurisdiction and service.

---

[118] *Actes 1900*, p. 207. Final Protocol, p. 239.

[119] *Actes 1900*, p. 207; Final Protocol, Art. 1; Convention, Art. 1. In the absence of a common *lex patriae* of the spouses, the law of their last common nationality was to apply (Art. 3). The case of spouses never having had a common nationality does not appear to have been of practical relevance at that time.

[120] *Actes 1900*, p. 207; Art. 3 of the 1894 draft was omitted.

[121] *Idem*, p. 209; Convention, Art. 2.

[122] *Ibid; idem*, Art. 3.

[123] *Ibid; idem*, Art. 4.

[124] Cass. 18 Mar. 1878, S. 1878.1.192; D.1878.1.201; Travers (1908) 6 R.D.I.P. 24, 32–33.

[125] *Actes 1900*, p. 216; Convention, Art. 5; Lewald, *op. cit. supra* n. 1, at p. 469; Buzzati (1901) 3 (2 ser.) Rev. dr. int. leg. comp. 269, 289 asks whether the *lex patriae* determines what is their domicile.

[126] Convention, Art. 5(1). The requirements under the Marriage Convention of a religious ceremony of marriage by the national law and the ensuing right not to recognise a marriage concluded in violation of this requirement prompted this complicated rule.

[127] *Actes 1900*, p. 212; Convention, Art. 6. It was designed as a counterpart to the exclusive national jurisdiction reserved by Art. 5.

[128] Convention, Art. 7. This provision was influenced by Scandinavian practice. For this reason the Convention speaks of *demand* and not of *action*.

The financial aspects of a divorce or judicial separation were not made the object of a special rule and remained to be determined according to the local rules of private international law. The problem of *lis alibi pendens* was not addressed, or that of public policy.[129]

The Convention applied if one party at least was a national of a contracting State.[130]

D. Guardianship of Minors

Guardianship of minors was first considered by the II Conference in 1894 and finally cast into treaty form by the IV Conference in 1902.[131]

Here, too, the *lex patriae* was chosen to apply as the law to govern guardianship. If the ward resided abroad and no guardian had been appointed, the diplomatic or consular representative of his home State was to be treated as such, if the ward's *lex patriae* allowed it (Article 2). If the *lex patriae* did not provide for the appointment of guardians for nationals abroad or did not empower its diplomatic representatives to exercise this power, or if the guardian appointed by the *lex patriae* had delegated his function to a person residing in the country of the ward's|residence, the local authorities were to apply their own law and appoint a guardian (Article 3) subject, however, to the ward's national law (Article 5). If the authorities in the ward's home State were subsequently to appoint a guardian, or its national diplomatic or consular representatives, the authority of the national guardian was to prevail over the local appointee.[132] The grounds and the periods for which a guardian was appointed were governed by the ward's national law (Article 5). The local authorities of the ward's residence were empowered to take the necessary interim measures.[133] The guardian's powers extended not only to the ward's person but also to his property at home and abroad, unless the *lex situs* of immovables provided otherwise (Article 7).

---

[129] Lewald, *op. cit. supra* n. 1, at p. 458.

[130] Convention, Art. 9; at the time when the petition is brought: Kahn, *op. cit. supra* n. 75, at p. 417, cf. Art. 4 with Art. 9. Consequently a change of nationality by one of the parties is irrelevant: *idem*, p. 425.

[131] *Actes 1894*, pp. 19, 121; Final Protocol, p. 3; Convention 12 June 1902 (*supra* n. 34); cf. Inst. dr. int. (Hamburg) (1891) 11 Ann. 87, 107 and *idem* (1895) 15; Lewald, *op. cit. supra* n. 1, at p. 472; Travers Rev. dr. int. privé (1912) 8 R.D.I.P. 140; Buzzati, *op. cit. supra* n. 75, at p. 290; Lehr (1889) 21 Rev. dr. int. leg. comp. 140; for the present position see XIV Conference, *Actes 1982*, t.2, p. 29.

[132] Art. 4, but the time of the cessation of the local appointment was to be governed by the law of the minor's habitual residence: Art. 4(3); *Fodero* v. *Massac*, Bordeaux, 6 July 1909, 30 May 1910 Rev. dr. int. privé (1910) 6 R.D.I.P. 884.

[133] Art. 6. For the practice see Lewald, *op. cit. supra* n. 1, at p. 292.

When the matter came up again in 1900[134] only formal changes were introduced. Articles 2, 3 and 4(3) were reformulated. A new Article 9 made it clear that while in general the Convention applied only to minors, nationals of other contracting States having their *habitual residence* in another State, any necessary protective measures could be taken even in the absence of a habitual residence.

E. Guardianship of Adults

Guardianship of adults[135] also figured in the programme of the conferences.[136] Its organisation followed the course adopted by the Convention on the Guardianship of Minors, limited, however, by the need to pay special regard to the personal law of the ward, having regard to the far-reaching and permanent effect of the measure. Consequently, the national law of the adult concerned applied in principle,[137] subject only to special exceptions (Article 1), and the local authorities were to exercise exclusive jurisdiction in accordance with the *lex patriae* (Article 2). The authorities of contracting States where an adult national of another contracting party was present were enabled to take provisional measures of which notice was to be given to the home State. Subsequent action by the latter State was to terminate any local measures (Article 3). If the | alien resided habitually in another contracting State, the local authorities were to notify the home State with the request to take action (Articles 4 and 5) while staying proceedings themselves (Article 6). Upon the failure of the home State to act, the State of the habitual residence was to initiate proceedings in its own courts, taking into account the reasons given by the adult's national authorities for not taking action (Article 6). In these circumstances the *locus standi* of petitioners for a guardianship order and the causes for making a decree appointing a guardian for an adult had to be recognised both by the national law of the adult and by the law of his habitual residence, but the procedure was to be that of the *lex fori* (Article 7). Such an appointment could be replaced by one made by the

---

[134] *Actes 1900*, pp. 103, 145, 199; Final Protocol, p. 242.

[135] 17 July 1905 (*supra* n. 36). For the categories of guardianship of adults see Art. 13 of the Convention.

[136] *Actes 1893*, p. 11; *1900*, p. 199; *1904*, pp. 17, 27–54 (report); 218 (text). Lewald, *op. cit. supra* n. 1, at p. 478; Inst. dr. int. (Geneva) (1892) 12 Ann. 71, 75; (Paris) (1894) 13 Ann. 261; (Cambridge) (1895) 14 Ann. 146.

[137] A change of nationality after a decree instituting a guardianship affects the latter – Lewald, *idem*, p. 481 – but such a situation is unlikely to arise in practice, except for prodigals: Trib. civ. Seine 11 Nov. 1905 (1906) Clunet 145; 31 Dec. 1910 (1911) Clunet 889; 6 May 1911 (1912) Clunet 503.

authorities of the adult's home State (Article 10). Similarly, the authorities of both countries could terminate the guardianship, those of the home State according to the *lex patriae* and those of the adult's habitual residence elsewhere by applying either the adult's *lex patriae* or their own law (Article 11). If the proceedings were to take place in the country of the adult's habitual residence, the administration of the wardship and the effect of its creation were to be governed by the law of the ward's residence, but any rule of the ward's *lex patriae* conferring guardianship on a specific person was to be respected as far as possible (Article 8(1), (2)), and immovables remained subject to their *lex situs*, if it provided a special regime for land (Article 12). A decision appointing a guardian in accordance with the Convention was to be recognised elsewhere, without exception (Article 9(1)). Although this provision speaks only of the recognition of the effects of the decree on the ward's capacity and guardianship, it also extended to his property (Article 8(1)), except immovables governed by Article 12, mentioned earlier. However, local requirements of publicity could be extended to proceedings abroad (Article 8(2)) – a provision which seems to have sanctioned the unilateral extension of domestic law anticipating the recognition of "self-limiting" rules of law (*règles d'application immédiate*) today.

Like the other conventions drafted during this period, the Guardianship of Adults Convention sought to reconcile measures taken by contracting States by maintaining them as far as possible.

IV. Activities between the Wars

A. Foreign Judgments

When the V Conference in 1925 considered a draft Convention on the Recognition and Enforcement of Foreign Judgments[138] the debates covered a broad range of problems which arise under this head.[139] Was | the form of a general convention or of a model treaty to be adopted?[140] Should an *exequatur* be required? Should only personal judgments be included or also property, and even matrimonial causes? Was the jurisdiction direct or indirect? Which law should serve to characterise the connecting factors? Could a *prorogatio fori* be tacit? What was the test of jurisdiction for legal entities?

---

[138] *Actes 1926*, pp. 97 *et seq.*; 161, 180, 183 (text).

[139] *Idem*, pp. 99, 101, 104–107, 109–115, 117, 119–120, 124–125, 127–130, 133–135, 139, 142, 144–145, 148, 168, 172.

[140] *Idem*, pp. 98, 127, 151, 156: Final Protocol, p. 345 (text). See also Inst. dr. int. (Vienna) (1924) 31 Ann. 127, 180; also (Brussels) (1923) 30 Ann. 393.

Was domicile to be the single test of jurisdiction for individuals or were additional tests to be accepted? Was exclusive jurisdiction to form an exception? Was the exception of public policy to be included and defined? What were the procedural requirements of notice, service, time and representation? Were provisions on default judgments and fraud necessary, and against a review on the merits? Was *res judicata* or enforceability required? What law governed the *exequatur* procedure? What was the effect of *lis alibi pendens*? Were protective measures and arbitral awards as well as *actes authentiques* to be covered?

The broad range open for discussion, prepared as for the other topics before the conference by a tentative draft and a well-thought-out questionnaire, only resulted in a short draft convention.

Judgments in civil and commercial matters were to be recognised unless the rules of the international jurisdiction of courts of the requested State excluded them, if the decisions were not contrary to the latter's public policy or public law, had the force of *res judicata* and did not contravene other treaty obligations between the contracting States (Article 1). An *exequatur* was required (Article 2). Arbitral awards, and settlements in face of the court, if enjoying the force of judgments in the country of origin, were also to be enforceable (Article 4). Article 3 dealt with the necessary documentation.

Given the extensive preparation and the length of the debates, it is surprising that the draft convention confined itself to the barest minimum and, in effect, left the test of recognising the jurisdiction of the original court in the hands of the requested court, thus perpetuating the status quo by a consensual formula. The same applies to the admission of the exception of public policy, which previous conferences had attempted to ban from the operation of the treaties, while maintaining the force of imperative laws (appearing as public laws in the present draft convention). The answer must be that the draft of 1925 sought to rely on the principles alone which had found the approval of the majority of participants, either out of conviction or as a concession, and had not attempted to take into account and settle, let alone to co-ordinate, the many problems set out above. In their absence the Convention, taken as a general|treaty, was too vague to attract signatures; as a model convention it added little to the existing bilateral conventions in force at the time.[141]

---

[141] France-Switzerland 15 June 1869 (1869) 139 C.T.S. 329; France-Belgium 8 July 1899 (1898–99) 187 C.T.S. 378; Belgium-Netherlands 28 Mar. 1925, 93 L.N.T.S. 431; see also Switzerland – Germany 2 Nov. 1929, 109 L.N.T.S. 273, France-Italy 3 June 1930, 153 L.N.T.S. 135.

B. Bankruptcy

When the subject of bankruptcy was taken up by the II Conference in 1894,[142] it had previously been discussed by two other bodies,[143] and had formed part of one treaty in Europe,[144] soon to be followed by another.[145] Unlike the other conventions before the Conference, which were concerned with choice of law, this draft concerned primarily jurisdiction, and choice of law only indirectly. However, at its final attempt the Conference did not formulate principles of jurisdiction of its own. Instead, jurisdiction to entertain bankruptcy proceedings was to be determined by the law of the court seised of the application (Articles 1, 3(a)). A bankruptcy order was not to be automatically effective abroad; instead, in order to be recognised abroad, it was to be subject to *exequatur* proceedings which controlled whether the order had been made by a court having jurisdiction as envisaged by the Convention (Article 3(b)), i.e. by a court which was competent according to its own law, was executory and not limited to the assets of a branch. The order was thus treated like a foreign judgment, but the procedure of recognition and enforcement was unusual in as much as the requested court had to follow the jurisdictional provisions of the original court. By failing to establish jurisdictional criteria of its own (direct jurisdiction) or to draw up the criteria compliance with which would have obliged to recognise and enforce foreign orders (indirect jurisdiction) the Conference sanctioned a multitude of proceedings with equal effect.

Application for an *exequatur* was to be made by the person appointed by the bankruptcy court, by any interested person or by letters rogatory (Article 4). The effects of the bankruptcy order upon the debtor, the powers of the administrator, the form of the proceedings including the|proof of claims, any compositions with creditors and the distribution of the assets were to be governed by the law of the court seised of the application for an *exequatur* (Article 5), but property rights including preferences were subject to the *lex situs* (Article 6). A foreign bankruptcy order accompanied by an *exequatur* was to prevail over a second order similarly rendered enforceable (Article 7), but the draft convention appears to have omitted to regulate the order of concurrent bankruptcy proceedings in the country where the *exequatur* is sought.

---

[142] *Actes 1894*, pp. 59–66; Final Protocol, pp. 6–7.
[143] Italian Law Conference, Turin, 1860, *Actes 1894*, p. 63; Inst. dr. int. (Paris) (1894–95) 13 Ann. 266, 279 – see also (Brussels) (1902) 19 Ann. 277, 300; (Cristiania) (1912) 25 Ann. 433, 462.
[144] Franco-Swiss Treaty, *supra* n. 141, Arts. 6–9.
[145] Franco-Belgian Treaty, *supra* n. 141, Art. 8, and Lipstein in I. F. Fletcher (Ed.), *Cross-Border Insolvency* (1990), p. 223.

By opening the way to several proceedings, the Conference rejected the unity of bankruptcy; by sanctioning the priority of a bankruptcy order accompanied by an *exequatur* it accorded restricted universality.

In its revision in 1900[146] the III Conference came out expressly in favour of the unity of bankruptcy by conferring exclusive jurisdiction on the courts of the country where the debtor had his principal establishment and, as regards companies (in a broad sense) where they had their seat (Article 1). It established also that the Convention was not limited to the insolvency of merchants (Article 13), while the earlier draft had left this matter to the contracting States.[147] A novel element was introduced by stating specifically, in Article 2, that public enterprises licensed by the State or a public authority were not included in the Convention, as well as enterprises subject to special legislative or administrative measures taken in the interest of creditors. The administrator was to have a *locus standi* to take protective measures immediately upon his appointment, while enforcement of the bankruptcy order remained subject to an *exequatur* (Article 5). The law governing the bankruptcy was also to determine the preferential status of creditors, but proprietary rights and preferences in respect of movables and immovables were to be governed by the *lex situs* (Article 9), and jurisdiction in this respect was to be exercised by the courts of the *situs* (Article 11). By Article 12 the law governing the bankruptcy was also to apply to subsequent compositions.

An attempt was made thereby to secure both unity and universality of bankruptcy. It covered branches elsewhere and avoided concurrent proceedings.

A further revision by the IV Conference in 1904,[148] prepared on the pessimistic assumption that for the time being the text would serve only as a model for bilateral agreements,[149] did not affect its substance in important respects.[150] Foreign creditors were to enjoy equal status (Article 5).

| When the Hague Conference resumed its sessions in 1925 the Draft Convention on Bankruptcy was the first item on the agenda.[151] Its extension to non-merchants was maintained, except in so far as the requested State entered a reservation limiting the Convention to merchants.[152] In the latter

---

[146] *Actes 1900*, pp. 147, 148, 151.

[147] *Actes 1894*, pp. 59–60.

[148] *Actes 1904*, pp. 55–59 (report), 191–192 (text); Final Protocol, pp. 222, 9.

[149] *Actes 1904*, p. 56.

[150] Arts. 4–11, i.e. bankruptcy of branches, appointment and power of liquidators, admission of creditors, compositions, distribution of assets, protective measures abroad and enforcement measures, order of preferences, maintenance of public services.

[151] *Actes 1925*, pp. 1 *et seq.*, 91 (text).

[152] *Idem*, pp. 29–39, 341 (Final Protocol); Convention, Art. 1(2).

case the test to be applied was to be furnished by the law of the requested State.[153] Faced with a choice whether to establish direct or indirect jurisdiction the V Conference appears to have opted for the latter.[154] It relied on the principal industrial or commercial establishment of the debtor and, in default of this, his domicile; in the case of a company or association this was the statutory seat, unless established fraudulently or fictitiously (Article 2). If jurisdiction was recognised by the Court in another Contracting State as having been exercised properly, the proceedings became exclusive,[155] subject to the necessary measures of publicity in the recognising country,[156] but the exclusivity remained relative and created a relative unity of bankruptcy only and no universality, seeing that Article 3 appeared to admit the existence of further bankruptcy proceedings in other contracting States and their recognition elsewhere. It reflects the view of the IV Conference in 1904 that the draft was to serve only as a model treaty.[157]

As in previous drafts the liquidator was accorded automatically a *locus standi* and the power to take protective action,[158] an *exequatur* was required for the sale of immovables and all measures of enforcement and the conditions for granting an *exequatur* were set out in Article 5 in greater detail than in 1904. The same principles applied to the effect of a bankruptcy upon the transactions of the debtor, subject to a power of reservation by other States in respect of assets situated in their territory.[159] As in previous drafts, preferential rights in movables and immovables were subject to the *lex situs* (Articles 10(1), 12(2)), but the new draft contained an interesting reference to the possibility of a *conflit mobile,* and incidental questions of title to these assets remained subject to the ordinary rules of the conflict of laws (Article 12(1)).

The usual provisions concerning compositions with creditors (Article 7) and the equal treatment of foreign creditors (Article 9) completed the |Convention, which was altogether more detailed and sophisticated than its predecessors.

The British delegation explained that for a variety of reasons, such as the doctrine of relation back, it could not accept the Convention, but favoured a

---

[153] Art. 1(3); *Actes 1925*, p. 67.

[154] *Idem*, pp. 39–41, 43.

[155] Art. 4, but only in respect of the country where the jurisdiction of the original court had been recognised: Art. 4(1).

[156] Art. 8; following the Dutch-Belgian Treaty, *supra* n. 141, Art. 22.

[157] See *Actes 1925*, pp. 60, 69 where the question of universal effect was raised but not finally decided; also whether the Convention included *"liquidation judiciaire"* (formerly French Law of 4 Mar. 1889), now *"Redressement Judiciaire"* (Law 85–98 of 25 Jan. 1985).

[158] Art. 4(1), (2) following Dutch-Belgian Treaty, *supra* n. 141, Art. 21(2).

[159] Art. 6, including those governed by maritime law: Art. 14; in a conflict between the law governing the bankruptcy and the *lex situs* the former was to prevail: see Art. 13.

solution whereby a bankruptcy in one country should be accepted as the basis of an ancillary bankruptcy in another.[160]

The draft of 1925 owed its clear and straightforward formulation to the excellent preparatory work: a tentative draft and a well-thought-out questionnaire angled on the individual proposals of the tentative draft. The failure to lead to a multilateral agreement owes much to the absence of readiness of some countries to accept either unity or universality of bankruptcies, whether on a general or a bilateral basis.

The Council of Europe prepared a draft convention[161] accepting the unity and controlled universality of bankruptcy in an attempt to coordinate proceedings in several countries, coupled with a detailed set of rules dealing with jurisdiction *ratione personae* and *materiae*, the effects of a bankruptcy, the powers of the liquidator, including set-offs, recovery of property, contracts, preferential claims, the capacity of the debtor, recognition of bankruptcy orders, especially as regards concurrent bankruptcies, their enforcement within the framework of the Brussels Convention and the power of the European Court to interpret the Convention. The Draft of an EC Convention still lies on the table.[162]

The highly technical and minute regulation presented by the draft (as explained in an attached commentary) appears to have deterred acceptance hitherto.

C. Succession

Succession[163] both testamentary and intestate, as well as (originally) *donationes mortis causa*, but not *"institutions contractuelles"*,[164] were the object of a series of drafts beginning in 1893[165] and coming to a temporary end in 1904 with an agreement signed on 17 July 1904, but not ratified by any signatory. The national law of the deceased was to apply[166] and not the law of the last domicile. No distinction was to be made between | intestate succession and

---

[160] Cf. Bankruptcy Act 1914, ss. 121, 122; Insolvency Act 1985, s. 213.

[161] European Convention on certain International Aspects of Bankruptcy of 5 June 1990, T.S. 136.

[162] E.C. Bull., Suppl.2/83.

[163] *Supra* n. 37. See Kahn, *op. cit. supra* n. 75, at p. 303; Buzzati, *op. cit. supra* n. 75, at p. 292; Inst. dr. int. (Oxford) (1880) 6 Ann. 53, 57. Asser in *idem* (1902) 19 Ann. 343.

[164] *Erbverträge*; contractual succession arrangements; Kahn, *idem*, p. 195.

[165] *Actes 1893*, pp. 29, 73–79; Final Protocol, p. 3.

[166] This was the law at the time of his death, even if he had the capacity at the time of making the will according to what was then his national law, but not at the time of his death. An exception was admitted if death occurred in a third State: Convention, Art. 8(2); Kahn, *op. cit. supra* n. 75, at p. 297; *Actes 1900*, Art. 11(2); *1904*, Art. 9(2).

wills.[167] By disregarding altogether the *lex situs* in so far as immovables were concerned, the draft adopted the unity of succession.[168] The accompanying report admitted that the *lex loci actus* governs the division of the estate, and the *lex situs* the vesting of interests, while the *locus standi* of compulsory heirs could raise a preliminary question (not expressed in these terms at that time).[169]

The *lex loci actus* was to govern the form of wills (Article 3(1)), but if the national law of the deceased required a particular form in order to comply with what were substantive conditions of the national law (characterised as *"formes substantielles"*, the national law was to prevail.[170] In addition, wills made in accordance with the deceased's national law before a diplomatic or consular representative were to be valid in form.

The question was faced how to reconcile the application of the *lex patriae* with the division of a State into separate legal units. Under the influence of Swiss and US practice, the application of the law of the district to which the deceased belonged was recommended.[171]

In abstaining from making provision for the reservation of public policy, the Conference suggested that a foreign *lex patriae* could be disregarded having regard to the public law and the social interest of the forum.[172] The question of jurisdiction involving a succession of a foreign national, the preservation of the estate and its collection and division was reserved for future treaties.[173]

The Conference of 1894 amplified the draft considerably. It amended the general rule governing form (1893 draft Article 3(1)) by adding that compliance with the formalities required by the *lex patriae*, if constituting a substantive condition, was also admissible,[174] and reversed its previous view that capacity to make a will was governed exclusively by the *lex patriae* at the time of the testator's death by referring alternatively to the law at the time of making the will.[175] Restrictions, whether absolute or within certain limits, on the power to dispose in favour of particular persons (*incapacités relatives*) were also to be governed by the testator's *lex patriae*.[176] The report shows

---

[167] Convention, Arts. 1, 2; Kahn, *idem*, p. 192.

[168] The principle of scission between the *lex domicilii* and the *lex situs* was described as "out of date": *Actes 1893*, p. 75 but see Kahn, *idem*, pp. 184 *et seq.*

[169] *Actes 1893*, p. 74; *1894*, p. 126(3), Kahn, *idem*, p. 193.

[170] Art. 3(2); Kahn, *idem*, p. 218; Buzzati, *op. cit. supra* n. 75, at p. 294.

[171] *Actes 1893*, p. 75.

[172] *Actes 1893*, Preamble, but see *1894*, Final Protocol, Art. 11 which contained a much more extensive catalogue.

[173] *Actes 1893*, pp. 77–79 (subsequently *1900* draft Art. 8), *1900*, pp. 121–122.

[174] *Actes 1894*, Final Protocol, Art. 3(2); Kahn, *op. cit. supra* n. 75, at p. 224 referring to Art. 992 of the Dutch Civil Code with lit. and further examples, *idem*, p. 228.

[175] *Idem*, Art. 4; see generally Kahn, *idem*, pp. 206, 242 *et seq.*; now Convention, Art. 5.

[176] Convention, Art. 5.

that this provision was aimed at gifts or legacies, e.g. to the testator's medical or spiritual advisers or the ward's | guardian.[177] The capacity of statutory beneficiaries, legatees and donees was to be governed by their national law.[178] The declaration of heirs limiting their liability for the debts of the estate or renouncing upon it was to be governed as to form by the law of the place where the succession was opened in order to protect third parties.[179] It was also recognised that immovables are subject to the *lex situs*, at least as regards formalities and publicity of transfer and in respect of rights of third parties.[180] The thorny problem of the civil law how to control the division of an estate between the beneficiaries (heirs) was to be governed, in the absence of an agreement between them, as to form by the *lex loci actus* and otherwise by the *lex patriae* of the deceased.[181]

The famous problem in civil law countries as to whether *bona vacantia* devolve upon the State of the *situs* exercising a *jus regale* or upon that of the deceased's nationality was solved in favour of the *jus regale*.[182] Anxious to avoid adopting the broad safety valve of public policy, the draft permitted the forum to apply its own law on what was believed to be more specific grounds to the effect that the public law of the forum or its rules on substitution, the capacity of public institutions, the liberty and equality of inheritances, the exclusion of beneficiaries on moral grounds, the unity of the succession or the rights of illegitimate children were concerned.[183]

Subject to these exceptions and the submission of immovables to the formalities of the *lex situs* the unity of succession was maintained.

The revision of the Draft Convention in 1900 was more formal than substantive.[184] The principle of unity of succession was rendered more pre-

---

[177] *Actes 1894*, p. 126(6); for a comment see Kahn, *op. cit. supra* n. 75, at pp. 199, 208 *et seq.*; also teachers, notaries, witnesses to a will.

[178] Art. 6, *Actes 1894*, p. 129; Kahn, *idem*, pp. 214, omitted by the draft of 1900, 214–215, 287 on the ground that this does not concern a question of succession but of general capacity, except the capacity of an unborn child. But note that in the case of a will a question of interpretation may be involved: *Re Schnapper* [1928] Ch. 42.

[179] *Actes 1894*, p. 126(7); Final Protocol, Art. 7.

[180] Final Protocol, Art. 8. Kahn, *op. cit. supra* n. 75, at p. 251; now Art. 6.

[181] *Actes 1894*, pp. 126–127; Final Protocol, Art. 9.

[182] *Idem*, p. 127 cf. *1904*, p. 131; Art. 9; for this problem see *Re Maldonado* 1954 P. 223 on the one hand and *Re Barnett's Trusts* [1902] 1 Ch. 847 on the other hand; Lipstein (1954) C.L.J. 22.

[183] *Actes 1894*, pp. 127–128; Final Protocol, Art. 11, relations. Today such provisions can be regarded as particular rules of public policy, anticipated by Kahn, *op. cit. supra* n. 75, at pp. 278, 282. Cf. the watered-down form in the Draft Convention on the Effects of Marriage, *Actes 1900*, p. 231, Final Protocol, Art. 7(1); infringement of imperative or prohibitive laws establishing or guaranteeing a social right or interest expressly applicable to the matrimonial property regime of aliens.

[184] *Actes 1900*, p. 244, Final Protocol; see also pp. 119 (report), 155, 262 (text).

cise.[185] At the same time it was relaxed in favour of laws of the forum which were of an express mandatory or prohibitive nature safeguarding | social rights or interests and of the *lex situs* protecting the integrity of rural estates as part of a succession.[186] By seeking to define the range of exclusionary laws, a reference to public policy was avoided again, but the attempt to obtain a list of such laws from each contracting State proved impracticable in the end.

A new provision amplified testamentary capacity by ensuring its retention on a change of nationality.[187] No preference was to be accorded to beneficiaries on the grounds of their citizenship of a contracting State.[188]

In 1904[189] the proposals in previous drafts relating to the incapacity to benefit certain persons, the capacity to take and the capacity to make a will, the manner and substance of the division of the estate, renunciation, limitation of liability and *bona vacantia* were omitted.[190] The range of the *lex patriae* was to include the determination of the share of beneficiaries, the duty to bring gifts and debts into hotchpot and the amount of the statutory portion as well as the essential validity of wills. The broad question as to the law governing the administration of wills was not resolved[191] and the contracting States retained their freedom to apply their own law to the separation of estates, the *beneficium inventarii*, renunciation and the liability of the beneficiaries (heirs) towards third parties (Article 1). The State where the succession was opened was to take protective measures unless the diplomatic or consular representatives had taken action by virtue of special agreements.[192] The right of *prélèvement* was restored in a limited form (Article 7(2)) in order to protect against discrimination on the ground of nationality but not for the purpose of balancing differences in the laws of inheritance.

By applying the *lex situs* to the exercise of a State to appropriate *bona vacantia*, the recognition of the *jus regale* was affirmed (Article 2). If the *lex patriae* of a testator required nationals abroad to observe certain formalities on pain of nullity, other contracting States could treat compliance with the

---

[185] Art. 1; the right of *prélèvement* was thereby excluded: Kahn, *op. cit. supra* n. 75, at pp. 289, 296; see Art. 7.

[186] Draft Convention, Art. 6(1), (2); Convention, 17 July 1904, Art. 6(3). Member States were to communicate a list of such laws to other contracting States: Art. 6(3). Kahn, *idem*, pp. 251, 279 *et seq.*; Buzzati, *op. cit. supra* n. 75, at pp. 269, 295; Offerhaus (1959) 16 A.S.D.I. 40; Makarov, op. *cit. supra* n. 91, at pp. 303, 307.

[187] Supplementing Art. 4(2) of the Draft Convention; Kahn, *idem*, pp. 200 *et seq.*

[188] Now Convention, Art. 7.

[189] *Actes 1904*, pp. 119 (report), 135 (text), 212 (Final Protocol); Missir (1906) 2 R.D.I.P. 644.

[190] 1894 draft Art. 3; 1900 draft Art. 5; Kahn, *op. cit. supra* n. 75, at p. 199 and see also pp. 283, 285 (esp.).

[191] See *supra* n. 173; Kahn, *idem*, p. 294.

[192] Convention, Art. 9; *Actes 1900*, Art. 5; Kahn, *idem*, p. 296, n. 170.

lex loci actus as sufficient[193] and the provisions on the | form of wills were extended to their revocation (Article 4). Most remarkable was the concession to the law of the domicile as a potential law to govern the succession. Foreshadowed by the 1900 draft (Article 11(2)) it was now made subject to bilateral arrangements (Article 9).

Although signed by seven States it was never ratified. The concentration on the national law and not on that of the domicile, the limited regard for the *lex situs*, the latitude given to the *lex fori* in all matters of the administration of estates, may have contributed to this lack of enthusiasm. Much further debate was needed.

In 1925, after a long and interesting discussion the V Conference produced a tentative draft[194] which differed somewhat from the Draft Convention of 17 July 1904. However, in the end it reverted to the text of 1905 with a few alterations (new Articles 2 and 3) and a rearrangement of the order of the articles. The Conference did so, notwithstanding the fact that a series of difficult problems had arisen; the unity of the succession by relying on the *lex patriae* had been criticised by those who wished to apply the *lex domicilii* alone, those whose law subjected successions to different laws for movables and immovables, and by those who regretted the absence of a rule on capacity, of more specific rules on *prélèvement*, the ability of corporations to take, and contractual arrangements between living persons instituting one contracting party heir on the death of the other.[195]

New proposals for the regulation of jurisdiction in succession cases were referred to a future conference.

On the other hand, the following amendments must be noted. The area in which the *lex patriae* was to apply was defined (Article 1). It covered the determination of the beneficiaries, their ranking, their shares, the duty to bring into hotchpot, the free part and the reserved or statutory portion. The duty of beneficiaries to bring into hotchpot any previous gifts by the deceased was declared (by Article 2) to be governed by the *lex patriae* of the *de cuius* at the time when the gift was made and not by that at the time of his death, in order to protect legitimate expectations.

More importantly, the V Conference in 1925 abandoned the approach adopted hitherto by the Hague Conferences which avoided the inclusion of a general clause protecting the public policy of other contracting States by inserting specific provision safeguarding social interests, such as laws regulating the regime of rural property and imperative or prohibitive laws to be

---

[193] Art. 3; Kahn, *idem*, pp. 236 *et seq.* See now the Convention on the Conflict of Laws relating to the Form of Testamentary Dispositions of 5 Oct. 1966, Art. 5.

[194] *Actes 1925*, pp. 197–204; report 277, text 283.

[195] *Idem*, pp. 212, 216 (now Art. 1(3)), 222, 230.

enumerated in lists to be communicated to other contracting States.[196] Instead, the Conference declared itself in favour of a general clause introducing a novel style which permitted courts to disregard a rule | of the *lex patriae* which was "manifestly incompatible"[197] with the law of the *lex fori*.

The new proposals for the regulation of jurisdiction on matters of succession were referred to the next conference. In view of the basic differences between the laws of the contracting States it is not surprising that the Convention remained a tentative one only.

In 1928 the VI Conference agreed on principles of jurisdiction to be added to the draft of 1925 on choice of law but the differences in the legal systems involved resulted in solutions based on compromises. Jurisdiction in contentious matters was entrusted to the courts of the State of which the deceased was a national *or* where he was domiciled. Both were to have exclusive jurisdiction, at the choice of the parties, if they agreed, or if the beneficiaries other than specific legatees were either all nationals of the State of the courts or domiciled there or if immovables or a business were located in that State.[198] For all other matters the jurisdiction of the courts of the deceased's nationality or domicile was also accepted. In a case of concurrent jurisdiction, that seised first was to oust the other.[199] Proceedings concerning succession to assets subject to a specific legal regime or where the *lex situs* was opposed on grounds of public policy to the regulation of the problems of succession covered by the choice of law provisions of Article 1[200] were to be subject to the *lex situs*. Decisions by these courts were to be recognised elsewhere subject to the usual safeguards.[201] Non-contentious jurisdiction was to be exercised exclusively by the national courts of the deceased on the same conditions,[202] in so far as this jurisdiction concerned the determination of the heirs, including the issue of certificates to this-effect and any notifications, any declarations challenging a will or contract of inheritance, the appointment and control of executors, the acceptance or rejection of a succession and distribution by agreement. Moreover, the courts where the as-

---

[196] Art. 6(1), *Actes 1904*, p. 213; *1925*, p. 354.

[197] Art. 3, *Actes 1925*, pp. 263, 283, replacing an earlier version which required that the foreign law must be "absolutely incompatible": *idem* (Art. 6), pp. 261, 262; Lewald (1928) R.D.I.P. 150; Offerhaus, *op. cit. supra* n. 186, at p. 41, Makarov, *op. cit. supra* n. 91, at pp. 301, 315; Plaisant, *Les règles de droit international dans les traités* (1946), pp. 90, 107 *et seq.*

[198] *Actes 1928*, pp. 100, 406; Art. 8(1).

[199] *Idem*, pp. 104, 407; Art. 8(3).

[200] *Idem*, pp. 100, 407; Art. 9.

[201] *Idem*, pp. 101, 407; Art. 10: existence of jurisdiction under the Convention, not contrary to the public policy or public law of the recognising court, *res judicata*, proper service, which included observation of the rules of the country other than that of the original court or of relevant treaties, if the defendant was not domiciled there.

[202] *Idem*, pp. 102, 407, 408, Arts. 12, 13.

sets were situated became the object of a third alternative jurisdictional choice.[203]

Further provisions dealt with the power of the country of the *situs* to take the necessary protective measures[204] and with the restriction of the | Convention in substance and in jurisdictional matters to the succession of nationals of contracting States or (for the first time) of stateless persons habitually resident there, and of dual nationals.[205] A reservation was included in favour of bilateral treaties.[206]

In view of the basic differences between the laws of the contracting States, in particular in exercising non-contentious jurisdiction,[207] it is not surprising that the Convention was not adopted by the participants and that another 60 years had to pass before satisfactory compromises could be found.[208]

D. Civil Procedure

The first draft Convention on Civil Procedure[209] was concerned only with the service of documents and letters rogatory.[210] Service of documents was to be effected between the authorities of the respective countries.[211] By Article 4, however, direct service by post or by the authorities of the requested country or by the diplomatic or consular representatives of the requesting State was not excluded, if permitted by the law of the requested State. The authorities in the requested State could refuse to carry out the service only if it affected its own sovereignty (Article 2). This formulation was chosen as being more precise than "public policy".[212]

---

[203] *Ibid.*

[204] *Idem*, pp. 102, 407, Art. 11.

[205] *Idem*, pp. 102, 408, Art. 15.

[206] *Idem*, pp. 103, 409, Art. 16.

[207] E.g. see *idem*, pp. 35 (Austrian *Einantwortung* in a German court); 84 (German declaration of challenging a will in a French court) or a French or Italian voluntary division of assets in Germany.

[208] See *infra*: Convention of 1 Aug. 1989.

[209] *Supra* n. 31; *Actes 1893*, pp. 63–68; Final Protocol, p. 2; cf. Inst. dr. int. (1877) 1 Ann. 125. Lewald, *op. cit. supra* n. 1, at p. 459; Heinsheimer, *op. cit. supra* n. 1, at pp. 487–491; Audinet (1905) 1 R.D.I.P. 208, 781; (1909) 5 R.D.I.P. 373.

[210] The term *"actes et documents"* is open to various interpretations including that of setting a time limit in contract according to French law: *Actes 1893*, p. 56.

[211] Art. 1. Following the Franco-Swiss Treaty, *supra* n. 141, Art. 20; abrogated 3 Feb. 1992 (1992) Rev, crit. d.i.p. 346 and the Franco-Baden Treaty of 16 Apr. 1846, Art. 5 (1845–1846) 99 C.T.S. 417. The Conference believed that the practice of service upon the Public Prosecutor's office at the court of the plaintiff's domicile was unsatisfactory: *Actes 1893*, pp. 63–65.

[212] See *Actes 1894*, pp. 52, 123, 127.

Letters rogatory were to be sent either through diplomatic channels or directly to the addressed authority (Article 3). The document had to emanate clearly from the requesting authority, had to fall within the jurisdiction of the requested authority or of another in the same State (Article 4) and, once again, had not to affect adversely the sovereignty of the requested State (Article 3). If incompetent, the requested authority was to inform the requesting authority immediately (Article 5).

| The law of the requested authority was to determine the form of execution of the request, but if the requesting authority demanded the observance of a special form not provided for by the local law, the request was to be followed, unless prohibited by the local law.

The draft was approved by the II Conference in 1894 with slight amendments of an explanatory nature.[213] It was supplemented by two chapters dealing respectively with security for costs and legal assistance in the case of alien plaintiffs and interveners (Article 1). A judgment condemning them to pay costs and expenses was to be enforceable in the other contracting States (Article 2) subject only to the control of its authenticity and its character of *res judicata* (Article 3). Legal assistance was to be granted to members of contracting States in accordance with the *lex fori*, subject to detailed scrutiny.[214] Execution against the person was excluded against nationals of the member States except where the *lex fori* permitted it.[215] Although it was realised that this method of execution was no longer available in most member States two provisions of the Netherlands Code of Civil Procedure gave rise to this prohibition.[216] In this form it was signed on 14 November 1896. The Convention of 1896 was revised in 1904 and signed in 1905.[217] Some changes were formal only and others more technical.[218] Despite certain attempts to the contrary[219] the Convention remained limited to civil and commercial matters, and a rearranged sequence of the rules conceals only lightly their identity in substance.

At the invitation of the League of Nations the VI Conference considered

---

[213] *Idem*, p. 53, Final Protocol, p. 4.

[214] Final Protocol, p. 6; Arts. 2, 3.

[215] *Ibid; Actes 1894*, p. 99.

[216] *Ibid*; Arts. 585(10), 768.

[217] See *supra* n. 31 and text; *Actes 1904*, pp. 81–108, 149–154, 197–200 (report); Final Protocol 205.

[218] Arts. 1, 2 (now including old Art. 4): service of documents; Arts. 9, 12, 5 (letters rogatory); Arts. 18, 19 (*cautio judicatum solvi*); Art. 21 (legal assistance); Art. 24 (corporeal restraint); Art. 3 (service of documents, language); Art. 7 (costs); Art. 10 (letters rogatory, language); Arts. 28, 29 (*cautio judicatum solvi*) – technical.

[219] *Actes 1904*, p. 84; that administrative decisions should be included. The Conference report stressed that the subject matter and not the type of court pronouncing on it forms the criterion.

once more the question of legal assistance.[220] For this purpose the Conference could seek either to revise the original text of 1904, thereby running the danger that some of the signatories of that text would not adopt the revised version thus opening the way to two separate conventions, or to adopt a new convention open to all, including any signatories of the 1905 version, thus opening again the way to duplication. In the end a twofold solution was accepted. A new separate Convention on Legal Aid was formulated side by side with a supplementary convention to that of 1904. The latter merely formulated the innovations produced by the | text of the VI Conference in 1928 with a view to incorporation in the Convention of 1905.[221]

The new draft convention followed on the whole that of 1905.[222] The following innovations may be noted: no *cautio judicatum solvi* was to be required and, where permitted, aid for administrative proceedings was included,[223] the power of the requested authority to control the grant of legal aid was slightly enlarged,[224] and a new provision (Article 4) on the transmission of the necessary certificates was added.

E. Conclusions

The Civil Procedure Convention, being procedural and little concerned with choice of law, was the most successful of the Hague Conventions concluded before the First World War and survived to form the basis of later revisions. The conventions dealing with marriage, divorce and guardianship found less favour and some of their original signatories denounced them within a few years. The basic reasons, then as now, were to be found in the strict adherence to the *lex patriae* and the *lex domicilii* with little give and take, except possibly by way of *renvoi*, the disregard of the *lex situs*, especially when immovable property was concerned, and of the contractual aspects of matrimonial property combined with the trend to co-ordinate systems of choice of law rather than by allocating them their own sphere. The cumulation of laws made the dissolution of marriages difficult for the States allowing divorce; the inclusion in capacity to marry of the need to obtain the

---

[220] *Actes 1928*, pp. 171, 216 (tentative draft), 249 (report), 259 (text); 410 (text).

[221] *Idem*, p. 263; Art. 19 was supplemented by a reference to the recovery of costs and expenses; Art. 20 was extended to administrative proceedings; Art. 22 allowed further enquiries; Art. 22 bis reproduced a new Art. 4 of the 1928 draft on the transmission of papers; Art. 23 replaced the old Art. 23 by the new version of Art. 7 of the 1928 draft concerning the reimbursement of costs and expenses; a new Art. 23 bis extended legal aid to obtaining certificates of civil status registers.

[222] See e.g. Art. 2 = Art. 21; 5 = 10; 6 = 12; 7 = 23, but excepting costs of experts; Art. 8.

[223] Art. 1(2), (3), supplementing 1905, Art. 20.

[224] Art. 3(2), supplementing 1905, Art. 22.

consent of the military authorities supervising compulsory military service resulted in the breakdown of the Convention on the Conclusion of Marriages.[225] The Draft Conventions on Guardianship of Adults, Bankruptcy and on Succession never reached the treaty stage.

The Peace Treaties of 1919 only restored the application of the Civil Procedure and Guardianship Conventions between the former enemies while other conventions remained in force between Germany and her former allies and some were subsequently brought into force again bilaterally.

|In the years between the two world wars the Hague Conferences revised and amended the Bankruptcy and Succession Conventions and supplemented the section on legal aid of the Civil Procedure Convention and of the Convention on the Recognition and Enforcement of Foreign Judgments – without, however, concluding any binding agreements.[226] It also discussed the problems arising from statelessness and dual nationality and specifically the retention or recovery of her previous nationality by a married woman whose husband possessed another nationality, so as to enable her to obtain a divorce excluded by the husband's national law.[227]

The VI Conference decided for the first time in 1928 to direct its attention to commercial law by attempting to draft a Convention on Sale. In this enterprise it had been preceded and influenced[228] by two drafts elaborated respectively by the Institut de droit international[229] and the International Law Association.[230] While the first of these two drafts covered the law applicable to contracts in general and the other restricted itself to the law of sale only, they both offered free choice, the former – in its Article 1 – as an autonomous principle of private international law, the latter as a subsidiary free choice of law forming part of the *lex loci contractus*.[231] In the absence of such an expression of choice the Institut offered (in Articles 2 and 3) objec-

---

[225] Denounced by France, 12 Nov. 1913; (1914) Clunet 301; by Belgium, 1 Nov. 1918; (1914) Clunet 778; (1915) 792; (1914) R.D.I.P. 364; (1917) Clunet 179.

[226] *Actes 1925*, Res. (a) and (b); *1928*, pp. 405 *et seq.* The British delegation stated that having only participated in the deliberations on bankruptcy, the adoption of the principle of unity of bankruptcy and the enforceability of foreign bankruptcy orders ruled out any UK acceptance of the Convention.

[227] *Actes 1928*, pp. 162–167, amending the following Conventions: Conclusion of Marriage 1902, Art. 8; Effects of Marriage 1905, Arts. 1(1), 4(1), 5(1), 9 bis (stateless), 9 ter (dual nationality); Divorce 1902, Arts. 3 bis (stateless), 3 ter (dual nationality), 8 (change of nationality or cumulation), 9 end; Protocol (wife retaining or recovering her original nationality); Guardianship of Minors 1902, Arts. 1(2)–(4) (stateless, dual nationality), 4 bis (change of nationality), 8 bis (information), 9(3) (stateless); Guardianship of Adults 1905 (provisions equivalent to those for minors).

[228] *Actes 1928*, p. 267.

[229] Inst. dr. int. (Florence) (1908) 22 Ann. 55–121, 255–292 (text 289–292).

[230] ILA 34th Report, Vienna (1926), pp. 482–519, esp. 490, 509 (texts).

[231] ILA Preamble, para. 2, Art. 3.

tive criteria selected according to the nature of the various types of contracts, thus anticipating the test of characteristic performance subsequently developed by the Swiss courts, while the International Law Association adopted a concise system of objective criteria[232] based on the distinction between immovables and movables (Articles I.A and I.B) and anticipating to a certain extent Article 5 of the Rome Convention, but permitting parties to contract out by selecting another law. Other provisions served to determine the place of contracting, if the parties reside in different countries, the sphere of operation *ratione materiae* of the law applicable and characterisation.[233]

| Given a difference of basic approaches by the contracting States on the question whether free choice was an autonomous test or admitted only within the framework of a system of law ascertained objectively, the VI Conference was able to prepare only three alternative versions concerning the choice of law relating to the sale of movables.[234] They all reflect the principal concern of the participants, which was whether mandatory laws, and if so which, restrict the unfettered free choice of law. For this purpose two alternatives were put forward: either the mandatory laws of the law chosen by the parties or those of the *lex loci contractus* apply.

Today it is realised[235] that the mandatory laws for consideration are either those laws forming part of the objectively applicable legal system which cannot be derogated from by the parties[236] or laws of an absolutely binding character which claim to apply in the forum including possibly those of other legal systems to which the former defers[237] no matter what law governs the contract. Faced with the need to choose between the two alternatives, as the Conference saw them, it prepared drafts restricted to the sale of movables which, like the International Law Association's draft, distinguished between the usual international sale, governed by the vendor's law, and the exceptional situation where the buyer's law applies because the seller operates directly or indirectly in the buyer's country.[238] However, if the parties select another legal system their choice was to be accepted.[239] Drafts I and II limited

---

[232] *Idem*, para.1.

[233] Inst. dr. int., Arts. 4–6; ILA Preamble, para.3 and Art. 3.

[234] *Actes 1928*, pp. 267 *et seq.*; report 364; text 385.

[235] See e.g. (1977) 26 I.C.L.Q. 885, 886; Hay (1982) 30 A.J.Comp.L. (Suppl.) 129.

[236] See e.g. Rome Convention on the law applicable to Contractual Obligations of 19 June 1980, Art. 3(3).

[237] *Idem*, Art. 7(2), (1).

[238] *Actes 1928*, pp. 376 *et seq.* Arts. 1 and 2 of all drafts; for contract on stock or commodity exchanges see drafts I, Art. 4; II, Art. 3; III, Art. 3; for ships, I, Art. 2; II, Art. 7; III, Art. 7.

[239] Drafts I, Art. 3; II, Art. 5 but see III, Art. 5; for aspects of contract to be included see I, Arts. 5, 11; II, Arts. 4, 9; III,4 (rejection) – and to be excluded, see drafts I, Arts. 8 (public policy), 9 (capacity); II, Arts. 9, 10; III, Arts. 8–10.

free choice by the application of the mandatory rules of the legal system chosen – a self-evident conclusion; Draft III relied on those of the *lex fori*.[240] Since in reality the application of the mandatory rules of both these legal systems is inevitable, at least as far as absolutely binding rules of the *lex fori* are concerned, the Draft Convention thus detracted from rather than added anything to the practice of States in force.

While none of the drafts reached the stage where a convention could be envisaged they all paved the way for a new drive after the Second World War.

V. 1951 and After

When the Hague Conference resumed its deliberations after the Second | World War it devoted its attention to three branches of the law: family law and succession, commercial transactions and procedure.

A. Family Law

The Conventions of 1902 and 1905 dealing with marriage, divorce and the personal and proprietary relations between spouses had outlived their period. Reliance on the national law of the parties, especially on that of the husband, and the many concessions to particular State interests requiring corresponding options for contracting out[241] had deprived these Conventions of their usefulness.

1. Marriage

The Marriage Convention of 14 March 1978,[242] intended to supersede that of 12 June 1902 (Article 22), covers both the celebration of marriages and the recognition of their validity,[243] but a contracting State is free to subscribe to the latter provisions alone.[244] As before, the form of marriage is governed by the *lex loci celebrationis*, but this time the rule is exclusive.

The wording of Article 2, which refers to "the law" and not to the "internal law" of the place of celebration, indicates that *renvoi* is admitted.[245]

---

[240] See drafts II, Art. 5(4); III, Art. 5(4).

[241] See Marriage Convention 1902, Arts. 2 (last two paras.), 3(2), 5(2).

[242] XIII Session, *Actes et Documents* (1978), Vol.3, pp. 269 (text), 115 (tentative draft), 289 (report); Batiffol (1977) Rev. crit. d.i.p. 451, 467 *et seq.*; Dutoit (1978) Riv. dir. int. priv. proc. 449, 465.

[243] Parts I, Arts. 1–6 and II, Arts. 7–23.

[244] Art. 16; *Actes 1976*, p. 292(7).

[245] *Idem*, p. 259(14); this reproduces the English practice in *Taczanowska* v. *Taczanowski* [1957] P. 301.

Essential validity is determined by two alternative choice of law rules. The first[246] reproduces the rule in *Sottomayor* v. *De Barros (No.2)*[247] with the slight modification that one of the parties must be a national of, or habitually resident in, the country where the marriage is celebrated. Moreover, a reservation permits member States not to apply this rule if the other spouse is neither a national nor habitually resident in that country,[248] thus effectively leading to the application of the second alternative rule. This relies for each of the spouses on the application of the choice of law rules of the *lex loci celebrationis* excluding *renvoi.*[249]

| Unlike the Convention of 1902, which was limited to the recognition of the formal validity of a Convention marriage, the new Convention adopts a jurisdictional approach.[250] A marriage which complies with the formal and substantive requirements of the *lex loci celebrationis* including *renvoi* is to be recognised in the contracting States (Article 9) irrespective of whether the issue is raised directly or as a preliminary question.[251] The report suggests[252] that such recognition must be accorded to marriages concluded in any country and not only in a contracting State. Following an established practice, consular marriages are recognised only if the *lex loci celebrationis* allows them (Article 9(2)). Recognition can therefore be denied on the ground that either the *lex loci celebrationis* or its choice of law rules or the applicable law have not been properly observed, but a subsequent validation remedies the defect[253] and the release of a marriage certificate creates a rebuttable presumption of validity (Articles 10, 23). Specific provisions of a substantive character exclude altogether certain types of marriages[254] and enable States, at their discretion, to refuse recognition if one of the spouses was already married under the Convention,[255] if certain impediments (consanguinity, adoption) applied, if nonage had not been waived, if mental capacity was lacking or consent was not freely given.[256] The power of refusal is further strengthened by the usual public policy clause.

---

[246] Art. 3(1), criticised by Batiffol, *op. cit. supra* n. 242, at p. 471.

[247] (1879) 5 P.D. 94.

[248] Art. 6, *Actes 1976*, p. 297(18).

[249] Art. 3(2) following *Sottomayor* v. *De Barros (No.1)* (1877) 3 P.D. 1. However, Art. 5 excludes foreign law which is manifestly incompatible with local public policy.

[250] Cf. Batiffol, *op. cit. supra* n. 242, at pp. 467, 473.

[251] Art. 12(1) with a discretionary exception if the main question involves the law of a non-contracting State; *Actes 1976*, p. 306(25), but see the critique by Batiffol, *idem*, p. 479.

[252] *Actes 1976*, p. 298(20).

[253] Art. 9; Batiffol, *op. cit. supra* n. 242, at p. 474; note that Art. 9 speaks of the "law" and not the "internal law".

[254] Art. 8: on board ships or aircraft, by proxy, posthumous and informal marriages, thus excluding common law marriages and marriages by habit and repute. The Convention fails to deal with unions between members of the same sex, which are sanctioned in some countries, such as Denmark; *Actes 1976*, p. 293(8).

[255] I.e. Arts. 1–6; subject to a subsequent dissolution: Art. 11(2).

[256] Art. 11(1); Batiffol, *op. cit. supra* n. 242, at p. 475, points out that the wording of

By omitting any reference to the requirement of parental consent – which may raise problems of characterisation (form or substance)[257] – the Convention has not necessarily adopted the view that form is always involved[258] but has only excluded this aspect from the discretionary power to refuse recognition and has relegated it to an issue of validity. However, member States are free to apply rules more favourable to the recognition of foreign marriages.[259]

| Unlike the Convention of 1905,[260] but following that of 1902, the Convention of 1978 does not touch upon the personal effects of a marriage.

2. *Matrimonial property*

In preparing the draft treaty on the choice of law in matters of matrimonial property, the Conference was not only preceded by its own earlier Convention[261] but by a series of others[262] and by a comparative survey of national choice of law solutions.[263] Confronted by its own earlier version, which relied on the national law of the husband, with conflicting national regimes which relied respectively on the express or presumed intention of the parties, nationality, domicile and a division between movables and immovables, the XIII Conference in 1978[264] attempted a compromise. The result is a series of interlocking rules of great complexity[265] which do not lend themselves to an easy application and which may have achieved little more than a restatement of existing contradictory practices. It is not surprising that hitherto it has been ratified by only three States.[266]

The Convention aims at the unity and universality[267] of the law governing matrimonial property. It awards first place to free choice of law,[268] limited,

---

Art. 11(1) is misleading since Art. 9 invites a general review of the validity of the marriage, let alone Art. 14.

[257] E.g. *Simonin* v. *Malac* (1860) 2 Sw. & Tr. 67; *Ogden* v. *Ogden* [1908] P. 46; *De Massa* v. *De Massa* [1939] 2 All E.R. 150n; *Galene* v. *Galene* [1939] P. 237.

[258] But see *Actes 1976*, p. 305(24e).

[259] Art. 13; for the problems arising therefrom see Batiffol, *op. cit. supra* n. 242, at p. 480.

[260] Art. 1; cf. Inst. dr. int. (Grenada) (1956) 46 Ann. 362.

[261] *Supra* n. 35.

[262] Lima, 9 Nov. 1878, Martens, *op. cit. supra* n. 2 (1891) 16 (2nd ser.) 293 (*supra* n. 23) Arts. 14–16; Montevideo, 12 Feb. 1889 (1896) Clunet 441, Arts. 40–43; Bustamante Code, 20 Feb. 1928, 86 L.N.T.S. 113, Arts. 187–190; Nordic Convention of 6 Feb. 1931, Arts. 3–5, 126 L.N.T.S. 121, 142; of 19 Nov. 1934, Art. 7, 164 L.N.T.S. 243, 279.

[263] *Actes 1978*, III (G.A.L. Droz).

[264] *Supra* n. 53.

[265] See also Batiffol, *op. cit. supra* n. 242, at p. 454.

[266] France (1979), Luxemburg (1989), Netherlands, 1 Sept. 1992. J.O. (France) 25 Sept. 1992; S.J. 7 Oct. 1992; 14 Oct. 1992 leg. § 5739.

[267] *Actes 1976*, pp. 331(13), 337(38); 332(15), Art. 2.

[268] Art. 3(1); for the form see Arts. 11, 13. *Quaere* whether the choice of one of several domestic matrimonial regimes constitutes a choice of law: Art. 7(2); Lipstein (1961) Clunet 1143 – cf. Art. 7(2); *Actes 1976*, p. 365(13); Batiffol, *op. cit. supra* n. 242, at p. 457.

however, to the national law or the law of the habitual residence of one of the parties at the time of the choice (Article 3(2)(I), (II)) or to the law of the first new habitual residence of one of them after the marriage.[269] Article 3(2) precludes a choice of different legal systems for different groups of their assets, except immovables, where the *lex situs* may be chosen for all or some of them, present or future.[270]

While purporting to establish the principle of immutability of the law so chosen,[271] the Convention permits the parties to replace the law selected by them with retroactive effect (Article 6(1)) by another legal system, | which must, however, be either the national law or that of the habitual residence of one of the spouses at the time or the *lex situs* for all or some of their immovables.[272]

In the absence of a free choice of law the law of the first common habitual residence of the spouses applies (Article 4(1)). Alternatively, the law of the common nationality of the spouses applies (Article 4(2)) if either a contracting State opts for that principle by an express declaration[273] no matter where the spouses have established their first habitual residence[274] *or* if the parties have the nationality of a non-contracting State *and* they reside in a contracting State which was made in the declaration *or* in a non-contracting State which applies the *lex patriae or* where the spouses have not established their first habitual residence after marriage in the same State (Article 4(2)(a)–(c)). In the absence of these common connecting factors the law most closely connected applies (Article 4(3)).

Unlike in the case of free choice – which can be altered – a change of the original habitual residence, when no choice of law had been made, at the outset or subsequently,[275] results prospectively[276] in a change of the law applicable to the matrimonial regime only by the assumption of the spouses' habitual residence in the country of which they are or have become nationals, or if they have resided habitually in a country for ten years after

---

[269] Art. 3(2)(III). For the reasons for this unusual provision see *Actes 1976*, p. 337(30); Batiffol, *idem*, p. 455.

[270] Art. 3(3); *idem*, p. 456.

[271] Art. 7(1); *idem*, p. 462.

[272] Art. 6(1), (2); *idem*, p. 460.

[273] Art. 4(2)(i) in conjunction with Art. 5, subject to the provisions on common nationality formulated by Art. 15 and to its exclusion if the spouses retain their habitual residence at the place where they both resided previously for five years, subject to the proviso that the State of their residence has not also made the required declaration or is a non-contracting State applying the *lex patriae*: Art. 5(2).

[274] *Actes 1976*, pp. 362, 363(150).

[275] Art. 7(1) – including a domestic matrimonial property regime: *supra* n. 268; Art. 7(2); *Actes 1976*, p. 365(163). *Quaere* if one of the local matrimonial property regimes applies by operation of law in the absence of an express choice.

[276] Art. 8(1), subject to the proviso in Art. 8(2).

the marriage or when the parties did not establish their first habitual residence in the same State after marriage.[277] It would seem that in this *"conflit mobile"* the conditions have been set too high.

However, like those who have selected expressly the law to govern their matrimonial property relations, spouses who have failed to do so can exercise an option to select another law,[278] but without retroactive effect[279] unless the form required by Article 8(2) is adopted.

Following existing practice in some countries, contracting States are empowered by Article 9(2) and (3) to require publicity of the selection of | the law to govern matrimonial regimes for the protection of third parties, and Article 14 contains the usual public policy clause.

The report suggests[280] that the Convention has achieved a reconciliation of the nationality and the domicile principle with a slant in favour of the latter but, leaving aside the opening in favour of the *lex situs* for immovables and a slight preference for the law of the habitual residence, it would appear as if each side had been enabled to retain its initial stance.

3. Divorce

When the XI Conference turned to divorce and judicial separation[281] in 1968 it had before it the previous treaty,[282] which had regulated both choice of law and jurisdiction by relying in substance on a combination of the national law of the spouses and the *lex fori* and for the purpose of jurisdiction on the courts of the nationality or the common domicile of the spouses, present or past, or that of the defendant, if separate.[283]

The Convention of 1 June 1970 followed the modern trend and concentrated on jurisdiction, but the influence of the substantive law continued to make itself felt in the provisions which offer the means for refusing recognition (Articles 7, 19–21) as part of the system which relies on indirect jurisdiction in contrast to that adopted in 1902 which regulated direct jurisdiction.[284]

The grounds of jurisdiction are of seemingly unusual complexity,[285] but

---

[277] Art. 7(2)(i)–(iii); *Actes 1976*, p. 367(170).

[278] Art. 7(2) first sentence; *Actes 1976*, p. 364(160). Cf. for a similar tendency Inst. dr. int. (Cairo) (1987) 62(2) Ann. 291, 293(3).

[279] Art. 8(1); *Actes 1976*, pp. 352(102), 353(106).

[280] *Idem*, p. 343(65).

[281] XI Conference Convention, 1 June 1970, *Actes et Documents* 1970 t.2.

[282] *Supra* n. 33.

[283] *Supra* Section III.C. See also Inst. dr. int. (Brussels) (1948) 42 Ann. 281.

[284] Direct jurisdiction comes into play only through the pleas of *res judicata* (Art. 9) and *lis pendens* (Art. 22).

[285] Much reduced in the UK by the Recognition of Divorces and Legal Separations Act 1971, s. 3, now replaced by the Family Law Act 1986, s. 46.

can be reduced to form the following scheme: the habitual residence of the respondent;[286] the habitual residence of the petitioner, if resident there for one year before the proceedings began or if last habitually resident there with his spouse (Article 2(2)), or if both nationals of the State (Article 2(3)) or if the petitioner is a national having his habitual or qualified residence there (Article 2(4)) or if present at the time of the proceedings and if the spouses had resided *together* in a State whose law did not provide for divorce (Article 2(5)).

The original jurisdiction includes cross-petitions and any subsequent conversion of judicial separation into a divorce (Articles 4, 5).

| The general obligation to recognise a foreign divorce in contested proceedings[287] is balanced by the need in all other cases to show that timeous notice was given (Article 8) and that it does not conflict with a previous decision requiring enforcement or recognition (Article 9). While the substantive law of the recognising State is generally irrelevant in so far as on the particular facts it would not have supported a divorce, or if according to the conflicts rules of the *lex fori* another law would have applied,[288] it can come into its own if at the time of the divorce the parties were nationals of a State which does not provide for divorce (Article 7) or if reservations have been made in favour of nationals of the recognising State and a law other than that applicable under the conflicts rule of the law of the recognising State had been applied, unless the result would have been the same (Article 19(1)), if at the time the parties had been habitually resident in a State which did not provide for a divorce,[289] or if a State called upon to recognise a divorce or judicial separation itself does not provide for them and one of the spouses was a national of a contracting State the law of which also does not recognise a divorce (Article 20).

In order to change the undesirable practice which had arisen in Switzerland, Germany and England,[290] whereby a Swiss divorce of an Italian national domiciled in Switzerland, recognised in these countries, did not enable him to enter into a second marriage, seeing that the Swiss divorce was not at that time recognised in Italy, whose law (under Article 1 of the 1902 Convention) governed his capacity to marry, the Convention provides that a State which must recognise a Convention divorce must not preclude either

---

[286] Art. 2(1) with which domicile is equated (Art. 3) to be characterised by the original court: Art. 3 *and Actes 1968*, p. 217(38).

[287] Art. 6(1), limited only by the power to control jurisdiction (Art. 2) and to refuse recognition on grounds of public policy (Art. 10), but not by reviewing the facts (Art. 6(2)) or the merits (Art. 6(3)).

[288] Art. 6(2)(a), (b), but see Art. 18(1).

[289] Art. 19(2) inserted at the request of Ireland: *Actes 1968*, p. 217.

[290] See the detailed account in (1973) Clunet 411–414; (1988) 809–813.

spouse from remarrying on the ground that the divorce is not recognised elsewhere.[291] The wording has caused difficulties since this provision mentions only divorces in other countries which must be recognised but seemingly does not cover divorces pronounced by the same court which is also called upon to consider the admissibility of a subsequent marriage.[292]

Faced with the question whether to incorporate the Convention *in toto* or to reproduce it in the form of a separate statute, the United Kingdom employed the latter technique. It made it possible in 1986 to extend the Convention's indirect regulation of jurisdiction to annulments[293] and | directly to divorces granted in the United Kingdom,[294] to include a provision on divorces, annulments and legal separations obtained otherwise than by legal proceedings[295] and, from the outset, in 1971, to reduce the complexity of the jurisdictional rules while complying with the Convention by treating the recognition of divorces and legal separations more favourably[296] and by following the Convention's basic provisions.[297] Connecting factors are characterised according to the *lex fori.*[298]

4. Maintenance obligations

When the VIII Conference approached the combined problems of the choice of law and the recognition and enforcement of maintenance obligations towards children, it was clear that two separate conventions were required,[299] but their range was to be limited exclusively to matters of maintenance between family members in the direct line of descent[300] without purporting to determine questions of family status.[301]

---

[291] Art. 11; *Actes 1968*, p. 221(54).

[292] See also Recognition of Divorces and Legal Separations Act 1971, s. 7; *Lawrence* v. *Lawrence* [1985] Fam. 186; Lipstein (1986) 35 I.C.L.Q. 179; but see now Family Law Act 1986, s. 50(a).

[293] Family Law Act 1986, ss. 44(2), 45.

[294] Domicile and Matrimonial Proceedings Act 1973, s. 5.

[295] *Idem*, s. 46(2), omitted by the Convention, *Actes 1968*, p. 212(12), (13), and the 1971 Act, s. 2; see Lipstein (1988) Clunet 824.

[296] Convention, Art. 17; the more favourable inclusion of the common law rules on recognition of foreign divorces (1971, Art. 3) was dropped.

[297] Convention Art. 1(2) = 1971 Act, s. 8(3), 1986 Act, s. 51(5); Arts. 2, 3 = s. 3, s. 46(1); Art. 4 = s. 4, s. 47(1); Art. 5 = s. 4(2), s. 47(2); Art. 6(1) = s. 5(1), s. 48(1); Art. 8 = s. 8(2), s. 51(3)(a); Art. 9 = 1986 Act, s. 51(1); Art. 13 = 1986 Act, s. 49.

[298] 1971 Act, s. 5(2); 1986 Act, ss. 46(5), 48(2).

[299] *Actes 1956*, t.1, p. 310, Choice of Law, Report de Winter, p. 348, text p. 314. Recognition and Enforcement, Report Jenard, p. 351 text. Petersen (1959) 24 Rabels Z 1, 31, 39; Neuhaus (1958) 23 Rabels Z 197.

[300] Choice of Law Convention, Art. 5(1); Recognition Convention, Art. 1(3) whether legitimate or not; adopted, unmarried and under 21: Choice of Law Convention, Art. 1(4); Recognition Convention, Art. 1.

[301] *Idem*, Arts. 5(2), 1(2) respectively.

As regards choice of law, the law of the child's habitual residence for the time being applied,[302] but if a declaration to this effect had been made by a contracting State, its *lex fori* applied if both maintenance creditor and debtor were nationals of that State and the maintenance debtor was habitually resident in that State.[303] If the law of the child's habitual residence denied him any maintenance at all, the law determined by the conflicts rules of the forum applied. The benefits of the Convention were to accrue if the laws of contracting States applied.[304]

In dealing with the recognition and enforcement of judgments concerning maintenance obligations towards children, the Conference had before it a draft convention prepared by the Rome Institute for the | Unification of Law[305] and the UN draft,[306] which resulted in the New York Convention of 20 June 1956 on the Recovery of Maintenance Obligations.[307] In following the Rome rather than the Geneva draft the Conference adhered to the orthodox method of international enforcement in preference to that favoured by the Geneva draft, which was influenced, at least in principle, by the English Maintenance Orders (Facilities for Enforcement) Act 1920, which divided the judicial function between the original and the requested court.[308]

Jurisdiction was to be exercised either by the court of the maintenance creditor's or the maintenance debtor's habitual residence,[309] or by the court to the jurisdiction of which the debtor either had submitted expressly or before which he had pleaded to the merits without questioning the jurisdiction (Article 3). The usual safeguards were provided.[310] A special provision ensured that periodic maintenance payments were enforceable even if ca-

---

[302] Art. 1(1), (2); no reference was made to the "internal law" since it was thought to be unnecessary: *Actes 1956*, p. 310. For the reasons for adopting this connecting factor see *idem*, p. 405(50).

[303] Art. 2; see the critique by Neuhaus, *op. cit. supra* n. 299.

[304] Art. 6; for a critique of this strange limitation see Verwilghen, Prel. Report, *Actes XII Conf.*, t.4, p. 103(20).

[305] *Actes 1956*, t.2, p. 169; (1947–52) 3 Inst. for Unification of Law 199.

[306] The so-called Geneva Draft, *Actes 1956*, t.2, p. 173; see Lipstein (1954) 3 I.C.L.Q. 125; Contini (1953) 41 Calif.L.B. 106, 119; Inst. U.L. *idem*, pp. 123, 163 *et seq.*

[307] *Actes 1956*, t.2, p. 178; 268 U.N.T.S. 3, 32.

[308] See now the Maintenance Orders (Reciprocal Enforcement) Act 1972, Part II of which embodies the New York Convention 1956, Cmnd.4485 (1956); Recovery Abroad of Maintenance (Convention Countries) Order 1975, S.I.1975/423; 1978/279; 1982/1530.

[309] But see the possibility of a reservation: Art. 18.

[310] Arts. 2, 5; need for jurisdiction under the Convention: for proper service upon the defendant or representation; if by default, proper notice or inability to present a defence; *res judicata*, unless provisionally enforceable in the original and the requested court; not contrary to a previous judgment between the same parties and the same object in the requested State and not manifestly contrary to its public policy. For the recent practice on public policy relating to maintenance claims see *Actes 1972*, t.4, pp. 45–48 (Pelichet Report).

pable of subsequent variation and not only accrued arrears, as English law holds.[311] This would appear to mean that the foreign award of periodic maintenance is to form the basis of a similar award by the requested court which can serve in subsequent internal proceedings in case of non-observance.

A significant feature of the two Conventions read together is that the identical test, i.e. habitual residence, is employed to determine jurisdiction and choice of law. Thus the way was opened for the future to concentrate on jurisdiction and to identify the latter with the applicable law (unless the latter should determine otherwise).[312] It also underlined the importance of the question whether the jurisdiction should be direct or indirect.[313]

When the XII Conference returned to the subject in 1978 with a view to replacing and extending the existing provisions to adults, it was presented | with a comprehensive comparative report.[314] Once again choice of law[315] and recognition and enforcement were regulated by separate conventions.[316]

The Choice of Law Convention of 2 October 1973 was extended to adults[317] and, like its predecessor, precluded any preliminary questions arising thereunder from forming *res judicata*.[318] On the other hand, its effect extended to the laws of non-contracting States.[319] The law of the habitual residence for the time being of the maintenance creditor was to apply once again,[320] but if it denied any maintenance, the common national law was to apply (Article 5)[321] and failing this the *lex fori* (Article 6).

In addition, the common national law could be invoked by the maintenance debtor or, failing a common national law the *lex fori*, in respect of claims of collaterals or based on affinity, if these legal systems denied

---

[311] Convention 1958, s. 7, reproduced by the Convention 1973, s. 11; contrast the English practice, *Harrop* v. *Harrop* [1920] 3 K.B. 386; *Beatty* v. *Beatty* [1924] 1 K.B. 807; *Actes 1972*, t. 4, pp. 49, 109(35), 137(114).

[312] *Actes, idem*, p. 109(37).

[313] *Idem*, p. 97(6).

[314] *Idem*, pp. 13–53 by Pelichet, at p. 13.

[315] *Idem*, p. 89: tentative draft; p. 95: Prel. Report Verwilghen; p. 377: text; p. 432: Report Verwilghen. See generally Batiffol (1973) Rev. crit. d.i.p. 243, 261.

[316] *Actes 1972*, p. 91: tentative draft; p. 127: Prel. Report Verwilghen; p. 268: text; p. 389: Report Verwilghen; U.K.T.S. 49 (1980) Cmnd. 7939.

[317] Arts. 1, 2; cf. 1956, Preamble and Art. 1(4); but permits far-reaching reservations: Art. 14; for the meaning of maintenance obligations see *Actes 1972*, pp. 391–394(18)–(25).

[318] Art. 2(2); 1956, Art. 5(2); but see the doubts expressed by Batiffol, *op. cit. supra* n. 315, at p. 266.

[319] Art. 3; cf. 1956, Art. 6.

[320] Art. 4; cf. 1956, Art. 2(1), (2); also 1973 Art. 10; contrast 1956 Art. 1(3); the wording of Arts. 4(1), (2), 7, 15 again excludes *renvoi*: *Actes 1972*, p. 453(168).

[321] Contrast 1956, Arts. 2, 3.

them.[322] Further innovations were provided by the rule that the law governing a divorce was to govern maintenance obligations between the spouses in the country where the divorce is being granted or is recognised[323] and by the provision that the right of a public authority to claim reimbursements of benefits paid to a maintenance creditor was to be governed by the law to which the authority is subject.[324] The safeguard of public policy was extended in Article 11(2) by allowing consideration of the needs and resources of the parties in determining the amount of maintenance, contrary to the applicable law. In its slightly amended and simplified form the Convention secured continuity.

The Enforcement Convention of 2 October 1973 was similarly extended[325] by including decisions of administrative authorities and claims by public bodies for the reimbursement of maintenance debtors | (Article 1(2))[326] as well as settlements in face of the court (Article 1(1)). The jurisdiction of the courts of the habitual residence of the maintenance creditor and debtor and of the *forum prorogationis* (Article 7(1), (3)) were supplemented by that of the courts of the common nationality of the parties (Article 7(2)) and of courts exercising jurisdiction in divorce, judicial separation and nullity (Article 8). The usual safeguards,[327] slightly augmented to exclude the possibility of ordinary forms of review affecting provisional judgments (Articles 4(2), 5(2) and (3)) and the defences of fraud and *lis pendens* were introduced. Findings of facts and on the merits were to be binding (Articles 9 and 12), and the provisions on the enforcement of decisions for the periodical payment of maintenance agreed in 1958 were taken over.[328] The Conventions of 2 October 1972 were to replace those of 1956 and 1958.[329] Enforcement in the United Kingdom is assured by the application of Part I of the Maintenance Orders (Reciprocal Enforcement) Act 1972.[330]

---

[322] Art. 7; doubtful Batiffol, *op. cit. supra* n. 315, at p. 267.

[323] Art. 8, but see the critique by Batiffol who argues that Art. 8 encourages conflicting decisions, if the maintenance creditor sues at his habitual residence and – it must be added – the divorce is not recognised there.

[324] Art. 9; Batiffol, *op. cit. supra* n. 315, at p. 264.

[325] Subject to the power to append far-reaching reservations: Art. 26(2).

[326] Subject to a reference both to its internal law and to the law applicable under the choice of law rules of the addressed authority: Arts. 18, 19.

[327] Arts. 4–6; contrast 1958, Art. 2.

[328] Art. 11; see 1958, Art. 7.

[329] Applicable Law Convention, Art. 18; Enforcement Convention, Art. 29.

[330] S. 40; Reciprocal Enforcement of Maintenance Orders (Hague Convention Countries) Order 1979 S.I.1979/1367; Magistrates' Courts (Reciprocal Enforcement of Maintenance Orders) (Hague Convention Countries) Rules 1986, S.I.1986/108.

5. Guardianship of minors

When called upon to reconsider the Convention of 12 June 1902[331] the Conference had the choice between a revision and the preparation of a new text. In deciding in favour of the latter,[332] the IX Conference (1960) had before it two previous attempts by other bodies[333] but in view of the strengthening of protective measures,[334] the exchange of information,[335] the provision on recognition and execution of measures taken or ordered elsewhere[336] and the dual characterisation of the concept of "minor",[337] to mention the major innovations, the revision was technical, even in its most important change: that of switching the emphasis from nationality to habitual residence (Articles 1, 8, 13(1)).

| While Articles 1, 2 and 4(1) of the Convention of 1902 had concentrated on nationality as the basis of choice of law and jurisdiction, and Articles 2–4 accorded the courts of the habitual residence of the minor only a subsidiary role, the Convention of 5 October 1961 concentrates on jurisdiction, treats jurisdiction and choice of law as identical[338] and accords pride of place to the courts of the minor's habitual residence.[339] However, the national courts of the minor come into their own on two grounds: if the guardianship arises by operation of law[340] and, generally, at their discretion if the interest of the minor demands it, after advising the authorities of the minor's habitual residence.[341] Thus a conflict of authorities is not excluded,[342] but by delegating their executive powers to the authorities of the other country rather than by entrusting them to their diplomatic or consular authorities[343] direct clashes can be reduced. In the end, while measures taken by the authorities in either

---

[331] *Supra* n. 34.

[332] *Actes 1960*, t.4, Prel. Report Marmol p. 18, text p. 213, English text: (1961) 10 I.C.L.Q. 53; (1960) 9 A.J.C.L. 708, Report von Steiger p. 220; see also Loussouarn (1961) Clunet 654, 681.

[333] Nordic Convention 1931, *supra* n. 262, Arts. 14 *et seq.*; ILA 48th Report (Hamburg 1960), p. 434.

[334] Arts. 8, 9; see also 1902, Art. 7; *Actes 1960*, p. 235; von Steiger (1960) 17 A.S.D.I. 30, 31, a *"Jugendschutzabkommen"*, Murad Ferid (1962) 27 Rabels Z 411, 429.

[335] Arts. 10, 11, *Actes 1960*, p. 236; see also Arts. 5(2); 4(1).

[336] Art. 7, *Actes 1960*, pp. 233, 237.

[337] Art. 12, *Actes 1960*, p. 237. C. Ganshof, Rev. dr. internat. et de dr. comparé 37 (1960) 279, 285. De Nova (1960) 14 Dir. internaz. 305, 310.

[338] Art. 2(1); de Nova, *idem*, p. 311; von Overbeck (1961) 8 N.T.I.R. 31, 50.

[339] Art. 1; on the ground that it represents best the social environment: *Actes 1960*, p. 220.

[340] Art. 3; *Actes 1960*, p. 227; see e.g. von Steiger, *op. cit. supra* n. 334, at p. 33.

[341] Art. 4(1), *Actes 1960*, p. 228; Loussouarn, *op. cit. supra* n. 332, at p. 691 believes that this power is exceptional only.

[342] Art. 4(3), (4); see also Art. 5(3). De Nova, *op. cit. supra* n. 337, at p. 309; von Steiger, *op. cit. supra* n. 334, at p. 32.

[343] See 1902, Art. 2. Art. 6(1): delegation by the national authorities; Art. 6(2): delegation by the authorities of the habitual residence.

country are recognised in the other country concerned, their enforcement as well as their recognition is determined by the conflicts rules of the other State.[344] Thus the possibility of a breakdown in the collaboration of the authorities is enhanced once more. The power of contracting States by way of a reservation to retain their jurisdiction in matters of guardianship arising in connection with proceedings in divorce or nullity of marriage[345] increases further the danger of concurrent guardianships, the more so since other contracting States are not bound to recognise it.

Two new provisions envisage, on the one hand, the exceptional and over-riding exercise of protective measures by the authorities of the minor's habitual residence if the person or the assets are seriously endangered[346] and, on the other hand, measures which are urgently required.[347] Here again reservations (Article 8(2)) and the power of other contracting States to replace these measures (Article 9(2)) encourage a conflict. Unlike previously the Convention applies to all minors habitually resi|dent in a Convention country, irrespective of their nationality,[348] unless a contracting State restricts it to its own nationals and to nationals of the other contracting States (Article 13(2) and (3)).

Contrary to the structure of the 1902 Convention, but in accordance with the current tendency, a public policy clause was included (in Article 16), possibly also in view of the opinions expressed in the *Boll* case, although the decision turned on whether the 1902 Convention precluded the application of the public law of the *lex fori*.[349]

6. Adoption

When the X Conference approached adoption,[350] it had before it a report and draft conventions placed before the Institut de droit international[351] and the International Law Association[352] as well as a treaty provision.[353] In keeping

---

[344] Art. 7; the generality of this provision may have rendered that of Art. 6(2) of the 1902 Convention unnecessary.

[345] Art. 15; *Actes 1960*, p. 239.

[346] Art. 8; *Actes 1960*, p. 234; this provision is a substitute for the general jurisdiction established by the Convention: *idem*, p. 235.

[347] Art. 9; they are said not to form a substitute for the general jurisdiction, but to fill a void with territorial effect only: *Actes 1960*, p. 235; contrast 1902, Art. 7.

[348] Art. 31(1); contrast 1902, Art. 9(1).

[349] I.C.J. Rep. 1959, 55. Lipstein (1959) 8 I.C.L.Q. 506, but see Batiffol and Francescakis (1959) Rev. crit. d.i.p. 259, Makarov, *op. cit. supra* n. 91, at p. 313, and the lit. cited by von Overbeck, *op. cit. supra* n. 338, at pp. 49, 232, esp. Lewald Rev. dr. int. privé, 1928, 149.

[350] *Supra* n. 62. X Conference 1964 (1965), t. 2; Prel. Report, p. 86 text: p. 399; Report 409.

[351] Inst. dr. int. (Rome) (1973) 55 Ann. 798.

[352] 50th Conference (Brussels 1962), p. 605; 51st Conference (Tokyo 1964), p. 822; see also Lipstein (1963) 12 I.C.L.Q. 835; (1965) C.L.J. 224.

[353] Nordic Convention 1931, *supra* n. 262, Arts. 11–13.

with the trend current in the post-war treaties prepared by the Conference the Adoption Convention concentrates on jurisdiction and, with a few important exceptions, identifies the *lex fori* with the applicable law.[354] Article 1 extends the exercise of jurisdiction to an adopter or to spouses who possess the nationality of a contracting State and who is or are habitually resident in one of the States, and a child possessing the nationality of a contracting State and habitually resident in one of them. Jurisdiction is excluded, in so far as the Convention is concerned,[355] where either the adopters do not possess the same nationality or do not have their habitual residence in the same contracting State (Article 2(a)), if the adoption is an internal one because all the parties are nationals of the State in which they habitually reside (Article 2(b)), or if jurisdiction is not exercised by the authorities of the State where the parties habitually reside or of which they are nationals (Article 2(c) in conjunction with Article 3(1)) – both at the time of the application and the grant (Article 3(2)).

| The authorities, while applying their own internal law, must take into account the national law of the adopter(s) in so far as it prohibits the adoption (Article 4(1), (2)) and the prohibition is incorporated in a declaration to this effect.[356] The national law of the child determines the necessary consents (Article 5(1)) as well as any grounds for annulling the adoption.[357] Recognition of an adoption, its annulment or revocation, is automatic,[358] subject to the usual safeguard of public policy (Article 15), which cannot, however, be invoked to disregard a declaration made in accordance with Article 13.[359] The Convention is silent as regards the law governing the effects of a Convention adoption.[360]

It is to be noted that unlike in Article 12 of the Convention on the Protection of Minors of 5 October 1961, no attempt was made to characterise the term "minor". Instead, the Adoption Convention provides its own autonomous characterisation.[361] It has failed to do so in respect of the types

---

[354] Arts. 4(1); 7(3); for the reasons see von Steiger, *op. cit. supra* n. 334, at pp. 33 *et seq.*, and see the lit. in Ficker, (1966) 30 Rabels Z 606, 613 n. 25, 625; Lagarde (1965) Rev. crit. d.i.p. 249, 253. Exceptions: Arts. 4(2), 5, 7(2)(a)–(c), 13.

[355] For the recognition of adoptions in accordance with the conflicts rules of the member States see *Actes 1964*, p. 93 and Convention, Art. 2(c); Graveson (1965) 14 I.C.L.Q. 528, 535; von Steiger, *idem*, p. 41; Ficker, *idem*, p. 620; Lagarde, *idem*, p. 251.

[356] Art. 13; Loussouarn (1965) Clunet 5, 10; Lagarde, *idem*, p. 254.

[357] Art. 7; the jurisdiction to revoke or annul an adoption is based on the adopter(s)' or the adoptee's habitual residence: Art. 7(1).

[358] Art. 8, subject to Art. 22; child habitual resident of non-recognising State and not national of State of adoption.

[359] *Actes 1964*, pp. 429–436.

[360] *Idem*, p. 411; Loussouarn, *op. cit. supra* n. 356, at p. 11; Graveson, *loc. cit. supra* n. 355; von Steiger, *op. cit. supra* n. 334, at p. 38; Ficker, *op. cit. supra* n. 354, at p. 629.

[361] Art. 1(2); Graveson, *idem*, p. 533.

of adoption available in the world, although in practice difficulties can arise.[362] The Convention has been incorporated into English law by a series of legislative provisions which have treated the Convention as one establishing direct jurisdiction.[363]

7. Civil aspects of child abduction

The XIV Conference, faced with the growing problem of the unauthorised removal of children, was called upon to complement the Convention of 5 October 1961 on Child Protection. At the same time the Council of Europe elaborated a convention on similar lines.[364] The Hague Convention[365] formulated for this purpose differs from all others dealing with family matters in as much as it is not concerned with choice of law, except | incidentally,[366] or the enforcement of private rights,[367] but forms an autonomous engagement not incidental to the other Conventions and taking precedence over that of 5 October 1961 (Article 34). It offers co-operation between bodies set up by contracting States to assist one another in tracing and generally in returning a child to its former guardians (Articles 6–11) and in securing access (Article 21).

Since the aim is to remedy a wrongful (Article 1(a)) removal or retention of a child,[368] it is evident that at some stage a breach of law must have been committed,[369] but the judicial or administrative authorities of the requested State are precluded from determining the merits (Articles 16, 19), irrespective of the existence or not of a previous custody order abroad,[370] unless and until they have decided not to return the child. Any legal question arising under the foreign law is therefore only a datum, determined by the law of the country from which the child was removed, but not to be enforced (Article 17). The requested authorities are called upon only to determine whether the

---

[362] Lipstein, ILA 55th Conference Report (Brussels 1962), p. 606 at p. 613 with cases; Graveson, *idem*, p. 536; von Steiger, *op. cit. supra* n. 334, at pp. 30, 31, 38, 40; Lagarde, *op. cit. supra* n. 354, at p. 250.

[363] Adoption Act 1968, ss. 1–4(1), (2), 9(5), 10, which were repealed by Children Act 1975, s. 24, replaced in turn by Adoption Act 1976, ss. 17, 52(3), 53, 59; see Dicey and Morris, *Conflict of Laws* (11th edn, 1987), Rule 109, pp. 884–889.

[364] Convention on Recognition and Enforcement of Decisions Concerning Custody and Enforcement of Decisions Concerning Custody of Children and Restoration of Custody, T.S. 105/1980.

[365] *Supra* n. 56. 24 Oct. 1980. *Actes 1982*, t. 3, p. 166: Prel. Report; p. 413: text; p. 426: Report Perez-Vera.

[366] Arts. 3(1)(a), (2), 5, 14, 15. See *infra*.

[367] Arts. 3(1)(b), 4, 8(1).

[368] Art. 4; in accordance with its factual approach a factual definition (16 years of age) was chosen in preference to a legal characterisation; *Actes 1982*, p. 449(76).

[369] *Idem*, pp. 441(64), 445(67).

[370] *Idem*, pp. 428(9), 430(17).

circumstances require the child to be returned. They must do so if less than a year has elapsed since the wrongful act (Article 12(1)), and should normally do so even after a year has passed, unless it appears that the child has settled in its new environment (Article 12(2)). Exceptionally, a return may be refused if the person charged with the care of the child did not exercise it or agreed or acquiesced in the removal or retention or if the child would suffer physical or psychological harm (Article 13(1)(a), (b)), if its fundamental rights or freedom would be violated[371] or, being of sufficient maturity, it objects to the transfer (Article 13(2)).

The ordinary remedies available to the person having the custody of the child according to the law of the country where he is found are not affected by the Convention (Article 18).

B. Succession

1. The form of wills

Inspired by the substance and proposals of the Report of the British Committee on Private International Law,[372] the British delegation to the VIII Hague Conference raised the question of the law governing the|formalities of wills.[373] In particular, the effect of a change of the testator's nationality, domicile or residence upon a previous will appeared to require attention.[374] The formalities governing a will had been considered in previous sessions of the Hague Conferences.[375] The conclusion had been that in principle the *lex loci actus* was to apply, but that the national law of the testator was to prevail if it required a particular form in order to comply with substantive conditions of the *lex patriae*. Subsequently, this rule was modified in as much as other contracting States were permitted to treat compliance with the *lex loci actus* as sufficient.[376] Moreover, wills made before consular or

---

[371] Art. 20; as interpreted by the law of the requested State. For the law of the United Kingdom see Child Abduction Act 1984.

[372] Cmnd. 491(1958). See *Actes 1956*, pp. 269, 276, 328; also 292, 357.

[373] In the UK the application of the law of the last domicile of the testator–*Stanley* v. *Bernes* (1830) 3 Hagg. Ecc. 373; *Bremer* v. *Freeman* (1857) 10 Moo. P.C. 306 – had been modified as regards wills of personal property of British subjects made abroad by the Wills Act 1861 (Lord Kingsdown's Act) which added compliance with the *lex loci actus*, the *lex domicilii* at the time of making the will and the law of the testator's domicile of origin in the dominions (s. 1) and by adding the *lex loci actus* if made within the UK (s. 2).

[374] A reference by way of *renvoi* to the national law of a British subject had brought this problem into the limelight: *Re O'Keefe* [1940] Ch. 124. S. 3 of the Wills Act 1861 dealt only with the effect of a change of domicile upon the construction and revocation of a will.

[375] See *supra* Section IV.C.

[376] *Supra* text to nn. 170, 174, 193.

diplomatic representatives were to be admitted.[377] These rules were to apply to the revocation of wills as well.[378]

The IX Conference[379] considered most of the arguments put forward previously and produced a convention which widened the range of laws, compliance with which renders a will or its revocation valid in form (Articles 1–4, 6, 8), but for this reason also extended the opportunities for making reservations (Articles 9–13). Intended to apply generally in substitution for the existing choice of law rules (Article 6), unless more favourable (Article 3), it was assumed that the Convention would be applied equally to contracting and non-contracting parties without modifications.[380] However, the wording of the Convention seems to permit, and the special needs of English law demanded, not simply incorporation but special legislation which satisfied both.[381]

The Convention speaks of "testamentary dispositions" in order to indicate that it is not limited to instruments in the nature of wills, but includes holograph documents, such as letters.[382] Joint wills are also | covered by the Convention,[383] but following a Swedish request the wording indicates that more than two persons may be involved, such as brothers and sisters.[384] In order to ensure on a broad range the formal validity of testamentary dispositions with an international element, the *lex loci actus*, the *lex patriae*, the *lex domicilii* and the law of the habitual residence were all made available to the testator – in the last three cases in the version either at the time of making the will or at the time of the testator's death.[385] At the request of the British

---

[377] *Supra* text to nn. 169–171, 174.

[378] *Supra* text following n. 193.

[379] *Supra* n. 63; *Actes 1961*, t. III, p. 18: Special Commission Report (H. Batiffol); 159 (Explanatory Report, H. Batiffol); 155: text. For the preparatory work see von Overbeck (1958) 15 Ann. suisse dr. int. 215.

[380] Art. 8; *Actes 1961*, pp. 28, 170.

[381] Wills Act 1963; references to the individual provisions of the Convention will therefore be accompanied by references to the provisions of the Act.

[382] *Actes 1961*, pp. 19, 160, 166; Art. 10, which contains a reservation in respect of oral dispositions, does not support the view that the Convention applies to oral wills. It was inserted on the insistence of the Yugoslav delegation: *idem*, pp. 28, 103. The Wills Act 1963 speaks of wills: s. 6(1).

[383] Art. 4. They are omitted by the Wills Act 1963 since their sphere is limited in English law, where they are useful only in exercising a joint power of appointment or on the unusual occasion of making mutual wills in one document; see *Williams on Wills* (6th edn, 1987), pp. 18–19; *Dufour* v. *Pereira* (1769) 1 Dick 419; see also Neuhaus and Gündisch (1956) 21 Rabels Z 551; prohibited in France: Art. 968 CC.

[384] *Actes 1961*, pp. 81, 87, 167. Any prohibition of a general or a restricted nature may raise a question of form or substance to be decided by the *lex fori*; Ferid, *op. cit. supra* n. 334, at p. 423.

[385] Art. 1(1)(a)–(d); Wills Act 1963, s. 1; this time, rather than that of the "opening" of the succession, was chosen since this phase was thought to be alien to the common law; *Actes 1961*, pp. 27, 100.

delegation, though with some hesitation, the *lex situs* was also placed at the testator's disposition – restricted, however, to immovables.[386] Although it sanctioned a scission of what were intended to be uniform single rules of choice of law,[387] it was believed that owing to its restriction to immovables the unity of the law of succession would be little affected by this concession to practical needs.[388] Any reference to a legal system is to its internal law and therefore excludes *renvoi.*[389] Apart from habitual residence and the *situs* of immovables,[390] which can be treated as facts, the other terms raise problems of interpretation. What is the law of the place of acting, if the act takes place on a ship or an aircraft?[391]

Nationality as a connecting factor causes difficulties if the country of the testator's nationality consists of a composite legal system. In a federal State it may be possible to identify nationality with the citizenship of a particular legal district,[392] but if a unitary State has a composite legal system, a subsidiary connecting factor must be called in aid. Such is the test of the "most real connection",[393] treated in Italian practice as the | place of residence of a British subject[394] in preference to that of the domicile of origin,[395] even if its abandonment was described as *"quasi exuere patriam".*[396] The Convention offers no direct guidance if the testator possessed dual nationality, but the *favor testamenti* expressed by it[397] should operate here as well.

The differing interpretations of domicile induced the drafters of the Convention to leave it to the law of the domicile in issue,[398] but on the insistence

---

[386] Art. 1(1)(e); *Actes 1961*, pp. 23, 71; Wills Act 1963, s. 2(1)(b). For a critique in principle see Cohn (1956) 5 I.C.L.Q. 395; Beitzke, *Festschrift für Lewald* (1953), p. 235.

[387] Art. 1 speaks of "a testamentary disposition" in the singular; *Actes 1961*, p. 18.

[388] Ferid, *op. cit. supra* n. 334, at p. 418. The application of the law governing the succession and that of the *lex fori* was ruled out as well as the law chosen by the testator and, contrary to the previous drafts, consular and diplomatic wills; von Overbeck, *op. cit. supra* n. 379, at pp. 228 *et seq.*

[389] Art. 1(1); *Actes 1961*, pp. 19, 160; Wills Act 1963, s. 6(1).

[390] *Actes 1961*, pp. 22, 23, 71.

[391] *Idem*, pp. 20, 161, but see Wills Act 1963, s. 2(1)(a).

[392] Art. 1(2); *Actes 1961*, pp. 21, 66. The text indicates the exceptional and limited character of this rule: *idem*, p. 162; Wills Act 1963, s. 6(1); dual nationality merely offers a choice.

[393] Art. 1(2); Wills Act 1963, s. 6(2)(b). Ferid, *op. cit. supra* n. 334, at p. 421.

[394] De Nova, *Il richiamo di ordinamenti plurilegislativi* (1940), pp. 108 *et seq.* with cases; *id. Festschrift für Leo Raupe* (1948), p. 67; *id.* (1950) 3 ser. 26 Ann. dir. comp. 25, 37; Falconbridge, *Conflict of Laws* (1947), p. 198 note (c); *id.* (1941) 19 Can. Bar. Rev. 320, 323 – Rev. crit. d.i.p. 1947, 45, 55.

[395] *Re O'Keefe* [1940] Ch. 124.

[396] *Moorhouse* v. *Lord* (1863) 10 H.L.C. 272, 283 and see *Whicker* v. *Hume* (1858) 7 H.L.C. 124, 159.

[397] Art. 3; *Actes* 1961, pp. 18, 21, 162; Wills Act 1963, s. 2(1)(c); Mann (1986) 35 I.C.L.Q. 423; see also von Overbeck, *op. cit. supra* n. 379, at pp. 218, 228.

[398] Art. 1(3); *Actes 1961*, pp. 22, 68.

of the British delegation a reservation was inserted in favour of the *lex fori*.[399] Since the rules of the Convention are apparently not intended to be applied *ex officio*[400] the beneficiaries are offered a choice of jurisdiction if a reservation is made to this effect – as it has been made by the United Kingdom.[401] It remains to be determined whether in respect of a joint will compliance with the law applicable to one of the testators will suffice, unless the will complies with the *lex loci actus* or, as regards immovables, with the *lex situs*.[402]

The same rules which apply to the formalities of a testamentary disposition apply also to its revocation.[403] The wording of Article 2(1) indicates that this notion has a restricted meaning and does not include factual situations, such as the effect of a subsequent marriage or divorce of the testator, the destruction of a testamentary disposition or its withdrawal from notarial custody.[404]

A number of substantive matters which raised problems of characterisation had to be solved in defining the ambit of the Convention. Successoral pacts,[405] considered originally for express exclusion,[406] are not mentioned specifically in the final version on the ground that they are contractual in character.[407] It would seem also that a reservation under | Article 12 would rule out their inclusion in a particular case. The requirement that nationals abroad must observe special formalities arising out of their age, nationality or other personal conditions demanded by their *lex patriae* when making a will abroad[408] was drastically deprived of its international effect by characterising such requirements as formalities.[409] However, the home State is allowed a reservation, limited to property in that State, subject to very stringent conditions.[410] Only legal provisions affecting the personal conditions

---

[399] Art. 9; *Actes 1961*, pp. 70, 132; for comments see Ferid, *op. cit. supra* n. 334, at p. 421.

[400] *Actes 1961*, pp. 23, 165.

[401] (1964) U.K.T.S. 5, 14.

[402] *Actes 1961*, p. 167.

[403] Art. 2; Wills Act 1963, s. 2(1)(c).

[404] *Actes 1961*, pp. 25, 75, 77.

[405] Admitted only in a limited number of countries, these are either general: Germany, BGB, para.2247, Swiss ZGB, Arts. 468, 494, 496, or limited to marriage settlements: France C.Civ., Arts. 1082, 1389 (*institution contractuelle*); Austria, ABGB, paras. 1249–1254.

[406] *Actes 1961*, p. 25; for the preparatory work, see von Overbeck, *op. cit. supra* n. 379, at p. 234.

[407] *Actes 1961*, p. 168.

[408] Netherlands Civil Code, Art. 992, now abrogated by a Law of 15 May 1981, Stb.284; Portuguese Civil Code, Art. 1961; as regards mentally ill persons, Austria ABGB, para.569; Spanish CC, Art. 688; Greek CC, Art. 1748, *Actes 1961*, p. 168 n. 3; minors, German BGB, paras. 2247(4), 2233; von Overbeck, *op. cit. supra* n. 379, at pp. 235 *et seq*.

[409] Art. 5; *Actes 1961*, pp. 95, 122; Wills Act 1963, s. 3; for the preparatory work see von Overbeck, *idem*, p. 233.

[410] Art. II. The will must be valid by virtue of the *lex loci actus* only, the testator must

are envisaged.[411] Consequently, factual impediments are not included,[412] or provisions which enlarge the range of formalities.[413]

A very broadly formulated Article 12 permits contracting States to reserve the right not to recognise testamentary clauses which under its own law do not relate to matters of succession.[414] The purpose is to separate those parts which are extra-patrimonial, such as an acknowledgement of paternity, legitimation, appointment of a guardian and adoption.[415]

The Convention makes no provision for the exercise of powers of appointment, which are unknown except at common law. The Wills Act 1963 could not disregard them and fitted them into the general scheme by enabling the donee of the power to rely on any of the legal systems applicable to testamentary dispositions[416] as well as on the law governing the essential validity of the power. At the same time the need to comply with any formal requirements contained in the instrument creating the power was removed.[417]

As had become a practice at the time a clause was inserted which permits member States to disregard any laws rendered applicable by the Convention if they are manifestly contrary to public policy.[418]

| The Convention applies if the testator died after its entry into force (Article 8), but States may reserve the right to apply it only to testamentary dispositions made after its entry into force (Article 13).

2. Administration of estates

In opening the XII Conference, the agenda of which included the administration of estates, the President (de Winter) observed that since the Conference had twice vainly tried to bring about a convention on the law of succession[419] the time did not seem ripe for another attempt. Instead an effort should be made to deal with those parts of the law of succession in most need

---

have been a national of the State concerned, domiciled or habitually resident there and must have died in a State other than that where he made the will. The reservation is therefore limited to cases sounding in *fraude à la loi*.

[411] *Quaere* which law determines the existence of this impediment; von Overbeck, *op. cit. supra* n. 379, at p. 239.

[412] *Actes 1961*, pp. 169; see also 41 (blindness); von Overbeck, *ibid.*

[413] *Actes 1961*, p. 99, soldier's will.

[414] *Idem*, p. 29.

[415] *Idem*, p. 173.

[416] S. 2(1)(d) in conjunction with ss. 1 and 2(1)(b).

[417] S. 2(2) superseding the rule to the contrary maintained for the exercise of powers governed by foreign law after the enactment of s. 10 of the Wills Act 1837: *Barreto* v. *Young* [1900] 2 Ch. 339.

[418] Art. 7; *Actes 1961*, p. 170.

[419] *Supra* Section IV.C.

of regulation and in respect of which the conclusion of an international agreement could be considered to be realisable.[420] The success of the Convention on the Form of Wills encouraged this course of action. Previous conferences had not touched this aspect of succession,[421] but the practical need for a uniform regulation had become recognised. In all countries the need to protect the holders of assets of the deceased and his debtors, when confronted with claimants representing to be entitled to the estate of the *de cuius* by virtue of the law governing his succession, has led to practices whereby the claimant's title is authenticated as a successor of the deceased.

In civil law countries, which follow the French legal system, the claimant beneficiary, who alleges he belongs to the category of beneficiaries who obtain possession (*saisine*) immediately,[422] establishes his right to succeed by setting out his title in a notarial document (*acte de notoriété*).[423] If not covered by this category, he must apply to the court to have his right to possession verified (*envoi en possession*).[424] A similar procedure *ex officio*, also limited to certification, obtains in Germany affecting either the entire estate, wherever situated, if the deceased was a German national[425] or limited to the assets in Germany, if he was an alien.[426] | Austrian law differs in as much the procedure in court supplements the passing of title by a formal transfer.[427]

Thus all the civil law systems embrace a system of publicity, semiofficial or official, available to beneficiaries who are universal successors in order to secure a dual purpose: if semi-official to safeguard holders of assets of the

---

[420] *Actes 1974*, Vol. I, p. 15; Lalive, *idem*, Vol. II, p. 286.

[421] *Supra* text to n. 191.

[422] See generally Droz (1970) Rev. crit. d.i.p. 184, 185, 209 *et seq.; Actes 1974*, Vol. II, p. 10.

[423] This includes *réservataires* (CC, Arts. 1004, 913–915); legitimate and illegitimate relatives (Art. 724); the surviving spouse (Arts. 724, 765–767) and *légataires universels* in the absence of *réservataires* (Arts. 1006, 1003).

[424] This includes *légataires universels* competing with *réservataires* (Arts. 1007, 1003); holders with *saisine* of a holograph or mystic will (Arts. 1008, 1003, 970, 976) and *légataires à titre universel* competing with *réservataires, légataires universels* or beneficiaries or intestacy (Arts. 1011, 1010) and the *Fiscus* (Arts. 768, 770). For Italy see Ferid and Firsching, *Internationales Erbrecht*, nos. 265 *et seq.*; Luxembourg, no.116; Netherlands, nos. 23, 24.

[425] BGB, paras. 2253 *et seq.*; in Alsace a *certificat d'héritier*; for Argentina see Ferid and Firsching, *idem*, no.96, Law No.17711 for the protection of purchasers of immovables; for Greece, nos. 274 *et seq.*, CC, Arts. 1956–1966 modified by Arts. 819 *et seq.* of the Law of Civil Procedure (1971); for Italy, Firsching and Ferid, s.v. Italien.

[426] BGB, para.2369.

[427] ABGB, paras. 797–799; Ferid and Firsching, *op. cit. supra* n. 424, s.v. Österreich, nos. 139 *et seq.*; for Switzerland see Art. 554 ZGB limited to a few cases, and compare for Denmark the Skiftelov n. 155 of 30 Nov. 1874; Ferid and Firsching, s.v. Dänemark, no.229; Norway, Lov om skifte of 21 Feb. 1930, para.12a – ff; Poland, Ferid and Firsching, s.v. Polen, nos. 174 *et seq.*; Switzerland, s.v. Schweiz, nos. 113, 118.

estate or debtors in paying or handing over these assets; if official, to secure in addition that certain testamentary provisions potentially conflicting with the statutory portion of beneficiaries are verified.

At common law, too, the estate passes directly, although to the personal representatives and not to the beneficiaries; where an executor has been appointed, the function of the court serves to verify the testamentary instrument, in appointing an administrator it replaces the immediate successor – the President of the Family Division – by a comparable act of publicity which is also constitutive.

It could therefore be stated confidently:[428]

The difference in the treatment of [the administration of the estate of a deceased person] according to civil and common law is functional rather than structural. In both the estate is made to vest immediately in a successor; in some formalities are required involving the cooperation of the courts, as e.g. in France, Austria, Germany and in Common Law countries, which indicate to the parties at large who is entitled to collect the assets and is liable to pay the debts.

In successions involving assets in several countries the first and foremost problem is to determine who is to be entrusted with the administration of the estate, the collection of the assets and the payment of debts. At present separate proceedings in some form or another must be initiated in many countries where there are assets. In some countries the device of recognising the foreign proceedings may be called in aid ...

It would greatly facilitate the process of winding up and distributing the estates of persons who died leaving assets in several countries if a uniform procedure could be established whereby the same person can be given the task of carrying out these functions in all countries where assets of the deceased are situated ... For this purpose it would suffice to establish a *principal jurisdiction* to determine this legitimation. Little difficulty should arise as regards choice of law *at this stage*. The acceptance of a principal jurisdiction would bring with it the acceptance of the choice of law rules of that country, at least for the purpose of conferring upon certain persons the power to take possession of the assets everywhere.

| In limiting the delivery of the certificate to the *locus standi* of the holder, as determined by the choice of law rules of the country of the principal place of jurisdiction, the question remains, at least at first sight, as to what law is to govern the distribution of the estate, for jurisdiction and choice of law are closely intertwined.[429] In practice, French courts have accepted a foreign

---

[428] Reply by the British government to the questionnaire, *Actes 1974*, Vol. II, p. 104, prepared by the present writer.

[429] *Idem*, p. 17 – see also pp. 23, 49 *et seq.* (*lex successionis, lex fori, lex situs, lex ultimi domicilii, lex patriae*); Droz (1970) Rev. crit. d.i.p. 183–206, esp. 224.

certificate issued by the courts of the foreign domicile of the deceased in so far as succession to movables[430] but not as to immovables[431] situated in France was concerned, thus tying recognition to the law governing the succession.[432] In England a local grant is always necessary, but if a grant (or possibly a certificate) has been obtained abroad in the courts of the last domicile of the deceased, an ancillary grant will be made on the same terms.[433] Alternatively, a local grant will follow as closely as possible the material provisions of the law of the last domicile of the *de cuius.*[434]

In attempting to meet the practical need experienced in most countries but either neglected or met by various devices of greater or lesser efficacy, the XII Conference embarked on a programme[435] which was both technical, though with legal undertones, and novel for many of the participating States, especially those whose background is formed by the civil law. A common lawyer, however, will detect familiar concerns and features.[436]

(a) Administration certificate. The centrepiece is an international certificate designating the person or persons entitled to administer the movable estate of a deceased person and indicating his or their powers (Article 1). Although limited in principle to movables, any express extension of the certificate's effect according to the law of the issuing State (Article 30(1); Annex D) to immovables abroad may be recognised by other contracting States in whole or in part if they so declare.[437] This extension is fraught with difficulties. In substance it opens up the question | whether matters of administering the estate of the deceased are involved or aspects of matrimonial property[438] and of the distribution of the assets; technically, it is not clear how and where a contracting State is to indicate which powers over local immovables will or will not be recognised (Article 30(3)).

---

[430] See the cases cited by Lipstein (1975) 39 Rabels Z 29, 33–35; esp. nn. 29, 30, 33, 37; Droz, *idem*, pp. 188–199; for this and other countries see Droz, *Actes 1974*, Vol. II, pp. 50 *et seq.*, 53; for Belgium, *idem*, p. 75.

[431] See Lipstein, *idem*, n. 28.

[432] For Switzerland see *Actes 1974*, Vol. II, p. 114.

[433] *J. b. Hill* (1870) L.R. 2 P. & D. 89–90; *I. b. Earl, idem*, p. 450.

[434] *Re Achillopoulos* [1928] Ch. 433, 444, 445; see also *I. b. Briesemann* [1894] P. 260, *I. b. von Linden* [1896] P. 148, *Groos* [1904] P. 269, 273.

[435] Prel. Report Droz, *Actes 1974*, Vol. II, pp. 7–19, 34–66; Special Commission Report Lalive, *idem*, pp. 136–151; Final Report Lalive, *idem*, pp. 285–308.

[436] See Goldman (1974) Clunet 256; Lalive (1972) 28 Ann. suisse dr. int. 61; Lipstein, *op. cit. supra* n. 430, at p. 29; Loussouarn (1976) Clunet 251; Droz (1969) 29 Comité fr. d.i.p. 319, 329 *et seq.*

[437] Arts. 30(2), 38(1); this provision was inserted at the request of the Irish and UK representatives.

[438] According to Belgian law the certificate could conflict with the right of the surviving spouse living in the regime of community of goods, and similar objections could arise under Danish, Norwegian and Swedish law, if the surviving spouse as co-owner opts to continue the matrimonial community regime with the heirs; Lipstein, *op. cit. supra* n. 430, at p. 43, but see *Actes 1974*, Vol. II, p. 109B.

(b) Holder's powers. The powers exercisable by the holder of the certificate must be set out in accordance with the model annexed to the Convention,[439] which offers a choice between three versions: power over all corporeal and incorporeal movables; over a particular asset or category of assets; or to carry out all or some of the acts set out in untechnical language in a Schedule.[440]

(c) Jurisdiction to grant the certificate. In determining which authority is to have jurisdiction to draw up the certificate if the deceased was a national of or domiciled in one State leaving assets in another, the Conference fell back on what had become a modern test, namely habitual residence.[441] The intimate relationship between jurisdiction and choice of law is acknowledged in as much as the *lex fori*, i.e. the law of the habitual residence of the deceased at the time of his death, applies in principle (Article 1). Faced with the old rivalry between the followers of the *lex patriae* and the *lex domicilii* (now reappearing in the form of habitual residence), a compromise was reached. The *lex patriae* at the time of death applies if either both the State of the habitual residence and that of the nationality of the deceased have made declarations to this effect (Articles 3(1), 31, 32) or if only the State of which he was a national has made such a declaration and the deceased has lived for less than five years in the country which had become his habitual residence.[442] A common lawyer can reconcile this situation with that in English law by identifying the continued application of the *lex patriae* with that of the law of the domicile of origin and its adhesion for five years after a change of residence with a somewhat rigid interpretation of the requirements for the acquisition of a domicile of choice. A second new solution accords the | deceased the faculty to select either of those two laws for the purpose of designating the holder of the certificate and in indicating his powers. Thereby the Swiss principle of *professio juris* is rendered applicable, albeit within the limited sphere of the administration of estates, as against that of distribution.[443]

---

[439] Art. 1(2); for the language in which it is to be expressed, see Art. 33.

[440] Annex C 10(a), (b).

[441] Arts. 2, 32; see also Recognition and Enforcement of Judgments concerning Maintenance Obligations (1958), Art. 3, (1973), Art. 7(1), (3); Guardianship of Minors, Art. 1; Recognition of Divorces and Legal Separations (1973), Art. 2(1)(a), (b); Adoptions, Art. 1; Lipstein, *op. cit. supra* n. 430, at p. 39.

[442] Art. 3(2); Lalive, *op. cit. supra* n. 436, at p. 64; Bucher (1972) 28 Ann. suisse dr. int. 76, 141 *et seq.* with lit.; Neuhaus (1955) 20 Rabels Z 52, 61; for earlier proposals to this effect see Asser (1906) 21 Ann. Inst. dr. int. 443, 457; Jitta (1912) 28 I.L.A. 322, 330(18).

[443] Art. 4; the Preliminary Report of Lalive, *Actes 1974*, Vol. II, p. 139 refers, *inter alia*, to the Swiss Law on Domiciliaries and Residents of 25 June 1891, Art. 22; also *idem*, Vol. I, p. 292; *op. cit. supra* n. 436, at p. 64. See also Jitta, *idem*, p. 331(19). See now the Swiss Law on Private International Law of 18 Dec. 1987, Art. 90(2) and the New York Decedents Estate Law, Art. 47; NY Estates Powers and Trusts Act 1968, s. 3.5.1(h).

A novel type of provision envisages that a legal system distinguishes *ratione personae* between rules of succession applicable to them.[444]

A series of provisions supplements the procedure for issuing the certificate. If it is to be drawn up in accordance with the national law of the deceased the authorities at the place of his habitual residence may ask those of his nationality for guidance in drawing up the contents of the certificate envisaged in the Annex and the Schedule.[445] The task of issuing the certificate is to be entrusted to "the competent judicial or administrative authority", to be designated in each State.[446] This seems to imply that a single authority is to be appointed, which in England could be the High Court and in civil law countries perhaps the Ministry of Justice. The Convention acknowledges, however, that in some countries the task of certifying the qualification of a beneficiary to take possession of the estate is in the hands of a body of specialised conveyancers known as notaries. In this case, the State concerned must designate this body and appoint a confirming authority (Article 6(2)). In addition, a measure of publicity and enquiry is to be provided.[447] In England the existing procedure for obtaining a grant should suffice, except perhaps in respect of publicity.[448] A further safeguard is provided for the benefit of interested persons or authorities in as much as upon their request the fact that a certificate has been issued, annulled or modified and its substance must be made available.[449] While each contracting State is at liberty to devise its own system of information, such as a public register, the task of identifying interested persons should once again create difficulties.

(d) Recognition. The certificate in the form in which it sets out the person of the holder and his powers is to be recognised by the other contracting States without further conditions[450] except that a procedure of | recognition may, but need not, be required.[451] This may be informal by providing publicity or by establishing a procedure comparable to that for obtaining an ancillary grant. In substance the powers set out in the certificate in accordance either with the law of the last habitual residence of the deceased or with his national law are made thereby part of the law of the State where the certificate is recognised subject, if need be, by means of a transposition.[452]

---

[444] It is concerned with laws of succession applicable to ethnic or religious groups, as is the case in Egypt and Israel; *Actes 1974*, Vol. II, p. 307.

[445] Art. 5; in conjunction with Arts. 3(1), (2), 37(1); *Actes, idem*, p. 293.

[446] Arts. 6(1), 37(1); *Actes, ibid.*

[447] Art. 7; *Actes, idem*, p. 294.

[448] Especially notice to interested parties, including the surviving spouse.

[449] Arts. 8, 37; *Actes 1974*, Vol. II, p. 295.

[450] Art. 10; *Actes, ibid.*

[451] Art. 10(1); it can be dispensed with, as is the practice in Scandinavian countries, if the deceased died habitually resident abroad.

[452] For this method see Lipstein (1972 – I) 135 Rec. des Cours 99, 207, 208. The question remains when and by whom this operation is to be performed.

Even before recognition has been granted the holder may take protective or urgent measures,[453] but here again the requested State may require an expeditious procedure of recognition to be observed.[454] Any protective urgent measures retain their validity after their preliminary period of recognition has expired, even if the certificate is subsequently refused recognition (Article 12(1)) or (it must be assumed) if no application for recognition was finally made. However, application may be made to confirm or to set aside the measures (Article 12(2)).

(e) Refusal to recognise. Recognition may only be refused on a limited number of grounds in accordance with a procedure to be determined by each State.[455] These are that, in the opinion of the requested State:

(1) the certificate is not authentic (Article 13(1));

(2) the certificate discloses on the face of it that it was issued by an authority lacking jurisdiction under the Convention (Article 13(2), apparently referring to Article 6(1));

(3) the deceased was habitually resident in the requested State (Article 14(1));[456]

(4) contrary to Articles 3, 4 and 31 the certificate has not been drawn up in accordance with the national law of the deceased (Article 14(2));

(5) the certificate conflicts with a decision on the merits rendered in or to be recognised by the requested State (Article 15);[457]

|(6) the certificate is manifestly incompatible with the public policy of the requested State (Article 17).

Recognition may also be restricted to certain of the powers indicated in the certificate.

A conflict between a prior administration in accordance with local law and a subsequent application for the recognition of an international certifi-

---

[453] Art. 11(1); the power expires after 60 days, unless the holder has initiated proceedings for the recognition of the certificate: Art. 11(3); moreover, it expires if a decision to the contrary is made: Art. 11(1).

[454] Art. 11(2); such proceedings would probably have to be observed in England.

[455] Arts. 10(1), 19. The wording of Art. 10(2) leaves it open whether the procedure of "opposition" or "appeal" against a grant may also be informal. The existence of any procedure and the designation of the competent authority are to be notified to the Netherlands authorities: Art. 37(1), (3).

[456] A different appreciation of the facts and conflicts of characterisation appear to be envisaged; see Art. 32.

[457] This could be a decision on the right to administer the estate or a decision determining the distribution. Excluded by the Brussels Convention, Art. 1 and by the Hague Convention on the Recognition and Enforcement of Foreign Judgments in Civil and Commercial Matters, Art. 1(4), the recognition of judgments of this kind appears to be of limited importance, if any. On the other hand, a conflict between two Convention, Art. 1, certificates issued in different countries could lead to difficulties if one of them had already been recognised. Art. 16 permits a flexible solution. See Lipstein, *op. cit. supra* n. 430, at p. 46.

cate appointing a different administration poses another difficulty. The Convention has sought to solve it by allowing the certificate to prevail, in so far as the two overlap, but no further (Article 20). It must also be considered whether recognition may be refused on any of the grounds enumerated in Articles 13–17, especially 14(2), 15 and 17.[458] Most importantly, the Convention has failed to take into account the likelihood that the local administrator has already made use of his powers under local law.[459]

(f) Power to control. The requested State may control the exercise of the powers of the holder in the same manner as it controls local administrators but may not curtail their extent.[460] The Convention permits the requested State to link the taking of possession of the assets with the payment of debts. This can be best achieved by requiring the holder to provide security, seeing that unlike a personal representative in English law the foreign holder may not be liable for the debts. The recognition of the holder's powers has as its counterpart the discharge of those who in good faith pay to him their debts due to the estate or hand over assets.[461] For the same reason the title of a *bona fide* purchaser of assets from the holder of the certificate is to be protected.[462]

(g) Challenge on the merits. If the designation or the powers of the certificate's holder is challenged on the merits, as distinct from the grounds set out in Article 13(2) or 14, the provisional effects may be suspended and the proceedings stayed until the court having jurisdiction has determined the issue. This will probably be a court in the requested | State.[463] If, on the other hand, the challenge occurs before the courts of the issuing State or in another contracting State, the effects of the certificate may be suspended until the dispute has been decided (Article 25). An annulment or a modification of the certificate or a suspension of its effects is not to affect previous acts by the holder and dealings in good faith with the holder (Articles 27–29). The usefulness of the Convention as a whole was doubted by Firsching at a time when only a preliminary draft was available, but the final version would not have satisfied him either. Instead, he advocated three principles:[464]

---

[458] *Actes 1974*, Vol. II, p. 361; Lipstein, *idem*, p. 47.

[459] See Kegel, *Internationales Privatrecht* (6th edn, 1987), § 21, p. 672.

[460] Art. 21(1), (3); Lipstein *op. cit. supra* n. 430, at p. 48; *Actes 1974*, Vol. II, p. 302.

[461] Art. 22; *Actes, idem*, p. 303. Questions of contract or property and not only of succession may be involved.

[462] Art. 23. This may require legislation by the *situs* or the provisions of the local law may be applied by way of analogy. Cf. Administration of Estates Act 1925, s. 27; German Civil Code, para. 2366.

[463] Art. 24. See also Art. 25(2). It will probably be for the law of that State to determine which court has jurisdiction; *Actes 1974*, Vol. II, p. 304. Lipstein, *op. cit. supra* n. 430, at p. 49 n. 89; for the effect of the annulment etc. elsewhere, see Art. 26.

[464] *Multitudo Legum Ius Unum, Essays in honour of Wilhelm Wengler* (1973), Vol. II, pp. 321, 327, 335.

(1) local law including its conflicts rules should apply to local assets;

(2) each State issues a certificate relating to local assets; if these certificates agree in their result, the surplus may be handed over in proceedings not very different from those where an ancillary administration exists;

(3) States which do not know the distinction between administration and distribution should not be forced to introduce it.

This overlooks the purpose of the Convention, which was to avoid the need for separate proceedings and to ensure a uniform application of law at least at the stage of winding up an estate before distribution, at a time when unity of succession in some countries was confronted by a scission in others and when the *lex patriae* applicable in some was met by the *lex domicilii* and the *lex situs* in others in what seemed a permanent and irreconcilable conflict of laws governinga succession.

Since the Convention was concluded,[465] the situation has changed completely since the principles of jurisdiction, and thus also of choice of law, limited to the administration of successions, have now been adopted by the XVI Conference to govern the choice of the substantive law of succession.[466]

Having prepared the way, the Administration Convention has served its purpose and can be said to have been merged in the Succession Convention for those States which adopt the latter.

|*3. Succession*

Between 1893 and 1928 the Hague Conferences had faced the problems involving choice of law in matters of succession in various drafts, some restricting themselves to a series of basic rules, others adopting a more extensive attitude which led to the adoption of detailed provisions concerning a considerable variety of aspects of the law of succession.[467]

Unity of succession centring on the national law of the deceased with only little regard to the law of his last domicile, the range of matters to be covered by the *lex successionis*, the effect of local mandatory laws in the place of a rule reserving public policy, but finally replaced by the latter, some concessions to the *lex situs* and the recognition of the *jus regale* in respect of *bona vacantia*, the exclusion of pacts of succession and of questions of capacity characterised the tendency of the proceedings. In the end a draft emerged which concentrated only on the fundamental aspects of succession, leaving

---

[465] For its subsequent fate see XVI Session t. II (1990), p. 115. Only two States have ratified it and it is not in force.

[466] Convention on the Law Applicable to Succession to the Estates of Deceased Persons of 20 Oct. 1988.

[467] *Supra* Section IV.C.

out administration, transmission and jurisdiction. Its failure to attract ratifications was probably due to two factors: a fairly rigid reliance on the principle of unity of succession in disregard of a scission which allots a place to
the *lex situs* and an equally rigid adherence to the principle of nationality.

When the XVI Conference resumed the work, it had before it a resolution
of the Institut de droit international[468] which regretted that it was unable as
yet to reach a uniform solution. Referring to the compromise reached by the
Convention on the Form of Testamentary Dispositions of 5 October 1961, it
proposed that capacity should be governed by the testator's personal law at
the time of making a will and that the essential validity should be governed
by the law governing the succession, as was the power of personal representatives. A limited *professio juris* was to be allowed. After much preparatory
work[469] agreement was reached on a convention which dealt in four parts
with its scope, the law applicable, pacts of succession and mutual wills, and
general provisions. Negatively, Article 1(2) provides that the Convention
does not apply to the forms of dispositions of property upon death (which
are covered by the Wills Convention of 5 October 1961), capacity to dispose
of property | on death (assumed to concern a matter of status), matters per-
taining to matrimonial property (which may raise problems of adaptation)[470] and property rights, interests or assets created or transferred otherwise than by succession. This category includes joint ownership (where the
right of the deceased accrues to the survivor) and transactions *inter vivos* at
common law which create equitable rights exercisable on the settlor's
death.[471] Positively, it applies (Article 7(2)) to the determination of beneficiaries, their shares and obligations arising under the succession, including
those under judicial orders,[472] loss of benefits through exheredation or dis-
qualification, the duty to bring in, or to account for, any benefits for the
purpose of determining the shares of beneficiaries, questions of legitimate

---

[468] (1967) II Ann. inst. dr. int. 563.

[469] *Supra* n. 65. XVI Conference, *Actes et Documents* t. II (1990), p. 19 (Droz, Commentary) = *Actes et Documents*, XII session, t. II, p.II 34; van Loon, Update on the Commentary on Succession in Private International Law, *idem* (1990), p. 107; Succession in private
international law. Prospective Study, *idem*, p. 41; Permanent Bureau, Conclusions of the
Special Commission on the law applicable to decedents' estates, Nov. 1986, *idem*, p. 189;
Rights of the State in matters of succession, *idem*, p. 203; Some suggestions on the possible
scope of the application of the Convention, *idem* p. 207; Preliminary Draft Convention
and Report (Waters), *idem*, p. 233; Explanatory Report (Waters), *idem* p. 526.

[470] *Actes 1990*, p. 543(45), (46); e.g. *Baudoin* v. *Trudel* [1937] 1 D.L.R. 216; [1937] O.R. 1
and the cases and lit. in Lipstein, *op. cit. supra* n. 452, at p. 209 nn. 70–72; Cansacchi,
(1953 – II) 83 Rec. des Cours 79, 111 *et seq.*; Batiffol (1967–1) 120 *idem* 169, 175; Steindorf,
Sachnormen (1958), pp. 81 *et seq.*; Kropholler, *Festschrift Ferid* (1978), p. 279.

[471] Art. 1(2)(d); e.g. *Matter of Totten* (1904) 179 N.Y. 112, 71 N.E. 748; *Maddison* v.
Alderson (1883) 8 App. Cas. 467.

[472] E.g. under the Inheritance (Provision for Family and Dependants) Act 1975.

portions reserved by law for certain beneficiaries[473] and the validity in substance of testamentary dispositions.[474] Other matters considered by a State
to fall into the law of succession can also be included (Article 7(3)). Notable
omissions are the construction of testamentary dispositions, but the difference in a factual approach to this question in some systems of law and a legal
approach in others precluded an agreement,[475] jurisdiction and the administration of estates, but the co-ordination of the choice of law rules between
the Succession Convention and that on the Administration of Estates of
Deceased Persons, if the former is ratified, renders further provisions unnecessary.[476]

The compromise offered by the Administration Convention[477] provided a
firm basis of the Succession Convention both for testate and intestate succession. No problem arises if the *lex patriae* and the law of the habitual
residence of the deceased coincide (Article 3(1)). If they do not, the *lex
patriae* applies as well, unless the deceased had been habitually resident
elsewhere for at least five years immediately before his death, but an escape
clause once again permits the *lex patriae* to apply if the deceased was manifestly more closely connected with the country of his nationality when he
died.[478]

| In addition, following the Swiss example,[479] but developing it further, a
person may designate the law of a particular State. This can apply, irrespective of whether the person died testate or intestate, only in one of four
situations: if either at the time of the designation or at the time of his death he
was a national of that State or was habitually resident there (Article 5(1)). A
reservation enables States not to recognise a designation if the person was at
the time of his death a national of and habitually resident in the reserving
State or if as a result of the designation the wife or a child of the deceased,
being a national of or habitually resident in the reserving State, is totally or
substantially deprived of a statutory portion or family provision which is
mandatory (Article 24(1)). The designation is presumed to comprise the
deceased's entire estate, even if partly testate and partly intestate (Article
5(4)), must be made in the form required by the designated law for a testa-

---

[473] Art. 7(2)(d); *Actes 1990*, p. 567(79).

[474] Art. 7(2)(e). For the use of this term see the Convention on the Form of Testamentary
Dispositions of 5 Oct. 1961, *supra* text to n. 382.

[475] *Actes 1990*, pp. 541(37), 569(81).

[476] *Idem*, p. 535(23), (24).

[477] Art. 3; foreshadowed in 1900 and 1904; *supra* text after n. 193.

[478] Art. 3(2); *Actes 1990*, p. 535(25); for the case that the close connection existed with a
third State see Art. 7(3); *idem*, pp. 547(49), 551(54).

[479] Formerly Law of 25 June 1891 on the Private Law Relations of Domiciliaries and
Residents, Art. 22(2), limited to a choice of the law of the deceased's home canton – now
Law on Private International Law, 18 Dec. 1987, Art. 88(2).

mentary disposition and must be recognised and valid according to that law (Article 5(2)).[480] An innovatory provision permits a person to designate by way of incorporation[481] the law of one or several States to govern the succession to particular assets, while the mandatory rules of the law governing the succession apply, whether that law has been chosen, designated or operates in the absence of a choice.[482] To that extent, but no further, the *lex situs* may come into its own.[483]

The uniform application of the Convention stipulated by it, even if the law applicable is that of a non-contracting State (Article 2), has led, exceptionally in the practice of the Hague Conferences, to the admission of *renvoi*, if the law of the non-contracting State contains a reference on.[484] Harmony of decision is said to have been its purpose, but the arguments adduced in support sustain it only if either the reference on is accepted without a further reference on or if a reference back can be established.[485] The effectiveness of this provision must remain uncertain given that a reservation is possible (Article 24(1)(b)).

The principle was confirmed that *bona vacantia* accrue to the local State by virtue of *the jus regale*,[486] but nothing seems to prohibit the State of the *situs* from conceding the estate to the national State of the deceased | on the ground that it regards that State as the *ultimus heres*.[487] In any circumstances the *lex situs* can only claim to apply, following previous proposals,[488] if certain immovables, certain bodies of persons or special categories of assets are subject to a particular order of succession based on economic, family or social considerations.[489]

Detailed provisions regulate successoral pacts and mutual wills, which are described as creating, varying or terminating rights in the future estate or estates of one or more persons parties to the agreement (Article 8). If the estate of one person only is involved (as is usually the case in a successoral

---

[480] For the sufficiency of an oral designation see *Actes 1990*, p. 557(65) and see *supra* text to n. 382.

[481] For English law see e.g. *Dobell & Co.* v. *SS Rossmore* [1895] 2 Q.B. 408, 412; *Ex p. Dever* (1887) 18 Q.B.D. 660, 664, 666; *Adamastos Shipping Co. Ltd* v. *Anglo-Saxon Petroleum Co. Ltd* [1959] A.C. 133.

[482] Art. 6 in conjunction with Arts. 3 and 5(1); *Actes 1990*, pp. 537(27), 559(69), 561(70), 565(75).

[483] *Idem*, p. 561(71).

[484] Arts. 4, 17; *idem*, pp. 551 (57), 593(117).

[485] *Idem*, pp. 551(58), 553(59).

[486] Art. 16; *idem*, p. 591(115); *supra* text to n. 182, but also to nn. 190, 193.

[487] *Idem*, p. 591(116).

[488] *Supra* text to nn. 168, 180, 186.

[489] Art. 15; *Actes 1990*, pp. 587, 589(110, 111). The reference to "enterprises" points to certain institutions stated to function under Belgian, German and Polish law. This article does not envisage restrictions based on alienage or public security. See *supra* text to n. 186.

pact), the choice of law rules of the Convention apply as they would have done if the promisor had died at the date of the agreement (Article 9(1)). If invalid under that law, *favor validatis* maintains the disposition if under the Convention the law applicable at the time of the promisor's death would have treated it as valid (Article 9(2)).[490] If the estates of more than one person are involved, as may occur in the case of marriage settlements or mutual wills, the laws applicable according to the choice of law rules of the Convention to each of the parties concerned must permit the dispositions, as if the parties had died at the time of the agreement (Article 10(1)). In addition, the parties may expressly select the law of the habitual residence or nationality at the time of the conclusion of the agreement of one or any one of the parties. Thereby a single law may become applicable in lieu of the cumulation envisaged by the basic provision for bilateral agreements; also, certainty is ensured for both unilateral and bilateral agreements.[491] If the law governing the succession at the time of the promisor's death does not coincide with that which is deemed to be that law at the time of the conclusion of the agreement, the latter is to prevail (Article 12(1)), subject to such rights as legitimate portion and the like which are indefeasible according to the law applicable at the time of the promisor's death (Article 12(2)).

Some marginal problems are also solved. Where on the death of two persons in the same occurrence the rules on *commorientes* conflict, or if none exists, neither party is to succeed to the other (or, in other words, they are deemed to have died at the same time without a presumption of survivorship).[492] A trust created by a testamentary disposition may be governed by a law other than that which governs the succession (Article 15). Finally, Article 16 includes the usual public policy clause.

| While seeking to be comprehensive, the Convention did not solve some of the questions addressed in previous drafts.[493] Others, such as that of the reimbursement by one beneficiary of debts paid by another beneficiary in excess of his quota,[494] were not noticed, while successoral pacts have been given a prominence which their very limited acceptance by the laws of few States only hardly seems to merit.

The success of the Convention will depend in the end on whether the compromise between the application of the *lex patriae* and the *lex domicilii* will be found acceptable, especially since the *lex patriae* remains preponder-

---

[490] *Idem*, p. 581(98). See *supra* nn. 405, 383.

[491] Art. 11; *idem*, p. 583(102).

[492] Art. 13; see e.g. BGB, para.20; *Re Cohn* [1945] Ch. 5.

[493] See *supra* text to nn. 189–192: capacity, the manner and substance of the division of the estate, limitation of liability.

[494] See for a comparable situation at common law *Re Scull* (1917) 87 L.J. Ch. 59; Franks (1954) 104 L.J. 504. See also *Re Collens* [1986] Ch. 505.

ant, and whether the neglect of the *lex situs* will be resented.[495] Perhaps acceptance would have been more palatable if the criterion of nationality had been replaced by that of the previous habitual residence until five years have elapsed since establishing a new habitual residence. Thereby even the domicile of origin might assume a new function and the need for a special provision for States having a composite legal system[496] could be avoided.

C. Commercial Law

1. International sale of goods

Continuing the work done in 1925 and 1928, a Special Commission of the Hague Conferences, at a meeting held on 28 May 1931,[497] produced a draft on the law applicable to the international sale of goods. This formed the basis of the discussions at the VII Conference, which accepted it with some modifications.[498]

The Convention applies only to international sale of goods. The test of the international character (in Article 1(1)) formed the object of critical comment,[499] which concentrated on the question whether this test was | subjective or objective. In the end the solution was found by excluding the exercise of an attempted choice by the parties to internationalise a contract by the submission to the jurisdiction of a foreign court or to an international arbitration (Article 1(4)).

A series of particular types of sales (of securities, ships, registered boats or aircraft, sales upon an order of a court or upon execution) are excluded (Article 1(2)). On the other hand, contracts which embrace a sale of raw materials in connection with an undertaking to manufacture or produce the finished object are covered by Article 1(3).

---

[495] For a recent rejection of the *lex situs* in matters of intestacy see Morris (1969) 85 L.Q.R. 339.

[496] Such as Art. 19 of the Succession Convention. The reference (Art. 20) to States having different systems of personal law is new and points to the enlargement of the Hague Conferences to include States where interpersonal conflicts can arise. See Lipstein and Szaszy, *International Encyclopaedia of Comparative Law* (1985), Vol. III, chap. 10. However, such States are free not to apply the Convention to internal conflicts (Art. 21).

[497] See *supra* text to nn. 228–240; VII Conference, *Documents 1952*, pp. 4 (text); 5 (report Julliot de la Morandière); VI Session, *Actes 1928*, pp. 265 *et seq.*; Extraordinary Session 1985, pp. 27 *et seq.*

[498] *Supra* n. 66, 15 June 1955, *Actes 1951*, pp. 18 *et seq.*; 360 (Report Julliot de la Morandière); Loussouarn (1986) Rev. crit. d.i.p. 271; McLachlan (1986) 102 L.Q.R. 591, 602 *et seq.*

[499] *Actes 1951*, p. 26; the draft of the Rome Convention on the law applicable to contracts caused the same reaction; see Lando, von Hoffman and Siehr (Eds), *European Private International Law of Obligations* (1975), pp. 3, 156; Piot (1957) Clunet 949, 959; Doelle (1952) 17 Rabels Z 160, 163.

The parties can select the law to govern their contract, which is the domestic law of the country concerned (Article 2(1)). *Renvoi* is therefore excluded. The choice must be express or must follow by implication unambiguously from the terms of the contract (Article 2(2)).[500] The law so chosen
applies also to questions of consent (Article 2(3)). Formulated thus generally, the Convention leaves no room for distinguishing between defects of
consent which render the contract voidable or void[501] or for the exception in
favour of the law of the habitual residence of a party if it would be unreasonable to determine the effect of his conduct by the law applicable to the
contract as a whole[502] because the latter, but not the law of the party's habitual residence, treats silence as consent to a proposed choice of law clause.
In the absence of an express or implied choice the contract of sale is governed
by the domestic law of the seller's habitual residence at the time when he
receives the order or by the law of the place where the seller maintains an
establishment, if the order is received there (Article 3(1)). On the other hand,
the law of the buyer's habitual residence or of the place where he maintains
an establishment applies, if the order is received there by the seller or his
representative (Article 3(2)).[503] A special rule (Article 3(3)) was devised for
sales on a stock or commodity exchange or by public auction.

The question whether the law applicable is that at the time of making the
contract or whether it can subsequently be changed was left open.[504] The
observations by the British delegate, indicating that the purpose of crystal-
lising the applicable law can be achieved (if only partly) by incorporating the
terms of the law so chosen into the contract which is|governed by its proper
law, deserve attention, however.[505] Although the possibility of selecting different laws to govern different parts of a contract was rejected, it was conceded that while some aspects of a contract might be governed by a law
chosen by the parties, others could be governed by the law applicable in the
absence of a choice.[506]

As an exception to the law applicable generally in the absence of an express
or implied choice of law, the form and the periods within which an inspec-

---

[500] The surrounding circumstances are irrelevant; cf. Art. 5 of the Convention on the
Law Applicable to Agency, *infra* text to n. 564.

[501] *Mackender* v. *Feldia* [1967] 2 Q.B. 590.

[502] Rome Convention of 19 June 1980, Art. 8(2); Cmnd.8489; Misc.5/1982; Contracts
(Applicable Law) Act 1990, s. 8(2); *Actes 1985*, p. 45 (Report Pelichet).

[503] See the Rome Convention, *idem*, Art. 5(2), second indent, but see Art. 5(3), the
additional protection of which in favour of the consumer did not feature at the time when
the Sales Convention was drafted.

[504] *Actes 1952*, pp. 39, 78, 80.

[505] *Idem*, p. 41.

[506] *Idem*, p. 40.

tion of goods delivered under a sale must be made as well as any notifications are governed by the *lex loci actus*.[507]

Four aspects of a contract of sale are excluded from the operation of the Convention (Article 5(1)–(4)): form does not require any comment. The exclusion of capacity, however, raises the question whether capacity always involves a question of status or is linked to the law governing the contract.[508] The exclusion of that part of a contract of sale which concerns the transfer of title to property left this matter to the choice of law rules of the contracting States[509] until a special convention on the law applicable to the transfer of title in sales has been concluded.[510] However, independently of any connection between the passing of title and the passing of the risk, all personal obligations including the passing of the risk are governed by the law governing the contract. In particular, the Scandinavian concern to protect the buyer's right against claims by the seller's creditors and to protect the unpaid seller's right to recover the object sold against creditors of the buyer[511] is treated as contractual.

By separating the question of the law applicable to the passing of the risk from that of the passing of title in sale, the Convention follows the modern trend in practice and legislation.[512] Finally, the usual reservation in favour of the intervention of the forum's manifest public policy appears here as well (Article 6).

A revision of the Convention of 1955 was envisaged by the XIV Session[513] resuming a discussion at the XIII Session,[514] having regard in particular to the UN Convention on a Uniform Law for International Sales.[515] The Convention of 1955 had not proved a great attraction.[516] It|was thought to be too simple, too inflexible in the choice of connecting factors[517] under the influence of civil law thinking, that the definition of a sale as international was deficient,[517a] that the requirement that a free choice must follow unambiguously from the terms of the contract was too narrow,[518] that the exclu-

---

[507] Art. 4; a fraudulent change of port in order to avoid an inconvenient inspection would constitute a breach of contract: *idem*, pp. 53, 55.

[508] See the lit. and practice cited in *idem*, p. 41 notes 76–78.

[509] *Idem*, pp. 62 *et seq.*

[510] *Idem*, p. 65; *infra* Section V.C.2.

[511] Art. 5(4); *idem*, p. 69 (report Ussing).

[512] See e.g. Rabel, *Das Recht des Warenkaufs* (1958), Vol. 2, p. 291 at pp. 296 *et seq.;* Beale, *Conflict of Laws*, Vol. 2, p. 977.

[513] XIV Conference, *Actes 1982*, I, 82, II, 180; Final Act B *ibid.* I, 60; Extraordinary Session 1985, *Actes*, pp. 18 (Report Pelichet), 175 (Prel. Report von Mehren).

[514] *Actes et Documents 1978*, Vol. I, pp. 176–178; also 184–186.

[515] Misc. 24(1980); Cmnd. 8074; 19 I.L.M. 671, esp. Arts. 1(1), 7(2).

[516] Nine ratifications; the UK had not signed this Convention.

[517] *Actes et Documents 1985*, pp. 37, 69 *et seq.*

[517a] *Idem*, pp. 39, 51, 65, 37.

[518] *Ibid*, 37.

sion of capacity on the ground that it concerned status failed to take into account the practice in many countries to include in their rules of conflict of laws a special rule on capacity to enter into contracts,[519] that the failure to include a rule on the formation and the form of a contract, including the choice of law agreement, was regrettable,[520] that an attempt should be made to establish a link between the passing of the risk and the enjoyment of proprietary rights,[521] and that the place of consumer sales had not been determined, that insufficient attention had been given to mandatory rules, to the possible limits of party autonomy and to partial choice of law.[522]

The XVI Conference produced a more far-reaching and detailed draft convention.[523] Unlike its predecessor, which relied on the vague test that a contract is international,[524] it applies to contracts of sale of goods which have an international character because the parties have their place of business (defined in Article 14) in different States or if a choice between the laws of different States is in issue.[525] As previously provided, a contractual choice of the applicable law is insufficient in the absence of a foreign element; a contractual choice of law clause even if coupled with a submission of any dispute to the jurisdiction of a foreign court or to arbitration viewed on its own does not attract the Convention either.[526] The narrowness of this provision is to be regretted since it excludes situations where a foreign element is indirect.[527] Once again a series of particular types of sales is excluded; some enumerated previously remain, but others are removed and yet others are added.[528] The problem | derived from antiquity as to whether an agreement to supply goods to be manufactured or produced is a contract of sale or of hire retained a prominent place and was solved in an orthodox manner.[529]

The parties can select the law to be applied,[530] which is the domestic law of

---

[519] *Idem*, p. 41 and notes 76–79.

[520] *Idem*, pp. 67, 41, 45; Piot, *op. cit. supra* n. 499, at p. 965.

[521] *Actes, idem*, p. 49 referring to the Hague Convention of 15 Apr. 1958 on the Transfer of Title in the case of International Sales of Movables, Art. 2, *infra* Section V.C.2.

[522] *Idem*, pp. 53, 99, 57, 59, 65.

[523] *Supra* n. 71; *idem*, pp. 691 (text), 167 (Prel. Report von Mehren); 710 (Explanatory Report von Mehren).

[524] *Actes et Documents 1978*, p. 179(21).

[525] Art. 1; it is irrelevant whether it is the law of a contracting State or not: Art. 6.

[526] Art. 1(b), subject to a possible reservation: Art. 21(i)(a). Cf. 1955, Art. 1(3).

[527] E.g. a chain of contracts of sale, the last of which takes place between parties having their places of business in the same State.

[528] Arts. 2 (sale by way of execution or otherwise by authority of law; securities, now described as stocks, shares, investment securities, negotiable instruments or money – remain); 3 (ships, registered boats, aircraft, electricity – removed): cf. 1955, Art. 1(1). Art. 1(c): goods bought for personal, family or household use, unless the seller knew of their destination at the time of the sale, are added.

[529] Art. 4; cf. 1955, Art. 1(2).

[530] Art. 7(1); cf. 1955, Art. 2.

the State concerned,[531] but the former requirement that the choice must be contained in an express clause or must unambiguously result from the provisions of the contract has been relaxed. By Article 7(1), the agreed choice must be express or clearly demonstrated by the terms of the contract and the conduct of the parties, seen as a whole. A new subsection (Article 7(2)) permits the parties subsequently to submit the contract as a whole or in part to a different law, irrespective of whether the contract was governed previously by a law chosen by the parties or by the law applicable in the absence of a free choice.[532]

The rule as to which law applies in the absence of a free choice was modified. In general the law of the State applies where the seller has his place of business at the time of the conclusion of the contract.[533] However, the law where the buyer has his place of business applies if *either* in the presence of both parties negotiations[534] were conducted and the contract concluded there *or* if the contract provides expressly that the seller must deliver there or if the buyer invited tenders and mainly determined the terms himself (Article 8(2)).[535] Article 8(3) permits, however, the application of another law with which the contract is manifestly more closely connected, but is in turn subject to a possible exception if the seller and the buyer have their places of business in States having made a reservation to this effect (Articles 8(4), 21(1)(b)) or their places of business are in different States which are parties to the UN Convention on Contracts for the Sale of Goods.[536]

Sales by auction or on a commodity or other exchange are governed by the law chosen by the parties, if the *lex loci actus* permits it; in the absence of an express choice by the parties the *lex loci actus* applies.[537]

Special choice of law rules apply also to the form of contracts, the inspection of goods, and consents and the validity of the contract.[538] Following accepted practice compliance either with the *lex loci actus* or with the law governing the contract satisfies the requirements of form|(Article 11(1)). A new feature (Article 11(2)) is that in the case of a contract between parties in different States, compliance with the *lex loci actus* of one of them suffices; in the case of an agent the *locus actus* is where the agent acts (Article 11(3)); when an act refers to an existing or contemplated contract, Article 11(4) (reproducing Article 9(4) of the Rome Convention) states that compliance

---

[531] Art. 15; *renvoi* remains excluded.

[532] Art. 7(2). The formal validity of the contract and the rights of third parties are unaffected.

[533] Art. 8(1) in conjunction with Art. 14; cf. 1955, Art. 3(1).

[534] Not necessarily all: *Actes 1985*, p. 729(65); cf. 1955, Art. 3(2).

[535] *Idem*, p. 731(78)–(80).

[536] Art. 8(5), p. 733(94).

[537] Art. 9; cf. 1955, Art. 3(3).

[538] Arts. 11, 13, 10 (cf. respectively 1955, Arts. 3(2), 4, 2(3)).

either with the law which governs the contract or would govern the contract (if concluded) or with the *lex loci actus* is sufficient. These rules do not apply, however, if the place of business of a party is in a State which has made a reservation to this effect (Articles 11(5), 21(1)(c)).

The *lex loci actus* applies to the inspection of goods, subject to an express clause in favour of the law chosen to govern the contract.[539]

The existence and the validity of consents to a choice of law clause are determined by the law so chosen.[540] The same applies to the contract of sale itself.[541] However, following Article 8(2) of the Rome Convention a party may rely on the law of his place of business if in the circumstances it would not be reasonable to determine the question in accordance with the law applicable to the contract if it were valid (Article 10(3)).

Overriding consideration is attributed to absolutely binding rules of the forum and to manifest incompatibility with local public policy (Articles 17, 18).

Leaving aside those matters to which special conflicts rules apply by virtue of the Convention, the general choice of law rules sanctioned by Articles 7–9 cover the following contractual topics: its interpretation; rights and obligations arising therefrom, performance; time for accrual of benefits; time for passing of the risk; reservation of title, its effect *inter partes;*[542] failure to perform and damages, subject to the prevalence of the *lex fori*, extinction of obligations including limitation of actions except in so far as it is procedural in character;[543] nullity and invalidity.[544]

The following remain outside the ambit of the law designated by the Convention to determine the sale of goods: capacity, agency, transfer of ownership except its contractual aspects, the effect of the sale upon third parties as well as prorogation of jurisdiction or arbitration agreements.

The new Convention shows many improvements over its predecessor, but apart from a novel choice of law rule on form if the places of business|of the parties are situated in different States it does little more than to give expression to existing practice, but it does so fairly comprehensively. Its main weakness is to be found in the restrictive treatment of the international character of the contract.

---

[539] Art. 13; *Actes 1985*, p. 743(138)–(141).

[540] Art. 10(1); cf. 1955, Art. 2(2).

[541] Art. 10(2); see the Rome Convention, Art. 8(1); for a critique see *supra* text to n. 501.

[542] These provisions take up those of Art. 2 of the Convention on Transfer of Title in the case of International Sales of Movables *infra*.

[543] This wording suggests that the measure of damages may be so characterised by the laws of some contracting States.

[544] Art. 12; but see Art. 5(a): nullity resulting from a lack of capacity falls outside the choice of law determined by the Convention.

It remains to be seen whether a specialised Sales Convention can hold its own within the area of States members of the Rome Convention.

2. *Transfer of title in the case of international sale of movables*

In close connection with the project of a convention on the international sale of goods, the VIII Conference concluded a draft convention on the transfer of title in the case of international sale of goods.[545] Confronted with the fundamental difference between legal systems which rely on the causal link between sale and transfer of title and those drawing a clear line between the two – as well as the Scandinavian approach, which seeks to protect the buyer against claims by the seller's creditors and the unpaid seller's right to recover the object against the creditors of the buyer[546] – the *rapporteur* prepared two drafts, one restricted to the parties to the sale, the other general.[547] The latter could refer to a previous project sponsored by the International Law Association.[548] Furthermore, the practical need for a convention on transfer of title was denied by the German and the British delegations, on whose behalf Professor Wortley pointed out that from the insurer's point of view the existence of an insurance, and not title, was relevant.[549]

In many respects the Convention on the Transfer of Title could build on that dealing with the Law Applicable to the International Sale of Goods. It is limited to international sales, it does not apply to securities, ships, registered boats, sales upon judicial authority or by way of execution but does apply to sales based on documents (Article 1(1), (2)). It applies to contracts to deliver goods to be manufactured or produced and neither a declaration of choice of law alone nor a submission to a foreign court or arbitration confers an international character upon the transaction (Article 1(3), (4)). The law governing the contract determines in relation to the parties until when the seller is entitled to the products and fruits of the goods sold and bears the risk, the validity of the clauses reserving title to the seller and until what time the seller is entitled to damages concerning the goods sold (Article 2).

| In relation to third parties not connected with the sale the passing of the title to the buyer is governed by the domestic law of the country where the goods are situated at the time of a claim by them[550] unless limited by a

---

[545] *Supra* n. 68. *Actes 1956*, p. 340 (texts); see also p. 83; Piot (1957) Clunet 949; Paschoud (1957) 4 N.T.I.R. 254, 258.

[546] See *supra* text to n. 511; Piot, *idem*, pp. 949, 959, 967; Paschoud, *idem*, pp. 254, 256, 259.

[547] VIII Conference, *Documents*, pp. 38, 39.

[548] *37th Conference* (Oxford 1932), p. 212; VIII Hague Conference, *Documents*, p. 37.

[549] *Actes 1956*, pp. 25, 33; Paschoud, *op. cit. supra* n. 545, at p. 261; *Leigh and Sillivan Ltd* v. *Aliakmon Shipping Co. Ltd* [1986] A.C. 785 seems to have given the lie to this statement.

[550] Art. 5(1); for the meaning of the term employed (*réclame*) see *Actes 1956*, p. 57.

reservation to the rights of the buyer in relation to the seller's creditors (Article 10(a)). However, in general the rights acquired by the purchaser according to the domestic law of a previous *situs* are preserved (Article 3(2)). Further, in a sale where the goods are represented by documents the purchaser retains the ownership of the goods acquired by virtue of the domestic law of the country where the documents were received (Article 3(3)). The special concerns of the Scandinavian countries are acknowledged in so far as the protection of the rights of the unpaid seller in the objects sold[551] in proceedings by creditors of the buyer is involved.[552] Where the goods are represented by documents, the rights of the unpaid seller against the creditors of the buyer are governed by the domestic law of the country where the documents are situated at the time of the seizure or when proceedings were begun (Article 4(2)).

The rights of a buyer against a third party claiming the goods are governed by the *lex situs* at the time when proceedings are begun by the third party,[553] subject to any rights of the buyer which he acquired under the *lex situs* at the time when he took possession of the goods (Article 5(2)). If the goods are represented by documents, the purchaser retains the rights granted by the law of the country where he received the documents, subject to the rights accorded to a third party in possession by the *lex situs* of the goods (Article 5(3)). Article 5 in its entirety can be excluded by a reservation (Article 10(b)). Except in the two last-mentioned situations goods in transit are governed by the law of the country of dispatch.[554] An old-fashioned public policy clause[555] (omitting the emphasis upon a *manifest* incompatibility with the *lex fori*) completes the Convention.

The structure of the Convention discloses that in order to satisfy everybody, it combined the two drafts, dealing respectively with the proprietary relationship *inter partes* and with the world at large. By the concession of reservations it has reduced its status to that of a model law which in one of its forms relies on the *lex situs*.[556]

| 3. Agency

As the Introductory Report prepared by Pelichet on behalf of the Bureau points out,[557] any attempt to formulate choice of law rules for agency is

---

[551] Described as privileges, the right to take possession or to ownership as exemplified by the reservation of title, or to rescind the transfer.

[552] Art. 4(1) Paschoud, *op. cit. supra* n. 545, at p. 269. See *supra* text to n. 511.

[553] Art. 5(1); Paschoud, p. 271.

[554] Art. 6; *idem*, p. 264.

[555] Art. 7; the relation of the Convention to the operation of bankruptcy was deliberately omitted from its ambit: *idem*, p. 274.

[556] See also Nial in *Liber Amicorum Algot Bagge* (1955), pp. 155–159.

[557] XIII Conference t. IV, (1979), pp. 9 *et seq.*

fraught with difficulties. It is necessary to regulate three separate relationships: principal and agent, agent and third party, and principal and third party. Furthermore, the task is complicated by the fact that agency shows many forms: direct (where the agent acts for a named or unnamed principal) and indirect (where the agent either acts in his own name only or where he acts for an undisclosed principal who can be indirectly involved). These various forms must all be taken into account.[558] In addition, a unitary concept of agency, which embraces principal and agent in all dealings as one, is to be contrasted with another which observes a separation. All these aspects have influenced the theory and practice regarding choice of law in matters of agency.[559] When the International Law Association submitted a proposal for a Convention on the Law Applicable to Agency[560] the XIII Hague Conference took up the matter.[561] While the International Law Association's draft had originally included both the relationship between principal and agent and that between principal and third party, the revised draft limited itself to the former.

The Convention concluded on 14 March 1978[562] dealt with the relationships between principal and agent (Articles 5–10), between principal and third party (Articles 11–14) and between agent and third party (Article 15). In a broad sweep the Convention applies to situations having an international character and includes brokers, direct and indirect agents (Article 1). The list of excluded topics comprises capacity, form, all types of agency of an involuntary character (by operation of law or by judicial order) as well as two exceptional cases (Article 2): of a shipmaster acting in this capacity and of any representative in proceedings of a judicial character. Those representing an incorporated or unincorporated entity as its organ or member and trustees representing a trust, its settlor or beneficiaries are also outside the ambit of the Convention (Article 3).[563]

As between principal and agent the law chosen by the parties applies in the first instance, but the choice must be express or follow with reason|able certainty from the terms of the agreement or the accompanying circumstances.[564] In the absence of a choice by the parties the domestic law of the place of the agent's business establishment applies or, failing this, that of his

---

[558] See Schmitthoff (1970–1) 129 Rec. des Cours 109–203.

[559] For a survey see *idem*, pp. 172–181.

[560] *ILA 44th Conference*, Copenhagen (1950), pp. 192, 195; modified *45th Conference*, Lucerne (1952), pp. 309–314; see Hague Conference, *Documents 1956*, pp. 81–119.

[561] At the request of the VIII Conference, *Actes 1956*, p. 323.

[562] *Actes 1976*, pp. 76 (draft text), 79 (Prel. Report Karsten), 371 (final text), 381 (Final Report Karsten).

[563] For the question of such persons acting outside their authorisation see *Actes 1976*, p. 413(144).

[564] Art. 5; see, however, the Sale of Goods Convention, Art. 2(2), *supra* text to n. 500.

habitual residence at the time when the agency was created (Article 6(1)). An exception exists in favour of the law of the principal's business establishment or of his habitual residence if it is also the law of the State where the agent is to act.[565]

The range of topics covered by the choice of law rules of the Convention is far-reaching: it includes not only the formation of the relationship, the obligations arising thereunder and their performance and extinction, but also the powers of the agent and specific problems arising in agency.[566] It must be noted that although the categories of damage for which compensation can be recovered are determined by the law declared to be applicable, the measure of damages and prescription and limitation of actions are left out.[567] Moreover, if the agency relationship forms part of a broader agreement, the Convention applies only if either the agency relationship represents the primary object of the agreement or is severable (Article 7).

The difficult question whether the relationship between agent and third party is governed by the law of the former or of the latter is solved in principle in favour of the law where the agent had his business establishment at the time of the relevant acts.[568] However, the law where the agent has acted[569] applies if that place coincides *either* with his principal's place of business establishment or his habitual residence *and* the agent has acted in the name of the principal[570] *or* with the principal business or habitual residence of the third party.[571]

These provisions are supplemented by another which permits the contracting parties (but not their agent) to contract out of the Convention | scheme by selecting another law.[572] The salient feature of this provision is that it applies one law both to the relationship between principal and third

---

[565] Art. 6(2); *Actes 1976*, pp. 392(52), 417(162). It would seem that in this case the international character of the agency agreement may be in issue but its absence should not alter the outcome. For the case where either the agent or the principal has more than one business establishment see Art. 6(3).

[566] Art. 8; in so far as the relationship between principal and agent is concerned, though not between principal and third party: Arts. 10, 11; *Actes, idem*, pp. 393(56), (57), 424(199).

[567] *Idem*, p. 394(59) in deference to the attitude of common law countries, contrary to the solution adopted by the Road Traffic and the Products Liability Conventions (Art. 8 respectively).

[568] Art. 11; *idem*, p. 398(74); Art. 12 provides an exception if the agent is an employee of the principal; in this case the law of the principal's business establishment applies; *idem*, p. 399(78).

[569] For the determination of the place of acting if the parties communicate with each other from places in different countries, see Art. 13.

[570] Art. 11(a). I.e. the representation must be direct; *Actes 1976*, p. 400(79), (80).

[571] Art. 11(b); also if the agent acted at an exchange or auction (Art. 11(c)) or has no business establishment: Art. 11(d); for the case where he has more than one business establishment see Art. 11, second para.

[572] Art. 15; *Actes 1976*, p. 429(222)–(225).

party and to the extent of the agent's powers as granted to him by the principal.[573] Nevertheless, difficulties can arise if the implied or apparent authority according to the law governing the relationship between principal and third party is either more or less extensive than that accorded by the law governing the relationship between principal and agent.[574]

A provision similar to that embodied in Article 7 of the Rome Convention of 1980 confers a discretion on the courts to give effect to the absolutely binding rules of any State with which the case has a significant connection.[575] The usual public policy clause appears in Article 17. Reservations are available (Article 18) to exclude the operation of the Convention where a bank is acting as an agent, agency in matters of insurance and where a public servant acts in his official capacity on behalf of a private person.[576] The Convention has followed orthodox lines as far as its basic principles are concerned. The technique of adapting these to a series of concrete situations has not altered the character of the basic rules but, like any diversification or complication, it may have rendered the Convention a little less palatable.

4. Trusts

When the XV Conference selected trusts as a topic of private international law, it was faced with a situation which had never presented itself before. The peculiar structure of the Anglo-American trust, which distinguishes between legal and economic ownership of the trust assets, giving rights to the beneficiary which operate *in rem* both in regard to the trustee by way of real subrogation (tracing) and against third parties (following), and the treatment of trust funds as separate property in the trustee's bankruptcy seem to confirm that the beneficiary has at his disposal an action *erga omnes* side by side with the trustee. At the same time the trustee is subject to duties towards the beneficiary which lead to a personal claim to have the assets administered in accordance with the terms of the trust and the general law governing trustees. The combination of proprietary interests of the beneficiary in the trust assets coupled with the personal relationship between trustee and beneficiary has obscured the nature of the institution of trusts. In fact these rights are not unitary in character, but based on a division of ownership according to the quality and not the quantity of the proprietary right; some are *in rem* and | others are *in personam*. The difficulties which had been experienced previously when Anglo-American trusts were found to be in issue in coun-

---

[573] Art. 15; *idem*, pp. 396(71), (72), 429(226).
[574] *Idem*, pp. 402(87)–403(90).
[575] Art. 16; *idem*, pp. 403(91)–405(95), 430(228).
[576] This last reservation was inserted in order to satisfy a particular situation in Spanish law: *idem*, p. 431(234).

tries of a civil law background[577] persuaded the Hague Conference in 1984 to adopt a new approach which combined the formulation of choice of law rules with a transposition into the domestic law of the contracting States of the substantive rules of a trust as part of a convention which avoided the technical use of Anglo-American trust notions.[578] It is replaced by a factual presentation of a trust and its effects.[579]

In substance the Convention applies to *inter vivos* and testamentary trusts created voluntarily or evidenced in writing.[580]

The parties are free to select the law to govern the trusts either expressly or by implication having regard also to the circumstances of the case.[581] The choice is ineffective, however, if the law chosen does not make provision for trusts or the particular type of trusts.[582] In the absence of such a choice the law most closely connected is to govern (Article 7(1)). A number of connecting factors are set out by way of example (Article 8): the place of administration, the *situs* of the assets, the place where the trustee resides or does business and the objects of the trust and where they are to be accomplished. Several aspects of the trust may be governed by different laws, as is often the case in respect of administration.[583]

The range of the law applicable to the trust as governed by the Convention is set out in detail (Article 8) and the safeguard of public policy is maintained (Article 18). Further, a State need not recognise a trust if, leaving aside the law chosen, the place of administration and the habitual residence of the trustee, the trust is more closely connected with another State which ignores either trusts altogether or the particular type of trust (Article 13). The choice of law, whether subjective or objective, can also be limited by the absolutely binding rules of the forum (Article 16(1)) and, in exceptional circumstances, by rules of the same character in force | in a State which has a sufficiently close

---

[577] See Lipstein, "Trusts", chap. 23 *of op. cit. supra* n. 496, nos. 39–59.

[578] *Supra* n. 70; *Actes et Documents 1985*, Vol. II, pp. 10 (Prel. Report Dyer and van Loon), 141, 352 (draft text), 172 (Prel. Report von Overbeck), 361 (final text), 370 (Explanatory Report von Overbeck); Hayton (1987) 36 I.C.L.Q. 260; Gaillard and Trautman (1986) Rev. crit. d.i.p. 1; (1987) 35 A.J.Comp.L. 307; Beraudo (1985/1986) Trav. Com. fr.d.i.p. 21; Jauffret-Spinosi (1987) Clunet 23; Kötz (1986) 50 Rabels Z 562; Gobin and Maerton, J.C.P. (ed. N.) 1985, 391 no.65ff; Pirrung (1987) IPRax 52.

[579] Arts. 2, 11, i.e. nature of fund, title to assets, trustee's power; separate fund represented by trustee; not available to creditors of trustee, including insolvency and bankruptcy, or as part of matrimonial property of trustee and spouse and subject to tracing, subject to third-party rights.

[580] Art. 3 but a State may include trusts declared by judicial decisions. For an explanation see Hayton, *op. cit. supra* n. 578, at pp. 267–268.

[581] Art. 6(1); see *supra* text to nn. 500, 564.

[582] Art. 6(2); the purpose is said to aim at avoiding *fraude à la loi*; also the Convention does not apply: Art. 5.

[583] Art. 9; the law applicable to the validity of the trust may itself refer different aspects to different laws but *renvoi* is excluded: Art. 17.

connection with the case.[584] Finally, States may limit the recognition of trusts to those the validity of which is governed by the law of a contracting State (Article 21).

The effect of the choice of law for trusts established by the Convention is restricted by the operation of other legal systems which may overlap as a result of other choice of law rules which are complementary. In the first place, preliminary questions concerning the validity of testamentary instruments and of conveyances and assignments involving assets which are to form the capital of a trust remain subject to the choice of law rules governing a succession or a transfer of property *inter vivos.* In the second place, the Convention acknowledges in some detail (in Article 15) that in a clash between the law governing the trust and the laws governing other private law aspects the latter may prevail. The mandatory rules of the laws applicable according to the conflict rules of the forum may take precedence in matters of succession, matrimonial property regimes, transfer of title to property and security interests therein, of creditors in case of insolvency,[585] of minors and incapable persons and, generally, in favour of third parties acting in good faith. A number of problems remain.

By treating the trust assets as a separate fund, the question arises whether it constitutes an "ownerless fund", a matter of importance if the trust fails or debts of the settlor are involved. A third party deriving rights on the death of the settlor to a compulsory share under the law governing the settlor's death can lay claim to a part, or possibly the entire substance of the trust, depending upon whether the settlor left other assets or beneficiaries. If the trust was established *inter vivos* the value of the trust assets may also have to be taken into account in computing the value of the inheritance and the respective shares in order to determine the compulsory shares.[586]

If the beneficiary is himself entitled to a compulsory share, he can take part or all of the trust fund absolutely, subject to a reduction in respect of the life interest remaining.[587]

The Convention has been very successful in accommodating the Anglo-American trust, even if the institution is unknown in local law. It does not define the legal position of the beneficiary, but the need can arise in order to determine in connection with the settlement of death duties on whom title has devolved, if these duties are charged to the heir or successor and not to the estate. By letting in the absolutely binding|prohibitory rules of the *lex fori* the Convention has potentially limited the life of the trust. It has also

---

[584] Art. 6(2) – subject to a right of reservation: Art. 16(3).

[585] E.g. setting aside a fraudulent conveyance in favour of third parties.

[586] Paris 6 Nov. 1967, (1968) Rev. crit. d.i.p. 508; Cass. civ. 4 Dec. 1990 (1991) Clunet 398.

[587] The doctrine of election does not appear to operate abroad, but see Art. 14: the law more favourable to the trust.

potentially exposed the trust assets to actions by the creditors of the settlor and of the beneficiaries. Finally, in taking a realistic view of the *lex situs* the Convention has endangered the integrity of the trust, if the rules of succession of the *lex situs* apply where the choice of law rules distinguish between succession to movables and immovables, even if the settlor died domiciled abroad and the trust is governed by another law.

None of these blemishes detracts from the real merits of the Convention, which has realistically taken note of the present position of Anglo-American trusts in civil law countries and has brought order into chaos.

5. Recognition of the legal personality of foreign companies, associations and foundations

In 1927 the Committee appointed by the League of Nations to consider the progressive codification of international law charged three experts[588] "to examine having regard to the solutions in international treaty practice the question of the recognition of the legal personality of foreign commercial companies".[589] In their report the experts advised that commercial companies validly constituted according to the law of a contracting State and having their real seat there will be automatically recognised in other contracting States; that the same applies to foreign commercial companies established in a contracting State; that foreign commercial associations which do not possess legal personality according to foreign law enjoy in other contracting States the same legal status accorded to them by their national law, but cannot avail themselves of a more favourable legal status in the host country, even if they fulfil all the conditions that confer legal personality upon local companies and associations; that foreign commercial companies and associations which are thus recognised will enjoy in other contracting States the rights derived from their recognition, to sue and to be sued in accordance with local law; and that, on the other hand, their recognition does not imply the right to establish themselves and to operate in other contracting States and, generally, to exercise permanently the activities envisaged by their statutes.[590]

The problem was taken up by the Hague Conference in 1951.[591] It enlarged the range considerably by including unincorporated associations and foundations[592] and dealt (in Article 2(3)) with the basic difficulty that some

---

[588] Rundstein, Guerrero, Schücking.
[589] Document Société des Nations C.206 M.80.1927, Hague *Actes 1952*, p. 128.
[590] *Actes, idem*, p. 135.
[591] *Supra* n. 67. *Idem*, pp. 198 (draft text), 385 (final text), 367 (Explanatory Report Nypels).
[592] Preamble and Art. 1(1); subject to the possibility of a reservation: Art. 9.

States attach legal personality to companies in consequence of | their incorporation in a country coupled with a statutory seat, while others rely on the law of the real seat (which is the centre of their administration). The draft convention recognises legal personality, if it is acquired by virtue of registration or publicity in a particular country where the organisation has its statutory seat, provided that the capacity conferred thereby includes not only the right to sue and to be sued, but also to own property and to enter into legal transactions.[593] Legal personality can also be recognised in the absence of registration or publicity, however, if local law confers it nevertheless (Article 1(2)).

It has been said that thereby the Convention sanctions the incorporation theory, but the wording of the two paragraphs of Article 1 suggests that the Convention gave equal weight to the seat theory. The critical test is whether legal personality so acquired will have to be recognised in another contracting State. The answer is in the negative if the real seat happens to be in another State which relies on the law of the real seat to confer legal personality or if it is in another State which also relies on this test (Article 2). However, a subsequent transfer of the real seat carried out within a reasonable time to a country which pays no attention to the locality of this seat maintains the previous legal status (Article 2(4)). This seems to cover the situation where the real seat of a company is transferred from one State relying on the test of incorporation to another using the same test.[594] The real seat is given primary consideration, but can give way to the test of incorporation.

If the statutory, as distinct from the real, seat is transferred to another contracting State, legal personality is allowed to continue, if both contracting States permit it but the company must transfer its statutory seat to the State of its real seat within a reasonable time (Article 3). Here again the test of the real seat prevails in the end.

Naturally a merger of companies in the same State is to be recognised. A merger between two companies in different States is to be recognised if it is recognised in these States (Article 4).

The recognition accorded to companies, associations and foundations possessing legal personality under their own law is also accorded to the legal status of such bodies which do not enjoy legal personality, in particular the right to sue and to be sued and their relationship with creditors; they cannot, however, benefit from any more advantageous rules available to similar bodies in the other contracting State (Article 6). Article 8, reserving the

---

[593] Art. 1(1); these powers will be recognised (Art. 5(1), (3)) subject to limitations: Art. 5(2), (3).

[594] Within Europe this situation can arise upon a transfer of the real seat from England to the Netherlands or possibly to Italy.

intervention of public policy, follows the traditional form before the modern version was established.

| Finally, Article 7 stresses that any recognition of status does not imply permission to carry on business on a permanent basis in the recognising State.

The Convention does nothing to bridge the gap between the law of countries which rely on the law of the place of incorporation and of those which require compliance with the law of the real seat. Concessionary time limits for establishing the company at its real seat do not eliminate the real problem. In particular, the Convention does not provide guidance as to how a transfer of the seat of a corporation from one country to another is to be carried out in practice if it is to operate there. Must the company be liquidated in the first country in order to be reconstituted in the second? Nor does the provision on cross-country mergers assist, seeing that they are effected either by a purchase of one company by another or by mutual liquidations followed by the creation of a new company.

The Draft Convention on the Mutual Recognition of Companies and Legal Entities (Goldman Report)[595] prepared for the European Community brought a considerable improvement. Civil and commercial companies and associations are recognised if established in accordance with the law of a member State and if their statutory seat is in one of the territories to which the Convention applies.[596] It suffices if the company is capable of having rights and duties, even if it is not granted the status of a legal entity by the law under which it was created.

If the real seat[597] is outside the territories of the contracting States, a contracting State can reserve the right not to apply the Convention if no effective link exists between the company and the economy of one of the territories of the contracting States (Article 3). Further, following a declaration a contracting State may apply its own laws, in so far as it regards them as *mandatory*, if companies established according to the law of another contracting State establish or have their real seat in the former State.[598] Any *directory* provisions of the laws of this State apply only if the articles of the company do not deviate from them either in specific matters or generally by referring to the law of the place of incorporation or unless the company proves that it

---

[595] (1969) 12 E.C. Bull (Suppl. No.2) 9; Campbell, *Common Market Law* (Suppl. No.1, 1970), Vol.1, chap. 9; Lipstein, *The Law of the European Economic Community* (1974), pp. 148 *et seq.* with lit.

[596] Art. 1. For their powers see Arts. 6–8; they are those of the law of the State of incorporation (Art. 6), but they must not exceed those under local law (Art. 7); the existence of legal personality is irrelevant (Art. 9).

[597] Defined as the place where the centre of control and management is situated: Art. 5.

[598] Art. 4(1); further safeguards are provided by a public policy clause (Art. 9).

has exercised its activities for a reasonable time in the member State in accordance with the law under which it was established (Article 4(2)).

| The Draft Convention avoids a confrontation between the law of countries favouring the principle of incorporation irrespective of the real seat of the company and those which require compliance with the law of the latter despite incorporation abroad. Instead, the *locus standi* of companies incorporated abroad and their powers are to be subject only to the mandatory laws of the latter without having their corporate existence challenged as such and within limits to the latter's directory laws. While welcome as a scheme of compromise, its practical feasibility must depend upon the elaboration of a set of rules in each contracting State which are to claim overriding authority in admitting the *locus standi* of those foreign companies and associations whose place of incorporation and real seat do not coincide. Moreover, the Draft Convention is restricted to questions of the *locus standi* and fails to address the question of a transfer of centre of control and management. However, perhaps the question should be put whether a transfer of the centre of management must necessarily attract the whole gamut of rules of the law of the new real seat. As the European Court of Justice has found recently,[599] no comprehensive arrangement has been reached as yet, but it left open whether it is really necessary.

D. Torts

1. Traffic accidents

An examination of the choice of law rules relating to torts was placed on the Conference agenda by the British delegation.[600] As the Introductory Report by Dutoit pointed out, the time had come for differentiated rules of choice of law to be developed to govern different types of torts by using a variety of connecting factors appropriate for each of them.[601] A survey showed that traffic accidents and products liability called for attention next.[602] The XI Conference undertook this task.[603]

The preliminary draft (1972) gave first place to the *lex loci delicti*, the law of the place of the accident, but took note of the social setting of the parties by the law of their habitual residence, if common to the victim, the author of

---

[599] *Reg.* v. *HM Treasury* 81/87 [1988] E.C.R. 5483, 5510–5511, 5512; [1989] Q.B. 446.
[600] X Conference, Final Act B IV 1(a).
[601] *Supra* n.72, XI Conference, *Actes et Documents 1970*, t. II, pp. 10(4), (7)–12(21).
[602] *Idem*, pp. 13(29)–14(31), 15(42)–17(54), 19(66), 65(4.1–4.3).
[603] *Idem*, pp. 62 (draft text), 65 (Prel. Report Essén), 193 (final text), 200 (Explanatory Report Essén).

the accident and the owner of the vehicle. Additional provisions dealt on similar lines with claims by gratuitous as well as paying pas|sengers. In adopting this approach the draft followed developments in both Europe[604] and the United States.[605]

The final draft followed the technique of its forerunner but sought to refine it and to introduce the place of registration of the vehicle or vehicles. Unlike its predecessor it covers civil non-contractual liability, not liability in tort, but this change of expression does not indicate a change of substance[606] and leaves characterisation to the *lex fori*. Article 1 excludes a number of aspects, however.[607] In principle the law of the place where the accident occurred applies (Article 3). However, the law of the State where the vehicle is registered applies, if different from the *lex loci actus*, to determine claims by the driver, owner or other person having control of, or an interest in, the vehicle, irrespective of their habitual residence; the same applies to claims by an injured passenger whose habitual residence is not in the State where the accident occurred, also by a victim outside the vehicle who is habitually resident in the State where the car is registered; if several victims make claims the choice of the applicable law varies according to the category into which the individual claim falls.[608]

If several vehicles registered in the same State are involved, the law of the State of registration applies. The liability of one or several persons outside the vehicle or vehicles is governed by the law of the place of registration, if they are all habitually resident in the State of registration. The same applies if they are victims of the accident as well.[609] These rules apply also to goods belonging to a passenger or entrusted to him and carried in the vehicle as well as those belonging to others. Damage to goods outside the vehicle is governed by the *lex loci delicti*, unless they are *personal belongings* of a victim habitually resident in the State of registration.[610]

Ancillary provisions deal with the situation where vehicles either have no

---

[604] C.A. The Hague 16 June 1955 (1959), Clunet 506; (1956) N.T.I.R. 219; German Decree of 7 Dec. 1942, RGBe 1942 1 706; BGHZ 57, 265, 267; 87, 95, 97; 90, 294, 297; 93, 214, 216; 108, 200, 202; also 7 July 1992 VI Z.R. 1/92; Benelux Draft Art. 18 (now Art. 14) (1951) Rev. crit. d.i.p. 710; (1952) 377.

[605] Beginning with *Babcock* v. *Jackson* (1963) 12 N.Y. 2d. 473, 191 N.E. 2d. 279, 240 N.Y.S. 2d. 743 and concluding in *Neumeier* v. *Kuehner* (1972) 31 N.Y. 2d. 121; 286 N.E. 2d. 454, 335 N.Y.S. 2d. 64.

[606] *Actes 1972*, p. 202 C.1.

[607] Products liability in a broad sense; liability for the maintenance or safety of public ways; vicarious liability other than of the owner of a vehicle and a principal or master, recourse against co-tortfeasor, recourse action or subrogation of insurers and similar actions by and against social insurance institutions or guarantee funds.

[608] Art. 4(a); *Actes 1970*, pp. 208(9.1)–209(9.4).

[609] Art. 4(b), (c); *idem*, p. 209(10–11).

[610] Art. 5(1)–(3); *idem*, p. 210(2–5).

registration or are registered in two countries. The law of the State where they are habitually stationed applies. The same applies if none of|the owner, possessor or controller or driver of the vehicle is habitually resident in the State of registration at the time of the accident.[611] Whichever law applies, by Article 7 the local standards of control and safety are to be taken into account as data. A novel provision allows a direct action by the person who has suffered injury or damage against the insurer of the person who is liable, provided that the law governing the latter's liability allows it. If this is the law of the place of registration and does not envisage the possibility of direct action, such a right is to be allowed nevertheless, if provided by the law of the State where the accident occurred. In the absence of such a right according to either law, resort is to be had to the law governing the contract of insurance, if it admits this remedy.[612]

In the attempt to pinpoint the law which best reflects the social setting in which it is to apply, recourse to what has been called the *lex stabuli* irrespective of whether the various parties involved are habitually resident in different countries or not may invite the question whether the *lex loci delicti* does not offer an adequate substitute. The reliance on direct action against the insurer does not introduce a new element, since it can operate only if the law referred to permits such an action. However, States may be deterred from adhering to the Convention if it obliges them to expose insurers to direct actions under legal systems which otherwise would not be applicable in their courts.

2. Products liability

Unlike the subject matter of all other choice of law rules which enables them to regulate in advance what law is to govern a particular situation, that which underlies the choice of law in matters of tort is always called upon to consider *ex post* what law is best to apply. Also, foreign torts have attracted attention much later than other legal institutions and, where they have, they concerned situations concentrated in one country only, albeit a foreign one.[613] The question was therefore only whether an action could be brought in another country and whether the fact that in the country where the tort took place the act was permitted, required or justified excluded an action abroad. The affinity with criminal law perceived at an earlier stage encouraged the development of rules drawing their inspiration from that law,

---

[611] Art. 6; the function of this provision is not self-evident.
[612] Art. 9. It follows the technique known as Kegel's ladder – see *infra* text to n. 622.
[613] *Mostyn* v. *Fabrigas* (1775) 1 Cowp. 161; *Scott* v. *Seymour* (1862) 1 H. & C. 219; *The Halley* (1867) L.R. 2 Adm. & Ecc. 3; (1868) L.R. 2 P.C. 193; *Phillips* v. *Eyre* (1870) L.R. 6 O.B. 1; *Chaplin* v. *Boys* [1971] A.C. 356.

including that of double criminality.[614] Modern choice of law rules in matters of tort are faced with a very | different situation; it involves cross-country torts which affect at least two countries and a variety of activities which may call for a set of differentiated choice of law rules.[615] One, several or indefinite connecting factors based upon equitable considerations may become available. Producing and merchandising goods are activities that have encouraged the development of new and separate rules. The XII Conference provided them.[616] The Convention, which addresses only international cases,[617] deals with the liability of manufacturers in a wide sense[618] for damage[619] including that resulting from misdescription, or to give adequate notice of the nature and methods of use of products.[620] A number of connecting factors came up for consideration: the place of manufacture, of injury, of consumption, of damage, of the effect of the act, of the best offer to the public, the place of the residence of the victim, the law which is foreseeable and insurable or the strictest law.[621] The preliminary draft adopted by the Special Commission proposed a choice based on a hierarchical preference of rules (also sometimes known as "Kegel's ladder").[622] According to this proposal, the law of the habitual residence of the injured person at the time of the accident was to apply, unless neither this product nor one of the same origin and type was available through commercial channels with the express or implied consent of the defendant.[623] If this law did not apply because the negative condition had materialised, the law of the State in which the accident occurred was to apply.[624] If this law did not apply because the same

---

[614] For these questions see Lipstein, *Ius Privatum Gentium, Festschrift für Max Rheinstein* (1969), Vol. I, p. 411.

[615] For a discussion of this tendency see *op. cit. supra* n. 496, at chap. 31; *Cheshire & North* (12th edn, 1992), pp. 554 *et seq.*

[616] *Supra* n. 73; *Actes et Documents 1974*, Vol. III, pp. 39 (Introductory Report Saunders), 107 (Prel. Report Willis Reese), 246 (text), 252 (Final Report Reese); for the extensive literature see Kegel, *Internationales Privatrecht* (6th edn, 1987), s. IV, para. 18, p. 473; Dutoit, Hague *Actes et Documents 1968*, p. 17(55); Ehrenzweig (1960) 69 Yale L.R. 794.

[617] Preamble. No attempt is made to enlarge on this aspect.

[618] Art. 3, namely of finished products, component parts, natural products, suppliers and others engaged in the commercial chain of preparation or distribution, including agents and employers, movables and immovables subject to a reservation in respect of agricultural products: Art. 16(2); de Nova (1973) 9 R.D.I.P.P. 297, 303.

[619] Art. 2(b); defined as injury to the person, damage to property and economic loss connected therewith, but not to the product itself.

[620] Art. 2(a); natural, industrial, new, manufactured, movable, immovable.

[621] *Actes 1974*, pp. 50–59.

[622] *Idem*, p. 105, Arts. 3–5.

[623] Art. 3; *ibid.*

[624] Art. 4; *idem*, p. 112: the term "accident" was to cover all occurrences in which a product may be considered to have caused the victim a relevant injury.

negative condition had materialised, the law of the State of the principal business of the defendant was to govern.[625]

| This simple scheme gave way to a more complicated one, favouring a solution owing more to American[626] than to German (Kegel's) thought.

Any claims for damages arising out of a direct relationship *inter se* whereby property or the right to use it was transferred are excluded from the operation of the Convention.[627] In all other cases a series of choice of law rules has been devised which show distinctive new features. Unlike previous provisions which envisage the application of several laws either cumulatively or alternatively,[628] the Products Liability Convention offers two principal conflicts rules in five permutations each of which combines the principal connecting factor with another, supplemented by a standby rule in case the first two fail to apply.

First, by Article 4 the law of the place of injury[629] applies if it *either* coincides with the habitual residence of the person directly[630] suffering damage (the plaintiff) *or* the product was acquired there by the plaintiff *or* is the principal place of business of the person claimed to be liable (the defendant).

Second, supplementing the first three alternatives, the law of the plaintiff's habitual residence applies it if [editorial note: if it] coincides *either* with the place where the plaintiff acquired the product *or* with the defendant's principal place of business (Article 5).[631] In the case of an overlap, the wording of Article 5 indicates that its provision is to prevail.[632] If, however, neither the law of the place of injury nor that of the plaintiff's habitual residence

---

[625] Art. 5; *idem*, p. 113.

[626] See Reese (1972) 25 Vand.L.R. 49.

[627] Art. 1 (2). The text refrains from characterising the relationship in legal terms, seeing that its nature as contractual or tortious as a result of implied warranties is open to dispute and that the exclusion or alternative use of either type of claim is regulated differently in the legal systems of some of the contracting States. *Actes 1974*, pp. 46, 257; de Nova, *op. cit. supra* n. 618, at p. 299. It also does not address the question of a collateral warranty of the qualities of a product to be acquired by some other supplier *Shanklin Pier Co.* v. *Detel Products Ltd* [1951] 2 K.B. 854.

[628] E.g. the English conflicts rule in matters of tort; as against the rules concerning form in matters of contract and wills.

[629] *Actes 1974*, p. 260; described as normally being the place where the defendant's wrongful act had its first impact upon the person directly suffering damage.

[630] For the reason for the distinction between persons suffering damage (Art. 1(2)) and directly suffering damage (Arts. 4–6) see *idem*, p. 257.

[631] These five permutations could also have been expressed in the following form: the law of the habitual residence of the plaintiff if also the principal place of business of the defendant, or the place of injury; the law of the place where the product was acquired if also the habitual residence of the plaintiff or the place of injury or the law of the principal place of business of the defendant if also the place of injury. As Loussouarn (1973) Clunet 32, 42(27) points out, the *locus delicti* has disappeared as a connecting factor.

[632] *Actes 1974*, p. 262.

applies, the plaintiff can choose between the law of the defendant's principal place of business and that of the place of injury.[633] Neither the law of the place of injury nor that of the plaintiff's habitual residence is to apply, however, if the defendant could not reasonably foresee that the | product or a similar product of his would be available in either of those places.[634] Consequently, only the law of the defendant's habitual place of business or (it must be asked)[635] the law of the place where the product was acquired may have to be considered, if the conflict rules of the forum should refer to either of them in the absence of a provision in the Convention.

By providing a cumulation of connecting factors, but not of laws, the problems have been avoided of having to opt for the better law or for the law which favours either the plaintiff or the defendant if a cumulation of connecting factors and laws is adopted.[636] On the other hand, it contributes an element of uncertainty.

While some legislation enables the plaintiff to make a clear-cut choice between the law of the place of acting and the law of the place where the damaging effect took place, the present Convention, by adding the need to rely on further connecting factors to the place of injury and that of the plaintiff's habitual residence, contributes to the possibility of further disputes between the parties before the appropriate choice of law rule can be ascertained.[637]

The range of the Convention in covering claims for damages based on products liability includes not only the bases of liability, exemption, or limitation or division of liability, damages and the *locus standi* to claim them, to mention only the principal heads, but also the burden, but not the methods, of proof.[638] A new and interesting provision (Article 9) states that rules of conduct and safety in the State where the produce was marketed can be taken into account in determining liability. The usual public policy clause (Article 10) completes the text.

It remains to be seen whether this Convention will prove to be of widespread use, given that as a result of EC Directive 85/374 the law on products

---

[633] Art. 6; de Nova, *op. cit. supra* n. 618, at p. 325.

[634] Art. 7; *Actes 1974*, p. 263. This idea stems from Ehrenzweig; for comments see de Nova, *idem*, p. 321.

[635] But see *Actes, idem*, p. 264.

[636] See Cavers, *Choice of Law Process* (1965) pp. 76 *et seq.*, esp. 113, 122, 146, 153, 156, 160; Leflar (1966) 41 N.Y.U.L.Rev. 267. For the various proposals made during the debates see de Nova, *op. cit. supra* n. 618, at pp. 316 *et seq.*

[637] For the alternative choice see: (Germany) Kegel, *loc. cit. supra* n. 616; (Switzerland) Law on Private International Law 18 Dec. 1987, Art. 133; see also in respect of jurisdiction under the Brussels Convention of 27 Sept. 1968: *Bier* v. *Mines de Potasse d'Alsace* [1976] E.C.R. 1735.

[638] Art. 8, in particular (8); *Actes 1974*, pp. 266, 267.

liability is assuming common features in the Community except in so far as member States exercise their power to abstain from adopting certain of its principles.[639] The range of the Convention[640] may be broader|than that of the Directive and national legislation following it, but overlaps as well as gaps must occur.

E. Procedure

1. Service of documents, taking evidence

The VII Conference (October 1951)[641] made the final touches to the amended draft of the Civil Procedure Convention of 1905 by adopting the proposals put forward in 1928.[642] No changes occurred in the first section (Articles 1–7), dealing with the service of judicial and extra-judicial acts and documents,[643] and in the second section (Articles 8–16), concerned with letters rogatory. The provisions on security for costs (*cautio judicatum solvi*) were slightly amplified.[644] Those on free legal aid were recast in order to accommodate the innovations introduced in 1928.[644a] As a result, Article 20 restricts legal aid to civil and commercial matters, but it can be extended to administrative proceedings; the competent authority asked to grant aid is authorised by Article 22(2) to make further enquiries. A new article (23) deals with the transmission of papers[645] and another (25) with the grant of legal aid for obtaining certificates of birth, marriage and death.

(a) *Service of documents abroad.* The X Conference (1964),[646] stimulated by a memorandum submitted by the International Union of Huissiers,[647] revised only part of the 1954 Convention (Articles 1–7: service abroad of judicial and extra-judicial documents), thus leaving some former contracting

---

[639] See e.g. Kelly and Attree, *European Product Liability* (1992).

[640] Art. 8, subject to a possible reservation in respect of Art. 8(9): prescription, limitations of actions; see Art. 16(1).

[641] *Supra* n. 45, *Actes 1952*, p. 390; *Documents 1952*, p. 61.

[642] *Supra* text to and the details set out in n. 221.

[643] Subject to a slight change in the first sentence of Art. 3 and a minor verbal modification of para. 2.

[644] Art. 19(2) by adding that a submission of duly authenticated documents suffices to prove *res judicata* and by formulating a new para.4 dealing with the competence of the authority to grant an *exequatur* to assess the total charges upon request.

[644a] See n. 221.

[645] The former Art. 23 now figures as Art. 24 and the old Art. 24 (no imprisonment for debt) becomes Art. 26.

[646] *Supra* n. 46; *Actes et Documents 1965*, t. III, pp. 63, 112 (prel. text), 74 (Prel. Report Taborda Ferreira), 345 (final text), 363 (Explanatory Report Taborda Ferreira). See Graveson (1965) 14 I.C.L.Q. 528, 538.

[647] *Actes*, p. 75, IX Conference, *Actes et Documents 1961*, t. I, p. 314.

parties bound by the 1905 Convention and others by that of 1954 (Article 22). The principal innovation consists in the establishment of a Central Authority in each contracting State[648] for the receipt of judicial and extra-judicial documents in civil and commercial matters.[649] The Convention, like its predecessors, does not offer guidance but | it was agreed, despite some doubts[650] that in practice dual characterisation according to the laws of the requesting and the requested States had proved to be the working test.[651] The Central Authority in the requested State must take the necessary steps under its own law to serve the documents on persons within its own territory,[652] but upon request may employ a particular method called for by the appli-cant.[653]

However, the new procedure for serving documents is not exclusive. First, a State remains free to effect service abroad directly through its diplo-matic or consular agents upon its own nationals and also upon others, but in this case the receiving State may object.[654] Second, a State may employ the traditional method of consular channels.[655] Third, unless the receiving State objects (Article 21(2)(a)), postal communications may be used to reach a person abroad, or the judicial or similar authorities concerned may act through the good offices of their counterpart abroad or any person interest-ed may effect service through the judicial or other competent persons abroad.[656] Other methods of service permitted by local law are not excluded (Article 19). The previous provisions on fees and their waiver, on the safe-guard of sovereignty and security and the settlement difficulties are preser-ved; likewise on the service of extrajudicial documents.[657]

Two new provisions of considerable importance add force to the purpose of the Convention, which is to bring proceedings to the notice of the ad-dressee of the document. If a writ of summons or an equivalent document has been transmitted abroad and the recipient (being the defendant) has not

---

[648] Arts. 2, 3 – or several: Art. 24.

[649] Art. 1. The wording of Art. 5 shows that the procedure is not open to individuals except those acting in a professional capacity (e.g. solicitors): *Actes 1964*, p. 84.

[650] *Actes 1964*, p. 307 (Prof. Anton).

[651] *Idem*, pp. 78, 159–168, 365, 366; but see *State of Norway's Application (No. 1 and No. 2)* [1990] 1 A.C. 723 (CA and HL); and see below text to n. 662.

[652] Art. 5(1)(a); cf. 1954, Art. 2.

[653] Art. 5(1)(b); 1954, Art. 3(2). According to Graveson, *op. cit. supra* n. 646, at p. 540, the second alternative was inserted at the suggestion of the Swiss delegation. The text does not make it clear whether the term "applicant" signifies the requesting authority. Detailed rules specify the procedure of certifying notification in accordance with a model: Arts. 6, 7 and Annex.

[654] Art. 8 in conjunction with Art. 21(2)(a); 1954, Art. 6(3).

[655] Art. 9 in conjunction with Art. 21(1)(c); 1954, Art. 1(1).

[656] Art. 10(a)–(c); 1954, Arts. 6(1), 1(4) see also 11, 6(2).

[657] Arts. 12–14, 17; 1954, Arts. 7, 4, 1(2), 25.

appeared, a stay of proceedings must be ordered until it has been ascertained that the document was properly served or was delivered to the defendant or to his residence by another method admitted under the Convention, and the defendant had sufficient time to arrange his defence.[658] Nevertheless, proceedings may continue and judgment be given, if transmission of the document was effected in accordance with the Convention, a period of not less than six months deemed adequate has elapsed and if despite reasonable efforts no certificate of|service could be obtained.[659] To balance this provision, a defendant who, without fault of his own, did not have knowledge of the document in sufficient time to defend or to appeal may be reinstated in the court's discretion, if a *prima facie* defence is disclosed.[660]

(b) *Letters rogatory.* The next (XI) Conference turned to the section of the 1954 Convention on letters rogatory,[661] now entitled "Taking Evidence Abroad". Its principal contribution consists in the fact that in distinguishing between letters of request and direct taking of evidence by consular or diplomatic officers and commissioners it divided the Convention into two parts: the first (Articles 1–14) reproducing in a modernised and modified form the provisions of the 1954 Convention (Articles 8–16) requesting the authorities of the addressed State to obtain evidence or to perform some judicial act; the second (Articles 15–22) sanctioning the taking of evidence by persons (consuls, diplomats, commissioners) appointed by the foreign authorities to take evidence elsewhere, subject to safeguards and reservations by the State where the evidence is to be taken.

Like the Convention on Service Abroad of Judicial and Extra-judicial Documents, the Evidence Convention is restricted to civil and commercial matters (Article 1(1)). Once again no definition was supplied on the ground that it was unnecessary, for:[662]

for over sixty years the Conference's Conventions had worked effectively without any need for a specific definition. The United Kingdom expert knew of no case in forty years in which there had been disagreement with any of its Convention Partners as to whether a particular request dealt with a "civil or commercial matter", this phrase being used in all of the United Kingdom's bilateral Conventions without definition.

---

[658] Art. 15(1); taken over by the Brussels Convention of 27 Sept. 1968, Art. 20(2) and (3).

[659] Arts. 15(2), 21(2)(b); urgent and provisional or protective measures may be taken without regard to these safeguards: Art. 15(3).

[660] Art. 16 but see Art. 16(3) in conjunction with Art. 21(2)(b).

[661] *Supra* n. 48; *Actes 1970*, t. IV, pp. 48, 178 (draft text), 55 (Prel. Report Amram), 191 (final text), 202 (Explanatory Report Amram).

[662] *Idem*, pp. 56 ad Art. 1, 203 ad Art. 1 – but see *supra* n. 651; the proposal to permit States to determine this question unilaterally was rejected. And see Lipstein (1990) 39 I.C.L.Q. 120; Knoepfler, *Mélanges Grossen* (1992), p. 1.

As in the Service Convention, the centrepiece of the first section is the Central Authority to which all letters of request must be sent for transmission to the competent authority.[663] Detailed provisions regulate the contents of the request, *inter alia*, as to the questions to be put to the person to be examined or a statement of the subject matter forming the enquiry, the property or documents to be inspected and whether evidence is to be|given on oath or any special form (Article 3), the languages to be used (Article 4), the refusal of the requested authority to act (Articles 5, 12) and the referral on to the competent authority (Article 6), notice to be given to the requesting authority of the place and time of the hearing (Article 7), the law to be applied, including any special procedure, if applied for and admissible (Article 9),[664] and methods of compulsion (Article 10). Most importantly, the privilege is established to refuse to give evidence by virtue of the law of either the State where the examination is to take place or the State of origin.[665] Articles 12 and 14 deal with the grounds for refusing the request and with fees and costs.[666]

The second section of the Convention regulates the direct collection of evidence by persons deputed by the foreign authority. A consular or diplomatic agent of a contracting State acting within the area to which he is assigned may take evidence without compulsion, firstly (Article 15), of nationals of the State which he represents,[667] unless the State where he acts requires him to obtain prior permission; secondly (Article 16), of nationals of the State in which he exercises his function or of third States, provided he has received permission, general or particular, and complies with the conditions specified in the permission,[668] except when the need to obtain permission has been waived. The latter status is also enjoyed by a person appointed commissioner by the requesting authority (Article 17). In all three situations, application may be made to the local authority for assistance to obtain evidence by compulsion, if the State where the authority acts has made a declaration to this effect.

The type of evidence taken must not be incompatible with local law or

---

[663] Art. 2. Although each contracting State must designate such an Authority, no need exists to use the Authority set up by the State of the requesting authority to dispatch the request.

[664] Unless incompatible with local law or incapable of performance in local conditions.

[665] Art. 11; States may also take into consideration other laws: Art. 11(2) – for an example see *Actes 1970*, p. 61.

[666] Special provision is made for the case where under its law the requested authority does not comply with the letters rogatory because it is a matter for the parties themselves: Art. 14(3).

[667] This wording was chosen because the consular officer or diplomat may represent nationals of a State other than his own.

[668] In all these cases further conditions may be imposed: Art. 19.

contrary to the permission given and may be taken in the manner laid down by the law of the State where the action is pending (Article 21(a), (d)). The privileges accorded to the witnesses where the request is addressed to the authorities of the requested State apply here as well (Articles 21(e), 11). If the witness refuses to give evidence when the proceedings are direct, the way under the first section of the Convention (Article 22) remains open.

The development of the provisions on direct taking of evidence by official or individuals representing the requesting State was motivated by the desire to maintain as far as possible the characteristic features of the | proceedings pending abroad by bringing in persons familiar with them, the language of the parties and the witnesses and their background.

How far this aim can be achieved depends upon the use made by the contracting parties of the need to obtain permission,[669] and the right to make derogations[670] or reservations.[671] In fact, the structure of the Convention gives it in many respects the character of a model law of the kind advocated over a period of years by the American delegation.[672]

(c) Recognition and enforcement of foreign judgments. The multitude of unsolved problems which had faced the 1925 Conference when considering the recognition and enforcement of foreign judgments (resulting in a preliminary draft which added nothing to and probably omitted much of what was current treaty practice at that time)[673] left the field open for a comprehensive review. The gap was filled on the suggestion of the Council of Europe[674] at an Extraordinary Session in 1966[675] by a draft treaty of considerable originality. A multilateral framework treaty is combined (in order to be effective) with the choice of a bilateral treaty, the component parts of which must be selected from a range set out by the framework treaty itself. The fact that it was drawn up at the same time as the agreement which became the Brussels Convention explains the similarity of the provisions notwithstanding the fact that the Hague Convention is a so-called simple one, regulating

---

[669] Arts. 15(2), 16(1)(a), (2), 17(1)(a), (2), 18, 19; also 8.

[670] Art. 27 (other kinds of transmission: Art. 2; less restrictive conditions for acts to be performed or methods of taking evidence under the Convention); by agreement: Art. 28 (concerning Arts. 2, 4, 8, 11, 13, 14 or s.II as a whole).

[671] Art. 23: pre-trial discovery; Evidence (Proceedings in Foreign Jurisdictions) Act 1975, s. 2(4)(a); see Collins (1986) 35 I.C.L.Q. 765.

[672] *Actes 1957*, pp. 266, 329; *1961*, pp. 209–223. The Evidence (Proceedings in Foreign Jurisdictions) Act 1975 appears to have been drafted with this trend in mind by consolidating thereby earlier British legislation and by including criminal proceedings.

[673] *Supra* text to nn. 138–141; *Actes 1925*, p. 344; *1928*, p. 421.

[674] IX Session (1960), t. 1 (1961), p. 71; see also the proposal of the ILA, *Report of the 49th Conference* (Hamburg 1958), p. 290 at p. 310 = Actes (*supra* n. 672) 73.

[675] *Actes 1969*; add (1967) 15 A.J.Comp.L. 362; (1968) 16 A.J.Comp.L. 601 (Recommendation), XI Session 1968, *Actes et Documents 1971*, t. I, pp. 110, 112 (Recommendation); see also IX Session (1960), t. 1 (1961), pp. 69–133.

only *compétence générale indirecte.* Thereby each contracting party is at liberty to establish its own jurisdictional rules while the treaty defines only the jurisdictional conditions in which a foreign judgment is to be enforced or recognised. The Brussels Convention, on the other hand, is a so-called double one, establishing a *compétence générale directe*: Thereby the original jurisdiction of the contracting parties is regulated for all by the same rules, and enforcement and recognition by the other contracting parties follow automatically. Despite these differences in function, the mandatory rules of the Hague Convention framework have much in common with the | Brussels Treaty, as a comparison shows (knowledge of the Brussels Convention is assumed).

Once again, the Convention applies to civil and commercial matters.[676] Again it excludes (with slight modifications) the same topics[677] and covers the same conditions for the recognition and enforcement[678] of judgments. The jurisdictional provisions, too, have their counterpart in the Brussels Convention.[679]

The mandatory provisions of the Judgments Convention remain inoperative, however, and the courts of the contracting States may not dismiss or stay the enforcement proceedings on the ground of *lis alibi pendens*,[680] unless the States concerned have entered, in addition, into bilateral arrangements (called "Supplementary Agreements") disposing of all or some of the matters set out in Article 23 (Articles 21–23).

It has been said that these matters, when included in a bilateral arrangement, serve only to extend and to integrate the Enforcement Convention[681] but not to restrict it by its reservations.[682] An analysis of these topics bears out this contention. Some involve definitions (Article 23(1), (2)). Others extend the Convention's range by including nuclear damage, provisional measures, provisional enforcement, default judgments, review of facts, ju-

---

[676] Art. 1 in conjunction with Art. 23(1), which invites the parties to define this and other terms; Brussels Preamble and Arts. 52, 53.

[677] Art. 1; Brussels Preamble; but family matters altogether and maintenance, legal persons and damage or injury in nuclear matters as well as *actes authentiques* are also excluded.

[678] Art. 2 = Brussels 24; Art. 3 = B.2(2); Art. 4 = B.26, 31, 30, 38; Art. 5(1) = B.27(1), 34(2), 27(2); new: Art. 5(2): procedural fraud; Art. 5(3) = B.21, 27(3), (5); Art. 6 = B.27(2); Art. 7(1) = B.29; Art. 7(2) = B.27(4); Art. 8 = B.29; Art. 9 = B.28(2).

[679] Art. 10(1) = Brussels 2, but substituting habitual residence and place of incorporation or principal place of business; 10(2) = B.5(5); 10(3) = B.16(1); 10(4) = B.5(3), but the damage to property must be tangible and the author of the injury must have been present there at the time; 10(5) = B.17; 10(6) = *Elefanten Schuh* [1981] E.C.R. 1671; 10(7), 11 = B.6(7); 12(1) = B.16(1), 17(1); 12(2) = B.19; 10(3) = *Marc Rich* v. *Soc. Impianti* (1991) 7 Arb. J. 251.

[680] Art. 20 = Brussels 21, 27(5).

[681] Droz (1966) 13 N.T.I.R. 225, 240; see also Panchaud (1968) 25 Ann. suisse dr. int. 359; Fragistas (1968) R.D.I.P.P. 745.

[682] Arts. 5, 9, 13, 19, 20.

risdiction of the courts of the domicile (Article 23(3), (4), (7)–(9)); judgments covered by another Convention without provision for enforcement or recognition, discretionary treatment of exclusive jurisdiction clauses and the inclusion of *actes authentiques* (Article 23(10), (12), (24)).[683] Still others deal with procedure in general, judgments other than for money, time limits for enforcement, rate of interest from date of judgment, form of documents, legalisation, the power to require security for costs and to deny legal aid and to render stay compulsory in case of *lis alibi pendens* (Article 23(14)–(21)).

|While the Brussels Convention excludes from its range jurisdiction based on the nationality (whether of the plaintiff or the defendant), the mere presence of the defendant or the presence of property belonging to the defendant, neither the mandatory provision of the Hague Convention (Article 10) nor the catalogue of provisions placed at the disposal of the parties in composing their Supplementary Agreement (Article 23) takes notice of the presence or absence of any of these bases of jurisdiction classified as "exorbitant".

However, by a Protocol attached to the Convention, the contracting parties sought to close what they clearly considered to be a gap by stating in its Preamble that the exorbitant grounds for assuming jurisdiction "can only exceptionally justify the international recognition and enforcement of judgments". Consequently, a judgment directed against a person having his habitual residence or domicile in a Contracting State is to be refused recognition or enforcement if the sole basis for assuming jurisdiction in the State of origin is any one of the following (Protocol, Article 4): the nationality of the plaintiff; the domicile, habitual residence or ordinary residence of the plaintiff;[684] the exercise of business by the defendant, if the action does not arise from the business; service of the writ upon the defendant during his temporary presence there; a unilateral choice of the forum[685] or the presence of property belonging to the defendant or its seizure, unless in respect of a claim to the property or if it constitutes a security for a debt which is in issue.

States were urged in signing the Convention to sign the Protocol as well, but failing this, to conclude a bilateral agreement in the exercise of the choice offered by Article 23.[686]

The structure of the Convention, which leaves a wide choice of solutions to contracting States, and the addition of a Protocol which is of a persuasive character, only show up the wide differences among the original parties to the Convention. Even if the principles of the Convention (which cover the

---

[683] For their meaning see Lipstein, *op. cit. supra* n. 595, at p. 281.

[684] Unless a permitted exception exists based on the particular subject matter of a class of contracts. The exception envisaged is probably that embodied in Arts. 7 *et seq.* and 13 *et seq.* of the Brussels Convention.

[685] Special reference is made to a specification in an invoice.

[686] *Actes et Documents 1968*, t.1; *1971*, p. 110.

broad range of the subject) should commend themselves to States in the end,[687] the likelihood of a great variety of Supplementary Agreements should leave the field much as it was before.

(d) Choice of court. Contemporaneously with the preparation of a Convention on the Law Applicable to the International Sale of Movables, the VII Conference formulated a preliminary draft of a Convention on the Contractual Choice of a Jurisdiction limited to International | Sales of Movables.[688] The subject was taken up by the VIII Conference,[689] apparently in order to satisfy a need arising out of the Sales Convention, since the range of the latter also delimits the Prorogatio Convention. The choice can be in favour either of a particular court or of the courts in general of a contracting State.[690] It must be express, a formula which evades adherence to the requirement of writing.[691] Instead a choice expressed orally must be confirmed in writing and be accepted (if only tacitly) by the other party. Thus the requirement of writing *ab initio* or *ex post* is accepted. The agreement can include present or future disputes and has an exclusive effect.[692] Nevertheless,[693] appearance by the defendant in an action brought in another State amounts to submission, unless the appearance is restricted to contesting the jurisdiction or in order to protect goods seized or in danger of being seized.[694] The jurisdiction of contracting States to take provisional or protective measures is unaffected (Article 4).

Judgments rendered by the courts thus seised are recognised and enforceable in the other contracting States subject to the usual conditions.[695] If recognition or execution is refused for failure to fulfil them, a new action may be brought on the same cause of action in the courts of the requested State.[696]

---

[687] The Convention came into force on 20 Aug. 1979, but has so far attracted only three signatories.

[688] VIII Session 1956, *Documents 1957*, pp. 44, 77 (text).

[689] *Supra* n. 49. VIII Session, *Documents*, p. 47 (Prel. Report Batiffol); *Actes*, pp. 139, 158 (draft text), 303 (Explanatory Report Frédéricq), 304 (same Batiffol), 344 (final text); Büllow, in *De Conflictu Legum, Mélanges Kollewiyn and Offerhaus* (1962), p. 89; Gottwald, *Festschrift für K. Firsching* (1985), p. 89.

[690] See e.g. *S.A. Consortium General Textiles* v. *Sun and Sand Agencies Ltd* [1978] Q.B. 279 and the comment in (1980) Clunet 420.

[691] Art. 2(1); *Documents 1957*, p. 48; *Actes*, p. 303.

[692] Art. 2(1) and (2); the specific mention of a broker is explained by Batiffol, *Actes, idem*, p. 303, as reflecting his position as an intermediary serving both parties.

[693] For the inclusion of this word see *idem*, p. 306.

[694] Art. 3; this formulation owes its origin to the Franco-British Convention of 18 Jan. 1934, Art. 4(1)(b), based in turn on s. 4(2)(a)(i) of the Foreign Judgments (Reciprocal Enforcement) Act 1933; *Documents 1957*, p. 49.

[695] Art. 5: proper notice and, if in default, reasonable time to appear, *res judicata* and enforceable, not contrary to a previous judgment having the force of *res judicata* in the requested State between the same parties in the same cause of action, not against public policy, not affected by fraud, not pleaded abroad and an authentic copy.

[696] Art. 6; *Actes*, p. 308.

At the instigation of the Austrian government and following some preparatory studies[697] the X Conference turned its attention to the formulation of a general convention on choice of court.[698] Faced with the question whether the new Convention was to be attached to its predecessor limited to sale of movables, to the Recognition and Enforcement | Convention or should stand alone, the Conference chose the last option.[699] A combination with the Recognition and Enforcement Convention was ruled out, because the latter was a simple or indirect convention, seeing that the contracting States had been unable to agree on a set out common rules of jurisdiction, while a Choice of Court Convention had to be a double or direct convention. In the end it was conceived as a separate agreement.

In substance the Convention applies to civil and commercial matters of an international character in general[700] except a broad range covering, *inter alia*, family law and succession,[701] and permits the selection of either the courts in general of a foreign contracting State or a specific court, which must, however, be competent according to the law or laws[702] of that State.[703] Nationality is irrelevant.[704] Unlike the Sale Convention it acknowledges clearly that the agreement requires at least a unilateral express written proposal to be accepted by the other party,[705] but not under duress (Article 4(3)). The choice is presumed to be exclusive in the absence of an agreement to the contrary[706] but the chosen court may nevertheless refuse to exercise jurisdiction on a number of grounds.[707] If the jurisdiction is non-exclusive, proceedings pending elsewhere likely to lead to a judgment which must be recognised may justify a stay elsewhere.[708]

---

[697] IX Session, *Actes et Documents 1960*, Vol. I, pp. 37, 31 (Memorandum), 141 (Committee Report).

[698] X Session, *Actes 1965*, t.4, pp. 11 (Introduction), 42 (prel. text), 195 (final text), 201 (Explanatory Report Welamson).

[699] *Idem*, pp. 12 *et seq.*, 202.

[700] Not of courts of third States; a reservation may except agreements between local residents and local branches of foreign business: Arts. 13, 14.

[701] Matters of status, family law, maintenance, succession, bankruptcy and immovable property are excluded: Art. 2(2).

[702] Arts. 1 and 2(1). The plural indicates that a contracting State may have a composite legal system.

[703] Art. 2(2) – cf. Sale, Art. 1.

[704] Art. 3 but States may make a reservation in respect of choice of court agreements made by their own nationals habitually resident in their own territory: Art. 12.

[705] Art. 4(1); national usages can be taken into consideration: *Actes 1965*, p. 212.

[706] Art. 5(1); distinguish Sale, Art. 5(1); *quaere* whether a waiver by submission to another jurisdiction is permitted: *idem*, p. 215.

[707] Arts. 5(2), 6: if it or a court in another contracting State has been granted nonexclusive jurisdiction; if the agreement could not oust the jurisdiction of the excluded court in view of the subject matter; if the agreement is void or voidable according to Art. 4 or if provisional or protective measures are involved.

[708] Art. 7; *quaere* whether the same cause of action must be in issue: *Actes 1965*, p. 219.

Recognition and enforcement of judgments given in accordance with the Convention are governed by the law of the requested contracting State.[709] This follows from the fact that, unlike the Recognition and Enforcement Convention, the Choice of Court Convention is a double one creating direct jurisdiction.[710] Conversely, a refusal of the chosen court to assume jurisdiction is not a bar to a new action in the same court (Article 9). Neither Choice of Court Convention contains a public policy|clause, but the power (Article 15) to make a reservation not to recognise choice of court agreements where the dispute has no connection with the chosen court or can be dealt with only with serious inconvenience by that court comes nearest to it.

As a workmanlike instrument the Convention, standing by itself, can fulfil a useful function. Standing side by side with the Recognition and Enforcement Convention it forms an exception conferring direct jurisdiction. However, within the difference between direct and indirect jurisdiction, the two Conventions can perhaps be reconciled.[711]

(e) Legalisation. Following a suggestion by the Council of Europe[712] the VIII Conference discussed[713] a memorandum prepared by the Netherlands State Commission[714] on the abolition of the requirement of legalisation. The IX Conference concluded this work[715] by reducing the somewhat cumbersome procedure to one of a single attestation.[716] Even this is not required if it is not required in the country where the document is produced or by virtue of an agreement between the States concerned (Article 3(2)). Moreover, the function of the attestation is restricted to ensuring the authenticity of the signature and the capacity in which the person signing the document has acted, but not the competence *ratione materiae* or *personae* of the author.[717] The Convention employs two different terms to describe the objects for which attestation may be required: the French text speaks of *"actes publics"*, the English text "public documents", seeing that no equivalent exists in the English language of the French expression.[718]

---

[709] Art. 8; settlements in face of the court are included: Art. 10.

[710] See *supra* text after n. 699; but see also the Sale Convention, Art. 5 where the chosen court has direct jurisdiction.

[711] Cf. General Choice Convention, Art. 8 in conjunction with Art. 6(2) with the Enforcement Convention, Arts. 10(5) and 12.

[712] *Actes 1952*, p. 277, proposed by the British government.

[713] *Actes 1957*, p. 235.

[714] *Ibid. Documents*, p. 205 with a list of treaties at p. 209.

[715] *Supra* n. 47. *Actes et Documents 1961*, t. 2, pp. 19 (Prel. Report Loussouarn), 133 (prel. text), 167 (final text), 173 (Explanatory Report Loussouarn).

[716] Art. 3(1). For the form see the Annex.

[717] Art. 2; *Actes 1961*, pp. 21, 178.

[718] *Idem*, p. 174.

The Convention enumerates the types of documents covered by it, which include instruments not known in this form in all countries,[719] and excludes not only documents executed by diplomatic or consular agents but also administrative documents dealing directly with commercial or customs operations (Article 1).

| *(f) Legal aid – security for costs.* Having revised those parts of the Civil Procedure Convention of 1 March 1954 dealing with the service of documents abroad and with letters rogatory,[720] the next step was to review the section on security for costs and legal aid.[721] The XIV Conference (1980) formulated as a general principle that nationals and persons habitually resident in a contracting State are entitled to legal aid in civil and commercial matters on the same basis as those of or in another contracting State.[722] The same privilege applies to those formerly habitually resident there, if the cause of action arose when they were resident there.[723] Where legal aid extends to administrative, social and fiscal matters, it must also benefit those covered by the Convention.[724] So does legal advice, if the applicant is present in the contracting State (Article 2).

For this purpose, machinery is provided by the establishment of a Central Receiving Authority (Article 3) and one or more Transmitting Authorities.[725] The rules on security for costs were amplified (Articles 14–17), the section on copies of entries and decisions was retained (Article 18) and that on physical detention enlarged by a provision (Articles 19, 20) on immunity of witnesses and experts from the jurisdiction of other contracting States.

F. General Principles

Inspired by a far-reaching survey by the famous Dutch writer Eduard Meijers of the problem of *renvoi*[726] the Hague Conference approached the problem where the connecting factors of nationality and domicile used by two different legal systems conflict leading to the acceptance or rejection of *ren-*

---

[719] Art. 1. Emanating from courts, public prosecutors, process servers, administrative documents, notarial acts, official certificates recording the registration or the existence of a document and notarial authentications of signatures (*certifications de signature apposées sur un acte sous seing privé*).

[720] *Supra* Section V.E.1 (a) and (b) of 1965 and 1970 respectively.

[721] Convention 15 July 1955, Arts. 17–24.

[722] *Actes et Documents 1982*, Vol.1, p.38; Art. 1(1).

[723] Art. 1(2); subject to a possible reservation.

[724] Art. 1(3). Legal aid in criminal matters is not included.

[725] Art. 4 – for the procedure see Arts. 5–13.

[726] (1938) 38 Bull. Inst. Juridique Int. 192, esp. 224 *et seq.*, preceded by Asser (1900) 2 (ser. 2) Rev. dr. int. legis. coup. 316, 317.

voi. Hitherto the questions whether *renvoi* is to be accepted, and if so why, had divided literature and practice and had been answered in accordance with the solution adopted by the laws of the forum. In the Netherlands this denied *renvoi* altogether.[727] Meijers offered an overriding solution which seemed both logical and practical as far as it went.

(1) If the forum refers to the national law and the national law refers to the domicile, which is in the State of the forum, the latter applies.

|(2) If the forum refers to the *lex domicilii* and the latter refers to the forum as being the *lex domicilii*, the law of the forum applies.

(3) If the forum refers to the law of the nationality and the law of the latter does so too, the law of the nationality applies.

These principles were adopted by the VII Conference.[728]

It is true that if the connecting factor is nationality in both legal systems the solution is clear: no conflict exists and no need for a reference back; when domicile is the connecting factor in both legal systems, again no conflict exists, unless the term domicile is characterised differently. If so, Meijers's preference for that of the *lex fori* needs an explanation, but this is lacking. If the forum refers to the law of nationality and the law of the nationality refers to law of the domicile, Meijers's acceptance again requires an explanation which is not forthcoming. Its absence in the only case given by Meijers where a conflict of connecting factors exists leaves the question of *renvoi* unanswered, the more so since Meijers's formula takes no notice of conflicts between the connecting factors: nationality or domicile and *situs.*[729]

VI. General Conclusion

It seems that the work of the Hague Conferences has been most successful when they handled practical matters of procedure and evidence, jurisdiction, formalities and all aspects of technical collaboration. The attempt to break down broad problems of private international law into specific topics ripe for international regulation is to be welcomed, but the need to reconcile divergent views has often led to compromises which have stifled development. It may even be asked whether the attempt to meet this dilemma, as was done by the Convention on the Recognition and Enforcement of Judg-

---

[727] Van Rooij and Polak, *Private International Law in the Netherlands* (1987), pp. 240–241.

[728] *Actes 1951*, pp. 202, 210 (Meijers), 236 (text). See also to a certain extent the Benelux Convention of 29 Nov. 1968, Art. 11: (1969) Clunet 358.

[729] The attitude of the Hague Conferences, which was generally negative, was discussed above in connection with the individual conventions. See now Graue (1993) 57 Rabels Z 26, who analyses in addition the practice of the courts in applying these conventions.

ments, by placing a choice of agreed solutions before the parties, should not be followed in the future. If clear-cut solutions of a uniform nature cannot be reached, the existence of parallel bilateral conventions formulated within the boundaries of a framework convention may pave the way for ultimate uniformity.

| Table of Signatures and Ratifications of the Hague Conventions

MEMBER STATES OF THE CONFERENCE		ARGENTINA	AUSTRALIA	AUSTRIA	BELGIUM	CANADA	CHILE	CHINA	CYPRUS	CZECH REPUBLIC	DENMARK	EGYPT	FINLAND
Statute	I												
Civil Procedure*	II	A	-	R	R	-	-	-	-	A	R	A	R
Sales of Goods*	III	-	-	-	R	-	-	-	-	-	R	-	R
Transfer of Title	IV	-	-	-	-	-	-	-	-	-	-	-	-
Sales–Choice of Court	V	-	-	S	S	-	-	-	-	-	-	-	-
National Law vs. Law of Domicile	VI	-	-	-	R	-	-	-	-	-	-	-	-
Recognition of Companies	VII	-	-	-	R	-	-	-	-	-	-	-	-
Maintenance Children–Applicable Law*	VIII	-	-	R	R	-	-	-	-	-	-	-	-
Maintenance Children–Enforcement*	IX	-	-	R	R	-	-	-	-	A	R	-	R
Protection of Minors*	X	-	-	R	-	-	-	-	-	-	-	-	-
Form of Wills*	XI	-	A	R	R	-	-	-	-	-	R	-	R
Legalisation*	XII	A	-	R	R	-	-	-	A	-	-	-	R
Adoption*	XIII	-	-	R	-	-	-	-	-	-	-	-	-
Service Abroad*	XIV	-	-	-	R	A	-	A	A	A	R	R	R
Choice of Court	XV	-	-	-	-	-	-	-	-	-	-	-	-
Enforcement of Judgments*	XVI	-	-	-	-	-	-	-	-	R	-	-	-
Protocol on Jurisdiction*	XVII	-	-	-	-	-	-	-	-	R	-	-	-
Divorce–Recognition*	XVIII	-	A	-	-	-	-	-	-	A	R	R	R
Traffic Accidents*	XIX	-	-	R	R	-	-	-	-	R	-	-	-
Taking of Evidence*	XX	A	A	-	-	-	-	-	-	A	R	-	R
Administration of Estates	XXI	-	-	-	-	-	-	-	-	R	-	-	-
Products Liability*	XXII	-	-	-	S	-	-	-	-	-	-	-	R
Maintenance–Enforcement*	XXIII	-	-	-	S	-	-	-	-	R	R	-	R
Maintenance–Applicable Law*	XXIV	-	-	-	S	-	-	-	-	-	-	-	-
Matrimonial Property*	XXV	-	-	S	-	-	-	-	-	-	-	-	-
Marriage*	XXVI	-	R	-	-	-	-	-	-	-	-	S	S
Agency*	XXVII	R	-	-	-	-	-	-	-	-	-	-	-
Child Abduction*	XXVIII	R	R	R	S	R	-	-	-	S	R	-	-
Access to Justice*	XXIX	-	-	-	-	-	-	-	-	-	-	-	R
Trusts*	XXX	-	R	-	-	R	-	-	-	-	-	-	-
Sales Contracts	XXXI	R	-	-	-	-	-	-	-	S	-	-	-
Successions–Applicable Law	XXXII	S	-	-	-	-	-	-	-	-	-	-	-

* = in force S = Signature R = Ratification A = Accession

FRANCE	GERMANY, FED. REP.	GREECE	HUNGARY	IRELAND	ISRAEL	ITALY	JAPAN	LATVIA	LUXEMBOURG	MEXICO	NETHERLANDS	NORWAY	POLAND	PORTUGAL	ROMANIA	SLOVAK REPUBLIC	SLOVENIA	SPAIN	SURINAME	SWEDEN	SWITZERLAND	TURKEY	UNITED KINDOM	UNITED STATES	URUGUAY	VENEZUELA	YUGOSLAVIA[1]
R	R	-	A	-	A	R	R	-	R	-	R	R	A	R	A	-	A	R	A	R	R	A	-	-	-	-	A
R	-	-	-	-	-	R	-	-	S	-	S	R	-	-	-	-	-	S	-	R	R	-	-	-	-	-	-
-	-	S	-	-	-	R	-	-	-	-	-	-	-	-	-	-	-	-	-	-	-	-	-	-	-	-	-
-	S	S	-	-	-	-	-	-	-	-	-	-	-	-	-	-	-	-	-	-	-	-	-	-	-	-	-
S	-	-	-	-	-	-	-	-	-	S	-	R	-	-	-	-	-	-	-	S	-	-	-	-	-	-	-
R	-	-	-	-	-	-	-	-	-	S	-	R	-	-	-	-	-	-	-	S	-	-	-	-	-	-	-
R	R	S	-	-	-	R	R	-	R	-	R	S	-	R	-	-	-	R	-	-	R	-	-	R	R	-	-
R	R	S	A	-	-	R	-	-	S	-	R	R	-	R	-	A	-	R	A	R	R	R	-	-	-	-	-
R	R	-	-	-	-	S	-	-	R	-	R	-	-	R	-	-	-	R	-	-	R	-	-	R	A	-	S
R	R	R	-	A	A	S	R	-	R	-	R	R	A	S	-	-	R	R	-	R	R	A	R	-	-	-	R
R	R	R	A	-	A	R	R	-	R	-	R	R	-	R	-	-	R	R	A	-	R	R	R	A	-	-	R
-	-	-	-	-	-	-	-	-	-	-	-	-	-	-	-	-	-	-	-	R	-	R	-	-	-	-	-
R	R	R	-	S	R	R	R	-	R	-	R	R	-	R	-	A	-	R	-	R	S	R	R	R	-	-	-
-	-	-	-	-	-	-	S	-	-	-	-	-	-	-	-	-	-	-	-	-	-	-	-	-	-	-	-
-	-	-	-	-	R	-	-	R	-	R	R	-	R	-	R	-	-	R	R	-	R	-	-	-	-	-	-
R	-	-	-	-	-	R	-	-	R	-	R	-	-	R	R	R	-	-	R	-	-	-	-	R	-	-	R
R	R	-	-	-	R	R	-	-	R	A	R	R	-	R	-	R	-	R	-	R	S	-	R	R	-	-	-
-	-	-	-	-	S	-	-	S	-	S	-	-	R	-	R	-	-	-	-	S	S	-	-	-	-	-	-
R	-	-	-	-	-	S	-	-	R	-	R	R	-	S	-	-	R	R	-	-	-	-	-	-	-	-	R
R	R	-	-	-	-	R	-	-	R	-	R	R	-	R	-	R	-	R	-	R	R	R	R	-	-	-	-
R	R	-	-	-	-	R	R	-	R	-	R	-	-	R	-	-	-	R	-	-	R	R	-	-	-	-	-
R	-	-	-	-	-	R	-	-	R	-	R	-	-	S	-	-	-	-	-	-	-	-	-	-	-	-	-
-	-	-	-	-	-	R	-	R	-	-	S	-	-	-	-	-	-	-	-	-	-	-	-	-	-	-	-
R	-	-	-	-	-	-	-	R	-	R	-	-	R	-	-	-	-	-	-	-	-	-	-	-	-	-	-
R	R	R	A	R	R	S	-	-	R	A	R	R	A	R	A	S	-	R	-	R	R	-	R	R	-	-	R
R	S	S	-	-	-	S	-	-	S	-	R	-	A	-	-	-	R	R	-	R	S	-	-	-	-	-	R
S	-	-	-	-	-	R	-	-	S	-	S	-	-	-	-	-	-	-	-	-	-	-	R	S	-	-	-
-	-	-	-	-	-	-	-	-	-	-	S	-	-	-	-	-	S	-	-	-	-	-	-	-	-	-	-
-	-	-	-	-	-	-	-	-	-	-	-	-	-	-	-	-	-	-	-	-	S	-	-	-	-	-	-

NON-MEMBER STATES		ANTIGUA & BARBUDA	BAHAMAS	BARBADOS	BELARUS	BELIZE	BOTSWANA	BRUNEI DARUSSALAM	BURKINA FASO	ECUADOR	FIJI	GRENADA	HOLY SEE
Statute	I												
Civil Procedure*	II	-	-	-	-	-	-	-	-	-	-	-	A
Sales of Goods*	III	-	-	-	-	-	-	-	-	-	-	-	-
Transfer of Title	IV	-	-	-	-	-	-	-	-	-	-	-	-
Sales–Choice of Court	V	-	-	-	-	-	-	-	-	-	-	-	-
National Law vs. Law of Domicile	VI	-	-	-	-	-	-	-	-	-	-	-	-
Recognition of Companies	VII	-	-	-	-	-	-	-	-	-	-	-	-
Maintenance Children–Applicable Law*	VIII	-	-	-	-	-	-	-	-	-	-	-	-
Maintenance Children–Enforcement*	IX	-	-	-	-	-	-	-	-	-	-	-	-
Protection of Minors*	X	-	-	-	-	-	-	-	-	-	-	-	-
Form of Wills*	XI	A	-	-	-	-	A	A	-	-	A	A	-
Legalisation*	XII	A	A	-	A	A	A	A	-	-	A	-	-
Adoption*	XIII	-	-	-	-	-	-	-	-	-	-	-	-
Service Abroad*	XIV	A	-	A	-	-	A	-	-	-	-	-	-
Choice of Court	XV	-	-	-	-	-	-	-	-	-	-	-	-
Enforcement of Judgments*	XVI	-	-	-	-	-	-	-	-	-	-	-	-
Protocol on Jurisdiction*	XVII	-	-	-	-	-	-	-	-	-	-	-	-
Divorce–Recognition*	XVIII	-	-	-	-	-	-	-	-	-	-	-	-
Traffic Accidents*	XIX	-	-	-	-	-	-	-	-	-	-	-	-
Taking of Evidence*	XX	-	-	A	-	-	-	-	-	-	-	-	-
Administration of Estates	XXI	-	-	-	-	-	-	-	-	-	-	-	-
Products Liability*	XXII	-	-	-	-	-	-	-	-	-	-	-	-
Maintenance–Enforcement*	XXIII	-	-	-	-	-	-	-	-	-	-	-	-
Maintenance–Applicable Law*	XXIV	-	-	-	-	-	-	-	-	-	-	-	-
Matrimonial Property*	XXV	-	-	-	-	-	-	-	-	-	-	-	-
Marriage*	XXVI	-	-	-	-	-	-	-	-	-	-	-	-
Agency*	XXVII	-	-	-	-	-	-	-	-	-	-	-	-
Child Abduction*	XXVIII	-	-	-	-	A	-	-	A	A	-	-	-
Access to Justice*	XXIX	-	-	-	-	-	-	-	-	-	-	-	-
Trusts*	XXX	-	-	-	-	-	-	-	-	-	-	-	-
Sales Contracts	XXXI	-	-	-	-	-	-	-	-	-	-	-	-
Successions–Applicable Law	XXXII	-	-	-	-	-	-	-	-	-	-	-	-

* = in force S = Signature R = Ratification A = Accession

LEBANON	LESOTHO	LIECHTENSTEIN	MALAWI	MALTA	MARSHALL ISLANDS	MAURITIUS	MONACO	MOROCCO	NEW ZEALAND	NIGER	PAKISTAN	PANAMA	RUSSIAN FED.	SEYCHELLES	SINGAPORE	SOUTH AFRICA	SWAZILAND	TONGA
A	-	-	-	-	-	-	-	A	-	-	-	-	A	-	-	-	-	-
-	-	-	-	-	-	-	-	-	-	A	-	-	-	-	-	-	-	-
-	-	-	-	-	-	-	-	-	-	-	-	-	-	-	-	-	-	-
-	-	-	-	-	-	-	-	-	-	-	-	-	-	-	-	-	-	-
-	-	-	-	-	-	-	-	-	-	-	-	-	-	-	-	-	-	-
-	-	-	-	-	-	-	-	-	-	-	-	-	-	-	-	-	-	-
-	-	A	-	-	-	-	-	-	-	-	-	-	-	-	-	-	-	-
-	-	A	-	-	-	-	-	-	-	-	-	-	-	-	-	-	-	-
-	-	-	-	-	-	-	-	-	-	-	-	-	-	-	-	-	-	-
-	A	-	-	-	-	A	-	-	A	-	-	-	-	-	-	A	A	A
-	A	R	A	A	A	A	-	-	-	-	-	A	A	A	-	-	A	A
-	-	-	-	-	-	-	-	-	-	-	-	-	-	-	-	-	-	-
-	-	A	-	-	-	-	-	-	-	-	A	-	-	A	-	-	-	-
-	-	-	-	-	-	-	-	-	-	-	-	-	-	-	-	-	-	-
-	-	-	-	-	-	-	-	-	-	-	-	-	-	-	-	-	-	-
-	-	-	-	-	-	-	-	-	-	-	-	-	-	-	-	-	-	-
-	-	-	-	-	-	-	-	-	-	-	-	-	-	-	-	-	-	-
-	-	-	-	-	-	-	-	-	-	-	-	-	-	-	-	-	-	-
-	-	-	-	-	-	-	A	-	-	-	-	-	-	-	A	-	-	-
-	-	-	-	-	-	-	-	-	-	-	-	-	-	-	-	-	-	-
-	-	-	-	-	-	-	-	-	-	-	-	-	-	-	-	-	-	-
-	-	-	-	-	-	-	-	-	-	-	-	-	-	-	-	-	-	-
-	-	-	-	-	-	-	-	-	-	-	-	-	-	-	-	-	-	-
-	-	-	-	-	-	-	-	-	-	-	-	-	-	-	-	-	-	-
-	-	-	-	-	-	A	A	-	A	-	-	-	-	-	-	-	-	-
-	-	-	-	-	-	-	-	S	-	-	-	-	-	-	-	-	-	-
-	-	-	-	-	-	-	-	-	-	-	-	-	-	-	-	-	-	-
-	-	-	-	-	-	-	-	-	-	-	-	-	-	-	-	-	-	-
-	-	-	-	-	-	-	-	-	-	-	-	-	-	-	-	-	-	-

Trusts

[Editorial note: first published in the International Encyclopedia of Comparative Law, Volume III, Chapter 23 (1994).]

| I. The Anglo-American Trust and its Derivatives

A. Definition

1. A trust is "a relationship which arises whenever a person (called a trustee) is compelled in equity to hold property, whether personal or real, and whether by legal or equitable title, for the benefit of some person or persons (of whom he may be one and who are termed beneficiaries or cestui que trust) in such a way that the real benefit of the property accrues not to the trustees but to beneficiaries ...[1] enforceable by the beneficiaries, not by the person who established the trust (called the settlor when the trust is established inter vivos and ... the testator in case of a trust set up by will.)"

"The remedies for the enforcement of the trust ... prevail against the trustee and against anyone into whose hands the trust property passes in breach of trust, except a bona fide purchaser for value of a legal title without notice of the breach. A beneficiary's equitable interest is assignable."[2]

B. Excluded Types

2. For the purposes of the present discussion, which is restricted to the place of the trust in private international law in favour of specified individuals,[3] no notice is being taken of socalled charitable trusts established for the benefit of some object permitted by law where the real benefit accrues to the objects of the trust.[4]

Nor will account be taken of trusts by operation of law, such as "constructive trusts",[5] which are more properly treated in connection with restitution, and of various institutions where the trust is used as a device to appoint trustees for creditors[6] or bondholders,[7] investment

---

[1] *Keeton and Sheridan* 2; also *Hanbury and Maudsley* 46; *Pettit*, Equity and the Law of Trusts (ed. 6 London 1989) 22; *Wortley* 699–703.

[2] *Keeton and Sheridan* 3.

[3] For the multitude of functions of trusts, see *Hornsey* 51–70; *Wortley* 706–709; *Lepaulle*, Validité 309.

[4] See *e.g., Keeton and Sheridan* 165–182.

[5] *Idem* 202 ss.

[6] *Hornsey* 49; *Fratcher* s. 45; *Simons and Radicati*, A Trustee in Continental Europe – The Experience of the Bank for International Settlements: Neth.Int.L. Rev. 30 (1983) 330–345, 330; *Garrigues* 29. Trib.civ. Seine 30 May 1873, Clunet 1880, 472 probably involved such a case.

[7] *Hornsey* 57; *Wortley* 706–707, FRENCH Cass.civ. 16 Feb. 1908, Clunet 1912, 243 on appeal from Cour Toulouse 18 July 1905, Clunet 1906, 451, Rev.d.i.p. 1907, 262 note *Nast.* Swiss BG 26 May 1936, BGE 62 II 140, 144; Trib.Arr.Luxembourg 21 Jan. 1971, Rev.crit.d.i.p. 1973, 51, note *Oppetit*, Le "trust" dans le droit du commerce international:

trusts,[8] business trusts,[9] land development trusts (UNITED STATES),[10] voting trusts,[11] letters of trust and trust receipts,[12] as well as trusts forming part of unincorporated associations.[13] These legal institutions, while retaining the figure of a trustee in his fiduciary capacity, lack the essential feature of the trust at common law which consists of a beneficiary or beneficiaries (as distinct from the settlor, who may, however be one) who can claim an interest of an equitable nature in the property vested in the trustee.[14]

C. Characterisation – Dual Character

i. At Common Law

3. *Characteristic features.* – The characteristic features of the trust in the narrow sense envisaged here are, firstly, that it is brought into existence by the intention of its creator, the settlor, either *inter vivos* or by a will, and is accepted by the trustee; secondly, that it creates rights by the beneficiary against the trustee, which are *in personam*; and, thirdly, that it gives the beneficiary equitable interests in the form of equi|table proprietary rights corresponding to legal estates[15] which operate in *rem* both in regard to the trustee by way of subrogation (tracing) and against third parties (following). Therefore "the beneficiary can properly be regarded as the owner of the beneficial interest ..."[16] but this conclusion remains controversial. The test would seem to be whether a beneficiary can assert a right in the trust property against third parties.[17]

---

ibidem 1–20, 3. And see the practice cited by *Nussbaum* 427 n. 94–97; *Loussouarn and Bredin* 384 no. 336.

[8] *Hornsey* 61; *Wortley* 706; *Fratcher* s. 52; *Bentivoglio* 105; *Van Gerven*, La forme juridique d'un "Investment Trust" en Belgique, en France et aux Pays-Bas: Rev.int.dr.comp. 1960, 527–558; *Würdinger* 39; *Reymond* 121a, 161a.

[9] *Hornsey* 65; *Fratcher* s. 44.

[10] *Hornsey* 67.

[11] *Idem* 69.

[12] *Ibidem; Fratcher* s. 48.

[13] *Fratcher* s. 49, s. 54–55.

[14] *Garrigues* 33, The so-called "common-law investment trust" (UNITED STATES Investment Company Act of 22 Aug. 1940, 15 U.S.C.A § 80a–1 to § 80a–52 (1981), § 80a–16 (c)) forms an exception: *Bentivoglio* 105, 107–109.

[15] *Hanbury and Maudsley* 17–22; *Scott*, The Law of Trusts (ed. 2 Boston and Toronto 1956) I 5–6; *Bogert*, The Law of Trusts and Trustees I (Kansas City, Mo. and St. Paul, Minn. 1935) § 17; but see *Maitland*, Equity (ed. 2 Cambridge, Engl. 1936) 106, 107, 115; *Waters*, The Nature of the Trust Beneficiary's Interest: 45 Can.Bar Rev. 219–283, 279 (1967).

[16] *Hanbury and Maudsley* 17.

[17] At common law the action for detinue, even when extended to ascertainable products of the original asset, resulted in a personal claim for damages with certain modifications and exceptions, see *Taylor v. Plumer* (1815), 3 M. & S. 562 (575), 105 E.R. 721.

4. *Beneficiary and trustee.* – The recognition of real subrogation in the hands of the trustee of the proceeds of the sale of trust property,[18] the right to trace trust assets into a mixed fund,[19] to follow them into the hands of persons other than a *bona fide* purchaser for value, namely an innocent donee[20] or a *mala fide* purchaser, and the treatment of trust funds as separate property in the trustee's bankruptcy,[21] seem to confirm that the beneficiary has at his disposal an action *erga omnes* in certain circumstances. In short, the beneficiary is the owner of the financial interest in the trust fund and is known as the equitable owner. The trustee is the owner of the administrative interests in the trust assets and is known as the legal owner.[22] At the same time he is subject to duties arising therefrom towards the beneficiary; the latter has a personal claim against the trustee to have the assets administered in accordance with the terms of the trust and the general law governing trustees.[23]

The combination of the proprietary interests in the trust assets coupled with the personal relationship between trustee and beneficiary has obscured the nature of the institution of trusts as a whole and has led to the ongoing dispute as to whether the rights of a beneficiary under a trust are *in personam* or *in rem*. In fact these rights are not unitary in character; some are *in rem* and some are *in personam*.[24]

ii. In Civil Law Systems

5. This difficulty has affected the ability of lawyers trained in systems other than Anglo-American law to allot a place to the trust in their own law and especially in applying their own rules of private international law. While a combination of attributes sounding *in personam* and *in rem* is not unknown, a division between legal and equitable ownership does not fit into a legal system which only knows ownership which is joint or in common, but ignores a division of ownership which is determined not by the quantity but by the quality of the right to ownership.[25]

---

[18] UNITED KINGDOM: Law of Property Act, 1925 (15 & 16 Geo. 5, c. 20) s. 2.

[19] *Re Hallett's Estate* (1880), 13 Ch. 696; *Hanbury and Maudsley* 635 ss.

[20] *Hanbury and Maudsley* 648; among codified systems the INDIAN Trusts Act, 1882 (no. II of 1882) s. 63–66, compared with s. 11–28 (duties of trustees) offers a good example.

[21] Bankruptcy Act, 1914 (4 & 5 Geo. 5, c: 59) s. 38 (1), now Insolvency Act 1986 (c. 45) s. 283 (3) (a); *Jennings v. Mather*, [1902] 1 K.B. 1 (C.A.); Restatement of Trusts 2d § 266; *Fratcher* s. 96–97.

[22] Split ownership: *Fratcher* s. 4, s. 95 and n. 728 (literature); *Schnitzer*, Treuhand 74 ss.

[23] *Fratcher* s. 92, 93, 96–97.

[24] *In personam*: trustee's duty to administer the trust; trustee's right to indemnity and compensation: *Fratcher* s. 77–80, 89, 92, 93.

[25] See *e.g.*, *Lepaulle*, in various contributions, namely Nature; Substitutes; Outsider; Traité; Civil Law; *Weiser; Kötz*, Trust 111–114.

D. The Common Law Trust in Civil Law Countries

6. The difficulty of analysing the notion of trust in terms of the conceptions current in legal systems other than ANGLO-AMERICAN law has had repercussions in three principal respects:

In the first place it has proved difficult to characterise claims based on ANGLO-AMERICAN law by or against a trustee according to the choice of law rules of the *lex fori*, other than actions *in personam* between beneficiary and trustee (which have occurred rarely). Is title to local property vested in the trustee or the beneficiary, in the executor and trusted or the heir or universal legatee, in the trustee under a marriage settlement or a spouse as beneficiary?

Secondly, do claims by a beneficiary to trace trust assets in the hands of the trustee or to follow them in the hands of a third party sound in contract, in tort or in property?

In the third place, many CIVIL LAW countries, in seeking to adopt the institution of the trust | for their own use, have created new legal categories which are called trusts but which have little in common with the ANGLO-AMERICAN trust. The notion of divided ownership is disregarded and title is vested in one person only, namely the trustee; the right of the beneficiary is reduced to one *in personam* and in some countries his position is passed over altogether in favour of the settlor's right to have the trust carried out properly (*infra* s. 7 ss.). Naturally this approach is reflected in the conflict of laws according as claims arising under one or another type of trust are involved. In the words of *Fratcher*,

"When courts of ... [civil law] jurisdictions have been confronted with attempts to create trusts of property subject to their law, they have not recognized that both the trustee and the beneficiary have rights *in rem* in the trust property. In some cases they have treated the trustee as the sole owner of the trust property, with only contract obligations to the beneficiary ... In others they have treated the beneficiary as the sole owner and the trustee as a mere *mandatarius* or managing agent."[26]

At this stage only this last aspect will be considered.

E. Indigenous Trusts in Civil Law Countries

i. Scotland

7. In SCOTS law the trustee is the sole and exclusive owner,[27] subject to the qualification that he is not entitled to the benefit or the enjoyment of the

---

[26] *Fratcher* s. 109; see *Ex Parte Milton*, 1959(3) S.A.L.Rep. 347, 349–350 (H.Ct.South.Rhod.).

[27] *I.R.C. v. Clark's Trustees*, 1939 S.C. (Ct.Sess.) 11, 22, 26; *McNair's Executors v. Litster*, 1939 S.C. (Ct.Sess.) 72, 77; *Walker* 4.

property,[28] which is held for trust purposes. The beneficiary has only a *jus crediti*,[29] which is enforceable against the trustee, is similar to, but distinct from, a right in contract, quasi-contract or both,[30] and can be assigned. A subsequent trustee or a beneficiary (suing in the name of the trustee[31]) can follow the assets, their identifiable proceeds or a surrogate in the hands of the original trustee or of a third party,[32] except a *bona fide* purchaser for value without notice of the trust.[33] The trust property does not form part of the assets in the trustee's bankruptcy[34] on the ground that "an apparent title to land or personal estate carrying no real right of property with it does not ... make such land or personal estate the property of the person who holds title."[35]

The trustee or trustees can be forced to lend their name or names to the beneficiaries who, in safeguarding their interests, rely on the proprietary right of the trustee.[36] However, in so acting the beneficiary has no vested equitable and co-existent right concurring with that of a trustee.[37] What is enforced in these circumstances is the proprietary right of the trustee. Only if the trust fails, the title to the assets reverts to the settlor.[38]

In effect, SCOTS law has succeeded in incorporating the trust as conceived in ENGLISH law by concentrating title to the assets exclusively in the trustee, thus avoiding the distinction between legal and equitable ownership, while maintaining its vestige by assigning to subsequent trustees and ultimately to the beneficiaries the original trustee's right in order to trace or to follow the trust assets. In the words of *Lord Normand* "it is a description of a typical

---

[28] *Camille and Henry Dreyfus Foundation Inc. v. Inland Revenue Commissioners*, [1956] A.C. 38, 47–48 (H.L.).

[29] *Walker* 4; *MacKenzie Stuart*, Law of Trusts (Edinburgh 1932) 1–2; *Wilson and Duncan* 14–15, 16, 119; *McCall-Smith* 204–206; *I.R.C. v. Clark's Trustees (supra* n. 27) 26.

[30] *Walker* 5 and n. 13; *Wilson and Duncan* 12, also 11, 26, 57; *Allen v. McCombie's Trustees*, 1908 S.C. (Ct.Sess.) 710, 716, 717; *Banff Magistrates v. Ruthin Castle Ltd.*, 1944 S.C. (Ct.Sess.) 36, 41.

[31] *Walker* 72; *Wilson and Duncan* 384; *Watt v. Roger's Trustees*, (1890) 17 R [1889–1890 S.C.] (Ct. Sess.) 1201, 1203–1204.

[32] *Walker* 72 and n. 80; *Wilson and Duncan* 121; *Jopp v. Johnston's Trustee*, (1904) 6 F [1903–1904 S.C.] (Ct.Sess.) 1028, 1035; *Heritable Reversionary Company, Ltd. v. Millar*, (1892) 19 R 43 (49–51), [1892] A.C. 598, 614 ss. (H.L.).

[33] *Wilson and Duncan* 15 with references.

[34] *Idem* 6, 7, 15, 120; *MacKenzie Stuart (supra* n. 29) 50, 121; *Anton* 470; *Heritable Reversionary Company, Ltd. v. Millar (supra* n. 32) 621; *Forbes's Trustees v. Macleod*, (1898) 25 R [1897–1898 S.C.] (Ct.Sess.) 1012, 1013; *Bank of Scotland v. Liquidators of Hutchinson Main Co., Ltd.*, 1914 S.C. (H.L.) 1, 15.

[35] *Heritable Reversionary Company, Ltd. v. Millar (supra* n. 32) 614.

[36] *Wilson and Duncan* 122; *Blair v. Stirling*, [1894] 1 S.L.T. (Ct.Sess.) 599; *Brown's Trustees v. Brown*, (1888) 15 R [1887–1888 S.C.] (Ct.Sess.) 581, 582–583.

[37] *Hetherington's Trustees v. Lord Advocate*, 1934 S.C. (H.L.) 19, 36; *Wilson and Duncan* 14.

[38] *Walker* 4, 11.

| trust according to Scots law, and it contains ... nothing repugnant to the English conception of trust ... it is a term which would be intelligible in reference to many other systems of law which do not derive from the law of England."[39]

ii. The Law of Quebec

8. The nature of the *fiducie* in QUEBEC law[40] is controversial.[41] Some regarded it as a legal entity of its own,[42] others fastened on the wording of CC art. 981 b that trustees are "seized as depositaries and administrators for the benefit of the donees or legatees of the property conveyed in trust."[43] It was, therefore, argued, although unsuccessfully, that the beneficiary is the owner and that the trustees as depositaries and administrators, acting on behalf of the beneficiaries, retain possession of the property until the *fiducie* comes to an end.[44]

The new Civil Code of 18 Dec. 1991 has put the problem to rest (art. 1260–1298). A *fiducie* arises when a person transfers some or all of his assets to another set of assets formed by him for a particular purpose and when a trustee undertakes, by accepting them, to hold the assets and to administer them (art. 1260, 1266). The assets form an autonomous unit which is distinct from the assets owned by the settlor, the trustee and the beneficiary and is not subject to proprietary rights by any of them (art. 1261). The settlor gives

---

[39] *Camille and Henry Dreyfus Foundation Inc. v. Inland Revenue Commissioners* (*supra* n. 28) 48.

[40] LOWER CANADA CC art. 981a – v, first introduced in 1879 (42 & 43 Vict., c. 29, as amended); *Civil Code Revision Office*, Report on the Quebec Civil Code II/1 (Books 1–4) (Quebec 1977) 523 no. 600 ss., 544 (literature).

[41] *Baudouin*, Le droit civil de la Province de Québec (Montreal 1953) 1241–1246; *Faribault*; Traité théorique et pratique de la fiducie ou trust du droit civil dans la Province de Québec (Montreal 1936); *Mignault*, La Fiducie dans la Province de Québec: Trav.sem.int.dr. 1937 V 35–55; *Mankiewicz*, Le fiducie québecoise et le trust de Common Law. Etude d'interprétation comparative: Rev.du B. 1952, 16–52; *Waters*, The Nature of the Trust Beneficiary's Interest: 45 Can.Bar Rev. 219–283 (1967); *Mettarlin* 190–198; *Caron*, The Trust in Quebec: 25 McGill L.J. 421–440 (1980); *Brierley*, Editor's *Post Scriptum*: *ibidem* 440–444.

[42] Following *Lepaulle*, Traité 31; see *Mettarlin* 211 ss. For SOUTH AFRICA, see *Honoré* 5 n. 21 with literature.

[43] *Mettarlin* 218 ss., 222; *Faribault* (*supra* n. 41) 101–103; for further literature see *Castel*, The Civil Law System of the Province of Quebec. Notes, Cases and Materials (Toronto 1962) 104.

[44] *Curran v. Davis*, (1933) Can.S.C.R. 283, 292 ss. (298, 302, 304 ss.), [1934] 1 D.L.R. 161, 170 (176, 179, 185) (Can.S.C.) on appeal from [1932] 53 Qué.K.B. 231 (235–236, 243, 245, 247), but see 251–252, 255; *McEwen v. Jenkins*, [1955] Qué.B.R. 785, 793; *Guarantee Trust Co. of New York v. The King*, [1948] Qué.S.C.R. 183, 205, 209 on appeal from [1947] Qué.B.R. 656; *Laverdure v. Du Tremblay*, [1937] A.C. 666, 681–682 (P.C.); *Fratcher* s. 112; *Caron* (*supra* n. 41) 426.

up the possession of the assets, the trustee must administer them, apply them for their expressed purpose and ensure that the rights of the beneficiary are protected (art. 1265). For these purposes he has the exclusive power to administer the assets, title to which is registered in his name, and he can exercise all proprietary rights necessary to carry out his task (art. 1278, 1307) as well as enter into obligations on behalf of the fund (art. 1275, 1276). Unlike in ANGLO-AMERICAN law, the beneficiary can himself be a trustee, albeit together with a third party (art. 1319, 1322).

iii. Louisiana Law

9. In LOUISIANA the Trust Code 1964, following its predecessors in 1882, 1914 and 1938 (Trust Estates Law) vests absolute title in the trustee and leaves the legal position of a beneficiary undefined.[45] The question is whether his nomination creates a *substitution* which leaves him in a position comparable in function, but not in time, to that of an equitable owner.[46]

F. Co-Existence of Fideicommissum and Trust

10. *General characterisation.* – In those countries where *fideicommissa* formed part of the traditional civil law and where trusts were intro|duced subsequently as an additional legal institution, the acknowledged division between present and subsequent ownership in the law of *fideicommissa* was not transported to the concurrent, but distinct, interests of trustee and beneficiary in the law of trusts.

11. *South Africa.* – In SOUTH AFRICA the trustee is the exclusive owner, but qua trustee he has no beneficial interest.[47] The beneficiaries share a legal position on an equal footing with creditors[48] except as regards immovable

---

[45] Trust Estates Law no. 81 of 1938, La.Rev.Stat. Ann. (1950) § 9:1791 – § 9:2212 (repr. 3A West 1965) Appendix no.R.S. 9; Trust Code, Law no. 338 of 1964, La.Rev.Stat.Ann. § 9:1721 – § 9:2252 (repr. 3A West 1965); *Wisdom* 83; *Oppenheim*, Limitations and Uses of Louisiana Trusts: 27 Tul.L.Rev. 41–58 (1953); *idem*, A New Trust Code for Louisiana: 39 *ibidem* 187–226 (1965); *idem*, The 1968 Amendment to the Trust Code of 1964:43 *ibidem* 34–45 (1968); *Lorio*, Louisiana Trusts – The Experience of a Civil Law Jurisdiction with the Trust: 42 La.L.Rev. 1721–1739 (1982); *Dainow*, The Introduction of the Trust in Louisiana:. 39 Can. Bar Rev. 396–407 (1961).

[46] *Stone; Foil*, Trust – Prohibited Substitutions: 22 La.L.Rev. 889–895, 891 (1962); *Oppenheim*, New Trust Code (preceding note) 198, 217; but see the critical observation of *Pascal*, Of Trusts, Human Rights, Legal Science and Taxes: 23 La.L.Rev. 639–661 (1963).

[47] *Honoré* 4, 43, 224 ss., 432 ss.; *McCall-Smith* 189, 207 ss.

[48] *Kemp v. McDonald's Trustee*, 1915 AD. 491, 499. But see *Estate Watkins-Pitchford v. Commissioner for Inland Revenue*, 1955 (2) S.A.L.Rep. 437, 460 (A.D.); *Greenberg v. Estate Greenberg*, 1955 (3) S.A.L.Rep. 361, 365, 368 (A.D.); *Braun v. Blann and Botha NNO and Another*, 1984 (2) S.A.L.Rep. 850, 859 no. (H), 865–866 (A.D.) which throw

property registered in the name of the trustee as such.[49] Opinion is divided as to whether, apart from particular legislation, the beneficiaries can exclude the trustee's private creditors in insolvency.[50] They cannot follow the trust property and can trace only when the disposition was lawful.[51] In short, generally speaking, beneficiaries only have a right *in personam*, but they enjoy also a right *ad rem*.

12. *Sri Lanka.* – In SRI LANKA, the statutory introduction of the trust has also resulted in a bifurcation.[52] The test as to whether a *fideicommissum* or a trust is involved is made to depend upon whether the donee or legatee acquired merely an administrative or a beneficial interest. In the former case the donee or legatee as owner is a trustee, in the latter case he holds as a *fideicommissarius.* The beneficiary, unlike a *fideicommissarius*, has only a right *in personam*.[53]

13. *Netherlands.* – The nature of the *bewind* in DUTCH law[54] is characterised by a division between administration and ownership of the assets, which is vested in the beneficiary.

G. Adapted Trusts

i. Restricted Use

14. *Central and South America.* – Similarly, legislation in CENTRAL and SOUTH AMERICA has resorted to the trust institution in name only when it created trusts for the benefit of bondholders[55] and *comisiones de confian-*

---

doubts on the legal construction in *Kemp's* case, but accept the trust, including a beneficiary's right *ad rem. Honoré* 14, 23, 447, 448, but see 412 ss.; *Hahlo*, The Trust in South African Law/El fideicomiso en el derecho sudafricano: 2 Inter. Am.L.Rev./Rev.jur.interam. 229–242 (Engl.), 243–258 (Span.) (1960), 78 S.A.L.J. 195–208 (1961); *Forsyth*, The Juristic Basis of the Testamentary Trust, the Principle of Non-Delegation of Will-Making Power and the Purism Movement: 103 *ibidem* 513–522 (1986); *Fratcher* s. 114.

[49] Trust Moneys Protection Act (no. 34 of 1934), amended by Act no. 57 of 1975, now superseded by the Trust Property Control Act (no. 57 of 1988) s. 12; see also Attorneys' Admission Amendment and Legal Practitioners' Fidelity Fund Act (no. 19 of 1941) s. 17.

[50] *Honoré* 14, 436, 441 ss.; *Joubert*, The Insolvency of a Trustee: 92 S.A.L.J. 22–30 (1975).

[51] *Honoré* 227, 447–448 and see 23; *McCall-Smith* 218 ss.

[52] Trusts Ordinance no. 9 of 1917, L.E.Cap. 87, amended by Acts no. 7 of 1968 and no. 30 of 1971; *Fratcher* s. 113.

[53] *Abdul Hameed Sitti Kadija v. De Saram*, [1946] A.C. 208, 216–217, (1946–47) 47 New L.Rep. 171, 175 (P.C.); *Honoré* 41.

[54] *Uniken Venema*, Trusts 70; *Honoré* 4 n. 12; 199 ss., 206, 412 ss; *Dyer and Van Loon*, Report 39; see draft of title 6 in Book 3 new CC art. 4 a and 4 b; title 6 did not yet enter into force, unlike the rest of Book 3.

[55] ARGENTINA: Law no. 19.550 on commercial companies (*Ley de sociedades comerciales*) of 3 April 1972 (BO 25 April), as revised by Law no. 22.903 of 9 Sept. 1983 (BO 15. Sept.) and consolidated by Decree no. 841/84 (BO 30 March 1984) arc. 338 ss. (*contrato de*

za^{56} whereby banks are enabled to accept funds which are | kept separate from their own assets, to be invested in authorized securities, unless the "trust" instrument provides otherwise. Thereby the bank can act as agent, executor or guardian in accordance with the relevant provisions of private law.[57]

15. *Luxembourg.* – The LUXEMBOURG Regulation of 19 July 1983,[58] like the legislation of some SOUTH AMERICAN states, is restricted to trust agreements in favour of banking institutions (art. 1). The trustee is the owner, the beneficiaries only enjoy rights *in personam* (art. 2), but like in LIECHTENSTEIN law (*infra* s. 17) the trust assets do not form part of the trustee's assets in case of his bankruptcy (art. 3 par. 1).

ii. General Application

16. Under the influence of *Ricardo J. Alfaro*,[59] who rejected the use of the *fideicommissum mortis causa* including substitution, an institution not re-

---

fideicomiso). CHILE (see next note): *Valdes,* Trusts in Chile: 81 Trusts & Est. 155, 156 (1945). BRAZIL: Decree no. 177 A of 15 Sept. 1893, amended by Decree no. 22.431 (*estabelece e regula a comunhão de interesses entre os portadores debentures*) of 6 Feb. 1933 (DO 16 Feb.). COLOMBIA: Law no. 5 on municipal budgets (*sobre presupuestos municipales*) of 26 July 1918 (Leyes de Colombia 1916–1918 (1939) 7) art. 4; PERU: Law no. 850 of 1931. *Goldschmidt* 41–42; *Patton* 430 ss.; *Fratcher* s. 119.

[56] BOLIVIA: Law no. 608 of 4 July 1928 art. 169; CHILE: Law no. 559 of 1925 art. 50; Law no, 4827 of 1930 art. 1–4. COLOMBIA: Law no. 45 on banking institutions (*sobre establicimientos bancarios*) of 19 July 1923 (Leyes de Colombia 1921–1923 (1941) 136) art. 107 par. 2; COSTA RICA: Law no. 15 of 23 Oct. 1936 art. 71 (now Comm.C art. 633–666); EL SALVADOR: Decree of 12 Nov. 1937 art. 13 = CC art. 1810; MEXICO: Trust Banks Law (*Ley de bancos de fideicomiso*) of 30 June 1926 (DO 17 July); General law of negotiable instruments and credit operations (*ley general de títulos y operaciones de credito*) of 26 Aug. 1932 (DO 27 Aug.) art. 346 and Law on banking and auxiliary organizations (*Ley general de instituciones de crédito y organizaciones auxiliares*) of 3 May 1941 (DO 31 May) art. 44 incorporating the Trust Banks Law; PERU: Law no. 7159 on banks (*Ley de bancos*) of 25 May 1931 (An.Leg.Peruana 25 (1930–1931) 320) art. 94 par. 13, *Patton* 424, 426; *Goldschmidt* 42; *Molina Pasqul* 70; *Fratcher* s. 119.

[57] See the laws, cited in the preceding note, of BOLIVIA (art. 170); CHILE (art. 50); COLOMBIA (art. 107 par. 2); COSTA RICA (art. 71); EL SALVADOR (art. 13); MEXICO (Gen.Law of negotiable instruments art. 356); PERU (art. 94 par. 14). VENEZUELA: Law of trusts (*Ley de fideicomisos*) of 26 July 1956 (G.O.spec.iss. no. 496 of 17 Aug. 1956) art. 12. *Patton* 414–419; *Wisdom* 80–81.

[58] Grand-ducal Regulation on fiduciary contracts of credit institutions (*Règlement grand-ducal relatif aux contrats fiduciaires des établissements de crédit*) of 19 July 1983, Memorial 1983 A 1334; *Witz,* Treuhandverträge von Kreditinstituten in Luxemburg – Das grossherzogliche Reglement vom 19.7.1983: RIW AWD 1984, 846–850.

[59] *Alfaro,* El Fideicomiso. Estudio sobre la necesidad y conveniencia de introducir en la legislación de los pueblos latinos una institución civil nueva, semejante al trust del derecho inglés (Panama 1920); *idem,* Adaptación del trust del derecho anglosajón al derecho civil: Acad.Interamer.Der.Comp.Int. 1 (1948) 1–108; *idem,* Trust; *Goldschmidt* 35; *Molina Pasquel* 54–78; *Batiza,* Tres Estudios sobre el Fideicomiso (Mexico 1954) 18–21.

stricted to banking was created in PANAMA[60] and PUERTO RICO[61] whereby the fiduciary (who may be an individual or a trust corporation) is owner, subject to an irrevocable mandate (a notion replaced subsequently by "act").[62] The beneficiaries are only his creditors.[63] The VENEZUELAN Law of trusts of 1956 (*supra* n. 57) follows the same lines,[64] not limited to banking institutions as trustees. It states clearly that the trust property and its surrogate is not available to the creditors of the fiduciary.[65] The MEXICAN legislation,[66] as interpreted in practice, regards the fiduciary institution as the owner, subject to the duty to account and to return the property which remains when the *fideicomiso* terminates.[67] Also the settlor and the beneficiary may obtain a separation of the trust property, if the trustee becomes bankrupt. It has been concluded, therefore, by some that the rights of the beneficiaries are *in rem*.[68]

In addition, VENEZUELAN as well as (probably) Mexican law enable the beneficiaries to bring an action to revoke dispositions of the trustee in contravention of his duties within five years from the time when they obtained knowledge of them.[69]

The *fideicomiso* in EL SALVADOR also vests the assets in the trustee, but is more restricted.[70]

---

[60] Law no. 9 of 6 Jan. 1925, as amended by Law no. 17 of 20 Feb. 1941 (see *General Secretariat of Organization of American States*, A Statement of the Laws of Panama (ed. 3 Washington, D.C. 1974) 241); *Wisdom* 80–82; *Patton* 414; *Garay Preriato*, El Trust Anglosajon y el Fideicomiso Panameño (Santiago de Chile 1941); *Fratcher* s. 121; also to a limited extent in EL SALVADOR under the Decree of 12 Nov. 1937 (*supra* n. 56), see the discussion at *Patton* 426.

[61] CC art. 2541–2581, formerly CC art. 834–874 (1930), incorporating Acts no. 40, 41 of 23 April 1928; *Patton* 419–423; *Goldschmidt* 41; *Sánchez Vilella* 388 ss; *Hendrickson*, Puerto Rico 345–348.

[62] *Patton* 418; *Sánchez Vilella* 384.

[63] *Goldschmidt* 50.

[64] *Idem* 32; *Fratcher* s. 123.

[65] Art. 18, 24 par. 2; *Goldschmidt* 47.

[66] *Supra* n. 56; Law on bankruptcy and suspension of payments (DO 20 April 1943) art. 169 par. via; *Goldschmidt* 31, 50; *Molina Pasquel*.

[67] Art. 346 states: "By virtue of the trust the settlor destines certain property to a specific lawful purpose entrusting the achievement of that purpose to a trust company" thus taking up the construction suggested by *Lepaulle*, Traité 31. For the characterisation of this institution see *Molina Pasquel* 73.

[68] *Ryan* 282; but see *Goldschmidt* 50, admitting exceptions.

[69] *Goldschmidt* 47.

[70] Decree of 12 Nov. 1937 (*supra* n. 56) art. 4; *Goldschmidt* 45–46.

H. Modern Comprehensive Legislation

17. *Liechtenstein.* – The LIECHTENSTEIN trust[71] resembles its SCOTTISH counterpart in many re|spects. The Law leaves the trustee's position fairly clear by stating that he is "that individual person, firm or corporation to which another (the settlor) donates a patrimony or any property right with the obligation to administer or apply it in his name as an independent owner of rights for the benefit of one or several third persons with effect against the whole world."[72] The trustee is the owner and can dispose of the assets,[73] but they do not form part of his assets for the purposes of bankruptcy and levy of execution (art. 915). The settlor's reversionary interest is given special attention (art. 917) and he can reserve the right to revoke the trust (art. 907 par. 1). A right to follow and to trace is accorded to the settlor, a co-trustee and a beneficiary (art. 912 par. 3). In all these respects the rights of the settlor against the trustee are contractual (art. 918, 926) as are those of the beneficiary (art. 927).

The LIECHTENSTEIN *Treuunternehmen* is a fund with or without legal personality in the nature of a private corporation which may issue shares,[74] has beneficiaries[75] and is administered by trustees.[76] As a corporation it is governed by the conflicts rules relating to legal entities[76a] which are not for discussion here.

18. *Jersey.* – The Trusts Law of JERSEY of 31 May 1983 and 14 March 1984, as amended on 21 July 1989[77] comes nearest among the laws of CIVIL LAW countries to introducing the ENGLISH trust in its entirety. In so doing it goes beyond the Hague Convention on the Law Applicable to Trusts and on their Recognition of 1985.

---

[71] Law on persons and business organisations (*Das Personen- und Gesellschafts-Recht*) of 20 Jan. 1926 (LGBl. no. 4) art. 897–932; *Ryan* 278; *Biedermann*, Die Treuhänderschaft des Liechtensteinischen Rechts, dargestellt an ihrem Vorbild, dem Trust des Common Law (Bern 1981).

[72] Art. 897; *Weiser* 51ss. therefore regards the trustee as the agent of the settlor.

[73] Art. 919 par. 3; see also art. 911 par. 3: subrogation.

[74] Law on persons and business organisations (*supra* n. 71) art. 932a (= Law on trust enterprises (*Treuunternehmen*) of 10 April 1928 (LGBl. no. 6) § 1).

[75] See Law on trust enterprises (preceding note) § 78, 102 ss., 124 ss.; for the protection of their interests against their creditors see § 136 ss.

[76] See Law on trust enterprises (*supra* n. 74) § 50 ss.; for constructive trustees see § 136 ss.

[76a] Law on trust enterprises (*supra* n. 74) § 83; *Schnitzer*, Treuhand 85; *Serick*, Anerkennung 624–642; *Schönle*, Die Anerkennung liechtensteinischer juristischer Personen in Deutschland: NJW 1965, 1112–1117, 1115 n. 17 with literature; *Borgioli*, Partecipazione di un' "Anstalt" ad una società italiana e art. 2332 c.c.: Riv.soc. 1977, 414–441; *idem*, Le Treuunternehmen nell'ordinamento italiano: Giur. comm. 1978 II 49–67; *Cassoni*, Anstalt 210–221; *idem*, Note 2002; *Picone* 83–163; AG Hamburg 31 July 1964, IPRspr. 1964/64 no. 29; OLG Frankfurt 3 June 1964, *ibidem* no. 22; OLG Stuttgart 9 June 1964, *ibidem* no. 23.

[77] See *Mathews and Sowden*, The Jersey Law of Trusts (ed. 2 London 1990) Appendix.

Foreign trusts are recognised[78] – and detailed rules set out the powers and obligations of the trustee of a JERSEY trust. It cannot consist of immovables, no matter whether the trust is local or foreign.[79] The assets are vested in the trustee as owner (art. 8), but unlike in other CIVIL LAW systems which recognise the trust, the interest of a beneficiary is characterised as representing movable property (art. 9 par. 10) which can be sold, pledged, charged or transferred otherwise (art. 9 par. 11). It is therefore treated as a right *in rem*. Following the property in the hands of third parties is thus possible and is allowed (art. 29) and a trustee, acting as such, is only liable *cum viribus* (art. 28).

The division of proprietary interests is reflected in the rule that foreign rules of succession applicable according to the law of a foreign settlor do not affect the creation or the validity of a JERSEY trust.[80]

Recent legislation in GUERNSEY and BELIZE follows the same model.[80a]

| II. Foreign Trusts in the Conflict of Laws

A. General Considerations

19. *Characterisation.* – Although none of the trust institutions adopted outside strictly common law countries introduced the ANGLO-AMERICAN trust in a form which can be completely identified with the latter they, and not only the ANGLO-AMERICAN trust, create problems for the courts elsewhere in applying their choice-of-law rules. If characterised as contractual relationships, the choice of law is determined; if characterised as proprietary, the *numerus clausus* of such rights in CIVIL LAW countries calls, at best, for a process of transposition[81] and, at worst, for a complete disregard of the trust on the ground that the institution is unknown,[82] unless the CIVIL LAW notion of ownership is rendered more flexible.

The relationship between trustee and beneficiary causes little difficulty: it is contractual. The legal position of a trustee towards third parties is more

---

[78] Art. 2, 45; foreign trusts for sale of immovables appear to be recognised.

[79] Art. 10 par. 2 *lit.* a (iii).

[80] Art. 8A par. 2 *lit.* b.

[80a] GUERNSEY: Law of 1989, 5 Trust Law International (1991) 19–23; BELIZE: Law of 1991, 6 *ibidem* (1992) 9–27.

[81] *Lewald*, Règles générales des conflits de lois – Contribution à la technique du droit international privé: Rec. des Cours 69 (1939 III) 1–146, 129; *Lipstein*, P.I.L. 207–208; *Neuhaus*, Grundbegriffe des internationalen Privatrechts (Beiträge zum ausländischen und internationalen Privatrecht no. 30) (ed. 2 Tübingen 1976) 353, 357.

[82] For an example drawn from the law of matrimonial property see *Phrantzes v. Argenti*, [1960] 2 Q.B. 19 and *infra* n. 162.

open to question, since the *lex situs* applies. Is he the owner or is title vested in the beneficiary who acts through him as an agent? If the trustee is the owner, how is another legal system to characterise the rights of a beneficiary to trace and to follow trust assets and to have them set apart in the trustee's bankruptcy, as ANGLO-AMERICAN law allows and some statutory legal systems provide in CENTRAL and SOUTH AMERICA as well as in EUROPE?

20. *Transposition.* – Since a division of ownership with several holders of title according to the quality (administrative or beneficial) of their title is unknown in CIVIL LAW systems, the usual process of characterisation (whether according to the *lex fori*, the *lex causae* or on a functional basis) is of no assistance. If a process of transposition is called for, interesting attempts have been made for this purpose.[83] Mandate, usufruct, emphyteusis, donation or heirship subject to a charge, stipulation in favour of third parties and curatorship have all been considered.[84] If a total disregard is ruled out, the only other alternative is a total incorporation; even then, however, the impact is not total as a result of *dépeçage*. Rights of succession and claims under matrimonial property regimes applicable in virtue of other legal systems may seriously curtail the operation of the trust.[85]

These possibilities must be kept in mind in examining the practice in a variety of countries. At the same time it is evident that the proprietary aspects of the position of a trustee and of beneficiaries do not present any difficulty, if proceedings take place in another COMMON LAW country where all acknowledge dual ownership, divided into legal and beneficial (*infra* s. 21–38).

B. Trusts in Anglo-American Conflict of Laws

i. Introduction

21. "If there should be any part of the conflict of laws free from confusion, it is not the treatment of trusts."[86] In the countries of the COMMON LAW, the difficulties in formulating choice of law rules for trusts are increased by the need to distinguish between trusts *inter vivos* and testamentary trusts and by the difference in the treatment of movables and immovables. On the other hand, the choice of law rules governing capacity to create a trust and the

---

[83] See *Wiegand*, Die Entwicklung des Sachenrechts im Verhältnis zum Schuldrecht: AcP 190 (1990) 112–138, 135–136.

[84] *Wisdom* 79.

[85] E.g., *Lepaulle*, Nature; *Weiser*; *Ryan* 265–283; *Kötz*, Trust 111; *de Wulf*; *Dreyer* 136, 158; sec also *infra* s. 71–73.

[86] *Rabel* 445.

required formalities are those which apply generally to transactions involving a foreign element. Since legal and beneficial interests are recognised, the principal question concerns the essential validity of the trust.

Finally, charitable and constructive trusts fall outside this survey since they invite respectively inclusion in the law of legal persons and restitution (*supra* s. 2). They are therefore also omitted when considering questions of choice of law.

|*ii. England and the Commonwealth*

22. It may be pointed out at the beginning that a trust may be intended to operate for a long time while certain legal systems impose time limits. According to the view taken by the late *J. H. C. Morris*, the desire to satisfy the broad expectations arising from trusts has led to the application of that legal system which is most favourable to its validity.[87]

a. Testamentary Trusts

aa. Essential Validity

23. *Movables.* – In principle, the law which governs the essential validity of a will of movables (*i.e.* the law of the testator's domicile at the time of his death) also applies to a trust set up by the will.[88] Although a testator is not free to select a law other than that of his domicile to govern the substantive law determining his succession, but only insofar as its interpretation and form is concerned,[89] it has been suggested that a testator domiciled in England can set up a testamentary trust governed by foreign law.[90] This liberty is said to be either general[91] or restricted to the law governing the administration of the trust.[92] Direct authority is lacking, but the decisions involving the

---

[87] *Dicey and Morris* (ed. 10, 1980) 674–675, omitted in ed. 11, 1987; *Macdonald v. Macdonald* (1872), 14 Eq. 60, 67; *In re Bankes*, [1902] 2 Ch. 333, 342–343; *In re Fitzgerald*, [1904] 1 Ch. 573, 588, 594 (C.A.); *In re Mitchner*, (1922) S.R. (Qd.) 252, 268–270; *In re Kehr*, [1952] Ch. 26, 30; *Jauffret-Spinosi* 46 with reference to the Hague Convention on Trusts of 1985 art. 14 (*infra* n. 260).

[88] *Thornion v. Curling*, (1824), 8 Sim. 310, 59 E.R. 123 (V.C.); *In re Annesley*, [1926] Ch. 692; *In re Ross*, [1930] 1 Ch. 377; *In re Lord Cable*, [1977] 1 W.L.R. 7, 20 (Ch.); *In re Adams*, [1967] Ir.Rep. 424 (S.C.); see also *Peillon v. Brooking*, (1858) 25 Beav. 218 (232), 53 E.R. 620 (M.R.); *Mayor of Canterbury v. Wyburn*, [1895] A.C. 89, 96 (P.C.); *Jewish National Fund, Inc. v. Royal Trust Co. and Richter*, [1965] Can.S.C.R. 784, 792, (1966) 53 D.L.R.2d 577, 584. *Sykes and Pryles* 663–665. It should be noted that secret and halfsecret trusts are not testamentary, even if made in contemplation of death, *In re Young*, [1951] Ch. 344, 350.

[89] *Dicey and Morris* (ed. 11) 1023 Rule 144; see *infra* s. 25, 26.

[90] *Dicey and Morris* (ed. 11) 1073 with cases in n. 14; *Forsyth*, Private International Law (ed. 2 Cape Town 1990) 312.

[91] *A.G. v. Campbell* (1872), 5 E. & I.App 524, 525, 530.

[92] *In re Aganoor's Trusts* (1895), 64 L.J. Ch. 521 may perhaps be cited for this proposition since the trust assets were situated and administered in ENGLAND; see Lipstein, P.I.L. 224. For the UNITED STATES see to this effect Croucher 115.

converse case of testators domiciled abroad provide some support.[93] Moreover, the greater freedom of choice of law for *inter vivos* trusts (*infra* b)
seems to favour this view, subject to the overriding force of the law governing a concurrent or subsequent succession.[94]

This last consideration is of paramount importance if the law governing
the succession is of the type which recognises the institution of *légitime* or
réserve not only when the trust operates on death, but also if established
inter vivos. It follows that in ENGLAND, where such an institution is lacking,
free choice has found unrestricted favour since in the normal case of a testamentary trust established in ENGLAND, the law governing the trust and the
law governing the succession will coincide. If they conflict, great difficulties
arise. The same is true if the law of the testator's domicile gives effect to the
trust, but the *lex situs* restricts it, and *vice versa*.[95] In the latter cases the law of
the place where the trust is administered may perhaps supply the law applicable to the essential validity of the trust as well.

24. *Immovables*. – In the case of immovables, even more than where
movables are involved, the *lex situs* has the final say. Here the law governing
the succession[96] is always identical with that governing the essential validity
of the trust.[97] It remains an open question as to | whether a free choice of law
permitted by the *lex situs* is to be recognised.

bb. Construction
25. Following the general principle concerning the construction of testamentary dispositions,[98] a testamentary trust, whether of movables or immovables, is to be interpreted in accordance with the law intended by the
testator.[99] In the absence of indications to the contrary this is presumed to be
the law of the testator's domicile at the time when the will was made.

---

[93] See *supra* n. 90–92.

[94] This would explain *In re Piercy*, [1895] 1 Ch. 83: estate duty.

[95] *Dicey and Morris* (cd. 11) 1019 citing *Fordyce v. Bridges* (1848), 2 Ph. 497, 41 E.R. 497
(Ch.); *In re Mitchner, supra* n. 87; *Jewish National Fund, Inc. v. Royal Trust Co. and
Richter, supra* n. 88.

[96] *Dicey and Morris* (ed. 11) 1021 Rule 143. In *Jewish National Fund Inc. v. Royal Trust
Co. and Richter, supra* n. 88, the CANADIAN Supreme Court relied also on the *lex situs* of
immovables to be purchased by the trust fund; and *cf.*, *Mayor of Canterbury v. Wyburn,
supra* n. 88.

[97] *Dicey and Morris* (ed. 11) 1076ss. Rule 157; *Nelson v. Bridport* (1846), 8 Beav. 547, 50
E.R. 215; *Fordyce v. Bridges, supra* n. 95; *Freke v. Lord Carbery* (1873), 16 Eq. 461; *Duncan
v. Lawson* (1889), 41 Ch.D. 394; *In re Piercy, supra* n. 94; *In re Hoyles*, [1911] 1 Ch. 179
(C.A.); *In re Miller*, [1914] 1 Ch. 511: *In re Ross, supra* n. 88; *In re Duke of Wellington*,
[1948] Ch. 118 (C.A.); *In re Mitchner* (*supra* n. 95) 265; Restatement 2d (1971) § 278
comment c; *Weintraub* 422, 423, 425 ss.
For the converse situation of *In re Piercy* (testator domiciled abroad, land in England), see
also *Master v. De Croismar* (1848), 11 Beav. 184, 50 E.R. 787.

[98] *Dicey and Morris* (ed. 11) 1022 Rule 144.

[99] *idem* 1073 Rule 157.

b. *Trusts Inter Vivos*

26. *Movables.* – A trust *inter vivos* is governed by its proper law both as to its essential validity and its interpretation. Few instances of such trusts are to be found outside marriage or family settlements.[100] In the absence of an express or implied choice,[101] the proper law is identical with the legal system with which the trust is most closely connected.[102] The situation of the trust funds, the trust document, the domicile and residence of the parties to the deed, the place where the day to day administration of the trust is to be carried out and the domicile and residence of the principal beneficiaries are the determining factors.[103] This offers a sufficient latitude for a finding in favour of the validity of such *inter vivos* trusts.

27. *Immovables.* – If the trust fund consists of immovables, the *lex situs* will normally apply – either because such a trust cannot be subject to any other law,[104] in particular because illegality by the *lex situs* will invalidate the trust,[105] or because a settlor will be presumed to have chosen that law. In the latter case the question remains open as to whether a settlor of immovables can select another law not only for the purpose of interpretation but also in respect of the trust's essential validity.[106] Although much speaks in favour of concentrating on a single system of law to govern the trust as a whole,[107] the realities of the various *leges situs*, if the trust should include immovables in several councries, militate against it.

---

[100] *Latham* 194, citing *Lindsay v. Miller*, [1949] Vic.L.Rep. 13 (S.C.).

[101] *Este v. Smith* (1894), 18 Beav. 112, 52 E.R. 44; *In re Hernando* (1884), 27 Ch.D. 284, 292; *In re Mégret*, [1901] 1 Ch. 547, 549; *In re Bankes* (*supra* n. 87) 345; *In re Fitzgerald* (*ibidem*) 587; *In re MacKenzie*, [1911] 1 Ch. 578, 586; *Montgomery v. Zarify*, 1918 S.C. (H.L.) 128, 132, 134, 138; *Duke of Marlborough v. A.G.*, [1945] Ch. 78, 83, 85 (C.A.); *Augustus v. Permanent Trustee Co. (Canberra) Ltd.* (1971), 124 Commonw.L.Rep. 245, 252 (H.C. of A.); *Lindsay v. Miller*, preceding note.

[102] *Dicey and Morris* (ed. 11) 1074; *Iveagh v. I.R.C.*, [1954] Ch. 364, 369 ss.; *Revenue Commissioner v. Pelly*, [1940] Ir.Rep. 122, 127 (H.C.); *Lindsay v. Miller, supra* n. 100; *Augustus v. Permanent Trustee (Canberra) Ltd.*, preceding note; *Perpetual Executors and Trustees Association of Australia Ltd. v. Roberts*, [1970] Vic.Rep. 732, 739ss. (S.C.).

[103] *Perpetual Executors and Trustees Association of Australia Ltd. v. Roberts*, preceding note.

[104] *Forsyth* (*supra* n. 90) 311.

[105] *In te Pearse's Settlement*, (1909) 1 Ch. 304 (unenforceable); *In re Piercy, supra* n. 94 (illegal); illegality under the personal law of a *beneficiary* does not affect the validity of a trust, governed by ENGLISH law: *Peillon v. Brooking* (1858), 25 Beav. 218, 53 E.R. 620.

[106] *Dicey and Morris* (ed. 11) 1077.

[107] *In re Fitzgerald* (*supra* n. 87) 588.

c. Administration

28. It was suggested hitherto that the administration of a trust is governed by the law of its place of administration.[108] This was said by *Dicey and Morris* to include

"the powers and duties of the trustees; their liability for breach of trust; their right to indemnity from the beneficiaries or to contribution from their cotrustees; their right to remuneration; the question what is income and what is capital; ... what are proper trustee investments; ... who can appoint a new trustee; ... what persons may be so appointed."[109]

The dividing line between the validity of a trust and questions of administration is, however, blurred. When dealing with a breach of trust the BRITISH COLUMBIA Court of Appeal applied the proper law of the trust, which differed from that of the residence of the trustees.[110] Upon analysis, matters of administration concern the | rights and duties of trustees which are regulated by the law where the assets are situated or the trustees reside, if that law is mandatory and purports to apply irrespective of what law governs the essential validity of the trust or in the absence of specific provisions in the trust instrument. The question remains as to whether a separate rule concerning administration of trusts is part of the ENGLISH conflict of laws or whether, like in *Ralli Bros. v. Compañia Naviera Sota y Aznar*,[111] the law of the place of administration is only taken into account by way of special connecting factor (*Sonderanknüpfung*), if mandatory.

The practice of the courts in ENGLAND and the COMMONWEALTH was thought hitherto to bear out the rule in *Dicey and Morris* as it appeared in the edition of 1980 (Rule 121)[112] which focussed on the law of the place of administration without necessarily considering whether the fact that the administration is situated in a particular country can often attract its law as the proper law of the trust.

Certain it is that the place of administration is determined principally by

---

[108] *Dicey and Morris* (ed. 10) 683 Rule 121; *Falconbridge*, Essays on the Conflict of Laws (Toronto 1947) 558; *Croucher* 112; *Nygh* 455; *Sykes and Pryles* 660; *Castel*, Conflict no. 360, 364, 368; but see *Dicey and Morris* (ed. 11) 1075.

[109] *Dicey and Morris* (ed. 10) 683; *In re Oldfield (No. 2)*, [1949] 2 D.L.R. 175, 179 (Man.K.B.); *In re Nanton Estate*, [1949] 56 Man.Rep.71, 79, [1948] 2 W.W.R. 113 (Man.K.B.); *In re Tyndall*, 1913 S.Aust. L.Rep.39 (S.C.); *In the Will of Gibson*, [1922] Vic.L.Rep.715, 719 (S.C.); *In re Kay*, [1927] *ibidem* 66, 69 (S.C.); *Betts Brown Trust Fund Trustees*, 1968 S.C. 170; but see *Sykes and Pryles* 660.

[110] *Harris Investment Ltd. v. Smith*, 48 B.C.R. 274, [1934] 1 D.L.R. 748 (B.C.C.A.); *Hoar* 1429.

[111] [1920] 2 K.B. 287 (C.A.).

[112] *Parkhurst v. Roy* (1880), 27 Gr. 361, aff. 7 Ont.App.Rep.614; *Vermont Loan and Trust Co. v. Ennis*, [1933] 2 W.W.R. 397, 405 (Sask.C.A.); *Harris Investment Co. v. Smith* (*supra* n. 110) 749.

the circumstance that the trustees reside there or carry on business,[113] that the assets (or an individual asset)[114] are situated there and, incidentally, by the presence of the beneficiaries.[115] It is noteworthy that most of these factors also determine what is the proper law of the trust.

It is significant that in ENGLAND the public trustee cannot be appointed, if the settlement is governed by foreign law;[116] on the other hand, no clear evidence can be adduced to the effect that as regards assets in England the ENGLISH rules on the appointment of trustees do not apply. *In re Hewitt's Settlement* does not support the view[117] that the foreign law governing the trust must apply to matters concerning the office of trustee.

Recently the doubts as to whether separate choice of law rules deal respectively with the proper law of a trust and its administration have been restated in *Chellaram v. Chellaram.*[118] The rule formulated by *Dicey and Morris* in the loth edition (*supra* n. 108, 109) was attacked on the ground, firstly, that the same law applied to the validity, interpretation and effect of a trust as well as to its administration seeing that all rights and duties existing between trustees and beneficiaries are interdependent.[119] Secondly it was held that the power to remove and appoint trustees is inherent in the jurisdiction of ENGLISH courts and may operate *in rem* or *in personam* as appropriate.[120]

While the legal reasoning underlying this decision is open to criticism,[121] it makes little difference in practice whether a separate choice-of-law rule (as *Dicey and Morris* formulated it in the loth edition) or the inherent jurisdiction of the ENGLISH court is called in aid to justify the application of ENGLISH law to a trust to be administered in England, except that the choice-of-law rule is not confined to the removal and appointment of trustees and includes all matters falling within administration. It remains also an open

---

[113] *In re Wilks*, [1935] Ch. 645; *Betts Brown Trust Fund Trustees, supra* n. 109; *In re Nanton Estate, ibidem.*

[114] *In re Tyndall, supra* n. 109; *Vermont Loan & Trust Co. v. Ennis, supra* n. 112.

[115] *Fordyce v. Bridges* (*supra* n. 95) 510 ss, 515; *In re Mitchner* (*supra* n. 87) 268; *Wilmot v. Thorpe* (1890), 16 Vic.L.Rep. 85 (S.C.); *Permanent Trustee Co. (Canberra) Ltd, v. Permanent Trustee Co. of New South Wales Ltd*, (1969), 14 F.L.R. 246, 252 (A.C.T.S.C.), rev. on different grounds *sub nom. Augustus v. Permanent Trustee Co. (Canberra) Ltd., supra* n. 101; *Jewish National Fund, Inc. v. Royal Trust Co.* (*supra* n. 88) 781, 782; 579, 583, respectively.

[116] *In re Hewitt's Settlement*, [1915] 1 Ch. 228, 234.

[117] See also *Danckwerts*, J. in *In re Kehr* (*supra* n. 87) 30.

[118] [1985] Ch. 409, 424; [1985] 2 W.L.R. 510, 519; [1985] 1 All E.R. 1043, 1051 ss. (Ch.D.); but see *Croucher* 112, with AMERICAN references.

[119] [1985] Ch. at 432, [1985] 2 W.L.R. at 526–527.

[120] *Ibidem* at 432 and 527, respectively.

[121] See *Lipstein*, Chronique de jurisprudence britannique (2e partie): Clunet 1988, 1051–1099, 1066–1068.

question as to whether in the absence of an express choice by the settlor, the residence of the trustees, the presence of assets, either of these or a combination of both, is necessary.

At first glance it would seem that the problem has been laid to rest by the Recognition of Trusts Act 1987 (c. 14), incorporating the Hague Convention on Trusts of 1985 which favours a uniform choice of law rule.[122] However, matters of administration may be governed by a different law (art. 9), if the law gov|erning the validity of the trust so permits (art. 10).

d. Foreign Trusts – Recognition and Variation

29. Trusts created in other countries following the COMMON LAW have been recognised in ENGLAND without difficulty.[123] ENGLISH courts have also enjoyed for a long time the power to appoint foreign trustees for ENGLISH or NORTHERN IRISH trusts.[124] It is not clear whether at the time when the earlier cases were decided, a change was only effected in the law governing the administration of the trust or whether perhaps the law governing its validity was also replaced when the new foreign trustees invested the assets abroad. It would now appear that no such change can occur without the consent of the beneficiaries.[125]

Now under the Variation of Trusts Act, 1958 ENGLISH courts have the power, to be exercised cautiously,[126] to approve an arrangement which revokes all or any of the trusts of an ENGLISH settlement in the event of the trust property becoming subject to the trusts of a settlement which will be recognised and enforced in some other jurisdiction.[127] It would seem that, as a result of this operation, the law governing the trust can be changed as well.[128] The same is possible if the trust is governed by foreign law.[129]

---

[122] Hague Convention on Trusts (*infra* n. 260) Sched. art. 7 (a) – (c), 8, whereby in the absence of an express choice of law by the settlor the place of administration, the *situs* of the assets and the place of residence or business of the trustee determine the law applicable both to the essential validity and the administration of a trust.

[123] *Nunneley v. Nunneley* (1890), 15 P.D. 186; *Forsyth v. Forsyth*, [1891] P. 363; *Goff v. Goff*, [1934] P. 107; *In re Ker's Settlement Trusts*, [1963] Ch. 553, 555.

[124] *Meinertzhagen v. Davis* (1844), 1 Coll.C.C. 335, 346, 63 E.R. 444; *In re Liddiard* (1880), 14 Ch.D. 310 (V.-C.M.); *In re Freeman's Settlement Trusts* (1888), 37 Ch.D. 148; *In re Simpson*, [1897] 1 Ch. 256 (C.A.); *Vestey v. Inland Revenue Commissioners*, [1979] Ch. 177, 192; *In re Seale's Marriage Settlement*, [1961] Ch. 574, 580; *In re Whitehead's Will Trust*, [1971] 1 W.L.R. 833 (Ch.).

[125] *Duke of Marlborough v. A.G.* (*supra* n. 101) 85.

[126] Variation of Trusts Act, 1958 (6 & 7 Eliz. 2, c. 53); *In re Weston's Settlement*, [1969] 1 Ch. 223, 230, 232; *In re Paget's Settlement*, [1965] 1 W.L.R. 1046, 1050 (Ch.).

[127] *In re Seale's Marriage Settlement* (*supra n.* 124) 579; *In re Windeatt's Will Trust*, [1969] 1 W.L.R. 692, 696 (Ch.).

[128] See preceding note.

[129] *In re. Pager's Settlement, supra* n. 126; *In re Ker's Settlement Trusts, supra* n. 123, but

The incorporation of the Hague Convention on Trusts into ENGLISH law in 1986 by the Recognition of Trusts Act 1987 (c. 14) has not, in general, affected the principles set out above. The reservation by the UNITED KINGDOM to art. 16 par. 2 of the Convention prevents the potential application of the absolutely binding rules of a third legal system with which the trust is more closely connected. On the other hand, the Act of 1987 extends its application to trusts other than those covered by art. 2 and 3 of the Convention (*infra* s. 64) arising under the law of any part of the UNITED KINGDOM or by virtue of judicial decisions in the UNITED KINGDOM or elsewhere.[130] The Act therefore extends to constructive and other trusts in the UNITED KINGDOM not necessarily entered into voluntarily or in writing as well as SCOTTISH trusts (*supra* s. 7) and to judicial trusts, even if created abroad (s. 1 (2)).

It is doubtful, however, whether a trust according to QUEBEC law (*supra* s. 8) envisaged in *In re Seale's Marriage Settlement* (*supra* n. 124) is a substitute by way of variation of the existing English trust, seeing that it alters the legal and economic balance between trustees and beneficiaries.[131] The same applies to the so-called trust under LIECHTENSTEIN law recognised in *Wyler v. Lyons*,[132] although in the particular circumstances the only issue was the *locus standi* of the defendant as a representative of a trust corporation as owner of the trust assets.

iii. United States[133]

a. General Considerations

30. In recent times the tendency in the UNITED STATES has been described as favouring compliance with the settlor's intention to secure the validity of a trust in selecting the law applicable to a trust, provided the elements of the trust are in some way connected with the law chosen.[134]

| As in the UNITED KINGDOM and the COMMON-WEALTH, the choice of law involves the essential validity of a trust and its administration. Equally a distinction is drawn, in selecting the law applicable, between trusts of mo-

---

see the critical observations of *Mann*, The Variation of Trusts Act, 1958, and the Conflict of Laws: 80 L.Q.R. 29–31 (1964).

[130] Using the discretion accorded by art. 20 par. 1 of the Convention.

[131] See *Buckley*, J. in *In re Seale's Marriage Settlement* (*supra* n. 124) 579 and the formulation of the Quebec settlement at 576; *Diamond* 307–308.

[132] [1963] P. 274.

[133] Restatement 2d (1971) § 267–282 (131–250). *Scott and Fratcher* § 533–664; *Scoles and Hay; Land; Beale* 969.

[134] *Scoles and Hay* § 20.14 p. 791; § 21.1 p. 800, 802 n. 11 with cases; *Scott and Fratcher* § 555, 591, 593 and 600; *In re Chappell's Estate*, 124 Wash. 128, 213 P. 684 (1923); *Ministers and Missionaries Benefit Board v. McKay*, 64 Misc.2d 231, 315 N.Y.S.2d 549, 560 (N.Y.Cty.S.Ct. 1979).

vables and immovables and between testamentary trusts and settlements *inter vivos*.

b. Essential Validity

aa. Testamentary Trusts

31. *Movables.* – Thus the validity of testamentary trusts of movables, while subject in principle to the law of the testator's domicile, is determined by the law which the testator has designated[135] and, failing this, by the law of his domicile[136] or the law of the place where the trust is to be administered.[137]

32. *Immovables.* – Testamentary trusts of immovables, being faced with the effective power of the *lex situs*, must accept the application of that law.[138] Certain escape mechanisms have been devised, however. These include an analysis of the *lex situs*, having regard to its purpose *ratione materiae* or *personae* and reliance on the equitable doctrines of conversion.[139]

bb. Trusts Inter Vivos

33. *Movables.* – Trusts of movables created *inter vivos* are governed by the law designated expressly or implicitly by the settlor and, in its absence, by the law of the place where they are situated and administered, but also by the law of domicile of the trustee and possibly of that of the beneficiaries.[140] In a conflict between the latter two the law upholding the validity of the trust is likely to prevail.[141]

---

[135] Restatement 2d (1971) § 269(b) comment f; *Scoles and Hay* § 20.14 p. 791 and n. 4 with cases; *Hutchinson v. Ross*, 262 N.Y. 381, 187 N.E. 65 (1933).; *Wyatt v. Fulrath*, 16 N.Y.2d 169, 211 N.E.2d 637 (1965). For a more restrictive approach allowing free choice to testators domiciled elsewhere only, see the NEW YORK Estates, Powers and Trusts Law of 1967 (EPTL) (17B McKinney 1981) § 3–5.1 (h); *Scott and Fratcher* § 554 A at 155, but see § 591.

[136] *Scoles and Hay* § 20.14 p. 791 n. 5 with cases: *Scott and Fratcher* § 555, 592; *Weintraub* 448;. *Hoar* 1417; *Matter of Tabbagh*, 167 Misc. 156, 3 N.Y.S. 2d 542 (Sur.Ct. 1938).

[137] *Scoles and Hay* (preceding note) n. 6 with cases; *Scott and Fratcher, ibidem*; Restatement 2d (1971) § 269, 278.

[138] *Scoles and Hay* § 21.2 p. 801; *Scott and Fratcher* § 651; Restatement 2d (1971) § 278; *Hoar* 1416.

[139] *Scoles and Hay* § 21.2 p. 862; Restatement 2d (1971) § 278 comment e and contrast *In re Berchtold*, [1923] 1 Ch. 192 for ENGLISH law, but note the similar approach in *In re Piercy, supra* n. 94 (*infra* s. 42).

[140] Restatement 2d (1971) § 270; *Scott and Fratcher* § 597–601 p. 298–311; *Scoles and Hay* § 21.3 p. 803; Hutchinson v. Ross, supra n. 135; Wilmongton Trust Co. v. Wilmington Trust Co., 26 Del.Ch. 397, 24 A.2d 309 (1942); Shannon v. Irving Trust, 246 A.D. 280, 285 N.Y.S. 478 (1936, aff. 275 N.Y. 95, 9 N.E.2d 792 (1937); Lewis v. Hanson, 36 Del.Ch. 235, 128 A.2d 819 (1937).

[141] Restatement 2d (1971) § 270 comment d, p. 165; *Scott and Fratcher* § 597 p. 301, § 600; *Weintraub* 421–422 with cases.

34. *Immovables.* – Trusts of immovables created *inter vivos* are subject to the *lex situs*,[142] but here again the interest-orientated interpretation of statutes has led to exceptions in favour of other legal systems.[143]

35. *Common solutions.* – The fact is irrelevant that the law of the settlor's domicile ignores trusts or prohibits them, provided that the trust assets are situated in a state of the Union where trusts are admitted.[144] The same applies if the assets are to be administered there.[145]

c. Construction

36. Unlike in ENGLISH law, the diversity of trust provisions in the UNITED STATES has given greater prominence to problems of construction. Testamentary and *inter vivos* trusts *of movables* are interpreted in accordance with the law chosen by the testator explicitly or by implication, while all matters of administration are interpreted with reference to the law governing the administration.[146] In the absence of an express or implied choice, the construction of trusts of *immovables* is governed in principle by the law of the *situs*, subject to any exceptions followed by the *lex situs*, especially if matters of administration are involved.[147]

|d. Administration

37. As in other COMMON LAW countries, the borderline in the UNITED STATES between matters of essential validity and administration is blurred.[148] Administration includes the duties of the trustees towards the beneficiaries, their powers, the liability of trustees for breaches of trust, their entitlement to compensation, especially for expenses, and their removal and replacement.[149]

A testator is free to designate the law governing administration of a trust of movables, whether *testamentary*[150] or *inter vivos*,[151] unless the choice is

---

[142] Restatement 2d (1971) § 278 p. 214; *Scoles and Hay* § 21.3 p. 803; *Scott and Fratcher* § 562 p. 571.

[143] *Scoles and Hay* (preceding note) at n. 4; Restatement 2d (1971) § 278 p. 214 and see *supra* n. 136.

[144] *Watts v. Swiss Bank Co.*, 252 N.Y.S. 2d 196, 198 (1964), mod. 24 A.D.2d 849, 264 N.Y.S. 2d 667 (1965).

[145] *Matter of Tabbagh, supra* n. 136; *Matter of City Bank Farmers Trust Co.*, 9 Misc.2d 183, 166 N.Y.S. 2d 772 (N.Y.Cty.S.Ct. 1957); *Scott and Fratcher* § 606.

[146] Restatement 2d (1971) § 268; *Scott and Fratcher* § 575, 576.

[147] Restatement 2d (1971) § 277; *Scott and Fratcher* § 648.

[148] *Scott and Fratcher* § 604 ss.; *Scoles and Hay* § 21.4 p. 807; § 21.2 p. 802–803 with cases.

[149] *Scott and Fratcher* § 664, 659; see for the similar approach in ENGLAND *supra* s. 28 text to n. 109.

[150] Restatement 2d (1971) § 271.

[151] *Idem* § 270.

clearly arbitrary for lack of any connection with the legal system so chosen.[152] In the absence of a choice the law governing the administration of a testamentary trust will normally, but not necessarily, coincide with the law of the last domicile of the testator.[153] In similar circumstances the law governing the administration of a trust *inter vivos* will be that where the trust assets are managed[154] on the ground that it reflects the most substantial connection.[155] The administration of trusts of immovables is governed in principle by the *lex situs*.[156]

On a minor scale than in ENGLAND, where the Variation of Trusts Act, 1958 (*supra* n. 126) enables the courts to revoke or amend trusts and to allow their transfer abroad, courts in the UNITED STATES have had to deal with the replacement of trustees by others resident in other states of the Union.[157] Such a change of the place of administration, if permitted by the court of the place of administration in pursuance of the settlor's intention or if in the best interests of the trust, may result in a change of the law governing the administration of the trust.[158]

e. Essential Validity and Administration – Conflicting Laws

38. Various solutions have been suggested if the law governing the essential validity of a trust of movables conflicts with that governing its administration. It would seem that the law governing the administration will prevail.[159]

---

[152] *Scott and Fratcher* § 598 p. 306; *City Bank Farmers Trust Co. v. Cheek*, 93 N.Y.L.J. 2941 (N.Y.S.Ct. 1935); see also 110 N.Y.S. 2d 434. 435, 437 (1952).

[153] Restatement 2d (1971) § 271; *Scoles and Hay* § 21.6 p. 809 and n. 3 and 4 with cases; *Rousseau v. United States Trust Co. of New York*, 422 FSupp. 447, 460 [13] (S.D.N.Y. 1976); see also *Dean* 493 ss.

[154] *Scoles and Hay* § 21.6 p. 810 n. 7 with cases; *Scott and Fratcher* § 612; *Swabenland* 449; *Beale* 972 n. 13 with cases.

[155] *Scoles and Hay* § 21.6 p. 810 n. 7 with cases; *Scott and Fratcher* § 612, but see p. 352; *Haberland v. Haberland*, 303 F.2d 345 (3 Cir. 1962); *Boston Safe* Deposit and Trust Co. v. Paris, 447 N.E.2d 1268, 1271 (C.A. Mass. 1983)

[156] Restatement 2d (1971) § 279; *Scott and Fratcher* § 659. Deposit and Trust Co. v. Paris, 447 N.E.2d 1268, 1271 (C.A. Mass. 1983).

[157] *Stoles and Hay* § 21.7; *Scott and Fratcher* § 613, 614.

[158] *Scoles and Hay* § 21.7 p. 811 with cases in n. 2; *Scott and Fratcher* § 615 with cases.

[159] *Cavers* 163 ss.; *Scoles and Hay* § 21.6 p. 810; *Farmers and Merchants Bank v. Woolf*, 86 N.M. 320, 523 P.2d 1346, 1348 (1974).

C. Anglo-American Trusts in Civil Law Conflict of Laws

i. Introduction

39. In subch. I it has been shown how some legal systems have sought to reproduce the ANGLO-AMERICAN trust in a form which fits into the structure of a CIVIL LAW system. The institutions so created do not correspond, however, to their ANGLO-AMERICAN models relying on divided ownership and will be disregarded in treating the position of an individual ANGLO-AMERICAN trust by the courts in a CIVIL LAW country and the power of persons in a CIVIL LAW country to create a trust on ANGLO-AMERICAN lines.

ii. Alternative Solutions

40. In countries where the ANGLO-AMERICAN trust does not form part of the legal system, the choice-of-law rules will also fail to make express provision for the recognition and enforcement of foreign trusts.[160] In these circumstances three approaches are open: Either a process of *transposition* must be attempted whereby the various aspects of a trust are translated into the corresponding terms of the conflict rules of the *lex fori*, before a choice of law is made;[161] or the|inability so to translate the foreign institution into the framework of the local system of conflict of laws results in the denial of its existence, in the absence of an apposite choice-of-law rule.[162] Alternatively, the foreign institution is transplanted bodily into the *lex fori* where it competes with the local private law.[163]

---

[160] But see *e.g.* Gutachten zum Internationalen und Ausländischen Privatrecht, 1967–1968 (Berlin and Tübingen 1970) no. 73 p. 795 (Köln).

[161] *Lewald* (*supra* n. 81) 129; *Lipstein*, P.I.L. 207; *Kegel*, Internationales Privatrecht (ed. 6 Munich 1987) 201–204, 216; *Kropholler* 279–289; FRENCH Cass.civ. 16 July 1971, Rev.crit.d.i.p. 1972, 612; GERMANY: OLG Köln 29 Oct. 1981, IPRspr. 1981 no. 67, IPRax. 1983, 73 note *Heldrich*. UNITED KINGDOM: *G & H Montage GmbH v. Irvani*, [1990] 2 All E.R. 225, 230, 235–236 (C.A.); ITALY: Trib.Orestano 15 March 1956, Foro it. 1956 I 1019, 1020 (*infra* s. 42).

[162] *E.g.* for the UNITED KINGDOM: *Phrantzes v. Argenti*, [1960] 2 Q.B. 19, 35, 36; *In re Macartney*, [1921] 1 Ch. 522, 527. For GERMANY: KG Berlin 20 March 1972, IPRspr. 1972 no. 123; AG Hamburg 31 July 1964, *ibidem* 1964/65 no. 29; OLG Stuttgart 9 June 1964, *ibidem* no. 23; OLG Frankfurt 3 June 1964, *ibidem* no. 22 And see for FRANCE: *Motulsky* 467; *Travers* 527, 529. *Schnitzer*, Treuhand 90 n. 40; *cf.*, *idem*, Trust 488–489; *Schönle*, Die Anerkennung liechtensteinischer juristischer Personen in Deutschland: NJW 1965, 1112–1117.

[163] The Hague Convention on Trusts and Their Recognition of 1 July 1985 (*infra* s. 60ss.) and the Trust Law of JERSEY (*supra* s. 18) provide examples.

iii. Characterisation, Transposition and Choice of Law

41. Once the relationship arising under an ANGLO-AMERICAN trust has been characterised or transposed, the existing choice-of-law rules of a CIVIL LAW system apply and the need for developing new choice-of-law rules does not occur. On the other hand, such a need does arise if the trust is transplanted into an alien system. Few, if any, cases have involved the liability of trustees towards the beneficiaries or the settlor which are treated as contractual.[164] On the other hand, the combination in the ANGLO-AMERICAN law of trusts of the formal title vested in the trustee and of equitable rights having effect against third parties, thus partaking of the nature of proprietary rights, has caused difficulties in countries which either entertain a different notion of a trust[165] or ignore the institution altogether.[166]

The reason is that CIVIL LAW countries do not know and cannot easily deal with the notion of divided ownership where one person has the legal title and the power to administer the property, while another has the right in equity to the economic benefits of the assets.[167] The *numerus clausus* of proprietary rights which does not permit a division of ownership according to quality, but only to quantity,[168] immediately poses problems if the trustee or the beneficiary incurs debts, becomes bankrupt or dies leaving persons entitled to a legitimate portion of the estate.

iv. Foreign Practice

a. Italy

42. The ITALIAN Court of Cassation in *In re Piercy*,[169] confronted with an ENGLISH testamentary trust for sale, which included land in Italy, with power to postpone, conferring a life interest on the testator's children with remainder to their issue, rejected the contention that it was an illegal substitution according to ITALIAN law. Following the decision of *North*, J. in the same matter[170] it held that, since the will was governed by ENGLISH law and

---

[164] But see BGH 15 April 1959; IPRspr. 1958/59 no. 49 at 188 no. 1, 189 no. 3.

[165] GERMANY: see *e.g.* RG 6 March 1930, RGZ 127, 341 at 344; *Würdinger* 32ss.

[166] FRANCE: Cass.req. 19 Nov. 1941, S. 1942.1.129, 131 note *Batiffol*; Cass.crim. 4 June 1941, S. 1944. 1.133 note *Batiffol*, D.C. 1942 J. 4 note *Nast*, J.C.P. 1942.II.2017 note *Maury*; Cass.civ. 3 Nov. 1983, Clunet 1985, 115 note *Ancel*, Rev.crit.d.i.p. 1984, 336 note *Revillard*; *Batiffol* 18–25; *Lepaulle*, Civil Law 26; *Motulsky* 467.

[167] *Supra* s. 5; *Droz*, Note (1976) describes at 329 the use of this technique by ANGLO-SAXON testators leaving assets in civil law countries as a "mania".

[168] But see *Schnitzer*, Treuhand 77.; *von Gierke*, Deutsches Privatrccht II (Munich and Leipzig 1905) 359.

[169] Cass. 21 Feb. 1899, Giur.it. 1899 I 216, Foro it. 1899 I 333.

[170] [1895] 1 Ch. 83; see also *supra* n. 94.

the trust was one for sale, ENGLISH law, and not ITALIAN law, the *lex situs*, determined the nature of the proprietary interest on the ground that according to the ENGLISH doctrine of equitable conversion the Italian land represented movables to be administered in ENGLAND.[171] Thereby the ITALIAN |court avoided the need to determine the effect of an ENGLISH trust upon title to land in Italy, but in so doing it overlooked the fact that in order to convert the land in Italy into movables, the title in the land and subsequently in the movables representing the proceeds had to vest in the trustee or the beneficiaries. By implication the Court regarded the trustee as the owner.

However, two generations later the land, having remained unsold, had become the object of expropriation, and the question was who was entitled to receive the compensation. The Tribunal of Orestano[172] did not find the solution an easy one and engaged in a detailed analysis of the legal nature of the position of trustee and beneficiary in ENGLISH law. It concluded that irrespective of the law governing the succession (which was ENGLISH) the nature of proprietary rights in land situated in Italy was governed by the *lex situs*. According to ITALIAN law the number of interests in property is limited and cannot accommodate a division between legal and equitable rights. A trust was not identical with an ITALIAN *fedecommesso*, since this involves successive, but not concurrent, interests. Faced with a choice between the formal title of the trustee and the substantive right of the beneficiary, the Tribunal of Orestano attributed ownership to the beneficiaries as heirs, while the trustee was regarded as an "*administrator sui generis* with the widest powers which come near to those of a mandatory, a representative, a commission agent, depositee and a fiduciary administrator."[173]

On the other hand, the Tribunal of Casale Monferrato, dealing with a will appointing an executor and trustee with power to sell the estate in Italy

---

[171] The rule in *In re Berchtold, supra* n. 139 was not in issue since it was thought that ENGLISH domestic law applied. When land in France was sold to a company whose shares the testator owned and had bequeathed to the defendant, the FRENCH Court of Cassation disregarded as fraudulent (*fraude à la loi*) the formal change of ownership which made the testator owner of movables governed by the law of the testator's domicile instead of an immovable governed by the *lex situs*, thereby depriving the plaintiffs of their legitimate portion according to FRENCH law: Cass.civ. 20 March 1985, Rev.crit.d.i.p. 1986, 66 note *Lequette*, affirming Cour Aix 9 March 1982, *ibidem* 1983, 282 note *Droz*; determined Cour Paris 23 Jan. 1990, Clunet 1990, 994 note *Niboyet-Hoegy*, J.C.P. 1991, II, 21637 note *Béhar-Touchais*; see also Cass.civ. 4 Feb. 1986, Rev.crit.d.i.p. 1986, 685 on appeal from Trib.gr.inst. Paris 24 Nov. 1983 and Cour Paris 12 July 1984, *ibidem* 1985, 514, 520 note *Lequette*.

[172] 15 March 1956, Foro it. 1956 I 1019, Riv.dir.int. 1959, 687; note *Bresch*, 6 I.C.L.Q. 169–175 (1957); *Jayme*, Die italienische Rechtsprechung zum internationalen Privat- und Prozeßrecht 1945–1966: RabelsZ 31 (1967) 446–536, 485; but see the critique by *Cassoni* (*infra* n. 174) at 757; see also Cass. 30 April 1955 no. 1217, Clunet 1957, 168.

[173] See also Cass. 29 March 1909, Giur.it. 1909 I 650, 652–653; *Kropholler* 280, 285.

consisting of movables and immovables and to hold the proceeds until the beneficiary reached the age of majority, found it easy to transpose the trust into ITALIAN law.[174] It was a *fiducia cum amico* or a testamentary *fiducia* (CC art. 627). Consequently the trustee held title to the land in Italy in virtue of the will which was governed by ENGLISH law and fulfilled the requirement of ITALIAN law relating to the character of the title.[175]

b. France

aa. Testamentary Trusts

43. *Judicial Practice.* – FRENCH courts agree that testamentary trusts validly created according to foreign law applicable in the circumstances[176] need not be transposed, and can be accommodated in FRENCH law, provided they do not offend against mandatory provisions of FRENCH law. A will by a testator subject to ENGLISH law leaving a life interest to his son with remainder to his grandchildren and appointing trustees does not constitute an illegal substitution under FRENCH law which is directed against a "dual testamentary gift of the same objects in full ownership for the benefit of persons appointed to receive them in succession."[177] While the remaindermen can be regarded as full owners with restricted powers prior to the death of a previous beneficiary, a life tenant cannot be compared to a legatee with full ownership encumbered by the right of a subsequent beneficiary. Instead, the will creates a restitutionary charge or *fiducie* in favour of the remaindermen imposed not on the life tenant, but on the trustees who "being a kind of mandatories are not really owners of the trust assets."[178]

The *Tribunal civil* of Nice[179] went even further. In similar circumstances it rejected not on|ly the suggestion of an illegal substitution according to FRENCH law, although the will purported to create an entail in respect of land

---

[174] 13 April 1984, Giur.it 1986 I 2, 754 with note *Cassoni*.

[175] Prelim. Prov. CC art. 22, 23.

[176] For earlier accounts see *R.L.*, Trust – Institution juridique anglo-saxonne – Jurisprudence française: Clunet 1911, 134–139; *Bates* 34; most trusts were given effect: *Motulsky* 454, 455.

[177] CC art. 896 ss.; Cour Douai 13 Jan. 1887, Clunet 1887, 57, 64; Trib.civ. Seine 5 March 1897, *ibidem* 1897, 594, 597; Trib.civ. Seine 19 Dec. 1916, *ibidem* 1917, 1069. See *infra* n. 178 and distinguish Trib.civ. Seine 9 March 1895, Clunet 1895, 628. FRENCH public policy is not involved: *Lepaulle*, Traité 32, 354 ss., 371 ss.; *Droz*, Note (1970) 528 ss.; but see *Motulsky* 467; *Travers* 527.

BELGIAN public policy is also not affected: Trib. civ. Brussels 27 Nov. 1947, Pas. 1948.III.51, 55 (II A). *Croo*, L'incidence du Trust anglo-américain en droit successoral français et belge: Trav.Conf.Univ. Bruxelles Fac.Dr. 1964 II 83–130, was not available.

[178] Trib.ciy. Nice 3 May 1905, Clunet 1911, 278, 281; also Trib.civ. Pau 3 July 1956 (*infra* n. 180); Trib.civ. Brussels 27 Nov. 1947 (preceding note) 56, and see note *Necker* 336; for an early example see Trib.civ. Seine 10 Dec. 1880, Clunet 1881, 435.

[179] Trib.civ. Nice 3 May 1905, preceding note.

in France, for the entail could be barred. Instead it regarded the trustees, who were also appointed executors as "testamentary executors of a special kind."

The *Tribunal civil* of Pau[180] took another step forward. It recognised that trusts, even if created by will, fall outside the law of succession and may be governed by a different system of law than the will itself.[181] They do not constitute a substitution. Title to the assets is vested in the trustee who has the widest powers, but not in his own favour. He does not represent the beneficiaries who are merely his creditors, but enjoy an "equitable right" in the exercise of their interests which is more potent than simple creditors' rights. In the eyes of the FRENCH court the trustee was only "a fiduciary executor furnished with a powerful control;"[182] the holder of a life interest enjoys the revenues within the temporal and other limits laid down by the settlor.

The fact that the tenant for life, the plaintiff's wife, had a special power of appointment (described as "a modality of the trust") to create another life interest before the assets devolved upon her children under the will of her mother did not, in the opinion of the court, render her the owner of the trust fund which under the will of the settlor, the mother, was to devolve upon the grandchildren absolutely. It followed that upon the failure of the wife to exercise the power of appointment no intestacy occurred which could enable the plaintiff husband to claim a usufruct under CC art. 767.

44. *Mandatory rules of the lex successionis.* – If the law governing the trust and the law governing the succession do not coincide, and the succession is governed by FRENCH law, the mandatory rules of the latter apply,[183] such as those concerning the compulsory share (*réserve*)[184] and the protection of minors. The same applies if the law governing the succession and the law governing the trust coincide and is FRENCH, while the trust is expressed in terms of ENGLISH law,[185] but in these circumstances it is unlikely to have come into being.

---

[180] Trib.civ. Pau 3 July 1956, Gaz.Pal. 1956.2.239; see also Trib.gr.inst. Bayonne 28 April 1975, Rev.crit.d.i.p. 1976, 330 note *Necker*, J.C.P. 1975.II.18168 note *Bonnais*, Rec.gén.lois 1976, 463 note *Droz*.

[181] Trib.gr.inst. Bayonne (preceding note) accepted this division by implication when it dealt with the trust independently of the law governing the succession; but see the reasons adduced by *Necker* 333–334.

[182] Trib.civ. Brussels 27 Nov. 1947 (*supra* n. 178) seems to have reached a similar conclusion.

[183] Cour Paris 29 Nov. 1952, Clunet 1953, 140; Trib.civ. Seine 19 Dec. 1916 (*supra* n. 177) in an *obiter dictum*; Trib.civ. Brussels 27 Nov. 1947 (*ibidem*) 56, 57; *Droz*, Note (1970) 527; *idem*, Note (1976) 330.

[184] Trib.civ. Alpes-Maritimes 22 Feb. 1928, Clunet 1928, 433; *Droz*, Note (1976) 330, who would regard the beneficiaries as owners.

[185] Cour Paris 18 Feb. 1909, Clunet 1910, 1144 (1168), D.P. 1909.2.273, Rev.d.i.p. 1909, 846 note *Donnedieu de Vabres*, aff. Cass.civ. 7 Feb. 1910, Rev.d.i.p. 1913, 454; Trib.civ. Seine-Inférieure (Rouen) 19 Dec. 1927, Rev.d.i.p. 1928, 511 note *Lepaulle*, Clunet 1928,

45. *Trustee's legal position.* – Leaving aside specific testamentary trusts,[186] executors and trustees appointed routinely by ENGLISH wills have been described as *exécuteurs testamentaires* since they lack any beneficial interest.[187] They have been allowed to sue and to be sued in respect of the estate in FRANCE and to dispose of it in this capacity as "fiduciary bailees" (*dépositaires fiduciaires*) or in virtue of a *mandat* entrusted to them.[188]

Upon a grant of probate in ENGLAND they can take possession of the estate in FRANCE without initiating new proceedings in the absence of persons entitled to a compulsory share.[189] If the ENGLISH executor abstains from acting, the beneficiaries themselves can take possession directly.[190]

bb. Foreign Marriage Settlements

46. *Characterisation – Contractual and proprietary.* – In dealing with foreign marriage settlements concluded in accordance with ENGLISH or AMERICAN law FRENCH courts have vacillated, when called upon to determine in whom title to the trust assets is vested.

| The marriage settlement as such could be accommodated easily. In an early decision it was described as containing at the same time features of the matrimonial regime of separation of goods and of a dotal regime.[191] Shortly afterwards it was said negatively that it does not constitute either a pact of future succession, a will, a *donatio mortis causa* or a substitution.[192] Subsequently, in conformity with the treatment of foreign testamentary trusts, a marriage settlement was treated as falling outside the ambit of the law of succession, but, if this was FRENCH, subject to its mandatory provisions, such as those concerning the compulsory share (*reserve*).[193]

For the purpose of characterisation it was identified with a synallagmatic contract partly for the benefit of third parties.[194] Irrespective of the law

---

1027. For the situation that both the succession and the trust are governed by foreign law, see *Droz*, Note (1970) 529; Cour Paris 7 Aug. 1883, Clunet 1884, 192.

[186] Trib.civ. Pau 3 July 1956, *supra* n. 180.

[187] Trib.civ. Seine 5 March 1897 (*supra* n. 177) 597.

[188] Trib.civ. Nice 5 May 1905, *supra* n. 177; Trib.civ. Alpes-Maritimes 22 Feb. 1928, *supra* n. 184; Cass.crim. 4 June 1941, *supra* n. 166; Cass.civ. 22 June 1954, Rev.crit.d.i.p. 1955, 123, 124 note *Loussouarn*.

[189] CC art. 1008; Trib.civ. Alpes-Maritimes. 23 Feb. 1928, *supra* n. 184; but see Cour Paris 25 Oct. 1952, D. 1954.J.255 note *Loussouarn*, S. 1953.2.124 with note, J.C.P. 1953.II.7544 note J.M., Gaz.Pal. 1953.1.190 with note, Clunet 1953, 370 with note.

[190] Trib.gr.inst. Paris 22 April 1976, Rev.crit.d.i.p. 1977, 324.

[191] Trib.civ. Seine 8 Aug. 1888, Clunet 1889, 635; Trib.civ. Seine 10 Dec. 1880, *supra* n. 178; but see Cour Paris 18 April 1929, *infra* n. 200, reversing Trib.civ. Seine 22 Dec. 1926, *infra* n. 198.

[192] Trib.civ. Seine 16 May 1906, Clunet 1910, 1229 (1241, 1245), Rev.d.i.p. 1907, 239 (251); Cour Paris 10 Jan. 1970, *infra* n. 194; *Droz and Revillard* no. 251.

[193] Cour Paris 10 Jan. 1970, following note.

[194] Cour Paris 10 Jan. 1970, D.S. 1972.J.122 note *Malaurie*, Gaz.Pal. 1970.1.313 note

governing the succession it could be governed by a legal system allowing trusts in the exercise of a free choice of law by the parties in accordance with the rules of conflict of laws of the *lex fori*.[195] In the particular circumstances of the case the Court of Appeal of Paris could so extend the free choice since the assets to be subjected to the trust and the trustee were located in the United States.

As a result it could hold that, having regard to the *lex situs* of the trust capital (in Pennsylvania), it did not form part of the estate of the wife, who had a life interest, although the wife had contributed the capital originally. Consequently it was not included in her estate on death.

47. *Mandatory rules of the lex fori.* – However, in virtue of CC art. 922 which applied to the succession, the capital of the trust originally contributed by the wife must be taken into account in order to calculate the portion of her estate of which she can dispose by will.[196]

On the other hand the fact of a divided title and the existence of powers of appointment under ANGLO-AMERICAN law does not offend against any mandatory rules of FRENCH law or FRENCH public policy, if the assets are situated outside France.[197]

In the same vein, dealing this time with an ENGLISH marriage settlement with assets in France, the *Tribunal civil de la Seine* (Second Chamber) decided in 1926 that the trust assets in the hands of the trustee, as distinct from the revenues due to the wife as tenant for life, are exempt from seizure by the life tenant's creditors.[198]

Shortly afterwards the Fifth Chamber of the same court concluded that neither the trustee nor the tenant for life could rely on the terms of the trust instrument unless it had been registered as a matrimonial property regime in order to protect purchasers.[199] In so deciding the court failed to realise that the restraint upon anticipation (now abrogated) did not affect accrued revenues and that any restrictions on disposal imposed upon the trustee by the trust instrument do not affect third parties.

On appeal the Court of Appeal of Paris denied that the trustee was the

---

R.S., Clunet 1973, 207 note *Loussouarn*, Rev.crit.d.i.p. 1971, 518 note *Droz; Woodworth*, Trusts and Estate Planning in France after *Epoux Courtois* and *Dame B*: 16 Int. Lawyer 704–711, 706 (1982); *Delattre and Tripet*, Trust inter vivos irrevocable et succession soumise à la loi française: J.not. 212 (1981) art. 56091.

[195] Trib.civ. Seine 16 May 1906, *supra* n. 192; Cour Paris 10 Jan. 1970, preceding note.

[196] Trib.civ. Seine 16 May 1906 (*supra* n. 192) 1244 and 254, respectively; see *Droz*, Note (1970) 529.

[197] Cour Paris 10 Jan. 1970, *supra* n. 194; Trib.civ. Seine 22 Dec. 1926, following note.

[198] Trib.civ. Seine 22 Dec. 1926, Rev.d.i.p. 1927, 70 with approving note *Lepaulle, ibidem* 309 at 314; see also Trib.civ. Seine 10 Dec. 1880, *supra* n. 178; Trib.civ. Seine 26 Dec. 1894, Clunet 3895, 587.

[199] Trib.civ. Seine 22 Feb. 1927, Rev.d.i.p. 1927, 263.

owner of the trust assets and treated him as a "mandatory or administrator" on the ground, firstly, that the trust instrument had not been registered and did not state expressly that title was conferred on him with the power of free disposal (thus reproducing the misconception expressed by the Fifth Chamber of the court below) and, secondly, that it sanctioned advancements to the remaindermen.[200] As a result both the trust assets in the hands of the trustees and the revenues in the hands of the life tenant became liable for the debts of the tenant for life in disregard of the rights of the trustees and of the remaindermen.

| The conclusion is inescapable that the Court of Appeal regarded the tenant for life as the real owner of the trust assets.

48. *Trustee as "mandatory or administrator"*. – It is to be noted that from an early time onwards FRENCH courts have stressed that the trustee of a marriage settlement or re-settlement is not the real owner, even if he has the right to employ the assets. He is merely "the legal representative of the person whose interest he must protect" and as a "mandatory or administrator"[201] with a *locus standi* to sue and to be sued. The trust assets are part of the assets of the beneficiary.[202] The equitable interest of the wife is thus elevated to legal title, in disregard of the fact that according to the marriage settlement governed by ENGLISH law the wife's equitable interest is postponed to the legal title of the trustee, if the assets are disposed in favour of a *bona fide* purchaser for value.[203]

cc. Conclusions

49. It follows that in FRANCE the legal position of a trustee and a beneficiary towards third parties is governed by the *lex situs*, FRENCH law, while the trust instrument itself is governed by the law which applies to the contractual arrangement. The consequences are clear: firstly, by incurring debts exceeding her revenues as a life tenant, the wife can frustrate the rights of the trustee and the expectations of subsequent beneficiaries since the trust assets are available to satisfy the life tenant's creditors. Secondly, if on the death of the life tenant the succession is governed by FRENCH law and no or only insufficient provision is made to satisfy those entitled to a compulsory share out of the life tenant's separate estate proportional to its value, the capital assets of the trust may be severely affected. The reason is that the extent of the

---

[200] Cour Paris 18 April 1929, Rev.crit.d.i.p. 1935, 149; *Bredin* 137–160.

[201] Cour Paris 18 April 1929, preceding note.

[202] Trib.civ. Seine 10 Dec. 1880, *supra* n. 178; Trib.civ. Seine 28 June 1901, D.P. 1902.2.361, Gaz.Pal. 1901.2.71, Clunet 1901, 812, rev. on appeal Cour Paris 27 Jan. 1904, D.P. 1905.2.356 on other grounds; Trib.civ. Le Mans 20 Nov. 1934, Clunet 1935, 651 note J.P.

[203] See *e.g.* Trib.civ. Le Mans 20 Nov. 1934, preceding note.

compulsory share may be calculated with regard to the value of the trust's capital assets, if treated as part of the life tenant's property.

At the same time it must be admitted that the FRENCH proprietary solution avoids the situation that the trust assets are available to the trustee's creditors. Moreover, a valid foreign marriage settlement affecting assets in France can be modified or rescinded in its synallagrnatic terms following a change of the personal law of the parties, if the latter permits a matrimonial regime to be varied.[204]

c. Switzerland

50. Although swiss writers have expressed themselves against the introduction of the ANGLO-AMERICAN trust and against its application in SWITZERLAND,[205] the SWISS Federal Tribunal made a strong effort to accommodate such trusts in SWISS practice, at least when the trust assets are situated in Switzerland. Confronted with an ANGLO-AMERICAN marriage settlement granting part of the income to the wife and the children with remainder to the children on the death of the settlor, who was also entitled to part of the revenues during his life, the Federal Tribunal was able to detect a fiduciary ownership by the trustee coupled with certain aspects of mandate, gift, promise of a gift, of a contract of succession and a contract in favour of third parties.[206]

According to SWISS law, which was applicable, the agreement did not offend against any of its mandatory provisions[207] and did not attract the operation of the SWISS law of succession.[208] Thereby the court solved both the proprietary[209] and the contractual aspects of the trust, but could leave open such questions as the effect of the law governing the succession and the matrimonial regime, if called in aid. When the assets of the settlement were situated in the United States the Federal Tribunal had no hesi|tation in treating the trustee as the exclusive owner.[210]

---

[204] Cour Orléans 24 Feb. 1904, Clunet 1904, 680, 683 on a reference by Cass.civ. 29 July 1901, Clunet 1901, 971; for the earlier proceedings see Trib.civ. Seine 28 June 1895, Clunet 1895, 847, 848; Cour Paris 2 Dec. 1898, Clunet 1899, 584; and *cf., Viditz v. O'Hagan*, [1900] 2 Ch. 87, 98 (C.A.), on appeal from [1899] 2 Ch. 569.

[205] *Reymond* 152a ss., 188a ss., 2093; *Gubler* 217a ss.; *Schnitzer*, Treuhand 70–73; *idem*, Trust 483.

[206] BG 29 Jan. 1970, BGE 96 II 79, Schw.Jb.Int.R. 27 (1971) 223 note *Vischer*, Clunet 1976, 695 note *Lalive*; critical *Gutzwiller*, Der Trust in der schweizerischen Rechtspraxis: Schw.Jb.Int.R. 41 (1985) 53–56; and see *Bloch* 67.

[207] BG 29 Jan. 1970 (preceding note) 92, 93.

[208] *Ibidem* 90.

[209] In SWISS law fiduciary ownership equals unrestricted absolute title; see *Gmür and Becker* (ed.), Berner Kommentar. Kommentar zum schweizerischen Privatrecht IV/1 (ed. 5 Bern 1981) prelim. comments to art. 646–654 no. 22; BG 20/27 Nov. 1913, BGE 39 II 800, 809 (4); BG 14 Nov. 1917, BGE 43 III 346, but see *Reymond* 165a, 166a (41), 174a (53).

d. Germany

aa. Introduction

51. *Little practice on trusts in general and inter vivos.* – GERMAN courts have been little concerned with trusts *inter vivos* arising from marriage settlements or in favour of relatives,[211] and only once with a trust for the benefit of creditors.[212] Nor were they called upon directly to determine the validity or the interpretation of a trust.[213] Instead, they have been confronted with the need to determine, with regard to assets situated in Germany of successions governed either by GERMAN or by foreign law, what place is to be accorded to foreign personal representatives. The latter either combined in their person the functions of executors and trustees or were executors with the broad status conferred on them by ANGLO-AMERICAN law.

52. *Specific problems.* – The need to face this question in detail arises in respect of all successions involving assets in Germany since a certificate of heirship or of executorship must be obtained from a GERMAN court.[214] If the succession is governed by GERMAN law, any appointments of trustees or of executors and trustees in a will drawn up in accordance with foreign legal terminology or law (as it may occur in the case of renvoi to GERMAN law) calls for a transposition into substantive GERMAN law.[215] If the will is governed by foreign law it is necessary to reproduce as closely as possible the status and powers of the foreign executor and trustee.[216]

---

[210] BG 18 Nov. 1949, BGE 75 I 315, 318 (3).

[211] BGH 15 April 1959, IPRspr. 1958/59 no. 49 at 190; note *Knauer*, Bereicherungsansprüche gegen einen trustbegünstigten Miterben: RabelsZ 25 (1960) 313–338.

[212] BGH 13 June 1984, IPRspr. 1984 no. 121; *Kötz*, Anknüpfung 206 n. 5.

[213] But see BGH 10 June 1968, IPRspr, 1968/69 no. 100 at 403; – 15 April 1959 (*supra* n. 211) 187; – 13 June 1984 (preceding note) p. 287 (c), (d).

[214] The certificate testifying to the rights of succession sets out the details of intestate rights, of testamentary appointments (CC § 2353), of what may be described as remaindermen (CC § 2363), and of executorship (CC § 2368), if the succession is governed by GERMAN law. It is limited to the assets situated in Germany, if the succession is governed by foreign law (CC § 2369).

[215] LG Kassel 25 Sept. 1958, IPRspr. 1958/59 no. 146; LG München 23 May 1958, *ibidem* no. 144, OLG Frankfurt 25 Sept. 1958, *ibidem* no. 145; – 29 Dec. 1962, *ibidem* 1962/63 no. 146, especially at 430; – 22 Sept. 1965, *ibidem* 1966/67 no. 168a; LG Nürnberg-Fürth 29 Dec. 1962, *ibidem* 1962/63 no, 148; BayObLG 1 Feb. 1980, *ibidem* 1980 no. 124; LG Hamburg 29 July 1980, *ibidem* no. 190; *Frankenstein* 492.

[216] LG München (preceding note) 479(3), 486, 487; LG Nürnberg-Fürth, *ibidem*; OLG Munchen 13 March 1967, IPRspr. 1966/67 no. 176; OLG Frankfurt 2 May 1972, *ibidem* 1972 no. 125; BGH 17 Oct. 1968, *ibidem* 1968/69 no. 161; KG 20 March 1972, *ibidem* 1972 no. 123: administrator.

bb. German Law Applies – Immovables in Germany – Renvoi

53. In most cases in which GERMAN law applied it did so by way of renvoi from ANGLO-AMERICAN law since succession to land in Germany was in issue.[217] Faced with a will made in the United States appointing an executor or an executor and trustee following ANGLO-AMERICAN practice and land in Germany governed by the *lex situs*, GERMAN courts could either disregard the trust on the ground that it is unknown to GERMAN law or transpose the institution so as to fit into the GERMAN framework.[218]

Using the latter technique the American beneficiaries under a will were held liable as heirs according to GERMAN law, although according to the law of the last domicile of the deceased the estate vested in the executors, and the beneficiaries were only legatees.[219] No reported cases have been found, however, certifying the beneficiaries as heirs according to GERMAN law.[220] Similarly, the existence of a claim to a compulsory share excluded the recognition of the appointment of an executor in the form of | a *Testamentsvollstrecker* even though he is limited to possession of the estate.[221] Quite generally, the applicable German law of succession extends not only to the determination of rights and obligations under the succession, but also to all questions within the ambit of the law of succession, such as the nature of the appointment of executors and executors and trustees.[222] For the latter purposes, however, the testator's intention reflecting his personal law must be taken into account so as to fit the personal representatives into the categories of GERMAN law either as simple *Testamentsvollstrecker* (CC § 2203) or as *Dauertestamentsvollstrecker* (CC § 2209).[223] It is admitted that the foreign executor or executor and trustee appointed in accordance with foreign (*in casu* MISSOURI) law, whereby legal title is vested in him, cannot be attributed this function in

---

[217] Renvoi is generally accepted by GERMAN law, see Introd.Law CC art. 4 par. 1. To this extent GERMAN courts recognise that different legal systems govern a succession: LG Kassel 25 Sept. 1958, LG München 23 May 1958, OLG Frankfurt 25 Sept. 1958, LG Nürnberg-Fürth 29 Dec. 1962, BayObLG 1 Feb. 1980, all *supra* n. 215; LG Wiesbaden 18 Jan. 1960, IPRspr. 1960/61 no. 138.

[218] For an excellent analysis see BFH 20 Dec. 1957, IPRspr. 1956/57 no. 153, esp, 502–504.

[219] LG Kassel 25 Sept. 1958 and OLG Frankfurt 25 Sept. 1958, *supra* n. 215; see generally *Graue* 178 no. 5.

[220] In LG Berlin 14 May 1961, IPRspr. 1960/61 no. 145 the succession consisting of movables was governed by foreign (ENGLISH) law, see *infra* s. 54.

[221] CC § 2306; LG München 23 May 1958, *supra* n. 215.

[222] OLG Frankfurt 25 Sept. 1958 and BayObLG 1 Feb. 1980, *supra* n. 215, therefore disregarded the fact that at COMMON LAW a subsequent marriage revokes a previous will (BayObLG at 397).

[223] OLG Frankfurt 25 Sept. 1958 (*supra* n. 215) 486–487; – 29 Dec. 1962 (*ibidem*) 498; see also – 22 Sept. 1965, IPRspr. 1966/67 no. 168a at 534, 536 with literature;. BGH 19 June 1967, *ibidem* no. 168b; *Schwenn*, Die Erteilung eines Erbscheins nach § 2369 BGB in deutsch-amerikanischen Nachlaßfällen: NJW 1953, 1580–1581.

GERMANY, where it is unknown in this form.[224] Nevertheless a transposition proved acceptable, although the GERMAN *Dauertestamentsvollstrecker* only exercises certain functions of an heir under GERMAN law while the estate vests in the executor and trustee.[225]

The latter has also been denied the character of an heir under GERMAN law, despite attempts to the contrary, although it is admitted that externally the trustee appears as the owner of the assets and may have been given powers of appointment. The fiduciary character of the trust is said to rule out his absolute title in GERMAN law.[226] An exception is admitted if the trustee is also the main beneficiary under the will[227] in which case the function of executor is merged with that of an heir.[228] On the other hand, an executor as such who has not also been appointed trustee has been denied the position of a *Testamentsvollstrecker*, wrongly it is believed,[229] on the ground that his office is limited in time and space and not charged with additional tasks.[230]

cc. Foreign Law Applies

54. If foreign law applies to the succession, the problem is different. The certificate of heirship or of executorship, which is limited in this case to the assets in Germany, must seek to restate as closely as possible the legal position of beneficiaries, executors and trustees according to foreign law. Thus

---

[224] OLG Frankfurt 25 Sept. 1958 (*supra* n. 215) 487; for the sequel see LG Wiesbaden 18 Jan. 1960, *supra* n. 217; OLG Frankfurt 29 Dec. 1962, *supra* n. 215; OLG Frankfurt 22 Sept. 1965, preceding note; but see OLG München 13 Oct. 1936, IPRspr. 1935/1944 no, 387 at 806 with literature.

[225] LG Wiesbaden 18 Jan. 1960 (*supra* n. 217) 448; LG Nürnberg-Fürth 29 Dec. 1962, *supra* n. 215; *Serick*, Behandlung 663: *uneigennützige Verwaltungstreuhand.*

[226] LG Nürnberg-Fürth 29 Dec. 1962 (*supra* n. 215) 446; the court disregarded the power of appointment as unknown in GERMAN law; it wrongly regarded special powers of appointment as limiting absolute title and was able to ignore general powers of appointment. The assertion to the contrary by *Serick*, Behandlung 662 does not appear to be borne out in practice.

[227] OLG Frankfurt 22 Sept. 1965 (*supra* n. 223) 536.

[228] OLG München 13 March 1967 (*supra* n. 216) 576.

[229] LG Hamburg 29 July 1980; *supra* n. 215; contrast BGH 17 Oct. 1968, IPRspr. 1968/69 no. 161; LG Frankfurt 25 Oct. 1935, IPRspr. 1935/1944 no. 385 at 800.

[230] BayObLG 1 Feb. 1980 (*supra* n. 215) 397; also LG Hamburg 29 July 1980, *ibidem.* In fact a personal representative is entitled to seek recognition in other jurisdictions – see also *Gottheiner* 40, but see *Graue* 176. The estate is vested in him until his duties in winding up the estate have been discharged. It is true that his liability for the debts, of the deceased is limited to the estate, and that the beneficiaries and legatees are not liable personally. This aspect may be decisive in denying the personal representatives in ANGLO-AMERICAN law the position of the GERMAN *Testamentsvollstrecker*. However, the enlargement of his powers in time, *e.g.* under the ENGLISH Administration of Estates Act, 1925 (15 & 16 Geo. 5, c. 23) s. 44 by making him also a trustee does not alter his position so as to concede him the character of a *Dauertestamentsvollstrecker*, if an executor is denied that of a *Testamentsvollstrecker*. In either case the beneficiaries will be treated as heirs, if German law applies.

the certificate to be issued to the executor as *Testamentsvollstrecker* is restricted spatially. In substance it must set out the powers which the executor enjoys according to foreign law in order to distinguish him from his |counterpart in GERMAN law.[231] If these powers are placed in the hands of the sole beneficiary, the latter has been treated as an heir according to GERMAN law in disregard of the applicable foreign law.[232] Generally speaking, however, the substance of the certificate has been determined in terms of foreign law.[233] It was therefore inappropriate to deny recognition to an administrator appointed by a NEW YORK court on the ground that he was neither an heir (*Erbe*) nor an administrator (*Nachlassverwalter*) under GERMAN law and could not be placed on an equal footing with an executor at COMMON LAW because he was appointed by a court and not by the deceased.[234]

Cases involving certificates of heirship as such figure in the law reports only exceptionally.[235] The existence of equitable ownership vested in the ultimate beneficiary has persuaded some writers that such a certificate should be issued to him.[236] It is doubtful whether this reflects the legal situation accurately. In the practice of the GERMAN Federal Tax Court, however, it became necessary to decide whether the trustee or the ultimate beneficiaries are liable to pay death duties. By GERMAN, as distinct from ANGLO-AMERICAN law where the estate is charged with the duty, these duties are payable by the heir in the meaning of GERMAN law. The Federal Tax Court has held consistently that the estate, although vested in the trustee or executor and trustee, is not subject to death duty until the legal title has vested in the ultimate beneficiary. Thereby the Federal Tax Court acknowledged the division between legal and equitable ownership and attached importance to the time of their merger.[237]

---

[231] LG München 23 May 1958 (*supra* n. 215) 479, 481; RG 18 Feb. 1926, JW 1926, 1988 note *E. Wolff* treats the ENGLISH executor as owner. *Gottheiner* 61 ss. does not distinguish between the cases where the certificate is expressed in terms of GERMAN or ENGLISH law; see also *Fetid and Firsching*, Internationales Erbrecht VI (Munich and Berlin 1955 ss., looseleaf) *sub* US Grundzüge C III no. 65b; *ibidem* III *sub* Grossbritannien C VI no. 82.

[232] OLG München 13 March 1967 (*supra* n. 216) 576.

[233] BGH 17 Oct. 1968, IPRspr. 1968/69 no. 161; OLG Frankfurt 2 May 1972, *supra* n. 216; *Ferid and Firsching* (*supra* n. 231) *sub* US Grundzüge C III no. 65a.

[234] KG 20 March 1972, *supra* n. 216 and *cf.* OLG Frankfurt 2 May 1972 (*ibidem*) 341, 342 with literature.

[235] LG Berlin 14 May 1961, *supra* n. 220.

[236] *Schwenn* 1115; *Gottheiner* 67, but see BFH 20 Dec. 1957 (*supra* n. 218) 503.

[237] RFH 29 Sept. 1935, IPRspr. 1935/1944 no. 384 at 792 ss.; – 9 Jan. 1936, *ibidem* no. 155; – 14 Oct. 1937, *ibidem* no. 391; BFH 20 Dec. 1957 (*supra* n. 218) 503; BFH 31 May 1961, IPRspr. 1960/61 No. 148; FinG Berlin 4 May 1976, IPRspr. 1976 no. 30; Müller, R., Der Erbausfall nach dem Recht der Vereinigten Staaten und die deutsche Nachlassbesteuerung: RabelsZ 7 (1933) 808–849, 833, 843; Schwenn 1115; Graue 179 part V; Gottheiner 38 n. 9, 10; Serick, Behandlung 664.

e. Netherlands

55. *Local settlement or will.* – The courts in the NETHERLANDS have had no occasion to consider marriage settlements and little occasion to deal with testamentary trusts. A trust *inter vivos* created abroad by a Netherlands national over assets in New York is likely only to raise questions as to its validity *inter partes*. For this purpose only contractual considerations count, and the DUTCH choice of law rules relating to contracts will apply.[238] The trust will be recognised in the NETHERLANDS.[239] The same applies to a testamentary trust made in similar circumstances except that a transposition is necessary, since the succession is governed by DUTCH law according to DUTCH conflict rules.[240] If the testator is a national of the United States, the result is the same, but no transposition is necessary.[241] If all the parties and the assets are situated in the Netherlands, DUTCH law applies and the arrangement will be treated merely as a contract in favour of a third party or as a *donatio mortis causa.*[242]

56. *Foreign trusts.* – If a foreign trust is to be recognised in the NETHERLANDS, difficulties arise since the legal position in DUTCH law of the trustee and of the beneficiaries is not clear.[243] Since split ownership is unknown in DUTCH law, leaving aside proposals *de lege ferenda*, the|legal status of trustee and beneficiary has to be transposed. Writers are divided. According to some the trustee bears the character of a fiduciary owner, although exceptionally of an administrator only, while the beneficiary has a *jus in rem*.[244] Others attribute ownership to the beneficiary and regard the trustee as a "special kind of testamentary executor or *bewind* holder";[245] still others seem to attribute to the trust rights equivalent to those of a legal entity[246] or admit

---

[238] *Henriquez* 253 ss., 261.

[239] *Idem* 262, 276.

[240] *Idem* 270, 278.

[241] *Idem* 277; *Uniken Venema*, Trusts 38, 41.

[242] *Henriquez* 276, 278.

[243] The only decision of the Hoge Raad (24 Nov. 1954, Bcsl.Ned.Bcl.rspr. 1955, 7) involved a revenue matter and merely determined that a beneficiary with a life interest is not to be treated as the owner of the trust assets. See also Rb. Utrecht 5 May 1956, aff. Hof Amsterdam 18 March 1960, cited by *Hijmans van den Bergh* 254 n. 5; Hof's-Gravenhage 5 Oct. 1962, Besl.Ned.Bel.rspr. 1963 no. 118, 119; Hof Arnhem 20 Dec. 1963, *ibidem* 1964 no. 117; Hof's-Hertogenbosch 24 April 1964, *ibidem* 1964 no. 265, cited by *Henriquez* 251 n. 1.

[244] *Hijmans van den Bergh* 260, 262, 267; *Uniken Venema*, Trusts 69, 72. The DUTCH new CC art. 3:84 par. 3 seems to rule out this solution: *ibidem* 45.

[245] *Kosters*, Het Internationaal Burgerlijk Recht in Nederland (Haarlem 1917) 631 ss.; *Van Brakel*, Grondslagen en beginselen van Nederlands internationaal privaatrecht (ed. 3 Zwolle 1953) 207; *Van Rooij and Polak*, Private International Law in the Netherlands (Deventer a.o. 1987) 242; but see *Uniken Venema*, Trusts 53ss.

[246] *Henriquez* 263, subject to rights to be exercised by the beneficiaries (at 264).

that under present conditions the trustee may have to be regarded as the absolute owner,[247] possibly subject to the limitations imposed by the law governing the trust.[248]

These difficulties are not eliminated if it is admitted that *inter vivos* settlements are governed by their proper law on an analogy with contracts[249] and that all claims arising under the law which governs the succession must take precedence.[250]

f. Jersey

57. The introduction of the ANGLO-AMERICAN trust in JERSEY eliminated most of the difficulties which beset the treatment of foreign trusts in CIVIL LAW countries.[251] While the distinction between legal and equitable ownership is not adopted as such, the treatment of the trustee as owner and of the beneficiary as a holder of a proprietary interest avoids the pitfalls which obstruct the accurate transposition of trusts in other CIVIL LAW countries.[252] At the same time the contractual element is given full reign inasmuch as the essential validity of a trust arid the relationship between the trustee and the beneficiaries are governed by the proper law of the trust.[253]

It is not surprising that the *lex situs* is allowed to protect *bona fide* purchasers and that mandatory provisions of the law governing the succession of the settlor are safeguarded.[254]

g. Quebec

58. A trust is governed by the law chosen expressly or by clear implication in the trust instrument. In the absence of such a choice or if the law chosen ignores the trust, the law applies which is most closely connected with the trust (CC art. 3107 par, 1). The place where the trust is administered, where the assets are situated, the residence or the establishment of the trustee, the object of the trust and the place where it is to be realised provide the elements for determining with which law the trust is most closely connected (art. 3107 par. 2). Specific aspects of the trust, *e.g.* its administration, may be governed by a law other than that which governs the trust as a whole (art. 3107 par. 3).

---

[247] *Uniken Venema*, Trusts 69.

[248] *Idem*, Trusts 47 no. 10, but 55 no. 16.

[249] *Idem*, Trusts 38, 68.

[250] *Henriquez* 270, 280.

[251] Trusts (JERSEY) Law (*supra* n. 77) art. 3, 4 and 37 (for Jersey trusts) and art. 45 par. 1 (for foreign trusts). In both cases the proper law applies; moreover, the proper law of a JERSEY trust can be varied subsequently (art. 37). See *supra* s. 18.

[252] Trusts (Jersey) Law art. 8, 9 par. 10, 11, art. 29.

[253] *Ibidem* art. 4, 37, 45.

[254] *Ibidem* art. 8 A par. 2 *lit.* b.

The law governing the trust determines whether an issue concerns the validity or the administration of the trust (art. 3108 par. 1). The same law also determines whether the law governing the trust as a whole or any specific aspects of it can be replaced by another (art. 3108 par. 2).

v. Conclusions

59. In CIVIL LAW countries choice of law problems in matters of trusts do not normally arise directly, unless the settlor or testator and, in some instances, certain assets are situated there.[255] Disputes between beneficiaries and trustees concerning the validity or interpretation of a trust do not appear to figure at all.[256] Instead, the recognition and consequential transposition of trusts created under foreign law | occurs incidentally, if questions are raised such as in whom title to local assets is vested, whether the trustees or the beneficiaries are liable for the debts of the estate and of the beneficiaries themselves as well as for succession duty, whether the trust assets are subject to claims for a compulsory share or *réserve*, whether a beneficiary under a testamentary trust must bring other gifts into hotchpot or whether the trust assets are affected by the rights of a surviving spouse arising out of a matrimonial property regime. At this stage the need for transposition arises, which may not be easy,[257] unless the institution of trust has been incorporated by law.[258]

In view of the structure of private international law, which relies on *dépeçage*, the recognition of a trust established under foreign law may therefore come face to face with other legal systems. The law governing the matrimonial property regime and the law governing the succession may not coincide with that governing the trust and, like the law governing the latter, may also differ from the *lex situs*. In these circumstances the capacity of settlors in CIVIL LAW countries to set up *inter vivos* or testamentary trusts has been questioned and denied, especially if the trust assets are situated in a country which does not incorporate the institution of the trust.[259]

---

[255] See *e.g.* Cour Paris 18 Feb. 1909, *supra* n. 185; Trib.civ. Seine Inférieure (Rouen) 19 Dec. 1927, *ibidem*; Cour Paris 10 Jan. 1970, *supra* n. 194; Trusts (Jersey) Law (*supra* n. 77) art. 5; *Henriquez* 259, 276, 270, 278.

[256] But see the reference to KG 16 May 1983 (not published), cited by *Kötz*, Haager Konferenz 573 n. 20.

[257] *Lion* 679; *Lepaulle*, Nature 969; *idem*, Validité; *idem*, Traité 53 ss.; *Batiffol and Lagarde*, Droit international privé II (cd. 7 Paris 1983) no. 515; *Bredin* 138; *Opetit* 7–8.

[258] Trusts (Jersey) Law (*supra* s. 18); Hague Convention on Trusts, *infra* s. 60 ss.

[259] See Trusts (Jersey) Law (*supra* n. 77) art. 8 A par. 2 *lit.* a: law of the domicile.

| III. The Hague Convention of 1985

A. General Characteristics – Incorporation

60. *Structure.* – The Hague Convention on the Law Applicable to Trusts and on Their Recognition of 1 July 1985[260] seeks to determine with effect for the contracting states,[261] firstly, what law is to apply to a trust and, secondly, how the institution of a foreign trust is to be integrated into the legal system of another country which either ignores or has a different conception of a trust. For this purpose two techniques are applied.

In the first place, the use of technical ANGLO-AMERICAN terminology is avoided, including any allusions to legal and beneficial ownership, tracing and following, and to rights *in rem* and *in personam*. It is replaced by a factual description of a trust and its effects[262] which appears to cover the modified types of trusts developed in some CIVIL LAW countries.[263]

In the second place, the Convention not only establishes rules of the conflict of laws, but having regard to the difficulties of transposition, once the existence of a valid trust has been ascertained, by transforming the quality of the rights arising thereunder without touching their quantity[264] it introduces instead a number of uniform rules of substantive law.[265] Thereby foreign trusts have become part of the law of those contracting states which possess CIVIL LAW systems.

61. *The fund.* – However, the characterisation of the trust as a "separate fund"[266] introduces the notion put forward 66 years ago by *Lepaulle* who

---

[260] Cited Hague Convention on Trusts of 1 July 1985, Act.Doc. La Haye 15 (1985) II 361, 23 Int.Leg.Mat. 1389 (1984). The Convention has been signed by CANADA, LUXEMBOURG, the NETHERLANDS, the UNITED STATES and been ratified by ITALY and the UNITED KINGDOM (Recognition of Trusts Act 1987, c. 14). See *Hayton*, Hague Convention; *Gaillard and Trautman*, Convention 1–31; *idem*, Trusts 307–340, respectively; *Jauffret-Spinosi* 65; *Kötz*, Haager Konferenz; *Béraudo; Maerten*; Dyer, Introductory Note on the Hague Convention on the Law Applicable to Trusts and on Their Recognition: Rev.dr.unif. 1985 I 274–284; *von Overbeck*, La Convention de la Haye du premier juillet 1985 relative à la loi applicable au trust et sa reconnaissance: Schw.Jb.Int.R. 41 (1985) 30–38; *Pirrung*, Die XV. Tagung der Haager Konferenz für Internationales Privatrecht – Trustübereinkommen vom 1. Juli 1985: IPRax. 1987, 52–55; *Steinbach*.

[261] Subject to the right of a contracting state to restrict recognition to trusts governed by the law of a contracting state (art. 21). In the present composition of the Hague Conferences this covers CANADIAN, ENGLISH, JERSEY, IRISH, SCOTTISH, AMERICAN and possibly ARGENTINE trusts.

[262] Art. 2, 11; *quaere* whether it constitutes a definition; see *Jauffret-Spinosi* 27 with a critique 27–29.

[263] See the Preamble par. 1 and *supra* s. 6–18.

[264] See *e.g., Nelson v. Bridport* (1846), 8 Beav. 547, 50 E.R. 215; *In re Aganoor's Trusts* (1895), 64 L.J. Ch. 521 (*supra* n. 92).

[265] Art. 11 par. 2 *lit.* a – d: *Gaillard and Trautman*, Convention 22, 29 (28).

[266] Art. 2 par. 2 *lit.* a, art. 11 par. 1.

presented the ANGLO-AMERICAN trust to FRENCH readers as a fund which is independent of a holder of legal rights and duties.[267] The question is, therefore, whether an "ownerless" fund has been created in the absence of the establishment of a separate legal entity, such as the LIECHTENSTEIN *Treuunternehmen* (*supra* s. 17). This is important where the trust has failed or where debts of the settlor are involved.

The doubts which have arisen in FRANCE, in particular, as to whether title is vested in the trustee or the beneficiaries (*supra* s. 48, 49) are not removed in substance by the provision that title stands in the name of the trustee, that he can manage the assets and may be a beneficiary himself.[268] The same applies to the provision that the trustee has an active and passive *locus standi* to represent the fund, including registration of assets "in his capacity as trustee".[269] A number of considerations militate against the assumption that he is the owner in the meaning of CIVIL LAW systems.

Provided that the law governing the trust so determines, personal creditors of the trustee cannot have recourse to the trust assets, for they do not form part of the trustee's estate upon his insolvency or bankruptcy, are not subject to his matrimonial property regime and are not included in his estate for the purpose of succession (art. 11 par. 2). From the point of view of EUROPEAN CONTINENTAL lawyers, his title comes nearer to that of one under a transfer of title for security purposes (*Sicherungsübereignung*) according to GERMAN law or a *mandataire* or *dépositaire fiduciaire* under FRENCH law (*supra* | s. 48, 49). However, these scruples are removed by the formal language of the Convention.

62. *Beneficiaries – Status.* – The legal position of the beneficiaries, though apparently treated as contractual subject to the trust instrument (art. 2 par. 3), is less than clear. The Convention, by inserting rules of substantive law providing for "tracing" but not necessarily for "following",[270] which is subject to the *lex situs*, adopts a proprietary approach to a certain extent, but probably not in principle.[271] It is unlikely that the Convention, unlike the legislation in JERSEY, wished to introduce dual ownership. However, the trustee is treated as having title to assets which are not to be regarded as his own property in the economic sense. It would seem, therefore, that the *numerus clausus* of proprietary rights has been broken. Nevertheless the

---

[267] "*Un patrimoine indépendant de tout sujet de droit*": *Lepaulle*, Civil Law 24; *idem*, Traité 31, probably inspired by the FRENCH construction of *fondations*: *Batiffol* 23. Henriquez 263; *cf.*, *Brinz*, Lehrbuch der Pandekten III (ed. 2 Erlangen 1886) 453–586.

[268] Art. 2 par. 2 *lit.* a – e.

[269] Art. 11 par. 1, art. 12.

[270] Art. 11 par. 2 *lit.* d; *Jauffret-Spinosi* 57; for doubts as to its effectiveness in German law see *Kötz*, Haager Konferenz 581.

[271] *Kötz*, Haager Konferenz 581.

question which exercised the Court of Appeal of Paris (*supra* s. 47) remains unsolved as to whether the trust assets are available to the settlor's or the ultimate beneficiary's creditors.

63. *Lex situs – Lex successionis – Control.* – In the third place, only a limited effort was made to supersede the property rules of the *lex situs*. Of the salient proprietary features of a trust only real subrogation by tracing has been safeguarded unconditionally.[272]

In the fourth place, reflecting the previous practice, a possible clash between the law governing the trust and the laws governing the succession of the settlor and his matrimonial regime, and possibly of the beneficiary as well, cannot be avoided, as the Convention admits.[273] The ANGLO-AMERICAN trust is thereby exposed to serious encroachments, but it must be remembered that, in COMMON LAW countries too, both testamentary trusts and marriage settlements have been successfully attacked on some of the grounds enumerated by the Convention,[274] *i.e.* when the law governing the trust clashed with the law governing the settlor's succession or the beneficiary's matrimonial property regime.

B. Choice of Law

i. Range

64. The Convention covers *inter vivos* and testamentary trusts (art. 2) created voluntarily and evidenced in writing (art. 3). A contracting party may also include trusts declared by judicial decision.[275] This provision is said to have been inserted *ex abundanti cautela* in order to safeguard the obligations of member states of the EUROPEAN ECONOMIC COMMUNITY under the Brussels Jurisdiction and Judgments Convention.[276] It only assists for the purposes of recognition, but not of choice of law under the Convention on Trusts. Within this limited ambit the wording "trusts declared by judicial decisions" may cover those incompletely constituted trusts which are imposed upon the parties by the court to be completely constituted subsequently, such as a decision of a court imposing a duty to settle property upon a divorce[277]

---

[272] Art. 11 par. 2 *lit.* d.

[273] Art. 15 par. 1; *ibidem lit.* e may affect protective trusts.

[274] *De Nicols v. Curlier*, [1900] A.C. 21 (H.L.); *In re De Nicols*, [1900] 2 Ch. 410; *Viditz v. O'Hagan*, [1899] 2 Ch. 569, [1900] 2 Ch. 87 (C.A.).

[275] Art. 20 par. 1; *Hayton*, Hague Convention 267–268.

[276] Brussels Convention on Jurisdiction and the Enforcement of Judgments in Civil and Commercial Matters, OJ EC 1972 L 299 p. 32.

[277] For the possible inclusion of trusts declared by judicial decision and the reasons for

Voluntary trusts clearly include resulting trusts but exclude constructive and statutory trusts. It must remain an open question as to whether conveyances or assents under a statutory trust for sale can be called voluntary.[278]

The practice of courts examined previously shows that trusts *inter vivos* rarely attract their attention,[279] while the bulk concerns testamentary trusts and the powers of the trustee thereunder, and mainly poses problems of their transposition. In the case of *inter vivos* trusts, their initial validity, subsequent modification, and the liability of the trust assets for the debts of the life tenant raised the main legal problems. Here the choice of law becomes important.

| *ii. Principles of Choice of Law*

a. General

65. Free choice of law by the settlor, whether express, implied or hypothetical is allowed under art. 6 par. 1. In the absence of such a choice of law, or if the law selected does not provide for trusts or the type of trust desired, the law most closely connected applies.[280]

b. Objective Connecting Factors

66. For the purpose of ascertaining this law, a number of significant connecting factors are provided, namely the place of administration, the *situs*, objects and places of execution of the trust as well as the place of residence or business of the trustee.[281] The typical legal situations or operative facts[282] to which these connecting factors are attached in order to determine the law applicable cover the appointment and removal of trustees, their rights and duties *inter se,* their powers and their delegation, restrictions on the trust itself, its variation and termination, and the relationship between trustees and beneficiaries (art. 8).

---

doing so, see *Hayton*, Hague Convention 266 n. 2; *Gaillard and Trautman*, Convention 10; but see *Jauffret-Spinosi* 35.

[278] *Hayton*, Hague Convention 267.

[279] FRENCH Trib.civ. Seine 10 Dec. 1880, *supra* n. 178; Cour Paris 10 Jan. 1970, *supra* n. 194; Cour Paris 18 April 1929, *supra* n. 200; Cour Orléans 24 Feb. 1904, *supra* n. 204. SWISS BG 29 Jan. 1970, *supra* n. 206.

[280] Art. 6 par. 2, 7 par. 1; the purpose of art. 6 par. 2 is said to aim at preventing *fraude à la loi.*

[281] Art. 7 par. 2 *lit.* a – d.

[282] For these and other terms see *Lipstein*, P.I.L. 197 n. 11.

c. Operation of Several Laws

67. While the law chosen by the parties to govern the trust may cover its validity, effects and administration, the parties are free to select different laws for different aspects, especially as regards administration.[283] The law governing the validity of the trust determines whether its operation or that of the law governing a particular aspect can be replaced by another law.[284] Renvoi is, however, excluded.[285]

d. Limits of the Applicable Law

68. The safeguard of public policy is maintained (art. 18). In addition, a state need not recognise a trust, despite its validity by the law chosen, if its place of administration and the habitual residence of the trustee are more closely connected with a state which ignores trusts altogether or the particular category of trust (art. 13). In substance this will cover the situation where the assets are situated in such a state or where the objects are to be fulfilled or, as it has been suggested,[286] where the beneficiary, the settlor or their creditors are to be found. The choice of law, whether subjective or objective, can also be limited by the absolutely binding rules of the forum[287] and, in exceptional circumstances, by rules of the same character in force in a country which has a sufficiently close connection with the case.[288] Finally, states may limit the recognition of trusts to those the validity of which is governed by the law of a contracting state.[289]

e. Dépeçage – Effects

69. *Complementary rules.* – The effect of the choice of law for trusts established by the Convention is restricted by the operation of other legal systems which may overlap as a result of other choice-of-law rules which are complementary.

70. *Preliminary questions* concerning the validity of testamentary instruments and of conveyances or assignments involving assets which are to

---

[283] Art. 9; for the attitude of the contracting states following the CIVIL LAW see *Jauffret-Spinosi* 43; *Gaillard and Trautman*, Convention 17.

[284] Art. 10; doubtful *Jauffret-Spinosi* 46–47, but see 55.

[285] Art. 17; *Gaillard and Trautman*, Convention 2 no. 2, 26 n.70.

[286] See *e.g.* FRENCH Cour Paris 18 Feb. 1909, *supra* n. 185; – 18 April 1929, *supra* n. 200; – 29 Nov. 1952, *supra* n. 183.

[287] Art. 16 par. 1; see also the Rome Convention on the Law Applicable to Contractual Relations of 19 June 1980 (OJ EC 1980 L 266 p. 1, 19 Int.Leg.Mat. 1492 (1980)) art. 7 par. 2; naturally the operation of a state's fiscal laws is safeguarded: art. 19.

[288] Art. 16 par. 2; see also the Rome Convention (preceding note) art. 7 par. 1; *Jauffret-Spinosi* 52–53.

[289] Art. 21; *Jauffret-Spinosi* 42 n. 41.

form the capital of a trust remain subject to the choice-of-law rules governing a succession or transfer of property *inter vivos* (art. 4).

71. *Conflicting legal systems.* – The Convention acknowledges in some
detail that in a clash between the law governing the trust and the laws governing other private law aspects the latter may prevail.[290] By way of illustration, but not of exhaustive enumeration,[291] the mandatory rules of the laws
applicable according to the conflict rules of the *lex fori* may take precedence
| in matters of succession, matrimonial property regimes, transfer of title to
property and security interests therein and, generally, of the protection of
third parties acting in good faith,[292] of creditors in case of insolvency and of
minors and incapable persons.

The protection of creditors in matters of insolvency would seem to cover
provisions such as setting aside a fraudulent conveyance in favour of third
parties. The protection of minors and incapable persons must be assumed to
concern the protection of settlors and beneficiaries. Of all these aspects the
operation of the law of succession is the most important.

iii. Unsolved Problems

72. *The beneficiary's rights.* – Three situations must be considered:[293]

(1) The beneficiary is not himself entitled to succeed to the settlor and to
claim rights of inheritance. In this case a third party deriving rights on the
death of the settlor under a system of laws granting a compulsory share can
lay claim to a part or possibly the entire substance of the trust, depending on
whether the settlor left other assets and beneficiaries.[294]

If the trust was established *inter vivos*, the value of the trust assets may
also have to be taken into account in computing the value of the inheritance
and the respective shares in order to determine the compulsory shares.

(2) The beneficiary himself is entitled to a compulsory share after the
settlor. Here the beneficiary can take part or all of the trust fund absolutely,
subject to a reduction in respect of the value of the life interest remaining.[295]

---

[290] Art. 15; see also art. 11 par. 2 *lit.* d sent. 2; *Gaillard and Trautman*, Trusts 330.

[291] See the wording of art. 15 sent. 2.

[292] See also PUERTO RICO: CC ch. 221; VENEZUELA: Law of trusts (*supra* n. 57) art. 3, 10,
11. The LOUISIANA Trust Code (*supra* n. 45) § 9: 1841–9: 1847 reconciles the conflicting
principles by permitting the compulsory share to be given in trust, but not matrimonial
community property. See *Oppenheim*, Limitations (*supra* n. 45) at 42 ss.; *Goldschmidt*
38–39. The JERSEY Trusts Law (*supra* n. 77) art. 8 A excludes the operation of foreign law
governing the succession upon a JERSEY trust.

[293] See the GERMAN BGH 15 April 1959, IPRspr. 1958/59 no. 49 at 190 no. II 1a – c.

[294] Cour Paris 6 Nov. 1967, Rev.crit.d.i.p. 1968, 508; Cass.civ. 4 Dec. 1990, Clunct 1991,
398.

[295] For problems of adjustment see FRENCH Cass. civ. 20 March 1985, *supra* n. 171;

(3) The beneficiary was given a general power of appointment and has exercised it in favour of a person other than a descendant either of the settlor or of himself.[296] Here a concurrence of claims is possible as well as a concurrence of laws. The succession to the settlor and to the beneficiary may be governed by different laws, and the exercise of general, as distinct from special, powers of appointment if the assets are mixed is governed by the law which governs the succession of the donee of the power (*infra* subch. IV).

73. *Choice of law.* – In cases where the testator lived in a common law country it is likely that the law governing the settlor's succession and the law of the trust as well as the law governing matrimonial property relations will coincide,[297] but the law governing the succession after the beneficiary may be different. If the succession includes land in a civil law country, the difficulties may become real.

Again, if the trust is *inter vivos*, the possibility exists that a legal system will govern the succession (and therefore the duty to bring into hotchpot) which was not contemplated at the time when the trust was constituted.

In all these circumstances, an adjustment favourable to the trust may be permissible, as the FRENCH: *Tribunal civil* Bayonne admitted[298] and the Convention encourages.[299]

C. Achievements and Drawbacks of the Convention

74. Firstly, the Convention has been able to accommodate the ANGLO-AMERICAN trust with its division between legal and equitable ownership as well as the so-called trusts developed in CIVIL LAW countries, and to give effect to it, even if the institution is unknown in local law, contrary to the earlier ITALIAN practice (*supra* s. 42).

Secondly, the Convention has done so by adopting the FRENCH, SWISS and later ITALIAN|practice of treating the trustee as comparable to a *"mandataire chargé de gérer et administrer les biens du trust"*,[300] with a *locus standi* to sue

---

GERMANY: LG München 23 May 1958 (*supra* n. 215) 478 no. 2; BayObLG 1 Feb. 1980 (*ibidem*) 391, 397–398; see also FinG Berlin 4 May 1976 (*supra* n. 237) 96; for cases where vesting is postponed: GERMAN BFH 20 Dec. 1957, IPRspr. 1956/57 no. 153; BFH 31 May 1961, IPRspr. 1960/61 no. 148 and *cf.* GERMAN BGH 10 Jan. 1968, IPRspr. 1968/69 no. 160 at 403; *Gaillard and Trautman* 26, 27.

[296] FRENCH Trib.civ. Pau 3 July 1956, *supra* n. 180.

[297] *Kötz*, Haager Konferenz 582.

[298] 28 April 1975 (*supra* n. 180) 331; Trib.civ. Seine Inférieure (Rouen) 19 Dec. 1927, *supra* n. 185.

[299] *Kötz*, Haager Konferenz 582.

[300] "Mandatory charged with the employment and the administration of the trusts assets": Hague Convention art. 3 *lit.* c; see *supra* s. 42, 45, 47, 48, 50.

and be sued, to register the assets in his own name as a trustee and to dispose of them. At the same time the assets are not available to execution by the trustee's creditors or in his bankruptcy, do not form part of his estate on his death and are not subject to his matrimonial regime. While holding a legal title which resembles that of an owner, the trustee is denied the economic or beneficial ownership.

However, the Convention has refrained from describing the legal position of the beneficiaries, while recognising their right to trace the trust assets in the hands of the trustee. It certainly does not confirm the somewhat isolated SOUTH AMERICAN view that the settlor is the owner. Nevertheless, it may be necessary to determine to whom the title of heir has devolved on the deceased settlor's death. This need arises not only if a legal system imposes death duties on the heir and not on the deceased's estate, as ANGLO-AMERICAN law does. It is also necessary if a grant of possession is required by heirs or a certificate of heirship. Quite generally, the need arises upon the death of the settlor.

Thirdly, the Convention has drawn up choice-of-law rules which limit the autonomy of the parties, if the trust is more closely connected with another legal system, *e.g.* if the settlor, the beneficiary or the creditors are to be found in the country of the latter.

Fourthly, the Convention has potentially curtailed the life of a trust by letting in the absolutely binding prohibitory rules (such as the rules against perpetuities) of the *lex fori* and, if a contracting state so decides, of other legal systems closely connected with the trust.[301]

Fifthly, the Convention has potentially exposed the trust assets to action by the creditors of the settlor and the beneficiaries, apart from permitting specific transactions to be avoided as a fraud upon creditors.

Sixthly, the Convention has endangered the maintenance and integrity of the trust by taking a realistic view of the operation of the *lex situs*.[302] This means that the rules of succession of the *lex situs* may apply, if the conflict rules of the *lex situs* so determine, even if according to the law governing the trust and the conflict rules of the *lex fori* another legal system applies to the succession. When this issue is raised in an ANGLO-AMERICAN court the trust assets remain intact, if a compulsory share is claimed under a CIVIL LAW system governing the succession of the settlor, because the settlor's assets are not regarded as including any interest in the trust assets, unless the settlor is also a beneficiary, as happens if a resulting trust ensues.

Since the same result is not assured if the claim is brought in a CIVIL LAW

---

[301] *Jauffret-Spinosi* 52–53.
[302] *Gaillard and Trautman*, Trusts 332 believe that this danger can be avoided by the courts; *Jauffret-Spinosi* 50–52.

country where the trust assets are situated, it has been suggested[303] that a *professio juris* should be allowed, at least in respect of successions (as is the practice in SWITZERLAND where foreign nationals are concerned) when these are linked to trusts. However, the FRENCH Court of Cassation has rejected this solution, at least *de lege lata*.[304]

The integrity of an ANGLO-AMERICAN trust in its entirety could only have been protected if, as part of its insertion into the substantive law of a CIVIL LAW country, the effect of a trust upon the title of the settlor and the beneficiaries had been set out specifically. This task would not have been easy and would probably have met with opposition by the CIVIL LAW states, parties to the Convention, whose practice had stressed all along the need to respect the mandatory character of the rules of succession applicable according to their conflict rules and the *lex situs*.

| IV. Powers of Appointment

A. Definition

75. A power of appointment is conferred by a person (called the donor) by an instrument, such as a settlement *inter vivos* or a will (called the instrument of creation), to appoint by deed or will (called the instrument of appointment) the person or persons (called the donee) who shall succeed to the property after the previous holder.

The power is called a general power if the donee can appoint to anyone he likes, including himself; it is called a special power if the donee can only appoint among a specified class of persons. In both types the donee, in exercising the power, affects not his own property but that of the donor.[305] However, if the power is general (but not if it is special) the donee can fuse or blend the assets which form the object of the power with his own by appointing them to himself, either by a disposition *inter vivos* or expressly or

---

[303] See note *Droz* on Cour Aix 9 March 1982: Rev.crit.d.i.p. 1983, 287–300, 296ss.

[304] Cass.civ. 22 Dec. 1970, Rev.crit.d.i.p. 1972, 467 note *A.P.*

[305] This is certainly true if the power is special: *Pouey v. Hordern*, [1900] 1 Ch. 492, 493; *In re Mégret*, [1901] 1 Ch. 547, 549; *In re McMorran*, [1958] Ch. 624, 634. It is also true of general powers: *In re Mégret (supra)* 549; *In re Waite's Settlement Trusts*, [1958] Ch. 100, 108; *In re Khan's Settlement*, [1966] Ch. 567, 578; *Rhode Island Hospital Trust v. Anthony*, 49 R.I. 339, 142 A. 531, 533 (1928); *Matter of Kelly's Will*, 161 Misc. 255, 291 N.Y.S. 860 (Westch.Cty.Sur.Ct. 1936); *In re Barnhart's Will*, 137 Misc. 131, 244 N.Y.S. 130, 133 (Niagara Cty.Sur.Ct. 1930), but see *Field*, J. (dissenting) in *In re Bauer's Trust*, 14 N.Y.2d 272, 200 N.E.2d 207 (210), 251 N.Y.S. 2d 23, 27, 28 (1964), as regards general powers.

Sykes and Pryles 707, 763; *Nygh* 512; but see *Scott and Fratcher* § 635; *Scoles and Hay* § 21.8 p. 812.

implicitly by will, thus making himself the owner. If exercised by will, the disposition combines in one act the formal exercise of the general power and the substantial transfer of the assets to himself before arranging for their distribution. The result is that, if the donee's will should be invalid, the entire fund passes to those entitled on his own intestacy. If, on the other hand, the donee in his will disposes separately of the fund subject to his power, or if he disposes of it by a separate instrument, the fund subject to his power remains separate and is not affected by the mandatory rules governing the donee's succession but by those of the donor. The same is true if the donee fails to exercise his power.

This principle has been adopted in the conflict of laws when the law governing the donee's succession differs from that of the donor.

B. *Choice of Law – General Rules*

76. Where only the laws of COMMON LAW countries are concerned, the ordinary rules of choice of law suffice to deal with what are identical institutions. Such is the position in the UNITED STATES where conflicts between the laws governing the donor's and the donee's succession are rare.[306] ENGLISH courts have had more than one occasion to deal with the situation that the formalities observed at the foreign place of acting did not provide for the exercise of powers or differed from those of ENGLISH law, especially since they can be exercised by will. Also, the mandatory rules of the law applicable to the donee's succession have sometimes clashed with the untrammelled freedom of testation under the COMMON LAW applicable to the succession of the donor. Courts in CIVIL LAW countries have taken little notice of powers.[307]

C. *Dépeçage – Exercise of Power and Blending*

77. Consequently it became necessary to distinguish between two questions: First, whether the donee had validly exercised his power by will; and second, whether by doing so the donee had disposed of the assets subject to his general power by combining them with his own in one disposition or separately. The latter aspect is easily overlooked if the sole assets disposed of by the will are those over which the donee has a general power of appointment.

---

[306] See *infra* n. 309–312; *Scott and Fratcher* § 636, except for rules against perpetuities.
[307] See *supra* s. 47 and n. 197; n. 226; *Frankenstein* 493–497.

D. Specific Choice-of-Law Problems

78. *The problems.* – From the point of view of the conflict of laws the following problems arise: which law governs (1) the form in which the power is exercised; (2) the capacity of the donee to exercise it; (3) the construction of the exercise of the power and (4) the effect of the mandatory rules of succession (such as a compulsory share) applicable on the death of the donee.

| Although ENGLISH and AMERICAN practice differ somewhat as a result of two factors – particular ENGLISH legislation in the past and the proximity of other legal systems embodying CIVIL LAW notions of mandatory rules of succession –, both practices will be considered together.

i. Validity and Effect of Power

79. The law governing the instrument of creation, whether *inter vivos* or testamentary, determines the formal and essential validity and the effect of the power upon its exercise.[308] If the power is created by will, this is normally the law of the donor's domicile,[309] or the *lex situs* for immovables,[310] but also sometimes the law of the place of administration[311] and, particularly if created *inter vivos*, the law selected expressly or implicitly by the donor.[312] However, if the exercise of special powers is invalid under the donor's law, it is irrelevant that it is valid under the donee's law.[313]

---

[308] *Scott and Fratcher* § 630, 631, 635; *Sykes and Pryles* 706–707; *Scoles and Hay* § 21.9 p. 813 with cases in n. 2.

[309] *In re Walbridge's Estate*, 33 N.Y.S. 2d 47, 50 [1, 2], [7] (Sur.Ct. 1942); *In re Fowler's will*, 31 Misc.2d 62, 225 N.Y.S. 2d 312 [1–5] (Westch.Cty.Sur.Ct. 1961); *In re Bauer's Trust* (*supra* n. 305) at 272, 209, 25 [1], respectively; see also *Amerige v. Attorney-General*, 324 Mass. 648, 88 N.E. 126, 132 [10] and n. 6 with cases (1949); *In re Wilde's Estate*, 222 N.Y.S. 2d 308, 310 [1–3] (N.Y.Cty.Sur.Ct. 1961). For the variety of solutions see *Wilmington Trust Co. v. Wilmington Trust Co.*, 26 Del.Ch. 397, 24 A.2d 309, 312 (2) (1942); *Mulford*, The Conflict of Laws and Powers of Appointment: 87 U.Pa.L.Rev. 403–425 (1938/39).

[310] *Amerige v. Attorney-General* (preceding note) 132, especially if combined with the place of administration; and see the practice cited by *Lipstein*, Conflict 442 n. 48.

[311] *In re Greenough v. Osgood*, 235 Mass. 235, 126 N.E. 461 (1920); *Wilmington Trust Co. v. Wilmington Trust Co.* (*supra* n. 309) 312 [2].

[312] *Amerige v. Attorney-General* (*supra* n. 309) 132 [10]; *Greenough v. Osgood*, preceding note; *Wilmington Trust Co. v. Wilmington Trust Co.* (*supra* n. 309) 313 [3]; *Dollar Savings and Trust Co. v. First National Savings Bank of Boston*, 32 Ohio Misc. 81, 285 N.E.2d 768, 775 (Mahoning Cty.Ct. C.P., Prob.D. 1972); for the provision of a substituted trust by the donee *Wilmington Trust v. Sloane*, 30 Del.Ch. 103, 54 A.2d 544, 550 [8] [9] (1947); and see the dissenting opinion of *Fuld*, J. in *In re Bauer's Trusts* (*supra* n. 305) at 279, 211, 27, 28, respectively.
For AUSTRALIA see *Augustus v. Permanent Trustee Co. (Canberra) Ltd.* (1971), 124 Commonw.L.Rep. 245, 255, 257 (H.C. of A.). And see generally *Scott and Fratcher* § 635.

[313] *In re Wilde's Estate, supra* n. 309; *Scott and Fratcher* at 454.

ii. Form

80. At COMMON LAW the formal validity of the exercise of a power of appointment was governed by the law of the donee's last domicile.[314] Moreover, if the donor so ordained, the requirements laid down by the instrument of creation had to be observed, if the donee died domiciled abroad, even if the donee's will was valid in form according to the law of his last domicile.[315] Upon the enactment of the ENGLISH Wills Act, 1861[316] concerning the formal validity of wills made abroad by British subjects, doubts arose as to whether the exercise of powers of appointment in a will of a British subject, itself validly made abroad in virtue of the Act, was invalid nevertheless for having failed to meet the formal requirements of the Wills Act, 1837 for the testamentary exercise of general powers of appointment.[317]

These doubts, first repudiated in later decisions,[318] were put to rest by the Wills Act 1963[319] which applies to all testamentary dispositions and relies alternatively on the law of the place of execution, or the law of the donee's domicile, habitual residence or nationality at the time of execution or death. In addition, the Act provides[320] that a power of appointment is properly executed if it conforms to the law governing the essential validity of the power (which is normally the donor's law at the time | of his death[321] or the *lex situs* in the case of immovables[322]), even if it fails to comply with any

---

[314] *D'Huart v. Harkness* (1865), 34 Beav. 324 (328), 55 E.R. 660 (661).

[315] *Dicey and Morris* (ed. 11) 1042 n. 23; *Barretto v. Young*, [1900] 2 Ch. 339, abrogated by the Wills Act 1963 (c. 44) s. 2(2).

[316] 24 & 25 Vict., c. 114, s. 9, 10; for similar legislation in AUSTRALIA see *Sykes and Pryles* 707 n. 32, 708 n. 33–35; *Nygh* 516 n. 71.

[317] 7 Will. 4 & 1 Vict. c. 26, s. 10, now abrogated by the Wills Act 1963 (*supra* n. 315) s. 7(3); *In re Kirwan's Trusts* (1884), 25 Ch.D. 373, 381; *Hummel v. Hummel*, [1898] 1 Ch. 642, 645, distinguishing *D'Huart v. Harkness, supra* n. 314, on the ground that the latter did not involve a will by a British subject validated by the Wills Act, 1861 (preceding note); *In re Price*, [1900] 1 Ch. 442, 450.

[318] *In re Price* (preceding note) 450; *In re Simpson*, [1916] 1 Ch. 502, 509; *In re Wilkinson's Settlement*, [1917] 1 Ch. 620, 626; *In re Strong* (1926), 95 L.J. Ch. 22, following *D'Huart v. Harkness* (*supra* n. 314) as representing the general rule; *In re D'Erste*, [1903] 1 Ch. 898 disapproved; *Sykes and Pryles* 710–711.

[319] *Supra* n. 315, s. 1; *Dicey and Morris* (ed. 11) Rule 149.

[320] Section 2(1) (d) and (2).

[321] Following *Murphy v. Deichler*, [1909] A.C. 446, 448 (H.L.); see also *Tatnall v. Hankey* (1838), 2 Moo. P.C. 342 (350), 12 E.R. 1036 (1039); *In the goods of Alexander* (1860), 29 L.J. Pr.M. & A. 93; *In the goods of Hallyburton* (1866), 35 P. & M. 122; *In the goods of Huber*, [1896] P. 209, 213; *In the goods of Tréfondt*, [1899] P. 247, 250; *In re Price* (*supra* n. 317) 451–452; *In re Baker*, [1908] W.N. 161 (Ch.D.); *In re Pryce*, [1911] 2 Ch. 286, 290 (C.A.); *Re Baeder* (1916), 36 Ont.L.R. 39, 44–45 (C.A.); *Re Hewitt*, [1918] 43 D.L.R. 716, 720 (Ont.S.C.); *Dicey and Morris* (ed. 11) 1042 n. 21; *Scott and Fratcher* § 634 p. 441. For AUSTRALIA, *Sykes and Pryles* 711, 712, 713; *Nygh* 514. For CANADA, see *Castel*, Conflict no. 356 p. 475; *McLeod* 429.

[322] Section 2(1)(b); *Scoles and Hay* § 21.11 p. 815 n. 2.

express requirements stipulated by the instrument of creation[323] The fact that the instrument of disposition is ineffective in dealing with the donee's separate property is irrelevant.[324]

The alternative use, in the exercise of a power of appointment, of the formal requirements of the law governing the donee's will or of the law governing the instrument of creation is also sanctioned by the practice in the UNITED STATES.[325] This seems to leave unaffected any exercise *inter vivos* of a power in local form, being that of the *situs* of the fund, by a separate instrument limited to this function, while the instrument of creation is governed by foreign law.[326]

iii. Capacity

81. According to ENGLISH law the law of the donee's domicile at the time of his death determines capacity to exercise a testamentary form of appointment.[327] In the UNITED STATES compliance with the law of the donor's domiciliary law appears to satisfy the requirement of capacity as well.[328] If exercised *inter vivos* compliance with either the donee's or the donor's law appears to suffice.[329]

iv. Construction

82. The instrument of creation must be construed in accordance with the donor's personal law or the *lex situs* (if immovables are involved)[330] unless

---

[323] Section 2 (2) abolishing the rule in *Barretto v. Young, supra* n. 315.

[324] *Scott and Fratcher* § 634 p. 447; *In the goods of Tréfond (supra* n. 321) 250. For the UNITED STATES see *Pitman v. Pitman*, 31 Mass. 465, 50 N.E.2d 69 (1943); *In re Winter*, 24 N.J.Misc. 172, 47 A.2d 548 (Union Cty.Orphan's Ct. 1946). For AUSTRALIA see *Sykes and Pryles* 711, 713 maintaining for AUSTRALIA the rule in *Barretto v. Young, supra* n. 315, if the danee's will is governed by *foreign* law.

[325] *Scott and Fratcher* § 634 p. 443; *Scoles and Hay* § 21.11 p. 816. Law governing donee's domicile: *First National Bank of Arizona v. First National Bank of Birmingham*, 348 So.2d 1041 (Ala. 1977); *Ward. v. Stanard*, 82 A.D. 386, 81 N.Y.S. 906 (1903); *Guaranty Trust Co. v. Stevens*, 28 N.J. 243, 146 A.2d 97 (1958). Law governing donor's domicile: *Fidelity Union Trust Co. v. Caldwell*, 137 N.J.Eq. 362, 44 A.2d 842 (1945); *Guaranty Trust Co. v. Stevens (supra)* as an alternative; but see *Harrison v. City National Bank*, 210 F.Supp. 362 (S.D. Iowa 1962) favouring the exclusive application of the donee's law.

[326] *Scott and Fratcher* § 634 p. 447–448; *Scoles and Hay* § 21.9 p. 813 n. 2; *Hanson v. Denkla*, 357 U.S. 235, 2 L.Ed.2d 1283 (1958), on appeal from *Lewis v. Denkla*, 36 Del.Ch. 235, 128 A.2d 819 (1957).

[327] Dicey *and Morris* (ed. 11) Rule 148; *In re Lewal's Settlement Trusts*, [1918] 2 Ch. 391. For this purpose it is irrelevant whether the power is general or special: *Pouey v. Hordern (supra* n. 305) 494; *In re Pryce (supra* n. 321) 296; *Castel*, Conflict 474–475; *McLeod* 428; *Sykes and Pryles* 716 confine this rule to the exercise of general powers; also *Nygh* 512.

[328] *Scott and Fratcher* § 633; *In the goods of Sloan*, 7 Cal.App. 2d 319, 46 P.2d 1007 (1935), but see NEW YORK EPTL (*supra* n. 135) § 3–5.1 (g); *Scoles and Hay* § 21.11 p. 816, 818.

[329] *In re Langley's Settlement Trusts*, [1962] Ch. 541, 552–553 (C.A.).

[330] *Dicey and Morris* (ed. ir) Rule 150; *Castel*, Conflict no. 358 p. 476; *Scoles and Hay* § 21.10 p. 814.

the construction is to be determined by some other system of law intended by him.[331] The exercise of a power of appointment including its construction is governed by the law applicable to the donee's succession,[332] but the donee can select another law to determine its interpretation.[333] Difficulties arise if the law governing the donee's succession does not|know powers of appointment,[334] or treats their exercise as a testamentary disposition of the donee's estate and subjects the will to restrictions by setting aside compulsory shares. In this case the law governing the instrument of creation is called in aid for the purpose of interpreting the testamentary exercise of the power including the question whether the donee intended to exercise the power.[335]

Conversely, the donee's will does not always indicate with sufficient clarity whether the will only expresses the exercise of a special[336] or general power, whether a general power is exercised separately in a will disposing of the donee's estate[337] or whether the exercise of such a power is included in the disposition of that estate.[338] In this last case, the assets subject to the power are caught by the restrictions on free disposition imposed by the law governing the donee's succession; in all the other cases they are not. The construction of the exercise of the power of appointment by the donee determines its separate validity or its merger with the donee's estate resulting in the attraction of the mandatory restrictions imposed by the law governing the donee's succession.

---

[331] *Dicey and Morris* (ed. 11) Rule 151; *Scoles and Hay* § 21.11 p. 817 n. 17 with cases; *In re Mégret* (*supra* n. 305) 549; *Augustus v. Permanent Trustee Co. (Canberra) Ltd.* (*supra* n. 312) 252, 255, 257.

[332] *Dicey and Morris* (ed. 11) Rule 150; *In re Price* (*supra* n. 317) 452; *In re McMorran* (*supra* n. 305) 634. For SCOTLAND see *Durie's Trustees v. Osborne*, 1960 S.C. 444. For NEW YORK see *In re Acheson*, 28 N.Y.2d 155, 269 N.E.2d 571, 320 N.Y.S. 2d 905 (1971); for CANADA, *Castel*, Conflict no. 357 p. 475; *McLeod* 431. For AUSTRALIA, *Nygh* 515.

[333] *In re Price* (*supra* n. 317) 452–453; thus the presumption declared in the Wills Act, 1837 (*supra* n. 317) s. 27 can apply if a foreign donee selects ENGLISH law.

[334] *E.g.* German CC § 2064, 2065; the French Cass.civ. 12. Aug. 1863, D.P. 1863.1.356, S. 1863.1. 446 has rejected a *"legs avec faculté d'élire"* since it would permit wills in favour of uncertain persons: note *Voirin* on Trib.civ. Cusset 12 Dec. 1962: J.C.P. 1963.II.13 056; note *Bihr* on Cour Aix 2 Oct. 1973: D. 1974.J.745, 746; *Marty and Raynaud*, Droit Civil. Les successions et les libéralités (Paris 1983) no. 563; *Planiol and Ripert*, Traité élémentaire de droit civil français III (ed. 4 Paris 1951) no. 2056–2059; *idem*, Traité pratique de droit civil français V (ed. 2 Paris 1957) no. 599–601. It would seem, however, that the same object can be achieved by a *charge d'hérédité* if only specific beneficiaries are envisaged. It is therefore comparable at best to a special power of appointment; *Planiol and Ripert*, Traité élémentaire (*supra*) no. 3680; *idem*, Traité pratique (*ibidem*) no. 599 with cases.

[335] *Dicey and Morris* (ed. 11) Rule 150, Exception.

[336] *In re Mégret* (*supra* n. 305) 549.

[337] *Ibidem*; possibly *In re Waite's Settlement Trusts* (*supra* n. 305) 108.

[338] *In re Pryce* (*supra* n. 321) 286, 299; *In re Khan's Settlement* (*supra* n. 305) 567, 569; *Barretto v. Young, supra* n. 315, may perhaps also furnish an example.

Upon analysis the problem resolves itself into two: firstly, did the donee exercise the power and, secondly, if he exercised it, did he merge or blend the assets subject to his power with his own? In ENGLAND the question whether a power of appointment has been exercised by a will of the donee is facilitated by the Wills Act, 1837[339] which provides that a general devise or bequest is to be construed to include any assets over which the testator may have a *general power* of appointment, unless a contrary intention appears in the will.

If the will of the donee of the power under an ENGLISH instrument of creation is governed by a law other than ENGLISH law, the intention to exercise the power can be stated expressly[340] or it can be implied by virtue of the Wills Act, 1837 s. 27, but in the latter case only if the donee testator domiciled abroad indicates, however slightly, that the instrument of disposition is to be construed as a will according to ENGLISH law.[341] It has even been suggested that a rebuttable presumption exists to this effect.[342] Moreover, if the donee's will is governed by a legal system which does not know powers of appointment or invalidates them (on the ground that they are powers of disposition over property not belonging to the disposing donee[343] and that the disposition of assets of the deceased cannot be left to the discretion of third parties), it has been assumed that the courts of the foreign domicile of the donee testator would refer to ENGLISH law as the law governing the instrument of creation.[344]

| This broad range of construction is also adopted in the UNITED STATES,[345] subject however to the requirements of the instrument of crea-

---

[339] *Supra* n. 317, s. 27; for an example of a COMMON LAW practice to the contrary in OHIO see *Dollar Savings & Trust Co. v. First National Savings Bank of Boston* (*supra* n. 312) 773 [4, 5].

[340] *In re Simpson* (*supra* n. 318) 502, 507; limited to an express reference: *In re Scholefield*, [1905] 2 Ch. 408, 416.

[341] *In re Price* (*supra* n. 317) 452, 453; *In re Baker's Settlement Trusts*, [1908] W.N. 161, 162 (Ch.); *In re Simpson* (*supra* n. 318) 507; *In re Lewal's Settlement Trusts* (*supra* n. 327) 397–398; *In re Fenston's Settlement*, [1971] 1 W.L.R. 1640, 1643–1644 (Ch.), but see *In re McMorran* (*supra* n. 305) 634; and see *Re Wilkison*, [1934] 1 D.L.R. 544, 546 (Ont.S.C.); *Re Woods, Re Browne*, [1947] Ont.Rep. 752, [1947] 4 D.L.R. 386 (Ont.H.C.).

[342] *In re Wilkinson's Settlement* (*supra* n. 318) 627; *Castel*, Conflict 469 n. 47, 482 n. 12; *McLeod* 432 n. 199, 200; *Sykes and Pryles* 709.

[343] *In re Simpson* (*supra* n. 318) 508 *per Neville*, J.

[344] *Ibidem*, not following *In re D'Este* (*supra* n. 318) 903, 905 and *In re Scholefield*, *supra* n. 340; *In re Lewal's Settlement Trusts* (*supra* n. 327) 397–398; see also the evidence concerning the attitude of FRENCH courts in *In re Scholefield* (*supra*) 417; *In re Price* (*supra* n. 317) 453 (*obiter*); *In re Pryce* (*supra* n. 321) 298 (DUTCH law); *In re Waite's Settlement Trusts* (*supra* n. 305) 107 (GUERNSEY law); *In re Khan's Settlement* (*ibidem*) 569, 580–581; with reservations: *In re McMorran* (*ibidem*) 633, 634 (validity and capacity only); *In re Fenston's Settlement* (*supra* n. 341) 1644; *Dicey and Morris* (ed. 11) Rule 150, Exception. For the FRENCH practice concerning powers of appointment in general, see Trib.civ. Pau 3 July 1956, *supra* n. 180; Cour Paris 10 Jan. 1970, *supra* n. 194.

[345] *Scott and Fratcher* § 642; *Scoles and Hay* § 21.11 p. 817 with cases, 819, 820 with cases.

tion.[346] The intention to exercise the power must be expressed in the law of some states and is implied in others.[347] The only question is whether the law of the donor or of the donee is determining.[348] According to a widespread practice the donor's law applies as it stands at the time when the power is exercised.[349] However, the law chosen by the donee to govern the exercise of the power has also been applied on occasions[350] and compliance with the *lex situs* is required in respect of immovables.[351] The principle of applying the law more favourable to the exercise of the power does not appear to have won favour.[352]

The law governing the instrument of creation has also been applied in South Africa;[353] the donee's law is called upon in SCOTLAND.[354]

v. Effect of Donee's Law of Succession or Matrimonial Property Regime

83. Since the exercise of a power of appointment as such, even if in the form of a testamentary disposition, does not involve the donee's property, it follows that the exercise of a special power of appointment will not attract the mandatory rules governing the donee's succession or matrimonial property regime.[355] The same applies in principle to the exercise of general powers, if the sole object of the testamentary disposition is to give effect to the power[356] or if it is clear that the property subject to the power is to be treated separately from the donee's own assets.[357] If, however, the donee makes his testamentary dispositions in such a manner that in accordance with the principles of construction set out above they can be interpreted as a contempo-

---

[346] *Scott and Fratcher* § 642 p. 486 n. 1 with cases; *Scales and Hay* § 21.11 p. 815 n. 1.

[347] *Scott and Fratcher* § 642 p. 489–490.

[348] *Idem* § 642 p. 490; *Sewall v. Wilmer*, 132 Mass. 131 (1882); *Farnum v. Pennsylvania Co. for Insurance*, 87 N.J.Eq. 108, 99 A. 145 (1916), aff. 87 N.J.Eq. 652, 101 A. 1053 (1917).

[349] *Rhode Island Hospital Trust v. Dunnell*, 34 R.I. 394, 83 A. 958 (1912).

[350] *First National Bank of Chicago v. Ettlinger*, 465 E2d 343 (7 Cir. 1972).

[351] *Scales and Hay* § 21.11 p. 815 n. 2 with cases.

[352] *Scott and Fratcher* § 642 p. 502.

[353] *Westminster Bank v. Zinn*, (1938) A.D. 57; for the structural differences between powers of appointment in SOUTH AFRICAN and ENGLISH law see *ibidem* 65–67, 71, 73; *Ladies Christian Home v. S.A. Association*, [1915] C.P.D. 467, *per Kotze, J.*

[354] *Durie's Trustees v. Osborne* (*supra* n. 332) 450 ss.

[355] *D'Huart v. Harkness, supra* n. 314; *In re Kirwan's Trusts, supra* n. 317; *Pouey v. Hordern* (*supra* n. 305) 394; *In re Pryce* (*supra* n. 321) 297, 299; *In re McMorran* (*supra* n. 305) 631; *In re Bald*, (1896) 76 L.T. Rep. 462, 66 L.J. Ch. 524 for SCOTS law; *Sykes and Pryles* 713 for AUSTRALIAN law.

[356] *In re Mégret* (*supra* n. 305) 549; *In re Hernando* (1884), 27 Ch.D. 284; possibly also *In re Waite's Settlement Trusts* (*supra* n. 305) 107–108; *In re Pryce* (*supra* n. 321) 296, 299; *Sykes and Pryles* 715. For the UNITED STATES see *In re O'Connor*, 82 N.Y.S. 2d 310, 312 [2] [3] (N.Y.Cty.S.Ct. 1948).

[357] *In re Khan's Settlement* (*supra* n. 305) 578; *Pouey v. Hordern* (*ibidem*) 494 (*obiter*), qualified *In re Pryce* (*supra* n. 321) 296.

raneous exercise of a general power taking the appointed property out of the instrument creating the power and merging the assets subject to the latter with his own by "blending" them, the ensuing single mass is subject to the rules governing the donee's succession (compulsory share)[358] and his matrimonial regime.[359]

This difference in the manner of exercising a general power explains why sometimes the law governing the donee's succession or his matrimonial property regime is applied and sometimes it is not. It is all a matter of interpreting the donee's will,[360] not of deciding a disputed rule of law.[361] In the UNITED STATES the same | problem could have arisen but did not in fact arise when the donee's succession was governed by swiss,[362] ITALIAN[363] and FRENCH[364] law or his matrimonial regime was governed by NEW YORK law.[365]

(Completed August 1992)

| List of Principal Works

(1)

1. COMPARATIVE LAW: *Alfaro*, The Trust and the Civil Law with Special Reference to Panama: 33 J.Comp.Leg. (N.S.) 25–31 (1951), cited Trust; *Amos,* The Common Law and the Civil Law in the British Commonwealth: 50 Harv.L.Rev. 1248–1274 (1937); *Bentivoglio*, Les "Investment Trusts" (1)/Investment Trusts (1): Unidroit

---

[358] *In re Pryce* (*supra* n. 321) 296, 299, 300; *In re Khan's Settlement* (*supra* n. 305) 578, 580, 583; *In re Fenston's Settlement, (supra* n. 341) 1647 (*obiter*); *Sykes and Pryles* 715.

[359] *Pouey v. Hordern* (*supra* n. 305) 494 (*obiter*) as explained in *In re Pryce* (*supra* n. 321) 296. For the AMERICAN practice see *e.g., Amerige v. Attorney-General* (*supra* n. 309) 131 [7–9]; *Rhode Island Hospital Trust Co. v. Anthony* (*supra* n. 305) at 348 and 535, respectively.

[360] See the wording of the dispositions in *In re Price* (*supra* n. 317) 443; *In re D'Este* (*supra* n. 318) 898; *In re Scholefield* (*supra* n. 340) 409; *In re Simpson* (*supra* n. 318) 503; *In re Pryce* (*supra* n. 321) 287; *In re Wilkinson's Settlement* (*supra* n. 318) 621; *In re Waite's Settlement Trusts* (*supra* n. 305) 108; *In re Khan's Settlement* (*ibidem*) 569; *Sykes and Pryles* 715.

[361] See, however, In *re Waite's Settlement Trusts* (*supra* n. 305) 108 with references to literature; *In re Khan's Settlement* (*ibidem*) 583.

[362] *In re Marsland's Estate*, 142 Misc. 230, 254 N.Y.S. 293, 296 [3] (Kings Cty.Sur.Ct. 1931). *Scott and Fratcher* § 636 p. 466.

[363] *In re New York Life Insurance and Trust Co.*, 139 N.Y.S. 695, 710 (N.Y.Cty.Sur.Ct. 1913); but see *In re O'Connor* (*supra* n. 356) 310 where the question was treated as one of construction.

[364] *Prince de Béarn v. Winans*, s.n. *Galard v. Winans*, 114 Md. 434, 74 A. 626, 631 (1909); *Scott and Fratcher* § 636 p. 466.

[365] *Austin Estate*, 38 Pa.D. & Cty.2d 79 (1966); *Scott and Fratcher* § 636 p. 467 (a matter of construction).

1957, 104–131; *Bolgar,* Why No Trusts in the Civil Law?: 2 Am.J.Comp.L. 204–219 (1953); *Buonincontro,* Trust e civil law (appunti di diritto comparato): Riv.dir.civ. (Padova) 1959, 680–688; *Droz,* Saisine héréditaire et administration de la succession en droit international privé français et comparé: Rev.crit.d.i.p. 1970, 183–225, cited Saisine; *Drucker,* Trusts on the Continent of Europe: 4 I.C.L.Q. 550–552 (1955); *Dyer and Van Loon,* Report on trusts and analogous institutions/Rapport sur les trusts et institutions analogues: Act.Doc.La Haye 15 (1985) II 10–108, cited Report; *Eder,* A Comparative Survey of Anglo-American and Latin-American Law (New York and London 1950) 86–118; *Fratcher,* Trust: *this* Encyclopedia Vol. VI ch. 11 (1973); *Garrigues,* Law of Trusts: 2 Am.J.Comp.L. 25–35 (1953); *Goldschmidt,* El Fideicomiso en los Países de la America Latina/The Trust in the. Countries of Latin America; 3 Inter-Am.L.Rev./Rev.jur.interam. 1–27 (Span.), 29–54 (Engl.) (1961); *Goldschmidt and Eder,* El fideicomiso en el derecho comparado (especialmente americano) (Buenos Aires 1948); *Goldstein,* Trust of Movables in the Conflict of Laws (Thesis Cologne 1966); *Hefti,* Trusts and Their Treatment in the Civil Law: 5 Am.J.Comp.L. 552–576 (1956); *Hornsey,* Rapport sur les possibilités d'utiliser certains principes du "trust" dans les pays dits de droit civil (1)/Report on Possible Uses of Certain Principles of the Trust in Civil Law Countries (1): Unidroit 1957, 44–103; *Jauffret-Spinosi,* La Convention de la Haye relative à la loi applicable au trust et à sa reconnaissance (1er juillet 1985): Clunet 1987, 23–73; *Klein,* A propos de la Convention de la Haye du 1er juillet 1985 relative à la loi applicable au *trust* et sa reconnaissance: Mélanges Piotet (Berne 1990) 467–483; *Kötz,* Trust und Treuhand (Göttingen 1963), cited Trust; *idem,* Die 15. Haager Konferenz und das Kollisionsrecht des trust: RabelsZ 50 (1986) 562–585, cited Haager Konferenz; *Lepaulle,* Civil Law Substitutes for Trusts: 36 Yale L.J. 1126–1147 (1926–1927), cited Substitutes; *idem,* Trusts and the Civil Law: 15 J.Comp.Leg. (N.S.) 18–34 (1933), cited Civil Law; *idem,* La notion de "trust" et ses applications dans les divers systèmes juridiques: Unidroit 1951, 197–208, cited Notion; *Lipstein,* Conflict of Laws and Comparative Law – Powers of Appointment in a Civil Law Sphere: Festschrift Wengler II (Berlin 1973) 431–442, cited Conflict; *idem,* The General Principles of Private International Law: Rec.des Cours 135 (1972 I) 97–229, cited P.I.L.; *Merryman,* Ownership and Estate: 48 Tul.L.Rev. 916–945 (1974); *Newman,* Trusts, Civil Law Concepts and Legal Realism/El fideicomiso, los conceptos de los sistemas de tradición romana y realismo jurídico: 3 Inter-Am.L.Rt v./Rev.jur.interam. 379–390 (Engl.), 391–404 (Span.) (1961); *Nussbaum,* Sociological and Comparative Aspects of the Trust: 38 Colum.L.Rev. 408–430 (1938), AcP 151 (1950/51) 193–208; *Patton,* Trust Systems in the Western Hemisphere: 19 Tul.L.Rev. 398–435 (1945); *Rabel,* Conflict of Laws IV (Ann Arbor 1958) 445–470; *Ryan,* The Reception of the Trust: 10 I.C.L.Q. 265–283 (1961); *Schnitzer,* Le trust er la fondation dans le conflit de lois: Rev.crit.d.i.p. 1965, 479–498, cited Trust; *idem,* Die Treuhand (der Trust) und das Internationale Privatrecht: Gedächtnisschrift Marxer (Zürich 1963) 53–113, cited Treuhand; *Serick,* Zur Behandlung des anglo-amerikanischen Trust im Kontinentaleuropäischen Recht: Festschrift Nipperdey II (Munich and Berlin 1965) 653–666, cited Behandlung; *Weiser,* Trusts on the Continent of Europe (London 1936); *Wilson* (ed.), Trusts and Trustlike Devices (London 1981); *de Wulf,* The Trust and Corresponding Institutions in the Civil Law (Brussels 1965).

2. AUSTRALIA: *Nygh*, Conflict of Laws in Australia (ed. 4 Sydney 1984); *Sykes and Pryles*, Australian Private International Law (ed. 2 Sydney 1987); *Wallace*, Choice of Law for Trusts in Australia and the United Kingdom: 36 I.C.L.Q. 454–482 (1987).

3. CANADA: *Castel*, Canadian Conflict of Laws (ed. 2 Toronto 1986), cited Conflict; *idem*, The Civil Law System of the Province of Quebec. Notes, Cases, and Materials (Toronto 1962), cited System; *idem*, La fiducie créée par donation entre vifs de biens meubles et le droit international privé québecois: Rev.not. 69 (1966/67) 271–286, cited Fiducie; *McLeod*, The Conflict of Laws (Calgary, Alta. 1983); *Mettarlin*, The Quebec Trust and the Civil Law: 21 McGill L.J. 175–241 (1975).

4. FRANCE: *Aghion*, Le trust juridique anglo-saxon 1: Rev.Inst.Belge 1930, 65–70; II (Les trustees): *ibidem* 1931, 49–57; III (La jurisprudence française): *ibidem* 1932, 4–13; IV (Le trust en droit fiscal français (1)): *ibidem* 1933, 1–6; *Aubert*, Trusts: Encyclopédie Dalloz. Répertoire de Droit International II (Paris 1969) 972–976; *Bates*, Common Law Express Trusts in French Law: 40 Yale L.J. 34–52 (1930); *Batiffol*, The Trust Problems as Seen by a French Lawyer: 33 J.Comp.Leg. (N.S.) 18–25 (1951); *Béraudo*, La Convention de la Haye du 1er juillet 1985 relative à la loi applicable au trust et à sa reconnaissance: Trav. Com.fr.d.i.p. 1985/86, 21–39; *Bredin*, L'évolution du trust dans la jurisprudence française: *ibidem* 1974, 137–160; *Decugis*, Note on Trib.civ. Seine 28 June 1901: D.P. 1902.2.361–362; *Droz*, Note on Cour Paris 10 Jan. 1970: Rev.crit.d.i.p. 1971, 525–531, cited Note (1970); *idem*, Note on Trib.gr.inst. Paris 22 April 1976: *ibidem* 1977, 327–334, cited Note (1976); *idem and Revillard*, Libéralités, Problèmes Communs, Testaments: J.Cl.Dr.Int. VIII (Paris, loose-leaf) Fasc. | 557 – B (5, 1988) no. 75–178; *Elland-Goldsmith*, The Trust and its Use in Commercial and Financial Transactions/Le trust et ses utilisations dans les opérations commerciales et financières: Rev.dr.aff.int. 1985, 683–719, (Part two/Seconde Partie) 945–968; *Gaillard and Trautman*, La Convention de la Haye du 1er juillet 1985 relative à la loi applicable au trust et à sa reconnaissance: Rev.crit.d.i.p. 1986, 1–31, cited Convention; *idem*, Trusts in Non-Trust Countries – Conflict of Laws and the Hague Convention on Trusts: 35 Am.J.Comp.L. 307–340 (1987), cited Trusts; *Gobin and Maerten*, Nouvelles perspectives du trust en France: J.C.P. (éd.N) 1985, 391 no. 65–95; *Lepaulle*, De la nature du trust: Clunet 1927, 966–982, cited Nature; *idem*, De la validité des trusts en France: Rev.d.i.p. 1927, 309–314, cited Validité; *idem*, An Outsider's Viewpoint of the Nature of Trusts: 14 Cornell L.Q. 52–61 (1928/29), cited Outsider; *idem*, Traité théorique et pratique du trust en droit interne, en droit fiscal et en droit international privé (Paris 1932), cited Traité; *idem*, Réflexions sur l'expansion du trust: Rev.int.dr.comp. 1955, 318–324, cited Réflexions; *Lion*, Un anglais constitue un trust, conformément à sa loi, sur ses biens situés en France – La loi française doit-elle reconnaître sa validité?: Clunet 1923, 677–683; *Loussouarn and Bredin*, Droit du commerce international (Paris 1969) 348–387; *Maerten*, Le régime du trust après la Convention de la Haye du 1er juillet 1985: J.C.P. 1988.I.3319; *Malaurie*, Note on Cour Paris 10 Jan. 1970: D.S. 1972.J.125–127; *Motulsky*, De l'impossibilité juridique de constituer un "trust" anglo-saxon sous l'empire de la loi française: Rev.crit.d.i.p. 1948, 451–468; *Nast*, Note on Trib.civ. Seine 16 May 1906: Rev.d.i.p. 1907, 254–262; *Necker*, Note on Trib. gr.inst. Bayonne 28 April 1975: Rev.crit.d.i.p. 1976, 332–337; *Niboyet*, Note on Trib.civ. Seine 8 Dec. 1924: Rev.d.i.p. 1925, 103–107, 105–107; *Opetit*, Le trust dans le com-

merce international: Rev.crit.d.i.p. 1973, 1–20; *Revillard*, La Convention de la
Haye du 1er juillet 1985 sur la loi applicable au trust et sa reconnaissance: Rép.not.
Defrénois 1986, 689–701; *Travers*, De la validité, au point de vue du droit français,
des trusts créés par des étrangers sur des biens soumis à la loi française ou par des
Français sur des biens situés hors de France: Rev.d.i.p. 1909, 521–5 35; *Wiederkehr*,
Biens: J.Cl. Dr.Int. VIII (Paris, loose-leaf) Fasc. 550 (11, 1984) no. 200–201.

5. GERMANY: *Coing*, Die rechtsgeschäftliche Treuhand im deutschen internationalen
Privatrecht: ZfRV 1974, 81–92; *Czermak*, Der Express Trust im Internationalen
Privatrecht (Frankfurt a.M. 1986); *Firsching*, Testamentsvollstrecker – Executor –
Trustee: DNotZ 1959, 359–373; *Frankenstein*, Internationales Privatrecht IV (Ba-
sel 1935); *Gottheiner*, Zur Anwendung englischen Erbrechts auf Nachlässe in
Deutschland: RabelsZ 21 (1956) 36–72; *Graue*, Der Trust im Internationalen Privat-
und Steuerrecht: Festschrift Ferid (Frankfurt a.M. 1978) 151–182; *Kötz*, Zur An-
knüpfung des unter Lebenden errichteten Trust: IPRax. 1985, 205–207, cited Anknüpfung; *Kropholler*, Die Anpassung im Kollisionsrecht: Festschrift Ferid
(Frankfurt a.M. 1978) 279–289; *Schönle*, Ist der englische Trustee einer deutschen
Treuhand gleich?: ZHR 121 (1958) 190–197; *Schwenn*, Die Anwendung der §§
2369 und 2368 BGB auf Erbfälle mit englischem oder amerikanischem Erbstatut:
NJW 1952, 1113–1116; *Serick*, Zur Anerkennung der liechtensteinischen Treuunternehmen in Deutschland: RabelsZ 23 (1958) 624–642, cited Anerkennung;
von Staudinger(-Stoll), Kommentar zum Bürgerlichen Gesetzbuch mit Einführungsgesetz und Nebengesetzen (EGBGB) Part 2 (ed. 10/11 Berlin 1976) no.
151–156 following art. 12 par. 1; *Steinbach*, Entwurf eines Übereinkommens der
Haager Konferenz über das auf Trusts anzuwendende Recht und über ihre Anerkennung: RIW/AWD 1986, 1–5; *Wengler*, Fragen des deutschen Erbscheinrechts
für Nachlässe, auf die englisches Intestaterbrecht anwendbar ist: JR 1955, 41–43;
Wohlgemuth, Der minderjährige Gesellschafter im Internationalen Privatrecht:
RIW/AWD 1980, 759–768; *Würdinger*, The German Trust: 33 J.Comp.Leg. (N.S.)
31–40 (1951).

6. ITALY: *Bernardi*, Il trust nel diritto internazionale privato (Pavia 1957); *Borgioli*, Le
Treuhandunternehmen nell'ordinamento italiano: Giur.comm. 1978 II 49–67;
Cassoni, Il "trust" anglosassone quale istituzione sconosciuta nel nostro ordinamento: Giur.it. 1986 I 2, 754–759, cited Trust; *idem*, L'Anstalt nel diritto internazionale privato italiano: Riv.dir.int. priv.proc. 1976, 210–221, cited Anstalt;
idem, Note on Cass. 28 July 1977: Giur.it. 1978 I 1, 2000–2005, cited Note; *Comoglio*, Il caso di "trustee" straniero che agisce in Italia per la vendita di beni
ereditari – un dubbio ricorrente di giurisdizione volontaria internazionale:
Riv.not. 1985, 243–252; *Gambaro*, Problemi in materia di riconoscimento degli
effetti dei *trusts* nei paesi di *civil law*: Riv.dir.civ. (Padova) 1984, 93–108; *Grassetti*,
Trust anglosassone, proprietà fiduciaria e negozio fiduciario: Riv.dir.com. 1936 I
548–553; *Palliccia*, "Trusts" testamentari inglesi riferentisi a beni siti in Italia:
Giur.it. 1933 IV 26–35, Riv.it. dir.int.priv.proc. 1932, 347–362; *Picone*, Diritto
internazionale privato delle società e riconoscimento di "Anstalten" e "Treuunternehmen" nell'ordinamento italiano: Com.e stud. 15 (1978) 83–163; *Vacirca*, Il
riconoscimento del Trust o della Anstalt del Liechtenstein nell'ordinamento italiano: Foro pad. 1977 I 349–350.

7. NETHERLANDS: *Driélsma*, Anglo-Amerikaans Trustrecht en Nederlands Successie-recht: W.P.N.R. 1963, 217 (no. 4767), cited Trustrecht; *idem*, Nogmaals Anglo-Amerikaans Trustrecht en Nederlands Successierecht: *ibidem* 1972, 169–173 (no. 5169), 181–187 (no. 5170), cited Nogmaals; *Dyer and Van Loon*, Anglo-Arneri-kaanse trusts en het Nederlandse recht. Preadviezen (Mededelingen van de Ne-derlandse Vereeniging voor Internationaal Recht no. 87) (Deventer 1983), cited Nederlandse recht; *Van der Grinten*, De trustee naar Nederlands recht: W.P.N.R. 1941, 321–347 (no. 3737–3741); *Henriquez*, Trusts in het internationaal privaat-recht: Ned.T.I.R. 12 (1965) 251–280; *Hijmans van den Bergh*, De Engclse "Trust" in het Nederlands internationaal privaatrecht: De Conflictu Legum. | Mélanges Kollewijn and Offerhaus (Leyden 1962) 254–267; *Meijers*, De Trustee en het Burg-crlijk Recht: W.P.N.R. 1927, 413 (no. 2998); *Offerhaus*, Aanpassing in het inter-nationaal privaatrecht (Mededelingen der Koninklijke Nederlandse Akademie van Wetenschappen, Afd. Lctterkunde Nieuwe Reeks Pt. 26 no. 5) (Amsterdam 1963); *Van der Ploeg*, Enkele erfrechtelijke hoofdstukken van internationaal privaatrecht. Preadviezen (Broederenschap der Notarissen in Nederland no. 74) (Utrecht 1961); *Uniken Venema*, In Nederland gelegene goederen, toebehorende aan Anglo-Amerikaanse Trusts: Ned.T.I.R. 14 (1967) 33–72, cited Trusts; *idem*, Trustrecht en Bewind (Zwolle 1954), cited Trustrecht.

8. SOUTH AFRICA: *Honoré*, The South African Law of Trusts (ed. 3 Cape Town 1984); *McCall-Smith*, Comparative Aspects of the Rights of the Beneficiary in the South African Trust: 5 Comp.& Int.L.J.South, Africa 188–223 (1972).

9. SPAIN AND LATIN-AMERICA: *Hendrickson*, The Puerto Rico Trust Code: 13 Int.Lawyer 344–356 (1979), cited Puerto Rico; *Martinez*, Trusts and the Civil Law: 42 La.L.Rev. 1709–1720 (1982); *Molina Pasquel*, The Mexican Fideicomiso – The Reception, Evolution and Present Status of the Common Law Trust in a Civil Law Country: 8 Colum.J.Transnat.L. 54–78 (1969); *Sánchez Villela*, The Problems of Trust Legislation in Civil Law Jurisdictions – The Law of Trusts in Puerto Rico: 19 Tul.L.Rev. 374–397 (1945).

10. SWITZERLAND: *Bloch*, Der Anglo-amerikanische Trust und seine Behandlung im internationalen Privatrecht: SJZ 46 (1950) 65–71; Dreyer, Le trust en droit suisse (Etudes Suisses de Droit International XXI) (Geneva 1981); *Gautschi*, Subroga-tion und Aussonderung von beweglichem Treuhandvermögen: SJZ 72 (1976) 317–328; *Gubler*, Besteht in der Schweiz ein Bedürfnis nach Einführung des In-stituts der angelsächsischen Treuhand (trust); ZSR 73 (1954) II 215a–476a; *Guisan*, La fiducie en droit suisse: Trav.sem.int.dr. 1937 V 13–116; *Huber*, Trust and "Treu-hand" in Swiss law: 1 I.C.L.Q. 64–66 (1952); *Meyer*, Trusts in Swiss Law: *ibidem* 378–381; *Reymond*, Le trust et le droit suisse: ZSR 73 (1954) II 119a–214a.

11. UNITED KINGDOM: *Anton*, Private International Law (Edinburgh 1967); *Cheshire and North*, Private International Law (ed. 11 London 1987); *Croucher*, Trusts of Movables in Private International Law: 4 M.L.R. 111–120 (1940); *Delaney*, Chari-table Trusts and the Conflict of Laws: 10 I.C.L.Q. 385–408 (1961); *Diamond*, The Trust in English Law: Riv.dir. int.priv.proc. 1981, 289–308; *Dicey and Morris*, see *infra sub Morris; Franceschelli*, Il "Trust" nel diritto inglese (Padua 1935); *Hanbury and Maudsley*, Modern Equity (ed. 13 London 1989); *Hayton*, The Hague Con-vention on the Law Applicable to Trusts and Their Recognition: 36 I.C.L.Q. 260–282 (1987), cited Hague Convention; *idem*, Trusts in Private International Law: 135 New L.J. 18–19 (1985), cited Trusts; *Hoar*, Some Aspects of Trusts in the

Conflict of Laws: 26 Can.Bar Rev. 1415–1436 (1948); *Keeton,* Trusts in the Conflict of Laws: 4 Curr.Lcgal Prob. 107–121 (1951); *idem and Sheridan,* The Law of Trusts (ed. 11 Chichester 1983); *Latham,* The Creation and Administration of a Trust in the Conflict of Laws: 6 Curr.Legal Prob. 176–195 (1953); *Morcom,* Trust Exporting: 126 New L.J. 1034–1036 (1976); *Morris* (ed.), Dicey and Morris on the Conflict of Laws (2 vol.) (ed. 10 London 1980, with cum.supp.) and *Collins* (ed.) (ed. 11 London 1987) with supp.vol. (yearly cum.), cited *Dicey and Morris; Newark,* Charitable Privileges and Restrictions and the Conflict of Laws: 15 N.Ire. Legal Q. 155–165 (1964); *de Pinna,* Variation of Trust and Foreign Elements: 111 New L.J. 579, 659, 752–753 (1961); *Walker,* Principles of Scottish Private Law IV/4 (Law of Trusts) (ed. 4 Oxford 1988); *Wilson and Duncan,* Trust, Trustees and Executors (Edinburgh 1975); *Wortley,* Le trust et ses applications modernes en droit anglais: Rev.int.dr. comp. 1962, 699–710.

12. UNITED STATES OF AMERICA: *American Law Institute,* Restatement Second of the Law of Trusts (St. Paul, Minn. 1959), cited Restatement of Trusts 2d; *idem,* Restatement Second of the Law of Conflict of Laws (St. Paul, Minn. 1971), cited Restatement 2d (1971); *Anon.,* Choice of Law – The Validity of Trusts of Movables – Intention and Validation: 64 Nw. U.L.Rcv. 388–406 (1969); *Beale,* Living Trusts of Movables in Private International Law: 45 Harv.L.Rev. 969–973 (1932); *Caldwell and Nagel,* Foreign Situs Trust: 6 Denver J.Int.L.Pol. 675–704 (1977); *Cavers,* Trusts *inter vivos* and Private International Law: 44 Harv.L.Rev. 161–202 (1930); *Dean,* Conflict Avoidance in Inter Vivos Trusts of Movables: 21 Law & Contemp.Prob. 483–498 (1956); *Hendrickson,* Change of Situs of a Trust: 118 Trusts & Est. 19–20, 26, 36–40, 109–110 (1979), cited Change; *Kroll,* Foreign Trusts: 112 *ibidem* 618–621, 647–648 (1973); *Lafer and Siegel,* Trusts of Movables in the Conflict of Laws: 36 N.Y.U.L.Rev. 713–722 (1961); *Land,* Trusts in the Conflict of Laws (New York 1940); *Scoles and Hay,* Conflict of Laws (St. Paul, Minn. 1982); *Scales and Rheinstein,* Succession Planning: 21 Law & Contemp. Prob. 499–532 (1956); *Scott and Fratcher,* The Law of Trust V A (ed. 4 Boston 1989); *Stone,* Trusts in Louisiana: 1 I.C.L.Q. 368–378 (1952); *Swabenland,* Conflict of Laws in Administration of Express Trusts of Personal Property: 45 Yale L. 438–451 (1936); *Weintraub,* Commentary on the Conflict of Laws (ed. 2 Mineola, N.Y 1980); *Wisdom,* A Trust Code in the Civil Law, Based on the Restatement and Uniform Acts – The Louisiana Trust Estates Act: 13 Tul.L.Rev. 70–98 (1938/39).

(2)

|*Aghion* 4; *Alfaro* 1; *American Law Institute* 12; *Amos* 1; *Anon.* 12; *Anton* 11; *Aubert* 4.
Bates 4; *Batiffol* 4; *Beale* 12; *Bentivoglio* 1; *Béraudo* 4; *Bernardi* 6; *Bloch* 10; *Bolgar* 1; *Borgioli* 6; *Bredin* 4; *Buonincontro* 1.
Caldwell 12; *Cassoni* 6; *Castel* 3; *Cavers* 12; *Cheshire* 11; *Coing* 5; *Collins* 11; *Comoglio* 6; *Croucher* 11; *Czermak* 5.
Dean 12; *Decugis* 4; *Delaney* 11; *Diamond* 11; *Dicey* 11; *Dreyer* 10; *Drielsma* 7; *Droz* 1, 4; *Drucker* 1; *Duncan* 11; *Dyer* 1, 7.
Eder 1; *Elland-Goldsmith* 4.
Firsching 5; *Franceschelli* 11; *Frankenstein* 5; *Fratcher* 1, 12.

Gaillard 4; *Gambaro* 6; *Garrigues* 1; *Gautschi* 10; *Gobin* 4; *Goldschmidt* 1, 4; *Gold-stein* 1; *Gottheiner* 5; *Grassetti* 6; *Graue* 5; *Van der Grinten* 7; *Gubler* 10; *Guisan* 10.

Hanbury 11; *Hay* 12; *Hayton* 11; *Hefti* 1; *Hendrickson* 9, 12; *Henriquez* 7; *Hijmans van den Bergh* 7; *Hoar* 11; *Honoré* 8; *Hornsey* 1; *Huber* 10.

Jauffret-Spinosi 1.

Keeton 11; *Klein* 1; *Kötz* 1, 5; *Kroll* 12; *Kropholler* 5.

Lafer 12; *Land* 12; *Latham* 11; *Lepaulle* 1, 4; *Lion* 4; *Lipstein* 1; *Van Loon* 1, 7; *Loussouarn* 4.

McCall-Smith 8; *McLeod* 3; *Maerten* 4; *Malaurie* 4; *Martinez* 9; *Maudsley* 11; *Meyers* 7; *Merryman* 1; *Mettarlin* 3; *Meyer* 10.; *Molina Pasquel* 9; *Morcom* 11; *Morris* 11; *Motulsky* 4.

Nagel 12; *Nast* 4; *Necker* 4; *Newark* 11; *Newman* 1; *Niboyet* 4; *North* 11; *Nussbaum* 1; *Nygh* 2.

Offerhaus 7; *Opetit* 4.

Palliccia 6; *Patton* 1; *Picone* 6; *de Pinna* 11; *Van der Ploeg* 7; *Pryles* 2.

Rabel 1; Restatement of Trusts 2d and Restatement zd (1971), see *American Law Institute* 12; *Revillard* 4; *Raymond* 10; *Rheinstein* 12; *Ryan* 1.

Sánchez Villela 9; *Schnitzer* 1; *Schönle* 5; *Schwenn* 5; *Scoles* 12; *Scott* 12; *Serick* 1, 5; *Sheridan* 11; *Siegel* 12; *von Staudinger* 5; *Steinbach* 5; *Stoll* 5; *Stone* 12; *Swabenland* 12; *Sykes* 2.

Trautman 4; *Travers* 4.

Uniken Venema 7.

Vacirca 6.

Wallace 2; *Walker* 11; *Weintraub* 12; *Weiser* 1; *Wengler* 5; *Wiederkehr* 4; *Wilson* 1, 11; *Wisdom* 12; *Wohlgemuth* 5; *Wortley* 11; *Würdinger* 5; *de Wulf* 1.

Characterization

[Editorial note: first published in the International Encyclopedia of Comparative Law, Volume III, Chapter 5 (1999).]

| I. History and Systematic Analysis

A. Historical Bases

1. – From the time when the question was first considered whether and when foreign law is to be applied it was evident, as the so-called statutists showed, that the extraterritorial application of foreign law must be determined by some criteria, if a discretionary and arbitrary choice of the "better" law is to be avoided. Early attempts to rely on the distinction between laws of a procedural and a substantive character, the former governed always by the *lex fori* while the latter were not, were followed by another. Laws were either real, and applied only locally, or they were personal and followed the person or were of a mixed kind and were based on the place of acting. As a result, the nature of rules of domestic law determined their application in space. It was only necessary to ascertain whether a rule was of a procedural, a real or a personal nature. However, in practice such distinctions proved artificial, as the famous English Question (the *quaestio aurea*) showed.[1] By denying the test of the nature of laws its universal dominance for determining the application of laws in space and by substituting an international element relying on territoriality the DUTCH school of the late 17th century was forced to formulate independent choice-of-law rules for the use of individual countries. These concentrated on broad categories of legal institutions (henceforth called "operative facts" for want of a better expression) which were combined with a territorial or personal link (henceforth called "connecting factors").[2] In this form they fashioned the development of choice-of-law rules in ENGLAND, SCOTLAND and the UNITED STATES in the 18th and the first part of the 19th century.

In CONTINENTAL EUROPE the critical exposition by *Waechter* (in 1841 and 1842) rejected the approach of the statutists and gave precedence to the *lex fori*, unless specific choice-of-law rules required the application of foreign law. Both he and, a few years later with greater emphasis, *Savigny* believed that "for each legal relationship that legal system must be ascertained to which this legal relationship pertains or is subject having regard to its particular nature."[3]

---

[1] *Lipstein*, Principles 117–118.
[2] See *Vischer*, Connecting Factors: *supra* ch. 4.
[3] *Savigny*, System des heutigen Römischen Rechts VIII (Berlin 1849) 28; *Lipstein*, Principles 195–196.

B. Systematic Analysis

i. The Seat – Unilateral or Bilateral Delimitation

2. – The legal relationship and its seat were thus made the elements of all conflict rules. The number of legal relationships which require to be connected with a particular system of laws is of course infinite, and it is conceivable that an almost infinite number of choice-of-law rules could be developed which are attached to individual rules of private law. Since they would be attached to the rules of private law of the *lex fori*, which often differ from those of their foreign counterparts, they would necessarily be unilateral choice-of-law rules restricted to the spatial or personal application of the *lex fori*.[4] In interpreting such rules no need would arise to consider any rules of foreign law.

Unless a country would be satisfied to entertain only those claims or defences to which its own domestic law applies, a need will present itself to take foreign law into account. Strict adherents to unilateral choice-of-law rules would leave the choice of its application to the choice-of-law rules of the country whose law is alleged to apply.[5] The need to take foreign law into account has led either to the bilateralization of local choice-of-law rules or to the adoption of local choice-of-law rules which are bilateral by nature. Consequently each legal system can only rely on its own approach when called upon to determine which of its choice-of-law rules applies to a claim or defence alleging that either local or foreign law applies.

ii. Relationship – Factual or Legal

3. – It might be objected that a legal relationship exists only in virtue of some system of laws and that an attempt to ascertain the law applicable to a particular (factual) situation by purporting to link an existing legal relationship to an as yet unknown legal system which is to | apply to it anticipates the choice of law. Ideally only a set of facts must be connected with a legal system before a legal relationship can be said to exist, and if the facts disclose a foreign element the need for a choice of law arises.[6]

In practice such a need arises because – as the pleadings will show expressly or by implication – the plaintiff frames his claim in the light of a particular legal system and the defendant does the same in his reply.[7] A choice of law does not arise in the abstract but only in respect of a specific

---

[4] *Bartin*, Principes I 223–224.
[5] *Niboyet*, Traité no. 922, 929, 931bis, 937, 940, 944, 945bis.
[6] *Plaisant* 56.
[7] *Bartin*, Impossibilité 232; *Gothot* 444 n. 2 with literature; *Falconbridge*, Renvoi 374; *idem*, Characterization 242; *Ancel* 258–261 who speaks of *"projet de disposition"*.

claim or defence. Therefore the legal relationship, as alleged and introduced by the parties is rightly regarded as the object of choice-of-law rules (*infra* s. 4, 6).

iii. Operative Facts

4. – At this stage the problem known as one of characterization or qualification poses itself. Modern choice-of-law rules (as shown above) focus on broad categories of typical legal institutions, each of which embraces sets of rules of substantive private law.[8] They are limited in number but capable of expansion. They include status (including legitimacy, legitimation and illegitimacy), capacity, marriage (validity, nullity), divorce and judicial separation, maintenance, guardianship, adoption, corporations (creation, existence, powers, dissolution), contracts (types, conclusion, validity, interpretation, discharge, damages), quasi-contracts (*negotiorum gestio*, unjustifiable enrichment and restitution), interests in movables and immovables created *inter vivos* or on death (including trusts, testamentary and intestate succession), formalities, procedure and foreign judgments (recognition and enforcement). For want of a better expression these heads of typical legal situations will here be called "operative facts".[9]

iv. Connecting Factors

5. – These categories of typical legal institutions are connected with specific systems of domestic law by personal, territorial or voluntary links. They are limited too and consist of nationality, domicile, residence (including ordinary and habitual residence), place of contracting or acting, place of performance, situation of an object, the centre of a relationship, the intention of the parties and the locality of the court. Since choice-of-law rules are national rules, any reference to the law applicable is determined by the notions attributed to the connecting factors by the *lex fori* (*infra* s. 22 ss.). Only nationality and any connecting factors employed by foreign law when renvoi arises form exceptions.

---

[8] *De Nova*, Glancing at the Content of Substantive Rules under the Jurisdiction-Selecting Approach: 41 Law & Contemp. Prob. no. 2, 1–9(2) (1977); *Cavers*, Critique 178; *idem*, Process 309; *von Mehren*, The Contribution of Comparative Law to the Theory and Practice of Private International Law: 26 Am.J. Comp.L. (suppl.) 31–41 (33) (1978); KG 20 June 1930, IPRspr. 1930 no. 70 (p. 154).

[9] *Rabel*, Conflict I 47; *Falconbridge*, Essays 44. Other terms in current use are *Rahmen-* or *System-, Sammel-, Rechts-* or *Verweisungsbegriffe: Neuhaus* 103, 126; catégories de rattachement synthéthiques: Rigaux, Thééorie no. 157 p. 244; Gruppenbegriffe: Weber 123.

Normally a choice-of-law rule consists of a set of operative facts coupled with one connecting factor, but sometimes two connecting factors are employed which may function alternatively or, more rarely, cumulatively.[10]

v. Interpretation

6. *Technique of Interpretation.* – A claim alleging the existence of a legal relationship based on rules of private law of some legal system – whether local or foreign – and similarly a defence must be tested in the first place as to whether the law applies on which the claim or defence relies. The choice-of-law rules of the court exercising jurisdiction carry out this task. For this purpose it is necessary to determine within the range of which category featuring in the conflict-of-law rules of the forum the specific rule of private law falls which underlies the claim or defence.[11]

| 7. *Incongruent notions.* – The difficulty is that the conflicts rules are expressed in terms of general typical categories of private law, while claims and defences in any one case are based on specific rules of a particular system of private law which may differ to a greater or lesser degree from comparable rules in other legal systems, especially from those of the *forum*, where they may even be unknown. Notions such as contract, tort, succession, capacity to marry, employed as the operative facts of conflict rules may appear to reflect broadly the complex range of rules of private law of individual legal systems. But the line as to whether a specific claim based on domestic law is to be treated as contractual or as sounding in tort, as involving a problem of matrimonial property or of succession in the meaning of the operative facts of the choice-of-law rules of the forum is not always easy to draw.

8. *Mutual adjustment.* – The operative facts making up the conflict rules of the forum and the claim or defence presented in terms of rules of a particular legal system must each be analysed in terms of the other. For this process the usual techniques of interpretation – whether those adopted by the *lex fori* or by the *lex causae* – have proved deficient since the interaction of two different types of rules is in issue – one formulated to determine the applicable law for a broad range of rules emanating from all the world's legal systems, the other based on the domestic law of a specific legal system.

---

[10] Hague Convention on the Form of Testamentary Dispositions, of 5 Oct. 1961 art. 1 and the national legislation based on it; also the practice concerning the form of contracts. See *e.g.* GERMAN Introd.Law CC: Cumulative: art. 38. Alternative: art. 10 par. 2, 11 par. 1, 13, 14, 15 par. 1, 17 par. 3, 18 par. 1, 20 par. 1, 25 par. 2, 26 par. 1 (wills), 28 par. 1, 29 par. 2, 30 par. 2, 31. Swiss PIL: Cumulative: art. 77, 95 par. 3, 137 par. 2. Alternative: art. 44, 54, 61, 68, 73, 78, 82, 90, 91, 93, 94, 105, 106, 110, 119, 120, 122, 124 par. 1, 130, 135, 138, 139, 145 par. 1, 156, 187 par. 1. *Kahn* 100 ss.

[11] *Bartin*, Impossibilité 226; *idem*, Principes I 222.

9. *Functional approach.* – It follows that the operative facts of the choice-of-law rules of the forum must seek to cover disparate types of rules of private law existing in other legal systems.[12] They must therefore be interpreted broadly.[13] At the same time rules of domestic private law must be identified by ascertaining their function in their *own* legal systems and not by their formal description or systematization. This process, known as characterization or qualification, relies both on the *lex fori* and the alleged *lex causae* in order to ascertain the applicable law in the light of each other.

vi. Technique of Interpretation

10. – It follows that reliance on the law of a particular country by the parties and by the court seized of the dispute occurs during two stages of the proceedings.[14] During the first stage the court is concerned with ascertaining which choice-of-law rule of its own system of private international law is activated. For this purpose it must not only consider the facts but also, since the matter before it is a legal relationship (*Rechtsverhältnis*), the rule or set of rules (either of the *lex fori* or of some system of foreign law) on which a party relies.[15]

The operation of the choice-of-law rule thus ascertained may or may not result in the application of the law alleged by a party to govern the case. At this second stage only the search for the law found applicable to the facts of the case concerns the court. It is irrelevant that in the courts of the country the law of which has been found to apply a different process of characterization would have attracted the operation of a different choice-of-law rule.[16] This aspect has already been taken into consideration by the forum during the first stage of the proceedings when it determined which law applies.

If only a factual situation were the object of the application of the choice-of-law rules of the forum by applying the private law notions of the *lex fori*, the need to modify their effect by taking also into consideration those of the *lex causae* thus ascertained might justify a duplication of the process of characterization (secondary characterization: *infra* s. 18).

---

[12] *Rabel*, Qualifikation 249 ss.

[13] *E.g.* RG 6 July 1934, RGZ 145, 121; LG Berlin 13 June 1989, IPRspr. 1989 no. 216, p. 485.

[14] *Batiffol and Lagarde* no. 294 p. 480; *Falconbridge,* Conflict 218; *idem*, Renvoi 371; *idem*, Characterization 236–237; *Despagnet*, Des conflits de lois relatifs à la qualification des rapports juridiques: Clunet 1898, 253–273 (258).

[15] See *supra* s. 4, 6. *Wengler*, Réflexions 667, 687.

[16] See *infra* s. 18. *Grundmann*, Qualifikation gegen die Sachnorm (Munich 1985); Heyn, Die „Doppel-" und „Mehrfachqualifikationen" im I.P.R. (Arbeiten zur Rechtsvergleichung no. 128) (Frankfurt a.M. 1986); *Allarousse*, A Comparative Approach to the Conflict of Characterization on Private International Law: 23 Case W.Res.J.Int.L 479 – 516 (1991). Were not available.

vii. Doctrinal Origins and Developments

11. *Introduction.* – The problem of characterization was first discussed by *Kahn* and *Bartin*, followed by many others, among whom *Despagnet, M. Wolff, Rabel, Beckett, Falconbridge* and *Robertson* figure prominently. By now the literature is enormous, allowing an entire volume to be devoted to an exposition of the various views expressed by writers.[17] Given that the problem of characterization is one of interaction|between the choice-of-law rules of the forum and a claim or defence conceived expressly or implicitly in terms of the substantive law of a particular legal system, it is not surprising that two principal and one subsidiary solution have been put forward. An autonomous solution is only indicated if the operative facts of the choice-of-law rule are based on an international convention.[18]

12. *Characterization by the lex fori.* – In the first place characterization according to the notions of private law of the *lex fori* has been advocated by what seems to be the main body of writers[19] and practice.[20] In so doing the court is applying its own notion of substantive law indirectly only by seeking to fit the claim into its scheme of typical categories of private law as it understands them in the light of its own notions of private law. The claim is treated as a set of facts expressed in terms of some legal system, and the operative facts, although interpreted sufficiently broadly to accommodate claims raising an issue of foreign law, are interpreted in the light of the legal notions of the domestic law of the forum.

An exception is recognized in some legal systems when interests in immovables or movables are concerned. The *lex situs* determines whether an interest in an asset is an interest in an immovable or movable.

13. *Characterization by the lex causae.* – In the second place characterization according to the *lex causae*, the applicable law, has been advocated by a few writers, notably *Despagnet*[21] and *Martin Wolff*.[22] It could have been formulated shortly after *Despagnet*'s article had appeared in response *inter*

---

[17] *Weber*; see also *von Overbeck* 90–126; *Lehmann* 534; *Vitta* 302–330.

[18] *Jayme*, Wandel 529–544; *Lagarde*, Observations sur l'articulation des questions de statut personnel et des questions alimentaires dans l'application des conventions de droit international privé: Mélanges Alfred E. von Overbeck (Fribourg 1990) 511–528.

[19] E.g., *Batiffol and Lagarde* no. 292, 293; *Kropholler* § 16 I; *Soergel and Siebert (-Kegel)* no. 65 preceding art. 7; *Vitta* 314; *Dicey and Morris (-Collins a.o.)* 36.

[20] FRANCE: Cass.civ. 22 June 1955, D.S. 1956, 73, J.C.P. 1955.II.8928, Rev.crit.d.i.p. 1955, 723; Cass.civ. 15 May 1963, Clunet 1963, 996 note *Malaurie*; Cour Paris 7 July 1954, Clunet 1955, 636 (642), Rev.crit.d.i.p. 1954, 552 (559), Gaz.Pal. 1954.2367. GERMANY: KG 22 Dec. 1936, JW 1937, 1947, IPRspr. 1935–1944 no. 220 p. 449; OLG Köln 11 Dec. 1991, IPRspr. 1992 no. 53 p. 110. SWITZERLAND: BG 29 Jan. 1970, BGE 96 II 79 (88); BG 22 March 1973, BGE 99 II 21 (24).

[21] *Supra* n. 14 at 261.

[22] *Selb, passim.*

alia to an ENGLISH judgment. Following the *lex fori* this characterized the question of parental consent to marriage as pertaining to form in all circumstances, thus attracting the operation of the *lex loci actus,* when according to the *lex causae* (the personal law) it would have been regarded as pertaining to capacity to marry.[23]

14. *Critique.* – It had already been questioned[24] how the *lex causae,* said to determine the characterization of an issue, can control the selection of the appropriate operative facts of a choice-of-law rule which is to determine in the first place the law which is to be the *lex causae.* The answer offered by *M. Wolff* was that "every rule takes its classification from the legal system *to which it belongs".*[25] In short, the applicable law determines the characterization of an individual rule, and a set of operative facts, part of the forum's choice-of-law rule, which normally create the problem, is not called in aid. Therefore *Wolff* offered the following reformulated choice-of-law rule as a prototype: "When a person dies the court applies all those rules prevailing at his last domicile which according to the law of that domicile are characterized as part of the law of inheritance".[26]

15. *A new "seat" theory.* – This formulation represents in effect a return to the quest for the "seat" of the relationship (in this case succession).[27] However before leaving it to the law of the last domicile of the deceased – the law of the seat – to decide whether a question of succession is involved, the *forum* decides itself whether the law of the last domicile applies because a matter of succession is involved and not (let us say) because a matter of community property is at stake. In other words the *lex causae's* characterization only operates indirectly after the *lex fori's* characterization has led to the reference to the *lex causae* itself as the law governing the succession. In fact a situation of *primary* and *secondary* characterization is brought into existence.

M. Wolff's suggestion can only succeed if *either dépeçage* is abolished and a single connecting factor (seat) determines with general effect all cases containing an international element *or* if every country's conflict rules are | unilateral only, as *Niboyet*[28] and *Gothot*[29] advocated.

16. *Critique.* – Even then the dilemma is not avoided, as the example set out below shows: Supposing *M. Wolff's* formulation concerning the characterization of the law of the deceased's last domicile is adopted by country A, and country B has a rule

---

[23] See *infra* s. 27. *Ogden v. Ogden,* [1908] P. 46.

[24] *Von Bar, C. L.* 167; see also *Raape* 519.

[25] *Wolff, M.,* PIL § 144 p. 154 (emphasis supplied); *Gothot* 3 with literature at 4 n. 2, 420.

[26] *Wolff,* M., PIL § 144 p. 156.

[27] *Gothot* 34, 419.

[28] *Niboyet,* Traité no. 959, 960, also 958bis.

[29] *Gothot* 412, 413, 438–444.

"when two persons have married the court applies all those rules prevailing at their first marital domicile which according to those rules prevailing at their first marital domicile are characterized as parts of the law of the matrimonial property regime,"

the forum elsewhere is once again faced with the problem which first inspired *Bartin* on noticing the conflict presented by the *Bartholo*case.[30] Gaps and overlaps may occur once again as a result of positive and negative characterization of rules (*infra* s. 17).

17. *Analysis – The problem.* – The problem discussed here takes its origin from two facts: firstly that the same formal description of a rule may conceal different functions in different legal systems and secondly that as a result of the universally followed technique of *dépeçage*, separate legal aspects of a case may be governed by different laws.

The different functions of the same rule can be illustrated by the following examples: consent to marry may constitute a formality or an aspect of capacity, the revocation of a will by a subsequent marriage or the continuation of a community property regime by a surviving spouse with statutory successors upon the death of the other spouse may concern succession or matrimonial property relations, the prohibition of gifts between spouses may concern capacity or matrimonial property.

18. *Analysis – Renvoi of characterizations.* – By characterizing a claim or defence by the *lex fori* alone, but by subsequently taking into account the characterization by the *lex causae* (secondary characterization) no reference back is made to the *lex fori*, contrary to the view held in the past by some writers and courts[31] and revived in the form of a *renvoi des qualifications* (*infra* subch. II). The essential feature of a reference back – a different connecting factor attached to *the same substantive issue* by the choice-of-law rules of the *lex causae* – is missing. Secondary characterization merely invites the forum to reconsider its previous characterization, an invitation which the forum accepted at the stage of selecting the proper choice-of-law rule after taking into account the claim brought in the light of a particular legal system (*supra* s. 3).

19. *The compromise: functional and teleological analysis.* – In the third place characterization based on the comparative method has been advocated increasingly in more recent times by what has been called the third school.[32] The operative facts of the *lex fori* must be interpreted broadly. Thus

---

[30] *Niederer* 243.

[31] *Kahn* I 29; see the discussion by *Rabel*, Qualifikation 263 ss.

[32] For a survey see *Zweigert* 42 ss. and see *Beckett* 54–60; *von Steiger*, Die Bestimmung der Rechtsfrage im internationalen Privatrecht (Bern 1937); *Niederer; Wigny*, Remarques sur le problème des qualifications: Rev.crit.d.i.p. 1936, 392–429 (426 ss.); *Kropholler* § 16 II 2 at p. 108; § 17 p. 110–113; *Cheshire and North* 45; *Dicey and Morris (-Collins a.o.)* 44; *Ancel* 251, 254, 258–261, 263.

the notion of contract is not confined to those agreements only which figure technically as enforceable agreements according to the *lex fori*.[33] Similarly, in order to be fitted into one of the types of operative facts of the *lex fori*, the claim or defence expressed in terms of a legal relationship according to some systems of domestic private law must not be strictly interpreted in accordance with the latter's technical notions but in the light of its function and purpose within its own legal system.[34] This approach underlies the exposition of the theory and practice of characterization attempted here.

20. *Statutory attempts.* – Characterization according to the *lex fori* is favoured by AUSTRIA,[35] EGYPT (CC art. 10), HUNGARY,[36] PERU (CC art. 2055), QUEBEC,[37] RUMANIA[38] and SPAIN (CC art. 12 par. 1). Characterization of immovables and movables according to the *lex situs* is sanctioned by QUEBEC[39] and BRAZIL (CC art. 8). Both HUNGARY[40] and QUEBEC[41] require in|stitutions which are unknown or known under a different name to be taken into consideration. The important fact must be noted that PORTUGAL[42] and YUGOSLAVIA[43] attach significance to the substance and function of a rule of foreign law referred to by the operative facts of the conflict rule of the forum in order to determine whether it is covered by the latter or by another provision.

The AUSTRIAN text requiring that foreign law is to be applied as it is in its original sphere of operation is probably limited to its interpretation and does not extend to its characterization;[44] the same applies to the PERUVIAN provision.

For the purpose of characterizing an issue as sounding in tort, ENGLISH law refers expressly to the *lex fori*.[45] Furthermore, if foreign law applies in ENGLISH proceedings, the limitation rules of that law apply, unless English law is also applicable, thus attributing a substantive and not a procedural character to foreign limitation rules.[46]

---

[33] *Re Bonacina*, [1912] 2 Ch. 394 (C.A.): contract; RG 13 Dec. 1929, IPRspr. 1930 no. 8 p. 22.

[34] SWISS BG 29 Jan. 1970, BGE 96 II 79: trust; FRANCE: Cour Paris 10 Jan. 1970, D. S. 1972.J.122, Rev.crit.d.i.p. 1971, 525, Clunet 1973, 207. GERMANY: OLG Hamburg 2 March 1979, IPRspr. 1979 no. 55 p. 189; *Wengler* 687.

[35] PIL § 3.

[36] Decree-Law no. 13/1979 art. 3 par. 1; Clunet 1980, 636.

[37] CC (1991) art. 3078 par. 1; see Rev.crit.d.i.p. 1992, 574 (591).

[38] Law no. 105 art. 3.

[39] CC art. 3078 par. 1 sent. 2; see *supra* n. 37.

[40] Decree-Law no. 13/1979 art. 3 par. 2.

[41] CC art. 3078 par. 2; see *supra* n. 37.

[42] Decree-Law no. 47344 art. 15, ZfRV 1970, 114–135.

[43] PIL art. 9.

[44] *Beitzke*, Neues Oesterreichisches Kollisionsrecht: RabelsZ 43 (1979) 244–276 (250).

[45] Private International Law (Miscellaneous Provisions) Act 1995 s. 9 (2).

[46] Foreign Limitation Periods Act 1984 s. 1.

C. Conclusions

21. – Today a fair amount of consensus seems to exist on two basic problems: firstly in facing the need to select a choice-of-law rule to cover the issue before the court involving a foreign element, a legal relationship, and not a set of facts, comes up for consideration.[47]

Secondly, in characterizing the legal relationship underlying the claim or defence before the court, not its technical connotation but its function and purpose is the object of the inquiry.[48] In the words of the GERMAN Federal Supreme Court:

"The subsumption of these rules [*i. e.* DUTCH CC art. 992 then in force] must be made in accordance with German law. In this connection the following principles of interpretation must be observed: the rules of foreign law must be examined with a view to their meaning and purpose, they must be analysed from the standpoint of foreign law and must be compared with the institutions of the German legal order. On the basis of this knowledge they must be subsumed by the German rules of private international law, the characteristics of which are shaped by the notions and definitions of German law."[49]

In the words of two GERMAN courts the nature and purpose of the rule,[50] the direct effects and not the classification[51] are determining.

The same approach can be observed in the PORTUGUESE legislation which provides: "A reference to a law encompasses only those rules which by their substance and function attributed to that law pertain to the sphere of the institution envisaged by the conflicts rule" (CC art. 15).

---

[47] *Kahn* I 92, 95; *Bartin*, Impossibilité 227, 232, 236, 733; *Rabel*, Qualifikation 243, 245; *Raape* 521.

[48] *Kahn* I 31, 72–73, 112, 119, 241; *Bartin*, Impossibilité 235 ss., 240, 241, 244, 252; *idem*, Principes I 224; *Lewald*, Règles 10–11, 77; *Batiffol and Lagarde* no. 294 p. 480.

[49] BGH 12 Jan. 1967, IPRspr. 1966–1967 no. 19 p. 64, NJW 1967, 1177; see also BGH 19 Dec. 1958, BGHZ 29, 137 (139), IPRspr. 1958–1959 no. 12 p. 389; RG 11 April 1940, RGZ 163, 367, IPRspr. 1935–1944 no. 233; also – 12 Nov. 1932, RGZ 138, 243; – 5 July 1934, RGZ 145, 85; – 6 July 1934, RGZ 145, 121, IPRspr. 1934 no. 29; BFH 8 June 1988, IPRspr. 1988 no. 134 p. 279; also – 7 May 1986, *ibidem* 1986 no. 112; – 20 July 1960, *ibidem* 1960 no. 70; OLG Hamm 25 May 1992, *ibidem* 1992 no. 100; OLG Hamm 3 Sept. 1973, *ibidem* 1973 no. 50 p. 125. For ENGLAND perhaps also *Macmillan v. Bishopsgate Investment Trust*, [1996] 1 W.L.R. 387 (399(c)), [1996] 1 All E.R. 585 (589(d – f), 596(e), 604(a – e)) (C.A.).

[50] RG 6 July 1934, preceding note; also *Ancel* 541, 542 to Cour Paris 3 March 1994, *infra* n. 195.

[51] OLG Hamburg 13 Jan. 1932, IPRspr. 1932 no. 28, JW 1932, 3823 note *Siebert*.

| II. Practice

A. Scheme of the Investigation

22. – An examination of the judicial practice in a number of countries must distinguish according as the process of characterization was based on the legal notions of the *lex fori*, the *lex causae* or on a combination of the notions of the *lex fori* and a functional analysis of the law pleaded by the parties. This examination will produce more instructive results if it is focused on the test whether the claim or the defence in a particular dispute

(i) is identical in form and in substance with similar claims or defences forming part of the *lex fori* (*infra* s. 23 – 26);

(ii) corresponds in form to a similar claim according to the *lex fori*, but the formal similarity conceals a material difference (*infra* s. 27–33);

(iii) differs in form from that under the *lex fori*, but is the same in substance (*infra* s. 34–35);

(iv) is unknown in substance and in form by the *lex fori* (*infra* s. 37–42);

(v) is known in substance and in form by the *lex fori* but unknown by the *lex causae* (*infra* s. 43–46);

(vi) results in the application of the same law whichever of any two choice-of-law rules of the *lex fori* is applied, no matter which of several characterizations is applied (*infra* s. 47);

(vii) differs in substance according as the characterization of the *lex fori* or the *lex causae* is followed, leading to gaps and overlaps (*infra* s. 48–58); but calls for exceptions in the case of renvoi (*infra* s. 50), movables and immovables (*infra* s. 51–54), and preliminary questions (*infra* s. 55–58);

(viii) relies on characterization by the *lex causae* (*infra* s. 59–61);

(ix) is presented before an International Tribunal (*infra* s. 65–67).

B. Typical Situations – Categories

i. Form and Substance Identical

23. *Marriage formalities.* – If the claim or the defence is identical in form and substance with that in force by the *lex fori*, only the application of a single choice-of-law rule of the *lex fori* is in issue. An example relying upon legal provisions no longer in force illustrates it clearly. A French national domiciled in France, of full age but under 30 years of age, married in England a French woman aged 22. According to FRENCH law as it then stood he was required to ask for his parents' consent (*acte respectueux*),[52] but failure to

---

[52] CC art. 154, now abrogated.

obtain it did not invalidate the marriage. By ENGLISH law no consent was required, but any consents, if necessary, would have been treated as pure formalities and governed by ENGLISH law as the *lex loci actus*, for ENGLISH law at that time did not distinguish between capacity to marry and formalities of marriage. The ENGLISH court applied the *lex loci actus* and held the marriage to be valid,[53] and so would have a French court if called upon to make a decision.[54]

24. *Interspousal – property, contract, tort.* – Claims between spouses to recover household furniture are characterized as concerning the effect of marriage[55] or maintenance[56] during the subsistence of a marriage and as concerning divorce during and after divorce proceedings.[57] The right to the matrimonial home also concerns maintenance both during cohabitation and after separation.[58]

The incapacity of a married woman, whether general or limited to standing surety for her husband,[59] may be counted as raising a question of the personal effects of marriage, or of matrimonial property relations or (infrequently) of contract. Good arguments may|be made out that the effect of marriage is involved.[60]

Similarly capacity or its lack to sue a spouse in tort is treated as relating to the effects of marriage.[61] Claims arising from a putative marriage are regarded as concerning the effects of marriage.[62]

A commercial partnership between spouses is by its nature more closely

---

[53] *Simonin v. Mallac* (1860), 2 Sw.&Tr. 67, 164 E.R. 917; *cf.* BELGIUM: Cass. 8 March 1963, Pas. 1963. I.754.

[54] *Ancel* 230; *Francescakis*, La théorie du renvoi (Paris 1958) no. 263 n. 1.

[55] OLG Celle 10 Sept. 1990, IPRspr. 1990 no. 89 p. 133; OLG Hamm 11 July 1989, *ibidem* 1989 no. 84 p. 183; OLG Stuttgart 10 April 1989, *ibidem* 1989 no. 85 p. 183; OLG Frankfurt 11 March 1988, *ibidem* 1988 no. 65 p. 135; also during separation (not maintenance): KG 5 April 1991, *ibidem* 1991 no. 146.

[56] As an alternative: OLG Celle, preceding note; OLG Koblenz 26 Nov. 1990, IPRspr. 1990 no. 115 p. 213 (also while living separately).

[57] OLG Hamm 27 May 1992, IPRspr. 1992 no. 101 p. 238.

[58] OLG Hamm 17 July 1992, IPRspr. 1992 no. 120; OLG Hamm 15 Nov. 1988, *ibidem* 1988 no. 90 p. 176; OLG Frankfurt 5 March 1991, *ibidem* 1991 no. 105 p. 196; OLG Düsseldorf 2 May 1990, *ibidem* 1990 no. 101 p. 193; OLG Koblenz 26 Nov. 1990, *ibidem* 1990 no. 115 p. 213.

[59] *Bank of Africa v. Cohen*, [1909] 2 Ch. 129 (C.A.).

[60] Cour Chambéry 19 Nov. 1877, S. 1878.2.5, Clunet 1878, 168.

[61] *Haumschild v. Continental Casualty* Co., 95 N.W. 2d 814 (Wis. S.Ct. 1959).

[62] Cass. 6 March 1956, J.C.P. 1956.II.9549 on appeal from Cour Paris 15 Feb. 1950, Clunet 1951, 190; Trib.civ. Seine 22 Dec. 1948, Rev.crit.d.i.p. 1949, 100; Cass. 8 Feb. 1963, J.C.P. 1964.II.13470 on appeal from Cour Paris 16 Dec. 1959, J.C.P. 1960.II. 11460.

identified with contract than with the effects of marriage both in GER-MAN[63] and ITALIAN law.[64]

25. *Succession – jus regale – commorientes.* – Claims by the Austrian fiscus and by the Crown in Great Britain to the assets in England of a *de cuius* who died domiciled in Austria intestate and without next of kin both assert a *jus regale.* In England that of the Crown in England prevails.[65]

In 1940 a mother and her daughter were killed in an air raid. They were German refugees who according to ENGLISH private international law were still domiciled in Germany. Therefore the succession to their movable property was governed by German law. In order to determine the beneficiary, two different rules had to be taken into account. According to GERMAN CC § 20[66] if two persons perished in the same accident they are deemed to have died contemporaneously. According to the ENGLISH Law of Property Act, 1925 (c. 20) s. 184, if it is uncertain which of them survived the other the younger is deemed to have survived the elder. If both provisions concerned substance, the German rule had to prevail; if the English rule was procedural it could exclude the German substantive rule.

An examination of the nature and functions of the respective provisions showed that they both contained irrebuttable presumptions (*praesumptiones juris et de jure*). Irrebuttable presumptions represent rules of substantive law. In the contest between German and English law of the same character, the German rule applied.[67]

26. *Summary.* – In all these cases either only the application of a single choice-of-law rule was in issue or the connecting factors of two choice-of-law rules were identical.

ii. Form Identical, Substance Different

a. Marriage – Form or Substance

27. – If the claim or defence is identical in form with a similar claim or defence under the *lex fori*, but is materially different, two choice-of-law rules of the *lex fori* with different connecting factors may lead to different results according as one or the other is followed.

---

[63] *Jayme*, Problemi 221–223; GERMAN CC § 1356; BGH 20 Dec. 1952, NJW 1953, 418; BVerfG 3 Sept. 1959, NJW 1959, 2277; BGH 28 Oct. 1959, NJW 1960, 428; but see RG 11 April 1940, RGZ 163, 367, IPRspr. 1935–1944 no. 223.

[64] *Communione di fatto* (factual community): Cass. 22 June 1932, Giur.it. 1933 I 1, 123.

[65] *Infra* s. 61; *Re Barnett's Trusts*, [1902] 1 Ch. 847; *Re Musurus*, [1936] 2 All E.R. 1666 (P.D.), but see *Re Maldonado*, [1954] P. 223 (see also at *infra* n. 225).

[66] As it stood then; now Law on missing persons (*Verschollenheitsgesetz*) of 4 July 1939 (BGBl. III 401–6) § 11.

[67] *Re Cohn*, [1945] Ch. 5.

The most striking example is provided by the counterpart of the first example given *supra* s. 23.

A French national, while under age (21 years at the relevant time), married in England an English woman without the consent of his parents, which was required by FRENCH law (CC art. 144), the law of his domicile. The marriage was void by FRENCH law on the ground of his incapacity to marry without it (CC art. 148). The ENGLISH court regarded every prescribed parental consent as a formality since in ENGLISH law it can be replaced on application by a court, and a marriage concluded without the required consent is valid nevertheless. Consequently it held the marriage to be valid. As a result the woman was treated as lawfully married in England while the man was free to marry again after the marriage had been annulled in France.[68] In the absence of a functional characterization[69] of the FRENCH rule as concerning capacity, only recognition of the French nullity decree could restore the balance.[70]

The constellation whereby the forum, following its own characterization, holds a mar|riage valid in form, and at the same time on a counter petition following a foreign characterization, declares the marriage invalid in substance only appears to have occurred once.[71]

b. Wills – Form or Capacity

28. – A comparable situation was presented, up to the recent reform of DUTCH law, by the problem of a holograph will made in France by a Dutch national in accordance with local law. According to DUTCH CC art. 992 (now abrogated), Dutch nationals abroad could only make a will in notarial form attested by two witnesses; lack of capacity rendered a holograph will invalid. According to FRENCH law, the *lex loci actus*, such a will was valid in form. As a result the will was invalid in the NETHERLANDS, but valid in form in FRANCE.[72] However a functional analysis by one FRENCH court led the will to be held invalid in substance by analysing the purpose of this provision.[73]

Such a functional analysis may well conclude that the former DUTCH pro-

---

[68] *Ogden v. Ogden*, [1908] P. 46; for the same conclusion in SCOTLAND see *Bliersbach v. McEwen*, 1959 S.C. 43.

[69] See also *supra* s. 19.

[70] *De Massa v. De Massa*, [1939] 2 All E.R. 150 n. (P.D.); *Galene v. Galene*, [1939] P. 237.

[71] LG Salzburg 1 March 1974, ZfRV 1975, 48.

[72] See note *Niboyet*, Rev.d.i.p. 1928, 105 with cases; *idem*, Traité III no. 956 p. 363; Cour Orléans 4 Aug. 1859, S. 1860.2.37. For ITALY, see *Vitta* III 160, 161 n. 189.

[73] Trib.civ. Seine 13 Aug. 1903, Clunet 1904, 166 (169), less clearly Trib.civ. Seine 10 Feb. 1927, Clunet 1928, 707, Rev.d.i.p. 1928, 101 (does not affect capacity, but prohibits a certain form). To the same effect: *Neuhaus* 148; *Lehmann* no. 92, 97. The former requirement of BELGIAN law that a claim can only be assigned by a public document, to be notified and accepted was held to concern substance and not form by OLG Hamburg 30 July 1934, IPRspr. 1934 no. 15.

vision aimed to ensure that reliable evidence is available to the Dutch authorities dealing with an estate of a Dutch national who had made a will abroad. If so, a question of formalities was envisaged; but in this case it might be asked why the provision is restricted to Dutch nationals, unlike the comparable provision of the FRENCH CC art. 999. However even so, the restriction imposed an incapacity. For the countries parties to the Hague Convention on the Form of Testamentary Dispositions of 5 Oct. 1961 drastic action has eliminated the problem; it provides that all limitations as to the forms of testamentary dispositions by reference to the age, nationality or other personal conditions of the testator shall be treated as matters of form (art. 5).

c. Limitation of Actions – Substance or Procedure

29. – What is believed to be the best known example, originated in Germany in 1882, and terminated in 1934. The GERMAN Supreme Court, faced with a contractual claim governed by the law of Tennessee and a plea that the time-limit for suing had expired, rejected the latter on the ground that according to TENNESSEE law statutes of limitation were procedural, and that procedure was governed by the *lex fori*, GERMAN law. Since the German law of procedure did not embrace limitation of actions, which was treated as touching substance, no time-limit whatever applied and perpetual liability ensued.[74] In 1934 this practice was reversed on the ground that the technical denomination of an institution according to the foreign *lex causae* was irrelevant.[75]

Firstly, reference to the foreign *lex causae* looks at the substance of foreign law and not its analytical denomination; secondly, despite its different denomination, the institutions of limitation of actions in GERMAN and ANGLO-AMERICAN law are functionally akin. Both include substantive as well as procedural elements. In GERMAN law, limitation of actions is also partly

---

[74] RG 23 Jan. 1882, RGZ 7, 21 (23); – 19 Oct. 1889, RGZ 24, 394; *cf.* – 19 Dec. 1922, RGZ 106, 82; but see – 8 May 1880, RGZ 2, 13; LG Berlin 24 Jan. 1930, IPRspr. 1930 no. 6; OLG Hamburg 13 Jan. 1932, *ibidem* 1932 no. 28, JW 1932, 3823 note *Siebert;* KG 5 Feb. 1934, IPRspr. 1934 no. 28; *Melchior*, Die Grundlagen des deutschen internationalen Privatrechts (Berlin and Leipzig 1932) 131 – 135.

[75] GERMANY: RG 6 July 1934, RGZ 145, 121, IPRspr. 1934 no. 29 p. 57; RG 20 March 1936, RGZ 151, 193 (201), IPRspr. 1935–1944 no. 701; RG 11 April 1940, RGZ 163, 367, IPRspr. 1935–1944 no. 223; BGH 10 Jan. 1958, IPRspr. 1958–1959 no. 37; BGH 9 June 1960, *ibidem* 1960–1961 no. 23; LG Bremen 10 May 1961, *ibidem* no. 50; OLG Hamburg 4 Jan. 1973, *ibidem* 1973 no. 27 p. 73; OLG München 27 March 1974, *ibidem* 1974 no. 26 p. 79.

The same approach prevails now in FRANCE: Cass.civ. 28 March 1960, Clunet 1961, 777, Rev.crit. d.i.p. 1960, 202; Cour Paris 13 March 1963, Rev.crit. d.i.p. 1963, 551; Trib.gr.inst. Seine 11 Feb. 1961, *ibidem* 1962, 741; Cass.civ. 21 April 1971, *ibidem* 1972, 74; Cour Paris 23 Jan. 1975, *ibidem* 1976, 97; Cass.civ. 7 June 1977, *ibidem* 1978, 119; Cass.civ. 8 Feb. 1983, Clunet 1984, 123.

procedural, for a remedy is withheld; in ANGLO-AMERICAN law the restriction imposed | upon a creditor affects also his substantive rights. No restitution is allowed, and securities are unaffected; but it is also procedural, for the period of limitation can be interrupted or suspended.[76]

The decision of the GERMAN Supreme Court in 1882 moved *Kahn*[77] to observe that reliance on a secondary characterization by TENNESSEE law had created a new type of renvoi which employed characterization by the *lex causae* rather than its use of a connecting factor different from that of the *lex fori*. Thereby *Kahn* anticipated the problem now known as *renvoi de qualifications* (*infra.* s. 50).

The test developed in GERMANY to determine whether a statute of limitations concerns substance or procedure found a similar expression in 1835 in England. In an action brought in ENGLAND on a promissory note governed by FRENCH law the defendant pleaded the French law of limitation of actions. In accordance with the distinction prevalent at the time (*supra* n. 77) the court considered whether by French law the contract had been extinguished altogether or whether only the remedy was barred. In the latter case, in the absence of evidence to the contrary,[78] English law applied on the ground that procedure was involved.[79]

The fact that in most countries statutes of limitation display a tendency to affect both rights and remedies without emphasizing the preponderance of one of them has rendered it more difficult to attribute to these statutes a particular effect.

It may perhaps be argued that the insistence in COMMON LAW countries on the procedural character of these statutes expresses a strict local policy in favour of a particular period of limitation. They apply exclusively as part of the *lex fori* and are spatially conditioned internal rules. By seeking to apply exclusively whenever the forum exercises jurisdiction they share a common feature with rules of procedure, but are not identical with the latter. Only a functional analysis can disclose whether they are of this nature. In the EURO-PEAN UNION the problem has been solved in form of a substantive characterization by the Rome Convention on the Law Applicable to Contractual Obligation art. 10 par. 1 *lit.* d. As a result the problem has ceased to exist in

---

[76] *Lipstein*, Chronique 417. GERMAN law before 1900 took a procedural approach: note *Siebert*, JW 1932, 3824; *Müller-Freienfels, Die Verjährung Englischer Wechsel vor Deutschen Gerichten*: Xenion. Festschrift J. Zepos II (Athens, Freiburg a.o. 1973) 491–534 (492 n. 4). Also FRENCH law: *Planiol and Ripert, Traité pratique* VIII (ed. 2 Paris 1950); *Michel, La prescription libératoire en droit international privé:* Rev.d.i.p. 1912, 302–330 (320).

[77] *Kahn* 106 n.

[78] *S.A. Métallurgique Prayon v. Koppel* (1933), 66 Sol.J. 800 (K.B.), but see now the Foreign Limitation Periods Act 1984 s. 1.

[79] *Huber v. Steiner* (1835), 2 Bing.N.C. 262, 132 E.R. 80, preceded by *British Linen Co. v. Drummond* (1830), 10 B.&C. 903, 109 E.R. 683.

the UNITED KINGDOM where the Foreign Limitation Periods Act 1984 declared all provisions dealing with limitation of actions to be substantive in character. SWISS law offers the same statutory answer (PIL art. 148). The Supreme Court of CANADA followed suit.[80]

d. External Manifestations – Form or Substance

30. *Greek orthodox marriages.* – The question whether a provision which requires a transaction to observe a certain external manifestation is one concerning formalities or substance has arisen in many spheres of law. When GREEK law[81] insisted on the conclusion of a marriage of orthodox Greek nationals to be celebrated by a Greek orthodox priest the fact that this requirement was treated in GREECE as one of substance affecting status was often disregarded abroad on the ground that it touched form and was governed by the *lex loci celebrationis.* A functional analysis will show that insistence on the sacramental character of marriage must rule out civil forms of celebration,[82] thus either attracting the personal law or restricting the range of form available to Greeks (*cf. supra* s. 28).

|31. *Contracts – in writing.* – The same method must be applied in determining whether FRENCH CC art. 1341[83] and ENGLISH Statute of Frauds s. 4[84] touch the form or the substance of a transaction.[85] Here the test must be whether the provision concerned seeks to protect a person against hasty action or seeks to perpetuate evidence or supports publicity.

When the FRENCH Law of 29 June 1935 art. 12 imposed a duty upon the vendor to include certain details in a contract of sale, the FRENCH Court of Cassation held that the requirement served to ensure certainty. The test was

---

[80] *Tolofson v. Jensen*, [1994] 3 Can. S. C. 1022, 120 D.L.R.4th 289; also Cour Paris 3 March 1994, Rev. crit.d.i.p. 1994, 532.

[81] CC art. 1367, abrogated on 5 April 1982.

[82] For an ambivalent view see *Wolff*, M., PIL § 151 p. 161. On the whole, literature and practice tended to characterize the provision as formal. For FRANCE, see *Batiffol and Lagarde* I no. 422; *Lehmann* no. 92; Cass.civ. 22 June 1955, D. 1956, 73, Rev.crit.d.i.p. 1955, 723, Clunet 1955, 682 with cases, J.C.P. 1955. II.8928. For a previous view to the contrary see Trib.civ. Seine 28 April 1906, Rev.d.i.p. 1906, 751; *idem* 25 Nov. 1907, *ibidem* 1908, 242 note *Niboyet*; see also note *Batiffol*, Rev.crit.d.i.p. 1955, 723 (725). For Germany, BGH 14 Dec. 1955, BGHZ 19, 266, IPRspr. 1955 no. 213 p. 586; OLG Frankfurt 23 Nov. 1970, *ibidem* 1970 no. 49 p. 135; OLG Köln 14. July 1976, *ibidem* 1976 no. 63 p. 204. swiss BG 29 March 1950, BGE 76 IV 109 (114 no. 3).

[83] KG 25 Oct. 1927, IPRspr. 1929 no. 7, JW 1929, 448; *Rabel*, Qualifikation 280; a similar problem is raised by RG 5 Nov. 1932, IPRspr. 1933 no. 20; BGH 23 Feb. 1983, *ibidem* 1983 no. 36 p. 102: notice of an assignment; substance or form.

[84] *Leroux v. Brown* (1852), 12 C.B. 801 (823), 138 E.R. 1119; later on Law of Property Act 1925 s. 40(1), now Law of Property (Miscellaneous Provisions) Act 1989 s. 2(1).

[85] Generally *Jayme*, Qualifikationsverweisung 93–106.

whether failure to observe it led to nullity (substance) or unenforceability (form).[86]

32. *Legitimation, interspousal gifts, procedural costs.* – Legitimation by acknowledgement according to ISLAMIC *Hanafi* law, unlike the same institution in CALIFORNIAN[87] and DUTCH law, does not introduce a man as the genetic father but constitutes a relationship akin to adoption open to an outsider[88] restricted, however, to the persons taking part in the process.[89]

The legal effect of gifts between spouses and their revocation occupied the attention of the FRENCH Court of Cassation. It regarded the question as one concerning the personal effects of marriage, *i.e.* the law of the common domicile of spouses of different nationality, which was FRENCH, and not as one touching matrimonial property relations, namely ENGLISH law alleged to have been chosen by the parties.[90] In favour of the first it may be argued that it serves to control any undue influence by one party on another,[91] while the second, in allowing a choice of law (at least according to FRENCH law) may encourage such a tendency. However, the effect of gifts between them upon the legitimate portion (*réserve*) of either party should also bring into consideration aspects of succession.[92]

A claim for an advance of costs made by the wife in proceedings against her husband was treated by a GERMAN court as concerning matrimonial property relations,[93] to be governed by Austrian law, although according to

[86] Cass.civ. 10 Dec. 1974, Clunet 1975, 542, Rev. crit.d.i.p. 1975,474,D.S. 1975 J.685,J.C.P. 1975.II.18249.

[87] *Cf* the ENGLISH and SCOTTISH decisions *Re Luck*, [1940] Ch. 864 (C.A.); *Kelly v. Marks*, 1974 S.L.T. 118 (Outer House): custody rights of grandparents.

[88] RG 12 Nov. 1932, RGZ 138, 243; KG 21 Oct. 1939, IPRspr. 1935–1944 no. 304 p. 637; BGH 14 Jan. 1971, BGHZ 55, 183 (193), IPRspr. 1971 no. 101 p. 310–312; AG Bonn 27 July 1988, IPRspr. 1988 no. 109 p. 214; OLG Köln 2 June 1986, *ibidem* 1986 no. 101; see also BGH 14 Jan. 1971, *ibidem* 1971 no. 101 p. 307; BGH 26 Oct. 1977, BGHZ 69, 387 (391), IPRspr. 1977 no. 98b p. 281; BVerwG 6 Dec. 1983, IPRspr. 1983 no. 79 p. 196.

[89] LG Tübingen 29 Sept. 1961, IPRspr. 1962–1963 no. 111; AG Hamburg 11 Jan. 1962, *ibidem* no. 112; LG Köln 25 May 1962, *ibidem* no. 114; AG Hamburg 19 April 1962, *ibidem* no. 121; AG Hamburg 25 March 1963, *ibidem* no. 120.

[90] Cass.civ. 15 Feb. 1966, Clunet 1967, 95; on appeal from Cour Paris 4 July 1963, Clunet 1964, 65, Rev.crit.d.i.p. 1963, 772; Cour Aix 17 May 1976, Rev.crit.d.i.p. 1977, 508; and see Cour Paris 27 May 1892, Clunet 1892, 940; Trib.civ. Seine 5 May 1900, *ibidem* 1901, 715 (old ITALIAN CC art. 1054); Cass.req. 15 March 1933, S. 1934.1.393.

[91] *Bartin*, Principes II 293, 215–216; KG 20 March 1939, IPRspr. 1935–1944 no. 215 p. 440 (GREEK law).

[92] Cass.req. 8 May 1894, D.P. 1894.1.358, Clunet 1894, 562; Cass.req. 7 May 1924, Rev.d.i.p. 1924, 206.

[93] OLG Dresden 16 March 1909, Annalen des Königlich Sächsischen Oberlandesgerichts 30 (1909) 321; *Lewald*, Privatrecht no. 133 p. 97, citing also KG 1 Oct. 1913, KGBl. 24 (1913) 120; LG Frankfurt II Sept. 1919, JW 1920, 168; book review *Lewald*, JW 1932, 2253; also *Rabel*, Qualifikation 274 ss.

AUSTRIAN law it sounded in maintenance. While the refusal of the GERMAN court to follow the characterization adopted by Austrian law is understandable it is difficult to regard a husband's obligation to finance his wife in an action against himself as covered by the regime of matrimonial property relations. It seems to be nearer in function to his obligation to support her[94] or to the personal effect of marriage.[95]

33. *Minor's and joint wills, effect of subsequent marriage.* – The provision of FRENCH CC art. 964 that a minor above 16 years of age can only dispose of his estate by will and is limited to one half of what a person of full age can leave raises | the question whether a matter of capacity or of succession is at stake.[96] Even if capacity is involved, its close and specific connection with succession identifies it with the latter.

The prohibition of joint wills to be found in some legal systems[97] once again raises the question whether substance or form is involved.[98] The practice is divided; both substance[99] and form[100] have found supporters. If the purpose of the rule should be to exclude undue influence – such wills occurring frequently among spouses – a substantive concern of succession underlies it.[101]

A contract between spouses included in a marriage settlement to leave their assets on death to the surviving spouse (*Erbvertrag*) may affect a legitimate portion and the future liberty of disposition. It concerns succession, not matrimonial property relations.[102]

If the effect of a subsequent marriage upon a previous will is in issue – as it can in ENGLISH law[103] – and the will becomes invalid thereby, the nature and

---

[94] OLG Düsseldorf 30 May 1969, IPRspr. 1968–1969 no. 81 b p. 174.

[95] OLG Düsseldorf 21 Jan. 1974, IPRspr. 1974 no. 54 p. 154, *in casu* identical with the law governing maintenance.

[96] Trib.civ. Nice 28 Dec. 1903, Clunet 1904, 713; *Rabel*, Qualifikation 266.

[97] FRENCH CC art. 968; ITALIAN CC art. 589, 635; but see GERMAN CC § 2265; AUSTRIAN CC § 1248.

[98] See *Rabel*, Qualifikation 259; *Fragistas*, Zur Testamentsform im internationalen Privatrecht: RabelsZ 4 (1930) 930–936; *Jayme*, Problemi 222 n. 16.

[99] GERMANY: BayObLG 13 Dec. 1957, IPRspr. 1956–1957 no. 149 p. 489; OLG Frankfurt 17 May 1985, *ibidem* 1985 no. 116 p. 299 with literature. Italy: Cass. 19 Dec. 1939, Rep. Foro it. 1949 v. Testamento no. 6.

[100] Cour Toulouse 15 May 1850, S. 1850.2.259; Cour Caen 22 May 1850, S. 1852.2.529; Trib.civ. Seine 23 Dec. 1882, Clunet 1882, 322; Trib.gr.inst. Paris 24 April 1980, Rev.crit.d.i.p. 1982, 684; for the conflicting older ITALIAN practice see *Vitta* III 158 n. 178, 180.

[101] Cass. 12 Nov. 1896, Giur.it. 1897 I 1,158.

[102] OLG Karlsruhe 20 March 1931, IPRspr. 1931 no. 96 p. 188; BayObLG 14 May 1981, *ibidem* 1981 no. 130 p. 308; *Rabel*, Qualifikation 284.

[103] Law of Property Act 1925 s. 177; Administration of Justice Act 1982 s. 18, esp. s. 18(3).

function of the ENGLISH rule provides the answer. At the time when the rule was formulated a woman upon marriage lost title to her movable property to her husband, who also retained the use of her immovables. Clearly the will is revoked as a result of the new matrimonial property regime, and the fact that a will is affected does not raise a question of succession.[104]

Identity in form, but difference in substance of the characterization of a claim in two legal systems has not created an obstacle to reconciling the functionally different foreign rule with the operative facts of the *lex fori* following an analysis of the function of the foreign rule. Only once the characterization by the *lex causae* was adopted, to be rejected later on (*supra* n. 86).

iii. Different in Form, Same in Substance

34. *Contract, tort and property.* – Where a claim brought for breach of promise to marry sounds in tort according to the *lex fori* and in contract according to the *lex causae* but the effect is the same in both, the quandary has stimulated various solutions. A cumulation or alternative application of the personal laws of the parties[105] or the application of the personal law of the defendant has been suggested where the particular issue concerns a breach of promise, on the ground that it is a matter of family law.[106]

Similarly a claim based on a contract in *favorem tertii* or with *Schutzwirkung für Dritte* (contracts with protective effects for third parties) may have as its counterpart a claim in tort for a breach of duty of care.[107] If the practice of the courts outlined above (s. 23–33) is followed, the technical denomination according to the foreign law is to be disregarded. What matters is that the same facts result in an action for damages, only the degree of fault, amount of damages[108] and the rules of prescription may differ.[109] Both legal

---

[104] *Re Martin, Loustalan v. Loustalan,* [1900] P. 211.

[105] *Lewald*, Privatrecht § 103 with cases; *Fedozzi*, Diritto Internazionale Privato (ed. 2 Padua 1939) 403; note *Cansacchi* to Trib. Turin 27 July 1948, Giur.it. 1949 I 2, 273 (276 n. 3); *Rabel*, Conflict II 284 ss.

[106] *Rigaux* no. 471; LG Frankfurt 9 May 1978, IPRspr. 1978 no. 43 and see OLG Frankfurt 5 July 1923, *ibidem* 1930 no. 62 p. 140; LG Düsseldorf 18 April 1967, *ibidem* 1966–1967 no. 56, Clunet 1971, 599; but see BGH 21 Nov. 1958, IPRspr. 1958–1959 no. 110, NJW 1959, 1032, note *Luderitz*.

[107] *White v. Jones,* [1995] 2 A.C. 207 (H.L.) and see generally note *Foyer* to Cass.civ. 18 Oct. 1989, Rev. crit.d.i.p. 1990, 712 (717 ss.).

[108] Trib.gr.inst. Chambéry 14 Dec. 1965, Clunet 1966, 110, Rev.crit.d.i.p. 1967, 110.

[109] ENGLAND: *Kremezi v. Ridgway,* [1949] 1 All E.R. 662 (663, 664) (K.B.), 26 Brit.YBInt.L. 483 (1949). GERMANY: LG Hamburg 29 Oct. 1975, IPRspr. 1976 no. 125 a p. 367; France: Cass.civ. 18 Oct. 1989, Clunet 1990, 415 (418), Rev.crit.d.i.p. 1990, 718 note *Foyer*.

institutions seek to enforce mutual promises focusing either on its initiation | or its breach. The dividing line is fluid,[110] but there is no gap.[111]

Culpa in contrahendo[112] may perhaps be treated similarly,[113] although the element of mutuality is less prominent here, and its occurrence has been identified as a unilateral breach of a duty of care in ENGLISH law.[114]

When referred to German law as the law applicable under the Hague Convention on the International Sale of Goods of 15 June 1955, the FRENCH Court of Cassation did not hesitate to include in it a claim for *violation positive du contrat* (*positive Vertragsverletzung*; breach of contract by faulty performance), although the claim might have been treated in FRANCE as sounding in tort. The basis of mutuality and the period of limitation were the same.[115]

Product liability sounds both in contract and in tort when restricted to the original parties to the bargain but the bond of mutuality emphasizes the contractual element.[116] It is therefore not surprising that the Hague Convention on Products Liability of 2 Oct. 1973 eliminated from its sphere the parties to the original bargain (art. 12 par. 2). The right of third parties to sue, construed as arising from a contract in favour of third parties or as flowing from a culpable infliction of damage, is functionally ambivalent, but any bond of mutuality is artificial.[117]

A claim for damages due to the loss of the services of a spouse which is treated the same, whether sounding in tort or as concerned with the effect of

---

[110] EuCJ 27 Sept. 1988 no. 189/87 (*Kalfelis v. Bankhaus Schroeder*), ECRep. 1988, 5565 (5585), Clunet 1989, 460.

[111] Contra *Jayme*, Qualifikationsverweisung 99; note *Dayant* to Cour Paris 23 Jan. 1975, Rev.crit. d.i.p. 1976, 97 (104 ss).

[112] *Keller a.o.* (*-Heini*), Kommentar zum Bundesgesetz über das internationale Privatrecht (IPRG) vom 1. Januar 1989 (Zürich 1993) art. 132–142 p. 1126; esp. *Stoll*, Tatbestände und Funktionen der Haftung für culpa in contrahendo: Festschrift Ernst von Caemmerer (Tübingen 1978) 435–474 (461); and see generally *Kessler and Fine*, Culpa in Contrahendo. Bargaining in Good Faith and Freedom of Contract. A comparative study: 77 Harv.L.Rev. 401–449 (1963–1964); *Nirk*, Rechtsvergleichendes zur Haftung für culpa in contrahendo: RabelsZ 18 (1953) 310–355; *Schmidt*, La sanction de la faute précontractuelle: Rev.trim.dr.civ. 1974, 46–73; *Piotet*, Nature et modalité de la responsabilité précontractuelle: ZSR 116 (1975) 253–270.

[113] LG Hamburg 29 Oct. 1975, IPRspr. 1976 no. 125 a p. 368; *Reithmann and Martiny* (*-Martiny*), Internationales Vertragsrecht (ed. 4 Cologne 1988) no. 190–191 with cases, but the practice cited there appears to have led to subsequent contracts.

[114] *Esso Petroleum v. Mardon*, [1976] Q.B. 801 (C.A.); *Ward v. Tesco*, [1976] 1 W.L.R. 810 (C.A.); it was, however, followed by a contract.

[115] FRANCE: Cass.civ. 18 Oct. 1989, Clunet 1990, 415 (418), Rev.crit.d.i.p. 1990, 712, 715 (717) note Foyer; *Viney*, La responsabilité. Conditions (Paris 1982) 193 ss. See also Germany: LG Hamburg 29 Oct. 1975, *supra* n. 113.

[116] OLG Köln 11 Dec. 1991, IPRspr. 1992 no. 53 p. 110.

[117] LG Berlin 13 June 1979, IPRspr. 1979 no. 216 p. 486.

marriage (as it is under the *lex causae*, AUSTRIAN law) allows the *lex fori* to follow its own interpretation.[118]

A GERMAN *Eigentumsvorbehalt* (reservation of title) and a FRENCH *pacte commissoire* involve the same legal rights,[119] but in a *conflit mobile* the GERMAN right has at best a contractual effect in FRANCE between the parties,[120] although its proprietary effects are acknowledged in bankruptcy[121] and in *protective* insolvency[122] proceedings.

A claim to *prestations compensatoires* (FRENCH CC art. 270) arising out of divorce proceedings in FRANCE has been characterized as concerning matrimonial property relations by a GERMAN court[123] and as pertaining to maintenance by the EUROPEAN COMMUNITY court.[124]

| 35. *Social payments – novel succession right.* – FRENCH *allocations familiales*, being social payments, have their counterpart in GERMAN *Kindergeld* (children's aid) in the meaning of the Federal Law on children's benefits.[125]

When special legislation granting "premature hereditary compensation" (*vorzeitiger Erbausgleich*, CC § 1934d) was in force for the benefit of illegitimate offspring, it was regarded as concerning succession and not status or maintenance, but a renvoi by the law governing the father's potential succession to GERMAN law resulted in the application of German law, whatever the characterization.[126]

JERSEY proceedings *en disastre* which involve an insolvent estate but exclude immovable property and do not discharge the debtor from unreco-

---

[118] BGH 27 April 1976, IPRspr. 1976 no. 37 p. 119.

[119] Cass.civ. 28 March 1934, D.P. 1934.1.151 note *Vandamme*; Cass.civ. 22 Oct. 1934, S. 1935.1.337 note *Esmein; Breitenstein*, Der Eigentumsvorbehalt im französischen Recht: RIW 1980, 680–691; *Terré and Simler*, Les biens (ed. 4 Paris 1992) no. 391 with literature.

[120] Cass.civ. 8 July 1969, Clunet 1970, 916 (917–919) note *Derruppé*, J.C.P. 1970.II.16182 note *Gaudemet-Tallon*; also Cass.req. 24 May 1933, D.H. 1933, 378, S. 1935.1.257, Rev.crit.d.i.p. 1934, 142, Clunet 1935, 381; Trib.civ. Strasbourg 19 June 1957, Rev. crit.d.i.p. 1959, 95; see also *Spellenberg*, Eigentumsvorbehalt in Frankreich: ZfRV 1994, 105–118; *Holzner*, Zur Sicherungszession im I.P.R.: *ibidem* 134–137.

[121] Law no. 80–335 art. 1; *Loussouarn*, Les conflits de lois en matière de réserve de propriété: Trav.-Com.fr.d.i.p. 1983–1984, 91–120 (102–106); *Mayer*, Les conflits de lois en matière de réserve de propriété: J.C.P. 1981.I.3019.

[122] Law no. 85–98 art. 121 par. 2.

[123] OLG Karlsruhe 18 Jan. 1989, IPRspr. 1989 no. 110 p. 251; *Hausmann*, Der Unterhaltsbegriff in Staatsverträgen des internationalen Privat- und Verfahrensrechts: IPRax. 1990, 382–389.

[124] EuCJ 6 March 1980 no. 120/79 (*Cavel v. Cavel* (no. 2)), ECRep. 1980, 731 (739 [5], 741).

[125] OLG Saarbrücken 30 June 1988, IPRspr. 1988 no. 86 p. 669, 670.

[126] BGH 19 Nov. 1985, IPRspr. 1985 no. 118 p. 303 (306). CC § 1934d was abrogated in 1997 and legitimate as well as illegitimate offspring are now treated equally, see Law on equal treatment of legitimate and illegitimate offspring at succession (*Erbrechtsgleichstellungsgesetz*) of 16 Dec. 1997, BGBl. I 2968.

vered debts correspond to bankruptcy proceedings in ENGLAND for the purpose of enforcement under the ENGLISH Bankruptcy Act 1914.[127] It is irrelevant that in ENGLISH law title to the assets must have vested in a trustee but not under the law of JERSEY.[128]

36. *Summary.* – The practice examined here shows that when a claim or a defence under foreign law is different in form but the same in substance as a similar claim or defence under the *lex fori*, the particular conflicts rule of the latter applies without the need to assess the function of the foreign rule on which the claim or the defence is based.

iv. Unknown in Form and in Substance by Forum

37. *Introduction.* – The fact alone that a claim or a defence is not known by the *lex fori* is not necessarily a ground for disregarding it, unless local public policy is affected.[129] The examples given here taken from the practice in several countries bear out these two considerations.

38. *Dowries, bride gift.* – The daughter of Greek parents domiciled in Greece claimed from them a dowry under GREEK law to be assessed in the discretion of the court having regard to the father's wealth and social position, the number of his children and the claimant's behaviour, but failed. The reason given was that the *lex fori* did not provide a remedy and not that the substance of the claim was unknown.[130] Although a comparable remedy, restricted however to divorce proceedings, which might have stimulated an analogous application, was only introduced in 1965,[131] previous legislation which enabled the courts to settle property to secure the payment of alimony[132] could have been called in aid by an imaginative gesture as well as that which enables the court to make provision for a discretionary payment out of the estate of a deceased spouse for the benefit of the survivor and for dependents.[133]

A claim under the law of VIRGINIA for the recovery in a French succession of immovables situated in France of a dowry, an institution unknown in modern FRENCH law, was admitted by the Tribunal de la Seine[134] but rejected

---

[127] Now Insolvency Act 1986 s. 426(4), (5).

[128] *Re a Debtor (no. 1 of 1979)*, [1981] Ch. 384 (400, 401).

[129] *Kahn* I 114–117, 183; cf., *Jayme*, Qualifikationsverweisung 91, 99.

[130] *Phrantzes v. Argenti*, [1960] 2 Q.B. 19 (36) with comments 9 I.C.L.Q. 508 (1960), 23 M.L.R. 446 (1960); *Shanaz v. Rizwan*, [1965] 1 Q.B. 390; *Stefanopoulos*, Das Recht der Mitgift in Griechenland: AcP 157 (1958/59) 494–511; cf. also *Slater v. Mexican Railways*, 194 U.S. 120 (128) (1904): alimony according to MEXICAN Law a part of a claim in tort.

[131] Matrimonial Causes Act 1965 s. 17, now 1973 s. 24(1).

[132] Matrimonial Causes Act 1950 s. 23; Matrimonial Causes (Property and Maintenance) Act 1958 s. 2 and 3.

[133] Inheritance (Family Provisions) Act, 1938, now Inheritance (Provisions for Family and Dependants) Act 1975.

[134] Trib.civ. Seine 24 Aug. 1877, Clunet 1882, 88.

by the Court of Appeal of Paris and the Court of Cassation because a proprietary right of this kind was unknown.[135] The same fate awaited the institution of a power of appointment in a GERMAN court.[136]

The claim of a wife married according to ISLAMIC law for the return of the bride gift (*Morgengabe*) upon the termination of the marriage has given rise to a number of different interpretations and therefore classifications.[137] Aspects of personal relations between spous|es,[138] maintenance,[139] matrimonial property[140] and divorce[141] have been the object of consideration. The personal rather than proprietary setting of the gift, having regard to the occasion when it is made, distinguishes it from a dowry and ranks it among the personal effects of marriage.

Since a prohibition of gifts between spouses is unknown in GERMAN law a GREEK rule to this effect examined as to its purpose appeared to protect the weaker spouse against the stronger. It therefore concerned the effects of marriage and not matrimonial property relations,[142] but might also concern succession.

39. *Proxy marriages.* – Foreign proxy marriages unknown as such in the forum relate to form and call for the application of the law of the place of celebration.[143] In an unconvincing decision the LG Hamburg distinguished between a proxy acting as a messenger and one acting as an agent, the former representing the party abroad, the latter appearing for himself. Having accepted the proxy as a messenger, the court applied contractual considerations and concluded that, in view of the unilateral nature of the act, its validity was determined by the law of the place where the document of proxy was issued, *i.e.* the law of the place of the party issuing the proxy.[144]

---

[135] Cour Paris 6 March 1879; Cass.civ. 4 April 1881, S. 1883, 166, Clunet 1882, 87 (88).

[136] LG Nürnberg-Fürth 29 Dec. 1962, IPRspr. 1962–1963 no. 148 p. 446.

[137] BGH 28 Jan. 1987, IPRspr. 1987 no. 48 p. 132–133, IPRax. 1988, 64 with note *Heldrich;* OLG Hamm 8 Sept. 1987, IPRspr. 1987 no. 55 p. 151; see the survey by *Jayme,* Identité 114.

[138] LG Berlin 8 Feb. 1992, IPRspr. 1992 no. 86 p. 197; see also KG 5 April 1991, *ibidem* 1991 no. 49 p. 146–147.

[139] KG 11 Sept. 1987, *ibidem* no. 73 p. 192; AG Memmingen 12 Dec. 1984, *ibidem* 1984 no. 73; but see OLG München 26 Nov. 1985, IPRspr. 1985 no. 67 p. 180–181.

[140] LG Tübingen 4 Feb. 1992, IPRspr. 1992 no. 93 p. 221; OLG Hamm 10 April 1992, *ibidem* no. 88 p. 201.

[141] AG Memmingen, *supra* n. 139; OLG Hamm 25 May 1992, IPRspr. 1992 no. 100 p. 237(4); OLG Frankfurt 14 March 1988, *ibidem* 1988 no. 70.

[142] KG 20 March 1939, IPRspr. 1935–1944 no. 215 p. 440; *Francescakis*, review of *Ancel,* Les conflits de qualification à l'épreuve de la donation entre époux (Paris 1977): Rev.crit.d.i.p. 1978, 804–816 (807).

[143] ENGLAND: *Apt v. Apt,* [1948] P. 83; Germany: BGH 8 Oct. 1981, IPRspr. 1981 no. 199 p. 483 (485); KG 19 Feb. 1973, *ibidem* 1973 no. 55 p. 151; OLG Bremen 31 Oct. 1974, *ibidem* 1974 no. 51 p. 147.

[144] LG Hamburg 29 April 1960, IPRspr. 1960–1961 no. 84, citing *Deuchler,* Die Hand-

On the other hand, a marriage celebrated in France between a German woman and her recently deceased French fiancé authorized by the President of the French Republic under the conditions set out in FRENCH CC art. 171 was held to concern the capacity of the wife and therefore the substantive validity of the socalled marriage. Unknown as such in GERMANY the marriage was void there.[145]

40. *Trusts, floating charges.* – The treatment of trusts by the courts of civil law countries provides what is perhaps the most outstanding example of the perplexing effect of an unknown foreign institution. Unless transposed bodily into a CIVIL LAW system[146] a functional analysis translated into terms of the *lex fori* broadly interpreted has led to the following classifications:

In the view of a SWISS court it is a fiduciary ownership by the trustee coupled with certain aspects of a mandate, a gift or promise of a gift, a contract of succession (*Erbvertrag, supra* s. 33) and a contract in favour of third parties.[147] In ITALY one court held that the title in the property was vested in the beneficiaries while the trustee was an administrator *sui generis* with the widest powers encompassing those of a mandatory, a representative, a commission agent, depositee and a fiduciary administrator.[148] Another court | regarded a trust as a *fiducia cum amico* or as a testamentary fiducia.[149]

One FRENCH court regarded the trustee as an owner subject to a *fiducie* "who being a kind of mandatory is not really the owner of the trust assets".[150] Two FRENCH courts held that title vested in the trustee with the widest powers as "a fiduciary executor furnished with a powerful control" while the beneficiaries were his creditors, exercising equitable rights more

---

schuhehe im Internationalen Privatrecht: Festschrift Raape (Hamburg 1948) 83–92 (85); for the German practice introducing this distinction see *Soergel and Siebert (–Kegel)* art. 13 no. 63.

[145] OLG Karlsruhe 22 Aug. 1990, IPRspr. 1990 no. 72 p. 141.

[146] By the Hague Convention on the Law Applicable to Trusts of 20 Oct. 1984 art. 2, 11; by legislation in JERSEY: Trust (Jersey) Law of 31 May 1983 and 14 March 1984, as amended 21 July 1984; see *Matthews and Sowden*, The Jersey Law of Trusts (ed. 2 London 1990); by legislation in GUERNSEY: Trusts (Guernsey) Law of 1989, see *Evans*, Trusts in the Island of Guernsey: 5 Trust L.Int. 19–23 (1991) and see *Matthews*, English and Channel Island Trusts Compared: 4 *ibidem* 2–6 (1988–1990); in BELIZE by the Trusts Act 1992; in the CAYMAN ISLANDS by the Trust Law 1967, revised 1976; *Lambert*, Cayman Islands Trusts to overcome the forced heirship problem: 4 Trust Law International 20 (1989–90); see also *Neocleous*, Cyprus – An Ideal Jurisdiction for Trusts: 5 Cyprus L.Rev. 3125–3146 (1987); *Spirou*, Une lacune de droit civil, Le Trust: Rev.hell. 45 (1992) 195–217 (213).

[147] BG 20 Jan. 1970, BGE 96 II 79, Clunet 1976, 695.

[148] Trib. Orestano 15 March 1956, Foro it. 1956 I 1019, Riv.dir.int. 1959, 687; see also Cass. 29 March 1909, Giur.it. 1909 I 1, 650 (652–653).

[149] CC art. 627; Trib. Casale Monferrato 13 April 1984, Giur.it. 1986 I 2, 754.

[150] Trib.civ. Nice 3 May 1905, Clunet 1911, 278 (281); also BELGIUM: Trib.civ. Brussels 27 Nov. 1947, Pas. 1948.III.51(55).

potent than those of simple creditors,[151] and a third that the trustee was a "mandatory administrator".[152]

In GERMANY the question was faced only in revenue cases when the Supreme Tax Court held that an estate vested in a trustee or an executor and trustee did not attract death duties in the person of the trustee but only in that of the ultimate beneficiary when title had vested in him.[153]

Despite analytical difficulties, courts in CIVIL LAW countries accommodated a totally alien institution by attributing its operation not necessarily to one choice-of-law rule of the forum but also to several thereby doing justice to the multiple facets of a trust which operate partly *in rem* and partly *in personam.*

A "floating charge" under ENGLISH law, the realization (crystallization) of which was pleaded in opposition to enforcement proceedings in France of an English judgment, presents an ambivalent image.[154] Unknown as such in FRANCE it is a shifting non-possessory security capable of being concentrated on a specific object on the occurrence of a certain event. The proprietary element predominates, coupled with an element of time. The *lex situs* applies and since in FRANCE such a charge is unknown and has no equivalent, its crystallization in ENGLAND was ineffective.[155]

41. *Consideration, causa, quantum meruit, aval, fideicommissum, factoring.* – The absence of the notion of consideration in CIVIL LAW systems, while its presence is essential at COMMON LAW (leaving out agreements embodied in deeds), has led courts in CIVIL LAW countries[156] to examine its function and to regard it as a formality rather than as an element affecting its material content as a contract, although upon a more detailed analysis it may be a substantive element.[157] The converse situation of an agreement unsupported

---

[151] Trib.civ. Pau 3 July 1956, Gaz.Pal. 1956.2.339; Trib.gr.inst. Bayonne 28 April 1975, Rev.crit.d.i.p. 1976, 330 note *Necker.*

[152] Cour Paris 18 April 1929, Rev.crit.d.i.p. 1935, 149.

[153] RFH 29 Sept. 1935, IPRspr. 1935–1944 no. 384 p. 792 ss. and the subsequent practice cited by *Lipstein*, Trusts: *infra* ch. 23 s. 237 (1994); see also BFH 31 May 1961, IPRspr. 1960–1961 no. 148.

[154] Cour Paris 19 Jan. 1976, Rev.crit.d.i.p. 1977, 126 (131).

[155] The note by *Lagarde* (*ibidem* at 135) points out correctly that any opposition under the FRANCO-BRITISH Treaty on the Reciprocal Enforcement of Judgments in Civil and Commercial Matters of 18 Jan. 1934 (171 LNTS 183) art. 5 par. 1 *lit.* a does not apply to assets in respect of which the charge had not operated at the time when the judgment had been rendered; reversed Cass.civ. 19 Oct. 1977, Revcrit. d.i.p. 1978, 369 note P.L., J.C.P. 1978.I.18805; Cour Rennes 6 Feb. 1962, Clunet 1963, 408 note *Jambu-Merlin* (esp. 423), Rev.crit.d.i.p. 1964, 486 note C. David; see *infra* n. 219.

[156] *E.g.* BGH 10 June 1969, IPRspr. 1969 no. 160 p. 402.

[157] For this problem see *Kessler*, Einige Betrachtungen zur Lehre von der Consideration: Festschrift Ernst Rabel I (Tübingen 1953) 251–277; *Neuhaus* 147; *Becker*, Gegenopfer und Opferverwehrung (Berlin and Frankfurt 1958); *Soergel and Siebert (-Kegel)* art. 11 no. 26; *Staudinger (-Firsching)*, Kommentar zum Bürgerlichen Gesetzbuch mit Einführungsge-

by consideration governed by ITALIAN law where liberality constitutes a good *causa*, was treated as an actionable contract valid in substance by the ENGLISH Court of Appeal.[158] When confronted with a claim for *quantum meruit* under NEW YORK law the *Landgericht* München described it as a "quasi-contractual supplementary basis of a claim applied when a contract is void or incomplete".[159] In fact a claim for *quantum meruit* combines elements of unjustifiable enrichment and *negotiorum gestio*.

A claim brought in ENGLAND based on an *aval* (a guarantee) added to a bill of exchange drawn in Germany on a debtor in France and accepted there was governed by GERMAN law according to the Bills of Exchange Act, 1882 s. 72(2). In the absence of a notice of protest required by s. 72(3) of the Act the problem was whether the signatory of an *aval* was subject to the require-|ments of the Bills of Exchange Act. An *aval*, being a guarantee, is unknown as such to the English Bills of Exchange Act. Under the Geneva Convention of June 1930 and the GERMAN Bills of Exchange Act of 1933 art. 30–32 it constitutes an independent guarantee, not accessory to the obligations covered by the law on bills of exchange and subject to the ordinary civil law in its relations with the subject of the guarantee. Consequently the provisions of the Bills of Exchange Act on notice of dishonour did not apply.[160]

If this functional division between provisions relating to bills of exchange and civil law obligations should be correct, the answer given by the court must be so as well. However there are signs that the opposite view was accepted in the 19th century.[161]

The personal representative of the tenant for life of land in Austria and Hungary subject to a *fideicommissum* was sued in England by his successor for waste. *Fideicommissa*, although sharing some features with settlements according to ENGLISH law, are unknown as such to the latter. Nevertheless an ENGLISH court was able to detect in the obligation under AUSTRIAN and HUNGARIAN law to make good any waste a comparable implied obligation according to ENGLISH law but not one arising in tort.[162]

A French *quittance subrogative* was treated by a GERMAN court, where it was not known in this form as evidence of a factoring transaction.[163] On the

---

setz und Nebengesetzen. Einführungsgesetz zum Bürgerlichen Gesetzbuch (ed. 12 Berlin 1984) art. 11 no. 85.

[158] In *re Bonacina*, [1912] 2 Ch. 394 (C.A.).

[159] LG München 22 Dec. 1980, IPRspr. 1981 no. 13 p. 44.

[160] G.&H. *Montage GmbH v. Irvani*, [1990] 1 Lloyd's Rep. 14, 2 All E.R. 225 (C.A.), on appeal from [1988] 1 W.L.R. 1285 (Q.B.); note *Lomnicka*: 39 I.C.L.Q. 914 (1990).

[161] ENGLAND: *Street v. McKinley* (1885), 5 App.Cas. 754 (764, 772), except in favour of the acceptor: *Jackson v. Hudson* (1810), 2 Camp. 447 (448), 170 E.R. 1213. For FRANCE: Cass.com. 4 Feb. 1997, J.C.P. 1997.II.22922.

[162] *Batthyany v. Walford* (1887), 36 Ch.D. 269 (278–279, 281).

[163] LG Kiel 18 Jan. 1984, IPRspr. 1984 no. 209 p. 507.

other hand a *lodo irrituale* was denied the character of an enforceable arbitral award by a GERMAN court which attributed to it a contractual effect only.[164]

42. *Summary.* – In practically all these situations an unknown institution of foreign law pleaded by a party is transposed so as to fit into the system of the *lex fori* unless considerations of procedure or of public policy make it impossible.

v. Unknown in Form and Substance by Foreign Law

43. *Introductory remarks.* – Just as the absence of the necessary remedy available to the forum because unknown may result in the rejection of a claim available according to the applicable foreign law, so the availability of a remedy according to the *lex fori* may not benefit a plaintiff's claim which is founded on foreign law which ignores it.

44. *Division of pension rights; adjustment of spouses' gains upon death.* – A claim for a *Versorgungsausgleich* (division of pension rights) in the meaning of GERMAN CC § 1587 brought in a GERMAN court in divorce proceedings between foreign spouses was rejected on the ground that it was unknown in foreign law which was applicable, whether classified as the law governing the divorce,[165] maintenance[166] matrimonial property[167] or the effects of marriage.[168]

A claim for a *Zugewinnausgleich* (post-marital division of spouses' gains during marriage) in GERMAN proceedings involving a succession governed by TEXAN law was held to concern matrimonial property and was rejected because the applicable matrimonial property regime was that of community of goods.[169] Had the claim involved a *Zugewinngemeinschaft mit pauscha-*
| *liertem erbrechtlichem Ausgleich* (flat-rate adjustment of spouses' gains during marriage upon death) it might have been treated differently[170] having

---

[164] OLG Hamm 7 Feb. 1980 and BGH 8 Oct. 1981, IPRspr. 1981 no. 199 p. 483 (485).

[165] OLG Hamm 2 March 1979, IPRspr. 1979 no. 59 p. 205; – 26 April 1979, *ibidem* no. 62 p. 210; – 10 April 1990, *ibidem* 1990 no. 83 p. 162; BGH 7 Nov. 1979, *ibidem* 1979 no. 75 p. 259; – 9 May 1990, *ibidem* 1990 no. 84 p. 167; – 3 Feb. 1993, *ibidem* 1993 no. 65 p. 152 (157); also OLG Hamburg 2 March 1979, *ibidem* 1979 no. 55; OLG Karlsruhe 22 Sept. 1988, *ibidem* 1988 no. 78 p. 157; OLG München 22 May 1979, *ibidem* 1979 no. 65 p. 221; OLG Stuttgart 12 July 1979, *ibidem* no. 68; OLG Düsseldorf 19 Nov. 1979, *ibidem* no. 77 p. 229; *Jayme*, Versorgungsausgleich in Auslandsfällen: NJW 1978, 2417–2420.

[166] OLG Koblenz 21 March 1991, IPRspr. 1991 no. 89 p. 116.

[167] OLG Hamm 14 Feb. 1979, IPRspr. 1979 no. 54 p. 187.

[168] OLG Hamburg 2 March 1979, IPRspr. 1979 no. 55 p. 190 obiter; OLG München 22 May 1979, *supra* n. 165.

[169] OLG Karlsruhe 29 June 1989, IPRspr. 1989 no. 164 p. 360; but see *Jayme*, Qualifikationsverweisung 105; *Schurig*, Erbstatut, Güterrechtsstatut, gespaltenes Vermögen und ein Pyrrhussieg: IPRax. 1990, 389–393.

[170] OLG Karlsruhe 9 Dec. 1987, IPRspr. 1987 no. 105 p. 262.

regard to the element of succession. However, such a claim had to fail when the succession was governed by DUTCH law which ignored this institution.

45. *Adoption.* – Even if adoption as such is unknown by the personal law of the child to be adopted, the required consent (*kafalah*) given by the child's representative has been held to be sufficient to support an adoption in FRANCE by French adoptors.[171] However, if the applicant for adoption belongs to a country which ignores the institution of adoption altogether, no adoption can take place in FRANCE.[172] This leaves it open whether the consent by the child's representative envisaged an institution comparable to a French adoption.[173]

46. *Summary.* – Generally speaking it would seem that the absence in the applicable law of an institution comparable to that of the *lex fori* will rule out any consideration of the latter. But the new Italian PIL art. 31 seems to let in ITALIAN law as the *lex fori*.

vi. Same Law Whatever the Characterization

47. – It can be argued that it is unnecessary to analyse the nature and function of a rule forming a claim or a defence, if the legal result is the same in both laws, whatever the characterization and whichever choice-of-law rule of the forum is applied (*supra* s. 34). However, the opposite view has also been supported[174] on the ground, it may be surmised, that for the purpose of a potential appeal the judgment below must not rely on alternative grounds and that whatever they are, they are reached upon an analysis of the nature and function of the rule pleaded.

For example, the law governing the consent of the wife to the sale of a house in Spain belonging to German spouses is the same irrespective of whether the consent is treated as an emanation of the personal effects of marriage or of agency.[175]

Similarly, whether treated as concerning maintenance or matrimonial property relations a claim for the return of an Islamic bride gift (*Morgengabe*) may result in the application of the same law.[176] Also a claim by a

---

[171] Cass.civ. 10 May 1995, Clunet 1995, 626 with note *Moneger*.

[172] Note *Moneger* (preceding note) citing Cour Dijon 12 March 1993, Rev.crit.d.i.p. 1994, 82 note *Muir Watt*.

[173] Cass.civ. 1 June 1994, Rev.crit.d.i.p. 1994, 654 note *Muir Watt*.

[174] *Nussbaum*, Deutsches Internationales Privatrecht (Tübingen 1932) 102; note *Bourel* to Trib.gr.inst. Chambéry 14 Dec. 1965, Rev.crit.d.i.p. 1967, 110 (117).

[175] BGH 24 Nov. 1989, IPRspr. 1989 no. 3; also OLG Zweibrücken 25 May 1993, *ibidem* 1993 no. 79 p. 189.

[176] OLG München 24 Nov. 1984, IPRspr. 1985 no. 67 p. 179 (180, 181); LG Münster 20 Dec. 1975, *ibidem* 1975 no. 108 p. 276; see also BGH 28 Jan. 1987, *ibidem* 1987 no. 48 p. 133.

Luxemburg mother against a German father for maintenance of an illegitimate child will be governed by GERMAN law, no matter whether it is treated
as delictual (in LUXEMBURG law) or for maintenance (GERMAN law).[177]

vii. Different in Form and Substance – Overlaps and Gaps

a. Matrimonial Property Relations and Succession

48. – If a surviving spouse's subsistence is assured as an aspect of matrimonial
property relations governed by the substantive law of A and as an aspect of
succession by the substantive law of B it may happen that as a result of an
intervening change of domicile or nationality the surviving spouse acquires
an excessive share in the estate of the deceased spouse due to an overlap.[178] In the converse case when the substantive law governing the matrimonial property relations relegates the surviving spouse's claim to the realm
of succession and the substantive law governing the succession treats it as
one concerning matrimonial property relations, a surviving spouse goes
away with empty hands.[179]

The answer in the first case, decided by the Court of Cassation, is to take
into account the share in the matrimonial property when assessing the share
in the decedent's estate. The functional approach, developed for the purpose
| of determining the appropriate choice-of-law rule, is thereby turned to a
new use, namely to determine the operation of a rule of substantive law
itself.[180] Nothing less than a legislative measure of correction can fill the gap
in the second case by adopting a subsidiary substantive rule, as occurred in
CALIFORNIA.[181]

When the leading FRENCH case was decided,[182] the law governing the matrimonial property relations (the MALTESE *Code Rohan*) was regarded as applying immutably and as intended to provide for the needs of a surviving

---

[177] *Jayme*, Identité 113; OLG Karlsruhe 20 March 1931, IPRspr. 1931 no. 96 p. 188;
OLG Frankfurt 5 July 1973, *ibidem* 1973 no. 62.

[178] *Beaudoin v. Trudel*, [1937] 1 D.L.R. 216 (Ont. C.A.), [1937] Ont.Rep. 1; and see the
examples given by BayObLG 31 March 1966, IPRspr. 1966–1967 no. 173 p. 533 (561 with
literature, also 556); *von Overbeck* 121; *Maury* 478 n. 3, 486, 488.

[179] *Cf.*, *Pouliot v. Cloutier*, [1944] 3 D.L.R. 737 (Can.S.Ct.).

[180] Cass.civ. 4 April 1881, Clunet 1882, 87. But see OLG Celle 10 Sept. 1959, IPRspr.
1958–1959 no. 148.

[181] CALIFORNIA Probate Code s. 201.5; *Lipstein*, Principles 209 n. 72; *Soergel and Siebert*
(*-Kegel*) no. 101–109 preceding art. 7; *Cavers*, Perspective 215 n. 57, 58; *Lewald*, Privatrecht 96 no. 132; *Lehmann* no. 114–116; OLG Celle 10 Sept. 1959, preceding note; *Rigaux*,
Droit no. 473 with literature. For the application of the CALIFORNIAN legislation, see *supra*
n. 178.

[182] *Bartholo*-case, Cour Algiers 24 Dec. 1889, Clunet 1891, 1131; *cf.* Cour Aix 21 March
1882, S. 1885.2.117; Cass.civ. 4 April 1881, Clunet 1882, 87; Cour Orléans 4 Aug. 1859,
S. 1859.2.529; *Lehmann* no. 107.

spouse while the law governing the succession as it then stood omitted the survivor.[183] It is therefore not surprising that the Court treated the widow's claim as one concerning matrimonial property relations in order to avoid a negative overlap.[184]

A positive overlap may occur if a surviving spouse's title to land in Germany is covered by foreign law governing the matrimonial property relations and by GERMAN law as the *lex situs* as the law governing the succession to immovables.[185]

b. Legacy and Forced Share

49. – A cognate problem is presented by a *legatum per vindicationem* of land in Germany left by a testator whose succession was governed by the law of Colombia. The proprietary effect of the legacy under COLOMBIAN law was met by its effect as an obligation in GERMANY.[186] Here the courts below sought to avoid an overlap by giving precedence to the proprietary nature of the institution according to the foreign law governing the succession. The GERMAN Federal Supreme Court rejected this view and accorded precedence in proprietary matters to the GERMAN *lex situs* and not to the foreign *lex successionis*. Upon functional considerations it argued that otherwise the *numerus clausus* of proprietary rights according to the German *lex situs* would be contravened and the rights of creditors of the deceased would be adversely affected. By way of adaptation it treated the legacy as creating an obligation only imposed upon the heir (*legatum per damnationem*).

The adaptation is justifiable on the ground that the holder of a *legatum per vindicationem* is not liable for the debts of the estate and is not an heir, unlike the holder of a *legatum per praeceptionem* in ROMAN law and a *réservataire* in FRENCH law.[187]

A similar question can arise in a GERMAN court if a succession governed by FRENCH law consisting of movables in Germany includes a forced share (*réserve*) having an effect *in rem* while the equivalent *Pflichtteil* in GERMAN law only imposes an obligation on the heir, or if a succession governed by SWISS law accords to the person entitled to a forced share (*Pflichtteil*, CC art. 470) the position of an heir.[188] Here, however, the proprietary nature places

---

[183] Old CC art. 767 before the reforms of 1891, 1917, 1925 and 1930.

[184] Cass.civ. 4 April 1881, Clunet 1882, 87.

[185] LG Bamberg 20 Nov. 1975, IPRspr. 1975 no. 215.

[186] GERMAN CC § 2147, 2174.

[187] BGH 28 Sept. 1994, IPRspr. 1994 no. 125 p. 275, IPRax. 1996, 39, reversing LG Münster 15 May 1992 and OLG Hamm 12 Feb. 1993, IPRspr. 1993 no. 114 p. 259; these latter decisions were in accordance with the earlier case law: OLG Hamm 3 July 1989, IPRspr. 1989 no. 162b; also BayObLG 29 Nov. 1974, *ibidem* 1974 no. 133; LG Köln 14 July 1992, *ibidem* 1992 no. 116 p. 273.

[188] *Lewald*, Questions 79; *idem*, Privatrecht 178–179.

the beneficiary in a different category, *i.e.* of an heir according to GERMAN law.[189] On the other hand, the SWISS Federal Tribunal, confronted with a division agreement by way of an assignment between Swiss co-heirs involving land in France which was treated as successoral in character by SWISS law (CC art. 635) and as contractual in FRANCE (CC art. 1696–1698) allowed SWISS law to prevail,[190] notwithstanding an attitude to the contrary of the *lex situs*.[191]

| *c. Exceptions*

aa. Secondary Qualification (Conflits de Qualifications)
50. – The GERMAN experience between 1882 and 1934 set out above (s. 29) confirms the following conclusion: When, after taking into consideration the nature of the legal claim pleaded, foreign law is applicable according to the relevant choice-of-law rule of the forum, an attempt to repeat this process by re-examining the nature of the provision pleaded in the light of the technical denomination (characterization) of the *lex causae* (secondary characterization)[192] may lead at first sight to a reference back (*i.e.* renvoi) and in practice to gaps and overlaps.[193]

However, this type of turning a reference to foreign law into a reference back differs from its classic prototype of renvoi inasmuch as the latter relies simply on a change of the *connecting factor*,[194] while the legal nature of the claim or defence remains the same. The type of seeming renvoi for discussion here is a *conflit de qualifications* (conflict of characterizations).[195] It results in a change of characterization of the claim or defence in the light of the *lex causae* inviting the application of a different choice-of-law rule of the forum – but no more – and is relevant only at the stage of choice of law by the forum in the light of the pleadings of the parties.

---

[189] BayObLG 12 Oct. 1917, NiemeyersZ 27 (1918) 377.

[190] BG 22 March 1973, BGE 99 II 21, Schw.Jb.Int.R. 30 (1974) 251, Clunet 1976, 478: for the constant practice of characterizing according to the *lex fori*, see BG 3 Dec. 1962, BGE 88 II 471 (473).

[191] BG 22 March 1973 (preceding note) 25(c) and see RG 7 July 1932, IPRspr. 1932 no. 6 p. 18.

[192] See *e.g.*, *Robertson; Jayme*, Qualifikationsverweisung 93; *von Overbeck* 101; for an early rejection: *Falconbridge*, Characterization 566; *idem*, Renvoi 697.

[193] See note *Legier, infra* n. 195.

[194] Naturally the connecting factor of the choice-of-law rule of the *lex causae* must be interpreted in accordance with the notions of the latter; *contra, Wengler*, Réflexions 689.

[195] For the problem of conflicts of characterization see Cour Paris 3 March 1994, Clunet 1995, 607 note *Legier*, note *Ancel*, Rev.crit.d.i.p. 1994, 532, comment *Audit*, D.S. 1994. Som. 355, note *Muir Watt*, J.C.P. 1995.II.22367 rejecting it for contracts and deploring a division of the *lex causae*; *Lequette*, Le renvoi de qualifications: Mélanges Holleaux (Paris 1990) 249–262. This problem is only touched lightly by *Sauveplanne, infra* ch. 6 s. 15 (1990).

In a different form the same problem was faced above (s. 48) when the substantive law applicable to the matrimonial property relations contained an element of succession and the substantive law applicable to the succession excluded certain potential beneficiaries on the ground that they were provided for under another heading. There the characterization is intrinsic in domestic law and cannot be adjusted by the techniques of private international law. Experience has shown that an analysis of the claim or defence pleaded in the light of foreign law before the forum engages in the selection of the appropriate choice-of-law rule anticipates and avoids any subsequent conflict of characterizations.

In practice the classic type of renvoi is mainly restricted to matters uniformly connected with status and succession and to the acceptance of the operation of a different connecting factor.[196] In the second place, renvoi occurs if the choice-of-law rule of the forum or of the law referred to emphasizes the importance of the *lex situs* for immovables. If so, the foreign *lex situs* may be called upon to determine whether an object is an immovable or not. Only this last case may perhaps rely on characterization according to foreign law for the reason given below (s. 51–54).

bb. Immovables – Nature and Interests in

51. *The problem.* – From the beginnings of private international law the notion of immovables, as distinct from movables, has supplied the substance of the operative facts of a choice-of-law rule which relies on the *lex situs*. Its basis is factual and its purpose is effectiveness both in respect of single and universal transfers. It is understandable that the aim to be effective has led to the suggestion that if the object is situated abroad and that foreign law applies the foreign *lex situs* and not the *lex fori* should determine the process of characterization. Criticism has been expressed because a pure question of fact is being made the issue and not a legal relationship, as in all other conflict rules.[197] Therefore the majority of writers[198] and the practice of the courts, especially in FRANCE,[199] but also to a certain extent in | GERMANY,[200] rejects a

---

[196] See my forthcoming report to the Fourth Commission of the Institut de Droit International.

[197] *Von Bar, Chr.* I 622–623.

[198] *Kahn* 73, 491, 494; *Niboyet*, Traité III no. 957 with an historical *excursus* p. 367 n. 2; *Lehmann* no. 69–71.

[199] Cass.civ. 28 July 1862, S. 1862.1.988; Cass.req. 15 July 1885, S. 1886.1.285; Cass.civ. 22 June 1955, D. 1956.J.73, J.C.P. 1955.II.8928, Clunet 1955, 728; Trib.gr.inst. Seine 12 Jan. 1966 (*Stroganoff-case*), Rev. crit.d.i.p. 1967, 120, J.C.P. 1963.II.15266.

[200] *Staudinger (-Hausmann)*, Kommentar (*supra* n. 157) art. 3–6 (ed. 13, 1996) art. 4 no. 65–69; *Staudinger (-Dörner)*, Kommentar (*supra* n. 157) art. 25, 26 (ed. 13, 1995) art. 25 no. 477–487; *Staudinger (-Firsching)*, Kommentar (*supra* n. 157) art. 24–28 a.F., 5, 6 n.F. (ed. 12, 1991) no. 226 ss. preceding art. 24–26; *Soergel and Siebert (-Kegel)* no. 75, 562 preceding

general exception in favour of characterization by the *lex situs*, although admitting that certain special situations may demand it[201] (*e.g.* fixtures, *quaere immeubles par destination*).[202] However, weighty voices to the contrary can also be heard.[203]

It should be added that if the reference by the *lex fori* results in foreign private international law being taken into account (renvoi) and if the foreign choice-of-law rule itself connects immovables with the *lex situs* elsewhere, a factual characterization according to the latter is open for discussion. In principle, however, the *lex fori* must determine whether an object is an immovable or not. Certain it is that in the leading English cases the *lex situs* was also the *lex fori*.[204]

It is another question whether the claim or defence before the court concerns a proprietary interest in land and not land as such. Here the nature of the legal (or equitable) interest in question is up for review, especially if it arises upon a reference back. In this case the need to attach to the notion of the particular interest involved a meaning which can be attributed to it by the *lex situs* (if foreign) may present a real problem (*infra* s. 52 – 54).

52. *Special function.* – In the ANGLO-AMERICAN practice[205] it is established that after finding that an object is an immovable for the purpose of private international law, and that a COMMON LAW system of law applies, a second question arises. It concerns the type of proprietary interest in issue seeing that at COMMON LAW property is either realty or personalty subject to different rules respectively.

No such question arises if the proprietary interest is governed by a CIVIL LAW system where the range of interests is limited by a *numerus clausus* and which applies equally to movables and immovables.[206] If both the *lex fori* and

---

art. 7, no. 92 preceding art. 24, art. 27 no. 36; RG 5 July 1934, RGZ 145, 85 (86), IPRspr. 1934 no. 5; *von Bar, Chr.* I no. 588.

[201] Trib.gr.inst. Seine 12 Jan. 1966 (*supra* n. 199) 121 note *Loussouarn* 125 ss.

[202] Cass.plén. 15 April 1988, Rev.crit.d.i.p. 1989, 100 note *Droz* 103, Clunet 1989, 86 note *Kahn*, D.S. 1988.J.325 note *Malaurie*, J.C.P. 1988.II.21066 note *Barbieri*, on appeal from Cour Montpellier 18 Dec. 1984, Rev.crit.d.i.p. 1985, 559 note *Batiffol*; D.S. 1985.J.210 note *Maury*, J.C.P. 1988.II.21066; Cour Paris 21 Sept. 1995, Clunet 1996, 683.

[203] AUSTRIAN PIL § 31 par. 2; Louisiana Code (1991) art. 353; QUEBEC CC (1986) art. 3078; *Bartin*, Impossibilité 249, 250, 253; *Lerebours-Pigeonnière (-Loussouarn)*, Droit international privé (ed. 7 Paris 1959) no. 361 p. 423(d); *Batiffol and Lagarde* I no. 288 p. 489; note *Batiffol*, Rev.crit.d.i.p. 1985, 563; Cass.civ. 5 April 1887, S. 1889.1.387; Trib.civ. Seine 14 March 1894, Clunet 1894, 815; Trib.gr.inst. Seine 12 Jan. 1966 (*supra* n. 199) note *Loussouarn* (except succession) with literature; *Jayme*, Qualifikationsverweisung 98.

[204] *Freke v. Lord Carbery* (1873), L.R. 16 Eq. 461; *Re Berchtold*, [1923] 1 Ch. 192.

[205] *Freke v. Lord Carbery* and *Re Berchtold*, both preceding note; *Toledo Society for Crippled Children v. Hickok*, 261 S.W.2d 692 (Tex.S.Ct. 1953), cert.den. 347 U.S. 334 (1954); *Story*, Conflict of Laws (ed. 8 Boston 1883) 629 note a.

[206] LG Wiesbaden 30 March 1973, IPRspr. 1973 no. 46; BGH 5 June 1957, BGHZ 24, 352, IPRspr. 1956–1957 no. 146; *Jayme*, Qualifikationsverweisung 101; see *supra* n. 191.

the law governing the alleged proprietary interest are COMMON LAW systems, the preliminary determination of the character of the object as an immovable or a movable can be dispensed with.[207] This leaves only the situation where the proprietary interest is created in a COMMON LAW country (*e.g.* a trust for sale) and a CIVIL LAW court has jurisdiction. The variety of legal or equitable interests will have to be transposed as best as is possible.[208]

The main reason why objections have been raised against the last mentioned solution seems to be that it creates a choice-of-law rule additional and complementary *pro tanto*, to the operation of the *lex situs*[209] in the limited conditions set out here.

The characterization by the *lex situs* of an object as land and as a particular type of interest in an immovable can therefore have a dual purpose. The first is whether or not it is land; it concerns the choice of law motivated by a specific reason – effectiveness. The second is whether it is an interest in the immovable which represents realty or personalty according to a system of COMMON LAW as the domestic law applicable. The first part of this process may however, be dispensed with if both the *lex fori* and the *lex causae* are COMMON LAW systems. The second involves a pure question of domestic law once the choice of law has taken|place which is to establish the nature of the proprietary interest.

53. *Examples – Common Law.* – The bifurcation of proprietary interests has occupied the courts both in COMMON LAW[210] and CIVIL LAW countries when the question came up for decision whether land held on trust for sale represents money and is therefore personalty,[211] or whether money, the product of a sale of land held under a strict settlement, is deemed to be realty and therefore an immovable.[212] Similarly the question has arisen in GERMANY and in FRANCE whether a building lease in Ireland is an interest in an immovable,[213] whether a mortgage of land abroad is an interest in an immov-

---

[207] *Re Hoyles*, [1911] 1 Ch. 179 (183, 185) (C.A.); doubtful *Dicey and Morris* 917.

[208] For a list of such interests see *Dicey and Morris (-Collins a.o.)* 918 ss.; *Cheshire and North* 780–783.

[209] *Batiffol and Lagarde* I no. 298 p. 488.

[210] See also *Kahn* 89–92; *Rigaux* no. 18 p. 24. In ENGLAND the Trusts of Land and Appointment of Trustees Act 1996 s. 3 has rendered most of these problems obsolete. For the problem itself see *Falconbridge*, Essays 513, 515.

[211] *Re Berchtold, supra* n. 204.

[212] ENGLAND: *Re Cutcliffe*, [1940] Ch. 565; for SCOTLAND: *Re Hewitt's Trustees v. Lawson*, (1891) 18 R. 793; *Macdonald v. Macdonald*, 1932 S.C. (H.L.) 79 (85); *Anton*, Private International Law (ed. 2 Edinburgh 1990) 352, 596, 599. For FRANCE: Cour Paris 31 Dec. 1889, D.P. 1891, 21, Clunet 1890, 121; Cass.civ. 14 March 1961, Rev.crit.d.i.p. 1961, 774 note *Batiffol*.

[213] GERMAN BFH 20 July 1960, IPRspr. 1960–1961 no. 70: similar to an *Erbbaurecht*, citing *Schuster,* Das englische Erbbaurecht in seiner juristischen und wirtschaftlichen Bedeutung: JW 1913, 625–629; *Mueller*, Englische Rechtsprechung 1929: RabelsZ 4 (1930) 808–825 (812).

able,[214] whether a floating charge is an interest in a movable,[215] whether land in France transferred fraudulently by the owner to a company of which he was the sole shareholder had lost the character of an interest in an immovable.[216]

54. *Examples – Civil Law.* – It has been shown that the need to characterize a claim as one concerning an immovable does not arise when both the *lex fori* and *the lex causae* are COMMON LAW systems (*supra* s. 52). However, it does arise if the claim concerns an object situated in a CIVIL LAW country whose conflict rules refer to foreign law which distinguishes between movables and immovables and applies different rules of choice of law and domestic law to them respectively,[217] the more so if a reference back has to be faced.

Thus a claim for a *Zugewinnausgleich* (*supra* s. 44) in respect of the wife's assets consisting of land in Germany was brought in divorce proceedings in Germany presented by the husband domiciled in INDIANA. The court in Wiesbaden characterized the claim as one concerning matrimonial property relations. Indiana law applied, which distinguished for choice-of-law purposes between claims affecting movables and immovables, the former governed by the law of the domicile (INDIANA), the latter by the *lex situs* (GERMANY). Since GERMAN law accepted the reference back, GERMAN law applied as the *lex situs*. The question was whether for the purpose of applying the apposite INDIANA domestic law the claim was one for personalty or realty and for the purpose of INDIANA conflict of laws the nature of the claim concerned was an interest in an immovable or a movable. This required the transposition of the claim to a quota of the *Zugewinngemeinschaft* to fit into INDIANA domestic law or the operative facts of the INDIANA conflicts rule by way of a second but not by a secondary characterization.

While INDIANA conflict of laws distinguishes between immovables (land) and movables its domestic law distinguishes between interests in realty and personalty, which may fall into either category of the conflicts rule. A claim to a share in a *Zugewinngemeinschaft* consisting of land in Germany may be

---

[214] OLG Karlsruhe 20 March 1931, IPRspr. 1931 no. 96 p. 189; *Jayme*, Qualifikationsverweisung 95 with literature n. 17, 105.

[215] Cass.civ. 19 Oct. 1977, Rev.crit.d.i.p. 1978, 369, J.C.P. 1978.II.18805, Clunet 1978, 617, on appeal from Cour Paris 19 Jan. 1976, Rev.crit.d.i.p. 1977, 126 note *Lagarde* 135; *Cabrillac*, La reconnaissance en France des sûretés réelles sans dépossession constituées à l'étranger: Rev.crit.d.i.p. 1979, 487–505 (497 n. 26); *cf.* Cass.com. 8 Aug. 1981, Rev.crit. d.i.p. 1983, 267; Cour Rennes 6 Feb. 1962, Clunet 1963, 408, Rev.crit.d.i.p. 1964, 486 note *C. David. Cf., Jayme*, Qualifikationsverweisung 105.

[216] Cass.civ. 20 March 1985, Rev.crit.d.i.p. 1986, 66 (74) note *Lequette* and see note *Droz* (*supra* n. 202) for various explanations.

[217] *Hay*, The lex situs rule: *Hoeflich* (ed.), Property Law and Legal Education (Urbana and Chicago 1988) 109–132 (116ss.).

regarded as a claim for the liquidation of a common gain and not as a proprietary interest in land. It concerns money, which is personal property and can count as an interest in movable property for the purpose of private international law. If so, Indiana law applied, and the claim had to fail. Such was also the conclusion reached by the court in Wiesbaden.[218]

| It could have been argued alternatively that directly or indirectly title to land in Germany was in issue – directly because under GERMAN law the claim inferred a duty to convey land or its proceeds, and indirectly because title to land formed the basis of the claim. GERMAN law would have applied, but the argument fails to convince.

This case shows that in the rare circumstances where a claim formulated in a CIVIL LAW court in proprietary terms of civil law leads to the application of foreign COMMON LAW which applies different choice-of-law rules for immovables and movables, and the civil court accepts a reference back, the nature of the claim may require transposition, before a choice can be made.[219] It occurs if the *lex fori* which is also the *lex situs* contains a single choice-of-law rule and the foreign law, being a COMMON LAW system, contains a dual choice-of-law rule according as the claim concerns an immovable or a movable after having been identified as an interest in realty or personalty.

d. Preliminary Question

55. *Choice of law and characterization of forum.* – It may happen that the right to succeed to an inheritance depends upon the legitimacy of the issue, a marriage in A by parties domiciled there followed by a divorce in B and a second marriage both valid by the law of B when the parties have become domiciled in B but not recognized in A. This may raise the problem whether a preliminary question is involved and whether the choice-of-law rules of the forum have to give way to those of another *lex causae*.

If the forum is in A, the law of A, including its choice-of-law rules and notions of characterization will determine the historical sequence of events including the validity of the divorce in B, the validity of the subsequent marriage and the ensuing legitimacy of the children. A sequence of questions must be answered by a series of choice-of-law rules and characterizations of the forum known as *dépeçage*.

56. *Choice-of-law rules of lex causae.* – If the legitimacy of the children of the marriage is treated as the principal question it is arguable that its choice-of-law rules and not those of the *lex fori* should determine the legality of the

---

[218] LG Wiesbaden, *supra* n. 206; *cf.* BGH 5 June 1957, *ibidem*.

[219] *Jayme*, Qualifikationsverweisung 94, 98, 105, also 95; *idem*, Identité 112; *Niboyet*, Traité III no. 967; BayObLG 31 March 1966 (*supra* n. 178) p. 559 III.2.

events leading up to it. In that case each intermediate question would have to be characterized according to the law of B, the *lex causae*. The result may well be different if the choice-of-law rules and the characterization of the issue differ.[220]

57. *Dépeçage and preliminary question distinguished.* – At this stage the different function of the choice-of-law rules in cases of simple *dépeçage* and in cases involving a preliminary question manifests itself. *Dépeçage* involves two concurrent elements of a case, *e.g.* in marriage, capacity and form. The choice-of-law rules of, and also characterization by, the *lex fori* apply to both. A preliminary question constitutes an antecedent question independent in substance and in time from that of the principal question.

58. *The principal question.* – According as the first (the historical) or the second (the independent) technique is employed the same legal question will either always receive the same answer or it will differ in line with the choice of law and characterization of whatever law governs the principal question.[221]

viii. Characterization According to the lex causae

59. *General considerations.* – It was argued above (s. 2) that apart from its possible application to preliminary questions characterization according to the *lex causae* is only required if the system of the conflict of laws adopted by the *lex fori* is a unilateral one in the sense that it only determines the spheres of application of the *lex fori*. If the conflicts system is bilateral, and takes | foreign law into account, two conclusions follow, one theoretical, and one practical (*infra* s. 60).

The forum is not directed automatically to the applicable law. It needs some guidance, and this is provided by its own choice-of-law rules, whether sophisticated or primitive. These rules make it possible to attribute a claim brought in the light of some legal system to one or other of its individual

---

[220] Opinion is divided:

In favour of the *lex fori*: *Raape* 485–495. *Batiffol and Lagarde* I no. 312 n. 8; implicitly Cass.req. 22 April 1986, J.C.P. 1987.II.20878 note *Agostini*, Clunet 1986, 1025 note *Sinay-Cytermann* (1036); Cass.req. 21 April 1931, S. 1931.1.377 note *Niboyet*, Rev.d.i.p. 1932, 526 (541) note *Niboyet*, Report *Pilon* at 527 (534); *Lehmann* no. 133; *Soergel and Siebert (-Kegel)* no. 78 preceding art. 7 with cases n. 7, art. 13 no. 17; *Shaw v. Gould* (1868), L.R. 3 H.L. 55.

In favour of the *lex causae* (if foreign): *Lagarde*, La règle de conflit applicable aux questions préalables: Rev.crit.d.i.p. 1960, 459–484 (471); Cass.civ. 3 June 1980, Clunet 1980, 327 note *Simon-Depitre* (328), Rev.crit.d.i.p. 1980, 331 note *Batiffol*, D. 1980, 549 note *Poisson-Drocourt; Soergel and Siebert (-Kegel)* no. 78 preceding art. 7, art. 13 no. 17, art. 19 no. 15; *Niboyet*, Traité III no. 966 ss.; *Schwebel v. Ungar*, [1965] Can. S.C.R. 148, 48 D.L.R.2d 644; and see following note.

[221] *Melchior* (*supra* n. 74) 249–263; *Wengler*, Vorfrage 161; *Raape* 485–495.

operative facts which may then refer to foreign law. Thus a characterization by foreign law must always be secondary because it operates only if foreign law has been found to apply, except where the choice-of-law rules of the forum are unilateral.

60. *Practical considerations.* – However, claims are brought in the light of some legal system, and if this should be foreign, with a view to inducing the forum to select that one of its choice-of-law rules which in the expectation of the party concerned will lead to the application of the law underlying its claim. The nature and purpose of the foreign rule underlying the claim determines which choice-of-law rule of the forum applies. This exhausts the process of characterization. The legal rule underlying a claim is found to be covered by one or other of the operative facts of the forum's choice-of-law rules.[222]

61. *Practice.* – Secondary characterization[223] has had a brief and checquered history until it was revived recently in the guise of *conflits de qualifications* (*supra* n. 195). Its sphere of operation is restricted to the characterization of objects and interests in immovables or movables for the reasons set out above (s. 50). Where secondary characterization of legal rules was attempted in other situations the ill-fated practice of the GERMAN Supreme Court between 1882 and 1934[224] disclosed that this technique leads to gaps and can lead to overlaps. Other instances are rare.

One case, however, deserves attention. *In re Maldonado*[225] faced a contest between the Spanish state and the British Crown, both claiming the movable estate in England of a Spanish national domiciled in Spain who had died intestate without any next of kin. According to ENGLISH domestic law the Crown in England might have succeeded on the strength of the *jus regale*. According to ENGLISH private international law, ENGLISH law applied, if the claim of the Spanish state disclosed a *jus regale*, but SPANISH law applied if the Spanish state claimed as *ultimus heres*. In the ENGLISH courts, the British claim was postponed since by the *lex causae*, the law of the deceased's domicile, the claim was one sounding in private law as being successoral in char-

---

[222] *Vitta* I 309.

[223] *Robertson* 239 ss.; *Batiffol and Lagarde* I no. 298 p. 349; *Holleaux*, Droit international privé (Paris 1987) no. 55 p. 276; *Vitta* I 308 ss. with literature n. 17; *Dicey and Morris* (*-Collins a.o.*) 918 ss.; *Schwind*, Neue Tendenzen im Internationalen Privatrecht: Mélanges Alfred E. von Overbeck (Fribourg 1990) 103–113 (111); *Siehr*, Rechtsangleichung im Internationalen Privatrecht durch nationale Kodifikationen: *ibidem* 205–243, and the literature cited by *Lipstein*, Principles 202 n. 42.

[224] *Supra* s. 29; see also Cass.civ. 18 Oct. 1989, Rev.crit.d.i.p. 1990, 712, 719 note *Foyer*, Clunet 1990, 415, 418, 419 note *Kahn*.

[225] *Re Maldonado, State of Spain v. Treasury Solicitor*, [1954] P. 223; *Lipstein*, Vacantia 22–25.

acter. However, the description of the state as ultimate heir falsely conjures up notions of family ties leading to claims of heirship in private law.

The successoral nature of the claim was first formulated in ROME by the Emperor *Augustus* and, after an interval when it was recognized as a *jus regale*, was revived by the GERMAN pandectists and taken up by many EURO-PEAN Codes.[226] However upon a functional analysis it cannot stand scrutiny. Even if the state is said to represent all nationals as heirs, their benefit is at best very indirect. Special administration proceedings are to be found, the liability of the state is limited in fact or in law, and the state cannot repudiate the inheritance.[227]

Another aspect must also be considered. The *jus regale* is a right of a public law nature. As such it is absolutely binding and operates territorially to the exclusion of all other claims to the assets of a deceased person.[228] In a clash between one state's *jus regale* and another state's ultimate heirship, the local *jus regale* should prevail.[229] In the converse situation a GERMAN court has rightly rejected the claim of the Swedish state to | the deceased's assets in Germany.[230] Naturally, in a clash between conflicting *jura regalia* each remains confined to its own territory.[231]

Of course it is open to states to seek to extend the operation of their *jus regale* to assets abroad and to accept such an extended claim by a foreign *jus regale*,[232] as was done by ITALIAN PIL art. 49.[233]

ix. International Conventions and International Tribunals

a. International Conventions

62. *General considerations.* – Problems of characterization of the kind arising in national conflict of laws by the need to consider the nature of foreign

---

[226] See *Lipstein, ibidem.*

[227] ANGLO-GERMAN M.A.T. 16 Oct. 1925, Rec. déc.T.A.M. 5 (1926) 632 (635–636), JW 1926, 2018; FRANCO-GERMAN M.A.T. 30 March 1926, Rec.déc. T.A.M. 5 (1926) 243 (248), JW 1926, 2021.

[228] *Lipstein,* Public Law 43.

[229] *Lipstein, ibidem;* also *idem,* Visions 376 n. 90 with literature; to the same effect the draft of a Hague Succession Convention of 11 July 1904 art. 9; and Hague Convention on the Law Applicable to Succession to the Estates of Deceased Persons of 20 Oct. 1988 art. 16; *quaere* if according to the law of the state claiming the *jus regale* more remote relatives would be entitled to succeed: *Wolff,* PIL par. 142.

[230] KG 3 April 1985, IPRspr. 1985 no. 115 p. 296 (298).

[231] *Re Barnett's Trusts,* [1902] 1 Ch. 847; *Re Musurus,* [1936] 4 All E.R. 1666 (P.D.A.).

[232] Hague Succession Convention 1988, Act.Doc. La Haye 16 (1988) II 591 no. 116; *Lipstein,* Hundred Years 615.

[233] See also Riv.dir.int.priv.proc. 1995, 905 –1279 (text) and comment *Clerici* on art. 49; *ibidem* 1148.

private law have only confronted International Conventions[234] and Tribunals[235] infrequently. In the words of an ENGLISH court,

"International conventions which are ... to be given effect by States with differing systems of municipal law, do not employ the terms of art of municipal law of any single country, but seek to express ... a general concept which can be translated into the terms of art of the municipal law of each country which becomes a party to the Convention."[236]

Instead, technical legal terms are either defined or, if undefined, are capable of being interpreted in terms of substantive law.[237] When necessary, an autonomous solution is preferred.[238]

Two good examples of undefined terms are provided by Bretton Woods Agreement art. VIII (2) (b) where the terms "exchange contracts" and "unenforceable" have caused a spate of conflicting comments. It provides:

"*Exchange contracts* which involve the currency of any member and which are contrary to the exchange control regulations of that member maintained or imposed consistently with the Agreement shall be *unenforceable* in the territories of any member" (emphases added).

Three possible notions could be attributed to the term "exchange contracts". In a narrow sense it could cover only an exchange of money of one currency for that of another; in a somewhat broader sense it could mean that money of one currency serves as payment for merchandise or services elsewhere, or in the broadest sense that it covers all transactions across borders which affect the economic resources of a member state.[239]

The term "unenforceable" excludes the notion of "illegality". It enjoins courts not to lend their aid to the enforcement of a contract.[240]

---

[234] *Niboyet*, Traité III no. 961–964 p. 389; *idem*, Problème; *idem*, Impositions 175; *Plaisant* 47–72 (75).

[235] *Lipstein*, Tribunals I 142–175 and II 51–83.

[236] *Post Office v. Estuary Radio Ltd.*, [1968] 2 Q.B. 740 (757), [1967] 3 All E.R. 666 (682 G) (C.A.).

[237] *Plaisant* 60.

[238] *Niboyet*, Traité III no. 694 p. 383 and n. 3; *Plaisant* 53; *Lehmann* no. 52(1); *Ginsbergen*, Qualifikationsproblem, Rechtsvergleichung und mehrsprachige Staatsverträge: ZfRV 1970, 1–15 (13); *Jayme*, Problemi 219–224.

[239] See *Lipstein*, Chronique 143 – 146; *Wilson, Smithett & Cope Ltd. v. Terruzzi*, [1976] Q.B. 683 (703) (C.A.) on appeal from [1976] Q.B. 683; BGH 8 Nov. 1993, IPRspr. 1993 no. 127 p. 283 (284); OLG Hamburg 9 Oct. 1992, *ibidem* 1992 no. 172 p. 373 (377). Comparative survey in *Ebke*, Internationales Devisenrecht (Heidelberg 1991) 202–246.

[240] *United City Merchants v. Royal Bank of Canada*, [1983] 1 A.C. 168 (H.L.); BGH 17 Feb. 1971, BGHZ 55, 334, IPRspr. 1971 no. 116b; BGH 14 Nov. 1991, BGHZ 116, 77 (84), IPRspr. 1991 no. 181; LG Hamburg 4 Sept. 1992, IPRspr. 1992 no. 171 p. 365; *Ebenroth and Woggan*, Einlageforderungen gegen Gesellschaften und Artikel VIII, Abschnitt 2(b) des I.W.F. Abkommens: IPRax. 1993, 151–154. Comparative survey in *Ebke* (preceding n.) 276–308.

Political treaties seldom contain private law terms which call for a characterization when translated into municipal law, unless they have to take into account status for jurisdictional purposes or private law claims of individuals.[241]

|63. *Hague Conventions on private international law.* – Among multilateral conventions the Hague Conventions on private international law form a notable exception by offering definitions. A single set of operative facts is employed by the treaty to cover all the legal situations envisaged by it. The only question is whether the legal question in issue is included. In national conflict rules normally the existence of several sets of operative facts forces a choice between them which is likely to raise a question of characterization of the individual claim framed in the light of a particular system of domestic law.

Thus the Convention on the Conclusion of Marriages of 12 June 1902 art. 1 conceded, albeit inadequately, to the *lex patriae* "the right to enter into a marriage". Did this include the consent of the military authorities in the case of a male liable to conscription?[242] The Convention concerning the Protection of Infants of 5 Oct. 1961 art. 12 leaves the determination as to who is a minor alternatively to the law of his habitual residence or of his nationality. The Convention on the Effects of Marriage of 17 July 1905 art. 6 par. 2 laid down that the requirement of a particular form for the choice of a matrimonial property regime as a substantive condition by the *lex patriae* of one of the parties was to be characterized as one of substance.[243] The wording of art. 9 par. 1, which allowed the parties to submit the matrimonial regime to another law, leaves it open whether it refers to modifications only or permits another contract. The Convention on the Form of Testamentary Dispositions of 5 Oct. 1961 art. 5 characterizes as matters of form any legal provisions limiting the permitted forms of testamentary dispositions by age, nationality or other personal conditions of the testator.

The Convention on the Law Applicable to Traffic Accidents of 4 May 1971 art. 1 par. 2 characterizes the range of traffic accidents by a description

---

[241] The Treaty of Versailles of 28 June 1919 (*Parry* 225 (1919) 188) art. 296 par. 1 no. 1–4 defined the types of claims to be considered by the Mixed Arbitral Tribunals; the Treaty of Lausanne of 24 July 1923 (28 LTS 171) art. 16, in dealing with the competence of the courts in TURKEY and EGYPT dealing with the status of persons went on to define it in detail; see also the Treaty of Montreux of 8 May 1937 (182 LTS 37) art. 28, going even into still greater detail.

[242] See *de Visscher*, La dénonciation par la Belgique des Conventions de la Haye: Rev.d.i.p. 1919, 624–630; *Anon.*, L'interprétation allemande de l'article 1 de la Convention de la Haye sur le mariage: *ibidem* 1912, 839–845 (840); Trib.civ. Brussels 21 June 1913, Pas. 1914.III.123; Cour Brussels 26 Nov. 1913, Pas. 1914.II.141; Cass.civ. 11 June 1914, Pas. 1914.I.317.

[243] *Lipstein*, Hundred Years 566 and n. 114.

but leaves the determination of noncontractual liability to the *lex fo-ri*,[244] while art. 2 adds a substantive exclusionary clause.[245] The Convention on the Law applicable to Products Liability of 2 Oct. 1973 characterizes the legal relationship envisaged by excluding contracts between the defendant and the plaintiff[246] while art. 2 contains a substantive exclusionary clause. The Convention on the Law Applicable to Maintenance Obligations of 2 Oct. 1973 also seeks to define its substantive area of application (art. 1,8). The Trust Convention of 1 July 1985 defines trusts (art. 2), whittles them down (art. 3) and contains an exclusionary clause (art. 5). The International Sales Convention of 22 Dec. 1986 defines the topic spatially and materially (art. 1 and 3) together with an exclusionary clause;[247] the Succession Convention of 20 Oct. 1988 only contains an exclusionary clause (art. 1 par. 2). The independent characterization as sounding in maintenance of claims for support arising as a result of divorce proceedings by the Convention on the Law applicable to Maintenance Obligations of 2 Oct. 1973, art. 8 has, however, met with objections.[248] The Convention on the Taking of Evidence Abroad in Civil and Commercial Matters of 18 March 1970 left the determination of what are "civil and commercial matters" open.[249] The Hague Convention on the Recognition and Enforcement of Foreign Judgments of 1 Feb. 1971 defines the notion of judgments (art. 2).

64. *Other conventions.* – The Rome Convention on the Law applicable to Contractual Obligations of 19 June 1980 art. 14 par. 1 treats all presumptions of law as substantive without distinguishing between presumptions *juris et de jure* and others. Art. 10 par. 1 *lit.* d does the same for limitation of actions. On the other hand, the Bustamante Code of 1928 left quite generally the question of characterization to the respective *leges fori* (art. 6).

| *b. International Tribunals*

65. *In general.* – International Tribunals do not possess a private law as a *lex fori*.[250] Consequently they are not faced with the usual problems of charac-

---

[244] Art. 1 par. 1: *Loussouarn*, La Convention de la Haye sur la loi applicable en matière d'accidents de la circulation routière: Clunet 1969, 5–19 (10).

[245] *Loussouarn*, preceding note.

[246] *Loussouarn*, La Convention de la Haye sur la loi applicable à la responsabilité du fait des produits: Clunet 1974, 32–47 (34, 38); *Batiffol*, La douzième session de la Conférence de la Haye de droit international privé: Rev.crit.d.i.p. 1973, 243–273 (254).

[247] The draft Consumer Sales Convention of 25 Oct. 1980 defined the type of transactions in substance (art. 1) and spatially (art. 15), consumers (art. 2) and excluded matters (art. 4).

[248] *Hausmann* 382–389.

[249] *State of Norway's Application*, [1990] 1 A.C. 723 (H.L.); *Lipstein*, Evidence 130–133; *idem*, Hundred Years 640 and 662 with literature.

[250] Mixed Arbitral Tribunals (M.A.T.), see *infra* s. 66. RUMANIAN-GERMAN M.A.T. 16

terization except when applying the terms of international Conventions.[251] Instead they have been able to develop their own rules. When dealing with claims involving state responsibility for denial of justice affecting property rights of aliens or breach of contractual obligations affecting them, international tribunals may have to determine questions of municipal private law as preliminary matters before dealing with state responsibility under international law. For this purpose international rules of the conflict of laws were developed by these tribunals independently of national rules. The tribunals did not follow any consistent line in matters of characterization.[252]

The absence of a *lex fori* in matters of private law including choice-of-law rules prevents the usual process of seeking to interpret the operative facts of the *lex fori* in the light of the claim brought according to some system of municipal law and thus explains the absence of any temptation to rely on the *lex fort's* legal concepts. In general these tribunals classify according to the law of one of the parties to the dispute.

66. *Mixed Arbitral Tribunals.* – The Mixed Arbitral Tribunals (M.A.T.) set up by the Peace Treaty of 1919 dealt with claims of a private law nature between individuals. They have sometimes chosen a domestic legal system without giving reasons[253] or have engaged in cumulating the laws of the parties[254] or in opposing such a cumulation to a third legal system.[255]

June 1925, Rec. déc.T.A.M. 5 (1926) 200 (211); *Lipstein*, Tribunals I 158–159, II 66; FRANCO-GERMAN M.A.T. 30 March 1926, Rec.déc.T.A.M. 6 (1927) 243 (246–247).

[251] See *supra* s. 59; SERBIAN and BRAZILIAN Loans Cases 12 July 1929, P.C.I.J.Rep. 1929 ser. A no. 20 and 21, p. 19–22; BELGIAN-GERMAN M.A.T. 13 June 1923, Rec.déc.T.A.M. 3 (1924) 305 (307); RUMANIAN-GERMAN M.A.T. 6 Nov. 1924, *ibidem* 4 (1925) 842 (847); ANGLO-TURKISH M.A.T. 10 April 1929, *ibidem* 9 (1930) 230 (233).

[252] *Dusenberg v. Mexico: Moore*, History and Digest of International Arbitrations III (Washington, D.C. 1898) 2157 (2158); *Knox v. Mexico: ibidem* III 2166; *Robert v. Mexico: ibidem* III 2468 (2471); *Rivlen v. Turkey: Nielsen* (ed.), American-Turkish Claims Settlement (Washington, D.C. 1937) 622 (626); *Gleadell v. Mexico*: Decisions of and Opinions of the Commissioners in accordance with the Convention between Great Britain and Mexico I (London 1931) 55, 57, 63; *The Enterprise: Moore* (*supra*) IV (Washington, D.C. 1898) 43 (49) (rights over slaves, AMERICAN law).

[253] BELGIAN-GERMAN M.A.T. 30 April 1923, Rec. déc.T.A.M. 3 (1924) 274 (277) (GERMAN *lex situs* to transfer of title to property, not BELGIAN law of contract); RUMANIAN-GERMAN M.A.T. 16 June 1925 (*supra* n. 250) 218, 224 (*lex loci contractus* or *executionis*); *idem* 17 June 1925, Rec.déc.T.A.M. 5 (1926) 235, 240; ANGLO-GERMAN M.A.T. 31 May 1926, *ibidem* 6 (1927) 540 (542) (limitation of action, *lex loci solutionis* – ENGLISH characterization disregarded); *idem* 24 Nov. 1926, *ibidem* 6 (1927) 635 (637–638) (assignment, ENGLISH law); also Anglo-German M.A.T. 8 March 1927, *ibidem* 7 (1928) 324 (326).

[254] FRANCO-GERMAN M.A.T. 22 March 1924, Rec. déc.T.A.M. 4 (1925) 390 (393) (insurance, annuities); RUMANIAN-GERMAN M.A.T. 16 June 1925 (*supra* n. 250) 211, 213–214; FRANCO-BULGARIAN M.A.T. 18 May 1925, Rec.déc.T.A.M. 5 (1926) 427 (429); ANGLO-GERMAN M.A.T. 5 Nov. 1925, *ibidem* 5 (1926) 670 (672); *idem* 7 April 1927, *ibidem* 7 (1928) 345 (354 (iii)).

[255] ANGLO-GERMAN M.A.T. 22 Feb. 1922, Rec. déc.T.A.M. 1 (1921/22) 730 (733); RUMANIAN-GERMAN M.A.T. 31 March 1927, *ibidem* 7 (1928) 738 (741).

Generally, two tendencies can be observed: one based upon general notions of law and another relying upon somewhat arbitrary tests. Tribunals classify according to "common juridical notions",[256] "*principes universellement admis en matière législative*",[257] "*principes généraux du droit international privé*"[258] "*portée générale*"[259] "*sens large*"[260] or "common ground".[261] The choice-of-law rules of the debtor's domicile have been called in aid,[262] and | a simple comparative approach can also be noticed.[263]

67. *European Court of Justice.* – The Court of Justice of the EUROPEAN UNION in exercising its interpretative jurisdiction under the Brussels, Lugano and San Sebastian Conventions concerning Jurisdiction and the Enforcement of Judgments in Civil and Commercial Matters has generally adopted an autonomous approach.[264] Exceptionally, if the terms of the Convention represent technical notions of private law or procedure the court will rely on a functional analysis of the national rule of private law involved.[265]

---

[256] ANGLO-GERMAN M.A.T. 7 April 1927 (*supra* n. 254) 353 (iii); FRANCO-TURKISH M.A.T. 13 Dec. 1927, Rec.déc.T.A.M. 7 (1928) 942 (947).

[257] BELGIAN-GERMAN M.A.T. 9 Oct. 1922, Rec. déc.T.A.M. 2 (1923) 395 (400).

[258] FRANCO-GERMAN M.A.T. 30 March 1926, *supra* n. 250.

[259] FRANCO-AUSTRIAN M.A.T. 30 Nov. 1921, Rec. déc.T.A.M. 1 (1921/22) 616 (619).

[260] FRANCO-GERMAN M.A.T. 23 Dec. 1921, Rec. déc.T.A.M. 1 (1921/22) 600 (605).

[261] ANGLO-GERMAN M.A.T. 7 May 1926, Rec.déc. T.A.M. 6 (1927) 60 (62); *idem* 14 June 1926, *ibidem* 6 (1927) 75 (76); *idem* 16 July 1927, *ibidem* 585 (587); *idem* 3 Dec. 1926, *ibidem* 643 (645); *idem* 4 Feb. 1927, *ibidem* 671 (674); *idem* 25 March 1927, *ibidem* 7 (1928) 330 (333); *idem* 8 April 1927, *ibidem* 369 (370); *idem* 9 Nov. 1927, *ibidem* 451 (453).

[262] ANGLO-GERMAN M.A.T. 15 July 1926, Rec. déc.T.A.M. 6 (1927) 564 (569); *idem* 7 April 1927, (*supra* n. 254) 348.

[263] ANGLO-GERMAN M.A.T. 24 July 1923, Rec. déc.T.A.M. 3 (1924) 223 (225); BELGIAN-GERMAN M.A.T. 22 April 1925, *ibidem* 5 (1926) 350 (352); FRANCO-GERMAN M.A.T. 16 May 1925, *ibidem* 397 (403) and see *Lipstein*, Tribunals I 159 n. 93 with further cases.

[264] Autonomous: EuCJ 30 Nov. 1976 no. 21/76 (*Bier v. Mines de Potasse d'Alsace*), EC Rep. 1976 1735 [19], [23]; EuCJ 7 March 1995 no. 68/93 (*Shevill v. Presse Alliance*), *ibidem* 1995 I–415 [24–29]; EuCJ 11 Jan. 1990 no. 220/88 (*Dumez v. Hessische Landesbank*), *ibidem* 1990 I–49, 80 [17] [20]; EuCJ 21 June 1978 no. 150/77 (*Bertrand v. Ott*), *ibidem* 1978, 1431 (1445 [14]); EuCJ 13 Nov. 1979 no. 25/79 (*Sanicentral v. Collin*), *ibidem* 1979, 3423 (3429) [5]; EuCJ 22 Feb. 1979 no. 133/78 (*Gourdain v. Nadler*), *ibidem* 1979, 733 (743 [3]); EuCJ 26 May 1982 no. 133/81 (*Ivenel v. Schwab*), *ibidem* 1982, 1891 (1900 [15], 1901); EuCJ 15 Nov. 1983 no. 288/82 (*Duijnstee v. Goderbauer*), *ibidem* 1983, 3663 (3675 [15] [17]); EuCJ 8 March 1988 no. 9/87 (*Arcado v. Haviland*), *ibidem* 1988 1539 (1545 [10] [11]); EuCJ 27 Sept. 1988 no. 189/87 (*Kalfelis v. Schröder*), *supra* n. 110; EuCJ 15 Feb. 1989 no. 32/88 (*Six Construction v. Humbert*), *ibidem* 1989, 346 (362 [10], 363 [15]); EuCJ 10 Jan. 1990 no. 115/88 (*Reichert & Kockler v. Dresdner Bank*), *ibidem* 1990 I–27 (41 [9]); EuCJ 26 March 1992 no. 261/90 (*idem* (no. 2)), *ibidem* 1992 I–2149 (2184 [35]); *Powell Duffryn v. Petereit*, [1992] Int.Lit.Proc. 300 (327 [14] [20]); *Jacob Handke v. Soc. Traitement Mécanomique*, [1993] Int.Lit.Proc. 5 (21 [10] [15]); *Mulox v. Geels*, [1993] Int.Lit.Proc. 668 (686 [10] [11] [14]); *Shearson Lehmann v. Treuhandgesellschaft*, [1993] Int.Lit. Proc. 199 (220 [13]); *Volker Sonntag v. Waidmann*, [1993] Int.Lit.Proc. 466 (484 [18]–[21] [25] [33]); *Marinari v. Lloyd's Bank*, [1995] Int.Lit.Proc. 737 (750 [18]).

[265] Domestic: EuCJ 6 Oct. 1976 no. 14/76 (*De Bloos v. Bouyer*), EC Rep. 1976, 1491

C. Conclusions

68. – The foregoing examination will have shown that in some way the *lex fori*, the *lex causae* and comparative law play a part in the process known as characterization: a claim presented in the light of some legal system (which may of course include the domestic law of the forum) raises the question as to which law applies. In the search as to which set of operative facts of the choice-of-law rules of the forum covers the claim, each – the set of operative facts and the claim – must be interpreted in terms of each other. Since the domestic law of the forum may not cover the type of claim formulated in terms of some foreign legal system which is alleged to apply, the operative facts of the choice-of-law rules of the forum must be interpreted broadly in order to accommodate the claim. The claim is formulated in terms of the legal system which the party alleges to apply, which is not necessarily the law which emerges finally as the *lex causae* after the claim has been characterized and been allotted the apposite choice-of-law rule. This must depend upon the process of mutual interpretation based on the extended range of the operative facts of the various choice-of-law rules of the forum and the analysis of the function and purpose of the rule of law pleaded by the party. For this investigation a technique is employed which can explain to each other the substance and not the formal categorization of each of them. Thus the process of characterization of a claim or a defence comprises the *lex fori* as expressed in the operative facts of its choice-of-law rules, the alleged (not the finally ascertained) *lex causae* and comparative expertise.

(Completed in March 1999)

(1508 [11] [13] [17]); EuCJ 6 Oct. 1976 no. 12/76 (*Tessili v. Dunlop*), *ibidem* 1976, 1473 (1486 [15]; EuCJ 17 Jan. 1980 no. 56/79 (*Zelger v. Salinitri*), *ibidem* 1980, 89 (97 [3]); EuCJ 7 June 1984 no. 129/83 (*idem* (no. 2)), *ibidem* 1984, 2397 (2408 [15]); EuCJ 15 Jan. 1987 no. 266/85 (*Shenavai v. Kreischer*), *ibidem* 1987, 239 (253 [6], 256 [17] [20]); EuCJ 3 July 1990 no. 305/88 (*Lancray v. Peters and Sickert*), *ibidem* 1990 I–2725 (2750 [29] [30], [1991] 2 Int.Lit.Proc. 99 (112 [31]); *Custom Made Commercial Ltd. v. Slawa*, [1994] Int.Lit.Proc. 515 (552, 626).
Cumulative: EuCJ 27 Nov. 1984 no. 258/83 (*Brennero v. Wendel*), ECRep. 1984, 3971 (3982 [13]); EuCJ 2 July 1985 no. 148/84 (*Deutsche Genossenschaftsbank v. Brasserie du Pêcheur*), *ibidem* 1985, 1981 (1992 [18]); EuCJ 3 Oct. 1985 no. 119/84 (*Capelloni v. Pelkmans*), *ibidem* 1985, 3147 (3159 [16]); EuCJ 4 Feb. 1988 no. 145/88 (*Hoffman v. Krieg*), *ibidem* 1988, 645 (667 [17] [18] [21] [30–32]); EuCJ 15 May 1990 no. 365/88 (*Hagen v. Zeehaghe*), *ibidem* 1990 I–1845 (1865 [19] [20]); *Danvaern Production v. Schuhfabriken Otterbeck*, [1995] Int.Lit.Proc. 649 (665 [18]); *Van der Linden v. Berufsgenossenschaft der Feinmechanik*, [1996] Int.Lit.Proc. 200 (216 [14] [16]); also *Six Construction v. Humbert* (preceding note) 364 [21].

| List of Principal Works

(1)

1. COMPARATIVE WORKS: *Ago*, Règles générales des conflits de lois: Rec.des Cours 58 (1936 IV) 243–469 (316–343); *von Bar, C. L.*, Theorie und Praxis des internationalen Privatrechts (ed. 2 Hannover 1889); *Bernasconi*, Der Qualifikationsprozess im Internationalen Privatrecht (Schweizer Studien zum internationalen Recht no. 101) (Zürich 1997); *Falconbridge*, Characterization in the Conflict of Laws: 53 L.Q.R. 235–258 and 537–567 (1937), cited Characterization; *idem*, Conflict of Laws. Examples of Characterization: 15 Can.Bar Rev. 215–246 (1937), cited Conflict; *idem*, Renvoi – Characterization and Acquired Rights: 17 *ibidem* 369–398 (1939), cited Renvoi; *idem*, Essays on the Conflict of Laws (Toronto 1947), cited Essays; *Hausmann*, Der Unterhaltsbegriff in Staatsverträgen des Internationalen Privatrechts: IPrax. 1990, 382–389; *Jayme*, Zur Qualifikationsverweisung im Internationalen Privatrecht: ZfRV 1976, 93 – 108, cited Qualifikationsverweisung; *idem*, Wandel des Unterhaltsbegriffs und Staatsverträge im internationalen Privatrecht: Mélanges Alfred E. von Overbeck (Fribourg 1990) 529–544, cited Wandel; *idem*, Identité culturelle et intégration. Le droit international privé postmoderne: Rec.des Cours 251 (1995) 9 – 268, cited Identité; *idem*, Problemi pratici della qualificazione nel sistema della Convenzione dell'Aja sugli effetti del Matrimonio: Dir.int. 1961 I 219–224, cited Problemi; *Kahn*, Gesetzeskollisionen: *Lenel and Lewald* (ed.), Abhandlungen zum internationalen Privatrecht (Munich 1928) 1–123; *Lewald*, Règles générales des conflits de lois: Rec.des Cours 69 (1939 III) 5–147, cited Règles; *idem*, Questions de droit international des successions: Rec.des Cours 9 (1925 IV) 1–125, cited Questions; *Lipstein*, The General Principles of Private International Law: Rec.des Cours 135 (1972 I) 99–229, cited Principles; *idem*, Conflict of Laws before International Tribunals I and II: 27 Trans. – Grot.Soc. 142–181 (1942) and 29 *ibidem* 51–83 (1944), cited Tribunals; *idem*, Bona Vacantia and Ultimus Heres: 1954 C.L.J. 22–26, cited Vacantia; *idem*, Chronique de jurisprudence britannique: Clunet 1980, 109–159 and 394–428, cited Chronique; *idem*, Conflict of Laws and Public Law (XIIth International Congress of Comparative Law, Sidney – Melbourne 1986 – General Report: *Banakas* (ed.), United Kingdom Law in the 1980s (London 1988) 38–58), cited Public Law; *idem*, Conflict of Public Laws – Visions and Realities: Festschrift I. Zaytay (Tübingen 1982) 357–378, cited Visions; *idem*, The Evidence (Proceedings in other Jurisdictions) Act 1973 – An Interpretation: 39 I.C.L.Q. 120–135 (1990), cited Evidence; *idem*, One Hundred Years of Hague Conferences on Private International Law: 42 *ibidem* 553–653 (1993), cited Hundred Years; *Lorenzen*, The Theory of Qualifications and the Conflict of Laws: 20 Col.L.Rev. 247 – 282 (1920), cited Theory; *idem*, The Qualification, Classification, or Characterization Problem in the Conflict of Laws: 50 Yale L.J. 743–761 (1940/1941), cited Qualification; *Makarov*, Quellen des Internationalen Privatrechts (ed. 3 Tübingen 1976), cited Quellen; *Martens*, Nouveau Recueil des Traités. Ser. 1: 1771–1871 (Göttingen 1817–1874), Ser. 2: 1874–1907 (Göttingen and Leipzig 1876–1908), Ser. 3: 1906–1941 (Leipzig and Greifswald 1908–1943); *Maury*, Règles générales des conflits de lois: Rec.des Cours 57 (1936 III) 329–567; *Neuhaus*, Die Grundbegriffe des internationalen

Privatrechts (ed. 2 Tübingen 1976); *Niederer*, Die Qualifikation als Grundproblem des Internationalen Privatrechts (ed. 3 Zürich 1961); *von Overbeck*, Les questions générales du droit international privé à la lumière des codifications et projets récents: Rec.des Cours 176 (1982 III) 9–258; *Parry*, Consolidated Treaty Series 1648–1919 (231 vol.) (Dobbs Ferry, N.Y. 1969–1981); *Raape,* Les rapports juridiques entre parents et enfants: Rec.des Cours 50 (1934 IV) 401–544; *Rabel*, Das Problem der Qualifikation: RabelsZ 5 (1931) 241–288, cited Qualifikation; *idem*, Conflict of Laws I (ed. 2 Ann Arbor, Mich. 1958), II (ed. 2 Ann Arbor, Mich. 1960), cited Conflict; *Rigaux*, La théorie des qualifications en droit international privé (Paris 1956), cited Théorie; *Weber*, Die Theorie der Qualifikation (Tübingen 1986); *Wengler*, Die Vorfrage im Kollisionsrecht: RabelsZ 8 (1934) 148–251, cited Vorfrage; *idem*, Réflexions sur la technique des qualifications en droit international privé: Rev.crit. d.i.p. 1954, 661–691, cited Réflexions; *Wolff, M.*, Private International Law (ed. 2 Oxford 1950), cited PIL; *Zweigert*, Die Dritte Schule im Internationalen Privatrecht: Festschrift Raape (Hamburg 1948) 35–52.

2. BELGIUM: *Gothot*, Le renouveau de la tendance unilatéraliste en droit international privé: Rev.crit. d.i.p. 1971, 1–36, 209–243 and 415–450; *Rigaux,* Droit international privé I (ed. 2 Brussels 1987), cited Droit.

3. FRANCE: *Ancel*, L'objet de la qualification: Clunet 1980, 227–268; *Bartin*, De l'impossibilité d'arriver à la suppression définitive des conflits de lois: *ibidem* 1897, 225–255, 466–495 and 720–735, cited Impossibilité; *idem*, Principes de droit international privé I (Paris 1930), II (Paris 1932), cited Principes; *idem*, La doctrine des qualifications et ses rapports avec le caractère national du conflit des lois: Rec.des Cours 31 (1930 I) 561–621, cited Doctrine; *Batiffol and Lagarde*, Traité élémentaire de droit international privé I (ed. 8 Paris 1993); *Lehmann*, Les qualifications: J.Cl.Dr.Int. VIII (Paris, loose-leaf) Fasc. 531 (11, 1988 (1)–(34)); *Niboyet*, Traité de droit international privé III (Paris 1944), cited Traité; *idem,* Le problème des "qualifications" sur le terrain des traités diplomatiques: Rev.crit.d.i.p. 1935, 1–34, cited Problème; *idem*, Les doubles impositions au point de vue juridique: Rec.des Cours 31 (1930 I) 1–103, cited Impositions; *Plaisant*, Les règles de conflits de lois dans les traités (Paris 1946).

|4. GERMANY: *Von Bar, Chr.*, Internationales Privatrecht I (1987), II (1991) (Munich); *Kropholler*, Internationales Privatrecht (ed. 2 Tübingen 1994); *Lewald*, Internationales Privatrecht (Leipzig 1930), cited Privatrecht; *Makarov*, Theorie und Praxis der Qualifikation: Vom Deutschen zum Europäischen Recht. Festschrift Dölle II (Tübingen 1963) 149–177, cited Theorie; *Neuner*, Der Sinn der international-privatrechtlichen Norm (Brünn and Leipzig 1932), cited Sinn; and *idem* [Commentary on his book]: RabelsZ 7 (1933) 733–735, cited Commentary; *Selb*, Martin Wolff und die Lehre von der Qualifikation nach der lex causae im internationalen Privatrecht: AcP 157 (1958/1959) 341–349; *Soergel and Siebert (-Kegel)*, Bürgerliches Gesetzbuch. Kommentar VIII (Einführungsgesetz) (ed. 11 Stuttgart, Berlin a.o. 1989); *Wolff, M.*, Das internationale Privatrecht Deutschlands (ed. 3 Berlin, Göttingen and Heidelberg 1954), cited Privatrecht.

5. ITALY: *Vitta*, Diritto internazionale privato I (Turin 1972), III (Turin 1975).

6. PORTUGAL: *Ferrer-Correia*, Das Problem der Qualifikation nach dem portugiesischen internationalen Privatrecht: ZfRV 11 (1970) 114–135.

7. SWITZERLAND: *Knoepfler and Schweizer*, Précis de droit international privé (Bern 1992); *Schnitzer*, Handbuch des internationalen Privatrechts (ed. 4 Basel 1957); *Vischer and von Planta*, Internationales Privatrecht (ed. 2 Basel and Frankfurt a.M. 1987); *Vischer*, Die rechtsvergleichenden Tatbestände im internationalen Privatrecht (Basel 1953).

8. UNITED KINGDOM: *Beckett*, The Question of Classification in Private International Law: 15 Brit. YB Int.L. 46–81 (1935); *Dicey and Morris (-Collins a.o.)*, The Conflict of Laws (ed. 12 London 1993); *Cheshire and North*, Private International Law (ed. 12 London 1992); *Robertson*, Characterization in the Conflict of Laws (Cambridge, Mass. 1940); *Unger*, The Place of Classification in Private International Law: 19 Bell Yard 3–21 (1937).

9. UNITED STATES OF AMERICA: *Cavers*, A Critique of the Choice of Law Problem: 47 Harv.L.Rev. 173–208 (1933), cited Critique; *idem*, The Choice of Law Process (Ann Arbor, Mich. 1965), cited Process; *idem*, Contemporary Conflicts Law in American Perspective: Rec.des Cours 131 (1970 III) 77–308, cited Perspective.

(2)

Ago 1; *Ancel* 3.
Von Bar, Chr. 4; *von Bar, C.L.* 1; *Bartin* 3; *Batiffol* 3; *Beckett* 8; *Bernasconi* 1.
Cavers 9; *Cheshire* 8.
Dicey 8.
Falconbridge 1; *Ferrer-Correia* 6.
Gothot 2.
Hausmann 1.
Jayme 1.
Kahn 1; *Kegel* 4; *Knoepfler* 7; *Kropholler* 4.
Lagarde 3; *Lehmann* 3; *Lewald* 1, 4; *Lipstein* 1; *Lorenzen* 1.
Makarov 1, 4; *Martens* 1; *Maury* 1; *Morris* 8.
Neuhaus 1; *Neuner* 4; *Niboyet* 3; *Niederer* 1; *North* 8.
Von Overbeck 1.
Parry 1; *Plaisant* 3; *von Planta* 7.
Raape 1; *Rabel* 1; *Rigaux* 1, 2; *Robertson* 8.
Schnitzer 7; *Schweizer* 7; *Selb* 4; *Siebert* 4; *Soergel* 4.
Unger 8.
Vischer 7; *Vitta* 5.
Weber 1; *Wengler* 1; *Wolff, M.* 1, 4.
Zweigert 1.

| List of Statutory Material

(Instruments arranged in reverse chronological order)

International Agreements

Hague Convention on the Law Applicable to Succession to the Estates of Deceased Persons of 20 Oct. 1988: Rec.Hague Conf. 1951–1988, 340, 28 Int.Leg.Mat. 146 (1989);

Hague Convention on the Law Applicable to Contracts for the International Sale of Goods of 22 Dec. 1986: Rec.Hague Conf. 1951–1988, 326, 24 Int.Leg.Mat. 1573 (1985);

Hague Convention on the Law Applicable to Trusts of 1 July 1985: Rec.Hague Conf. 1951–1988, 314, 23 Int.Leg.Mat. 1388 (1984);

Rome Convention on the Law Applicable to Contractual Obligations of 19 June 1980, in force 1 April 1991, OJ EC 1980 L 266 p. 1;

Hague Convention on the Recognition and Enforcement of Decisions Relating to Maintenance Obligations of 2 Oct. 1973: Rec.Hague Conf. 1951–1988, 202, 1056 UNTS 199;

Hague Convention on the Law Applicable to Products Liability of 2 Oct. 1973: Rec.Hague Conf. 1951–1988, 192, 11 Int.Leg.Mat. 1283 (1972), 1056 UNTS 187;

Hague Convention on the Law Applicable to Traffic Accidents of 4 May 1971: Rec.Hague Conf. 1951–1988, 142, 965 UNTS 411;

Hague Convention on the Recognition and Enforcement of Foreign Judgments in Civil and Commercial Matters of 1 Feb. 1971: Rec.Hague Conf. 1951–1988, 106;

Hague Convention on the Taking of Evidence Abroad in Civil and Commercial Matters of 18 March 1970: Rec.Hague Conf. 1951–1988, 152, 847 UNTS 231;

Hague Convention Concerning the Powers of Authority and the Law Applicable in Respect of the Protection of Infants of 5 Oct. 1961: Rec.Hague Conf. 1951–1988, 42, 658 UNTS 143;

Hague Convention on the Conflict of Laws Relating to the Form of Testamentary Dispositions of 5 Oct. 1961, Rec.Hague Conf. 1951–1988, 48, 510 UNTS 175;

Hague Convention on the Law Applicable to International Sale of Goods of 15 June 1955, Rec. Hague Conf. 1951–1988, 12, 510 UNTS 147;

Bretton Woods Agreements of 27 Dec. 1945, 2 UNTS 29;

Geneva Convention Providing a Uniform Law for Bills of Exchange and Promissory Notes of 7 June 1930, 143 LNTS 257, 172 UNTS 412;

Bustamante Code of 20 Nov. 1928, 86 LNTS III;

Hague Convention on the Effects of Marriage of 17 July 1905: *Martens* 6 (3rd ser. 1913) 480, *Parry* 199 (1905) 17;

Projet d'une Convention sur les conflits de lois en matière de successions et de testaments (Draft of a Convention on the conflict of laws concerning successions and last wills) of 4 July 1904, Act.La Haye 4 (1904) 212;

Hague Convention on the Conclusion of Marriages of 12 June 1902, *Martens* 31 (2d ser. 1904) 706, *Parry* 191 (1902) 253.

Austria

PIL – Federal Law on private international law (*Bundesgesetz über das internationale Privatrecht*) of 15 June 1978, BGBl. no. 304/1978, Rev.crit.d.i.p. 1979, 174, RabelsZ 43 (1979) 375.

Belize

Trust Act 1992, 6 Trust L.Int. II (1992).

France

Law no. 85–98 on bankruptcy (*Loi relative au redressement et à la liquidation judiciaires des entreprises*) of 25 Jan. 1985, JO 26 Jan. p. 1097;

Law no. 80–335 on the effects of reservation of title in sales contracts (*Loi relative aux effets des clauses de réserve de propriété dans les contrats de vente*) of 12 May 1980, JO 13 May p. 1202;

Law concerning the fixing of the sales price for enterprises (*Loi relative au règlement du prix de vente des fonds de commerce*) of 29 June 1935, JO 30 June p. 6914.

Germany

Introd.Law CC – Introductory Law to the Civil Code (*Einführungsgesetz zum Bürgerlichen Gesetzbuch*), as proclaimed on 21 Sept. 1994, BGBl. I 2494, corr. 1997 I 1061;

Federal Law on children's benefits (*Bundeskindergeldgesetz*) of 31 Jan. 1994, BGBl. I 169;

Law on bills of exchange (*Wechselgesetz*) of 21 June 1933, RGBl. I 399, BGBl. III 4133–1.

Hungary

Decree-Law no. 13/1979 on private international law (*Törvényerejű rendelet a nemzetközi magánjogról*) of 31 May 1979, M.K. no. 33/1979, Rev.crit.d.i.p. 1981, 158.

Italy

PIL – Law no. 218 on the reform of the Italian regime of private international law (*Riforma del sistema italiano di diritto internazionale privato*) of 31 May 1995 no. 218, in force since 1 Sept. 1995, GU 3 June no. 68.

Portugal

Decree-Law no. 47344 on private international law provisions of the new Civil Code (*Código Civil Direitos dos estrangeiros e conflitos de leis* [CC Title I | cap. 3]) of 25 Nov. 1966, D.Gov. I no. 274, Rev.crit. d.i.p. 1968, 369, RabelsZ 32 (1968) 513.

Rumania

Law no. 105 on private international law (*Lege cu privire la reglementarea raporturilor de drept international privat*) of 22 Sept. 1992, M.of. no. 245 of 1 Oct. 1992, amended M.of. no. 254 of 26 Oct. 1993, Rev.crit. d.i.p. 1994, 167, RabelsZ 58 (1994) 534.

Switzerland

PIL – Federal Law on private international law (*Bundesgesetz über das internationale Privatrecht*) of 18 Dec. 1987, BBl. I 5, AS 1988, 1776 (in force 1 Jan. 1989).

United Kingdom

Trusts of Land and Appointment of Trustees Act 1996, c. 47;
Private International Law (Miscellaneous Provisions) Act 1995, c.42;
Law of Property (Miscellaneous Provisions) Act 1989, c. 34;
Insolvency Act 1986, c. 45;
Foreign Limitation Periods Act 1984, c. 16;
Administration of Justice Act 1982, c. 53;
Inheritance (Provisions for Family and Dependants) Act 1975, c.63;
Matrimonial Causes Act 1973, c. 18;
Matrimonial Causes Act 1965, c. 72;
Matrimonial Causes (Property and Maintenance) Act 1958, 6 & 7 Eliz. 2, c. 35;
Matrimonial Causes Act 1950, 14 Geo. 6, c. 25;
Inheritance (Family Provisions) Act 1938, 1 & 2 Geo. 6, c. 45;
Law of Property Act 1925, 15 & 16 Geo. 5, c. 20;
Bankruptcy Act 1914, 4 & 5 Geo. 5, c. 59;
Bills of Exchange Act 1882, 45 & 46 Vict., c. 61;
Statute of Frauds 1677, 29 Car. 2, c. 3.

The British Islands

Guernsey: Trusts (Guernsey) Law 1989, Ordres en Conseil 31 (1988–1989) 217.
Jersey: Trust (Jersey) Law of 31 May 1983 and 14 March 1984, as amended 21 July 1984, Rec.Lois 1984, 27, 11 Commonw.Bull. 238 (1985), Rev.dr.aff. int. 1987, 419.

Dependent Territories

Cayman Islands: Trust Law 1967, rev. 1976, Cayman Islands Gaz. 1976 no. 23.

United States of America

California: Probate Code 1990, Stat. 1990, c. 79, 52–54A West's Ann.Cal.Codes. Probate (1991).

Yugoslavia

PIL – Law on private international law (*Zakon o rjesavanju sukoba zakona s propisima drugih zemalja u odredenim odnosima*) of 15 July 1982, Sl.l.Y. no. 43 pos. 525, Rev.crit.d.i.p. 1983, 353, IPRax. 1983, 6.

Two Basic Problems of
Private International Law Revised*

Ronald Graveson entertained a particular interest in general problems of private international law. It is therefore fitting, in remembering Graveson's contribution to the subject, to present a revision of two problems which have attracted constant attention for more than a hundred years: *renvoi* and characterisation.

Renvoi

Let us turn first to *renvoi*, which extends a reference to foreign law to include foreign private international law. Although every student of the topic had to define his position, the result has been meagre: either an acceptance or rejection of the technique and its variants, sometimes combined with an enumeration of the practice of the courts in applying it. The question *why* and *when* foreign private international law is to be taken into consideration had been neglected until the *Institut de droit international* took it up in 1993.[1]

[Editorial note: first published in King's College Law Journal 10 (1999), 167–176.]

* [Kurt Lipstein] Emeritus Professor of Comparative Law, University of Cambridge and Fellow of Clare College, Cambridge. This article is based on a lecture which was delivered in memory of Professor R H Graveson CBE QC at King's College London on 7 May 1998.

[1] (1994) 65.ii *Annuaire de l'Institut de droit international* 17, 115.

Two previous discussions between 1896 and 1900[2] and again between 1957 and 1965[3] had proved inconclusive. Only a wider examination, advocated by the late Professor Wilhelm Wengler, which seeks broadly to analyse when foreign private international law is to be taken into consideration, was expected to yield concrete results.[4]

A preliminary survey of any relevant legislation carried out on a global basis showed that a considerable number of countries either accepted *renvoi* unconditionally, or limited its operation to a reference on or back, or circumscribed it by general provisions, such as "if reasonable or equitable", or "unless it contravenes the purpose of a reference on or back", or "*sauf indication contraire*". Equally the legislation in a considerable number of countries either rejected any reference on or back, while a | considerable number ignored the problem altogether. Only four countries provided specifically when foreign private international law is to be taken into account. In Germany these detailed specific provisions appear to cover only matters of status, matrimonial property and succession. At the same time an impressive list which cuts across that permitting *renvoi* excludes it.[5] Swiss law comprises more or less the same topics by more general and less elaborate legislation.[6] In Portugal a sophisticated combination of general principles, modifications and exemptions throws the burden on the *lex causae* and envisages principally cases involving status and succession. If, however, the application of foreign private international law results in the invalidity or ineffectiveness of an act valid according to the applicable domestic law, foreign private international law is to be disregarded.[7] This formulation reflects in negative terms the general opinion that foreign private international law is to be taken into consideration if it results in the validity or the effectiveness of an act or a transaction. Louisiana legislation in 1991 combines the American technique of "approaches" with the orthodox use of rules as applied elsewhere. Foreign private international law is only to be considered in three

---

[2] (1895) 14 *Annuaire de l'Institut de droit international* 284; (1896) 15 *Annuaire* 188; (1897) 16 *Annuaire* 14, 181. 184; (1898) 17 *Annuaire* 14, 36, 212, 230; (1900) 18 *Annuaire* 34, 41.

[3] (1957) 47.ii *Annuaire de l'Institut de droit international* 1, 176; (1961) 49.ii *Annuaire* 272, 282, 295, 318, 320. 327; (1965) 51.ii *Annuaire* 145, 150, 258.

[4] (1994) 65 *Annuaire de l'Institut de droit international* 115.

[5] Law of 25 July 1986, arts. 4(1), 7, 9–11, 13–15, 17(1), 19–26; noted in (1986) 50 *Rabels Zeitschrift für ausländisches und internationales Privatrecht* 663, and in (1987) 76 *Revue critique de droit international privé* 170.

[6] Law of 18 December 1987, arts 14, 37(1), 91(1), 119(3), 124(3); noted in (1988) 52 *Rabels Zeitschrift für auslädisches und internationales Privatrecht* 378, and in (1988) 77 *Revue critique de droit international privé* 409.

[7] Law of 25 November 1964, arts. 17–19, noted in (1968) 32. *Rabels Zeitschrift für ausländisches und internationales Privatrecht* 513, and in (1968) 57 *Revue critique de droit international privé* 369.

cases, namely those concerning the form of wills of immovables, succession to immovables situated abroad and proprietary rights in immovables abroad. In all other circumstances considerations of the preponderant impairment of the policies of the laws of the countries concerned are to determine the discretion whether to consider foreign private international law or not.[8]

Among the countries where the question has not been the object of legislation those which favour taking foreign private international law into consideration also appear to limit it to status (Belgium, France, England, possibly the Netherlands), matrimonial property (Belgium, France) and succession (Belgium, France, England, possibly the Netherlands, but probably not Scotland), all understood in a broad sense. While the legislatures and the courts have faced the question whether foreign private international law is to be applied in particular situations, they have not focused on the broader issue of the purpose and the usefulness of relying on the principle that a reference to foreign law includes the latter's rules of private international law.

Ronald Graveson has written that the purpose of private international law is justice,[9] but so is the purpose of all law. That of private international law in particular may be said to be to ensure certainty, effectiveness, uniformity and compliance with the common intention of the parties.

Certainty, in the sense of an identity of solutions globally, is only achieved if the connecting factors of the conflict rules of the *lex fori* and the *lex causae* are identical and not subject to different interpretations, or lead to the same result (a British sub|ject dies domiciled in Italy leaving immovables in England; English law applies in both countries) or if in a conflict between the connecting factor nationality and the connecting factor domicile, the latter is to prevail. This solution was advocated in 1938 by Meijers,[10] adopted by the Hague Renvoi Convention of 15 June 1955, and envisaged in the abortive Benelux Convention of 3 July 1969. In order to be complete a similar hierarchy between situs and other connecting factors would have to be devised. In the situations described here, certainty also ensures uniformity and effectiveness. Unfortunately the conditions in which global certainty, uniformity and effectiveness can be achieved are limited.

Normally the *foreign* rule of private international law will contain a dif-

---

[8] Law 923 of 1991; Code Civil, arts. 3515–3594. See Symeon Symeonides, "Problems and Dilemmas in Codifying Choice of Law for Torts: The Louisiana Experience in Comparative Perspective" (1990) 38 *American Journal of Comparative Law* 431; also Symeonides "Les grands problèmes de droit international privé et la nouvelle codification de Louisiana" (1992) 81 *Revue critique de droit international privé* 223.

[9] R. Graveson, *Conflict of Laws* (7th edn., 1974) at 7.

[10] E.M. Meijers, "La Question de Renvoi" (1938) 38 *Bulletin de l'Institut Juridique International* 192 at 224.

ferent connecting factor from that of the forum and the initial choice of jurisdiction will determine which of the two rules of private international law forms the *lex fori* and which is part of the *lex causae*. Thus the ultimate choice of law depends on which jurisdiction has been seised in the first place. No global and at best a relative uniformity can be achieved. Instead a reference back to the *lex fori* at least assures effectiveness in the country of the forum which exercises factual control and may support the validity of an act or a transaction. Thus it can be argued that even if no global uniformity and certainty is achieved in the great majority of cases where foreign private international law is taken into consideration, unquestioned ultimate applicability of the *lex fori* constitutes an element of effectiveness, since the attitude of foreign law is respected. This is so especially if taking foreign private international law into consideration leads to a reference on. Moreover the original relative effectiveness may assume a broader dimension if the reference back or on is incorporated in a judgment which can be recognized abroad.

Particular instances favouring taking foreign private international law into consideration include the following:

(1) When the parties, in the exercise of the right of free choice, have chosen a particular system of law, including that system's rules of private international law, the normal rule (to be mentioned later on) that a lawful choice of law nominating a particular system of law is not to be tampered with by outside forces may require a qualification. Naturally the parties themselves can make a choice of law by referring to the rules of private international law of the law chosen, and the law thus rendered applicable will represent the law freely chosen by them, albeit by a strangely circuitous route. Thus, the new German Law on Arbitration Proceedings of 22 December 1997[11] envisages it expressly. Moreover, if in the absence of express choice the proper law is applied as selected by implication or on objective grounds, the objective approach may perhaps justify taking into consideration the rules of private international law of the law applicable in the absence of an express choice of law.

(2) Further, if in a conflict of laws in time an act or transaction valid according to the choice of law rules of the law applicable in the courts of State | A is questioned incidentally in later proceedings in State B in which a reference to the law of A is normally restricted to the domestic law of A, nevertheless the respect of acquired rights demands the application of the rules of private international law of A. For example: marriage of Swiss uncle and niece in Russia, invalid according to Swiss domestic law but valid by Swiss private international law which refers to Russian law, challenged subsequently in proceedings in Italy, at a time when *renvoi* was excluded.

---

[11] BGBl 1997 i 3224. at 1051.

(3) More generally, if the main question in proceedings involves a preliminary or incidental question, the law governing the main question, including its rules of private international law, may have to give way to the law governing the preliminary or incidental question including its rules of private international law treated as a separate main question, especially if the validity of the institution or relationship which is the subject-matter of the preliminary issue is safeguarded thereby.[12]

On the other hand, foreign private international law should not be considered in the following situations:

(1) If the parties are accorded a free choice of law and have exercised it by selecting a particular system of domestic law without expressly including the latter's rules of private international law. If the law allows the parties to determine their legal relations by freely adopting any one of the world's legal systems the principle would be defeated by the imposition by the same law of another legal system. As stated before, the parties, for reasons of their own, however circuitous, can of course include in their choice of a particular legal system its rules of private international law. Moreover, as stated before, it can be argued that in the absence of an express choice of law, the proper law objectively ascertained may include its rules of private international law.

(2) If the forum contains alternative choice of law rules these may operate either on an equal footing or as substitutes for each other, an arrangement known as "Kegel's ladder".[13] Similarly a cumulation of laws invites the same conclusion.

(3) If mandatory rules of a third legal system are applied supplementing the applicable law.[14] Their purpose would be frustrated by the inclusion of that law's rules of private international law.

(4) A tendency has made itself felt in continental Europe to discern what has been called a "hidden *renvoi*" when the forum refers to foreign law and the applicable foreign, mainly common, law regards the issue (e.g. of divorce) as one of exclusive jurisdiction based on domicile or habitual residence and treats jurisdiction and applicable law as co-extensive. If the foreign court refuses to assume jurisdiction in the absence of a local domicile or |habitual residence, that court is said to have referred to the substantive law of the state where in its opinion the party concerned is domiciled or habitually resident. However, by declining jurisdiction English or similar law does not call for the exercise of jurisdiction by what it regards as the competent courts (even if it grants recognition). Still less does it designate the law of the

---

[12] E.g. *Shaw v Gould* (1868) LR 3 HL 55; R. v *Brentwood Superintendent Registrar of Marriages ex parte Arias* [1968] 2 QB 956; *Schwebel v Ungar* [1965] 48 DLR (2d) 644.

[13] French Code Civil Arts. 311.14, 311.16, 31 1.17 and German EG-BGB 1986, paras. 13(2), 14(1), 14(3).

[14] Rome Contract Convention 1980 Art. 7.

foreign domicile or any other law as the law applicable. In short: "the refusal to assume jurisdiction is not equal to a reference back or on to another jurisdiction, and, *ex hypothesi*, the English [or similar common law] court has never been seized at all".[15]

(5) Finally, if the *lex fori* contains rules of domestic law which are identical with those of the *lex causae*, and the latter's private international law refers back to the *lex fori*, resulting in what is sometimes called a false conflict, the forum, in its discretion, may reject the reference back. In exercising it the forum may perhaps be influenced by the consideration that in applying its own law the way is open to appeals on point of law; in applying the *lex causae*, only questions of fact present themselves and, save in exceptional circumstances, the interpretation of foreign law is not subject to an appeal.

Characterization

Leaving aside recent currents which revive statutist notions (Currie and other American writers[16]) and unilateral choice of law rules (which leave the choice of foreign law open: Niboyet, Gothot[17]), there exists general agreement that modern conflict rules focus on broad categories of typical legal institutions, each of which embraces whole sets of substantive private law, limited in number, but capable of expansion. They include status (including legitimacy etc.), capacity, marriage, divorce, judicial reparation, maintenance, guardianship, corporations, contracts, quasi-contracts, including unjust enrichment and restitution, interests in movables and immovables, formalities and foreign judgments. These kinds of typical situations will here be called "operative facts"; they are connected with specific systems of domestic law by personal, territorial or voluntary links, called "connecting factors". Together they constitute choice of law rules.

---

[15] Kurt Lipstein, "General Principles of Private International Law" (1972) 135 *Hague Recueil* 104, at 213.

[16] Brainerd Currie. *Selected Essays in the Conflict of Laws* (1963); also B. Currie, "The Disinterested Third State" (1963) 28 *Law and Contemporary Problems* 754; Amos Shapira. *The Interest Approach to Choke of Law* (1970); William Baxter, "Choice of Law and the Federal System" (1963) 16 *Stanford* LR 6; Russell Weintraub, "The Emerging Problems in Judicial Administration of a State-Interest Analysis of Tort Conflict of Laws Problems" (1971) 44 *Southern California LR* 877; Leonard Ramer. "Choice of Law: Interest Analysis and Cost-Contribution" (1974) 47 *Southern California LR* 817; Robert Sedler, "The Governmental Interest Approach to Choice of Law: An Analysis and a Reformulation" (1977) 25 *UCLA LR* 181.

[17] Jean Niboyet, *Traité de droit international privé français*. Vol. III (1944) *passim*, esp. 959–960; Pierre Gothot, "Le renouveau de la tendance unilatéraliste en droit international privé" (1971) 60 *Revue Critique de droit international privé* 1, 209, and 415.

These choice of law rules serve to test whether a claim or defence alleging or denying the existence of a relationship based on the private law of some legal system, local or foreign, is governed by that law or the law of some other system. This depends | upon which category of the forum's conflict rules covers the issue. Since the conflict rules are formulated in general terms of categories of private law familiar to the forum – contract, tort, succession – while individual claims or defences rely on specific rules of a particular system of private law, which may be foreign, it is *necessary to interpret the operative facts of the forum's conflict rules and the claim or defence in terms of each other* by the process known as "characterization" or "qualification". The three basic methods advocated hitherto: interpretation according to the *lex fori* (Kahn[18]), the *lex causae* (Despagnet[19]) or broadly on a comparative basis (Rabel[20]) have proved deficient since the interaction of two different types of rules is in issue. One is designed to indicate the applicable law for broad categories of rules of any foreign legal system; the other reflects the domestic law of a specific legal system. Both must be interpreted broadly, but while the operative facts of choice of law rules can be subjected to a *comparative analysis*, claims formulated in the light of a particular domestic law must be classified according to their *function* in their *own* legal system and not according to their formal placement within it. It will therefore be argued here that the law of a particular country, although not necessarily the same country, becomes relevant during two separate stages. The first seeks to ascertain which set of operative facts of the forum's choice of law rules is called upon by the domestic rule – either of the *lex fori* or of foreign law – on which a party relies. This may or may not lead to the application of the law on which the party relied in its initial pleadings.

The second stage is limited to the proof and the application of the law so found. It is of no concern that according to the applicable foreign law a different characterization would have led to application of a different choice of law rule of the forum. This aspect was already considered during the first stage, when the function of the rule supporting the claim was analysed.

It follows that the two stages identified here involve different legal processes: the first may require an exercise in comparative law to assimilate claims based on foreign law involving, on the one hand, a broad interpretation of the operative facts of the choice of law rule, and, on the other hand, a functional analysis of the rule of domestic law pleaded by the party. The second is concerned with evidence. The following survey of the practice bears out this conclusion.

---

[18] Franz Kahn. *Abhandlungen zum Internationalen Privatrecht* (1928) 1–123.

[19] Frantz Despagnet, "Des conflits de lois relatifs à la qualification des rapports juridiques" (1898) 25 *Journal de droit international* 253.

[20] Ernst Rabel, "Das Problem der Qualifikation" (1931) 5 *Zeitschrift für ausländisches und internationales Privatrecht* 241.

Identical in Form and Substance

The simplest situation exists if the claim or defence is identical in form and substance with similar claims and defences known in the domestic law of the forum's choice of the rule. Only one set of operative facts is involved.

Some examples are: (a) the marriage in England by a Frenchman over 21 but under 30 years old to an Englishwoman required the consent (*acte respecteux*) of his parents according to French law, but the absence of such a consent did not affect the validity of the marriage. In English law, consent by parents to the marriage of a minor can|be replaced by permission given by a court, but the absence of consent does not render the marriage invalid. Both types of consent concerned formalities. Consequently the *lex loci actus* applied, being the English choice of law rule dealing with formalities.[21]

(b) The right of the state to the estate in England of a *de cuius* domiciled in Austria, who died intestate without next of kin, is a *jus regale* in both countries. The Crown in England takes the assets in England in virtue of its sovereign right and the choice of law rule concerning succession does not apply.[22]

(c) On the contemporaneous death in London of a mother and her daughter, both domiciled in Germany, the younger was deemed to have survived the elder according to English law;[23] by German law the parties were deemed to have died at the same time.[24] Both English and German law establish an irrebuttable presumption amounting to a substantive rule of succession, not merely a rule of evidence. German law applies as the law governing the succession.[25]

Identical in Form, Different in Substance

(a) The requirement of parental consent under French law to the marriage of a child under the age of 21 is an essential part of the marriage ceremony. In its absence the child lacks capacity to marry. The child's personal (French) law applies and the marriage is void.[26] In *Ogden v Ogden*[27] an English court mistakenly treated this requirement of consent as equivalent to parental consent in English law, which is a formality governed by the *lex loci actus*.

---

[21] *Simonin v Mallac* (1860) 2 Sw. & Tr. 67.
[22] *Re Bamett's Trusts* [1902] 1 Ch. 847; *Re Musurus* [1936] 4 All ER 1666.
[23] Law of Property Act 1925 s. 184.
[24] BGB para. 20.
[25] *In re Cohn* [1945] Ch. 5.
[26] French Code Civil Art. 148.
[27] [1908] P 46.

English law was applied to the marriage in England. As a result the wife was regarded as validly married in England while her husband was free to marry again after the marriage had been annulled in France.[28]

(b) The requirement under the old Article 992 (now abrogated) of the Dutch Civil Code that a will made abroad by a Dutch national must be in notarial form to be valid was treated in France as a formality governed by the *lex loci actus*, French law, while in the Netherlands it may have concerned the capacity to make a will.[29]

(c) In *Huber* v *Steiner*[30] limitation of actions was treated as procedural and therefore governed by the *lex fori*. In reality the alleged procedural character is influenced by its binding character which may express a spatially conditioned internal rule or public policy, but it also contains certain aspects of substantive law which may prevail in foreign legal systems.[31] In Germany a contract governed by Tennessee law was held to include that law's limitation of actions rule, which were treated as relating to substance although regarded as procedural in Tennessee[32] Such laws were both substantive and procedural; partly procedural in Germany (striking out); partly substantive | at common law; securities remain unaffected; the substance counts, not its formal denomination.

(d) Further, is the requirement that certain contracts must be in writing[33] a question of substance or form? The test is whether the requirement serves to protect against hasty action or to perpetuate evidence (publicity).

Different in Form, Same in Substance

Breach of promise to marry (where still actionable) may sound in contract at common law and in tort in France; damages, the degree of fault and the limitation of actions may differ, but the existence of mutual promises is common and turns the scales towards mutuality and contract Contracts in favour of third parties and the liability in tort of the solicitor in *White* v *Jones*[34] show the same features; the same applies to *culpa in contrahendo*.[35] Product liability sounds both in contract and in tort when applied between the original parties to the bargain, but in tort to the outsiders claiming under the Hague Convention 1973.

---

[28] *Cf. De Massa* v *De Massa* [1939] 2 All ER 150.

[29] Niboyet, *Traité*, Vol. III. n. 18 above, 363.

[30] (1835) 2 Bing. NC 202.

[31] See now the Foreign Limitation Periods Act 1984 s. 2(1).

[32] RGZ 145.121, 6 July 1934.

[33] E.g. Law of Property Act 1925 s. 40(1); French Civil Code Art. 1341.

[34] [1995] AC 207.

[35] *Esso Petroleum* v *Mardon* [1976] QB 801; see also *Ward* v *Tesco* [1976] 1 WLR 810.

Unknown in Form and Substance by the Forum

When a claim, such as that under Greek law, for a dowry to be assessed in the discretion of the court, having regard to the father's wealth and social position, came before an English court it failed. The reason given was that the *lex fori* did not provide a remedy, not that the substance was unknown.[36] It is possible that an analogous application of the Matrimonial Causes Act 1965 section 17[37] (relief on divorce) or of the Matrimonial Causes Act, 1950 section 17, 1958 sections 2, 3 (alimony), could have filled the gap. The recognition of foreign proxy marriages did not cause a problem, although the form is unknown in England.[38] On the other hand a posthumous marriage validly concluded in France was not recognised in Germany, not because this form of marriage was unknown in Germany but because the surviving German spouse lacked the capacity to enter into such a marriage.[39]

Unknown in Form and Substance by Foreign Law

A claim to a *Versorgungsausgleich* (division of pension rights) according to German law brought in divorce proceedings governed by Italian law had to fail since no such institution existed in Italian law. In Italy this situation has now been regulated in a positive sense.[40]

Same Law, Whatever the Characterization

The consent of a German wife to the sale of a house in Spain belonging to German spouses is governed by the same (German) law irrespective of whether the consent|is treated as concerning the personal effects of marriage or agency.[41] A claim by a Luxemburg mother against a German father for maintenance of an illegitimate child is governed by German law no matter whether it is treated as sounding in tort in Luxembourg or as a claim for maintenance in Germany.[42]

---

[36] *Phrantzes* v *Argenti* [1966] 2 QB 19.
[37] Now Matrimonial Causes Act 1973 s. 24(1).
[38] *Apt* v *Apt* [1948] P 33.
[39] OLG Karlsruhe, 22 August 1990 [1990] IpRspr no 72.
[40] Law on Private International Law of 31 May 1995, art. 31.
[41] German Federal Supreme Court 24 November 1989 [1989] IPRspr no 3.
[42] OLG Karlsruhe, 20 March 1931 [1931] IPRspr no 96; OLG Frankfurt, 5 July 1973 [1973] IPRspr no 62.

Different in Form and Substance – Overlaps and Gaps

In a conflict of laws in time it may happen that the claim of a surviving spouse was characterised initially as one relating to matrimonial property according to the personal law of the spouses but as one relating to the law of succession following a change in the personal law, be it of nationality or domicile. As a result the surviving spouse may acquire an excessive share in the estate of the deceased. In the converse case, the same claim may be characterised originally as relating to succession and, upon a change of nationality or domicile as one relating to matrimonial property relations. In this case the surviving spouse receives nothing. The quandary in the first case can be resolved by treating the share obtained under the regime governing the matrimonial property relations as part of the share in the decedents estate. Illogically, but justly, the substantive law, and not the choice of law is adjusted. In the converse case only a legislative measure can fill the void.[43]

Secondary Characterization

The present analysis can dismiss secondary characterisation because the functional, not the formal, denomination of the claim or defence has been taken into account during the first stage when the claim or defence is being interpreted in the light of the operative facts of the forum's conflict rule. *Re Maldonado* provides a serious deterrent against engaging in this practice.[44] The present analysis does not touch, either, upon the characterisation of movables and immovables. Reliance on characterisation by the *lex situs* favoured in common law countries is not favoured in continental Europe. The reason is probably that at civil law a uniform notion of ownership coupled with a *numerus clausus* renders the distinction unnecessary. At the same time the difference between interests in land and personalty in common law countries invites a first investigation as to whether land is involved, unless two common law countries are involved.[45]

To conclude our remarks on the subject of characterisation, the classic controversy as to whether the *lex fori*, the *lex causae* or comparative law serves to resolve problems of characterisation fails to face reality. In fact a claim or defence based, as it must be, upon an alleged *lex causae* seeks to attract the application of one of several possible operative facts of a conflict

---

[43] Compare *Beaudoin* v *Trudel* [1937] 1 DLR 216 with California Probate Code s. 201.5.8.

[44] [1954] P 223.

[45] *Re Hoyles* [1911] 1 Ch. 179, 181.

rule of the *lex fori* expressed in categories fashioned within the framework of the *lex fori*. For this purpose each must be interpreted in terms of the other. This means that the function and not the denomination of the rule of domestic law pleaded must be analysed in order to fit it into the categories | (operative facts) of the conflict rules of the *lex fori*, interpreted broadly, and not limited to technical notions of the *lex fori*. Both must draw on comparative law to achieve this goal. Only then it emerges which choice of law rule of the forum is affected and which legal system is applicable.

Unusual Bedfellows – Renvoi and Foreign Characterization Joined Together

1. Basic Premises

For the purpose of the present investigation it may be useful to set out the premises on which it is based.[1]

Renvoi can arise when the choice of law rule of the forum employs one connecting factor to the operative facts[2] of the forum's choice of law rule in order to determine the applicable law, while the choice of law rule of the law referred to employs a different connecting factor to its operative facts. Any different characterization of the latter has been taken into account when the function of the rule of foreign law pleaded by a party has been analysed in order to determine which conflicts rule of the forum operates (see *infra*). The forum recovers the power to apply its own do|mestic law but need not do so.

[Editorial note: first published in Basedow et al. (eds.): Private Law in the International Arena. From National Conflict Rules towards Harmonization and Unification – Liber Amicorum Kurt Siehr (2000), 405–412.]

[1] Lipstein, *International Encyclopedia of Comparative Law*, Vol. III Ch. 23, nos. 1–21 (in course of publication).

[2] The term "operative facts" indicates that part of a choice of law rule which represents a category of typical legal situations, such as contract, tort, succession. The term is used for want of a better expression. See Rabel, *Conflict of Laws*, 2nd edn. (1958) Vol. I, 47. For other terms see Neuhaus, *Die Grundbegriffe des internationales Privatrechts*, 2. Aufl. (1976) 103, 126; Rigaux, *La théorie des qualifications en droit international privé* (1956) p. 244.

Characterization affects the interpretation of the operative facts of the forum's choice of law rules in the light of a claim or a defence formulated and pleaded in accordance with some system of laws, foreign or local. It is a preliminary process which determines which operative facts among two or more choice of law rules of the forum are involved leading to the application of a particular system of law to the issue in question.

2. Consequences

Renvoi determines the ultimate choice of the relevant connecting factor attached to a single category of operative facts embodied in the choice of law rule both of the *lex fori* and of the law referred to.

Characterization results in the selection of one of several operative facts, forming part respectively of two or more choice of law rules of the forum after an analysis of the function of the legal provision pleaded by the party or parties coupled with a broad interpretation of the operative facts in issue. Once this process has been concluded the appropriate choice of law rule has been ascertained and proof of foreign law can begin.

Thus, at most, the choice of law process in the forum may comprise first a characterization of the claim or defence resulting in the choice of the appropriate choice of law rule of the forum leading to a reference to a particular legal system. Subsequently the application of the legal system so found may end in a reference back, if the forum accepts the substitution of its own connecting factor by another referred to, if foreign.

In the normal type of case, once characterization by the forum of the claim or defence has taken place by analysing the function of the law pleaded coupled with a broad interpretation of the operative facts of the forum's choice of law rule, a secondary characterization according to the law found to be applicable is not called for. The reason given by this writer is that, as shown above, the function of the rule pleaded by the party has already been taken into account during the process of selecting the applicable law. A repetition of this exercise fails in its purpose for it only represents an invitation to the forum to reconsider – now in the light of the law found to be applicable – the selection of the appropriate choice of law rule reached already in the light of the law pleaded by the parties.[3] This may, or may not, be the law found to be applicable at the conclusion of this process.

---

[3] Lipstein (supra n. 1) no. 50.

|3. Movables, Immovables; Unitary or Separate Treatment

Complications can arise, however, on two levels when the question before the court involves property.[4]

Firstly, in some countries the notion of property is a unitary one, in others (common law countries) it distinguishes between interests in land (realty) and other interests (personalty) which latter notion includes not only interests in tangibles but also in intangibles (choses in action).

Secondly, independently of this division of substantive legal interests, the choice of law rules in some countries (mainly but not exclusively common law countries) distinguish between movables and immovables and between interests in either of them.

4. Effect Upon Connecting Factor and Operative Facts

This distinction between reliance on the factual nature of immovables and movables on the one hand and interests in immovables and movables on the other hand has been little noticed in the practice and in literature.[5] This is not surprising since in the relevant choice of law rules, such as "succession to immovables is governed by the *lex situs*", "matrimonial property relations between spouses are governed by their personal law if the property is movable and by the *lex situs*, if immovable", the inclusion of a reference to immovables and movables serves a dual purpose.

Firstly, taken alone they form part of the operative facts and thus represent a *legal category* of *rights* (or *interests*) in *immovable* or *movable prop-*

---

[4] Jayme, "Qualifikationsverweisung im internationalen Privatrecht", 17 *Zeitschrift für Rechtsvergleichung* (1976) 93–107.

[5] Dicey and Morris, *Conflict of Laws*, 9th edn. (1973) Rule 77; (12th edn. (1993)) Rule 113 cited by Jayme, supra, at pp. 93, 98, 101, 104, but see 95 (now 13th edn. (2000) rule 111). The English practice suggests it to a certain extent; as regards the legal interests in the object:

Chatfield v. *Berchtold* (1872) L.R. 7 Ch. App. 192, 193; *Re Fitzgerald* [1904] Ch. 573, 588, 589; *Re Cutcliffe* [1940] 565, 571; *Re Ritchie* [1942] 3 D.L.R. 330, 335; *Re O'Neill* (1922) N.Z.L.R. 468, 474; *Hacque* v. *Hacque* (1964–1965) 114 C.L.R. 98, 106, 119–120, 125, 135.

As regards the factual nature of the object:

Freke v. *Lord Carbery* (1873) L.R. 16 Eq. 461, 467; *Duncan* v. *Lawson* (1889) 41 Ch. D, 394; *Re Hoyles* [1911] 1 Ch. 179; *Hacque* v. *Hacque* (supra) 107–109; *Macdonald* v. *Macdonald* (1932) S.C. (H.L.) 79, 84, 85, 88.

Confusing: *Freke* v. *Lord-Carbery* (supra) 466; *Hacque* v. *Hacque* (supra) 98, 105–106; 109, 123, 133, 134, 136.

The account given by Rabel, *Conflict of Laws*, Vol. IV (1958) 15ff is inconclusive; see also Niboyet, *Traité de droit international privé* III (1944) no. 967; IV (1947) nos. 1153, 1190.

erty. They cover the legal claims or defences relating to property. The notion has a legal connotation. As in all operative facts it signifies rights or interests in immovables or movables.[6]

| Secondly, at the same time, read in conjunction with the reference to the *lex situs* it *represents a fact* and displays some of the characteristics of a connecting factor.

The quandary is now clear. Possessing the characteristics of both parts of a choice of law rule the terms immovables and movables may become subject to two different processes of characterization according as their character as a legal interest or as a connecting factor is in question. As shown above, the practice of the courts shows little appreciation of this difference.[7]

5. As a Connecting Factor

The combination of a reference to the factual character of immovables or movables with a reference to the *lex situs* results in a connecting factor of a mixed nature. It is therefore not easy to call in aid directly the test which serves to interpret connecting factors, namely the domestic law of the forum and not that of the *situs*. The present dispute as to whether the *lex fori* or the *lex situs*[8] must determine the factual nature of the object bears out this distinction.

---

[6] The following are interests in immovables: Rentcharges, *Re Berchtold* (1872) 7 App. Cas. 193, 199; Mortgages, *Re Hoyles* [1911] 1 Ch. 179, 187; *Hacque* v. *Hacque* (supra n. 5) 114 C.L.R. 88, 100ff.; *Re Ritchie* [1942] 3 D.L.R. 330, but see to the contrary the cases cited by Dicey and Morris, *Conflict of Laws*, 13th edn. (2000), esp. *Re O'Neill* [1922] N.Z.L.R. 468; Leaseholds: *Freke* v. *Lord Carbety* (1873) L.R. 16 Eq. 461, 466; *Duncan* v. *Lawson* (1889) 41 Ch. D. 394, 398; Debenture Stock: *Re Cutcliffe* [1940] Ch. 565, 571; Scots Heritable Bonds: *Re Fitzgerald* [1904] 1 Ch. 573, 588, 589.

[7] See supra n. 5.

[8] *Lexfori* Kahn, Abhandlungen zum internationalen Privatrecht I 73, 491, 494: Niboyet, Traité III (supra n. 5) no. 957; Lehmann, *Juriscl. dr. int.* VIII Fasc. 531 (1988); Staudinger(-Hausmann), *Kommentar zum Bürgerlichen Gesetzbuch mit Einführungsgesetz und Nebengesetzen: Einführungsgesetz zum Bürgerlichen Gesetzbuch*, 13th edn. (1996) art.3–6; art. 4 no.65–69; Staudinger(-Dörner) same, 13th edn., (1996), art. 25, 26; art. 25 nos. 477–487; Staudinger (-Firsching), same, 12th edn. (1984) art.24–28 a.F. 5, 6 n.F., 12th edn. (1991) no.226ff. preceding art.24–25; Soergel Siebert(-Kegel), nos. 75, 562 preceding art.7, no.92 preceding art. 24; art. 27 no. 36.

France: Cass. civ. 28 July 1862 S. 1862.1.988; Cass. req. 15 July 1885, S. 1886.1.285; Cass. civ. 22 June 1955, D. 1956 J. 73, J.C.P. 1955 II 8928, Clunet 1955, 728, T.I.J. Seine 12 Jan. 1966, Rev. crit. d.i.p. 1967, 120, note Loussouarn 125 ff, J.C.P. 1968 II 15266, Germany: R.G. 5 July 1934, R.G.Z. 145, 85, 86.

With Exceptions: Cass. plén 15 April 1988, *Rev. crit. d.i.p.* (1989) 100 (note: Droz); Clunet 1989, 86 (note: Kahn); D.S. 1988 J. 325 (note: Malaurie); J.C.P. 1988. II. 21066 (note: Barbieri) on appeal from Montpellier 18 Dec. 1984, *Rev. crit. d.i.p.* (1985) 559 (note: Batiffol); D.S. 1985 210 (note: Maury); J.C.P. 1988 II 21066; Paris 21 Sept. 1995, Clunet 1996, 683.

| In principle the *lex fori* must determine the meaning of any connecting factor, for the *lex fori* determines in what circumstances a legal system is to be applied. On the other hand, reliance on the *lex situs* is supported by considerations of effectiveness in the realm of property. This consideration must clearly prevail when legal interests in immovables or movables are in issue. It is, however, doubtful when it comes to interpret the connecting factor which relies on the nature of a movable or an immovable. Little difficulty exists where the object is land, a fact recognized equally by the *lex fori* and the *lex situs*. Accessories such as *immeubles par destination* (chickens on the land) create difficulties, but it would seem that even then the *lex fori* rather than the *lex situs* (if different) must be called in aid for only the factual aspects of the asset are in issue.

6. As a Legal Interest

It is different when the legal interest in the asset must be determined. Here the question as to whether the claim or defence is based on an interest in a movable or immovable must follow the usual pattern. The claim presented in the light of some legal systems and the operative facts of the choice of law rule of the forum must be interpreted in terms of each other in order to decide whether a legal interest in an immovable or a movable is involved.

7. Conflicts Situations

The problems discussed here do not, however, present themselves always in the same form when a conflicts rule distinguishes between immovables and movables and applies different laws to them respectively.

In the first place, their solution is simple when the conflict rules of the *lex fori* themselves incorporate the division between immovables and movables and the interests in them. The question whether an immovable or a movable is in issue will be solved in the usual way by relying on the *lex fori*. The function of the legal provision pleaded by a party, examined in the light of the operative facts of the *lex fori* interpreted broadly will show whether the

---

Lex situs: Austrian P.I.L. para. 31(2); Louisiana Code (1991) art. 353; Quebec, C.C. (1986) art. 3078; Bartin Clunet 1897, 225, 249, 250, 253; Principes de droit international privé I (1930) para. 888, p. 236; Lerebours-Pigeonnière (-Loussouarn), *Droit international privé*, 7th edn. (1959) no. 361 p. 423(d); Batiffol and Lagarde, *Droit international privé* I, 8th edn. (1993) no. 288 p. 489; Batiffol, *Rev. crit. d.i.p.* (1985) 563; Cass. civ. 5 April 1887, S. 1889.1.387; Trib. civ. Seine 14 March 1894, Clunet 1894, 815; T.I.G. Seine 12 Jan. 1966 (supra); Jayme (supra n. 4) at pp. 93, 98.

claim or defence falls within the ambit of the forum's conflict rule on immovables or movables as understood by the latter.

In the second place, when the choice of law involves a court and parties which are both subject to a common law system which distinguishes between realty and personalty and therefore do not differ from each other, the English Court of Appeal held in 1910[9] that it is unnecessary to have recourse to private international law and | to determine whether an interest in a movable or an immovable is involved. In terms of modern parlance, the conflict is a false one. This solution has not found universal approval. Not only the domestic rules of the two legal systems may differ in details. It also remains unclear whether the law applied in the end is that of the forum or of foreign law. On the answer to this question may depend whether an appeal is possible, because the *lex fori* is being applied or foreign law in which case no appeal is possible.

This leaves the situation where the forum has a unitary rule of private international law (e.g. succession is governed by the *lex patriae*, matrimonial property relations are governed by the law of the parties' domicile) while the foreign law referred to contains a conflict rule which is binary and distinguishes between immovables and movables as connecting factors and between interest in immovables and movables as operative facts governed respectively by the *lex situs* or the personal law of the parties. If the forum accepts a reference back and the claim concerns land situated in the country of the forum, the problems discussed above become reality.

8. The Problem in Practice

Such was the case which faced the Landgericht in Wiesbaden (Germany).[10]

An American domiciled in Indiana, while serving with the Army in Germany, married a German woman: separation of goods applied. During the marriage the wife acquired valuable land in Germany. In the course of a divorce the husband, basing his claim on German law which provided for a division between the spouses of the increase of their respective fortunes during marriage (*Zugewinngemeinschaft*), brought an action in Germany.

The German court applied its choice of law rule concerning matrimonial property which referred to the personal law of the husband, which turned out to be Indiana. According to Indiana law movable matrimonial property

---

[9] *Re Hoyles* [1911] 1 Ch. 179.
[10] L.G. Wiesbaden 30 March 1973, I.P. Rspr. 1973 no. 46; *Fam. R.Z.* (1973) 657; Jayme (supra n. 4) at p. 94.

was governed by the law of the husband's domicile, Indiana, and immovable property by the *lex situs,* Germany. The German court accepted the reference back and held that the *lex situs* determined whether an object was an immovable or a movable. It then found that according to German law the claim concerned an interest in a movable being in the nature of an economic rather than of a proprietary kind. Thus the personal law of the husband, Indiana law applied, which ignored a claim of the kind allowed by German law.

|If the principles developed above are applied, a critical examination of the decision of the court in Wiesbaden must start from two questions:

(i) Is land in Germany subject to a *Zugewinngemeinschaft* an immovable?

(ii) Is the right in a *Zugewinngemeinschaft* consisting exclusively of land an interest in an immovable?

For the forum, which was the court in Wiesbaden, the first question to be decided according to the *lex fori,* which also happened to be the *lex situs,* was therefore whether land constituted the connecting factor (see *supra* para. 4). In fact, the Court disregarded this aspect and faced immediately the second, which was whether the interest in issue concerned an immovable or a movable. For the purpose of characterizing the interest in issue, the German court held that it was more economic than proprietary in nature and was therefore an interest in a movable. This characterization was unnecessary at this stage, since it was clear that, for the purpose of the German conflict rule, the claim concerned matrimonial property and that the personal, i.e. Indiana, law applied. In short, the German court anticipated without good reason a characterization according to Indiana law, the applicable law, including its conflict rules which distinguishes in matters of matrimonial property whether the claim in issue concerns an interest in a movable or an immovable.

Since German law was prepared to accept the reference back by Indiana law, it now became necessary to determine firstly, what was the connecting factor of the Indiana conflicts rule which distinguished between immovables and movables? Secondly, since unlike in normal cases of a reference back, where only the connecting factor changes but not the operative facts, another question arose. Was the interest represented by the *Zugewinngemeinschaft* consisting exclusively in land in Germany an interest in an immovable or a movable, having regard to the Indiana conflicts rule that immovable matrimonial property is governed by the *lex situs* and movable property by the *lex domicilii.*

As regards the first question, it was suggested above (para. 4) that the *lex fori* determines the connecting factor. In a case of a reference back this must be the foreign law referred to, i.e. in the present case the law of Indiana. It was also suggested above (para. 4) that this is a question of fact. Thus the proceedings concerned land in Germany. The second question should have been whether the interest in a *Zugewinngemeinschaft* consisting exclusively of land in Germany is an interest in an immovable or a movable. The court in Wiesbaden answered it by characterizing it according to German law. In fact the problem was one of characterization according to Indiana law in order to decide whether the choice of law rule concerning immovable or movable of Indiana conflict of laws applied. In a German court this should have been one of proof of foreign law. The answer would have depended upon whether according to Indiana law a *Zugewinngemeinschaft* creates a commu|nity of goods in the combined increase in the value of the separate fortunes of husband and wife brought into the marriage irrespective of the movable or immovable nature of the assets, not unlike a partnership. If so, the interest therein of a spouse is not an interest in an immovable. If this were accepted, the Indiana choice of law rule on matrimonial property relations concerning movables (which term includes choses in action such as rights in a partnership) would apply. This points to the law of the domicile of the parties (Indiana). The answer to this question is, however, disputed. It must depend upon whether the economic or the proprietary character of the interest is regarded as predominant by Indiana law. Whatever the answer, this is not an instance of *secondary characterization*. It is a second, additional characterization.

9. Conclusions

To sum up: the conclusion reached here and the conclusion reached by the court of Wiesbaden may lead to the same result, but not necessarily. According to the method set out here,

(a) the German court characterizes the claim as affecting matrimonial property and refers to the national law of the parties – found to be Indiana law;

(b) the Indiana court finds that land is concerned and applies its rule that matrimonial property relations concerning immovables are governed by the *lex situs*;

(c) the Indiana court characterizes the claim arising out of a *Zugewinngemeinschaft* in German land;

(d) according as the Indiana court finds the economic interest to predominate over the proprietary one, its characterization of the claim will result in the application of Indiana or of German law.

The situation is unique. It occurs only if the choice of law rule of the forum is unitary and the choice of law rule of the law referred to is binary, distinguishing between immovables and movables and interests in them respectively.

Conflict of Laws Before International Tribunals Sixty Years Later

I. Choice of Law Problems in the 1940's

Some sixty years ago, in 1941 and in 1943 in an address to the Grotius society, I examined the technique by which International Tribunals approach problems of choice of law.[1] As the American-Mexican Claims Commission said in the *Illinois Central Railroad Co. Case*,[2] claims needing decisions in accordance with the principles of international law may belong to any of four types:

(i) "Claims between a national of one country and a national of another country. These claims are international even in cases where international law declares one of the municipal laws involved to be exclusively applicable."

This type of claim was the subject of my study in 1941. It noted that international tribunals have developed rules of the conflict of laws of their own. They lack a *lex fori* and *renvoi* and show difficulties in characterizing the nature of claims. Also public policy is determined by international and not by domestic law.

(ii) Claims as between two national governments in their own right.

The Boll case illustrates the type of problem when an international Convention raises a question of private international law.[3]

[Editorial note: first published in Basedow et al. (eds.): Aufbruch nach Europa. 75 Jahre Max-Planck-Institut für Privatrecht (2001), 713–723.]

[1] Transactions of the Grotius Society 27 (1942) 142–175; 29 (1944) 51–83.

[2] Opinions of the Commissions under the Convention concluded September 8, 1923 between the United States and Mexico I 187, RIAA IV 21, 23–24.

[3] ICJ Reports 1958, 52; Lipstein (1959) 8 ICLQ 506, 520 and the lit. cited 135 (1972 I) Hague Rec. 99, 169 n. 13.

| (iii) "Claims as between citizens of one country and the government of another country in its public capacity."

They include claims by concession holders if the concession is curtailed or revoked or when the principal question involves state responsibility according to International Law and rights of a private law nature, alleged to have been violated, must be established as a Preliminary Issue or Question. Early instances of this kind were examined in my study of 1943.

(iv) "Claims as between a citizen of one country and the government of another country acting in a civil capacity. These claims, too, are international in character and they, too, must be decided in accordance with the principles of international law, even in cases where international law should merely declare the municipal law of one of the countries involved to be applicable."

Such are the claims presented under the Convention on the Settlement of Investment Disputes between States and Nationals of Other States of 18 March 1965[4] and in virtue of Article VII para. 3 of the Claims Settlement Declaration by the United States and Iran of 19 January 1981.[5] Here the defendant State, by an agency, instrumentality or entity controlled by it, has either entered into the private transaction or has assumed the obligations arising out of a private law transaction by succeeding to a private person or entity.

II. The 1940's Revisited

The present study examines: whether the conclusions reached in 1941 concerning the problems outlined above (i) and (iii) have been affirmed or further developed; whether the issues formulated above (ii) and (iv) have been raised before international tribunals in the intervening period.

Turning first to the practice of International Tribunals for the determination of claims between nationals of one country and nationals of another, it is noteworthy that the rich run of examples provided by the Mixed Arbitral Tribunals set up after the First World War and examined in 1941 has never been equaled. The United States-Iranian Tribunal established by the Declaration of 19 January 1981 dealt with claims between private parties on both sides, but the Iranian party stepped into the shoes of the private Iranian party as a result of a general measure of nationalization. Thus the few cases which may be relevant can be regarded as falling either under head III or head IV of the present exposition.

---

[4] UNTS 575, 159.
[5] Iran-US Claims Tribunal Reports 1 (1981–2) p. 9 cited Iran-US CTR.

| III. Claims Between Citizens of one Country and the Government of Another Country Acting in a Public Capacity

1. The choice of law was prescribed by Article V of the Declaration by the United States and Iran.[6] The Tribunal was to apply the rules and principles of commercial and international law held to be applicable, trade usage and contract provisions and to have regard to changed circumstances. In so doing the Tribunal was not bound by particular choice of law rules, but was able to apply whichever law it deemed appropriate.[7] The broad and imprecise provision naturally gave rise to an uncertain and imprecise practice, interpreted autonomously.[8] However, it was admitted that the choice between the various alternatives will not affect the result.[9]

Free choice of law was accepted as the first principle for contracts on the ground that it contributes to a general principle of law.[10] The proper law of a contract was applied to its formation[11] and formalities[12] and to limitation of liability[13] subject to the power to deviate from it.[14] Agency and the effects upon the principal of a contract concluded by the agent were held to be subject to the law freely chosen;[15] in the absence of an express choice of law the law of that country was applied where the agency was constituted and where the agent was to perform his functions.[16] Promissory notes were governed by the law of the country where they were drawn or issued.[17] The broad formulation of the Declaration's choice of law provision also enabled the Tribunal to rely on the substantive rules of unjust enrichment ascertained by the comparative method[18] without engaging in a choice of law.[19] Similarly in characterizing a legal claim the Tribunal was free to rely by an exercise in comparative law on the legal system deemed suitable in the absence of a *lex*

---

[6] Supra n. 5 at p. 11.
[7] *Harnischfeger v. Mort* 8 Iran-US CTR, 119, 140–141; *American Bell International v. Iran* 6 ibid, 74, 98.
[8] *Oil Fields of Texas v. Iran, National Iranian Oils, Oil Service Company of Iran, ibid* 347, 377; *Harnischfeger v. Mort*, supra n. 7.
[9] *American Bell International v. Iran*, supra n. 7 at p. 98.
[10] *American Bell International v. Iran*, supra n. 7 at p. 97–98.
[11] *Oil Fields of Texas International* (supra n. 8) at 377.
[12] *Economy Forms Corp. v. Iran et al*, 3 ibid 42, 48.
[13] *American Bell International* (supra n. 7) at 98.
[14] *Alan Craig v. Iran et al*, 3 ibid 280, 287: 78 ILR 658, 666.
[15] *Harnischfeger v. Mort*, supra n. 7 at 140.
[16] *Utterwyk Corp. v. Iran et al*, 19 ibid 106, 126 [64].
[17] *Sedes v. Iran Industrial Co. et al*, 21 ibid 31 at 44 [29], 63 (4), 78 ILR 658, 666.
[18] *Schlegel Corp. v. NICI*, 14 ibid 176, 180 [12]; also *Sea Land Service Inc. v. Iran et al*, 6 ibid 149, 168; *Shannon and Wilson Inc. v. Atomic Energy Organisation of Iran*, 9 ibid 397, 402; *Flexi-Van Leasing v. Iran* 12 ibid 335, 352–353.
[19] *Isaiah v. Bank Mellat*, 2 ibid 232, 236, 237; 72 ILR 716, 721.

fori.[20] In *Rexnord v. Iran* a dishonoured bill of exchange was held to be governed by English law without | analyzing why English law was applied.[21] It was in fact an obligation entered into in England by an operating branch of a Texan company. A lease of land in New York attracted the law of that State.[22] The Tribunal was ready to enforce a provision of an International Convention such as the Bretton Woods Agreement art. VIII (2)(b) if both parties to the proceedings are nationals of Member States.[23]

2. The Convention on the Settlement of Investment Disputes between States and nationals of other States of 18 March 1965 (ICSID) like the Iranian-United States Declaration (supra) contains its own choice of law rules. Article 42(1) offers free choice of law in the first instance and, failing this, calls for the application of the law of the contracting state including its choice of law rules and of International Law, as it may be applicable. The addition of International Law as the law applicable to claims of individuals against states acting in a private capacity (above Case IV) deserves special attention.[24]

Normally reliance on the choice of private law will suffice.[25] In one set of cases in which private law governed the contract, International Law served to supplement the law governing the contract in its character of rules containing general principles.

This occurred in the first place when the existence of "contractual relations of a complex nature" did not fall "within well developed ... doctrines of law".[26] Here International Law supplied principles which were applicable in analogous circumstances; thus it served to fill in *lacunae.*[27] The same applies where a contract touches the sphere of administrative law by

---

[20] *Harnischfeger v. Mort* (supra n. 7) 136.

[21] 2 *ibid* 6 at p. 12; 71 ILR 603, 610; for cheques see *Dallal* v. *Iran and Bank Mellat,* 3 *ibid* 10, 14, but see 19; *Esphahanian v. Bank Tegarat* 2 *ibid* 157, 168.

[22] *Queens Office Tower Associates v. Iran National Airlines Corp,* 2 *ibid* 247, 250. See also *BP v. Astro Protector Co,* 77 ILR 543, 547.

[23] *Dallal v. Iran and Bank Mellat,* (supra n. 21) at 13, 16.

[24] For earlier use of the technique to apply Public International Laws as a subsidiary means of filling gaps in Private International Law see Neuhaus (1978) 28 *German Yearbook of International Law* 60 with further literature.

[25] *Agip v. Government of the Popular Republic of the Congo,* 67 ILR 319, 331–332 [43], [45] (1979); see also *Benvenuti and Bonfante v. Government of the Popular Republic of the Congo,* 67 ILR 6 345, 366 (1986).

[26] *Oil Fields of Texas v. National Iranian Oil Co* (1982), (supra n. 6) 69 ILR 565, 594; Mann et al, Contrats entre Etats et Personnes et Personnes Privées étrangères, Rev Belge de droit international 1975, 562, 570 per Seidl-Hohenveldern.

[27] *Ameco v. Republic of Indonesia* (1986), 89 ILR 89, 520–521 [20]–[22]; *SPP (Middle East) and Southern Pacific Properties (Middle East) v. Arab Republic of Egypt* (1992) 106 ILR 502, 608 [84]; see also *Amoco International Finance Corporation v. National Iranian Oil Co.* (1990) 83 ILR 500, 541–543 [112]–[117]; *SPP (Middle East) Ltd and Southern Pacific Properties v. Egyptian General Company for Tourism and Hotels* (1983), 86 ILR 435, 456–458 [49]; 22 ILM 752.

reserving to the State a | measure of discretionary powers[28] such as that to terminate the relationship for reasons of public interest or welfare.[29] Cp. Texas 465 [56] where a negative clause (not to vary the contract) deprived the contract of an administrative character. It occurred in the second place if compensation for expropriation became an issue in the course of proceedings raising claims of a private law nature.[30] This situation will be treated below in the discussion of Case 3.

An unusual technique led the Iran-US Tribunal in one case[31] and an *ad hoc* Commission set up by the ICC in another[32] to annul an arbitral award on the ground of excess of power. In *Klöckner v. Republic of Cameroon*[33] failure to give reasons supplied the ground for annulment when the contract in question was governed by French law (being the law in force in that part of the Cameroons) and the issue was whether in contracting a party owed a duty of full disclosure (p. 208). This was affirmed by the original Tribunal not by the citation of French legislation or practice but by reliance on an alleged general principle of law. The reviewing *ad hoc* Commission acting in virtue of the Declarations art. 52(1)(b): – manifest excess of powers due to a violation of art. 42(1): failure to consider the applicable law; art. 52(1)(e): failure to state reasons – stigmatized the reliance on general principles of law, unaccompanied by references to practice as imprecise.

It accused the original Tribunal of having acted in excess of its powers not only by deciding questions not submitted to the arbitration but also in misinterpreting the express provisions of the agreement in respect of the way in which they are to reach their decisions, notably in regard to the legislation and the principles of the law to be applied.[34] In other words excess of power may consist in the non-application by the arbitrator of the rules contained in the arbitration agreement or in the application of other rules. Failure to apply the rules referred to by the compromise as distinct from mere misconstruction of that law constitutes the excess of power.[35]

---

[28] *Ameco v. Republic of Indonesia* (supra n. 27), (1984) at 453, 460, 466, 468 [189]; see also *Southern Pacific Properties v. Egyptian General Company for Tourism and Hotels* (supra n. 27) at 628 [165].

[29] *Ameco v. Republic of Indonesia* (supra n. 27) at 468; *Texaco v. Libyan Arab Republic* (1977) 53 ILR 389, 465 [56]; *Government of Kuwait v. American Independent Oil Company* (1982) 66 ILR 519, 588 [91].

[30] See the cases cited supra n. 28.

[31] *Klöckner Industrie-Anlagen GmbH et al v. Republic of Cameroon* (1985), 114 ILR 153, 243, 287–302.

[32] *Ameco v. Republic of Indonesia* (supra n. 27) 521, 527 [43].

[33] Klöckner Industrie-Anlagen GmbH et al v. Republic of *Cameroon* (supra n. 31) 208–10; *Klöckner v. Cameroon* (supra n. 31) 268 [64] – 273 [79].

[34] *Klöckner v. Cameroon* (supra n. 31) p. 266 [59] – 273 [79] following *Orinoco Steamship Company*, Scott, Hague Court Reports (1916) 226, 230.

[35] *Ameco v. Republic of Indonesia* (supra n. 27) 521, 522 [23].

While in the *Klöckner* case the formal disregard of the specific provisions of French law constituted the excess, in the *Ameco* case factual errors or omissions | were the cause.[36] In both cases the *ad hoc* Commissions stressed that an annulment for excess of power had to be clearly distinguished from an ordinary appeal.[37] As the Commission in the *Klöckner* case said: "an error in law, even an essential one, does not generally constitute an excess of power, at least if it is not manifest".[38]

In an ICC arbitration, International Law alone served to confer legal personality upon the Arab organization for Industrialization which had been set up by four Arab states without incorporating the new entity according to the domestic law of one of the Member States. In *SPP (Middle East) Ltd and Southern Pacific Properties v. Egyptian General Company for Tourism and Hotels*[39] – another ICC arbitration – a joint venture agreement did not contain a choice of law clause. The presumption that the law of the State party to the contract applies was contested on the ground that the nature of the agreement had "denationalized" it with the result that the principles of international law, international practice and trade usages supplemented national law. Without deciding this question the tribunal found that the formulation of art. 42(1) of the ICSID Convention was not limited to a particular category of state contracts and was relevant in the circumstances. Moreover, International Law formed part of Egyptian law.[40] Thus International Law was applicable whatever the technical approach.

Similarly in *Government of Kuwait v. American Independent Oil Co (AMINOIL)*, art. III (2)[41] of the Agreement provided: "The law governing the substantive issues ... shall be determined by the Tribunal, having regard to the quality of the Parties, the transnational character of their relations and the principles of law and practice prevailing in the modern world." A later addition stated: "... the agreements ... shall be given effect and must be interpreted and applied in conformity with principles common to the laws of Kuwait and the State of New York ... and in the absence of such common principles in conformity with the principles of law normally recognized by civilized States in general, including those which are normally applied by international tribunals."[42] It followed that since one of the parties was a State, Kuwait law applied coupled with the general principles of law forming

---

[36] *Ibid* p. 531 [57], 532 [60], 534 [66], 538 [79], 539 [83], 540 [86], 541 [88], 542 [91], 543 [95], 545 [98], 546 [103].

[37] *Klöckner* (supra n. 31) 267 [61]; *Ameco* (supra n. 27) 527 [43].

[38] *Klöckner* (supra n. 31) 268 [61].

[39] 86 ILR 435, 456 [49] (1983) 22 ILM 752 (1983) for the annulment proceedings see supra n. 27.

[40] *Ibid* p. 458.

[41] 66 ILR 519 (1982) at 561 [8].

[42] *Ibid* 560.

International Law to solve problems arising out of the contractual character of the Concession.[43] In the absence of any pleadings of Ghanaian law in a joint venture between a citizen|of one State and the government of another (Ghana) and in the absence of evidence that Ghanaian law differed from International Law, the Arbitral Tribunal in *Biloune & Marine Drive Complex Ltd v. Ghana Investment Centre and the Government of Ghana*[44] applied International Law as the law governing the Tribunal. And in *Elf Aquitaine v. National Iranian Oil Co.*[45] also concerning a common venture, the agreement (art. 41(5)) provided that the Tribunal was not bound by any specific rule of law, but could rely on "considerations of equity and generally recognized principles of law, and in particular International Law" (p. 262). Based on a broad trend in recent literature, the Tribunal relied on International Law[46] (p. 266 [20]). Consequently the principle *pacta sunt servanda* defeated the defendant's attempt to rescind the common venture.

IV. Claims Between Citizens of one Country and the Government of Another Country Acting in a Public Capacity

Claims between citizens of one country and the government of another country acting in a public capacity arise if a commercial enterprise jointly undertaken with a government or its agencies involves certain public law aspects touching the conclusion or execution of the agreement. Such aspects include *ultra vires* acts of the government or its agents, concessions, hiring of foreign mercenaries, stabilization clauses and expropriations. While the substance of such an agreement may be of a private law nature, the discretionary or sovereign power inherent in a government creates a certain disequilibrium between the parties. Contractual relations of a complex nature were found – as was shown above – to have attracted supplementation by International Law to fill *lacunae* or to control discretion.

In the specific instances falling under head 4 a combination of a domestic and international law or of general principles of law has become current. In *Revere Copper and Brass Inc v. OPIC*[47] a long term economic development agreement with the government of Jamaica contained what is now known as a stabilization clause.[48] Thereby the government was to do nothing to in-

---

[43] *Ibid* 561 [9], [10].
[44] 95 ILR 184 (1989) at 207.
[45] 96 ILR 252 (1982) at 262.
[46] *Ibid* p. 266 [20].
[47] (1978) 56 ILR 258, 263.
[48] Weil, Melanges Rousseau, 301, 319–320 (1975); see also *Texaco v. Libyan Arab Republic* (1977) 53 ILR 389, 423, 464–65, 476 (clause 16); *BP v. Libyan Republic* (1974) 53 ILR 297 at 298, 322; *Libyan American Oil Co, LIAMCO v. Libya* (1977) 62 ILR 141, 142.

crease taxation or to derogate from the company's rights in the project, the agreement to remain in force for twenty-five years. Nevertheless the government greatly increased the levies. The repudiation of the terms of the contract was held to constitute an expropriation to be judged according to International Law. This | applied when action taken by a government contrary to the economic interests of an alien conflicts with previous undertakings and assurances notwithstanding that the underlying agreement was governed by domestic law.[49]

Previously in *Sapphire International Petroleum v. National Iranian Oil Co.*[50] the Tribunal had only concluded that a choice of law of the States party to the agreement was not to be presumed in view of the nomination of an arbitration abroad. The wording of the original agreement which referred to the duty to observe good faith indicated a choice of the general principles of law. A Concession proper had previously been considered in *Saudi Arabia v. Arabian American Oil Co. (ARAMCO)*[51] which contained a choice of law clause.[52] Saudi Arabian law was to apply to all matters within the jurisdiction of Saudi Arabia. Reading this clause as a reference to the nature of the matter under consideration[53] and to the principles of Private International Law, the law most closely connected applied in virtue of general principles of law in the absence of a domestic *lex fori* and in the presence of an express rejection of Libyan law.[54] However, in a Concession public rights were held to be inevitably mixed with private rights granted to the holder of the Concession. Thus Saudi law, insofar as it applied, was to be interpreted and supplemented by the general principles of law.[55]

Finally International Law applies to the effects of a Concession, if certain matters cannot be governed by any rule of municipal law of any State (e.g. state responsibility, acquired rights).[56]

In *EP v. Libyan Republic*[57] the Concession, which contained a stabilization clause[58] provided that the principles of the law of Libya common to the principles of International Law shall apply and, in the absence of such common principles, then in accordance with the general principles of law as have been applied by international tribunals.[59] While admitting the absence of a

---

[49] (1978) 56 ILR at 271.
[50] (1963) 35 ILR 136, 173.
[51] (1958) 27 ILR 117.
[52] *Ibid* 154–155.
[53] Ibid 154, 156; see also *BP v Libyan Republic* (supra n. 48) at 326 [46].
[54] *Ibid* 157–166; see also *BP v. Libyan Republic* (supra n. 48) at 327 (2); *Texaco* (supra. n. 48) 478; *LIAMCO* (supra n. 48) 169.
[55] *Ibid* 166–168; see Cie d'Electricité de Varsovie RIAA vol. 3, 1679 at 1687.
[56] *Ibid* 171–172, 205.
[57] (1973, 1974) 53 ILR 297.
[58] *Ibid* 324.
[59] *Ibid* 328: clause 28 (7).

lex fori, the Tribunal relied on the conflicts rules of Danish law (the seat of the Tribunal) as the most suitable. It found that in the case of a conflict between the applicable law and International Law, the general principles of International Law applied.[60] The revocation of the Concession was to be disregarded as an | *abuse of sovereign power*[61] and as a violation of International Law. Following the wording of the choice of law clause the general principles of law applied, with the result that International Law came into operation once again,[62] this time to determine the remedies.[63]

Another Libyan Concession was the object of *Texaco v. Libyan Arab Republic.*[64] Again a stabilization clause was included.[65] The choice of law clause (clause 28) was identical with that in the *BP* case.[66] The arbitrator adopted what he regarded as the leading principle in ARAMCO.[67] Considering the Concession to be a contract, although not as an administrative one,[68] of an international and not of a domestic nature, a new approach was required which differed from the classical one taken by the Permanent Court of International Law in the *Serbian and Brazilian Loans* Cases.[69] The freedom to select the law to govern the contract had to be sanctioned by a particular system of laws. For an international arbitration this was International Law and a new tendency permitted to "delocalize" a contract.[70] The cumulation of laws in clause 28 supported this conclusion.[71] Agreements other than Treaties were capable of falling within the ambit of 12 International Law. In the absence of conformity between Libyan and International Law the reference in clause 28 led to the general principles of law and thus to the sources of International Law.[72] This protected the private party to the contract against abrupt unilateral modifications of the legislation of the contracting State, especially in the case of Concessions.[73] It also accorded the private party certain international powers in interpreting and performing the contract.[74] It followed that an Agreement between a State acting in an

---

[60] *Ibid* 328.

[61] *Ibid* 331 b(1).

[62] *Ibid* 334.

[63] *Ibid* 334 et seq.

[64] (1977) 54 ILR 389.

[65] Supra n. 48: p. 423.

[66] 53 ILR 389, 442; see supra n. 59 and see *Libyan America Co v. Libya LIAMCO,* supra n. 48 p. 142.

[67] Supra n. 51.

[68] *Ibid* 440. 463 et seq.; but see *Libyan American Oil Co, v. Libyan Arab Republic* (supra n. 48) 189.

[69] PCIJ see A nos. 20, 21.

[70] 53 ILR at 445, 448 with lit; especially 460 [50].

[71] *Texaco* supra n. 48, p. 445 [29]; 450 [36] as modified in 1961 p. 451 [38]; 474 [67].

[72] *Ibid* 453 [41], 462 [52].

[73] *Ibid* 454, 456, 457 citing Sapphire supra n. 50.

[74] *Ibid* 458 [47], 459 [48], 460 [50]; *eg pacta sunt servanda see also Libyan American Oil*

official capacity and a private person may be governed by domestic law and international law in respect of certain aspects, depending upon the nature of the contract as characterized by the Tribunal.

The most recent case, *Sandline international v. Government of Papua New Guinea*[75] involved a contract to supply mercenaries to a government fighting a | revolt. The contract stated that it was "to be construed and governed in accordance with the law of England".[76] The government denounced the contract. The claimants plea that English law applied was dismissed by the Tribunal on the ground that in a contract between a State and an individual International Law applied, which also formed part of English law.[77] Without stating it expressly, the Tribunal appears to have followed the choice of law principles developed previously which granted the parties a free choice of law (i.e. English law) subject to the proviso that International Law (which also happened to be part of English law) could cover certain aspects of the agreement. In the present instance International Law supplied the remedy of estoppel in face of the government's defence that the contract was illegal under English law.

V. Conclusions

The present survey shows that the conclusions drawn in 1941 and 1943 to the effect that International Tribunals which apply in principle International Law have developed their own autonomous choice of law rules have retained their validity in part only.

Firstly, if the International Tribunal has to deal with claims between a national of one country and a national of another country, the thesis developed sixty years ago still holds good. An International Tribunal can elevate domestic law into the international sphere.

Secondly, the same is true if the claim between two States concerns a question of Private International Law.

Thirdly, a new trend exists where claims of a private law nature arose originally between a national of one State and a national of another State and the latter's State subsequently assumed the obligations of its own nationals. The same trend exists where an Investment Dispute exists between a national of one State and another State assuming or supporting an investment. In these circumstances special agreements provided their own choice of law

---

Co *(LIAMCO) v. Libyan Arab Republic* (supra n. 48) 190–193; *Clausula rebus sic stantibus.*

[75] (1998) 117 ILR 552.
[76] *Ibid* 561.
[77] *Ibid* 560.

rules which included international law within its own rights or part of domestic law. The US-Iranian Declaration added little new and led to the adoption of traditional choice of law rules. The ICSID Convention also added a reference to International Law which served to supplement the domestic law applicable and to fill a *lacuna*.

Fourthly, where claims between citizens of one State and another State acting in its public capacity are concerned a variety of choice of law clauses culminated in a combination of domestic law (that of the State concerned), international law and general principles of law. Mainly applied to Joint Ventures, Concessions and to contracts of a complex character, having regard to |their dual nature, these clauses enabled the Tribunals to apply different laws to different aspects of the claim and not only to supplement the applicable domestic law in the case of *lacunae* or of issues of a general character such as *pacta sunt servanda rebus sic stantibus*, international public policy, estoppel[78] or State responsibility.

---

[78] For an early example see *USA v. Norway (Norwegian Shipowners Claims)* RIAA vol. 1, 309, 330.

The Law relating to the movement of companies in the European Community

I. Background

It has long been established and is well known that in some countries the law of the place of incorporation applies to the creation, existence, the powers and the internal and external management of legal entities while in others the seat, the place the central administration is situated determines the law applicable. Nor does this division coincide with the division of civil and common law countries.[1]

Difficulties exist when a legal entity established according to the law of incorporation or established according to the law of its seat wishes to transfer its seat to another country, for according to the law of the former or future seat the corporation ceases to exist or will not be recognized. Hitherto nothing but the creation of a new local entity and the accompanying liquidation of the old one could bridge the gap, unless the creation of a branch or of a sister association could satisfy the need, if a country following the test of the law of the seat was involved.[2]

[Editorial note: first published in Mansel et al. (eds.): Festschrift für Erik Jayme (2004), 527–531.]

[1] *Staudinger/Grossfeld*, Internationales Gesellschaftsrecht (1998) Rz. 22–28; *Zimmer*, RabelsZ 2003, 298, 302ff.

[2] For a good survey see *Halbhuber* (2001) Common Market Law Rev. 1385 (C.M.L.Rev.) with lit.

II. The effect of community law

The establishment of the European Economic Community posed the question as to how the newly introduced freedom of establishment within the community (art. 52, now art. 43) which extends to companies (art. 58 old, 48) was to be put into practice. Art. 220 (now 290) provided the answer. A Convention to be concluded by the member states was to secure the mutual recognition of companies or firms, the retention of legal personality in the event of a transfer of their seat as well as the possibility of mergers. However, the transfer of the centre of administration from one country to another was not included. Two attempts were made to deal with this need.

1. An abortive Hague Convention of 1951[3] recognized a company's legal personality if acquired by registration or publicity in a particular country where the company had its statutory seat, provided that the capacity conferred thereby included not only the right to sue and be sued, but also to own property and to enter into legal transactions.[4] Recognition could be denied if the real seat happened to be in another state which relied on the law of the real seat to confer legal personality, or if it was established in another state which relied on this test. A subsequent transfer of the real seat carried out within a reasonable time to a country which disregarded the locality of the seat was to preserve the|previous legal status, i.e. if both the law of the place of incorporation and that of the seat adopted the law of the place of incorporation. Recognition was not to imply the right to carry on business on a permanent basis in the recognizing country.

This Convention, by concentrating on the duty to recognize foreign companies, failed to address, except in very limited circumstances, the question as to whether the law of the place of incorporation or that of the new seat applies after recognition.

2. Under the auspices of the European Community the so-called Goldman Report[5] concerning the Mutual Recognition of Associations and Legal Entities faced with the conflicting reliance on the law of the place of incorporation and the law of the seat realized the need to harmonize or to unify the conflicting choice of law rules. It did so by requiring the recognition of all associations of civil or-commercial law established in accordance with the law of the member states and having their registered seat in a Convention country[6] – not necessarily in the same – and of legal entities of a public law

---

[3] Conférences de la Haye, Actes de la 7 session 1951, 126; (1951) Rev. crit. d.i.p. 727.

[4] Art. 2(3) in conjunction with art. 1(1), 5; Lipstein (1993) 42 International and Comparative Law Quarterly 554, 629 ff.

[5] (1960) 12 Bull E.E.C. Suppl. 2; (1968) Rev. trim. dr. eur. 400, 405; (XIII) Communicazioni e Studi 623 (1969) and the comment by *Lipstein*, The Law of the European Economic Community (1974) 148–157.

[6] Art. 1.

character exercising an economic activity normally carried out for remuneration.[7] If the real seat was located in a country not a party to the Convention, a Convention country, following a declaration, was to be entitled to disregard the Convention, unless a serious link existed between it and the company.[8] Similarly, the existence of a real seat in a Convention country entitled that country to apply its own mandatory provisions to community countries.[9] Soft law was to be governed by special provisions. If recognized, the associations were to enjoy the status and capacity conferred by the law of the place of incorporation, subject to the limitations and contained in arts. 3 and 4.

Recognition of associations in virtue of the Convention was not necessarily to imply the recognition according to the entity's law of its rights and capacities.[10] Instead a *transposition*[11] was permitted, irrespective of the law of incorporation.

In envisaging the mutual recognition of the associations incorporated in one Convention country and having its statutory seat in another, the Convention did not address the problem of a change of seat from one country to another.

III. Community law and choice of law – the European Court

This problem presented itself only gradually when in a series of three decisions the European Court in Luxemburg was called upon to apply the Community legislation on freedom of establishment to the movement of corporations.

The first[12] dealt with the right of a corporation according to law of the State where it was incorporated and had its central seat of administration, to leave the country of its seat. The court confirmed the right of the State to control the move (for fiscal reasons). In the|second case[13] the admissibility of establishing a branch in the country by an association incorporated in another was in issue. On the strength of Community law this step was approved by requiring the host country to recognize the corporate status of the moth-

---

[7] Art. 2.

[8] Art. 3.

[9] Art. 4; see also *Überseering v Nordic Construction Co.*, (infra n. 15) para. 60.

[10] Art. 7.

[11] For transposition see Lipstein, Hague Recueil 135 (1972 I) 99, 207.

[12] *The Queen v Treasury and Commissioners of Revenue, ex parte Daily Mail and General Trust* [1980] ECR 5483.

[13] *Centros Ltd v Erhvers-og Selskabsstyrelsen* [1999] ECR I 1459 leading to an extensive literature which need not be reviewed here in view of the conclusions reached in this article.

er company. However the legal status of the branch according to Private International Law was not considered.[14] In the third case[15] the European Court was faced with the basic question: the admissibility under European Community Law of a transfer of a company's central seat of administration to another country which submitted companies to the law of their seat and treated the company as having ceased to exist under the law of its incorporation without having been re-established according to the law of the new seat. Once again the answer was positive. In the light of the relevant provisions of Community Law the corporate character acquired by the corporation under the law of its previous seat was to be recognized in the country of its new seat, but the question whether apart from recognition in a limited sense by the courts of the new seat of the law of the old or the new seat or a combination of both applied, remained open to speculation.[16] As the following considerations will show, recognition of the law of the previous seat in a broad sense so as to apply the law of the previous seat of the corporation is ruled out.

The duty of courts in a Community country applying Community Law to recognize the corporate status of a legal entity, its status and capacity, established in the country of its previous seat, operates independently of domestic choice of law rules (which fall outside the competence of Community law). Within the limits of Community Law the sphere of Private International Law is not impaired.[17]

If this interpretation is accepted, the dispute as to whether the practice of the European court has resulted in the abrogation of the application of the law of the seat of an association in favour of the law of incorporation is baseless. Countries are free to apply the law of incorporation or that of the seat, provided that the previous status and capacity of a legal entity incorporated or having its centre of administration abroad is recognized upon a change of seat.

---

[14] *Ebke*, JZ 1999, 656, 658 (iv); *Ulmer* ibid 662 (ii); *Sonnenberger*, RIW 1999, 721, 722 (2), 727 (3); *Halbhuber*, ZEuP 2003, 418, 429; *Roth*, IPRax 2003, 117; *Kindler*, RIW 2000, 644, 651 (IV.1) ibid 2003, 1073, 1076, 1079 (VII); *Behrens*, IPRax 1999, 323, 334 (ii); *Forsthoff*, Eur. R. 2000, 167, 173, 175.

[15] *Überseering BV v Nordic Construction Co. Baumanagement GmbH*, N.C.C. C.208/00, NJW 2002, 3614; RIW 2002, 945; JZ 2002, 903.

[16] *Lutter*, BB 2003, 9 (iii); *Zimmer*, ibid, 1, 3, 4; *Roth*, IPRax 2003, 119, 120; *Halbhuber*, ZEuP 2003, 419, 423.

[17] *Überseering* (supra n. 15) paras. 67–73 and especially 79; distinguish 92, foreshadowed by *Kindler*, RIW 2000, 648.

IV. New choice of law problems

Instead the difficult question arises how to define the relationship between the range of Community Law demanding recognition by the courts of Community countries of the status and powers of a corporation established in another Community country and the range of the relevant domestic law determined by the choice of law rules of the country to which it has transferred its seat. Is the recognition restricted to the obligation to observe | the personality and the capacity of the entity – or as it has been put: to respect its corporate attributes[18] – or does it extend to the legal consequences of corporate status, i.e. does it include the observance of the corporate law of the country of the original seat, or some of it?

Since Community Law imposes the duty for the purpose of moving the establishment[19] to recognize the association as a legal entity but remains incompetent to pronounce a choice of law, the legal effects of the recognition must be restricted.[20] The existence of corporate personality, its status and capacity must be recognized, but the internal and external relations are governed by the choice of law rules of the host country – which may rely either on the law of the association's incorporation or on the law of the seat of the entity. If by the law of the new seat a foreign entity loses its status upon changing its seat, the combination of the duty to recognize its previous status according to Community Law and the choice of law of its seat preserves the previous status.

As far as the obligation of recognition is concerned little difficulty exists if it is restricted to accepting the status and capacity of a foreign entity – as is suggested here. If, however, recognition should embrace the law of the transferring entity as a whole, or if the choice of law rules of the host state refer to the law of the place of incorporation, considerable difficulties present themselves. The structure and organization of the entity as incorporated may differ from those of any corresponding association in its powers and liabilities so as to impede its realization and enforcement by the courts of the new seat.

In these circumstances the technique known in the Conflict of Laws as *adaptation and transposition*[21] must be employed whereby the original *lex causae* is adapted and results in the application of a comparable institution of the *lex fori*. Known in German practice as the recognition of a *Scheingesell-*

---

[18] *Knapp*, DNotZ 2003, 571.

[19] *Überseering* (supra n. 15) paras. 56, 57.

[20] *Halbhuber* (supra n. 14) 403.

[21] See supra n. 11; the two processes can coalesce when what amounts to an adaptation of the original *lex causae* by the *lex fori* results in the integration of some of the latter's institutional rules.

schaft,[22] it has resulted in the treatment of a German *Offene Handelsgesell-schaft* as the equivalent of a Dutch or English private limited company, in the absence of incorporation in the country of the new seat.[23]

It may be objected that given the original creation of a legal entity abroad, it is likely to have attracted subscribers who relied on the structure of the company according to the law of the place of incorporation (shareholders' rights and obligations – restricted risk, board meetings, capital, director's liability; bankruptcy) exclusive reliance on the law of the new seat may require limitations *ratione materiae* either by excluding internal management control from the operation of the law of the new seat or by an attempt to rely on the law relating to a GmbH, a S.A.R.L. or its equivalent as mandatory provisions.[24]

| When in *Überseering BV v Nordic Contraction Company Barmanagement GmbH* C.208/00 the European Court of Justice pronounced that a foreign corporation desiring to move its centre of administration from the country of its incorporation to another country in the European Community retained its corporae character, the Court did not indicate whether any or all aspects of its internal and external relations remained subject to the original law of incorporation or became subject to the law of the new seat.

The question is now partly resolved by the European Court in *Kramer v Kamer van Koophandel en Fabricken voor Amsterdam* C.167/01 of 30 September 2003. It gives effect to the Council Directive on Coordination of Safeguards which for the Protection of the Interests of Members and Others are required by Member States of Companies – with regard to the formation of Public Limited Liability Companies and the Maintenance or Alteration of their Capital. Leaving aside the provisions on future harmonization they all cover the protection of the public by requiring certain measures of publicity for foreign companies on the Company register. They are: a file containing certain obligatory information (First Directive) which must be mandatorily given in the statutes or instruments of incorporation and the minimum amount of share capital required (Second Directive); annual accounts (Fourth and Seventh Directives), and in the case of branches, their address, the activities, the register where the file referred to in the First Directive is kept, the name and the legal form of the company and, if necessary, the

---

[22] For this concept see *Sonnenberger and Grossrichter*, RIW 1999, 722 (2), 725, 726; Lutter, BB 2003, 7, 9 (iii); Zimmer, BB 2000 at 5 (3); RabelsZ 2003, 298, 301 n. 13 with lit; Kindler, NJW 2003, 1073, 1074 (2); *Halbhuber*, ZEuP 2000, 48, 330; *Schanze and Jüttner*, AG 2003, 36; BGH 1 July 2002, NJW 2002, 3539.

[23] Recognition as demanded by the European Court is only relevant in the narrow sense according to Community Law but not in respect of the ensuing choice of law, but this absence may not prevent its reconstruction as a GmbH. See BGHZ 146, 342.

[24] *Eidenmüller*, ZIP 2002, 12; *Überseering* para. 92.

different branch name, details concerning the position of the persons authorised to represent the company in outside dealings, and legal proceedings as company organs or permanent representatives in winding up and liquidation of companies, insolvency proceedings, accounting documents and closure of the branch and, on a discretionary basis, the signature of representatives, the original constitution, memorandum and articles, a statement of encumbrances of company property in a member state, the requirement of the use of another Community language and the certification of transactions as well as an indication in the letter heading where the basic information is to be found (First, Eleventh Company Directive).

It followed that while Dutch legislation (the law of the host state) complied with certain formal requirements or publicity of European Community law (*Kramer v Kamer van Koophandel* at para. 51) it did not in respect of substantive requirements (paras. 65, 76), such as minimum capital and penalties (paras. 73, 100, 109). The result is the recognition of a company incorporated abroad, even if the act of incorporation abroad sought to evade the requirements of the less favourable conditions of the law of the prospective host state (para. 96) in the absence of overriding grounds of public policy (paras. 132, 143). However it leaves it to the host state to decide which law applies to the external relations of the transferring company.

Intellectual Property: Parallel Choice of Law Rules

I. England

In a previous article[1] it was contended that for the purpose of the conflict of laws the structure of immaterial property law (which term is used here to include patents and the like) is exceptional. Due to its privileged character accorded by the sovereign local authority it is territorial in the dual sense that such laws are strictly confined in their operation to their country of origin and that within that territory the application of foreign immaterial property law is excluded by its inherent limitation.[2] In English and Commonwealth law this insight was concealed until recently by the assertion that the courts could only exercise jurisdiction in respect of claims based on their own national intellectual property law. Jurisdiction was thus functionally linked to the exclusive sphere of the applicable law.[3]

Two factors have changed this conclusion. First, the Brussels Convention of 1968 does not restrict proceedings concerning immaterial property to the courts of the country of origin, *i.e.*, of registration of patents as well as in the case of copyrights, except when the validity of the right is in issue (art. 16(4)),

---

[Editorial note: first published in Cambridge Law Journal 64 (2005), 593–613.]

[1] "Intellectual Property: Jurisdiction or Choice of Law?" [2002] C.L.J. 293.

[2] See generally K. Lipstein "Inherent Limirations in Statutes and the Conflict of Laws" (1977) 26 I.C.L.Q. 884, 885.

[3] *Fort Dodge Animal Health Ltd.* v. *Akzo Nobel NV* [1998] F.S.R. 222, 226 *per* Laddie J., but see the Court of Appeal on other grounds *ibid* 251, [1998] ILPr 732. 741 [22]. For an example outside the law of immaterial and industrial property in England see the German *Rabattgesetz* as interpreted by the OLJ. Munich IPRspr 1995 no. 129; German Law on Unfair Competition: OLG Frankfurt *ibid* 1995 no. 125; for France: P. Véron, "Trente Ans d'Application de la Convention de Bruxelles" (2001) 128 Clunet 805, 808.

now art. 22(4) of Reg. 44/2001. Second, it is now being contended that in its inception a question of a particular choice of law is involved. The first has not, however, changed the territorial and substantively restricted character of intellectual and industrial property law as Laddie J. seems to suggest.[4] The second is ruled out by the parallel existence of mutually exclusive rules of substantive law with the result that the court seized must dismiss the claim in the absence of | an enforceable cause of action. The court is incompetent *i.e.,* indirectly it has no jurisdiction.

While choice of law instead of jurisdiction confers its special imprint on claims when local or foreign immaterial property rights are raised in English courts, the jurisdictional aspect has not been eliminated completely. It has changed: while effectiveness was the consideration previously which guided the courts to the proper jurisdiction the substantive law of which applied, now the *lex originis* and the *lex protectionis* determine the jurisdiction of the court which applies its own law. To initiate proceedings elsewhere than in the courts of the *lex originis,* means to rely on the *lex protectionis* of the court addressed which applies its own intellectual or industrial property law in virtue of treaty obligations. As Kekewich J. realized in 1895,[5] English courts cannot apply English law to claims based on a violation in Germany of an English immaterial property right and German courts cannot do so either if a German immaterial property right is alleged to have been infringed in England.[6] It is not a matter of convenience as Aldous J. assumed in the *Plastus* case (at 447) but of necessity, given the special character of immaterial property law.

Influenced by the extension of jurisdiction rendered possible by the Brussels Convention which eliminated the rule in the *Moçambique* case[7] in respect of trespass to land, previously also applied by way of analogy to the infringement of immaterial property rights, and by the abolition of the rule in *Chaplin* v. *Boys*[8], the practice changed. Lloyd J. in *Pearce* v. *Ove Arup Partnership*[9] accepted jurisdiction based on the defendant's domicile in Eng-

---

[4] [1998] F.S.R. 222, 227.

[5] *"Morocco Bound" Syndicate Ltd.* v. *Harris* [1895] Ch. 535; also *Norbert Steinhardt & Son* v. *Meth* (1961) 105 C.L.R. 440, 443–444; Roch LJ. in *Pearce* v. *Ove Arup* [1999] 1 All E.R. 769. 797.

[6] *Def Lepp Music* v. *Stuart Brown* [1986] R.P.C. 273. 275; *Apple Corporation Ltd.* v. *Apple Computer Inc.* [1992] F.S.R. 431, 470; *Mölnlycke AB* v. *Procter & Gamble Ltd.* [1992] 1 W.L.R. 1112, 1117–1118; *Plastus Kreativ AB* v. *Minnesota Mining and Manufacturing Co.* [1995] R.P.C. 438, 444, 447.

[7] Civil Jurisdiction and Judgments Act 1982, s. 30.

[8] [1971] A.C. 35C.

[9] [1997] Ch. 393; upheld on this point by the Court of Appeal [2000] Ch. 403; W. Cornish, "Intellectual Property Infringement and Private International Law: Changing the Common Law Approach" [1996] Gewerblicher Rechtsschutz und Urheberrecht, 285–289. For the Dutch practice see P. Véron, "Trente Ans d'Application de la Convention de Bruxelles". 809ff.

land in respect of a breach of copyright in the Netherlands, despite the fact that the relevant Dutch and UK legislation was territorial and substantively exclusive. In his words, the court would otherwise be in the "quixotic position" of accepting jurisdiction, but denying a remedy.[10] In fact this situation is not unusual. In denying a remedy in England the court supports the defence, which normally relies on an exclusive jurisdiction elsewhere, but which in|the case of immaterial property relies on its territorial and substantive restriction to the country of its origin,[11] unlike in an action based on a civil tort such as passing off.

Laddie J. followed suit in *Coin Controls Ltd.* v. *Suzo International (UK) Ltd.*[12] in proceedings against a group of UK, Dutch, German and Spanish companies by assuming jurisdiction in respect of related actions by complying with art.6(1) of the Brussels Convention. This allowed him to join the Dutch defendant which had participated in the infringement in England, but the assertion that art.6(1) may perhaps also permit the assumption of jurisdiction in respect of the violation by another defendant of a foreign patent identical in substance with the UK patent is open to doubt.[13]

To call Private International Law in aid is admissible when the infringement in England of English immaterial property is the result of an act committed abroad with effect in England,[14] for in this case it is committed in England and only English law is involved. It is quite another matter if it is alleged, without questioning the validity of the alleged right, that an infringement has occurred abroad affecting foreign immaterial property law and that according to English Private International Law the *lex loci delicti* is applicable. Such was the situation in *Pearce* v. *Ove Arup* faced by Roch LJ. in the Court of Appeal[15] as to whether the application of foreign immaterial property law is possible irrespective of a foreign territorial and substantive restriction.[16] While it is acknowledged that English immaterial property law cannot apply in respect of an infringement abroad and that foreign immaterial property law is restricted to acts within its own territorial sphere of operations, the question was put squarely by the Court of Appeal in *Pearce* v. *Ove Arup*,[17] nevertheless, as to whether an English court can entertain an action when according to English Private International Law a

---

[10] But see Vinelott J. in *Tyburn Productions Ltd.* v. *Conan Doyle* [1991] Ch. 75, 89.

[11] See *Coin Controls Ltd.* v. *Suzo* [1997] 3 All E.R. 45. 58, 59: see also C. von Bar, *Internationales Privatrecht II* (Munich 1991), no. 707.

[12] [1997] 3 All E.R. 45, [1997] F.S.R. 660.

[13] See also *Mölnlycke* v. *Procter & Gamble* [1992] 1 W.L.R. 1112. 1117–1118.

[14] *Abkco* v. *Music Collection* [1995] R.P.C. 657, 660: see also BGH 16 June 1994. BGHZ 126. 252, 256 with literature.

[15] [2000] Ch. 403. 439. 440.

[16] [2000] Ch. 403. 437, 438, 441.

[17] [2000] Ch. 403, 423, 436, 437, 438, 440.

foreign immaterial property right has been infringed in the country of its origin.

On proof in the English court of the applicable foreign law, its territorial and substantive character, which restricts its application to courts of its origin, must result in its failure to be applied in an English court: can this result be avoided by relying on the fiction admitted by English Private International Law that the court in | England is sitting as a foreign court or that foreign law is applied as a fact in English courts?[18] The answer must be negative. The fiction developed in *Collier* v. *Rivaz* served to introduce foreign private international law to supplement foreign domestic law, but the forum remains the same. And foreign law is only treated as a fact for the purposes of proof. Nor can any abstention from proving foreign law, resulting in the application of English law, assist. If English immaterial property law applies, its territorial and substantively restricted nature precludes its application to the infringement abroad of a foreign immaterial property right.

A distinction has been sought to be drawn between disputes in which the complaint of an infringement is linked to doubts concerning the validity of the immaterial property rights and infringements. This point was raised by Laddie J. in *Coin Controls Ltd.* v. *Suzo*[19] quoted with approval by Lord Woolf M.R. (as he then was).[19a] Relying on the test developed first in *Potter* v. *Broken Hill*, a case involving the validity of a patent, it has been stated that the courts of the country granting the right alone can determine its validity by virtue of the *lex originis* and equally in proceedings for an infringement, if the validity of the immaterial property right is questioned incidentally. In simple cases of infringement no such exclusive jurisdiction is said to exist. Since it is accepted that immaterial property law is strictly territorial and inherently limited it is not surprising that the courts of the country of origin must have exclusive jurisdiction to determine its existence and extent, a principle now reiterated by art. 16(4) of the Brussels Convention (now art. 22 Reg. 44 2001), except for copyrights if the uniform protection in all the Convention countries is to be assured. The exclusive jurisdiction of the courts of the country of origin is a means to an end. When infringement alone is in question in any one of the Convention countries, protection available there is based upon a parallel local law, but does not constitute a universal protection based upon the *lex originis* in any one of them. The territorial and substantively limited character of the local law restricts protection geographically and qualitatively. Substance and jurisdiction go hand

---

[18] *Collier* v. *Rivaz* (1842) 2 Curt. 855; *Re Anneslev* [1926] Ch. 692.
[19] [1997] 3 All E.R. 45.
[19a] *Fort Dodge Animal Health* v. *Akzo Nobel* [1998] ILPr at 742 [29].

in hand. Foreign intellectual and industrial property law excludes itself, and the local court, relying on its own law, must determine the measure of local protection, except, it is believed, insofar as the claimant's title to the right is concerned.[20]

| II. France

Neither French nor German practice relies expressly on the test of jurisdiction or attaches much importance to the territorial and the inherent limitation of immaterial and industrial property.[21] At the same time the ordinary rules of choice of law are not applied.[22] Despite this silent abstinence the same factors of territoriality and inherent limitation reappear in another guise. In France the leading case concluding the development over a century is the decision of the Court of Cassation dated 20 December 1959, *Soc Fox Europa* v. *Soc Le Chant du Monde*.[23] Filling what was perceived as a gap in the Berne Convention by relying on French *droit commun* to supplement it, holders of foreign intellectual property rights created in the country of their origin (*i.e.*, published or created there[24]) were held to enjoy in France in accordance with French law the protection of such rights for infringements committed there.

This brought to an end an evolution which had begun by a grant of local protection for publications in France by French nationals. Alien title owners had been excluded, and foreign intellectual property law had been irrelevant.[25] After a relaxation in 1810 in favour of French assignees of rights of foreign owners of works to be published in France, a judgment of 20 August

---

[20] See also Cornish, "Intellectual Property Infringement and Private International Law", esp. 288, 289.

[21] But see *e.g.*, Bartin. Clunet 1934, 780, 783, 787: Holleaux (below n. 23) 95.

[22] Cass 21 January 1936. Rev. cnt. d.i.p. 1936. 510, 514, 515 note Niboyet, S. 1937, 81, note Niboyet; GP 1936, I, 445 Paris; TGI Rev. crit. d.i.p. 1974. 112. note Bonet.

[23] Rev. crit. d.i.p. 1960. 361. note Terré, Clunet 1961, 420, note Goldman. D 1960, 93. note Holleaux on appeal from Paris 13 January 1953, Rev. crit. d.i.p. 1953, 739. JCP 1953 II 7667. note Loussouarn, GP 1953 1 191. It was followed for design by Paris 14 March 1991, Clunet 1992 148, 150, 151, 153 note Pollaud-Dulian 168, and for models note Ginsburg, JCP 1992 II 21780.

For a similar approach previously by Trib. civ. Seine, 14 February 1931. Clunet 1932, 420: 6 December 1933, Clunet 1934, 97; Rev. crit. d.i.p. 1934, 420, foreshadowed Cass. 14 December 1857, S. 1857 I 145: D 1858 I 161 (Verdi). A. Lucas and H.-J. Lucas, *Traité de la Propriété Littéraire et Artistique* (2nd ed., Paris 2001), nos. 928. 933.

[24] In the absence of publication and therefore of a local connection, attempts have been made to refer to the author's personal law: Lucas and Lucas. *Traité de la Propriété Littéraire et Artistique*, nos. 979–982.

[25] Terré (n. 23 above) 363.

1852 removed the incapacity of aliens to enjoy French intellectual property rights.[26]

By eliminating the aspect of discrimination against aliens in respect of works published in France,[27] only the problem of contact with a foreign country remained limited to whether protection extended to works of foreign origin. This protection was conceded in 1857[28] except for musical works, until the Franco-Italian Treaty|of 29 June 1862,[29] followed by others, ensured the reciprocal recognition of the right to all types of intellectual creations.[30] The recognition of the foreign privilege, not its local application, coupled with the concession of the available local remedies marks the insight that immaterial property rights, whether foreign or local, and therefore rights created by them, are strictly territorial.[31] This substantive territorial limitation eliminates reliance on choice of law rules.[32] Instead, immaterial property laws operate side by side with incidental regard to the law of the place of origin. This incidental regard manifested itself in the requirement that in the country of origin a *droit privatif* must have come into existence.[33] The requirement assumed a fundamental role, being a right to the work, its title or attribution, combined with the grant of the remedies accorded by the law of the country where protection is sought. Now the

---

[26] Cass cnm 20 August 1852. D 1852 1 335, S 1853 I 234. reiterated by Cass 27 July 1948, D 1948, 535. Rev. crit. d.i.p. 1949 75. note Batiffol.

[27] Law of 22 March 1852.

[28] Cass req 14 December 1857, S. 1858.1.145, D 1858.1.161 (Verdi).

[29] (1862–1863) 126 Parry, Consolidated Treaty Series 115. For a list of similar treaties concluded by France see Clunet 1878, 454–456; France-Russia (1911–1912) 215 Parry Cons. Treaty Ser. 91.

[30] *Grus* v. *Ricaldi* (Donizetti) Cass 25 July 1887, S 1888.1.17 note Lyon-Caen. D 1888 I 5, Clunet 1888, 245, 246, 248, 267–268 note Célica; Paris 22 November 1888, S 1890.2.121, Clunet 1890, 673: Cass 22 December 1959 at 362 and note Holleaux D 1960, 95; Cass 7 April 1998, Rev. crit. d.i.p. 1999, 76. 81 note Bergé; see also Trib. civ. Seine 20 December 1929, Clunet 1930. 681, 683; Paris 28 July 1932, Rev. crit. d.i.p. 1932, 671, 673 note Trachtenberg, Clunet 1934, 64, D 1934 2 139 note Lepointe; Cass 15 December 1975, Rev. crit. d.i.p. 1976, 575, Clunet 1976 421, Paris 14 March 1991, Clunet 1992, 148, note Pollaud-Dulian, JCP 1992.II.21780 note Ginsburg; Cass crim 29 March 1924, Clunet 1924, 708, 711, GP 1924.I.684, D Hebd 1924, 322; Cass 4 January 1964, D 1964, J. 321 (Furtwängler); Pollaud-Dulian, Jurisct. dr. internat. Fasc 563–60 nos. 44, 62, 67; Lucas and Lucas, *Traité de la Propriété Littéraire et Artistique*, no. 906; generally Renault, Clunet 1878, 117, 454, 463.

[31] Note 30 above, esp. Paris 14 March 1991 (Almak) Clunet 1992 133, 148, 150, note Edelmann, JCP 1992.I.21780 note Ginsburg; CA Rennes 17 June 1996; Cass 7 April 1998, Rev. crit. 1999, 716, Lucas and Lucas, *Traité de la Propriété Littéraire et Artistique*, no. 976.

[32] H. Schack, "Kolorierung von Spielfilmen: Das Persönlichkeitsrecht des Filmregisseurs im IPR" 1993 IPRax, 46, 48.

[33] Trib. corr. Seine 20 December 1929, Clunet 1930, 681, 683; Trib. civ. Seine 14 February 1931, Clunet 1932, 113, 140; same 6 December 1933, Clunet 1934, 907. Rev. crit. d.i.p. 1934, 420, 423; Cass 29 April 1970. Clunet 1970, 936 note Françcon; Lucas and Lucas, *Traité de la Propriété Littéraire et Artistique*, no. 906; see also no. 42.

combination of a foreign *lex originis* with a local *lex protectionis* raised the question as to which of these aspects of a claim affecting immaterial property fell within the sphere of either of these laws.[34] The former is concentrated on the place of first publication, creation or registration, the latter on the *lex fori* if it coincides with the *lex loci delicti*.[35]

The parallel jurisdiction of more than one country facilitates proceedings in more than one of them, if the infringement took place in several. If the same infringement affects two jurisdictions, one of which relies on the tortious act, the other on the tortious effect, a duplication becomes inevitable.

| In reaching this stage little attention was paid to the reasons why in the case of immaterial property law two legal systems are to be taken into account and why the ordinary rules of private international law do not apply. The answer is to be found in the particular structure of intellectual as well as industrial property law. It is the uniquely territorial character of immaterial property law. It is not only exclusive in the positive sense that it applies always in the country where it is in force, but also in the negative sense that it cannot operate in any other country side by side with its local equivalent.[36] By its nature an immaterial property right is not a right in a movable or an immovable but an exclusive privilege of a temporary kind conceded by local public law[37], the creation of a statute.[38] However, the demand for pro-

---

[34] Goldman, Clunet 1962, 985 (2) note to Lyon 16 February 1961; Paris 3 June 1961, Rev. crit. d.i.p. 1962, 299, 307. 309 note Desbois.

[35] Lucas and Lucas, *Traité de la Propriété Littéraire et Artistique*, nos. 976 ff. 987–991.

[36] For an early insight see Celliez, cited by Renault, Clunet 1878 at 465; for a later view Bartin, Clunet 1934 781, at 788, 794, 801; for a comparable approach in Germany see Staudinger – von Hoffman, BGB vol.10 (3rd ed., Berlin 1998) – nach art.38 Anhang II Rz 13 n. 29; Soergel-Kegel, BGB vol.10 (12th ed., Stuttgart 1996) Anhang vor art.12 Rz 16, 17.

[37] Cass 25 July 1887 Grus, Trib. corr. Seine 20 December 1929, Clunet 1930, 681, 684, GP 1930. 1.376, 377; Trib. civ. Seine 14 February 1931 Clunet 1932, 113, 140; same 6 December 1933 Rev. crit. d.i.p. 1934, 420, note Niboyet at p. 425: "like a bird the right settles in many places": *i.e.*, the right remains the same, but the remedies are local; Cass 21 January 1936, Rev. crit. d.i.p. 1936, 510 note Niboyet; see also Terré, note to Cass 22 December 1959. Rev. crit. d.i.p. 1960, 361, 367; Holleaux note DP 1960, 95 (ii) and the pungent remarks by Renault, Clunet 1878 at 466, but see E. Bartin, *Principes de Droit International Privé, III* (Paris 1935), nos. 379–383; Clunet 1934 (above n. 36) at 791, 800; Lucas and Lucas. *Traité de la Propriété Littéraire et Artistique*, nos. 961, 982–85. For a conflict in time see Trib. civ. Seine 14 February 1931, Clunet 1932, 114.

[38] It is a different question whether for the purpose of certain aspects of domestic law an intellectual property bears a proprietory or a personal character. See *Campbell Connelly* v. *Noble* [1963] 1 W.L.R. 252; whether on the death of the owner such a right is to be treated as property falling within the matrimonial property regime of community of goods or as a personal right falling into the succession: Paris One February 1900 S. 1900.2.121 note Salleiles, Cass 25 June 1902, S. 1902.1.103, note Lyon-Caen; also Trib. corr. Seine 20 December 1929, GP 1930.1.376; Mazeaud D 1959 Chron. 139.

tection abroad has led to unsuccessful attempts to rely on choice of law and jurisdiction rules. Instead modern needs have led to foreign immaterial property rights being given effect either in virtue of treaties or of local law by a novel technique. An equivalent local parallel right was conceded which provides local protection in the absence of the possibility of giving effect directly to foreign immaterial property law with the help of Private International Law. This protection is accorded not because it supports a right under foreign law (which is strictly territorial and cannot be applied elsewhere) nor because a new right is brought into being by local law. Instead the foreign claimant is accorded protection in accordance with the form and the extent of the remedies of local law in favour of the holder of the comparable foreign right or privilege. This ensures that, despite the parallel treatment of intellectual and industrial | immaterial property in several jurisdictions according to local law uniformity is safeguarded.[39]

It could be argued – and has recently been suggested again[39a]– that in order to provide protection in France (or for that matter in any country) according to local law it is only necessary to show either publication abroad or at least the creation of an original work.[40] Such was the position before the requirement of a *droit privatif* was established in 1887 by the *Verdi* case. Only French immaterial property law was believed to be in issue, and no need existed to face the question of foreign law. More recently the same tendency reappeared when it was said that in fact the differences between existing legal systems are not fundamental, leading to a gradual convergence.[41]

However, the task of the courts, as the French courts rightly perceived, is not to apply and enforce a foreign immaterial property right, but only to recognize a foreign title, its limits and extensions and to accord to the holder of a foreign title the same procedural and substantive protection as a local title holder would receive.[42] In other words, the ordinary rules of choice of law do not apply, since foreign immaterial property rights cannot apply. The foreign *lex loci delicti* ousts the jurisdiction of the court seized (see I above)

---

[39] Lucas and Lucas, *Traité de la Propriété Littéraire et Artistique*, no. 1060 ff.

[39a] See p. n. 41, 45 below.

[40] See the defendant's argument in TGI Seine 19 March 1964, Rev. crit. 1965, 89, 93; TGI Lyon, 3 June 1961, Clunet 1962, 974, note Goldman 985 (2): Global application of local law, Pans 14 March 1991, Clunet 1992, 148, 150, note Pollaud-Dulian, Rev. crit. d.i.p. 1962, 299, note Desbois at 310; Cass 29 March 1924 DH 1924, 332, Clunet 1924, 707: GP 1924.I.684.

[41] Goldman (n. 40 above); Desbois (n. 34 above); Lucas and Lucas, *Traité de la Propriété Littéraire et Artistique*, nos. 977, 978.

[42] Cass 25 July 1887 (Grus), n. 30 above); Cass 22 December 1959 (n. 23 above), Paris 14 March 1991, Clunet 1992, 148, note Pollaud-Dulian, JCP 1982 I 21780 uote Ginsburg; Paris 22 November 1888, S. 1896 2 221, Clunet 1890, 673, 675 (Chopin); Trib. civ. Seine 20 December 1929, GP 1930 I 376, Clunet 1930, 681, 683; also Cass crim. 15 June 1899, Clunet 1899, 818, 821; Cass 29 March 1924 (n. 40 above); Desbois, note Rev. crit. d.i.p. 1965, 97.

and renvoi cannot apply. Therefore the Court of Cassation required as early as 1857 evidence of a *droit privatif* (an exclusive privileged title according to the law at the place of literary or industrial creation before protection could be made available in France). In the words of the Court of Cassation, the protection of foreign copyrights "presupposes pre-existing rights and only provides authors the means to enforce those which they have acquired in the country of origin". However, in recent times a general shift away from the *lex originis* has been observed towards the *lex loci delicti* as the *lex protectionis*.[43]

The *lex originis* assumed a function in forming the basis for an award of judicial protection in France (here *lex protectionis*).[44] The|strictly territorial character of intellectual property law was not breached since the foreign title was only recognized and the remedies are provided locally in parallel proceedings arising out of a local infringement. Thereby the foreign immaterial property right is not translated into a local one: at the same time regard to the *lex originis* does not pose a Preliminary Question since the existence of parallel proceedings constitutes a unity of proceedings.[45]

The reference to a *droit privatif* according to a foreign *lex originis* is not a reference to a foreign *lex causae* by observing ordinary rules of Private International Law followed by procedural protection by the *lex fori*, if it is the *lex loci delicti*. Instead it is a reference to a concrete statutory concession or privilege. After acknowledging the territoriality of the French *lex protectionis*, the question became how to ascertain the range *ratione personae* and *ratione materiae* of the privilege according to the foreign *lex originis* which requires protection, if the protection is not to be equated with the same personal and material privileges of the *lex protectionis* and thereby substituting a local privilege for a foreign one. In the words of Niboyet, the foreign intellectual property right had to be nationalized.[45a]

While thereby the *lex originis* was assured a place in the process of protecting foreign intellectual property rights, it became necessary to observe the range of the foreign *droit privatif*. In the words of one commentator, "all that is necessary is that a state recognizes a certain exclusive right over the work".[46] In the practice of the courts this recognition covers title (*titularité*)

---

[43] Note Goldman (n. 34 above).

[44] See the cases cited at n. 42 above.

[45] Pans 14 March 1992, Clunet 1992, 148, 160–161, 162, note Pollaud-Dulian.

[45a] J.P. Niboyet, *Traité de Droit International Privé Francpais*, IV (Paris 1947), no. 1315 p. 733.

[46] Goldman (n. 34 above); Trib. civ. Seine 20 December 1929, Clunet 1930, 681. 684, GP 1930.I.376 ca Gautier Rev. cnt. d.i.p. 1989. 379, Lucas and Lucas no. 971. 10 63. Trib. civ. Seine Six December 1933, Clunet 1934, 907, Rev. crit. d.i.p. 1934, 424.

to the work,[47] its duration,[48] the right to translate the work[49] (which however, involve a contract assigning this right), the capacity to | assign the right[50], an employer's right to assign copyrights arising from work by employees[51] and the right to succeed to the privilege.

While therefore the measure of the protection of a foreign immaterial property right is determined exclusively by the *lex protectionis*, aspects of the *locus standi* of the claimant are determined by the *lex originis*.[52] By these means the country where protection is sought makes it clear that the protection is not offered to a right created by the *lex fori* or *delicti* but in parallel proceedings to a privilege created abroad.

However, when the foreign privilege is identical with the concession granted by the holder to translate the work or to have it assigned, a trend can be noted to rely on the law most closely connected with the transaction, which, however, happens to be identical with the *lex originis*[53] or, in the case of a *droit moral* with the *lex protectionis*.[54] However, the Court of Cassation, on 7 April 1998 has affirmed the original bifurcated principle.[55] Difficulties were created by the author's *droit moral* described as the enjoyment of his "droit au respect de son nom, de sa qualité et de son oeuvre".[56] It embraces

---

[47] Paris, 14 March 1992, Clunet 1992, 148, 151, 160–161, note Pollaud-Dulian, Cass 7 April 1998; Rev. crit. d.i.p. 1999, 76 ff, for the early development see Renault, Clunet 1878, 454, 462. but see 465 unless the work is unpublished; note Desbois Rev. crit. d.i.p. 1962, 299. 308, 309 pleading for the application of the personal law.

[48] TGI Seine 19 March 1964, Rev. cnt. d.i.p. 1965, 89, note Desbois, at 92. 93. 97; Cass 15 February 1975, Rev. crit. d.i.p. 1976, 515, note Bonet, Clunet 1976, 440; JCP 1976.II.18394, note Françcon on appeal from Paris 24 April 1974, D 1975, 67, Rev. crit. d.i.p. 1975. 440, 449, 450, note Bouet; also Cass 25 July 1887 (above n. 30); Paris 21 November 1888, Clunet 1890, 673; see also Renault, Clunet 1878, 454, 463; Goldman, Clunet 1960 at 149, note to Paris 29 April 1959; Bartin (above n. 36); Berne Convention, art.7(8), 18(1); Law 27 March 1997 art.123(12), Lucas and Lucas, *Traité de la Propriété Littéraire et Artistique*, uo. 958.

[49] Cass 29 April 1970, Clunet 1970, 936, 938 B, note Françcon, Rev. crit. d.i.p. 1971, 270, 272, note Batiffol; TGI Lyon, 16 February 1961, Clunet 1962, 974, 983(1), note Goldman, Rev. crit. d.i.p. 1962, 299, note Desbois, 305, 307, 411.

[50] Pans, 3 January 1961, Clunet 1962, 981, 983; GP 1962, 16; Trib. civ. Seine 6 December 1933, Rev. crit. d.i.p. 1934, 421, 422; Cass. crim. 29 March 1924, Clunet 1924, 708, 709, GP 1924.I.684 (n. 30 above) and distinguish the contract to assign: Trib. civ. Seine 15 February 1958, Clunet 1959, 146; GP 1958.1.421; JCP 1958.2.11193, Calice, Clunet 1924, 616 and *cp.* *Campbell Connelly Noble* (n. 38 above); Pollaud-Dulian (n. 30 above) nos. 53, 54–59.

[51] Paris, 1 February 1989, Clunet 1989, 1005, note Edelman.

[52] Pans, 22 November 1888, S. 1890.2.121, Clunet 1890, 673; Trib. civ. Seine 20 December 1929, Clunet 1930, 681, 683, 684, GP 1930.1.376; Cass 7 April 1998 at 150 (above n. 47); also Cass. crim. 28 May 1875, DP 1875 I 329, 334; Rouen, 25 February 1876, DP 1876 2 67; Cass. req. 20 November 1877, DP 1878 I 309; Cass 20 February 1882. DP 1882.1.465.

[53] Paris, 29 April 1970 (n. 49 above); Lucas and Lucas no. 966, 967, 968.

[54] See the cases cited by Lucas and Lucas, *Traité de la Propriété Littéraire et Artistique*, no. 968 n. 183 and n. 63 below.

[55] See n. 47 above.

[56] It is an "enumeration of the author's personality": *Fox Europe* v. *Luntz*. D 1973, 363,

the right to control new issues of the work, to modify it or to alter it completely. The author's thought remains alive, attached to the person coupled with some material interests, even if the intellectual property right has been assigned.[57]

The *droit moral* is part of the *droit privatif* by representing one aspect of the statutory privilege or concession or, more precisely, by representing either a *quality of title* determined by the *lex originis* or part of the *extent* of an author's right to be defined and enforced by the lex protectionis. It has long been recognized that a copyright embraces both personal and material interests.[58]

|*Huston* v. *Turner*[59] offers the most recent example. A claim by the heirs of an American copyright owner against film producers in France, assignees of the copyright, based on the right to prohibit alterations of the original was allowed by the TGI Paris[60] on the strength of French law as the *lex protectionis*, even if no comparable right existed under the *lex originis*. The relevant French provision was held to apply always. Such provisions may therefore either be described as specific "règles d'application immediate" (Francescakis),[61] called in the case discussed here "lois d'application impérative" or as general rules of public policy. On appeal the claim was dismissed by the Court of Appeal of Paris[62] on the ground that no such right existed in the United States, the *lex originis*, but it was allowed by the Court of Cassation.[63]

---

366 (ii B), note Edelman, Lucas and Lucas, *Traité de la Propriété Litteraire et Artistique*, no. 927 p. 740, no. 1108.

[57] Paris, 1 February 1989, Clunet 1989, 1005, 1008–1009, note Edelman: for the comparable right of a performer: 4 January 1964, D 1964.J.321, note Pleyette (Furtwängler); TGI Seine 10 January 1990, D 1991, J.206, 207 (Rostropovich), Lucas and Lucas, *Traité de la Propriété Littéraire et Artistique*, nos. 812, 906, 1026.

[58] Paris, I February 1900, S. 1900.2.121, 122, 126, note Saleilles, Trib. civ. Seine 15 February 1958, D 1958, 682, 684 (The Kid), note Lyon-Caen and Lavigne at 687 (ü), Clunet 1959, 146, GP 1958.I.421, JCP 1959.III. 11 113, note Lavigne, and Lyon-Caen; on appeal Paris, 29 April 1959, Rev. crit. d.i.p. 1959, 484 note Loussouarn; Clunet 1960, 129, 137, note Goldman 147. D 1959, 402. 406(b), note Lyon-Caen and Lavigne. S. 1959, 185; GP 1959, 624, note Gombaldieu; Cass 28 May 1963, Clunet 1963, 1005; D 1963.J.677 on other grounds; see also Pollaud-Dulian n. 45 above.

[59] See below n. 60–63 for the judgments in the various instances. For the previous practice see Paris 28 July 1932 DP 1934.2.139. 141 B, 145, note Lepointe; and the cases cited n. 58 above. Pollaud-Dulian, Jurisclasseur de droit international, no. 61; Schack, "Kolonerung von Spielfilmen" 1993 IPRax, 46.

[60] 22 November 1988, Rev. crit. d.i.p. 1989. 372, 379. note Gautier, Clunet 1989, 67, note Edelman, DS 1989, 343 note Audit.

[61] Ph. Francescakis, *La Théorie du Renvoi* (Paris 1958) nos. 7. 10, 12, 13, 26–39. Rev. crit. d.i.p. 1966, 1.

[62] 6 July 1989, Rev. crit. d.i.p. 1989. 706, 708. note Gautier; Clunet 1989. 979, 992, note Edelman; DS 1990 J. 152, note Audit; JCP 1990.II.21410, note Francçon, foreshadowed by Goldman, note to TGI Lyon 16 February 1961, Clunet 1962 at p. 984(2).

[63] 28 May 1991, Rev. crit. d.i.p. 1996, 752, note Gautier. Clunet 1992, 133 note Edelman;

The outcome is not clear since reliance on a *droit moral* of French law, the *lex protectionis*, in the absence of such a right by the *lex originis* does not appear to exclude the recognition of such a right, had it existed according to the *lex originis*. It seems to affirm, however, that the *droit moral* is treated, at least in principle, as constituting an aspect of the privilege itself as created by the *lex originis* and does not merely focus on the extent of the protection of the intellectual property right, which is always determined by the *lex protectionis*. The latter applies only in a substitution for the *lex originis*, if the latter fails to include it. Doubts have, however, been expressed as to whether a *droit moral* according to the *lex protectionis* is to be recognized if it does not exist by the *lex originis*.[64]

| III. Germany

It has been stated by courts[65] and by writers[66] in Germany that in matters of intellectual and industrial property the ordinary rules of Private International Law do not apply. Instead the *lex protectionis* (the law of the state where redress is sought) applies. The question remained whether such law takes the place which the *lex loci delicti* occupied in Private International Law or whether it was restricted territorially.

As early as 1914 the court stated that in the matter of patents there are "as many patent areas as there are states".[67] The court concluded that in respect of the same invention the right to a patent for the invention in Switzerland is independent of the right to the patent in Germany, even if vested in the same person. Therefore a product lawfully manufactured in one country must not be introduced or used in another, even if the same person enjoys the patent in

---

DS 1993.J.197, note Raynard, JCP 1991.II.21731, note Francçon; Lucas and Lucas, *Traité de la Propriété Littéraire et Artistique*, nos. 959, 1001.

[64] Goldman note to Paris, 29 April 1959, Clunet 1960. 128 at 146; Bergé note to Cass, 7 April 1998, Rev. crit. d.i.p. 1999, 85; Ginsburg note to Paris, 14 March 1991 (above n. 47) JCP 1992.I.21780 II; Lucas and Lucas, *Traité de la Propriété Littéraire et Artistique*, nos. 973–975, 1108; Berne art.6 bis; Schack, "Kolorierung von Spielfilmen". 49 (n. 32 above).

[65] BGHZ 118, 394, 397: 126, 252, 255; 136, 380, 385–386; Schack, "Anmerkung zu BGH 2.10.1997 – I ZR 88/95 – Spielbankaffaire (zum 1PR des Filmurheberrechts)", 1998 JZ 1018: Martiny (1967) 40 Rabeis Z 218, 220 with lit. at n. 7.

[66] Von Bar, *Internationales Privatrecht II*, no. 705 with cases at note 362; Kreuzer in Münchener Kommentar zum BGB vol.10 nach Art. 38. Anhang II Rz 7–15. 26, Von Hoffman, Stoll. Staudinger Kommentar zum BGB (12th ed.) Article 38 Rdz 591. 592, Siehr IPRax 1992, 29, 31 n. 16, note to LG Düsseldorf 31 October 1990 now BGHZ 126, 252 (n. 65 above).

[67] RGZ 84, 371, 375, previously RGZ 30, 52, 54, 55, BGHZ 16 April 1975, GRUR 1975, 361, 364.

both countries, except in virtue of a licence. The court said "The effects of a right granted by a patent are restricted to the territory of the country the competent authorities of which have conferred it ... each of these rights operates locally independently of all others." The same was ultimately also acknowledged for trademarks.[68]

This conclusion follows from the nature of immaterial property law, which is territorial in the dual sense, that positively it has exclusive application locally and negatively that foreign law cannot be considered.[69] The territorial character of immaterial property laws results in their parallel operation, if admitted in several states[70] but cannot lead to the application of the law of A to infringements in B or law of B to infringements in A.[71] Thus a "bundle of local rights" protects the same immaterial property interest originally | established in one country.[72] Only acts within the territorial range of the local immaterial property law (the *"Schutzland"*) are subject to it.[73]

The absence in German law of recourse to the *lex originis* to determine the nature and extent of what French law described as the *"droit privatif"* forming the core of the immaterial property right appears to be due to the difference in approach to the function of the "bundle of rights" representing the local effect of a foreign immaterial property right. It would seem that at one time the territorial character of foreign immaterial property law was also thought to exclude the *recognition* of such laws by the country of protection.[74] By excluding the *lex originis* to circumscribe the nature and limits as distinct from the effects (governed by the *lex protectionis*), the "bundle" of parallel rights[75] consists of a conjunction of immaterial property rights which may differ not only in the measure of protection provided in several countries but also in the quality of the rights sought to be protected.[76] In short, protection is provided not for the same immaterial property right,

---

[68] RGZ 118, 76, 80–82 overruling RGZ 18, 28; 45, 145; 51, 267; 108, 9 which had envisaged suits in Germany for violations abroad by a German of a foreign patent, subject to the effect of exhaustion: BGHZ 41, 84, 88(a).

[69] See section 11, above.

[70] RGZ 118, 76, 81; BGHZ 41, 89. 91, subject to the proviso that foreign acts may affect local trademarks – see above n. 68.

[71] RGZ 118, 71, 81; BGHZ 49, 331. 334 (a); also BGHZ 41, 84, 89; 126. 255. 256: L. Raape, *Internationales Privatrecht* (5th ed., Berlin 1961) para. 64 II, p. 641; A. Nussbaum, *Internationales Privatrecht* (1932), 338 n. 2.

[72] BGHZ 18, 1, 13; 22, 1, 14; 49, 331, 334 (a); OLG Frankfurt 27 January 1966, IPRspr 1968–69 no. 166a; B Verf G 23 January 1990; GRUR 1990, 438, 441 IV (1), (2).

[73] BGHZ 49, 331, 334–335; Siehr, IPRax 1992, 29. 32 (b).

[74] OLG Hamburg 27 March 1958, IPRspr 1958–59 no. 152, Kreuzer, n. 66 above Rz 17, 20.

[75] Eg OLG Koblenz 14 July 1967, IPRax 1966–1967 no. 182; OLG Hamburg 27 March 1958 (n. 74 above); OLG München 29 January 1959 *ibid* no. 153 p. 512.

[76] Siehr IPRax 1992, 29. 31 (b).

albeit with different effects in different countries, but for different immaterial property rights. Such a right in one country may trigger off protection in another country which differs not only in extent but also in substance from the original right.

It is therefore not surprising that some learned commentators[77] regretted the omission to isolate the original immaterial property right and instead to delegate the questions of authorship, assignability and title in general to the basic *lex originis*. However it would seem that, in respect of the related right given in German law to a performing artist the German Federal Constitutional Court may have recognised that a performer has a *"droit moral"* which constitutes a proprietary right[78] limited territorially by the *lex protectionis*. The practice of the German Federal Supreme Court, as formulated in 1914 observing strict territoriality, suffered a change when the Court treated an infringement in Norway of a Norwegian trademark by a German defendant[79] subject to German jurisdiction | as a tort to which a German court could apply the German rules of Private International Law relating to torts (art. 12 EGBGB then in force). According to art. 12 such claims addressed to a German defendant were not to be entertained by German courts to a greater extent than German law would have allowed. Since no German trademark existed in the name of the defendant, for which it could have demanded exclusive territorial application, and although the Norwegian trademark legislation was territorial and the judgment obtained in Norway against the defendant could not be enforced in Germany, the German defendant who had infringed the foreign trademark abroad could be sued in Germany for a tort committed abroad. Thus, while the court recognised the exclusive territoriality of German immaterial property law, even if in the particular case no equivalent German trademark existed, it was prepared to disregard the same character of Norwegian trademark law – which should have precluded its application in Germany – and was willing to apply the latter in German proceedings as a result of a reference to Norwegian law by the German rule of Private International Law relating to torts.[80]

In 1956 the Federal Supreme Court sought to improve on this practice.[81] Assuming that the court had jurisdiction, the objection that the German court was dealing with a foreign (Portuguese) trademark of a territorial

---

[77] Drobnig (1974) 40 Rabels Z 195, 200, but see Ulmer *ibid* (1977) 41, ¡*bid* 479, 481; H. Schack, "Zur Qualifikation des Anspruchs auf Rechnungslegung im internationalen Urheberrecht" 1991 IPRax 347, 348 and "Kolorierung von Spielfilmen", 48 (b).

[78] B Verf G 23 January 1990, GRUR 1990, 438 I 1, 439 III, 440 II, 1 a, 441 b, aa, bb, 2 III 3 a.

[79] RGZ 129, 385, 386–387, JW 1931, 428 note Nussbaum; also OLG Hamburg 12 May 1933, IPRspr 1933 no. 102: LG Munich 4 July 1972, IPRax 1973 no. 108.

[80] RGZ 129, 385, 386. 387, esp. 388.

[81] BGHZ 22 I 13–14; the question had remained outstanding in RGZ 118, 76, 81.

character was dismissed on the ground that the effect of the judgment could only be felt in Germany and did not violate foreign sovereignty (*i.e.* the exclusive territoriality of Portuguese law).

In fact Portuguese sovereignty was not in issue, but the German court failed correctly to interpret Portuguese law, which is territorially restricted. While referred to as the *lex loci delicti* it would appear that Portuguese law was not applied. In the view of the German court the question was whether in the light of article 12 of the Introductory Law to the Civil Code a claim against a German defendant for an infringement of Portuguese law was justified to the extent assessable if a German trademark corresponding to that abroad had been violated. The court held on the strength of the German choice of law rule (art. 12 of the Introductory Law to the Civil Code) that a claim for an infringement abroad of a foreign trademark was admissible in Germany to the extent that such a claim was actionable in Germany. What was designed as a choice of law rule including a comparator was turned into a rule of substantive law by way of|what appears to be a fiction.[82] This made it possible to treat an infringement of a foreign immaterial property right as a tort committed in Germany, thus avoiding the territorial limitation of *the foreign law*.

After the German Federal Supreme Court had relied in 1956[83] indirectly on the assistance of the German choice of law rule in tort the balance was restored in 1994[84] when the court returned to the practice followed in 1927.[85] The competent legal system to deal with immaterial property law is the law of the country in respect of whose territory protection is sought (*Schutzland*), given its exclusive territorial character having only limited effect. This law (the *lex protectionis*) embodies the "unfettered economic law" of the country concerned.[86] The necessary connecting factor consists in the alleged act of infringement which took place in the country where protection is sought.[87] The court of protection's jurisdiction is identical with the *lex fori* (which is normally the *lex loci delicti*), subject to possible exceptions to be considered later on. However in BGHZ 136, 381 (1997) the *lex fori* was not identical with the *lex protectionis* (the law of the *Schutzland*) which was Luxemburg.

The Federal Supreme Court in an action for the infringement of a copyright (acquired in accordance with the law of the former German Democrat-

---

[82] Kreuzer, *Münchener Kommentar* Rdz 114 with lit.
[83] See n. 81 above.
[84] BGHZ 126, 252, 255 with lit, also 118, 394. 397; Katzenberger, IPRax 1983, 158; Ulmer (1973) 37 Rabels Z 499.
[85] RGZ 118, 76, 81.
[86] BGHZ 126, 252, 256; Siehr, IPRax 1992, 219, 220.
[87] BGHZ 126, 252 at 256. 258 (4).

ic Republic) and a licence thereunder to exercise the right in Luxemburg, held that Luxemburg law was applicable as the *lex protectionis* and not German law.[88] The court stated expressly that in relying in German proceedings on Luxemburg law as the law of the (foreign) State of Protection, the German court was not applying Luxemburg law as the *lex loci delicti* by following the German rules of private international law, but as the foreign *lex protectionis*.

The *explanation* for the deviation from the normal practice which identifies jurisdiction with the *lex protectionis* (which is the *lex loci delicti* of the specific local right) must be found in the Brussels Jurisdiction Convention which enables the court to assume jurisdiction on the defendant's residence (in Germany). Thereby the main problem of the present study was being touched, which is whether rules of foreign immaterial property law can be applied by courts elsewhere as part of the *lex protectionis* or *lex loci delicti* notwithstanding their territorial character which restricts their effect | to the country of their enactment. The only difference between the BGH 136, 386 case and *Pearce* v. *Ove Arup*[89] is that in the latter English Private International Law served to determine the applicable law expressly to support the application, while in the case under consideration Luxemburg Law was purported to be taken into account as the *lex protectionis* (the *Schutzland*) – which was also the *lex loci delicti*. In both cases the parallel operation of immaterial property legislation was disregarded in favour of a reference to foreign law where the infringement had taken place. However, while an infringement of a protected interest, such as by way of passing off, may attract the operation of the local private law rules of tort and their application by courts elsewhere in virtue of their rules of private international law, an infringement of an immaterial property is an illegal act incapable of being prosecuted outside the country where protection is sought. In BGHZ 136, 380 the German court referred to the "*Schutzland*" and its law as the *lex protectionis* – which was also the *lex loci delicti*. In *Pearce* v. *Ove Arup* a rule of English Private International Law had the same effect. Although the territorial nature of Luxemburg law did not conflict in substance with the corresponding German law, the problem remains the same. It is whether with the extension of jurisdiction by the Brussels Convention the application of foreign territorial law has been accepted and is possible. However, the reference by the German Federal Supreme Court[90] to the control to be exercised in applying foreign (*i.e.*, Luxemburg) law may perhaps indicate that the court had doubts whether Luxemburg immaterial property law could be applied in Germany.

---

[88] BGHZ 136, 386, 385(1), 386(1) citing BGHZ 118, 394, 397; 126, 250, 255 with lit. at p. 256.

[89] [2000] Ch. 403.

[90] BGHZ 136 at p. 386.

If the nature of the foreign law involved precludes its application by courts in other countries, the courts in these countries are unable to adjudicate in the absence of a local cause of action. Local law cannot be substituted in view of its own territorial nature. Expressed in procedural terms, local (German) courts lack jurisdiction of necessity.

IV

The foregoing survey shows that while French courts strictly observe the territorial character of immaterial property law, English and German courts have shown a willingness to assume jurisdiction and to apply foreign immaterial property law alleged to have been infringed abroad. In England, and to a certain extent in Germany, the extension of jurisdiction by the Brussels Convention had this|effect, and the foreign *lex protectionis*, being also the *lex loci delicti*, was applied without expressly referring to the relevant choice of law rule.[91] In Germany in BGHZ 136, 380 local jurisdiction existed in virtue of art.2 of the Brussels Convention and the foreign (Luxemburg) *lex protectionis* was applied, which was also the *lex loci delicti*, but the court brushed aside this consideration (at p. 386). On the other hand in BGHZ 22 1 at 13 the court relied on a choice of law rule (art. 12 EGBGB) as a means to apply German law by way of a fiction although the *lex protectionis* was foreign.

It emerges, therefore that the time honoured territoriality of immaterial property law and its parallel enforcement on the strength of the Berne and Paris Conventions and the Madrid Agreement or of "droit commun" is being undermined by its transcountry protection, based on the Brussels and Lugano Conventions (now Reg 44/2001) with or without reliance on Private International Law. At present this development appears to be impeded by the combined positive and negative character of territorially limited legislation. The question is whether this character will be lost, and with it the structure of the relevant treaties.[92]

Recent practice has not deviated from the general observance of the territoriality of immaterial property rights, and the extension of jurisdiction in *Pearce* v. *Ove Arup*[93] to infringements of domestic immaterial property rights abroad has remained unique. In an action in another country the courts in the country of protection can therefore only succeed if the local law is applied as the *lex loci delicti*.

---

[91] *Pearce* v. *Ove Arup* [2000] Ch. 403.
[92] Approving Staudinger 2 rz 594; but see 595.
[93] [2000] Ch. 403.

The classic treatment by Ulmer[94] starts from the position that the protection of immaterial property rights in countries other than that of the country of origin is determined by an infringement (*Eingriffshandlung*)[95] which alerts the local law. This law is not to be identified with the *lex fori*, including possibly, the rules of the conflict of laws, but with the *lex loci delicti*,[96] in the sense that the action is for damages, not to enforce a right based on foreign[97] territorial law, but a local, territorially limited right provided that a | sufficient connection exists between the country of the *forum* and the infringement.[98]

A distinct feature is, however, that unlike in the conflict of laws in general, where choice of law and jurisdiction operate independently of each other, the territoriality of immaterial property law[99] precludes its application elsewhere than in the country of origin. Since it cannot apply elsewhere, courts in other countries cannot either apply other than their own rules, and on the failure of foreign immaterial property law to apply, the local court must of necessity cease to exercise jurisdiction in the absence of a cause of action, unless its own law provides any relevant remedies.

The legal basis of the support offered by the country of protection is stated to be that the infringement constitutes a local tort. However, the protection by the law of tort in the country of protection is dependent on the violation of a protected right (which in the case of a copyright is the law where the work was first published) and the territoriality of this type of right cannot support an action in tort elsewhere.

The answer why protection is granted nevertheless is to be found for copyrights in art. 5(1) of the Berne Convention which provides that, leaving aside the protection provided by the country of origin, the benefit of protection accorded in each Convention country is that of the local law (as the *lex loci delicti*), with exceptions in favour of the law of the country of origin for the period of protection and the *droit de suite*.[100] Outside the range of the

---

[94] E. Ulmer. *Die Immaterialgüterrechte im Internationalen Privatrecht* (Munich 1975).

[95] Ulmer, *Immaterialgürerrechte*, p. 13 para. 22, p. 15 para. 26.

[96] *Ibid*, p. 15 para. 27, p. 68 para. 29. This disability cannot be overcome by an artificial extension of jurisdiction, *e.g.* by reliance on the Brussels Convention: Lipstein, "Intellectual Property: Jurisdiction or Choice of Law?".

[97] This disposes of the problem whether in reality a tort has been committed – see Sir Peter North and J.J. Fawcett, *Cheshire and North's Private International Law* (13th ed., London 1999), p. 618 n. 13 with lit.

[98] J. Carrascosa González. "Conflict of Laws in a Centenary Convention: Berne Convention 9th September 1886 for the Protection of Literary and Artistic Works", in H.-P. Mansel *et al.*, (eds.), *Festschrift für Erik Jayme, I* (Munich 2004), 105, 111 (23), 112 (26), 116 (37) with lit. at 110 n. 16, 17, 18, p. 116 n. 31.

[99] Ulmer, *Immatertalgüterrechte*, p. 50 para. 68.

[100] Ulmer, *Immaterialgüterrechte*, p. 31 para. 41, p. 39 para. 53: see also p. 32 para. 42; p. 33 para. 43.

Berne Convention the creation, effect and extinction of a copyright is simi-larly governed by the law of the protecting country,[101] including its vesting in the author.[102]

As stated before, the territoriality of a foreign copyright precludes its application as a protected interest in support of an action *in a country of protection* for damages in connection with an infringement. The choice of the *lex originis* is precluded by its territorial character, and the ordinary rules of the conflict of laws fail to support an action *in the country of origin* for damages for the violation of the copyright elsewhere. An action in another country – the country of protection – can therefore only succeed if | the *local* law is applied as the *lex loci delicti*. However, this raises the problem outlined before: the local immaterial property law of the country of protection ap-plies only to violations of local immaterial property law and what is required here is the protection of what is in substance a foreign right.

The solution adopted by the Convention and by national choice of law rules is this: a unilateral choice of law rule of the country of origin referring to its own copyright law with territorial effect is bilateralized by another which *introduces the same law in the country of protection in the guise of the corresponding law of the country of protection.* In other words: A parallel remedy is introduced. In contrast to the classic solution of conflict of laws whereby the *forum* introduces foreign law as the law governing the tort abroad by assuming a broad jurisdiction, the specific choice of law solution for the infringement of immaterial property law is to assume exclusive ju-risdiction and to apply the law of the country of protection as reflecting the *lex originis.* While the classic solution favours the importation of foreign law, *the specific solution for copyright is to export the lex originis by giving it effect within the framework of the lex protectionis by a parallel remedy.* Choice of law and territoriality have been reconciled. With justification Ulmer has stressed that the ordinary principles of the conflict of laws do not apply in the area of immaterial property law.

For patents the Paris Convention, art. 2(1) offers the same remedy as the Berne Convention art. 5(1), but unlike in the latter, the existence of the same patents in several countries is reflected in the local treatment.[103] The law of the country of protection alone governs the acquisition, the effect and the cessation of the right in question.[104]

Thus the two Conventions provide a remedy for copyright holders by offering parallel protection in other Convention countries and for patent holders, if the remedy sought in the *forum* other than the *forum originis* is a

---

[101] Ulmer, *Immaterialgüterrechte*, p. 37 para. 50.
[102] Ulmer, *Immaterialgüterrechte*, p. 39 para. 54. p. 40 para. 55.
[103] Ulmer, *Immaterialgüterrechte*, p. 61 para. 86.
[104] Ulmer, *Immaterialgüterrechte*, p. 74 para. 110, p. 75 para. 112.

procedural one, such as discovery,[105] probably if the patent granted by the law of the country of *origin* is identical with that in the country of protection,[106] as in the case of copyrights, or if the joint action by two or more alleged infringers represent a common design resulting in a common law tort.[107] It would seem that in the absence of | conventional or statutory provisions, references to the *lex originis* are ruled out for copyrights.

V. Conclusion

In all three countries it was realised early that the law of copyright and industrial property is territorial in character in the sense that within the same country only the local law of immaterial property can hold sway and that consequently equivalent foreign legislation is precluded. Protection in a country other than that of origin must rely on parallel protection in accordance with local law, if any such protection is sanctioned by international agreement or by local law. The ordinary rules of the conflict of laws do not assist since a reference to foreign immaterial property law is to law which is selflimiting territorially. In France, but not in England or Germany, the law of the country where the immaterial property right came into existence (*lex originis*) determines the right in a broad sense, such as title, leaving the law of the country where protection is sought to furnish the remedies available there.

It is believed that this limited reliance by the *lex protectionis* on the *lex originis* serves a necessary function, if it is to be maintained that a foreign immaterial property right is being protected and not a local right in substitution for a foreign right.

In recent times the notion that the infringement of an immaterial property right constitutes a tort, so that the system of conflict of laws includes the protection of such claims arising from torts committed abroad, has inspired the enforcement by the forum of claims concerning infringements of immaterial property rights abroad, for tort laws are not territorially exclusive and are capable of application in other jurisdictions. As a result the long established insight was disregarded that the infringement of immaterial property rights is sanctioned by laws which are strictly territorial and incapable of application by courts abroad, and with it the refusal to assume jurisdiction by courts in countries other than that where the infringement occurred refuse to assume jurisdiction (the country of protection).

---

[105] *Mölnlycke* v. *Procter & Gamble* [1992] 4 All E.R. 47, 58.

[106] The jurisdictional aspects of art. 21 and 22 of the Brussels Convention are not being considered here; see *Coin Controls* v. *Suzo* [1997] 3 All E.R. 45, 53.

[107] *Mölnlycke* v. *Procter & Gamble* [1992] 4 All E.R. 47, 53.

The absence of jurisdiction on the ground of *necessity* and not, as it is usually justified, on grounds of procedural convenience, has been disturbed by the enlarged jurisdiction offered by the Brussels and Lugano Conventions, now Reg. 44/2000. Can the extended jurisdiction apply where foreign exclusively procedural or political territorial law is involved? The answer must be: Foreign territorial law is exclusive in a positive sense in being the only law applicable within its bounds. In a negative sense it is excluded elsewhere by | the existence of equivalent local law. Consequently the use of Private International law, resulting in a total application of foreign immaterial property law or of the right of the state concerned to make an equivalent protection available must be ruled out.

The fact that the exclusive character of immaterial property law precludes proceedings abroad for the enforcement of claims for infringements elsewhere can result in considerable inconvenience, especially if the same activity constitutes identical infringements in several countries. It is suggested here that the drafters of the Berne and Paris Conventions sought to provide one or several other effective remedies when Private International Law is unable to offer assistance, if the infringement of an immaterial property right in one country cannot support an action in another having regard to the territorial character of the law pleaded in support of the claim.

While Private International Law serves to introduce a claim based on foreign law in proceedings brought in another country, the Berne and Paris Conventions seek to ensure *parallel* protection of the identical course of action. This operates without difficulty if the jurisdiction and law of the protecting country coincide with one *lex loci delicti*.

If the infringement has occurred elsewhere or in several countries the vexed question of territoriality might be thought to arise again. However, the Conventions would seem to aim at the *parallel protection* of an identical right. They seek to achieve this when either a single or a multiple infringement in one or several foreign countries is sought to be remedied without resort to multiple jurisdictions. In the case of multiple infringements in more than one country it is suggested that art. 28 of Reg. 44/2001 provides the means on the basic assumption that no choice of law is involved, if the country of protection assumes jurisdiction in respect of all of them and therefore also on the strength of the local *lex protectionis*.

Instead of relying on the foreign *lex loci delicti* the Conventions start in this case, by way of parallel protection of the foreign claim, by identifying it with an identical claim arising from a local infringement.[108]

---

[108] It is an entirely different matter if *in personam* proceedings involve a contract concerning an immaterial property right by a purchaser with notice of a prior equitable interest. In this case choice of law is affected, but not jurisdiction. See *Griggs Group Ltd.* v. *Evans* (2000) F.S.R. 939, paras. 28. 57, 60, 110.

Original Places of Publication